ALEXANDER
TO ACTIUM

PETER GREEN

ALEXANDER TO ACTIUM

THE HELLENISTIC AGE

THAMES AND HUDSON

First published in Great Britain in 1990 by
Thames and Hudson Ltd, London
This paperback edition 1993
First published in the U.S.A. by University of California Press

Printed and bound in the United States of America

Dis manibus
F. E. Adcock
G. T. Griffith
W. K. C. Guthrie
J. E. Raven
with gratitude for much wisdom freely
shared, and in affectionate memory

The historian may well interest himself in the state of things, the condition of society, the principles underlying a system of government or a system of thought. But if he is to understand historically and practice historical writing, he will have to think of such analyses as steps in a chain of events, as matters explanatory of a sequence of happenings. He will have to concentrate on understanding change, which is the essential content of historical analysis and description. History treats fundamentally of the transformation of things (people, institutions, ideas, and so on) from one state into another, and the event is its concern as well as its instrument.

G. R. Elton,
The Practice of History

Chorus of all. All, all, of a piece throughout:
Thy Chase had a Beast in View;
Thy Wars brought nothing about;
Thy Lovers were all untrue.
'Tis well an Old Age is out,
And time to begin a New.

*Dance of Huntsmen, Nymphs,
Warriors, and Lovers*
John Dryden, *The Secular Masque*

ἆ μάκαρ, ὅστις ἔην κεῖνον χρόνον ἴδρις ἀοιδῆς,
Μουσάων θεράπων, ὅτ' ἀκήρατος ἦν ἔτι λειμών·
νῦν δ' ὅτε πάντα δέδασται, ἔχουσι δὲ πείρατα τέχναι,
ὕστατοι ὥστε δρόμου καταλειπόμεθ', οὐδέ πῃ ἔστι
πάντῃ παπταίνοντα νεοζυγὲς ἄρμα πελάσσαι.

Choerilus of Samos

CONTENTS

MAPS

PREFACE AND ACKNOWLEDGMENTS

The Hellenistic age has one great advantage for us: it is easily definable. Its unity was first perceived, its limits set, even its name invented, by the nineteenth-century German historian Johann Gustav Droysen. For him, as for most subsequent students of the period, it began with the death of Alexander the Great in 323 B.C., continued through the rise, decline and fall of the great kingdoms carved by his marshals (known as the *Diadochoi*, or "Successors") from the empire he left, and ended with Octavian's dissolution of the last of these, Ptolemaic Egypt, in 30 B.C., just under three centuries later. This is a modern perspective: it is highly doubtful whether any ancient writer, from the Augustan age onwards, ever recognized the problem in these terms. Rome's triumph encouraged an innate natural tendency to take short views.

It follows that to attempt a historical survey of the Hellenistic period means, in effect, writing the history of the Greek world, the *oikoumenē*, during that period: not only of the Greek-speaking cities and states (as opposed to those that merely employed the vernacular Attic *koinē* as a *lingua franca*), but also of those far larger areas, profoundly alien in speech and culture to the Greek spirit, that were forcibly taken over, and in a very real sense exploited, by foreign overlords: Greek, Macedonian, and, later, Roman.* It became clear to me during my researches that the degree to which this Graeco-Macedonian diaspora spread its much-vaunted culture, its reasons for doing so, and the audience it reached, especially in the East, had been in ways badly misrepresented. Thus one of my objects in writing the present work is to draw a more realistic picture of the impact, nature, and limitations of this diffusion.

I must state plainly at the outset that I regard the whole notion of a conscious, idealistic, missionary propagation in conquered territories of Greek culture, *mores*, literature, art, and religion—much less the undertaking of such conquests, whether by Alexander himself or any of his successors, with this ulterior end in view—as a pernicious myth, compounded of anachronistic Christian evangelicism and Plutarch-inspired wishful thinking, and designed (whether consciously or not) to provide moral justification for what was, in essence, despite its romantic popularity, large-scale economic and imperial exploitation. Edouard Will points out how much the

---

*Cf. Davies, *CAH* VII².1 263, for a good analysis of the problems involved in defining the field of inquiry.

prewar attitude to Hellenistic imperialism was conditioned by "la 'bonne conscience' colonialiste," and to what an extent "le choc de la décolonisation nous a fait prendre conscience de ce qu'étaient les réalités coloniales," with a very similar impact on the thinking of the Hellenistic historian.*

I must also, at the same time, emphasize that this does not—since I am old-fashioned enough to prefer operating with a free intellect, an open rather than a closed mind—mean that I am either a declared or a covert Marxist, as should become abundantly clear in the course of this book. Throughout I have been in pursuit of the truth, an aim much ridiculed today, for their own partisan purposes, by committed ideologists; and though neither I nor any reasonable person would believe that Ranke's ideal of writing history *wie es eigentlich gewesen sei* is attainable—what ideal is?—that does not release the historian from the harsh obligation of striving for it to the best of his or her ability. To do otherwise is as though (to draw a theological parallel) the concept of inherent human sinfulness and fallibility were taken as a self-evident reason neither to pursue virtue, nor to avoid error; or, worse, as indicating that the terms "virtue" and "error" had no significant meaning.

When I first embarked on the vast task that I had, with incurable optimism, set myself, my primary aim was simple enough: to provide an up-to-date and unified survey of a period heavily worked by specialists, but still too often ignored by those (including many professionals) in the habit of skipping adroitly from Alexander—if not from the defeat of Athens in 404—to the rise of the Roman Republic. Such a synthesis must of necessity rest, to a great extent, on foundations laid by the great pioneers in the field. Hellenistic history as we know it would be inconceivable without the work of such scholars as Droysen, Niese, Berve, Wilcken, Tarn, Rostovtzeff, Holleaux, Bouché-Leclercq, and Préaux, not to mention countless others still living, all of whom have contributed so much in understanding to every aspect of this multifaceted age. Yet, at intervals, a time arrives, for this as for other periods and areas, when it becomes desirable to pull all the threads together in the light of a mass of new discoveries and changing interpretations, and to attempt an interim overview, governed by a single outlook.

Specialists are, more often than not, loath to undertake such a task, for which, by temperament and training, they tend, in any case, to be ill suited; when others perform it, they label it "popularization" or, with rather more charitable contempt, *haute vulgarisation*. This of course at once raises the question of the audience for which such books are written. The most common answer is, for the "intelligent general reader," and loose though this definition is, I would agree that if the findings of ancient historians have any validity at all, they should most certainly be disseminated among thinking people—especially if, as will be seen in a moment, they have some application to the problems of our own world today. At the same time, close and profitable contact, over nineteen years, with colleagues in a large, energetic, and variegated Classics Department has convinced me—not entirely on the *quis custodiet* principle—that specialists, too, benefit at times from an attempt to impose some sort

---

*Will, in Eadie and Ober, eds., 281–82.

of coherent perspective on their activities. It is no bad thing, once in a while, to stand back, take the long view, and meditate upon the sum of things.

I have, thus, written this book with both audiences always in mind. The main text throughout remains free (I hope) of all arcane allusions, historiographical jargon, specialist shorthand, and quotations—familiar commonplaces apart—in foreign languages. In the Notes and References, on the other hand, my one concession to lay readers is to make it easier for the curious to hunt down references to fragments by directing them, whenever possible, to the actual source of the quotation rather than to the collections of Jacoby, Müller, Diels and Kranz, and others, which may be in every academic library, but remain inaccessible to nonspecialists and baffling even when found. Similarly, I have taken it for granted that my colleagues will know which editions of ancient authors are the most reliable, whereas the general reader will, nine times out of ten, simply go to the relevant Loeb or Penguin volume, if available, and take potluck. But for both categories I have made my documentation of sources, both primary and secondary, as full and scrupulous as I could. Too many Hellenistic commonplaces—*experto crede*—are surprisingly hard to run down. For the sake of precision, I have also frequently made citations in the original Latin or Greek where an important point was at issue, and I have always quoted foreign scholars in their own languages, having suffered in the past from translations that were artfully slanted for partisan ends.

Inevitably, however, my own investigations were shaped and influenced by preconceptions and judgments often very much at odds with those of my predecessors. It is, of course, a truism that every historian remains at heart a revisionist, and I am no exception to the rule. My synthesis is squarely based on its own axioms. Some of my revisionist views (e.g., my treatment of Hellenic cultural diffusion, referred to above) emerged only during the course of writing. Others took the form of conscious principles that I brought to my task *ab initio*, which it is only fair to set down at the outset. My original impulse to write this book came some years ago, when, being required to give a course of lectures on Hellenistic civilization, and having already a clear idea in my head of just what demands the subject would properly make on the historian, I scoured the libraries for such a work, and failed to find it. Surveys indeed existed, and more have appeared since; but none, in my view, met the essential conditions. To the best of my knowledge, no survey of quite this kind on the Hellenistic age exists in any European language. George Leigh-Mallory climbed Everest because it was there. I have written *Alexander to Actium* because it was not there, and needed to be.

The principles I brought to its composition are set out briefly below. First, I regarded it as essential to emphasize—very much against recent trends in historiography—the linear, diachronic, evolutionary development apparent in the three centuries of the Hellenistic era. The general absence of such treatment has been one of the most striking features of the scholarship devoted to the period.* Professor

---

*This was written before I saw *CAH* VII².1, in which the joint editor, Professor F. W. Walbank, writes (p. xi): "General surveys, whether of particular kingdoms or of the whole area of

Elton's lapidary pronouncement on this topic, reproduced as one of my epigraphs, has been in my mind throughout. The implementation of his advice sent me back to the now-unfashionable business of writing narrative history. This does not mean that I have not learned a very great deal from the tradition of the *École Annales*, from socially oriented scholars such as Lefebvre or Braudel; but I have also taken to heart the recent animadversions on French education made by that formidable historian and *philologue* Jacqueline de Romilly, who remarked, *inter alia*, that while schoolchildren today could tell you just how Louis XVI dressed, or what he ate for breakfast, they more often than not had only the haziest notion of who he was, when he lived, and what he achieved. Even when, inevitably, I break the chronological flow of the narrative to survey special topics, I have always tried to keep in mind the Heracleitan flow and change of events, the far-reaching transformations that the Hellenistic world continually underwent throughout its existence.

Second, I felt it essential that I should treat every significant aspect of cultural development in the Hellenistic age, from the visual arts to literature, from mathematics to medicine, from philosophy to religion, and evaluate each as a significant aspect, not of civilization in a static sense, much less *sub specie aeternitatis*, but of the continually evolving totality, or plenum, that constitutes a civilization's history. This, of necessity, led me into a number of fields where I am no expert, and for which—though I have always studied the ancient evidence to the best of my ability—I am more than usually dependent on the work of other scholars. The deep debt of gratitude I owe them is, I hope, adequately acknowledged in my Notes and References. It is important to emphasize, however, that my intention on such occasions has not been, in the first instance, to rehash specialist conclusions at second hand, but rather to relate the general patterns that emerge from those conclusions to the social and political developments of the age. Thus, for example, the Greek treatment of quadratic equations or conic sections is not, in detail, my business; but the fact that the Greeks (some arguments to the contrary notwithstanding) had no true grasp of algebra until the Christian era most certainly is. In the same way, Stoic cosmology, say, or the scientific principles of Epicurus do not fall, technically speaking, within my competence; but both offer crucial evidence for any historian of the late Hellenistic world, to be ignored at one's peril.

Such an approach is bound to be idiosyncratic, not least in its selectivity. My approach to the sciences and the visual arts is, first and foremost, sociohistorical throughout: I am no scientist, nor is art criticism in the strict sense my professional concern. Even in literature, where I am a good deal more at home, the historian has always perforce taken precedence over the critic. The poet-playwright Menander (who has always struck me as a classic example of a growth industry created by papyrological accident) thus becomes a valuable social witness without any necessary

---

Hellenistic civilisation, do not provide a substitute for a chronological narrative of events, for without such a framework a general sketch may well fail to convey the sense of historical development." He himself and Professor Edouard Will now offer us, accordingly, three chapters of narrative history covering the period from Alexander's death to the battle of Raphia (217 B.C.), but the general tone of the volume remains synchronic and separatist.

reference to the quality of his work. Further, since my emphasis is on change and evolution, I discuss static institutions only insofar as they show signs of significant development. Hence the reader will find no separate chapter on sex, marriage, and private life, though references to such matters occur, where appropriate, in other contexts. Nor, perhaps more controversially, do I devote specific sections either to law or to school education, on the grounds that during our period the first (where not merely municipal or parochial) was little more than an elaborate sham masking the realities of power, while the second offered nothing, in essence, but literary rote learning, elementary mathematics, music, athletics, and—most important—a rhetorical grab bag that would enable men at the top to talk their way into, or out of, anything.

It has also been suggested to me that I should include a discussion of Hellenistic historiography apart from Polybius (who gets full treatment in Chapter 17), down to, and including, Diodorus Siculus in the first century B.C. The trouble here is that Polybius remains the only worthwhile historian of the Hellenistic period whose work substantially survives. Diodorus, as we are too often reminded, is a third-rate compiler only as good as his source: this makes him, at times, of great value, but not on his own account, and I have no wish to burden an already overlong book with yet another imaginative analysis of his chronological inconsistencies and synthetic rhetoric. Like Plutarch, he believed that one virtue of history lay in "recording the nobility of distinguished men, publicizing the vileness of the wicked, and in general promoting the good of mankind" (1.2.2). Successful statesmen, he thought, were righteous, while evil ones met with frustration: nothing, in short, succeeds like success. None of this inspires confidence. Those Hellenistic historians who might have been worth discussing (e.g., Hieronymus of Cardia, Poseidonius, Timaeus, or Phylarchus), not to mention memoirists of events in which they themselves were involved, such as Aratus of Sicyon, are extant only in tantalizing fragments. While I admire the scholarly acumen and ingenuity that enables scholars such as T. W. Africa or Jane Hornblower to convert these fragments into bricks with a minimum of straw, it is not a talent I share. I do have brief discussions of all the historians here mentioned at appropriate points in my text or notes, but hesitate to theorize in general about a tradition almost wholly lost to us. This reticence, I notice, is shared by most recent authors (Ussher, Brown, Grant, Fornara) of general works on ancient historiography.

Third, as far as lay within my technical command, I was determined to avoid any unnecessary disruptive fragmentation of the interwoven elements that went to make up the Hellenistic plenum. This applied in particular to the political history (a notable stumbling block in the past), where any misguided attempt to deal separately and successively with Ptolemies, Seleucids, Attalids, Antigonids, Greek *poleis*, and so on, not only made for hopeless confusion and irritating repetitions, but also, much worse, kaleidoscopically distorted, to an acute degree, what was in fact an admittedly complex, but still unified and interdependent, Mediterranean scene. I cannot pretend to have solved this problem completely, but I have done my level best to bear it in mind at every stage. If the result at times verges on polyphony, I hope the voices, and their relationships, remain tolerably clear. The importance of political history has, it is true, been overstressed in the past (though not nearly so much as the sociologists would like us to believe); at the same time, until the political threads have been satisfactorily unraveled, it must remain doubtful whether anything else can be understood in any meaningful sense at all.

Fourth, it seemed extremely important to avoid missing the wood for the trees. This is a danger endemic to Hellenistic studies by reason of the nature, and limitations, of our evidence. For Ptolemaic Egypt in particular we have a vast mass of epigraphical and, above all, papyrological material, on which a succession of notable scholars have done epoch-making work. The risks here are comparable to those inherent in the locally concentrated work of European historians such as Le Roi Ladurie, but without the same counterbalancing plethora of national-level testimony to offset them. Our general narrative sources for the Hellenistic period are for the most part either late, or local, or both; even the best historian, Polybius, is not only circumscribed in period, but *parti pris* to a disconcerting extent (below, pp. 269 ff.).

Further, while some of the papyrus finds, most notably the so-called Zenon Archive, are of real national importance, most of them remain local, minor, and particular. This is not for one moment to deny their enormous, and compelling, sociological interest, but the very nature of the material has, inevitably, dictated the pattern assumed by specialist work in the area: where particularism is rated as a high academic virtue, the *disiecta membra* of village bureaucracy come as a welcome boon. This trend is not encouraging to international historiography on a broad canvas. Infuriatingly, the records of Alexandria and the waterlogged Delta are lost; what we have instead, for the most part, is material from the garbage dumps and mummy cartonnage of bone-dry Philadelphia or Oxyrhynchus; and using this to interpret Ptolemaic Egypt is, all too often, like sifting the municipal waste of Rochdale or Kansas City with a view to writing the history of England or the United States. I hope I have exploited this material adequately; on the other hand I have always done my best not to use local evidence to draw unwarranted larger inferences. This is one of many places where the (anyway suspect) rule of *ex pede Herculem* most definitely does not apply.

Several critics have suggested that my treatment of the Greek *poleis* in the Hellenistic era is flawed beyond redemption by what I suppose might be defined as creeping Droysenism. I have, they argue, underestimated both the autonomy enjoyed by the *poleis*, and the importance, even in conditions of limited freedom, that should still be attached to their affairs. I also (it is claimed) exaggerate the degree of freedom enjoyed by city-states in the classical era, and, in particular, take a rose-tinted view of the role of Athens in the maintenance of freedom, a charge that may surprise those familiar with my earlier work (see e.g., *The Shadow of the Parthenon*, pp. 75 ff.). I underestimate the power and reality of *Völkerrecht*, it is said; I am insensitive to Hellenic political traditions, not to mention "the practical limitations upon Seleucid sovereigns." I strive for *Realpolitik* but succumb to reductionism. And so on. As Diaghilev said to Cocteau, "Etonne-moi, Jean": I am quite ready to be convinced by sound arguments and good evidence, and in one or two cases I have modified my views accordingly. But on my central thesis I stand firm. The *poleis* were not wholly free in the fifth century, but at least they were fighting each other, and that not all the time. Not to be subject, in the last resort, to the dictates of a bureaucratic monarchy does make a difference to one's outlook, as the exceptional case of Rhodes (see pp. 378 ff.) demonstrates with peculiar clarity. Of course the *poleis* had autonomy to the extent that they ran their own municipal affairs: so do the cities of the Soviet Union today. The passionate pursuit, against all odds, of *eleutheria* was not a mere political gimmick. Would the Greeks have fought with such desperate fury at Crannon, or in the Chremonidean War, or for Mithridates VI, or at Corinth in 146, if they had not seen something infinitely precious at stake, something for which municipal self-government, flourishing commerce, and empty public honors were no adequate substitute? The answer is self-evident.

There is one further point that should, perhaps, be stressed. As my work proceeded, it acquired an unexpected and in ways alarming dimension. I could not help being struck, again and again, by an overpowering sense of *déjà vu*, far more than for any other period of ancient history known to me: the "distant mirror" that Barbara Tuchman held up from the fourteenth century A.D. for our own troubled age is remote and pale compared to the ornate, indeed rococo, glass in which Alexandria, Antioch, and Pergamon reflect contemporary fads, failings, and aspirations, from the urban malaise to religious fundamentalism, from Veblenism to *haute cuisine*, from funded scholarship and mandarin literature to a flourishing dropout counterculture, from political impotence in the individual to authoritarianism in government, from science perverted for military ends to illusionism for the masses, from spiritual solipsism on a private income to systematic extortion in pursuit of the plutocratic dream. Contemporary cosmological speculation seems to be taking us straight back to the Stoic world view, while Tyche has been given a new lease of life by computer analysts, who prefer to describe it, with pseudo-Hellenic panache, as "stochasticism." I have, however, steadfastly tried to avoid drawing such factitious parallels in my text, or coloring ancient phenomena with modern associations. Wherever possible I was determined to let the evidence speak for itself. What this parallelism signifies I do not pretend to know, and think it wiser not to speculate; but it does suggest, forcibly, that there may indeed be something more in the Hellenistic age for concerned modern readers than mere antiquarian interest.

The final revision of the fourth and last draft of this book was completed during a year's leave from my duties in the University of Texas at Austin, while I was primarily and officially engaged upon a very different (and far more particularist) project. I am profoundly grateful both to the National Endowment for the Humanities (which elected me a Senior Fellow for 1983–84), and to the Research Institute of my own university, for thus enabling me to spend my leisure moments, as well as my working days, uninterrupted by those multifarious claims on a teacher's time that, in the ordinary way, make sustained work on this scale so difficult of achievement. The superb holdings of the Classics Library and the Perry-Castañeda Library in the University of Texas at Austin have been my prop and stay throughout: I would like to express my warmest thanks to the Classics Librarian and the Classics Bibliographer, Bernice Dawson and Goldia Hester, for their consistent courtesy and helpfulness. Nor is it easy to find sufficient praise for the always overworked yet unfailingly cheerful staff of the Inter-Library Loan Department, who procured me innumerable recherché volumes that I had despaired of ever finding, at a speed that constantly belied their own pessimistic prognostications.

Both Professor Erich S. Gruen and the University of California Press, and Professor K. D. White and Thames and Hudson Ltd, made available to me, well in advance of publication, proofs of their then-forthcoming new books, *The Hellenistic World and the Coming of Rome* and *Greek and Roman Technology*, respectively. A similar courtesy was extended to me by Professor Stanley M. Burstein in respect of *Translated Documents of Greece and Rome, vol. 3, The Hellenistic Age from the Battle of Ipsos to the Death of Kleopatra VII*, by Pauline Hire of the Cambridge University Press in respect of Professor J. J. Pollitt's *Art in the Hellenistic Age*, and by Doris Kretschmer of the University of California Press in respect of *Hellenism in the East*, edited by Amélie Kuhrt and Susan Sherwin-White. This most generous courtesy on their part was of inestimable benefit to my own work.

Dr. B. J. Bardsley read each chapter of my final draft in typescript, and saved me from a variety of errors and infelicities. Further stringent professional scrutiny of the entire text was provided by Professor Eugene N. Borza and an anonymous reader for the University of California Press. My chapters on Hellenistic art have been read and annotated by Professor A. F. Stewart, and further benefited from correspondence with Professor Brunilde Ridgway. On numerous occasions all the above-named readers made illuminating suggestions, and more often still did their best to save me from my own perverseness; they should not be blamed for those occasions on which the author's idiosyncratic obstinacy remained deaf to their admonitions. My meticulously accurate, thorough, and learned copyeditor, Paul Psoinos, rescued me from more slips, confusions, inconsistencies, and inaccuracies than I care to think about, and will always remain in my mind as the living embodiment of Zeno's favorite paradox. In London, Jamie Camplin and Suzanne Bosman went far beyond the call of duty in ensuring that I got, finally, just about every illustration I wanted. Mary Lamprech and Doris Kretschmer have been towers of strength and reassurance throughout what proved a longer haul than any of us originally envisaged. Last but far from least, I am immensely grateful to my old friend Dr. August Frugé, Director Emeritus of the University of California Press, for the endless time and trouble he took in reading a gargantuan manuscript, and the unfailing tact, sympathy, and wisdom with which he strove to tone down my purple patches and overstated views. How far he succeeded in this laudable endeavor is another matter.

Modified versions of Chapters 6, 10, and 37 have previously appeared in *Grand Street*, and of Chapters 13, 27, and 33 in *Southern Humanities Review*. Chapter 19 was originally delivered as a lecture at Mount Allison University, New Brunswick, Canada, and afterwards published by the Crake Institute in that university as part of *The Crake Lectures 1984* (1986).

All translations in this work (including those of Cavafy) are, unless otherwise attributed, my own. I am, further, conscious of having been more than usually inconsistent in the transliteration of Greek names. Having lived in Greece for the best part of a decade, I find it hard to tolerate any but the most insistent of Latinized or Anglicized names (e.g., Athens, Piraeus, rather than Athenai, Peiraieus—or Peiraiefs); at the same time, many Latinizations have become so firmly rooted that it would be pure pedantry to reject them. In the end I simply chose, in each case, the spelling with which I felt most comfortable, without any attempt at consistency. Thus the reader will find Piraeus, but also Kerameikos (rather than Ceramicus); Cassander and Antigonus, rather than Kassandros and Antigonos; while Anglicized Ptolemy (as opposed to Greek Ptolemaios) has an orthodox Hellenic title in Philadelphos. My attitude in this matter was inspired by the dealings of T. E. Lawrence with his proofreader, over variants of Arabic orthography, in *The Seven Pillars of Wisdom*. Walt Whitman's best-known apothegm also applies.

The length of time between the original submission of my manuscript (fall 1984) and publication has, inevitably, prevented me from taking full account of much useful work published during the intervening period. However, I take comfort from the fact that nothing I have read to date has persuaded me of the necessity to make major substantive revisions to my text. There is, I do not doubt, much of value that I have missed: the flow of scholarship on the Hellenistic period is now so strong that it has become virtually impossible for one man to master it all, and I have not attempted to do so. I have, however, wherever possible added fresh material to my notes in particular, and modified some points of detail as a result.

The accident of major retinal surgery meant that this preface was written— ideally as I now perceive—without access to books, and in the perfect conditions provided by Seton Medical Center in Austin: I would like to thank the unfailingly friendly nursing staff who looked after me so well, and made my stay such a pleasant one, despite its antecedent cause. I owe, further, an eternal debt of gratitude to Dr. Coleman Driver, Jr.: scholars and writers live by their eyes, and Dr. Driver's great skill saved mine, literally, at the eleventh hour.

My wife, as always, has been a source of encouragement, loving support, and sensible advice (not always sensibly taken) throughout. My deepest long-term debt, however, must always be to those great Cambridge scholars under whom, a more than usually irritating ex-service undergraduate, I studied in the halcyon years immediately after World War II. Some of them, now gone from us, are commemorated in my dedication. I do not for one moment flatter myself that they would have entirely approved of my present undertaking; but anything of real value in it I owe to them, and I gratefully offer it to their memory.

Peter Green
Austin, Texas
August 1984–May 1988

Preface to the second printing

For the second American printing of this book, and for the French, Greek, and German translations, I have taken the opportunity to correct a number of errors and misprints, and to make minor revisions in the light of criticisms offered by reviewers and fellow scholars. For their careful and exhaustive scrutiny I am especially grateful to Dr. Paul Cartledge, Prof. Christian Habicht, Prof. Jørgen Mejer, Prof. Andrew Stewart, and Prof. Frank W. Walbank. It goes without saying that they should not be held responsible for any errors remaining.

Peter Green
Austin, Texas
November 1992

PART ONE
ALEXANDER'S FUNERAL GAMES, 323–276 B.C.

CHAPTER 1

PERDICCAS, EUMENES, CASSANDER, 323–316

When Alexander lay dying in Babylon, in June 323 B.C., Perdiccas, now his senior commander,[1] spent much time at his bedside. The question of the succession was in everyone's mind. It was to Perdiccas, reportedly, that Alexander gave his ring, its seal the symbol of imperial authority; but the ultimate source of that report must have been Perdiccas himself, a fact that does not inspire confidence. And what, even if true, did the gesture signify? Was Perdiccas to be the king's heir, his regent, or nothing more than the supervisor of what he hoped would be a peaceful succession? Perdiccas himself claimed that he was to be *epimelētēs tēs basileias*,[2] a nicely ambiguous phrase that could be—and has been—translated as either "regent of the kingdom" or "guardian of the monarchy," thus ensuring its bearer's position whether or not the predominantly royalist Macedonians actually put a king on the throne. Perdiccas may well have invented the title; in any case, his interpretation of Alexander's dying gesture left him in an unchallengeable position of authority.[3]

It was probably to Perdiccas—again, if Perdiccas did not invent both statements on his own behalf—that Alexander uttered his two last famous apothegms. He was asked to whom he left his kingdom. Since he had no obvious heir, this was an urgent question. "To the strongest," he replied.[4] He also declared—his last recorded words—that "all his foremost friends would hold a great funeral contest over him."[5] True or invented, that was a shrewd assessment. Waiting in Babylon was a group of tough, battle-scarred, ambitious commanders. Their eyes were fixed on the glittering prizes of empire, and their ideals were a good deal more mundane than Alexander's own. Not for them, in any form, the fusion of East and West. When Alexander was dead they repudiated, almost to a man, the Iranian wives wished on them in that bizarre mass-marriage ceremony at Susa.[6] Not for them Persian court protocol or high-flown plans to change the shape of the world.

Indeed, the very fact of their Macedonian background—with all that this implied—was to prove a major determining factor in all that followed. Macedonia had always been, and to a great extent remained, an ambiguous frontier element of the Balkans. Despite the assertions of *parti pris* advocates, there is insufficient linguistic

3

Fig. 1. Babylon: the Ishtar Gate. Painting by Elizabeth Andrae of the 1914 excavation.
Vorderasiatisches Museum, Berlin

Fig. 2. Alexander the Great, wearing
ram's horn and elephant-scalp
headdress. Silver tetradrachm minted at
Alexandria by Ptolemy I ca. 305 B.C.
British Museum, London. Photo: Leonard
von Matt.

evidence to identify what the Macedonian language, and, hence, Macedonian ethnicity, really was. Macedonia formed, as it were, a buffer enclave between the Thessalians (whose Hellenism was never in doubt) and a range of variously hostile and dubiously civilized tribes such as the Epirotes, the Illyrians, and the Paeonians. At least since the early fifth century the lowland royal house of the Argeads had been at some pains to establish its Greek identity, in a cultural no less than an ethnic sense. Alexander I, at the time of the Persian Wars, was held eligible to compete in the Olympic Games on the basis of a family tree (almost certainly fictitious) deriving the Argeads from Argos. By the time of Archelaus (413–399), the Argead court at Pella had acquired a considerable veneer of Attic sophistication, and some distinguished resident Athenians, including Euripides. Yet Macedonian society remained, in essence, sub-Homeric and anti-Greek, a rough and vigorous monarchy ruling, by main force, over ambitious barons (many of them former princes in their own highland cantons) whose chief interests in life were fighting and drinking. Southern Greeks never lost an opportunity of sneering at Macedonian barbarism, nor Macedonians at Greek effeteness; and though it would be unwise to take all Demosthenes' insults at face value, there can be no doubt that Alexander's marshals, all of whom sprang from Macedonian baronial families, were a breed apart.

Xenophobic (Peucestas was the exception that proved the rule) and grasping imperialists, these old soldiers had no intention of sharing real power with the locals—Persian officials advanced under Alexander were to get short shrift in the years ahead, doing most of the bureaucratic donkey-work and getting few of the plum jobs—or of learning native ways, or even of speaking the languages, much less studying the literature. It was the last Lagid monarch, Cleopatra VII, who was also the first to learn Egyptian (see below, p. 663). Insofar as they cultivated the local population at all, the Macedonian generals set their sights on the wealthy, the conservative, the influential elite (both civil and religious), those who were most likely to support their rule in return for special concessions, speciously disguised as *eunoia*, good will, *euergesiai*, benefactions, or *philanthrōpia*. What these marshals wanted was colonial power, and the enormous fringe benefits that such power gave. Under their charismatic leader they had done what generations of panhellenists had advocated: they had conquered the Achaemenid empire of Persia. It had been a long, fierce, eleven-year struggle, and for all that time they had played subordinate roles to a new Achilles in pursuit of his heroic destiny. Now they wanted something more. Most of the gold and other loot had already been shared out, to flood the Mediterranean markets and provide the ostentatious brand of conspicuous consumption that the Hellenistic monarchs made peculiarly their own. What these Macedonian commanders now sought was to get their hands on the empire itself.

They did not, to begin with, all have the same ideas about how this gigantic prize should be handled. Some wanted to maintain a unified kingdom on behalf of the legitimate royal heirs. Others made no bones about wanting to win control of it on their own account. Others, again, greed limited by cautious pragmatism, hoped to carve up the cake to their measure, to settle for lesser but still profitable fiefs—

surely this vast imperial mass could accommodate them all? The real, central contest was between the unitarians and the separatists, those who wanted to preserve the monarchy and those eager to go it alone. This was the main result of Alexander's death—inevitable when the entire empire had been won, and held together, by one man's unique and irreplaceable personality. The crisis was the more intense for the lack of an obvious successor: uncertainty spurred ambition; ambition bred paranoia.

Roxane, Alexander's Bactrian wife, was pregnant, but even if she bore a son, that would mean a long regency—ideal for ambitious would-be usurpers. What was worse, the child would be half-Bactrian, a point heavily exploited by Ptolemy.[7] The only other possible blood-successor was Arrhidaios, Philip II's son by a Thessalian dancing girl. Arrhidaios was reputedly weak-minded and epileptic;[8] certainly Alexander had not entrusted him with any responsible command, civil or military. For traditional royalists the choice was uninspiring.[9] While many of the future contenders for empire must have foreseen, from the start, that no one could hold Alexander's conquests together *en bloc*—and indeed that even Alexander himself might have found the task beyond him when the momentum of his quest finally slackened—there were others who feared anarchy, bloodshed, and chaos if the direct succession were lost, and others, again, who simply could not envisage a continuation of Macedonian power except through Alexander's descendants.

The true conflict, in other words, would come between the rival Macedonian commanders, with little influence from outside, and heavy reliance on the loyalty, or purchasability, of private, professionalized, quasi-mercenary armies. Persian and Iranian allegiance, if "allegiance" is the right word, would go to whoever came out on top in the struggle to be Lord of Asia: it is significant that only two native risings occurred on the news of Alexander's death,[10] and both of these, as we shall see in a moment, involved Greeks; there were otherwise no indigenous revolts against the colonial government. As for the sixty thousand–odd mercenaries, of various nation-

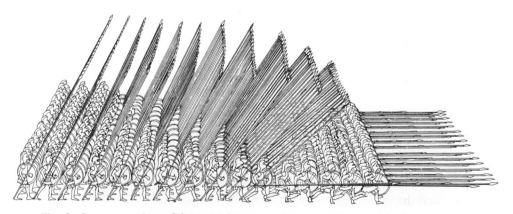

Fig. 3. Reconstruction of the Macedonian phalanx, armed with the famous sarissa, a heavy lance resembling the medieval Swiss pike.
Drawn after P. Levi, *Atlas of the Greek World,* 1980.

alities, who had been serving under both Alexander and Darius, they would throw their support to whoever paid them most generously and promptly. If the Macedonian barons wanted power, the mercenaries would settle for cash; and below the top echelons Macedonian veterans also had loot as their prime concern. The soldiers of Alexander's old Guards' Brigade (*Hypaspistai*), now renamed the Silver Shields (*Argyraspides*), many with over forty years' continuous service, not only enforced what amounted to employment contracts on their general, Eumenes,[11] but were quite capable, even in the moment of victory, of selling him off to the other side, for inevitable execution (below, p. 20), in order to ransom their camp, baggage, loot, and women, captured by a diversionary action (316/5 B.C.). But then, Eumenes was a Greek, and Macedonian troops, especially the old sweats who had served under Philip II, were never really comfortable being led by non-Macedonians. ("That pest from the Chersonese" was how the Silver Shields dismissed Eumenes when he was pleading for his life as a prisoner.)[12] The Greek cities invoked the name of freedom and fought wars and revolts in the name of self-determination and autonomy. Yet even here the motives were seldom as simple as they sometimes look; the autonomy motif was soon cynically exploited by the Successors (*Diadochoi*) for propaganda and divide-and-rule purposes, as it would be again later by Rome.

Even at the initial conference in Babylon after Alexander's death, the debate concerning the succession sparked off a confrontation, nearly a civil war, between the Macedonian cavalry and infantry. The elite cavalry commanders, including Perdiccas himself, wanted to wait for the birth of Roxane's child, and, if it proved to be a boy, to acclaim him king under a regency.[13] The bid of the fleet commander, Nearchus, to have Heracles, Alexander's son by Barsine, acclaimed as the heir apparent got nowhere:[14] why choose a bastard over legitimate offspring? In any case, despite his seniority under Alexander, Nearchus never came to much among the Successors; but then he, like Eumenes, was a Greek; worse still, he was a Cretan, and thus a proverbial liar.[15] Ptolemy's quintessentially Macedonian proposal for a ruling council of the King's Friends was killed by the supporters of Perdiccas, whose ambition was held in check only by the consideration of Roxane's unborn child. Even so, a proposal to make Perdiccas king was actually advanced at the meeting (not, one supposes, without his prior knowledge), and made some impression:[16] this was what most provoked the representatives of the infantry phalanx. Their spokesman, Meleager, urged the acceptance of Arrhidaios as a candidate[17]—an act that must, even if Arrhidaios lacked the drive or personality ever to achieve true independence of action, make one wonder just how mentally incapable he really was. Xenophobia also played its part here: the Macedonian rank and file did not relish the prospect of kowtowing to a half-Oriental monarch.

Arrhidaios, who had clearly been waiting in the wings, was now brought in by Meleager, and the infantry acclaimed him vociferously.[18] They then stormed the palace, and the Bodyguard, including Perdiccas, barely escaped a lynching and withdrew, taking the cavalry with them.[19] Meleager now briefly held the key to the succession, but lost his nerve when the cavalry cut off food supplies to the city. In the end

Eumenes, still acting as Alexander's chief secretary, managed to talk Meleager's troops into a less belligerent attitude, and proposed a compromise by which Arrhidaios should be made king, and Roxane's son, if son the child proved, should be made joint king with him. This proposal was accepted. Arrhidaios was given the title of Philip III, while Alexander's child by Roxane—who was indeed a boy—became Alexander IV.

Perdiccas, bent on reasserting his somewhat shaken authority, announced a "purification" of the army after Alexander's death. At the public parade to perform this ritual, the ringleaders of the infantry revolt were rounded up, without effective protest, for immediate execution—in one account by being trampled to death by war elephants.[20] Meleager was, diplomatically, spared, and was even appointed Perdiccas's deputy (*hyparchos*); but as soon as the crisis died down, and the situation was once more under control, he was murdered while seeking sanctuary in a temple.[21] So, for the time being at least, the unity of the empire was preserved. But the omens were not good. Arrhidaios, at best, was no forceful ruler: it is symptomatic of the realities of power that Perdiccas, though officially now acting in the name of the new kings, nevertheless retained all the authority of a regent. It would, too, be fifteen or sixteen years at least before Roxane's child—even if a boy who took after his father—became a force to reckon with. Whatever happened, and despite any traditional Macedonian loyalties to the throne, the empire was going to be dependent, for the crucial next decade or so, on regents and advisers who had their own ambitions to satisfy.

This was at once clear when Perdiccas—in his new capacity as *epimelētēs*, either guardian or regent, or, when convenient, both,[22] and with the authority of Alexander's seal ring as further support—summoned a council in Babylon to announce the various key commands that had been agreed on.[23] Here we find almost all the great marshals. Three, however, were absent. Antipater, who during Alexander's expedition had held the key post of regent or viceroy in Macedonia, was still at Pella. A few months before his death Alexander had summoned him to Babylon; but Antipater, sensing that if he obeyed he was a dead man, had remained at home, sending out his son Cassander to negotiate on his behalf.[24] It proved a wise decision. Craterus, whom Alexander had appointed to replace Antipater, was on his way back to Europe with Polyperchon, his second-in-command, leading ten thousand of the veterans:[25] he had got as far as Cilicia, and sensibly stayed there until the situation clarified itself. A genial bear of a man, in his broad-brimmed Macedonian slouch hat, he was popular with the troops; but he lacked that fine edge of ruthlessness necessary for supreme rule. A third key figure, Antigonus One-Eye (*Monophthalmos*), who almost from the beginning of the Persian expedition had held the appointment of commander in central Phrygia, responsible for keeping Alexander's lines of communication open, also, for the time being, remained where he was, in his fortress at the crossroads city of Celaenae.[26] He too, like Craterus, was larger than life: a towering, corpulent figure, with a harsh parade-ground voice and a shatteringly hearty laugh[27]—not to mention the physical deformity for which he was nicknamed.

When the appointments were announced, they were revealing. Antipater was reconfirmed as Macedonian viceroy: this could be construed as a direct blow at Craterus, thus robbed of the post for which he had Alexander's own authority.[28] Perdiccas was well aware of Craterus's popularity with the infantry; he may now have given him his problematic, and in any case largely honorary, guardianship (*prostasia*, as opposed to *epimelēteia*) of the monarchy, as a sop to this not-so-dangerous military Cerberus.[29] Meleager's appointment as *hyparchos* can be viewed in much the same light. Even if Craterus was technically guardian (*prostatēs*) of one or both kings, he never stood in a position to exercise that office;[30] whereas Perdiccas retained both Alexander and Arrhidaios in Asia, where he could keep a watchful eye on them.[31] Among the other appointments, the most important were those of Ptolemy, Lysimachus, Antigonus One-Eye, and the Greek, Eumenes. Ptolemy was one of the few to realize that limiting his ambitions would actually get him farther in the long run. He asked for Egypt, and got it. He had no cause to regret his choice. Lysimachus was given Thrace, while Antigonus was confirmed in his existing command of Pamphylia, Lycia, and Greater Phrygia.[32] Whether this was "really a political setback" for Antigonus is debatable, but certainly he and Perdiccas had never cared for each other, and renewed conflict between them was, in these circumstances, a foregone conclusion.[33] Eumenes, who was resented by the Macedonian old guard, but like all shrewd administrators knew far too much about his colleagues to be discounted, got Cappadocia and Paphlagonia. This could not be described as generous, since neither area had yet been conquered; they were held by a local monarch called Ariarathes, and the appointment was contingent on Eumenes' ousting him. Alexander's old friend Leonnatus was allotted Hellespontine Phrygia. All these men were either Macedonian or Greek: the era of Persian equality had died with Alexander. The dead king's other projects, as costly as they were grandiose, also now met their demise, voted down by the army assembly.[34] They had included a fleet of a thousand large warships for a North African campaign, the encouragement of racial fusion by mass transfers of populations, and the construction of transcontinental highways, numerous temples, and a tomb for Alexander's father, Philip, "to equal the biggest of the Egyptian pyramids."

When all the appointments had been made, the new satraps at once took off for their fiefs and dug themselves in, removing all the cash and troops they could from Babylon. Perdiccas was left with the two kings, the remnants of the imperial army, and a rather shaky control of things. He had won the first round, but his power base was still uncertain. As Arrian says, "everyone was suspicious of him, and he of them."[35] The first thing he had to do was look for allies. The likeliest candidates were Craterus, Ptolemy, and Antipater. He was also forced to dispatch one of his Eastern satraps, Peithon, to put down a huge mutiny and revolution of the Greek military settlers in Bactria. Peithon, an ambitious man, played with the idea of joining the rising himself, but dropped it when he found his troops obstinately loyal to the Macedonian throne. The rebellion was crushed, violently, for the moment;[36] but Bactria remained difficult territory, and later broke away from Seleucid control altogether (see p. 332). It was now, too, that Rhodes expelled its Macedonian garrison and regained its independence.[37]

Fig. 4. Lysimachus of Thrace(?).
Roman copy of a Hellenistic bust,
tentatively identified through similarity
to a coin portrait, itself uncertain.
Musée d'Art et d'Histoire, Geneva.

Most serious of all, Craterus, Antipater, and Leonnatus were almost at once (? Sept. 323) caught up in a revolt of some mainland Greek states, precipitated by Alexander's death, and culminating in the so-called Lamian or Hellenic War. The leading rebel was, once again, Athens. Here Alexander's decree enforcing the recall of exiles (324), all removed on political grounds and thus hostile to the democratic government, had caused violent resentment; and his death without viable heirs, by seeming to place Macedonian control over Greece in jeopardy, provided the Athenians with an irresistible opportunity to make one more bid for freedom. Sparta, still smarting from her defeat by Antipater in 331, held aloof.[38] Funds—including the treasure of Alexander's absconding paymaster Harpalus, who had fled to Athens— were spent on hiring mercenaries, now easily available from the mass of unemployed soldiers of fortune (mostly paid off and sent home after the winding-up of the Persian expedition) gathered in the southern Peloponnese, near Cape Tainaron.[39] A brilliant Athenian general, Leosthenes, took charge of operations.[40] The Aetolians and Thessalians joined Athens as allies. In the winter of 323–322 Leosthenes occupied Thermopylae, Corinth and Argos joined the revolt, and Antipater found himself blockaded in the Thessalian town of Lamia. Demosthenes came home from exile in triumph; hopes ran high. But then things began to go wrong. Leosthenes was killed during the siege of Lamia by a sling stone from the walls. Antipater sent out emergency appeals for help, and some of them were answered.

Lysimachus was tied up by a local insurgence in Thrace, and Craterus, in Cilicia, preferred for the moment to play a waiting game. However, in the spring of 322 Leonnatus brought his army across the Hellespont, with ambitions of his own in mind, since Alexander's sister, Cleopatra, had written him with an offer of marriage, and he planned to "lay claim to Macedonia."[41] At the same time Cleitus, one of Craterus's commanders, was sent to take charge of the Macedonian fleet in the Aegean—a sensible move, since control of the sea was essential for victory in this campaign. Leonnatus was killed in a hard-fought cavalry engagement against the Thessalians,[42] the first of many Macedonian marshals to be eliminated from the power struggle; but Cleitus annihilated an Athenian fleet of over two hundred vessels off the island of Amorgos,[43] and Craterus himself—now free to cross the Aegean unimpeded, and perhaps sensing that the tide was on the turn—arrived in time to help defeat the allied Greek land forces at Crannon, in Thessaly (August 322). Athens, rather than stand siege, surrendered unconditionally to Antipater.[44]

Amorgos and Crannon marked the end of Athens as a serious political or military force in Greece. Her cry of "Freedom for the Greeks" had failed.[45] It is significant that the propertied classes, as a whole, had been against the war and in favor of Macedonian collaboration; it was the common people, the *plēthos*, who forced what they proudly called a Hellenic war. The division was symptomatic, and a foretaste of things to come.[46] The orator Demades, characteristically, had been angling, in secret, for an intervention by Perdiccas; Antipater found out about this only when Perdiccas's papers became available after his death. It has been suggested that Perdiccas must have already had wide secret contacts in Greece among the opponents of Craterus and Antipater.[47] Antipater, conscious of where his best support lay, went easy on wealthy Athenians in the terms he dictated: they kept their lands and possessions; he limited the franchise by making citizenship conditional on the possession of a minimum fortune of two thousand drachmas, thus slashing the voting population to a mere nine thousand. So much for freedom and democracy. He also shipped out twelve thousand impoverished Athenians to Thrace, and installed a Macedonian garrison in Piraeus.[48] Hypereides, who had been a passionate advocate of armed resistance, was hunted down and killed; Demosthenes escaped execution only by committing suicide.[49] An oligarchic government was imposed, led by Demades and the aged conservative Phocion (below, p. 40).

The Aetolians continued to resist in their mountain retreat, and Olympias, Alexander's mother, watching events from her homeland in Epirus, now (322/1) made them an offer of support—probably because Antipater and Craterus had taken the field against them.[50] Olympias cordially detested Antipater, who as viceroy had continually thwarted her during Alexander's lifetime. She also had every intention of seeing that young Alexander IV succeeded to the throne. Her best ally for this purpose was Perdiccas, who at least claimed to be maintaining the monarchy, and who certainly, at this point, was in charge of the kings. She therefore sent her daughter, Cleopatra, to Perdiccas in Sardis. The death of Alexander of Epirus had left Cleopatra an eligible widow (330); the death of Leonnatus, to whom she had made a written offer of marriage in return for aid against Antipater,[51] meant that she had no prior commitments. Dynastic marriages play a large part in this story: a union between Perdiccas and Cleopatra would have suited Olympias very well. Cleopatra, as Alexander's sister, was a prize worth winning, and in fact at one time or other was courted by most of the Successors; it is one of history's more piquant ironies that in the end she married none of them.[52]

Eumenes, for whatever motive, encouraged Perdiccas in this new matrimonial venture, and served him as a diplomatic go-between. The risks were high. Perdiccas, in the course of his rise to power, had courted and married Antipater's daughter Nicaea.[53] (Antipater, a true dynastic power-broker, disposed of his two other daughters, Phila and Eurydice, to Craterus and Ptolemy: a shrewd hedging of bets.)[54] But the offer of Cleopatra came as a fatal temptation. Perdiccas was convinced that "through her he could work on the Macedonians to help him gain supreme power."[55] At the same time he was anxious, for obvious reasons, to keep this new intrigue from Antipater's ears.

Enter now, on the Sardis scene, that redoubtable lady Cynane (also sometimes referred to as Cynna), Alexander's half-sister and the widow of Philip II's nephew Amyntas IV, with her hoydenish, ambitious daughter Adea in tow, whom she planned to marry off—as very much the dominant partner—to Philip Arrhidaios. Perdiccas took fright: this was a challenge to his own control of the kings. His adviser and friend Alcetas, who had sensibly steered him into marrying Nicaea, and was already in a highly nervous state over the Cleopatra affair, now lost his head completely and had Cynane assassinated.[56] At this point the Macedonian troops, who retained a strong and loyal affection for Philip II's kin, mutinied. Perdiccas was forced to let Cynane's daughter marry Philip Arrhidaios after all, adopting the traditional Macedonian royal name Eurydice when she did so. Still, Perdiccas's position in Asia, at least, was now greatly strengthened. After military victories in Pisidia and Cappadocia, where he won Eumenes' firm support by conquering his satrapy for him,[57] Perdiccas turned his attention to Antigonus One-Eye in central Phrygia. He knew—and Antigonus knew he knew—that Antigonus had, unforgivably, informed Antipater in advance of his son-in-law's plans to marry Cleopatra. Thus when Perdiccas called on Antigonus for an administrative and financial accounting of his stewardship, and followed this with a barrage of (probably trumped-up) charges, Antigonus, in alarm, left for Europe to join Antipater (Nov./Dec. 321). The news he brought of Perdiccas's activities—not least the threat that, on marrying Cleopatra, he would march on Macedonia as king, and rob Antipater of his office there—had immediate results.[58] Craterus and Antipater patched up a truce with the Aetolians, and at once set out for Asia. They also sent envoys to Ptolemy asking for his support. Antigonus seems to have crossed separately to Halicarnassus, perhaps as a diversionary tactic.[59] Eumenes, dispatched by Perdiccas to hold the Hellespont against Antipater and Craterus, made a great show of raising troops, but was mysteriously elsewhere when the invading armies arrived—for part of the time, at least, dancing attendance on Cleopatra at Sardis, and bringing her Perdiccas's gifts.[60] The crossing went off flawlessly: most of Perdiccas's supporting troops and allies, including Neoptolemus, another of Alexander's old marshals, now governor of Armenia, seem to have gone over *en masse* to the invaders.[61] Eumenes remained loyal, but he had showed a remarkable talent for not being in the wrong place at the wrong time.

Perdiccas at this point had every reason to feel paranoid suspicion, since it was clear to everyone, not least because of his marital intrigues, that he was planning a bid for the throne, and they reacted accordingly. By early 320 he had Antipater, Craterus, Lysimachus, and Antigonus One-Eye all lined up against him. This is a pattern that recurs several times during the initial struggles of the Successors: a bid for power by one leading marshal; a coalition of the rest to stop him. However, this coalition was not Perdiccas's only problem: he found it urgently necessary to deal with Ptolemy as well.[62] Ptolemy had not been idle since reaching Alexandria: he had already, without authorization, annexed the rich North African state of Cyrenaica, on his western marches.[63] He had also, very neatly, foreseen, and spiked, Perdiccas's ambitions. Macedonian custom decreed that to be king meant, *inter alia*, burying your predecessor. Ptolemy may have bribed the commander of the funeral cortege; we do not know. But in the end Alexander's body was neither taken home to be buried in the royal tombs at Aigai (mod. Vergina), nor was it conveyed—despite Alexander's own supposed last wish[64]—to the Siwah oasis. Ptolemy got it (? late summer 321), and kept it: first at Memphis, for a pharaoh's burial, and latterly in Alexandria, where it was kept on permanent display in a gold coffin, a quasi-magical good-luck charm and legitimizer of power.[65] Now, with impeccable timing, Ptolemy

Fig. 5. *Alexander's Funeral Cortege* by André Bauchant (1874–1958), an imaginative reconstruction painted in 1940, and loosely based on the ancient descriptive evidence (DS 18.26–28 *passim*).
Tate Gallery, London.

also threw his very considerable support behind the anti-Perdiccan coalition. Perdiccas, wrongly, suspected Ptolemy of aiming for sole control of the empire himself, a potential rival who had to be dealt with at once.

First, Perdiccas tried to get the army to condemn Ptolemy,[66] but this time-honored gambit failed. Ptolemy, too, was married to one of Antipater's three daughters. More important, he possessed vast reserves of treasure, taken over from his predecessor as satrap of Egypt, the Greek Cleomenes, who on Ptolemy's arrival had been demoted to the position of deputy.[67] Cleomenes, in the hope of getting his lucrative post back, had offered his services to Perdiccas as a secret agent. Ptolemy found this out, and thus had a nice excuse (if he needed one) for eliminating the mole in his entourage—not to mention for taking charge of the more than eight thousand talents of gold and silver (the talent being roughly 57 lbs. in weight) that Cleomenes had accumulated.[68]

So Perdiccas, in the spring of 320, left the government and defense of Asia in Eumenes' hands and marched south on Egypt, his confidence in the Greek apparently still unshaken after the fiasco at the Hellespont.[69] It seems likely that Ptolemy maintained an effective fifth column among his rival's troops.[70] In any case two thousand soldiers of the invading force were drowned in an attempted crossing of the Nile Delta, many more fell prey to crocodiles, and as a result Perdiccas, never the most personally popular of men, was murdered in his tent by a group of his own officers while Ptolemy and his army sat across the river and waited.[71] The incident can be dated sometime between 21 May and 19 June.[72]

The day after Perdiccas's murder, Ptolemy (who may well have been privy to the plot from the beginning) came over, provided the hungry Macedonians with fresh supplies, and in return was offered Perdiccas's position as guardian of the kingdom.[73] Being a canny survivor, he turned this tempting offer down; two of those responsible for Perdiccas's assassination, including Peithon, the satrap of Media (see above, p. 9), were appointed *pro tempore* to the supreme command instead.[74] Ptolemy's luck, as always, had held: only two days later news came through that on the borders of Cappadocia Eumenes had fought a great battle with Craterus and Neoptolemus, the renegade governor of Armenia, and had not only defeated them but had left them both dead on the battlefield, having himself slain Neoptolemus in single combat.[75] As Diodorus says, "if this news had broken two days before Perdiccas's end, no one would have dared raise a hand against Perdiccas, because of his great success."[76] So Leonnatus, Perdiccas, Craterus, and Neoptolemus were all gone now: the field was narrowing. The Macedonian army assembly in Egypt formally condemned Eumenes and fifty of his chief supporters to death—a neat piece of propaganda, since it meant that not only Eumenes himself, but all supporters of the Perdiccan faction, could henceforth be treated as rebels.[77] The condemnation also gave the other marshals, in particular Antigonus One-Eye, a quasi-juridical right of execution against Eumenes, though it took no less than five years to carry the sentence out.

The deaths of Perdiccas and, to a lesser extent, Craterus left a gap in the power structure, and in July 320 another meeting of the Successors was held, this time at Triparadeisos ("Three Parks"), in Syria.[78] The Macedonian army was in an awkward mood, apparently having marched north from Egypt without pay. Philip Arrhi-daios's ambitious young wife, Eurydice, stirred them up to demand immediate cash payments. Peithon and Arrhidaios, the temporary supreme commanders, wisely re-signed, and Antipater—the obvious, logical choice—was appointed guardian of the kings "with full powers" even before his arrival.[79] When he did appear, despite his great age he took prompt and vigorous action. He could not work miracles: there were no immediate funds available to pay Perdiccas's former troops, and Eurydice lost no time in exploiting the fact. But—after a near-lynching of the new *epimelētēs*—order was restored by Antigonus and Seleucus, using a mixture of firmness and con-ciliation; Eurydice was got under control, and Antipater worked out his settlement. The main plums he had to dispose of were, of course, the satrapal commands.[80]

Ptolemy he left where he was, "for it was impossible to shift him, because he appeared to be holding Egypt through his own prowess, as though it were land won by the spear."[81] Since Eumenes had been condemned by the army, and was in any case Perdiccas's sole surviving supporter of the first rank (some other Perdiccans now retreated to Tyre),[82] Antipater stripped him of his command in Cappadocia. At the same time he made Antigonus One-Eye commander-in-chief of the Macedonian army in Asia, with the specific assignment of winding up the war against Eumenes.[83] It may also have been now that, as an extra safeguard, Antipater married off his daughter Phila, Craterus's widow, to Antigonus's son Demetrius, the future Be-sieger (*Poliorkētēs*),[84] though without any great optimism about how long this would ensure Antigonus's support. Antipater was suspicious—rightly, as things turned out—of Antigonus's own ambitions: during the recent campaign he had shown him-self disturbingly independent. In the end, however, Cassander persuaded his father of Antigonus's loyalty, and Antipater left him most of his existing army in Asia Minor—with Cassander himself attached to the staff as cavalry chiliarch and watchdog, "to prevent Antigonus from pursuing his private interests undetected."[85] Antipater then set off back to Macedonia "to return the kings to their homeland." His outlook had always been European, indeed Macedonian: he had stayed at home during Alexander's Eastern expedition; at heart he wanted no truck with Asia. Superficially, the fiction of a single royal empire had been maintained. But in reality this balance-of-power deal already foreshadowed the triangular breakup of the empire, with Macedonia, Egypt, and Asia at the three points of the triangle. Ptolemy, Lysimachus, Cassander, and Antigonus One-Eye—not to mention Seleucus, the ex–cavalry commander (*hip-parchos*) now allotted the satrapy of Babylon (which appointment under Alexander would have meant demotion, but was now, in the new, less centralized climate, a distinct step up)—were none of them men to sit still and carry out orders for long, if at all.

Antigonus, to begin with, was quite happy in his allotted task of eliminating Eumenes, not least since this gave him ample opportunity to establish himself firmly in the Anatolian and eastern satrapies. One less rival, especially this slightly built, clever, elegant Greek,[86] who was regarded with something less than enthusiasm by Alexander's old guard, would be all to the good.

Eumenes is a fascinating and ambivalent figure. Our knowledge of him derives,

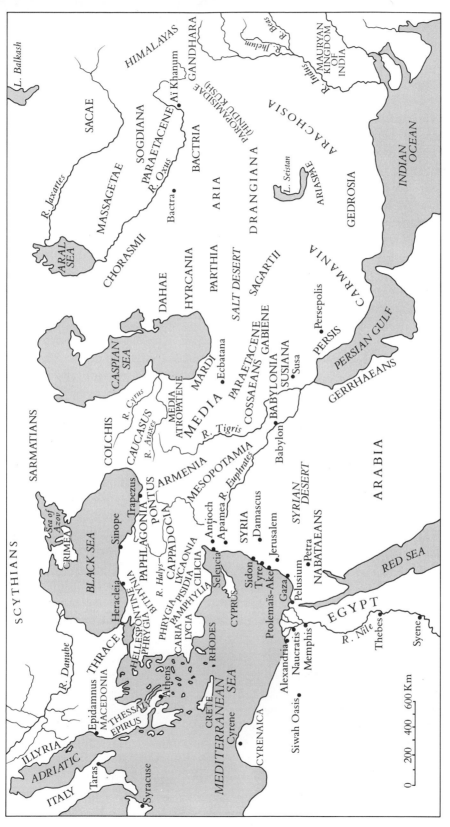

Map 1. Alexander's empire: the inheritance of the Successors.

ultimately, from his ultrapartisan friend (and possible kinsman) the historian Hiero-nymus of Cardia, who never loses an opportunity of singing his praises, highlight-ing his exploits, or denigrating his enemies.[87] Much of this material may well be true; even so, the overall record suggests that Eumenes, for all his virtues, was a more devious and self-seeking character than Hieronymus is disposed to admit. But then, the ambitious patriot, venal yet honorable, is no rare phenomenon in Greek history: Themistocles offers only the most striking example of the breed, while students of modern Greek politics have a whole range of candidates from which to choose. As chief secretary Eumenes had files on everyone, kept Alexander's correspondence, and probably knew more of his master's plans—not to mention his colleagues' weaknesses—than anyone else, now that the king himself was dead. He was married to a sister of Barsine, the Persian by whom Alexander had Heracles (see p. 7). He worked with genuine loyalty to preserve the royal succession, but this by no means precluded his advancing his own position in the process. Indeed, he seems even to have used his Greekness to some advantage.[88] Earlier, in 323, when Leonnatus had talked loosely to him about seizing power in Macedonia,[89] Eumenes had lost no time in informing on him to Perdiccas. His allegiances do sometimes have an air of *ad hoc* opportunism about them: when he backed Perdiccas in 322, did he really believe the *epimelētēs* in his protestations of loyalty to the kings?

Nevertheless, the modern fashion for discrediting all ancient testimony that sup-ports his honorable intentions can be overdone.[90] At the lowest level of self-seeking *Machtpolitik* it is clear that Eumenes, as a Greek, had to throw in his lot with the kings, since unlike a blue-blooded Macedonian baron he could not, short of emulat-ing Alexander, usurp the throne himself. However, some men are loyalists and roy-alists by conviction, and all the evidence at our disposal suggests that Eumenes was just such a man. What was more, despite jibes from the Macedonians about his cam-paigning with stylus and writing tablet,[91] he turned out a more than competent field commander. He was destroyed in the end only by repeated betrayals (the price of reliance on over-independent and quasi-mercenary commanders), and by the funda-mental greed-*cum*-xenophobia of Macedonian troops, who at heart resented being led by a smooth Greek intellectual, especially one who failed to bring them loot as well as victories. They may on one occasion have greeted him in Macedonian, as a kind of backhanded compliment, but they let him down badly during their first campaign against Antigonus in Cappadocia.[92] Left with no more than six hundred faithful followers, Eumenes was forced to flee to the impregnable hill fortress of Nora (spring 319), in the northern Taurus range, where he could hold out indefi-nitely.[93] Antigonus at once took over both his troops and his satrapy, and laid siege to Nora.

Further successes against Eumenes' colleagues Alcetas and Attalus (summer 319) now put Antigonus into so strong a position that he began seriously to envisage taking over the whole empire.[94] His dream was given powerful encouragement when, late in 319, he learned that the septuagenarian Antipater had finally died. On his deathbed he had arbitrarily bequeathed his office as *epimelētēs* to a loyal old Mace-donian officer, Polyperchon, a man of no great intelligence or achievement. (His intelligence may be judged by the fact that he promptly invited Olympias, of all people, back to Macedonia from Epirus as royal guardian of the young Alexander—a move he soon had cause to regret.)[95] Antipater's son Cassander, who had expected the appointment himself, and was not prepared to settle for the secondary post of chiliarch,[96] at once formed a coalition against Polyperchon. Its members included Ptolemy, who made a habit of opposing all strong, ambitious rivals, and now saw a chance to shore up his always-disputed frontier in Coele-Syria; Antigonus, who regarded himself as Alexander's destined successor; and Lysimachus, who quite simply wanted a bigger slice of the imperial pie than Thrace.[97]

Antigonus's first task, before any more ambitious undertaking, was to settle, one way or the other, with Eumenes. The Greek could be a very useful lieutenant, so Antigonus offered him alliance (318). Eumenes had already been making strenuous efforts to negotiate some sort of deal with Antipater: despite his difficult relations with the old viceroy, he clearly found Antigonus a far more threatening figure. Even before sending the historian Hieronymus to negotiate terms with Antipater in Macedonia, he had hinted broadly at his willingness to surrender to the right person.[98] But with Antipater's death and the defeat of the other Perdiccans, Eumenes was no longer in any position to bargain. Antigonus's offer of alliance, then, dictated by personal ambition though it clearly was, must have come as a godsend—just as Cassander's approach had to Antigonus himself.[99] Eumenes swore allegiance to Antigonus, and the siege of Nora was lifted (early summer 318). Clearly the army-imposed death sentence could be invoked or ignored as circumstances might dictate. Two or three months later, however, the Greek received letters in Cappadocia from Polyperchon and Olympias, offering him high office in the royalist forces being mustered against Antigonus and Cassander. Eumenes, whose natural sympathies (and best advantage) lay with the kings—or perhaps, more specifically, with Alexander's son—accepted.[100] The coalition patched up at Triparadeisos had now, to all intents and purposes, been abandoned: a new round in the struggle was beginning.

Despite a counteroffer from Antigonus, Eumenes finally made up his mind to throw in his lot with Polyperchon and play for the high stakes. Among the incentives offered him were a five-hundred-talent *douceur*, the title "general of Asia," which Antipater had bestowed on Antigonus in 321, and the command of the veteran Macedonian Silver Shields—the latter, as things turned out, a poisoned gift.[101] Eumenes and Antigonus fought a duel for the next two years (318–316/5): Eumenes had obviously calculated that if he could raise the Macedonian barons against Antigonus—and, incidentally, build up a record of victories sufficient to overcome the handicap of his being a mere Greek—he might well succeed to the substance, as well as the title, of Antigonus's command.

The campaign was a divided one, with Polyperchon operating in Greece, Eumenes in Asia. Polyperchon tried to whip up Greek support against Antipater's son Cassander by having the kings proclaim the restoration of the constitutions that Antipater had abolished after his victory at Crannon,[102] and thereby offer the prospect of peace for Hellas. The Greeks rightly interpreted this move as pure propaganda, since it ignored the key question of autonomy, and in effect reverted to the *status quo* of 323 rather than that prevailing before Chaeronea.[103] They therefore sided with Cassander, who rewarded their trust by returning Athens to a plutocracy nine months after its brief reversion to democratic rule in 318/7, notable chiefly for a series of vengeful purges (see p. 41). At least, as so often, the propertied classes benefited. Polyperchon, meanwhile, having lost his fleet to Antigonus and Cassander, campaigned in the Peloponnese. Eumenes won the good opinions of Macedonian troops in Asia by insisting that he, as a mere foreigner, had no claim to royal power himself, but was rather defending the kingdom in the name of the deified Alexander (claiming to have had dreams in which Alexander was alive and presiding over his council). Yet even so his position was a balancing act, and could not be sustained for ever. He even resorted to the trick—borrowed from Perdiccas, who had already played it at Babylon—of meeting with his commanders in the presence of Alexander's empty throne and regalia, as though the dead king were indeed still in command.[104] At the same time Polyperchon's fumbling campaign in Greece made little headway, and Antigonus realized that the quickest way to finish off both Polyperchon and Eumenes was to cut their communications by sea. This he accomplished with a crushing victory over Cleitus, in a naval battle off Byzantium (summer 317).[105] After this severance their final defeat was merely a matter of time.

Polyperchon, who now had physical control of young Alexander IV, was not helped by the intervention of that dreadful, and still dangerous, matriarch Olympias, hell-bent on seeing her grandson safely on the throne.[106] Unfortunately Philip Arrhidaios's wife, the too-ambitious Eurydice, had declared (early 317) for Cassander as regent, thereby provoking Olympias to invade Macedonia. Eurydice came out in full armor at the head of her troops to meet Olympias at the Macedonian-Epirot frontier. This was no masquerade: like her mother before her, Eurydice had been, most unusually, trained as a warrior.[107] But at the sight of Alexander's mother, backed by her Epirot levies and some of Polyperchon's troops as well, the Macedonians with Eurydice laid down their arms. Olympias, now unstoppable, lost no time in executing Philip Arrhidaios and forcing Eurydice to commit suicide (Oct.

Fig. 6. Olympias, mother of Alexander the Great. Gold medallion from Aboukir, Egypt (third century A.D.?). British Museum, London.

317), stating as her justification that she was avenging the supposed murder by poison of her son, Alexander. Antipater's son Iolaus (who had, it was rumored, given Alexander the poison as his cupbearer) was exhumed from his grave, and his ashes were scattered.[108] Using the same excuse, Olympias also executed about a hundred of Philip Arrhidaios and Eurydice's supporters.

This was horrible publicity: Polyperchon must have cursed himself for ever letting the dowager queen return from retirement in Epirus. Cassander, too, who had been campaigning in the Peloponnese, and had earlier that year (317) negotiated a settlement with Athens,[109] was now spurred into action. He invaded Macedonia, got a sentence of death pronounced by the Macedonian army on Olympias, drove her back into the city of Pydna, and there starved her into surrender (spring 315). His promise, made during the negotiations, to spare her life he ignored, and she was executed, perhaps by stoning.[110] Of Alexander's direct line only the young Alexander IV survived, and he was now in Cassander's custody. This in itself was a kind of long-term death sentence, since Cassander, however informally, had begun to act as king of Macedonia, and had no intention whatsoever of stepping down. He underlined his position by giving Philip Arrhidaios and Eurydice royal burial at Aigai, marrying Philip II's morganatic daughter, Thessalonike, and restoring Thebes, the city Alexander had destroyed in 335 *pour décourager les autres*.[111]

Meanwhile in Asia Antigonus had devoted two years (318–316) to hunting down Eumenes. Both rivals claimed to be "supreme commander in Asia," a nice instance of the emptiness of such titles during a power struggle unless backed up by superior force.[112] Despite the Greek's skill as a general and diplomat, Polyperchon's setback left him dangerously isolated. He was driven into the eastern satrapies, where despite other military support the Macedonian help he hoped for from Bactria-Sogdiana failed to materialize. The battle of Paraetacene (fall 316) proved indecisive. Finally (see above, p. 7), though still undefeated in the field, Eumenes was betrayed by his own men to Antigonus at Gabiene, and—after some hesitation on Antigonus's part—executed (316/5).[113] With his death, and that of Philip Arrhidaios, the struggle for the succession entered on a new phase, as Antigonus One-Eye made his final bid for supreme power, and the fiction of the unified empire was exploded once and for all.

CHAPTER 2

ANTIGONUS ONE-EYE'S
BID FOR EMPIRE, 316–301

By defeating Eumenes, Antigonus had consolidated his grip over a vast area extending from Asia Minor to the uplands of Iran. The fiction of special commands under the kings was still maintained, but Antigonus began to act uncommonly like an independent monarch. He removed Peithon from his office as satrap of Media, and had him liquidated, on a charge—possibly true—of planning revolt. To replace him he reverted to Alexander's old pattern of appointing a native satrap, in this case one Orontobates, but he also installed a Macedonian garrison commander.[1] The satrap of Persia, Peucestas, another of Alexander's old personal friends, had, uncharacteristically, gone native in dress and custom, and was immensely popular locally as a result: Antigonus discreetly kicked him upstairs with the promise of high office, and made sure he was kept from then on at headquarters, where he could not get up to any mischief.[2] Other veteran officers were executed on various pretexts, or killed while attempting alleged insurrections.

More alarming still were Antigonus's systematic raids on the treasuries of Ecbatana, Persepolis, and Susa, from which he removed a total of no less than twenty-five thousand talents.[3] Nor was the lesson of Eumenes' betrayal lost on him. The Silver Shields, who had sold Eumenes to Antigonus in return for their loot, could never be trusted again. A new mercenary age was dawning, in which an army would regularly sell itself, as a matter of course, to the general who defeated it; but even among mercenaries the Silver Shields were a special case. Antigonus posted the more reliable of these veterans to his phalanx brigade, and then had a quiet word with Sibyrtios, the satrap of Arachosia, a tough frontier region south of the Hindu Kush, on the borders of modern-day Afghanistan and Pakistan. In return for confirmation in his office, Sibyrtios was to dispose of the hardest cases among the Silver Shields. They were to be posted to Arachosia, and sent out, a detachment at a time, on garrison, scouting, or other front-line duties in which they were sure to be killed.[4] Finally, the axe seemed about to fall on Seleucus, the satrap of Babylonia. Ordered to give an accounting of his office by Antigonus (who had clearly learned

21

Fig. 7. Aerial view of Susa.
Oriental Institute, University of Chicago.

Fig. 8. Aerial view of the palace terrace, Persepolis.
Oriental Institute, University of Chicago.

something from Perdiccas's methods), Seleucus prudently fled to Ptolemy in Egypt (late summer 315).[5]

Antigonus was thus left controlling virtually the whole of Alexander's Asian empire; he was, further, supported by numerous mercenaries, and could afford to pay them on a long-term basis. Needless to say, his high-handed moves caused great alarm among his fellow marshals. Seleucus lost no time in warning Ptolemy—not to mention Cassander in Macedonia, and Lysimachus in Thrace—that Antigonus was purging all Alexander's old officers, had acquired immense wealth, "and as a result had displayed overweening arrogance, so that his ambitions now embraced the entire Macedonian kingdom."[6]

Meanwhile Antigonus himself marched down into northern Syria (315/4). On the way he raided another ten thousand talents from the treasury at Cyinda, in Cilicia; since he held the kings' commission as commander-in-chief, it was hard to argue with him (whatever counterclaims Cassander might make in Greece), and the Persians were already treating him as "the acknowledged lord of Asia." He also received eleven thousand talents in the form of annual tribute.[7] In Syria he was met by envoys with an ultimatum from Lysimachus, Ptolemy, and Cassander.[8] He was to restore Seleucus to his Babylonian satrapy; he was to surrender Syria to Ptolemy, and Hellespontine Phrygia to Lysimachus. This last was a particularly outrageous condition, since it would have given Lysimachus—whose titular claim to this area was nonexistent—a stranglehold over the Hellespont. There may also have been a clause (the text of Diodorus is uncertain) requesting the cession of Lycia and Cappadocia to Cassander. Antigonus was, further, to share out all treasures taken since the death of Eumenes. He gave the envoys, not surprisingly, "a somewhat rough answer." His flat rejection of their terms was inevitable: it also meant war.

Confident and aggressive, Antigonus pressed on south to Phoenicia.[9] If there was to be war, he would be ready for it. His vast cash reserves—over 45,000 talents—dwarfed those of his opponents. He had one great weakness, the lack of a fleet: Seleucus could—and did—sail past his camp with impunity. Nothing daunted, Antigonus now set up shipyards at Tripolis, Byblos, and Sidon, as well as on the Cilician coast; he also made a deal with the Rhodian government to build vessels for him from imported timber (see p. 32).[10] Like Alexander, he bivouacked near Old Tyre, and laid siege to Tyre itself, though to begin with he made little headway against the citadel; that was strongly held by Ptolemy's troops, many of them formerly in the service of Perdiccas. Antigonus secured alliances with some of the princes of Cyprus, a counterweight against Nicocreon and other local kings, who since 321 had had treaties with Ptolemy.[11] He stormed Joppa and Gaza. He sent his nephew—another Ptolemy—to settle affairs in Cappadocia and to guard the Hellespont against a possible crossing by Cassander. He even sent a mission to Polyperchon in the Peloponnese,[12] naming him generalissimo there, for what that was worth,[13] sweetening the offer with a thousand talents (which by now he could well afford), and encouraging the old commander to carry on the war against Cassander in Greece. He set up a system of beacons and dispatch carriers throughout the eastern Mediterranean to speed up communications.[14] His energy and determination were boundless.

Fig. 9. The cedars of Lebanon: one of the few remaining stands, at Bsharre, 1,960 meters above sea level. Throughout the Hellenistic period, they provided ambitious conquistadors—such as Antigonus—with an ample supply of shipbuilding timber.
National Council for Tourism, Lebanon.

Perhaps most important, from Old Tyre Antigonus issued a public political (and, from his own viewpoint, juridically binding) manifesto before his assembled troops, who gave it a semblance of Macedonian legitimacy by acclaiming it.[15] The main points of this so-called Decree of the Macedonians were as follows. First, Cassander—who, Antigonus asserted, had murdered Olympias, married Philip II's illegitimate daughter, Thessalonike, by force, and was trying to make a bid for the throne of Macedon—was to be declared a public enemy unless he destroyed the cities of Cassandreia (Potidaea) and Thebes, both of which he had rebuilt,[16] released Roxane and Alexander IV "and gave them back to the Macedonians" (whatever that meant; presumably to Antigonus himself and his supporters), and "in short, obeyed Antigonus, the properly appointed general, who had taken over the guardianship [*epimeleia*] of the monarchy"—a peculiarly brazen claim, since young Alexander IV and his mother had been in Cassander's keeping ever since 317/6 (see p. 20). Second, all the Greek cities were to be free, autonomous, and ungarrisoned: this clause applied both to those on the mainland and to the cities of Asia.

It is this second provision that was of real significance. The perennial, and virtually insoluble, problem it enshrined was that of somehow reconciling the cities' pas-

Fig. 10. Aerial view of Tyre, seen from the west-northwest. Alexander's original
causeway (top left) has widened over the centuries through the accumulation of silt.
From P. M. Green, *Alexander the Great,* London and New York, 1970.

sion for self-determination with the autocratic powers exercised by the great
Hellenistic monarchies.[17] Polyperchon had handled the question by means of a reversionary amnesty decree from which the words "freedom" and "autonomy" were
conspicuously absent (see p. 18). Antigonus's gesture, then, was something new.
How far he and his son Demetrius after him were sincere in their championship of
Greek freedom is debatable. The propaganda value to them, and the embarrassment
to their rivals (Cassander in particular), were both immense. What was more, the
good will of the Greek cities not only eased the collection of revenues, but also mad
available a vast pool of skilled labor. Both rulers, for whatever reason, held fast to
the new slogan throughout their lives. We should note that neither freedom nor autonomy meant exemption from taxes or tribute (*aphorologēsia*): it was the Roman
general Flamininus who made that welcome addition to the formula (see p. 311).[18]
Autonomy was indeed synonymous with *polis* rule, and a vital condition for its survival;[19] but the anomalous, not to say paradoxical, position of these cities in the context of a bureaucratic and authoritarian central government meant, in the vast majority of cases, that their much-touted freedom was illusory, a matter of empty
honorific titles, parochial offices, municipal privileges, votes that lacked power,

form without substance. There were exceptions (Rhodes is a notable instance, but Rhodes was a special case: see p. 378); exceptions, however, they remained.

As soon as he heard what Antigonus had done, Ptolemy issued (fall 313) a similar proclamation, "wanting the Greeks to know that he, no less than Antigonus, had their autonomy in mind."[20] There is an interesting contrast here. Antigonus could make his offer look plausible enough, since the Greek cities of Asia were already free, democratic, and ungarrisoned. On the other hand, Cassander, Lysimachus, and Ptolemy all held cities down with garrisons and oligarchies. It is interesting to speculate just why Ptolemy—who was, after all, Cassander's ally—should have come out with so embarrassing a pronouncement at this point. The most likely explanation is, Ptolemy had already foreseen that his ultimate adversary would be whoever triumphed in the confrontation between Cassander and Antigonus:[21] no bad thing, then, to furnish himself good propaganda as a defender of liberty well in advance.

Needless to say, none of these ambitious rivals hesitated for one moment to trample on every Greek liberty in sight when the situation called for tough or emergency measures. Even if we concede Antigonus, as I think we must, both consistency and sincerity in his policy of freedom for Greece, it still remains true that his prime concern was the strategic consolidation of his own power.[22] In furtherance of this aim he now promoted, as a counterweight to Cassander's Athens, the so-called League of Islanders (314?). This organization drew its membership from the Cycladic islands of the central Aegean, and had its center on Delos.[23] (Whether Delos itself was a member is disputed, though the island remained under Antigonid control until 286.) The League offered useful reinforcement to Antigonus's still-weak naval arm: there is evidence that the islanders defended their territories against his enemies. At the same time Antigonus kept up a flow of cash, troops, and agents into Greece, attempting to rouse the Greek cities against Cassander. Finally, after a lengthy siege, he also forced the capitulation of Tyre (June 313).[24]

The first round of the struggle lasted until 311. Antigonus, like Perdiccas in 321, found himself fighting a war on two fronts, around the Hellespont and in Syria. There was, as well, inconclusive activity in mainland Greece and in parts of the eastern Mediterranean, where Antigonus and Ptolemy vied for control of Rhodes and Cyprus. Revolts in Cyprus and Cyrenaica kept Ptolemy busy until 312,[25] but he was then persuaded by Seleucus—impatient to recover his command at Babylon—to chance a showdown against Antigonus's son Demetrius in the Gaza Strip. Demetrius, young, tall, exceptionally handsome, was married to Craterus's widow, Phila (see p. 15), one of those brilliant, forceful women whom we meet again and again among the Hellenistic ruling classes.[26] At Gaza he proved no match for Ptolemy (late 312),[27] losing five hundred of his best troops killed and eight thousand captured, with Ptolemy's war elephants wreaking havoc among his cavalry.[28]

This victory gave Seleucus the chance (borrowing troops from Ptolemy for the purpose) to return to his fief in the East. Encouraged by oracles and dreams that hailed him, Macbeth-like, as a future king, Seleucus, in quick order, recaptured Babylon, won over Media and Susiana, and began writing to Ptolemy with some-

Fig. 11. Seleucus I Nicator (?). Silver
tetradrachm minted at Susa
ca. 305/4–301 B.C. The bull's horn and
ear are symbolic of superhuman
strength. The panther skin may allude
to Dionysus's conquest of India,
emulated both by Alexander and by
Seleucus himself: some scholars identify
the portrait as Alexander.
British Museum, London.

thing very like royal panache about his achievements.[29] Ptolemy himself did not
capitalize on his victory at Gaza. The news of it at once drew Antigonus down to
Syria from Asia Minor; but Seleucus's successes made an immediate campaign undesirable. Antigonus was reunited with his son Demetrius, who had extracted himself from his defeat with reasonable skill, and a general peace began to look attractive
to all involved—not least to Ptolemy, who had no liking for another round in Syria
with Antigonus. The terms of the treaty (311) were little more than a rationalization
of the *status quo*.[30] Cassander was to be "general of Europe" until Alexander IV came
of age: the royal succession was, officially at least, still being kept alive, though the
signatories to the treaty dealt with each other as *de facto* independent rulers, and Cassander was shortly to lay the whole pious fiction to rest—along with the surviving
Argeads. Lysimachus was confirmed in Thrace, Ptolemy in Egypt and the adjacent
regions, while Antigonus was to be "first in rank in all Asia," a significantly vague
phrase[31] that took no account of Seleucus's aggressive campaigning in the eastern
satrapies.

Seleucus, in point of fact, now very much master of his own fief again, was not a
party to the peace treaty at all: he and Antigonus remained at war until 309/8.[32] Nor,
we may note, was Polyperchon, that blunt old royalist officer out of his depth in
these new power games, but doing his level best to learn the tricks of blackmail,
murder, and betrayal along with his juniors. Bribed by Antigonus, as we have seen,
with the offer of the command in the Peloponnese against Cassander, he found himself deserted by his own son Alexander (who went over to Cassander's side: 315/4?),
and seems to have followed him in 313. We have not yet heard the last of him.

Finally, by the peace of 311 the Greek cities were formally declared autonomous,
and were required, on oath, to preserve each other's freedom at need. We possess an
official (and in places carefully vague) letter from Antigonus to the city of Scepsis, in
the Troad, touting the peace as a triumph, stressing his concern with the citizens'
freedom, and, predictably, making no allusion to Demetrius's humiliating defeat at

Gaza.[33] (Scepsis in return promptly offered Antigonus, now over seventy, divine honors.)[34] The oaths sworn by all contracting parties may well have persuaded Antigonus that he could use the Greek *poleis* as a powerful extra political or military force if he could claim infringement of the treaty by any of his rivals. He would, on the other hand, have no hesitation about taking a tough line with any city that used its freedom against *him*. In any case, the treaty lasted almost no time at all, and the freedom clause proved to be little more than a political chimaera. All the marshals by now controlled various Greek cities—Antigonus in Anatolia and the Aegean, Lysimachus in Thrace, Ptolemy in Cyrenaica and on Rhodes and Cyprus, Cassander in Greece itself. None of them would ever let these power bases revert to true independence: in other words, each signatory to the treaty would have a fine excuse for war whenever he needed it. Once again, despite the preservation of the regency, it was clear—clearer than ever—that there were five virtually independent fiefs, those of Ptolemy, Antigonus, Lysimachus, Cassander, and Seleucus. Yet at least three of the five lords—Antigonus, Lysimachus, Seleucus—still nursed the ambition of winning the whole of Alexander's empire. In this they were, to some extent, abetted by the treaty of 311, with its diplomatic fiction of an undivided inheritance under Alexander IV.[35] It was to be another decade before that dream was finally laid to rest.

For both Antigonus and Ptolemy, in fact, the peace of 311 was no more than a truce, a breathing space. Ptolemy was eager to recover the whole satrapy of Syria, and with it Phoenicia, where Demetrius had been quietly reestablishing his power. Though Antigonus wanted to take advantage of peace in the West to deal with Seleucus, he remained in hot competition with Ptolemy for the islands and ports of the Aegean and eastern Mediterranean. By 310 Ptolemy was accusing Antigonus of infringing on the freedom of the Greek cities of Cilicia,[36] while Cassander, tired of playing royal guardian, brought some honesty into the power struggle by having the young Alexander and his mother, Roxane, executed. (Theories that they were only executed much later or that Cassander contrived to keep their deaths secret until 306 [!] lack persuasiveness.)[37] From now on, as Diodorus says, "all those who ruled nations or cities nursed royal hopes."[38] But the Argead mystique died hard, and it was four years before a new claim to kingship, based primarily on achievement, emerged and was upheld. Antigonus, with opportunistic cynicism equal to Cassander's, furnished old Polyperchon with one final ace to play in the royalist stakes: Heracles, Alexander's illegitimate son by Barsine, now about sixteen years old.[39] Polyperchon, with this new claimant to the throne in tow, made a spirited bid to invade Macedonia. Cassander, who had not cut short the legitimate bloodline in order to have his well-laid plans disrupted by a bastard, promptly sized up Polyperchon's limitations with uncommon finesse, and did a deal with him. He confirmed him in the Peloponnese, and left him the empty title of general (*stratēgos*); what he asked in return was the murder of Heracles.[40] Polyperchon duly obliged, and from that moment, like the old soldier he was, faded away. His bargaining counter gone, he languished in subordinate positions, and by 302 was dead; how or when we do not know. But with Heracles' death, and the murder—on Antigonus's orders—of Alexander's marriage-hunting sister, Cleopatra, in Sardis a year later (309/8),[41] the Argead line of Philip and Alexander was finally at an end. The time was ripe to recognize a few new royal dynasties; but they still took their time in appearing.

Antigonus's attempt to deal with Seleucus failed, and that failure led to the old marshal's undoing.[42] Antigonus's general Nicanor met Seleucus in a great battle: we can pinpoint neither its exact location nor its date, but it was somewhere in the eastern satrapies about 309/8, and Seleucus was victorious. If 312 was afterwards remembered as the first regnal year of the Seleucid dynasty[43]—being the year in which Seleucus retook Babylon from Antigonus's forces—then this victory finally assured the dynasty's survival, even though Seleucus did not officially assume the diadem till 305. Antigonus was forced to abandon any hope of recovering Alexander's eastern conquests beyond Anatolia. He seems, indeed, to have made a nonaggression pact with Seleucus, since from 308 Seleucus was in conflict with Chandragupta (known to our Greek sources as Sandrakottos), the Indian founder of the Mauryan empire, and in 303 ceded him the satrapies of Gandhara, eastern Arachosia, and Gedrosia in exchange for intermarriage rights and a gift of five hundred war elephants.[44] When the final showdown came between Antigonus and his rivals, those elephants played a crucial part in securing the victory (see p. 34).

The struggle between Antigonus and Ptolemy for the control of the Mediterranean continued. Ptolemy—who seems earlier to have been at least in diplomatic communication with Seleucus[45]—accused Antigonus of garrisoning supposedly free cities (310), though at the same time he was setting up a command post of his own on Cos. Antigonus, ignoring the complaint, strained every nerve to build up a large fleet.[46] Events in the years between 310 and 306 are confusing, since Cassander's deal with Polyperchon produced, by way of reaction, a brief alliance between Ptolemy and Antigonus, the main rivals. This, however, was a mere expedient aberration. Ptolemy made an abortive invasion of the Peloponnese (308), his sole venture on the Greek mainland,[47] gaining little except some garrisoned keypoints near the Isthmus (Corinth, Sicyon, Megara): bad propaganda, in any case, for a self-styled liberator of Greece. Soon afterwards Antigonus sent Demetrius to free Athens from Cassander, which he did (307), to freedom-loving cheers from the populace. The city was now refortified and strengthened in anticipation of the coming conflict with Macedon (the so-called Four Years' War, 307–304).[48] Though an attempt at this time to organize the Greek states into an anti-Cassandran league, reminiscent of that set up by Philip II, proved premature, Athenians had no qualms about offering their new earthly savior divine honors—perhaps because of the timber for a hundred triremes that he promised them from Syria. Had Cassander, as seems likely, cut off Athenian imports of Macedonian lumber? At all events the wood (probably Cypriot pine) was delivered, and Athens paid 14,040 drachmas for its transport.[49] The puppet dictator Demetrius of Phaleron (see p. 48) went into exile, and a democratic government (but one under Antigonus's control) was set up.

This venture, however, marked the limits of the cooperation between Antigonus and Ptolemy. Warfare broke out between them again almost immediately, first

Fig. 12. Demetrius Poliorcetes ("the Besieger"). Silver tetradrachm struck in the mint at Salamis (Cyprus) after 301 to commemorate his naval victory there in 306 B.C. The obverse shows Victory (Nike) on the prow of a warship, blowing a trumpet. The reverse carries the inscription "King Demetrius" and shows Poseidon, chlamys folded on one arm, trident poised to strike.
British Museum, London. Photo Hirmer.

off Cyprus, where Demetrius, fresh from the fleshpots of Athens, equipped with new, large vessels, and posing once more as a liberator,[50] inflicted a crushing and immensely significant defeat on Ptolemy's forces (306); and then in Egypt, where Ptolemy, rallying gamely from the greatest setback of his career, was lucky to beat off a full-scale invasion.[51] He might write jauntily to his allies, Cassander in particular, "about his successes and the mass of deserters who had joined him,"[52] but he made no mention of Cyprus, which for the next decade passed under Antigonid control. Demetrius struck coinage at the Cypriot mint in Salamis that showed Poseidon wielding his trident and, on the reverse, Nike (Victory) alighting on the prow of a trireme.[53] The point was well taken.

Demetrius's victory in Cyprus also marked the final step in the emergence of the independent Hellenistic kingdoms of the Successors, the establishment of new royal dynasties.[54] The delay in taking such a step (it was, after all, four years since the murder of Alexander IV) has often been remarked, and is indeed significant. It is surely to be explained by the profound differences observable between the old Macedonian national and territorial kingship and the new reliance on simple military achievement: the Ptolemies and Seleucids had been brought up under the old regime, but they claimed their thrones on the new terms established by Alexander. The change took time to work out, let alone get used to. But now, to celebrate their Cypriot victory, which was made the clear justification for such pretensions, Antigonus took the title of king (*basileus*), and bestowed it also on his triumphant son. The affair was skillfully stage-managed. From now on both wore the diadem and the royal purple.

Fig. 13. Ptolemy I Soter. Silver tetradrachm minted at Alexandria ca. 305–300 B.C. The diadem indicates a period after Ptolemy's assumption of kingship.
Bibliothèque Nationale, Paris. Cabinet des Médailles. Photo Jean Roubier.

Thus, even if Antigonus did not lay claim to the heritage of Alexander, which is debatable,[55] he at least formally established the concept of the Antigonid dynasty, and on the basis of military achievement rather than territorial claims. Not to be left behind, within a year or so both Ptolemy and Seleucus had each also proclaimed himself king (305/4);[56] so, apparently, did Lysimachus. Even Cassander, despite Plutarch's reservations as to whether he claimed the title officially,[57] is referred to as "King Cassander" on coins, and is described on a bronze statue base at Dion as "Cassander, King of the Macedonians."[58] That he was now recognized as king seems certain (306; see below). At last, after almost two decades, Alexander's officers were reaching out beyond his gigantic shadow.

It is usually said that, of all these crowned heads, only Antigonus still dreamed of ascending the throne of a united empire, and thus fiercely contested the claims of his fellow monarchs. It is true that not only Antigonus, but also Demetrius, refused the title of king to the rest; it is also true that the Antigonids persisted in claiming kinship with the Argeads.[59] But while the others—if territorial claims came into it at all—were primarily serving notice of ownership on specific areas (e.g., Ptolemy in Egypt, Lysimachus in Thrace), and were thus quite happy to recognize one another's titles, did that mean that they would refuse imperial supremacy if the chance offered itself? And were they not, in any case, anxious to avoid being thought inferior to Antigonus? As we shall see, the dream of empire could still overpower Lysimachus and Seleucus, even if they were ready, as good pragmatists, to settle for shorter horizons until, or unless, fortune smiled on their endeavors.[60]

The future was to lie with the separatists; but Antigonus, for one, still cherished greater hopes. After all, his kingship at present remained a rather elusive concept, and his son Demetrius was to be for some years a king virtually without a physical kingdom. The title "king," not least in the East, could still compel obedience in a way that other names could not;[61] but these new monarchies seem not only to have been predicated on the dynasty rather than the territory, if any, that it controlled, but also to have been seen as personal prizes for military and diplomatic success. The entry "monarchy" (*basileia*) in the *Suda*, a Byzantine lexicon, enshrines this tradition: "It is neither descent nor legitimacy that gives monarchies to men, but the ability to command an army and to handle affairs competently." It is surely no accident that Ptolemy refrained from assuming royal status at least until he had beaten Antigonus back from the gates of Egypt.[62] The nearest of them all to a traditional territorial monarch was Cassander, who in at least two inscriptions, as we have seen, is described as "King of the Macedonians."[63] And it was Cassander against whom Antigonus and Demetrius soon concentrated their forces.

First, however, Antigonus was anxious to establish complete control of the sea lanes, and to achieve this end there was one island bastion, still fiercely independent, that he would have to reduce: Rhodes. Officially neutral, the Rhodians had made treaties with all the competing dynasts,[64] and by trading undisturbed all round the Mediterranean had become immensely wealthy, putting down pirates—which got them in everyone's good books—and carefully avoiding commitment in the matter of Alexander's funeral games.[65] However, they did in the end lean toward Ptolemy, since the bulk of their revenues came from trade with Egypt, and since they got most of their food there. But though they had refused to take part in the Cyprus campaign,[66] their plea of neutrality cut no ice with Antigonus, who was ready to find any excuse to reduce the island, and to jettison fine talk of freedom and autonomy in the process. This is perhaps not surprising, since earlier he had won valuable concessions from the Rhodians (315–312; see p. 23), including the operation of a shipyard, the use of warships, and some kind of military alliance.[67] He nearly scared them into surrender without a fight, but then insisted both on getting a hundred of their noblest citizens as hostages, and on having access to their harbor for his fleet (summer 305). The Rhodians decided to resist, and Antigonus sent Demetrius with a strong force to reduce them.[68] Demetrius had nearly four hundred ships, as well as great siege towers—including the famous city stormer (*helepolis*), over a hundred feet high and with a sixty-foot base[69]—torsion catapults, rams, fire arrows, and other new mechanical devices. The siege dragged on inconclusively for a year,[70] and in the end there was a compromise peace: the Rhodians finally surrendered their hundred hostages, and agreed to ally themselves with Antigonus except in any war against Ptolemy. In return they were left autonomous, ungarrisoned, and (what was for them most important) in possession of their own revenues. This successful defense was the basis for the influence they were to exercise, as a free and independent naval power, for the next century. In gratitude to Ptolemy, who had not only kept them victualed throughout the siege but had also sent them valuable military aid,

Fig. 14. Demetrius Poliorcetes ("the
Besieger"), horned and wearing
diadem. Silver tetradrachm minted
at Amphipolis, 290/89 B.C.
British Museum, London. Photo Hirmer.

they established a cult of Ptolemy the Savior (*Sōtēr*);[71] and to commemorate the raising of the siege they commissioned a giant statue of Helios, the so-called Colossus of Rhodes, which stood at the entrance to the harbor and was numbered among the Seven Wonders of the ancient world. This short-lived monument to gigantism (it was shaken down by an earthquake ca. 227 B.C.) stood 105 feet high, took twelve years to complete, and cost three hundred talents, the proceeds from the sale of Demetrius's siege engines. Few people, we are told, could embrace its thumb. A convenient oracle, doubtless to the Rhodians' great relief, forbade its reerection, though the *disiecta membra* long remained a tourist attraction.[72] Contrary to general belief, it did not bestride the mouth of the harbor.

One reason Antigonus and Demetrius had raised the siege of Rhodes was to have a free hand in Greece against Cassander, who from his base on Euboea was making constant raids on Athens and the surrounding countryside.[73] Demetrius, now tagged with the ambivalent title "the Besieger" (*Poliorkētēs*), seized the Isthmus of Corinth (304/3), robbed Cassander not only of Corinth, but also of Chalcis in Euboea, won all Arcadia except for Mantinea, wrested Sicyon from Ptolemy's garrison, conquered Achaea, and installed a Macedonian garrison on Acrocorinth, which remained there over sixty years as a permanent safeguard, until Aratus removed it in 243 (see p. 151). Sparta, however, he prudently left alone.[74] Meanwhile Antigonus was busy with administrative problems in Asia Minor. We possess two letters he wrote—*qua* adviser, but nevertheless clearly expecting compliance—about the proposed merger (*synoikismos*, "synoecism") between the communities of Teos and Lebedos in Ionia. The population of Lebedos was to be transferred *en bloc* to a new common site, and the letters go into endless detail—fiscal, legal, economic—about just what such a move would entail. Even if Antigonus merely endorsed plans drawn up by a corps of secretaries, these interminable recommendations on ground rents and allocation of houses, civil lawsuits and public services by individuals (*leitourgiai*), the grain-reserve fund and the assessing of taxes, strongly remind us that he—like other Hellenistic rulers—was a good deal more than a mere condottiere, the warlord suggested by our literary sources.[75] But this particular synoecism was never in fact carried out. In 302 Teos was conquered for Cassander, and in the following year Antigonus's death at Ipsus left all his administrative plans void.

By the spring of 302 Demetrius was, after his successes, at last in a position to revive something like the old League of Corinth, which Philip II and Alexander had established and controlled—though whereas Philip's league had been an alliance of Macedon with the Greeks, what Demetrius envisaged was a Greek alliance against Macedon.[76] He saw it as excellent propaganda; besides, to establish, if not a common peace (*koinē eirēnē*), at least a general alliance (*symmachia*) through the League not only would facilitate the subsequent control of Greece, but—more immediately important—would serve as a political base from which to launch an all-out attack on Cassander and Macedonia.[77] To organize Greece in such a way that it would willingly defend itself against their rivals was a regular policy of the Macedonian kings.[78] Idealistic attempts to interpret the League of 302 as the instrument for creating a "United States of Greece" are fundamentally mistaken.

The League duly elected Demetrius the Besieger its captain-general, and he marched north with the intention of finishing off Cassander. Here he and his father missed a great opportunity. Cassander desperately sued for peace, but Antigonus, to whom he applied, held out for unconditional surrender.[79] This Cassander understandably balked at; and his refusal left him with only one possible option, a coalition with Antigonus's other opponents, Ptolemy, Seleucus, and Lysimachus. They welcomed him with open arms.[80] The allies had a bold strategy: the defense of Macedonia was abandoned in order to draw both Demetrius and Antigonus together into Asia Minor. Antigonus, now over eighty and vastly corpulent, seeing final success at last within his grasp, took the bait and summoned Demetrius from Europe for a decisive test of strength. While Ptolemy, in a (largely self-serving) diversionary tactic, invaded Syria,[81] Lysimachus, Cassander, and Seleucus brought Antigonus and Demetrius to battle at Ipsus, in Phrygia (301).[82] Seleucus's Indian war elephants carried all before them.[83] Demetrius, though he led a successful cavalry charge, was so carried away with the excitement of victory that he left the main body, and was never able to get back (partly, again, because of Seleucus's elephants) to rescue his father, who fell, mortally wounded. Without Demetrius, and with Antigonus dead, the battle was lost.

Demetrius fled to Ephesus. Apart from the powerful fleet that Antigonus had built up with such care, his assets were now limited to Cyprus and a scatter of coastal cities. The allies were left to parcel out Antigonus's domain among them, "cutting it up like a huge carcass," as Plutarch says, "and each taking his slice."[84] Lysimachus took most of Asia Minor (thus at last gaining control over both sides of the Hellespont) as far as the Taurus Mountains, except for parts of Lycia, Pamphylia, and Pisidia, which were variously held by Demetrius and Ptolemy. Ptolemy's Palestinian campaign had netted him the whole of Syria and Phoenicia south from Aradus and Damascus; Seleucus soon arrived, insisting that under the victors' agreement Coele-

Syria should be his, and hinting fairly broadly (when Ptolemy complained that he had been omitted from the share-out) that those who fought at Ipsus should have the sole right to dispose of the spoils.[85] For the moment this frontier problem was settled amicably; but Coele-Syria, as we shall see, was destined to become a bone of contention between Ptolemies and Seleucids for centuries. Cassander made no claims in Asia, but expected a free hand in Europe.

The removal of Antigonus One-Eye, it is often said,[86] marked the end of an era. Yet the ghost of Alexander's empire proved singularly hard to lay, and it was to be another twenty years and more before the final bids for supreme power were made and defeated. Only then did the lasting pattern of the Successor kingdoms become clear, and the overriding mood of the Hellenistic age—dynastic autocracy in public affairs, commercial or intellectual disengagement in private life—begin to establish itself throughout the Greek world. At this point it may be advantageous to look back a little, to see how these conflicts affected a single city that had once, but no longer, stood at the center of Aegean affairs: Athens.

CHAPTER 3
DEMETRIUS OF PHALERON: THE PHILOSOPHER-KING IN ACTION

Athens has entered this narrative so far only in a tangential way. We have watched the conflicts of the Successors in Greece, and seen their impact on Athens, but exclusively from the outside. It will be beneficial now to alter the perspective and the viewpoint, to see how a once-dominant Greek *polis*, now subject to Macedonian overlordship and torn by crippling class enmities, reacted to the larger struggles that followed Alexander's death. When Antipater imposed the new oligarchy on Athens after the defeat at Crannon in 322, when an activist like Hypereides was tortured before execution while Antipater looked on,[1] when Polyperchon claimed to have restored the old constitution, when Cassander in his turn imposed new restrictions, when Phocion fell victim to the vengeful mob, when Demetrius of Phaleron ruled as a Macedonian-backed puppet dictator (with, what was worse, Peripatetic pretensions of being the "Good Tyrant"),[2] when Antigonus's son, that other, more famous Demetrius, once more restored the democracy, such as it was by then, only to billet his smart mistresses in the back chamber of the Parthenon[3]—how did Athenians react? What was their attitude toward the old burning questions of free speech, majority government, self-determination, the claims of the state, the rights of citizens?

The bitter truth, which they concealed from themselves as long as they could, and to a quite striking extent, was that they had become politically impotent. How, after long years of power, did that impotence manifest itself? One inevitable result of the Macedonian victory was an exacerbation of the long-simmering hostility between the Athenian *dēmos* and those wealthy, aristocratic ultras and commercial entrepreneurs who emerged as natural collaborators with Macedonia and, later, with Rome. Antidemocratic feeling in this powerful, articulate minority (which included the bulk of Athenian intellectuals) can be traced back well into the fifth century. Until the defeat at Chaeronea (338) a vigorous, if at times irresponsible, system of democracy had held the counterurge toward authoritarian rule well in check: both in 411 and in 404 the triumph of the extreme oligarchs was of surprisingly brief duration. Even immediately after Chaeronea, a decree was passed imposing stringent penalties upon any person attempting to subvert the democracy.[4] But with Anti-

Map 2. Attica.

pater's rule in Greece, above all with the drastic constitutional changes that he imposed on Athens after Crannon, the checks were removed, and the authoritarians and plutocrats came into their own.

Predictably, the periods of their ascendancy were almost always associated with the intrusion of an external power: in turn Persia, Sparta, Thebes, and, now, Macedonia came to count on their willing cooperation. The rich, who for long had had a tradition, both official and private, of spending their money on conspicuous public services and benefactions (Cimon is a good example),[5] and in return expected the privileges of office, did not take kindly to egalitarianism. One list of those who per-formed such liturgies (*leitourgiai*) at this time is headed with the aristocratic slogan *eutaxia* ("good order," "discipline").[6] The intellectual tradition established by Aris-totle and his successor Theophrastus in the Lyceum had, inevitably, strong pro-Macedonian associations: not for nothing had Aristotle been hired by Philip II as Alexander's tutor. In his famous *Characters* (see p. 70) Theophrastus enjoys some sly digs at the expense of anti-Macedonian aristocrats; he also had Demetrius of Pha-leron as a student. The whole elitist tradition of education, from Plato's *Republic* on-wards, favored—not least under a government that encouraged the elite—what one modern scholar-turned-politician memorably termed a "dictatorship of the virtuous Right."[7]

Some contemporary juxtapositions are eloquent. Increased silver production from the Laurium mines now supported civic as well as military projects. It is no accident that the defeat at Chaeronea coincided with a great burst of public building in Athens: the Panathenaic stadium and theater, the stone dockyards and arsenal of Piraeus, the Southwest Fountainhouse, an elaborate water clock, the Lyceum gym-nasium.[8] It was after Chaeronea, too, paradoxically, that total conscription was, briefly, introduced,[9] and the Athenian fleet was increased to almost four hundred tri-remes—a case, though patriots like Lycurgus and Demosthenes did not see it that way, of locking the stable after the steed was stolen. Too late the Athenians reorga-nized their military command, having learned, the hard way, "that the Athenian mi-litia was too amateurish, that a divided responsibility was often no responsibility at all."[10] By 305/4 ephebic service (military training undertaken during the two years between the ages of eighteen and twenty) had ceased to be compulsory, and the *ephēbeia* soon degenerated into a smart upper-class club: nothing could more clearly illustrate the harsh realities of the loss of true political freedom at Athens.[11] Me-nander's *Bad-Tempered Man* (*Dyskolos*; see p. 75) won first prize at the Lenaea in the same year that Demetrius of Phaleron came to power (317/6).[12] The two men were close friends, to the point that, after Demetrius's fall, Menander was in serious dan-ger of prosecution simply on the grounds of their association.[13] Nothing in his plays makes this anecdote unlikely. Finally, in 306, a year after the "liberation" of Athens by Demetrius, the future Besieger, Epicurus opened his philosophical school there, with its message of self-sufficiency, noninvolvement, and individualistic quietism.

Politically, the loss of real power tended to emphasize two unfortunate charac-teristics that can be observed in the Athenian *polis* from very early on: anarchic dem-agoguery and the strongman *Führerprinzip*, the one frequently alternating with the other. Until the fourth century the anarchy, though recurrent, was always soon brought under control: one thinks of the conflict between Isagoras and Cleisthenes (510–508), the hysterical episodes of the Mytilene debate (427), when genocide was only averted by a last-minute reprieve, and the execution of the victorious generals after Arginusae for failing to pick up survivors in a severe storm (406).[14] The *Führerprinzip* in a sense was the obverse of this: the urge to let some leader take the destiny of Athens in hand and work miracles with it. Themistocles and Pericles are the two obvious examples in the fifth century; Alcibiades, given a little more luck,

Fig. 15. Comic actor portraying a slave
carrying a basket of fruits to an altar.
Fourth-century Italian red-figure
phlyakes vase.
Musée du Louvre, Paris. Photo Archives
photographiques.

would have been another. In the fourth century the thaumaturges still appear at crucial moments, but now, as we might expect, they tend to be financial officers rather than statesmen in the old sense. The moment Eupolis and Aristophanes in their comedies (*The Demes*, 412; *The Frogs*, 405) started raising the illustrious dead to advise the living *polis*, the Periclean age was over. Eubulus (405–335), who put Athenian finances on a solid footing in the mid-fourth century, and his successor Lycurgus, who raised revenues to over a thousand talents a year (hence all the public buildings)—these are the new heroes.

It would be easy, but somewhat misleading, to suggest that the ambitious middle-class Athenian, shut out of effective politics, turned to commerce instead, since Athens in Alexander's day showed an enormous economic boom; but the truth is that the increasing preoccupation with personal rather than public matters, in every area of life, long predated Chaeronea. We can see business expanding at a dizzy rate throughout the first half of the fourth century: the private speeches of the orators provide excellent evidence for this. We also have evidence of a vast surge in local (as opposed to Athenian) deme activity from about 360 onwards—evidence of parochialism, if not, indeed, of withdrawal from national, let alone international, affairs.[15] Already in Aristophanes' latest plays, in particular the *Plutus* (388), we find a clear foreshadowing of the nonpolitical social and domestic trivia, the lovesick youths and rapacious elderly skinflints who form the stock-in-trade of Middle and New Comedy. Solipsistic neutralism in philosophy was not invented by Epicurus: Antisthenes was ready to contract out half a century earlier (see p. 612). The growing fashion for hiring mercenaries to do one's fighting rather than serve in the ranks oneself is yet another phenomenon with its roots in the fifth century. In other words, the movement toward a private rather than a public existence may have been intensified by the removal of full political freedom, by subservience to autocratic (and, more often than not, external) government; but such things did not of themselves *cause* this change. Nor was it universal: for whatever mixed motives, many Athenians, like Demosthenes and his friends, fought the trend desperately. Nor should we underestimate the counterinstinct, most prevalent among aristocrats and intellectuals, that looked down in contempt on all mundane and banausic occupations from the vantage point of inherited capital or estate income (cf. p. 470). Yet this too proved, in the long run, socially disruptive, promoting an ivory-tower cult of philosophical mandarins who (as Callimachus was to put it; cf. p. 182) abhorred all things public.

Athens in the Hellenistic age presents a psychologically and socially complex picture. For every diehard rebel fighter there is a pro-authoritarian apologist. Most people—as always—stood somewhere between these two extremes. They would enjoy liberty, but did not mean to jeopardize their lives or careers overmuch in order to get it. They disliked, and for the most part intellectually despised, Macedonians; but after the disastrous defeats of Crannon and Amorgos they were prepared, by and large, to settle for the best Macedonian government they could get. Political attitudes were noted and acted on. For example, it escaped no one's notice in Athens that whereas Cassander favored the oligarchs and authoritarian methods, Demetrius had inherited from his father, Antigonus, a general committal to Greek freedom that at least gave democratic principles more leeway. This distinction explains much of the maneuvering in Athens during the twenty years between Crannon and Antigonus One-Eye's death at Ipsus (301).

The politicians who come to the fore in Athens under Macedonian rule offer an interesting spectrum of conservatism, pragmatic opportunism, hysteria, subservience, and cynical *Realpolitik*. We have Phocion, known (though not by the lower orders) as "the Good," antidemocratic, antipopulist ("that Pétain-like figure," one scholar calls him),[16] a skillful general who advised Athens to keep out of military showdowns with Macedonia and to negotiate instead, both before Chaeronea and at the time of the Lamian War: the natural opponent of Demosthenes and Hypereides, a master of *Realpolitik*, the darling of the conservatives. Yet in 322 he beat off a Macedonian attack on Attica, a nice case of political calculation being ousted for once by the territorial imperative.[17] He negotiated peace terms with Philip, and later with Antipater. In Plutarch's *Life* he emerges as a stiff-necked, overly righteous, singularly unlikable character, much given to aphoristic one-liners and moral putdowns. His advice against embarking on the Lamian War may, in retrospect, have been sound, but is totally undercut by his contemptuous, patronizing denigration of that courageous commander Leosthenes.[18] There is a meanness of spirit about Phocion for which no amount of rectitude can compensate: his readiness to urge acceptance of Macedonian requests for the surrender of various Athenians (who would be going to almost-certain death) conveys an unpleasant mixture of cold indifference and creeping servility. In 322/1, working with Antipater, he limited the Athenian franchise to the nine thousand or so with capital in excess of two thousand drachmas;

when, in 318, the democracy was briefly restored, those who for three long years had been deprived of their cherished civic rights took a bloody revenge on him (see below), the hysterical violence of which testifies eloquently to the outrage they felt.[19]

Phocion forms an interesting contrast (the more so since their policies were not dissimilar) to the potbellied, devious Demades, often his fellow envoy to Macedonia. An unprincipled and cheerfully viscerotonic opportunist of low origin,[20] Demades brought to his office the certainty that Athens had to come to terms with Macedonia, and a populist gift of the gab that manifested itself in memorable aphorisms. Macedon without Alexander, he said, would be like the Cyclops minus his eye; and when the news of Alexander's death reached Athens, Demades pooh-poohed it, on the grounds that, had it been true, the whole earth would have stunk of his corpse.[21] He regularly took bribes from the Macedonians (but then so did Demosthenes), and was fined ten talents for proposing to recognize Alexander as a god.[22] He also stopped Athens from becoming involved in an abortive Spartan revolt against Antipater, in which King Agis III was defeated and killed outside Megalopolis (330).[23] His profile is (to put it mildly) prudent rather than heroic. After Alexander's death he was stripped of his civic rights; however, when Antipater seemed about to attack Athens in 322, Demades was hastily brought back to negotiate.[24] Antipater had no illusions about him. Demades in old age, he said, was like a victim after the sacrifice—nothing but tongue and guts.[25] But the tongue could be mean: Demades was good at paying off old scores, and in fact used his Macedonian connections to get both Demosthenes and Hypereides condemned to death.[26]

With Demades, unlike Phocion, the Athenian *dēmos* was balked of its victim. Early in 319 Demades, together with his son Demeas, was put to death by Antipater and Cassander, who uncovered correspondence showing that Demades had intrigued with Perdiccas and (it seems) was also in touch with Antigonus One-Eye. Demades obviously believed in playing the field and hedging his bets. It may, though, have been his sharp turn of phrase that undid him. In one letter to Perdiccas he had, characteristically, urged him to save the Greeks from Antipater, "that rotten old thread on which they hung." Antipater, who in fact died very soon afterwards, was not amused. Nor was Cassander, who according to one account with his own hands butchered both father and son together, in a rain of blood, screaming insults at Demades for his treachery and ingratitude.[27] Ironically, Demades was, at the time, on an embassy to seek the removal of the Macedonian garrison from Piraeus.[28] His case, even more than that of Phocion, nicely captures the Athenians' ambivalence toward politicians in these traumatic times. If Phocion marks a sharp swing toward the conservative principles espoused by men of wealth and rank, Demades' career reveals, with unpleasant clarity, the ease with which principles of any sort could be abandoned, under external pressure, by politicians and electorate alike.

In the fraught negotiations with Antipater and, later, Demetrius the Besieger, we can see yet another round being played, on the domestic front, between authoritarians and populists, a rather nasty variation, under Macedonian overlordship, of the perennial Athenian class war: *kaloi k'agathoi*, landowners and businessmen, arrayed against the now uncertainly enfranchised lower orders. Class and property, of course, went together.[29] We know the whole pattern from Plato and, particularly, Aristotle, whose influence is strong here through his successor Theophrastus. The man of property was also the man of education, the man freed from banausic concerns with making a living, the responsible citizen fit to discharge the duties of government. Such skills, the aristocrat had argued, could not be taught; *arete*, a man's full potential, was innate. (It is a mark of changing *mores* in the Hellenistic age how completely, and how soon, this ideal came to be abandoned, though of course the plutocrats who had bought an education yielded to none in their conviction that *arete* was innate, once they had it.) This responsible figure was contrasted with the ignorant, emotional voter in a mass assembly, the cat's-paw of unscrupulous demagogues. Strong and authoritarian rule came naturally to such thinkers. If Aristotle had reservations about Plato's *Republic*,[30] they were not on the grounds of social illiberalism.

So, in the fall of 322, with a Macedonian garrison in Piraeus to keep the many-headed rabble subdued, Antipater and the *kaloi k'agathoi* ("the brightest and best" would be a fair equivalent) of Athens put the propertied classes in control. The Board of Generals (*strategia*) contained some members, like Phocion, who were only too ready to collaborate (indeed Phocion was afterwards named as the man responsible for "the dissolution of the *demos* and the laws"); the rest went along with their colleagues.[31] The picture is all too familiar. We should at the same time remember, to Demades' credit, that the reason he at this point opened private negotiations with Perdiccas (cut short by the latter's death in Egypt) was to try to win more popular, democratic concessions from Antipater. The actual constitution established by the end of 322 was anything but liberal. As we have seen, the 2,000-drachma property qualification disfranchised well over half the population. The nine thousand men left with the vote were, roughly speaking, the hoplite census, those eligible for service in the heavy-armed infantry. Over twelve thousand Athenians by this device were swept into a kind of civic limbo,[32] on the charge that they were "troublemakers and warmongers,"[33] a stock political all-purpose accusation with a long history. Many, to avoid trouble, were shipped out to Thrace, where Antipater found them land and a city—striking testimony to the danger they were thought to represent by the authorities. We may doubt if those who went did so willingly. Others, later, joined Ophellas's short-lived expedition in Cyrenaica (see p. 222):[34] service as mercenaries was one obvious solution, like the French Foreign Legion in the nineteenth century, for the various victims and misfits of the Hellenistic age. Those who remained felt, not without cause, "that they were suffering outrageous and ignominious treatment."[35]

The populist hold on the jury courts was broken,[36] and the abolition of pay for attendance at the Assembly as well as for jury service can be seen as further anti-populist measures. The new regime claimed to be following the laws of Solon in its theory of government, which was that property and education gave that privileged minority held to possess enough of both (with the leisure and intelligence they implied) the right to make policy and conduct administration.[37] Since this was, in effect, a meritocracy, it was thought only logical also to abolish sortition, the lot, and with it rotation among the ten tribes in making appointments to office. One hostile inscription, made in the short period of the restored democracy (318/7), and honoring a Sicyonian, Euphron, for his services to the Athenian *dēmos* during the Lamian War, complains that "those holding office in the oligarchy" (i.e., between 322 and 318) annulled Euphron's privileges and removed the stelae recording them.[38] The Macedonian garrison, a focal point of resentment, was all that kept this group in office. Phocion, now leader of what was in effect a Macedonian-backed junta, though he had tried to keep the garrison from being installed, soon came to realize its advantages, consistently—and with good reason—refusing to ask for its withdrawal.[39] It is no accident that a factor contributing to Demades' execution was his strenuous but ill-timed attempt to have the Macedonians evacuate Piraeus altogether.

The death of Antipater in 319 produced an interesting situation in Athens. Cassander, smarting at not succeeding his father (see p. 18), began intriguing for power. Like Antipater's, his horizon was essentially Macedonian, and he had a similar authoritarian streak in his notion of government. His first step, a shrewd one, was to replace the garrison commander in Piraeus with a close and loyal friend of his own, Nicanor, Aristotle's son-in-law—one more link in that Peripatetic chain between Macedonia and the Athenian conservatives. With the conservatives supporting Cassander, it followed that Antipater's official successor as *epimelētēs*, Polyperchon, was obliged to appeal to the democratic Greek city-states for support. What this old soldier really thought about Greek freedom is open to doubt; but he badly needed some counterweight against Cassander's ambitions. Hence his famous proclamation (see p. 18), in the name of the kings,[40] offering an amnesty for past political offenses, the restoration of exiles, and a return to the constitution as it had existed before the Lamian War. The vexed question of garrisoning was carefully ignored: there could be no thought of shifting the Macedonian garrison out of Piraeus except by force. At the same time Polyperchon's move was, *inter alia*, as Plutarch says, aimed at Phocion, who had not only transferred his allegiance from Antipater to Cassander, but had sanctioned Nicanor's appointment as garrison commander.[41]

This public proclamation, with its royal backing, constituted a direct appeal, and promise, to the disenfranchised, now at one stroke of the pen restored to citizenship by the kings' fiat. Polyperchon anticipated action in the Assembly as a result, and he was right. But the clumsy blend of inadequate force and incompetent diplomacy that he brought to the situation could not hold back the *dēmos* now: in fact his bungling brought things to a head. Nicanor, who had been quietly strengthening his defenses, refused to budge. In the autumn of 318, after an abortive assault on Piraeus by Polyperchon's son Alexander, and subsequent rumors of a private deal between Alexander and Nicanor, Athenian patience snapped.[42] The pro-Macedonian group was thrown out of office, strong democrats were elected in its place, and various oligarchic leaders, Phocion included, were condemned to death or exile. Phocion, who had been on a diplomatic mission to Polyperchon, was eventually brought back (April 317), to be dragged before the Assembly on a cart, through a hooting mob. The Assembly was packed: not only with citizens, it was alleged, but also (though this sounds like an oligarchic canard against the reenfranchised)[43] with women, slaves, and aliens. A letter from Philip Arrhidaios was read, clearly drafted by Poly-perchon, stating that in the king's opinion Phocion and his supporters were traitors, but that the free citizens of Athens should pronounce sentence on them. This the Assembly did, with cheering. The violence of feeling, the vindictiveness, the sense of outrage, all come across unmistakably in Plutarch's account.[44] The procedure was as illegal, and as fraught with hysteria, as the mass condemnation of the comman-ders at Arginusae in 406. Only the men of substance sympathized with Phocion; the populists (i.e., those he had disenfranchised) reviled him bitterly. So, after being howled down without a hearing,[45] Phocion the Good was made to drink the hem-lock,[46] and his remains were cast out beyond the frontier of Attica. He had been an Athenian general and administrator for almost half a century.

The democratic government lasted only about nine months; it is surprising, in the circumstances, that it survived so long. Even more surprising, perhaps, is the failure of the Macedonian commanders directly concerned to make any move to anticipate or immediately to scotch the coup. However, they did take effective long-term action. Cassander brought thirty-five ships and four thousand men from Antigonus (now campaigning in the eastern Aegean) into Piraeus (spring 317), and made it impregnable, so that Nicanor's garrison now needed only to man the fortress of Munychia.[47] Nicanor himself took on the role of admiral, and by the fall of 317 Polyperchon had suffered severe defeats both on land and at sea. Cassander, who clearly balked at a direct assault on Athens, had other, equally effective methods. First he cut off the Athenians' seaborne supplies, and then he systematically set about the reduction of Attica. That meant starvation for Athens, and envoys—after an ini-tial heated discussion—were sent to negotiate terms with Cassander.[48] Nothing could have suited him better: his prime objective was not the conquest of Athens, but the throne of Macedonia; thus he was ready to show himself accommodating.[49] But Athens was to be placed under a single ruler, whom Cassander was to choose. The result, he hoped, would be a stable, reliably pro-Macedonian government. To this end he appointed (July 317) Demetrius of Phaleron, a handsome Athenian phi-losopher then in his early thirties, a Peripatetic product of Theophrastus's Lyceum, a prolific writer,[50] who had been associated with Antipater's junta but had fled at the time of the countercoup.[51] Cassander, himself no mean scholar,[52] must have chuckled at the thought of giving the Athenians, in uncomfortable practice, a taste of their own theoretical Platonic—or in this case Aristotelian—medicine, a real philosopher-king.

The Athenians were left city, countryside, revenues, and navy: Cassander did, however, insist on holding Piraeus, at least "until the war against the kings [i.e., Polyperchon] was over." Once again a property qualification for citizenship was im-posed, though this time it was halved, to ten minas (= 1,000 drachmas), a significant reduction. The dangerous resentment and violence caused by Antipater's earlier, doubly strict disenfranchisement were, this time, to be avoided.[53] Demetrius, in the best Aristotelian tradition, was to have a broader social base for his constitution. He had been trained by Theophrastus (and probably by Aristotle himself) to believe that men had to be educated for civic duties, that political responsibility was not

Fig. 16. Demetrius of Phaleron (?).
Roman copy of a Hellenistic bust;
identification tentative.
Museo Archeologico, Florence.

innate.[54] He also felt it his job to halt wastage by legislating against excessive luxury. Absolute ruler in fact (though a Macedonian appointee), he was technically *epi-melētēs* of Athens, as Perdiccas and his successors had been of the kings. He had himself elected annually to the Board of Generals, and once, in 309, to the post of archon also, so that he would afterwards qualify for *ex officio* membership in the Areopagus.[55] In connection with the new franchise law he conducted the first full census ever held in Greece. The figures reported are twenty-one thousand citizens (before the law was changed), ten thousand metics (resident aliens), and four hundred thousand slaves.[56] The number of slaves is far too large, though not so exaggerated as has sometimes been argued: for this period a figure of one hundred thousand is quite possible, including perhaps thirty thousand working in the mines.[57] As a symptom of new wealth even the reduced figure is striking. Lastly, Demetrius had himself assigned the task of revising the legal code, a suitable undertaking for an Aristotelian, and one that he left a reputation afterwards for having carried out well.[58]

The ten years of Demetrius's rule are chiefly remarkable as evidence for what was liable to happen when a philosopher-king got a free hand in real life. As we might expect from the static, authoritarian blueprints laid down by Plato and Aristotle, there was a freeze, a moratorium, on natural political evolution. What happened was, nothing happened: it is remarkable how much of Demetrius's legislation was merely negative, a series of prohibitions with no positive, dynamic program behind them. One point regularly made about this regime is that it enjoyed financial stability. But since Athens was not now involved in war, had a fleet of only twenty vessels, did not need mercenaries for defense (the Piraeus garrison performed that

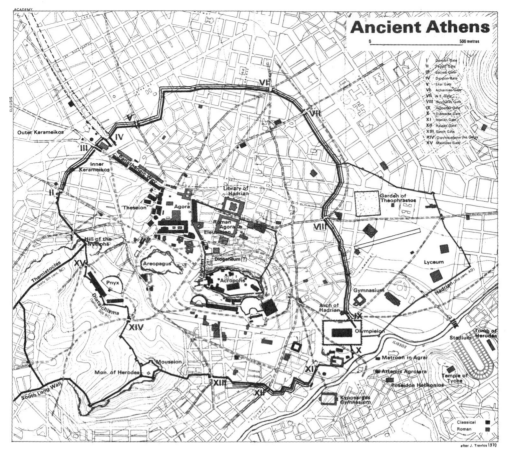

Map 3. Ancient Athens in relation to the modern city.
From the *Blue Guide* to Athens, 2d ed. (1981), maps 10–11.

function), and was no longer paying jurors or assemblymen—and had indeed even discontinued the so-called Entertainment Fund (*theōrikon*), which paid for indigent citizens' admission to the theater—there was no reason why the finances should have been anything but flourishing. They were no longer being swallowed up by swollen military or civic budgets. The mines were still working at full capacity; the state could even afford to take over the so-called liturgies—that ancient equivalent of supertax—by which wealthy citizens had paid for the equipping of triremes or the training of dramatic choruses: one more nail in the coffin of individual civic pride, of personal involvement in the affairs of the *polis*.

Over this scene, so remote, now, from the beliefs and practices of the classical city-state, there presided a dandified intellectual in his mid-thirties who—as hostile critics were not slow to point out—led a life at startling variance with the rules he imposed.[59] An elegant fop, he dyed his hair blond, made himself up, and cultivated courtesans and pretty boys with cheerful bisexual impartiality. (The boys used to lie in wait for him during his afternoon walk along the Street of the Tripods, in what is now the Plaka.) His enemies were not slow to allege that he seduced the wives, sons, and daughters of Athenian citizens, and led a life of luxury himself while drafting sumptuary laws for Athens as a whole; but I do not think we are therefore entitled to dismiss all the stories about him as mere rhetorical propaganda designed to point up a "Do as I say, not as I do" contrast. Had Demetrius been a puritan of rigidly monastic habits (a true Platonic Guardian, in fact), the stories would have been very different. The resentment against him would pick on what it could, and sometimes we can catch the exaggerations. Demetrius was, for example, accused of neglecting the Athenian army. All this meant, in fact, was that he restricted ephebic enrollment in accordance with the new franchise laws[60]—what else was there to neglect? His worst fault was probably a certain harmless exhibitionism: when he became archon, for instance, he had his praises sung in procession, at the Dionysia, by a somewhat camp-sounding chorus that compared him in brightness and beauty to the sun. This was nothing, as we shall see (p. 55), to the unsolicited compliments that his namesake the Besieger was to receive in Athens a decade later.

But his sumptuary laws were certainly real enough. Demetrius put an end to the beautiful (but horribly expensive) funerary monuments that adorned the Street of the Tombs and still make the Kerameikos the most enjoyable ancient site in Athens. He also severely restricted the extravagance of the funerals themselves. He set up a board, the *gynaikonomoi*, whose job it was to enforce the regulations restricting expenditure on women's dresses, jewelry, servants, and carriages. There were to be no more than thirty guests at any wedding breakfast or dinner party.[61] (Needless to say, stories of his own huge and wildly luxurious banquets were legion.) Real-estate laws were promulgated to protect business investors. It seems possible that, economies apart, one object of the sumptuary laws was to keep the common people quiet by demonstrating some sort of restrictive control over their social superiors. Certainly Demetrius took great care to ensure that the whole populace got an abundance of consumer goods at cheap prices—and was duly sneered at for priding himself on doing so: the attitude of a common exciseman, snapped one historian. Why he should have had donkeys paraded through the theater, or a giant mechanical snail trundling along at the head of his public processions, spitting out saliva, must remain a mystery. Bread and circuses? Perhaps. Polybius says he claimed it was to show that Athens had given up her old ambitions to spearhead the glory of Greece, and now danced to Cassander's orders.[62] At one level this is a shrewd comment. Athens was certainly not the last society, and probably not the first, to be corrupted by the lure of conspicuous consumption and expensive novelties. The honorific statues and decrees that Demetrius collected during his term of office suggest that those, at least, who could afford such things were happy to collaborate.[63]

There was, nevertheless, a strong opposition group, and its hopes were pinned, naturally, on Antigonus One-Eye, who not only was in conflict with Demetrius's master, Cassander, but also, as we have seen, had a reputation for liberalism where Greeks were concerned. Athenians were quite happy to cooperate with Cassander in the rebuilding of Thebes, which they took to be a slap at Alexander's memory and (from their point of view) an anti-Macedonian gesture in favor of *polis* rule;[64] but when it came to a basic choice between Cassander and Antigonus, Antigonus looked by far the more preferable candidate, not least after his famous proclamation from Old Tyre (see p. 24). Encouraged by this, in 314 the islands of Lemnos, Imbros, and Delos broke away from the Demetrian regime,[65] but Antigonus was in no condition, then, to capitalize on their secession. After the peace of 311 it was another matter. Once again he began making vigorous propaganda on the well-tried basis of free-dom for the Greeks, a natural gambit since Cassander operated with oligarchic sup-port. Antigonus, who had consolidated his military position during those crucial years, now looked a far more attractive champion to the Greeks than the vacillating and ineffectual Polyperchon; what was more, that clause in the 311 agreement calling for Greek self-determination gave Antigonus a perfect excuse for attacking the Athens of Demetrius whenever he felt ready (see p. 28).

In spring 307 the time was ripe. Antigonus fitted out a fleet of 250 ships at Ephesus, and entrusted it, together with five thousand talents in cash, to his son De-metrius—not yet the Besieger, but full of youthful dash and energy. His brief was "to liberate all the cities in Greece, but Athens first."[66] Young Demetrius descended on Piraeus without warning, caught the defenders off guard, and was welcomed with wild enthusiasm by the mob. The fortress at Munychia capitulated after a brief siege: its garrison was evacuated, and the fortress itself destroyed. Demetrius entered Athens in triumph: "assembling the people he gave them back their ancestral system of government,"[67] and made lavish promises of grain and timber. Demetrius of Pha-leron was given a safe-conduct to Thebes, and spent his latter years in Ptolemaic Egypt (see p. 85). There he helped organize the Museum and Library, wrote a defen-sive monograph—like any out-of-office politician—about his own ten-year rule, claiming that far from destroying the democracy he actually improved it, and com-posed, of all things, a hymnal for the worship of the new deity Sarapis, apparently in gratitude for being cured of temporary blindness.[68]

The Athenians, predictably, revoked the decrees in his honor, and removed all his statues (except one, on the Acropolis) and melted them down: for chamberpots, said some. Then, in one of their too-characteristic fits of excess, and egged on by sedulous apes such as Stratocles (who may, nevertheless, have been working for Athenian independence), they voted to have gold—not bronze—statues of Antig-onus and Demetrius set up at public expense next to those of the tyrannicides, Har-modius and Aristogeiton.[69] As if this were not enough, they decreed their Savior Gods, as they now called them,[70] other, still more flattering honors: the title of king was to be conferred on them, two new civic tribes were to be created and named after them, their likenesses were to be woven into the Panathenaic robe along with those of the twelve Olympian gods, an altar was to be set up at the spot where De-metrius first stepped from his chariot in Athens, and the year was henceforth to take its name not from the eponymous archon, but from the annually elected priest of the Savior Gods' cult. (The cynical noted that the ground round their altars teemed with hemlock.) It comes as a relief to learn that the envoys conveying these respects to Antigonus were also instructed to ask, in return, for those large subventions in grain and timber that Demetrius had promised. These, together with the return of Imbros, they duly obtained.[71]

Though the usual round of prosecutions was launched against supporters of the fallen regime,[72] the transition back to democracy was made without undue fuss. Not that it was the old kind of independent, and highly politicized, democracy that the fifth century would have recognized. For one thing, it was underwritten, and thus in the last resort still controlled, by the Antigonids.[73] For another, many radical administrative changes, such as the centralization of finances and the state's assumption of liturgies, had come to stay. Nevertheless, the reaction meant a period of populist extremism, encouraged by Demetrius, who enjoyed the atmosphere of heady adulation that surrounded not only himself but also his wife, Phila (she too was given divine honors, being associated with Aphrodite). In 306, however, Antigonus recalled his son to the eastern Mediterranean for the campaign against Ptolemy (see p. 29).[74] Thirty triremes from the brand-new Athenian navy accompanied him.

Distaste for Aristotle and his Peripatetic associates, Demetrius of Phaleron not least (the Lyceum being firmly, and understandably, tagged in the public mind as a hotbed of traitors, oligarchs, and Macedonian collaborators), probably also lay behind the proposal, in 307, to ban the establishment of new schools of philosophy in Athens without prior authorization from the Council and the Assembly (see p. 61).[75] This proposal, made by one Sophocles of Sunium, came before the legislative committee charged with the revision of Demetrius of Phaleron's laws. In the heat of the moment, and with the horrible example of the Aristotelian ex-dictator fresh in mind, the legislators (*nomothetai*) wrote in the restriction, clearly not appreciating either the threat it presented to the Athenians' much-cherished freedom of speech or the conflict it constituted with the laws of Solon (since the Lyceum was a religious foundation dedicated to the Muses, and thus to interfere with it was nothing less than *asebeia*, impiety). Yet the move was a popular one, as we can see from the following fragment of a play by Alexis:[76]

> So this is the Academy, and this Xenocrates?
> May the gods grant many blessings to Demetrius
> And the legislators, for casting out of Attica
> As garbage the men who claim to endow our youths
> With the powers of argument, of dialectic!

Wiser heads, taking the long view, had Sophocles of Sunium prosecuted on the popular all-purpose charge of proposing an unconstitutional measure (306).[77] Demochares, Demosthenes' nephew, defended him, with a rousing rhetorical assault on the immoralism and treachery and chicanery that the philosophers encouraged, a favorite conservative charge ever since Aristophanes' play *The Clouds* (423).[78] It is worth noting that not only the Lyceum, but also Plato's Academy, and its current head, Xenocrates, came in for this kind of abuse: in his speech Demochares, like Alexis, attacked the corrupting influence of "the fine *Republic*, the lawless *Laws*."

Nevertheless, the prosecution against Sophocles was successful, and the principle of free association was finally reestablished in Athens. Theophrastus, who had fled the city in 307, now returned, and soon Epicurus arrived from Lampsacus to establish his own school (see p. 60).[79] Zeno of Citium, the founder of Stoicism, was not long in following him (see p. 61). The extreme democrats were opposed by a more moderate group—led by Phaedrus of Sphettos, a mining magnate—whose concern for independence did not wholly eclipse their sense of property, and who were thoroughly alarmed by the populist excesses of the extremists. (It is interesting, and significant, that about this time the remains of Phocion were brought back to Athens, given a public burial, and honored with a statue at the state's expense.)[80] However, while the war between Antigonus and Cassander sputtered on, there was not much that the moderates could achieve. An Athenian force scored some minor successes against Cassander, but soon lost the initiative. Panic when Cassander looked like winning was replaced by another outburst of fulsome gratitude to those protecting deities, Antigonus and Demetrius, when they rescued Athens from crisis. In 304 Cassander captured the passes north of Attica, and actually occupied Salamis:[81] the Athenians, foreseeing another winter of famine, desperately appealed to Demetrius. He raised the siege of Rhodes (see p. 33), landed at Aulis, and forced Cassander into retreat. Athens was saved, and her passes were once more secure.

Demetrius, together with a large fleet and army, spent the winter in Athens.[82] Here he demonstrated, in memorable fashion, just what Greek freedom suggested to him. Having acquired the rear chamber of the Parthenon as living quarters for himself and his prize collection of courtesans, all under the command of a rapacious elderly madam known as Lamia, he spent the winter in a continual round of parties and orgies. Athena, the wits said, had received him in person: in his capacity as Savior God he habitually referred to the goddess as his elder sister, a relationship that, in his view, gave him a perfect right to raid her treasury. He struck coins bearing, variously, his own features and Athena's head; it has even been suggested that some issues, as a kind of private joke, combined the two, offering an Athena-style head with Demetrius's profile.[83] The realities behind the democratic façade were made all too plain when Demetrius intervened, personally, on behalf of an Athenian crony subjected to a stiff fine, and got the sentence quashed. A decree was, it is true, passed forbidding him to act in this way, but when he lost his temper the Assembly quickly reversed the decision, and ratified a counterproposal (made by Stratocles) that whatever Demetrius proposed in future was to be endorsed. The moderates were outraged; but Demetrius was still the protector of Athens against Cassander.

In 302 the Besieger was admitted, uninitiated and at the wrong time of year, to the Eleusinian Mysteries (a month was intercalated for his benefit); this was also the time when he and Antigonus resurrected the old device of the League of Corinth, so that thenceforth Demetrius campaigned as the League's generalissimo (see p. 34).[84] But when Antigonus summoned him back to Asia for the fatal showdown at Ipsus in 301, the moderates got their chance. With Antigonus dead and Demetrius, for the moment, a fugitive, a change of government became possible. The interesting thing is that this time there was no swing back to the extreme oligarchs. The moderate faction opted for neutrality and peace. As we have seen, compulsory conscription had already been abandoned, and the period of training for ephebes, even as volunteers, had been reduced from two years to one. There were no heroics, no attempt to restore Athenian independence in any substantive sense. Phaedrus of Sphettos and his associates took the middle road, and Cassander lost no time in making a peace settlement with them.[85] Though there were to be at least two further catastrophic attempts to win back the city's freedom (see pp. 147, 562), plutocracy, in one shape or other, had come to stay.

CHAPTER 4

ZENO, DIOGENES, EPICURUS,
AND POLITICAL DISENCHANTMENT

All societies, it has been said, get the philosophers and the architects they deserve, on the grounds that these tend to furnish a peculiarly accurate reflection of the *Zeitgeist*. Athens in the late fourth century B.C. is no exception to the rule. Her major buildings then were secular and commercial: Philo's great arsenal in Piraeus (329), the Panathenaic theater and stadium, the large but unfinished peristyle on the northeast side of the Agora, probably designed to accommodate (in that ever-litigious city) an overflow of law courts. In the more traditional mode she patched and developed. A new temple of Apollo Patroös, on the site of the old sanctuary, was built during Lycurgus's administration as public treasurer (337–325/4); he was also responsible for completing the extensive alterations carried out in the Theater of Dionysus, as well as the half-built Piraeus shipsheds, and for building the Lyceum's gymnasium.[1] Such activities, however, could hardly count as innovation.

In many ways the Athenian creative impulse—certainly the form of it that we associate with the Periclean era—seems to have run dry during this period. As early as 386 we find plays by the old masters—Aeschylus, Sophocles, Euripides—being performed at the great festivals along with less-regarded new productions; after 339 the same seems to have been true of Attic Old Comedy.[2] Lycurgus also passed a law authorizing the erection of bronze statues to the three great fifth-century tragedians, and establishing a canonical text of their works (later purloined by the Ptolemies; see p. 89), from which actors were not permitted to deviate.[3] When Aristotle, later in the fourth century, wanted to define the perfect tragedy, he went back a century, to the *Oedipus Tyrannus*.[4] The mood was retrospective; there was a sense, instantly recognizable today, of being overwhelmed by one's own classics. Though the architecture of the Agora was later to be transformed at least twice, it is noteworthy that neither of these changes would have taken place without external stimulus, in this case enlightened patronage by the wealthy, and quintessentially Hellenistic (i.e., nonclassical, non-Athenian), kings of Pergamon. "The Athenians were to create no more great buildings in their own manner and out of their own resources."[5] In literature, as we shall see, the mood had shifted, rapidly, from one of civic involvement to escapism, by way of fantasy, ivory-tower scholarship, and half-hearted social realism heavily laced with romance. The happy ending, by no coincidence, arrived in art about the same time that it seemed to be disappearing in real life. As we might expect, these trends are also faithfully mirrored in early Hellenistic thought.

It is often stated as a fact that Stoicism and Epicureanism were designed to support thinking men who had been disoriented by the collapse of the city-state, as a kind of "ring-wall against chaos."[6] This claim has to be scrutinized with some caution. The *polis*, it is argued, had "never given security," whereas "Hellenism was a world of cities, and Hellenistic Greeks were making money, not worrying about their souls."[7] This is at best a half-truth. Though the *polis* may not have given security in the sense that a welfare state does, it did, until the end of independence, make each citizen in the assembly feel conscious of participation—full, practical participation—in the business of government. Aristophanes might make a joke of it, but Demos really did rule. The cities of the Hellenistic world, certainly those, like Athens, that had lost control of their own destinies, might keep up their ceremonies and traditions (the Athenian Panathenaic procession was still going strong under the Roman empire),[8] but they had lost the special kind of confidence that only self-determination can produce.

The loss of external political freedom inevitably drove men inward on themselves. Not all were looking for the same thing, but a remarkable number of those who did not opt for financial, material success (and indeed, some who did) were on a quest for freedom of the soul. If they could not have true political *eleutheria*, at least they would achieve inner release, a mastery of the self. Now, this self-searching for the idea of spiritual liberation (endocosm, as it were, rather than exocosm) is the most noticeable feature that all Hellenistic systems of thought have in common. Just as earlier, in the archaic world of the eighth century B.C., Hesiod had had nothing to offset his impotence, when confronted with rapacious and unscrupulous local barons, apart from the force of moral principle,[9] so now the loss of political autonomy impelled men to seek self-sufficiency (*autarkeia*). The disruption of old certainties, the subversion of traditional patterns and values, in particular those associated with the world of the *polis*, led to an obsession with Tyche—Chance, Fortune (see p. 400). Intellectuals who scoffed at anthropomorphic deities interfering with human affairs were (perhaps by way of compensation) hopelessly vulnerable to the random-numbers game, the unpredictable swerve (*parenklisis, clinamen*) in an atomized world.

In his treatise *On Tyche* Demetrius of Phaleron, reflecting on the eclipse of the Greek states by Macedon, and perhaps also on the vicissitudes of his own career, wrote: "Fortune does not correspond to our mode of life . . . and regularly demonstrates its power by confounding our expectations."[10] Virtue, in other words, was no guarantee of prosperity; Tyche (in this resembling any archaic Greek deity) was wholly indifferent to good works, much less good intentions. The Macedonians, Demetrius mused, had been given the prosperity previously enjoyed by the Persians, but only on loan. That was a shrewd assessment. Polybius, who lived to see the triumph of Rome, knew all about the mutability of Fortune: it took him as a hostage from his homeland and led him to make his life's work writing, and explaining, the

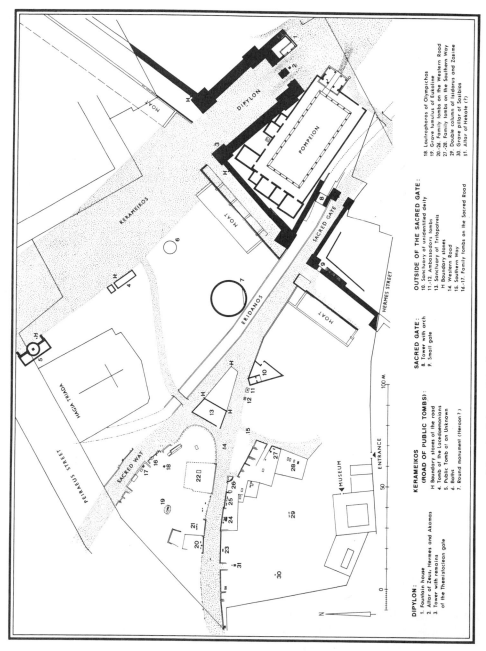

Map 4. Athens: Dipylon, Kerameikos, and Sacred Gate.
Kerameikos Museum, courtesy of the Greek Archaeological Service.

DIPYLON:
1. Fountain house
2. Altar of Zeus, Hermes and Akamas
3. Tower with remains
   of the Themistoclean gate

KERAMEIKOS
(ROAD OF PUBLIC TOMBS):
H Boundary stones of the road
4. Tomb of the Lacedaemonians
5. Public Tomb of an Unknown
6. Baths
7. Round monument (Heroon ?)

SACRED GATE:
8. Tower with arch
9. Small gate

OUTSIDE OF THE SACRED GATE:
10. Sanctuary of unidentified deity
11.-12. Ambassadors tombs
13. Sanctuary of Tritopatreis
H Boundary stones
14. Western Road
15. Southern Way
16.-17. Family tombs on the Sacred Road

18. Loutrophoros of Olympichos
19. Grave tumulus of Eukoline
20.-26. Family tombs on the Western Road
27.-28. Family tombs on the Southern Way
29. Double column of Isidorus and Zosime
30. Grave pillar of Sosibios
31. Altar of Hekate (?)

achievement of his conquerors (see pp. 269 ff.). Theophrastus was much criticized by intellectuals for endorsing Chaeremon's claim that "Tyche, not reason, is what guides the affairs of mankind."[11] We will find the same sense of human impotence reflected in the plays of Menander (see p. 73). "Stop going on about intelligence," says one character. "Human intelligence is that and nothing more. It's Fortune's intelligence that steers the world. . . . Human forethought is hot air, mere babble."[12]

In his idiosyncratic monograph on Epicurus, the French scholar-priest Fr. A. J. Festugière wrote: "How was it possible not to realise that, from the day when the Greek city fell from the position of autonomous state to that of a simple municipality in a wider state, it lost its soul? It remained a home, a material background: it was no longer an ideal."[13] The migrants who drifted to Alexandria, to Antioch, to Pergamon or Ephesus, cut off from their roots, were alone, ciphers, like modern provincial newcomers to London or Paris or New York. Small wonder if their materialism took the logical step of deifying men on the basis of power and achievement. Ruler worship was to become one of the most characteristic phenomena of the Hellenistic period. When Demetrius the Besieger returned to Athens from Corcyra in 291 (see p. 127), he was greeted with a paean including the words:[14]

> The other gods are far away,
> Or cannot hear,
> Or are nonexistent, or care nothing for us;
> But *you* are here, and visible to us,
> Not carved in wood or stone, but real,
> So to you we pray.

Those who had elevated Demetrius to the status of Savior God, the younger brother of Athena, could hardly do less than address him in these or similar terms; and the Parthenon then became his only logical habitat. Neither they nor modern critics should have been surprised at the consequences.

Nor was it an accident that Euhemerus of Messene, a philosopher-fabulist in Cassander's circle (ca. 311–298), achieved such extraordinary popularity. In his best-known work Euhemerus described Panchaia, a utopia in the Indian Ocean, where the Olympian gods, it transpired, had been great kings and rulers deified by their grateful subjects.[15] It would have been hard, at this time, to formulate a notion with greater epidemic appeal. Euhemerus became the Hellenistic equivalent of a best-seller: his work was one of the first Greek texts to be translated into Latin prose, and by none other than Ennius.[16] Small wonder: it blurred the line between gods and human heroes; it could be used by intellectuals as ammunition to support atheism, or by propagandists at the royal courts to enhance the prestige of monarchy. If the common man, throughout the *oikoumenē*, the civilized Greek world, was to be subjected to autocratic rule, he might at least satisfy one side of his emotions by making a cult of it. Meanwhile he could pursue, in private, all those significantly negative virtues we find touted by Hellenistic philosophers: *aponia*, absence of pain; *alypia*, avoidance of grief; *akataplēxia*, absence of upset; *ataraxia*, undisturbedness; *aprag-*

mosynē, detachment from mundane matters; *apathia*, non-suffering (or, freedom from emotion); and, positive for once, *galēnismos*, the tranquillity of a calm sea. Like Eliot's women of Canterbury, they did not want anything to happen: their good, like Demetrius of Phaleron's, was negative, predicated on the consistent avoidance of present troubles. Indeed, all of them except the Stoics made it a prime rule to avoid any kind of political involvement. The change from the values of the Periclean age, when those who contracted out were known, contemptuously, as the *apragmones*, the do-nothings, or the *idiōtai*, private people and, hence, idiots,[17] is fundamental.

Yet the interesting thing is how far back before the onset of the Successor monarchies we find all these symptoms developing. They are not—this cannot be over-stressed—simply and solely the result of the loss of political autonomy. The cultivation of the individual soul was propounded in turn by Pythagoras, the Orphics, and Plato. Escapism meets us in many forms well before the end of the fifth century. Euripides' choruses are always wishing themselves somewhere else, remote and romantic, preferably metamorphosed into birds. The ornithological motif reappears in Aristophanes' comedy *The Birds* (414), where two disgruntled citizens want out of Athens, with its never-ending lawsuits and fiddling bureaucrats; Eupolis in *The Demes* (412), as we have seen, turned to dead leaders to solve Athenian problems.[18] As early as Aristophanes' *Plutus* (388) we find the assumption that wealth "is both the final cause and the prerequisite of all activities."[19]

The world of the *polis*, in fact, was being attacked by intelligent moralists for its shortcomings long before it was rendered obsolete by external aggressors like Philip of Macedon. Demagoguery and mass hysteria were the populist vices, balanced by totalitarian violence on the part of oligarchical extremists, such as those intellectual aristocrats who in 411 spearheaded the revolution of the Four Hundred. If it was men like Critias, Plato's uncle, who formed the Spartan-backed authoritarian junta of the Thirty, it was the free democracy that in 399, after several years of scarring civil war, was provoked into condemning Socrates. Plato himself reveals, in his *Seventh Letter*, how he became disillusioned with both forms of government.[20] Relatives were eager for him to join the witch-hunting activities of the Thirty, and this shocked his sensibilities; yet how, on the other hand, could he accept, much less work with, a system that executed his philosophical master? Many responsible, intelligent men must have felt as he did; many must have shared his belief that the only solution was to jettison the old forms and concepts, to plan society anew. Hence, of course, the *Republic*. Hence, too, the Theory of Ideas, that striving to find eternal perfection and pattern somewhere behind the appalling flux of mundane appearances. Yet Plato was an aristocrat born and bred, and the brave new world he fashioned was itself, inevitably, a totalitarian and elitist utopia. Worse, his idealist theorizing proved itself a rather more subtle version of the prevalent escapist mood. When put to the practical test it either failed through ignorance of human nature, as Plato himself failed at the court of Dionysius in Sicily, or else, when effectively implemented, as by Demetrius of Phaleron, emerged as nothing but (more or less enlightened) authoritarianism.

The urge to reject the *polis* took other, more striking forms, of which the most significant was the counterculture preached, and practiced, by the Cynics, and by those Socratics, like Antisthenes, who influenced them (see pp. 612 ff.). Personal asceticism, simplicity of life, the rejection of material possessions and the pleasures of luxury, as well as of all accepted social conventions: these were the characteristics of the Cynic. He was called a "follower of the Dog" from the group's founder, Diogenes of Sinope (400–325?), known as "the Dog" because he believed that all natural functions were proper, and therefore could and should be performed in public, as a dog performs them, all *physis* and no *nomos*. Plato is said to have described him as "Socrates gone mad." What most people know, or think they know, about Diogenes testifies to the kind of character that breeds legends: that he lived in a tub, that he went through Athens carrying a lamp in broad daylight, in search of a "real man," and that he told Alexander to stand out of the way because he was keeping the sun off him.[21]

There was a mythic quality to Diogenes: his personality bred anecdotes, and he collected more of them than almost anyone else in antiquity. The legend, it has been well said, "is a vector of reality."[22] His contempt for the civic side of Athenian life was total. He called "the Dionysiac competitions great spectacles for fools, and the demagogues the mob's menials," and thought most men were only a finger's breadth short of madness. He refused all local allegiances, calling himself a "citizen of the world" (*kosmopolitēs*).[23] When asked what the finest thing in the world was, he replied, promptly, "Freedom of speech."

With their profession of poverty, not to mention their more exhibitionistic habits, the Cynics were liable to attract some rich dilettanti, but they had comparatively little effect on the fabric of Hellenistic life. Their chief importance is as a psychological symptom, an index of social malaise; and as we have seen, that malaise—the trend toward commercialism, the reaction against the affluence that came with it—had begun long before Alexander's day. The opening-up of the Persian empire, the subjection of the Greek city-states to external control, simply accelerated and intensified an already existing process. Even Hellenistic ruler cults had their roots in the secular humanism of the Periclean *polis*. If, as Protagoras claimed, man was the measure of all things, why not of divinity? Lysander, Alexander, Demetrius the Besieger: their achievements and glory were palpable, visible, of this world. Small wonder that, as the years went by, the traditional civic gods were not so much rejected—public ritual has always been the most stubbornly conservative of phenomena—as shunted off into a vague, blissful, remote Elysian heaven, and left with no direct impact on, or interest in, human existence (see pp. 622 ff.). Real men had, in the end, outperformed their own anthropomorphic deities. Menander was well aware of this attitude:[24]

> *Onesimos:* Smikrines, do you think the gods have so much leisure
> That they dish out each individual's daily ration
> Of good and bad?
> *Smikrines:*   What d'you mean?
> *Onesimos:*   I'll tell you.
> Say there are—what?—a thousand cities, more or less,

> With thirty thousand inhabitants in each. Do the gods
> Worry their heads over each single soul's salvation?
> *Smikrines:*   What?!
> That sounds like a headache of a life to me.

Thus we find the Hellenistic thinker inheriting and developing these various anti-civic, self-regarding modes of thought: the Socratic cultivation of the soul; the Cynic contempt for material wealth, and rejection of social norms; the cultivation of a personal rather than a collective *autarkeia*, self-sufficiency in the face of political powerlessness and social unrest. To avoid suffering, pain, disturbance (*alypia*, *apathia*, *ataraxia*, and the rest of the negative objectives), to attain and preserve inner calm: these were the chief aims of Hellenistic philosophy. To its ultimate loss, it concentrated on ethics and metaphysics, leaving more practical scientific work to be done by others (see p. 453); thus there is always a certain faint aura of unreality clinging about it. The two systems that came to dominate the Hellenistic world (and indeed the Graeco-Roman culture that succeeded it) were neither Platonism nor the post-Aristotelian thinking of the Peripatetics, but those of the Stoics and Epicureans, the Garden and the Porch. We shall look more closely at their tenets later (see Chaps. 35 and 36); for now, it may help to examine, briefly, the lives and personalities of the two sects' founders, who both took up residence in Athens toward the close of the fourth century.

Epicurus, son of Neocles, a Philaid aristocrat (and hence a remote descendant of Miltiades), was born in 341, on the island of Samos,[25] where his father had been an Athenian cleruch. The Athenians were expelled from the island by Perdiccas shortly after Alexander's death (323).[26] With his expropriation Neocles seems to have lost all his capital, and to have eked out a living thereafter as a village schoolmaster. Stories of his mother being a spell-chanting herbalist, and his brother a pimp, though possibly slanderous inventions, similarly suggest sudden impoverishment in Epicurus's family. Prior to this disaster Epicurus had, as an adolescent, already shown a strong interest in philosophy, spurred on by irritation at his teacher's inability to answer the question "If, as Hesiod says, Chaos was created first, what was Chaos created from?"[27] He studied Plato with a master named Pamphilus, and may (whether now or later is unclear) have been introduced by Nausiphanes to the Democritean atomic theory that we find outlined in Lucretius's great Roman poem *De Rerum Natura* (*On the Nature of Things*). Pleasure, said Democritus, was the ultimate goal, absence of dread the state of mind to achieve. Epicurus was later to modify this to absence of care: it is possible that his views were to some extent shaped by his family misfortunes.

In 323/2, shortly before the outbreak of the Lamian War, and prior to his family's expulsion from Samos, Epicurus, now eighteen, went to Athens to do his compulsory two years' military service as an *ephēbos*: one of his fellow ephebes, in the next year's intake, was the future poet Menander. How much time Epicurus had for philosophy during this period of conscription is doubtful. In any case Aristotle had by now—since anti-Macedonian feeling was running high—withdrawn from Athens to retirement in Chalcis.[28] If the young conscript attended the immensely

Fig. 17. Portrait bust of Epicurus.
Roman copy of a third-century
original.
Capitoline Museum, Rome.

popular lectures of Aristotle's successor Theophrastus now rather than later, he clearly did not find them congenial.[29] He is said to have heard Xenocrates lecture in the Academy.[30] It is also possible that more practical matters left their mark on him. When Leosthenes died on the battlefield, when Hypereides was executed with ignominy and Demosthenes was driven to suicide (see pp. 10, 11, 36), an intelligent thinker could not but reflect on the advantages of withdrawal, of the nonpolitical life. One of Epicurus's more famous aphorisms—the subject of a peculiarly silly essay by Plutarch[31]—was *lathe biōsas*, which means, in effect, "Get through your life without attracting attention." During the wars of the Successors this was a piece of advice with practical as well as ethical implications.

The lesson, in the event, came even nearer home. From garrison duty in the forts of Attica Epicurus would, in the normal course, have rejoined his family on Samos in 321. But by now history had overtaken them. The war against Antipater had been fought and lost. Alexander's decree recalling all exiles had been implemented, and Neocles had lost his Samian estate: Athens (as we know from epigraphical evidence) did not treat the island gently.[32] A new, bleak world was dawning for him and those like him. There now began for Epicurus the years of exile and poverty. Philosophy in Greece was a wealthy rentier's pursuit until the Cynics staked a claim in it, but Epicurus proved himself (as in so many other things) an exception to the rule. He was, in essence, self-made. From 321 until 306 he lived first with his family in Colophon, then alone in Mytilene on Lesbos (311/10), and finally at Lampsacus by the Hellespont (310–306). During this last period he made the permanent friendships of his life—with Metrodorus, who became his deputy, with Her-

Fig. 18. The Attic frontier fort of Eleutherai, on the Gyphtokastro pass over
Mt. Kithairon.
Photo Alison Frantz.

marchus, who succeeded him, and with the wealthy Idomeneus, who gave him financial backing—and worked out his philosophical system (which might perhaps be more accurately described as a way of life). But all the while politics pursued him: to live without attracting attention, not least for so outspoken a man as Epicurus, proved difficult. His teaching spell in Mytilene (which was under Antigonus One-Eye's control) coincided with Antigonus's brief truce with his rivals (see p. 27); the truce once over, Epicurus's position became difficult. He had antagonized many of the local intellectuals, and seems to have been expelled from the city. He later wrote a pamphlet *Against the Philosophers of Mytilene*: he had a sharp polemical manner,[33] and sometimes it got him into trouble. From Mytilene he moved on to Lampsacus, now held by Antigonus's adversaries.

Doubtless he could have survived in this peripheral wandering scholar's existence indefinitely; but by now he had worked out his creed, and if he meant to disseminate it beyond a merely local audience, he had to go to Athens. However much a backwater now in other respects, Athens still remained the unchallenged philosophical center of the Greek world. Moreover, by establishing a cooperative commune of contributing friends, Epicurus had to a great extent remedied his financial problems. In 306, at the age of thirty-five, he moved to Athens, and bought the house and garden by which he is known, where he and his group took up permanent residence. Apart from occasional visits to Lampsacus, where he had formed many friendships, he stayed there until his death (271/0). Outside events largely dictated the timing of his move. He was, predictably, hostile to Cassander and his supporters. He was also in competition with the established schools of Plato and Aristotle. The Lyceum, of course, enjoyed Macedonian support, and from 317 till 307 Athens had been ruled by a puppet dictator who was not only Macedonian-sponsored but also a Peripatetic.

After the change of regime brought about by Demetrius the Besieger a natural reaction against both the Lyceum and the Academy led, as we have seen (p. 49), to a law forbidding the establishment of philosophical schools without prior permission from the Council and the Assembly. But with the rescinding of this law (spring 306), freedom of association was once more recognized, and this time for good.[34] Theophrastus had left Athens in 307, in fear of prosecution; when he returned, Epicurus felt safe to make his own move. Once established in Athens he began a lifelong advocacy of his ideals: freedom from fear, whether of the gods or of death; freedom from vain desires and public ambitions. Amid wars, commercial greed, and an increasingly materialistic culture, he preached peace of mind, the unregarded life, withdrawal, the contemplative existence. His ideal, as we shall see, was the nearest thing to medieval monasticism that the ancient world had to offer; and it was similarly reviled and misrepresented by its enemies.

About the same time, a twenty-two-year-old Phoenician named Zeno, from Citium on Cyprus, the son of a merchant, arrived in Athens. Tradition reports that he was shipwrecked near Piraeus. The traditional date of his arrival is 312, during the regime of Demetrius of Phaleron, which may or may not be significant.[35] A tall, dark, lean man, it is said: serious of mien, thick-legged, fond of green figs and a place in the sun. Attempts to give an Oriental slant to his thinking have not been successful: Citium, though cosmopolitan, was a Greek city, and there is nothing in the Zenonian corpus that could not be derived from Greek tradition. Indeed, we hear that as a precocious adolescent he had had his father bring back the latest philosophical treatises from Athens along with his more commercial freight. Now he shopped around the lecture halls, tried the Academy, was converted for a while to Cynicism, came to Socrates by way of Antisthenes' writings, and finally worked out his own system. He is said to have been in a bookseller's shop one day, soon after his arrival, reading Xenophon's *Memorabilia*, and to have asked the bookseller where he could find men like Socrates. Crates the Cynic (see p. 616) was walking past outside, and the bookseller simply said, "Follow that man."[36]

Though he always lived frugally,[37] Zeno seems to have been solidly well off. The tradition that he arrived with a thousand talents as capital, which he thereafter lent out on bottomry, may be exaggerated, but there is nothing about him that suggests Cynic poverty, and much to support the contention that he was a prudent rentier: he never lacked money for gifts or purchases.[38] He began to teach in the Stoa Poikile, or Painted Colonnade (so called because it was used as an art gallery), where he soon became a familiar part of the Athenian scene. Because of this his followers were known as Stoics, or "Colonnaders," like the poets who had formerly met there. He was much cultivated by King Antigonus Gonatas, whose attentions he seems to have found intermittently tiresome, not having a taste for royal reveling.[39] Antigonus in-

Fig. 19. Portrait bust of Zeno of
Citium. Roman copy of a Hellenistic
original.
Museo Nazionale, Naples (Farnese
Collection). Photo Alinari/Anderson.

vited him to his court (see p. 141), as Archelaus had invited Euripides over a century
earlier: Euripides went to Pella and wrote *The Bacchae*, but Zeno, like Socrates,
made polite excuses.

He acquired remarkable respect and admiration in Athens during his lifetime—
no easy thing for a philosopher to do, but Zeno was a byword for consistently practicing what he preached. He was honored with a bronze statue and a gold crown;
there is even a tradition that the keys of the city were at some time left in his possession for safekeeping.[40] When he died, in 262/1, Athens gave him a public tomb,
complete with commemorative inscriptions, though he had never become an Athenian citizen, and indeed prided himself on his Cypriot birthright.[41] As Kurt von Fritz
wrote, "his ethical doctrine gave great comfort to many during the troubled times of
the successors of Alexander. According to this doctrine the only real good is virtue,
the only real evil moral weakness. Everything else, including poverty, death, pain, is
indifferent. Since nobody can deprive the wise man of his virtue he is already in possession of the only real good and therefore happy."[42]

Yet in many ways Zeno was an extremely odd cultural hero for the respectable
citizens of early third-century Athens. During his Cynic period he advocated unisex

dress, upheld sexual freedom between men and women—more specifically, the right of men to joint ownership of women (*koinōnia gynaikōn*) for purposes of intercourse—was against monogamy, and firmly tolerant of homosexual relations.[43] This we learn from surviving references to his early treatise *The Republic (Politeia)*,[44] which was well in line with countercultural tendencies, and influenced so powerfully by Cynic ideas that it was said in jest to have been written on Cynosura—Cynosura being not only the name of a well-known local headland, but also, literally interpreted, "the Dog's tail."[45] Zeno wanted everything that characterized the organized *polis*—temples, law courts, gymnasia, money, local allegiances—swept away. This

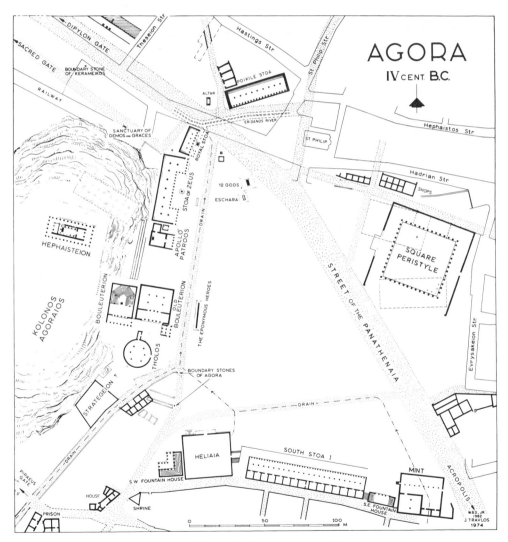

Map 5. The Athenian Agora ca. 300 B.C.
From Camp, *The Athenian Agora*, p. 155.

constituted a frontal assault on Plato and Aristotle, who both, in their different ways, sought the ideal ruler in the context of the *polis*, whereas the Cynics held the *polis* in contempt, not least now that its real power was broken, and saw the wise man as the outsider, the world citizen (*kosmopolitēs*) standing apart from all regional ties.[46] We should, Zeno said, "think all men our fellow demesmen and fellow citizens"—a hint, here, of the later Stoic notion of living in harmony with the cosmic world order (see p. 634). Like Epicurus, like Diogenes, what he offered in those troubled times was not so much a fully reasoned philosophical system as a way of life. It is a nice paradox that this Phoenician iconoclast should have been accepted as a resident guru by the Athenians, as a master who taught their young men "self-fulfillment and self-restraint";[47] an even nicer one that his system should, in the fullness of time, have become an instrument for the instruction of rulers and men of action, from Cato to Marcus Aurelius. Few can have foreseen, as they heard Zeno discourse, striding up and down in the Stoa Poikile, that here was the nucleus of the Greek system of ethics that would take Rome captive—that Stoics, men of the Stoa, would eventually come to include generals, provincial governors, even emperors among their number.

CHAPTER 5

THEOPHRASTUS, MENANDER, AND THE TRANSFORMATION OF ATTIC COMEDY

The literature that has survived from the late fourth century and subsequent Hellenistic period shows some striking contrasts with that of the classical era.* In ways these can be misleading. It might appear, for instance, at first sight, as though there had been a total collapse of tragedy, but of course this is not true. Just as many hopeful tragedians, in Athens and elsewhere, were as busy as ever, but for whatever reason—ranging from the vicissitudes of Byzantine taste to plain lack of talent—their work has, except for snippets and fragments, failed to survive. Lycurgus, as we have seen (p. 52), enshrined the triad of Aeschylus, Sophocles, and Euripides with bronze statues in the Theater of Dionysus (itself now enlarged and frozen in stone, as though by Medusa), as well as the establishment of a canonical text for their plays. Retrospective hagiolatry does not argue for a strong original movement in any art, and it does look very much as though the aim of tragedy from the fourth century onward was imitative, an attempt to emulate the old masters through skilled *mimēsis*.

The stress laid on *mimēsis* by Aristotle in the *Poetics*, as indeed by Plato in his *Republic*, is significant.[1] The borderline between portraying life and imitating art was, and is, far less clear than is often supposed: from the fourth century onwards successful techniques in realistic depiction at once attracted what is rightly known as

---

*Apart from the texts that have survived intact, and the fragments of well-known (and much copied) authors such as Callimachus, a whole host of minor elegists, tragedians, epic poets, epigrammatists, and others were busily at work throughout our period. Till recently—the tragedians excepted—Powell's *Collectanea Alexandrina* (Oxford, 1925) was the only accessible collection of this material, or what survived of it. Now the field has been extended almost beyond recognition by the publication of Hugh Lloyd-Jones' and Peter Parsons' magisterial *Supplementum Hellenisticum* (Berlin and New York, 1983), containing the remains of about 150 little-known authors (in addition to those assembled by Powell) and numerous unattributed fragments and excerpts. To browse through this collection gives one the median flavor, as it were, of Hellenistic poetry in a way nothing else could do. A translation of even a representative selection from this wide-ranging material would be a real service to literature.

the sincerest form of flattery. Just as the stimulus for new architecture now came from external sources (see p. 52), so the social and religious tension between tribe and *polis* that had fueled Attic tragedy was largely dissipated. Tragedies were produced, but failed to catch fire. They bear about the same relation to a Sophoclean or Euripidean play as do those relentlessly second-rate survivals from the Epic Cycle to Homer's *Iliad* and *Odyssey*, or the forgotten Victorian three-deckers moldering in major libraries to the work of Trollope, Dickens, and George Eliot.

There was a group of much-touted tragedians, the so-called Pleiad, in Ptolemy Philadelphos's Alexandria (see p. 177), but their fame seems to have been largely due to royal propaganda and sedulous self-promotion: only one, Lycophron (see pp. 177–79), has any real claim to fame, or notoriety, and that not as a dramatist.[2] We know the names of over a hundred fourth-century and Hellenistic tragedians, and possess fragments, substantial in some cases, of their work.[3] There were occasional oddities, or historical dramas (e.g., Moschion's *Themistocles*), but for the most part these forgotten playwrights went on working the same old mythic plots, perhaps with a certain preference for the exotic. Among the titles credited to Lycophron, for instance, we find an *Andromeda*, a *Heracles*, a *Suppliants*, and a *Hippolytus*. Literature was now too often feeding exclusively on literature. Many of these plays, significantly, were written to be read rather than acted.[4] The general mood is caught to perfection by an anecdote about the fourth-century actor Parmenon, famous for his imitation of a squealing pig: when a real pig was brought on stage, the audience found its squealing sadly inferior, and yelled for Parmenon.[5] Those high-voltage civic and tribal conflicts that had sustained fifth-century tragedy's dialectic were gone for ever, and Attic tragedy became, from the mid-fourth century if not earlier, little more than a fashionable literary exercise. It is a nice paradox that the tradition of Athenian high drama best survived in later comic playwrights' numerous parodies of famous scenes from tragedy.[6]

The drama most characteristic of the Hellenistic period—and the sort that most profoundly influenced not only Rome but the whole subsequent course of European theater—was neither tragedy nor comedy in the fifth-century sense of those terms, though it derived elements from both, late Euripides and late Aristophanes in particular, and bore a closer generic relationship to comedy than to anything else. The metamorphosis of Attic Old Comedy, as we can see it in Aristophanes' *Plutus*, points the way directly toward Menander; so do the florid excesses and melodramatic romanticism of a tragedy such as Euripides' *Orestes*. The transformation is organic and progressive, involving no conscious break.[7] Plots become more domestic; increased prominence is given to slave characters (e.g., Cario in the *Plutus*); there is an incipient tendency to stylize and typologize. What emerges—something wholly predictable in the light of political and social developments—is new to Greek literature: the private comedy of manners. Citizen status in Menander is important only in terms of social prestige (compare all those municipal honorific decrees): there is no real sense of civic involvement.[8] Whether comedy by ceasing to be topical became *ipso facto* universal is quite another matter.[9]

The plots of this New Comedy are complicated and improbable, littered with long-lost foundlings, twists of mistaken identity, and supposed courtesans who turn out to be virtuous middle-class virgins, more often than not heiresses into the bargain. In sexual matters Aristophanic outspokenness (*aischrologia*, "dirty talk," as the fourth century labeled it) has been replaced by coy insinuation (*hyponoia*), the sure mark of an emergent bourgeois-genteel culture.[10] There is always a happy ending. The characters are stereotypes—the crusty old father, the vacuous juvenile lead (head buzzing with romantic yearnings), the cunning slave, the aphoristic cook, the braggart soldier. They are even given stock names.[11] Frustrated love is the recurrent theme. The moralizing asides thrown in to give these puffball plays extra weight should not blind us to the fact that they were the precise ancient equivalents of modern situation comedies or soap operas.[12] A contemporary reader may find some difficulty in appreciating the reasons for the high status Menander, for instance, enjoyed throughout antiquity (though not, interestingly, during his lifetime). Quintilian praised his rhetorical expertise; Plutarch, who detested Aristophanes, could not think of any better reason for going to the theater than to watch Menander, adding: "When else do intellectuals pack the house for a comedy?" The Alexandrian scholar Aristophanes of Byzantium exclaimed: "Menander, Life—which of you imitated the other?"[13] He was the "star" of New Comedy, the "siren of the theaters"; his work was replete with "wit's holy salt."[14] The only objections raised were to his vocabulary, regarded by some purists as overly colloquial—the cost, one assumes, of imitating life.

Obviously even Hellenistic Greek society was not chiefly remarkable for kidnappings, coincidental rape, and contrived happy resolutions. What, then, did Aristophanes of Byzantium mean when he praised Menander for so skillfully imitating life? The compliment cannot but strike us as paradoxical, since to our way of thinking Menander's plays are remarkably formulaic and artificial. The truth, I suspect, is that we badly underestimate the staying power of those iron social-*cum*-literary conventions governing fifth-century Attic drama—conventions that laid down, *inter alia*, what social class of person could be presented in what type of play, as well as what range of actions, reactions, opinions, language, and vocabulary were appropriate or acceptable for them. Euripides must have raised a few shocked eyebrows by making the husband in his *Electra* a peasant farmer.[15] What stirred admiration for Menander was the (to us, gingerly) way in which he set about broaching these conventions, to put on stage something at least approaching life as it was actually lived, some features of everyday Athenian existence. To borrow a phrase from Dr. Johnson, it was not so much that he did it well as that he did it at all.

As the Hellenistic period proceeds we shall find other characteristic experiments in verse, in particular those of urban pastoral (Theocritus), literary epic (Apollonius Rhodius), or epigram and aetiology (Callimachus). But for the earlier years, the late fourth and early third centuries, poetry is almost exclusively associated with drama. Most serious writing was now in prose, and here we find an enormous amount of ephemeral trash being churned out. Historians, philosophers, epistolographers, rhetoricians, biographers, political pamphleteers, gossipmongers—all were busy. Much of what they wrote was either of little importance *per se* or else superseded by later work, which cannibalized it ruthlessly. (One critic, perhaps with an axe to grind, wrote no less than six books on the alleged plagiarisms of Menander.)[16] Scientists and medical historians developed their own tradition (see pp. 480 ff.), largely independent of the philosophers: physics took one road, metaphysics another, to their mutual loss. In oratory, manner increasingly outstripped matter. Epideictic displays, the *logos* for its own sake, became all too prevalent. A society that saw an increasing alienation between rural or urban rentiers and actual producers (the so-called banausic element, despised by all those of gentlemanly education) was bound to witness a growth of unreality in its literature: the Golden Fleece pursued in the library, sheep and goats observed at more than arm's length from behind a thicket of bucolic conventions, literary battles, mock blood. A direct concern with politics was largely restricted to the pamphleteer or the historian, and even then seldom took the form of personal involvement—though Polybius was a striking exception to the rule (see pp. 269 ff.).

Theophrastus (371/0?–288/5), Aristotle's successor as head of the Peripatetic school based on the Lyceum, forms an interesting transitional figure between the old and the new styles in literature. Old enough to have known Plato, he was also a typical *epigonos* of the great thinkers in that, like so many Hellenistic intellectuals, he was more a synthesist, continuator, and teacher than an original pioneer, largely carrying on and developing work begun by Aristotle (though his thought was independent in some areas, e.g. the concept of the soul). He was a popular lecturer, attracting, it is said, crowds of up to two thousand; and Aristotle, deciding that his given name, Tyrtamos, was ugly, renamed him Theophrastus, "Divine Speaker."[17] We have a description of him on the podium, pomaded, dressed in the height of fashion, extravagant and dramatic in his illustrative gestures ("once, mimicking an epicure, he stuck out his tongue and licked his lips").[18] He never married, indeed spoke slightingly of all human passion, and seems to have poured all his energy into his work; we know of well over two hundred books attributed to him, though few have survived.[19] We also possess his will, a remarkable social document, dealing with everything from the manumission of favorite slaves to the replacement of explorers' maps in the Lyceum cloister. Bury me, he said, anywhere convenient in the garden: an interesting sidelight on his personality. A conservative and a man of means, he cultivated Cassander and (perhaps in consequence) enjoyed the friendship and support of Demetrius of Phaleron. This enabled him, though a noncitizen, to own property in Athens, but also got him prosecuted for impiety (without success) by his political enemies. The charge was that he had declared the sovereignty of Tyche in human affairs.[20] Like the rest of the philosophers at Athens, he left the country while Sophocles' restrictive legislation remained in force (above, p. 49).[21]

Theophrastus's most solid work was done on botany: we still possess his treatises on the classification and aetiology of plants. It is very tempting to regard his more famous *Characters* as an essay in the same genre, an attempt to apply the principles of botanical classification to human beings, to typologize men as one would flowers. This reveals an interesting tension between two equally well-marked characteristics of the period. On the one hand we find an increasing tendency toward mimetic realism, which emerges with greatest clarity in the visual arts (see pp. 92 ff.); on the other, there is a drive to abstract and generalize, leading directly to the stock

Fig. 20. Portrait bust of Theophrastus.
Roman copy of a Hellenistic original.
Villa Albani, Rome. Photo Alinari.

characters of New Comedy. The lively sketches that Theophrastus produced—hardly later than 319, to judge from their topical allusions, the year of Antipater's death[22]—contain elements of both, plus strong echoes, both in characterization and in colloquial language, of early Aristophanic characters such as Strepsiades in the *Clouds* or the Sausage Seller in the *Knights*. Aristotelian universals are thus offset with quirky, personal details that bring Theophrastus's portraits instantly to life. Nothing quite like them seems ever to have been produced before; and though they started a long tradition carried on by such figures as Samuel Butler and La Bruyère, nothing quite like them was ever achieved again.

Their purpose is uncertain. It now seems unlikely that (as was once supposed) they had an ethical object, much less that they were put together to show Theophrastus's student Menander how to illustrate *ēthos* in his plays—an engaging instance of economy in utilizing sparse available evidence—but I find the currently more fashionable theory that they formed illustrative matter for Theophrastus's lost *Poetics* (or, alternatively, his monograph on comedy, also lost) no more convincing.[23] Loose similarities with Aristotle's ethical exempla prove nothing, and the *Characters* hardly read like models for budding rhetoricians. Jebb's old theory that Theophrastus wrote these sketches for the private amusement of his friends, and that they were only collected and published after his death, seems no longer to be taken seriously by scholars; but it has, I think, a great deal to be said for it.[24]

Like most work from this period, the *Characters* shows comparatively little concern with contemporary events.[25] Once or twice, though, we catch a glimpse of what it was like to live in Athens after Crannon. The braggart (23) "will tell you he has had three letters in a row from Antipater, inviting him to Macedonia, and that he's been offered a license for tax-exempt export of timber from Macedonia, but has refused it, not wanting anyone to run him down as pro-Macedonian" (the most probable date, historically, for this fictional scene is 320/19).[26] We sense at once the currents of pro- and anticollaborationist feeling that must have torn Athens in those difficult days. The rumormonger (8), purporting to have witnesses straight from the battlefield, tells a circumstantial story, replete with wishful thinking (cf. p. 19), of how "Polyperchon and the king [i.e., Philip Arrhidaios] have won a battle, and Cassander is a prisoner" (again, the likeliest date for such a rumor is 319, soon after Antipater's death and Cassander's revolt). Finally, Theophrastus's portrait of the oligarch, or authoritarian (26), with his "arrogant taste for power and gain," his scorn for "the rabble" and "democratic agitators," his complaints that the rich are being bled to death by obligatory state services (he would clearly have supported Demetrius of Phaleron, who abolished them),[27] that the working classes are irresponsible and ungrateful, must have borne a recognizable resemblance to many who supported the oligarchic regime installed by Antipater. As Ussher says, "one feels often that Theophrastus is dealing with flesh-and-blood Athenians, eccentric, puffed-up, or merely nasty—contemporaries well known in the city and recognizable by any reader."[28]

What *we* get from the *Characters*, on the other hand, is a vivid mosaic of Athenian social life. Athens under Macedonian control, with Phocion and the oligarchs still in power, springs to life here as nowhere else.[29] We are given glimpses, as rare as they are valuable, into private homes, the market, the baths, the theater, the gymnasia, temples, and law courts. We meet barbers, bankers, nursemaids, musicians, flute girls and wine merchants, parasites and informers. Pets (as we might guess from the *Greek Anthology*) are in great demand. Social life, with its dinner parties and public festivals, pays very little attention to the political uncertainties of the day. It is hard to remember, reading Theophrastus's sketches, that he is portraying the life of a recently defeated, junta-ruled city, with a Macedonian garrison quartered in Piraeus. That provides the historian with a salutary corrective. But above all there is his marvelous, and unending, procession of offbeat, eccentric, nonconformist personalities: the flattering toady patting his patron's cushions in the theater; the rattlepate running on by free association; the bore whose own children ask him for a story to put them to sleep; the oaf who sings heartily in the public baths, hammers hobnails into his shoes, and forks hay to the cattle while gulping his own breakfast; the low fellow who shrinks from "no disreputable trade, town crier or hired cook"; the flasher who exposes himself to respectable women (presumably the other sort are regarded as fair game); the absent-minded stumblebum who contrives, after a midnight visit to the outhouse, to lurch down the wrong path and get bitten by his neighbor's dog; the superstitious man walking around all day with a mouthful of bay leaves; the boil-ridden hairy oaf with black decaying teeth, who not only fails to wash before going to bed with his wife, but even "burps at you in the middle of a drink"; the grossly jovial dinner companion who assures you that his diarrhea was "blacker than this soup"; the military coward who pretends he has to go back for the sword he's forgotten, and spends his time playing nurse to the wounded; the foot-in-mouth master of tactlessness who watches your servant being flogged and tells you about a slave *he* had, who—after just such a whipping—went and hanged himself; the slanderers, the ambitious, the misers, the cheeseparing freeloaders.

This fascinating gallery, quite apart from illuminating the whole complex structure of Athenian society in the late fourth century—its idiosyncratic no less than its perennial elements—also forms a significant literary analogue to the new realism in portraiture so characteristic of the whole Hellenistic age (see pp. 107 ff.). Aristotelian *mimēsis* applied to all forms of artistic expression. When Sophocles claimed that Euripides drew men as they were, whereas he himself portrayed them as they ought to be,[30] he was foreshadowing an era when the Euripidean thesis would be treated as axiomatic. How far the rejection of idealism in favor of things-as-they-are can be correlated with the loss of true autonomy is a moot point; it could equally be argued that the new trend was, rather, implicit in Promethean (or Protagorean) humanism, the dangers of which had already been foreseen by Sophocles in the closing lines of a famous chorus from the *Antigone*.[31] What remains incontrovertible is that when we come to the work of Menander, who himself studied under Theophrastus, and seems to have shared his teacher's typologizing preoccupation with the *comédie humaine*,[32] we find ourselves in a bourgeois world of moneymaking and matchmaking, of comfortable cliché and romantic fantasy, where accuracy of type is matched only by implausibility of plot, and we seem light-years (rather than a bare century) distant from the great moral and political issues that preoccupied the tragedians of fifth-century Athens. Universalism now rested on a solid basis of family values and shared commercial interests.[33]

Menander, son of Diopeithes of Cephisia, was a wealthy and well-connected Athenian.[34] Born in 342/1, he was about five when Philip defeated the Greeks at Chaeronea, and twenty at the time of Crannon and Amorgos (322/1). It was now, while still completing his two years' service as an *ephēbos*, that Menander put on his first play, the *Orgē* (*Wrath*), and won his first victory with it.[35] His instructor in playwriting was the prolific and long-lived Alexis (ca. 375–ca. 275), whose working career spanned both Middle and New Comedy, and from whom Menander borrowed a good deal—the concept of the *parasitos* (originally a blend of dinner companion, private jester, and freeloader: hence our "parasite"),[36] the coining of pseudo-profound aphorisms (marriage as slavery, the virtues of moderation, life as a carnival, old age as the evening of life),[37] and, possibly, some of his plots (e.g., *Into the Well* at once brings Menander's *Dyskolos* to mind).[38] But Menander totally lacks the satirical pungency that makes the loss of Alexis's work, except for tantalizing fragments, particularly regrettable. "Everyone agrees," he once wrote, "that all top people are rich: you never see a blue-blooded beggar."[39]

Menander wrote over a hundred plays, yet won first prize only eight times.[40] He was drowned in his fifties while swimming off Piraeus (292/1): Pausanias locates his tomb beside the Athens–Piraeus highway, near Euripides' cenotaph.[41] He is said to have been a handsome man, and his surviving portraits support this;[42] but there is

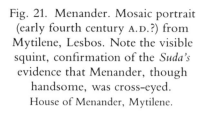

Fig. 21. Menander. Mosaic portrait (early fourth century A.D.?) from Mytilene, Lesbos. Note the visible squint, confirmation of the *Suda's* evidence that Menander, though handsome, was cross-eyed. House of Menander, Mytilene.

also a tradition that he suffered from a pronounced squint, now strikingly confirmed by the famous mosaic found in Mytilene.[43] It was probably through his connection with Theophrastus that he came to be an intimate friend of Demetrius of Phaleron. Phaedrus, in one of his fables, draws an unpleasantly plausible picture of the Athenian elite hastening to pay court to Demetrius, to "kiss the oppressor's hand" while privately grumbling about their loss of freedom. Among the last in line, Phaedrus says, who came sneaking in only because "absence might be a mark against them," was Menander: elegant, languid, pomaded, mincing along in a loose flowing robe. "And who," Phaedrus makes Demetrius exclaim, "is that screaming queen who has the nerve to approach me in such a getup?" "That," his attendants told him, "is Menander, the playwright." At which Demetrius, instantly changing tack, exclaimed: "The most handsome man I ever saw!"[44] If we relate this fable to what we know of Demetrius's own dandified, not to say epicene, habits (above, pp. 46–47), it is hard to resist the conclusion that Menander, like many an artist since, was out to win influence in high places, and knew, in this case, just how to do it. Far from being homosexual, he was "absolutely crazy about women"; but the same source to which we owe that description reminds us that he had "sharp wits."[45] In any case, his intimacy with Demetrius was such that after the dictator's fall he only just avoided prosecution simply (so far as we can tell) on the basis of guilt through association.[46]

How far he should be assumed, because of these associations, to have been himself an advocate of authoritarian or plutocratic rule is an open question. As one scholar put it, "pupils may be transitory or inattentive, and friends do not necessarily think alike."[47] Yet it is hard to visualize this crowd-pleasing middle-of-the-roader, platitudinous if ironic,[48] as a liberal crusader. He would seem rather, on what little evidence we have, to have shared the chameleon qualities attributed to Alcibiades,[49] and to have worked hard to ingratiate himself with whatever regime might be in power. It has even been suggested that his sympathy with pro-

Macedonian government was one reason why his plays, at least during his lifetime, lacked more popular success. This I doubt: while the fuss about P. G. Wodehouse's German broadcasts was at its height, his books continued to sell in undiminished quantities. The parallel is interesting in other ways, too, since the world Menander portrays is almost as stylized as that of Blandings Castle or the Drones Club, and indeed contains many very similar characters: Bertie Wooster is not at all unlike one of Menander's well-heeled young suitors, potty with innocent passion and misunderstood good intentions, while his clever, manipulative slaves have many characteristics in common with Jeeves.[50] Both writers, moreover, lived in highly disturbed times; both, except in the most oblique ways, ignored these disturbances in their work. One scholar wonders whether the *Dyskolos* (see below) may not carry political overtones, with the old curmudgeon of the title symbolizing the Athenian *dēmos* forced to accept the unwelcome regime of Demetrius of Phaleron:[51] I find this a grotesquely improbable notion.

The keynote, rather, is (as in those late Euripidean choruses) escapism. What the members of an Athenian audience wanted, in 316,[52] was to get away from their own grim condition, a not-unfamiliar phenomenon today. It had not been all that long since the defeat at Crannon, Phocion's hysterically orchestrated execution, the brief but violent restoration of democracy. To that extent these Athenian spectators are much more like a modern soap-opera audience than the constantly involved, and politicized, *dēmos* of the fifth century, on whose vote the fate of Athens hung daily. Also, the abolition of the state subsidy (*theōrikon*) for theatergoing must have substantially modified the composition of the audience as such, restricting it for the most part to prosperous bourgeois citizens and their would-be emulators, all only too eager to forget, for a while, the harsh realities of public life, and[53]

> to be entertained instead by the consoling and idealised picture of stable, middle-class family life, where the problems of money and sexual desire, of misunderstandings and flawed relationships, were more limited in scale, always fathomable, and always resolved in the inevitable happy ending which celebrated and cemented family unity.

It is quite possible that in those anarchic times, when the reduced fleet of Athens could no longer adequately police the Aegean, and law and order too often went by default, there in fact were kidnappings of heiresses by pirates, especially from the more exposed coastal districts of Attica. It is certain that exposure (in addition to abortion and primitive contraception) was practiced by Greek families, and the rescue of foundlings by rural peasants, childless or not, may have been a more common phenomenon in real life than we suppose. Yet when all allowances have been made, the world we enter here is immeasurably remote from that of Oedipus or Antigone. Technically, too, we have come a long way from the obscenity, political involvement, and episodic vaudeville structure of an Aristophanic comedy. *Agōn* and *parabasis*, choral lyrics integrated with the action—all are gone. Instead we have the sequence of five acts familiar from later European drama, divided by choral interludes that have little if anything to do with the action, and do not survive in our manuscripts, which merely mark the points where they occur.[54]

The escapist motif is unmistakable. For most Athenians of the classical era the Agora, the hub of the *polis*, formed the center of the world, whereas Menander as often as not sets his scene out in the Attic countryside. His characters, rustic or urban, are concerned with their own rather than the state's affairs, with money and marriage, not with politics. The nearest we come to civic factionalism is the tired exchange of stereotyped insults ("You drivel-spouting troublemaker"; "You authoritarian bastard") between two characters in the *Sicyonians*.[55] Menander's soldiers—Polemon in the *Perikeiromenē* (*Shorn Woman*), Thrasonides in the *Misoumenos* (*Unpopular Man*)—are figures of fun, their lust well contained by romantic yearnings;[56] but the real unemployed mercenaries and soldiers of fortune who roamed the countryside (see p. 313) tended to be unpleasant toughs much given to rape and larceny. Murder and serious illness, similarly, are taboo subjects in the plays.[57] Rape is a recurrent motif, but only as a stylized determinant of plot: it normally takes place at a nocturnal festival, and more often than not the rapist later, all-unknowing, marries his victim, who regularly bears a child as the result of his earlier attentions.[58]

Pimps and parasites, gold-hearted whores, mysterious pregnancies, mistaken identities, complex and ill-motivated social deceptions, family legacies—these are the ingredients that go to form Menander's stock in trade. There is the same quiet yet stubborn preoccupation with good (i.e., financially profitable and socially improving) matches that we find in, say, Jane Austen, though without her incomparable psychological insight. No one in this world, with very few exceptions, has a job or does any serious work except on his own estate: Menander's society consists, in essence, of rural landowners, rentiers, and their employees, slaves, or hangers-on (e.g., the recurrent high-class cooks). We meet the occasional merchant, but his line of merchandise, as in Dickens, tends to remain vague. Metics, resident aliens, though an influential group, are conspicuous by their absence.[59] The element of Chance or Fortune, Tyche, tends as always to be overworked,[60] though this may in some degree be because Menander is dealing with an agricultural society where (political vicissitudes quite apart) luck formed an integral element of the year's balance sheet, and technological foresight remained minimal (see p. 469).

Till 1907, the date of Lefebvre's publication of the Cairo codex,[61] our verdict on Menander had to rest on brief quotations and the opinions of ancient critics: his works were all lost (except through the indirect medium of Roman adaptations) before the eighth century A.D. Three plays, *The Arbitrators* (*Epitrepontes*), *The Woman of Samos* (*Samia*), and *The Shorn Girl* (*Perikeiromenē*, variously rendered as *The Rape of the Locks* or *The Unkindest Cut*), were well enough represented in the codex to give a general idea of their plot, structure, and, above all, their language and style. The overall impression was of relentlessly low-key colloquial dialogue, recreating (with a discreet infusion of popularized ethics) the platitudinous exchanges of day-to-day life, and written in an unpretentious Attic already well on its way to becoming *koinē*—that bastardized vernacular *lingua franca* of the Hellenistic world, now enshrined for ever in the New Testament.[62]

Finally, in 1959, came the most important find: virtually the whole of an early play by Menander, the *Dyskolos* (variously translated as *The Curmudgeon, The Bad-Tempered Man, The Peevish Fellow, The Grouch,* or even *Grumpy*).[63] It is now possible to form a fair picture of his work as a whole, since there exist also numerous citations and fragments from other plays: the total body of surviving work—including the bulk of *The Woman of Samos* and of a further play, *The Shield* (*Aspis*), published in 1969 from the same papyrus book as the *Dyskolos*[64]—fills a fat volume.[65] Yet far from enhancing our opinion of a playwright on whom earlier judgments tended, because of the fragmentary corpus, either to be held in abeyance or else to echo the eulogies of antiquity, the publication of the *Dyskolos* leaves us all too aware that the standards of the late fourth century B.C. are very different from ours. Produced in January 316, a few months after Demetrius of Phaleron became *epimelētēs* of Athens, it won the young playwright what was probably his second victory. The play's situation and characters—not by accident, I would maintain—bear even less direct relation than is usual with Menander to contemporary affairs.[66] A fifth-century audience had had no qualms about relegating Sophocles' *Oedipus* to second place (it was defeated by a production of Aeschylus's nephew Philocles);[67] this new generation of Athenians was, clearly, easier to please.

Since the *Dyskolos* is our only complete play by Menander, and since opinions are fairly sharply divided as to its merits, it may be advantageous, at this point, to give a fairly detailed description of its plot. After an introductory prologue by the god Pan, setting the scene and explaining the action (1–49), we are presented with a stock Menandrian situation (50–188): a rich young man, Sostratos, sighing with love for a girl he has encountered, while his companion, Chaireas, works out a plan for her conquest. If she's a whore, Chaireas says airily, we'll burn her door down. If, on the other hand, she turns out to be a freeborn girl with marriage in view, then "find out about her family, income, personal habits" (65–66). Sostratos has sent off his huntsman, Pyrrhias, to make just such inquiries. Pyrrhias now enters, very much in disarray, but with the information that the girl is, indeed, freeborn. His disheveled state is due to the fact that he has just been run off her father's farm by the father himself, Cnemon, the curmudgeon of the title, and the kind of farmer who today would carry a prominently racked rifle or shotgun in his pickup. Hardly has Pyrrhias got this information out before Cnemon storms in, mangling mythology and ranting about trespass. From the opening lines every character seems both under-motivated and, for no good or sufficient reason, in a permanent hysterical frenzy.

At this point it might seem a simple solution to Sostratos's problem if he were to tell Myrrhine, Cnemon's daughter, and, if it comes to that, Cnemon himself, just what he has in mind. But instead (since with Menander tortuous gambits must do duty for a plot) he goes off to consult with Geta, a clever slave of his father's (181 ff.). Enter then Myrrhine, the daughter, complaining that their old servant has dropped a bucket down the well. Sostratos, dizzy with love, gets water for her. The scene between them is observed by Daos, the slave of Cnemon's stepson, Gorgias, who just happens to own the only other house in the immediate neighborhood, where (to complicate things further) he lives with the curmudgeon's separated wife. Daos, thinking Sostratos is aiming to seduce Myrrhine rather than marry her, goes and tells his master. Gorgias, an overeducated rhetorician who talks like a book, in elaborate bipartite sentences,[68] confronts Sostratos with this suspicion. Sostratos manages to convince Gorgias that his intentions are strictly honorable.

The two young men now concoct an improbable plan for Sostratos to work in the fields alongside Gorgias, the point being that Cnemon cannot stand the sight of gentlemen of leisure. Sostratos agrees, but is soon complaining that the mattock he has been given weighs a ton (390). This scene is followed by the appearance of Geta, together with Sikon, a cook, dragging a sheep: Sostratos's mother has had a bad dream about her son, and is going to sacrifice to Pan (393 ff.). The dream, of course, is that Sostratos was in farm clothes and working his neighbor's land with a mattock. Cnemon sees the sacrificial procession arrive, and decides, with no good reason given, that it is unsafe to leave his house unattended (427 ff.). His endemic suspicions and ingrained rural sourness are not provided with any adequate roots in the action; he is simply a walking embodiment of crabbed misanthropy, a Theophrastan humor, the eternal angry farmer swearing at trespassers. (As Pan explains early in the prologue, Cnemon lives in a hill region "where those who can, farm the rocks": perhaps that should suffice.) Meanwhile Geta and Sikon try to borrow pots and pans from him, with predictable results; Sostratos staggers in half-dead from fieldwork, and not even having had the chance to talk with Cnemon; everyone talks, boringly and irrelevantly, about the sacrifice;[69] and Cnemon discovers that his mattock is down the well. This takes us to the end of the third act.

The fourth act at least provides a little fortuitous action (620 ff.). Cnemon falls down the well, where, I cannot help feeling, it would have been more sensible to leave him. Gorgias and Sostratos, however, haul him up offstage, Sostratos in erotic ecstasy because Myrrhine is there beside him, making a loud Greek female fuss about her poor father. The rescue is described by Sostratos in a brisk little parody of a tragic messenger speech (666–90). The rescued Cnemon now delivers a portentous harangue about realizing for the first time that "a man needs someone, someone there and ready to help him out" (708–47).[70] He then promises to adopt Gorgias, already his stepson, as his legal son—a move that makes me wonder about the claim that "Gorgias's motives in saving him from the well are purely disinterested"[71]—and tells him to find a husband for Myrrhine. "*I* won't be able to," Cnemon admits, a trifle disingenuously; "not a single one will *ever* please me." Finally he comes out with one statement, however platitudinous, that has interest, because it suggests Cynic influence: "If everyone was like me, there'd be no courts, men wouldn't drag each other off to prison, there'd be no war—everyone would be happy with middling possessions" (743–45).

This direct assault, in a prize-winning play, on everything from civic involvement to due process under law—everything, in fact, that characterized the *polis* in its heyday—is of considerable social significance. The rejection of war, once the favorite inter-*polis* sport, is particularly interesting. Yet nothing comes of this interpolated sermon in any dramatic sense; it bears no more relation to the substance of the play than does a commercial to the program it interrupts. Instead, the last act is devoted to a perfunctory knotting-up of the various frustrated betrothals. Gorgias talks Cnemon into letting Sostratos marry Myrrhine (Myrrhine herself, characteristically, is not consulted). Sostratos's father, Callippides, arrives for the sacrifice and balks at the idea of letting *his* daughter marry Gorgias, saying he does not intend to have two paupers in the family at once (775 ff.). Sostratos, suddenly acquiring Gorgias's rhetorical prolixity for the occasion, then reads his father a mini-lecture on not being stingy—"Fortune will take everything from you and bestow it on someone else, who may well not deserve it" (797 ff.). Invest in everyone, Sostratos says. Then if you ever come a cropper, you'll get help in return (809–10). Instead of dressing his son down, not only for gross impertinence but also for the appallingly cliché-ridden form that his impertinence takes, Callipides at once gives in. The double betrothal will take place. The cook Sikon and Geta the slave then have a little rough horseplay with the sleeping Cnemon; after a rude awakening he is finally worn down by their jolly violence and agrees to attend the feast, grumbling as he goes. (And who could blame him?) So the play ends, and we are left with the problem of whether Menander imitated life or vice versa.

Now it is, I would concede, often easy enough to make a serious writer look ridiculous by merely potting his plots: Clifton Fadiman's demolition of the novels of Faulkner is a classic case in point.[72] On the other hand, it is also undeniable that Menander stands as ancestor to the whole European comedy of manners, from Molière and Goldoni by way of Sheridan to Shaw, Wilde, and their modern *epigonoi* such as Coward, Simon, and Ayckbourn. The near-unanimous verdict of antiquity may be hard to understand, but it is also hard to argue with it, to insist that the emperor may, after all, lack the gorgeous apparel claimed for him. There is, too, something infinitely ironic—Tyche in one of her more malicious aspects—about the mere possibility that now, at last, that the miracle has happened, and a whole Greek prize-winning drama has been resurrected from the sands of Egypt, it could conceivably be regarded as second-rate hackwork. One can hardly blame the papyrologists and textual critics who have labored so long and so minutely on Bodmer Papyrus IV for not being disposed to admit that their collective intellectual endeavors have been expended on such lightweight matter. Yet Sir William Tarn—a formidable Hellenistic scholar, though neither a papyrologist nor a textual critic—dismissed Menander and his imitators as "about the dreariest desert in literature," and that verdict cannot be lightly set aside.[73]

Menander's defenders have naturally done their best to disprove it. Their regular line is to ignore the substance of the attacks, and to stress that Menander should really be admired for something quite different, such as the social and psychological realism of his characterization,[74] his Platonic, even Aeschylean, concern with humanity,[75] his elegance, emotional subtlety, and complex dramatic skills,[76] his energy, power, and sense of purpose,[77] or his significant realistic detail, *anti*-typical characterization, clever word games, and deflating parody ("secularization").[78] The list could be extended: most of the qualities selected for praise, we may note, are hard to prove or disprove. Yet sooner or later even Menander's most devoted admirers are forced to concede many of those faults we have already noted: the hackneyed recurrent motifs, the artificial coincidences, the repeated use of grotesque devices (e.g., rape at a festival) to precipitate action. These are then excused by a timely reminder that Menander had, after all, a very different audience to deal with from that of his fifth-century predecessors, and needed (despite his large private income!) "to pamper and not antagonise them in his competitive struggle for success," an argument that Euripides, for one, would have treated with the contempt it deserves.[79]

In other words, we are being asked to accept as fact that the soap-opera plots, the popular aphorisms, the commonplace moral values, stock characters, stereotyped opinions, and cliché-ridden dialogue were all concessions made by this intellectual and creative paragon to the Aunt Ednas of the Athenian bourgeoisie, whereas any flashes of brilliance that can be detected in his work are ascribed to the genius he was forced to restrain while pursuing the bitch-goddess success. In that case, quite apart from the innate immorality of such a proceeding (once a whore, always a whore, as Orwell remarked in a very similar modern context), one can only point out that Menander's essay in self-prostitution did him singularly little good. Eight victories in over a hundred attempts is hardly the record of a clever crowd-pleaser: Hugh Walpole did far better. Alternatively, a diametrically opposite case has been argued (at least one scholar has, on different occasions, tried both approaches), which asserts that Menander's comedies were caviar to the general, that he did not make enough concessions, and was, indeed, defeated so often because "his audiences did not appreciate the delicate nuances and individualised refinements of his art."[80]

Examination of the surviving *oeuvre* reveals a good deal of special pleading and hyperbole in all these claims. The supposedly subtle characterization is both broad and one-dimensional, based on generalized ethics rather than psychological insight. The wise aphorisms turn out to be crackerbarrel commonplaces. Too much of the dialogue is flaccid and colloquial pseudorealism, little relieved by occasional references to such things as decaying battlefield corpses,[81] a phenomenon with far less shock value for that harsh age than for our own, and anyway already familiar in previous literature from Homer and Archilochus onwards. Significant transformations (e.g., Cnemon's change-of-heart speech in the *Dyskolos*), are badly undermotivated.

The rest of the corpus similarly abounds in situational idiocies. Take the *Arbitrators* (*Epitrepontes*), another much-praised Menandrian torso: a young stud, Charisios ("Charmer"), having raped one Pamphile ("Darling") during the inevitable night festival, gets married, only to discover, first, that the girl he married has a baby five months later, and then, as a dénouement, that she was also the girl he raped, and that the child is therefore presumptively his. We get the usual array of wisecracking cooks and smart slaves, rings and tokens, implausible coincidences. Disbelief, though suspended, keeps breaking in. Why, we may legitimately ask, did Charisios not have the problem of her five-months' child out face-to-face with his wife instead of listening to the servants? Why, instead, does he simply walk out on her in a huff and take up with Habrotonon, a guitar-strumming floozy with the usual heart of gold? No play otherwise, the cynic might answer; rational plots are not exactly Menander's forte.

Perhaps more important than the ongoing debate about Menander's literary value to us is any attempt we can make to explain his appeal to his contemporaries and, *a fortiori*, to succeeding generations in the Hellenistic and Graeco-Roman world. We will not attain this end by upgrading his aims, or outlook, to satisfy our own preoccupations. There is, now, more than enough material on which to form a judgment, and it all tells the same story. While his Athenian spectators appreciated *mimēsis* insofar as this delineated popular character types, from grouchy old farmer to braggart soldier, from conniving slave to lovesick youth, they had no time at all for tragic involvement in the old fifth-century sense, much less for political satire or for broad Aristophanic humor. Realism, *mimēsis*, became, indeed, a far preferable alternative to what Gregers Werle in *The Wild Duck* described as "the claims of the ideal." The passion for achieving a likeness, in literature as in the visual arts,[82] repudiated everything that Daedalic sculptors or Platonic thinking had stood for. It is no accident that from Aristophanes' *Plutus* onwards the scene of each comedy is normally restricted to that *ne plus ultra* of mundane realism, a street with house-fronts, or that plays are named after professional types (*Farmer, Doctor, Parasite*), or courtesans.[83]

The free spirit no longer explored Cloudcuckooland, harrowed Hades, or soared heavenwards on giant dung beetles; it moved, now, at the discretion of Macedonia, and in Pella, notoriously, creative endeavor was an imported commodity. The mood was both genteel and escapist: a middle-class obsession with money, offset by a coy, almost prim, rejection of peasant obscenity; resignation, or indifference, to the loss of political independence; an upgrading of family values; a sanitization of unpleasant realities such as rape or abduction; the deployment of romantic fantasy to camouflage unpalatable social facts. When we read Aristophanes or the fifth-century tragedians, we know, instantly, that we are in the presence of something astonishing and unique, both socially and in literature. Even the fragments of Menander's teacher, Alexis, crackle with originality and life.[84] But what Menander himself mirrors for us, with deadly accuracy, is something at once less uplifting and more familiar: the flawed, self-seeking nature of our own common humanity.

All this perhaps lends a rather unexpected overtone to the famous anecdote in Plutarch about Menander still not having written his play as the festival for which it was meant approached.[85] When a friend inquired, in some anxiety, about his progress, Menander replied: "Oh, the comedy's finished: I've got my theme—all I have to do now is write the dialogue." That, alas—formula dressed out in platitude—is just how his work reads. The notion of all else being secondary to plot is, of course, a staple of Aristotelian criticism;[86] but critics who apply it to Menander do so at their peril.[87] Daos, the slave in the *Aspis*, may be as full of sly literary quotations as Aeschylus and Euripides in the *Frogs*,[88] or the characters in the *Epitrepontes* may cite Euripides himself at one another, and on occasion philosophize in his manner;[89] the overall result is still a sad falling-off from Attic Old Comedy, let alone the fifth-century tragedians. But it was (a fact of prime historical importance) what, in his lifetime, the people who mattered, that is, the theatergoing propertied classes, wanted; and it caught the admiration of ancient critics after his death. If we can appreciate why—and part, at least, of the answer should emerge during the course of this book—our understanding of the Hellenistic age will be immeasurably enhanced.

CHAPTER 6

THE POLITICS
OF ROYAL PATRONAGE:
EARLY PTOLEMAIC ALEXANDRIA

We have seen much evidence of a move away from involvement with the classical *polis* during the late fourth century: commercialism, lack of real political power, and intellectual alienation all played their part in this process. What Plato, with odd pre-science, referred to as "doing your own thing" became increasingly the norm for thinking Greeks rather than, as earlier, a term of social abuse.[1] Another major factor was the rapid development of urbanism. The collapse of one sort of city, and political system, heralded the emergence of another, which had far stronger roots in the future: it is, indeed, still with us today. The establishment of the great Successor kingdoms under autocratic monarchs working through a centralized bureaucracy brought with it urbanization on a far larger and more cosmopolitan scale than anything hitherto known. Pergamon, Antioch, Seleucia-on-Tigris, above all Alexandria: these vast cities, focal points for international trade and cultural development, are more like London or Paris or New York today than were Periclean Athens or even Knossos at the height of its glory. The megalopolis had arrived on the European scene for the first time: cities, that is, of polyglot population and enormous resources, their interests not limited by merely local or ethnic considerations. Foreshadowed in ways by Near Eastern cities such as Nineveh, Babylon, and Mari-on-Euphrates, or, within the Greek cultural sphere, by early Ionian foundations—Miletus, for instance, or the Halicarnassus of Herodotus—they nevertheless marked a completely new stage in Mediterranean history, culminating, three centuries later, in what Horace was to describe as "the smoke and wealth and clamor of Rome."[2]

Of these Hellenistic cities the most important—and certainly the most enduring: it still flourishes today—was, is, Alexandria in Egypt. Poised between Africa and Europe, the meeting place of all races and creeds,[3] Alexandria has survived almost two and a half millennia of violent, colorful history. Here lay Alexander's body, on display, embalmed, in a golden coffin—till a late Ptolemy, short of funds, exchanged it for one of glass or alabaster (see p. 553).[4] Here Caesar, while busy im-

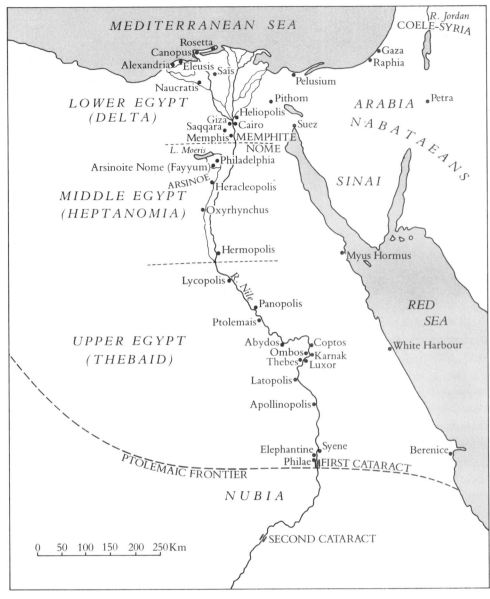

Map 6. Egypt.

pregnating Cleopatra with male offspring and vast political ambitions, found himself fighting an *opéra bouffe* campaign against the troops of a court eunuch and the always violent, always unpredictable Alexandrian mob (see pp. 664 ff.). Here the Septuagint was translated,[5] and—our present concern—the greatest center of learning in the ancient world brought into being. (During Caesar's brush with the locals in 48 B.C. some part of the famous Library's main book collection was burned, accidentally but irretrievably: one instance of the pen *not* being mightier than the sword.

Mark Antony allegedly presented Cleopatra with two hundred thousand volumes commandeered from the Pergamon library by way of compensation, but how far they coincided with those lost is anyone's guess.)[6] The cynical Alexandrians transferred their flattery, like their hatred, from one conqueror to another without embarrassment. The modern Alexandrian poet Constantine Cavafy has a delectable comment on Antony and Cleopatra's defeat:[7]

> The news about the outcome of the sea battle off Actium
> Was indeed unexpected.
> But there's no need for us to draft a new address.
> Only the name need be changed. There,
> In the last lines, instead of *having freed the Romans*
> *From the ruinous Octavian,*
> *That parody of a Caesar,*
> We'll now put *having freed the Romans*
> *From the ruinous Antony.*
> The whole text fits in beautifully.

Disputatious by nature, the Alexandrians became adept at theology (having, according to tradition, been converted by St. Mark, whose body was later filched from the Moslems by some Venetian privateers, in a barrel of pickled pork) and at the riots that, in those early, heady days, went with arguments over dogma.[8] Satirists abounded in the city, and showed scant respect for the great: it was in Alexandria that the various nicknames for reigning Ptolemies were first coined. When Ptolemy II married his full sister (see p. 145)—by some sexist oddity it was she, not he, who, while they both lived, was known as Philadelphos—the Greek poet Sotades, who seems to have made a habit of attacking the Successors, published a lampoon that included the stinging line "You are pushing the prong into an unholy fleshpot." For this he was first imprisoned, and later hunted down by Ptolemy's admiral Patroclus, who drowned him in a lead coffin: even the modes of execution tended to be exotic.[9] In A.D. 215 the Roman emperor Caracalla suffered similar attacks (though not on the grounds of incest) from local scribblers during a state visit, and retaliated—despite lavish sacrifices made in his honor—by ordering a general massacre of the young men of military age.[10] Small wonder that Alexandria became a hotbed of heresies: the great Athanasius, bishop of Alexandria during the fourth century, had his work cut out.[11]

As the Roman empire declined, so did the commerce on which Alexandria depended. In 616 the city was captured by the Persians, and thirty years later by the Arabs. The development of Cairo and the discovery of the eastern trade route round the Cape left Alexandria a backwater. Its renaissance came only in the nineteenth century with Mahommed Ali, who restored it as a major port and naval station: in both World Wars it served as the main Allied naval base in the eastern Mediterranean.[12] Thus we see that despite its vicissitudes—at one point the canal supplying the city with fresh water silted up—Alexandria has had a continuous, organic, living

Fig. 22. Roman lamp (first century A.D.)
with a schematized view of the
harbor of Alexandria.
Leningrad Museums.

history in a way that Pergamon, say, has not. Though subsidence of the land and silting have changed the city's appearance (few ancient remains survive, and only the western quarter, the least important in antiquity, seems to have been continuously occupied), the heritage of Alexandria has survived unbroken.[13] In that sense the streets that witnessed the pomp of the Ptolemies are also those that brooded over Cavafy's furtive amours: Alexandria has remained, even in the twentieth century, what Lawrence Durrell, in *The Alexandria Quartet*, called "the great winepress of love." Since 1956, however, the city has lost most of its cosmopolitan, non-Islamic inhabitants—Greeks, Italians, Coptic Christians—and with them a great deal of its perennial magic. But Alexandria has survived previous lean years, and may well do so again. No one should underestimate its capacity for passive resistance.

The city lies on a narrow bar of land between Lake Mareotis and the sea, about 130 miles northwest of Cairo. In 331 B.C., after finally reducing the island fortress of Tyre, and being crowned pharaoh in Memphis, Alexander the Great decided to found a new city here.[14] There had been an earlier settlement on or near the site, known as Rhacotis, but now Alexander, accompanied by a Greek architect named Deinocrates, personally went over the ground, marking out the site of the agora, the perimeter of the city walls, the location of temples. It seems clear that commerce was the main object he had in mind; but Alexandria also provided a fine complex of deep-water harbors, better than any other existing port in the Delta, and was blessed with a healthy climate and cool prevailing winds, a boon during the summer season.[15] A dike and mole were constructed, linking the offshore island of Pharos to the mainland; the mole became known as the Heptastadion, or "Seven-Stader," because it was almost a mile long (eight stades to the mile). From the start Alexandria was, inevitably, cosmopolitan, since it had no Greek background or roots, no Hellenic founder (*oikistēs*) to give it a firm ethnic tradition. Laid out on an axial grid so oriented that it caught the coolness of the sea breeze,[16] Alexandria was, first and last, Alexander's creation, the nearest thing to that racial melting pot he is sometimes alleged to have envisaged. His prophet Aristander declared that the city would have "most abundant and helpful resources and be a nursing mother to men of every nation." For once Aristander showed true prescience: the city developed and flourished with extraordinary speed.[17]

While Alexander was conquering the East, his governor in Alexandria, the rapacious Cleomenes (see p. 14), was encouraging trade and exploiting the fellahin in time-honored style: he had, after all, an age-old pharaonic tradition on which to draw, and to the Egyptian peasant it made little difference who was calling the tune. When Ptolemy son of Lagus was allotted Egypt as his satrapy after Alexander's death, Alexandria, rather than Memphis, became his natural center of operations. Ptolemy, as a Greek-educated Macedonian, preferred not to be out of sight of the Mediterranean. He also determined, from very early on, that Alexandria was to be not only a great commercial port, but also the new home, and breeding ground, for the best in Greek art, science, and scholarship.

It is interesting to speculate on what gave him this impulse, and drove him to pursue it with such resolution, to sink so much capital into fulfilling his dream. He was, of course, a historian himself (his account of Alexander's campaigns is the one on which Arrian later most relied), just as his son and successor, perhaps as a result of Strato's encouragement (below, p. 88), dabbled in science. Such amateur interests can be a powerful inducement to patronage: it was Charles II's scientific dilettantism that made him grant a charter to the Royal Society. The Greek world had had a long history of enlightened cultural support from kings and tyrants. Peisistratus fostered and developed the dramatic festivals of Athens, and was probably responsible for a standard revised text of Homer being made public property.[18] Wealthy rulers such as Hieron or Gelon in Sicily, and Arcesilas IV in Cyrene, had commissioned victory odes and entertained poets and artists. In Macedonia itself, King Archelaus (r. 413?– 399) had brought such celebrities as Euripides and Agathon to his court (Socrates got an invitation, but turned it down), and commissioned the great artist Zeuxis to paint his palace murals.[19]

However, one man more than any other influenced the specific form that Ptolemy's patronage took, and that was Aristotle. Hitherto poets and artists had been encouraged and given commissions, and kept around court, primarily as status symbols. Now there emerged a new ambition: to support learning for its own sake.[20] The implications of such a decision are far-reaching. Most important is the new, and significant, preoccupation with the past that we have already noted in other contexts (see, e.g., p. 52). Not only did Ptolemy's project involve a crucial value judgment— namely, that the art, science, and literature of earlier Greek civilization were of an unequaled standard, and, thus, of supreme cultural importance for the future—but, because of the hazards of transmission, it also meant, in the first instance, a major rescue operation on the texts embodying this heritage.

The obvious model for an undertaking of this size and scope was Aristotle's research center at the Lyceum. The foundation and continuing support, in Alexandria, of the Museum and Library owed a great deal to the pioneering work that Aristotle, and, to a lesser extent, Plato's Academy, had already undertaken, not only in the establishment of something very like universities, but also by working out, and publicizing, "distinctive theories of lifelong learning, which were supported by metaphysical arguments of considerable complexity."[21] At this point we should perhaps consider just what a museum (*mouseion*) was before it acquired modern connotations. Originally, as its name implies, it had been a shrine or center dedicated to the service of the Muses,[22] and hence often—though by no means always—also associated with literary studies. The Muses had, similarly, been connected with thinkers and philosophers at least as early as the time of Pythagoras; but it is particularly in Aristotle's case that we find a museum embodying all the features of an intellectual, and primarily scientific, community: the cult center; the buildings for residence, common meals, library holdings, and research; the surrounding cloisters and garden where students and teachers could stroll and talk. The cloister (*peripatos*) gave its name to Aristotle's followers, who were known as Peripatetics.

There was also a more direct influence. Aristotle's immediate successor, as we have seen (p. 68), was Theophrastus. Ptolemy tried to lure Theophrastus away from Athens to help plan his new center of learning;[23] Theophrastus declined, but instead encouraged Ptolemy to take on a former student of his, now in exile: none other than the former dictator Demetrius of Phaleron (above, p. 48).[24] Thus direct Peripatetic influence was paramount in the establishment of the new Museum and Library. Yet there was, at the same time, a sense of freedom and experiment in the air. Ptolemy had to bring in his Greek intellectuals from outside: there was no local talent—certainly none of the kind he wanted—on which he could draw. Erosion of political autonomy in the Greek city-states had left many writers and scholars in a *déraciné* mood, no longer anchored to the *mores* and loyalties of their own local communities. To such men Ptolemy's offer must have looked extremely attractive. Paradoxically, in one sense their loss of freedom had released them: the old rules no longer applied; new patterns had to be worked out.

As Fraser says, "such circumstances clearly provided a receptive background for patronage."[25] Alexandria, with its polyglot immigrants and diverse traditions, had no true ethnic or even religious center: one aim of the Ptolemies in fostering the cult of the new (or at least revamped and syncretized) deity Sarapis was to offer the Greeks in Egypt some common focus of devotion (see pp. 406 ff.). The artist or writer might feel adrift, but at least if he had an original bent he could pursue his own ideas, uncramped by powerful socioesthetic restraints. This in part explains the marked trend toward individualism and naturalism that we find in all branches of Hellenistic culture. At any rate, Ptolemy soon began scouring his new-found empire for talent: Cyrene, Cos, and Samos provided him and his immediate successors with

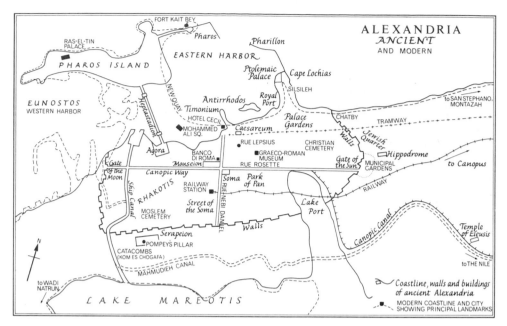

Map 7. Alexandria, ancient and modern.
From Jane Lagoudis Pinchin, *Alexandria Still: Forster, Durrell, and Cavafy*
(Princeton Univ. Press, 1976), frontis.

a surprising proportion of it. Callimachus came from Cyrene (see pp. 179 ff.), while Philetas, the first tutor selected for Ptolemy's son and heir, was a native of Cos. Young Ptolemy II (the future Philadelphos) was himself born on Cos (309), and thus will have enjoyed being given a Coan tutor. This practice of getting the best scholars or poets available to educate the crown prince was something that Ptolemy had had occasion to observe in Macedonia, where the young Alexander had been taught by no less a figure than Aristotle himself.[26] Ptolemy II's other tutors included the physicist Strato of Lampsacus,[27] who later went back to Athens and succeeded Theophrastus as head of the Lyceum (287), and Zenodotus of Ephesus, who was also appointed the first librarian, a post he held until 270 (see p. 89). It became a common, though not invariable, practice for the chief librarian also to serve as royal tutor: Apollonius and Aristarchus certainly did so.[28]

Philetas was that interesting, and very characteristic, new phenomenon, a scholar-poet, critic and creator at once; he was immensely influential, though his work was surprisingly soon lost.[29] This double function, synthesis and analysis, may have been encouraged by the general feeling, among intellectuals, that the impulse of *polis* art had somehow failed, that creation was in the doldrums, that a new approach had to be sought—and yet, at the same time, that the process of rebuilding meant looking back to the achievements of the classic past, examining them, using their skills and technique as a base for the development of any new artistic endeavor.[30] There had been a fundamental break with the past—and yet the past had to be recaptured, in all its complexity, before the new art could be realized. This thesis, of which Rudolf Pfeiffer has been the leading proponent, is highly attractive, even though some of us may doubt whether imitation, *mimēsis* in the wider sense, was really "regarded as impossible, or at least as undesirable," whether there had really been quite so total a repudiation (and in so short a time) of Aristotle, quite so radical a shift in literary perspective. Yet the *Zeitgeist* is certainly one familiar to a modern reader: it is very much the mood in which Eliot put together his famous cento of quotations at the conclusion of *The Waste Land: These fragments have I shored against my ruins.* No accident that the Hellenistic poets, like Eliot or Pound, tended to be allusive, literary, obscure, preoccupied with semantics, eager to "purify the dialect of the tribe." Prolixity became suspect, perfection in limited space was the new ideal to aim for: succinctness (*oligostichiē*), the jewellike phrase, the perfect epigram. "Big book, big evil," said Callimachus, succinctly.[31] Philetas, apart from his polished poetry (epigrams, elegies, epyllia), compiled a manual, or glossary, of odd words, rare dialectical terms, and obsolete or technical usages (*Glōssai Ataktai*) that achieved instant fame throughout the Greek-speaking world. Nothing could have been more characteristic of the age than this work and the *succès fou* it enjoyed. Unlike most recipients of Ptolemy's patronage, Philetas did not stay permanently in Alexandria, but retired to fresh laurels on Cos. He died and was buried there, and the Coans erected a bronze statue in his honor.[32]

Museum and Library, it seems clear, operated independently, much in the manner of a modern residential institute such as All Souls, or the Institute for Advanced Study at Princeton. Though the primary emphasis, as in these two modern centers, was on individual research, nevertheless teaching did, clearly, form part of the program, though it may have been largely unofficial and informal, discussion group rather than lecture. Nor, when Ptolemy I set up the Museum,[33] did he forget the traditionally religious antecedents of such a foundation: its head was also a priest, and members were vowed to serve the Muses. The resident community of scientists, thinkers, and scholars led an enviable life: "free meals, high salaries, no taxes to pay, very pleasant surroundings, good lodgings and servants."[34] On the other hand, since they were academics with leisure, and dependent on patronage, backbiting jealousy and paranoia were endemic. In one iambic poem Callimachus, using the persona of an old long-dead satirist, Hipponax, counseled the men of learning not to be so suspicious of one another.[35] Timon of Phlius, a bitter lampoonist who also satirized Heracleitus as a "riddling, noisy, rabble-baiting cuckoo,"[36] wrote of Ptolemy's Alexandrian think tank: "In the polyglot land of Egypt many now find pasturage as endowed scribblers, endlessly quarreling in the Muses' birdcage."[37] Perhaps he had failed to get a sinecure there himself. The Museum faculty also developed a reputation for symposia, frivolous research topics, and alcoholism:[38] to anyone in the same profession there cannot fail to be a certain sense of *déjà vu.*

Then as now, too, some degree of political *savoir-faire* was essential for survival. Demetrius of Phaleron rashly advised Ptolemy I to favor his children by Antipater's daughter Eurydice over those by his later wife, Berenice:[39] a lunatic move, since whichever way Ptolemy decided the matter, Demetrius had made enemies for life, and doubly dangerous in the event, since Ptolemy decided to ensure the succession through Berenice's line after all. Naturally, one of the first things that Ptolemy II did on his succession was to confine Demetrius to prison *sine die*: he died, perhaps a suicide, about 280. In happier days he had counseled Ptolemy I to study treatises—probably including his own—on kingship;[40] a wiser man would have stuck to such generalized topics, and left the thorny matter of the succession severely alone. Most of the quarrelsome bookworms were sensible enough to stay well clear of palace intrigue: they knew better than to risk offending their patrons. Besides, their very existence was, in a sense, improbable. Outside the enchanted circle of the royal court, Alexandria was a fairly philistine city. Many of the successful men of affairs that we hear about had little interest in anything but commerce.

The city, like most Hellenistic *poleis*, was, nominally at least, a democracy,[41] but one in which Ptolemy made all the key appointments and controlled the treasury, so that its democratic privileges were—as usual—little more than honorific and municipal top-dressing. A bureaucratic court hierarchy of innumerable officials developed. The king enjoyed a wide range of commercial monopolies (see p. 366), on, *inter alia*, oil, papyrus, and perfume,[42] and imposed high tariffs on foreign imports. The range of exports included such key products as grain, papyrus, drugs, glassware, scent, and unguents, and luxury articles in gold, silver, or faience.[43] The Ptolemaic dynasty ran Egypt, in effect, as a private estate, at a profit. This profit went into the rulers' pockets (and those of a minority of favored supporters) and was used precisely as they pleased, to support scholarship, mercenaries, extravagant processions, or anything else that caught their royal fancy. Patronage paid well. Strato of Lampsacus was paid a total fee of eighty talents to tutor the future Ptolemy II in science and mathematics (above, p. 86).[44] For the first three generations of Ptolemies, at least, relations with the Alexandrians were good. When Ptolemy II floated the time-honored Egyptian custom of royal incest there was, as we have seen, a certain amount of shock; but surprisingly soon people got used to the idea.

This, then, was the atmosphere in which Ptolemaic scholars, poets, and scientists operated. Curiously, though we know a good deal about the running of the Museum,[45] with its priest-president and lay director (*epistatēs*), its communal meals and intellectual atmosphere, there is not a single academic or literary figure of distinction that we actually know to have been a member of the community. Doubtless many of them were, but we cannot be certain of this, and our judgment of Ptolemy's achievement must, as a result, in one important area be held in abeyance. Our knowledge concerning the Library is a good deal more specific. It includes the names of the successive chief librarians, their main tasks, and even the number of books that the Library is supposed to have amassed in its heyday, 490,000—a fleabite when compared to the thirteen million or so volumes held by the Library of Congress, but for its day and age startling.[46] Here again we see the influence of Aristotle's Lyceum: the stress throughout is on the collection and comparison of material evidence. The Museum could very easily, like Plato's Academy, have taken instead the highroad of metaphysical speculation, but this it never did.

The Library, then, was originally planned by Ptolemy I Soter, with advice from the exiled Athenian philosopher Demetrius of Phaleron (who was not, however, as has sometimes been supposed, the first chief librarian: that honor went to Zenodotus).[47] The chief librarian, as we have seen, often also held the responsible post of tutor to the heir apparent (though not invariably: Eratosthenes, for one, did not). Yet his responsibility to the Library itself weighed equally heavily on him. There was a strong feeling that the literary heritage of archaic and classical Greece, from Homer to the great Attic dramatists, was in danger, whether physically or culturally, of being lost, of vanishing beyond recall through indifference and neglect. When we look at the subsequent history of the transmission of texts, and ponder the losses that in fact occurred,[48] the fear seems well justified, not least in an age when the multiplication of books remained a matter of supply and demand, and the hazards threatening their survival (whether through war, accident, or mere lack of public interest) were proportionately far higher than today. You might be able, as Socrates claimed,[49] to buy a copy of Anaxagoras in Athens for one drachma, but an unpopular and obscure writer like Heracleitus would attract neither scribes nor booksellers. Indeed, we are told that Heracleitus deposited the text of his treatise in a temple for safekeeping:[50] the implication is that there were few, if any, other copies.

The scholars who staffed the Library saw their mission as nothing less than the rescue of all past Greek literature, and set themselves to obtain copies of every known work. If in sociological terms this undertaking was merely the logical conclusion of a trend that had begun with Eupolis's *Demes* over a century before (above, p. 39), we nevertheless owe its agents an immeasurable debt of gratitude for what they preserved. Royal purchasers combed the book marts of the Aegean and Asia Minor, the best of which were located in Athens and Rhodes.[51] Since they paid good prices for rare titles, it was inevitable that numerous forgeries began to circulate for their benefit.[52] With such an influx of material, the chief librarian's first major task was to organize accessions and cataloguing.[53] Ptolemy II's son and successor, Ptolemy III Euergetes I, had the collector's mania so well developed that he ordered all books unloaded on the Alexandria docks to be seized, and copies made of them: the Library kept the originals (marked "from the ships"), while the owners were fobbed off with the copies.[54] The same Ptolemy borrowed from Athens the official copies of all three tragedians (Aeschylus, Sophocles, Euripides) in order to correct the texts in the Library (above, p. 52). Before the Athenians would part with them, they insisted on a fifteen-talent deposit; but once having got his hands on these prize exhibits, Ptolemy decided to forfeit his deposit and keep them.[55]

Such anecdotes testify to the second, and perhaps the most important, of the chief librarian's responsibilities: the establishment, insofar as this could be achieved, of sound texts, free from spurious matter such as forged interpolations, and purged of scribal errors made during the process of transmission.[56] Like the great modern public libraries, the Royal Library of Alexandria—together with its smaller offshoot, housed in the Sarapieion, and boasting a mere 42,800 volumes—was open to all those who could read, and wished to learn. In this regard the democratic constitution of Alexandria was a fact. The Greek alphabet (as opposed to hieroglyphs or

Fig. 23. Two Pompeian wall paintings showing writing materials, coins, and moneybags. In the center of the upper painting, a cylindrical container full of papyrus rolls, with a "white board" (*album*) to its left. In the lowest row of the lower painting, from left to right, an inkpot and pen, a half-unwound papyrus roll, an open set of wooden-backed wax tablets (diptych: also at left in upper painting), and a carrying case (*capsa*) suspended from a nail.
Museo Nazionale, Naples.

syllabaries accessible only to a scribal elite) was one of the great democratizing forces in ancient culture: with less than thirty symbols it could be learned, and was, by almost everyone.[57]

A new, more bookish age was dawning; and the devoted labors of Ptolemy's corps of scholars should not be underestimated when we look at the body of classical literature that has survived time's vicissitudes, and consider the state of each author's text. Not only did they use their scholarship to standardize texts; they also invented basic aids to punctuation, and introduced a system of accents. (Aristophanes of Byzantium is credited with both innovations.) Not surprisingly, a swift and startling improvement also took place in handwriting: scribes broke free from the angular restraints of epigraphical models to develop a more elegant, flowing script, which made for both easier copying and quicker, more comfortable reading.[58] Finally, the elucidation of texts led to commentaries, a body of exegetical work based on sources for the most part now lost to us, and transmitted with the manuscripts of authors' works in the form of marginal comments (scholia). Some of these scholars, like scholars in any age, were third-rate pedants, given to crazy theories and, worse, perversely ingenious emendations; but we can still be grateful to them, and their royal patrons, for the work they did. It is no small tribute to them that, for four hundred years or so after the Renaissance, classical scholars could find no higher goal than to follow in their footsteps, and conclude the great work that they had begun.[59]

CHAPTER 7

EARLY HELLENISTIC ART AND ITS ANTECEDENTS, 380–270: SPACE, PATHOS, REALISM; OR, THE HORSE AS CRITIC

When Alexander the Great was in Ephesus (334), he sat for his portrait, astride his warhorse, Bucephalas, for the famous Greek painter Apelles,[1] who had worked for Alexander's father, Philip, and was later to serve Ptolemy—a tribute, one feels, to his diplomatic no less than his artistic skills. When he painted Antigonus One-Eye, he executed the portrait in three-quarter profile to mask the old general's empty eye socket;[2] perhaps he had done the same for Philip. The finished picture of Alexander, however, did not meet with the king's approval: Alexander believed, to put it mildly, in self-alignment with the ideal (whether divine or merely Achillean), and expected his portraitists to convey that quality in their work. Apelles, by way of self-justification, had Bucephalas brought into the studio and placed in front of the finished work— probably a panel painting on wood, a more popular medium by that time than the mural. When the live horse neighed at its painted likeness, Apelles said: "You see, O King, the horse is really a far better judge of art than you are."[3]

Apelles' comment enshrines the central criterion of visual art throughout the Hellenistic and Graeco-Roman period: deceptively realistic naturalism (*alētheia, veritas*).[4] Anecdotes of this kind abound. We hear, for instance, of birds pecking at one picture by Zeuxis because they mistook his painted grapes for the real thing.[5] (He afterwards painted a "Boy with Grapes," and the same thing happened: Zeuxis remarked, in irritation, that he must have painted the grapes better than the boy; otherwise, the birds would have been scared off.) *Ars est celare artem*: those later *trompe-l'oeil* effects in which, with cunning perspective, doors, windows, whole landscapes were painted on blank inner walls, as though on a stage backdrop, simply took the principle one stage further, emphasizing that obsession with theatrical imagery—masks, actors, scenes from plays in performance—that formed so prominent a feature of the Hellenistic cultural scene.[6] Such effects could sometimes be al-

Fig. 24. *Trompe-l'oeil* wall painting from Boscoreale (first century B.C.).
The Metropolitan Museum of Art, New York, Rogers Fund, 1903.

most too successful. Protogenes is said to have painted a satyr scene with a partridge in it: the bird was so realistically done that no one had eyes for anything else—tame partridges are said to have besieged it with mating calls—and the artist, infuriated, painted it out.[7]

Perspective provided the link between the real world and artistic illusion,[8] a divergence from the "true" *mimēsis* that Plato, for one, regarded with intense suspicion.[9] Realism was thus very literally in the eye of the beholder,[10] and could be manufactured by an expert at will: here the visual artist was simply doing, in his own terms, what a rhetorician like Gorgias, equally given to the art of illusion (*apatē*), had recommended. Lysippus of Sicyon, the late fourth-century sculptor, said that, whereas his predecessors had portrayed men as they were, he made them as they appeared to be,[11] a nice variation on Sophocles' comparison of himself and Euripides (above, p. 71). Since it always hovered on the edge of caricature (see p. 109), *trompe-l'oeil* realism could without difficulty be reconciled with the era's countertrend, baroque fantasy, a progressive cultivation of the grotesque, already discernible in Aristophanes' later comedies, from the *Birds* (414) onwards.

As in literature and philosophy, so in architecture and the visual arts we find social and political change faithfully reflected by new styles, new themes, new conventions.[12] The trend is away from classicism, away from an art that "had taken group experience and a faith in the attainments of an entire culture as its principal theme."[13] These changes are, again, noticeable from an earlier date than is often supposed, and, as in other fields, the crucial period is, roughly, between 380 and 370. In a remarkable survey, Blanche Brown lists many of the factors leading to the erosion of the *polis*: autocratic takeovers in Sicily, Thessaly, Caria, and elsewhere; the rise of federations; the spread of panhellenism; the emergence of Macedonia as a strong and successful military monarchy; the association of the new rulers' courts with cultural patronage on a large scale, and (through the same channels) with self-promoting propaganda in the form of grandiose architecture or encomiastic literature.[14] Professionalism—military, political, financial, legal, theatrical, athletic—replaced the old civic ideal of amateur all-rounders. The cult of personality, long shunned, and with good reason, in the *polis* (see p. 108), began to gain ground very soon after the Peloponnesian War. Honorific portraits of the Athenian admiral Conon and his son Timotheus were set up—on the Acropolis, too!—in 393,[15] and the Spartan general Lysander had festivals in his honor and was actually worshipped as a god.[16] Such a trend not only paved the way for Hellenistic monarchy and ruler cults; it also, inevitably, brought a new realism to representative art.

Some of the most significant, and most easily explained, departures can be found in the new building programs of the late fourth and early third centuries. As we have seen (above, p. 52), the Greek city-states of the mainland, Athens in particular, largely abandoned those major religious-*cum*-civic constructions that had been the hallmark of the fifth century. One obvious reason for this was financial stringency: as mere satellites of Macedonia, stripped of their old revenues, they could no longer well afford such gestures. Besides, major monuments like the Parthenon had been an expression of civic self-confidence, of pride in supremacy, a tribute to the city's guardian deities and human resources. After Chaeronea, who could make such a claim in Athens? So when the fourth-century finance minister Lycurgus (390–325/4), in direct emulation of Pericles, launched *his* building program to offset Philip's victory, he concentrated on more secular and commercial matters.[17] Such a step was, in a sense, the *reductio ad absurdum* of Protagorean humanism.

It was in this mood that the Athenians, during Antipater's regency (above, p. 8), built the Panathenaic stadium and the arsenal, and began an ambitious peristyle on the northeast side of the Agora, to embellish their new law courts. We may note that the peristyle was never finished: indeed, the number of grandiose projects begun in Athens about this time, but never brought to completion, is in itself significant. The restyling of the Pnyx, with stoas to shelter citizens from the rain, was one such aborted project; the portico for the Hall of the Mysteries (*telestērion*) at Eleusis was another.[18] In all cases the drying-up of funds was probably a major factor, though the renovation of the Theater of Dionysus seems to have been due, in part at least, to the belief that it would make a more convenient place of assembly than the Pnyx, and was therefore (following a decree of 342) duly completed.[19]

Sport, commerce, litigation, entertainment, and debate: the secular (and predominantly private-sector) emphasis is clear, and the other main building projects confirm this. We find increasingly ornate and gargantuan private tombs, which at times (as in the case of the famous Mausoleum at Halicarnassus) come almost, by a logical extension of private memorials into the public domain, to usurp the functions of temples. This, together with the progressive tendency toward the deification (or at any rate the worship) of human beings during their lifetime, was an inevitable development. Gigantism, though not yet reaching the heights it was later to scale

Fig. 25. Athens: the Theater of Dionysus, seen from the Acropolis, looking south.
Photo Alison Frantz.

under the patronage of the Ptolemies and the Seleucids (below, pp. 158, 164), is already noticeable during the fourth century, for example in the huge theaters now being constructed. The theater at Epidaurus could accommodate fourteen thousand spectators; the rebuilt Theater of Dionysus in Athens, by close-packing and banking the seats (only about sixteen inches' width for each bottom), and by replacing all wooden supports with permanent stone blocks, increased its capacity to an amazing seventeen thousand.[20]

Stoas, or colonnades, originally attached, like covered cloisters, to temple enclosures, became increasingly secular and commercialized, often now containing shops, warehouses for grain storage, and similar features. The huge South Stoa in Corinth,[21] facing on the agora, had two aisles and was no less than 525 feet long, with Doric columns outside (71 to the façade) and Ionic inside. It contained thirty-three shops, each with a storeroom behind it. Every shop was equipped with a deep well, drawing water from the fountain house of Pirene, itself enlarged and embellished at this time. Private edifices, such as the choregic monuments (319 B.C.) of Lysicrates and Thrasyllus in Athens[22]—the latter, significantly, adapted from the unfinished Propylaea on the Acropolis, a neat instance of the shift from civic to personal emphasis in building[23]—become, like the funerary stelae, extraordinarily elaborate and grandiose: as we have seen (p. 47), this trend was cut short only by Demetrius of Phaleron's sumptuary laws (316/5). Sometimes the distinction between private and public monument is lost altogether. A classic instance is the circular tholos building at Olympia known as the Philippeion (begun by Philip II in 339, and completed after his death by Alexander),[24] which contained gold-and-ivory statues of Amyntas III, his wife Eurydice, Olympias, Philip, and Alexander, executed by the great sculptor Leochares, and which seems to have been designed for ancestor worship in the manner of a Shinto shrine.

Private houses, too, became more luxurious. Already in the mid-fourth century Demosthenes felt impelled to complain, not only about municipal projects to clean up Athens, with improved street paving, whitewash, and new water fountains, but also that some get-rich-quick politicians had "built homes for themselves that were more impressive than public buildings"[25]—for a diehard city-state conservative, the ultimate act of hybris. *Katagōgia*, hotels, began to appear at the great cult centers such as Epidaurus.[26] The Piraeus arsenal, built by Philo, the same architect who designed the façade for the Hall of the Mysteries at Eleusis, was over 433 feet long and nearly 59 feet wide, with a triglyph frieze and cornice, thirty-five columns down each side, and great doorways more than 9 feet wide by 16 feet high.[27] This extraordinary edifice honored no god; indeed, no man: it was, rather, a storehouse for the rigging, sails, ropes, and other gear of the Athenian navy. Equally elaborate, and also stoa-like in appearance, were the shipsheds for the triremes themselves.[28] As Roland Martin says, "A vigorous brand of functionalism, directed towards commercial ends, integrated itself with the purely religious and civic architecture which had been characteristic in the classical period."[29]

Temples, it is true, were still being built, but in prosperous Asia Minor rather than on the Greek mainland: in cities such as Ephesus, Sardis, Didyma, where there

Fig. 26. Colossal statues of members of the Hekatomnid family, often identified as Mausolus of Caria and his consort Artemisia, (Halicarnassus, mid-fourth century B.C.).
British Museum, London.

was still a powerful sense of continuity, mainly expressed in Ionic architecture, though Doric or Attic features began to creep in after a while. These temples, again, tended toward gigantism. One pleasant exception is the superbly sited temple of Athena Polias at Priene, begun about 340, designed by Pytheos, who later wrote a book on its architecture,[30] and dedicated in 334 by Alexander himself; his dedicatory inscription still survives.[31] More characteristic of the age were the huge temples of Artemis at Ephesus (built on an old base, but raised nearly 9 feet higher: volume was all) and at Sardis.[32] Above all, there was the temple of Apollo at Didyma, an oracular shrine near Miletus. In 335 the temple had been in ruins for over a century, its shrine empty, the god's archaic bronze image away in Ecbatana, looted by Xerxes as early as 494. But (miracle of miracles!) on Alexander's whirlwind approach down the coast, the oracle was heard to speak again, proclaiming Alexander's name.[33] About 300 Seleucus recovered the image from Ecbatana, and began a new temple. Building on it continued sporadically until A.D. 41: even then it was still unfinished. It was so

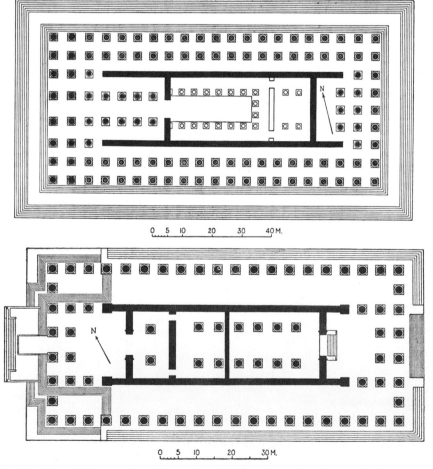

Fig. 27. Plans of the temples of Artemis at Ephesus (upper) and at Sardis (lower). From Dinsmoor, p. 226, fig. 81, and p. 228, fig. 82.

Fig. 28. Model of central Priene in the second century B.C., seen from the southeast.
The temple of Athena is at the upper left, and the theater toward the upper right,
with the main agora immediately below them, and the gymnasium (*palaistra*)
at the bottom left.
Staatliche Museen zu Berlin.

Fig. 29. The temple of Apollo at Didyma, begun ca. 300 B.C. by Seleucus I and
abandoned, still incomplete, about the middle of the first century A.D.
Photo Hirmer.

large, Strabo reports, that to roof it proved impossible; so the central cella was left open, an unpaved court planted with laurel, Apollo's sacred tree, and containing a little Ionic shrine housing the god's image and oracular spring. Such details remind us that Apollo was the Seleucids' patron deity. There is a striking contrast here between the self-advertising art underwritten by a Seleucid monarch, and the backwater of nostalgia, commercialism, and private esthetics to which the old mainland city-states had retreated. The nearest thing to Didyma on the mainland was perhaps the temple of Olympian Zeus in Athens, abandoned from Peisistratus's day till the reign of Antiochus IV Epiphanes, and finally completed only by Hadrian.[34]

As a component of sculpture and painting the old classical reverence for order and geometric pattern still persisted; but it was increasingly undercut by the new realism, which preferred anatomical accuracy to organic harmony of structure, the world as it was, or appeared, rather than as it ought to be. The progressive loss of idealistic canons, combined with sophistic inroads on the old religion, brought divinities, already uncompromisingly anthropomorphic, down into the marketplace, where they rapidly became indistinguishable from market shoppers. The mid-fourth-century Piraeus Athena is as much society matron as goddess; the slightly later Artemis A (also from Piraeus) looks for all the world like a 1930s German film star, while with Artemis B (early third century) we have a clear case of individual, indeed, powerful, portraiture, a kind of Hellenistic Lady Bracknell.[35]

Heterosexuality, too, came into its own from the fourth century onward. Aphrodite was progressively stripped of her draperies, finally emerging nude in the famous statue made by Praxiteles, and bought by the city of Cnidos (after Cos had turned it down in favor of a more chastely traditional draped version). This statue—set in an open circular shrine, where it could be viewed from all sides—became a famous tourist attraction. Its appeal lay in qualities utterly remote from that earlier collective pride—compounded of athleticism, the warrior code, family loyalties, civic honor, and homosexual idealism—that underlay the great nude male statues of the archaic and classical eras.[36] No accident, either, that the goddess who attracted this exposé was Aphrodite. The swing from public to private and personal preoccupations, combined with a post-Euripidean interest in the (often morbid) psychology of passion, made sex a subject of increasing interest as the Hellenistic age progressed. Among the mythological figures represented in Greek art from now on, on jewelry in particular, Eros and Aphrodite predominate. The market had been flooded with gold, taken by Alexander from the vast treasuries of Susa and Persepolis, and carelessly scattered as pay, largesse, and bribes. Much of it ended up adorning wives or mistresses in the shape of necklaces, earrings, bracelets, and pendants.

Menander's obsession with affairs of the heart and the pursuit of profitable marriages is exactly matched by the record in the so-called minor or decorative arts, where a kind of overriding greed, sensuality blended with avarice, now becomes visible. Ours is by no means the first age to have suffered from what Thorstein Veblen, in his *Theory of the Leisure Class*, labeled "conspicuous consumption." From the mid-fourth century—indeed, in many cases earlier—jewelry, clothing, luxury food, funerary monuments, entertainment, furniture, housing, all tell the same

Fig. 30. Aphrodite of Cnidos. Roman copy of an original by Praxiteles executed ca. 360–350 B.C.: the sculptor first offered it to Cos, which refused the statue because it portrayed the goddess undraped. Taken instead by Cnidos, it became one of that city's prime attractions.
Vatican Museums.

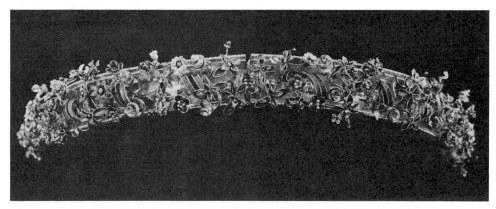

Fig. 31. Gold diadem from Canosa, in southeastern Italy (Hellenistic era).
Museo Nazionale, Taranto.

Fig. 32. Bronze warrior A, found in
the sea off Riace, near Reggio, in 1972;
executed ca. 460–450 B.C.
Museo Nazionale, Reggio Calabria.

story: self-indulgence as a classic substitute for power. Though Demetrius of Phaleron's sumptuary laws were no sort of real solution (above, p. 47), it is all too easy
to understand the reason for their imposition. Always hovering on the very edge of
ostentatious vulgarity, yet never quite succumbing, Hellenistic jewelry in particular—the stone of choice seems to have been the garnet—offers a unique blend of
daring extravagance and dazzling technical skill. From Egypt came the Heracles
knot, known there as an amulet since the second millennium B.C.; from Asia Minor,
the crescent, sacred to the moon goddess, and adapted by Greek goldsmiths as a
pendant; from the north, about 330, the hoop earring with an animal or human
head.[37] The conversion of religious motifs to secular use is symptomatic. Diadems,
perhaps through association with the new royalty, became popular from about 300,
and continued in vogue, complete with matching bracelets, for at least two centuries, going out of vogue when the Hellenistic monarchies were eclipsed by Rome.

If the female statue shed its clothes (when appropriate) toward the end of the
fourth century, the male nude became softened to a remarkable degree, in both
bronze and marble: the feminine element is clearly emergent here too, and the con-

cept of the hermaphrodite, increasingly prevalent from the early third century on,[38] would seem its logical conclusion. In bronze especially, the young male statues from Marathon, Ephesus, and Antikythera, even the victorious athlete in the Getty collection, all reveal a mood of sensitive introspection that sets them in sharp contrast to the magnificent, bearded, heroic fifth-century warriors of Riace Marina, the embodiment of self-confident masculinity, with their heavy musculature and great, firm, rounded buttocks.[39] But then the art favored by wealthy rentiers with the leisure for self-analysis and the cultivation of good taste—dependent, moreover, on hired mercenaries to do their fighting for them, their political activity limited to municipal affairs—is unlikely to bear much resemblance, whether physical or psychological, to that associated with the citizen-soldiers of a genuinely independent *polis*.

There was, however, another side, in late fourth-century sculpture, to this yearning, delicate, sensuous element—perhaps best expressed in Praxiteles' famous group of Hermes with the Young Dionysus[40]—and that was a realism that set out to capture the roughness and brutality of everyday life. If Praxiteles was the begetter of the first genre, Lysippus (late fourth century) can surely be traced behind the second. "As the smooth, podgy loves and Venuses stem from the one, the muscle-bound, pin-headed bruisers are the other's no less degenerate progeny."[41] Thirty years be-

Fig. 33. Hermes with the Young Dionysus. A possibly original work by Praxiteles (343 B.C.?) discovered *in situ* in 1877 during the excavation of the temple of Hera at Olympia, where the travel writer Pausanias had seen it in the second century A.D. (Paus. 5.17.3). Some modern scholars (e.g., M. Robertson) argue that it is a late Hellenistic copy of a bronze original. Olympia Museum. Photo Hirmer.

Fig. 34. Bronze head of the boxer
Satyros, probably by Silanion (ca. 335
B.C.); found at Olympia in 1880.
National Museum, Athens.

fore, Silanion had made a still-idealized portrait of Plato; now, at Olympia, he set himself to tell the truth about a professional boxer,[42] including "the characteristic marks that his career has left" (ca. 335).[43]

There was still idealism in portraiture, as the various heads of Alexander by Lysippus make plain; but Lysippus, too, was not only a traditionalist but also a great technical innovator, who, as Pliny says, preserved proportion (*symmetria*)[44] while modifying "the squareness of the figure of old sculptors."[45] What, precisely, did this imply? If Lysippus pursued an ideal canon of proportions, wherein did his naturalism consist? A suggestive model is the design of the Parthenon, where subtle curves (*entasis*) were employed to give the appearance of verticality. Lysippus applied this principle to sculpture: he wanted his statues not only to *be* tall, but to *look* tall. Hence (as Pliny remarks) his reduction in the size of their heads. He also used torsion in such a way as to eliminate the foursquare flatness that had characterized earlier statues, producing a multiplanar composition that could be fully appreciated only by walking all round it. A good example of this is the so-called Apoxyomenos ("Youth Scraping Himself Off")[46]—a nice instance, says one scholar, of how realistic an eye Lysippus had when kings and gods were not in question.[47] We may also compare the Pothos ("yearning Desire") by Scopas of Paros (? mid-fourth century), not only for its technique, but also for the skillful way it catches the half-sublimated eroticism that becomes such a characteristic feature of the Hellenistic period.[48]

This trend had begun at least half a century earlier. Leochares was not the only artist to portray Zeus as an eagle (ca. 370), carrying off Ganymede, but he may well have invented the motif,[49] which recurs frequently in the minor arts. A bronze relief copy on the back of a folding mirror shows Ganymede clinging to the eagle in erotic

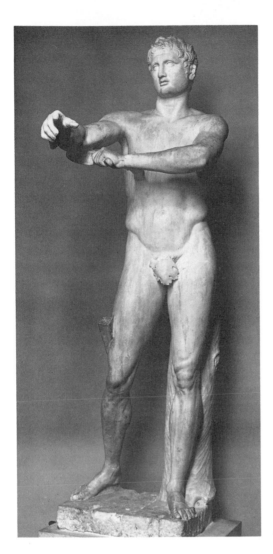

Fig. 35. The Apoxyomenos, or "Youth Scraping Himself Off." Roman copy of an original executed by Lysippus ca. 340–330 B.C.
Vatican Museums.
Photo Deutsches Archäologisches Institut, Rome.

Fig. 36. Bronze mirror-back showing the abduction of Ganymede by Zeus in the form of an eagle (ca. 300).
Staatliche Museen zu Berlin.

ecstasy:[50] whether this represents Leochares' original intention it is impossible to determine, but the notion would be well in tune with the *Zeitgeist*. More suggestive still is Timotheus's "Leda and the Swan"—another highly popular Hellenistic motif—in which the swan is scaled down to harmless domestic size, as though it were a pet goose, while Leda protects it with her robe against, once more, the attacking eagle (a nice reversal of the more common iconography, which has a huge swan towering over Leda in Olympian majesty);[51] but then one sees the Beardsleyish *double-entendre* of the swan's upstretched neck and head, which have been arranged so as to resemble a gigantic erect phallus.[52]

Equally interesting, though more for the light it sheds on ethical values than because of any direct psychological association, is the group of Eirene and Ploutos, Peace and Wealth allegorized, executed by Praxiteles' father, Kephisodotos, between 372 and 368, and carrying clear associations with Aristophanes' main theme in his *Plutus*.[53] Once again we find a dominant Hellenistic motif prefigured in the early fourth century. Peace is now associated with wealth, profit, rather than with the prowess of victory (Nike): statues of Nike were still produced, but I do not consider it fortuitous that the most famous example, the Winged Victory of Samothrace, was

Fig. 37. Leda and the Swan. Roman copy of an original work tentatively attributed to Timotheus (ca. 370 B.C.). Capitoline Museum, Rome. Photo Hirmer.

Fig. 38. Eirene and Ploutos (Peace and Wealth). Roman copy of an original by Kephisodotos, made for the Athenian Agora ca. 375–370 B.C. Staatliche Antikensammlungen und Gyptothek, Munich.

possibly executed by a Rhodian sculptor, Pythokritos, at a time (early second century) when Rhodes was still a free and independent naval republic, and that Pythokritos executed at least one other, similar Nike on behalf of his own countrymen.[54] The Rhodians, at least, were prepared to man their own ships, whereas a far more characteristic feature of the fourth and succeeding centuries was the professional mercenary soldier (see p. 74), hired by free citizens to do their fighting for them while they got on with their moneymaking and private erotic interests.

But naturalism, the determination to convey reality in both choice and treatment of subject, was the dominant mood; and where we can most easily study the fluctuations of this trend is in portraiture. Pliny notes that Myron, the mid-fifth-century sculptor, did not seem "to have given expression to the feelings of the mind" (*animi sensus non expressisse*).[55] The lead seems to me to have come in painting, with Polygnotus's search for *ēthos*. A generation or so later the psychological breakthrough was already well under way, not only in painting or sculpture (early portraits of Socrates are revealing from this viewpoint), but also in literature, as the late

Fig. 39. The Winged Victory (Nike) of Samothrace, possibly the original sculpted by (?) Pythokritos ca. 190 B.C.(?) to celebrate the Rhodian naval victory over Antiochus III off Myonnesos; but a date as early as 250 is possible. Musée du Louvre, Paris. Photo Alinari.

plays of Euripides make very clear.[56] Xenophon gives a fascinating account of Socrates' discussions with Parrhasios and Cleiton on the artist's ability to reproduce not physical traits alone, but also the semblance of character (*ēthos*) and emotion (*pathos*)[57]—most notably, the visual arts suggest, suffering and pain. Here the painter had the advantage, it was felt, being able to portray both *ēthos* and *pathos*, whereas the sculptor was restricted to the latter.[58] Yet here, still, we find the striving for idealization behind the realism. Sometimes the realism is generic, as in the famous Tanagra terra-cotta figurines, which look for all the world like miniature representations of the characters in Menander's plays;[59] more often we have reasonably firm ascriptions, and can identify the subjects portrayed.

We have to bear in mind that during the classical era "the erection of a portrait statue was the exception, not the rule."[60] The cult of personality was frowned on: when Pausanias, in 479, as captain general of the Hellenes put his own name on the base of the serpent column commemorating the Persian Wars, he provoked an international incident.[61] Portraiture was for the gods; even if they were shown in human guise, that was no reason for men to climb up beside them. No fifth-century Greek, for instance, was ever represented on a coin. Obviously, with a shift in the public mood toward deifying (or otherwise enskying) human leaders, or, with Euhemerus (p. 55), explaining even the Olympian gods as, originally, heroes elevated to divine status, the barriers between gods and men were going to blur, and the boundaries of permissible iconography to grow wider, in both the public and the private domain. Nor was it only the great who demanded commemoration: the lost individual, too, would not be slow to fight the anonymity of megalopolis by having his own features shaped in stone to defy consuming time.[62]

Portraiture, with idealizing restrictions, had certainly existed in the fifth century, and perhaps even earlier: the famous Calf Bearer (ca. 570) offers a representation, if not the likeness, of the (named) dedicator.[63] One interesting piece of evidence pointing in the same direction is the fact that the brothers Boupalos and Athenis, sculptors on Chios around 500, are said to have incurred the undying wrath of the satirist Hipponax by making a caricature of him in marble:[64] the very idea of a caricature presupposes that of a likeness, the features of which can then be exaggerated or distorted. Pliny refers to a self-portrait by the sculptor Theodoros of Samos (*fl.* ca. 560–520).[65] We have portrait busts of Themistocles and Pericles, both probably based on full-length originals made during their lifetimes.[66] Demetrius of Alopeke (early fourth century) was well known for his individualized portraits, including one of a Corinthian general described by Lucian as bald, potbellied, and with varicose

Fig. 40. Draped lady with a fan.
Tanagra terra-cotta figurine, fourth or
third century B.C.
Musée Borély, Marseille.

Fig. 41. The Calf Bearer
(Moschophoros) from the Athenian
Acropolis (ca. 570 B.C.).
Acropolis Museum, Athens. Photo Hirmer.

Fig. 42. Themistocles. Portrait herm
from Ostia, perhaps copied from a
Greek original made during
Themistocles' lifetime (? in the 470s).
Ostia Museum. Photo Deutsches
Archäologisches Institut, Rome.

veins, and another of Lysimache, priestess of Athena and perhaps the model for Aristophanes' Lysistrata.[67] The urge to deny likenesses in this period has, I think, been overdone.

On the other hand, it is certainly true that the dawn of the fourth century reveals a new attitude. The barriers between mortal and immortal were breaking down. Grateful cities, as we have seen, were quite ready to worship Lysander as a god, just as Asclepius the healer could now be portrayed as human, sympathetic, accessible.[68] By the time of Alexander's death the urge for realism and individualism had created circumstances in which portraiture could flourish. It has often been pointed out how loath most of the early Successors were to portray themselves on coins.[69] Lysimachus, for instance, despite his consuming ambitions (p. 28), was still using the legitimizing portrait of Alexander at the time of his death. Pyrrhus, similarly, never used his own image on his coins. It is significant that not until the time of Philip V and Perseus was royal portraiture used on coins circulating in the cities of mainland Greece. The prejudice against Macedonian overlordship ran deep, and was long-lasting. Yet there is a difference between overt and covert self-promotion, and the Macedonians, to look no farther, had done a good deal of the latter. An ostensible Zeus can look very like Philip II (or, earlier, Amyntas); an ostensible Heracles is, beyond any doubt, Alexander. The earlier Argeads show remarkable facial individualism in their supposed portrayals of deities.[70]

Philip, we remember, had not been above having his image carried in procession, a thirteenth god, along with the twelve Olympians.[71] (He was assassinated the same day: serve him right for impiety, said traditionalists.) There was also the matter of that circular family shrine at Olympia (above, p. 96), with all its gold-and-ivory portrait statues—a medium hitherto reserved for cult figures. New discoveries of ivory miniatures in the royal Macedonian tombs at Vergina suggest, again, a well-developed tradition of realistic portraiture by the closing decades of the fourth century.[72] Yet the sheer diversity of Alexander's likenesses[73]—even though they duly record the upward glance, the twist of the neck, the supposed *pothos*—cannot encourage us in the hope that any of the alleged portraits we possess are what today we would think of as a true representation. The official monopoly granted to Lysippus was no guarantee of verisimilitude. If I hazard a guess that the Issus mosaic comes closest to the truth, that is no more than a subjective impression, partly inspired by the matching portrait of Darius and the generally realistic detail of the picture. Features that can be caricatured seem, paradoxically, most likely to survive without serious distortion. Ptolemy I's hooknose and cracker jaw at once carry conviction.[74] On the other hand, the portraits we have of Aeschylus, Sophocles, and Euripides are in all likelihood those commissioned by Lycurgus long after their deaths, and copies at that.[75] Both the Demosthenes and the Aristotle best known to us are posthumous, and the Demosthenes, like most of our surviving portraits, is also a late Roman copy. Both offer marvelous appreciations of temperament and character; but are they likenesses in the modern sense? Many scholars doubt it.[76] Yet, obstinately, a sense of individualism persists.

Fig. 43. Demosthenes. Roman copy of an original statue by Polyeuktos(?) made ca. 280 B.C. for erection in the Athenian Agora.
Ny Carlsberg Glyptotek, Copenhagen.

When we turn to painting, we are confronted with one unfortunate but incontrovertible fact: though the period covered by this chapter was held in antiquity to mark the apogee of this medium,[77] very little of the original work has survived, so that scholars are too often reduced to arguing retrospectively from what may, or may not, be accurate Roman copies, reinforced by the testimony of hit or miss literary sources such as the elder Pliny. A good deal has been inferred from painting on pottery, but this is chancy. During the fourth century, red-figure conventions were progressively abandoned in pursuit of greater depth and realism. Yet the quest for spatial freedom never broke away from an essentially linear technique until red-figure ran its course (by 320 in Attica; a couple of decades later in Italy). It remained throughout a conservative medium, its moves toward modernization always cautious in the extreme.[78]

Till comparatively recent times evidence of what the great mural and panel painters had achieved in this period was, to say the least, inadequate. There was the Alexander Issus mosaic, probably copied from a lost fourth-century mural by Philoxenos of Eretria. There were marginally relevant and ill-preserved tomb paintings from Etruria and Kazanlak and Alexandria. There were those late Roman copies and adaptations; but what, precisely, had they been copied from? During the past half-century, however, the excavation of a number of Macedonian tombs, some containing well-preserved murals, has shed steadily more light on the nature of Hellenistic painting, and done much to confirm both its classically based conservatism and its now-undoubted links with the Romano-Campanian tradition. The tomb of Lyson and Callicles (third or second century) reveals an illusionist style of architectural painting that looks forward to the so-called Roman Second Style. The impressionist brushwork of the portrait of Rhadamanthys in the Great Tomb at Lefkadia (ca. 280 B.C.) anticipates that in the "Satyr and Maenad," a painting of Nero's reign in the House of the Epigrams at Pompeii, just as its composition suggests the wall paintings of Boscoreale (first century). The Tomb of the Palmettes, also at Lefkadia (late third century) has yielded marvelous complex floral patterns that, again, belong in a tradition dating back to the fourth-century painter Pausias and continuing through the Pompeian period.

But the most remarkable discovery came in November 1977, when Manolis Andronikos opened up two royal Macedonian tombs at Vergina (ancient Aigai) with fourth-century frescoes: a hunting scene, a portrait of a mourning woman in the Polygnotan tradition, above all, a splendidly vigorous mural showing Pluto's rape of Persephone, with Persephone desperately stretching out her arms to her agonized companion Cyane as the god's chariot whirls her away. The hunting scene, over-hopefully attributed, by some, to the original artist of the Issus mosaic,[79] was in bad condition when excavated, and has since suffered further deterioration; but the other two are excellently preserved. Since then, in 1981, the excavation by Andronikos of three more tombs at Vergina has provided further striking proof of continuity between the early Hellenistic tradition and that known to us from Pompeii, as the full-length portrait of a young warrior from the second of these tombs (early third century) demonstrates.[80]

There is a clear link here, too, with the fine mosaics from the royal Macedonian palace at Pella,[81] and all belong to the category of court art, which assumes so important a role later in Alexandria and Pergamon. Mosaic work, by its very nature, was always an art that catered to the wealthy and powerful. From the first quarter of the fourth century onwards (as we know from examples at Olynthus and Eretria as well as Pella) it displays a fashionable, and recurrent, iconography: griffins, sphinxes, panthers, Nereids, Dionysiac motifs.[82] We may note that the Pella mosaics are made with natural pebbles, black, white, or colored, whereas the use of tiny cut cubes (tesserae) seems not to have been introduced until sometime after Alexander's conquests. (Where the technique originated is still uncertain: competing theories argue

Fig. 44. Mourning woman, perhaps
Demeter. Wall painting from Tomb I,
Vergina (ca. 340–330 B.C.).
Photo courtesy Professor M. Andronikos.

Fig. 45. Wall painting of the rape of Persephone by Hades. On the right,
Persephone's distraught companion Cyane. From Tomb I, Vergina (ca. 340–330 B.C.).
Photo courtesy Professor M. Andronikos.

Fig. 46. Mural portrait of a young Macedonian warrior. From the Bella Tomb, Vergina (late fourth century B.C.).
Photo courtesy Professor M. Andronikos.

Fig. 47. Dionysus riding a panther. Pebble mosaic from Building I of the royal palace, Pella (ca. 330–300 B.C.).
Photo Ph. M. Petsas.

Fig. 48. Royal lion hunt. Pebble mosaic from Building I of the royal palace, Pella (ca. 330–300 B.C.).
Photo Tombazi, Athens.

Fig. 49. The so-called Alexander Sarcophagus, probably that of Abdalonymus, the last king of Sidon (appointed by Alexander in 332 B.C.). From the Sidon royal necropolis, executed ca. 325–311 B.C.(?) before Abdalonymus's death.
Archaeological Museum, Istanbul.

Fig. 50. Lion hunt from the Alexander Sarcophagus (cf. above, no 49). Abdalonymus
spears a lion that has attacked his horse, while Alexander (center) rides in to
assist him.
Archaeological Museum, Istanbul. Photo Hirmer.

for Sicily, the East, or Greece itself.) We also find marble chips being used (e.g., at
Olynthus before 348), or irregular stone fragments, or several of these in combination.[83] Pella's lion-hunt mosaic matches the fresco adorning Philip's tomb at Vergina:
both look forward to the relief work on the so-called Alexander Sarcophagus from
Sidon.[84]

We are reminded that from now on it was, primarily, monarchs who had both
the urge and the resources to celebrate their own achievements, who were ready to
exploit art or architecture in any way that would effectively promote the royal message.[85] Those compelled to live under such regimes—especially those who remembered a different way of life—found different solutions. For the most part, as we
have seen, they turned inward for their freedom, or to the world of private and sensual pleasure for their escape from involvement: the world of Eros and Aphrodite in
all its manifold enticements;[86] or, at a lower level, an epicure's obsession with *haute
cuisine*,[87] which was responsible for good cooks' fetching such high prices in the
Hellenistic age, and for the endless lip-licking allusions to food in the comedians.
Intoxication (*methē*) was also allegorized, and by no means in a hostile manner.[88]

Zeuxis experimented with chiaroscuro early in the fourth century, while his
contemporary Parrhasios was achieving unprecedented subtlety and expression of
line.[89] The latter painted a picture of the Athenian *dēmos* that Pliny, rightly, calls "an
ingenious subject-piece," since Parrhasios portrayed the Athenian people as, at one
and the same time, inconstant, unjust, bad-tempered, merciful, compassionate, open
to persuasion, vainglorious, proud, humble, fierce, and cowardly, a description with
which few historians would quarrel, but that must have taxed even Parrhasios's re-

Fig. 51. Still-life with eggs and game. Wall painting from the House of Julia Felix,
Pompeii.
Museo Nazionale, Naples.

sources.[90] Perspective, first discovered in the fifth century by Agatharchus, was
steadily refined.[91] Perhaps the most significant innovation, apart from portraiture,
was the discovery of landscape painting, a precise romantic analogue in the visual
arts to the urban passion for piping shepherds and bucolic peace. The painters who
portrayed, as Vitruvius says, "harbors, headlands, woods, hills, and the wanderings
of Odysseus,"[92] scenes of sunny pastoral escapism, were catering to precisely the
same *déraciné* audience of city intellectuals as a poet like Theocritus (see p. 235), writing idylls on the rivalries of rural goatherds. Escapism and realism were now two
sides of the same coin. Menander had done no more than foreshadow a general
trend. What politically conscious artist of the fifth century could ever have brought
himself to paint a still life, that hymn to things-in-themselves, that total and delectable rejection of all social awareness? (It is clear that Hellenistic artists did paint still
lifes: unfortunately, only Roman copies or variations survive, though even these are
striking enough.) When I try to summarize the private vision of the Hellenistic era, a
still life or a genre scene—a marine-life mosaic, a bowl of fruit, a hare—is what instantly flashes into my mind. But as Louis MacNeice well knew, "even a still life is
alive," so that "the appalling unrest of the soul / Exudes from the dried fish and the
brown jug and the bowl."[93] Zeuxis and Chardin inhabited uncomfortably similar
worlds.[94]

CHAPTER 8

THE DIVISION OF THE SPOILS, 301–276

The final quarter-century of the drawn-out struggle between Alexander's successors was notable (even in that age of violent and cynical *Machtpolitik*) for some cold-blooded dynastic marriages, and the even more cold-blooded dynastic murders that several of these produced: Olympias was by no means the last Macedonian queen determined at all costs to see her son or grandson on the throne. It was also a period of tantalizing bids for power, frustrated at the last moment either—according to the way one looks at it—by Chance, Tyche, or by the human frailties and errors of judgment inherent in the protagonists. Even after Antigonus's death at Ipsus (301: above, p. 34), the dream of Alexander's empire (or, at the very least, all that could be spear-won from it) remained a potent lure, not only for Antigonus's surviving son, Demetrius, but also, and more improbably, for old Lysimachus—even, arguably, for Seleucus. Each forced a showdown and was, in one way or another, destroyed by it, while Ptolemy the Savior waited, prudently, in Egypt for their losses to fall into his patient hands. Ptolemy was the only one of all Alexander's marshals who had seen, right from the beginning, that limited ambitions, a safe power base, a prudent division of the spoils, and canny diplomacy—including dynastic intermarriages[1]—offered the only viable solution.

It was not by mere serendipity that the Ptolemaic dynasty outlasted all its rivals, or that, almost alone of the Successors, Ptolemy died peacefully in his own bed, of old age (283),[2] having set up a smooth transition of power to Ptolemy II, later known as Philadelphos, his son by Berenice. This ambitious Macedonian widow[3]—probably Ptolemy's half-sister and his previous wife Eurydice's niece[4]—originally became the king's mistress (317/6) and in due course his wife. Ptolemy's third marriage need not have waited for his repudiation of Antipater's daughter Eurydice and her son Ptolemy Keraunos ("the Thunderbolt") in 287/6: the Successors made their own rules, and Philip II had set a good Macedonian precedent for diplomatic polygamy. Theocritus claims that Ptolemy's marriage to Berenice was a love match:[5] love, the Greeks held, was a species of madness, and the consequences in this case certainly suggest a degree of imprudence, of less than logical thinking, on Ptolemy's part. To

119

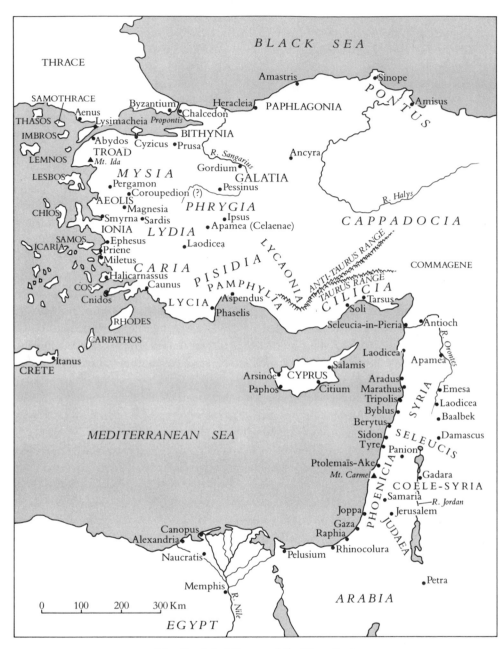

THRACE

BLACK SEA

SAMOTHRACE

THASOS

IMBROS

LEMNOS

LESBOS

CHIOS

AEOLIS

IONIA

SAMOS

ICARIA

COS

RHODES

CARPATHOS

Itanus

CRETE

Aenus

Lysimacheia *Propontis*

Byzantium
Chalcedon

Heracleia

Amastris

Sinope

PONTUS

Amisus

PAPHLAGONIA

BITHYNIA

Abydos Cyzicus •Prusa

TROAD
▲*Mt. Ida*

Gordium

Pergamon

R. Sangarius

Ancyra

MYSIA

GALATIA

•Coroupedion (?)

•Pessinus

Magnesia

PHRYGIA

Smyrna •Sardis

•Ipsus

•Apamea (Celaenae)

LYDIA

R. Halys

CAPPADOCIA

Ephesus

Priene

Miletus

•Laodicea

CARIA

PISIDIA

LYCAONIA

ANTI-TAURUS RANGE

COMMAGENE

Halicarnassus

Caunus

PAMPHYLIA

TAURUS RANGE

CILICIA

Cnidos

LYCIA

Aspendus

Phaselis

•Soli

Tarsus

Seleucia-in-Pieria

•Antioch

R. Orontes

MEDITERRANEAN SEA

Arsinoe

Paphos

CYPRUS

Salamis

Citium

Laodicea

Apamea

Aradus

Marathus

Tripolis

Byblus

SYRIA

•Emesa

•Laodicea

•Baalbek

SELEUCIS

Berytus

Sidon

Tyre

Panion

•Damascus

PHOENICIA

Ptolemaïs-Ake

▲*Mt. Carmel*

•Gadara

COELE-SYRIA

Samaria

~*R. Jordan*

JUDAEA

Joppa

Jerusalem

Gaza

Raphia

Rhinocolura

Canopus

Alexandria

Naucratis

Pelusium

Petra

Memphis

R. Nile

ARABIA

EGYPT

0   100   200   300 Km

Map 8. Asia Minor and the Near East.

disinherit Keraunos made for a great deal of trouble later, as we shall see (pp. 131 ff.). However, arguably the most dangerous thing that Ptolemy ever did in his life was to beget on Berenice that extraordinary woman Arsinoë II,[6] the wife in turn of Lysimachus,[7] whose existing male heirs she induced him, fatally, to have murdered; of Ptolemy Keraunos, her half-brother; and finally of Ptolemy II, her full brother. Corruption, intrigue, greed, luxury, ambition, the temptations that so often proved fatal to Alexander's other successors, came as naturally to the Ptolemies as the Egyptian air they breathed: they seemed positively to thrive on them.

The settlement made after Ipsus, like the Treaty of Versailles, might have been calculated to cause trouble later. Antigonus One-Eye had been eliminated, but his son Demetrius the Besieger, though in retreat, was still very much alive. He took an army of nine thousand men with him to Ephesus.[8] He still possessed the strongest fleet in the Aegean, paid for, one may surmise, with the residue of Persia's looted treasures: it stayed remarkably loyal, as did his forces in general, and this argues for regular pay as well as the personal devotion elicited by charisma. Asia Minor, except for a few scattered coastal cities, was now lost to him, and so was the East. But Demetrius still held Cyprus, Tyre, and Sidon,[9] and the League of Islanders maintained its allegiance (above, p. 26). In Greece itself the situation looked less encouraging. The Hellenic League of 302 was a dead letter (p. 34). Demetrius had hoped to base himself on Athens. But his excesses there had not been forgotten; his friends were out of office, and a delegation met him during his voyage across the Aegean to let him know that he would not be welcome, that Athens would, indeed, close its gates against him. His wife Deidameia had already been escorted across the border to Megara.[10] A recent decree banning all kings from Athens was cited in justification.

The heady days of Demetrius's enskyment as an Athenian savior god were clearly over (for the moment, at least: as we shall see, changed circumstances would later bring them back again). Now, however, he was even obliged to petition the Athenians for the return of the squadron he had left in Piraeus, not to mention his cash deposits. Then he set out for the Isthmus, and based himself instead on Corinth, one of the very few strongholds on the mainland that he still controlled (301/0).[11] It is noteworthy that he still regarded himself as a king, as his father's royal successor, even though he held almost no land, and was at this point little more than a naval condottiere. Kingship for him, as for his son Antigonus Gonatas, was primarily a personal rather than a territorial attribute. He also now faced some formidable enemies. These included Cassander, in Macedonia; Lysimachus, who after Ipsus had seized most of Anatolia as far south as the Taurus Mountains (and, perhaps more important, had at last got the stranglehold he coveted over the Hellespont and the Bosporus); and Ptolemy, who would join any coalition against an overambitious would-be empire builder who looked like upsetting the balance of power in the Near East. The one unknown factor after Ipsus was Seleucus, whose elephants had largely won the battle, and who had, on the face of it, got very little in return for his help.

Ptolemy, scared as always that Seleucus might attempt to encroach on his frontiers in Syria—this region, known as Coele-Syria, in fact remained a bone of conten-

Fig. 52. The temple of Apollo at Corinth (mid-sixth century B.C.), seen from the
south. Acrocorinth is in the background.
Photo Deutsches Archäologisches Institut, Athens.

tion as long as the two dynasties continued in existence—now set up marriage alliances with both Lysimachus and Cassander.[12] The elderly Lysimachus, whose territories Demetrius had invaded, was without difficulty persuaded to discard his wife Amastris, Dionysius of Heracleia's widow, whom he had married in 302, after Nicaea's death, mainly to provide himself with strategic support against Antigonus,[13] and to take on instead his naval ally Ptolemy's young daughter Arsinoë (300/299),[14] a choice he lived—but not long—to regret: the sex kitten had sharp claws. Another of Ptolemy's daughters, this one by Eurydice, was bestowed on Cassander's son Alexander. Seleucus, alarmed, and with good reason, by these combinations,[15] found himself driven, willy-nilly, to patch up an alliance with his recent enemy Demetrius.[16] Old Seleucus married Demetrius's daughter Stratonice, briefly reconciled Demetrius with Ptolemy (whose daughter Ptolemaïs in turn became betrothed to Demetrius; but the reconciliation was over before they could marry),[17] and in effect brought the Besieger back, however uneasily, into political circulation.

One significant side effect of Demetrius's temporary *rapprochement* with Ptolemy involved a hitherto little-known princeling who was destined to play a crucial role in Mediterranean affairs during the next two decades. This was Pyrrhus, the youthful (b. 319) yet already twice-exiled king of Epirus, in northwest Greece.[18] Demetrius, with whom he had done distinguished service at Ipsus,[19] and who had become his protector, sent him to Ptolemy's court as a hostage (299/8). (Despite their new alliance, Ptolemy clearly wanted insurance against Demetrius, whom he saw, with good reason, as both slippery and unpredictable.)[20] Ptolemy took an instant liking to the young Pyrrhus, realized he was a natural soldier, and saw in him a marvelous chance of acquiring a counterweight against Cassander.[21] After Cassander's death, in 298/7,[22] Ptolemy supplied Pyrrhus lavishly with arms and men, restored him to his Epirot throne, and married him off to the ominously named Antigone, Berenice's daughter by a previous marriage. A new player, and by no means a negligible one, now joined the Macedonian power game as, in effect, Ptolemy's lieutenant in mainland Greece.[23] In due course Pyrrhus also became his ex-patron Demetrius's deadly enemy; but gratitude for favors received was liable, then as now, to be strictly in proportion to the present and future benefits they might generate—which probably explains why (as the cynical Lysimachus well knew) Pyrrhus "was eager to show Ptolemy no ingratitude and to deny him nothing."[24] Pyrrhus named his son by Antigone after Ptolemy; he also, with urbanizing zeal, built a city, near the site of modern Preveza, which he named after his mother-in-law. It did not prove a success.

Cassander had probably died of consumption, and his eldest son, who succeeded him as Philip IV, soon succumbed to the same disease.[25] His two younger sons, Antipater and Alexander, now became rivals for the succession, under the far from impartial eye of Cassander's widow—and Philip II's daughter—Thessalonike.[26] She was rash enough to set aside considerations of primogeniture, and to insist that both sons—the younger being her favorite—should divide the realm: the elder one, Antipater, promptly murdered her.[27] His brother Alexander, hard pressed, appealed to the two nearest warlords, Demetrius and Pyrrhus. Cassander's death had already tempted Demetrius into action. His first move was to mount an expedition against Athens: strategic considerations apart, he had neither forgotten nor forgiven the rebuff her envoys had handed him after Ipsus.

From 301 the Athenians had enjoyed a brief spell of quasi-independence. As we have seen (p. 51), a moderate conservative group led by Phaedrus of Sphettos had gained power, with a policy of what today we would call third-world neutralism.[28] At the same time it is clear, from an important papyrus fragment,[29] that the city was torn with violent factionalism: conservatives, as always, against populists, while the hoplites of Athens found themselves fighting the city's hired mercenaries. The commander (*stratēgos*) of the hoplites, one Charis or Charias, seized the Acropolis, also using foreign troops for the purpose. Lachares, the commander of the mercenaries, and described by Pausanias as "the people's champion,"[30] finally managed to evict him, though only after a long period of anarchy, during which there had been severe food shortages. Charis's non-Athenian troops were released under safe-conduct, but he himself and his Athenian aides were condemned to death by formal vote in the Assembly. Piraeus at some point (the papyrus is highly fragmentary here) seceded: Lachares may well have got help from the radicals there.

All this took place before Cassander's death (May 297), which is referred to subsequently in the papyrus; we know, indeed, that Cassander not only was Lachares' friend, but also urged him to seize power as tyrant himself. This, in due course, he did.[31] The question is, when? Ferguson and others argued for 300,[32] but recent scholarship has advanced the theory that Lachares' coup did not take place till 295.[33] Such evidence as there is, however, suggests strongly that he was at the very least planning a takeover as early as 298/7, about the time of Cassander's death, or perhaps sooner.[34] I am therefore going on the assumption that he was already in power before 296, at the very latest during Cassander's final months, and conceivably as early as 300, though the argument for this date is shaky. It depends on the assertion (cf. Chap. 5, n. 47) that Lachares "the tyrant" stopped Menander's play *The Imbrians* from being put on, in 301 or 300.[35] Even if the statement is true, we cannot be certain what it implies. It is assumed that Lachares (in whatever capacity) banned the production, but this remains pure speculation; one could equally well argue that the violent factional fighting on and around the Acropolis necessitated the cancellation or postponement of the entire festival.

On all counts Lachares must have been anathema to Demetrius, who saw in him not only a dangerous radical, but, far worse, a creature of Cassander and his successors. Demetrius accordingly gathered an amphibious expeditionary force (297/6?). However, many of his ships were lost during a severe storm off the coast of Attica, after which he wasted much time waiting for reinforcements and campaigning inconclusively in the Peloponnese.[36] It was not until 296 that he amassed a force sufficient to blockade Athens and Piraeus;[37] but once he was in position, the siege proved highly effective. Athens held out, desperately, on starvation rations, hoping for relief from Ptolemy. Ptolemy dispatched a fleet of 150 vessels (early 295?), but it failed to break the blockade, and his international prestige suffered a setback in consequence.[38] Though Lachares stripped the Acropolis of its gold dedicatory shields, even removing the gold plates from Athena's great chryselephantine statue in an effort to raise funds, finally, just as in 404, Athens was starved into surrender (spring 295). It is possible that Demetrius received covert aid from inside the city.

Lachares escaped through the lines to Thebes, taking much of the Acropolis gold with him.[39] The Athenians opened their gates, though earlier they had decreed death for anyone even proposing negotiation with the Besieger,[40] and Demetrius once again entered the city in triumph. While an armed guard stood by, he made a public address in the Theater of Dionysus. To everyone's relief, he was in a generous mood. Grain and other supplies were brought in; no one was exiled or executed. Demetrius is said to have arrested those who persistently bad-mouthed him in the Assembly, but then to have released them unharmed, citing Pittacus to the effect that "pardon is better than punishment."[41] A motion was formally proposed and carried that Piraeus and Munychia should be turned over to Demetrius, who lost no time in establishing a strong garrison there.[42] It was to be many years before it was removed.

What type of government did Demetrius impose at this point? This, again, is a question that has generated much argument. The currently prevalent view is that it was, in effect, an oligarchy,[43] of which there are indeed clear signs from spring 294 onwards.[44] Unfortunately, Plutarch's testimony, usually translated "he [Demetrius] appointed those officials most friendly to [or: popular with] the people," which would be compatible with an oligarchic dispensation, can also mean "he established the offices most acceptable to the people," quite a different matter.[45] The chronological dispute is vital here, since in the spring of 295 we have clear epigraphical evidence for an unquestionably democratic change of regime.[46] It does not seem at all unlikely to me that Demetrius would make initial concessions, political no less than economic, after his victory, and that the changes of 295 were in fact carried out under his auspices. A later progressive tightening-up would have been warmly approved by all the men of property, moderate or extreme, who would, in any case, hardly have supported Lachares; perhaps only dedicated hard-line anti-Macedonian democrats like Demochares would have opposed such a measure. The same government that Demochares labeled an oligarchy would be quite ready to refer to itself, in all sincerity, as democratic. What it thought of Demetrius became abundantly clear in 290 (see below).

Ptolemy, watching these events, and still smarting from the rebuff of his fleet, must have congratulated himself on having an obligated ally in Pyrrhus on the western marches of Macedonia,[47] since it was by now abundantly clear that, even if Demetrius's long-term aim was the reconquest of Asia, he meant, first, to secure himself the Greek mainland (as Philip II had done) by way of a springboard. There were, too, compensations for the other Successors in Demetrius's current preoccupation with Greece and Macedonia. He could not be everywhere at once, and his troops were spread thin: thus his rivals lost no time in taking over his few remaining overseas possessions. Seleucus got Cilicia, and Lysimachus the Ionian ports, while Ptolemy himself acquired Cyprus, a notable prize.[48] Despite such losses, the anarchic situation in Macedonia presented Demetrius with an irresistible opportunity; it also soon became very clear to him that the main danger there was his ex-protégé Pyrrhus. When Cassander's young son Alexander, hard pressed by his elder brother, appealed to Pyrrhus (after drawing a blank with Demetrius, who was busy elsewhere), the Epirot monarch did indeed get him his throne back, but also—acting very much in the character of Achilles, whose descendant he claimed to be[49]—took over several of his western frontier cantons by way of payment, together with Ambracia, Amphilochia, and Acarnania, thus gaining a splendid bridgehead into central Greece, and undoing much of the protective frontier work achieved by Philip II and Cassander.[50] Ptolemy, whose agents also seem to have been stirring up revolt against Demetrius in the Greek cities, must have been pleased.

The pleasure, however, was short-lived. Demetrius, who had been winning back lost ground in the Peloponnese, and was indeed on the verge—after defeating King Archidamus IV in two pitched battles—of capturing Sparta itself, nevertheless abandoned the investment.[51] He came north in tardy response to Alexander's appeal, only to find that the job had already been done, all too well, by Pyrrhus, and to have Alexander tell him, in nervous embarrassment, that he was no longer needed. This dismissal proved, to put it mildly, an error of judgment. At Larissa, after a little diplomatic sparring, Demetrius had the upstart Alexander assassinated. What he really seems to have feared, and with reason, was that the two brothers might achieve a reconciliation and unite against him: Lysimachus, who backed Antipater, the elder brother, had been working toward just this end, with the declared object of keeping Demetrius out.[52] Demetrius now, after a testily self-defensive harangue justifying his essay in regicide,[53] got himself acclaimed king, *faute de mieux*,[54] by the Macedonian army assembly (autumn 294).[55]

They soon regretted their choice. Demetrius, with that incurable flamboyance that marked all his actions, put on Oriental airs like Alexander the Great in Babylon: he wore a double crown symbolizing Europe and Asia, and a robe that represented him as a sun among stars; he put his portrait on his coinage, perhaps the first living ruler to do so. There was a staginess, a theatrical panache about all Demetrius's actions, which has been recognized as a highly characteristic feature of the whole Hellenistic age.[56] He could hardly have proclaimed his ambitions more clearly. The resentment and fear he built up as a result proved, in the end, his undoing. Meanwhile he reconquered Thessaly (293), establishing there a new royal city and port, Demetrias (mod. Volos).[57] He also won back most of central Greece.[58] Boeotia proved troublesome, and he was forced, together with his son Antigonus Gonatas, to reduce Thebes twice in successive years (292–291); nevertheless, probably recalling the bad propaganda made by Alexander's destruction of that city, he did not take extreme measures. Thirteen ringleaders died, the Cadmea was garrisoned, Thebes lost its autonomy.[59] That was bad enough; at least no worse followed. Sparta still held out, and between 292 and 289 Demetrius had some inconclusive brushes with Pyrrhus and the newly formed Aetolian League, in west-central Greece: a disquieting omen of things to come.[60]

In 291 Lanassa, Pyrrhus's ex-wife (see n. 10), whose dowry was the great island of Corcyra, controlling the Adriatic and the sea route to Italy, offered herself in marriage to Demetrius (still regarded as the handsomest man in Greece), "understanding that, of all the kings, he was the most inclined to marry wives."[61] Demetrius jumped at the chance. Though this alliance may, later, have done him harm by alienating the loyal Phila's Macedonian supporters,[62] the prospect of a western *apertura* was something Demetrius found irresistible. He also, we may surmise, was not averse to scoring against Pyrrhus in a more personal sense. He sailed for Corcyra, and the marriage took place. Meanwhile Greek resistance against him solidified. In 290 Pyrrhus's allies the Aetolians seized Phocis and banned all Demetrius's supporters from the Pythian Games, at Delphi: war was clearly in the air.[63]

These supporters now included the Athenians—or, to be more accurate, the Athenian oligarchs, since 294 given increasingly direct support by Demetrius, and secure in the backing of his garrisons, now not only in Piraeus, but also on the Hill of the Muses. In 292, moreover, Demetrius had ordered the restoration of all exiled Athenian oligarchs, thus strengthening the conservatives' power still further.[64] There was no specific constitutional change at this time: there did not need to be.[65] If the amnesty extended to anti-Macedonian democrats, men like Demochares and Phaedrus of Sphettos's brother Callias (which seems *prima facie* unlikely), they certainly did not take advantage of it, but chose to remain in exile. They called the regime an oligarchy: to all intents and purposes, external formalities apart, they were right.[66]

Demetrius got back from Corcyra in September 290, and kept his Athenian supporters happy with a rival version of the Pythian Games, held in Athens itself. He also, evoking memories of headier days in 307, entered the city with Lanassa, in deified pomp once more, Demetrius and Demeter, the Savior God accompanied by his consort. (Presumably Phila had instructions to stay home.) This was the occasion on which Demetrius was welcomed, not only with incense and garlands and libations, as Demochares scornfully recalled afterwards,[67] but also by an ithyphallic chorus praising his beauty, offering him prayers, and making the notorious claim that he was the only true god, for the others were "far away, or cannot hear, or are nonexistent," and mere wood or stone, as opposed to a presence manifest in flesh and very truth.[68] The flattery, however, came as preamble to a demand: let the god put down these thievish Aetolians, always bent on robbing their neighbors "and now seeking more distant prey," together with the new Sphinx (i.e., Pyrrhus) ravaging Greece. Our source for much of this is Demochares, who, naturally enough, relates it only to pour scorn on it. Demetrius's support now came almost exclusively from the conservative, and pro-Macedonian, propertied classes; it was opposed by all outspoken and committed democrats or nationalists[69]—as subsequent events were to make all too clear.

Despite all his frenetic activity, Demetrius's base in Greece remained anything but secure. "Threatened in the west by Pyrrhus, in the east by Lysimachus and Seleucus, and in the islands by Ptolemy, he saw his authority declining."[70] It was true that Demetrius had the strongest, and most modern, fleet in the Mediterranean, and could count on an army of up to 100,000 men.[71] But the lure of empire had destroyed better men than the Besieger, and now it was his turn to learn bitter truths the hard way. His lavish preparations, in particular his shipbuilding activities, and the bull's horns with which he was adorned on his royal coin portraits, left no doubt as to what he was about. Lysimachus, who knew just how shaky Demetrius's Greek foundations were, reactivated against him the old coalition of 302: that is, himself, Seleucus, and Ptolemy.[72] Between them they had already annexed most of Demetrius's Asiatic strongpoints while he was busy in Greece (p. 125), and the League of Islanders also now passed under Ptolemy's control.[73] Lysimachus had no trouble in persuading Pyrrhus to abrogate (289/8) the peace treaty he had recently made with Demetrius, and in the spring of 288 the two leaders staged a bilateral invasion of Macedonia from east and west, catching Demetrius completely off guard.[74]

Demetrius's support in Macedonia, confronted by a threat of this magnitude, crumbled with appalling speed: not surprisingly, when one considers his vast ambitions, offensively luxurious lifestyle, and arrogant treatment of his Macedonian subjects.[75] By midsummer it was all over. The Macedonians went over to Pyrrhus, the great fortress of Amphipolis on the Strymon fell to Lysimachus, and Demetrius— the actor deprived of his role, as both Plutarch and Cavafy portray him—stripped off his royal robes, donned a black cloak, and fled to Cassandreia in the Chalcidic peninsula.[76] Here his first wife, the Macedonian Phila, Antipater's daughter, who had stood by him through everything, at last lost heart, and committed suicide. Yet

Demetrius himself remained indomitable: a few months spent whipping up support in the Greek cities brought solid results. It is amazing, not how many deserted his cause, but how many still stood by him when all seemed lost: whatever Demetrius lacked, it was not charisma. He rallied his mercenaries, swept down into central Greece, restored the independence of Thebes, and then passed into the Peloponnese, probably basing himself on Corinth.[77] Meanwhile Pyrrhus and Lysimachus shared out the Macedonian royal domains between them.[78]

A democratic revolution that had been simmering for some while in Athens now, predictably, came to a head.[79] The date was April or May of 287.[80] Grain was hastily brought in from the Attic countryside,[81] before Demetrius could move from the Peloponnese. The situation was afterwards described, in retrospect, as an emergency.[82] Macedonian garrisons still occupied Piraeus and the Hill of the Muses: there may have been local skirmishes. The Athenians stripped Demetrius's officials of their powers, "and voted to elect archons once more, in the traditional manner." Previously (as later under Antigonus Gonatas, after the Chremonidean War: p. 147) archons had been appointed by the king.[83] The Hill of the Muses was put under siege, and its fortress finally stormed by a commando under the Athenian general Olympiodorus. This operation was carried out at the loss of only thirteen men, including the heroic Leokritos, who was the first over the wall and into the fortress.[84]

Demetrius, however, marched north with a far larger army than the Athenians were expecting, and an appeal for immediate help went out to Pyrrhus in Macedonia—also, surely, to Ptolemy, since the appearance once more of his powerful fleet off Piraeus was a by no means negligible factor in subsequent peace negotiations,[85] even though it failed, again, to save Athens in an emergency. Demetrius, as in 294 (p. 124), put the city under siege, "in a fury."[86] Attacks on the besieging forces by Athenians and mercenaries seem to have been unsuccessful.[87] The philosopher Crates was sent to negotiate with Demetrius, and made him see (Plutarch reports) where his own best advantage lay: in other words, the presence of Ptolemy's fleet, and the impending arrival of Pyrrhus with his army, argued for a settlement rather than war à outrance.[88] Demetrius agreed: he was itching to get off to Asia and deal with Lysimachus, and had no desire, as yet, to tangle with either Pyrrhus or Ptolemy. Formal peace negotiations were held in Piraeus, between Ptolemy's ambassador and the envoys of Demetrius, with Callias and his brother Phaedrus of Sphettos representing Athens, probably as mere observers.[89] It tells us a lot about the pressures under which Athens existed during this period that Phaedrus, who had been associated with the moderate conservatives ever since Ipsus (p. 50), and who had, indeed, served as general under the tyrant Lachares, should not only have been entrusted with this duty, but should later have received a warm tribute from a democratic government for his various services to the state.[90] Even so, his specific recommendation to make peace with Demetrius was afterwards (? 200) chiseled off the commemorative stone.[91]

The terms of the agreement were concluded by July 287, and the peace was, in essence, a bilateral agreement between Ptolemy and Demetrius, with the Athenians as incidental beneficiaries.[92] Demetrius kept the fortresses of Corinth, Chalcis, Piraeus, Eleusis, Salamis, and Attica;[93] but the price was acknowledgment of a return at Athens to free and independent democratic government, which in the event endured, however precariously, for over twenty years. One immediate result of this was the return from exile of Demochares,[94] an intransigent Gaullist somehow now accommodated among the more pliable men of Vichy. Though the concession to Athens cost Demetrius little but his pride, what he yielded to Ptolemy was another matter. The maintenance of the new *status quo* left Ptolemy—with his naval base on Andros, his control of Cyprus, his suzerainty over the League of Islanders—in firm control of both the Aegean[95] and the eastern Mediterranean, and looking forward to "a generation of imperial dominion."[96] Though not a party to the agreement, Pyrrhus made a brief visit to Athens about this time, offered sacrifice on the Acropolis, and told the Athenians that if they had any sense, they would never again admit any king within their walls.[97] He made a separate peace with Demetrius before the latter's departure for Asia Minor, but this was no more than a brief truce of convenience.

Demetrius, leaving his son Antigonus Gonatas to hold his possessions in Greece, crossed over to Asia Minor late in 287 and began a series of inroads into Lysimachus's territory.[98] At first he scored some successes. In Miletus he was met by Ptolemy's former wife Eurydice, together with her daughter Ptolemaïs (see p. 122), whom Ptolemy had offered him in marriage during their brief reconciliation (299): they are possibly represented in a famous Boscoreale fresco, copied from some contemporary third-century painting.[99] Demetrius now—better late than never—married Ptolemaïs, and, after a period spent recruiting fresh troops, began attacking those Ionian cities that did not come over to him voluntarily (spring 286). He captured Sardis; he even won over some of Lysimachus's local commanders. But when Lysimachus sent a strong army south against him, Demetrius made his fatal mistake. Instead of staying by the coast, and relying on his formidable fleet, he turned inland, with Lysimachus's son Agathocles in hot pursuit.

Demetrius did not want a showdown at this point. Like Eumenes before him (p. 20), he hoped to raise the great eastern satrapies on his side; and like Eumenes, he failed in this endeavor. He had lost command of the sea, and Seleucus's vassals stood firm: as early as 294/3 Seleucus had raised his son Antiochus to the co-kingship (a significant precedent), and sent him east as his viceroy. Lysimachus's army cut off Demetrius's supplies and severed his lines of communication. Demetrius's troops were furious and dispirited at being taken on what they regarded, reasonably, as a wild-goose chase, and deserted in increasing numbers. Famine and disease also took their toll. Demetrius abandoned his eastern project, and crossed the Taurus range into Cilicia. Here, after one abortive attempt to conciliate Seleucus, he scored some initial military successes. But at the critical moment he fell ill, lost his momentum, and with it yet more of his support. Defeated by Seleucus, and still defiant, he contrived to escape, but finally was starved into surrender (spring 285).[100]

Seleucus, nothing loath at having so useful a trump in his hand, set Demetrius up in luxurious captivity at Apamea, on the Orontes, and talked airily of releasing him. This so alarmed Demetrius's old enemy Lysimachus that he offered Seleucus no less than two thousand talents to murder his prisoner. For once a Successor showed, or affected, moral scruples: Seleucus referred to Lysimachus, because of this suggestion, as a "dirty savage,"[101] and though his motives for keeping Demetrius alive may have been strictly pragmatic, this at least suggests that he had some notion of what dirty savagery was. In any case Demetrius very soon produced a solution of his own by drinking himself to death (late summer 283).[102] A frenetically energetic man, he was obviously bored witless by inactivity, and must also have realized that he had come to the end of his long road at last. He was only fifty-four when he died: a brilliant if erratic general, a lover of women, a classic overreacher.[103] Plutarch, inevitably, compared him to Mark Antony: each, as he says, was responsible for his own downfall.[104] If Demetrius failed to perceive that "it was no longer an age for vast dreams, but for limited ambitions," he was by no means the only Successor to retain this tempting illusion. Alexander's legacy of virtually limitless Eastern conquest—compare the modern American myth of the Open Frontier—still cast its potent spell over those who had campaigned with him, and indeed inspired many of their descendants.

For a while it looked as though Lysimachus might succeed where Demetrius had failed. Antigonus Gonatas, isolated by his father's death, his only hope to hold fast to his Greek fortresses, found himself up against constant Athenian efforts to wrest them from his control. To this end the new democratic government sent envoys to Lysimachus, Ptolemy, and Antipater (probably, but not certainly, Cassander's nephew rather than his son) seeking cash subventions, and to the native rulers of Paeonia and Bosporus in search of grain (286/5). Their efforts raised a total of two hundred talents and 22,500 *medimnoi* (roughly, bushels) of wheat.[105] An attempt in 286 to recover Piraeus proved abortive;[106] four hundred Athenian hoplites were betrayed to the garrison by a supposed Macedonian turncoat, and massacred as the gates were thrown open to them. The surviving epitaph of one of these soldiers, Chairippos, speaks of his "losing his life under Munychia's walls while staving off the day of slavery for his beloved country":[107] as Shear rightly insists, "day of slavery" was, in this case, no mere cliché of elegiac verse, but an all-too-real subjugation, "which Athens had recently known and now had reason to fear might be swiftly reimposed." On the other hand, a few months later Demochares succeeded—perhaps on a wave of enthusiasm caused by the news of Demetrius's surrender—in winning back Eleusis. Antigonus's assumption of the title of king after his father's death thus had a certain hollow ring to it.

Lysimachus, for whom Pyrrhus had now outlived his usefulness (indeed, he showed signs of becoming a dangerous rival), proceeded to seize both western Macedonia and Thessaly from him (285).[108] Pyrrhus retreated to his old kingdom of Epirus, and for the next four years, apart from the recovery of Corcyra,[109] concentrated his energies on local affairs.[110] If Cassander's son Antipater had expected Lysimachus to restore him, as he had promised, he was in for a rude surprise. The shrewd old marshal was himself acclaimed king of Macedonia by a compliant army, and when Antipater protested, he was put to death.[111] This virtually ended the claims of Cassander's line on the Macedonian succession. Nor, at this point, would any prophet have laid out much money on the chances of Antigonus Gonatas, who in 285 had little to his account except a useless treaty with Pyrrhus, trouble in Athens, a group of garrisoned and fortified Greek cities—Corinth, Chalcis, Demetrias, the so-called Fetters of Greece—and a mercenary corps, to pay which he was forced to tax the cities, a procedure that hardly enhanced his popularity.[112] His military record showed as many failures as successes. He had a sharp tongue, perhaps acquired from his philosophical training under Zeno of Citium. He was also the first, though by no means the last, commander to describe his retreats as strategic withdrawals.[113] Had anyone at this point predicted for Antigonus a reign of nearly forty years as unquestioned king of Macedon, and a dynastic legacy lasting till the Roman conquest, he would surely have been laughed out of court.

Lysimachus, for one, clearly did not take Antigonus seriously. His own power was now extensive and solid, reaching from Macedonia to Cilicia: Pyrrhus, to look no farther, was well aware of it. So was Ptolemy, who seems, like Lysimachus, to have discounted Antigonus in his calculations. He also was the beneficiary of an unexpected windfall: on the news of Demetrius's death the latter's ally in Miletus, the Phoenician prince Philocles, had taken the pick of his naval squadrons to Ptolemy, together with the sovereignty of Tyre and Sidon; never had Ptolemy's gift for sitting still and waiting paid off better.[114] Ptolemy also, like many others, now saw clearly that the removal of Cassander and Demetrius, the apparent impotence of Antigonus, and Lysimachus's expansion in Asia were factors that made a final test of strength between the last two Successors outside Egypt, Lysimachus and Seleucus, almost inevitable.

Now though Lysimachus underrated Antigonus, his potential challenger Seleucus did not. This was why, as a gesture of friendship, in 283 he sent Demetrius the Besieger's ashes home in state to his son,[115] escorted by envoys briefed to show Antigonus where he might find a new, and far more powerful, ally than any he had enjoyed hitherto. Pyrrhus, as we have seen, had retreated to Epirus, and in any case from 281 onwards was to be wholly occupied with affairs in Italy and Sicily (see p. 230): for the time being, at least, he could be discounted as either ally or rival.

What finally spoiled Lysimachus's chances, however, was a remarkable error of judgment on his domestic front.[116] Like Ptolemy, he married more than once; like Ptolemy, again, this gave him serious problems over the succession, not least since his current wife was the redoubtable Arsinoë (above, p. 122). We have already seen how Ptolemy repudiated Eurydice in favor of her niece Berenice, and made his son by the latter, Ptolemy II Philadelphos, his co-ruler and destined successor (285), two years before his own death (pp. 87–88). But this move left out of account, and effectively debarred from the throne, that violent, dangerous, and intensely ambitious man, Ptolemy Keraunos, the aptly named Thunderbolt, Eurydice's eldest son. Keraunos took his grievance to Seleucus, who temporized, offering to get him the throne when his father died. Impatient, Keraunos tried Lysimachus instead. But on old Ptolemy's death, in 283, Lysimachus, ever the canny diplomat, began to renegotiate alliance with Ptolemy II by offering him yet another daughter in marriage; so Keraunos, inevitably, began to think in terms of the *Macedonian* succession, a siege perilous for which there already existed too many potential candidates—Lysimachus's eldest son, Agathocles, popular and a fine soldier (above, p. 129); Antigonus Gonatas; Pyrrhus; and no less than three sons of Arsinoë's by Lysimachus.

In Macedonia, however, candidates for a throne could vanish very fast. Pyrrhus, for one, was *hors de concours*, and Antigonus at this stage remained a non-starter. Arsinoë, a lethally ambitious woman now in her mid-thirties—Tarn talks about her "remote and spiritual beauty":[117] she was as remote and spiritual as a rattlesnake disturbed—talked her elderly husband, with Keraunos's all-too-willing help, into executing Agathocles on a treason charge (283/2). (Pausanias asserts that, on top of everything else, Arsinoë had played Potiphar's wife to Agathocles' Joseph, pursuing him sexually and then arranging for his death when he rejected her advances.)[118] This act not surprisingly caused serious unrest; Lysimachus responded by ordering an indiscriminate purge, which made matters worse. He had been a harsh and exacting ruler, and his subjects were ripe for revolt. A stream of refugees, headed by Agathocles' widow, Lysandra (Arsinoë's half-sister: no love lost there), now sought asylum with Seleucus, begging him to intervene. Keraunos, on the other hand, having helped to eliminate Agathocles, stayed on with Lysimachus as his lieutenant, eyes still fixed on the throne of Macedon.[119]

In 282 Seleucus, only too glad of an excuse to take action, marched on Asia Minor, and town after town opened its gates to him. By 281 Lysimachus—now over eighty—was forced to counterattack: most of Anatolia had gone over to Seleucus. Perhaps the most significant defection was that of Philetairos, the governor of Pergamon, who—in alarm at Agathocles' murder, and his own possible fate at Arsinoë's hands—not only allied himself and his great hill fortress with Seleucus, but impounded no less than nine thousand talents of Lysimachus's treasure left in his charge, thus laying the foundation for the future Attalid dynasty (see p. 166). Like Antigonus at Ipsus, Lysimachus staked everything on a set battle, this time at Corupedion, near Magnesia-by-Sipylos (Feb. 281), and lost it, himself (again like Antigonus) dying on the field.[120] Lysandra was so bitter against her father-in-law that it was all his son Alexander could do to persuade her to give up the old man's body for burial.[121] Arsinoë, in Ephesus (renamed Arsinoeia in her honor by Lysimachus), heard of the defeat, and the mass desertions by Lysimachus's forces that followed it, and knew that only prompt action could save her. While a favorite maid of honor, dressed in her royal robes, was left behind as a decoy (and was, indeed, killed when mistaken for her), Arsinoë herself, disguised as a beggar, slipped away to the port and took ship for Macedonia, carrying her very considerable wealth with her.[122] She took up residence in Cassandreia, a logical enough move: after his defeat of Pyrrhus (p. 130), Lysimachus not only had been recognized as king of Macedonia, but had been worshipped there as a god. She had got all three children away with her; now she waited on events.

Ptolemy Keraunos was captured by Seleucus, and well treated;[123] but a few months made it very clear to the Thunderbolt that Seleucus, even at seventy-seven, had his own ambitions, now, to spend his old age on the Macedonian throne, and showed no signs of helping his loyal supporter Keraunos to the throne of Egypt, either. So when Seleucus, after his great victory, finally set out for Europe, and stepped ashore at Lysimacheia to reclaim his Macedonian heritage, Keraunos stabbed him to death (281/0).[124] His title of Nicator ("Conqueror") had not lasted long. Alexander's dream of world empire had claimed its last victim. Antipater apart, of all Alexander's marshals only Ptolemy had stayed the course and died of natural causes. Seleucus stood, at the moment of his assassination, within an ace of winning the whole hand; but with his removal the natural tripartite division of Europe, Africa, and Asia soon reasserted itself, and this time for good. Ptolemy Keraunos, riding a wave of popularity with Lysimachus's more loyal veterans, actually got himself acclaimed king of Macedonia. He then sent messages to Arsinoë in Cassandreia, offering to marry her, make her queen of Macedonia, adopt her children, and entail the throne to the eldest, Ptolemy of Telmessos (above, p. 132).[125] Arsinoë insisted on marriage before the army assembly, outside Cassandreia. Keraunos agreed. Young Ptolemy, after vainly warning his mother against this importunate suitor, fled to Illyria, and the wedding took place.[126] Keraunos at once murdered Arsinoë's two remaining children, and she herself only just contrived to escape, seeking sanctuary on Samothrace. As we shall see (p. 145), her astonishing career still had a long way to go.

Keraunos was not left to enjoy his ill-gotten gains for long. After soundly thrashing Antigonus Gonatas when the latter tried conclusions with him at sea, he secured all Macedonia and Thessaly except for Demetrias;[127] but early in 279 he had to face something new, a mass invasion by the Gauls, hitherto held in check by the strong northern defenses of Lysimachus.[128] On his first encounter with them he was killed, and his head, stuck on a spear, accompanied the Gauls as they plundered Macedonia, a derisive *memento mori* that, we may suppose, afforded Arsinoë a certain cold comfort when she learned of it.[129] Anarchy ensued: it was at some point during this period that Cassander's nephew Antipater "Etesias"—so called, derisively, because of the duration of the Etesian winds—enjoyed his forty-five-day reign.[130] The Gauls thrust south, into Thrace, Asia Minor, the Balkans. Walled towns were reasonably safe, but the countryside was gutted. One horde was finally turned back, at Delphi, by a mixed army under the leadership of the Aetolians, who very soon saw that these hulking broadswordsmen were dangerous only at close quarters, and highly vulnerable to guerilla tactics.[131] Driven north, in blinding snow, they suffered heavy losses, and it is from this time on that the Aetolians (in a very real sense the saviors of Greece) began to acquire their reputation as a political and military force in the Greek world.

Curiously, this invasion by the Gauls was also the making, at long last, of Antigonus Gonatas's reputation. In 279, after Keraunos's death, Antigonus was only barely maintaining his already precarious hold on Demetrias, Chalcis, Piraeus, and Corinth. An abortive attack on Aetolia by the Spartan king Areus, who had reconstituted the old Peloponnesian League, had had the indirect but momentous effect of forcing four Achaean cities into federation as a breakaway movement, thus resuscitating the earlier Achaean League in opposition to Sparta (280). This seemingly unimportant chain of events was to have immense repercussions in Peloponnesian politics for the next hundred years and more. In Athens an ultrademocratic government, including Demochares, was in power.[132] Seleucus's son and successor (p. 129),

Antiochus I, had designs on the throne of Macedonia, and a war broke out between him and Antigonus at this time: as Tarn says, "each claimed Macedonia; each thought the other his most dangerous rival."[133] Meanwhile the throne itself remained vacant. Antipater Etesias was ignominiously deposed by a middle-class general, Sosthenes, who staved off the Gauls for a while, and kept some kind of rudimentary government going, but flatly refused the title of king.[134] He died, probably fighting the Gauls, c. June 277. Antigonus Gonatas now moved north on Thrace, with a fleet and a strong force of mercenaries (summer 277). It may have been during his absence that the Spartans expelled his garrison from Troezen,[135] and that other cities of the Peloponnese, including Argos and Megalopolis, recovered their independence.

We can only guess at Gonatas's motives in launching this expedition. He may have been preparing for a bid to recover Macedonia; more probably he was hoping to benefit from the uncertain conditions following Lysimachus's death, and to acquire a little extra territory, of which he stood much in need. But whatever the reason for his presence near Lysimacheia in the late summer of 277, in the event it gave him the greatest stroke of good fortune in his entire career. A vast column of Gauls, estimated at eighteen thousand or more, was marching through Thrace toward the coastal cities of the Chersonese.[136] By a clever ruse Antigonus outmaneuvered, trapped, and massacred them all, winning what Tarn rightly calls "a great and bloody victory." As after Marathon two centuries before, the psychological repercussions were enormous. Before the year was out,[137] Antigonus Gonatas had been recognized again, and this time for good, as the rightful king of Macedonia, and had won back the throne that his grandfather Antigonus One-Eye had coveted, in vain, for so long.

His victory seemed to give Gonatas fresh confidence and energy. In 277/6 he finally drove out Antipater "Etesias" and Arsinoë's one surviving son, Ptolemy, won back Thessaly, and stormed Cassandreia.[138] Pan, the god who, it was claimed, had turned his foes back in panic rout, was now established as a patron deity in the Macedonian capital of Pella, and represented on Antigonus's coins: seemingly, the king's own features—snub-nosed, if not horned—bore a noticeable resemblance to the demigod's traditional iconography.[139] The lame-duck son of Demetrius the Besieger had, in the end, proved himself a worthy scion of Antigonus One-Eye. Now finally established, though with one perilous trial of strength against Pyrrhus yet to come (p. 143), Gonatas was to rule Macedonia for more than thirty-five years. Antigonids, Seleucids, and Ptolemies had established a balance of power at last. By 276 Alexander's funeral games were over.

PART TWO
THE ZENITH CENTURY
276–222 B.C.

CHAPTER 9

PTOLEMY PHILADELPHOS AND ANTIGONUS GONATAS, 276–239

The third century B.C. witnesses the acme of Hellenistic culture, just as the fifth witnessed that of the classical era; yet both, paradoxically, are very short, during their most crucial years, on solid historical documentation, and for once the later period is worse off than the earlier.[1] We have no continuous narrative of events except for Justin's miserable (but at times, alas, indispensable) epitome of Trogus Pompeius, a Gaulish historian who wrote under Augustus: it takes Justin to make us properly appreciate Diodorus, lost, except for fragments, after Ipsus (301). Trogus's own work was derived, at third or fourth hand, from the lost history of Phylarchus, who picked up where Duris of Samos (281) and Hieronymus of Cardia (Pyrrhus's death in 272?) left off, and carried the story through to Cleomenes III's defeat at Sellasia (222). If Hieronymus had a bias in favor of the Antigonids, whom he served,[2] Phylarchus seems to have been a puritan idealist with a strong distaste for Hellenistic luxury, and a corresponding romantic admiration for the last bastions of Greek city-state individualism, above all for the Sparta of Agis IV and Cleomenes III.[3] This made him critical of the Achaean League's statesman Aratus of Sicyon (below, p. 151), and brought down on his head, in consequence, some of Polybius's most rancorous and partisan disapproval.[4] Plutarch, on the other hand, who idolized the free *polis*, identified its demise with that of Demosthenes, and disliked Hellenistic kings, and their courts, to the point of not writing about them (an omission the modern historian can only regret),[5] found Aratus and Phylarchus equally attractive writers, a fact that has created some nice problems in source criticism.

Phylarchus survives in Plutarch's *Lives* of Pyrrhus (reinforced by Pyrrhus's own memoirs), of the Spartan kings Agis IV and Cleomenes III, and of Aratus of Sicyon. Aratus also left memoirs, which, again, Plutarch used in his biography. Since Aratus and Cleomenes, as we shall see, pursued directly conflicting policies, and since Plutarch's criteria are moral rather than historical, the Achaean leader's pact with Antigonus Doson against Sparta (below, p. 259) provoked Plutarch to charge him, more in sorrow than in anger, with moral inconsistency. How could any good man oppose those who sought to bring back the disciplinary virtues of the Spartan *ancien régime*?[6] The historical digressions in Pausanias and Strabo are also in all likelihood ultimately derived from the same sources.[7] It is only from 220 that we once more have a contemporary narrative voice, and key witness, in Polybius, who also devotes an important digression to the origins of the Achaean League.[8] Polybius is by no means an impartial witness, but remains notwithstanding a full and eloquent one, whose firsthand experiences as statesman and soldier stood him in good stead as a historian (below, pp. 273 ff.). The papyri and inscriptions provide much help in dark places, but all too often of a local (and, in Egypt, parochial) nature: minor honors, village tax returns, details of municipal government that can only with difficulty be fitted into any overall pattern.[9] Coins are useful as a guide to regal propaganda; in the case of the Indo-Bactrian kings (pp. 330 ff.) they provide almost our only evidence.[10]

Thus the history of the period, from Corupedion (281) to the accession of Philip V in Macedonia (221), has to be patched together from shreds and snippets: much of it, especially the chronology, remains problematic to a degree. Yet to qualify every statement becomes tedious and, ultimately, self-defeating. If, then, the following narrative on occasion sounds a good deal more assured than the facts warrant, the reader should bear in mind throughout that the evidence is shaky, and the hypotheses remain fragile.

The period with which this chapter is concerned, up to Antigonus Gonatas's death, in 239, reveals a round of frontier wars between the three major dynasties—Antigonids, Seleucids, Ptolemies—in which, as usual, "each side supported the enemies or revolted subjects of the other."[11] Antiochus I, Seleucus Nicator's son, by now over forty, was chiefly concerned with holding his vast, heterogeneous eastern kingdom together, and seeking to prevent (generally without success) a whole string of internal secessions, from Pergamon in the west to Bactria in the far east.[12] Though his official Eastern capital was Seleucia-on-Tigris, his focus of interest tended toward the Mediterranean, as his concern for Antioch and its great port, Seleucia-in-Pieria, makes very clear. He expended far more effort and investment on Asia Minor and the always elusive foothold in Europe than he did on his vast Oriental satrapies, and this in the long run was to prove a major factor in the collapse of the Seleucid empire. Ptolemy Philadelphos, in Egypt, was, like his father, a defensive counterpuncher rather than an aggressor, a trait he passed on to subsequent generations:[13] no accident that after Actium, in 31 B.C., the Ptolemaic domains were still almost exactly what they had been when defined at Babylon and Triparadeisos. A series of Syrian wars emphasized the obvious friction that was bound to exist between Ptolemies and Seleucids; they also hinted at Ptolemaic interest in controlling the trade routes of Asia Minor, the eastern Mediterranean, and the Aegean.[14] This last concern probably lay behind the Ptolemies' perennial diplomatic meddling in the affairs of mainland Greece, their unswerving hostility to Macedonia, and their readiness to support any anti-Macedonian faction, from Pyrrhus to the Achaean League.

Antigonus Gonatas, on the other hand, was largely concerned to secure Macedonia's frontiers and to establish some kind of *status quo*, a measure of political and economic stability, after long years during which the country had been stripped of its manpower and its resources, a no-man's-land fought over by a succession of sav-

Fig. 53. Antiochus I, wearing the royal diadem. Silver tetradrachm struck at Antioch ca. 256–246 B.C.
Private collection. Photo Hirmer.

agely ambitious warlords. But such an aim required firm control of the Greek mainland, and hopes of independence were by no means yet dead in the city-states. First Athens made a bid for freedom in the so-called Chremonidean War (268?–263/2?: below, pp. 147 ff.); then came the rise of the Achaean League under the leadership of Aratus of Sicyon (from 251/0: pp. 151 ff.). Later, as we shall see (pp. 258 ff.), Sparta—aggressively independent, even in reduced circumstances, and now straining to recover old glories, virtues, and privileges by way of what passed for social revolution—made a fierce bid to smash the power of Macedonia in Greece once and for all, a bid that was destroyed at Sellasia (July 222: see p. 261).

The establishment, development, and organization of the Achaean and Aetolian Leagues present interesting features: they are, first and foremost, almost the only successful examples of Greek federation as a working political device. This involved, *inter alia*, the concept of *sympoliteia*, a division of authority within the federal structure, between local and central government, the latter being responsible for such key areas as foreign policy, military affairs, and court cases involving treason. A citizen of any member state might be restricted to his own city in the exercise of political rights, but would enjoy civil privileges throughout the federation. Another significant feature of the system, particularly in the case of Achaea, was the admission of non-ethnics on equal terms, essential if the *sympoliteia* was to develop strongly: as we shall see, this policy led to Achaean confrontations with Sparta and, later, with Rome. Though some sort of Achaean confederacy had been in existence during the fourth century, the true development of the League can be dated to 280, when the first four cities federated, and, more particularly, to 251 (see below, p. 151), when Aratus brought Sicyon in as a member, and himself very soon became the leading Achaean statesman. The Aetolians had federated as early as 370, probably in response to the expansionist activities of Thebes.[15] During the third century the organization of both Leagues was along roughly similar lines: an annually elected general (*stratēgos*), a council (*boulē*, *synedrion*), and an assembly (*ekklēsia*), together with a smaller steering committee (*dēmiourgoi, apoklētoi*), which dealt with much of the day-to-day work. The Aetolian League was more chary than the Achaean about granting full membership to peripheral *poleis*, and always kept firm control over their activities, in many cases offering them *isopoliteia*, reciprocal rights without unification, rather than *sympoliteia*. Since brigandage and piracy formed a regular line item in its budget, the Aetolian League's guarantee of *asylia*, freedom from reprisals or seizure of property, was highly valued.

Meanwhile separatism of a different sort was in evidence in Asia Minor. The powerful fief of Pergamon, which, under its governor Philetairos, had transferred its allegiance from Lysimachus to the Seleucids after Corupedion, was soon to break away altogether, as an independent kingdom (p. 148). About the same time a string of cities along the southern shore of the Black Sea, including Byzantium, Chalcedon, and Heracleia Pontica, declared their independence and formed themselves into a "Northern League."[16] Bithynia and Cappadocia became autonomous states under native dynasties. The tendency of the Seleucid domains to fragment was there from the very beginning. One last curious enclave in Anatolia was that occupied by the Gauls—or Galatians, as they were generally known to the Greeks of Asia from now on—who, after their various defeats, had been pushed off by Antiochus I and his war elephants into a kind of reserve in Phrygia (275/4),[17] from where they could be drawn on at need as mercenaries by the various contending parties. Their uncouth violence and migrational mass descent had thoroughly scared the Greeks:[18] it followed that one sure badge of ascension in the battle of Hellenistic power seekers was a good, clean, certified victory over these peripatetic bogeymen. Antigonus Gonatas, Antiochus I, the Aetolian League, even Attalus I of Pergamon (p. 150), all acquired such a certificate, to their immense advantage.

Let us first consider the position of Antigonus Gonatas, that most unlikely of Macedonian monarchs: short, snub-nosed, knock-kneed, earnest patron of intellec-

Fig. 54. War elephant attacking a Celt, probably a group commemorating Antiochus I's "Elephant Victory" over the Galatians in 270 B.C. Terra-cotta statuette from Myrina (Asia Minor). Musée du Louvre, Paris. Photo Giraudon.

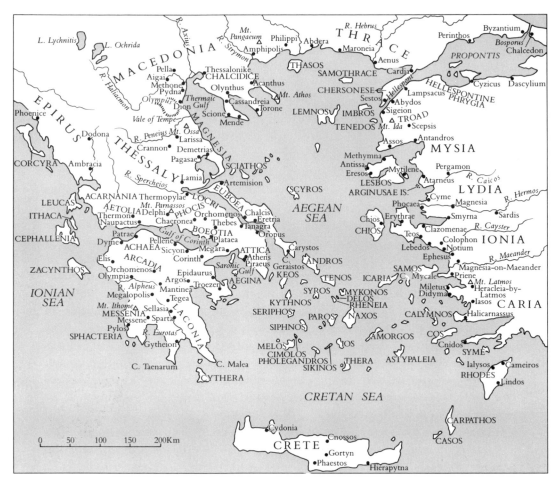

Map 9. Mainland Greece and the Aegean basin.

tuals, a Stoic with a taste for the worship of Pan, and a ruler whose concept of his duties (similar in this to that other Stoic, Marcus Aurelius) verged on the masochistic.[19] In 276, largely as the result of his victory the previous year over a Galatian horde outside Lysimacheia (p. 134), he was reestablished as king of Macedonia. He had a nonaggression pact with Antiochus I, whose half-sister (and stepdaughter) Phila he now married (276), an alliance that was to last throughout his long reign.[20] The wedding hymn, composed by Aratus of Soli, celebrated the rout of the Gauls by Pan's divine agency, but could not, of course, fail to shed a little glory on the bridegroom also, as Pan's human avatar.[21]

Antigonus now set up his court—a notably intellectual one—in Pella.[22] Having spent a good deal of his career as a king without a kingdom, he had been forced to seek his strength internally, to the lasting benefit of his own character; and here, clearly, his early training under Zeno of Citium was invaluable. The influence of Stoicism at Antigonus's court was strong, indeed fundamental. Zeno himself refused

Fig. 55. Aratus and the Muse Urania, with a globe of the heavens between them. Mosaic from Trier, third century A.D. Landesmuseum, Trier.

an invitation to go there, but he sent his disciple Persaeus instead, to tutor Antigonus's son, Demetrius, and to provide the proper theoretical backing for Antigonid kingship.[23] It is a mark of Stoic involvement—unique among Hellenistic thinkers—in affairs of state at a practical level that Persaeus should have died defending Corinth on Antigonus's behalf against Aratus (243).[24] Antigonus's notion of kingship as "noble servitude" undoubtedly stems from his Stoic attachments,[25] though it has a Cynic tinge to it as well: kingship brought suffering rather than pleasure; the diadem, Antigonus declared, was a bauble that most men would never so much as retrieve from the midden if they knew all that it entailed.[26]

Among the writers and thinkers at Antigonus's court the best-known undoubtedly was Aratus of Soli, author of the *Phaenomena* (see p. 184), an astronomical poem that presents Zeus as the consciousness of the world, as reason personified, a development of Anaxagorean *Nous*, the agent and instrument of cosmic order. As goes the god, so should the king go. The stars in their courses serve mankind (navigational aids, the agricultural year cycle); the supreme being sees to the good of his creatures. No accident that Aratus was the nearest thing to a scientist in Pella, or that his science was primarily moral in its application. The true Stoic was not interested in pure science (p. 634); such banausic matters, he felt, could be left to the hedonists and moral imbeciles who thronged to Ptolemy's antechambers in Alexandria. Pella was now a serious, dedicated court—though not above Hellenistic-style flattery of its ruler's virtuous achievements: Aratus wrote an encomium of Antigonus as well as his wedding hymn, and it was the king's old teacher Menedemus who moved the honorific decree on his behalf after that first famous victory over the Gauls.[27] Self-complacency is an endemic hazard of virtuous living.

In addition to Aratus, Pella provided a base for the distinguished historian Hieronymus of Cardia (p. 137), who had served Gonatas's father and grandfather before him as officer and garrison commander, and now in his old age wrote for the Antigonids—therefore, inevitably, both stressing and favoring their actions—the history of the Successors' wars.[28] There was also that plain, blunt Cynic philosopher,

Bion of Borysthenes: caustic, vulgar, arrogant, exhibitionistic, perhaps an ex-slave, yet also tenderhearted, appalled at the notion of a god who could visit the sins of the father on the children, ready to take pity even on a tortured frog—this last evincing a disposition most uncharacteristic in any Greek, ancient or modern.[29] He scoffed at religion, was fond of boys, gave popular public lectures (for a stiff fee), and seems to have enjoyed the role of licensed philosophical buffoon at Antigonus's court. ("Why tear your hair out in bereavement?" he asked. "Sorrow isn't cured by baldness.")[30] He and Zeno's disciple Persaeus both hint at that strain of radicalism, on occasion leading to something very like social revolution, that tended to show up where Stoic or Cynic advisers were in evidence. (Cleomenes III of Sparta was another Stoic, guided by the philosopher Sphaerus; and he, as we shall see [pp. 257 ff.], planned just such a revolution—though for highly suspect motives—and came very close to bringing it off.) If a man demands justice, not merely as an abstract concept, but in setting up the life of a society, and if he holds, further, that within that society (however defined) all men have equal rights, then the odds are that his views, sooner rather than later, are going to set something or someone on fire.

Antigonus Gonatas, then, may fairly be called the first Stoic king. Unlike the Ptolemies and some others, he never sought divinization, whether for self-aggrandizement or as an instrument of political propaganda. Macedonia was not a receptive country for ventures of that sort. Philip II's attempt to present himself as a thirteenth god in the Olympian pantheon had not proved auspicious,[31] and Alexander's request for deification had met with a scandalized refusal from Antipater.[32] Gonatas modestly argued that he lacked the charisma for such a step, and, considering the number of times he was defeated, he may well have been right. Even after 276 his position remained questionable so long as Pyrrhus was still alive.

In late 275 Pyrrhus at last returned from Italy (see pp. 228 ff.), and early the next year invaded Macedonia.[33] His primary objective was loot: he had 8,500 men in his army, and no money with which to support them. But at the same time it is plain that he was making a genuine bid to recover the throne. He also bore a personal grudge against Antigonus, who had refused him support during his war with Rome. His forces engaged those of Gonatas in the passes of Aoös, near Antigoneia. When, after a stubborn rearguard action, Gonatas's mercenaries were defeated, his demoralized Macedonian troops went over to Pyrrhus *en masse*. Gonatas himself had no choice but to flee, accompanied only by a small cavalry escort, to the safety of Thessalonike. Pyrrhus now recovered most of Macedonia and Thessaly (274), leaving Antigonus only one or two coastal cities and a still-powerful fleet. To Pyrrhus's chagrin, his defeated opponent still maintained the royal purple: like his father before him, Gonatas did not equate loss of territory with loss of kingship, even after a second drubbing in the field, this time at the hands of Pyrrhus's son Ptolemaeus.[34]

Pyrrhus could now, briefly, claim to be king of Macedon once more: the Macedonians had shown whom, in the moment of victory, they preferred. But the preference was fleeting. Pyrrhus lost popularity by letting his Gauls plunder the royal tombs at Aigai,[35] and by leaving his son Ptolemaeus to hold Macedonia on his behalf while he plunged into a pointless, and finally fatal, campaign in southern Greece.

Fig. 56. Bust probably portraying
Pyrrhus of Epirus. Roman copy of a
third-century original.
Museo Nazionale, Naples. Photo Alinari/
Anderson.

Early in 272, on the invitation of that disgruntled royal Spartan exile, Cleonymus
(see p. 223), Pyrrhus invaded the Peloponnese,[36] his excuse being that he aimed to
liberate all cities still held by Antigonus's garrisons. Athens, always eager to support
any anti-Macedonian power—the occupation of Piraeus still rankled—offered him
alliance, for what that was worth.[37] A stubborn defense by Sparta bogged Pyrrhus
down,[38] and Antigonus took the opportunity to recapture most of Macedonia.[39] He
then took his fleet down to Corinth (summer 272), and marched on Argos. Those of
the Argives who preferred Pyrrhus to Antigonus sent an urgent message to the Epirot for help.[40]

Pyrrhus promptly raised the siege of Sparta and came north. Both armies seem
to have been let into the town by different factions.[41] During the street fighting that
ensued, Pyrrhus was knocked unconscious by a tile an old woman lobbed at him
from a rooftop. An enemy soldier, seeing who he was, hacked off his head as he lay
there, and sent it to Antigonus, who—like Alexander with Darius, or Caesar with
Pompey—professed shock and sorrow, but must also have felt considerable relief.[42]
This was in the autumn of 272: resistance to Gonatas collapsed instantly, and this
time for good. He might have won all Greece now, but, like Ptolemy, he preferred
limited gains: he was, first and foremost, king of Macedonia.[43] He still held Piraeus;
on his way back to Macedonia he garrisoned Eretria and Chalcis. Henceforth his rule
was virtually undisputed in Macedonia, though, as in Philip II's day, there was to be
vigorous opposition, not only from Athens and Sparta, but also, now, from the
Aetolian and Achaean Leagues: his support for *tyrannoi* did not endear him to
would-be democrats. But so long as Antigonus held Acrocorinth, Piraeus, and the
key cities between central Greece and the north, his position was hard to shake.
Athens, despite her approaches to Pyrrhus, he treated with courtesy, and respect for

her culture; it would not be all that long before propertied moderates were offering him official sacrifices (245/4), and stelai were erected commemorating his victory over the Gauls.[44] But the last word was with his Macedonian garrison in Piraeus, and Athenians still chafed under that alien restraint.[45] It was, ironically, Ptolemaic Egypt that gave them the illusory chance for another bid to regain their freedom.

The reign of Ptolemy II Philadelphos (283–246) almost exactly coincided with that of Antigonus Gonatas (276–239). During the same period we find two successive kings in Seleucid Asia: Antiochus I Soter (281–261), and Antiochus II Theos (261–246). The period thus possesses a certain unity,[46] underlined by the consistency throughout it of Ptolemaic policy. At home this policy was one of cultural ostentation and self-advertisement, by way of such things as the Museum and Library (above, pp. 84 ff.), even the Pharos (p. 158). It was in 279/8 that the indefatigable Arsinoë, bored with sanctuary on Samothrace, finally returned to Egypt. Here she cultivated her brother, Ptolemy II, her junior by eight years, to such effect that he repudiated his existing wife—another Arsinoë, and, to confuse matters further, the returned Arsinoë's former stepdaughter—on a charge of conspiracy, exiled her, and then proceeded to marry his own full sister. She promptly adopted his first wife's children, took the title "Philadelphos," and began to appear with her brother-*cum*-husband on his gold and silver coinage.[47] The date of this marriage is uncertain: all we know is that it must have taken place before 274/3, when Arsinoë appears as regnant queen on the Pithom stele.[48]

Arsinoë was undeniably beautiful as well as determined, and the mass of honorific material that has survived suggests that Ptolemy's incestuous marriage was something more than a mere act of calculated policy. At the same time, calculation undoubtedly entered into it. Ptolemy I had already been deified, and the more divinity that hedged the royal succession the better. Ptolemy II probably figured on playing Osiris to Arsinoë's Isis for the benefit of his Egyptian subjects, and Zeus to

Fig. 57. Ptolemy II and Arsinoë II, the Theoi Adelphoi, represented on a gold octadrachm minted at Alexandria(?) by Ptolemy III ca. 246 B.C.(?). British Museum, London.

her Hera for any Greeks who, like the scurrilous poet Sotades (above, p. 82), were unwise enough to query the propriety of the relationship.[49] Sailors were already praying to Arsinoë during her lifetime, a sign that she was regarded in some sense as the avatar of Isis, and she was promptly deified after her death (July 270). Though there is no reason to doubt her influence over Ptolemy, her role as the political power behind the throne has probably been exaggerated: historiography is no more immune than any other discipline to the insistent claims of feminism.[50] We need not suppose, for example, that the First Syrian War (274/3–271), against Antiochus I, was won only by her energy and brains:[51] Ptolemy could be a forceful enough ruler when force was called for.

In his foreign policy economic as well as political considerations applied. Ptolemy wanted control over the Aegean, the eastern Mediterranean trade routes, and the sea passage through to the Black Sea, and seems to have profited by the death of Seleucus to strengthen his position in these areas.[52] He already, as early as 279/8, had a bridgehead at Miletus.[53] Despite a revolt in the buffer state of Cyrenaica, engineered by his half-brother Magas,[54] Ptolemy by 272/1 had won back the best part of coastal Syria and large parts of southern Anatolia, some as far west as Caria, and including most of Cilicia. His devoted court poet Theocritus (pp. 235 ff.) celebrated these conquests in his *Encomium of Ptolemy*:[55]

> Over all [Egypt] Lord Ptolemy rules as king: in addition
> He cuts himself slices from Phoenicia and Arabia,
> From Syria, Libya, and the swarthy Ethiops' lands;
> Over all Pamphylia his word is law, and among the Cilician
> Spearmen, the Lycians and the warlike Carians,
> And the isles of the Cyclades, for the finest vessels
> That sail the seas are his, all the sea and land
> And the echoing rivers are ruled by Ptolemy, while about him
> Swarm horsemen and shieldmen, agleam in brazen armor.

He also put out feelers to the West with an embassy to Rome:[56] trade beyond the Straits of Messina would be, from now on, increasingly dependent on Rome's good will.

Ptolemy's hopes of establishing long-term control over the Aegean were not encouraged, however, by the resurgence of Macedonia under Antigonus Gonatas. Ever since the days of Philip II, Greece and the Aegean had been Macedonia's natural sphere of influence, and Gonatas showed no signs of abandoning that role. In particular, once firmly in power he seems to have worked hard to restore the naval supremacy that Macedonia had enjoyed under his father, Demetrius.[57] To Alexandria, nothing could have looked more potentially alarming. It followed that for years the Ptolemies actively subsidized all Macedonia's enemies in this area. After Pyrrhus's death (272) Ptolemy concentrated his efforts on Athens. He was already supplying a large proportion of the city's wheat.[58] He also knew just how to exploit Athenian longings for freedom and autonomy. The dream of regaining effective control of Piraeus was hard to resist.[59] Potential anti-Macedonian allies—including the Spartan king Areus, ever ready to switch sides in furtherance of his inflated royal ambitions—were carefully nursed into a coalition. When he judged the time ripe, Ptolemy, through his agents, encouraged the Athenian nationalists to throw out the pro-Macedonian party,[60] and, a little later, assured of Egyptian support, and backed by a variety of Peloponnesian allies, to declare war on Antigonus (autumn 268?).[61]

The ringingly patriotic motion for war was made by an idealistic, and hand-some, Athenian citizen, Chremonides, who not only gave his name to the war,[62] but also—like Antigonus, like Cleomenes—was a professed Stoic, a student of Zeno's. Thus we have the piquant situation of a war being fought out between the philoso-pher's former disciples, though in neither case, it would seem, on Stoic principles:[63] Antigonus meant to consolidate his power, while Athens was in pursuit of that ever-receding *polis* dream, genuine self-determination—a goal conditional, in the first in-stance, upon the recovery of Piraeus.[64] There was much talk of a new crusade against the barbarian, of Greek freedom, of Sparta and Athens fighting side by side (with the help of an Egyptian fleet, but this was not stressed). Ptolemy, so the Chremonidean Decree claimed, "conspicuously shows his zeal for the common freedom of the Greeks": in fact he was doing no more than exploit that old and potent slogan with a view to limiting Antigonid naval expansion—both strategic and economic—in the Aegean,[65] and the substantive help he gave the Athenians was minimal. It is, never-theless, significant how many Greek cities were ready to throw their weight against Macedonian domination.

There was inconclusive campaigning during 266, to which Antigonus Gonatas's possession of Corinth remained the strategic key. Then, in 265, Antigonus met the ambitious Spartan king Areus outside Corinth and left him dead on the battlefield.[66] Despite ineffectual diversionary tactics by his opponents, Antigonus now put Athens under siege. Ptolemy had other claims on his attention just then: perhaps because he had won control of Ephesus (ca. 262/1), Antigonus's powerful fleet was now threat-ening his position in the Aegean, and indeed soon scored a major victory over the Ptolemaic squadrons off Cos (261?).[67] Thus the Egyptian fleet did not break An-tigonus's blockade, and Ptolemy, who had instigated the rising, did nothing, just as his father had done nothing, to save Athens.[68] Once again the city was starved into surrender (262/1?). This time there was no polite talk about autonomy. Antigonus put his own Macedonian officials in to run the city.[69] Piraeus kept its garrison (the precise role, and effectiveness, of which during the siege remains uncertain); the Hill of the Muses was reoccupied. Troops were also posted at strategic points along the coast of Attica.[70] Athens lost the right to appoint her own magistrates (and possibly to mint her own coins),[71] becoming

> a mere university city
> And the goddess born of the foam
> Became the kept hetaera, heroine of Menander,
> And the philosopher narrowed his focus, confined
> His efforts to putting his own soul in order
> And keeping a quiet mind.

Antigonus Gonatas was now "the undisputed master of Greece."[72]

While all this had been going on, Antiochus I in Asia had had his own problems—mostly, as always, those of secession. Not only was the Seleucids' control over their outlying dependencies uncertain, but at the same time they took no firm steps to limit or rationalize their frontiers. Pontus, Bithynia, and Cappadocia were all now either independent of, or breaking away from, the unwieldy eastern empire. The satrapies of Bactria and Sogdiana were soon to achieve independence *en bloc* (ca. 250: see p. 332). The movement that ultimately led to the secessionist kingdom of Parthia was already under way in 247, when Parthia was invaded by Parsa tribesmen under their leader Arsaces (hence the Arsacid dynasty). Thus Antiochus's famous proclamation, "I am Antiochus, the Great King, the legitimate king, the king of the world, king of Babylon, king of all countries. . . . May I personally conquer [all] the countries from sunrise to sunset, gather their tribute, and bring it [home]," [73] has a certain ironic ring to it in 268. With the death five years later of Philetairos, the elderly, possibly eunuch, governor of Pergamon, Antiochus found himself faced with trouble much nearer home. [74] Philetairos's nephew and adopted son, Eumenes, decided to make his own bid for independence. Antiochus sent out a punitive expedition against him, and Eumenes defeated it near Sardis. [75] Another fragment of empire was ready to break loose.

Then, in June 261, Antiochus himself died, at the age of sixty-four. [76] He was succeeded by his son Antiochus II Theos, co-regent since 266, when he had replaced his elder brother, Seleucus, executed on suspicion of disaffection. [77] The new king was reputedly an alcoholic and a playboy, [78] but he had enough political sense to seek a concordat (*homonoia*) with Macedonia. Antigonus Gonatas welcomed this new support. If he wanted to drive Ptolemy out of the Aegean he would need an even stronger fleet; and now, with a general peace giving all contestants a much-needed breathing space, he set about building it. [79] Undercover agitation continued in the background: Cyrene was once more maneuvered into revolt, and Ptolemy only recovered it in about 246. With Macedonia's tacit support, Antiochus II launched yet another campaign against various Ptolemaic outposts of empire, the so-called Second Syrian War. [80] Our information concerning this war remains minimal. Antigonus may also have had trouble on his northern frontier, [81] and in any case he was faced with a crisis much nearer home: his nephew Alexander, governor of Corinth and Chalcis, rebelled against him (253/2), possibly with Egyptian backing, and proclaimed himself king (252? 249?). [82] Ptolemy seems to have lost ground in Cilicia, Pamphylia, and Ionia—where Antiochus II regained Ephesus (ca. 258), and picked up the sobriquet of *Theos* ("God") after his liberation of Miletus. [83] In 253 the king of Egypt was hard-enough pressed to make his peace with Antiochus, through that favorite Ptolemaic device, a dynastic alliance. Antiochus married Ptolemy's daughter, Berenice Syra, who brought him "a vast dowry," arguably the revenues of Coele-Syria. [84]

In order to make this match Antiochus II had been obliged to repudiate his prior wife, Laodice, turning over considerable domains to her at the same time. [85] Remar-

Fig. 58. Antiochus I, wearing the royal diadem. Silver tetradrachm minted at (?) Apamea or Antioch between 255 and 246 B.C. Private collection. Photo Hirmer.

Fig. 59. Ptolemy III Euergetes, wearing radiate crown and aegis, with trident scepter over his left shoulder. Gold octadrachm struck at Alexandria(?) ca. 246–222 B.C. British Museum, London.

Fig. 60. Seleucus II, wearing diadem. Gold stater minted at Antioch ca. 243–226/5 B.C. British Museum, London.

riage was always risky for a Hellenistic ruler, and the *douceurs* with which Antiochus tried to buy Laodice off had singularly little effect. However, both parties to the arrangement died shortly afterwards, Ptolemy II in January 246, and Antiochus II that same August. Antiochus died, apparently from illness but, some said, as the result of poisoning, at Ephesus, where Laodice happened to be in residence.[86] The scene was now set for a new showdown, between two ambitious queen mothers, Laodice and Berenice Syra, each competing on behalf of a potentially regnant son. It also seems likely that two rival foreign policies, Laodice's of competitive independence and Berenice's of cooperative alliance, also lay behind the hostilities that now followed.[87]

Laodice's son Seleucus had, so she claimed, been designated heir by Antiochus on his deathbed. However, Berenice had also borne the late king a son, and meant to enforce the child's claim as sole legitimate successor after Laodice's repudiation. From Antioch she appealed to her brother in Alexandria, the new king Ptolemy III Euergetes ("Benefactor"). Ptolemy at once left for Antioch, only to find when he got there that both Berenice and her child had already been assassinated, probably by Laodice's agents, if not, as one source suggests, by Seleucus in person.[88] The Third Syrian (or Laodicean) War, which resulted from these events, dragged on until 241, with Seleucus—now Seleucus II Kallinikos ("Gloriously Triumphant")—campaigning in Asia Minor and Syria,[89] and Ptolemy grandiloquently claiming victories from the Hellespont to the Euphrates.[90] He did briefly occupy Antioch (246–244). Perhaps in 246/5 he also fought a naval battle off Andros, though the evidence is highly ambiguous;[91] he appears to have lost it, which will have done little to restore his much-diminished role in the Aegean, and even less to assuage his political and economic problems in Egypt itself. The peace certainly extended his northern frontier in Syria, leaving him with one first-class prize, Seleucia-in-Pieria, the port of Antioch, which remained in Lagid hands till the time of Antiochus the Great;[92] but many of his other claims seem to have been ephemeral or exaggerated. Seleucus II had his own problems. His mother, Laodice, had insisted on his giving co-regency, together with the territory north of the Taurus Mountains, to his younger brother, Antiochus Hierax ("the Hawk"). With typical Seleucid aplomb, the Hawk—who did not, any more than Ptolemy Keraunos, acquire his title by accident—lost no time in setting himself up as an independent sovereign.[93] What with provincial rebellions and internecine dynastic rivalries, the unwieldy Seleucid empire was to prove itself fatally susceptible to fission.

In that same year Eumenes of Pergamon died (241), to be succeeded by his adopted son, Attalus I.[94] The most interesting thing about Eumenes was perhaps his support (indiscriminate, if we can trust Diogenes Laertius) for the philosophical schools of Athens—an indication that the Pergamene dynasty, even at this early stage, envisaged itself as the patron and preserver of Greek culture.[95] Attalus seems to have decided that a victory over the Galatians, still the uncontrollable scourge of Asia Minor, was, as always, the best and quickest way to win solid international prestige. He duly met and defeated them in a pitched battle: only after this success

Fig. 61. The middle reaches of the Euphrates River.
Photo André Parrot.

(237?) did he formally lay claim to the title of king (as well as that of Savior, *Sōtēr*), which his predecessor, although *de facto* monarch, had always carefully avoided.[96]

Also in 241 Antigonus Gonatas, now the elder statesman of Greece (and indeed known, like that not-dissimilar character Konrad Adenauer, as "the Old Man"),[97] was forced to make an unsatisfactory peace with the newly powerful Achaean League (pp. 139–40). Though his rebellious nephew, Alexander (above, p. 149), had died in 246/5, it was not until the winter of 245, and then in somewhat bizarre circumstances, that Gonatas had recovered the fortress of Acrocorinth,[98] and even then he did not hold it for long. Two years later, in 243, Aratus of Sicyon, the Achaean League's powerful and dynamic general, who had brought Sicyon (freed by him in 251 from a brief but violent tyranny) into the League,[99] now had also wrested Corinth once more from Antigonus's control, thus establishing the Achaean Confederacy as a major force in Greek affairs.[100] Corinth, though garrisoned on its acropolis by four hundred Achaean troops (not to mention no less than fifty watchdogs), for the first time since Philip II's day held its own city keys, and joined the Achaean League on a voluntary basis. Megara, Troezen, and Epidaurus followed suit, so that League territory now had a common boundary with Attica.[101]

Antigonus, who earlier in Aratus's career had hoped to patronize him or turn him into a subservient *tyrannos*,[102] saw, too late, the caliber of the man he was up

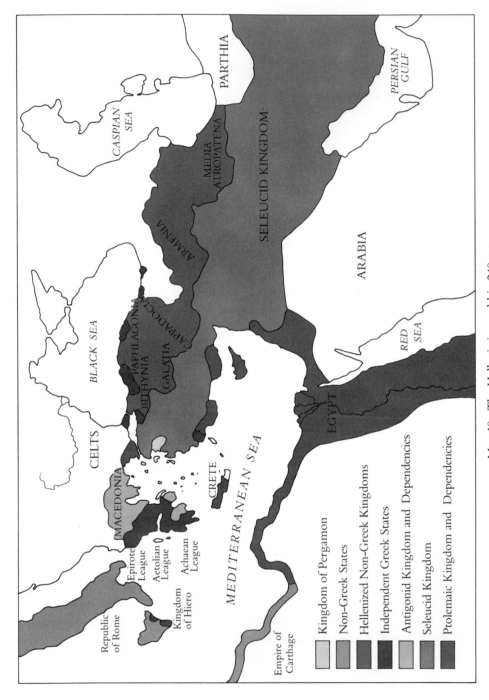

Map 10. The Hellenistic world in 240 B.C.
From Ferguson, *The Heritage of Hellenism*, p. 155

against. Something of a vendetta followed. With the Achaean League, inevitably, getting support from Egypt, Antigonus had no option but to turn to their rivals the Aetolians (243/2), thus incurring a good deal of moral opprobrium from those, Polybius included, who regarded the Aetolians, with good reason,[103] as little better than opportunistic condottieri and pirates.[104] However, Polybius's claim that these unlikely allies planned an invasion of the Peloponnese, with the partition of Achaea as its objective, has been disproved by modern research.[105] The Achaean League made an alliance with Sparta, and also, hopefully, appointed Ptolemy III the League's honorary admiral (242).[106] The Aetolian assault was driven back by Aratus,[107] and Antigonus, his support gone, found himself with no option but to negotiate (241/0).[108] Corinth remained independent; all that Macedonia still held in the Peloponnese were the cities of Argos and Megalopolis. Meanwhile Aratus kept busy. He planned the assassination of the tyrant of Argos, and, when that failed, made an abortive raid on the city (240?).[109] More interestingly, having moved in on Attica, he now "in his zeal to liberate the Athenians" tried to assault Piraeus,[110] for which he was censured by the Achaeans, since the armistice with Macedonia had already been ratified (242). Afterwards, in his memoirs, he blamed a subordinate for the attack. This earned him the scorn of Plutarch, who tells us that Aratus made many other unsuccessful assaults on Piraeus, "like an unlucky lover."[111] It is worth noting that Athens did not join the League, but chose to remain neutral.

But perhaps the most significant result of this abortive conflict involved Sparta. The twenty-odd years after the death of Areus (265) form an obscure period in Spartan history. His son and successor, Acrotatus, was killed in battle outside Megalopolis (260), and there seem to have been other reverses. But now a young and active Eurypontid king, Agis IV, had taken the field with Aratus. During the four years of his reign (244/3–241) he had, for reasons we will consider later (p. 250), proposed a whole series of drastic social reforms, including the two time-honored steps of debt cancellation and redistribution of land. These proposals, though they could be justified in terms of the ancient Lycurgan constitution, and were probably essential if Sparta was to reemerge as a major Hellenic power, aroused intense opposition among a wealthy minority into whose hands the larger part of the land of Sparta had fallen. These found their natural leader in Leonidas II, the Agiad king whom Agis had deposed (on extremely flimsy grounds), exiled, and replaced with Cleombrotos, Leonidas's son-in-law but a supporter of Agis. Leonidas's unforgivable act had been that of persuading the Spartan council of elders (*gerousia*) to reject Agis's reformist proposals. One constitutional illegality begets another. Successive boards of ephors challenged and repudiated each other's acts, with increasing violence. Finally, during Agis's absence at the Isthmus, Leonidas and his group seized power; and when Agis came back, he was put through a travesty of a trial, and then summarily executed.[112] That, however, was by no means the end of his reforms.

What Antigonus Gonatas made of these developments it is hard to tell. His Stoic training must have given him a certain sympathy with the aims of the Achaean League and of men like Agis: he certainly went out of his way to try to conciliate Aratus, though Aratus himself was notably cool toward Agis, whom he saw, with reason, as a threat to stability in the Peloponnese. But politically, in the last resort,

Gonatas stood on the other side, against all radical or ideological reform: he was an Antigonid first, a philosopher second. However, his dilemma, if dilemma there was, did not last long. Early in 239 Antigonus Gonatas died, at the ripe old age of eighty. His real achievement was to have lasted so long, to have given Macedonia a chance to recuperate from the years of anarchy, to build up some economic reserves once more. His son, who succeeded him as Demetrius II, was a tough and ambitious prince, and, unlike Gonatas, by no means content with the *status quo*.

CHAPTER 10

THE NEW URBAN CULTURE: ALEXANDRIA, ANTIOCH, PERGAMON

We have already seen something of the great new Hellenistic cities: their shift away from the ideals of the Greek *polis* (though many of them obstinately retained the political institutions, now for the most part meaningless, of council and assembly under ultimate royal domination), their cosmopolitan commercialism, their swarming crowds of entrepreneurs, bureaucrats, agents, craftsmen, slaves.[1] Even a small state such as Pergamon reveals the same pattern, indeed in an acute form: despite *phylai* (tribes), *dēmoi* (demes), *prytanis* (chief magistrate), and elected offices, the city was in practice wholly subject, both financially and administratively, to five *stratēgoi* (generals) appointed by the king.[2] The Attalids never let their (essentially self-promoting) philhellenism interfere with the working of an autocratic regime, and were quick to punish *lèse-majesté* by impertinent scribblers:[3] in this they resembled the Ptolemies. What is less often appreciated is that foundations like Alexandria, Antioch, and Pergamon were not really a new phenomenon, but a reversion to something very old: the great royal (and, more often than not, theocratic) cities of the Near East—Nineveh, Babylon, Tyre, Uruk, Mari-on-Euphrates.[4] The shift to authoritarian rule, based on flourishing international commerce, thus had a solid ancient tradition on which to model itself.

The pharaonic system of Egypt underlay the new, quasi-divinized exploitative rule of the Ptolemies. Behind the Seleucid foundation of Antioch we can glimpse earlier flourishing cities: Ugarit (mod. Ras Shamra), Poseideion (? Ras-el-Basit) on the Orontes.[5] Pergamon, in Asia Minor, looks back to Lydian, even to Hittite rule: Eumenes and Attalus used their wealth in ways very similar to that characteristic blend of self-aggrandizement, patronage, bribery, and entrepreneurism Croesus displayed.[6] We should always bear in mind that the age of the city-states, however remarkable and admirable a phenomenon, was, in historical terms, a marvelous anomaly. There had been nothing like it in Aegean history till then; it lacked any models. With the establishment of the Successor kingdoms of the Hellenistic era, the Near

Fig. 62. The lighthouse of Alexandria,
represented on the reverse of a coin of
Antoninus Pius (r. A.D. 138–61).
Private collection.

East settled back into the age-old patterns it had known from the dawn of civilization. The Ptolemies and Seleucids even produced, with their royal deifications
(pp. 396 ff.), a politicized, quasi-secular version of the pharaonic or Babylonian god-
king, priest and prophet of his people. At the same time the flourishing commercialism of these great kingdoms led, inevitably, to a degree of public ostentation—
coupled with bread and circuses for the increasingly restive urban proletariat: the
dividing line between religious spectacle and popular entertainment is often blurred—
that would have astounded a civic promoter like Pericles. No one, it is worth stressing, ever thought of including the Parthenon among the Seven Wonders, which are,
essentially, a Hellenistic tribute to gigantism: the Pyramids, the Mausoleum, the
Colossus of Rhodes, the Temple of Artemis at Ephesus (p. 98), the Hanging Gardens of Babylon, the Pharos of Alexandria (see below).[7] The only fifth-century
Athenian work included is Pheidias's statue of Zeus at Olympia; and we can be certain that what earned that its place was, as in every other case, its stupefying size.

The agora, not surprisingly, now lost its political associations, and became an
exclusively commercial center, surrounded by godowns, banks, and shopping ar-
cades: religion, in the form of temples, was more often than not relocated elsewhere,
while culture retreated to private or royally patronized institutions.[8] Even here the
commercial factor was all-pervasive. The poets who praise Ptolemaic Alexandria
do so almost exclusively in terms of its size and affluence. Long before Thorstein
Veblen, this great capital—by Egypt, as it was, significantly, always described, not
of it—stood as a dazzling monument to conspicuous consumption, of which the
Ptolemies themselves, with their taxes, tariffs, and royal monopolies, accounted for
a major part. Herodas (see p. 245), in his first mime,[9] lists as Alexandria's attractions
wealth, power, public spectacles, philosophers, elegant youths (so Cavafy: *plus ça
change*), a glut of available women, the Museum, good wine. This was the Alex-

Fig. 63. Arsinoë II, veiled and
crowned. Gold octadrachm minted at
Paphos on Cyprus ca. 270 B.C.
Photo Hirmer.

andria of Ptolemy II and Arsinoë, the Sibling Gods (*Theoi Adelphoi*): Theocritus describes it in almost identical terms.[10] Here the divinized Ptolemy Soter is enthroned
in splendor beside Heracles and Alexander. Egypt, because of the Nile, exceeds all
lands in fertility, and is an inexhaustible source of labor. Besides, Theocritus goes
on, the gold, the wealth are not left to lie idle in the royal palace: a clear allusion to
the Persian Achaemenid empire, which tended to stockpile its bullion, creating an
artificial shortage,[11] till Alexander took over the accumulated treasures of Susa,
Ecbatana, and Persepolis, and in a few short years flooded the Mediterranean
with them.

But if we expect Theocritus, in the course of his encomium on an exploitative
economy, to sing the praises of wise reinvestment, then we know nothing about ancient economics. Since the ideal was stability rather than growth (see p. 363), for the
ancient Greek, and, *a fortiori*, for the Hellenistic ruler, there were only three things to
be done with a cash surplus. It could be spent on public or private promotion (generally defense, municipal display, or, in the widest sense, self-adornment); it could be
laid up in the vaults as a comforting bulwark against the unpredictable vicissitudes of
Tyche; or it could be given away to charitable causes, the arts and sciences included,
that would reflect well on the donor's greatheartedness, altruism, and cultural sophistication. Not for nothing did two Ptolemies adopt the title Euergetes, "Benefactor." Theocritus goes on to list the recipients of Ptolemy II's generosity: the temples
and their priests, other kings and cities, personal friends, creative artists. The pattern
of patronage is clear. Moreover, as he says, "What's better for a prosperous man than
to get himself a good reputation [*kleos*] among his fellows?"[12] The commercialism is
not, after all, a sufficient end in itself. Through Alexandria the Ptolemies were to
achieve their lasting memorial, their apotheosis.

Alexandria was the Queen of the Sea, and indeed symbolically portrayed as such, a nice blend of maritime self-promotion and civic cult.[13] If Ptolemy I was the Savior, and Ptolemy III the Benefactor, it remained the deified Arsinoë to whom men prayed, as to Isis, when in peril on the sea. The role of the Sibling Gods was nothing less, as Theocritus sees it (and doubtless he was giving expression to official policy), than to "succor all mankind."[14] There is a clear motif here that leads directly to later cults emphasizing salvation (*sōtēria*).[15] When the Athenians welcomed Demetrius the Besieger as a god present and tangible, incarnate (p. 55), they were formulating concepts, and releasing forces, the ultimate embodiment of which they could scarcely have imagined (cf. pp. 408 ff.).

Perhaps, too, the cultured obsession with miniaturism that we find expressed by Hellenistic jewelers, by Callimachus, by innumerable elegant epigrammatists, was, in part at least, called into being as a direct reaction against Ptolemaic gigantism in public display. Sometimes, it is true, as in the case of Alexandria's famous lighthouse, the Pharos, unprecedented size was not only practical, but of real public benefit.[16] This ancestor of all modern lighthouses, built of white marble or limestone, stood on a flat rock at the eastern extremity of Pharos Island, at the entrance to the east harbor and the royal port. It was polygonal, built in three stages, tapering toward the top. The fire maintained there gave a light that was directed out to sea by a system of mirrors. The whole edifice was crowned with a statue of Zeus the Savior. Other manifestations of Ptolemaic munificence, however, were not so clearly functional. Ptolemy II's zoo might perhaps be thought to have had educational value; but the royal palaces and their land occupied, in all, between a quarter and a third of the city, and most of this area was taken up with shrines, statues, elaborate fountains, and other works of art, interspersed with pleasure gardens, the Museum and Library, and the royal necropolis, centered on Alexander's mausoleum. None of these survives today.[17]

Alexandria, that humming center of mercantile activity, was also, looked at in another way, a monument to consumerism. A top-heavy, luxury-loving, exploitative court and bureaucracy sucked in the produce of the countryside—the papyri tell us of huge cargoes of grain, as well as oil and honey, being shipped to the capital; and we know that, at least in the late Ptolemaic period (2d/1st c. B.C.), failure to channel all available supplies thither carried the death penalty[18]—but gave little in return except the occasional sumptuous spectacle, like the procession of Ptolemy Philadelphos (275/4) recorded by Callixeinos of Rhodes in Book 4 of his *Alexandria*.[19] This Dionysiac extravaganza is worth studying in detail. It is sometimes suggested that the Ptolemies only became really corrupt and overblown in the later period of the dynasty. Here is a detailed and circumstantial account showing that Ptolemy II, early in the third century, could beat his spendthrift successors at their own game. Callixeinos begins with a detailed description of the pavilion erected for distinguished guests: 130 couches set in a circle, under pillars seventy-five feet high, the roof draped with a scarlet-and-white canopy, and a portico running round the pavilion outside, in the shade of which guests could stroll at their leisure. Animal furs hung between the pillars; the floor was strewn with flowers, and the walls were decorated with ceremonial shields. The whole pavilion was full of statues and paintings,

Fig. 64. Reconstruction of the Pharos
lighthouse, Alexandria, erected ca.
285 B.C.
From Hermann Thiersch, *Pharos. Antike
Islam und Occident,* Leipzig and Berlin, 1909.

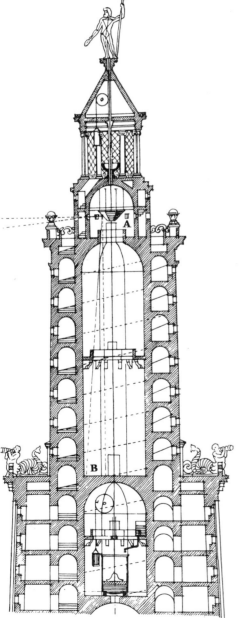

Fig. 65. Technical reconstruction of
the Pharos lighthouse, Alexandria. In
addition to the signal fire, the tower
contained an ingenious optical system
(*A*) by means of which the horizon
could be scanned from a platform
(*B*) a hundred feet below.
From Hermann Thiersch, *Pharos. Antike
Islam und Occident,* Leipzig and Berlin, 1909.

including those of the important Sicyonian school:[20] Ptolemy's eclecticism had an eye for quality—and fashion. Gold was everywhere: gold cups, gold jugs, gold tables, gold tripods, gold couches and eagles. Whatever the initial distribution of the bullion looted from Susa and Persepolis, a good proportion of it must have found its way to Alexandria.

The procession, held in the city stadium, showed the same kind of ultramontane extravagance. Nike (Victory) figures with gold wings, satyrs with gilt leaves of ivy on their torches, 120 boys carrying saffron on gold platters, gold-crowned Dionysiac revelers, a Delphic tripod eighteen feet high, a four-wheeled cart twenty-one feet long by twelve feet wide, a gold mixing bowl that held 150 gallons, a wineskin stitched together from leopard pelts, with a 30,000-gallon capacity (dribbling out its contents along the route), a giant float with fountains gushing milk and wine, the biggest elephants, the tallest actors, six hundred ivory tusks, and goats, camels, ostriches, peacocks, three bear cubs, a giraffe, and an Ethiopian rhinoceros. And gold, gold, gold all the way. The Dionysiac theatrical element, so marked a feature of later Ptolemaic iconography, is already prominent.[21] Perhaps to our way of thinking the most *outré* item was a gaudily painted gold phallus, almost two hundred feet long—how did it negotiate corners?—and tied up, like some exotic Christmas present, with gold ribbons and bows. No wonder an intellectual like Callimachus said big books were a big evil: elegant miniaturism was one of the few permissible outlets against this relentless and all-pervasive ostentation.[22]

Though Alexandria was the most extreme instance of the self-promoting megalopolis, the showcase of a royal dynasty, it by no means stood alone. Wycherley writes of "the mass-production of new Hellenistic cities in Asia which took place under Alexander and his successors,"[23] their axial-grid plans as monotonously repetitive as those of the American Midwest,[24] and it is clear that this was another recognized mode of acquiring prestige. Antioch is a good example of the trend. Its site is arrestingly dramatic,[25] in the fertile coastal plain linking Palestine with southern Anatolia, on the left bank of the Orontes River and under the towering peaks of Mt. Silpios. Unfortunately the side of the mountain away from the city offers an easily negotiable slope to invaders, and in fact the Persians twice breached the walls of Antioch by this route. Antioch also suffered, during the winter months, from torrential seasonal rains, which washed down tons of topsoil and made major engineering precautions essential.[26] But the position, clearly, like that of San Francisco on the San Andreas Fault, was held to be well worth the risk. (Antioch, too, has a history of seismic activity.) The suburb of Daphne, five miles outside Antioch proper, offered not only a beautiful tree-shaded landscape, but abundant natural springs that kept the capital supplied with water.

This was one reason why, in 300, Seleucus decided to build an inland adjunct at Antioch to his coastal capital of Seleucia-in-Pieria—that, plus Antioch's access to the inland caravan routes, and the cool breeze off the sea from May to October, which brought down the temperature, and decreased the humidity set up by the heavy winter rains. The land around was rich: oil, wine, grain, and vegetables were

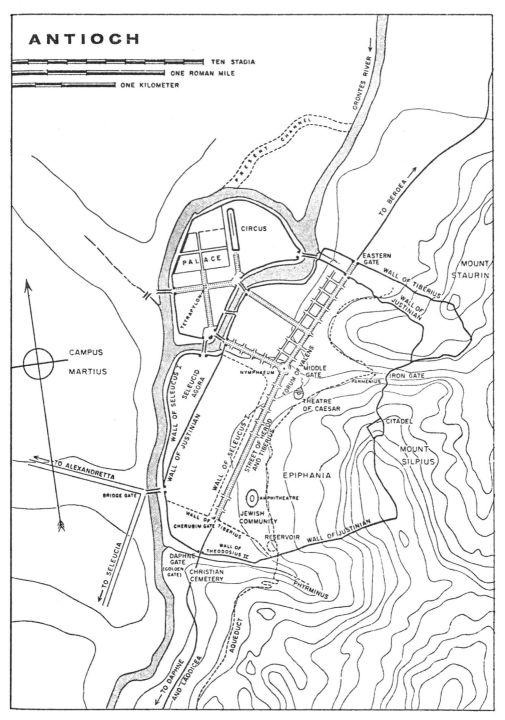

Map 11. Ancient Antioch.
From Downey, *Ancient Antioch*, fig. 3.

produced in abundance. The area was thickly forested, and had a plentiful timber supply. Fish and shellfish swarmed offshore. There were also Greek legends attached to the area, a great advantage—as Cavafy pointed out—for Greek immigrants seeking ethnic roots.[27] Io was said to have died there, and the sons of Heracles to have founded Heracleia near Daphne. The element of insanity that recurs in these stories seems to have bothered no one. It is possible, though far from certain, that Alexander, on his way south to Egypt in October 333,[28] saw the site's potential: he enjoyed the spring water, said it reminded him of his mother's milk.[29]

The first of the Successors actually to build in the area was Antigonus One-Eye.[30] He set up his own eponymous capital of Antigoneia about five miles northeast of the future site of Antioch, in a good defensive position (307).[31] However, when Seleucus acquired northern Syria in 301, after Ipsus, he decided, as a propaganda move, to obliterate his predecessor's city (or at least reduce it to village status), and to build one of his own instead: arguably a mistake, since Antioch's superior water supply did not offer adequate compensation for strategic vulnerability and seasonal flooding.[32] In fact Seleucus founded two linked pairs of inland and harbor cities in this region, as part of a military colonization scheme to establish, and maintain, firm control over the territory that formed the heart of his empire:[33] Antioch with its port of Seleucia-in-Pieria, and Apamea, similarly served by Laodicea-on-Sea, and all four named after members of the royal family.

So, in April 300,[34] Seleucus made his sacrifice, and an obliging eagle bore off the sacrificial meat to the site of Seleucia. Three days later he sacrificed on Antigonus's altar in Antigoneia, and asked for a sign as to whether he should occupy the site and change its name, or begin a new foundation elsewhere. Once again an eagle flew off with the burning meat, and (even more obligingly) deposited it on the altar that Alexander had set up at the site of Antioch while marching south. The city was duly built there. Aetiological legends of this sort, however fictitious in detail (unless we assume that the seers trained an eagle like a homing pigeon, which is not impossible), nevertheless have considerable significance as propaganda. Some of the details, moreover, sound very like those associated with the foundation of Alexandria. In both cases, for instance, the perimeter of the city wall was supposedly traced in flour or wheat,[35] and in both the axial-grid system of streets was so aligned as to catch the best of the prevailing winds, and to get the most shade in summer and sun in winter.[36]

Seleucus had statues set up of the dynasty's protectors and supposed founders, Zeus and Apollo; but by far the best-known statue in the new city, commissioned by Seleucus from Lysippus's pupil Eutychides of Sicyon about 296/3, was the image of Tyche, the "Fortune" of Antioch, at first merely a symbol of good luck, but soon regarded as Antioch's personal protectress, her patron deity.[37] Eutychides' concept became—and not only in Antioch—a popular Hellenistic image of "success, fertility, and prosperity":[38] the uncertain ambivalence of Fortune, the chanciness of Chance, were forgotten in this upsurge of determined optimism. Luck and good luck became synonymous. There sat Tyche the goddess on Mt. Silpios, holding a

Fig. 66. The Tyche of Antioch.
Eutychides' famous group (ca. 300–295
B.C.) showing a crowned Tyche with
her foot on the (allegorized) river
Orontes was commissioned shortly
after the city's foundation in 300, and
often copied, as in this Roman version.
Vatican Museums. Photo Alinari.

sheaf of wheat, the city wall incorporated in her turret crown, with a naked swimmer below her symbolizing the river Orontes. Reproductions of this statue were popular souvenirs with visiting tourists.

The population of the city, like Alexandria's, was ethnically mixed. It included, besides Macedonians and Greek immigrants, a Jewish community (including many retired mercenaries), local Syrians, and some five thousand Athenian and Macedonian settlers from Antigoneia, whom Seleucus forcibly transplanted, and whom the citizens of Antioch later took pride in as their true ancestors: the spell of Athens remained potent.[39] A statue of Apollo, the size (it goes without saying) of Pheidias's Olympian Zeus, was commissioned from the Athenian sculptor Bryaxis for Seleucus's new temple in Daphne. Bryaxis also executed a bronze statue of Seleucus himself: its size is not recorded.[40] The Seleucids, like the Ptolemies, inaugurated a dynastic cult. Seleucus Nicator, the founder, was duly deified by his son Antiochus,[41] though chiefly as a political measure (and so regarded by the Seleucid cities), without that extravagant ceremonial at which the Ptolemies showed themselves so adept.[42]

Again like Alexandria, Antioch may have preserved the traditional features of a Greek *polis*, the council and council-chamber, the educational system;[43] but even if this is true—and there is much to suggest that Antioch was, *ab initio*, subject to a Macedonian governor[44]—these were concessions without substance, however much citizens might cherish them. The true power lay elsewhere, and as the Hellenistic period advanced, even the pretense of maintaining democratic institutions was given up. Nor were the Seleucids especially distinguished for their patronage of the arts. For one thing, they were too busy fighting most of the time; for another, they lacked the immense financial resources of the Ptolemies. They had no margin to support projects such as the Library and Museum, and, it would seem, no taste, as Antigonus Gonatas did, for intellectuals who made up in moral fervor what they lacked in expensive habits. On the evidence it looks rather as though the Seleucids felt they had to emulate the Ptolemies as a matter of prestige. The one big name they caught was Aratus of Soli, the astronomer-poet (pp. 183 ff.), and they only got him for a couple of years (274–272), during which he prepared a critical edition of the *Odyssey* for Antiochus, and began work on the *Iliad*; after that, significantly, he went back to Pella and the company of Antigonus, whom he had probably left only for the duration of Pyrrhus's final invasion (above, p. 143).[45]

It seems to have been Antiochus I who, soon after his accession, shifted the capital from Seleucia-on-Tigris to Antioch, which was, among other advantages, much better protected against attack from the sea.[46] It was not, however, invulnerable. During the Laodicean War we find the Ptolemies in possession of Antioch between 246 and 244, and of Seleucia-in-Pieria until 219 (above, p. 150).[47] Under Antiochus IV Epiphanes (r. 170–163) the city was developed and expanded—he added a new quarter, Epiphania[48]—and from 175 onwards its luxury began to rival that of Alexandria. When the Roman general Aemilius Paullus celebrated victory games after beating the Macedonians at Pydna, in 168 (see p. 415), Antiochus decided to hold a rival show (despoiling friends and temples in the process), and Polybius's description shows that the same kind of ostentation as Ptolemy II had affected was clearly a crowd-pleaser in Antioch too.[49] We find the same thousands of extras with gold shields and crowns, the same horses and elephants and ivory tusks, the gold jars of saffron ointment, the twelve-pound silver dishes, the thousand-table banquets, gigantism and vulgarity triumphant.

Our last example is the fortress of Pergamon, set high (335 m) on a trachyte spur of the Pindasos range, overlooking the isolated and fertile Caicos valley, in northwest Asia Minor. The site is at once dominant, impressive, and forbidding.[50] Pergamon formed part of ancient Mysia. It had good access to the sea; Lesbos lay westward of it, and the Gulf of Adramyttion to the north.[51] In 399 the remnants of the Ten Thousand who had retreated with Xenophon from Cunaxa made a halt there, and were given support by some local Greek dynasts.[52] Pergamon also, for some

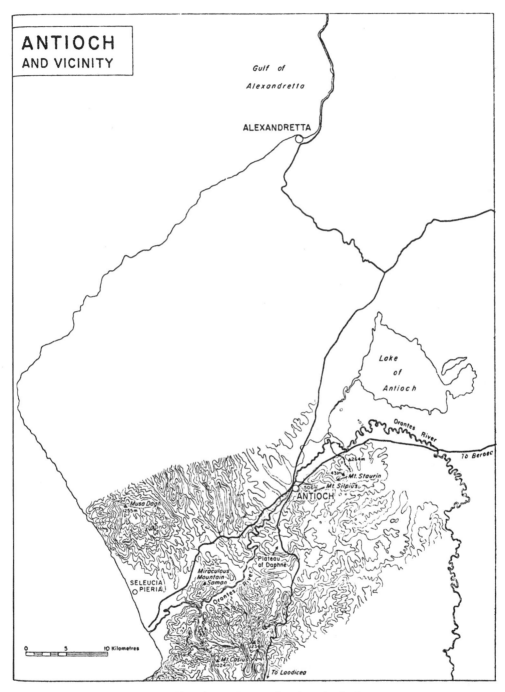

Map 12. The environs of ancient Antioch.
From Downey, *Ancient Antioch*, fig. 5.

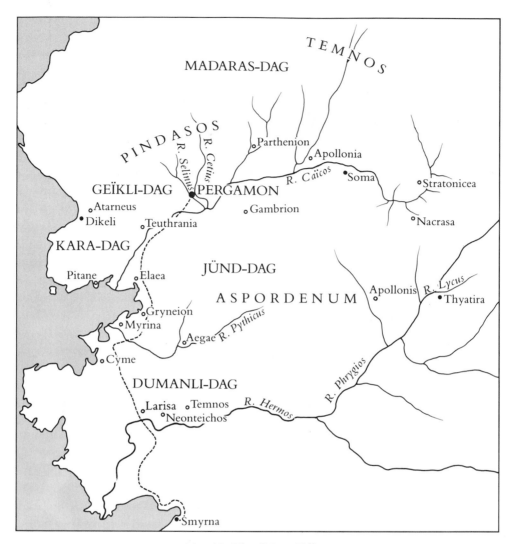

Map 13. The Caïcos Valley.
From Hansen, *The Attalids of Pergamon,* xxii.

years, formed the home of Alexander the Great's bastard son, Heracles, and of the child's Persian mother, Barsine.[53] In 302 Lysimachus deposited personal spoils to the amount of nine thousand talents in the Pergamene stronghold. The Paphlagonian in whose charge he left this treasure was Philetairos, whose career we have already had occasion to notice (pp. 132, 148 ff.). A faithful vassal for years, he finally ran foul of Lysimachus's wife Arsinoë over her machinations regarding the succession, and shrewdly then offered his fortress, treasure, and services to Seleucus. The latter's victory at Corupedion showed how wise a decision this had been. After Seleucus's death, however, as we have seen, Philetairos began moving, cautiously, toward the idea of secession.[54]

At the same time he spent a good deal of his considerable funds on courting favor, not only with the powerful, but with all his immediate neighbors in Asia Minor.[55] A fragmentary inscription from Cyzicus records a whole series of his benefactions to that city: twenty talents for public games, fifty horses for cavalry defense, consignments of wheat and barley, exemption of duty on flocks, and so on.[56] Delphi, which was not normally given to issuing favors except in return for very tangible benefits, gave Philetairos and his nephew Eumenes a whole string of privileges, including front seats at public functions and priority for oracular consultation. Philetairos toyed with the idea of independence, moved up crabwise on it.[57] First his coins bore the image of Seleucus; then, when Seleucus was murdered, they reverted to the Alexander head for a while; next Ptolemy Keraunos succumbed to the Gauls (p. 133), and back came Seleucus's head again; presently Philetairos added his own name.[58] It is a fascinating progression.

Pergamon's wealth did not depend solely on Persian loot embezzled from Lysimachus, or, indeed, on tribute and taxation, profitable though these undoubtedly were.[59] The principality's exports were as solid as Alexandria's, and of much the same sort: the country produced an abundance of wine, oil, grain, horses, hogs,

Fig. 67. Pergamon: aerial view of the Asklepieion, from the south.
Staatliche Museen zu Berlin.

sheep, and dairy products. In addition, the local gray-blue andesite made excellent building material; the potting clay was good; timber and pitch were available for ships; there was a flourishing woolen-goods industry; gold, silver, and lead were mined; and Alexandria's virtual monopoly on papyrus was matched by Pergamon's equally flourishing trade in parchment (the name in fact is derived from the place), though the popular legend that parchment was invented there,[60] because the Ptolemies banned the export of papyrus to the Attalids, is a legend pure and simple, since parchment was known in Asia Minor, and elsewhere, as a writing material long before.[61]

When the dynamic Attalus I (269–197) defeated the Galatians (p. 150), and claimed, at last, the title of king, a new era in the city's history opened. The laurel wreath of victory appeared on Pergamon's coinage; it was, too, this Galatian triumph that provided much of the impulse for the sculpture and public architecture with which Attalus and his successors adorned the great acropolis of Pergamon. We will examine this in more detail later (pp. 351 ff.); in the present context what is important to appreciate is the contrast between Pergamon and either Alexandria or Antioch as cities. Pergamon's commanding position, rising over a thousand feet from the plain, and the four great terraces composing it, both shaped its building patterns and linked it (as the other two cities could not be linked) to a specifically Greek rather than Near Eastern tradition: that of the civic acropolis.[62]

The acropolis of Pergamon was fundamentally different from that of Athens; yet its buildings, in the last resort, fulfilled a very similar function. The royal library might be second only to Alexandria's, but Pergamon stood more in the Athenian tradition. It is interesting that in the mid-third century the Attalids supported the Academy—Attalus II set up a statue in Athens to Carneades—and that from then on Pergamenes not only attended the Academy as students, but provided more than one of its directors.[63] The gymnasium of Pergamon is the largest and most complete to

Fig. 68. Philetairos, first Attalid ruler of Pergamon, laureate and wearing the diadem. Silver tetradrachm minted by Eumenes I ca. 260 B.C.(?). British Museum, London.

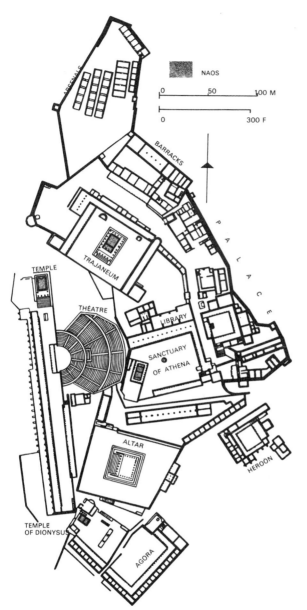

Fig. 69. Plan of the acropolis
of Pergamon.
From Charbonneaux, Martin, and
Villard, fig. 405.

survive from antiquity.[64] Yet the scholars at the Attalids' court could not match the Alexandrians' brilliance and flair. Niggling erudition seems to have been the ideal; most of the group were "critics, summarisers, interpreters rather than creators."[65] Not surprisingly, the Attalids were primarily interested in the visual arts: hence the art critics who thronged the circle round the ruling family.[66] Pergamon itself, it might be argued, was a work of art, Malraux's museum-without-walls on the grand scale; it has been compared, inevitably, to Versailles.[67] What defies the imagination is how it must have been to live there. We can without difficulty picture ourselves in

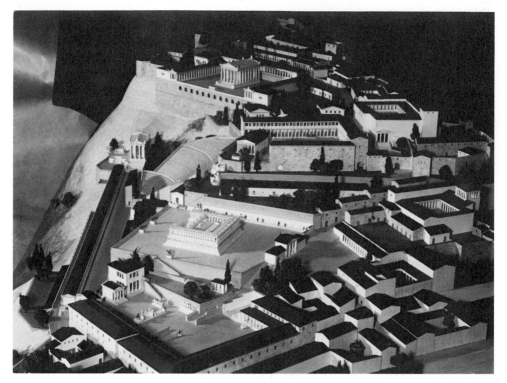

Fig. 70. Scale model of the acropolis, Pergamon.
Staatliche Museen zu Berlin.

Alexandria: Theocritus's gossiping Syracusan ladies, picking their way through crowded streets on their way to a public recital in the palace, nearly being ridden down by the royal household cavalry.[68] But who, except for the occupants of the palace, new-style Macedonian barons, and the troops who guarded them, actually lived on the acropolis at Pergamon? Barracks, theater, temples, library, the Great Altar below: only the agoras strike one with a touch of common humanity; the rest is unrelentingly monumental.

The severance of public and private worlds has no more striking formulation in the whole Hellenistic era. The Athenian acropolis, under a democracy, was for the gods alone, though by Pericles' day man-the-measure-of-all-things had left his civic mark on the god's dwelling place, and a little later Demetrius the Besieger was more than willing to exploit his honorary godhead by using the Parthenon as a private residence (p. 50). The same trend can be observed in Hellenistic Pergamon, where, once more, human and divine are inextricably confused; and the result, oddly, is one of the loneliest places on earth. From that great rock, as from the Athenian acropolis, one can see, far below, the sprawl of rooftops, the smoke of human habitation stretching across the plain. The monuments strike chilly in the sunshine; life, real life, is going on somewhere quite different.

CHAPTER 11

THE CRITIC AS POET: CALLIMACHUS, ARATUS OF SOLI, LYCOPHRON

A preoccupation with the past, a sense of being overshadowed by one's own classics, an elevation of the critic to an integral role in the establishment of new creative canons, even in the creative process itself—these are all phenomena that we recognize today, and to which we therefore have no difficulty in responding when we meet them in the literature of the Hellenistic period, from the third century onwards. Ransacking the past for preservable fragments, allusions, or verbal usages is a practice familiar to us from the work of Eliot, Pound, David Jones in *The Anathemata*, or the Kazantzakis of the *Odyssey* sequel.[1] Today both poetry and fiction are being firmly moved into the control of academic critics, who dispute each others' views as fiercely as ever the occupants of the Muses' birdcage in Alexandria did (above, p. 87). Scholarship has become a necessary adjunct to creation: allusiveness and symbolism are prized, while it is by no means uncommon for the creative artist to double as a university professor, so that, like John Hawkes or John Barth, he can, if he so wishes, feed his output straight into the academic hopper for critical evaluation, without any intervening stage.

All this irresistibly recalls the practice of writers such as Callimachus or Lycophron: the ideal of the poet-as-critic (or vice versa), a label first attached to Philetas (above, p. 86), proved immensely popular. It also was one of many factors that helped to create a mandarin elite, dependent on state patronage, contemptuous of the common man, heir to all those Platonic and Aristotelian sneers at the banausic occupations, what Shakespeare was later to label as the business of "rude mechanicals," "base, common, and popular." These hypereducated intellectuals were writing for—and very often about—each other, and thus, like Pound or Eliot, prided themselves on their richly exotic literary or mythological references. At the same time an active distaste for the vulgarly accessible ("I abhor all public things," Callimachus asserted)[2] drove them to reject or modify those genres, the epic in particular, that had been associated with large audiences. They were, in essence, fundamentally

171

elitist. Just as Pound embraced Italian fascism, and Eliot proclaimed himself an Anglo-Catholic royalist, so the Hellenistic poets sought lucrative patronage from absolute monarchs, in return for which even the most intellectually abstruse of them were expected, at intervals, to glorify their patrons with palpable flattery and hints of divine status. In his first hymn Callimachus associates, indeed virtually equates, Ptolemy II with Zeus (78–87), and in the second with Apollo (26–27). "From Zeus come kings," he wrote, "for than Zeus's princes nothing is more divine." Zeus bestowed abundance on them, but not to all equally. "We can judge this from our lord, since he has outstripped the rest by a wide margin. What he thinks in the morning he accomplishes by evening—by evening the greatest projects, but the lesser ones the moment he thinks of them." And again: "Whoso fights with the blessed gods would fight with my king; whoso fights with my king would fight with Apollo."

The attacks on popular or accessible literary forms tended to be not just elitist, but also xenophobic. At the end of *Hymn* 2 Callimachus makes Apollo tell Envy (who has been supporting poetic prolixity): "The Assyrian river [i.e., the Euphrates] has a broad stream, but carries down much dirt and refuse on its waters."[3] Polyglot, cosmopolitan, above all Oriental influences are to be deprecated (cf. pp. 317 ff.): stick to the pure unsullied spring of the Greek Muses. Centuries later the Roman satirist Juvenal, who had very little time even for native Greeks, was to make an identical complaint about the filth washed down by the Orontes.[4] Oriental syncretism, already having a huge impact on Hellenistic society, was (for that very reason) to be rejected, together with epic and the heroic *ēthos* that epic presupposed (p. 202).

In scholarship, as in other fields of human endeavor, Parkinson's law applies: critics will expand their activities as far as they are subsidized to do so. Cultural *parvenus* like the Ptolemies or the Seleucids still looked over their shoulder to Athens for guidance. Libraries and research institutes are, by definition, dedicated to the recovery of the past. The object may be to create a platform from which to launch new discoveries, but first the existing heritage must be made secure (p. 89). The heritage in the present case was, with good reason, identified as that of fifth-century Athens, and the process of recovery and embalming had begun, like so many of these trends, long before the Hellenistic age proper. The fourth-century canonization of the three great Athenian tragedians, as early as 386 (above, p. 52), shows this very clearly; Aristotle's attempts, in his *Poetics*, to define the genre according to fifth-century terms and examples merely confirm it. All the collecting, cataloguing, textual criticism, and literary evaluation that went on, century after century, in the Alexandrian Museum and other subsidized establishments was, in the last resort, backward-looking, a retrospective genuflection to classical supremacy. Athenian cults, Athenian myths, the Attic dialect, Athenian literary genres—all were researched, promoted, imitated.

At the same time this process was influenced by new social, political, even religious trends. The notion of Euhemerus (above, p. 55), that the Olympian gods were really ancient kings divinized in recognition of their achievements on earth, was one that fitted in well with the deification of Alexander the Great, or of Ptolemy Soter and Arsinoë, the pragmatism that had led even Athens to greet Demetrius the

A

B

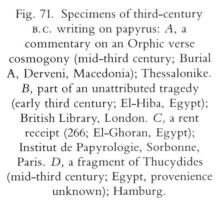

C

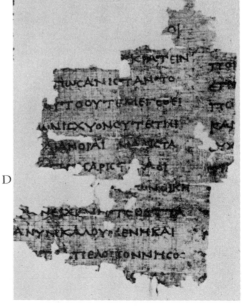

D

Fig. 71. Specimens of third-century
B.C. writing on papyrus: *A*, a
commentary on an Orphic verse
cosmogony (mid-third century; Burial
A, Derveni, Macedonia); Thessalonike.
B, part of an unattributed tragedy
(early third century; El-Hiba, Egypt);
British Library, London. *C,* a rent
receipt (266; El-Ghoran, Egypt);
Institut de Papyrologie, Sorbonne,
Paris. *D,* a fragment of Thucydides
(mid-third century; Egypt, provenience
unknown); Hamburg.

Besieger as a god manifest. This treatment inevitably found its way into all Hellenistic court poetry (not always as open flattery), since, after all, it was the new god-kings who handed out the patronage and footed the bills for poetry and research. On that basis elitism was inevitable: the political involvement of citizens under a democracy had become no more than a theory for intellectuals, rather like those Republican dreams nursed by opulent Stoic senators in Rome under the Julio-Claudians.

Further, since the academic world involved, then as now, an element of teaching—was, indeed, didactic and prescriptive by nature—we also find, along with the self-defensive smokescreen of learned obscurantism and allusiveness, a counterurge to explain things: old customs, puzzling myths, the archaic byways of art and literature; and the more recondite, the better. This aetiologizing urge stemmed in part from a genuine, if unacknowledged, longing among *déraciné* urban skeptics and rationalists for emotional, even religious roots that were in danger of being lost; but at the same time a kind of in-group freemasonry was also at work. A similar phenomenon is offered today by those ingenious scholars who compile keys or commentaries for Pound's *Cantos* or Joyce's *Finnegans Wake*. Learned scholiasts flourished, while, by inverse snobbery, the idea of a simple, straightforward concept, name, or reference, a direct and unambiguous statement, became anathema. Lewis Carroll parodied this recurrent trend in a poem in which he characterized the attitude as learning to look at everything "with a sort of mental squint."[5] A would-be young poetaster asks his older mentor:

> "For instance, if I wished, Sir,
>   Of mutton-pies to tell,
> Should I say 'dreams of fleecy flocks
>   Pent in a wheaten cell'?"
> "Why, yes," the old man said: "that phrase
>   Would answer very well."

Thus the pleasure of puzzles is reinforced by the superior sense of knowing the answers to them. Further, the scholarly passion to find out what songs the Sirens sang, obscure erudition for its own sake, was in part to mask the fact that the original emotional force of the old myths was rapidly being lost in an increasingly secular, skeptical, and commercial age. Yet the emotional *need* was as strong as ever—nobody, in one way or another, could leave the myths alone—and attempts to satisfy it can be glimpsed here and there: the syncretic evolution of new or revamped gods through the assimilation of foreign cults (e.g., Sarapis), or the use of ruler worship to knit together the cosmic order, with dead kings and queens identified by court poets as constellations—one more reason, along with the rise of astrology (p. 595),[6] for the amazing popularity of a poem like Aratus's *Phaenomena*—or fancies such as the rediscovery of the lost dedicated lock from Berenice's hair as, again, a group of stars, near the Great Bear, a comforting juxtaposition of heaven and earth. The historicization of myth, the reconciliation of old variants in credible form, was one of the main tasks the Alexandrian scholar-poets set each other.[7]

Epigrams, being primarily concerned with sex or death, as well as meeting the new literary requirements of jeweled brevity, flourished as never before. A genre once largely restricted to tombstones now blossomed in a wealth of literary allusion, imitation, and subtle variants for the *cognoscenti*.[8] During the first half of the third century, besides Callimachus, we find exponents of the epigram such as Asclepiades of Samos (b. ca. 320), an innovator who broke away from old epigraphical conventions to pioneer the personal, emotional, and, more often than not, erotic epigram (also one of the "malignant gnomes" castigated by Callimachus in his prologue to the *Aitia*);[9] and the bitter, brooding pessimist Leonidas of Taras,[10] first of the vagabond poets.[11] Between them Asclepiades and Leonidas sum up the antithetical extremes of early Hellenistic society. In Asclepiades, whose hedonism found sharp, controlled focus with mostly four-line epigrams, we see, *inter alia*, the desexualization of Eros, from elegant youth to pretty cherub,[12] an evolution exactly matched in the visual arts (compare the Eros of Praxiteles with that by Lysippus),[13] and culminating in the small winged *putti* so popular throughout the Graeco-Roman period,[14] armed with the arrows that now objectified the pangs of ardent desire.

Asclepiades' attitude to passion is on the whole lighthearted, bisexual, and cheerfully inconstant: the act, the moment of ecstasy, achieved or in prospect, is paramount.[15] The agonies of frustrated love now have their own, at times somewhat masochistic, attraction, not least in the *paraklausithyron*, when the beloved's door is fast shut, the suitor outside, and (a nice extra touch) the rain pouring down.[16] If this poet wants, as has been suggested, "the private, the exclusive, the uncompeted-for,"[17] that does not stop him writing kiss-and-tell squibs about innumerable partners of both sexes—even if he objects to a courtesan like Hermione openly professing an identical creed (in a message embroidered in gold on her sash), or mocks two Samian girls who have turned lesbian.[18] (Callimachus's erotic epigrams, in sharp contrast, are never obscene, invariably homosexual, and reveal a consistent delicacy of feeling—reasons, perhaps, why he numbered Asclepiades among the hostile gnomes.)[19] Yet there is also in Asclepiades a sense of *Weltschmerz*, the inevitable overspill from that pathos with which he gilds his sensuality:[20]

> I'm not yet twenty-two, and I'm weary of living:
>   Oh Loves, why this plague, why burn me so?
> For if something should happen to me, I know your reaction—
>   You'll go on playing knucklebones, you'll not give a damn.

Even the vanity of transience cannot here keep Asclepiades, characteristically again, from adapting a euphemism popular in wills to skirt round the fact of death.[21]

Here he stands in sharp contrast to Leonidas, whose concerns are (as Auden once wrote of A. E. Housman) "something to do with violence and the poor,"[22] and whose Cynic possession by death not only matches Webster's, but is expressed in language that foreshadows every *memento mori* in subsequent European literature:[23]

> Endless, O man, the time that elapsed before you
>   Came to the light, and endless time there'll be

> In Hades: what share of life remains but a pinprick, or whatever's
>   Less than a pinprick? A brief spell
> Of affliction is yours, and even that lacks sweetness,
>   Is more hateful a foe than death.
> Compacted from such a framework of bones, O man, can you, do you
>   Still reach out to air and sky? See, man,
> How useless your striving: by the half-woven fabric
>   A worm sits over the threads, till all
> Wears thin as a skeletal leaf, is more abhorrent
>   By far than the spider's web.
> Search out your strength, O man, at each day's dawning,
>   Bow low, be content with a frugal life, in your heart
> Always remember, so long as you mingle with the living,
>   From what jackstraw you're made.

The expected *carpe diem* motif ("life's too brief, so enjoy it while you can") is given a savage reversal: we see here, in embryo, the self-flagellant puritanism that would culminate, centuries later, in the Desert Fathers of the Thebaid. Leonidas knew, too well, the price that hedonism could exact: there are few poems more savage than his contemptuous epigram on Anacreon (probably suggested by a well-known statue):[24] drunk, gray-bearded, robe trailing, one shoe lost, "a lecherous look in his leaky eye." Yet Leonidas could also be moved by rocks and waterfalls, by the rural simplicity of a cool spring sacred to the Nymphs, by a shepherd's whittled dolls.[25] This pastoral vision, as we shall see (pp. 233 ff.), had an increasing (and increasingly unreal) attraction for urban intellectuals.

In many ways progressive secularization, which had gained impetus as a result of the fifth-century sophistic movement, had come to undermine all the old comforting certainties. People were beginning to have serious eschatological doubts: was the whole concept of Hades, now under heavy rationalist assault, no more than an old-wives' tale? Oddly—perhaps not so oddly—this caused serious worry. At least Hades was a place, with a traditional geography: it might be scary, but it fostered the sense of continued existence, if only as a shade, and in a conceivable locale below. "What of the underworld?" the interlocutor in one of Callimachus's epigrams inquires of a dead man.[26] "Much darkness," comes the reply. "And resurrection?"[27] "A lie." "And Pluto?" "A fable." "We are undone." It is a heartfelt cry, and one that goes far to explain the salvationist cults that gain steadily in popularity from now on. The dead man's final comment is also worth noting. He says, in effect, "I'm telling you the truth, but if you just want to hear what suits you, lies come cheap in the underworld." By Juvenal's day, again, things had gone farther, and, as he says, then not even small children believed in Hades any longer.[28] It was left for another scholar-poet, in our own day, Louis MacNeice, to resurrect a really terrifying Charon ("his hands / Were black with obols, and varicose veins / Marbled his calves"), who announces to the would-be traveler over the Styx: "If you want to die, you will have to pay for it."[29]

The whole business of rescuing the past through books has always had an oddly eclectic quality about it, and the Hellenistic operation was more idiosyncratic than most. One might suppose that what would emerge would be an age of great historiography; but even allowing for massive losses of key texts, this does not seem to have been the case. The historians, such as Phylarchus or Hieronymus of Cardia, may have existed, but they did not provide the dominant mode of inquiry (*historia*). This mode, in its reliance on the pre-historiographical instrument of myth, was, indeed, profoundly antihistorical. To systematize, syncretize, and expound the whole surviving corpus of Greek myth became one of the prime aims of the Hellenistic *littérateurs*; and that corpus (as becomes abundantly clear from Roman poets like Propertius or Ovid) was then regularly employed as a kind of exotic secular Bible, to provide precedents, exempla, warnings, or moral guidelines for human activities on earth. Throughout Ovid's vast output of poetry, the referral—across the whole range of social or moral conduct—to mythical precedent or justification remains constant. No other comparable court of appeal existed. Thus it is clear that the antiquarianism involved in the rescue (and, where possible, reconciliation) of variant mythic traditions was dictated, also, by a species of moral quandary that urgently needed some less coldly rational solution to ethical problems than those proposed by the philosophers. It was very far from being merely an academic game, though many academics, Callimachus not least, may have treated it as such: in various ways—by erudite systematization, by deliberate hermetic obscurantism, by literate irony and disarming ambivalence—Hellenistic writers were trying to rescue not only the mythic heritage as such, but the whole supportive moral world view, long savaged by sophists and scientists, that this heritage implied. Lycophron, Aratus, and Callimachus well illustrate the three different approaches to this pressing problem.

Just how recherché the process could become, and how obsessed with the mandarin pursuit of referential allusiveness and obscurity for their own sakes, we can see at once in that extraordinary poetic *tour de force*, the *Alexandra* of Lycophron. Lycophron of Chalcis (b. ca. 330–325) came to Alexandria about 285/3, eventually to work in the Library for Ptolemy II,[30] cataloguing the collection of comic playwrights, and writing a treatise on comedy as such;[31] he was also a prolific tragic poet, one of the seven included in the so-called Pleiad.[32] But it is his "obscure poem," as it was described even in antiquity,[33] for which he was, and still is, remembered. The *Alexandra* is a slave's report to Priam of Cassandra's prophecies concerning the destruction of Troy, the subsequent fortunes of the Greeks, the struggle between Europe and Asia, and, interestingly, the rise of Rome (this last probably stimulated by Pyrrhus's defeat in southern Italy and the Roman embassy to Ptolemy in 273).[34] The poem is 1,474 lines long, a messenger speech taking up the space of an entire play, and written in rather flat, conventional iambic trimeter verse, piquantly at odds with the exotic matter it has to convey.[35] Cassandra, who "apolloed the voice from her bay-fed throat, reproducing the utterance of the dark Sphinx" (5–8), is the excuse for all the allusive periphrasis that follows; even the slave introducing her takes thirty lines to say, in effect, that on the morning Paris set sail, Cassandra began to prophesy. "The centipede lovely-faced stork-colored daughters of the Bald Lady struck

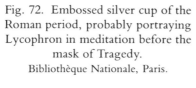

Fig. 72. Embossed silver cup of the
Roman period, probably portraying
Lycophron in meditation before the
mask of Tragedy.
Bibliothèque Nationale, Paris.

maiden-slaying Thetis with their blades" (22–24) simply means that Paris's hun-dred-oared ships, built of timber from Bald Mountain (*Phalakra*) in the Troad, painted with the apotropaic eye on their bows, hulls pitch-black, like storks (more plausible than white, the other prevalent color of European storks), dipped their oars in the sea, more particularly the Hellespont (since this claimed the life of the maiden Helle), Thetis *qua* sea nymph being used by synecdoche to represent the sea itself.

Every line requires this kind of exegesis, and the vocabulary is as exotic as the allusions: out of a 3,000-word total for 1,474 lines, over 500 are found nowhere else (*hapax legomena*), and more than a hundred appear here for the first time:[36] compare Joyce, and Kazantzakis in his *Odyssey*. Lycophron anticipates the advice given to the young would-be versifier in Carroll's "Poeta Fit, Non Nascitur" (above, p. 174): "And evermore be sure / Throughout the poem to be found / Consistently ob-scure." At the same time it is important to note that the puzzles or enigmas (*griphoi*) that produce Lycophron's obscurity have nothing to do with the *Alexandra*'s struc-ture, poetic vision, or style, which, far from being baroque, is in the old classical tradition of tragic narrative. The mystification applies exclusively to content,[37] and consists, for the most part, of simple periphrastic substitutions in nomenclature, ap-plied frequently to mythical persons, less often to places or objects. There is a nice parallel here with Orwell's view of Salvador Dali's painting, which, he remarks, is highly conventional, not to say Pre-Raphaelite, in technique, and only truly bizarre in its choice and treatment of subject.[38]

Such an exercise is, clearly, aberrant, the idea of the sovereign power of the *logos* carried to more than logical extremes. One also gets the impression from the *Alex-andra* that straightforward traditional myth was felt to be too frail a growth to sur-vive unprotected in a skeptical world, and therefore had to be hedged about with impressively arcane mystery. As a phenomenon, this kind of allusive word play, again, has its roots back in the fifth century. The rhetorical excesses of Gorgias, the punning fantasies and self-sustained verbal utopia created by Aristophanes as Cloud-cuckooland in *The Birds*,[39] both clearly foreshadow this kind of literary venture, where the word is, in effect, cut loose from any dependence on its social context. We know this trend today; and I suspect the underlying cause in both cases is the same. On the one hand we find a sense of political impotence, the inability to control or influence public events, leading to a withdrawal from involvement into a private world: solipsism has its verbal functions no less than its social or philosophical dimensions. On the other, there is this deliberate emphasis on arcane mystery, the assimilation of myth to a hermetic discipline.[40] For Hellenistic thinkers one motive here was surely an attempt to revalidate the moral and existential macrocosm of a worldview that had found its last great exponent in Pindar, its nemesis in the sophists of the post-Periclean era.

Callimachus (ca. 305–ca. 240), like Ben Jonson, has always had a rather better press than he deserves, and for much the same reason: his academic ideals and credentials can hardly fail to appeal to those other academics, in antiquity or modern times, who have been called upon to evaluate him.[41] Besides, anyone who so prides himself on restrained good taste is bound to pick up votes from latter-day hopefuls not quite sure in their own minds just what the latest criteria of good taste may be. Callimachus has always been a firm favorite among scholarly *littérateurs*, who, like Odysseus Elytis's young Alexandrians in the *Axion Esti*, tend to mock the out-of-step dissenter. Counterattacks are rarer; but we find the Roman epigrammatist Martial contemptuously telling an acquaintance with a taste for the byways of mythology that instead of reading his, Martial's, verse, which is about real life (*hominem pagina nostra sapit*) he should, obviously, bury himself in Callimachus's *Aitia*.[42] Nothing shows better how far, beginning in the fourth century, literature moved away from the public arena, to become the property of a private, very often subsidized, intellectual minority, than the pervasive educated taste for Callimachus throughout the Hellenistic period. He is more quoted on papyrus, by grammarians, critics, lexicographers, metricians, and editors, than any other poet except for Homer. A North African from Cyrene, with strong Dorian roots, Callimachus never, as far as we know, visited Athens; but then, Arthur Waley never set foot in China. As a young man Callimachus was an obscure schoolmaster in a suburb of Alexandria, but somehow caught the attention of Ptolemy II, who gave him substantial backing for life.[43] One tradition asserts that he got his start as "a youth around the court,"[44] a claim that has puzzled scholars;[45] looked at in a context of homosexuality (below, p. 182) and literary patronage, it seems clear enough.

Callimachus may have frowned on big books, but can hardly have objected to multiplicity of titles, since his own overall literary output was enormous: eight hundred volumes (i.e., papyrus rolls), according to that catchall Byzantine lexicon the *Suda*. Though this total is almost certainly exaggerated, he undoubtedly wrote a great deal: hymns, epigrams, iambics, epyllia, and, inevitably, occasional court poetry for his patrons, ranging from an epithalamium for Arsinoë's wedding to the ode describing her death and subsequent deification, or the related elegy on the enskyed Lock of Berenice, written not long before his death (ca. 240).[46] His long and rancorous feud with Apollonius, who favored, and wrote, literary epic (below, pp. 201 ff.), did not stop him, in his first *Iambus*,[47] from advising his literary colleagues to avoid quarrels and backbiting. His own lampoons are full of literary allusions, but lack the real bite of an Archilochus or a Hipponax. Though given the enormously responsible task—which he carried out with distinction—of producing a *catalogue raisonné* of the Library's holdings, the famous *Pinakes*, or "Tablets," in 120 volumes,[48] he never held the post of chief librarian.

Again and again in his mannered explorations of the Greek mythic heritage Callimachus attacks stale themes and bloated rhetoric, extols the virtues of restraint, good taste, purity, brevity.[49] As a program this wins our respect, but its execution is often disturbing. Its author is also constantly engaged in polemics, both attacking others and justifying himself against criticism. Students of Pound will find themselves in familiar territory. *Hymn* 2, after its slash at ornate and diffuse Orientalism, ends with a direct appeal to Ptolemy: "Farewell, my lord: may Criticism dwell where Envy is."[50] He returns to the attack in his prologue to the *Aitia* ("Causes"), a longer poem of which only tantalizing fragments survive.[51] This odd work, recently claimed as a kind of countergenre to epic,[52] is in fact little more than a loose rag-bag offering a series of aetiological explanations for odd customs. The lock of Berenice, the myth of Acontius and Cydippe, ekphrastic accounts of various archaic statues, puzzling temple rituals, even the invention of the mousetrap (fr. 177): all are dragged in somehow. The obsession with the past is all-consuming. Sometimes—a recurrent problem ever since Xenophanes, in the sixth century, censured Homeric and Hesiodic morality[53]—the past can be embarrassing: on the verge of describing Hera's sacred but incestuous marriage to Zeus (fr. 75.4 ff.), Callimachus apostrophizes himself: "Dog, dog! Restrain yourself, my shameless spirit! . . . Much knowledge is a sore ill for anyone who cannot control his tongue; he is like a child with a knife." The heritage sometimes calls for diplomatic sanitization: certain archaic crudities are hard to swallow in this more genteel age. Discussion of the *aitia* is hung on various fairly lame devices, such as a drinking party where the abstemious narrator asks his neighbor,[54] as the wine is going round for the third time, "Why is it the tradition of your country to worship Peleus, king of the Myrmidons?" In the prologue, a late addition, he slashes away at malignant gnomes like Asclepiades,[55] who decry his poetry because he failed to produce an epic, preferring the pared-down poem, the "back roads" of literature (not originality so much as the rare and exotic). By the time that prologue was written, the quarrel had been going on for thirty years, a literary analogue to the Funeral Games. I find this a sobering thought.

The *Aitia* is no fuller of recondite scholarship than Callimachus's one venture into epic subject matter, the *Hecale*,[56] which describes how Theseus spent a night in the hut of an old woman, the Hecale of the title, on his way to subdue the bull of Marathon. The actual feat seems to have been briefly, even casually, described (frr. 258–60): with demure wit Callimachus characterizes the captive bull, being dragged back to Athens, as a "sluggish traveler." What really interests him is the evening discussion between Theseus and Hecale, a peg on which he can hang endless snippets from early Attic legend, the raw pabulum for yet more of that aetiologizing, which exerted as powerful a lure on the scholar-poets of Alexandria as allegory did on the medieval schoolmen. It has recently been suggested that there is social significance in the choice of protagonist here, that the socially inferior (but morally shining) Hecale represents a conscious rejection of Aristotle's insistence on the lower orders' being fit for presentation only on the comic stage.[57] There may be something in this, but it would be unwise to press it too far: Callimachus's conservative, anti-democratic nature makes him an unlikely candidate for radical innovations of a socially progressive sort (below, p. 182). On the other hand, it was widely believed, even in antiquity, that with the *Hecale* Callimachus was consciously counterattacking those who had long mocked his apparent inability to produce a long (i.e., epic) poem.[58] This too is possible, though the mockery can hardly have been stilled by a work that took up no more than one book in the collected edition, and was probably little more than a thousand lines in length. More important, I think, is the impulse that sent Callimachus in pursuit of this somewhat obscure topic at all, grubbing through volumes of local Attic history (possibly including Philochorus, who also supplied material to Plutarch)[59] to give the myth a new lease of life.

By comparison the *Hymns*, though they too never miss an opportunity for exotic aetiological glossing, stand in a more conventional tradition. They also make good propaganda. It was politic to celebrate Delos in the 260s, when the Ptolemies controlled the island and its cult:

> Windscoured that island, untilled, wavebeaten, fixed
> In the deep, better running for gulls than horses; the sea
> Roiling fierce round it sloughs out a mass of scurf
> From Icarian waters; sea-voyaging fishers have made
> Their home there.
>
> (*Hymn* 4.11–15)

But such passages of straight description are rare, the poem being for most of its length clotted with mythological detritus and aetiological signposting; even visiting merchant seamen

> do not return on board
> Till they have been whipped around the circuit of your Great
> Altar, to gnaw at the olive tree's sacred trunk,
> Hands bound behind their backs, something the nymph of Delos
> Thought up for fun, as a joke for young Apollo.
>
> (Ibid. 320–24)

Hymn 1, the *Hymn to Zeus*, in addition to a whole mass of erudition on divine origins, and some not-so-sly digs at the conflicting traditions of Zeus's birth, also portrays kings as the god's vicegerents on earth, and stresses that "than Zeus's princes nothing is more divine." But some kings, of course, are more equal than others, and the wisdom of Ptolemy is *sans pareil*.[60] Earlier precedent for this kind of literary genre must be sought not only in the *Homeric Hymns*, but also in that last archaic repository of privilege and kingly status, Pindar. There is an interesting similarity between the encomia of Callimachus and those that Pindar lavishes on his clients, the Sicilian nabobs, or that ill-fated monarch Arcesilas IV of Cyrene, Callimachus's own birthplace. Callimachus in fact adapted the Pindaric epinician ode as an elegy to celebrate a victory in the boys' double race by Sosibius.[61] Sosibius went on to become a famous, indeed notorious, minister under Ptolemy IV (below, p. 289): he was suspected not only of complicity in the murder of Ptolemy's mother, Berenice II (the same whose lock of hair reappeared as a constellation), but also of forging the king's will to his own advantage.[62]

Callimachus's waspishness to his rivals was matched only by his servility to the great: not for him Samuel Johnson's definition of a patron. Sosibius is described as being "friendly in his relations with the people, and not forgetful of the little man, a thing one rarely finds in the wealthy."[63] Knowing Callimachus's constant preoccupation with his own alleged poverty, we may suspect that the argument was, as so often, *ad hominem*. Callimachus has had plenty of praise in the past. A. W. Bulloch, in the *Cambridge History of Classical Literature*, lauds him to the skies: "The most outstanding intellect of his generation, the greatest poet that the Hellenistic age produced" (p. 549), though the precise nature of this greatness remains elusive. Professor Hugh Lloyd-Jones eulogizes him as "a wit, a dandy and an ironist," whose impact on Roman literature (and here I would agree) was incalculable: "Without Callimachus it is hard to imagine what Augustan poetry would have been like."[64] Conceivably, less artificial. Despite such glowing testimonials, I cannot help finding him at once pretentious and faintly distasteful, a literary exhibitionist with an unpleasant groveling streak about him, a sycophant implacable in his attacks on rival sycophants, a baroque and overworked scholar-poet who, even allowing for occasional flashes of mordant wit, and a handful of fastidious erotic epigrams, wears his erudition with self-conscious panache, and succeeds, when he does, in spite of it.[65] Perhaps his most striking virtue, apparent even in his most pedantic and allusive passages, is his precise economy of language.

Yet at the same time his value as a witness to social trends is enormous. His abhorrence of "all public things" was political and class-based as well as literary. Such an attitude never functions in a void, not even for occupants of ivory towers; and in this case it reveals a shrewd sense of accommodation to the *status quo*. The poor schoolmaster from Cyrene could not only justify his position as royal client, but also satisfy his high social aspirations, by associating himself with a line of blue-blooded, antipopulist poets and thinkers from Theognis and Heracleitus through Plato to Cleanthes. Nor is it any accident that he staked his claim to exclusivity in an erotic epigram (see n. 2, p. 775). Homosexual rather than bisexual by temperament (some of his erotic verse foreshadows the Alexandrian *amitiés particulières* of Cavafy), he could cite excellent precedent for regarding his sexual preferences, too, as socially and culturally superior to the heterosexual *ēthos* now rapidly gaining ground throughout the Greek world.[66] Here he is harking back, antiquarian as always, to that aristocratic tradition so jealously cultivated by the old-fashioned Athenian *kalos k'agathos* (aristocratic gentleman), the tradition associated with the *kalos* vases and other, more explicit, painted scenes of upper-class pederasty in the late archaic pe-

Fig. 73. Aristocratic pederasty: scene from the Attic red-figure "Peleus and Thetis" vase by Peithinos (late sixth century). Note the fashionable, and costly, Ionian robes.
Staatliche Museen zu Berlin.

riod (570–470), and which later provided the elitist homoerotic mystique underpinning Platonic dialogues such as the *Charmides*, the *Phaedrus*, or the *Symposium*.[67]

Women, for Callimachus, were clearly one of the "public things" (*dēmosia*) that he had rejected, together with populist democracy. At the same time, a sinecure under the Ptolemies exacted other, less palatable compromises. To swallow authoritarian government was easy enough, a mere acceptance of the *Zeitgeist*. However, the security of the Museum also meant coming to terms in some way with the ostentation, vulgarity, and gigantism inherent in the Ptolemaic *ēthos*, and without fatally offending one's royal paymaster. This may possibly in part explain Callimachus's big-book-big-evil doctrine, his sustained assault on the literary gigantism of his rivals: it is tempting to see in Apollonius a displaced substitute target for the Ptolemies themselves. Callimachus, and many lesser literati like him, were natural candidates for admission to an intellectual enclave whose members were learning to live—and, at a price, to live well—off the surplus income of commercial absolutism. There is a nice irony about the fact that the liaisons of this social aspirant, this fastidious nondrinker from public fountains, should nevertheless have been with youths who, if not actual prostitutes, were still unpleasantly mercenary and rapacious,[68] and in the Athens of Demosthenes or earlier could well have been liable to prosecution.[69]

Aratus of Soli (ca. 315–240/39)[70] was in ways a very different character from

Fig. 74. Pebble mosaic floor of the royal palace(?), Pella (late fourth or early third
century B.C.).
Photo Tombazi, Athens.

Callimachus and Lycophron, though he won high praise from the intellectuals of the
Alexandrian court, Callimachus himself included.[71] His patronage came from Antigonus Gonatas (above, p. 142), and thus had a Stoic core, which shows clearly in his
surviving work. (It is true that between 274 and 272 he moved to the court of Antiochus I, but this was merely because during those years Antigonus had been ousted
from Pella by Pyrrhus, and was battling to win back his kingdom: scholarship and
philosophy had to be suspended for the duration, while the scholars themselves
sought less *mouvementé* areas. As soon as Antigonus was reestablished, Aratus returned to Pella: it seems to have been his natural center.) It was, traditionally, at the
request of Antigonus himself that Aratus composed the *Phaenomena*, essentially a
versification of two prose treatises, one by Eudoxus (see p. 459),[72] a name meaning
"of good repute" (Antigonus claimed that Aratus had made Eudoxus's repute better,
had improved his *doxa*),[73] and the other, on weather signs (*sēmeia*), by Theophrastus.
The versification was skillfully and at times imaginatively done, though the astronomical knowledge proved to be shaky in places, as Hipparchus and others lost no
time in pointing out.[74] But for us there are two fundamental questions: first, why
was it done at all? And second, what gave the poem its immense, and enduring,
popularity, so that Cicero, Germanicus, and Avienus all translated it (even though
Cicero sniffed at Aratus's actual expertise)?[75]

As regards the first issue, it remained true that, in an age when the communication of knowledge was still predominantly oral rather than literary, a didactic poem of any sort was easier to memorize than a treatise in prose. More to the point, the movements and positions of stars had been of crucial importance to sailors and farmers for centuries. (The litany of epitaphs for drowned sailors is a leitmotif running through our corpus of Hellenistic epigrams.)[76] But this was by no means all. On the one hand the Hellenistic period witnessed a great advance in scientific astronomy (pp. 459 ff.): stars were, so to speak, very much in the air. This, however, was not Aratus's prime interest in the topic—nor, it is safe to say, the chief concern of his readers. What attracted them was something in fact fundamentally antiscientific, a trend very much associated with Stoicism: the use of the constellations to demonstrate cosmic order and morality. It is noteworthy that when Aratus gets to Eudoxus's investigation of the complex stellar movements of the planets he simply omits the whole section (453 ff.), with the offhand comment that they are all vagrant and unpredictable, and beyond his competence:[77] "With these, my courage fails; may I prove adequate / To describe the circles of the non-wandering stars and their signs in the firmament" (460–61). One obvious reason for his avoidance of such a topic, apart from its technical difficulty, was the Stoic search for universal cosmic order as a model reflecting ideal right government on earth: viewed in these terms, the wandering planets were anomalies, and indeed too uncomfortably like Hellenistic politicians for his or his patrons' tastes. Hence his excursus on Justice (98–136), and his highly Stoic, not to say pantheistic, opening invocation to Zeus:

> From Zeus be our commencement, whom we mortals never
> Leave unnamed: full of Zeus are all the highways,
> All men's market centers, full the ocean
> And harbors: in all ways we all have need of Zeus.
> For we are also his offspring, and he in his compassion
> For mortals gives favoring signs [cf. 772], rouses nations to work,
> Reminding them of their livelihood, says when the soil is fittest
> For oxen and mattocks, says when the seasons favor
> Tree-planting, the sowing of every kind of seed.
> Himself it was that fixed signs in the heavens,
> Sorted the constellations, figured out the year—
> Which stars above all should mark each changing season
> So that all things might flourish unfailing: wherefore
> Men ever set him first and last in their prayers.
>
> (*Phaen.* 1–14)

Following Hesiod[78]—Callimachus said, perhaps a little waspishly, that Aratus had skimmed off the honey from Hesiod's work[79]—he sketches the Gold, Silver, and Bronze Ages; but despite the "maiden Justice" of Hesiod,[80] it seems to have been his own (Stoic?) notion to equate the constellation Virgo with *Dikē*, Right Justice, now in retreat from earth among the stars, and thus to promote an essentially optimistic view of divine government.[81] Again and again the *Phaenomena* demonstrates an all-pervasive belief in the rule of divine wisdom, rational and symmetrical, throughout the universe. This highly unscientific way of thinking not only developed ideas taken from the Platonic (?) *Epinomis*, but also opened the way toward another characteristically Hellenistic phenomenon, the pseudoscience of astrology (below, pp. 595 ff.), since one central tenet in this tradition was the belief that the stars could somehow record, reveal, or even influence human conduct. "Not yet have we mortals learned everything from Zeus," Aratus observes, "but much is still hidden, of which Zeus will give us later if he so wills" (768–71). How anyone could describe this as "the confident voice of the man who recognizes the march of science" eludes me:[82] it is the voice of religious obscurantism personified, the abrogation of reason.

What is historically significant about this poem, of course, is its best-selling impact. It highlights for us, as nothing else could, the other face of Hellenistic culture. What it offers is everything that scientific progress ignored: belief, faith in an ordered cosmos divinely set up and maintained, moral and ethical guidance to match practical instructions covering the regular, recurrent, and predictable year cycle. It not only borrowed from Hesiod; in many ways it was a throwback to modes of thought that Hesiod himself, with his primitive taxonomies, was struggling to slough off, a reaction against the freethinking rational inquiry that had been the mainstay of classical intellectual progress. While a minority of (often atheistic) scholars continued their priceless work in astronomy and mathematics (pp. 453 ff.), the majority—including the Stoics, and thus those kings and rulers who were advised by them—listened with increasing fervor to the music of the spheres. "The multitude," said Cleanthes, Zeno's successor in the Stoa, "has no intelligent judgment . . . you will find such only in the few";[83] yet it was Cleanthes, too, who argued that the Greeks should prosecute the great astronomer Aristarchus of Samos for impiety, because of his heliocentric theory, that "the fixed stars and the sun remain unmoved, and that the earth revolves about the sun."[84] Till Galileo's day the moralists, theologians, and astrologers held the field. Aratus offered that immensely attractive temptation, a morally certain universe; no one was eager to believe Aristarchus's psychologically disruptive theories.

CHAPTER 12

KINGSHIP AND BUREAUCRACY: THE GOVERNMENT OF THE SUCCESSOR KINGDOMS

The Diadochoi found themselves Alexander's heirs in more ways than they had anticipated, and the legacy proved itself—in every sense—a taxing one. Except in Macedonia, which had its own idiosyncratic problems (below, pp. 198 ff.), the new rulers were forced to deal with dilemmas inherent in Alexander's career of conquest, and to adopt solutions very similar to those he himself had outlined. They stood, long after his death, in his tremendous shadow still. He had made them what they were; and however consciously they might try to jettison his alleged ideals—above all, the military and administrative fusion of races in universal empire—their fierce ambitions forced them to follow where he had led. The enormous prize he had left to them, the Achaemenid empire from Asia Minor to the Hindu Kush and beyond, was in effect spear-won territory, the spoils of conquest. That one central fact conditioned the conduct, outlook, and administration of both the Ptolemaic and the Seleucid dynasties for the entire course of their existence: they treated the territories they controlled, however they might assign them, as royal estates.[1]

Neither empire, moreover, had any kind of a national foundation; neither was viewed with anything more positive than resentful acquiescence by the bulk of its indigenous inhabitants. The Seleucid empire, as we have seen, began to fragment as soon as it was formed: Bithynia, Pontus, Pergamon, Bactria, Cappadocia all split off, and not even the brilliant military-*cum*-diplomatic imperialism of Antiochus III (ca. 242–187) could reverse this trend for long (pp. 293 ff.). In Egypt it needed only a weakening of control at the top, from the time of Ptolemy IV (221–204), to produce a whole string of violent native insurrections (pp. 323 ff.), with the object of restoring Egypt's own age-old pharaonic tradition, and shifting the cultural center of gravity back from Hellenic Alexandria to Egyptian Memphis. Thus in both cases (though the details varied considerably) we have the same fundamental situation: an occupying imperial minority of Graeco-Macedonian administrators and settlers, backed by a Macedonian-officered force of mercenaries, whose main object was to maintain their own powers and privileges, while at the same time making sizable fortunes. To do this involved them in an economically static cycle of extortion, bribery, and sweated labor. The key to their continued rule—since that rule did not in any sense depend on a willing consent, much less an active choice, by the governed—lay, of necessity, in the maintenance of a large standing army and paramilitary police force. These, the former especially, were also made essential by the nonstop border feuding and competitive warfare that went on between the dynasties, as each tried to strengthen its position, and to ward off encroachment, by extending its frontiers and overseas possessions.

Now, full-time armies are an expensive luxury, a vast drain on any exchequer, as Philip II and Alexander each discovered to his cost (Alexander landed in Asia Minor with no more than a fortnight's pay for his men, and thirty days' provisions: from the Granicus onwards, conquest balanced the books).[2] It followed that the primary administrative activity of both Ptolemies and Seleucids was, in one way or another, financial. Even though their territories were wealthy estates, to be milked as they saw fit, much of the profits, far from being reinvested (not in itself a natural Greek activity; see p. 469), was of necessity spent on preserving and perpetuating the *status quo*. In particular, this self-perpetuating need fully explains the complex system of tariffs, monopolies, excise duties, and heavy taxation that characterizes the Successor kingdoms (pp. 368 ff.). It also, indirectly, explains their concern, at every level, with the exercise of justice. This has sometimes been taken by the guileless as proof of a punctilious respect for the rule of law and, above all, for *Völkerrecht* (below, p. 196). However, a piecemeal study of cases suggests, with some force, that the motivation was not so much concern for the individual's rights, much less defense of interstate treaties—both of which were regularly ignored and abused—but a determination to impose, by force if need be, a legal code that consistently worked to the government's advantage.

This, of course, included the repression of any kind of social revolution; but the intensity of official concern with this particular problem cannot escape our notice. While it remains a truism that no government ever encourages opposition, the degree to which that opposition is perceived as dangerous or disruptive will vary a good deal depending on circumstance, even in a world where any change is held to be for the worse. Now, if there is one common feature shared by all the authoritarian regimes of this period, in Greece as well as in Egypt or Asia (and indeed by some on the face of it not authoritarian at all, like the Greek leagues), it is a quite hysterical determination to prevent economic or political upset by any sort of populist movement (see below, Chap. 22, pp. 390 ff.). The regular slogans of such movements called for the abolition of debts and reallotment of the land, rallying cries that were anticapitalistic only in the sense that others wanted a slice of the capital, but antioligarchic in that fundamental social sense that always made of Greek politics a moral, rather than an economic, issue. As for the class problem, that was there too, but less in evidence from the third century on because of steadily increasing universal commercialism. If the peasantry was consistently exploited, if the division between city (*polis*) and countryside (*chōra*) grew ever wider, there was, by the same token, an ever-increasing number of ex-peasants on the make, only too willing to grind the faces of the poor from whose ranks they had risen.[3] What we see here is the rise of the true Greek bourgeoisie—subsequently encouraged and abetted by its Roman counterpart—which systematically destroyed all those precarious, but genuine, advances in democracy and freedom for which earlier ages had fought so hard and so long.

Thus in both Alexandria and Antioch, and subsequently in minor kingdoms such as Pergamon or Bactria, we find a Macedonian, or less often a Greek, ruling dynasty, primarily dedicated to its own perpetuation, and draining both the economy and the public fiscal resources for this purpose. If we do not bear in mind the paradox of Hellenistic finance, the workings of the administration will often be very hard to fathom. Yet at the same time, human nature being what it is, these dynasts were most anxious to justify their rule on a religious, even on a philosophical basis.[4] Some, like Antigonus Gonatas, were more sincere about this than others. It is no accident that the early Hellenistic period saw a proliferation of treatises on kingship.[5] By a series of historical accidents, monarchy had once more come to be the most generally viable system of rule, and, as usual, intellectual justification had to be found for a political *fait accompli*. The trend is already apparent early in the fourth century, with the pamphlets of Isocrates[6] and Aristotle's somewhat embarrassed discussion of monarchy in the *Politics*:[7] however personally congenial, it went against the intellectual democratic *Zeitgeist*. Still, Pella was funding Aristotle's work, and he had, after all, been the young Alexander's tutor; not only he but also Theopompus seems to have written a "Letter of Advice" to the crown prince.[8]

One thing that emerged from all this was the concept of the morally responsible ruler. Demetrius of Phaleron urged Ptolemy Soter to read treatises on kingship (p. 88), hinting that he might find there advice such as his courtiers would not dare to give him face to face.[9] Not the Stoics only, but also the Peripatetics, even the Neo-Pythagoreans,[10] began to promote the idea of meritocracy in kingship, the notion of the crown as something to be earned by noble deeds, coupled with a sense of royal responsibility to one's subjects, Antigonus Gonatas's creed of noble servitude.[11] It is not hard to see how such an approach could also embody the Euhemeristic concept of deification as the reward for great deeds on earth: had not Heracles pointed the way? Kingship and divinization thus became a linked upward sequence in the same process, something akin to the later official Roman career plan, the *cursus honorum*.

It is interesting, especially in view of their economic preoccupations, that these rulers tried to avoid the historical justification—namely, that they wore their crowns by right of their, and Alexander's, conquests—and preferred by far either the philosophical justification of power through good works, or, even more convenient, the concept, said to have been declared by Seleucus Nicator, that "it is not the customs of the Persians and other such races that I shall impose on you, but rather this law, common to all, that the king's decrees are always just."[12] The best man is king; whoever becomes king has therefore proved himself the best, and, since he embodies the law (below, p. 200), can do no wrong, is inevitably just—a most useful syllogism for any royal *arriviste*. None of this was really new, except for the intellectual rationalization: most of it, in fact, was something more than archaic.[13] The whole concept of right subsisting in the will of an anointed or otherwise specially privileged ruler went right back to primitive tribal custom. Compared with this, the Athenian achievement—nearly five centuries of painfully won civic justice, of legal codes, of equality under a common law (*isonomia*)—remained an anomaly. But then, it was even longer ago that Athens, for one, had got rid of her kings.

The pattern now evolving was, like so much else in the Hellenistic world, syncretic. With the extinction of the Argead line (above, p. 28), blood succession was, for a moment at least, in abeyance; however, all three main dynasties, once established, perpetuated themselves by filial inheritance. (The Ptolemies, who habitually practiced sibling incest, kept an even closer grip on the dynastic succession, though at the price, eventually, of a somewhat erratic gene pool.) The other sure route to kingship was conquest. Here the models that all Alexander's marshals had to emulate were Philip II and Alexander himself. The Macedonian monarchy had retained numerous archaic, even Homeric traits:[14] the prestige of the triumphant warrior; the symbolic use of the diadem, the royal robe, and the seal ring; personal command in war; a group of privileged and, most often, aristocratic Companions, or Friends (*hetairoi*, *philoi*), in battle, at dinner, to give advice as a royal council; the right to distribute booty (and to control looting); the duty, in general, of being what Homer called the "shepherd of the people," handing out gifts and charitable patronage, winning renown as fighter and hunter, and through philanthropic generosity and cultural enhancement.[15]

This generosity also implied a great fund of wealth on which it could draw at will without impoverishing the donor; and the king's style of life, with palace, pomp, display, and numerous servants, was expected to reflect his exalted status. At the same time excessive luxury was frowned on, in particular by Stoic theorists: moderation and self-control, a sense of justice in accordance with the divine harmony of things—such was the ideal at which a Hellenistic monarch, in theory at least, was expected to aim. Once a basis for the king's function had been established, it was not hard for court moralists and philosophers to formulate more or less tactful rules of royal conduct. A king must honor truth; he must also be accessible to his subjects. Plutarch tells a famous anecdote about an old woman with a petition to Demetrius the Besieger. He brushed her aside with the excuse that he was too busy to attend to her. "*Too busy?*" the old woman snapped. "In that case, stop being king."[16] Hellenistic kings also, as we have seen, regarded themselves as guardians of culture—Greek culture, understood, though Ptolemy Soter did order the Egyptian priest Manetho to write, in Greek, a history of Egypt, perhaps because Seleucus Nicator had earlier commissioned Berossos (also a priest) to set down, again in Greek, a digest of Babylonian wisdom. The two works were finally dedicated, on completion, to Ptolemy II Philadelphos and Antiochus I.[17]

All this should be borne in mind when we consider the problems of the individual dynasties. Nothing so exposes the glory-seeking and xenophobia behind Alexander's supposed Hellenizing mission to the East as the stubborn refusal of the civilizations he invaded to appreciate the higher things he offered them in return for their subjugation.[18] The parallel with British India is inescapable. What the indigenous population got, in both cases, was technical expertise, a strangling bureaucracy, and a useful *lingua franca*—English in one case, the *koinē* in the other. The government was, similarly, imposed by the conquerors rather than nationally based. We must suppose that the likelihood of Ptolemy I's ever advancing native non-Greek-speaking Egyptians to positions of high office always remained minimal, especially when we consider the total failure of Alexander's experiments in this direction the moment he was dead. It was inevitable, from the beginning, that Ptolemy would employ a cadre of Macedonians and Greeks, who would then in turn transmit their orders—in the first instance via a corps of interpreters—to a largely unchanged system of Egyptian scribal administration, the infrastructure of local government.[19]

Ptolemaic Egypt offers us most of our firsthand evidence of the bureaucracy at work, though since the papyri deal in detail with one particular area (Philadelphia in the Fayyum), and information for Alexandria itself is largely lacking, the effect can be to drown us in a sea of local municipal detail—surveys, petitions, receipts, accounts, nominal rolls, petty litigation—rather than to afford us a broad overview. During the reigns of the first three Ptolemies, for which our evidence is fullest, the administration and economy were maintained in reasonable equilibrium. Egyptians were used to the notion of a king who personally owned their country; the early Ptolemies were still to some extent influenced and restrained by Greek precedent. Even so, there were no fewer than four dating systems employed simultaneously by Philadelphos's officials, so that the recipient of a letter, like the modern scholar, had to work out, or guess, which system applied in each particular case.[20]

Regulations tended to be specific, rational, and, above all, efficient. Where Ptolemaic control took on a thoroughly un-Greek appearance was in its cavalier treatment of private property, its encroachment on *laissez-faire* economics with an all-pervasive system of state control. Such control, however, had to be competently as well as forcefully applied; and from the time of Ptolemy IV onwards, the Lagid monarchy's declining prestige abroad was matched by faltering administrative machinery in Egypt itself. It is hard to decide whether constant dynastic intrigues, minority regencies, military reverses, and economic crises were primarily responsible for the breakdown of the system, or whether simmering anarchy and sullen antigovernmentalism (especially in the rural areas) contributed more, in the first instance, to this decline by substantially diminishing the royal revenues. In any case the two trends seem to have been symbiotic. After the battle of Raphia (217: see p. 289), when for the first time native Egyptian troops were recruited in large numbers, riots and revolts became endemic, and a good many concessions officially touted as *philanthrōpia* in fact represented tacit surrenders to *force majeure*.

Right from the beginning, as satrap, fifteen years or so before he declared himself king, Ptolemy I had seen very clearly that he was faced in Egypt with several intractable conditions that he might or might not be able to make work for his advantage. Because of the nature of Egypt's fertility, which was wholly dependent on the Nile floods, the pharaohs had very early established a powerful centralized bureaucracy (essential for adequate irrigation and flood control), aligned with an equally powerful priesthood.[21] Ptolemy had to take over the first, and avoid alienating the second (see below). Then as now, it paid to have the support of the mullahs.

At the same time he could not rely on local resources to maintain his rule in any way; nor is it probable that such a notion ever occurred to him. He would have to retain a strong Graeco-Macedonian army, besides importing, or encouraging, a large, active colony of Greek businessmen, willing, initially, to invest Greek capital in the country. One primary reason for granting what amounted to privileged mass immigration, on very favorable terms, would be to ensure a flourishing and profitable export trade.[22] Egypt produced no silver, and now, with the progressive exhaustion of the Nubian mines, very little gold of her own, either.[23] That large, expensive army had to be paid, cash on the barrel, or else it became a dangerous liability; the export flow of grain, and papyrus, and other commodities (pp. 366 ff.), was essential to keep the royal exchequer in adequate funds, a goal that excise and direct taxation could not achieve unaided. As for Egypt's agricultural and other home production, the Ptolemies took very good care to ensure that it was geared, first and foremost, to paying *them*. If Egypt was a royal estate, they were its landlords.

What kind of loyalty could the Ptolemies count on? Their Friends (who gradually expanded into a large administrative class) formed the original base of their support. The military, in every sense mercenaries, served for pay, while Macedonian regulars were further indebted to the crown for grants of land (*klēroi*) and free billets or lodgings:[24] very often a family would serve in the army for generation after generation (again, the parallel of British India comes to mind). Foreign civilians granted citizenship and privileges would likewise support the regime with some enthusiasm. But with the native Egyptians it was quite another matter. Despite a policy (initiated by Alexander, and regularized by Ptolemy III and his successors) of the king's also being consecrated as pharaoh on accession,[25] the priesthood and population would very naturally have preferred Egyptian rulers. The priests could be, and were, won over temporarily by lavish concessions and benefactions, including the building of temples;[26] but it seems clear that during the violent insurrection that erupted against Ptolemaic rule after Raphia the priests, like their Orthodox counterparts in the Greek War of Independence, played a leading role.[27] The toiling fellahin—on whose constant labor the economy, in the last resort, has always depended[28]—had no say in the matter, but undoubtedly preferred indigenous to foreign masters. Adoption of the pharaonic cult, in fact, never reconciled Egypt to these adventitious Macedonian rulers. The Hyksos dynasty had, in the end, been driven out;[29] might not the Lagids one day suffer the same fate?

Symbolic of their alien quality, of course, in sharp contrast to the age-old pharaonic city of Memphis, was Alexandria itself, the new foreign capital on the Mediterranean—polyglot, alien, whoring after strange gods, its tall lighthouse casting radiance far out over the waters of what the Egyptians, with parochial suspicion, described as the "Great Green."[30] Ptolemaic rule never really caught on in Egypt. That is significant, since the Ptolemies, unlike their Persian predecessors, were actually resident in the country—in it, yet not of it: insulated by their Greek-speaking court and bureaucracy, largely indifferent to Egyptian culture, exploiters in an alien world. Small wonder, in the circumstances, that no Ptolemy before Cleopatra VII learned to speak Egyptian. Modern parallels suggest themselves.

Fig. 75. Glass vase from Begram, Afghanistan (first century B.C.), with a much-oversimplified representation of the Pharos lighthouse, Alexandria. The figure crowning the edifice is traditionally supposed to have been Zeus the Savior. Trumpet-blowing Tritons may also have been located at the next lowest level to provide foghorns for shipping. (See also figs. 64 and 65.) Kabul Museum. Photo Josephine Powell.

A great deal has been made of the complexity and centralization of Ptolemaic administration: it is often suggested that this (like it or not) was yet another example of Greek rational efficiency at work. Efficient at first it was (above, p. 191); but all too soon the bureaucracy became top-heavy, indecisive, and with a fatal tendency to strangle in its own red tape. The centralization, far from being the result of administrative streamlining, tended to be caused by a nagging (and well-justified) fear of fraud at every level. Everyone was on the take; each petty official was bent on feathering his own local nest. The result was a mass of directives, returns, and memoranda that equals anything a government agency can turn out today. Every department, from the state treasury to the ministry of justice, had as its prime objective the increasing of the king's power and revenues. A nice instance of this is the famous oil monopoly enjoyed by Ptolemy II, and detailed at length in his revenue laws.[31] Every price is specified; also what oil plant (sesame, castor, linseed, etc.) shall be sown in which area, how and where the oil workers are to register locally (it is a criminal offense for them to move from one nome, or district, to another). There are endless fines, for anything from buying non-government oil on the sly to withholding wages or seed at the prescribed time. We glimpse a whole swarm of petty officials in charge of this cumbersome operation: tax farmers, clerks, village headmen (*kōmarchai*), overseers, government agents, excisemen. Once again, the goal is the maintenance of the *status quo*. "The intention of these elaborate regulations was clearly purely fiscal: to ensure the king's revenues, not to improve production."[32]

Alexandria, as we have seen (above, p. 88), enjoyed titular independence: at least it possessed a council and assembly, though they probably exercised jurisdiction over municipal affairs only, and with notable exceptions even there.[33] The royal palaces, the harbor, the army, and the foreign communities generally were under the direct control of the crown, and answerable to Greek laws. The Egyptian country-side (*chōra*), split up, as under the pharaohs, into nomes (*nomoi*, districts), was directly administered by a royal bureaucracy, the main concern of which was to screw tax quotas out of the inhabitants.[34] The government of external possessions such as Cyprus, Cyrene, or Coele-Syria—which formed a closed-currency zone with Egypt (p. 373)[35]—was carried out by *stratēgoi* (military commanders) directly responsible to the throne: this system showed the Ptolemaic blend of central control and delegated authority at its most successful.[36] The main value of these areas was strategic, though the copper mines, forests, and wheat of Cyprus also offered an economic bonanza.[37] The *stratēgoi* were not, for obvious reasons, given too much financial independence: a strong commander still had to depend on the local treasurer (*oikonomos*) for funds, and the *oikonomos* was a crown appointee, reporting to Alexandria. Thus overambitious or would-be rebellious provincial administrators found it hard to build up any kind of independent power base against the central government. This may also have been one reason why, in Cyprus especially, democratic institutions were encouraged in the cities: a decentralized system of government was far harder to organize for effective rebellion.[38]

There seems, also, as we might expect, to have been some distinction between the long-term imperial holdings, such as Cyrene, and other, less permanent, areas of influence, especially those with a predominantly Greek population and a tradition of independence, such as the Cycladic islands or the coastal cities of Asia Minor. The latter tended to keep their own mints, and in general enjoyed a greater degree of real autonomy.[39] The overall impression, however, certainly throughout Egypt itself, the heartland of the Lagid kingdom, is one of strangling royal interference in every area, of heavy taxation, of bureaucratic illiberalism run riot. Alexandria, with its luxury, culture, commerce, public shows, and relentless ostentation, was the playground and front window for an occupying power that never came to terms with, much less assimilated, the age-old native civilization on which it had imposed itself. Ironically, after a harsh period of Persian rule, punctuated with violent nationalist uprisings, the Egyptians in 332 had welcomed Alexander as a deliverer—a fundamental error of judgment with appalling consequences for the future.[40] Too late, they found that what Macedonia brought was not freedom but systematic exploitation.

The Seleucid East, like Ptolemaic Egypt, was another case of spear-won territory held down by right of conquest, and similarly at the monarch's arbitrary disposal, to veterans, cities, or private individuals, as gifts, or in return for cash or services.[41] Again, there was no national power base, and no ethnic support. The Seleucids' problems were worse than those facing the Ptolemies in that they did not control one well-defined and well-protected area, unified ethnically and virtually safe from invasion; what they had was a loose, heterogeneous, and rapidly shrinking mass of old Achaemenid satrapies, where communications were, at the best of times, hazardous. Macedonian by birth, the ruling dynasty always had its eyes to the west; yet even there its position was tenuous. The Seleucids never controlled the Royal

Road from Susa to Sardis for all its length; from Antioch they were forced to loop south by way of Cilicia and the Taurus range, through lower Phrygia.[42] Their administrative and military control was never as effective as the Ptolemies', despite their policy of covering their vast territories with a network of Greek-controlled strongholds and post roads, once again in the hands of privileged immigrants, including numerous Ionians.[43]

These settlements ranged from military colonies (*katoikiai*), largely concentrated in Lydia and Phrygia, to villages (*kōmai*), garrison outposts (*chōria* or *phrouria*), and cities proper (*poleis*): the distinctions are those conferred by municipal status. The *katoikiai* never seem to have evolved into *poleis*, perhaps because the constant local warfare endemic to the area made too much autonomy seem undesirable in the eyes of the authorities.[44] In any case even the *poleis*, being subject to the imposition of governors, garrisons, taxes, and arbitrary royal edicts, did very little better than the less-privileged communities. Just as the Ptolemies had a viceroy in southern Egypt at the new city of Ptolemaïs, so the Seleucids ruled their eastern satrapies from Seleucia-on-Tigris, leaving Antioch as their capital in the west (above, p. 164). The size of these imperial fiefs made secession by the local satrap—very often a member of the royal family—an ever-present possibility, as the cases of Antiochus Hierax and Achaeus all too clearly demonstrate (pp. 263, 291):[45] a compelling reason for the regular separation of military and civil authority that, again, both Ptolemies and Seleucids practiced, a lesson learned (along with so much else) from the example of Alexander.[46]

The Seleucid royal court, household, and administration, insofar as evidence is available for them, seem to have closely resembled the Ptolemies'.[47] Once again we find an independent Graeco-Macedonian cadre, its habits perhaps somewhat more Orientalized than those prevailing among Ptolemy's bureaucrats. The chain of military settlements described above was capable of providing, in an emergency, up to about 47,000 infantry and 8,000 to 8,500 cavalry: it also had a very similar system of land grants for regular soldiers.[48] The fleet seems to have been maintained by trierarchies, in the old Athenian manner. The Seleucids not only kept up a strong cavalry arm (one reason why they clung so desperately to the horse-breeding satrapy of Media),[49] but also had a large corps of war elephants—another royal monopoly—stationed at Apamea.[50]

The Seleucids, again like the Ptolemies, also instituted a royal cult: the worship of kings was well acclimatized in the East. The Babylonians, for example, were quite ready to worship Seleucus Nicator (officially, now, descended from Apollo) along with their other gods.[51] Ilion, similarly, offered him monthly sacrifices, and instituted quadrennial games in his honor.[52] In various cities he had his own priest, was given the title of *theos*, and provided with a divine genealogy.[53] It was only later, when Antiochus III and his successors began raiding native temples for their tithe as "gods manifest,"[54] that they, like the later Ptolemies, ran up against a blank wall of religious hostility, once more with a strong nationalist ingredient to it. The Seleucids, like the Ptolemies, could conciliate a native priesthood, for the time being, by what amounted to large-scale bribery; but the moment they infringed unacceptably on religious or ethnic prerogatives, they were rapidly, and forcibly, reminded that they ruled only on sufferance, and by right of conquest. It is no accident that whenever the various parts of the empire felt they had a chance to break away they invariably did so (cf. p. 263).

At this point it will be convenient to examine the ambivalent position of the officially autonomous Greek *poleis*. Though various kings, as we have seen, talked a good deal about freedom and self-government in their dealings with the Greek cities under their control, it is safe to say that genuine liberty was never in question— certainly no more than suited the king's policies. *Eleutheria*, in short, remained conditional upon the will and coercive strength of the sovereign.[55] This was especially true in the cities of mainland Greece and western Asia Minor, where a tradition of autonomy had been long established (p. 25): all three Successor dynasties played variations on a complex freedom-charade in their dealings with these foundations. Small wonder that in Euhemerus's utopia the inhabitants were specifically declared to be not only autonomous, but also kingless (*abasileutoi*).[56]

The degree to which the *poleis* enjoyed actual independence was directly dictated by one of two principal factors: their proven loyalty, or, in a case like that of Rhodes, their strength to resist attack. Both factors were predicated on the relative power or weakness of the individual monarch.[57] This lesson had been strikingly demonstrated during Alexander's march of conquest southward from the Granicus to Caria: surrender and cooperation were rewarded; resistance met with violent punitive measures, and in all cases Alexander himself was the judge, indeed often the creator, of that international law (*Völkerrecht*) on which, in theory, the relationship between monarch and city was to rest.[58] The same remained true for the Successors. Technically, the Greek cities were left not only free, but in most cases democratic. Cassander's rational experiment in governing through oligarchic juntas had proved immensely unpopular (above, p. 48),[59] and while no autocrat would willingly surrender the realities of power, most of them (as should by now be clear) saw the advantages of catering to the nostalgic *amour propre* of local civic government. It cost nothing, provided excellent publicity, and, by decentralizing authority (above, p. 194), created an extra safeguard against sedition.

All this produced a kind of political mirage that it was in the interest of both sides to maintain.[60] While the king, in the last resort, regarded the Greek cities as more or less privileged enclaves in territory over which his final word was law, the cities themselves, as has well been said, "while not disputing the sovereignty of the kings over their Macedonians and over the barbarians whom they had conquered, liked to regard themselves as sovereign states in alliance with the king."[61] The king, alert to public opinion, did not press the constitutional issue, and in any case saw autonomous local government as a useful instrument for simplifying his own administrative responsibilities.[62] The cities went through the motions of freedom, but in the last resort they did so on sufferance. What they really felt about their *de facto* subjection can be inferred from the carefully euphemistic terminology employed in decrees of the early to mid-third century honoring Greek officials who served the Successors.[63] Such service, though popular (Callias of Sphettos offers a good example), was felt to be a trifle embarrassing. Thus we find it said of such persons, in decrees intended for Greek public consumption, that they had "spent time with" the king, or had "gone abroad" with him, or had "enjoyed his friendship": anything to circumvent the notion of paid service, and perhaps a residual unwillingness to face the grim fact of political impotence.[64] It is significant that later this objection fades: by 200 the honorand's court title is being expressed openly, without circumlocution.

It is surprising how many scholars till comparatively recent times showed themselves ready, indeed eager, to accept the mirage as sober fact. Today the mood is different. Wolfgang Orth's *Königlicher Machtanspruch und städtische Freiheit* spells out, in detail and from a whole series of individual instances, the regular exercise of *force majeure*, by Seleucus Nicator and his immediate successors, upon Greek *poleis* that were in no position to resist. *Sois mon frère, ou je te tue*: behind the façade of theoretical freedom we find extortion, blackmail, press-ganging, and other similar practices,[65] all predicated upon *Machtpolitik*. As Ernst Badian nicely put it, "*Völkerrecht*, in the world of the Hellenistic kings, was always a mixture between what we might call the balance of interests and the balance of terror."[66] The reluctance of earlier writers to recognize such unpalatable truths sprang in part from a quite remarkable faith in, and preoccupation with, the sanctity of *Völkerrecht* as an internationally accepted juridical force before which even the most powerful monarch must bow in acquiescence.

Undeterred by the modern example of the International High Court of Justice at the Hague (not a body famous for enforcing its beliefs, let alone its decisions, on anyone), Tarn took this thesis well beyond its logical conclusion, a *reductio ad absurdum* in every sense, by arguing that the reason why—in 324, after conquering the Achaemenid empire!—Alexander the Great requested deification was because otherwise, in insisting on the return of all exiles to their cities, he would be overstepping his legally constituted authority as *hēgemōn* (leader) of the League of Corinth.[67] Unreal pedantry could scarcely go farther. Yet the most influential prewar monograph on the relations between cities and rulers in the Hellenistic period, Heuss's *Stadt und Herrscher des Hellenismus*, is full of similar sophistries. It should scarcely need emphasizing at this point that even if we could trace a coherent system of international law covering the relations of the Seleucids, or any other Hellenistic power, with the Greek cities—which we cannot—its importance would still be limited to the degree to which the monarchs chose to observe it. In this respect Bikerman's *Institutions des Séleucides* is a model of pragmatic realism.[68]

If the situation permitted, some cities could at least be relieved of those embarrassing outward signs of subjugation, for example garrisons and tribute quotas, under which many of them labored.[69] The tribute, in any case, could always be made good by calling it something else, whether taxes or contributions (*syntaxeis*): where juridical autonomy, even in the technical sense, ended and arbitrary royal benevolence (*eunoia*) began was sometimes hard to determine. On the other hand, genuine freedom (once again the example of Rhodes comes to mind) could be a distinct embarrassment to any Hellenistic ruler whose airy talk about autonomy came up against the harsh realities of the power struggle. Antigonus One-Eye offers a good example. When he needed the Rhodian fleet to fight Ptolemy (above, p. 32), and Rhodes—whose leaders were in any case sympathetic with the Ptolemaic regime, for commercial if for no other reasons—preferred to stay neutral, he sent Demetrius to reduce the island stronghold by force.[70] Even the titular democracies of the Greek cities, that of Rhodes included (p. 378), were to some extent a sham, since throughout the Hellenistic period their government was increasingly weighted in favor of the propertied classes, and as a rule ignored not only slaves and metics, but also, in colonial foundations, a substantial body of disfranchised indigenous inhabitants.[71]

This makes it even harder to understand the still-prevalent emphasis on the "self-governing" *poleis*, and the "formal complexities of Greek international life in the hellenistic period."[72] If this period is, in fact, "unthinkable without the *poleis*," if "no contribution to the history of *Völkerrecht* which ignores the basic community-form in which most Greeks lived can claim to have more than scratched the surface of the complex legal, moral and traditional relationships which regulated inter-state intercourse in the hellenistic world," if it was, finally, "the *poleis* which survived," what does all this in fact mean? Merely that towns, whether in Hellenistic Greece, medieval England, middle America, or the Soviet Union, are more often than not (whatever their relative degree of bottom-line freedom) left to run themselves, at least at a municipal level, because to run them from outside is simply too much trouble. The minutiae of local government can be fascinating in their own right, but to treat them as the larger world in microcosm is to court disaster. The plain truth of this at once becomes apparent when we study the actual exchanges between, say, the cities of Asia Minor and the Seleucids. In pursuit of autonomy (i.e., the privilege of being left alone), and of sizable land grants attached, via their individual recipients, to civic territory, local embassies would lavish flattery, gold wreaths, birthday honors, and every kind of sycophantic toadyism on the monarch concerned.[73]

Last, a brief word—brief, because the evidence is minimal[74]—about Antigonid Macedonia. The great difference between the kingdom of Antigonus Gonatas and that of his Seleucid or Ptolemaic contemporaries is, of course, that unlike them he had a national power base: he was a Macedonian ruling Macedonians, and with a fair line of descent from Antigonus One-Eye and Antipater to justify his kingship. Alone among the Successors, the Antigonids were not, by and large, dependent upon spear-won territory, though now they held Chalcidice, Paeonia, Thessaly (where since Philip II's day the Macedonian king had been *ex officio* archon for life, a pleasant, face-saving fiction),[75] a buffer in Thrace, and a handful of important Greek cities. Thus they were not, in the full sense of the word, Hellenistic. Even though their own cities were by now standard Greek *poleis*, with mixed commercial populations, they did not carry their rule or their language abroad and attempt to impose them on a subjugated alien people. Nor were they prone to those devastating family intrigues that so weakened the Ptolemies and Seleucids. There was some, though not much, royal land available outside Macedonia for the ruler's friends (such fiefs reverting to the crown upon the donor's death), or for settlers, but no large-scale imperial exploitation.

The old Macedonian nobility that had been so powerful a force under Philip II and Alexander was now no more than a shadow of its former self. Many of the old-guard barons had fallen in battle, or been purged, during Alexander's Eastern campaigns. Of those who survived, some stayed abroad, whether in or out of office, and the bulk of those who came back, as well as Antipater's friends who stayed in Macedonia throughout, had died either during the wars of the Successors, or else fighting the Gauls. In any case by the mid-third century they were no longer a serious factor in Macedonian politics.[76] This, together with the smaller territory involved, kept Macedonia free, by and large, from the complex court bureaucracies, and court intrigues, that plagued the Ptolemies and Seleucids. The country was split up, for administrative purposes, into cities or groups of cities, under overseers or governors (*epistatai*) directly responsible to the king.[77] Antigonid control over the rest of Greece was now one of dominant influence rather than direct rule. The only points south of Thessaly where Macedonia still maintained such direct rule—and garrisons—were the so-called Fetters of Greece: Demetrias, Chalcis, Acrocorinth, and, intermittently, Piraeus, similarly governed by *epistatai*, but with overall control vested in two military commanders. This, however, was a defensive arrangement only, aimed at preserving the *status quo*, and a certain degree of superiority through the possession of strategic fortresses—which had, indeed, more than justified the collective name by which they were known.

One effective check on any taste a Macedonian king might have for renewed expansionism was a shortage of funds. The Pangaeum mines had declined in productivity from about 300, after Philip II's vigorous exploitation,[78] till by the second century the Macedonian land tax (which included state revenue from the mines) yielded no more than two hundred talents.[79] The vast wealth brought back after Alexander's campaigns had been largely dissipated,[80] and the prolonged ravages of the Gauls had further impoverished the economy. What remained was the timber and ship-chandling trade, plus a margin of exportable grain, which at least enabled Gonatas to maintain full production of an excellent gold and silver coinage,[81] with regular commercial outlets via Rhodes and Delos.[82]

Antigonus Gonatas was also heir to the well-established pattern of the Argead dynasty whereby the king was *primus inter pares*, ruled by virtue of his bloodline, but exacted only as much respect as his personal charisma could command, and made no fuss about pomp and circumstance.[83] He wore a purple cloak, a broad-brimmed hat, and on occasion a simple blue-and-white headband as diadem. His scepter was a staff, and he did not require prostration of his subjects, who addressed him without flowery honorifics. As for royal deification, the Macedonians had had quite enough of that with Alexander. Perhaps no other ruler could have got away with a request to be worshipped as a god among his own Macedonians; even so, Antipater for one flatly refused to accede (p. 143). Antigonus, the Stoic, preferred his kingship to be based on philosophical justification rather than on any supposititious assumption of godhead (p. 143)—which is not to say that the Ptolemies or the Seleucids would not take a good philosophical argument if it came their way: Antigonus was simply a little more scrupulous about it. Indeed, most of the philosophical schools, as we have seen (p. 189), were eagerly scrambling aboard the authoritarian bandwagon, finding proofs, to their own satisfaction, that monarchy was the best form of government, that the king embodied the state—*L'état, c'est moi* two millennia ahead of itself—and was, indeed, "law incarnate."[84]

On all this Antigonus turned a cool eye, sardonic in the wisdom that only harsh experience can bring. To the flatterers who assured him that his deeds had made him divine he replied, drily, "My pisspot-bearer knows better."[85] Antigonus's attitude looks forward to that of the dying Emperor Vespasian, well aware that he would automatically be deified on expiry, and muttering to those around him, *in extremis*, "Oh dear—I think I'm turning into a god."[86] There is a fundamental sanity about Antigonus's attitude (whatever we may think of his Stoic pretensions) that comes as a relief after all the cultural and theocratic propaganda the Seleucids and Ptolemies employed to justify the territorial exploitations that they owed, in the last resort, to dead Alexander's conquests.

CHAPTER 13

ARMCHAIR EPIC:
APOLLONIUS RHODIUS
AND THE VOYAGE OF *ARGO*

Few things are more enjoyable, for the uninvolved spectator, than a good (i.e., really rancorous) literary quarrel, and that between Callimachus and Apollonius—even allowing for the dubious nature of much of the evidence[1]—has to be accounted one of the best bookish battles on record.[2] It is full of picturesque personal insults; patronage and job competition may well have fueled its flames. It involved charges of plagiarism, incompetence, and bad taste. In short, it is irresistible. We have an epigram that Apollonius wrote against Callimachus,[3] in the form of two mock encyclopedia entries: "*Callimachus*: Trash, cheap joke, blockhead. *Original Sin*: Writing Callimachus's *Origins*" (a pun on *aitios*, "responsible," and *aitia*, "causes," "origins").[4] Callimachus in turn wrote a tirade, a curse poem (*katadesmos, devotio*) against Apollonius, "a deliberate exercise in obscurity and abuse."[5] The poem, unfortunately, does not survive; but we know quite a lot about it, both from the scholiasts and from Ovid, who imitated it.

Its title was *The Ibis*, this being the name Callimachus chose to designate his rival. The sacred ibis (*Tantalus aethiopicus*) was a common bird in Egypt, and an object of interest to ancient writers.[6] Venerated by the local inhabitants,[7] the ibis was a foul feeder of gluttonous and indiscriminate voracity, scavenging any kind of filth or carrion: Strabo observes that "every crossroads is crowded with them." It was also popularly believed to offset its diet by giving itself water enemas and colonic irrigation *per anum* with its own beak, besides copulating orally, nesting in date palms to avoid cats, and having a gut over forty yards long.[8] The application is not hard to fathom. Callimachus was saying, in effect, that Apollonius lacked all taste and discrimination in his use of material, that he was an uncritical vulgarian who collected and passed on every kind of cheap trash. Worse, he was a plagiarist, who stole the pure Hippocrene water of the true poet's inspiration, added this to his own waste products, and then discharged the whole mess on the public, at gross and unjustifiable length. "Omnivorous and unclean," says Strabo, "the ibis is only with diffi-

Fig. 76. Bronze bust rescued from the sea near Livorno, Italy, and tentatively identified as Apollonius Rhodius. Museo Archeologico, Florence.

culty kept away from things that are clean themselves, and alien to all defilement."[9] So Apollonius, on top of everything else, was probably being attacked as a corrupting influence.

It is interesting, and significant, that, insults apart, what tradition remembered as the core of the quarrel was a matter not of content but of form, of style. Callimachus was the apostle of concision, of erudite miniaturism, of pungent irony. Apollonius, on the other hand, wanted to revive the epic—perhaps not, to begin with, in so typically Alexandrian a dress as he finally gave it. He may even (the ultimate heresy) have been advancing behind the shield of Aristotelian authority, since each of the *Argonautica*'s four books is about the size of an average tragedy, and the whole would precisely meet Aristotle's demand for "poems on a smaller scale than the old epics, and answering in length to the group of tragedies presented at a single sitting."[10] Since I have a good deal of sympathy for Apollonius, and thoroughly enjoy his *Argonautica*—much of which I absorbed as a child, without knowing it, through Andrew Lang's *Tales of Troy and Greece*—I perhaps should emphasize, at the outset, that in their original quarrel Callimachus was arguably right all along the line.

The conditions that created and sustained Homeric epic were long gone, and beyond recall. Bookish literacy had replaced the oral tradition (books now had private individual readers, one more encouragement for introspection); heroic *gestes* were, to put it mildly, out of fashion, and Callimachus saw that any epic produced in Alexandria that ignored these facts would be artificial and sterile to a degree. What he objected to in the big book was perhaps not so much mere bulk—though his allusion to the fat *Lyde* of Antimachus, another of Apollonius's favorites, suggests objections on that score too[11]—as the epic *ēthos*, inflated heroic posturing inappropriate to his own time and place. It is also worth bearing in mind that, as Konrat Ziegler long ago pointed out, the third-century poets best known to us were all a small minority amid a terrible crowd of propagandists and encomiasts, pumping out sedulous epic rubbish in honor of Alexander, or the Attalids, or (going back a little) Philip II of Macedon, or the Spartan Lysander, or even those who distinguished themselves in the Persian Wars. Platitudinous rhetoric, bloated with post-Gorgianic tropes, had reached epidemic proportions: Callimachus's complaints were well justified.[12] Further, though this depends on a much-debated question of literary priorities, it does look very much as though Apollonius borrowed from his immediate predecessors—Aratus, Lycophron, Theocritus,[13] and, above all, Callimachus himself—to a degree that today would at once incur the charge of plagiarism.[14] This goes well beyond linguistic borrowings and adaptation of phraseology: it extends to specific topics and episodes, and general subject matter, including a number of *aitia*, for example the rites to Apollo on the island of Anaphe.[15] The crows that jeer at Mopsus in Book 3 of the *Argonautica* are at once recognizable from Callimachus's *Hecale* and *Iambus* 4, while the crow's speech seems to be lifted from Callimachus's *Hymn to Apollo*.[16]

Questions of literary judgment and piracy apart, there are signs that Callimachus had more personal reasons to resent Apollonius.[17] The facts of Apollonius's life have been disputed, and the evidence remains ambiguous in certain areas; but the main outlines seem clear enough. He was born about 295, an Alexandrian Greek (unlike Callimachus, the poor if well-bred schoolmaster from Cyrene). He is regularly described as having been taught by Callimachus,[18] and in some sense this may well be true: Callimachus was his senior by about a decade. Probably while still a very young man he composed an early draft,[19] perhaps incomplete,[20] of the *Argonautica*, and recited it in the literary salons of Alexandria, where it was greeted with a storm of ridicule and abuse, doubtless orchestrated by Callimachus and his literary followers, the antiheroic, counterinflationary, big-book-bad-thing group. Piqued, Apollonius retired for some time to Rhodes, and worked on a second version of his epic there: at a guess, undercutting the Homeric *ēthos*, increasing the stress on *aitia*, reducing the heroic component in Jason's character, and reevaluating his encounter with Medea more strictly in terms of Hellenistic erotic psychology. In short, what had begun as mere Homeric pastiche was to be refurbished, as far as possible, to suit the prevailing canons of literary taste.

The significance of Apollonius's choice of retreat has never, I think, been properly appreciated. In the third century Rhodes was the last bastion of genuine freedom (if of modified democracy) left in the Aegean world, a powerful, independent maritime republic that had stood off Demetrius the Besieger (p. 133), and left its famous Rhodian sea law as a legacy, by way of Byzantium, to Venice.[21] Its atmosphere must have offered a welcome contrast to that of the Ptolemaic court, while its culture cannot have helped but be more sympathetic to the epic mode, above all to a poem that in its final form laid such stress on maritime exploration.[22] At all events it was on Rhodes that the *Argonautica* took its final shape, and on Rhodes that Apollonius won the international fame, as poet and scholar, that finally enabled him to stage his triumphant return to Alexandria (ca. 270–265?). Like Cavafy, he found himself irresistibly drawn by the Ptolemaic capital, the center of his intellectual world; yet till his dying day he commemorated both his early rejection, and his gratitude to the city that had adopted him, by his style of address: he was known to his contemporaries, and is still known today, as Apollonius, not of Alexandria, but of Rhodes.

On his return he was appointed chief librarian (*prostatēs*) in succession to the first holder of that office, Zenodotus, the Homeric scholar.[23] We may surmise that Zenodotus had some say in the choice of his successor, and approved of Apollonius's epic interests—which did not stop Apollonius, in true Alexandrian style, from publishing a monograph that attacked Zenodotus's edition of Homer root and branch.[24] Apollonius held this post till about 246/5, when Ptolemy III Euergetes (who had been tutored by Apollonius as a boy) appointed the great mathematician and geographer Eratosthenes in his place.[25] Apollonius then retired, for the second time but under more auspicious circumstances, to his beloved Rhodes.

What is now clear is that though Callimachus worked in the Library—was indeed responsible for establishing its catalogue, the *Pinakes* (above, p. 180)—he never held the coveted post of chief librarian. That he was in the running is certain, and the late suggestions of his actual appointment confirm this. But the list of librarians we now possess on papyrus clinches the matter.[26] The clear inference is that Apollonius and Callimachus were in competition for the job sometime between 270 and 265, and that Apollonius got it. This would make Callimachus, his former teacher, technically his subordinate. Apollonius would not have forgotten those early slights and snubs. Callimachus, in turn, would not forgive the rival who, by way of revenge,

Fig. 77. Papyrus fragment from Oxyrhynchus (second century A.D.) listing the earliest directors of the Library in Alexandria: Zenodotus, Apollonius Rhodius, Eratosthenes, Aristophanes of Byzantium, Apollonius ("the Classifier"), Aristarchus. The Board of Trinity College, Dublin.

first plagiarized his work and was now his superior. There was a tradition that in old age the two men were reconciled, and indeed buried beside each other.[27] Acquaintance with literary feuds suggests that this was pure wishful thinking on the part of scholiasts anxious for a happy ending.

When we first read the *Argonautica*, one inescapable point that strikes us is that some of the original objections, and others that have been made since, are well grounded. Apollonius may have led off with Apollo (1.1), and may have involved the Muses as his interpreters (1.22: *hypophētores*, a hint at the refinement through art of divinely inspired utterance), but the Muses do not seem always to have been paying attention. An endless procession of modern scholars has repeated, generation after generation, the same criticisms of Apollonius's work. It is structurally feeble, falling into a series of loosely connected episodes (or short epyllia, if we want to justify the practice). The ending has been described as "hurried and trivial."[28] The characterization is sketchy, except for that of Medea, which is inconsistent. The action is again and again held up while the bookish author explains quaint local customs (*aitia*), or inserts geographical digressions, or treats us to potted digests of new Alexandrian discoveries in science and medicine.[29] The gods are turned into commonplace nagging Greek relatives, Hellenistic style, while at the same time their actions are conducted, as it were, on an upper stage, with no direct reference to human events. There is too much detail crammed into too little space. Above all, Jason, the expedition's leader, is no Homeric hero in pursuit of renown (*kleos*), but a lachrymose and indecisive Everyman, acted on rather than acting, taking a kind of masochistic pleasure in his own despair.[30] He has even been described as an antihero.

There is some truth in all of these criticisms. Yet in the last resort what is most striking and important about Callimachus and Apollonius is not so much their differences as their similarities. When we look at the surviving fragments of Callimachus's *Hecale*, for example, we could well be reading some lost epic by Apollonius: there is the same innovative concern with language, the same insistence on *aitia* (and that specialized form of *aition*, the etymological gloss),[31] the same loose hold on narrative, the same preoccupation with personal reactions. What both poets in fact reveal is an identical, and ineradicable, Alexandrianism, with its twin temptations of scholarship and naïveté,[32] which emerges, as a kind of social index and correlative, whether the genre be epic, epigram, hymn, mime, or pastoral. Its features are worth examining in more detail.

One of the most striking, and most pervasive, is the influence of the visual arts on these writers. Again and again they might be describing—indeed, very often are describing—a picture or statue. This practice was, and still is, known as *ekphrasis*.[33] Think of the departure of *Argo*,[34] "long wake ever gleaming white behind her, / Like a track seen stretching away across green savannah" (1.545–46), watched by gods, nymphs, and old Chiron himself, "feet splashed by the waves' white breaking, / Waving them *bon voyage* with massive hoof, while beside him / His wife held up, for Peleus, the child Achilles" (1.554–58: note now the domestic, indeed familial, slant);[35] or the glimpse of Hephaestus, leaning on his hammer as *Argo* threads her way through the Clashing Rocks, while Hera and Athena hug each other for fear

(4.956 ff.); or the decoration of Jason's cloak (1.725–67), rightly described as "a rich Hellenistic textile,"[36] an obvious borrowing from Homer's Shield of Achilles, and almost certainly depicting, in the various scenes described, well-known local works of art.[37]

Alexandria was full of artists, and their commissioned work could be seen everywhere. We catch glimpses of this in Theocritus, who sketches a pair of chattering Syracusan ladies admiring the tapestries and their artwork in the royal palace,[38] and in one of Herodas's *Mimes*,[39] where, again, we find two silly women praising the realism of various paintings and sculptures in the great temple of Asclepius on Cos. (The realism, clearly, extends to the viewers as well as what they view.)[40] This ubiquity of public murals, tapestries, and reliefs may also help to explain Apollonius's remarkable awareness of the play and effect of light: dawn glow, the sun's rays glancing off water, the chiaroscuro of fields under mountain peaks. No other Greek poet (with the notable exception of Pindar) has quite this sensitivity. With Hellenistic developments in the visual arts, especially the new portraiture (which was no respecter of persons, relentlessly stressing Ptolemy I's cracker jaw, or Arsinoë II's prominent eyes and double chin, regardless of deification),[41] we can also correlate Apollonius's vivid realism of description, and, perhaps more significant still, his pursuit—all the more striking in an epic or heroic context—of the mundane, the commonplace, the *anti*-heroic, for which he has often been faulted, but which emerges as a key element in the understanding of Hellenistic art as a whole.[42]

This antiheroic attitude runs through the entire fabric of the Hellenistic poet's world outlook. In part it is socially based, one more index of political impotence: in a world of kings and mercenaries, money-grubbing, and introspection, who could treat the urge for heroic renown, *kleos*, as anything but a bad joke? After the Macedonian conqueror, even the old gods looked shabby. Worse, urban sophistication had brought acute awareness of the arbitrary, sometimes childish, often embarrassing nature of the old myths, without reducing by one iota the equally acute emotional need for them. The aetiologist in his study was uneasily aware that each myth had an archetypal core, to be explained or tactfully bowdlerized, but never to be altered in essence. Thus the scholar's cynicism concentrated, where possible, on the machinery of epic convention. In the new climate of the third century it was also safe to reject the old Homeric code, since no one any longer really wanted it, even if pious lip service was still paid to its more famous aphorisms.[43] Aspiring to a heroic ideal had become *vieux jeu*, along with the risibly anthropomorphic Olympian deities; better to cultivate your garden, tend your soul, amass wealth, hone your esthetic sensibilities, let your horizon be limited by matters familial and philosophical.

All this perhaps helps to explain the constant scaling-down of the divine, the numinous, the terrible to a series of domestic commonplaces. It tells us why, in Apollonius, "the terrible but alluring magician of Homer [i.e., Circe] has become a nervous aunt,"[44] full of suburban outrage at her eloping (and, come to that, homicidal) niece; or why Hera, visiting Aphrodite and her child, Eros, remarks brightly on parting, "Don't get cross and fight with your boy; he'll change his ways in time,"[45] for all the world as though she were an Alexandrian matron paying a social call. In a sense, of course, she is; Euhemerus had done his work all too well. In this new age, if mortals, as Heracleitus put it long before, are immortal, then immortals are mortal too[46]—often highly bourgeois mortals, at that. A genteel sense of middle-class propriety had been at work on gods and myths alike ever since Xenophanes' day (see p. 180), and now reached its acme. Alexandrian critics fastidiously suppressed the more robust or otherwise embarrassing characteristics of Homer's deities. The gods could not be arrogant, or suffer physical pain, or fear; Aristarchus found Thetis's advice to her son, Achilles, that he should assuage his grief by having intercourse with a woman, intolerably indecorous.[47]

We should also remember in this context the Epicureans' treatment of the gods (below, p. 622), which was to sidetrack them altogether from the real business of human life, and confine them to some remote Elysian never-never land, as a kind of genuflection to tradition. As Lesky saw, though without seeing why, there is no essential or organic connection in Apollonius between the divine and the human spheres of action.[48] The scholarly obsession with Homer that so many of the Alexandrians displayed has paradoxical elements.[49] It is a quest for roots, for ultimate authority; it is also an exercise in escapism, a retreat into the academic womb of the Library and its books, into "the security of the known past, with a mind folding in on itself and turned away from the new and the uncertain."[50] But to embrace this past necessitated, as we have seen, a radical revaluation of the too often starkly archaic *mores* that it assumed—hence Apollonius's suburbanization of epic convention. The characters in Hellenistic epic have no formulaic epithets; if the gods behave like censorious aunts and uncles, the protagonists often seem to exemplify the virtues of togetherness, of collective activity. What chance did *kleos* stand in a world whose ideal was *ataraxia*?[51]

It has been argued that the *Argonautica* is an attempt to present a group hero, *Heldengesellschaft* rather than *Hauptheld*.[52] No accident that instead of Homer's *klea andrōn*, the deeds of heroes, Apollonius proposes to describe *klea phōtōn*, the deeds of ordinary men. His language is an odd amalgam that suits this ambivalence. Homer's artificial epic speech remains the base, but this has been overlaid with later literary words, from prose and verse, including neologisms and unique formations, plus an infusion of the Alexandrian vernacular.[53] Even verbally, the Hellenistic epic hero is *déclassé*. His horizon, similarly, had widened since the archaic age, and the world he knew was no longer the unknown and terrifying outback that Homer's audience still faced. The blank spaces on the map had mostly been filled in, even if at times wrongly: one reason, perhaps, why for their return voyage Apollonius sent the Argonauts on that fantastic—and for stretches impossible—voyage up the Danube, Rhône, and Rhine, chasing the age-old northern European amber routes that still possessed the merit, for a Mediterranean audience, of misty, romantic unfamiliarity.[54]

The gods of this new epic were not, could no longer be, frightful and unpredictable sources of limitless and arbitrary power. Developing science had long since robbed them of their meteorological prerogatives; no one in Apollonius's day would, in his heart of hearts, attribute the thunder to Zeus, much less suppose that if he scaled Olympus he would find a pantheon of deities ensconced on the summit.

From Aristophanes' day on the sophistic snigger made itself felt. Conflicting theo-logical variants provoked sly send-ups, artful protestations of ignorance, from the scholar-poets. How celebrate Zeus? Under which title or avatar? Where was he born? Ida? Arcadia? Cretans showed his tomb, but, of course, all Cretans were liars: good Greeks knew (did they not?) that he was immortal.[55] Thus we find no real mo-tivation for the divine support accorded to Jason's expedition, and little of substance in the support itself. Similarly, there is no substantial opposition from the gods, ei-ther; all the real trouble is caused by mortals or inanimate nature—the Clashing Rocks, Amycus the boxer, Aeëtes and his *Flammenwerfer* bulls.

Romantic antiquarianism is mixed with academic cynicism, a bad compound. The *aitia* have a wistful quality—Alexandrian scholars would like to believe in these strange old traditional customs—but all the time one senses the new post-Aristotelian scholarship at work too, classifying and cataloguing, so that *aitia* be-come, in effect, vehicles for early social anthropologizing, the stance adopted by Margaret Mead among the Polynesians, investigating tribal customs from a position of sympathetic cultural superiority. Aristarchus has a fascinating discussion, apropos a textual reading by Zenodotus of which he disapproves, on the restriction of equally shared meals, by definition, to civilized human beings, on the grounds that sharing is a characteristic beyond the comprehension of animals or savages.[56]

This is the cultural burden that Jason has to bear: small wonder if he emerges as a version of the common man, unheroic, passive, barely competent, too often the mere victim of events, a negative leader whose main goal—one he shares with many thinkers of the day—is to reach a haven of inaction, to avoid pain and trouble. The old ideals of physical prowess, courage, honor, may get polite acknowledgment, but little more. All the Argonauts, it has been noted, possess each his own special quality, but are otherwise unremarkable; and Jason's outstanding characteristic, like Paris's, is his sexual irresistibility. What is more, this remains an inherent, indeed a passive, attribute: it involves (as George III said of the Order of the Garter) no damned nonsense about merit. Jason does not need to *do* anything to seduce Hyp-sipyle or Medea; he simply shows up in his splendid cloak, looking like a star, and any eligible woman in sight runs after him. If he resembles any Homeric hero, it is, surely, Paris.[57]

Such dominant sexuality, and the psychological insights that naturally accom-pany it, are quintessentially Hellenistic phenomena, Euripidean in origin, but taken now to their logical conclusion. Political-*cum*-social alienation always leads to vari-ous private preoccupations, of which by no means the least important, or demand-ing, is the erotic, since it offers an (often deceptive)[58] sense of being in charge of one's own life. We do not need the anthropomorphic byplay, with a personalized Eros shooting his arrows into Medea's heart, to understand Apollonius's intentions: once again, the Homeric convention has been overtaken by social developments. In Book 4 the poet directly apostrophizes Eros: "Merciless passion," he calls it, "great calam-ity, great abomination for mortals" (445 ff.), showing at once that it is the inner force, not some mythological *putto*, that he has in mind. Thus the famous scene in Book 3, Hera calling on Aphrodite to further Jason's plans by having Eros make

Medea love him (52 ff.), is mere decoration, functionally otiose, since Medea can lose her heart, and is shown losing her heart, quite well on her own, without any external divine assistance.

Book 3's delineation of that sudden, shy, bright, adolescent incandescence of Medea's—bringing with it all the physical and psychological agony that is the penalty of intense passion—has been rightly recognized as one of the *Argonautica*'s main achievements:[59]

> Like a flame that shaft burned under   286
> Her maiden heart: endless bright sidelong glances
> She darted at Jason, her breath fetched quick and labored
> In her heaving breast, all else was forgotten, her spirit
> Melted in that sweet ecstasy.

> So Love the destroyer   297
> Blazed in a coil round her heart, her mind's keen anguish
> Now flushed her soft cheeks, now drained them of all color.

> Quick beat the heart in her breast, as a shaft of sunlight   755
> Will dance on the housewall when flung up from water
> New-poured into cauldron or pail: hither and thither
> The circling ripples send it darting, a *frisson*
> Of brightness—just so her virgin heart now beat a
> Tattoo on her ribs, her eyes shed tears of pity, constant   760
> Anguish ran smoldering through her flesh, hotwired her finespun
> Nerve ends, needled into the skull's base, the deep spinal
> Cord where pain pierces sharpest when the unresting
> Passions inject their agony into the senses.   765

This is not the only passage where Apollonius, like Callimachus (p. 777 n. 48), reveals familiarity with medical symptoms;[60] but it is surely the first description in European literature of the unmistakable symptoms that herald the onset of a migraine. Hellenistic poets and artists may have become sudden experts in small children and young love,[61] but they were too sophisticated to miss the dark side of their new emotional freedom.

Apollonius's very success in his portrayal of Medea's innocent and overwhelming passion inevitably makes it all the harder for him to justify the metamorphosis of this dazzle-eyed girl into a murderous witch, who without compunction will let her paramour butcher her brother, Apsyrtos (4.450–81).[62] Indeed, he balks at the far grimmer version of events, described by Pherecydes (*fl.* 5th c.) and known to the Apollonian scholiasts, according to which Medea herself cut Apsyrtos into bloody pieces and scattered them behind *Argo* to delay pursuit.[63] Yet the one violent passion is the inverted analogue of the other. It is psychologically right that the tongue-tied silence of that first confrontation between Medea and Jason ("like oaks or tall pines /

That stand stilly side by side, earthrooted in the mountains / On a windless day")[64] should be picked up by their later, very different speechlessness,[65] when they throw themselves as suppliants on Circe's mercy, and Circe knows, instantly, as Jason grounds his great sword, that the trouble here is murder.

Jason is scared of Medea when she rounds on him with charges of betrayal (4.355 ff., esp. 395 ff.); but then Jason, at intervals, is scared of everything. He sheds tears as he sails (1.535); his mother begs him not to go (1.268 ff.), in antiheroic contrast to Thetis's treatment of Achilles. When Idas taunts him, he is lost for words (1.460). More than once he is accused of shiftlessness, resourcelessness: he is *amēchanos*.[66] After the incident of the Clashing Rocks in Book 2 he says he should never have accepted the quest at all (624 ff.). He had, in fact, only been elected leader by default; Heracles was the obvious choice, but told the Argonauts to choose Jason instead, since the expedition had been mounted on his account. When Heracles is left behind, and a mutiny ensues, Jason sits there in tears, taking insults from Telemon: it requires the intervention of Glaucus the sea god to restore discipline (1.1284–1343). While Polydeuces is settling the boxer Amycus's hash (style and skill matched against mere muscle-bound brutality), while Zetes and Calaïs are chasing the Harpies (2.1–300), Jason is inactive. Phineus's prophecies unnerve him; the prospects ahead leave him hopeless.

It is true that Jason does snap into action when the Fleece is at last within reach, facing down Aeëtes and passing the tests—fiery bulls, dragon-teeth men—to which he is subjected (3.173 ff.). Yet at first he is so alarmed at the thought of these ordeals that a whole string of fellow Argonauts offer to take his place (3.491–520), and he only in the end wins through by courtesy of Medea and her magic. Like so many ancient magicians, Medea can save others, but not herself: Jason, radiant with sex, one calculating eye on the Fleece (which, with a pleasant touch of pre-Freudian symbolism, gets to be spread, gold and all, on their wedding couch),[67] has no difficulty in knocking off this infatuated virgin, for all her spells. This—apart from winning the Fleece, a part of the *Ur*-myth that could hardly be omitted—remains his only positive achievement, except for impregnating Hypsipyle and accidentally killing his own recent host during a night battle (1.1032–35). What was Apollonius thinking of when he created such a character?

My own guess is that he was venturing an essay in realism, analogous to those unflattering portraits that were now all the rage (above, p. 104): the battered boxer, the drunken old slattern. How, he must have asked himself, would a voyage of this sort *really* have been, minus the heroic and formulaic conventions? How would a sensitive, weak-willed, mildly impractical man—a man, in fact, not entirely unlike an Alexandrian scholar—react to that series of strange circumstances presupposed by the traditional legend as, say, Pindar knew it? Probably, if the truth were told, much as this Jason does. The age of heroes is over: fighting is more often than not left to the professionals, and most adventures are the inner ones of the mind. There is ample evidence in the *Argonautica* of such a mind at work. The awareness is, in essence, romantic, even though this romanticism has to work against the ingrained

Fig. 78. Dragon disgorging Jason while Athena looks on: red-figure Attic cup by
Douris (ca. 480 B.C.). Note the tutelary but lively owl in Athena's left hand, and the
Golden Fleece hanging in the background. This Jonah-like episode, despite
Apollonius's liking for exotic motifs, never made it into the *Argonautica*.
Vatican Museums. Photo Alinari.

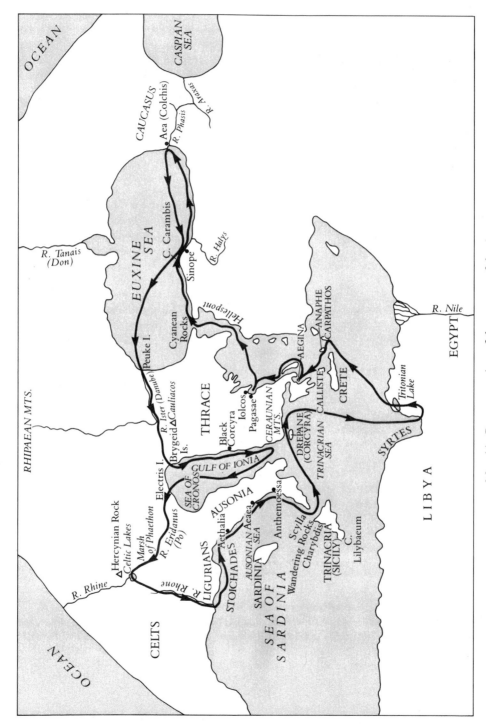

Map 14. Reconstruction of the voyage of the Argonauts.

skepticism of a scholar who knows very well that there is an explanation, an *aition*, for everything: the Golden Fleece was really used for panning by prospectors; the Harpies were kites and buzzards; *Argo*'s voyage to Colchis was part pirate raid, part trading venture.

Paradoxically, what holds Apollonius's epic venture together, the powerful colloid behind his fragmented library research, is the old traditional legend with which he had to work: the adventure-studded voyage along the southern shore of the Black Sea, the winning of the Fleece and of Medea, the Argonauts' perilous homeward journey. As quests go, this is a winner: the story grips us, whatever digressions there may be along the way, however improbable the details. (Apollonius himself seems incredulous at the thought of *Argo*'s twelve-day portage, and firmly attributes responsibility to the Muses.)[68] Medea's passion might be less striking with a more sympathetic hero. As it is, we do not need to have the story continued once the Argonauts step ashore again at Pagasae, and the unifying fellowship engendered by *Argo* herself is broken up. We know, only too well—and so, *a fortiori*, did Apollonius's original audience—just how this Jason, this Medea, will behave under the stresses of ambition and desire and jealousy in Corinth.

To that extent Apollonius succeeded, I think, better than he knew, or most modern scholarship has been disposed to admit. We devour the story: the *Argonautica* is almost impossible to put down once you start it, pedantries, digressions, *aitia* and all. At one level that episodic quality of which critics have complained is built into any quest legend from its foundations. Adventures getting there, adventures coming back: that, *au fond*, is not so very different a formula from the *Odyssey*'s. Many of the adventures, too, are no less intriguing. There is the interlude among those homicidal, but presumably no longer malodorous, ladies of Lemnos: "You aren't coming back," says Hypsipyle; and Jason, with the politician's instinct for ignoring awkward statements, concedes the point by instructing her, if she bears a son, "Send it to my parents."[69] There is the rape of Hylas by the water nymphs;[70] there are the episodes of Phineus and the Harpies and the Clashing Rocks;[71] above all, there is that strange incantatory flight of the Argonauts, pursued by the men of Colchis, that forms the bulk of Book 4.

What Apollonius achieved here was a classic of escape literature not only in the physical sense, but as the apotheosis of all those Euripidean choruses that wanted to be somewhere else, somewhere mythical and romantic, away from the grim realities of life here and now. At one level it is a nightmare, an anxiety dream: however far they retreat into the watery and labyrinthine womb of those interconnecting European waterways, sometimes by nonexistent routes, the pursuers always head them off.[72] But it is also, at a still-deeper level, a paradigm of the whole Alexandrian search for *ataraxia*. To return to one's familiar first beginnings (and perhaps, as Eliot hinted, to know the place for the first time), to close the circle at last, *diminuendo*, on the beach at Pagasae, is an achievement in itself. It reminds me of Parer and M'Intosh, Day Lewis's two heroic aviators in "A Time to Dance," who, their epic flight to Australia at last achieved, their flimsy plane a wreck, "stepped out of the broken / Body, and went away."[73]

Fig. 79. J. W. Waterhouse's *Hylas and the Nymphs:* Greek mythology as refracted
through late-Victorian English prurience and gloomy summer weather.
Manchester City Art Gallery.

Another point that needs stressing is the rootlessness of these Greek writers,
living in Egypt yet never assimilated to the indigenous culture, and creating their
own, in a sense, at second hand. I suspect that Apollonius had some interest, antiquarian or otherwise, in Egyptian matters: hence, in part, Callimachus's label for
him, "Ibis." How, asked the Psalmist, shall we sing the Lord's song in a strange
land? And how, in their luxurious enclave or ghetto, were these Egyptian (or
Cyrenaic) Greeks to maintain the matrix of sustaining myth that grew up amid warring Mycenaean baronies in central Greece and the Peloponnese? The retreat from
reality into a complex aetiological obscurantism must, for such *déraciné* intellectuals,
have offered an almost irresistible temptation, aptly symbolized by *Argo*'s flight.
Their intellectual superiority to the mythic heritage was equaled only by their desperate psychological need for the comfort that it offered: the linkage between earth
and heaven, a sense of cosmic perspective, of chthonian roots. It was by assuaging
this hunger that Stoicism later achieved its greatest success (pp. 631–32).

So the Argonauts, after trials and tribulations, end where they set out, and (in a
rather different sense from Odysseus) are happy to do so. *In my end is my beginning.*
They have challenged the exclusive validity of the old heroic *ēthos:* their own successes have been based on group cooperation. If home as the goal echoes the *Odyssey*
(and with Alexandria such a hive of Homeric scholarship it would be odd if that
pattern, at least, did not survive), the group venture is a wistful echo, equally obsolete, of the lost democratic ideal. In either case the attitude is retrospective, nostalgic, a search for *temps perdu*, the marvelous journey vouchsafed by Cavafy's Ithaca.[74]

But, as readers of Proust well know, such explorations can be highly enjoyable for the reader, and the *Argonautica* is no exception. Even the peripheral just-so stories have their own weird charm: why the Etesian winds blow for forty days, how the bronze giant, Talos, had an Achilles' heel (or ankle), what causes the formation of amber, how Sinope outwitted her divine would-be lovers.[75] Even at the very end of the poem, when the Argonauts—only ten lines of text away from Pagasae—land on the beach at Aigina, we get a quick *aition* to explain why the islanders have a footrace in which the contestants carry full waterpots (4.1765–72). Sometimes the mythic digressions are not even aetiological, but simply inserted for local color, like the glimpse of the eagle on its way to attack Prometheus, and then "the agonized cry of Prometheus as his liver was torn away" (2.1247–59). Orpheus's song, similarly, begins, for no very compelling reason, with an Empedoclean cosmogony (1.496 ff.).

The visual effects hinting at artwork—for example, Eros and Ganymede playing at knucklebones (3.115–27)—come out strikingly in the similes. Unlike so much that affects Homeric dress in this epos, the similes—which, like Apollonius's descriptions of nature, another Alexandrian trait (p. 233), are generally, and rightly, praised—almost always echo some Homeric original: Jason as the bright but baleful star Sirius, doves fleeing before a hawk, oxen under the yoke, bees swarming from their hives, a boy caught in a flooded river.[76] There are occasional original flashes, for example the dead giants that are like ships' timbers laid by the shore to be softened for wedges (1.1003–5). Apollonius's predilection for star imagery, his frequent references to the sun and sunlight, to clouds, storms, and landscape, suggest not only strong Pindaric influence, but what might be termed a proto-Wordsworthian attitude to nature.[77] This is one regular, almost inevitable, characteristic of a developing urban society. Man has a margin of leisure, understands (and up to a point can organize and control) his environment; the forces that beset him are no longer totally unmanageable—a lesson that must have struck home with especial force in a city like Alexandria, so close to the Nile valley.

So nature, for the city-bred scholar (as opposed to the toiling peasantry), begins to take on a romantic hue, and this is faithfully reflected in the literature. Callimachus could write in his *Hecale* of[78]

> the frost-rimed first dawn, when footpads' hands are no longer
> Hunting their victims, already the morning lamps are aflicker,
> And somewhere a water-drawer is chanting his well-song,
> And those who dwell close to the highway are shot from their sleep
> By the sound of axles screeching under wagons,
> While blacksmiths firing up their forges deafen the neighbors.

Apollonius, similarly, sees the dew on the rose—an essentially romantic image—where Homer, more practical, had seen it on the wheat:[79] the impulse is now esthetic rather than utilitarian; art is breaking farther away from a working symbiosis with life. The stage is set for the full flowering of that most Hellenistic of all literary forms: the pastoral.

CHAPTER 14

EVENTS IN THE WEST:
SICILY, MAGNA GRAECIA, ROME

Despite regular economic and commercial links, the eastern and western ends of the Mediterranean had very little political contact, in any serious sense, until the middle of the third century, and even then this was largely brought about through the expansionist activities of Rome. It was Rome that steadily encroached on the wealthy cities of Campania and southern Italy, Rome whose embroilment with the great commercial empire of Carthage in the First Punic War (264–241) led to the absorption of Sicily as a Roman province, Rome whose concern to halt the depredations of Adriatic piracy brought about a Roman intervention in Illyria, and, very soon, a confrontation with Antigonid Macedonia. The impact of Alexander's conquests could not leave the West untouched, but their effect was secondary, and for the most part restricted to attempts, by local condottieri, to ape the royal pretensions of the Ptolemies and the Seleucids while operating in the old Sicilian tradition of military tyranny.[1]

The Sicilian so-called monarchies of Agathocles (317/6–289) and Hieron II (269–215) in Syracuse, though the latter in particular reveals a certain Ptolemaic panache, were not really Hellenistic, but rather an extension of the quasi-benevolent autocracy practiced in the fifth century by Hieron I and Gelon, and early in the fourth by Dionysius I. At the same time these rulers were well aware of what was going on in the eastern Aegean, and in ways sought to emulate it. When Agathocles proclaimed himself king, in 305/4, it was a deliberate bid to join the select club recently established by the Diadochoi (pp. 30–31).[2] Contacts between West and East certainly existed, for the most part in the form of a succession of Greek generals who either were invited across the Straits of Otranto by hard-pressed Greek settlers (caught between Rome and the mountain tribesmen of southern Italy), or else decided to try their luck there independently. Some of them, like Timoleon of Corinth, who liberated Syracuse from the despotic tyranny of Dionysius II (344), were reasonably enlightened men; but mostly they come over as savage, and savagely ambitious, military thugs.

The sheer record of atrocities during the fourth and third centuries, in Sicily particularly, is worse than for almost any other period of ancient history: a grisly chronicle of mass executions, public torture (on one occasion in the theater, with schoolchildren brought in to watch, since the punishment of a tyrant was held to be a highly edifying spectacle),[3] rape, pillage, and enslavement, with the Romans as the worst, but by no means the only, habitual offenders. The period with which we are here concerned, from the mid-fourth to the late third century, is chiefly important, in terms of Hellenistic history, for the progressive emergence of Rome as a powerful, and, very soon, dominant factor in the affairs of the Greek and Macedonian world. Roman involvement was directly contingent upon the military adventurism, in Sicily and Magna Graecia, of successive foreign captains: Timoleon, Alexander of Epirus, Agathocles, Pyrrhus. Hieron II, a native Syracusan (and onetime lieutenant of Pyrrhus) falls into a slightly different category (see p. 224).

By the end of the First Punic War (241), with Greek Sicily firmly in her grasp and a growing appetite for international trade, Rome was bound, sooner rather than later, to be drawn into the politics of the Hellenistic world. Political caution could not hold out for ever against commercial greed; the private sector was sure, in the long run, to force a change of policy. At the same time it seems clear that the original policy was not (as has sometimes been assumed) one of imperial expansionism. Illyrian piracy formed no more than the immediate excuse for what can be seen, in retrospect, as inevitable intervention on a major scale. Rome's *ad hoc*, initially reluctant involvement in Greek and Macedonian affairs nevertheless destroyed the delicate diplomatic balance between Ptolemies, Seleucids, and Antigonids, thus radically transforming the nature of power politics in the eastern Mediterranean. From about 200 onwards the Hellenistic kingdoms—and *a fortiori* the smaller surviving principalities or Greek *poleis*—found themselves combining, with progressively less success or confidence, to stem the tidal encroachments of this great new power, imperial despite itself. One by one the independent monarchies surrendered or were destroyed: when in 133 Attalus III of Pergamon, anxious to preempt the ambitions of his illegitimate half-brother, Aristonicus, bequeathed his entire kingdom to Rome (p. 529), he was merely being realistic (and, arguably, avoiding unnecessary bloodshed). What we must examine now is the background to this expansionism: the struggle for power in Sicily and southern Italy between about 345 and 220.

Democracy, in the Sicilian cities, with their tradition of commercial expansionism and enormous wealth (combined with bitter poverty), was an uncertain and intermittent luxury. More characteristic were the tough oligarchies and military tyrannies that we so frequently find dominating the scene.[4] Class warfare, more violent and more bloody in Sicily than elsewhere because of a huge gap between haves and have-nots, produced a volatile, unstable political pattern, with the cities largely incapable of long-term mutual cooperation. Devastation was widespread. Divide and rule, as innumerable foreign conquerors learned, offered the simplest key to control of this rich but turbulent island. The situation in Syracuse was typical. In 346, after a ten-years' ouster, Dionysius II, in vengeful mood, and not noticeably improved in his moral or philosophical outlook by Plato's tutelage, finally regained control of Syracuse, only to be blockaded by various rebels, not to mention a Car-

Map 15. Sicily.

thaginian fleet.[5] The aristocrats of Syracuse appealed first to Hicetas, the Syracusan tyrant of nearby Leontini, and then to their mother city, Corinth. The second choice proved wiser than the first.

Hicetas intrigued with Carthage, and was plainly bent on extending his own absolute power. The Corinthians, ignoring his bland assurances that no help was needed, dispatched to Syracuse a middle-aged ex-condottiere named Timoleon to restore order and deal with the Syracusans' various pressing problems.[6] Against all odds, Timoleon proved the most extraordinary success. He got rid not only of Dionysius (who was shunted off to retirement in Corinth, where he became a walking tribute to the fate of tyrants),[7] but also of several other would-be usurpers, Hicetas among them. He freed Syracuse, and beat off the Carthaginians, with whom, after the great battle of the Crimisos River, he made a working peace based on spheres of interest (339/8): the Carthaginians kept the western part of the island, but all Sicily east of the Halycus River was now under Greek rule.[8] He introduced democracy, of a sort, once more; he even got the cities of Sicily back into some kind of federation. Colonists were invited from mainland Greece—no less than sixty thousand new citizens came to Syracuse alone—and a flood of prospectors arrived to take over deserted land (e.g., at Megara Hyblaea),[9] and to boost the population of the cities with a strong, fresh Hellenic input.[10] Corinth, perhaps also acting as a middleman for other cities (and as an exchange center for their currencies), now began to import enormous quantities of Sicilian wheat and dairy produce into mainland Greece at competitive prices.[11]

Dictatorial powers over Syracuse were conferred on Timoleon by acclamation. Despite his extraordinary successes, and self-proclaimed moderation, he was really no more than a benevolent tyrant in the Peisistratean tradition. It is significant that after the Crimisos victory his ambitions became more obvious, and his rule a good deal tougher, more palpably authoritarian.[12] While no more a democrat by conviction than any of the Successors, he was, like them, more than ready to play the democratic game for so long as he found it either necessary or advantageous. Like Peisistratus, again, he depended on mercenaries, who had helped to establish his power in the first place. Though the assertion that "he was autocratic and ruthless and brutal and faithless (otherwise known as 'diplomatic')" is too strong a reaction in the other direction,[13] there can be no doubt of his unscrupulous determination in pursuit of his goals.[14] Further, though born lucky—and a true child of his age in his cultivation of Random Fortune (*Automatia*)[15]—he was not quite the genius that his own propaganda endeavored to make him out.[16]

Timoleon's good press is due in part to the historian Timaeus (ca. 356–ca. 260), whose father, Andromachus, was one of Timoleon's closest allies, and whose praise of Timoleon himself earned him a stinging reproof from Polybius.[17] This seems to have depressed Timoleon's stock a little too far, in antiquity as among modern historians.[18] Though his methods may have been fundamentally those of a *tyrannos*, he did get rid of rival minor tyrants; he did revise the laws of Syracuse on a democratic basis;[19] he symbolically destroyed the palace-fortress of Ortygia in Syracuse, home of too many despotic rulers; and even if his "restored democracy" was in fact (as has been argued) nothing but oligarchy in disguise,[20] at least he was moving in the right direction. For eight years he struggled against formidable opponents: final victory looked, and was, far from certain. The worst of his cruelty was reserved for local brigands or would-be despots, whom he determinedly stamped out. He took an unswervingly hostile line against Carthage. He knew how to win popularity while never relaxing his grip on government, an enviable talent. When he began to go blind he stepped down from office, and died a year or two later (337/6), shortly after Chaeronea, as Syracuse's most honored elder statesman.[21] At his funeral his achievements were enumerated: the overthrow of tyrants, the defeat of Carthage, the repopulation of devastated cities, the restoration of the rule of law in Greek Sicily.[22]

Immediately after his death, however, all his work was undone. His Council (*synedrion*) of Six Hundred,[23] originally an echo of Cleisthenes' Council of Five Hundred in democratic Athens, soon degenerated into a mere oligarchic faction (*hetairia*) of the wealthiest and most blue-blooded families,[24] and monopolized power in Syracuse. The result was a renewal of feuding and *stasis* (factional warfare). Throughout this period the Syracusans remained, as so often, their own worst enemies. Yet despite all this internecine fighting, both our literary and our archaeological sources confirm the growing prosperity of Sicily in the late fourth and early third centuries.[25] Agricultural production, in response to increased demand for exports, was up,[26] and the capital reserves thus acquired went into a spate of public building:[27] temples, theaters, town walls, municipal offices were all renovated or enlarged, and the cities of Gela and Acragas were refounded.

Yet the political base remained, as always, uncertain. The independent, self-determined *polis* had, as we have seen, lost all its real power in mainland Greece; in Sicily, on the other hand, it had never taken really firm hold. There was a weakness here to be exploited, a power vacuum to be filled. Predictably, Syracuse, under the uncertain control of the Six Hundred, soon fell into the hands of a military adventurer whose continuing support came from the lower classes (317/6). This was Agathocles (b. 361 at Thermae in Sicily),[28] who had first come to Syracuse at the age of eighteen, with his father, an immigrant potter from Rhegium.[29] Once again we have to be careful about our evidence, though this time in an inverse sense: the same historian, Timaeus, who glorifies Timoleon, also paints as black a picture as one could conceive of Agathocles[30]—but then, Agathocles was responsible for exiling him, just as Cleon was for exiling Thucydides a century earlier.[31] Agathocles, as a native Sicilian, seems to have modeled himself, as we might expect, on Dionysius I rather than on the Successor dynasts.[32] Though his father made good in Syracuse as a prosperous ceramics manufacturer,[33] Agathocles himself spent his early years as a mercenary, heading his own private army, a skillful and daring soldier of fortune. This did not stop him making much political capital out of his reputed skill as a potter: he was never slow to exploit the common touch. Also, like so many populist politicians, he ensured his future by marrying money: in his case the immensely wealthy widow of Damas, his patron and ex-lover.[34] Though Justin is probably wrong to present his early career as that of a pretty boy who graduated from minion

Fig. 80. Colonnade of a Doric temple of Athena (ca. 480–460 B.C.) built into the
south wall of Syracuse Cathedral.
Photo Hirmer.

to bandit by way of professional gigolo,[35] the exaggeration is perhaps not so great as some scholars have supposed.[36]

Agathocles' takeover of Syracuse was accompanied by a mass slaughter of propertied oligarchs—some four thousand died in one day[37]—and wholesale looting. He offered to resign his generalship, but was confirmed in sole power by an assembly of his elated *sans-culotte* supporters, who made him in effect dictator, with a mandate to cancel debts and redistribute land. The Spartan-led opposition to him collapsed ignominiously.[38] His ferocious cruelty seems to have been class-based throughout (it was always the oligarchs whom he decimated in his Sicilian forays, always the radical exiles whom he reinstated), and in any case abated as soon as he felt himself firmly established, from about 305 onwards. His "pretense"[39] to champion democracy was probably neither more nor less sincere than the Successors' claims to be promoting Greek freedom: what it primarily indicates is the source of his support. To get that support he must have fulfilled some, at least, of his pledges: it would be interesting to know (though the evidence is lacking) just what happened to the property of those four thousand dead oligarchs. Certainly his main opponents were the rich and the well-connected, identified in Diodorus's account as the Six Hundred, who numbered among them "all the most respectable and largest property owners," who had "governed the city during the oligarchy."[40] It is also clear that he enjoyed genuine popularity (offset by the occasional brutal purge) with the common people, since he had no bodyguard and was easily accessible at all times.[41] It is interesting that his success signaled a resurgence in Syracusan imperial ambitions.[42]

What makes Agathocles of special significance in a Hellenistic context, indeed, is his extension of activity into North Africa.[43] Driven back from Acragas to Gela, and thence to Syracuse, where he was blockaded by a Carthaginian fleet, Agathocles thereupon, with cool impudence, eluded the blockade,[44] sailed from Syracuse with a moderate-sized squadron (August 310), crossed the Libyan Sea, burned his boats, and marched on Carthage—"the first European to invade North Africa in force."[45] The odd result was that Carthage and Syracuse now found themselves faced with each other's forces simultaneously. It was at this point that Agathocles made an alliance with Ophellas, Ptolemy I's governor in Cyrene (see p. 42). There is no reason to suppose that he was deliberately abetting Ptolemy's own anti-Carthaginian policy;[46] Ophellas was an ambitious maverick, and each man probably figured on using the other for his own purposes. If so, Agathocles won hands down. He waited till Ophellas obligingly brought him cavalry, chariots, and a large infantry force. Then, with cool aplomb, he attacked and killed his new ally, and took over his entire army (309/8).[47]

After this promising start, however, Agathocles' subsequent progress was less spectacular. Forced by trouble at home to return to Sicily (an inevitable hazard) he found himself shuttling to and fro between his Syracusan and North African spheres of action, to the detriment of both. Rebellion in Sicily was followed by mutiny in his army, probably due to arrears of pay. In 306 he was forced to abandon his African venture. He made peace with Carthage on the basis of the *status quo*:[48] though his expedition had proved a failure, it was not forgotten, as the subsequent actions of

Fig. 81. Aerial view of ancient
Carthage, showing the harbors.
Photo Dr. Gus van Beek.

Pyrrhus and Rome make very clear. Then he returned home to Syracuse, where (on the basis of a war indemnity and a consignment of grain he had received as part of the deal) he gave himself the airs of a conqueror.[49] Indeed, it was soon after this that, in imitation of the Diadochoi, he declared himself king (305). Will is surely right in seeing this as a purely personal affectation, a "superficial decoration calculated to enhance the tyrant's prestige,"[50] with no imperial implications, since Agathocles' power was now by and large restricted to Syracuse.[51]

Yet his ambitions were by no means dampened. From now on he did his best to involve himself in the affairs of Greece and Egypt, perhaps as part of an ongoing effort, still, to create a strong anti-Carthaginian Greek bloc in the West under his leadership.[52] About 300 he married, as his third wife, Theoxene, the sister(?) of Magas, Ptolemy's new governor of Cyrene, and in all likelihood Ptolemy's own daughter or stepdaughter.[53] We may surmise that Ptolemy was not ungrateful to him for eliminating Ophellas, who had been showing dangerous signs of independence. Shortly after this, in any case, Agathocles moved to keep Ptolemy's enemy Cassander out of Corcyra, that key island controlling the Straits of Otranto and the Adriatic: he burned the Macedonian fleet, and occupied the island himself, displacing the royal Spartan condottiere Cleonymus, who had made it his base.[54] In a further bid for useful Greek connections he married off his daughter Lanassa to Pyrrhus (295), with Corcyra as her dowry (above, p. 126).[55] However, in 290, perhaps in renewed hope of a final confrontation with Carthage, Agathocles broke with Pyrrhus, to ally himself instead with Demetrius the Besieger.[56] Lanassa thereupon also left Pyrrhus, and went back to Corcyra, her dowry, where, and for which, Demetrius, as we have seen, in turn married her (p. 126).

All these maneuvers were in vain. Demetrius had offered to guarantee the succession of Agathocles' son, but could not prevent him being assassinated by a disgruntled half-brother, the son of the king's first wife. Agathocles, surrounded by family intrigue and, like Freud, suffering from cancer of the jaw, packed his Ptolemaic wife, Theoxene, off back to Egypt, and (since he now had no heir designate) as a last gesture before his death restored the democracy in Syracuse (289), a good way of annoying all his relatives at once, and a sure guarantee of anarchy and factionalism the moment he was gone.[57] The worst charge that can be brought against Agathocles, it has been claimed, "is that he was a mere opportunist who lived by improvisation and had no fixed policy."[58] But he was also an anachronism, the old-style local *tyrannos* with a populist following, murderous and repressive, in a new world of expansionist superpowers. His forays into southern Italy never achieved anything of value; he conquered Bruttium, but could never control the Greek cities of the mainland.[59] He was thus a transitional figure between Sicily's Greek past and Roman future.[60] Indeed, he appealed to the Romans rather more than he did to the Greeks: Scipio, the conqueror of Carthage, named him, together with Dionysius I, as the supreme example of boldness and intelligence in a statesman.

This hyperbolic claim, it is safe to say, tells us rather more about Scipio, and Roman values generally, than it does about Agathocles (or, for that matter, Dionysius). Though Agathocles made a considerable effort to learn the new rules for ambitious would-be monarchs, he never fully assimilated them. His Carthaginian expedition marked the highlight of his career, and after it he relapsed for too long into mere bloody-minded Sicilianism, a virus from which better men than he were not immune. Any larger objectives he might have had were invariably conditioned by his *idée fixe* over Carthage. At the time of his death, for instance, he was planning, and had already made extensive preparations for, another North African campaign, one object of which was to prevent the Carthaginians' importing wheat from Sicily or Sardinia.[61] The natural condition of Sicily—at once wealthy past belief in physical resources, yet isolated from the major centers of Hellenic culture and commerce—meant that if it was to move with the times, it would most probably be under external rule. Pyrrhus is reported as saying of this period that Sicily was ripe for the plucking—"for ever since Agathocles' death the whole island has been riddled with factionalism; law and order have broken down in the cities, and the demagogues are having a field day."[62]

It is a nice paradox that the last, and arguably the best, of Sicily's independent tyrants, Hieron II (ca. 306–215)—an ex-lieutenant of Pyrrhus who rose, by way of a Syracusan command, to kingship through victory[63]—should have ruled Syracuse for half a century, from 269, as a purely domestic fief, without any trace of external military adventurism; and an even nicer one that from 263, after six years of progressively less effective resistance to Roman armies (during which time he was allied with Carthage),[64] he should have switched sides, thereafter appearing as the Romans'

Fig. 82. Hieron II of Syracuse. Silver thirty-two-litra piece minted at Syracuse between 269 and 265 B.C. British Museum, London. Photo Hirmer.

Fig. 83. Philistis, wife of Hieron II. Silver sixteen-litra piece minted at Syracuse between 269 and 241 B.C. Private collection. Photo Hirmer.

sedulous client-king, regularly supplying them with grain, timber, and other basic necessities during their long struggle against the Carthaginians.[65] By the time Hieron died, what he ruled—perhaps a quarter of the island—had become a privileged enclave under treaty (renewed 247 *sine die*) in the new Roman province of Sicily; but in this way he had avoided the massacres and depredations from which the rest of Sicily had suffered, and indeed derived enough profit from his dealings with Rome (his ports and naval yards were open to Roman warships) to achieve regular representation, and victories, at the Olympic Games, to rebuild and extend Syracuse's stone theater, to erect temples, gymnasia, stoas, not to mention a splendid palace for himself on the harbor island of Ortygia, and a gigantic altar (199 × 23.5 m) on which no less than a thousand beasts could be slaughtered simultaneously.[66]

This cultural ostentation, while highly Hellenistic in flavor—we recall how he built that monstrously large ship for Ptolemy II (p. 774 n. 22)—did not make him a Hellenistic monarch. *Philanthrōpia* of his sort had been long established with those early fifth-century Deinomenid rulers Gelon and (his namesake, but probably no relation) Hieron I. Most of his public works were carried out after Rome's occupation of Sicily at the end of her first war with Carthage (241), and in a sense under the Roman aegis.[67] An early believer in the protective arm of the *pax Romana*, Hieron sold off his catapults and siege engines to the Rhodians, and concentrated on civic promotion schemes instead. He might, and did, wear the diadem, use the title of king, and represent his queen, Philistis, on his coinage (a clear borrowing from Ptolemaic practice: the case of Arsinoë II springs to mind),[68] but these practices did not *per se* make him a genuine Hellenistic monarch. He spent most of his reign, in effect, as Rome's client—privileged, but a client nevertheless. Polybius pays lavish tribute to his singlehanded success against odds, his most un-Sicilian avoidance of bloodshed, his modesty and personal temperance in the midst of luxury, his popularity with his subjects.[69] It is, nevertheless, arguable that what most appealed to Polybius about Hieron was, precisely, his wholehearted cooperation with Rome. Perhaps his most lasting contribution was the so-called *lex Hieronica*, Hieron's law, a system of tithes on grain and other products, widely regarded as equitable, and taken over by the Romans when Sicily became a province.[70] Though his overseas trade with Egypt and Rhodes enriched him and his city, it could never give him true independence.

Fig. 84. The Greek theater, Syracuse, built ca. 475 B.C. and renovated by Hieron II ca. 230.
Photo Edwin Smith.

Fig. 85. The murder of Archimedes by a Roman soldier during the capture of Syracuse, 212 B.C. This mosaic, of uncertain provenience, was once thought to be a Roman copy of a Greek painting contemporary with the event, but is now generally dated to the Renaissance.
Liebieghaus, Frankfurt am Main. Photo Marburg.

Hieron remained faithful to his Roman patrons till the end. His last known public acts were the dispatch of grain, cash, and auxiliaries to Rome after the crippling defeats at Lake Trasimene (217) and Cannae (216).[71] Soon after his death—he lived to the ripe old age of ninety-two[72]—even the semblance of freedom vanished.[73] His grandson and heir, Hieronymus, a spoiled adolescent, was maneuvered by the two leading regents into negotiations for an alliance with Carthage. This caused such alarm that opponents of the move had Hieronymus assassinated.[74] However, the pro-Carthaginian populists,[75] mistakenly assuming that Rome had been finished by Cannae, not only consolidated their power in the backlash of feeling against Hieronymus,[76] but also began to conduct raids against Roman-held territory.[77] In very short order they saw Leontini sacked (213), and Syracuse itself put under siege by a far-from-defeated Roman proconsul, Marcus Claudius Marcellus. Though that scientific genius Archimedes (p. 465) had made the city walls virtually impregnable, in

212 Syracuse was betrayed; the gates were opened, and the city sacked: Archimedes himself was one of the casualties.[78] From now on Sicily was a Roman province, and its administrators bled it even whiter than its home-grown rulers had done. As Cicero said at the trial of the island's most notorious governor, Gaius Verres, Sicily was "the first to teach our ancestors what a fine thing it is to rule over foreign nations."[79] The lesson was soon learned, and put to increasingly enthusiastic use as time went by.

We must now look back for a little to see what had been happening during these decades in Magna Graecia. At the time of Timoleon's activities in Sicily, and of Alexander the Great's expedition against the Persian empire, Alexander's brother-in-law, Alexander of Epirus, received an appeal from the people of Taras (Roman Tarentum, mod. Taranto) for help against the Messapian and Lucanian tribesmen of the hinterland, who coveted their rich plain and seaport. This was in 334, and the expedition that Alexander of Epirus mounted set a pattern. Once in Italy, the Epirot king began to get ambitions (if he had not been nursing them from the start) to conquer worlds in the West as his brother-in-law was doing in the East. He led a very similar type of army, a royal tribal muster reinforced by mercenaries, which was more than a match for any local levies. His conquests and, worse, his *rapprochement* with Rome (for a campaign against the Samnites) scared the Tarentines, and they were by no means sorry when, in 330, he got himself killed.[80]

It is true that genuine Hellenizing schemes of conquest were rare in the West. The most notorious, the Athenians' Sicilian expedition (415–413), had resulted in a catastrophic defeat for the invaders, which also served to discourage others from any similar attempt. Even so, one might have thought that the Tarentines would think twice before risking a repetition of the dangers to which they had exposed themselves by importing Alexander of Epirus: could they not see that any mercenary captain was liable to turn conquistador on his own account? Yet in 282 they sent an embassy to solicit the assistance of Pyrrhus (of all frustrated and ambitious warlords), and this time against Rome herself.[81] The Roman fleet, in defiance of an existing treaty, had trespassed in Tarentine waters; hostilities had been declared, and the Greeks wanted a first-class general to deal with Rome's legions. On this score Pyrrhus was their obvious choice. He was a brilliant and seasoned commander; he was also available—too available, they might have reflected, had they not been so eager for his services, and full of imperial dreams that would not be satisfied with service as a mere hired generalissimo. His present situation also should have given them pause for thought. After invading Macedonia with Lysimachus he had been driven out of his new fief in 285 by Lysimachus himself, and retired to his own small western kingdom (above, p. 130).[82] This was a man who would be king with a vengeance, and of considerably more than the Molossian kingdom of Epirus.

When the Tarentine ambassador reached him, early in 281, Pyrrhus nevertheless found himself in a quandary, since Lysimachus had recently been eliminated at Corupedion (p. 132). Which road should his ambition take? Should he accept this timely offer, follow where his former father-in-law Agathocles had pointed the way, and work to carve himself an empire in the West?[83] Or should he rather stay in Greece,

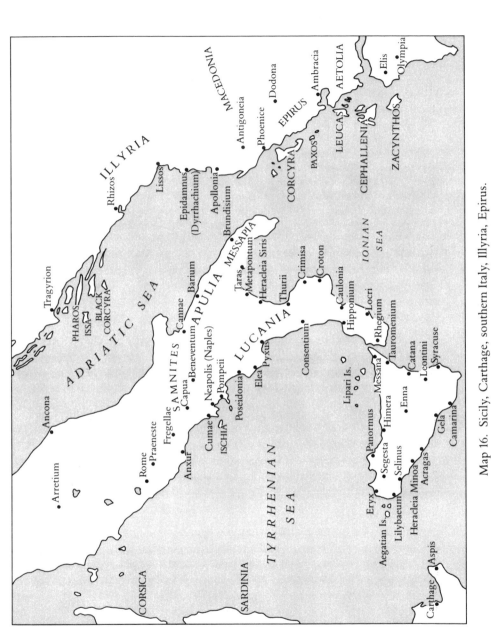

Map 16. Sicily, Carthage, southern Italy, Illyria, Epirus.

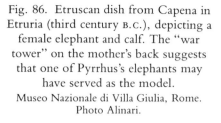

Fig. 86. Etruscan dish from Capena in Etruria (third century B.C.), depicting a female elephant and calf. The "war tower" on the mother's back suggests that one of Pyrrhus's elephants may have served as the model.
Museo Nazionale di Villa Giulia, Rome.
Photo Alinari.

and make one last bid for the Macedonian throne? In the end he accepted the Tarentine offer, perhaps with a view to having it both ways by establishing a base from which he could, eventually, return to Greece in strength.[84] It may be doubted whether he had any true appreciation of just how formidable an enemy he was up against in the Romans; worse, by 280 it was already too late to reverse Rome's progressive absorption of Magna Graecia.[85] His rivals at home—Ptolemy Keraunos, Antigonus Gonatas, Antiochus I—all heaved a collective sigh of relief at his decision, and lost no time in providing him with troops and equipment (including elephants) in order to get him out of Greece as soon as possible.[86] In return Pyrrhus gave up—at least for the moment—his designs on the Macedonian throne.

He landed in Italy in May 280. The Tarentines, who had bid for a mercenary general, found themselves invaded by a vast foreign army as well.[87] Pyrrhus, who meant business, also occupied the acropolis and garrisoned the city: this did not make him popular. It also sent a warning signal to his official opponents. For Rome, the war against Pyrrhus became the turning point in a drive to control the whole Italian peninsula,[88] whereas for Pyrrhus, that skillful yet feckless condottiere, it was simply one more episode in a hand-to-mouth career of military adventurism. To begin with he was remarkably successful, defeating two Roman consular armies in succession, at Heracleia-by-Siris and Ausculum. At one point he was actually in Latium, near Praeneste, no more than a few miles from Rome.[89] But at the urging of old Appius Claudius Caecus, who clearly understood the immense potential value of Magna Graecia, Pyrrhus's offer, made very much in the spirit of the Diadochoi, to partition Italy (with the south going to him) was rejected,[90] and soon afterwards Pyrrhus himself was lured south by an offer from Sicily to lead a campaign against the Carthaginians.[91] Ptolemy Keraunos's death almost drew him back to Greece (p. 133), but the offer of Acragas, Syracuse, and Leontini was one he could not resist. In 278, with ten thousand veterans at his back, he answered the call.

His initial reception was enthusiastic, and he soon scored up such a string of victories in western Sicily that he was hailed in some quarters as king. The Carthaginians, meanwhile, driven by a well-justified fear of Pyrrhus's ultimate intentions, sought, and obtained, a firm alliance with Rome,[92] a move that should have given him pause, but clearly did not. By 277 the only strongholds still eluding him were the western port of Lilybaeum, still firmly in Carthaginian hands, and Messana (mod. Messina), where the Mamertines—a group of independent mercenaries rather like the Catalan Grand Company in the Middle Ages—had dug themselves well in. Pyrrhus, who was no diplomat, when offered peace by Carthage (with Rome by now at her back) on the basis of the *status quo*, refused the offer, and then failed to take Lilybaeum by siege.[93] Having thus ignominiously thrown in an all-but-won hand, he returned to Italy, after quarreling rancorously with the Sicilians he had gone to help (fall 276),[94] who were in no mood to encourage another potential tyrant,[95] much less now—with Rome in the game—to support his plans for carrying the war into North Africa. The Carthaginians damaged his fleet severely during the crossing.

Once again Pyrrhus was answering an appeal for military assistance from the hard-pressed Tarentines and Samnites; once again, incredibly, there was the same basic *malentendu* between the contracting parties. What the locals wanted was a professional general who stuck to his commission; what they got, as with Alexander of Epirus, was an ambitious conquistador, and, worse, this time one who proved no match for the opposition. Pyrrhus spent the winter in Taras, getting his army ready for a spring offensive. But in the summer of 275 he was soundly beaten at Beneventum (then Maleventum, but renamed in honor of the Roman victory) by Manius Curius Dentatus, who had taken the trouble to learn how elephants should be dealt with.[96] It was in these less than auspicious circumstances that Pyrrhus returned to Greece to try his luck against Antigonus Gonatas (above, pp. 143 ff.). He had not abandoned his Western dream altogether: he left his son Helenus and a garrison force behind in Taras. But he himself never came back, and the following year he withdrew most of his troops from Italy. In 272, answering one appeal for help too many, he was knocked out by that old lady's well-aimed tile in Argos (above, p. 144).[97] In the same year the Romans took Taras, which was surrendered to them by Pyrrhus's skeleton garrison.[98]

Both Rome and Carthage benefited from Pyrrhus's removal; and with his going the last chance for a Greek recovery in the West vanished. The unification of all Italy under Rome was now only a matter of time. Ptolemy II, always alert to Mediterranean realities, promptly sent an embassy to this rising, indeed risen, power, becoming the first of the Hellenistic monarchs to cultivate a policy of friendship toward Rome, or to recognize her growing importance in international affairs.[99] As subsequent events made plain, Ptolemy had displayed shrewd foresight. Rhegium fell in 270, and Brundisium (mod. Brindisi) three years later. Sicily beckoned alluringly. In 264, partly through greed, partly by accident, Rome lurched into the first of her three drawn-out wars with Carthage.

The course of that great and draining struggle does not directly concern us here. But Rome emerged from it the ruler of Sicily, proceeded to occupy Sardinia and Corsica, and in 229 turned, at last, eastward to Illyria. If the Greeks of the West played no great role, either politically or culturally, in the development of the Hellenistic world—but then there had been no Alexander to open up a vast empire for their exploitation—at least, through a series of accidents, they had been in part responsible for bringing about the confrontation of that world with its ultimate nemesis: Rome.

CHAPTER 15

URBANIZED PASTORALISM, OR VICE VERSA: THE *IDYLLS* OF THEOCRITUS, THE *MIMES* OF HERODAS

There is a pleasant paradox about pastoral poetry: it is set in the countryside (or at least in a formalized idyllic landscape), its ideals are rural and bucolic, it glorifies summer ripeness—and it is invariably produced by urban intellectuals who have never themselves handled a spade, much less herded sheep, goats, or cattle, in their lives. It is, clearly, a perennial form of literary and social escapism, and one that may have concealed political undertones. It grafts a kind of yearning idealism onto a reality that was, in fact, peculiarly harsh and unrewarding. Thanks to Virgil, we tend today to think of Arcadia as Poussin saw it, the symbol of happy innocence, a golden dreamland of timeless shepherds (and even in Virgil a composite idealization of the Po valley and the hills of southern Italy).[1] The real Arcadia was, and is, one of the remotest and most stubbornly backward areas in all Greece. It is possible that this very remoteness attracted Hellenistic poets searching for country roots, archaic customs, exotic *aitia*. The association of Arcadia with Pan will also have helped.[2] Elements of the lost Golden Age were thought to survive among Arcadians: their simplicity and egalitarianism (a plain diet, community at feasts between master and slave) were regularly singled out for comment.[3] Their homeland was distant, unwalled, mysterious, "an ancient Shangri-La."[4]

The contrast between reality and symbol is instructive. We have to admit, urban mutations that we are, that the myth possesses immense durability and power: its antirealism has never interfered with its appeal, and may indeed have enhanced it. The cliché image of nymphs and shepherds—the former decorative and peripheral, the latter often homoerotic—in a stylized pastoral setting has lasted through centuries of European literature, and spilled over into the visual, even the musical, arts. The piping in Theocritus, the wind whispering through the pine trees, is the direct ancestor of *L'Après-midi d'un Faune*.[5] Such a vision is closely bound up with the

233

equally seductive dream of a lost Golden Age, or indeed of the millennium still to come: the nostalgia, or hope, for simple virtues, uncomplicated living, plain home-grown food, basic country values. The dream still haunts us today: the popularity of the western is one manifestation of it.[6] We yearn for some kind of prelapsarian para-dise. Today this haven has acquired familiar characteristics. It is ecologically bal-anced, free of industrial pollution and acid rain, full of stone-ground bread (if not homespun clothes), not to mention homespun platitudes. It is the motivating force behind the commune and, in one sense, the kibbutz. It explains all those executives who, in one way or another, go back to the land over the weekend or during vaca-tions. That this should be an exclusively urban phenomenon is no accident. The real shepherd or farmer knows, too well, that his life is poor, dangerous, backbreaking, and without respite. Leisure plays little part in it. Hesiod was under no illusions whatsoever on this score,[7] and a modern Greek shepherd, a poor dirt farmer any-where, will echo his sentiments.

The pastoral dream, then, is the special property of the gentleman poet, living on patronage from a Ptolemy or an Augustus: when Marie-Antoinette played at being a milkmaid, the charade did not require her to get up at four in the morning and milk obdurate cows in freezing weather with chilblained hands. Yet—and this is the odd thing—the pastoral tradition did derive, originally, from a genuinely rural and traditional folk art (piping, dancing, singing competitions), and the moral ideal it propounds has a good deal to be said for it. It probably, in the last resort, *is* better to drop with fatigue from hoeing potatoes than to be poisoned, slowly, by synthetic food additives and carbon monoxide. Simple life, simple values do have the edge in many ways over cultured urbanism. What has always tended to cloud the issue is the fact that the ideal projected by city-dwelling intellectuals tended, very soon, to be-come formalized in a literary genre with its own rules, which floated it free, in a somewhat rootless fashion, from its actual origins.

The country has always generated its particular functional art forms. In Greece, both ancient and modern, we know of milling songs, sowing songs, reaping songs, songs for harvest and grape treading: these are, strictly speaking, agricultural rather than pastoral, the distinction being between the life of plowing and arable cultivation on the one hand, and the breeding of herds, whether cattle, sheep, or goats, on the other. All formal pastoral poetry stems from the latter activity (Theocritus has plenty about herding, only one idyll involving reapers). Since one of the essential ingredients of the myth is leisure (literary rentiers tend to bring their own luggage with them when they go exploring), this is not altogether surprising. No one could even pretend that a field laborer has an easy time of it; but there are plenty, field laborers included, who will cheerfully tell you that the herdsman's life is almost as ideal as the bucolic poets make it out. To correct this misapprehension one need only study the primitive shepherds and goatherds, often seasonally transhumant, of Greece and Yugoslavia and Albania.[8] Sleepless nights in midwinter during the lamb-ing season, the ravages of wolves and disease, long hours exposed to bitter cold and driving rain, the rescue of beasts from deep and dangerous crevasses, the setting of broken limbs—these are not activities that feature in the literary pastoral tradition, where the sun is always shining and the flocks, for long stretches, can take care of themselves.

Yet the sun did shine, and not only in summer; there were times, for long stretches, when the pastoral scene was much as the poets represent it. Herding is a lonely business, and the shepherd's pipe must be one of the oldest forms of solo entertainment in the world. (Modern shepherds carry transistor radios, even sport the occasional Sony Walkman, another symbolic confrontation of cultures.) A herdsman played to while away the time. If he had a companion, they would play together or in turn, sing rival songs, cap one another's efforts. There is no reason to believe that Theocritus was doing anything but picking up common tradition when he made his swains exchange gossip about their sex lives, or even have sex with each other.[9] The nexus of associations between goats, sex, shepherds, and Pan is assuredly no accident. Nor is the connection of Pan with the dangerous noon hour, when the sun is high, shade limited, the air in summer sultry, and the siesta liable to bring bad dreams, often of an erotic sort.[10] Panic terror and the sexual drive are inextricably linked. There is also, of course, that other solace of the lonely, no less popular with herdsmen than with any other isolated group: no accident, again, that among his other attributes Pan should have been associated with masturbation.[11]

Most of these phenomena show up, to some extent formalized, in the *Idylls* of Theocritus. Thus he is drawing on a genuine tradition, not merely rehashing literary models: in that sense his roots go deep. He is an early pioneer (if not the originator) of the pastoral idyll, at a point when reality can break in still: today it is generally assumed that it was he who "established and codified the landscape,"[12] though in antiquity he was regarded as preeminent in the genre rather than as its originator.[13] It seems indisputable that he based his inspiration on the actual habits, observed at an impressionable age, of Sicilian herdsmen.[14] The patterned repetition of key lines is "characteristic of folksongs, games, wedding-songs, lullabies, spells and other substitute categories of poetry,"[15] and Theocritus may well have adapted this kind of traditional oral poetry for his own purposes. Singing matches, for instance, are a genuine feature of the pastoral tradition in Sicily.[16] Yet the process of codification was literary enough, and we can see how soon formal sclerosis set in by a comparison with the later work of Bion and Moschus—or indeed of Virgil in the *Eclogues*. Despite his originality, Theocritus was no more immune than his contemporaries from the curious attitude to literature that we have already noticed among Hellenistic intellectuals (p. 172), "as if its province had been defined at some date in the past and it had been forbidden to advance in certain directions or to penetrate below a certain phenomenological level."[17]

In a sense what Theocritus created was a subbranch of epic, crossed with mime.[18] Like Callimachus, he was adept at reducing heroic material to a mundane or quotidian level, while at the same time also introducing touches of low-life realism or colloquial speech, and "surrounding his lowly characters with a literary dimension by citing mythological precedent for their humdrum, prosaic activities."[19] At the same time, the genesis of Theocritean country song is probably not altogether remote from that of American country-western. We certainly find Theocritus's herdsmen engaged in all the traditional pursuits: competing in song or on their pipes, whittling away at woodcarving to pass the time, serenading girls while some friend watches the flock, exchanging reminiscences and good-natured (or not so good-natured) banter, talking about, or practicing, barnyard sex of the sort popular in rural areas. They drink, they are malicious gossips; they are not above beating up women out of jealousy.[20] They know all about hopeless passion, which, as good Greeks, they feel to be an encumbrance: to be really enjoyable, sex should stand on a par with eating and drinking. The example of the animals they herd is a clear inspiration to them. If half the joy of the pastoral myth derives from its emotional simplicity, half also depends on its obsession with rude productive plenty, the Cockaigne vision: pailfuls of milk, sweet dripping honeycombs, sheepskin jackets, great round cheeses, apples and plums galore, wine in brimming bowls, Demeter "with wheatsheaves and poppies in either hand."[21]

This ideal had been established long before Theocritus's day. The plays of Aristophanes, especially those from his earlier period, emphasize the pleasures of rural peace against the harsh demands of war. A striking example is *The Acharnians* (425), in which a simple, but far from *simpliste*, old countryman, Dicaeopolis, makes his own private peace with Sparta, while the chorus talks nostalgically of the pleasures of planting vines and figs and olives.[22] Other comedies of the period have numerous references to the kind of never-never land where the rivers run with wine or soup, and thrushes pop themselves, grilled, into people's mouths of their own accord, and automation, of a purely magical kind, has removed the need for hard work.[23] If there is a core of historical truth behind the Golden Age myth, it probably looks back to the Paleolithic and Mesolithic periods, when the nomad hunters, who lived off wild fruit and crops and berries as well as the animals and fish they speared or trapped, were slowly being replaced by agriculturalists living in settled communities, plowing, sowing, bound to a year-long calendar of backbreaking toil, faithfully reflected in Hesiod's *Works and Days*.[24]

It is surely no accident that the ideal is always pastoral, never agricultural (at least not until Virgil's day, and only then as propaganda for Augustus's back-to-the-land movement):[25] nymphs and shepherds, not nymphs and field hands, much less the three-tined rectitude of Grant Wood's *American Gothic*. To peasants scratching a bare living from the soil, the herdsman's or hunter's life must have seemed idyllic indeed, Arcadian in the ideal sense. To chase deer, spear fish, or, later, to sit on a warm thyme-scented hillside piping about Amaryllis or Galatea while the sheep and goats got on with feeding themselves—what bliss. Hesiod faced the grim facts of a Greek winter, the searing cold northers that could "skin an ox";[26] the Theocritean tradition conspired to pretend that winter did not exist, that the Greek countryside was bathed in eternal sunshine, a fiction maintained to this day by the National Tourist Board. Even Aristotle regarded the shepherd's life as one of supreme idleness, with hunters, brigands(!), fishermen, and fowlers coming next, in descending order, and the wretched peasant, as always, the drudge among food gatherers.[27]

This, then, was the formal genre that Theocritus crystallized, and passed on, ultimately, to Sannazzaro, Shakespeare, Milton, Spenser, and their ever more artificial and literary successors, till the Industrial Revolution burned the heart out of such sugary conceits. Theocritus himself had not acquired the stylized sentimentality that makes Virgil's *Eclogues* so offensive in places; but he was a city dweller, a poet, an intellectual, whose love affair with the countryside was conducted in vacation time. He may have longed for the simple life, may have dreamed of getting back to nature; but he was not dependent on nature for his livelihood. In one sense this enskyment of rural simplicity was really an attack on the vast, impersonal cities of the Hellenistic world. Ever since Socrates' day the Cynics, to look no farther, had been attacking the values of *polis* and, *a fortiori*, megalopolis, urbanism. As real political power declined, individualism and quietism, contracting out of the rat race, became increasingly attractive, and were symbolized by the physical rejection of town for country.

Despite their realistic associations, Theocritus's shepherds, it has been well said, remain "idealised types unencumbered by real herds or interests beyond their erotic fancies. Their song flows forth in faultless hexameters. They are better lovers and poets than shepherds."[28] Not that this conscious stylization prevented quite a few delicate—and class-conscious—Alexandrian critics and their successors from asserting that Theocritus's herdsmen were too real, that their cheerful chat about sheepskins and sodomy gave off an improper smell of the midden, that they were not literary enough. This probably explains the curious and, to my mind, wholly erroneous modern determination to make Hellenistic pastoral poetry the begetter of the pathetic fallacy, that odd habit (first labeled by Ruskin)[29] of attributing to nature, both animate and inanimate, human characteristics or reactions, especially in response to the vicissitudes of living persons.[30]

Yet two points strike one instantly about such a claim. First, cases of the true pathetic fallacy in Hellenistic pastoral are surprisingly rare. The *Lament for Bion*, a late work, wrongly attributed to Moschus (*fl.* 150), and in fact probably composed (ca. 50?) by some follower of Bion himself, is the best-known, and most often cited, example.[31] The whole of nature—rivers and orchards, rocks, flocks, and birds—is here summoned to lament the dead poet. It is the pathetic fallacy run wild. Yet this poem cannot be duplicated anywhere else: it is unique. Bion's own *Lament for Adonis*[32] contains only one instance of the figure,[33] with mountains, woods, and springs weeping for Adonis; and Theocritus is almost equally sparing: Daphnis is mourned by his herds, by mountains, by oaks, but also howled over, in natural style, by wolves and jackals.[34] When the poet invites all nature, in a familiar *adynaton*,[35] to reverse the rules of the natural order through grief, with owls hooting to nightingales, brambles bearing violets, and pears growing on pines,[36] there is no indication that this bizarre appeal is answered. Theocritus, indeed, goes out of his way to avoid the pathetic fallacy, and at least one salutary warning has been voiced against the dangers of applying "the nineteenth-century yardstick, product of realism and scientism" in an ancient Greek context.[37]

Second, and in contrast, there is no evidence to support, and much against, the theory that the pathetic fallacy had its true beginning in the Hellenistic period. Insofar as the concept can be isolated, it would seem to have been around (exactly as we might suspect, given its animistic flavor) since the very dawn of history. Fifteen hundred years before Homer, in the *Epic of Gilgamesh*, mountains and rivers, wild ass and gazelle, lion and leopard, all weep—wild answering to wild—for the dead Enkidu.[38] Anthropomorphism allows the river Xanthus every kind of human reaction in its fight with Achilles;[39] the lovemaking of Zeus and Hera induces joyful fertility in the blossoming earth,[40] a passage with strong undertones of sympathetic magic. This last example has particular importance for us, since in the Hellenistic period it was, precisely, that aspect of the pathetic fallacy as index of a universal sympathy between nature and mankind, microcosm and macrocosm, that was picked up and developed by Stoicism (below, p. 633). The absolute fatalism in the notion of the *heimarmenē*, man's ineluctable impermanence, the brief life sparked from an eternal sleep,[41] was to be offset by the sympathy for that impermanence supposedly inherent in the natural order:[42]

> Begin, Sicilian Muses, begin your lamentation!
> Ever when mallows perish along the garden rows, or
> Green parsley, or curly sprouting dill, thereafter
> They come back to life, enjoy another year's growing: yet
> We men, big and strong though we are, yes, and clever,
> That first death we die, we sleep on, deaf, heedless,
> In the hollow earth, a long sleep, sans end or waking.
> (*Lament for Bion*, 98–104)

The Stoic world order, aiming to fill a gap left by the now largely discredited (and uncomfortably anthropomorphic) Olympians, reverted, in paradoxical fashion, to something in essence much older, a numinous universal pantheism, in which the natural order was bonding agent as well as generic force. To describe this world view in terms of Ruskin's pathetic fallacy involves severe limitations, and can be, on occasion, very misleading.

As a pioneer in the pastoral genre, Theocritus enjoyed certain real advantages. Largely spared the problem of reshaping a literary heritage, he was in a good position to dictate that heritage himself, to achieve "an Alexandrian rationalisation of loosely established forms."[43] He stands at the very edge of the formal, romanticized pastoral landscape, with Hesiod's real-life drudgery still lurking in the background. He knows a good deal of genuine country lore, including a whole mass of *Märchen*, proverbs, popular songs (still flourishing in Greece today as *laïkà tragoúdhia*), and, most interesting of all, popular magic.[44] Even if this is simply an aspect, comparable to Kazantzakis's regional borrowings in his *Odyssey*, of the Alexandrian quest for realism, it is singularly convincing. At the same time the dark side of the herdsman's life is played down: destructive mercenaries, famine, freezing sleet, buzzards, spontaneous abortions do not figure prominently in the *Idylls*. Instead we are treated to the harvest-home dream of fertility and abundance, a perpetual shimmering cloudless noontide. The pastoral dream was what appealed to the Graeco-Roman world: of all the Hellenistic escape routes, this one proved by far the most popular.

Rightly or wrongly, the piping sunlit shepherd was associated with the idea of leisured idleness, what the Greeks called *hēsychia* and the Romans *otium*—"vacation, freedom, escape from pressing business, particularly a business with overtones of death."[45] From here it was only a short step to Epicurean *ataraxia*, freedom from stress and worry in an idealized utopian landscape.[46] The connection between Epicureanism and pastoralism lies in the remoteness from the mundane world of commerce and politics that the pastoral scene presupposes; and leisure, of course (as every novelist, not to mention every experimental psychologist with a cageful of rats at his disposal, is well aware), begets love, or, more particularly, sex. Fontenelle was not the only critic to see that "pastoralism is the product of a marriage between idleness and love," with hillside or riverbank as a backdrop to seduction, of boys and girls alike.[47] Theocritus's idylls addressed to boys by an aging homosexual (29, 30) have an oddly moving, Cavafy-like quality about them, a terrible consciousness of *temps perdu*:

> By your soft lips I beseech you,
> Remember that you, too, were younger
> A year ago, that before we can spit we're old
> And wrinkled: youth once fled can never
> Be caught back again, it wears wings on its back
> And we are slow to run down things that fly.
>   (*Id.* 29.25–30)

The urban–rural tension sometimes intrudes, and it can have a timeless, class-conscious component. In *Idyll* 20, for instance (whether spurious or not makes no difference to this particular argument: the idea was in the air), a city girl rejects a herdsman because of his chapped lips, black hands, and filthy smell (9–10); nearly two centuries earlier, in Aristophanes' *Clouds* (423), the rich old farmer Strepsiades' socially superior wife was faced with an identical problem: money may talk, but it can also stink, sometimes strongly enough to turn the stomach of even the hardiest gold digger.[48] Such flashes of uncomfortable realism, however, are comparatively rare. For the most part Theocritus's pastoral characters have no real interests except their own intense emotions: in this they foreshadow the attitudes and behavior patterns common in nineteenth-century European fiction, and probably reflect similar bourgeois assumptions in their creators.

The concept of the countryside as an ideal retreat, embodying a kind of basic vitality unattainable by man in the *polis*, can be traced back at least as far as Plato's *Phaedrus*, but it took Theocritus to get the pastoral dream launched on its long literary career.[49] By Virgil's day, as we have seen, sentimentalized and symbolic shepherds—non-smelly, esthetic, sheepless—were highly fashionable. The late (2d c. A.D.?) Greek romance *Daphnis and Chloë* even has a young pastoral couple too innocent to know about sex, the ultimate paradoxical joke to anyone brought up within reach of a farm. The way was being made ready for Marie-Antoinette and her Watteauesque milkmaids. Theocritus, right from the beginning, offers a mannered complexity of style in elegant contrast to the simple life that he is ostensibly celebrating: many of his idylls are as richly ornamented as fine Hellenistic jewelry. John Ferguson draws a fascinating parallel between the mannered pseudo simplicity of Theocritus and a famous diadem from Canosa, in southeastern Italy, "covered with exquisite ornamentation in the form of artificial flowers and leaves formed of gold, enamel, and precious stones."[50] Those familiar with the later work of Yeats will at once connect such a phenomenon with his great Byzantium poems, and reflect that pastoral mannerism has an odd history, and crops up in unexpected places.

We know little about Theocritus himself, and even that is both confused and ambivalent.[51] He was probably born between 310 and 300, and died about 260:[52] his career thus coincided with the golden age of Alexandrian culture under Ptolemy II, and Callimachus, Aratus, and Apollonius were his near-contemporaries. He was a native of Syracuse in Sicily,[53] spent some time on the island of Cos,[54] and rather more in Alexandria. On Cos he came under the influence of Philetas:[55] *Idyll* 7—a program piece set on the island, and referring to Philetas as an already established poet (40)—purports to be autobiographical, and describes a group of literary friends celebrating harvest festival with songs and good cheer. It has been suggested that the first seven idylls, with their predominantly bucolic mode, form the output of Theocritus's "Cos period,"[56] and the theory is in many ways attractive, since no early work can be shown to have been written in Sicily, but almost all show acquaintance with the eastern Aegean.[57] This does, however, leave the early Syracusan period an unavoidable blank. On the other hand, the highly disturbed conditions prevalent in Sicily during Theocritus's lifetime (above, p. 217), with devastation and brigandage matters of common occurrence, would not be conducive to pastoral fantasy—hungry mercenaries being all too liable to slaughter sheep or cattle[58]—and may well have brought about Theocritus's emigration.

In 275/4, when Hieron II first came to power in Syracuse (as generalissimo but not, as yet, king),[59] Theocritus made a bid for his patronage with *Idyll* 16.[60] In these hexameters echoes of Pindaric and Simonidean lyrics abound, loaded flattery for Hieron, since his namesake in the fifth century had been a great patron of the arts, commissioning work from Pindar, among others. The approach suggests expertise in the business of landing patrons: this is no prentice work. However, Hieron remained obdurate: he had more urgent matters on his mind just then, including an imminent campaign against the Carthaginians,[61] duly noted by the hopeful poet, who portrays them as trembling for fear, while Hieron himself (80–81) "girds him like the heroes of old, with horsehair crest shadowing his helmet." (His victory, and subsequent Carthaginian alliance, were still clearly in the future at the time of writing.) Not even Theocritus's picture of his poems as Graces, come home empty-handed from their quest for patronage, and crouching in the bottom of their box (5–12), stirred Hieron's heart. The poet's attack, in the process of touting for patronage, on contemporary commercialism is both vivid and socially revealing, a confirmation of trends we have already observed:

> Where's such a patron today? Who'll reward his praise-singer?
> I cannot tell, for no longer, as in old times, are men zealous
> To be praised for fine deeds, but by gain are overmastered.
> Each keeps hand close in pocket, casting round for new income,

Wouldn't rub off the very tarnish from his cash as a present,
but is quick with the old excuses: "Charity starts at home; I'd
Be glad of a handout myself," or "The gods reward poets,"
Or "Homer's enough for all; who'd listen to anyone
Else?" or "The finest poet's the one who duns me for nothing."

(*Id.* 16.13–21)

When Theocritus turned his attention to Ptolemy II, however, he was far more successful. Ptolemy brought him to Alexandria, and supported him:[62] in return Theocritus began to turn out poems that were less purely pastoral, more grandiose propaganda for Ptolemy's monarchy. *Idyll* 17 is entirely devoted to this theme (see p. 146): the clear parallel drawn between Ptolemy and Zeus (1–4, 131 ff.) cannot but remind us of Callimachus (p. 172).[63] It is odd that the unsuccessful bid for Hieron's support should have turned out so much better a poem than the "stiff, conventional, sycophantic" tribute to Ptolemy,[64] including the careful handling of his incestuous marriage (128 ff.), here legitimized by reference to the *hieros gamos* of Zeus and Hera. There is similar blatant flattery inserted elsewhere: in *Idyll* 14, for example, we find Thyonichus advising his lovelorn friend Aeschinas that if he wants employment as a mercenary (that regular fallback for the Hellenistic unemployed), or indeed patronage of any kind, Ptolemy is his man—generous, kind, cultured, gallant, a reliable paymaster (58–64). In *Idyll* 15 (which reveals close personal familiarity with Alexandria) there is no less starry-eyed a description of entertainment put on in the royal palace by Queen Arsinoë (21–23, 78 ff.).[65] It is all a long way from the earthy rural innocence that forms a leitmotif in the earlier, more truly bucolic, idylls, where literary sophistication never interferes with the promotion of country matters. In *Idyll* 4, for instance, characters get thorns in their feet (50–55: "What a tiny prick, and still it undoes a man my size!") or are caught "milling" some pretty little piece behind the barn (58 ff.), and indulge in cattle-chat (12–25) while their calves are nibbling the olive shoots (45). Theocritus has become, in effect, a court poet. There is always a price to be paid for patronage.

Where did Theocritus stand in the great literary quarrel between Callimachus and Apollonius? Very much, it would seem, on the side of Callimachus.[66] He not only avoided the large (or inflated) book, but severely limited his overall production: it is unlikely that much, if any, of his work is lost, while quite a few poems in the canon may well be spurious.[67] The key passage is in *Idyll* 7. The narrator, probably (though not certainly) a persona for Theocritus himself, seems to be under the tutelage of Philetas (40–41), and mock-modestly describes himself as no match—yet—for his teacher, but rather a frog to Philetas's sweet-singing cricket. Lycidas replies endorsing this stand, and adds:

I find about equally loathsome the builder who struggles
To raise his house as high as some tall mountain,
And those barnyard cocks of the Muses who lose their labor
Crowing away against the bard of Chios.

(*Id.* 7.45–48)

In other words, keep it short; don't try to compete with Homer. It is even possible that *Idyll* 5, ostensibly a contest, complete with insults, between Comatas the goatherd and Lacon the shepherd, carries some veiled allusions to the great literary quarrel. The accusations of theft—sheepskin coats, pipes, and whatnot (1–19)—could hint at literary plagiarism. Comatas says at one point how sad he is to see Lacon, his pupil since childhood, turn against him in this way (35 ff.), and we remember that Apollonius was said to have been taught by Callimachus (p. 203). "And when can I recall having heard or learned anything worthwhile from you, you vile and envious wretch?" Lacon inquires. To which the brief and pithy retort is: "Last time I buggered you." The contest is turned over to a third party to adjudicate: we have a match on, Lacon tells Morson, to see who's the better *boukoliastas*, singer of country songs (67–68). Comatas insists that it is his opponent who picks the quarrels (77). It is clear enough where Theocritus's sympathies lie.

Yet in the last resort, like so much Theocritean criticism, such interpretations remain no more than speculative. Seldom can any poet have put less of himself, in any direct sense, into his poetry. This impression is only reinforced by his formalism. Even his descriptions of scenery and artifacts—the cool spring, the shady pine tree, the hum of bees round the hive[68]—have an artificial quality about them. It has been suggested that what he often does is describe not so much the physical world around him as various examples of contemporary art, reality at one remove: the practice known as *ekphrasis* (p. 205). One famous, and fascinating, instance of this occurs in *Idyll* 1.[69] A shepherd's rustic cup of ivy wood (*kissybion*) is described in detail (27–55): deep, two-handled, freshly carved and waxed, with a decoration of ivy and vine leaves. The *kissybion* seems to have been something of a literary confection, as the passage devoted to it by Athenaeus makes clear.[70] It has one handle, or two, or none; it is the same as a *skyphos*, or, alternately, a *kypellon*; it is a small cup, or again, as Homer knew it, a large bowl.[71] About all that Athenaeus's sources agree upon is that it was made of ivy wood, and essentially a lower-class vessel, being used by "swineherds, shepherds, and rustics."

Thus Theocritus's description of the elaborate carving with which this *kissybion* is embellished offers one more example of epic convention refigured (above, p. 206), the more striking since there is no earlier example in literature of a mere *kissybion* being decorated at all,[72] and in particular since the scenes on the cup cannot but recall those on Homer's Shield of Achilles and the pseudo-Hesiodic Shield of Heracles.[73] The contrasts of theme are piquant and subtle. There is a glittering amplitude about the world portrayed by Homer (and imitated by pseudo-Hesiod): the circle of earth and heaven are there, marriages, the exercise of justice, warfare, and cattle-lifting, but also reapers, vintners, herdsmen, sheep at pasture, lords and ladies dancing, all ringed with the stream of Ocean. It will be noticed that Homer's picture includes the domain of Theocritus (rather than standing in simple antithesis to it), so that the effect in the *Idylls* is one of self-imposed limitations. Homer is no stranger to two men quarreling over one woman, Theocritus's opening scene (32–38), but here the erotic has wholly eclipsed the heroic, and in what follows all the scenes are of private, rural endeavor: the old fisherman gathering his net, neck muscles swelling with the effort; foxes raiding a vineyard while the boy left to guard it plaits a cricket cage. On top of this low-keyed naturalism, Theocritus has deliberately, for his own literary benefit, confused two kinds of cup, a *skyphos* and a Megarian bowl, ignoring the handles of the first in order to get in two extra scenes and an acanthus decoration, and indifferent to the fact that the second would not stand steady for milking.[74] So much for the literary visual eye in action. But the consciousness of the visual arts remains strong.

This is equally true of Theocritus's landscapes and genre scenes. In *Idyll* 15 the Adonis bower, part of the festival tableau in Ptolemy's palace, has Erotes, Amorini, flying from branch to branch, wreathed and beribboned (120–21), all just as we find them in Graeco-Roman painting.[75] Bowers, grottoes, nymphs, goats: this kind of formal pastoral landscape is instantly familiar to us from the Pompeian wall paintings.[76] A remarkable number of the Theocritean epigrams seem to be, precisely, descriptions of, or accompaniments to, painting and statues.[77] There is, once more, a paradox about the constantly reiterated criterion of realism in the visual arts (we find this in Herodas, too)—the grapes so lifelike that birds peck at them (above, p. 92)— since, of course, the technique is pure artifice, an ingenious *trompe-l'oeil* deception. False perspectives, literary pastoral: the retreat from reality greets us on every side. The bucolic scene is out of place and time, an eternal bee-loud noontide.[78] Amid oaks, willows, elms, bays, myrtles, near the obligatory cave and spring (or waterfall)—their innocence counterpointed against the sophistication of his audience[79]— Theocritus's characters compete, converse, and, intermittently, copulate, only being "recalled to business occasionally by the antics of their animals."[80]

Yet the pursuit of genuine realism existed, as we have seen, both in literature and in art: the interesting (but by no means surprising) thing is that it tended to concentrate on the city rather than the country. Good examples in Theocritus are *Idylls* 2 and 15, in which we move away from the formalized rural setting to a dramatized scene or monologue involving urban characters. An obvious visual parallel here is provided by the street scenes of the mosaicist Dioscorides of Samos, who worked in the second century B.C. but probably drew on third-century models.[81] In *The Magicians* (*Id.* 2) we watch Simaetha—whose name, interestingly, resembles those elsewhere given to cows or she-goats, with a hint of sexual libidinousness implied[82]— performing an authentic magical ritual to recover her lost lover, Delphis, slowly shifting from the obsessional circularity of passion (well symbolized by the revolving wryneck on its frame) to a mood of stoical survival and endurance, come what may.[83] In *Idyll* 15 we follow the two Syracusan housewives, Gorgo and Praxinoa, from their meeting in Praxinoa's house (complete with baby and nursemaid), through the crowded streets of Alexandria, past mounted guards and jostling Egyptians, to Ptolemy's royal palace.[84]

These idylls are, in effect, mimes,[85] the mime being a short dramatic interlude, Sicilian in origin, with emphasis on characterization rather than plot or narrative: a music-hall sketch, a slice of (usually low) life, sometimes with a single performer, sometimes with two or more. Mimes in antiquity were divided into two categories, pantomimes (*hypotheseis*) and farces (*paignia*), the former being longer, more serious, and more elaborate, the latter short, comic, and "stuffed with coarse ribaldry and scandalous gossip."[86] Plutarch's narrator in his *Dinner-Table Discussions* argues that such characteristics make mime (and Old Comedy) unsuitable as postprandial entertainment, whereas Menander is praised as highly moral (no homosexuality; vice punished, virtue rewarded), and lowbrow enough for even a soused guest to understand.[87] The most important early mimographer, Sophron of Syracuse (*fl.* ca. 450), who in literary terms was probably the founder of the genre, wrote on topics very similar to those treated by Herodas (they both, for instance, share an interest in dildos), and was actually adapted by Theocritus, who is said, in particular, to have lifted the maid, Thestylis, in *Idyll* 2 from the earlier writer:[88] the one sizable fragment of Sophron found on papyrus also, significantly, describes a sorceress and her assistant.[89]

Herodas, on the other hand, professed to be influenced by the sixth-century iambic satirist Hipponax,[90] the inventor of the choliambic ("limping") trimeter, or scazon, a line remarkable for its thumping reversed final foot; and it is true that he used both Hipponax's meter and an artificial approximation to his Ionian dialect (whereas Sophron had written in Doric shaped to a kind of rhythmic prose). Fortunately—since little of either Sophron or Hipponax survives—these progenitors are not essential to an immediate appreciation of either Herodas or Theocritus in his mimetic idylls.[91] When we compare either with some of the tantalizing papyrus fragments of mimes that have survived from antiquity,[92] it is clear that his literary standards are markedly superior to theirs. These were popular, lowbrow entertainment, frowned on by the morally serious; whereas Sophron won high praise from no less an admirer than Plato, who borrowed his methods of characterization and kept his *Mimes* as a favorite bedside book.[93] Yet the fragments possess a marvelous vulgar vitality that makes one wish we had more of them, regardless. They tend to be brassily obscene, with a more than Aristophanic relish for taboo words. One is set in India, is spoken partly in pseudo-native gibberish, and involves a native deity called *Pordē* (Fart). In another a woman is yelling to her slave "Come and fuck me," and showers him with exotic insults when he refuses ("You found my cunt too rough a proposition?").[94]

We sometimes forget how much our overview of Greek literature is conditioned by the morally costive Graeco-Roman and Byzantine pundits who sifted out what they thought worth preserving (especially as school texts, a selection process that always sets a premium on virtuous platitudes), and trashed, or ignored, the rest. Sometimes an oddity will survive from the trash heap to shift our perspective, and remind us how much we have lost, how perilous our generalizations about ancient literature must always remain. Herodas is very much a case in point.[95] Despite his gift for graphic thumbnail sketches, he is not a writer of consistent dramatic skill or poetic achievement, and the greasy amorality that exudes from almost every line of his work would probably have ensured his literary demise even if he had been.[96] Yet for us his sociohistorical value is immense; his total indifference to improving attitudes comes as a great relief, and his scabrous worm's-eye view of life can, on occasion, be extremely funny. In 1891 a papyrus was found that contained seven of his *mimiamboi* virtually intact, and sizable (if baffling) fragments of several more. Scholars have been arguing over them ever since.

All we know of Herodas himself (*fl.* ca. 280–270) is that he was a contemporary of Callimachus and Theocritus in Alexandria, and working during the reign of Ptolemy II.[97] Though the younger Pliny praised him,[98] he does not seem to have been widely known or read. There is no good evidence either that he was a farmer or that he came from Cos (as the literary histories sometimes claim), though he may, like Theocritus, have spent time there.[99] His realism needs careful watching, since his little dramatic interludes are highly artificial, written, as we have seen, in a bad literary imitation of Hipponax's archaic Ionic salted with touches of Attic, even of Doric, and a (typically Hellenistic) mixture of two genres, the mime and the iambus, employing the matter of the first and the language and meter of the second—the iambus, especially the scazon, being originally the verse form regarded as appropriate for ridicule, satire, or declarations of private love. This, presumably, is why Knox translated Herodas into a fake archaic jargon so obscure that it often requires the Greek to elucidate what Herodas is actually saying.[100]

In *Mime* 1 we watch an old go-between or bawd attempt—unsuccessfully—to interest a grass widow in a new lover: her pitch shows Herodas at his best:

> Child, how long is it now you've played the widow,
> Tossing alone on your single bed? Since Mandris
> Went off to Egypt it's been ten long months,
> And not one syllable has he written you, oh no,
> He's forgotten you, he's drinking from some new cup!
> And that's where the Goddess is housed—why, every object
> That grows or is made abounds in Egypt: wealth,
> Wrestling schools, power, tranquility, renown,
> Gaudies, philosophers, gold, pretty young boys,
> The shrine of the Sibling Gods—our noble King!—
> The Museum, fine wine, every luxury you could want,
> And women (by our Lady!) in more numbers
> Than the heavens boast stars, for comeliness the equal
> Of the goddesses who came to angle for Paris's judgment
> In his beauty contest (hope they missed *that* little whisper!).
> You silly girl, what's going on in your mind? Why on earth
> Keep warming that stool of yours? Before you know it
> You'll be old, your bloom will be burned away, dead ash.
> Look around, change your tack for two or three days,
> Have some fun with another man—a ship can never ride safely
> On just a single anchor.
>
> (*Mim.* 1.21–42)

The arguments, temptations, and veiled threats all fail: Metriche announces her intention of remaining faithful to Mandris (about the only show of virtue in our surviving text), but still, with wry humanity, breaks out a pot of wine for her ever-thirsty visitor.

Few of the other mimes achieve this level of creative vividness. We listen to a pimp, in court, making his case against a rowdy sailor for abduction of one of the brothel girls (and parodying legal oratory in the process: *Mim.* 2). We meet a loquacious, prematurely aged, poverty-stricken mother lugging her no-good son off to be beaten by the local schoolmaster: the exchanges of mother and son offer a glimpse into that perennial problem, the generation gap (*Mim.* 3).[101] We eavesdrop on a group of women, as featherbrained and talkative as Theocritus's Syracusan matrons, making *ex voto* offerings in the temple of Asclepius, and praising, like so many Aunt Ednas, the realism of the artwork on display (*Mim.* 4; cf. above, p. 206). Eavesdropping, in fact, is what the audience seems to be doing more often than not, most obviously with the two bored housewives' wink-and-snigger chat about dildos in *Mime* 6. (Cerdo the cobbler, who makes the dildos, shows up again in *Mime* 7, this time selling shoes, again to ladies: his public, as opposed to his under-the-counter, role.)[102] A sadistic mistress, learning of her slave-lover's infidelity with a neighbor, first wants him whipped, then decides on branding, and is only talked out of both by her maid (*Mim.* 5). Comparison may be made with an anonymous papyrus fragment on a very similar theme (the protagonist is the same foul-mouthed lady cited earlier): the slave here is punished for rejecting his mistress's advances because he prefers a fellow slave.[103] There is an unpleasant and obsequious slave named Malakos ("Softy," or "Faggot"), and the mistress also attempts to poison her husband. *Mime* 8, badly mutilated, shows us, exceptionally, Herodas himself, telling a symbolic dream (16 ff.), in the context of a Dionysiac ritual, about his work's harsh treatment by the critics, and his confidence in his own ultimate triumph.

It is all very Hellenistic, and, ultimately, very depressing. From the literary viewpoint, Herodas is a typical Alexandrian: he has found a species of art hitherto ignored by the intellectuals; he has revamped old meters and dialect forms; his works are pithy and brief. Low life, in fact, complete with vernacular platitudes, cleverly sauced up for Alexandrians with a certain *nostalgie de la boue.* It would be interesting, and valuable, to know just what sort of social cross section formed the audience for such entertainment. I cannot share the confidence of most modern scholars that Herodas was catering to select *littérateurs,* capable of picking up the most recondite allusions, rather than to the popular audience that enjoyed a lowbrow mime.[104] At the very least I suspect there was something in Herodas for both categories to enjoy. Nor am I by any means convinced (though here there is wider disagreement) that performances of the *mimiamboi* were limited to one-man recitations, much less that such works were mere *Buchpoësie.* The alternative need not be an elaborate stage production with scenery (as Cunningham seems to imply),[105] but rather the equivalent of the quick vaudeville sketch, which similarly lasts about five minutes, and can involve two, three, sometimes four actors.

But whatever our views on such topics, it is hard to deny that there is an awful void here at the heart of things. Extreme wealth on the one hand, grinding poverty on the other; stonily unself-conscious brutality, relentless commercialism; in particular, too many bored, stupid, and intermittently vicious middle-class women with time on their hands and no sense of purpose, more than ready to treat their slaves as animated tools in a way that might have surprised Aristotle. Here we hit on a central leitmotif of the period (see pp. 597 ff.). With Tyche supreme, and deified kings for gods (reflecting, on a more palatial scale, precisely the same materialist aims as the new bourgeoisie), it is not to be wondered at that Simaetha, in a desperate attempt to control at least her private life, should resort to magic, or that the magic should have erotic compulsion as its goal. What Simaetha, like most of the other characters that we meet, has on her mind is sex: more or less romanticized, but still compulsive and obsessional, the appetite of a spoiled consumer. It is no accident that the magic ritual described by Theocritus is authentic to the last detail, and has ample parallels in the magical papyri (see pp. 598 ff.): it was a deadly serious business, on a par with the discovery of a good cook.

Among consumer appetites, as any student of Athenaeus's sources from this period is well aware, gourmandizing also ranked very high. Like the pursuit of sex, infatuation with *haute cuisine* became, at least among the propertied classes, a kind of substitute religion: "Give me sensation, and then again sensation" is a creed with a long history. Then, as later, it also produced its own backlash. The poor, as we shall see (pp. 590 ff.), turned rather to salvationist cults: if there was no hope for them in this world, at least the next one might offer rewards, not the least of which would be the spectacle of their temporal masters in torment for all eternity. But such cults also had something to offer a jaded bourgeoisie. In this world of relentless sensual self-gratification, it is not surprising that the Cynics should have found adherents among the well-to-do. Here was a need that, in the long term, pastoralism could never fill. The rentier might be glad, for a while, to dress his *scholē*, his idleness, in pseudosignificance by conjuring up a dream of Arcadia; but his heart was in the city, where his livelihood lay, and the herdsman's piping, however literary, in the end still left him unsatisfied. To pay the piper presented no problem; but to call the right tune was a very different matter.

CHAPTER 16

THE ROAD TO SELLASIA, 239–222

At the time of Antigonus Gonatas's death in 239, Aratus—a general of great energy and vision, though reputedly prone to diarrhea before every major engagement[1]— had made the Achaean League a force to be reckoned with in mainland Greece. His capture of Acrocorinth in 243 (brilliant, though not preceded by any declaration of war, and carried out at the expense of a nominally friendly power)[2] had fatally weakened Macedonia's control over the Peloponnese.[3] The rival Aetolian League had already put Boeotia *hors de concours* (245) and now controlled most of central Greece.[4] In terms of local Greek power politics they were bound, sooner rather than later, to try their luck against Aratus. In 241 they did so, and were soundly beaten: Aratus allowed them an easy victory and then, knowing their lax discipline, took them by surprise while they were plundering the suburbs of Pellene.[5] A year or so later the two confederacies were uneasily allied against Macedonia (239/8?). The relationship rested on nothing but temporary convenience, and could not last: it took a really undaunted political idealist to describe it as "the most hopeful Greek alignment of Hellenistic times," and by 230 it was a dead letter.[6]

Antigonus, old and ill, made peace with Aratus in 241/0. Tarn, with fine hyperbole, writes of "a general truce throughout the Greek world,"[7] but the treaty did little to check Aratus's disruptive activities. These included abortive attacks, in the name of anti-Macedonian "freedom," on Argos and Piraeus; for the latter he afterwards tried, in some embarrassment, to throw the blame on a colleague.[8] The Athenians were in no mood to exchange their easygoing Macedonian control for Aratus's brand of confederate adventurism. Aratus himself was regularly elected (every alternate year, the prescribed maximum) as commander-in-chief of the Achaean League— the League consisting of a group of cities united in a confederacy (*sympoliteia*), that is, with a common federal citizenship but retaining independent control of their internal affairs (cf. above, p. 139). This constitution has been the cause of much scholarly debate (its written terms do not survive), but the modern, if more complex, parallel of the United States is inescapable.

Map 17. Central Greece and the Peloponnese.

The alliances in Greece during the next couple of decades display a labile quality in which immediate convenience is the paramount factor, and principle conspicuous by its absence. In 240/39, before Antigonus Gonatas's death, Macedonia and Aetolia were allied against the Achaean League; the League itself was largely financed by Ptolemy III (an encouragement to anti-Macedonianism) and uncertainly allied with Sparta. The Aetolians, however, though for long Macedonia's allies,[9] fell out with Antigonus's successor, Demetrius II, over their aggressive policy in Epirus, and promptly, as we have seen, allied themselves instead with the Achaean League (239): the so-called War of Demetrius, which followed, lasted until 229. Aratus's expansive plans for the League also, before long, came into collision with the ultra-Lycurgan ambitions of Cleomenes in Sparta: by 228 Sparta and the League were at war. Ptolemy III, calculating that a resurgent Sparta would prove a more effective ally against Macedonia than the League, transferred his backing from Aratus to Cleomenes, and the Aetolians, in effect, followed suit (though in their case there was always the likelihood of their selling their swords to the highest bidder). Finally, in a *volte-face* the shock of which still reverberates through our surviving sources, the League called in Antigonus Doson of Macedonia in order to crush Spartan imperialism before it got out of hand. This completed the *ronde*.

It is a melancholy progression, made worse by the fact that any trace of purported idealism, revolutionary or other, that we encounter during these fraught years turns out, on investigation, to be mere camouflage for the most squalid class warfare or ruthless *Machtpolitik*. This does not, however, imply total cynicism. Equality, even if it was equality for a privileged elite only, remained an ideal that men in Sparta would still fight and die for, not least when it was inextricably linked to the recovery of the old, proud, warrior regime associated with the name of Lycurgus. Even so, at times one momentarily sympathizes with the impatience of Arnold Toynbee, who, despite having lived through half a century of totalitarianism, both fascist and communist, found all this parochial squabbling distasteful in the extreme, and argued that the best possible solution for the Greek states was another strong external leader like Philip II.[10]

Sparta, in any case, was dangerously weakened by her peculiar internal stresses, both social and economic. There is daunting irony in the fact that this ultraconservative Greek state should have been the one to turn into what was widely regarded at the time as a hotbed of social revolution, though the change in question was actually a counterrevolution, or even, it has been argued, a mirage. We have already seen how her young king Agis IV got himself killed while trying to deal with the situation (p. 153).[11] It would be misleading to suppose that either Agis or his later successor, Cleomenes III, was any kind of a radical in the modern sense. Most of their "revolutionary" moves (e.g., their repeated, and often illegal, attacks on the ephors, that group of five annually elected commissars who formed a constitutional counterweight to the monarchy)[12] were primarily designed to increase their own unchallenged power. The violent opposition to their reformist movement was a case of conflict between degrees of elitism: it stemmed from a small caucus of ultraconservative property owners, perhaps not more than a hundred or so all told, into whose hands had fallen the best of the land and a vast preponderance of wealth, and who had not the slightest intention—despite the Lycurgan tradition—of surrendering their privileged status without a fight. It was this group, under Leonidas II, Cleomenes' father, that not only killed Agis and fought Cleomenes, but also had Agis's brother Archidamus assassinated, when Cleomenes in 227 tried to strengthen his hand by recalling him from exile in Messene (below, p. 257).[13]

The curious sense of unreality that permeates the so-called Spartan revolution during these decades (ca. 244–222) is directly due to the fact that its main object—reform rather than revolution—was to restore a near-fatally crippled elite.[14] The famous *homoioi*, the "Equals," the Spartiate warriors whose business was national defense (and, on occasion, national aggression), and who lived off the produce of their serf-worked estates, had by the third century fallen from an original (mid-seventh century) figure of some eight or nine thousand to no more than seven hundred.[15]

This fact alone at once suggests a new and dangerous vulnerability of the elite to all those inferiors, helots above all, who had for centuries been held down by well-organized *force majeure*. Not only were the numbers of the Spartiates diminished: their famous, and rigorous, Lycurgan training, the *agōgē*, had, perhaps in consequence of Sparta's collapse as a leading Aegean power, largely gone by the board. The influx of wealth had played its part in the decline; it had also played havoc with Sparta's always ramshackle ancient economy. More and more of the ancestral land, as we have seen, had fallen into the hands of a powerful minority, including women—a factor that seems to have been regarded as one of their major stumbling blocks by the reformists.[16] Countless Spartiates had lost their landholdings (*klaroi*), and as a result, under Spartan law, had either lost their citizenship altogether, or had been reduced to the status of second-class citizens (*hypomeiones*). Others were hopelessly in debt.

In short, Sparta had at last reached the same agrarian-social crisis that had faced Athens three and a half centuries earlier, in Solon's day. (At the same time it should be borne in mind that throughout Greece, by the mid-third century, almost nonstop warfare, with its accompaniment of rapine, cropburning, wanton destruction, and, above all, slave trading on a massive scale, had made fearful inroads into the agricultural economy, striking especially hard at the free smallholder, and sending a steady stream of destitute, desperate men into the great cities. The erosion of the yeoman class, the concentration of wealth in fewer and fewer hands, the degradation of once-independent farmers or landowners to proletarian status—all these phenomena, though observable in acute form at Sparta, formed part of a more general malaise.)[17] When we hear of seemingly radical-sounding schemes to abolish debts in Sparta, to redistribute the land on a massive scale, even to free helots, we should not be misled. Short-term, these were preemptive, and sometimes desperate, measures designed to forestall and choke off a true revolution from below by making the fewest concessions possible. Long-term, they were all promoted in furtherance of a paradoxically reactionary dream: the reestablishment of a strong and privileged elite, the purging of Sparta's new and effete luxuries, the return of the Lycurgan regime, complete with black broth, flogging, and barrack life; above all, the resurgence, in significantly increased numbers, of a matchless standing army.

The chief malcontents were, precisely, those *déclassé* Spartiates who wanted their privileges back, who deeply resented the economic collapse that had been helped on its way by Sparta's crushing defeat at Leuctra in 371, her loss of Messenia with its free granary and rich *klaroi*, the establishment of Messene and Megalopolis as rival powers on her frontiers.[18] The fierce conservative opposition to the reformers' plans has a certain piquancy in that those plans aimed, by and large, at a full restoration of the *ancien régime*.[19] It is also significant that when the reform bill came to a vote in the *gerousia* (council of elders), it was defeated by only one vote: Agis had substantial backing for his plans. No less ironic, in a different way, was the use of Stoic notions of concord (*homonoia*), with its program of equality, fellowship, and the abolition of class war, to provide intellectual justification for what Agis and Cleomenes were doing. (On the other hand, the Stoa had been heavily influenced by Sparta from the beginning in its formulation of the ideal state,[20] and it seems clear that Cleomenes' Stoic adviser, Sphaerus, was as eager as anyone for the restoration of the Lycurgan constitution.)[21] *Homonoia* was, essentially, for the *homoioi*: what happened to the second-class citizens of Laconia, the dwellers round about (*perioikoi*), or, *a fortiori*, the helots, was quite another matter. The manpower shortage among Spartiates was so acute that numerous *perioikoi* of the "best sort" were indeed offered citizenship, but primarily, as Cleomenes himself stressed, for purposes of defense, not through any principle of brotherhood.[22] Admission to the club would *per se* ensure their grateful loyalty to its founding members.

All animals might in theory be equal, but for Spartiates some were definitely more equal than others. Here the Stoic partiality for strong, wise, reasonable royal rulers—the rational earthly analogues of Zeus ordering the universe—will have very much worked to the advantage of a monarch such as Cleomenes.[23] The common messes, the equal lots (*klaroi*), the rigorous training, the whole Spartan legend, applied solely to a minority, an elite cadre. It was in *their* interests that land was to be redistributed; it was *their* debts that were to be canceled (in any case the Spartan treasury could not have paid them). Freeing the helots had no place in the Lycurgan system, which indeed relied on their labor to survive; and even Stoic thinkers were chary of advocating mass emancipation, since until the Industrial Revolution there was no obvious alternative source of cheap labor. Sphaerus (b. 290?), the Stoic thinker from Olbia who advised Cleomenes, and had been one of Zeno's most brilliant students, doubtless supplied his movement (if that is the right word for it) with such ideology as it had, besides constituting a major source for Phylarchus.[24] He may well have utilized that fine old Stoic bromide about even the most downtrodden slave being a king over his own soul, and enjoying spiritual if not physical freedom. What the helots thought about this is not on record.

It is no accident that the Hellenic Leagues of both Philip II and Demetrius the Besieger (above, p. 34) had provisions for using all their federal resources to crush social revolutions from below: from first to last, this was a property owners' world. Third-century conditions for the poor were appalling: the gap between wealth and indigence had widened dangerously with the emergence of large urban centers under authoritarian rule. It is thus symptomatic of the age that, despite its crypto-fascist motivation, Agis's attempt at reform should have been countered so strongly by a wealthy propertied minority. His murder in 241 was almost inevitable. In the calculations of Macedonia, the Achaean League (chiefly in the person of Aratus), and the Aetolians, then, comparatively little part was played by Sparta—at least from Antigonus Gonatas's death until the sudden career of conquest and reform embarked on by Cleomenes in 229/8.

Gonatas's son and successor, Demetrius II (ca. 275–229), was a vigorous activist who had probably been co-regent with his father during the last few years of the latter's reign. He had taken a leaf out of Philip II's book by marrying an Epirot princess, Phthia, in 239—perhaps as insurance against the Illyrians, and in general to shore up his western frontier[25]—and in 238/7 naming the child of their marriage Philip also.[26] This was the future Philip V: Greece was not slow to take the hint. The

Aetolian and Achaean Leagues, as we have seen, now allied themselves, briefly but effectively, against Demetrius.[27] The course of this war is obscure, its details unimportant. But Aratus was successful enough to make the tyrant of Megalopolis, Lydiades, think twice about his support of Demetrius, and in 235 bring Megalopolis over to the Achaean League.[28] Lydiades, a shrewd and ambitious politician, at once became Aratus's personal rival, alternating with him as elected League commander-in-chief for the next six years. He also argued that the League would be well advised to move against Cleomenes rather than, as Aratus wanted, Argos. His motivation was obvious and preemptive: any Spartan king with aggression in mind might be expected to make Megalopolis his first target for attack, and Cleomenes was no exception.[29] Aratus, who had been allied with Agis IV against Aetolia less than a decade before, saw no advantage, and much danger, in supporting the Megalopolitan's notorious (if understandable) anti-Spartan crusade.[30] Personal pique also may have played its part here: Aratus was jealous, and it was at his insistent urging that Lydiades' proposal was turned down.

The polarization of anti-Spartan and anti-Macedonian groups within the League had disruptive consequences later. When Argos was finally brought into the League, in 229, it was at the cost of cutthroat intrigue between Aratus and Lydiades: if her leader Aristomachus finally "achieved Aratus's dream, he then took the pleasure out of it by firmly aligning himself with Lydiades' anti-Spartan policy, and since he was elected League general for 228/7, the result was a dangerous split in the confederation's leadership."[31] At the time, though, it must have looked very much as though Aratus—that inveterate opponent of all things Macedonian[32]—was right. In 233 Demetrius's attempt to regain a position of strength in the Peloponnese looked like succeeding. His general Bithys defeated Aratus at Phylacia: this turn of events so delighted the Athenians, no lovers of the Achaean League, that they made Bithys an honorary citizen on the spot.[33] Times had changed indeed since Demosthenes' day.

Demetrius got no chance to follow up this success. That constant Macedonian hazard, a tribal invasion from the north, now intervened. Demetrius lost his western allies in Epirus, where a civil war, with revolutionary undertones, had broken out.[34] With the assassination of its queen, Deidameia, the Epirot royal house was toppled, and the new republic federated itself with Acarnania (once part of the Epirot kingdom, then taken over by Aetolia, now independent).[35] Demetrius, hard pressed, turned to the Illyrians for military aid. Their levies made short work of Epirus, still weak from internal dissension; then, under their queen, Teuta, and with no major naval power available to contain them, they embarked on such an orgy of looting and piracy down the Adriatic coast as to attract the attention of Rome (229). With Illyrian corsairs controlling both the Straits of Otranto and the Corinthian Gulf, Italian trade began to suffer. Worse, these successes gave Teuta imperial ambitions for the Illyrian royal house. Already in 231 Illyrian troops (paid for by Demetrius) had routed the army of the Aetolian League besieging Medeon, in Acarnania.[36] A year later Teuta attacked Elis and Messenia, and joined with a band of roving Gauls to briefly capture Phoenice, the port of Epirus.[37] The Epirotes and Acarnanians, ungratefully, then concluded alliances with Illyria against their rescuers, the Aetolian and

Achaean Leagues, while Teuta, having put down a rebellion at home, toyed with the idea of invading Greece, of making Illyria a major Greek power.[38] "The Illyrians were transforming themselves from disreputable buccaneers to respectable imperialists."[39]

Italian traders complained, and the Greeks resident along the Adriatic coast panicked; the Romans sent a mildly irritated embassy "to investigate."[40] Our understanding of what the envoys actually accomplished is clouded by Polybian rhetoric. They do not seem to have issued any sort of immediate ultimatum, since Teuta went straight on with her aggressive campaign regardless, attacking Epidamnus, Apollonia, and the vital island of Corcyra (early summer 229). Reinforced by an Acarnanian squadron, she then defeated a combined Achaean-Aetolian fleet, whereupon Corcyra surrendered.[41] Epidamnus was already under siege. Only now, with the Adriatic Greeks in a state of sheer hysteria, did the Romans move. It is worth noting that, throughout this whole furor, neither Demetrius II nor his successor Antigonus Doson made any move to involve Macedonia.[42] Why should they, when the Romans, eventually, cleared up a dirty and dangerous situation for them? Far from regarding the Roman intervention with hostility, as was once thought,[43] they surely welcomed it.[44] They will also have noted that when the Romans attacked, they did so with devastating speed, violence, and professionalism, not to speak of crushing numerical superiority.[45] The Illyrians, whose forte was privateering rather than formal warfare, collapsed ignominiously, and a treaty was signed by early spring 228.[46]

Three points are worth noting about this so-called First Illyrian War. First, Rome was clearly loath to intervene, and would not have done so for the sake of a few disgruntled Italian merchants alone. It was only when the whole complex of trade and communications between the eastern Adriatic, the Corinthian Gulf, and the wealthy cities of Magna Graecia was seriously threatened with disruption that her expeditionary force went into action. Second, having dealt with Teuta, the Romans showed no signs of wanting to establish any kind of permanent presence in Illyria. They mulcted the Illyrians of a war indemnity to cover their expenses; they forbade them (in the interests of peaceful commerce) to send warships anywhere near the Straits of Otranto; they trimmed back Illyria's frontiers in favor of their local ally Demetrius of Pharos (see p. 296), an act they afterwards had cause to regret. But that was all. There was no occupation; no "protective" garrisons remained behind. For the time being, at least, Rome disclaimed any acquisitive interest in the Balkans. Third, the significance that Polybius attaches to this otherwise unimportant intervention, as being essential for the understanding of Rome's rise to power, has nothing to do with imperialism, as has so often been supposed.[47] Its real importance lies, simply and solely, in the crushing military superiority and disciplined skill of the Roman legions—a lesson that two far from negligible Macedonian kings, Philip V and Perseus, were to learn the hard way.

That same year Demetrius was defeated and killed in a great battle against the Dardanians (229): his son and heir, Philip, was still only nine.[48] He had as guardian Demetrius's cousin, Antigonus, nicknamed Doson. The meaning of this epithet is uncertain. Since Antigonus undertook to step down in Philip's favor when the boy came of age, "Doson" is often interpreted as the future participle of the verb *didōmi* (i.e., "he who will give"); he was also known as Epitropos, "Trustee" or "Guardian."[49] At one point, threatened by an angry mob, he came close to resigning his thankless office altogether.[50] It is also sometimes alleged that he took the Macedonians, as represented by their army assembly, into some kind of constitutional co-partnership (*koinon*), so that his authority was shared with them, and that in return he was elected king as Antigonus III (228/7?). But this is highly speculative: Doson's power would seem, from his career, to have been unhampered by any such restraints. His main handicap was that, like so many of his line, he suffered from inherited tuberculosis (above, p. 123).[51]

Macedonia's weakness had immediate repercussions in Greece. Still in 229, after some lean years made tolerable only through the public munificence of her millionaire leader Eurycleides,[52] Athens finally got rid of her Macedonian garrison in Piraeus. Since the Chremonidean War (above, p. 147) Macedonian control over Athens had been continuous, but seems to have varied considerably in strictness. In 256 Antigonus had lifted most restrictions, but a few years later they were back again (253/2), and remained in force, apart from a brief spell between 247 and 245, until the death of Demetrius.[53] It was typical of the period that what, sixty-five years on from its installation, finally shifted the Piraeus garrison was hard cash. It cost 150 talents in soldiers' pay to make the Macedonians go quietly.[54] Part of this sum (20 talents) came as a gift from Aratus. Nevertheless, though Athens had broken with Macedonia, and taken Aratus's money, her leaders still refused to join the Achaean League, opting instead for a watchful neutrality. Such cool pragmatism was more than understandable in a city that had been impoverished by constant wars; and it worked. Athens contrived to stay on good terms both with Macedonia and with Ptolemaic Egypt. The price was a violent falling-out with Aratus,[55] but the Achaean League—over which Aratus's control was now far from assured—took no action, for fear that Eurycleides and his associates might then bring Athens over to the League's enemies. As a result Athens was largely left alone, an intellectual cul-de-sac of philosophers, a tourist city living on past glories (see p. 147).

Antigonus Doson meanwhile set about stabilizing Macedonia's position. The invading Dardanian tribesmen—who reputedly came near washing-water only three times in their lives, at birth, marriage, and death[56]—were driven off. Thessaly, which had revolted, was won back, and Antigonus recovered the traditional office of chief (*tagos*) of the Thessalian League, held by most Macedonian kings since Philip II.[57] Aetolia's neutrality he bought, with damaging concessions in central Greece. He knew his own limitations; he was no overreacher. In Greece as a whole he certainly achieved, and probably hoped for, no more than a shaky maintenance of the *status quo*. Throughout most of his reign the chief focus of concern on the Greek mainland was the dangerously renascent Sparta of Cleomenes.

Cleomenes III (265/60–219) was an ambitious man, and the subject of violently partisan judgments during and immediately after his own lifetime, which makes any evaluation of his character or career hazardous.[58] Leonidas II, his father, the Agiad king who had ruled with, and after, the Eurypontid Agis IV—had, indeed, been primarily responsible for his death—forced a marriage between Cleomenes and Agis's widow, Agiatis, a wealthy heiress: to secure her holdings, it is said,[59] but doubtless also to win added control over the dual kingship. Agiatis apparently shared her late husband's reformist notions; and the young Cleomenes, so the tradition goes, fell deeply in love with her. We do not have to believe that he simply took over Agis's plans, and wife, to forward his own ambitions for himself and his peers: anti-Spartan propaganda may well have been at work in the attribution of motives and responsibility. This is more than likely as regards the death of Agis's infant son by Agiatis. Cleomenes was said to have had the child murdered; but, as has long been recognized, it is far more probable that Leonidas was responsible, and then put the blame on his son.[60] Cleomenes, in any case, was, on his record, no killer.[61] Nevertheless, the full truth in all likelihood can never be recovered.

Certainly many people in and around the Peloponnese came to believe, for a while, that what Cleomenes had in mind was populist revolution. The first few years of his reign, however, he waited, worked with the ephors, realistically recognizing them as the true power in the state,[62] and consolidated his own backing. He knew, very well, not least with Agis's fate to remind him, that what he wanted could be won only by force. The Aetolians ceded him several cities, including Tegea and Mantinea, and he may have set up an unofficial alliance with them.[63] In 229, with Macedonia weakened by Demetrius's defeat and death, and Argos, at last, a member of the Achaean League, he moved against Lydiades' city of Megalopolis—a promising *apertura* into southern Arcadia.[64] It was this, coupled with the widespread fear that he might be promoting social anarchy, that finally persuaded the Achaean League to declare war against him (spring 228?).[65] Even so, the initiative once more came from Lydiades: Aratus did everything he could to avoid open conflict with Sparta, even to the point of avoiding engagements when they presented themselves.[66] If he was really eager to extend the League's territories,[67] he had an odd way of showing it. Lydiades, who was serving as his cavalry commander, in fury made—without permission—a death-or-glory cavalry charge against Cleomenes' troops, and as a result got himself killed.[68] Aratus may well have felt that the censure he incurred at home for his lack of initiative was worth being thus rid of his most irksome political rival.

At the same time the tensions between various members of the League—Achaea, Argos, Megalopolis—remained deep and divisive. At one point during the campaign Megalopolis, under heavy pressure from Cleomenes, was persuaded by Aratus and authorized by the League synod to appeal for aid to Antigonus Doson in Macedonia; the appeal was duly made, and Antigonus, sensibly, agreed to intervene in the event of a formal request from the League.[69] Such a request was brought forward for immediate discussion; but Aratus, who had been quite happy to use Megalopolis as a stalking-horse to sound out Antigonus's plans, shied away from committing the League—at this stage—to the Macedonian connection. Let League members, he urged, save their own cities. The League synod voted accordingly.[70] These are facts to be borne in mind when considering just how and why, four years later, the League reversed its decision, and indeed allied itself—at a price—with Macedonia in order to finish off Cleomenes.

Cleomenes now went back to Sparta to secure his own position (late summer 227), carefully leaving his Spartiate troops behind, and taking with him only his mercenaries, whose loyalty was to him personally rather than to the Spartan state. He might have learned something about the economics of primitive (and elitist) communism from his wife, or from Sphaerus, his Stoic tutor, or even, in a general way, from the Cynics;[71] but what he wanted and needed, above all else, was a reborn Spartiate army with himself in sole command of it.[72] Idealizing talk about the Lycurgan reforms or the ancestral constitution (*patrios politeia*) did not for one moment blind Cleomenes to the simple truth that the *ancien régime* could only be restored by a strong autocrat: the lesson of Agis's failure had not been lost on him. His specious claim to win friends through persuasion rather than bribery (but see below, p. 259) was probably, in his impecunious state, making a virtue of necessity.[73] It is notable that in 227/6 Sparta was conspicuously absent from the list of powers contributing to the restoration of Rhodes after that city's near-total destruction by earthquake (see p. 381).

With the prestige of his military successes to help him, Cleomenes set about clearing the opposition.[74] As soon as he got back to Sparta he carried out a lightning *coup d'état*. The ephors he simply eliminated: four of the current board of five were killed fighting, along with their supporters, and the office was abolished. Cleomenes seems also to have replaced, or possibly augmented, the *gerousia* (council of elders) with a new official, the *patronomos*, "paternal legislator," a suggestive term.[75] Cleomenes exiled some eighty of his main opponents, clearly the big property owners, and redistributed their land, together with his own and that of his supporters, into four thousand lots (*klaroi*).[76] Exiles were recalled, and given holdings. Debts were rescinded. Citizenship was bestowed on a select group of foreigners and *perioikoi*: from the epithets used in our source, it is clear that the chief criterion was good family.[77] Bearing in mind the Spartan tradition, this is exactly what we might expect: even in an emergency Cleomenes went by the studbook. Sphaerus was assigned the task of reviving the ancient Lycurgan training system (*agōgē*). That this crucial responsibility fell to a non-Spartan intellectual has occasioned surprisingly little comment: at the very least it hints eloquently at the degree to which the tradition had been abandoned.

None of this should distract us from the central fact that before the end of 227 Cleomenes had made himself sole ruler of Sparta. Polybius remarks, with complete accuracy, that Cleomenes turned legitimate kingship into a tyranny.[78] His persistent monarchist propaganda only serves to confirm this (though one has a certain sympathy, when considering his successors, with Pausanias, who described him as the last king of Sparta).[79] So does the strong possibility that he enrolled mercenaries as citizens, and put them through the *agōgē*, thus in effect (a point that would not have been lost on his opponents) procuring himself a private army within the state.[80] There was to be no possible opposition. Cleomenes, as a counterstroke to the opposition's murder of Archidamus (above, p. 250), even filled the vacant second kingship by appointing his own brother Eucleidas, as opposed to a Eurypontid candidate: as Plutarch observes, "this was the only time that the Spartans had two kings from the same house."[81] His sole aim in restoring the *agōgē* was to revivify Sparta's legendary invincible army. His offer of citizenship to *perioikoi* and foreigners was essential if the depleted Spartiate body was to be brought back up to effective strength.[82]

Yet the immediate effect on the surrounding states (and in this deliberate propaganda must have played some part) was a conviction, doubtless encouraged by Sphaerus and his Stoic friends, that a real social revolution was in the air.[83] Cercidas the Cynic seems to have been convinced of this,[84] and it is easy enough to see why. Debts were being canceled in Sparta; *perioikoi* were being enfranchised; the land had been redistributed. Wishful thinking will have done the rest. It may even, for a while, have obscured the brutally obvious fact that Cleomenes at heart was an ambitious old-style imperialist, that social reform for him was no more than an instrument with which to achieve Spartan mastery over the Peloponnese, perhaps over all Greece.[85] To begin with he seemed to be near achieving his ambition. He certainly impressed Ptolemy III, who by now had become convinced that Cleomenes was a far more promising ally against Macedonia than the Achaean League—rumors of a possible League *rapprochement* with Antigonus Doson cannot have failed to reach Alexandria—and had transferred his funding to Sparta as a result.[86] We may note that he avoided open conflict with Antigonus by not giving Sparta any military aid; and how far he actually trusted Cleomenes can be judged from the fact that, as a condition of his support, he demanded—and got—the king's mother, together with his children, as hostages.[87] Cavafy, paraphrasing Plutarch (who in turn based his account on the Stoic-tinged version of Phylarchus), made two of his best poems out of this odd incident.[88]

In 226/5 Cleomenes and his now greatly strengthened standing army, equipped with the long Macedonian pike (*sarissa*), recaptured Mantinea from Aratus, and beat the Achaean League's forces at Hecatombaion.[89] As a result he came within an ace of forcing the League to make terms with him before he moved on Corinth and Argos. The League had already made contact with Antigonus Doson, probably in the winter of 227/6 (above, p. 256).[90] An emergency embassy, with Aratus's son as one of its members, now went north to appeal for Macedonian aid. Antigonus was willing enough to help, but his price of support was Acrocorinth—the most important of Macedonia's lost Fetters of Greece—and that was a sacrifice the League was not, yet, prepared to make. The embassy confirmed the earlier alliance, but for the moment Antigonus stayed put.[91] In the circumstances the League felt compelled to open negotiations with Cleomenes. A treaty was arranged, and only illness prevented Cleomenes from ratifying its terms.[92] What these terms were remains uncertain: the relative success of Aratus and Cleomenes as negotiators depends very much on which source we follow. But it does look very much as though what Cleomenes wanted was permanent League leadership for himself, and unquestioned hegemony of the Peloponnese for Sparta, in return for no more than the cession of prisoners and occupied territory.[93]

Over the winter of 226/5 Aratus seems to have regained some of his dominance over the League: he was elected generalissimo for 225/4; he then tricked Cleomenes into breaking off negotiations (spring 225), presumably in the expectation of winning a better deal by force of arms. Clearly, too, Aratus was against any real *rapprochement* of Cleomenes with the League, since this would have weakened his own position. Arguably Aratus's diplomatic tactics were mistaken, since in the campaign that followed Cleomenes had very much the best of it (summer 225).[94] Further negotiations proved hopeless (late 225). Cleomenes now, understandably, wanted too much: not only hegemony of the League, but also joint control of Acrocorinth.[95] The crude bribe he offered Aratus at the same time merely added insult to injury, and may well have been no more than a device to undermine his reputation in the League.[96] Aratus himself, though *strategos* with emergency powers, was in despair at the turn events had taken, the shipwreck of his policies. Yet at the same time he, like all Greek men of property, was desperately scared of the Spartan's revolutionary reputation, and the hopes this had aroused among the dispossessed. "The most dreadful charge he brought against Cleomenes," Plutarch wrote, with Aratus's *Memoirs* before him, "was his abolition of wealth and correction of poverty."[97]

Cleomenes' sweeping military successes in Achaea and the Argolid eventually forced the League's hand. He pressured Argos into accepting a garrison and an alliance; he captured Corinth, and seemed all too likely to capture Acrocorinth as well.[98] When he demanded its surrender from Aratus (it still had an Achaean garrison), Aratus replied, and afterwards recorded the reply in his *Memoirs*, that he "did not control events, but was rather controlled by them," a response that Cleomenes regarded as frivolous, and that angered him into further aggression, this time against Aratus's own home town of Sicyon.[99] Aratus, who twenty years earlier had wrested Acrocorinth from Macedonian hands for the League (243/2: above, p. 151), now faced a bitter choice between losing that great stronghold to Cleomenes, or giving it away to Antigonus Doson as the price for his assistance, since no other help was forthcoming. (Both the Aetolian League and Eurycleides' Athens had turned down the League's appeals.) Under the iron pressure of circumstance, which Cleomenes had dismissed as mere mockery, Aratus finally chose Antigonus, and the pact with Macedonia was at last made operative. At the same time Aratus was made emergency dictator (*strategos autokrator*) and provided—like any tyrant—with a bodyguard.[100] Antigonus at once marched south, and Cleomenes broke off the siege of Sicyon to deal with this new threat.

The irony of a situation that could induce the League's most embattled anti-Macedonian to bring in his archenemy, make him a present of Acrocorinth, and use his troops against a Spartan king—whatever the circumstances—was lost neither on Aratus's friends, nor on his detractors, nor indeed (if we take his remark to Cleomenes at its face value) on Aratus himself, who was no more inclined, other things being equal, to destroy Cleomenes than he was to truck with Antigonus. In his *Memoirs* he complained of being driven by Necessity,[101] a harsh taskmaster familiar to all Greek thinkers and statesmen. That surely is no more than the simple truth. Yet admirers and detractors alike regarded this *volte-face* as a supreme act of betrayal. The first group was desperately anxious to justify the decision as a planned and conscious act of policy; the second, equally eager to regard the decision as deliberate, used it to blacken Aratus's name in retrospect, to dismiss him as a cynical exponent of *Machtpolitik*, a plausible long-term hypocrite using words like "freedom" and "democracy" for his own selfish ends.

Both sides were therefore ready to play up, in different ways, the rumors that claimed Aratus had been conducting secret diplomatic negotiations with Antigonus Doson ever since 227/6.[102] For Phylarchus, the defeat of his hero Cleomenes was sheer disaster, and Aratus became the traitor whose unholy collusion with Macedonia had brought this disaster about, whose fear (and envy) of Cleomenes had made him, in effect, sell out the Greeks to Antigonus.[103] Phylarchus would, obviously, see Aratus's secret hand in the negotiations from the very beginning. Polybius took the same facts, but gave them a very different interpretation.[104] For him the enemies of freedom were the Aetolians and Cleomenes (cf. below, p. 283), with the Achaean League as the champion of Greek liberties, and Antigonus Doson as a generous, honorable, high-minded monarch, whose intervention in the Peloponnese was made as a matter of principle, and who in effect freed Sparta from tyranny.[105] The truth seems to have been that Aratus detested the solution forced on him, and had no illusions about the authoritarian tactics that Antigonus would employ once given a free hand in the Peloponnese; but he was by then in too vulnerable a position to make any other choice. Presumably he salved his conscience with the argument that, since it looked as though Cleomenes would capture Acrocorinth in any case, it might at least be turned over to a potential ally.

The masses everywhere saw what Cleomenes was doing in Sparta, misinterpreted his program completely, and thought (to begin with, at least) that he meant to carry the banner of social revolution through the length and breadth of the Peloponnese.[106] This was even made a motive, in Plutarch's account, for Aratus's surrendering Acrocorinth to the Macedonians. Antigonus, too, must have dreaded something of the sort. Once having got the promise of Acrocorinth, he took the field with twenty thousand troops, to confront Cleomenes at the Isthmus.[107] It soon became all too clear—not least in Argos—that whatever Cleomenes had in mind to achieve, social reform outside Sparta was not it.[108] As a result, his mass support melted away as rapidly as it had grown: town after town changed sides.[109] Cleomenes' resurgent power had always been in a sense illusory, since it depended on mercenaries, and Cleomenes paid his mercenaries with the subventions he got from Ptolemy. Antigonus, who was well aware of this, may have ceded some territories in Asia Minor to Ptolemy to persuade him to withdraw his support from Sparta. In any case, Ptolemy must have seen for himself which way the wind was blowing in the Peloponnese: at all events, he stopped payments to Cleomenes.[110] The results were immediate and dramatic. Cleomenes, in a desperate effort to raise both money and troops, is said to have sold six thousand helots their freedom at a flat rate of five minas (= 500 drachmas) a head, though where they got the cash from remains a puzzle.[111] It should scarcely need emphasizing that this emergency act of manumission in no way constituted part of Cleomenes' reform program, and cannot be construed as showing concern for helot equality.

Antigonus now reconstituted the Hellenic Leagues of Philip II and Demetrius the Besieger as a League of Leagues (autumn 224), including the federations of

Macedonia, Thessaly, Achaea, Boeotia, and Epirus (but not, of course, that of
Aetolia), with himself as *hēgemōn*.[112] Members seem to have been left an unusual degree of autonomy, even in the matter of war or peace.[113] For Antigonus, nevertheless, this new league remained primarily an instrument for the furtherance of Macedonian power. His insistence on the surrender of Acrocorinth (not to mention the
destruction of the statues of those—Aratus alone excepted—who had liberated it),[114]
and the garrisons that he installed (see below), make that clear enough. To sweeten
this somewhat bitter pill he carefully emphasized that his quarrel was not with
Sparta, but with Cleomenes: in other words, this was a crusade to put down social
revolution or tyranny, according to one's viewpoint. Polybius certainly subscribed
to such a view. Though he conceded Cleomenes some admirable qualities,[115] he
nevertheless condemned him politically as an ambitious, headstrong, violent, and
perjured *tyrannos*, while regarding Aratus's *Memoirs* as "exceptionally truthful and
clear."[116] Pausanias, too, followed the pro-Achaean line.[117]

A string of reverses, and shortage of money for his troops, neither of which
could be offset by the capture, and savage sack, of Megalopolis,[118] drove Cleomenes—
like Antigonus One-Eye in 301, or Lysimachus in 282—to stake everything on a
major pitched battle. It took place in hilly terrain at Sellasia, some eight miles north
of Sparta, in July 222.[119] Cleomenes was outnumbered and, despite a brave stand,
finally beaten. Accompanied by Sphaerus and others, he fled to Gytheion,[120] and
there took ship for Egypt.[121] Ptolemy III received him and his party, gave them
smiles and promises, but carefully left them powerless. When Euergetes died, his
son Philopator did not prove so accommodating.[122] A voluptuary ruled by women,
Ptolemy IV was scared (and therefore resentful) of Cleomenes: the Spartan's enemies
soon had him under house arrest. His request to be allowed to return to Sparta and
reclaim his throne fell on deaf ears: he knew far too much, now, about the Ptolemies'
weaknesses.[123] A year or two later Cleomenes and his friends, in fine Stoic style,
committed suicide after an abortive (and ludicrous) attempt to raise the Alexandrian
mob against its new monarch (219).[124]

Antigonus Doson entered Sparta in triumph, the first foreign conqueror ever to
do so. A flatterer assured him that his fortunes had been "Alexandrized": the dead
conqueror's *tychē* was felt to rub off on his favored successors. A young Achaean
cavalry commander called Philopoemen, of whom we shall hear more, distinguished
himself in the battle.[125] The Spartan Ephorate was restored, indeed given supreme
power; but the kingship, predictably, was left in abeyance. Some at least of the social
reforms seem to have survived.[126] Antigonus kept Macedonian garrisons on Acrocorinth and in Orchomenos, and left a senior officer in charge of Peloponnesian affairs:[127] he meant to make the most of his opportunity. Sparta's bid for freedom and
hegemony (if not, yet, her hope for a return to the old Lycurgan regime) was over.
Instead, she was forced by Antigonus into alliance with—though not membership
in—his new Greek confederacy.[128] If Sellasia "signified the success of the new movement towards freedom and unity over the particularist imperialism of Sparta,"[129] a
claim that is, in whole or part, debatable, it remains a sad truth that the success was
bought at an appallingly heavy price, and proved transitory in the extreme. In any

case Antigonus was given no time in which to enjoy his victory. He was called back north at once by another barbarian invasion, suffered a severe consumptive hemorrhage on the battlefield, and survived long enough only to make all arrangements for the young Philip V to take his place. He died in the early summer of 221,[130] still in his forties, leaving an invaluable fund of popularity and good will behind him.[131]

What, meanwhile, was the position in Egypt, and the vast, unmanageable empire of the Seleucids? Ptolemy III, as we saw earlier (p. 150), had lost command of the sea to Antigonus Gonatas—perhaps one among many reasons why he eventually switched his support in Greece from Sparta to Macedonia, cynically advising Cleomenes, at the same time, to come to terms with Antigonus Doson[132]—but still had a large fleet with which to harass the Seleucids in the eastern Mediterranean. He also retained control of Ephesus and Lebedos (now renamed Ptolemaïs), as well as cities in Thrace and on the Hellespont.[133] His prudent rule at home is demonstrated (with due allowance made for flattering hyperbole) by the famous Canopus Decree of 4 March 238, made by the Egyptian priesthood in honor of the king and his wife, Berenice, as *Theoi Euergetai*, "Benefactor Gods."[134] (This Berenice, daughter of King Magas of Cyrene, and known to Hellenistic historians as Berenice II, was the battle-seasoned equestrienne who raced victorious chariot teams at Nemea, and whose dedicated lock of hair [p. 179] was immortalized as a constellation by Callimachus.) Ptolemy wins praise, not only (as we might expect) for benefactions to the temples and promotion of Egyptian cults[135]—especially those involving sacred animals—but also for maintaining peace by means of a strong national-defense system, and in general for good government. As an instance of the latter the decree singles out Ptolemy's importation, at his own expense, of grain for the populace when an inadequate Nile flood threatened nationwide famine—"in return for which things the gods have granted stability to their royal rule, and will give them all other good things for ever hereafter." It all smacks, not surprisingly, of paternalist estate man-

Fig. 87. Berenice II, wife of Ptolemy III, with veil and diadem. Gold octadrachm minted at Alexandria(?) ca. 240–230 B.C. Photo Hirmer.

agement; but at least it can be said of the first three Ptolemies that they managed their estates with prudence, if not with foresight.

Ptolemy III also got credit for recovering, during a campaign abroad, certain sacred statues that the Persians had removed, and returning them to their temples. The campaign in question was the long, drawn-out Third Syrian (or Laodicean) War, against Seleucus II (above, p. 150). In 241 this war had finally ended in a peace treaty that ceded to Ptolemy an enclave including the great naval base of Seleucia-in-Pieria.[136] Seleucid Syria still retained Laodicea-ad-Mare as a viable seaport. The vexed question of the Syrian frontier was to remain in abeyance, greatly to Alexandria's benefit, for another twenty years, until the accession of a weak Ptolemy was offset by that of a strong and dynamic Seleucid (below, p. 288).

The decades following the Laodicean War had witnessed further erosion of the Seleucid empire. Seleucus II, having been forced by his mother, Laodice, to cede Asia Minor to his brother, Antiochus Hierax, found himself—inevitably—engaged thereafter in a fratricidal struggle with this all-too-hawkish sibling rival (above, p. 150). Ptolemy III, that adroit fisher in other men's ponds, seems to have supported Hierax, doubtless hoping to strengthen his own position in Asia Minor and the Aegean.[137] Seleucus, preoccupied by this War of the Brothers (239–236), had little time to attend to the great eastern satrapies: it was about now that Bactria and Sogdiana seceded, under Diodotus, the Seleucid general appointed by Antiochus II (ca. 250?), and that Parthia made its first moves toward independence. About 236 Seleucus made peace with Hierax, surrendering to him all Asia Minor north of the Taurus Mountains.[138] The concession did nothing to assuage the Hawk's ambitions. He was by now hand-in-glove with the Gauls (Galatians), who had taken to exacting protection money from all the Greek states of Asia Minor: this act of *de facto* brigandage on his part was not forgotten. He then compounded his offense by conspiring with the same Gauls to overthrow Attalus I of Pergamon.

Fig. 88. Antiochus Hierax ("the Hawk"). Silver tetradrachm minted at Sigeion in the Troad ca. 240–230 B.C. Private collection.

Fig. 89. Attalus I Soter(?). Marble head found at Pergamon (third century B.C.). Staatliche Museen zu Berlin.

Here, at last, Hierax had met his match. Attalus, as we have seen, had already once defeated the Gauls (above, pp. 150–51), and proclaimed himself king (237?); he now pursued Hierax (231–229?), with deadly and unrelenting hatred, from Phrygia to Lydia, from Lydia to Caria, then eastward, beating him in three major battles.[139] By 228 Attalus had taken over all the Hawk's briefly held territories in Asia Minor. A fine propagandist, he let no one forget his triumph, but—like Augustus after Actium (below, p. 679)—stressed only his victory over the forces of barbarism, not his defeat of a fellow countryman. Both in Athens and in Pergamon his ceremonial sculpture and architecture caught the prevalent mood by presenting him as a god manifest on earth (below, pp. 339 ff.).[140] Do not climb the sky, Alcman had advised mere mortals in the sixth century; do not attempt to marry Aphrodite.[141] As the Hellenistic age progressed, more and more rulers evinced an incurable determination to do both. The frontiers between the human and the divine, breached with arrogant panache by Alexander and the aetiologizing propaganda of Euhemerus (above, p. 55), were now being steadily further eroded.

Antiochus Hierax made one last desperate bid to recoup his fortunes. He approached, or was approached by, his aunt Stratonice, the ex-wife of Demetrius II (she had left Demetrius when he married Phthia, the future mother of Philip V).[142] Between them they devised a scheme to overthrow Seleucus. While Stratonice led an insurrection in Antioch, Hierax moved eastward into Babylonia. Seleucus was forced to abandon his Parthian campaign by this diversion; but when he moved, it was to some effect. He drove Hierax out—the Hawk fled, first to Ptolemaic territory, probably Ephesus, where he was imprisoned but escaped; and then to

Thrace, where he was soon murdered by the Gauls (227)[143]—and, this done, captured and executed Stratonice (who had seemingly nursed hopes of marrying her peccant nephew). His next target, predictably, was Attalus; but before he could move against him he died after an accidental fall from his horse (226).[144] He was succeeded by his first son, who reigned as Seleucus III Soter for three years, and was then murdered by one of his own officers while conducting an ineffectual campaign against Attalus.[145] (He was known by his troops, with heavy military irony, as Thunderbolt.)

At this point the Seleucid fortunes seemed to have reached their nadir. But Seleucus III's cousin Achaeus, nominated as governor of Asia Minor, proved a man of remarkable energy and vision, coupled, unexpectedly, with apparent freedom from the usurper's ambition. He had Seleucus III's younger brother proclaimed king as Antiochus III (223). Achaeus then set about Attalus so vigorously that by 222 he had driven him back to Pergamon and recovered all the lost territories of Asia Minor.[146] With the accession, now, of new young monarchs—two of them, Antiochus III and Philip V, men of great talent and personality—in all three Hellenistic kingdoms (Ptolemy III was succeeded by the weak and vacillating Ptolemy IV Philopator in 222/1),[147] a watershed had been reached, as Polybius recognized, in the history of the Greek-speaking world. Yet—and he recognized this too—what in the long run was to have the greatest effect, and most radical impact, on that world was the intervention of Rome.

PART THREE
PHALANX AND LEGION
221–168 B.C.

CHAPTER 17

POLYBIUS AND THE NEW ERA

"The starting point for my treatise," Polybius wrote, "will be the 140th Olympiad [= 220–216 B.C.]. . . . In earlier times the affairs of the inhabited world [*oikoumenē*] had been, as it were, scattered, since enterprise, consummation, and locality remained separate in each instance; but from this turning point onwards history emerges as an organic whole: the affairs of Italy and of Africa are interwoven [*symplekesthai*][1] with those of Asia and of Greece, and all things point in concert to a single end."[2] That end, of course, was the rise of Rome to supremacy in the Mediterranean, and to achieve its delineation meant writing "universal" or "general" history (*ta katholou graphein*), a virtually new concept.[3] "Who," Polybius asks, "is so indifferent or indolent that he would not want to know how, and under what form of government, almost every part of the *oikoumenē* came under Rome's sole rule in less than fifty-three years, an unprecedented phenomenon?"[4] Who indeed? It was to answer this question, in the first instance, that Polybius wrote his *Histories*—or at least the first part, covering the period down to 168; the second part (167–146) sought rather to evaluate Rome's achievement for future generations, not in terms of success or failure (over which there could be no argument), but according to moral criteria.[5] Significantly, he seldom implies that that achievement is good himself.

Of the forty books into which the *Histories* were divided, we have the first five intact, and substantial fragments from all the rest except 17, 19, 37, and 40 (which consisted of the general index). The structure of the first thirty books seems to have been loosely hexadic, with Books 6 and 12 as natural dividing points, presenting two general discussions, on political systems and historiography, respectively, and the next two hexads (Bks. 19–24, 25–30) each covering a period of four Olympiads (146–149, 150–153).[6] The apparent modification of structural plan, especially in the last ten books, is almost certainly due to Polybius's decision, *in mediis rebus*, to continue his work beyond the watershed of Pydna (June 168: see p. 430) and take account of the destruction of Corinth and Carthage in 146. The precise point at which the plan was revised, the number of books already written (and published), the degree to which the change necessitated revisions in books previously written, and the date at which the complete work became available are questions that have all been fiercely debated and to which no final answers can be given.[7] It seems likely that the

Fig. 90. Commemorative portrait of Polybius(?). Cast of a
stele, now lost, found at Kleitor, Arcadia, and identified by an
inscription matching that for a homonymous probable later
descendant of the historian, with an identically named father.
Staatliche Museen zu Berlin. Photo Alinari.

point at which Polybius changed his mind was after Corinth fell; that Books 1–5, and perhaps 6, had been published by about 150; that the last ten books were not finished till after 129;[8] that he was still revising and adding to the *Histories* at the time of his death (ca. 118; passages in Books 1–15 appear to have been added after 146, and there are traces of revision throughout);[9] and that in consequence the finished work only appeared posthumously.[10] Even these assumptions are far from certain, and anything beyond them is pure guesswork.[11]

Polybius called his study a *pragmateia*, a practical treatise or guide. Not for him the aim of some Hellenistic historians, to give enjoyment (*terpsis*); what he offered was useful advice (*ōpheleia*). His work was to be *pragmatikē*, realistic, rational, Thucydidean,[12] politico-military, shorn of genealogical and mythical fictions, and based, where possible, on autopsy;[13] but also *apodeiktikē*, analytical, demonstrative, scientific in method.[14] Despite polite genuflections to his Roman readers, he was really aiming at Greeks. His declared purpose was to provide useful matter for statesmen (he had been one himself); to chronicle the course of events between Philip V's clash with Rome in 200, the final Macedonian defeat at Pydna in 168, and the sack of Corinth and loss of Achaean and Macedonian independence in 146 (he had been either eyewitness or participant in much of the history he wrote); and, finally, to teach men how to face disaster (a lesson, again, that he had learned from bitter personal experience). The powerful *ad hominem* motivation that, despite disclaimers, pervades Polybius's approach to his task as a historian is everywhere in evidence.

As an individual, an Arcadian, a Greek, a former soldier and statesman, he had to swallow the bitter humiliation of defeat, loss of independence, eclipse by an alien power, deportation *sine die*. He had to come to terms with new realities, to learn how to live with the Romans while, at the same time, still being able to live with himself. To that extent his history cannot help being an attempt to rationalize as inevitable what he had been powerless to prevent. History minus truth, he proclaimed, is as useless as an eyeless creature;[15] but the vision in his case remains astigmatic. Hence his intriguing, and at times self-contradictory, obsession with that characteristically Hellenistic concept Tyche[16]—by turns, and often simultaneously, Chance, Luck, Fortune (both malign and benevolent), Providence: the random factor, Fate's guiding hand, the unpredictability of things. Polybius quotes Demetrius of Phaleron on the downfall of Persia, the astonishing rise of Macedonia. "But notwithstanding," Demetrius wrote, from equally harsh experience, "Tyche never accommodates herself to our life, always comes up with some new twist to defeat our calculations"; and he went on to predict the fall, in time, of Macedonia also, a prediction, trite enough in itself, that made a deep impression on Polybius.[17] It also provided him with a unifying theme. If Tyche brought the *oikoumenē* under Roman control, then Polybius could write the universal history of that process. Tyche, in short, is crucial to his historiography.[18]

His escape clause is that Tyche can be invoked as an explanation only when no rational cause for an event appears possible:[19] those "acts of God" that are the nearest approach by insurance companies to theology.[20] In practice, however, he does not

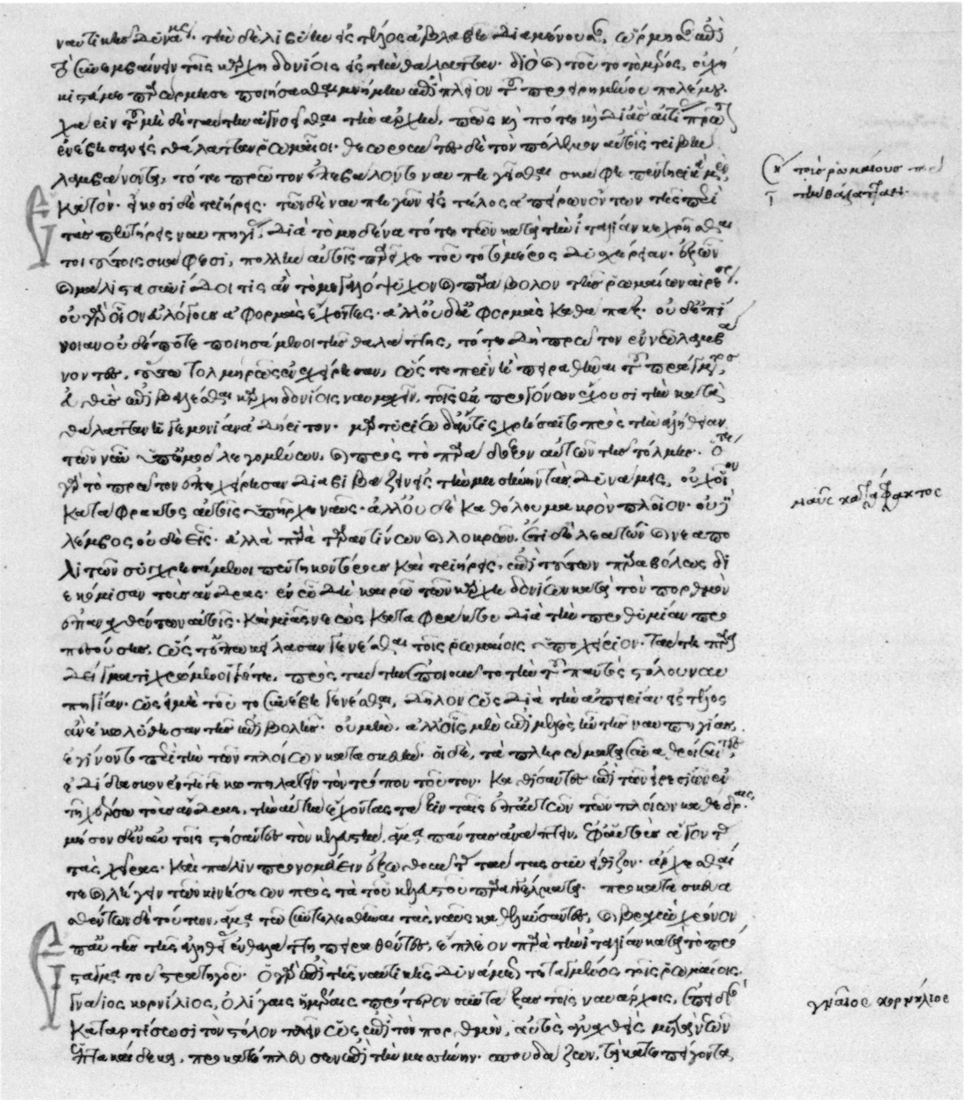

Fig. 91. Early fifteenth-century manuscript of Polybius from Constantinople
(Polyb. 1.20.7–21.4).
British Library, ms. add. 11728, London.

always stick with this working rule, least of all when dealing with Rome. Tyche, he
implied, willed Rome's meteoric rise in half a century;[21] yet the Romans also, or alternatively, brought this result about by their own merits, qualities, and efforts. We
sense a psychological double bind here. Polybius had seen the Romans in action: he
knew at first hand, better than many, just how their formula for success worked. Yet
at the same time, as a Greek, he needed some palliation for defeat. So extraordinary a
phenomenon as the triumph of Rome had to be providential; and if providential,

then, by mere mortals, irresistible.[22] Thus, though men frequently attribute to Tyche what is really the result of human action,[23] rational causation and the workings of Tyche are interdependent, and best invoked together. Tyche may dictate the overall shape of events, but within this pattern man can, up to a point, make his own decisions.[24] Polybius's position here is not all that far from the cautious stand on *Moira* (Fate) taken by Herodotus.

What is more, having created a device to relieve his countrymen of ultimate responsibility for succumbing to the Roman takeover, he can then be as rational as he pleases in dealing with excesses of religious or superstitious credulity. Predecessors who claimed that no snow or rain ever fell on a certain open-air statue of Artemis, or that anyone entering the holy of holies in Zeus's mountain shrine in Arcadia at once lost his shadow, are given very short shrift. To believe what is not only unreasonable but impossible, Polybius argues, has to indicate either "childish naïveté" or a "feeble intelligence."[25] This does not mean that he was a consistent intellectual rationalist. Like Herodotus again, he reveals an odd mixture of credulity and skepticism. His general attitude might most charitably be described as incoherence tempered by Euhemerism,[26] with the political cynic preponderant, though not always in complete control. His attitude to Roman religion is predictably ambivalent. He is well aware (how could he not be?) that Rome swarms with religious ceremony, that *numen* is all-pervasive: in fact he describes superstition (*deisidaimonia*) as "the thing that holds the Roman state together."[27] This admission he hastily justifies by the claim that the Romans "have acted thus for the sake of the common people," who, being "flighty and full of lawless urges, irrational passion, and violent rage," need to be "restrained by impalpable fears and suchlike mummery"—an opium-for-the-masses thesis that recurs elsewhere,[28] and is strikingly reminiscent of the ideas propagated by that fifth-century authoritarian Critias in his *Sisyphus*.[29]

Polybius, in short, comes across, for various reasons, as a historian whose center is not quite in the middle; and it is worth looking at his career with this in mind, not least since for over half a century of crucial Hellenistic history he remains by far our most serious witness. He was born about 200 in the Arcadian city of Megalopolis,[30] some twenty-two years after it had been destroyed by Cleomenes (above, p. 261: it was rebuilt soon after the Spartan defeat at Sellasia). Cleomenes, as we have seen, gets very short shrift in the *Histories*. Polybius's father, Lycortas,[31] was a distinguished Megalopolitan statesman, several times generalissimo (*stratēgos*) of the Achaean League, and a close friend of Philopoemen, another Megalopolitan, whose career in the League followed an identical course. Both men represented a limited, and somewhat intransigent, attitude in politics: they sought a united Peloponnese under Achaean leadership, with Sparta neutralized and made a member of the League. (In 188 Philopoemen, with Rome's tacit approval, was actually to demilitarize Sparta, and abolish the old Lycurgan constitution: see p. 423).[32] They also favored alliance with Ptolemaic Egypt in return for regular financial support, and a somewhat ambivalent policy of neutrality toward Rome in her dealings with Macedonia and Greece.[33]

This was the atmosphere in which the future historian grew up, and it left an indelible mark on him. He was perhaps four or five when a Roman proconsul, Titus Quinctius Flamininus, proclaimed the freedom of the Greeks at the Isthmian Games of 196 (p. 311), and seven at the time of the Roman military evacuation (194). Throughout his early adolescence the Achaean League was fighting both the Aetolians (for whom, again, he seldom has a good word) and the Seleucid Antiochus III. Since his father was a wealthy gentleman landowner as well as a League politician, Polybius grew up with a passion for riding, hunting, and the outdoor life[34]—pursuits that later stood him in good stead when dealing with Roman aristocrats. He also was constantly exposed, from an early age, to the world of practical politics. He tells us of an occasion during his adolescence when he heard, and had very sharp moral reactions to, an angry debate between Philopoemen and the current League general.[35]

It is clear that he early adopted as his own the views of Lycortas, Philopoemen, and their circle, which called for collaboration with Rome "only within the strict conditions of the Achaean laws and the Roman alliance." This he terms an "honorable" attitude, as opposed to the "specious" subservience of pro-Roman extremists such as Aristaenus.[36] In fact, a point that Polybius himself elsewhere makes clear, during Aristaenus's year as *stratēgos* (188/7) Achaean policy abroad was aggressively independent, and conducted largely without reference to Rome:[37] Polybius's local prejudices need careful watching. Similarly, the impression he gives that from 180 Achaean policy was dictated by the pro-Roman group is simply untrue: the Lycortas caucus retained all its influence,[38] and suspicion grows that what Polybius is really trying to do is exculpate his father from association with the decisions that led to Pydna. His position is made abundantly clear by the fact that, aged eighteen, he was chosen to carry the urn containing Philopoemen's ashes at the latter's state funeral (183/2),[39] and afterwards composed, in three books, an encomiastic biography of the dead statesman, probably his first published work.[40]

He was also, as Lycortas's son, being groomed for high office. The mere fact of belonging to his father's circle constituted a political education in itself. Polybius must, from childhood onwards, have heard the arguments for and against coexistence and compromise with Rome thrashed out a thousand times. In 181/0, though still well under the official age limit of thirty,[41] he was chosen, together with his father and the grandson of Aratus, to serve on an embassy to Ptolemy V Epiphanes. Ptolemy had renewed the old Lagid alliance with the League (p. 249: 182/1?),[42] negotiating through Lycortas for the supply of arms and cash, and now promised a naval squadron, for the acceptance and delivery of which the Achaean delegates were to be responsible.[43] The mission was canceled because of Ptolemy's death, but the honor, for a young man in his early twenties, remained outstanding. By 170/69—presumably after considerable experience of soldiering in the field, though for this we have no direct evidence[44]— Polybius had, at the youngest possible age, been appointed cavalry commander (*hipparchos*) of the League:[45] this position was political as well as military, and normally formed the stepping stone to election as *stratēgos*.

Thus Polybius was deeply committed both to the League and to his own career within it. As we have seen, his political group favored an independent neutralism with regard to Rome, an attitude that made its members suspect both to the pro-

Roman Achaean party and to the Romans themselves.[46] The times were to test this policy severely, and Polybius was to modify his own attitude enough by 170, whether on principle or for more pragmatic reasons, to oppose his father in the Achaean assembly.[47] Since 172 Rome had been at war with Macedonia (the so-called Third Macedonian War), a conflict that was to end in 168 with the total defeat at Pydna of the Macedonian king Perseus (pp. 427 ff.). The attitude of the Achaean League was, from Rome's viewpoint, by no means satisfactory. Its leaders were not only divided among themselves, but also, clearly, hedging their bets, since as late as 171 a standoff between Rome and Macedonia did not strike even Polybius as wholly out of the question.[48] Two Roman envoys who visited the Peloponnese in 169 found that, in their opinion, certain leaders of the League were unfriendly to the Roman cause, and named, among others, Lycortas and Polybius.[49] They had not, in point of fact, actively promoted defection from the Roman alliance; but their support for it had been, at best, lukewarm.[50]

It is true that the Roman definition of "unfriendliness" (*inimicitia*) seems to have included anything short of total and sycophantic collaboration, the kind of attitude encouraged (if we are to believe Polybius) by the Achaean pro-Roman group under the leadership of Callicrates. Now in 180 Callicrates had been the spokesman of a notorious embassy to Rome—notorious largely through Polybius's venomous account of it.[51] In his version, Callicrates urged the Romans to wake up to the hostility and intransigence of the dominant party of Lycortas; were Callicrates, Hyperbatus, and their group in power, they would ensure that Achaean policy—indeed the very law of the land—was wholly subordinated to Rome's will. The offer, Polybius claims, was enthusiastically endorsed, and from then on Rome consistently supported such sycophants while ignoring wiser if less toadying friends in Achaea. In this version the opposition to Rome is associated with populist politicians and the mob; its removal, with Callicrates and his upper-class supporters.[52]

There is, clearly, much to arouse suspicion in this account, and its widespread acceptance at face value as a turning point in Roman-Greek relationships—with liberal scholars denigrating Callicrates, while conservatists or realists praise him as "a far-sighted statesman whose actions were conducive to the welfare of Achaea," what might be termed the Laval syndrome[53]—comes as something of a surprise. In the first place, Polybius had powerful motives for doing a hatchet job on Callicrates, who was not only his father's leading opponent, but also (as we shall see) the person directly responsible for Polybius's own seventeen-year exile. Second, the narrative bristles with inconsistencies and implausibilities. Can we really believe that any Achaean politician would urge his fellow countrymen to place the interests of Rome above their own laws and constitution, or, if he did so, that he would then be delegated to go to Rome and present the opposition's case?[54] Further, though Callicrates, as spokesman, claims that his party is out of favor in Achaea, the mere fact of his presence there before the Roman Senate, as ranking member of an Achaean embassy, officially delegated, *ipso facto* disproves such an assertion.[55] What is more, the *stratēgos* for that year (181/0) was his henchman Hyperbatus.[56]

We need not doubt, then, that Callicrates' speech was conciliatory to Rome (by no means a new departure),[57] nor that it pleased the Senate, nor that it aimed, *inter alia*, to embarrass Lycortas and the Achaean opposition, which there are some signs that it did.[58] But just as Polybius erred from the truth in claiming that Callicrates and his group were out of power at the time of the 180 embassy, he is equally misleading in his suggestion that from then on they, hand in glove with Rome, dictated Achaean policy. It is true that Callicrates himself was elected *stratēgos* at some point after his return from the embassy (taking bribes in the process, Polybius sneers):[59] but it so happens that all the *stratēgoi* known to us from the following decade are Callicrates' opponents.[60] The most we can say is that the embassy may have encouraged hard-liners in Rome, and undoubtedly tended to deepen the divisions in Lycortas's own party between the advocates of intransigence and those who preferred cautious compromise. Callicrates' most concrete achievement would seem to have been the restoration of the Spartan and Messenian exiles.[61] The real lesson for a modern reader is the degree of *parti pris* manipulation that Polybius's narrative reveals.

After ten further years of such public political bickering it is hardly remarkable that the Roman envoys who visited Achaea on a fact-finding mission should have detected anti-Roman sentiments in some of the League politicians. What *is* surprising is that at the time no action was taken against any individuals on the basis of such complaints because (says Polybius) no convincing excuse for doing so could be found.[62] The envoys clearly knew nothing about the brisk debate on future policy, involving Lycortas and his associates, that had taken place a few months previously.[63] On that occasion some firebrands had actually spoken out in favor of disciplining the pro-Roman extremists. Lycortas himself wanted strict neutrality, while Polybius and others felt they should keep their options open, and offer the Romans aid—but only if circumstances made it desirable or advisable for the benefit of Achaea. This last view prevailed, and it was as a member of the then-dominant group that Polybius became *hipparchos* (170/69).

In fact the Achaeans passed a decree placing their forces at the disposal of the Roman consul in Macedonia;[64] but the consul, Quintus Marcius Philippus, declined the offer when Polybius, after careful delay, acquainted him with it.[65] Since the delay was obviously engineered in hope of just such a rejection, it is hard to tell (a thought that also occurred to Polybius) whether Marcius's refusal was dictated by kindness or suspicion. A more likely motive is self-interest. Polybius himself stayed on with Marcius when the other envoys left, and (on the Roman's secret instructions) subsequently managed to get the Achaean assembly to veto the dispatch of five thousand troops to Marcius's opposite number, Appius Claudius Centho, in Epirus. This act pleased Marcius, who seems to have wanted to keep a rival out of action, and also saved the League something over 120 talents; but at the same time it gave Polybius's political enemies the chance to represent him as less than enthusiastic for the Roman cause[66]—and who is to say that at the time they were wrong?

In any case, when, after Perseus's defeat at Pydna (p. 430), the Romans conducted a purge of unreliable leading men in Achaea, deporting no less than a thousand of them to Rome,[67] among those thus exiled was Polybius.[68] His father, Lycortas, must already have been dead; otherwise he too would have been listed among the more distinguished exiles. From now on, as Polybius wrote, and had learned the hard way, it was accepted that everyone (which for him meant the Greeks of the Peloponnese) must obey Rome's orders.[69] Such control, despite the Roman partiality for legalism, could be arbitrary to a degree: neither Polybius nor any of his fellow deportees was ever put on trial, or even accused, though ostensibly they were in Italy to answer charges of not having aided Rome against Perseus. In actual fact they were partly regarded as hostages for the good behavior of those left in the Peloponnese, and partly had been shipped off out of the way to stop them making any trouble in future themselves. The list of victims was drawn up by Callicrates and his associates: Polybius is, understandably, no kinder to Callicrates than Thucydides, for a like reason, had been to Cleon.[70]

The position of Polybius in this group was exceptional. Most of the Achaeans were kept well clear of the capital, on various Etruscan estates. But Polybius remained in Rome, and was clearly free also to travel. This privilege he owed to the intercession, as he himself tells us, of the eighteen-year-old Scipio Aemilianus, son of Aemilius Paullus, the victor of Pydna: they had first met through "the loan of some books and conversation about them."[71] Scipio, Polybius tells us, begged for his company and intellectual guidance: there is a Socratic flavor about the whole episode. When the other deportees were being moved to provincial cities, Scipio and his elder brother, Fabius, petitioned the praetor on Polybius's behalf, and he was allowed to remain behind, becoming a constant companion and adviser to Scipio, just as the young man had hoped.[72] It is likely that Lycortas and his son had, in an official capacity, already made the acquaintance of Aemilius Paullus, perhaps when the Roman visited Megalopolis during his tour of Greece. It is even possible that Polybius actually took up residence in Scipio's household.[73]

The literary and philhellenic friends whom Scipio gathered round him in the so-called Scipionic circle offered the kind of company that Polybius found most congenial: intellectual, but at the same time tough-minded and aristocratic. They included Furius, Laelius, and, later, the Greek philosopher Panaetius (below, p. 639), who probably fostered in the historian a taste for Stoicism.[74] Scipio and Polybius shared a passion for hunting: this was how Polybius also made the acquaintance of a hostage of a different sort, the Seleucid prince Demetrius I, whose escape from Rome he helped to organize, almost certainly with the connivance, if not the active assistance, of his Roman patrons (p. 440).[75] There was also a mildly puritanical streak of self-betterment and self-control in Scipio that appealed strongly to Polybius, who goes out of his way to emphasize how different the moderate, altruistic, brave, generous Scipio was from the common run of upper-class young Romans, many of whom were willing to pay a talent for a boy lover, or three hundred drachmas for a pot of caviar.[76]

Yet, again, there is something disturbing about this long and uncharacteristic hymn of praise to a patron. How far did Polybius remain objective over Scipio, and the public events with which he and his family were involved? It has been noted that almost all the Roman speeches in the *Histories* are made by connections of Scipio's family, not an encouraging sign.[77] Once again the *ad hominem* motif is detectable. Despite his insistence on historical impartiality, his declared contempt for writers who inflate local or personal interests on their own behalf,[78] one gets the constant nagging suspicion that Polybius's grandiose scheme of universal history conceals, at one level, an extended apologia for his own career and the aims of the Achaean League. This does not make him any the less interesting. He knew his Thucydides and Xenophon well, and can hardly have failed to reflect on what he had in common with his two famous predecessors. All three of them spent long years in exile—exile, moreover, that in one way or another brought them into sharp conflict with groups of their own countrymen in power. All three were strongly conservative land-owners, at odds with the more radical democrats of their own cities. Like Xeno-phon, Polybius was a country gentleman who rode, hunted, and had very consider-able military experience. Last, all three were conditioned, as historians, by the events that had shaped their lives, even though Thucydides hardly protests his impartiality more than Polybius does, and Polybius's declared methods of work—his respect for firsthand information, his safeguards on speeches, his care with documents—at times almost verbally echo those of his great Athenian forerunner. Like Thucydides, Polybius was obsessed by the idea of truth; but as has been well observed of him, he was clearly "a man who has persuaded himself of the truth of matters in which he has a strong personal commitment, and is not prepared even to envisage the possibil-ity that there may be another point of view."[79]

Polybius spent seventeen years as an official detainee. He seems to have had re-markable freedom of movement, especially when in Scipio's entourage. Yet "he had come to Italy under a cloud and he stayed on under compulsion."[80] Inevitably, his picture of Roman public life was affected by his ambiguous status, mostly toward discretion. He tells us nothing about the murderous rivalries between the great Ro-man families, the sulphurous lawsuits, the scandals, the corruption. This kind of tactful omission is precisely what we might expect in an ambience where "to disap-prove of Rome was to perish."[81] He can analyze Rome's rise to world domination, but he cannot afford either to query her motives or to challenge the rise itself, much less take apart the machinery of government or scrutinize the internecine power struggles he witnessed. He also had to take it as axiomatic, whatever evidence to the contrary he might observe, that the ruling class was firmly in control both of its own lower orders and of the Italian allies.[82] As a result his Roman characters tend to be one-dimensional, or at best seen out of their social context (Cato is a nice instance: all the old curmudgeon's jokes at Polybius's expense are quoted, but we hear not a word about his endless feuding and litigation),[83] while the single theme of imperial progress eclipses all else. Though individuals may be criticized, this policy is never questioned.

What Polybius was up against can be judged by his fate and that of his fellow Achaeans. It was not until 150, after at least four previous petitions had been refused (the first written decision declared that "we do not consider it in the best interests either of the Romans or of your own peoples that these men should return home," a perennial bromide),[84] that Scipio, whose influence was now at its height, persuaded the Senate to rescind the deportation order. By this time no more than three hundred of the original thousand were left alive. Yet despite all this the proposal still encountered fierce opposition. Polybius, relying on his privileged status, pressed for re-instatement with all former honors. Cato the Censor, who had supported the Achaeans' plea to go home, with jovial asides about turning them over to the Greek undertakers, told Polybius, twinkling (but the joke had its sharp edge), that he ought to learn from Odysseus, and not go back into the Cyclops' cave to retrieve the hat and belt he had left behind.[85] Clearly Polybius, however influential his friends, could not count on Rome beyond a certain point. Even after his release he remained, like any Roman client, under serious obligations to his patron,[86] and in reading his work it is important to bear in mind that "he was never completely free to express his real opinions."[87]

Interestingly, he was in no hurry to return home after his release; and even after he had done so, he was soon back in the company of his Roman friends once more. Probably in 150 he accompanied Scipio to Spain and North Africa, where he interviewed the aged Numidian ruler Masinissa for his recollections of Hannibal ("very avaricious").[88] Scipio also seems at some point to have sent him on an exploratory voyage round the coast of northwest Africa.[89] Back in Achaea he ran into a wave of rabid separatism that was fast moving toward a direct confrontation with Rome (pp. 448 ff.). His appeals for peace and unanimity fell on deaf ears, and (one suspects) his own position as, in effect, Rome's protégé did not make him popular with the nationalists of the day. Thus when (149) he received an official invitation to proceed to North Africa "as there was need of him for public service," he accepted with alacrity, and the Achaeans voted to send him.[90] If he foresaw the coming disaster—and he must have been blind if he failed to—he probably figured that he would rather be elsewhere when it happened.

Though this first journey proved abortive—he turned back from Corcyra because he mistakenly thought the war was over—Polybius in 146 stood with Scipio and watched Carthage burn, duly recording for posterity his patron's prescient *obiter dicta* about Rome one day suffering a like fate, his noble tears over the transience of empire.[91] That same year the Achaean League went down fighting Rome's legions, and Corinth, at the Senate's express command, was sacked and razed to the ground.[92] Polybius returned to Greece as Rome's postwar liaison officer, in time to see the looted art treasures stacked outside Corinth for removal to Italy, while soldiers sat playing draughts on priceless paintings.[93] The League had been abolished: Polybius's new role was that of a Roman commissioner—commissar, almost—who had, in effect, to sell the new regime to the various individual cities, regulate the relations between them, and in general make the transitional period as smooth as possible.[94]

Despite the role he performed, it is clear that he found Rome's actions in 146 both alarming and unpalatable, and tried, in the *Histories*, to convey to his masters something of what the Greeks felt about this new fire-and-sword policy. Two of the four types of Greek reaction to the destruction of Carthage that he records—tucked away tactfully between others that acknowledge the logic or necessity of Rome's "final solution," in terms of imperial self-defense or legitimate coercion[95]—speak of ruthlessness, treachery, and the lust for power (*philarchia*).[96] About Corinth, on the other hand, he kept discreetly quiet. He had already made his feelings on terrorism very clear when discussing Philip V's destruction of Thermon in Aetolia, and his Greek readers would not be slow to apply the lesson for themselves: [97]

> Violent and gratuitous destruction of temples, statues, and all such gear, since it offers absolutely no advantage to one's own side in a war, and does nothing to cripple the enemy, can only be described as the act of a deranged mind and attitude. Decent men should not make war on the ignorant and wrongheaded with a view to stamping them out and exterminating them, but should rather aim to correct and remove their mistakes. Nor should they lump the innocent and the guilty together, but rather treat those they regard as guilty with the same merciful compassion that they extend to the innocent. Wrongdoing as an instrument of terrorization, to coerce unwilling subjects, belongs to the tyrant, who hates his people as much as they hate him; but a king's business is to treat everyone well, to win men's love by his humane and generous conduct, and thus to rule and preside with the consent of those he governs.

Fine words; but they stand in piquant contrast to the latter-day career of their author, whose actions, if not his private thoughts, were dictated by a bitter consciousness of the inevitability of Roman overlordship.[98]

Polybius might have been treated as a traitor by his fellow countrymen, but the *fait accompli* of defeat made him rather appear in the guise of a savior. His services to Achaea in the difficult years after 146 were gratefully recognized—not only by the pro-Roman aristocratic government—with statues and other marks of honor. He did his job honorably, refusing all gifts. One inscription claimed that if Greece had followed Polybius's advice, she would never have fallen; and that, having fallen, it was only through his aid that she survived. In his own city of Megalopolis it was written as a tribute that "he had been the Romans' ally, and had stayed their wrath against Greece."[99] Those words alone show how radically the Greek spirit had changed, even since the days of Aratus and Cleomenes. The nationalists who had died fighting for Achaea, playing their last desperate hope (and suspected by the *bienpensant* of revolutionary aims), get little sympathy from Polybius—or, one suspects, from the citizens who had to live with the consequences of their failure. This is what really arouses Polybius's anger. Their aims, he declared bitterly, had been unrealistic; they did not understand Roman methods, they completely misjudged the situation, and because of this obdurate, indeed criminal, stupidity, they had brought disaster on themselves and their people.[100]

The dream of independence was ended at last: it was not to be fully renewed for another two millennia and more. Polybius himself lived on for nearly thirty years after the sack of Corinth, years mostly spent working on his *magnum opus*. He still traveled. He visited (145 or later?) the Alexandria of Ptolemy VIII, nicknamed *Physkōn*, "Potbelly," "Bladder" (p. 538), and, predictably, found it an unpleasant sink of gross luxury.[101] He may have accompanied Scipio during the siege of Numantia in

Spain (133).[102] He also at some point apparently traced Hannibal's route through the Alps. He visited Locri in southern Italy on several occasions, and claimed to have won the Locrians exemption from service in Rome's Spanish and Dalmatian campaigns.[103] But for the most part he probably worked and hunted to a vigorous old age at home in Arcadia. He is said to have died at eighty-two, of a fall from his horse, returning from a day's excursion in the countryside.[104]

What kind of a history would such a man create, looking back over his long and strangely fragmented life? How far, and in what way, would his views have changed between his highly politicized youth in Achaea and his Romanized old age? We have already seen his bias at work: how far can we trust him over the events he describes? And, perhaps most important, how literally are we to take his endless explanatory asides, telling us what his intentions are, what he regards as the function of a historian, the value of history? Why so much self-justification? And if, as Buffon insisted, the style reveals the man, what are we to make of his prose, no bad place to start in any evaluation of a historian? The first thing one notices is his terrible weakness for abstractions, a habit that Orwell regarded as a telltale symptom in the historical propagandist anxious to camouflage a bad case. The sentences are long, clumsy, and overloaded: Polybius may be trying to emulate the thorny complexities of Thucydides, but what he actually conveys has been well described as "the flat and prosy verbosity of a government department."[105] His grasp of periodic structure is rudimentary, and his bureaucratic muddiness has been compared with the style current in the Hellenistic chanceries, what German scholars refer to as his *Kanzleisprache*.[106]

He nowhere describes himself as a realist (though the pursuit of *pragmatikē historia* strongly implies it); he does not need to. His vision is flat, relentlessly two-dimensional; he never thinks of himself as an artist. If he was aware of the way in which imaginative Roman writers were assimilating Greek models to create a new kind of literature, he gives no signs of it. He is a politician setting the record straight to his own satisfaction, in the wearily portentous prose of his kind. He is not only deficient in creative imagination himself—a trait he shares with Xenophon, and one that offers certain advantages to the modern scholar evaluating his evidence—but also, we find, irritably suspicious of those historians who possess it, on the grounds (not entirely mistaken grounds, either) that they will produce a distorted, romantic version of events. He himself, on the other hand, is prickly because he is using these same events to justify himself. He was not exactly a quisling:[107] despite his friendship with Scipio—whose equal he would have considered himself, socially if not in wealth[108]—he must have deeply resented the destruction of his career and country, his unjust deportation, his uneasy client status.

Yet there was ambivalence in his attitude, and more than a touch of the pragmatic *collabo* about him. He belonged to the ruling class; he had held high office. As a member of the property-owning elite he could not fail, at one level, to sympathize with the aims of Roman government, which were, inevitably, slanted in favor of wealthy upper-class provincials, and against insurrection, whether national or social.[109] He had a vested interest, after the fact, in Roman rule, and the scholar who labeled his role in Achaea from 146 as that of a "Roman commissar" was not exaggerating.[110] As Momigliano says, he "paved the way for the other Greek intellectuals who accepted Roman rule and collaborated with it."[111] He could justify this role only by working to limit Rome's growing appetite for unilateral exploitation (uncomfortably apparent after 146), her increasing use of force to maintain her supremacy—and, to a lesser extent, by appointing himself the interpreter of the New Order to his fellow Greeks. When we read him we should always remember that he is explaining Rome to a Greek audience; though he keeps one eye on his Roman readers too, he remains above all Rome's spokesman, "interpreting Rome to Greece, explaining that the empire had come to stay and could not be resisted, and indicating that this was such a vast historical design that it absolved his own compatriots from any slur of failure or impotence."[112]

The Stoic philosopher Panaetius, a Greek from Rhodes, similarly tried to reconcile Greeks to Roman rule: no accident that Panaetius too was an intimate of Scipio, that they and Polybius had long discussions together on the Roman constitution.[113] (The logical end of this trend was reached by another Greek thinker, Poseidonius of Apamea, who identified the Roman empire with the Stoic world state.) This matter of the constitution, discussed at length in Book 6, is revealing. Behind it lies the belief (which has something to be said for it) that a nation's destiny is inseparable from its system of government. On the other hand, Polybius's actual analysis of that system is, to put it mildly, bizarre. He praises Rome for her supposed "mixed constitution," an adaptation of Plato's and Aristotle's blend of monarchy (the consuls), aristocracy (the Senate), and democracy (the popular or plebeian element).[114] Such a mixed constitution was conceived to be the evolutionary climax of a process that had begun with Romulus and his successors, continuing by way of Tarquinius Superbus, the tyrant, to aristocratic rule and the oligarchy of the decemvirate.[115] It was also thought to have saved Rome, about the mid-fifth century, from the eternal repetitive sequence (*anakyklōsis*) of kingship/tyranny–aristocracy/oligarchy–democracy/ochlocracy.[116] This ingenious fantasy—a classic example of what happens when literary authorities, however irrelevant, are preferred to direct observation, however convenient—was finally nailed for the nonsense it was only by Mommsen.[117]

It is clear from this, and indeed has often been noted, that for a man who spent seventeen years among Roman statesmen, in a crucial period of Roman history,[118] Polybius is surprisingly obtuse about how the Roman system actually worked. His thinking, both practical and theoretical, never really breaks loose from its Greek conditioning. His view of Rome's imperial activities overseas is colored by the innate assumption that what he was dealing with was something very much akin to a Hellenistic monarchy. The niceties of provincial government through magistrates either eluded or failed to impress him: perhaps he saw the whole thing as an elaborate sham.[119] He, of all men, should have understood the subtleties of Roman political life, of patronage and clientship, the dominant role of the Roman nobility, "the nuances of public life."[120] Perhaps in his heart of hearts he did; perhaps it was all too close to the bone for comfort. But perhaps, too, the theoretical model he set up was designed, by way of comfort or parochialism, for Greek readers, who would instantly recognize Aristotelian theory when they saw it.[121] Whatever the influence on him of the Scipionic circle, his intellectual premises remained firmly set in a Greek mold,[122] and it seems all too likely that, like most educated Greeks, he still privately regarded the Romans as semibarbarians. He may even have had the Achaean League in mind as a model for Rome: it was certainly his ideal.[123]

Thus despite his claims to universalism, Polybius remained at heart a Peloponnesian Greek, who constantly exaggerated the importance both of the Leagues and of Macedonia in the Mediterranean at large (and *per contra*, found it hard to forgive Timaeus for doing precisely the same with Sicily and Magna Graecia). He attacked the habit of self-promoting parochialism in others, but was far from immune from it himself. This is not entirely surprising. Polybius was no intellectual in the formal sense: his ideas about religion were muddled; his philosophical concepts, thirdhand commonplaces. As a result, his approach to history was both confident and *simpliste*. Facts were facts, and could, with proper care, be retrieved, along with their causes.[124] Epistemological doubts never assailed him:[125] like Ranke, he sought to recover the past *wie es eigentlich gewesen sei,* in his own words "to record with complete fidelity what was actually said and done, however banal it might be."[126] The aim was utilitarian: past exempla would enlighten future readers, particularly statesmen.[127]

Polybius's limitations can be seen as an inevitable consequence of his upbringing. His formative years had been spent in the narrow, feuding environment of the Leagues of central Greece: nor was it so very long since Arcadia, Aetolia, and Achaea had been among the most backward, primitive communities south of Thessaly. Polybius made a hero out of that rabid local nationalist Philopoemen (though he was not above criticizing him on occasion);[128] his virulent distaste for the Spartan king Cleomenes was not only political but social, Cleomenes in his view—generally shared at the time—being a dangerous would-be subverter of the established order.[129] He had all of Thucydides' admiration for success, and Xenophon's self-alignment with the rural aristocracy. When, in his early thirties, he was forcibly removed to Rome, these various traits must have made him, for all his resentment, as susceptible to Rome's powerful allure as a nineteenth-century Fiji Islander to the measles. He tries to suggest that the young Scipio hero-worshipped him;[130] elsewhere he makes it clear (what no one could doubt) that it was really the other way round.[131] Whether he wholly approved of the policies that Scipio was called upon to implement is, as we have seen, quite another matter. In any case the process of assimilation and change must have been traumatic, and there are signs that Polybius never fully recovered from it. The efficiency, power, order, and discipline that he found in Roman government and Roman military affairs appealed to him in the way that the administration of British India appealed to Kipling. Yet, like Kipling again, he had his moments of doubt. How, he must have asked himself, did Scipio's sack of Numantia differ from the destruction of Corinth or Carthage? He also seems to have foreseen the convulsions of the late Republic, which, like Cato and others, he saw as the necessary outcome to moral decay engendered by long prosperity.[132] Worse, despite all the manifest benefits to his own class from a *clientela*-like relationship to the dominant power, despite his personal position of precarious privilege, his Greekness could never quite swallow the plain fact of defeat. Here was where fate stepped in. The concept of

Tyche took responsibility off his, and his countrymen's, shoulders. His thinking here is blurred, and small wonder. Tyche smiled on the Romans because of their achievements; their achievements were due to Tyche. The argument achieves its own *anakyklōsis*.

Within the definable limits of his prejudices, Polybius is, by and large, a conscientious historian. In his speeches he follows the Thucydidean example of trying to get as near as possible to the gist of what was actually said.[133] He stresses the historian's need for practical political experience, for topographical autopsy.[134] He worked hard to get his facts right, even if he did not always follow his own precepts. He talked to survivors; he made use of memoranda specially prepared by himself or others; he consulted archives and inscriptions;[135] he tried to take the long view. Ultimately he is best on military action, straight narrative, the day-to-day minutiae of diplomacy. His character analyses, though they often make shrewd points, are *parti pris* and too prone to great-man motivation. His attacks on various fellow historians would carry more weight were he not guilty of most of the same faults himself. He dismisses Timaeus as a niggling fault-finder, in two long and vicious digressions in which he himself niggles and carps with the best of them.[136] The animus here is that of the experienced statesman and soldier faced with a typical intellectual of the day, remote from practical affairs, dependent on books rather than experience, and liable to substitute rhetoric for passion. Yet, Timaeus might have retorted, was not Polybius's own description of the Roman constitution the merest Aristotelian mishmash? Did he not on occasion have recourse to books, with erroneous results, instead of using his own eyes when that would have been easy enough—for example, in his description of a Roman military camp?[137]

His underlying motives are sometimes concealed. It seems pretty clear that whatever he alleges against Timaeus, the strongest animus he felt was caused by natural jealousy of Timaeus's huge success.[138] Similarly, he criticizes Phylarchus for overdramatized sensationalism, in particular for his harrowing descriptions of how half-naked women and children were led off into slavery, sobbing and wailing, after a town's capture.[139] But what he really resented was Phylarchus's sympathetic portrayal of Cleomenes. Once again, too, pot is calling kettle black, since Polybius himself was quite capable of pulling out the rhetorical stops when it suited him. Good examples are the mutiny in Alexandria after Ptolemy V's accession; Hasdrubal's surrender, cursed by his comrades, reproached by his wife, at the fall of Carthage; and the long elegiac lament over Greece's downfall and ruin—fair Greece, sad relic—which he witnessed in 146.[140] He must rationalize his own actions by making Rome a more than human force, and duly does so; but he is also not above defending his own position as a historian by denigrating the competition with whatever criticism comes to hand.

The fact that Polybius never entirely lost his Greek sense of local, Hellenocentric superiority, even after seventeen years of watching Greece's nemesis in action at close quarters—let alone with Alexander's example to ponder—tells us more about Greek irredentism in general than it does about Polybius *qua* historian. At least Polybius grasped the concept of universalism—or at any rate of Mediterraneanism, which in the Graeco-Roman world tended to be regarded as the same thing: one reason for the failure of the Seleucid empire, too much westward squabbling while the eastern pot boiled over—and left us an invaluable narrative, based as much on personal experience as on research, of the events accompanying Rome's rise to supreme power in the ancient world. We may challenge his general explanations for this phenomenon, we may pick holes in his much-vaunted objectivity, we may charge him with personal prejudice or camouflaged self-exculpation, and all these criticisms will have considerable force. Yet in the last resort his faults are venial, and for long stretches forgotten both in our sympathy for his protracted ordeal (however successfully he conformed to his new world), and in our gratitude for the very existence of his *Histories* as such. Over the eighty-odd years that he covers he remains our best, and at times our only substantial, source of evidence. Ancient historians, perhaps a stronger breed today than Dionysius of Halicarnassus, who could not bear to read him from cover to cover[141]—but then Dionysius was more concerned with style than substance—continue to criticize his failings while using his material. Since that is just what Polybius himself did to Phylarchus and Timaeus (whose chronological system of Olympiads he took over), he has no real cause for complaint.

CHAPTER 18

ANTIOCHUS III, PHILIP V, AND
THE ROMAN FACTOR, 221–196

In June 217 the news of Rome's defeat by Hannibal at Lake Trasimene reached Greece. Philip V of Macedon read the dispatch in eloquent silence at Argos while attending the Nemean Games.[1] He showed it only to his Illyrian confidant, the ambitious freebooter Demetrius of Pharos, who had sought refuge at Philip's court when driven from Illyria by the Romans (p. 296).[2] Demetrius instantly advised him to wind up the local war then occupying his attention, and to devote his full energies to the West. This war, known as the Social War or the War of the Allies, had been spluttering on intermittently since 221.[3] After Antigonus Doson's death, the Aetolians saw their support in the Peloponnese crumbling, and felt themselves—not without reason—to be surrounded by enemies, most notably Macedonia and the Achaean League. Fighters by nature, they decided to take the initiative: vigorous raids were carried out against Messenia and a whole string of Achaean-held frontier posts. Messenia appealed to the Achaean League; both the League and Philip—in his capacity as heir to the leadership of Doson's Greek alliance (*symmachia*: above, pp. 260–61)—declared war on Aetolia, with lavish promises that the cities under Aetolian control would, on liberation, enjoy their ancestral laws and constitutions, ungarrisoned, free, and tributeless (*aphorologētoi*). It was the Roman Flamininus who ensured maximum publicity for this tempting package deal (below, p. 311); but he almost certainly borrowed the idea from Philip.

The news of Cleomenes' death led to yet another royalist coup in Sparta (ca. 219): the ephors were murdered, a legitimate Agiad was deposed, and the new king, Lycurgus, allied himself with the Aetolians. A *Putsch* in Messene about 219 seems to have toppled the oligarchic regime there, which had been friendly to the Aetolians, and to have replaced it with a populist, pro-Achaean government.[4] Yet another installment of the Graeco-Macedonian *ronde* was now under way. In the campaigns that followed, Philip and his allies consistently outfought and outmaneuvered their opponents. Discipline in the Macedonian army was strict.[5] Philip's speed, energy, and dash,[6] his strategical flair, his use of siege equipment, all provoked comparisons with Alexander the Great[7]—with whom, on rather flimsy evidence, he claimed rela-

Fig. 92. Philip V of Macedon. Silver
tetradrachm, provenience uncertain,
minted ca. 190–180 B.C.
Photo Hirmer.

tionship.[8] Like Alexander, too (or indeed any new Macedonian monarch), he had
lost no time in purging his predecessor's overly influential advisers, partly with the
help of Aratus and Demetrius of Pharos.[9] Like Philip II, he had an inordinate passion
for wine and women; his relationship with Aratus did not, characteristically, stop
him seducing the wife of Aratus's ineffectual son—whose lover, equally characteristically, he had also been.[10] His prestige was now enormous: dedications were made
to him; he was even known as the "darling [*erōmenos*] of Hellas,"[11] a title to be recalled in irony when later he earned a reputation as a bloody butcher.

Soon after the incident at the Nemean Games, peace negotiations took place at
Naupactus, on the north coast of the Corinthian Gulf.[12] Philip had clearly found Demetrius's advice attractive,[13] and that shrewd politician Aratus was only too glad to
pick up what he could at the conference table. An armistice was concluded on the
basis of the *status quo*. But during the talks the speech that stuck in everyone's
mind—if we are to believe Polybius—was that made by the Aetolian negotiator,
Agelaus, who had earlier raided Achaea with the Illyrians,[14] but was now sounding a
warning of a very different sort:[15] "If it's action you want, then look to the west, pay
heed to the war in Italy. . . . For if you wait till these clouds, now gathering in the
west, come to rest in Greece, I am mortally concerned lest we may, every one of us,
find these truces and wars, and all such childish games that we now play against each
other, so abruptly cut short that we shall find ourselves praying the gods to leave us
at least this power—to fight and make peace with each other when we please, in
short, to have control over our own disputes."

While flattering Philip's warlike ambitions, the speech—if genuine, which is
doubtful[16]—also carried an implicit plea to the young Macedonian king not to rush
impetuously into a conflict with Rome. Greek unity was more important. Despite
Polybius, it is unlikely that such a warning was needed—yet. Philip may have been
headstrong and ambitious, with the temper of his ancestor Pyrrhus,[17] but he had a
very firm grasp on logistical realities. To attempt an invasion of Italy with no harbor

from which to operate, and while Macedonia's own frontiers were still threatened, would be suicidal.[18] Even after Cannae, when the temptation was far greater,[19] such an undertaking still remained, in essence, an impractical dream. War fever and hysteria will have lent the threat a kind of spurious reality at the time, and this shows clearly in our sources. Just what Agelaus really said at Naupactus we cannot determine, but it is unlikely to have been as prescient as Polybius claims. Even if he did not fabricate it *in toto* to fit his theory of history, this speech remains to a great extent the product of historicizing hindsight.

The occasion, at least, was appropriate enough. Naupactus was the last peace settlement that the Greeks ever made without Roman participation: little more than twenty years later the Roman Flamininus (see p. 417), despite his philhellene pretensions, was laying down the law for Greeks and Macedonians as though he were a *paterfamilias* and they the fractious, ill-behaved children that at times they so uncomfortably resembled.[20] Like most momentous changes, this one came about by a series of apparent accidents. Yet behind the events lay an ineluctable pattern: the fatal inability of the Greeks to unite in common action, the quarrelsomeness that Rome learned, all too well, how to exploit; the ambition and greed (commercial no less than military) of the great senatorial families, the alluring wealth of Egypt and Asia; the awesome superiority of the Roman military machine, the resilience in the face of disaster that enabled Rome to survive, not only Trasimene, but Cannae and the Trebbia, and still, ultimately, to thrash Hannibal (202), to burn Carthage (146: above, p. 279). Despite her own serious internal conflicts, Rome was strong and united in a way that Greek separatism could never match. If Agelaus ever really called on his fellow Greeks to close ranks against the threat from the west, the cry fell on deaf ears. Where was Antiochus, where were the Achaeans, when in 197 Philip V of Macedon went down to defeat at Cynoscephalae (p. 310)?

But this is to anticipate. In 221 the new young monarchs who had come to the thrones of all three Successor kingdoms—Antiochus III, Ptolemy IV Philopator, Philip V—had other problems on their minds. That Rome, a still largely unknown power, had in 229/8 become, briefly, involved in Illyria was regarded as a matter of small importance (above, pp. 253 ff.). Even Rome's so-called First Macedonian War, which followed (below, pp. 297 ff.), "misnamed what was basically a contest among Hellenes and Macedonians, a revival of the Social War, a reflection of Hellenistic politics."[21] Antiochus and Ptolemy both inherited the endless ongoing quarrel over their Syrian frontier; Antiochus, in addition, was plagued, throughout his unwieldy empire, with secessions and would-be usurpers, and Ptolemy (at least from 207, and probably much earlier) had to deal with a series of dangerous native insurrections and the loss of the Thebaid. Macedonia was at least as much preoccupied with the nagging problem of the Greek leagues as with Illyria. Yet before long all three of them—even Antiochus, whose interests, on the face of it, lay in a quite different direction—had become dangerously embroiled in the Roman issue.

It will be convenient, in fact, to begin with Antiochus, whose driving ambition, probably from the moment he ascended the throne, was to restore the lost imperial possessions of his great-great-grandfather, Seleucus I Nicator (above, p. 31). This program aimed, ultimately, at the reconquest of Coele-Syria as far as the gates of

Egypt, the repossession of the great eastern satrapies, and firm control not only over the seaports of Asia Minor, but also of the Hellespont itself, and of eastern Thrace on its European side. It is a mark of Antiochus's stature (and at least some justification of his title, "the Great") that in appearance at least, even if only for a brief period, he succeeded in all these projects. It is worth noting that his most ambitious undertaking, the great expedition to Bactria and India, with its unmistakable echoes of Alexander, bothered the Romans not at all; it was only his comparatively minor campaigns in western Asia Minor and, above all, in Thrace to which they took exception (pp. 304 ff.).

When we consider the troubled realm he inherited, it is surprising that he had as few initial setbacks as he did. (How far even these were due to the supposedly malign and brutal influence of his vizier Hermeias, a Carian Greek in whose assassination the king eventually connived, remains uncertain: Polybius is our sole source for Hermeias's activities, and his account reeks of hostile propaganda.)[22] His general Achaeus, the conqueror of Antiochus Hierax (above, p. 264), and the master mind behind Antiochus's own accession, continued as a tower of strength in Asia Minor, driving Attalus I back till he held little more than Pergamon itself (spring 222), and overall, Polybius claims, acting "with intelligence and generosity."[23] Having dealt with a major revolt by Molon, his successor as governor of Media (221–220)[24]—a difficult campaign that got off to a shaky start—Antiochus decided to begin his program by invading Syria; he had no doubt heard, through his intelligence sources, that Egypt was crippled by court intrigue and public unrest. An earlier attempt had never got off the ground (221): this time he launched a major expedition (the Fourth Syrian War, 219–217). The excuses given were the standard ones: Syria and Phoenicia had originally been conquered by Antigonus One-Eye, and promised to Seleucus Nicator after Ipsus in an agreement with Cassander and Lysimachus; Ptolemy Soter, both during the war of 315–311 and at the time of Ipsus, had been, officially, campaigning for Seleucus rather than on his own account.[25]

Antiochus got off to a good start. He captured Seleucia-in-Pieria, thus winning back a major port on the eastern Mediterranean littoral (above, p. 263).[26] Tyre and Ptolemaïs-Ake surrendered to him: the road through Palestine to Egypt lay open. Had he been Alexander he would have followed it—probably with success, since Ptolemy's defenses were in no sort of preparation.[27] But he preferred a more cautious and methodical approach, consolidating his position in Galilee and Samaria.[28] Meanwhile Ptolemy's diplomats stalled him with peace talks—chiefly remarkable for the tangled web of claims and counterclaims over Coele-Syria that Polybius's account of them reveals[29]—while a large army was got together by the king's Greek adviser Sosibius. Sosibius not only put these troops through a rigorous training program under professional Greek officers (a step that paid off handsomely); he also took the novel step of enrolling no less than thirty thousand native Egyptians as hoplites. Advantageous in the immediate emergency, this decision was, in the long run, to destablize the regime more than any external threat.[30]

Between leisurely negotiations and Antiochus's own weakness for local siege warfare, Ptolemy held up the Seleucid invasion until the summer of 217. Then, at the head of fifty-five thousand men, and accompanied by his young sister Arsinoë III,[31]

Fig. 93. *A,* Ptolemy IV, wearing the royal diadem (gold octadrachm minted at Alexandria[?] ca. 220–210 B.C.). *B,* Arsinoe III, sister-wife to Ptolemy IV, wearing royal coronal and necklace, and carrying the scepter, visible over left shoulder (gold octadrachm minted ca. 215–210 B.C.).
British Museum, London.

he took the field in person, to face Antiochus's army, now sixty-eight thousand strong, at Raphia, in Palestine, just beyond the Egyptian frontier.[32] It was the biggest formal battle since Ipsus, which it also resembled in another way: Antiochus, like Demetrius the Besieger before him, shattered the enemy's left wing (his combination of cavalry and elephants proved irresistible);[33] but—again like Demetrius—he could not resist pursuing his advantage, so that Ptolemy's commanders were able to organize a counterattack and shatter the Seleucid phalanx while its general was still on his death-or-glory charge.[34]

Resounding triumph though it was—Coele-Syria was safe, and Egypt relieved of the threat of invasion—Raphia brought little good to the victors, and some unlooked-for troubles as well.[35] Ptolemy IV, despite recent attempts to credit him with an active foreign policy,[36] was clearly an indolent character, dominated to a great extent by his advisers and womenfolk, if not the complete sensual fribble portrayed by Polybius.[37] There is an interesting contrast, in the latter's account, between Sosibius's energetic preparations, which brought victory at Raphia,[38] and the king's dilatory disinclination to follow that victory up, ascribed by Polybius to his urge to get back to the fleshpots of Alexandria—even though he then admits that Ptolemy spent a further three months settling affairs in Coele-Syria and Phoenicia.[39] His concern for family affairs also extended to acquiescence in the murder of most of his close relatives, including his mother.[40] At all events, having won the battle he was quite happy to settle for the *status quo*; he even let Antiochus keep the naval base of Seleucia-in-Pieria. Coele-Syria, at least, stayed in Ptolemaic hands for almost another two decades. Ptolemy also now married his sister Arsinoë (October 217), and the two received a cult as the Father-Loving Gods (*Theoi Philopatores*).[41] But his

Egyptian troops had tasted blood, and sensed their own power: on the domestic front the king had won what was to prove an expensive victory.[42]

In this connection there may have been more pressing motives than self-indulgence for the terms he allowed Antiochus. A fall in population and a shrinkage of overseas trade had brought about so acute a shortage of silver in Egypt that the silver currency was debased; a bronze coinage was introduced during the reign of Ptolemy III, and in 210, only seven years after Raphia—and Trasimene—silver seems to have been abandoned altogether as Ptolemaic Egypt's standard currency.[43] In the circumstances it would be understandable if Ptolemy balked at hiring the extra mercenaries needed to pursue an aggressive foreign policy; financial considerations may similarly have dictated the enrollment of Egyptian troops at cut-price rates. Raphia doubtless brought in a fair amount of the plunder that constituted a major source of regular income for any Hellenistic monarch; but after Raphia the supply dried up. The problem is complex;[44] it does, however, seem more than likely that events in Egypt now tended to follow a vicious circle. The native troops in Ptolemy's army stimulated a strong nationalist movement; the nationalists at first restricted themselves to a long, and successful, guerilla campaign, but then rebelled so effectively against the central government that for a long period Upper Egypt achieved total independence under a series of native pharaohs (205–186/5?);[45] the loss of Upper Egypt deprived Ptolemy of a substantial proportion of his revenues, besides necessitating an increased army of mercenaries to fend off the constantly marauding rebels; the resultant drain on capital meant a serious cutback in overseas trade, which in turn exacerbated an already difficult economic situation.[46]

All these factors should be borne in mind when considering Ptolemy's lackluster foreign policy. It is true that the real deterioration only set in about the time of Philopator's death, or shortly before (205/4): until then the Ptolemaic empire remained more or less intact. Then came open revolt and anarchy, backed by the native priests, and disrupting administrative communications throughout the kingdom: even the famous elephant-hunting expeditions had to be discontinued (see below, p. 329).[47] The Ptolemaic government had worse dangers to face than Antiochus III's depredations in Coele-Syria, and the equally conciliatory treaty made with him after the Fifth Syrian War reflects this all too clearly (below, p. 305). The surviving honorific decrees from Canopus (March 238) and Memphis (March 196) reveal an increasing effort to conciliate the powerful native priesthood, to create some kind of acceptable common ideology of power for Greek rulers and privileged Egyptians alike.[48] But the economic crisis led, inevitably, to harsher taxation and greater bureaucratic stringency, thus giving fresh animus, and further recruits, to the nationalist movement.[49]

Three years before Antiochus's defeat in Syria (220), his hitherto loyal commander (and maternal uncle) Achaeus[50]—presumably encouraged to play his own hand, if not by Molon's example, at least by his own reconquest of Asia Minor—had proclaimed himself king, and assumed the diadem.[51] However, his mercenary army, recognizing a no-win situation when they saw one, refused to follow him to Antioch,[52] and he ended up as a freebooter in the Anatolian highlands: Antiochus judged,

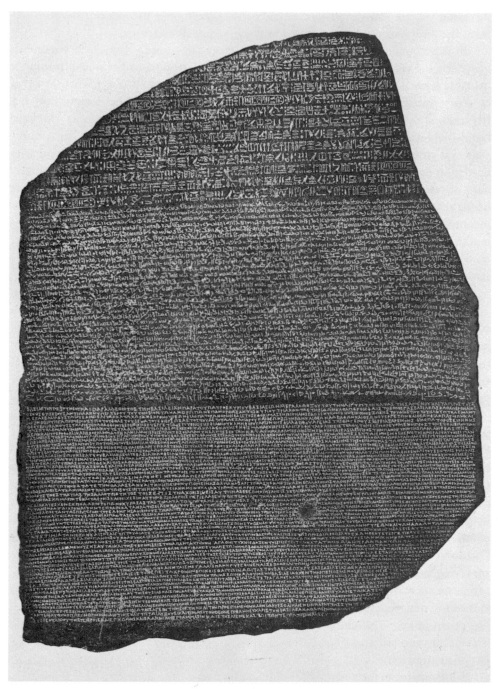

Fig. 94. The Rosetta Stone. This trilingual inscription (hieroglyphic and demotic Egyptian; Greek) on black basalt, embodying a decree by the Egyptian priesthood in honor of Ptolemy V Epiphanes (27 March, 196 B.C.), was the key to Champollion's decipherment of hieroglyphic in 1824.

British Museum, London.

Fig. 95. Antiochus III ("the Great"). Silver tetradrachm minted at Ecbatana ca. 205–200 B.C. On the reverse, a war elephant and the inscription "King Antiochus." British Museum, London.

correctly, that Achaeus and Attalus of Pergamon, old opponents already, would keep each other busy for a year or two. In 216 Antiochus moved back into Asia Minor himself, blockaded Achaeus in Sardis, and in 213 caught him trying to escape. The pretender was mutilated and his corpse crucified, an Achaemenid practice that suggests Antiochus was rehearsing his chosen role as Great King of Asia.[53] It also made an example that discouraged civil war in the Seleucid domains for the next fifty years.

Antiochus now was ready to move east, on an extraordinary campaign—as much propaganda as actual conquest—that lasted seven years (212–205), was impressive rather than substantial, and came to be known as his anabasis. Its object was the recovery, or, failing that, the amicable co-option, of lost territories in the upper satrapies, including Bactria and Parthia, both now ruled by independent dynasts. The situation in the satrapies of southern Iran—Carmania, Gedrosia, Drangiana—is unknown, but in all likelihood they too had seceded. Antiochus in 212 can have been sure of very little beyond Persis (Parsa) and Media. Yet what he planned was to win back control over all territories to which Seleucus Nicator had, however briefly, laid claim.[54] Now he was looking eastward, as far as the Indian satrapies long relinquished to the Mauryan Chandragupta (above, p. 29); but later, as we shall see, he also moved on disputed territory in Asia Minor, even in Thrace, simply and solely because the founder of his dynasty had been there before him.[55]

There may, again, have been economic considerations behind the anabasis: Rostovtzeff plausibly suggested that one reason for Antiochus's pressing interest in the eastern satrapies was the need to regain access to the gold mines of Siberia and India via the Bactrian caravan routes.[56] Be this as it may, the dominant impetus throughout was, beyond any doubt, provided by Antiochus's passionate dynastic dream, his

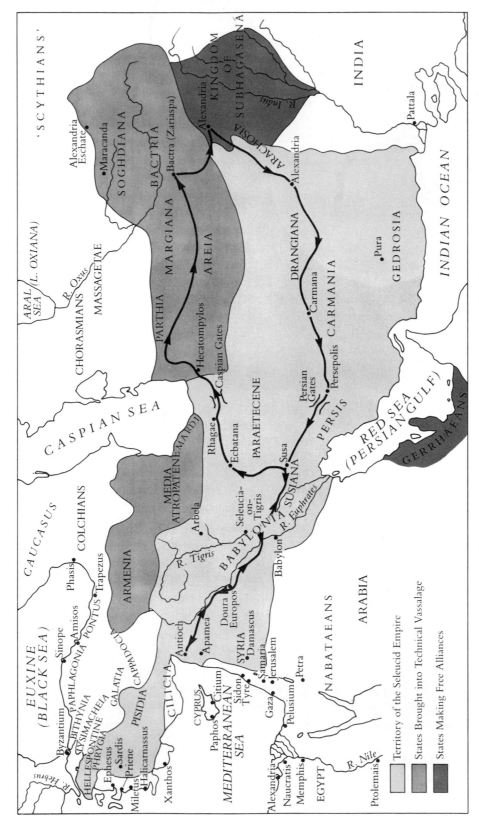

Map 18. The Anabasis of Antiochus III (the Great), 212–205 B.C.

determination to restore the Seleucid empire in its full and pristine glory. He had at his accession found a realm greatly weakened by territorial losses and internal rivalries. In eleven years—years of stress and maturation—he had suppressed two major rebellions (those of Molon and Achaeus), and recovered Media, Persis, Susiana, and Babylon, not to mention large areas of western Asia Minor. His only failure had been in Phoenicia and Coele-Syria (217). Now he was ready to assault the eastern satrapies.[57] Having first secured Armenia[58]—he had taken care of Media Atropatene (mod. Azerbaijan) as early as 220[59]—he marched east into Media, where he spent the years 211 and 210 assembling and preparing his army;[60] he also raised four thousand talents to pay his troops by taking over the accumulated treasures of the great temple in Ecbatana.

In 209 he was ready, at last, to set out on his anabasis proper: the intimidating news of his massive preparations had clearly traveled ahead of him, as perhaps was his intention. Arsaces II of Parthia came to terms with him.[61] After besieging the Graeco-Bactrian king Euthydemus in Zariaspa (mod. Balkh) for two years (208–206), he made a deal with him too: Euthydemus convinced him that they both had more to fear from incursions by nomads than from one another.[62] He crossed the Hindu Kush, as Alexander had done, signed a treaty of friendship with a local Indian ruler named Subhagasena (Sophagasenus)—perhaps, *inter alia*, to encourage trade[63]— and returned home by way of Arachosia, Drangiana, and the Persian Gulf (206– 205).[64] He also found time for an expedition against the Gerrhaean Arabs, who purchased their freedom with tribute in cash and spices.[65] Antiochus came back to Seleucia-on-Tigris the most famous eastern campaigner since Alexander (205), the champion who had restored Seleucid imperial hopes.[66] Yet if the propaganda was good, the actual achievement was insubstantial. The eastern satrapies were not in

Fig. 96. Arsaces II of Parthia. Silver tetradrachm, provenience uncertain (Hecatompylos?), minted ca. 210–190 B.C. The reverse shows the king sitting on an omphalos(?) beside a palm tree, testing his bow. The inscription reads: "The Great King Arsaces Made Manifest [Epiphanēs]."
British Museum, London.

any real sense subdued: what he had acquired there were friendly neighbors, *amici* in the loose Roman sense, certainly not vassals. The title of Great King, which Antiochus now assumed, or encouraged others to bestow on him,[67] was to a great extent wishful thinking. He still had to recover Coele-Syria, the Anatolian coastal cities, and the Hellespontine area; and it was while pursing this part of his dream of empire that he found himself on collision course with Rome (p. 421).

What, meanwhile, of Philip? As we saw earlier, the new young Macedonian king had very soon found himself engaged in two areas: Illyria and central Greece. In Illyria Demetrius of Pharos, once Rome's protégé in the Dalmatian archipelago (above, p. 254),[68] had set himself up as, in effect, the pirate king of the Adriatic, raiding as far afield as Pylos and the Aegean. He also enjoyed Macedonian protection (from ca. 225), through probably not an official alliance. He had contributed troops to Antigonus Doson for the Sellasia campaign:[69] for some reason both Antigonus and Philip treated him as a valued adviser (he was, however, probably not quite the catastrophic *éminence grise* that Polybius tries to make him out).[70] Demetrius's piratical activities contrived to annoy not only the Rhodians, who expelled his squadrons from the Cyclades,[71] but also Rome, which had to deal with repeated complaints from Italian traders in the Adriatic, and may have been anxious to protect grain ships from molestation not only by Demetrius, but also by another, equally vigorous Illyrian corsair, Scerdilaidas,[72] who at one point had been similarly contracted to Philip, but broke with him in 217 over alleged nonpayment, and thereafter plundered Macedonian shipping as readily as the rest.[73]

In 219—the same year, we may note, that Hannibal began the siege of Saguntum—Rome took steps to eliminate this nuisance, and Demetrius sought refuge with Philip (above, p. 286),[74] who was then preoccupied by his joint campaign with Aratus against the Aetolians (above, pp. 286–88). Demetrius urged peace, arguing in effect that Philip needed more elbowroom to deal with the Illyrian question,[75] and with a shrewd eye to his own reestablishment on the Adriatic coast. The result was the treaty of Naupactus (217: above, p. 287). Philip duly moved into southern Illyria, drove out Demetrius's rival in piracy, Scerdilaidas, and enabled Demetrius himself to recover his fief there.[76] Scerdilaidas, with characteristic effrontery, appealed to Rome. A patrol of ten quinqueremes came to investigate. Intervention by Rome was the last thing Philip either wanted or expected at this point, and he at once retreated. But if he was anxious to avoid a showdown, so, clearly, were the Romans.[77] There could be no question of using the Illyrian front to counter either Macedonian or Roman plans for imperial expansion, since such plans simply did not exist. Philip had no ambitions, certainly no immediate ambitions, in Italy; he was far more concerned, as subsequent events showed, to stabilize his always volatile western frontier by subjugating all Illyria and establishing a permanent port on the Adriatic.[78] If he dreamed, perhaps, of emulating his ancestor Pyrrhus, he will have been well aware, like everyone else, of how that ill-fated venture turned out (above, p. 231). Since Pyrrhus, no other Greek had looked westward.[79] That was not fortuitous. As a result, Rome had been left undisturbed to master the whole of southern Italy and Sicily by the end of the First Punic War (above, p. 232).

If Philip had no ambitions in the West, it was equally true that Rome did not envisage serious intervention in the East. But after Philip's tentative moves toward creating a Macedonian outlet on the Adriatic were blocked by a Roman squadron, he took a step that brought him no substantial advantage, and made him permanently suspect at Rome. In 215, again, apparently, on the advice of Demetrius, he signed a treaty with Hannibal the Carthaginian.[80] This carefully vague treaty was, it is obvious, drafted by Carthage. It required Philip to act as an ally of the Carthaginians, if and when called upon in their war against Rome (which he never was), though to do specifically what, if anything, is not made clear. In return, the Carthaginians undertook, if they won the war, to make the Romans abandon their sphere of influence in Illyria in Philip's favor—small gain, it might be thought, for a most perilous commitment. The implication of a possible second front made good propaganda in Greek Italy, and was calculated to embarrass the Romans, but remained, in practical terms, a chimera.[81] At this point the real likelihood of Philip invading Italy was nil, and even when he finally acquired his Adriatic staging post by capturing Lissos (below, p. 298),[82] there was no serious concern in Rome, merely a decision to take routine preventive measures. Indeed, the so-called First Macedonian War, which followed (215–205), was remarkable for Rome's initially lackadaisical attitude: it is not even certain whether a formal declaration of hostilities was made.[83]

The course of events shows that Philip's focus of interest continued to be Illyria: an entanglement with Rome was still something he preferred to avoid. The only time that a Roman squadron appeared on the eastern shore of the Adriatic, to defend the cities Philip was harassing in 214, a similar scenario to that in 217/6 promptly played itself out. The young king, taken by surprise, at once withdrew, burning his own fleet of 120 vessels, and retreating over the mountains.[84] The Roman commander, Marcus Valerius Laevinus, now stationed his squadron in Illyria, at least for the following winter (214/3), as a safeguard against future raids.[85]

The Macedonian threat, as always, looked more serious from the viewpoint

Fig. 97. Coin portrait identified as Hannibal, in the role of Melkart-Heracles. Silver shekel minted at New Carthage ca. 221 B.C. British Museum, London.

of the Peloponnese. Aratus in particular was alarmed by Philip's increasingly in-dependent policy, the professionalism of his army,[86] and the greater ruthlessness he had begun to display under Demetrius of Pharos's influence. (At some point now Rome demanded Demetrius's surrender: Philip ignored the request.)[87] When in 215 civil strife again flared up in Messene, Philip, with an eye to conquest, incited the factions—"government" (*stratēgoi, archontes*) and "champions of the people" (*dēmagōgoi, proestōtes*)—against each other.[88] Since the oligarchs had been driven out around 219 (above, p. 286), it follows that (unless another countercoup had taken place meanwhile) a moderate democratic regime was now under attack by radical, and probably pro-Aetolian, extremists. Aratus, alerted to what was going on, hur-ried to the scene, arriving a day after the *dēmagōgoi* had defeated their opponents in a bloody *Putsch*, killing more than two hundred of them.

Philip, accompanied by Demetrius of Pharos, asked leave of the victors to sacri-fice on Mt. Ithome, and took Aratus and his son along as well. It seems likely, from what followed, that they had a strong armed escort. Polybius, echoed by Plutarch, records a discussion that supposedly took place on the mountain summit, after the sacrifice.[89] Demetrius advised Philip to seize Mt. Ithome, saying that whoever held the two horns of the Peloponnese (Ithome and Acrocorinth) controlled the bull. Ara-tus was horrified by such talk. If Philip could take Ithome and still keep faith with the Messenians—who had, clearly, given him access to the mountain on condition that he respect its territorial integrity—then, Aratus said, he might keep it. An im-possible condition, and so meant. Otherwise, his reputation as an oath breaker would neutralize any immediate advantage that possession of the citadel might offer. Grumbling, Philip conceded the point—for the moment. His abortive meddling in the affairs of Messene had resulted in much bloodshed, but little success.[90]

He soon, however—perhaps irritated with himself for having given in to Ara-tus, and, more immediately, by the loss of his fleet—began to ravage the Messenian countryside "as though motivated by passion rather than reason."[91] This may have been his frustrated reaction to a full-scale, but unsuccessful, assault on Ithome led by Demetrius of Pharos, who got himself killed during the action (215).[92] From being the "darling of the Greeks" at his accession (above, p. 287),[93] Philip came very soon to be feared as a wild, cruel, and politically unpredictable adventurer.[94] He and Ara-tus from then on had little use for each other; and though Achaean propaganda must have painted Philip in progressively more lurid colors, it did not have to invent, *ex nihilo*, his choleric temper, unruly physical appetites, and weakness for impromptu massacres. It is an index of the new atmosphere prevalent after the treaty with Car-thage that when Aratus finally died, in 213, of what sounds like consumption, Philip was widely believed to have had him poisoned.[95]

For the next two years (213–212), consistently with his policy, Philip kept up his remorseless pressure on the cities of Illyria. To begin with, while he repaired his naval losses, and to avoid unnecessary provocation of Rome, he was careful to stay clear of the coast, where Laevinus, the Roman commander, was now firmly in con-trol of key points such as Dyrrhachium, Apollonia, and Corcyra (which from 213 became his naval base).[96] Instead he attacked the hinterland, driving north and cut-

Fig. 98. Aerial view of Messene, in the southwestern Peloponnese.
Photo Raymond V. Schoder, S. J.

ting deep into Scerdilaidas's territory.[97] It was only then that he made his successful descent on Lissos (above, p. 297), and thus established himself on the Adriatic. So far the Romans had largely ignored his activities; but now—though fears of a Macedonian invasion of Italy can confidently be discounted as, at best, free-floating Roman hysteria that found its way into our annalistic sources[98]—a situation had arisen in which a first-class power, rather than mere local chieftains and pirates, was now able to menace the trade routes of the southern Adriatic.[99] More positive measures were called for.

The Romans, casting around for allies of their own who could deal with this situation, picked, *faute de mieux*, the Aetolians (212/11): arguably a mistake. The treaty now made between them—the oldest original Roman treaty surviving, and the first document illustrating Rome's relations with the Greek world—stipulated that Rome would restrict herself to removable booty (a point that Flamininus and his men doubtless recalled later when, with philhellenist zeal, they raided the country for works of art), while Aetolia would get any territorial concessions that might be going.[100] The Romans prudently set Corcyra as the northern boundary for this arrangement: they knew the kind of allies they were dealing with, and had no wish to see further potential corsairs preying on shipping in the sea lanes between Greece and Italy.[101] The proper function of the Aetolians was to distract Philip. Unfortunately, they overdid it, proving so unbelievably brutal in their habits—the Romans, too, got a bad reputation for atrocities[102]—that the effect was to create a *rapprochement* between Philip and the Achaean League.

The relationship, however, being bred of necessity, remained cool. For a long time Aratus's son (with all the nervous irritation of a cuckolded ex-lover) kept the Macedonian at arm's length: when we remember Philip's conduct in Messenia it is not hard to see why. The course of the war between 211 and 208 is confused. Sporadic fighting took place all over and around Greece: in Illyria, Thrace, Thessaly, Acarnania. Philip still could not face the Roman fleet; he did better on land, driving the Aetolians back from Thessaly—an area nominally independent, in fact very much under Macedonian control[103]—and making short work of an incursion by Attalus of Pergamon (his sole appearance in Greece), who had joined the Roman-Aetolian coalition, and in 209 was actually appointed Aetolian *strategos*.[104] Philopoemen, the Achaean League's general, leading brigades that he had spent some time reorganizing and training, crushed a resurgent Spartan army at Mantinea (207), after which Sparta took no further part in the fighting—though it was not long, as we shall see (p. 302), before her new king made his presence felt in the Peloponnese. Philip was called back to Macedonia, and Attalus to Pergamon, by barbarian invasions.[105] Though Laevinus's successor, Galba, soon earned some notoriety for his Aetolian-style cruelties,[106] Rome, having lost interest in these internal squabbles, left the Aetolians to get on with the war from now on.[107]

This they very soon tired of doing without adequate support. In 206/5 they broke their treaty with Rome and made a separate peace with Philip, which gave him back all he had lost.[108] (The previous year he had sacked the Aetolian capital of Thermon, and looted its temples, something that may have given those licensed buccaneers pause for thought.)[109] The Romans, at last, were stirred into action. With the Hannibalic war still not settled (despite a recent victory at the Metaurus in 207), Philip could not be left to ravage Illyria unopposed. Complaints from Rhodes and Chios, that the war in Greece—which was in fact the so-called First Macedonian War—was disrupting international commerce, had also made some impression at Rome. In the spring of 205 a Roman task force of thirty-five ships and no less than eleven thousand men landed at Epidamnus.[110] This was a considerably larger force than the agreement with Aetolia had envisaged. In fact the whole operation smelled of crude blackmail, since its prime object was not so much to fight as to pressure the Aetolians back into the war. The Aetolians, rightly calculating that this move was a bluff, refused to budge. Thereupon the Romans, refusing an offer of battle by Philip, negotiated a peace of their own. The result was the treaty of Phoenice (summer 205), which finally brought the First Macedonian War to an end.[111]

There were minor territorial concessions on either side, though the status of Lissos remains uncertain.[112] Both sides' allies were included in the treaty. Philip did well enough out of the negotiations, consolidating his acquisitions in inland Illyria. Rome had ensured the safety of the southern Adriatic, and there may have been those in the Senate who also felt (unlikely as this may seem in retrospect) that the campaign had staved off an active partnership between Philip and Hannibal. In any case, for the next five years or so it was in North Africa, with no Macedonian intervention, there or in southern Italy, that Rome's legions had to face the Carthaginian; and the affairs of Greece were let slide: the Senate did not even leave holding troops in the Balkans. Philip, too, seems to have felt that Phoenice had finally settled his brush with Rome.

In 205, as always, there were other problems nearer home than the Hannibalic war to occupy all three Successor monarchs, who still thought primarily of the *oikoumenē* without reference to Italy.[113] In Sparta, where all the conditions for social upheaval still existed in acute form, a tyrant named Nabis had recently assumed control of the country (207), after a decade and more of disorganized rule, during which the old dual kingship was ended, and a non-royal military adventurer, Lycurgus— ironically named—bribed his way into a sole monarchy (219: above, p. 286). He died about 211, and his young son Pelops succeeded him, under the guardianship of another ambitious officer, Machanidas. Machanidas perished at Mantinea in 207, apparently in single combat with Philopoemen, and Nabis became king. The tradition is uniformly hostile to him, and should be taken with more than a grain of Attic salt.[114] Of his background and activities till his assumption of power nothing is known: his very name, it has been argued, is foreign, a Greek version of the Hebrew *nabi*, a divinely inspired prophet.[115] On the other hand, unlike his immediate predecessor, the mercenary Machanidas, he was no proletarian usurper: certainly a Spartiate, perhaps even a legitimate Eurypontid, descendant of that King Demaratus who was driven from Sparta by Cleomenes I, and ended at the Persian court as adviser to Darius (ca. 491).[116] In 205, when he is named in the treaty of Phoenice, Nabis was about forty years old—one coin portrait shows a heavy-jowled, fleshy, bull-necked man in middle age, with a sharply imperious nose[117]—and apparently guardian to the boy-king Pelops, son of Lycurgus.

How Nabis himself seized power is unknown: probably with the aid of the mer-

Fig. 99. Nabis of Sparta. Silver tetradrachm minted at Sparta(?) in the late third or early second century B.C. British Museum, London.

cenaries who figured so prominently in his regime, and are described by Polybius as a crowd of murderers, burglars, cutpurses, and highwaymen. Technically, the description of him as a *tyrannos* is correct.[118] That he did away with Pelops is all too likely, and though his brutality may have been exaggerated by his opponents, we need not doubt that he secured his position by the usual methods: banishment, extortion, judicial murder. He is accused, *inter alia*, of killing off all surviving members of both royal houses, of exiling distinguished citizens and handing out their womenfolk to his mercenaries, of robbing temples in the style of Antiochus Epiphanes, and of collusion in piracy with the Cretans.[119] A single, financial, thread can be detected running through most of these charges. Nabis was desperately short of money: for economic no less than sociopolitical reasons the axe fell, above all, on men of property.[120] Nabis had no outside financing, from Egypt or anywhere else—the withdrawal of Ptolemy III's subsidy had been what sealed Cleomenes' fate (above, p. 260)—and was thus reduced to imposing taxes in order to fund his mercenaries, a familiar problem. He also needed cash to develop a fleet, turn Gytheion into a naval base,[121] and complete the building of a fortified city wall round Sparta, now no longer the unwalled yet proudly inviolable capital of the great days before Leuctra.[122] The total army he raised, including Lacedaemonian contingents, numbered somewhere between fifteen and eighteen thousand men.[123] The cost of all this must have been exorbitant; no wonder he was charged with robbery.[124] Yet the Delians, interestingly, greeted him as a benefactor,[125] which suggests that they at least had not suffered from his depredations.

All this caused great alarm in the Peloponnese and beyond. Nabis was busy, so report went, not only slaughtering the well-to-do, but also enfranchising foreigners, including mercenaries, and freeing the helots wholesale, moves probably dictated by the depletion of the population through warfare.[126] Sparta was becoming a refuge for brigands, runaway slaves, and adventurers of every sort: Nabis encouraged them to use his territory as a base from which to raid surrounding cities, for the most part those of the Achaean League.[127] He even supposedly had an iron maiden, fashioned (a nice psychological touch) in the likeness of his wife, Apia, the daughter of an Argive *tyrannos*, and studded inside with sharp nails, which he employed to torture and kill his opponents: the evidence for this device is so oddly circumstantial that I suspect it may indeed have existed, scholarly incredulity notwithstanding.[128]

When in 201 Nabis treacherously attacked his current ally Messene (perhaps at the invitation of a populist group within the walls),[129] even though he was soon driven off by Philopoemen and a levy from Megalopolis, property owners throughout the Peloponnese took fright. The war that followed was viciously fought (200–198/7),[130] with the League forces, to begin with, under Philopoemen's leadership; but when he was defeated in the autumn election for the 200/199 *stratēgia*, he left the country to take up a mercenary command in Crete.[131] The League had the better of it on the whole so long as Philopoemen remained in command;[132] but after his departure Nabis was soon besieging Megalopolis once more.[133] In 195 it took Flamininus to disarm—and even then not permanently—this last, and most disconcerting, of Spartan social firebrands (below, p. 417).[134] Yet Nabis represented nothing new. In

Fig. 100. Aerial view of the theater, Megalopolis (late fourth century B.C.).
Photo Raymond V. Schoder, S. J.

the last resort he was little more than a strong-arm version of Agis or Cleomenes, with even fewer scruples (and indeed unable to afford them). Like his predecessors, he was a nationalist king aiming to restore an elite, this time without even the pretense of maintaining the Lycurgan constitution. Like other Hellenistic monarchs, he ruled alone, and through mercenaries: thus the charge of tyranny brought against him was technically sustainable. He was also hand in glove with the Cretan and Laconian pirates.[135] He had the common ambition of late Spartan kings, to revamp his country as a strong, independent, and aggressive power; in the pursuit of this goal he achieved a quite uncommon degree of success, and it was this aspect of his policy that Flamininus, who understood power better than most men, effectively cut short.

At the same time Antiochus III, back from his extended anabasis through the eastern satrapies, was moving on the Hellespont by way of Asia Minor and the Aegean (204–203),[136] while in Alexandria the death of Ptolemy IV Philopator, in the summer of 204,[137] had been followed by a more than usually bloody conflict over the regency, Ptolemy V Epiphanes being still a child.[138] Ptolemy IV's widow and sister,

Arsinoë III, was eager for it; but so were his two most powerful ministers, Sosibius and Agathocles, who had Arsinoë murdered. Sosibius's fate is uncertain; Agathocles held the regency briefly (but long enough to make contact with Rome in 203) before being lynched by the Alexandrian mob, now emerging as an active, if not organized, political force.[139] (Polybius describes these events at great length and in vivid, not to say gory, detail, and then assures us that his account is neither too long nor too sensational! *Also sprach* . . .)[140] The five-year-old king was passed from the control of one ambitious adviser to another, and the state of the regime—secession in Upper Egypt, near-anarchy throughout the *chōra* (above, p. 192)[141]—positively invited external aggression. Antiochus, for one, could not fail to be eyeing the scene with uncommon interest. Frantic embassies were sent off in all directions: to Antiochus, urging him to respect the peace of 217 (p. 290); to Rome, seeking diplomatic representations to Antiochus; to Philip, offering alliance and marriage; to Greece, to hire mercenaries against the Seleucid threat.[142]

Bearing in mind Antiochus's known, and by now highly visible, ambitions on the European front, one might have expected Philip to take this bait. Instead, he and Antiochus made a secret pact to conquer, and share out between them, Ptolemy's various overseas possessions (203/2)[143]—a piece of greedy wishful thinking rather than the serious, not to say Machiavellian, statecraft as which it has sometimes been represented. The immediate result was to leave each monarch, for the moment, free to pursue his own aggressive interests: Philip in the Aegean, Antiochus in Coele-Syria and Phoenicia, where he promptly unleashed what is now known as the Fifth Syrian War (202–195). Nor did the pact keep these two royal thieves from very soon falling out with one another: betrayal is more in evidence than mutual aid.[144]

Antiochus swept down through Coele-Syria (202/1), and after some temporary reverses (most notably at Gaza) inflicted a crushing defeat on the Ptolemaic forces at Panion, near the headwaters of the river Jordan, in a whirlwind campaign that also netted him the key port of Sidon (200/199).[145] It was about this time that the same Roman mission as had already issued a stern warning, if not an ultimatum, to Philip (below, p. 307) advised Antiochus to refrain from the invasion of Egypt.[146] Since this, on the face of it, was not Antiochus's immediate intention, there was no reason why he should not return an accommodating answer, and he duly did so. The envoys' aim was to reconcile Antiochus with Ptolemy, to pour oil on troubled eastern waters. Armed with the Seleucid's assurances, they proceeded to Alexandria.[147] Antiochus was left to complete the subjugation of Coele-Syria at his leisure (198), to raid Ptolemy's coastal strongholds from Caria to Cilicia, handing out *douceurs* in the shape of grain consignments and dowries for the daughters of the poor in cities such as Iasos that he "liberated," and to invade the territory of Pergamon (197/6). Attalus's outraged delegation to Rome produced no more than a friendly request to Antiochus to avoid territorial infringements.[148] But when Antiochus crossed the Hellespont in 196, and began to rebuild the abandoned city of Lysimacheia as a military base and residence for his son Seleucus, the Romans, alarmed at last, treated him as they had earlier treated Philip: he was to relinquish the territory he had won in Asia Minor, refrain from attacking "free" Greek cities, and, above all, keep out of Europe: what Rome had freed, no Hellenistic monarch was to conquer or enslave.[149]

Antiochus, correctly deducing that this was no ultimatum, and that the Senate had no wish to fight him, took very little notice. Lysimacheia remained his outpost at least till 191/0. He ratified a treaty with Ptolemy that left him in possession of Coele-Syria (195);[150] young Ptolemy himself was betrothed to Antiochus's daughter Cleopatra, and in due course married her (194/3).[151] The treaty, coming as it did in a period of internal insurrection and attempted military coups, was greeted in Alexandria with relief. It was later asserted there that Cleopatra's dowry had included Coele-Syria,[152] but this can be seen as yet another hopeful court fantasy. When a further Roman mission arrived in Lysimacheia, repeating the Senate's earlier admonitions (in particular over the matter of Antiochus's presence in Europe), the king—a smooth diplomat who knew how to utilize public opinion[153]—challenged Rome's authority to intervene anywhere in Asia Minor, justified his presence in Thrace by Seleucus I's defeat of Lysimachus in 281 (above, p. 132), and produced, like a rabbit out of the proverbial hat, his treaty with Ptolemy and his daughter's forthcoming marriage into the Ptolemaic house as proof of his pacific intentions.[154] This constituted a splendid propaganda victory, but it left Antiochus a permanent object of suspicion at Rome.

Meanwhile Philip, after the treaty of Phoenice (205), had decided to build himself a really large and powerful fleet—a notable gap in his armament ever since he had been forced to burn his boats and retreat overland in 214 (above, p. 297). Earlier efforts in this direction had apparently not got very far.[155] By 201, however, the fleet was built and in action.[156] Philip could now once more hold his own at sea with the navies of Rhodes or Ptolemy or the Attalids. In the anarchic conditions then obtaining throughout the Aegean, he may well also have fancied his chances as a large-scale quasi-official condottiere, a better-organized Demetrius of Pharos. This, indeed, was how he financed his shipbuilding program in the first place (204/3). He commissioned an Aetolian freebooter, Dicaearchus, who embarked on a kind of piratical *razzia* around the Aegean,[157] Illyria and the Adriatic now being off limits. He backed

Fig. 101. Ptolemy V Epiphanes. Gold octadrachm minted at Alexandria(?) ca. 200–190 B.C.
British Museum, London.

Crete's pirates against the Rhodian fleet.[158] The islands of the Cyclades were terrorized.[159] City after city was raided and plundered. Dicaearchus, who finally met his
death in Alexandria in 196, had a certain bizarre humor: wherever he anchored his
pirate vessels he set up two altars, one to Impiety (*Asebeia*), the other to Lawlessness
(*Paranomia*).[160]

By 203 the resultant loot was being poured into the construction of warships,
and a year later Philip's fleet was ready.[161] It was now, by no coincidence, that he set
up his secret pact with Antiochus. His subsequent activities suggest a continuation
of Dicaearchus's freebooting activities on a larger scale, with a simultaneous eye to
strategic advantage. Philip captured Thasos, a useful staging post, and sold the
whole population into slavery.[162] He systematically raided the Black Sea grain route
through the Hellespont and the Propontis,[163] which suggests not only economic
motivation but also a traditional Macedonian endeavor to extend control in the
Thraceward regions toward the Bosporus.[164] In 201/0 he captured Ptolemy's naval
base at Samos[165]—the vessels he captured there brought his fleet up to over two hundred—beat the Rhodian fleet off Lade,[166] invaded Ionia, and ravaged the territory of
Pergamon.[167] Hair-raising atrocities were reported: that febrile, wolfish streak in
Philip chronicled by Polybius,[168] and clearly visible in the surviving coin portraits,[169]
was now given free rein.

If Philip was in fact aiming at establishing a general Aegean thalassocracy, over
and above raising a little quick capital, his policy was intelligible but his methods can
only be described as suicidal. It is doubtful whether any immediate gains he made
outweighed the damage that these piratical activities did to his reputation.[170] The
combined squadrons of Rhodes, Chios, Byzantium, and Pergamon finally put a stop
to Philip's foray in a naval engagement off Chios, where the Macedonian king suffered a crippling and costly defeat, losing almost half his fleet and more men killed
than in any previous battle, by land or sea.[171] From here he withdrew south to
Miletus.[172] He regrouped his forces in Caria (where he retained an enclave till 196, the
only lasting result of this campaign), but during the winter of 201–200 his fleet was
blockaded in Bargylia by Attalus and the Rhodians, and he came within a hair's
breadth of being starved into surrender.[173] While he was thus immobilized, envoys
from Rhodes and Pergamon hurried off to Rome to denounce his activities.[174] It is
interesting how quickly Rome, not long since a disregarded barbarian interloper,
had become a kind of general arbiter of Aegean affairs. Her defeat of Hannibal at
Zama in 202 must have greatly enhanced her prestige and aggressive self-confidence.

By the spring of 200 Philip, having broken through the blockade by a trick,[175]
was back in Europe, where he promptly got himself involved in a war between
Athens and Acarnania: his vision was still fundamentally local. To oblige his Acarnanian allies he sent an expeditionary force to help them ravage Attica.[176] He also dispatched a Macedonian squadron, which coolly captured four Athenian triremes
from Piraeus. But the Rhodian and Pergamene squadrons that had chased Philip
across the Aegean now reappeared from their base on Aigina, and rescued the stolen
triremes, to the great delight of the Athenians.[177] The septuagenarian Attalus, always
on the lookout for opportunities to enlarge his kingdom, was invited to Athens:

knowing that a Roman delegation had lately arrived in the city, he accepted. The Athenians, who had just abolished the two tribes, Antigonis and Demetrias, that they had created in a fit of pro-Macedonian enthusiasm a century or so before (above, p. 48), now replaced one of them with an Attalid tribe in honor of the king of Pergamon.[178] But it was not until they received assurances that Rome, as well as Rhodes and Pergamon, was committed against Philip that they went beyond giving their guests a good time and actually declared war on Macedonia.[179]

This was a move they quickly had cause to regret, since no sooner had they made it than their allies found good reasons for needing to be somewhere else. The Rhodian fleet took off to prize loose Philip's recent acquisitions in the Cyclades, and Attalus returned to Aigina:[180] diplomatic cooperation with Rome soon brought him the island of Andros, though, ironically enough, it was at Rhodes's expense rather than Philip's.[181] Philip's reaction to the Athenian declaration of war was prompt, vigorous, and characteristic. He set up an advance headquarters on Euboea, and dispatched his general Nicanor to ravage Attica—which Nicanor did to such effect that his troops penetrated as far as the Academy while the Roman mission was still in Athens. Faced with this contemptuous gesture, the Romans had no choice but to deliver an ultimatum to Philip: he was to war on no Greek state, and to settle the wrongs done to Attalus by arbitration.[182]

Quem Deus vult perdere, prius dementat. Philip, to all appearances not in the least perturbed by the prospect of taking on the military machine that had so recently thrashed Hannibal, and confident that Rome, without even a formal alliance, was in no position to act as protective guardian on behalf of the Greeks, responded to this ultimatum just as he had done to the Athenians' declaration of war—with a major raid on Attica, led by Philocles, his commander in Euboea.[183] Meanwhile he himself led an all-out attack on the cities of the Hellespont, one object clearly being to throttle the Athenian Black Sea grain route.[184] So much for not warring on the Greeks. His siege of Abydos proved unexpectedly difficult, and it is a mark of the terror his methods inspired that the inhabitants, facing defeat, preferred suicide to surrender.[185] It was here that the senatorial envoy Marcus Aemilius Lepidus caught up with him, carrying a second, and final, ultimatum (summer 200).[186] This repeated the first, with two further clauses tacked on. Philip would now have to submit at arbitration to paying damages to Rhodes as well as to Attalus; and, interestingly, he was required to refrain from encroaching on Egypt or Egypt's possessions.

That Philip actually intended to invade Egypt at this point is out of the question. On the other hand, since a similar warning was issued to Antiochus (above, p. 304), it is more than possible that the Senate had got wind of the secret pact between the two rulers. There was a sharp exchange with Lepidus over the responsibility for aggression: Philip stood his ground, refused to be intimidated. After his undignified retreat before Roman squadrons in 217/6 and 214, this may have come as a surprise. If there had to be war, he said, then the Macedonians would give a good account of themselves. At this point Lepidus broke off the discussion and left. Philip, still unperturbed, pressed home his assault on Abydos, announcing to the inhabitants, with mordant irony, that if they wanted to commit suicide, they had three days in which to do so. They took him at his word, to the last man.[187] Never can gallows humor have fallen flatter. Philip then set out for Macedonia. Meanwhile, after one rejection, the proposal for war was finally, on resubmission, ratified by the Roman *comitia centuriata*.[188] Philip was not yet home when news reached him that a Roman army had already landed at Apollonia (autumn 200), and a Roman fleet was wintering in Corcyra.[189] The wanton destruction of Abydos, the insolent rejection of a conciliatory Roman envoy, had finally brought Roman public opinion round—too soon after the long Punic struggle—to the prospect of yet another conflict.[190] A new, and ultimately fatal, phase in Macedonian affairs had begun.

The great question, of course, is why Rome, at this juncture, should have gone to war with Macedonia at all. From the Roman viewpoint there had been no change of situation in Illyria since 205: Badian's picture of "Roman fear and Roman hatred" is, at best, an exaggeration.[191] Philip's pact with Antiochus, even if known, was hardly of real interest to Rome, and certainly not that threat to the balance of power in the Hellenistic world as which it has sometimes been represented.[192] Philip and Antiochus were too busy cheating each other to form a stable Seleucid-Antigonid coalition,[193] and in any case the history of the Successors had shown just how fragile such alliances tended to be. No concern for the Senate there. A war in defense of allies, then? But the allies, in any formal or technical sense, did not exist: Polybius never mentions them, and he was the last man in the world to suppress evidence so favorable to a portrayal of Rome as the honest broker fulfilling her legal commitments.[194] Could Philip have been regarded, or indeed (bearing his ancestry in mind) have vaunted himself, as the new Pyrrhus?[195] But Pyrrhus had looked westward, had indeed invaded Italy (above, pp. 228 ff.), whereas Philip's interests had all been in Illyria and the Aegean, areas for the most part (and not least since the peace of Phoenice) remote from Rome's immediate interests. There was, as we have seen, no conceivable risk of a Macedonian seaborne invasion of Italy, least of all since Hannibal's defeat. Nor is it plausible that Rome should now seek revenge on Philip for his deadletter treaty with Carthage, much less go to war with Macedonia on behalf of Athens. (In the event, the Athenians found themselves fighting on their own, since neither Rome, Attalus, nor the Rhodians gave them adequate support.)[196] There is no evidence for a renewed threat to the Adriatic: Philip was now concentrating all his efforts on the Hellespont.

Indeed, a state of war was reached only with extreme reluctance, certainly on the Roman side: many in Rome did not want it at any price. It was too soon after Zama for another major conflict. On the other hand, no one had expected such defiance from Philip, who had been cast, in senatorial eyes, for the familiar role of obligated client-prince;[197] and Philip, for his part, had good reasons for believing that Rome would avoid war at all costs. Both sides, in the event, were wrong: neither would back down. "Miscalculations are no small factor in the creation of war."[198] It is, of course, always possible that the Senate, after briefing by Lepidus, saw Philip as a dangerous and ambitious lunatic who would, when the time came, stop at nothing, a view to which his behavior at Abydos must have lent some plausibility.[199] Certainly no one had forgotten the treaty he struck with Hannibal; even if that in itself did not offer an adequate *casus belli*, it was an eloquent indication of untrustworthiness.

Face-saving, then, combined with a preemptive strike against a potential, and growing, menace?[200] The miscalculation once granted, this seems at least possible; nor was the time badly chosen. After his ruthless freebooting activities in and around the Aegean, Philip was, not surprisingly, strapped for allies. Rome had ensured the nonintervention of Antiochus, who in any case was only too ready to profit by Philip's misfortunes. The Achaean League, itself now at war with Nabis of Sparta (above, p. 302), was seriously divided. It began the war as Philip's titular ally,[201] though in effect maintaining neutrality, and not encouraged by rumors that Philip was trying to have Philopoemen assassinated.[202] Philip's main supporter in Achaea was exiled; his successor as *stratēgos*, Aristaenus, was eager for a *rapprochement* with Rome.[203] Dissension ran deep. Eventually a divided League voted for Aristaenus's proposal.[204] The deciding factor in choosing Rome over Philip was almost certainly the better chance Rome offered of dealing with Nabis and strengthening the League's position in the Peloponnese: the outlook, as always, remained parochial.[205] The League's defection left Philip highly vulnerable.

In 199 the Aetolians too, after cautious hesitation, finally committed themselves to Rome, but only because it looked by then as though Philip would lose.[206] A similar belief encouraged Athens, long restrained by fear, and the anxiety of dealing on her own with Macedonian incursions, to enact (200/199) a hysterical reversal of all the lickspittle honors that the Council and the Assembly had previously voted Philip: the statues were to be pulled down, the feast days and priesthoods were to be abolished; the priests, whenever they prayed for Athens and her allies, were also bidden to "curse and execrate Philip, his children and kingdom, his sea and land forces, and the entire race and name of the Macedonians"; any anti-Philip decree was to be adopted *nemine contradicente*, anyone making a proposal that could be construed as favoring him could be killed with impunity as an outlaw; finally, all the antityrannical legislation enacted against the Peisistratids should be reactivated to deal with Philip.[207] "It was," Livy remarks, "with writings and words, their only strength, that the Athenians waged war against Philip."

It is sometimes argued that Philip also alienated his own upper classes by promising better conditions for the underprivileged;[208] but for this there is no serious evidence, certainly not his habit (familiar in many other earlier Macedonian monarchs, not least Philip II) of wearing ordinary clothes and affecting to be a man of the people.[209] Philip's favor, like that of his predecessors, always went to the aristocrats on whom he primarily depended. Setbacks certainly did not improve his temper. In the fall of 200, having failed to capture both Eleusis and Athens, he subjected Attica to the kind of wholesale pillaging and devastation that had not been seen since the Persian Wars.[210] For the next two years his fearsome energy, coupled with an indifferent opposition, kept him well in control of the situation. He was here, there, and everywhere. He bottled up a Roman army in the mountains of Illyria, drove back the Aetolians to the south, crushed a Dardanian invasion from the north.[211] But in 198, with the arrival in Greece of the young consul Titus Quinctius Flamininus, the tide at once began to turn.

What Edouard Will describes as "militant philhellenism"[212]—whether genuine on Flamininus's part, or, more probably, a mere new instrument of anti-Macedonian political pressure[213]—was now to be the order of the day. A meeting between Flamininus and Philip at the Aoös River in Illyria proved abortive: Philip stormed out in a rage on hearing the Roman terms—peace only if he evacuated his Greek strong points (Thessaly, Euboea, Corinth), cities to be ungarrisoned and autonomous.[214] According to Diodorus, Flamininus claimed, already, to have a senatorial commission to liberate Greece, but this seems unlikely.[215] The emphasis was still all on getting Philip out of Greece rather than deciding the status of the Greek states when he was gone.[216] Flamininus, after the breakdown of the talks, lost no time in driving Philip's forces back into Thessaly, where Philip carried out a desperate scorched-earth policy in sharp contrast with the Roman's carefully calculated restraint: no looting, no atrocities.[217]

By the later summer of 198 Rome's legions were on the Gulf of Corinth. Flamininus worked hard on the dissident members of the Achaean League: most came over, though one or two, Argos in particular, held out for Philip. In November Philip, thus robbed of his allies, tried once more for peace.[218] In a conference at Nicaea near Thermopylae he once more was presented with terms that virtually restricted him to Macedonia, and negotiations stalled. But this was election year for Flamininus: he told Philip to send an embassy to Rome—where (as he had anticipated) negotiations broke down over Philip's retention of Demetrias, Chalcis, and Corinth, the Fetters of Greece[219]—while he himself spun out discussions till he was confirmed in his proconsulship, then took the field again. Philip, desperate, now sought alliance where he could find it, which meant with Nabis of Sparta, and, as a bait, turned over Argos to him; he also betrothed his daughters to Nabis's sons. The Spartan subjected his new possession to a reign of terror (a nice reward to the Argives for their loyalty), and then added insult to injury by promptly turning round and making a deal with Flamininus. This stipulated an armistice between Sparta and the Achaean League till the war with Philip was over, and bound Nabis to supply Flamininus with auxiliary troops for the prosecution of the war itself.[220] Rome throughout this period remained extremely cavalier about such *ad hoc* wartime associations, and indeed always avoided any more binding commitments in Greece: the Achaean League, for instance, was repeatedly put off in its quest for a written alliance.[221] Nabis could expect nothing better.

Philip's army was by now reduced to some twenty-five thousand men: like Antigonus One-Eye, like Lysimachus, like too many of his predecessors, he decided to stake everything on a single battle. At Cynoscephalae ("The Dogs' Heads"), in Thessaly, he came within an ace of destroying Flamininus's legions with a massed charge of the Macedonian phalanx (June 197)—a terrifying spectacle, even for battle-hardened Romans—and indeed one phalanx was completely successful. But the other overreached itself, lost formation, and was cut to pieces; the rest of the army was then broken up by a flank attack, something to which the phalanx proved highly vulnerable. In close formation, and on level ground, the charge of the phalanx was regarded as all but irresistible; but its flanks and rear remained open to attack, even when screened by cavalry or light-armed troops. The Romans used variations on this type of attack not only at Cynoscephalae, but also later against

Antiochus III at Magnesia (p. 421) and the Achaean League troops outside Corinth in 146 (p. 452). Another technique available to a seasoned legionary commander was to loosen the compact formation of the phalanx, with its bristling hedge of leveled pikes (sarissas), by tempting it onto uneven or otherwise unfavorable terrain (a good example of the tactic is its use by Aemilius Paullus at Pydna in 168; cf. p. 430). It was the adaptability of the disciplined legionary to changing tactical requirements, as Polybius saw,[222] that gave him the edge over his counterpart—equally disciplined, but far less flexible—in the phalanx.[223]

Cynoscephalae was the first victory over a Greek army by Romans in a major pitched battle; but it left Rome absolutely in control of the situation in Greece. After his defeat Philip agreed perforce—having burned the royal archives at Larissa to avoid embarrassing diplomatic revelations—to rather stiffer terms than those he had earlier rejected.[224] He would evacuate Greece. He would pay a thousand-talent war indemnity. The Greek cities of Europe and Asia (this last clause for Antiochus's attention) would be free; at the same time—again because of Antiochus[225]—Rome judged it prudent to keep garrisons in Demetrias, Chalcis, and Acrocorinth, the Fetters of Greece.[226] However, at the Isthmian Games of 196, after considerable Greek pressure on the Senate,[227] Flamininus, as part of his commission, solemnly proclaimed the freedom of the Greeks, with a roll call of all those—Corinthians, Phocians, Locrians, Euboeans, and others—who were henceforth to be autonomous, ungarrisoned, exempt from tribute, in possession of their ancient laws.[228] His knowledge of the language may have been less than perfect, his cultural aspirations dubious, his philhellenism primarily a persuasive instrument with which to implement Roman *Machtpolitik*;[229] but his timing, on this occasion, was impeccable. The Greeks assembled for the games greeted his proclamation with delirious enthusiasm. Titles and honors were showered upon him.[230] We have heard the same slogan often enough, and so had they, but never before from a Roman.

And what, in the last resort, did it mean? Perhaps Livy came nearest the mark when he defined this *libertas* as a *munus*, a privilege bestowed by Rome as part of the benefits accruing to a foreign client.[231] Flamininus's evacuation of Greece in 194 is so described (below, p. 418): his announcement of it, in Livy's version, is heavy with paternalism, with a lively awareness of mutual obligations. Formal Roman clientship (*clientela*) is too narrow a term; once again, as in his public acknowledgment of *eleutheria*, the Roman is drawing on a well-established Hellenistic custom, that of *euergesia*, benefaction. It should have escaped no one's notice that, despite all the heady talk of freedom, Eretria in Euboea had been made over—the reward for a faithful client-prince—to Eumenes of Pergamon.[232] (Old Attalus had had a stroke the previous year while making a speech in Thebes, and died some months later: his son succeeded him without incident.)[233] From now on—as every Greek diplomat knew, and however unwilling senators might be still to tie their country to Eastern commitments—it was to be Rome that exercised the patronage.

CHAPTER 19

THE SPREAD OF HELLENISM: EXPLORATION, ASSIMILATION, COLONIALISM; OR, THE DOG THAT BARKED IN THE NIGHT

Hellenization, the diffusion of Greek language and culture that has been defined, ever since Droysen's *Geschichte der Diadochen* (1836), as the essence of Hellenistic civilization, is a phenomenon calling for careful scrutiny.[1] Its civilizing, even its missionary aspects have been greatly exaggerated, not least by those anxious to find some moral justification for imperialism; so has its universality. On the other hand, despite the labors of scholars such as Rostovtzeff, this trend has been matched by a persistent tendency to underplay the lure of conquest, commercial profits, and generous land grants (below, p. 371), which provided the main driving force behind this Greek diaspora—not to mention the stubborn refusal of allegedly inferior races to embrace the benefits of Greek enlightenment thus rudely thrust upon them. It was, significantly, no king or conqueror, but wandering Cynic philosophers such as Diogenes—dropouts from the affluent bourgeois society of the Successor kingdoms—who described themselves as "citizens of the world" (*kosmopolitai*),[2] and talked about an equality based on the common nature (*physis*) of the human animal. Whatever their mission may have been, it was not to promote the ethics, morality, and political organization of a system they had rejected.[3] Yet such odd men out remained an insignificant minority. Despite the widespread adoption (by the *kosmopolitai* among others) of Attic *koinē* as a Hellenistic *lingua franca*, it is notable—and symptomatic—how resistant it remained to foreign loan words.[4]

An analysis of the extant evidence is revealing. The Greeks had long assumed in themselves, partly on environmental grounds, a cultural superiority over all alien societies[5]—a superiority that even extended, in the visual arts, to idealizing themselves, while portraying outsiders with a realism often not far this side of caricature[6]—yet this never manifested itself as a compelling urge to convert or enlighten the *barbaroi*, whom no less an intellectual than Aristotle regarded as slaves by nature,

312

to be treated like animals or plants.[7] In classical drama—for example, Aristophanes' *Acharnians* (425) or *Thesmophoriazusae* (411), and Euripides' *Orestes* (408)—the jabbering foreigner had always been good for a laugh.[8] No one ever thought of educating him. Isocrates in the fourth century might argue—in deference to the sophistic notion that *aretē* (that quintessentially Greek quality, virtue and natural capability combined) could be taught as well as inherited—that Greekness was a matter of attitude, not blood, to be got from a proper training in Greek culture (*paideia*);[9] but he still shouted louder than anyone for a crusade against the barbarian. Curiosity about the rest of the world undoubtedly existed, but was not, perhaps mercifully, accompanied by any inclination to improve it.

Thus the dissemination of Hellenism, when it came, was incidental rather than conscious or deliberate, an important point. Further, those Macedonian soldiers and Greek businessmen who exploited the indigenous populations of the great Successor kingdoms could not, by any stretch of the imagination, be regarded as a cultural elite. The stupid, bombastic, drunken, cowardly *miles gloriosus* who appears in literature from Menander's day onwards (above, p. 74), with his toadying servant and chestfuls of Persian plunder, had all too real a basis in fact. Such men were massively indifferent to the language and civilization of any country they happened to be occupying, an attitude that their victims, for the most part, reciprocated. Even in the heavily Hellenized areas of Syria, Phoenicia, and Cyprus bilingual inscriptions are common; Aramaic remained the second language of Antioch, and was spoken as the vernacular throughout Syria long after the Roman conquest.[10] It was the polyglot poet and anthologist Meleager of Gadara (*fl.* ca. 100 B.C.) who wrote, sardonically, "What's so surprising about my being a Syrian? You and I, friend, inhabit one country—the world," a fine Stoic sentiment, and then ended his own epitaph with the Syrian, Phoenician, and Greek words for "farewell," not perhaps quite what the Stoics had in mind.[11] Alexander's racial fusion *de haut en bas* died with its begetter, but the cosmopolitanism of Diogenes had come to stay.

Any Egyptian who wanted to get anywhere under the Ptolemies had to speak, and preferably also write, *koinē* Greek. We have a letter of complaint (ca. 256/5) to an official from his (probably Egyptian) native servant about the contemptuous ill treatment he has received "because I am a barbarian," and petitioning for regular pay in future "so that I don't starve because I can't speak Greek."[12] Similarly, an Egyptian priest is resentful at a Greek settler who "despises me because I am an Egyptian."[13] Though later, as we shall see, a certain degree of low-level acculturation took place, in the fourth and third centuries imperial racism was rampant among the Greeks and Macedonians of Alexandria, and never entirely died out. The King's Friends excluded all non-Greeks from their circle. Alexandrian marriage customs remained, as several scholars point out, ultra-Greek for the Greeks; it is also remarkable how many residents clung to the citizenship of their own *polis* rather than assuming that of Alexandria. The list includes most of the major third-century poets and scholars except for Apollonius, who was in any case Alexandrian by birth (*pace* Professor Lefkowitz; cf. p. 783). No Macedonian of note before Cleopatra VII, and very few Greeks, would ever learn Egyptian, so that the administration (still, ironically, in

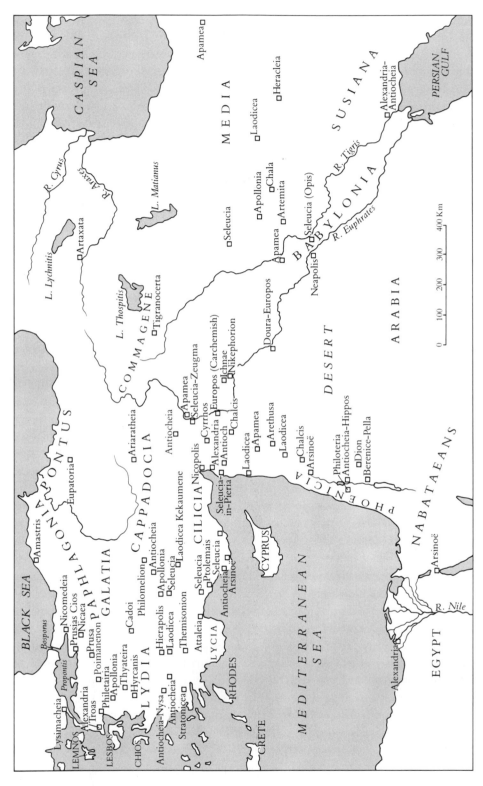

Map 19. Hellenistic foundations.

essence pharaonic) functioned, at middle level, through a corps of more or less bilingual native interpreters and scribes.[14] Competition for such posts, now as in the earlier pharaonic period, was intense. On the other hand the Hellenized Egyptian was not required to read, much less to enjoy, Greek literature, any more than his masters knew, or cared about, the age-old literary heritage of Egypt. Such assimilation as took place tended, in the first instance, to be among the illiterate or culturally indifferent lower classes; and here it was the alien Greeks, who, by intermarriage and religious syncretism, slowly became Egyptianized,[15] a pattern that repeats itself elsewhere in the *oikoumenē* from the second century onwards.

Borrowings and adaptations, then, we would expect to find in those areas that, first, required no linguistic skill, and, second, were commonly accessible without conscious intellectual effort: that is, the visual arts, architecture, and music. Apart from music, for which there is only sketchy literary evidence (suggesting possible Oriental influence on Greek modes and instruments rather than vice versa),[16] this is precisely the case. Yet even in the area of art and architecture, what is often pointed to as evidence for cultural dissemination is, in the sense proposed, nothing of the sort. I am thinking particularly of the export of Greek building styles, pottery, statuary, gymnasia, temples, theaters, and the rest of the civic impedimenta essential for any self-respecting *polis*, into areas as far afield as, say, Bactria. Aï Khanum, on the Oxus, is a good case in point (cf. below, p. 332). Probably founded by Alexander as Alexandria Oxiana,[17] Aï Khanum, like all such cities, was settled exclusively by Greek and Macedonian colonists. In Bactria, colonists apart, no less than 13,500 troops were left behind by Alexander, more than enough to form what has been accurately described as "the nucleus of a central Asian Greece."[18] Thus, far from any kind of diffusion, what we find in such cases is an alien enclave, an artificial island of Greek social and cultural amenities almost totally isolated from the indigenous population that it dominated. There were areas of contact, even of interpenetration, but these were few, and brought about by special circumstances.

That much-touted respect for exotic alien wisdom occasionally found in Greek literature—for example, Herodotus's astonishment, later shared by Plato and Aristotle, at the hoary, unchanging, Egyptian priestly tradition[19]—depended in the main on unfamiliarity (because of the language barrier) with the literature in which such wisdom was enshrined. Nor do we find, *per contra*, any substantial evidence in the Seleucid East or India for local interest in Greek literature or Greek ideas, but rather a great deal to suggest implacable hostility, with a religious and ideological no less than an ethnic basis.[20]

Local acclimatization tended, inevitably, to be restricted to two well-defined categories. On the one hand we find those still-independent rulers who went Greek for their sociopolitical advancement. On the other, there were the intelligent and ambitious collaborators who set out to make a career in the administrative system of the occupying power: in the Seleucid empire, it has been calculated, not more than 2.5 percent of the official class, and that only after two generations.[21] These were the men who became interpreters, who acquired jobs as clerks, tax collectors, accountants, or other categories at subexecutive level in the bureaucracy, with an outside chance of clawing their way up the ladder of advancement to positions of real power as senior administrators or military officers (including police). By so doing they committed themselves to the foreign regime they served in a social no less than a professional sense. Like Indians under the British Raj angling for the *entrée* to European club membership, they developed the taste for exercising naked,[22] for worshipping strange gods, for patronizing the theater; they courted municipal kudos by the lavish generosity of their benefactions. The prime motive in such cases was, clearly, social and professional ambition, even if a little genuine acculturation took place at the same time. Against this must be set that deep resentment and hostility felt by most of their fellow countrymen toward an occupying power (not to mention the angry contempt, mixed with jealousy, that they themselves would attract), and, on the Graeco-Macedonian side, a powerful distaste for those who in any sense went native.[23] It took a liberal intellectual like Eratosthenes, even in the Hellenistic age, consciously to challenge such an entrenched attitude.[24]

When all these factors are taken into account, a radically modified picture of Hellenization emerges, restricted, for the most part, to some curious instances of architectural and glyptic hybridization; some social assimilations among non-Greek rulers and in the administrative sector of the major kingdoms (particularly the Ptolemaic); a few religious syncretizations that transmuted their borrowings out of all recognition (e.g., Isis and Sarapis); and the establishment of the Attic *koinē* as a useful international language, primarily for administrative and commercial purposes, but also, later, for religious propaganda. This does not mean that the Greek and Macedonian colonists failed to have a profound impact on the societies they controlled, particularly through the widespread colonization of the Seleucid empire (cf. p. 372); but this impact was, first and foremost, economic and demographic rather than cultural. As we shall see, it is hard to track the conscious diffusion of Greek intellectual ideas in the Hellenistic East with any real confidence, and of genuine literary interpenetration between Greek and other cultures there is virtually no trace. For one thing, literary translations—as opposed to those of medical, mathematical, astronomical, or similar practical treatises (p. 325)[25]—seem to have been nonexistent, a sure sign of esthetic indifference.

Thus whatever the Greeks and, *a fortiori*, the Macedonians were up to (over and above financial exploitation) in the kingdoms ruled by Alexander's heirs, spreading cultural light formed a very small part of it. Itinerant sophists might peddle the latest philosophical clichés of Academy or Stoa at street corners, and the local-boy-made-good, with his Greek-style education,[26] would have a stock of well-worn quotations from Homer, Euripides, and Menander at his disposal. It does not add up to very much. To what extent the locals would patronize a Greek theater (e.g., that of Aï Khanum in Bactria), and what they absorbed, or even understood, if they did, remain highly problematic questions.

The failure of Hellenism to catch hold among the indigenous inhabitants of the Ptolemaic and Seleucid kingdoms thus has nothing to do with its intrinsic intellectual or cultural merits as a system of ideas, a creative matrix, a way of life. It failed for several good and compelling reasons wholly unrelated to the criteria by which we would assess it: the bitter resentment of defeat, which found expression in passionate ethnocentrism; a theocratic temper that subordinated arts and sciences alike to the requirements of religion,[27] and was chary of translating religious texts; a language barrier that no one cared to break except for the immediate requirements of commerce and administration. This general rejection throws into prominent relief the two striking exceptions for which we have evidence, and in both cases, as is at once apparent, special circumstances apply.

The first concerns the large and influential community of Jews in Alexandria, perhaps originating as prisoners of war settled there by Ptolemy I.[28] This community, though ethnically debarred by its own religious laws from intermarriage, contained a high proportion of intellectuals, and, equally important, became bilingual in Greek. To a surprising extent, the external aspects of synagogue ritual were adapted to Greek custom.[29] In the third century the Torah was translated into Greek, an act with far-reaching consequences. Even more important was the production, perhaps begun under Ptolemy II, but not completed till the second century, of the Septuagint, the Greek version of the Hebrew Bible.[30] It is noteworthy that the prime motive for translation in this case was the increasing inability of the Greek-speaking Alexandrian Jews to understand either Hebrew or Aramaic. As a result, a considerable body of Helleno-Judaic literature passed into circulation.

Yet, once again, despite favorable conditions for direct mutual influence—they were all living in the same city, must often have passed one another in the street—the evidence reveals an almost total lack of contact, certainly in the third century and arguably for much longer, between this Jewish Alexandrian literary movement and the contemporary tradition of Callimachus, Theocritus, and their successors. The *cognoscenti* of the Museum reveal no interest in, or knowledge of, the prophetic mode of discourse so characteristic of Jewish thought,[31] while the dominant influence on Jewish Alexandrian literature is not Homer, much less Callimachus, but the Sep-

Fig. 102. Mid-first-century B.C. papyrus of the Septuagint (Deut. 31.28–30, 32.1–7; Egypt, provenience unknown).
Cairo, Société égyptienne de papyrologie.

tuagint. The form and substance of those works that survive remain Jewish, prophetic, religious-inspired throughout. The nearest we come to classical influence is
an extraordinary fragment of tragedy, in flat iambic trimeters, entitled *Exodus,* and
covering most of the life of Moses, which has little literary merit, but does at least
reveal familiarity with the language and meter of Euripides. There are also some unremarkable fragments of epic: Philo Senior on Jerusalem, Theodotus on the Jews,
filtered through to Eusebius by way of Alexander Polyhistor. This could hardly be
described as an impressive cross-cultural record.[32]

The one shining exception to all these predictable, if depressing, conclusions is,
of course, provided by the greatest, and most historically significant, cultural confrontation of them all: that between Greece and Rome. Though the lack of a home-
grown intellectual tradition has probably been exaggerated, the familiar picture of
"captive Greece captivating her savage conqueror, and bringing the arts to rustic
Latium" remains true enough in essence.[33] The Roman attitude to the Greeks was,
predictably, ambivalent. On the one hand they swallowed Greek culture whole (a
feast that gave the more old-fashioned among them severe indigestion), imitated
Greek literature, rehashed Greek philosophy in ponderous, awkwardly abstract
Latin, sedulously pastiched Greek art. On the other, perhaps not least because they
"had eaten of the apple of knowledge and knew themselves to be culturally naked,"[34] a
situation always liable to arouse resentment, they despised and mistrusted the Greeks
themselves as slippery, unreliable, unwarlike, covetous mountebanks, confidence
tricksters with no moral principles and a quicksilver gift of the gab.[35] Paradoxically,
it was (as Horace notes) on the one occasion when the Greeks came as a defeated
nation rather than as conquerors that their culture had most influence. The ambivalence is shared by Polybius, who identified Rome's moral decline with the hedonistic
ways her *jeunesse dorée* picked up from the Greeks after Pydna, but was well aware of
the need to emulate them in cultural matters.[36] Though they could not fight like
Spaniards or Carthaginians, it was felt, they understood the power of words.[37] Con-
descension of this sort could cut both ways: Philip V somewhat patronizingly announced himself impressed by the military organization of these "western barbarians," a term that Cato the Elder later found Greeks still applying, along with other
ethnic slurs, to the Romans, and to which he took great exception.[38]

No accident, either, that it was the Romans—the most enthusiastic promoters
of Hellenizing standards, perhaps because they were so morbidly conscious of being
cultural *parvenus* themselves—who were seriously worried about the real or fancied
decline of those standards. After all, as Cicero reassured them, they themselves had
either shown more inventiveness than the Greeks, or at the very least had improved
anything the Greeks had taught them to which they cared to turn their minds.[39] Livy
puts into the mouth of the consul Gnaeus Manlius remarks that suggest he has very
little time for the latter-day Macedonians of Alexandria and Seleucia and Babylon:
they had, he observed acidly, "degenerated into Syrians and Parthians and Egyptians."[40] Juvenal in his notorious anti-Greek tirade makes precisely the same point.
What proportion of the dregs that are washed across from Orontes to Tiber, he asks
rhetorically, is really Greek anyway? In they swarm, with their unintelligible native

lingo and disgusting habits and weird musical instruments and gaudy prostitutes, to corrupt decent Romans.[41] Long before the end of the first century A.D. Rome had taken over the Greek xenophobic attitude to *barbaroi*, and was applying it, with gusto, to the Greeks themselves.

This ingrained sense of superiority, whether masquerading as panhellenism to sanction the rape of the East, or, later, helping to keep Ptolemies and, to a lesser degree, Seleucids in cultural isolation, century after century, from the peoples they ruled and exploited, is an extraordinarily constant factor in the history of the Hellenistic era. The Macedonians in particular began with a total indifference to, and contempt for, the cultures on which they imposed their government, even though in the interests of profit they were more than willing to take over, not only existing modes of production, serf labor, and land tenure (particularly throughout Asia), but also the (sometimes familiar) forms of municipal government they found.[42] Alexandria was "by" Egypt, yet not of it:[43] Alexander's attempts at racial fusion were abandoned immediately after his death, and Egyptians in Alexandria suffered from constitutional discrimination. Seleucus, alone of his marshals, remained faithful to the "Persian" (actually Bactrian) wife, Apame, wished on him at the time of the Susa mass marriages,[44] so that the subsequent dynasty was by blood *mixobarbaros*; but this had less influence on Seleucid policy than has sometimes been supposed.

In all instances what the Successors set up were enclaves of Graeco-Macedonian culture in an alien world, governmental ghettos for a ruling elite.[45] When we come to assess the ubiquitous Greek temples, Greek theaters, Greek gymnasia, Greek mosaics, and Greek-language inscriptions scattered throughout the *oikoumenē*, we should never forget that it was for the Hellenized Macedonian ruling minority and its Greek supporters, professional or commercial, that such home-from-home luxuries—not to mention the *polis* that housed them[46]—were, in the first instance, provided. In Egypt, and probably elsewhere, the gymnasium resembled an exclusive club: entry was highly selective, by a scrutiny (*eiskrisis*) designed to keep out undesirables (i.e., non-Greeks) and to foster Hellenism. There was a waiting list, and children from suitable families were put down on it from a tender age.[47] Only by the very end of the Ptolemaic period were wealthy local citizens sometimes admitted.[48] In the Seleucid East the racial barrier was less strictly applied, though a non-Greek gymnasiarch was still a rarity,[49] and athletic victories—apart from those won by hired jockeys in the horse and chariot races on behalf of rich local nabobs—were restricted almost without exception to Greek competitors. In Greece itself, in the third century, we find the occasional Hellenizing non-Greek winning chariot or athletic races at Nemea or on Delos (e.g., an Aramaic Sidonian who called himself Diotimus), and Romans doing likewise at the Isthmus; but these isolated instances have less cultural significance than has sometimes been claimed for them. It is hard to argue with the assertion that "on the whole, the gymnasia did little to further an understanding between the Greek settlers and the native population, and did a lot to keep them apart."[50]

Against the degeneration alleged by Livy and Juvenal we can set the remarkably pure Greek still written in Doura-Europos even after a century of Parthian rule, and

Tacitus's admission that the Greeks of Seleucia-on-Tigris had not, even in his day, "declined into barbarism."[51] It is also true that a fair number of the local inhabitants, especially those who were socially or politically ambitious, took full advantage of such openings as the Greek gymnasium culture offered. A native eager to get on in this new imperial world had to cooperate with the regime, just as a local princeling would often be eager to show himself *au fait* with Greek manners. In some of his most mordant poems Cavafy exactly catches the nervous, snobbish cynicism that inevitably characterized such *arrivistes*:[52]

> Since so many others more barbarous far than us
> Make this sort of inscription, we'll inscribe it too.
> Anyway, don't forget that sometimes
> Sophists from Syria come our way,
> And verse-cobblers, and other such fribbleheads,
> So that un-Hellenized we're not, I think.

Cavafy is satirizing, *inter alia*, the regular use by Asiatic dynasts of the title "Philhellene," only appropriate for someone who in fact stood outside the Greek world, looking in.

Again, the parallel of British India springs to mind, where the acceptance of English as a *lingua franca*, and the appetite of numerous educated Indians for such plums of power as they could grab within the system as it stood (along with the social *mores* of club or cantonment), in no way mitigated the deep-abiding resentment of British rule, much less made any inroads against India's own long-standing cultural and religious traditions. Another interesting parallel is the way in which the scions of Anatolian royal families, for example Ariarathes V of Cappadocia or Nicomedes IV of Bithynia, were sent west for their education, normally to sit at the feet of the reigning philosophers in Athens, "like the vassal princes of the Indian empire who were sent to Harrow and Sandhurst;"[53] it is symptomatic that what these two took home as a result of their experiences was a superficial taste for Greek theatricals.[54] Further, just as a surprising number of Englishmen, despite their own rigid caste system and xenophobic assumptions, were fatally seduced by the lure of Eastern mysticism, so the Indo-Greeks, in a very similar situation, capitulated to some highly un-Greek local influences before they were done. Indian legends and Indian scripts invaded their coinage. Even if the notion of portraying the Buddha in human form was a Greek innovation,[55] their sculpture and reliefs and architecture absorbed far more than they imposed.

Menander, perhaps the greatest king of the Indo-Greeks (r. ca. 160–130), and the only one remembered in later Indian tradition, may have set Pallas Athena on the reverse of his coins,[56] but he was also, in some sense, a convert to Buddhism (traditionally because of discussions with the Buddhist priest Nagasena)[57] who employed the Dharma-Chakra (Wheel of Law) symbol, and was associated in tradition with the building of stupas and the original iconography of the Buddha image.[58] Greek sculpture adapted itself to the lotus posture, and—after a gap of four centuries—

103. Greek-influenced statue of
Bodhisattva, from Gandhara (second-
third century A.D.).
Museum of Fine Arts, Boston.

Fig. 104. The Indo-Greek king Menander. Silver tetradrachm, provenience unknown, minted ca. 160–130 B.C. On the reverse, the fighting Athena of Pella, aegis on left arm, thunderbolt poised, with the inscription "Menander the Savior King."
British Museum, London.

came up with a new and more enduring version of the mysterious "archaic smile." The ghost of Apollo still lurked behind the Buddha's features, but it was a losing battle.[59] Absorption was slow but inevitable; by the time that the Indo-Greek and Graeco-Bactrian kingdoms finally vanished amid the incursions of Sacas, Parthians, and Kushanas (130–100), their inhabitants had been thoroughly Orientalized. By then—but not till then—Narain's verdict had come true: "Their history is part of the history of India and not of the Hellenistic states; they came, they saw, but India conquered."[60]

If it had not been for the Romans, whose strong obsession with Greek culture formed part of the overall imperial legacy that Rome disseminated throughout her far-flung provinces, the impact of Hellenism might well have been less fundamental, less widespread, and less enduring. As it was, Rome achieved a larger, and certainly a more cohesive, empire than Alexander had won—yet one that remained, in essence, a Mediterranean phenomenon. When we talk about the *oikoumenē*, this should always be borne in mind. Even before Rome's ascendancy, the *oikoumenē* was for the most part limited and defined (certainly in the minds of those who exploited it) by Alexander's conquests. In other words, it was an eastern Mediterranean complex, with large but ill-defined Oriental extensions. Northern Europe and Asia, the whole vast African continent south of Egypt and Cyrene, whatever lay beyond the Pillars of Heracles in the west, or the Mauryan empire in India—these areas lay outside the frontiers of the *oikoumenē*, and had no part in it. Even western Europe and the western Mediterranean were assimilated to it only through Rome. Contact between Magna Graecia or Sicily and the Greek East was, as we have seen, limited to commercial transactions, and from the time of the First Punic War these Greek enclaves became Roman fiefs: when Carthage's hold over the West was broken, it was not by Greek action.

With unimportant exceptions, Hellenization meant the interpenetration of Greek and Oriental culture—that was certainly how Droysen saw it[61]—and where Greek rulers did not have the strong arm of Rome to maintain their institutions, they made a less lasting impression than is often supposed. As we have seen, the customary method of diffusion was by way of imposed rule, military settlements, commercial exploitation, by men who brought their language, culture, and administration with them, and enforced their authority by means of a mercenary army. Exploitation exacerbated poverty, so that resistance was often felt at all social levels, with an abused peasantry rallying behind a dispossessed aristocracy or priesthood.[62] The conquerors' artificial islands of culture were at first no more acceptable than a wrongly matched heart transplant. Again, the piecemeal Roman takeover from the beginning of the second century tends to obscure this.

The Ptolemies never cared about Egyptian civilization as such, even though they took over the Egyptian administrative system largely unchanged (p. 191), and regularly went through the mummery of a pharaonic coronation (placating the powerful priesthood was another matter); and the Egyptians rebelled against them whenever they could. In this connection we should note a remarkable document, the so-called *Oracle of the Potter*, an anti-Greek, anti-Macedonian nationalist manifesto from the early Ptolemaic period, which in apocalyptic language foretells the downfall of these hated and blasphemous foreign overlords, the destruction of irreligious Alexandria, the resurgence of Memphis as Egypt's pharaonic capital. It thus seems likely to have been produced in secessionist Upper Egypt, about 200 (above, p. 304).[63] Its appeal is to the downtrodden fellahin: it graphically portrays the starvation and misery of the *chōra* under Ptolemaic rule, and looks forward to a Golden Age to be ushered in by the restored Egyptian pharaohs, a regime so delectable that men will wish the dead alive once more. There is a resemblance here, at least in tone, to the somewhat later third *Sibylline Oracle*, produced perhaps around 150, in the reign of Ptolemy VI Philometor, by Jewish zealots: an incoherent attack on the Seleucids (especially for their activities in Palestine), the Romans, and Greek *mores* generally, which nevertheless reserves praise for Ptolemy himself, who had shown favor to the Jews. It is significant that by the mid-second century, with increasing assimilation of the middle and lower Greek social strata in Alexandria to Egyptian customs,[64] this nationalist violence has largely subsided, and the new tension is between Graeco-Egyptian and Jew.[65]

The extent and passion of Iranian resistance—passive, militant, messianic, or proselytic[66]—to Alexander's conquest and occupation can be gauged from the considerable body of surviving material (again, mostly prophetic and oracular) attacking it. Alexander is the Evil Invader; above all, like the Ptolemies in Egypt, he is presented as a blasphemous disrupter of religion. In both cases what has been destroyed is a system of divine kingship:[67] for the Persians, part of the world order created by Ahura Mazda, and involving not only the priestly caste of the Magi, but also a long-established secular aristocracy, for whom the recovery of Achaemenid theocratic rule is a passionately held article of faith. This counterpropaganda, with nice irony, was disseminated in *koinē* Greek. As early as 320 we find a cuneiform *Babylonian Chronicle* attacking Antigonus One-Eye for his brutal depredations;[68] Seleucus I took the hint, and got Babylonian support in consequence (312: above, p. 29). This was not the kind of atmosphere, to put it mildly, that encouraged acculturation across formidable religious and linguistic barriers.

Neither in Iran nor in India did Greek culture, arguably, leave any substantial trace beyond its own enclaves—certainly not in the literature, where Alexander and his conquistadors figure as "the demons with disheveled hair of the race of wrath."[69] Attic *koinē* did indeed, as we have seen, become a useful *lingua franca* in regions not too far from the traditional site of the Tower of Babel; but this was, first and foremost, for commercial and administrative reasons. As a medium for propaganda, on the other hand, it was, more often than not, employed against Graeco-Macedonian rule. Indeed, what has sanctified the *koinē* (in more senses than one), and given it by association a cultural *réclame* that it scarcely deserves *per se*, is, of course, its key role in the dissemination of Christianity.

It could be argued, with only minimal hyperbole, that the whole concept of Hellenization as a beneficial spreading of light among the grateful heathen was a self-serving myth, propagated by power-hungry imperialists, and rooted in the kind of contemptuous attitude (crystallized by Aristotle: above, p. 312) that saw Greeks as the embodiment of all intelligence and culture, while the rest of the world consisted of mere barbarians, that is, people whose speech was an unintelligible, non-Greek, *ba-ba-ba*. Alexander's rape of the East rested very largely on this premise. Nothing is more eloquent of the enclave mentality than the export of Macedonian place names, wholesale, to northern Syria, so that the port of Seleucia-in-Pieria commemorates not only a ruling monarch, but also a local mountainous coastal range renamed after a loosely comparable site back home. The idea of a missionary crusade to spread superior culture among the unenlightened formed a useful propaganda adjunct to panhellenism, and was later popularized by Plutarch, who argued that those whom Alexander defeated were luckier than those who escaped him, since the former got the benefits of Greek culture and philosophy, while the latter were left to stew in their ignorant primitivism.[70] Bullying people for their own good has a long and depressing history.

I wish I could share the optimism of the late Moses Hadas, who in his study *Hellenistic Culture* painted a roseate picture of the East's enthusiasm for Greek ideas. Yet even he had to admit, significantly, that the enthusiasm was largely restricted to the "upper classes" (i.e., the professionally or socially ambitious), and that the Middle East was not nearly so anxious to see the light as the already more westernized Syro-Phoenician littoral.[71] Those who wore Greek dress (and removed it in the gymnasium), who aped Greek accents, attended Greek plays, and dropped their pinch of incense on Greek altars, had good and sufficient reasons for their behavior, into which esthetic or moral considerations seldom entered. Genuine cultural conversions did undoubtedly take place; but they seem to have been very much in the minority. What we find instead, more often than not, is a steely determination to get on in the world: the eagerness of some locals to acquire Greek names should not necessarily be attributed to philhellenism.[72] Modern parallels suggest themselves. Once again Cavafy has drawn us some marvelous pictures of the mixed motives governing such behavior.[73]

Hadas reminds us that even though the Bible was translated into Greek by Alexandrian Jewish scholars (above, p. 317), "we know of no case where a Greek work was translated into an oriental language," the clear implication being that this is a proof of the superiority of Greek literature as such.[74] The significance of this interesting fact is not, I think, quite what Hadas took it to be. Hostility, ignorance, and plain indifference played a large part in the matter. The hostility was not to Greek culture *per se* (though its secular nature did not appeal to fundamentally theocratic minds) so much as to foreign occupation and everything associated with it. Those few intellectuals who did take the trouble to investigate Greek culture tended to borrow its style (as Ezekial from Euripides) or scholarly techniques and methodology (as Jewish historians from the Museum of Alexandria) or formal logic (as the Pharisees from the Stoa or the Academy), husking out the theoretical insights and discarding the substance as irrelevant. Such attitudes should remind us that the Greeks brought with them neither a powerful proselytizing religion, like the Arabs, nor, like the Jews, a close-knit theocratic tradition of their own.[75]

To take your own superiority for granted does not necessarily, or even commonly, imply that you are altruistically eager to give others the benefit of it, especially when you are busy conquering their territory, exploiting their natural resources and manpower, taxing their citizens, imposing your government on them, and unloading their accumulated gold reserves onto the international market in the form of military loot. The main, indeed the overwhelming, motivation that confronts us in these Greek or Macedonian torchbearers of Western culture, throughout the Hellenistic era, is the irresistible twin lure of power and wealth, with sex trailing along as a poor third and cultural enlightenment virtually nowhere. Among all those in Alexandria who could boast aulic titles and high political, military, or even religious preferment, those in the arts and sciences are by a very long way the least prominent.[76] While all three Successor dynasties patronized scholarship and the arts for reasons of prestige, such activities remained exclusively a court function, pursued by Greeks for the benefit of Greeks (above, p. 84). There is no hint of fusion or collaboration with the local culture: this omission is particularly striking in the case of Ptolemaic Egypt, since the (unwilling) host nation had a long and distinguished cultural history of its own.

Prosopographical research shows something over two hundred literary figures in Ptolemaic Egypt: all are foreigners.[77] Even in medicine and science, where we would expect a higher proportion of native practitioners, out of more than a hundred known names only about a dozen are Egyptian (it is true, of course, and too seldom stressed, that an unknown proportion of these Greek names may in fact conceal Egyptian owners). There is not one Egyptian gymnasiarch or athlete; on the other hand, about one-fifth of the musicians, actors, dancers, painters, and sculptors known to us—again, about a hundred in all—have unmistakably Egyptian names. These statistics, fragmentary and uncertain though they are, nevertheless still tell their own story. The only cases of scholarly acculturation we know about are the compilations of a Manetho or a Berossos, Greek-language digests of local science or history made by compliant priests for their new overlords: Manetho's history of Egypt to 323 was commissioned by Ptolemy II Philadelphos, while Berossos dedi-

cated his account of Babylonia to Antiochus I. Amélie Kuhrt argues that both Manetho and Berossos "helped to make accessible the local ideological repertoires and
historical precedents for adaptation by the Macedonian dynasties, which resulted in
the formation and definition of the distinctive political-cultural entities of Ptolemaic
Egypt and the Seleucid empire." The first part of this claim is a euphemism for sedulous imperial bootlicking; the second is a wild exaggeration.[78] When Callimachus
wanted a really insulting tag for Apollonius, he referred to him as an *Egyptian* ibis
(above, p. 201). Despite the low-level Egyptianization of Alexandrian Greeks from
the early second century onwards (above, p. 316),[79] the indifference of all Ptolemies
before Cleopatra VII to the Egyptian language, let alone to what was written in it,
testifies eloquently to a persistent, deep-rooted, all-pervasive cultural separatism in
the upper echelons of Ptolemaic society.

It is also often asserted that this was a great age of exploration, another cliché
that deserves closer scrutiny than it usually gets. Since transshipment at regular
stages was the rule for ancient cargoes, and since, furthermore, very few travelers in
antiquity (or indeed in any period before the nineteenth century) shared the passion
of Flecker's pilgrims in *Hassan*—"For joy of knowing what may not be known / We
take the Golden Road to Samarkand"—but went abroad only in pursuit of handsome profits, it follows that their ignorance about what went on farther down the
line remained profound. Trading embargoes such as that imposed by the Carthaginians on the western Greeks, who were effectively barred from Gaul, Spain, and the

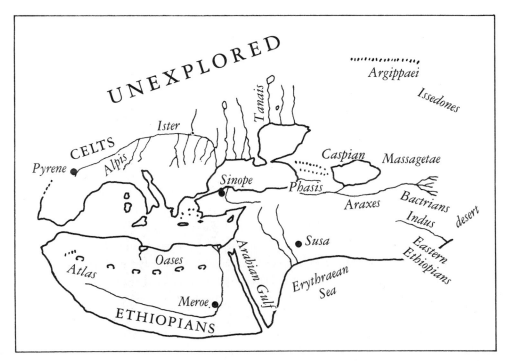

Fig. 105. Herodotus's concept of the world, ca. 450 B.C. (Redrawn.) From O. A. W.
Dilke, *Greek and Roman Maps* (London, 1985), 58.

Atlantic, merely exacerbated this trend. As soon as the known boundaries are passed, the tall stories begin: tales of gold-digging Indian ants, of the Hyperboreans in the far north, up the amber routes (above, p. 207), of tribesmen with feet large enough to use as parasols to keep off the sun (Skiapods), or a penis reaching to their ankles, or born minus an anus, only acquiring this useful addition at puberty.[80]

Worse, such genuine explorers as there were tended to be disbelieved by the pundits at home. Seleucus I sent Megasthenes to visit the Mauryan emperor Chandragupta at Pataliputra (mod. Patna), on the Ganges: as a result of his journey Megasthenes wrote the best and most comprehensive account of India known to the ancient world, only to be dismissed as a liar by the later geographer Strabo.[81] In much the same way Herodotus, earlier, had ridiculed the claim of certain Phoenicians to have circumnavigated Africa, because they "said what I do not believe, though others may, that while sailing round Libya [i.e., westward] they had the sun on their right"—a piece of evidence that in fact clinches the truth of their claim, and places their route clearly in the southern hemisphere, probably round the Cape of Good Hope. Apart from an abortive venture in the second century B.C. by Eudoxus of Cyzicus, this feat was not to be repeated till the Renaissance.[82] Alexander believed to his dying day that the Caspian was an arm of the northern ocean.[83] At some point between 320 and 240 a remarkable explorer called Pytheas, either eluding or postdating the Carthaginian blockade in the Mediterranean, crossed the Bay of Biscay to Ushant and Cornwall, and then circumnavigated Britain, making frequent forays ashore, and sailing as far north as the Faeroes (he mentions nights of 2–3 hours only, which gives a latitude of about 65°).[84] At one point he entered a region where "there was no longer any separate land or sea or air, but a kind of mixture produced from these, resembling a jellyfish": perhaps ice-sludge accompanied by an exceptionally nasty Norwegian sea fog.[85]

Again, the oddities of genuine experience excited disbelief. We find Polybius (of all people) sneering at Pytheas's claims;[86] but then Polybius had done some exploring outside the Pillars of Heracles himself (above, p. 279), and may have disliked competition. Pytheas is also unusual in that, if we discount the lure of the Cornish tin mines, he seems not to have been following a commercial route. He was a skilled astronomer and mathematician, who investigated tides, and whose calculations of latitude achieved unprecedented accuracy.[87] Most of the exploration done in the Hellenistic period, however, followed the lines of age-old trade routes, and very often (because of the transshipment principle) failed to pursue even them far beyond the early staging posts. The fantastic geography in Book 4 of Apollonius's *Argonautica* reveals a fundamental ignorance of the rivers of central and northern Europe (above, p. 213). Despite Alexander's expedition and Ptolemaic exploration of the sea routes to the East, it was not until the reign of Tiberius that a Greek merchant, one Hippalos, caught on to the simple secret of the Indian monsoon winds (known, and kept secret, by Arab middlemen for centuries): that from May to October there was a steady prevailing wind from the southwest to carry a ship to India, and that from November to March it reversed itself, and blew with equal steadiness from the northeast.[88]

The conflict of Seleucid and Ptolemaic rulers over Syria did not—predictably—

Fig. 106. World map accompanying Book 7 of Ptolemy's *Geography* (second century A.D.). British Library, London.

lack its element of commercial competition (cf. p. 372). The trade routes from the East mostly converged at Seleucia-on-Tigris:[89] they included the sea lane up the Persian Gulf, and the overland caravan routes from the Hindu Kush. From here, by two alternative routes, they reached the Mediterranean at Antioch's port of Seleucia-in-Pieria. From Antioch consignments were dispatched through Anatolia to Ephesus by way of Tarsus and Apamea, along the western section of the old Achaemenid royal road. This road was nominally under Seleucid control, but at various times the Ptolemies disrupted it (Ephesus itself changed hands more than once), until Antiochus III's victory at Panion in 200 finally eliminated Ptolemaic competition from this area altogether (above, p. 304). The Ptolemies thus became dependent exclusively on the southern sea route from India, which made port at Aden. From Aden goods were transported by caravan north to Palestine or Alexandria. However, the loss of Coele-Syria made the northern end of this route equally problematic of access; so we find second-century Ptolemaic traders moving south in search of a link route that would bypass Arabia altogether, from some point along the shores of the Red Sea.

The Ptolemies were also in search of what had become an increasingly highly valued arm in ancient warfare: elephants. (Whether they were in fact worth the time, money, and trouble expended on them is another matter altogether.) The elephants that the Ptolemies' hunters rounded up in what is now Somalia were not the large African bush elephant, but the smaller forest elephant:[90] at Raphia, in 217, the huge Indian elephants of Antiochus scared them off even before battle was joined.[91] Inscriptions and literary sources alike suggest exclusively commercial reasons for opening up this route south and east of Egypt; the same is true of Seleucid control over the Oriental caravan routes. We hear of both dynasties commissioning explorers, but only to secure or establish openings for profitable trade. The scientific curiosity that (perhaps through Aristotle's urging) stimulated Alexander to take geographers and botanists on his expedition is almost wholly absent here. Yet at the same time geographical theory was advancing. By about 300 Dicaearchus of Messene had produced a map of the known world embodying, in crude form, the principles of latitude and longitude; so, somewhat later, did Eratosthenes, Apollonius's successor as chief librarian in Alexandria, aided by a surprisingly accurate formula for measuring the circumference of the earth (below, p. 480).[92]

If Greeks and Macedonians did not promote their culture with the object of converting their new subjects to Hellenism, at least their post-Alexandrian diaspora carried that culture—certainly its more visible and socially indispensable elements—to the four corners of the Mediterranean world and beyond, so that there developed (for example) something of an international style in Greek art. It has been claimed that "a middle-class Greek, settling down in the Fayyum . . . might hire Egyptian workmen to decorate his walls with murals—but the pictures themselves would be crude imitations of what was being painted at Athens or Syracuse or Antioch."[93] The basic inspiration remained Greek. Generalizations in this area are dangerous. The evidence is patchy, while those with the money to commission murals obviously made sure that they got what they wanted, and some patrons will have had

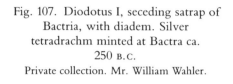

Fig. 107. Diodotus I, seceding satrap of
Bactria, with diadem. Silver
tetradrachm minted at Bactra ca.
250 B.C.
Private collection. Mr. William Wahler.

more adventurous taste than others. But the phenomenon described certainly existed:
my impression is that it was commoner in the third century than later. This would
agree with the patterns of absorption we have noted, which show (in Egypt as elsewhere) a slow progressive surrender to local influences from about 200 onwards.

Perhaps the most extraordinary example of Greek enclave culture—finally absorbed by something larger than itself—is that of the isolated Greek kingdoms in
Bactria and India. For over two centuries, beginning with the renegade Seleucid satrap Diodotus shortly before or after 250, a series of more than forty Greek kings
ruled in the East, from Bactria to the Punjab. There are a few scattered literary references—we have already seen how Antiochus III besieged Euthydemus for two years
in Zariaspa (above, p. 295)—but most of the story has been pieced together from
these rulers' self-promoting and highly idiosyncratic coinage. Though there is a
great deal of scholarly dissension concerning the chronology, relationships, and conquests of individual monarchs, the overall picture is clear enough.[94] Greeks had been
settled in Bactria by the Persians long before Alexander left colonists there:[95] some
were time-expired mercenaries, who chose these fertile uplands rather than the unpredictable future of a retirement in Greece. They also formed a handy buffer against
the constant threat of incursion by northern nomads (above, p. 295).[96] Alexander,
recognizing the difficulties inherent in a Bactrian satrapy, earmarked a remarkably
large body of troops for the policing of the area (above, p. 9). Two years before his
death the Greek colonists revolted (325),[97] and in 323 it took a major campaign by
a picked body of Macedonian veterans to subdue them.[98] At the settlement of Triparadeisos, in 320 (p. 15), the satrap placed in charge of Bactria was, significantly,
a Cypriot Greek, Stasanor. The choice arguably reflects an attempt to conciliate
these restless and intractable Greek settlers, though we are also told that no Macedonian would touch the job. Stasanor's presence certainly quieted things down, but
at the price of encouraging a separatist movement. By 316, indeed, Stasanor was so
well entrenched in his bailiwick that not even Antigonus One-Eye would attempt to
shift him.[99]

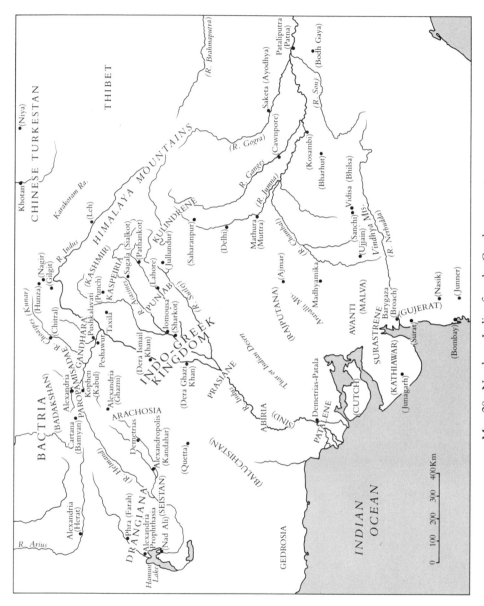

Map 20. Northern India after the Greek conquest.
From Tarn, *The Greeks in Bactria and India*, 2d ed., endpaper map 2.

A few years later, after his capture of Babylon, Seleucus I reconquered Bactria:[100] clearly the only way to hold it was by force of arms. Whether in the circumstances he continued the practice of encouraging Greek settlers[101]—the prime cause of trouble in the region—seems highly doubtful. At all events, shortly before or after 250 yet another satrap, Diodotus, finally broke away from the Seleucid empire, and established a Bactrian kingdom. Bactria was a frontier province, and it must have occurred to Diodotus, very early on, that he got little from his Seleucid overlords in exchange for the tribute payments that they were seldom powerful enough to enforce. Even so, as in the similar case of Pergamon (p. 168), he seems to have continued to acknowledge Antiochus II's sovereignty on his coins long after his *de facto* secession.[102] The large number of Greek colonists in Bactria gave his rule powerful support, and created an ethnic enclave of a most unusual sort.

There has been much debate as to whether the Greek empire of Bactria and India was, in essence, a fifth Hellenistic state, or rather "part of the history of India."[103] The simple answer is that it began as the first and ended by being absorbed into the second (cf. above, p. 322). Just how persistent Greek separatism was has been strikingly demonstrated by a decade and more of excavation at Aï Khanum. This city ("Lady Moon" in Uzbek) lies at the confluence of the Oxus (Daria-i-Panj) and Kokcha rivers, on the northern Afghan frontier with Soviet Russia. It occupies a natural strategic site, well placed to guard the northeastern approaches to Bactria.[104] Founded about 329/8, during Alexander's campaign in the upper satrapies, it finally succumbed, about 100, to a barbarian incursion from across the Oxus (in December 1979, by one of history's coincidental ironies, its French excavators were cut off from their site in precisely the same way) and saw its desecrated temple turned into a Kushana storage magazine.[105]

Despite its remoteness, Aï Khanum was in every respect a Greek city throughout. The great palatial complex with its peristyle courtyard, the funerary cult shrine (*hērōön*), the lush Corinthian capitals of the hypostyle hall—though the hall itself is an interesting Achaemenid throwback—the pottery, the bronze and terra-cotta figurines, perhaps above all the Delphic maxims inscribed, in Greek, on a base in the *hērōön* (copied at Delphi, set up, and paid for by a loyal globe-trotting citizen), all form "a stunning testimony to the fidelity of these Greek settlers of remote Bactria to the most authentic and venerable traditions of Hellenism."[106] That verdict was given in 1967: subsequent seasons of excavation have not merely confirmed but intensified it.

The area was peaceful and well guarded: Aï Khanum's long-undisturbed state is a tribute, in this wild frontier region, to highly efficient policing. Probably Euthydemus made full use of the famous Bactrian cavalry to keep the Saca hordes in check: he was able to raise no less than ten thousand horsemen against Antiochus.[107] Outside the walls Paul Bernard and his team found not only a large funerary mausoleum of Hellenistic type,[108] but also a wealthy Greek colonist's villa, probably the home of some landowner who lived on, and by, his estates, using local labor in much the same way as was done in other parts of the Seleucid empire.[109] The gymnasium or palaestra covered an area of nearly a hundred square yards.[110] There was

Fig. 108. Aï Khanum, on the southern bank of the Oxus in northern Afghanistan.
View (before excavation) of the central area of the city, including the palace
and theater.
French Archaeological Delegation in Afghanistan.

a beautiful public fountain with carved gargoyles and waterspouts in the form of
lions' and dolphins' heads.[111] A temple, a palace, an arsenal: these were predictable
enough;[112] on the other hand, the discovery of a Greek theater beside the Oxus came
as something of a surprise, a striking symbol of Hellenic cultural vigor in this remote
region.[113] It may not suffice to justify Plutarch's romantic picture of Persian or
Gedrosian children happily declaiming the choruses of Sophocles,[114] but at least it
forms a logical companion to the fragments of what appears to be a post-Aristotelian
philosophical treatise,[115] not to mention a sophisticated sundial.[116]

Behind its constantly renovated city walls, well defended and ethnocentric, the
enclave of Greek Aï Khanum held the outer world at bay.[117] The isolation, however,
was never total, and indeed by the end Aï Khanum had become more effectively cut
off from the Greek West than from the indigenous culture of Bactria. One arresting
symptom of this severance is the large pebble mosaic, dated to about 150, found in
the palace bathing quarters.[118] It is not only the poor, provincial quality of the execution that attracts attention—large, coarse pebbles, a total absence of defining lead
strips and even of black pebbles set to create outlines—but the remarkable fact that
elsewhere in the Greek world pebbles had, for a century and more (i.e., just about

since the establishment of the Bactrian kingdom) been replaced by cubes (tesserae), which made possible a far more subtly modulated technique. This suggests that the mosaicists who went east handed down their skills without any fresh infusion of outside talent, finally suffering a degeneration comparable to that we find, over a similar period, in the gold staters originally struck by Philip II, then copied and re-copied as far afield as Gaul and southwestern England, till the quadriga and chari-oteer on the reverse became a meaningless jumble of lines and blobs.[119] At the same time, local influences can be detected *ab initio* in the architecture (e.g., the hypostyle hall) and the visual arts, growing, as we would expect, progressively stronger with time.[120] A non-Greek temple was found outside the walls.[121] A silver-gilt medallion of Cybele in her chariot, from the mid-third century, already reveals a subtle fusion of Greek and Oriental elements, with the latter ultimately predominant.[122]

After Diodotus I's death, perhaps as early as 248,[123] his son of the same name succeeded him, and ruled till about 235, when he was killed during a coup. Its leader was Euthydemus, in all likelihood a relative of Diodotus, and perhaps the satrap of Aria and Margiana, who thus founded the second dynasty of Graeco-Bactrian

Fig. 109. Reverse imprint left on clay floor by a papyrus (now perished) of the mid-second century B.C. in the library(?) of the palace at Aï Khanum.
Kabul Museum.

Fig. 110. The Indo-Greek king
Demetrius I, wearing diadem and
elephant-scalp headdress. Silver
tetradrachm, provenience uncertain,
minted ca. 190 B.C.
British Museum, London.

kings.[124] He enjoyed a long reign (it was toward the end of it that he stood off Anti-ochus), but details are lacking. His son Demetrius I (r. ca. 200–190),[125] a strong, heavy-jowled man portrayed wearing the elephant-scalp headdress (as a conqueror of India), and possibly married to a daughter of Antiochus III, crossed the Hindu Kush into the Punjab, and established himself at Taxila;[126] he had already made in-roads on the old Seleucid satrapies around the Caspian.

In India now as well as Bactria, these Greek dynasts—Demetrius, the great Menander, Euthydemus, and the rest—maintained their improbable rule. "Against all imagining, almost entirely cut off from the Greek world, for more than a hundred and fifty years they and their descendants ruled in western India. They lived, spoke and thought as independent Greek kings long after Greece itself had fallen wholly under the power of Rome."[127] Bactria held out till about 140, when the last regnant Graeco-Bactrian king, Heliocles I, went down fighting the Saca hordes from the Asiatic steppes, leaving his descendants as a landless dynasty. The Indian king-dom persisted almost another century; then, about 55, its king Hermaeus likewise vanishes from history, to be replaced by the Saca chieftain Azes I. Yet Menander, the Buddhist convert, was the only one of these legendary rulers to survive in Indian literature, under the name of Milinda: there is, surely, a moral of a sort to ponder here. Far more important than his prowess as a warrior was his status as a sage and a thinker, who had embraced Eastern ways: when he died, he was revered as a saint, and his ashes were divided between the chief cities of his kingdom.[128] Whatever im-pressed Menander's Indian subjects, it was not his superior Greek culture.

CHAPTER 20

MIDDLE-PERIOD HELLENISTIC ART, 270–150: *SI MONUMENTUM REQUIRIS . . .*

Goethe once remarked, shrewdly, that "scholarship without any notion of art is one-eyed" (*Philologie ohne Kunstbegriff ist einäugig*), but failed to provide any adequate guidance as to how the art could be related to an overall interpretation of society. This is a particularly pressing problem in the period under discussion, where for long stretches our evidence is skimpy at best, and the chronology in consequence chaotic.[1] Such literary statements as we possess tend to be puzzling. We have a nice instance of this in the elder Pliny (A.D. 23/4–79), whose chapters on the history of art are among the few writings on this topic to survive from antiquity. Pliny says, quite bluntly, of the period between 295/2 and 156/3 (in effect, the whole High Hellenistic phase), that the sculptor's art in Greece came to a halt then (*cessauit deinde ars*).[2] A modern reader, conditioned to admire the intellectual realism of Hellenistic portraiture, and, above all, the powerful baroque achievements of Pergamon's sculptors and architects, may well wonder what on earth Pliny meant.

Now the compiler of the *Natural History* was a scissors-and-paste polymath, industrious but unoriginal, and the most likely answer is that he was simply parroting the congenial views of some conservative Greek critic—perhaps Pasiteles, a Romanized Greek sculptor of the first century B.C. Pasiteles, as an energetic and dedicated neoclassicist, rejected all art that stood formally outside the classical tradition.[3] This explanation, if true, illuminates one symptomatic cultural trend from the mid-second century onwards (to which the Roman takeover in Greece provides an important, though not the only, antecedent cause): a recurrent, academic urge to turn one's back on innovation, to exhume and resuscitate the past—the classical past, *bien entendu*—as the only correct approach to literature or art. This movement reached its apogee with the so-called Second Sophistic of the second century A.D., when dilettanti such as Lucian or Herodes Atticus, the first Aramaic by birth, the second an Athenian who became a Roman consul, vied with one another in writing "pure," that is, classical, Attic Greek.

Such an attitude might at first sight, when viewed against its broad historical background, seem something of a contradiction in terms. Innovation was fundamental to this new age. The enormous expansion of horizons that followed Alexander's conquests, an expansion as much sociocultural as geographic, had involved, inevitably, an abandonment of parochial restrictions, a willingness to experiment. The conquistadors, as we have seen, neither wanted to jettison the basic concept and attributes of the *polis*—they would as soon have denied their own Greekness—nor, in all likelihood, could have done so had they been so inclined. Nevertheless, the focus of perspective now shifted to areas outside mainland Greece, often either hostile or indifferent to Hellenism (above, p. 323), where quite different standards were current, and even the *polis* very soon began to undergo a subtle metamorphosis. Despite the ingrained xenophobia of Graeco-Macedonian colonists, external influences, as we have seen, began to creep in. More important still—if harder to quantify—were the inner changes wrought on the Greek psyche, both at home and abroad, by those tremendous social and political upheavals that followed Alexander's death, which we have observed in earlier chapters: loss of self-confidence and idealism, displacement of public values, the erosion of religious beliefs, self-absorption ousting involvement, hedonism masking impotent resentment, the violence of despair, the ugliness of reality formalized as realism, the empty urban soul starving on pastoral whimsy, sex, and *Machtpolitik*.

All this could not fail to leave a deep impression on the visual arts. "Expressionism" or "baroque" is simply polite academic shorthand for the result. It was against such trends, which even before the third century had made amazing inroads, at every level, into the conventions and iconography of traditional Greek art (even while, as in the case of the Pergamene sculptures, looking directly to fifth-century inspiration), that the classicizing reaction—regarded by Pliny in the first century A.D. as the only legitimate form of artistic expression—eventually produced so violent, and long-lasting, a counterrevolution. Pliny, as we have seen, was talking about statuaries; and for the period under discussion that meant, above all, portraitists.[4] Stewart explains this concentration primarily in economic terms—a decline in prosperity meant a decline in public commissions of a religious (or, he might have added, civic) nature, the replacement of the *polis* as a patron by wealthy individuals or the private society (e.g., the philosophical schools). But this shift in emphasis, as should by now be clear, was, in the first instance, social and psychological, the consequence of, among other things, political collapse: what is really significant is that those who had the money (and there were plenty of them) no longer chose to channel it into public, collective gestures of religious or civic pride. This swing away from involvement toward individualism, accompanied, in the grim decades that followed the Chremonidean War (above, p. 147)—the years of neglected shrines, of seedy dilapidation, of what has been described as "almost total cultural hiatus"[5]—by a mood that blended *Angst* and self-indulgence, could not fail to have a strong impact on portraiture, not least since so many of the finest sculptors were still Athenians.

It certainly helps to explain both the baroque emotionalism, above all in sculpture, that now emerges as a dominant motif—the Pergamene kings, as we shall see,

Fig. 111. Bronze figurine of a rachitic
dwarf (provenience unknown;
? ca. 200 B.C.).
Museum für Kunst, Hamburg.

employed Athenian artists—and the revulsion that it ultimately engendered. The writhing, struggling, twisted bodies, racked with pain or ecstasy; the violence and hysteria, the lowlife genre scenes, the brutal Gillray-like caricature of physiognomy; the taste for portraying *putti*, cripples, grotesques, drunks, and geriatric flotsam; self-promotional gigantism and allegory in public art, quasi-surrealism and domestic, not to say pathological, trivia in the private commission—all this, inevitably, in the end inspired a retreat into what can only be described as passionate academicism. The whole third-century sculptural experiment was to be swept away, forgotten. *Cessauit deinde ars.* Art stopped then. An era that had begun when the Successor kingdoms were settling into their final form, when money was plentiful, patronage lavish, and old rules everywhere being discarded, drew to a close amid massive Roman depredations and, worse, the ubiquitous establishment of Roman authority. Men like Flamininus, Aemilius Paullus, and Mummius looted the Greek world wholesale for art treasures; in return they brought the administrative tidiness and commercial exploitation of the *pax Romana.* The neoclassicist reaction in Greek art might have been made to measure for them and all wealthy Roman collectors, who were deeply suspicious of any hint of modernism, but would pay the earth for a genuine Old Master (below, pp. 567–69), and good money for a skillful copy. The Graeco-Roman hybridization that followed created a profitable mass market in nostalgia (below, pp. 566 ff.).

What this movement ousted had its faults: much of it was brash, vulgar, overblown, emotionally self-indulgent to the point of melodrama, and obsessed with the more pathological aspects of realism. But despite everything it was immensely alive, with a crackling vitality that gave the lie to all those tired sneers about decadence. A good point to start from is the subtly changing attitude to *barbaroi*, the modifications that world conquest produced in traditional Hellenic xenophobia. Just as Euhemerus had blurred the dividing line between men and gods, so the cosmopolitanism that followed in the wake of Alexander's conquests had lessened, not the Greek's sense of superiority to the *barbaros*—who had, after all, whether Gaul or Persian, collapsed before higher discipline, intelligence, and *force majeure*—but at least the sense of alien otherness that the *barbaros* always evoked. Besides, having vindicated the forces of civilization—gods once again triumphant over giants, Lapiths over centaurs—the Greeks could now afford to be generous in victory. It had to be admitted, moreover, that these Gauls possessed many of the Homeric qualities—physical bravery, simplicity, a strict code of honor—that were sadly wanting in the new world of commerce, urbanism, and mercenary armies. The myth of the Noble Savage was well launched. There was a tension, a contradiction here that found vivid expression in art: who was truly civilized? Where, in the last resort, did honor lie?

From being treated as a dumb brute, risible or beneath contempt, the barbarian now graduated to the familiar role, given wide currency by Rousseau in the eighteenth century, of uncorrupted surrogate hero. The great series of Pergamene sculptures[6] commemorating Attalus I's victory over the Galatians (238/7?)[7] at the headwaters of the Caicos River is, first and foremost, a tribute to the courage and dignity of these shaggy, mustachioed, gold-torqued primitives in defeat: if Diodorus is right, their clean-shaven condition shows that they were chieftains.[8] Such a concept would have been wholly unthinkable in the Periclean age, though Herodotus, that non-Athenian cosmopolitan, would have understood it very well. Attalus was inordinately proud of his achievement. He had put a stop to the nightmare of raiding and Danegeld (his predecessors paid tribute to be spared the Gauls' depredations); he had struck a decisive blow for Greek civilization against barbarism. Not only did he now take the titles of king and savior, but he also commissioned at least four commemorative monuments:[9] (1) a statue, probably of Athena Polias Nikephoros, on a huge circular base in the precinct of Athena's temple in Pergamon; (2) a later monument, a large *bathron* (the so-called long base), the creation of Epigonos, a native Pergamene sculptor, which seems to have carried bronze battle groups commemorating various victories, over Galatians and others, including one over Seleucus III's generals,[10] thus giving us a *terminus post quem* of 226/3; (3) a rectangular monumental base located on the south side of the Athena sanctuary, celebrating the final defeat of Antiochus Hierax and his Galatian mercenaries in 228; and (4) one among the four groups of half-size statues that he presented to Athens (the other three taking as their themes the battle of gods and giants, Theseus's victory over the Amazons, and the defeat of the Persians at Marathon[11]—a nice diplomatic balance between piety, flattery, and self-promotion), perhaps on the occasion of his state visit to Athens in 200 (above, p. 306), and observed by Pausanias, centuries later, on the south side of the Acropolis.[12]

Thus the Pergamenes, and in particular their king, were presented as the new saviors of Greek culture, who had not only held the forces of darkness at bay, but were enlightened enough to commemorate the fact by a major investment in first-class Greek public art. At the same time, the defeated Gauls were to be given their full due for courage, defiance, and the moral—one had almost said Stoic—certainty that led them, without hesitation, to choose death above dishonor. Though Schober's reconstruction of (1) as a group is now generally repudiated,[13] the famous individual pieces assigned to it and to the *bathron* are impressive enough separately: the dying warrior (not, as was once thought, a gladiator) commemorated by Byron, blood pouring from a deep gash in his breast, his broken trumpet beside him, propped on one arm in the instant before losing consciousness for the last time; the proud Gaul at bay, who has just killed his wife and now, with head averted and sword poised high, is in the act of driving the keen point down vertically, into his ribcage at the juncture of shoulder and torso, defiant—and flamboyant—to the last. This, the so-called Ludovisi Group, is at pains to recall the great classical sculptors; yet its effect is profoundly unclassical. The mood is melodramatic, the expressionism violent, yet the human dignity overwhelming. Once again, the tensions of the age reveal themselves.

Here—among other things—we see the beginning of that long, frequently disastrous, at times ridiculous obsession with earthy, primitive, peasant values that has bedeviled urban intellectuals down the ages: D. H. Lawrence's ithyphallic gamekeeper, even that appalling old village bore, Kazantzakis's Zorba, stand, at however

Fig. 112. The Dying Gaul. Roman copy in marble of a bronze original, probably by Epigonos of Pergamon, executed at Pergamon ca. 230–220 B.C.
Capitoline Museum, Rome.

Fig. 113. The so-called Ludovisi
Group, a Gaul committing suicide after
killing his wife. Roman copy in marble
of a bronze original executed at
Pergamon ca. 230–220 B.C.
Museo Nazionale, Rome. Photo Hirmer.

many removes, in the same tradition. There is an element of guilt involved, over the
loss (indeed, the destruction) of simple, strong moral values, uncontaminated by
more corrupt and sophisticated worldliness; the Hellenistic preoccupation with children springs in part from this mood. There is also, bound up with the guilt, a rejection of urban life as the fountainhead of corruption, a yearning for uncluttered rural
innocence. This trend, of course, is closely linked to the emphasis on the pastoral
scene that we saw developing with Theocritus (above, p. 235). Subsidized by international trade and royal monopolies, the scholar-poet comforts himself in megalopolis with dreams of goatherds and waterfalls, milkmaids and harvest home, bucolic
life sanitized in the manner of Poussin.[14]

The literary convention is faithfully reflected in the visual arts, which now similarly begin to explore landscape, to develop an iconography of the countryside. Yet
whatever this pastoral scene may imply, in neither literature nor art could it by any
stretch of the imagination be described as realistic. Urban anxieties betray themselves: in every such scene known to me wild nature is offset, however inappositely,
by a piece of ultracivilized architecture. This is true even of that famous Pompeian
wall painting, clearly derived from a Hellenistic original, with goat and goatherd set
in a brooding, artificial, almost surrealist scene, with lurid lighting and an oddly

ominous mood.[15] Landscape has arrived, is indeed dominating its human inhabitants, but the effect could hardly be described as Wordsworthian: "Gothic," even "apocalyptic," are the epithets that come to mind. Vivid expressionist brushwork is combined with a cunning displacement of topographical realities. We have here a premonitory hint of those recessive *trompe-l'oeil* effects so familiar from later Graeco-Roman murals, where, again and again, an illusion of reality is created on a flat surface: the painted window opening on a painted vista, architectural perspectives that might be the backdrop for a play. The resemblance is not accidental. The theater, and theatrical conventions, played a key role in Hellenistic art. The theater itself was changing in structure to match the special requirements of New Comedy. With dialogue all-important, and the chorus gone, a shallow raised stage, the proscenium, now appeared, direct ancestor of the conventional curtained stage with which we are familiar today.[16] If all the world was a stage, the stage in turn became a picture, and artists were not slow to take the hint. Their realism, again and again, is theatrical realism; the truest face is the stage mask, the *persona*, grinning blindly at us across the centuries even from so remote an outpost of empire as Aï Khanum.[17]

New levels of reality encouraged more daring experiments in realism, which was now extended to cater for a flourishing *nostalgie de la boue*. Low life artists like Piraeicus, known as the *rhyparographos*, "depicter of sordid subjects" (such as barbershops, cobblers' stalls, donkeys, food, and the like, Pliny tells us: class prejudice remained constant and virulent),[18] were not only popular, but commanded a good price. Rich dilettanti, as always, enjoyed going slumming at one remove. Realistic work of this sort has survived in the later mosaics of Sosus and Dioscurides, copied from earlier third-century Hellenistic paintings, with their street musicians, gossiping players, and still lifes, and, later, in the Pompeian murals.[19] The tradition of large-scale impressionistic paintings on mythical themes that we found in the Vergina royal tombs (above, pp. 113–15) seems to have continued, with only minor modifications, throughout the Hellenistic era.[20] Realism of one sort or another—the three-dimensional effects of chiaroscuro and perspective, a new concern with physiognomy as a guide to character—was the prime aim throughout. Even *trompe-l'oeil* set out to deceive the observer with a semblance of verisimilitude. The mid-third-century changeover from pebbles to fine cubes (tesserae) for mosaic work (above, pp. 333–34) had no other reason but to create a technique more nearly able to emulate the painted mural (which it often copied: witness the brilliant *opus vermiculatum* reproduction of the fourth-century mural depicting Alexander's encounter in battle with Darius).[21] The exploration of emotional extremes, more noticeable in the plastic arts, required, and got, enhanced technical virtuosity to let the artist match his subject; yet behind the experimentation, even in its most baroque excesses, a bedrock of traditionalism can always be sensed. When the classicizing reaction came, it had ample material on which to work. In the long run the real innovations depended on enlightened patrons; and here, as we shall see, the Attalid kings stood virtually alone. It would, after all, be surprising if the men of property who kept Greek artists, precariously, in business were of a temper to encourage genuine radicalism in

Fig. 114. Genre or comedy scene with street musicians. Mosaic by Dioscurides of
Samos, ca. 100 B.C., in the Villa of Cicero, Pompeii; probably a copy of a Greek
original of the third or second century.
Museo Nazionale, Naples. Photo Alinari.

art any more than they did in politics. But contemptuous caricatures of drunks,
dwarfs, cripples, old crones, and other such *canaille* from the lower orders, warts and
all, were quite another matter.

The collapse of the city-state ideal manifests itself in odd ways. One of the most
suggestive is the lessening of interest, from the beginning of the third century, in the
formal standing male nude in sculpture. Heroes are now, clearly, at something of a
discount (the revival of the convention in the second century was to portray, and
promote, living rulers: below, p. 359). Male statues tend to be, more and more, of

Fig. 115. Preparations for a concert. Wall painting from Stabiae, first century A.D.
Museo Nazionale, Naples.

poets and thinkers, of private individuals—the uninvolved, the nonpublic, the uncommitted—and they are, as a rule, clothed and seated. The gymnasia, it is true, still
flourished, and indeed remained the educational keystone of the Graeco-Roman
world. Their importance can be judged from their increasing size, complexity, and
formal magnificence, with huge courts for athletics as well as lecture halls, dining
rooms, baths, theaters, colonnades, and sun bays (*exedrai*). At Pergamon the gymnasia for adolescents, ephebes (men aged 18–20), and adults spread over three successive giant terraces up the hillside: the ephebes' was 500 feet long and about 118 feet
deep.[22] Physical training was still regarded as vitally important; but "what had given
these images of naked god or athlete their characteristic quality was the fact that they
blended individual and city, city and god, in the same glorification of the male ideal:
now far-reaching social and political changes had drained this symbol of its
substance."[23]

The most popular nudes now were of Aphrodite, or of human models who might be regarded as her devotees (though personal portraits of respectable ladies remained decorously draped): the progressive secularization of Hellenistic art is significant. The dominant ideal was sensuous gratification: we find an increasing emphasis on the private, domestic haven, the semidetached world of blank courtyards turning its back on the public male involvement of the agora. Political despair or indifference is breeding a new concern with familial values. Now, by no accident, sculpture (and, we may infer, painting) displays a preoccupation with children— and, in particular, with Eros as the formalized link between passion and its natural end product. At the same time we cannot escape, here as elsewhere, that pathological extremism of private emotion apparent—and strongly criticized—as early as Euripides' day: an extremism that emerges in the visual arts as physical violence, baroque expressionism. When Medea kills her children (almost as popular a theme with Hellenistic painters, it would seem, as Leda's impregnation by Zeus as swan) it is, at one level, all too eloquent a comment on the whole third book of the *Argonautica*, on the virgin heart that fluttered in her breast like sunlight dancing on a wall, ekphrasis in reverse (above, p. 209). Painters and poets alike were well aware of that ironic foreshadowing, the chiaroscuro of passion.

The new Hellenistic quasi-rococo awareness of children (nothing could be less heroic than the sculpture of the traditional *putto*, muscle replaced by baby fat) is thus linked with an acute awareness of sexual passion, pleasure, and pleasure's obverse, pain. The hermaphrodite, an idealization of the most desirable qualities in boy or woman, fused in a single body, is, as we have seen (above, p. 103), perhaps the most characteristic innovation of the Hellenistic age. Violence, too, is all-pervasive, a natural legacy of the Successors' disruptive power struggles, appearing even in the iconography of childhood: myth may sanction the infant Heracles strangling snakes, but what was the special appeal that made the image of an ordinary little boy throttling a goose so uncomfortably popular? The two women whom Herodas shows us on a visit to the temple of Asclepius on Cos, examining the works of art displayed there (above, p. 246)—a small girl looking up at the apples on an orchard tree, an old man, the portrait of a woman friend—are especially taken by this chubby little goose-choking urchin; and since fidelity to life is their repeatedly emphasized criterion, one can only assume it to be the realistic stranglehold that attracts them.[24] Violent, indeed sadistic, emotion is a commonplace in Hellenistic sculpture: Marsyas suspended, ready for flaying, Laocoön writhing, agonized, in the serpents' coils, Gauls dead or dying; and the common denominator, too often, is pain or horror. *Timor mortis conturbat me.* But the sensuality is there too: Pan fumbles a suburban Aphrodite while Eros plays pander, Eros (child molesting child) knowingly embraces Psyche, satyrs chase all-too-willing nymphs. Ripeness is all.

Court art leans, at one level, toward the personal and the allegorical. The great sardonyx cameo known as the Farnese Cup, probably made between 180 and 176 in Alexandria,[25] offers on the back a wild-haired Gorgon, and in the tondo (it is shaped like a flat cup) a symbolic demonstration of the benefits derived from the Nile flood.

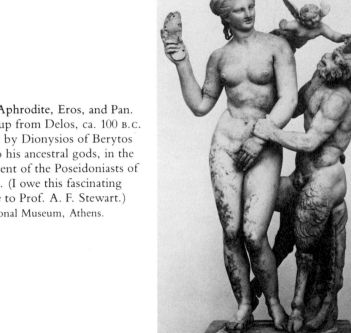

Fig. 116. Aphrodite, Eros, and Pan.
Marble group from Delos, ca. 100 B.C.
Dedicated by Dionysios of Berytos
(Beirut) to his ancestral gods, in the
Establishment of the Poseidoniasts of
Berytos. (I owe this fascinating
reference to Prof. A. F. Stewart.)
National Museum, Athens.

Fig. 117. Eros and Psyche. Roman
marble group, copied from a Hellenistic
original of ca. 150–100 B.C.
Capitoline Museum, Rome. Photo Alinari/
Anderson.

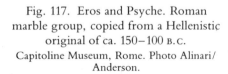

Fig. 118. The Tazza Farnese (Farnese Cup). Sardonyx cameo bowl, probably from
Ptolemaic Alexandria (ca. 180–170 B.C.; date disputed).
Museo Nazionale, Naples. Photo Alinari.

That flood was thought to be ensured through the intercession of a dead and di-vinized king, in this case (if Charbonneaux is right) Ptolemy V Epiphanes, here shown as the sphinx of Osiris. Above the sphinx, with one elbow resting on its head, reclines the deified Nile's wife, Euthenia ("Abundance"), robed as Isis, and bearing the features of Cleopatra I, co-regent with her son Ptolemy VI Philometor; the latter stands behind her in the guise of Horus-Triptolemus, complete with seed bag and knife, one hand grasping a plowshare. On the left, the Nile in person, a large, benevolent figure complete with cornucopia. On the right, two seated ladies representing the Egyptian seasons of harvest and flood. One is topless; the other sips unconcernedly from a winecup while presenting ample naked buttocks to the viewer, amid a studied disarray of dress.[26] In the air we see the Etesian Winds, which cause the flood, and are thus ultimately responsible for fertility. With such quasi-theological conceits did the Ptolemies wrap up the secular underpinning of their re-gime. Ptolemy IV's endowment of the Homereion in Alexandria had been alle-gorized in much the same way (below, pp. 355–58). The city of Alexandria was similarly depicted by Sophilus (late third century) in personified form, as a woman crowned, somewhat grotesquely, with ships' prows, and clutching a rudder to indi-cate the source of her international wealth.[27] There is, clearly, a wide gap between this kind of allegorizing propaganda and the trend toward violent realism in the pri-vate sector.

Perhaps what comes closest to bridging the gap is the officially sanctioned coin portrait: here we find a well-established tradition of faithful, and often far from flat-tering, verisimilitude. Euhemerism has done its work well: no longer, even in the more formal royal marble bust, do rulers show any hesitant qualms about self-pro-motion. It is also noticeable that the farther afield we travel from the old centers of Hellenic civilization, the fewer traces of even minimal idealization appear in these representations. Both the Louvre bust and the numismatic portraits of Antiochus the Great show the same psychologically penetrating likeness: intelligent, fine-boned, even ascetic, the air of cold command offset by a certain subtle weakness around mouth and chin.[28] Attalus I of Pergamon reveals an interesting streak of conceit: the Berlin bust not only portrays him as a heavier, slab-faced Alexander, in the style made popular by the Azara herm, but was at some point reworked to cover his own limp and scanty hair with a wig.[29] This contrasts interestingly with the coin portraits of the dynasty's founder, Philetairos, which show the plump, bull-necked, beard-less, smooth face of an enormously fat and possibly eunuchoid man (p. 167).[30]

The Ptolemies formalized their portraits more, sometimes utilizing a modified version of Ptolemy I Soter's features as the stamp of legitimization; but the self-indulgent Ptolemy IV Philopator (p. 290) issued what is clearly a realistic portrait: big football head, thick fleshy features, an expression of petulant and hysterical anxi-ety.[31] In contrast to all the male Ptolemies of this period, who seem to have been uniformly overweight, their moonfaces emphasized still further by the huge radiate crowns they wear,[32] the powerful women behind, or co-occupying, the throne— Arsinoë II and III, Berenice II[33]—look as thin as whippets, with the air of nuns suf-fering simultaneously from indigestion and anorexia. By the time of Ptolemy VI

Philometor this trend has reversed itself. On a gold ring bezel from the Louvre this king appears as thin, nervous, and exophthalmic as any of the Lagid women; he has, besides, acquired a scanty beard, and substituted the Egyptian double crown for the radiate monstrosity of his predecessors, thus emphasizing the pharaonic claims of the later Ptolemies (p. 192).[34] We have already noted the portraits of Philip V (above, p. 287); his son Perseus shares his wolfish expression, combined with a small, mean mouth in eloquent contrast to the Alexander-like thrusting profile and disarrayed hair.[35] There is an odd facial resemblance between Perseus and his father's Roman nemesis, Flamininus:[36] perhaps the latter was careful to accentuate his declared Hellenizing interests as part of his public physiognomy.

But it is when we move eastward, away from the stabilizing (and, still, idealizing) influences of tradition, that the portrait gallery really becomes fascinating, a tribute to the massive assurance of self-made men unhampered by Greek narcissism,

Fig. 119. Perseus, last king of Macedon. Silver tetradrachm minted at Amphipolis or Pella ca. 179–168 B.C. Private collection. Photo Hirmer.

Fig. 120. Prusias I of Bithynia. Silver tetradrachm minted at Nicomedia(?) ca. 200 B.C. British Museum, London.

who took a tough, sardonic pleasure in presenting themselves to the world as they really were. Prusias I of Bithynia (r. ca. 230/28–ca. 185/2) is porcine, crass, and self-satisfied.[37] The early kings of Pontus resemble nothing so much as a family of escaped convicts: Pharnaces I (r. 185/3–170) has the profile of a Neanderthaler, and Mithridates IV (r. 170–150) that of a skid-row alcoholic.[38] The Greeks who ruled Bactria and India, though more civilized in appearance, were equally pragmatic about warts-and-all representation: there is a stylistic link here with the Republican portraits of Romans—by Greeks—that begin about the mid-second century (below, p. 576).[39] Diodotus I (r. ca. 256?–ca. 248) is lumpish.[40] Euthydemus I (r. 235–200?), in both his coins and the Villa Albani bust, emphasizes his age and decrepitude: the slack jowls, the toothless mouth.[41] Many of these monarchs sport the solar topee (or a topeelike helmet) latterly associated with the British Raj: colonialism breeds its own symbols of continuity. Antimachus I (r. ca. 190–175?) is coarsely jovial;[42]

Fig. 121. Mithridates III of Pontus, father of Pharnaces I and Mithridates IV. Silver tetradrachm minted at Amaseia(?) ca. 220–185 B.C. British Museum, London. Photo Hirmer.

Fig. 122. Pharnaces I of Pontus. Silver tetradrachm minted at Amaseia(?) ca. 185–170 B.C. Bibliothèque Nationale, Paris. Cabinet des Médailles. Photo Hirmer.

Fig. 123. Mithridates IV of Pontus.
Silver tetradrachm minted at
Amaseia(?) ca. 170–150 B.C. Note the
family resemblance between
Mithridates IV, his brother Pharnaces I
(fig. 122), and their father, Mithridates
III (fig. 121).
Private collection. Photo Hirmer.

Demetrius I (r. ca. 200–185) looks pompous and determined, every inch the heavy Indian conqueror;[43] the renegade Eucratides I (r. ca. 170–155) comes across as a leathery old long-service officer,[44] while the great Menander Soter (r. ca. 160–130), gaunt and austere, his features reminiscent, in different ways, of both Pope and Lord Curzon, is the only one of these kings instantly identifiable as a serious thinker, if not as a potential convert to Buddhism (above, p. 320).[45]

The Farnese Cup, the "Child Strangling a Goose" (or perhaps hugging it to death, love and death as opposite sides of the same coin),[46] realistic royal portraiture—all these forms of expression, though profoundly different from one another, are still farther removed from the proud public art of fifth-century classical Athens. One of the Hellenistic age's oddest paradoxes lies in the fact that it was the kings of Pergamon who, with conscious deliberation, came closest to recapturing that mood, style, and coherent civic sense of exultant pride. We saw earlier how they set out to build the terraces of Pergamon's great acropolis into one vast monumental architectural complex (p. 168)[47]: this kind of "organic" acropolis, featuring colonnaded stoas, became very popular in the third and second centuries. We find good examples at Lindos and Camiros on Rhodes; the buildings that Seleucids, Ptolemies, and Attalids presented to the cities of Old Greece such as Athens or Corinth all tended in the same direction. There could be an element of competition in these donations: Philip V's stoa on Delos, over seventy yards long, built on the avenue between harbor and precinct, was carefully designed "to mask the portico of Attalus and hide it from pilgrims arriving on the quay."[48]

The classically inspired yet profoundly anticlassical execution and iconography of the statues commissioned to commemorate Attalid victories over the Gauls (above, p. 339) show to even more striking effect in Pergamon's largest, and in ways most impressive, memorial, the Great Altar, a startling baroque extravaganza commissioned by Eumenes II (r. 197–160/59), and at the same time often turning to Athens for inspiration.[49] The reconstruction in the Berlin Staatliche Museen is misleading in at least two ways. First, it takes the entire structure out of context. One's initial view

Fig. 124. Reconstruction of the Great Altar of Pergamon, erected by Eumenes II
ca. 180–160 B.C.
Staatliche Museen zu Berlin.

of the actual site, on a shallow plateau immediately below the uppermost level of the
acropolis, comes as something of a surprise. That gigantic foursquare stepped
base—stripped bare now by the German archaeologists, and with large trees growing out of it—has no functional relevance to anything else in sight. It was designed
for no other purpose than to be monumentally, overwhelmingly impressive. One
honest travel writer, lacking the scholar's ingrained respect for this grandiose Attalid
advertisement, wrote that it resembled "a peculiar, monstrous open-air megaron."[50]
He had a point.

Second, the Berlin reconstruction gives only a foreshortened view of what in
fact was an almost square complex (base 112 × 120 ft.), round three sides of which,
five steps up, and set on a course of smooth facing slabs (orthostats), ran a great
continuous frieze, or relief band, over seven feet high and almost four hundred in
length, with a strong projecting cornice above and crowned with a colonnade, but
offset by no frame or molding. The frieze's figures, carved in high relief, actually
intruded, with foot or knee or hand, onto the steps by which the worshipper ascended to the altar. "The two worlds intersect and at this point are one."[51] On the
fourth side the frieze and colonnade formed two enclosing wings, framing the ascent
to platform level, where a transverse colonnade enclosed the altar area itself. On the
wall round the altar was a second, smaller frieze, depicting, in continuous narrative
form, the legend of Telephus, son of Heracles and Auge, and king of Mysia, whose

history was treated by the Attalids as their own foundation myth. This pictorial narrative technique seems to have been a Hellenistic invention. The main frieze, in conscious emulation of Athens—and the very use of a frieze, since friezes had gone out of fashion in the third century, can be seen as deliberate classicizing—dealt with that time-honored symbolic theme of civilization triumphant over barbarism, the battle of gods and giants. It belongs to the final, greatest period of Pergamene expansion as an independent state.[52]

A passionate Hellenist born too late, Eumenes II was devoted to the cause of reactivating the old Hellenic spirit in Asia Minor; he was also a skillful and energetic propagandist for his own regime. The Great Altar, perhaps a *hērōön* for Telephus, was also associated with Athena, Pergamon's patron goddess; and Eumenes, predictably, made the most of the connection with Athens. "The Athena who appears on the Gigantomachy of the Great Altar (east frieze) is shown in the same pose as the one on the west pediment of the Parthenon—clearly a deliberate and significant reference."[53] But in Pergamon she has Zeus, not Poseidon, for her companion. Eumenes gave her the title "Bringer of Victory" (*Nikēphoros*), and established both a shrine (the Nikephorion) and a public festival (the Nikephoria) in honor of Attalus's defeat of the Gauls.[54] The festival lasted five days, with games, and achieved international standing. Like Peisistratus in sixth-century Athens, Eumenes "was inviting the Attic genius and Olympic Panhellenism to take up residence on his acropolis." Furthermore, by linking his dynasty to the Telephus legend (and royal line), Eumenes was pursuing a favorite objective of Hellenistic monarchs: the establishment of divine descent. Telephus was the son of Heracles, who in turn had been (*pace* Amphitryon) the son of Zeus.[55] The Attalids, too, had put down barbarism; now they were to promote themselves as torchbearers of Hellenic culture. Like the Ptolemies, the Attalids had their library—into which, another echo of Athens and the Parthenon, they inserted an outsize statue of Athena.[56]

Thus it should not be surprising that, emulating Athens in this too, Pergamon now likewise had its team of monumental sculptors and architects, some of them Athenian. In concept and execution the frieze of the Great Altar was, beyond any doubt, planned to rival that of the Parthenon, not least by being more immediately accessible to the viewer. There are numerous thematic and stylistic echoes of the Parthenon reliefs, including an emotional violence and intensity of expression common to the centaurs on the Parthenon metopes and the giants of the Pergamon frieze.[57] Yet somehow, for all its brilliance of technique and conscious attempts at classicizing, again and again the Pergamon frieze betrays its time and place of genesis. A better description of its theme might be the battle of gods and gigantism. As has well been said, "anatomy in the frieze almost becomes a vehicle for abstract expressionism."[58] Intensity, even savageness, of passion was nothing new in Greek art or literature; but the florid, rhetorical, almost rococo expression of that intensity and savageness, with cracking muscles and rolling eyeballs, a distortion not only of features but of fundamental form, marks the Pergamon reliefs, despite their classicizing mode, as a product of their own age and no other. They are also very uneven. So

Fig. 125. The Great Altar of Pergamon, east frieze. Gigantomachy: the winged giant
Alcyoneus.
Staatliche Museen zu Berlin.

vast an undertaking must have called for a whole team of sculptors—forty is the top estimate—ranging from enthusiastic baroque innovators to dull and platitudinous academicians.

What is more, self-conscious erudition of a very Hellenistic sort has been at work here. Someone did their homework on this frieze beforehand, digging out a whole slew of meticulously characterized mythical figures, aiming for the most exhaustive of iconographies. Animal traits suggest Oriental influence rather than pristine Atticism. Giants sprout serpent coils, bull's horns, lion's paws or heads. Poseidon's marine horses have equine quarters, but also fins. The fighting is graphic, and, at times, bloody. Artemis's hound sinks its fangs into the neck of a dying giant; the giant contrives to gouge out one of the dog's eyes. Zeus, protected by shield and huge eagle, blasts away at his attackers with thunderbolts: presumably he was meant to suggest the Attalid dynasty embattled against Galatian hordes. There is a quite extraordinary and sustained violence about this frieze: fierce diagonal tensions, the crimp and strain of knotted muscles, huge, lumpish wrestlers snorting and heaving, faces set in the rictus of rage or agony. (The major deities, however, maintain a certain Stoic calm.) Once again, and this time at almost unbearable length, we are confronted with pain, hatred, frenzy, berserk physical outrage. Those who hired mercenaries to do their fighting for them clearly needed some surrogate.[59] The long and bloody decades of Alexander's Funeral Games had left their mark: we can see here a clear foreshadowing of the roaring crowd that later packed the stands of the Coliseum.

The Great Altar in its concept, its techniques, and its sculptural expertise is purely Greek, and very often classical Greek at that; yet the overall effect remains profoundly alien from the world of the mainland *polis*, and far less classical in spirit than the equally famous Winged Victory of Samothrace, set up by the still-independent Rhodians after their victory over Antiochus III in 191/0 (p. 106). More subtly than in Bactria, the East is moving to absorb Hellenism at the source. Nor should this surprise us. However the Attalids might spend their millions to revivify the ghost of the classical spirit, the culture they lived and breathed was something very different: Anatolian rather than Hellenic, at once more autocratic and less involved than the political crucible of the *polis*, a world of court patronage and academic fribblers, of powerful merchant bankers, imperial ambition, and dynastic intrigue, where the still small voice of wisdom, or what passed for wisdom, came, more often than not, from the anti-establishment figure, the wandering sage (above, p. 312).

All the porticoes, poets, and patronage in the world could not bring back the creative intensity, the heady excitement of political arrogance, free enterprise, and passionately anarchic collectivism that had thrown up a Sophocles or an Aristophanes, built the Parthenon, fought—and lost—the Peloponnesian War. Yet the nostalgia, the editing, the retrospective scholarship went on unabated. Ptolemy IV Philopator, a literary dilettante as well as a libertine (he wrote a tragedy entitled *Adonis*, and presumably played the lead),[60] actually founded a Homereion, a shrine

Fig. 126. The Great Altar of Pergamon, north frieze. Gigantomachy: the figure of
Nyx (Night).
Staatliche Museen zu Berlin.

Fig. 127. Marble votive relief by Archelaus of Priene (ca. 150 B.C.), found at Bovillae, near Rome, and chiefly remarkable for its bottom panel, which shows Homer being crowned by the World and Time during a ceremony in the Museum at Alexandria. On the top three levels, Zeus, Apollo as cithara player, and the choir of the Muses. British Museum, London.

honoring Homer, with inside it a statue of the poet surrounded by personified figures of the cities that claimed to be his birthplace. A remarkable relief of a stylized Hill of the Muses, by Archelaus of Priene, shows on its lowest level Homer being crowned by the World and Time: Time has the features of Ptolemy IV, and the World those of his sister-wife Arsinoë III.[61] Though the relief is later (ca. 150–125, but perhaps a copy of a third-century original) the implication is clear: it took the Homereion, and, thus, Philopator, to give Homer true immortality—an eerie foreshadowing (if one cares to look at it that way) of modern critical theory, with the critic a key element in the creative process. A painter called Galaton contrived a really dreadful allegorical picture for this shrine, in which Homer figured as a kind of river-god-*cum*-fountain, spouting the water of inspiration from his mouth; lesser poets queued up with their jugs to catch what they could, a liquid version of Aeschylus's metaphorical claim, that his plays were slices cut from Homer's great feasts.[62]

Those who argue that this kind of atmosphere, at once artificial and sycophantic, was unlikely to produce good original work, whether in art or literature, should relish the story of Ptolemy IV judging a poetry competition: he needed one more judge, and the Library supplied Aristophanes of Byzantium *ex officio*. The other judges, presumably courtiers, classed the poetry by the amount of applause it got. Aristophanes, however, gave his vote to the poet who was applauded least. When asked to explain himself, he brought texts from the Library to show that his candidate was the only really original poet: the others had simply been plagiarizing wholesale from their predecessors.[63] This was not, I suspect, a popular position to assume. Whichever side of the Great Debate a *littérateur* took in the third or second century, the clear assumption was that his material, form, technique, and inspiration would be drawn from the great poets and the mythic heritage of the past. Two hundred years later Horace, in his *Art of Poetry*, was still drumming home the same message, urging poets to handle Greek models by day and night: *uos exemplaria Graeca / nocturna uersate manu, uersate diurna.*[64] I cannot think of another critic, apart from Aristophanes, who set originality as a prime criterion of merit. Horace's attack on surrealist painting fits in precisely with the neoclassicist mode that from the mid-second century came to dominate both Greek and Roman art.[65] (There were fascinating exceptions; but exceptions, as we shall see, they remained.) It was only the impact of the accumulated Greek experience on the *tabula rasa* of Roman creativity that made possible the brief, if intense, artistic efflorescence in the late Republic and early Augustan period; from then on academicism (allied, as so often, with covert political censorship) closed in stiflingly, despite the protests of writers such as Persius and Petronius.[66]

The trends noted in this chapter were neither tidy nor clear-cut. When Pliny talked about art stopping, his rhetorical hyperbole was doubly misleading, since not only did art of a kind he disapproved flourish then, but the classicism that for him (as for Horace) *was* art never really stopped. While the Pergamene kings promoted organic public architecture, allegorizing propaganda, and baroque statue groups or reliefs, while more mundane artists found a promising market in the exotic and the grotesque, nevertheless many painters and sculptors continued to work in a more conventional (i.e., classical) tradition, in particular for the representation of those endless mythic scenes that provided the Greek, as later the Roman, mind with its basic psychological—one had almost said spiritual—underpinning: its archetypal perspectives, its religious iconography, above all its divinely sanctioned moral precedents. When, about the middle of the second century, the standing male nude began to portray kings as deified heroes (p. 343), the technical expertise was ready.[67]

Yet it would be idle to pretend that the art of the third and second centuries, though enjoying a transient freedom while the shadows lengthened in the west, did not at the same time reveal symptoms of a deep and ultimately self-destructive malaise. We have seen how political impotence (or, at best, parochial insignificance) re-channeled energies into private concerns: the family, children, a philosophical or, too often, merely hedonistic absorption in the self, the pursuit of wealth, an urge to

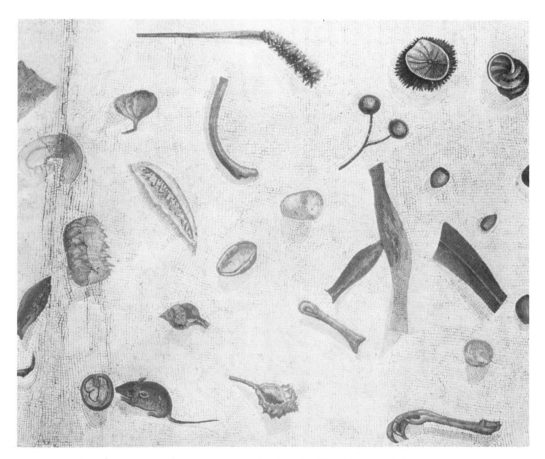

Fig. 128. Second-century-A.D. copy or adaption, by Herakleitos, of the *Asarōtos Oikos* ("Unswept House") mosaic executed by Sosus at Pergamon in the early second(?) century B.C.
Vatican Museums.

Fig. 129. The punishment of Laocoön and his sons. Marble statue group by
Hagesander, Athenodorus, and Polydorus; from the Baths of Titus, Rome. (First
century A.D., but perhaps based on a late second-century-B.C. two-figure original.)
Vatican Museums. Photo Fototeca Unione.

contract out of the world's grim and insoluble problems, to cultivate one's garden, Epicurean or other. Pollitt offers a splendid example of this trend in a bronze statuette of Epicurus's successor Hermarchus, in which sagging body, protruding paunch, and eloquent body language combine to convey a graphic impression of the absent-minded, asocial thinker in pursuit of *ataraxia*.[68] At the same time a lurking self-contempt for lost virtues promoted the compensatory, yet guilt-ridden, myth of the Noble Savage, while unconscious resentment fired the terrible streak of violence and sadism that emerges in a flayed Marsyas, a rachitic dwarf. Realism and escapism are everywhere in contrapuntal tension. The minutely lifelike—for example, that extraordinary mosaic floor at Pergamon by Sosus, known in part from copies, which portrayed the miscellaneous detritus (a fig, a dormouse, a sea urchin, a bird's clawed foot) dropped by dinner guests[69]—can acquire a mythic quality by uneasy juxtaposition: the realism is that of a Bosch or a Dali painting.

Those theatrical backdrops and *trompe-l'oeil* vistas, careful distancings (as in Callimachean literature) from the abrasive problems of life as lived, are nevertheless given meticulously accurate and realistic treatment, as though part of a palpable looking-glass world. If classicism continued to flourish as a medium for the interpretation of myth, the demons of suffering and social disruption that we see at work in the Pergamon frieze were not exorcised by the slow, ineluctable spread of Roman *auctoritas*. Perhaps in the late second century B.C., perhaps in the first century A.D., there appeared that apotheosis of tortured expressionism, the famous Laocoön group.[70] Winckelmann, studying the group in Rome, praised its noble simplicity and calm grandeur, perhaps the most perverse judgment ever made on a work of art, and a jolting testimony to the subjectivism of an ideologically committed vision, which will see only what it wants to see.[71] Muscles knotted and straining, face drawn into a rictus of pure agony, the Laocoön has always seemed to me a terrible symbol of Hellenistic civilization at its last gasp, caught inextricably in the viselike coils of a new world from which neither athleticism nor fine words could free it.

CHAPTER 21

PRODUCTION, TRADE, FINANCE

It has always been a cause for puzzlement as to why the Greeks, intellectual pathfind-ers in every branch of pure science (below, p. 465), should have revealed so stubborn a streak of tribal naïveté when it came to economics.[1] It is true (and has often been remarked) that economic theory never progressed beyond the level of estate manage-ment till the Middle Ages, that the principle of "buy cheap, sell dear" was about the sum of its achievement in antiquity. Yet why was this? Homer, the secular equivalent of a Bible for traditionalists, may have been partly responsible: the economics of a heroic age have little to do with production. What we find instead is a system of gift exchange for rare commodities, and an ingrained habit of acquiring the fruits of other men's sweat through plunder.[2] This was a habit that died hard. Aristotle re-garded warfare as a natural mode of income,[3] and his pupil Alexander took the lesson to heart, plundering what has been estimated at 180,000 talents of accumu-lated Persian gold (p. 366), and then releasing it, as booty and coined money, on the Mediterranean market, driving down the gold-to-silver ratio from 1:13 to 1:10, and halving the value of both metals in relation to copper. Hitherto the Persian kings (and, on occasion, their satraps) had struck coins, both gold and silver, only on a very limited scale, more often than not to bribe Greek politicians or pay Greek mer-cenaries. It was Alexander and his successors who in effect converted the East to a Greek-style money economy, keyed exclusively to the Attic-weight silver standard, and creating what has been well described as "a monetary *koinē* for the eastern Medi-terranean." This standard was adopted as far afield as Bithynia, Pontus, Parthia, and Greek Bactria: only the Ptolemies rejected it (p. 194). It is no accident that 79.6 per-cent of all known Greek coin hoards are datable to the Hellenistic period.[4]

However, both Ptolemies and Seleucids, and the Romans after them, counted on booty as a major line item in their accounts. Ptolemy III made fifteen hundred talents of silver, or what amounted to 10 percent of his annual income, from the capture of Seleucia-in-Pieria. Antiochus IV seized eighteen hundred talents from the Temple in Jerusalem. The Gerrhaean Arabs bought off Antiochus III with five hundred talents of silver and twice that weight of incense (above, p. 295).[5] The di-viding line between this kind of exploitation and unofficial piracy (e.g., the habitual running-in of grain ships for their valuable cargoes) was often very thin indeed.[6] There was also a deeply rooted tendency to regard acquisition by force as in some sense both socially and morally preferable to production and, in particular, to commerce. A Phaeacian in Homer's *Odyssey* sneered at the ungentlemanly, unathletic merchant, trading for profit, as though that were some sort of social solecism.[7] Throughout Greek history, while farming one's own land was a legitimate source of income, indeed the normal way of life for an agricultural aristocracy, neither working for others (at whatever occupation, farming included) nor going into business was ever entirely free of class-based prejudicial associations. By the fourth century, moreover, at least a vocal minority of the elite—Plato and Aristotle are prime examples—had come to condemn all manual labor, as well as commerce, on the grounds that it was "banausic": a word that, originally describing the handicrafts of artisans, came to mean "mechanical," and then "base," "common," or "in bad taste."[8]

It has often been pointed out, correctly, that this gave no sense of the actual economic scene in Athens, where the vast majority of the population worked very hard indeed, slaves, free men, and metics (resident aliens) side by side, and for very similar wages; but that is not the point. It was an ideal, a moral article of faith, cherished by the fortunate few, aimed at by the many. As we shall see (e.g., below, Chap. 30, p. 526), throughout the Hellenistic period a large section of the population became increasingly devoted to commerce, and some made large fortunes out of it; but they were not, by and large, the people who exercised their minds with the reiteration of such traditional, ethical shibboleths. That was the prerogative of the (mostly rentier) intellectuals, who cared no more than Plato had done about the lifestyle of the despised commercial classes, or how it might seem to contradict their own beliefs. Among the many consequences of their attitude was a complete removal of the best theoretical brains in Greece from the field of economics. It is by now a truism that the remarkable scientific advances of the Hellenistic period contributed virtually nothing to society's technological or economic betterment (below, p. 470).[9] It would have been surprising if they had. Not only was the subject largely ignored; when faced at all, it was misunderstood. Persians and Greeks alike, in their different ways, had failed, in effect, to make the transition from a status-distributive to a market economy. What we find from the fourth century onwards is a piecemeal struggle to come to terms with new international realities while still thinking largely in terms of a heroic-age economy.

One marked characteristic of this phenomenon is the tendency to frame economic problems in moral terms. There was little or no attempt, throughout our period, to come to grips with what we would see, instantly, as the central dilemma, namely, how to improve and streamline production methods. Indeed, Alan Samuel has recently argued, with considerable persuasiveness, that the predominant economic ideal in antiquity was not growth at all, but rather stability:[10] one more instance of the ubiquitous cast of mind that regarded change of any kind as degeneration, and concentrated on the maintenance, at all costs, of the *status quo*, be it

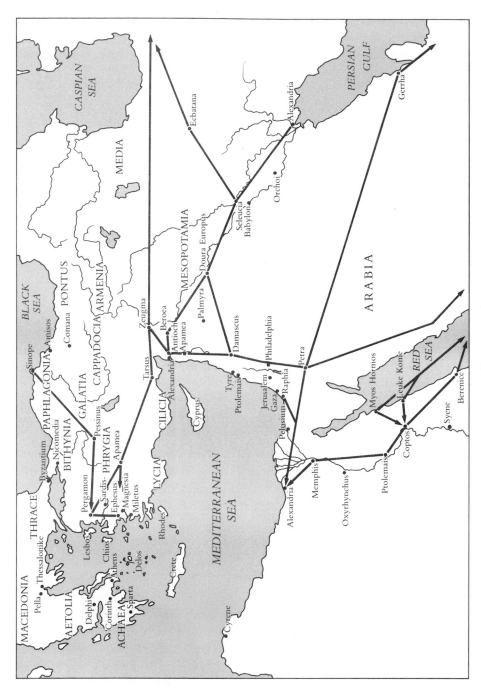

Map 21. Hellenistic trade routes.
From Ferguson, *Heritage of Hellenism*, pp. 158–59.

economic, political, social, or cultural. Production was for the despised getters and spenders, the *banausoi*, Plato's *tiers état*: the business of theorists was the art of government, of philosophical (meaning ethical) thinking and eloquent speech, how to lead the good life in mind and body. This induced a quite extraordinary blindness to what we would see as obvious economic realities; it also stunted technological advance, which was bound to suffer from the absence of an investment-oriented, free-market economy.

On the first point, we can take a splendid example from Isocrates' pamphlet *On the Peace*, of about 355.[11] Isocrates asks how is it that the Megarians, with scanty natural resources, no fertile land, no silver mines, no fine harbors, "farming bare rock," nevertheless own the largest and most luxurious houses in Greece. We would answer, instantly, that they owed their wealth in part to a flourishing manufacture of cheap woolen goods,[12] and even more to their carrying-trade, with linked ports on the Saronic and Corinthian gulfs (Isocrates underestimates Megarian harbors), and, equally important, control of much land traffic between the Peloponnese and northern Greece. This solution never occurs to Isocrates for one moment. As we can see from the terms in which the question is posed, his only notion of legitimate profit is through natural, primarily agricultural, direct resources. Old aristocratic modes of thought are hard to shake. Beyond this, his sole criterion for success or failure is a moral one. Failure is the result of intemperance (*akolasia*) or overreaching (*hybris*), while success—in Megara's case as in others—can be explained by prudent moderation or self-control (*sōphrosynē*)!

While it is plainly true that Alexander's Eastern conquests transformed the economic realities of the Mediterranean world, they did not, could not, eradicate this mode of thought altogether. All that happened, as we might expect, was a progressive erosion of the original moral criteria. Fourth-century thinkers had spent much time arguing, in a kind of moral vacuum, as to just how much wealth the good man might possess, and in what ways it was proper to acquire it; they did not consider studying, in any fundamental sense, the means of production. The prejudice against commerce ran very deep. Sparta's ideology had rejected it altogether, and the warrior Spartiate, living off the income of his serf-run estate while he devoted himself to athletics and militarism, touched a deep chord in the psyche of every well-connected Greek. Thebes at one point made all those who had not abstained from trade for *ten years* ineligible to serve in public office, as though the taint, the *miasma*, of business were so lingering and all-pervasive that it took a decade to eradicate its effects.[13]

So while the Hellenistic age sharpened the taste for affluence, and rapidly destroyed all moral scruples against avarice, it did not, in the last resort, bring any intellectual appreciation of the economic forces by which that avarice was gratified. To understand this one need only read that amazing collection of "ingenious expedients, most of them bordering on fraud or violence" found in Book 2 of Pseudo-Aristotle's late fourth-century treatise the *Oeconomica*.[14] The author, inquiring how statesmen went about replenishing their treasuries, provides some revealing answers. Dionysius I of Syracuse, among other schemes, used to pilfer gold and silver from temples (a fairly widespread habit in an emergency). Cleomenes, Alexander's governor in Egypt, used his position to corner the wheat trade and make a killing out of the famine in Greece (ca. 330): we know from Xenophon and Lysias that this kind of thing was common among grain merchants.[15] Clazomenae reduced its capital debt by striking an iron coinage with the face value of the same weight in silver. The governor of Phocaea made money hand over fist by taking bribes from both sides in arbitrations. Mausolus of Caria, alleging a threatened Persian invasion, got large subventions from his citizens to fortify the capital, Mylasa. "But though he kept the money, he announced that heaven, for the time being, forbade the walls to be built."[16]

In all this we see no perception of economics beyond more or less ingenious (and shady) schemes for direct emergency levies. Thus it seems clear that it was the partial collapse of the Ptolemaic economy in the second century, with loss of territories abroad, insurrection at home, and devaluation of the currency (above, p. 291), that stimulated the frantic development of the Nubian gold mines so graphically described by Diodorus.[17] Egypt had the potential for a flourishing market economy; but in the last resort, though they were forced to look abroad for a short list of essential imports, it was only the direct exploitation of natural resources that her Macedonian rulers really understood. The Ptolemies' exorbitant system of customs dues and protective tariffs (up to 50 percent on imported olive oil or fine wines),[18] their restrictive currency laws (below, p. 373), and their stunning 24 percent interest rate on loans, double that in force anywhere else at the time, undoubtedly combined to curtail international trade severely,[19] except for those commodities (e.g., papyrus) that were essential everywhere, and sold at reasonable prices abroad to pay for equally essential imports.[20] Lack of silver can only partly explain this deliberate policy. The strongest motive seems to have been political, the urge for complete and self-sufficient independence. It is no accident that the Ptolemaic copper coinage exactly matched in weight the ancient pharaonic *deben*,[21] or that copper rings had, similarly, been used under the pharaohs as a measure of value.

Let us now consider the question of technological stagnation. Alexander's violent disruption of the static Persian economy had at least provided a strong, indeed a frenetic, stimulus for trade. Whereas the Achaemenid rulers had, by their fiscal policies, drained the Near East of gold and silver as tribute, which they then melted down and kept as bullion, out of circulation except for the darics used to pay mercenaries, or for similar noncommercial purposes (above, p. 362), Alexander released the accumulated specie of centuries onto the market in a matter of months: the total sum has been variously assessed at somewhere between 170,000 and 190,000 talents, with a purchasing power of 285 billion dollars (1978 calculation).[22] The result was rapid inflation, followed by a fall in prices about the mid-third century.[23] He also gave Egypt and Mesopotamia their first mints, introducing a monetary economy where none had existed before (a hedge against the worst consequences of inflation, though he was probably unaware of this at the time), together with the Greek banking system,[24] now advancing from age-old notions of land-tied income and unproductively stored bullion to a point where credit was at least understood, payments could be made by bookkeeping entry (*diagraphein*), and capital was regularly invested at interest to produce a cash income.[25] To that extent he broke an impasse, since otherwise without new land or advanced technology little change was possible; nor, as we have seen, was change of any kind looked on with general favor. Economic growth and technological innovation tend to advance *pari passu*; throughout the Hellenistic world both remained at a discount. The danger about stability, as an ideal, is that all too often it slides into, and is indistinguishable from, mere stagnation.

The opening-up of the East was, despite panhellenic propaganda, little more than Homeric raiding on a grand scale, so that the Achaemenid empire became, in effect, one vast mass of spear-won booty. The new territories thus acquired were for the prime benefit of their conquerors and the conquerors' hangers-on, a simple transfer of ownership that brought only very limited economic advances. Thus (to turn to my second main point) it should come as no surprise that the actual list of known technological advances is minimal.[26] Double or even triple crop rotation was a fair index of the greed felt by rentiers anxious to exploit yet further already overworked soil. Some sugar and cotton were now produced, but made very little economic impact. The iron plowshare was widely employed, and the ox-driven water wheel appeared, around 200, as a more efficient alternative to the swing beam or *shaduf.*[27] The peach, cherry, and apricot were domesticated in Asia Minor. Improvements on the saddle quern for hand-grinding wheat or barley can be dated to the fourth century, while donkey-driven grain mills began to bring the grinding of grain out of the home, and saw the emergence of the professional miller.[28] By the first century the rotary quern was in regular use. Improved screw presses were developed for crushing grapes and olives.[29] The compound pulley appeared for lifting heavy weights, in particular by crane, though precisely when is uncertain.[30] The screw seems to have been an invention of the third century.[31] Archimedes' screw was used to pump up water from mines: it was, predictably, operated by slaves.[32] Another type of suction pump, invented by the third-century engineer Ctesibius (below, p. 475), was employed to raise irrigation water for the kitchen garden.[33] Despite the crucial importance of seaborne commerce, the only useful development in naval technology seems to have been the lateen sail:[34] the enormous vessel built by Ptolemy IV was for show only, and in fact virtually immovable (below, p. 774 n. 22).[35] A far more useful—and enduring—innovation was the camel, first imported into Egypt by Ptolemy II: today it seems as quintessentially Egyptian as the Sphinx or the Pyramids.[36]

Even when all proper allowances have been made, this is not exactly an overwhelming list. "Except for a new quick-growing wheat which gave a double harvest and a higher yield . . . most of the novelties were intended to provide luxury products for a small minority without making undesirable payments abroad."[37] It should be noted, too, that such double harvesting was a limited experiment, and by no means evidence for increased land exploitation on a wide scale. The soil still lay fallow every other year in most areas. Such advances "were not the sort to change the relations of industry to commerce or the social dominance of the landowner over the town and the commercial classes."[38] Nor were the attitudes they represented liable to stimulate financial adventurousness or sophisticated notions of credit. Banking still bore very little relation to our modern definition of the word. Capital, as we have seen, might now be invested; but merely to deposit it with a *trapezitēs* for safekeeping did not, as a rule, produce interest,[39] and (more surprisingly) neither the banks nor anyone else normally lent money for commercial purposes, whether agriculture, trade, or manufacture.[40] The exception might seem to have been in the area of maritime loans (bottomry); but this was an area the banks kept clear of, on the grounds of high risk, and the loans were also, as we shall see, a form of insurance policy (below, p. 375).[41] In general, loans tended to be short-term, and usually for nonproductive, consumer purposes. Nor can we find any trace of "machinery for the creation of credit through negotiable instruments."[42] Payments and loans were limited by the amount of cash on hand, and thus there could be no such thing as a public or national debt, a consideration that leads me to feel there may be more to be said in favor of this supposedly primitive system than many modern economists would allow.

When we consider the political structure of the Successor kingdoms, with an exploitative Graeco-Macedonian elite maintaining its rule by force—and bureaucracy—over a native labor pool, such conservatism is hardly to be wondered at. It is true that the market increased enormously in size, so that vast private fortunes were made and lost;[43] but we should never forget that for Ptolemies, Seleucids, and Attalids alike (the case of Antigonid Macedonia is somewhat different)[44] all land was crown land, in effect a private estate to be worked and milked for the owner's direct profit (cf. above, pp. 187 ff.). Like Trimalchio some centuries later, these entrepreneurs had few creative outlets for their cash in hand: what did not go out on real estate, luxuries, or short-term loans more often than not ended up in the strongbox.[45] Yet the extraction of this endless cash flow was a major ongoing operation. We have already seen some of the devices employed to implement it: widespread, heavy, and often arbitrary taxation—taxes on aliens' houses, on baking establishments (25 percent), death duties, a vintage tax (*apomoira*, 16.7 percent), tithes on sacrifices; fees for maintaining herds, owning slaves, practicing handicrafts; a 5 percent combined sales, transfer, and inheritance tax (*enkyklion*)[46]—not to mention tariffs both direct and indirect, and the ubiquitous state monopolies. These tariffs and monopolies applied even to the Ptolemies' own foreign dominions: nothing, least of all legal niceties, must be allowed to interfere with the maximum consumption of domestic products, above all those governed by royal protectionism.[47]

As for agricultural production, that, as in most dirigist economies, was subject to the most detailed bureaucratic planning, at every level: what seed was to be sown where, what dues were to be paid by lessees, and when—every step in the procedure, from the renting of royal storehouse equipment to the assessment of harvest returns, was subject to scrutiny by a swarm of local or governmental officials.[48] The resultant *papyrasserie* suggests that an ancient planned economy was no more efficient than its modern counterpart, producing little on time except for a mountain of otiose documentation. The monarch could, and as time went on almost invariably did, lose his grip on the direction of a system that tended to acquire a diffuse and impalpable life of its own. Senior officials feathered their own nests as a matter of course; dishonesty was rampant at all levels. Weights were falsified, accounts manipulated; petty extortion, in cash or kind, became the norm. Fines and arrests proliferated, but did nothing to improve matters. Further losses were incurred as a result of pure incompetence or disorganization: stored wheat went bad through official negligence, tax payments were entered for the wrong year. Protectionism, not surprisingly, flourished. The wretched fellahin, exploited and abused, had their own traditional ways of getting back at their oppressors: skimped or sabotaged work at sowing and harvest, or, worse, on the dikes and irrigation canals. Pilfering was endemic, mass strikes by no means rare, and fugitivism a commonplace.[49] As in the comparable modern case of Soviet Russia, what really surprises is that agricultural production did not seize up altogether. Could the argument often advanced today also hold good for Ptolemaic Egypt, namely, that a certain degree of inefficiency and chaos was vital if the managerial *apparatchiks* were to stay in power? If so, we have a nice case of the Ptolemies creating a bureaucratic monster that in the end they were quite unable to control, since the whole *raison d'être* of the Ptolemaic economy was to feed the royal treasury: it was not even state capitalism, properly considered, but rather personal profiteering on a nationwide scale.[50]

It cannot be sufficiently stressed that Egypt in particular (for which our evidence is by far the best)[51] was not concerned, under the Ptolemies, to improve the economy and, hence, the general standard of living. (Indeed, since it was an article of faith in antiquity that what kept the lower orders hardworking and malleable was, precisely, their poverty, such a policy would have been regarded as a virtual invitation to social revolt.) The prime object of this outsize "household economy" was, by preserving the *status quo*, to service the court and the bureaucracy,[52] to fill Ptolemy's coffers, above all to pay the Ptolemaic fleet and a vast standing mercenary army. Since Egypt had no silver of her own, limited international trade became an essential, if unwelcome, part of this process, as we have seen. The prime exports—wheat, papyrus, unguents—were offset against necessary imports that all, in one way or another, had to do with defense: iron, tin, copper, timber, horses, elephants. Hence a good deal of Ptolemaic foreign policy.[53] The opening-up of Somalia was linked both to the expansion of eastern trade and to the hunting of elephants (p. 329), while Cyrene bred horses, the Nubian mines furnished gold, and Cyprus could provide both copper and timber. An attempt to grow fir trees on a large scale in Egypt (as a supplement to the native acacia, sycamore, and persea, none of them tractable timbers, and the soft, fibrous palm),[54] with a view to shipbuilding, seems to have been unsuccessful.[55] The vine and olive were everywhere introduced into Egypt by the Greeks, with the added inducement not only of protectionist tariffs but also of concessions such as heritable leases and reduced taxation.[56] The results, again, were not spectacular.

Ptolemaic Egypt also maintained close links with Carthage, chiefly but not exclusively commercial: the two countries shared a common frontier, remote and ill defined, in western Cyrenaica, on the Gulf of Sidra. Tyre, the mother city of Carthage, was under Ptolemaic control for most of the third century. Through Carthage Alexandria could import not only horses but, more important, Spanish silver, over which Carthage exercised a monopoly (lost by 202: Rome's increasing ascendancy in this area may have helped to drive Ptolemaic Egypt off the silver standard). During

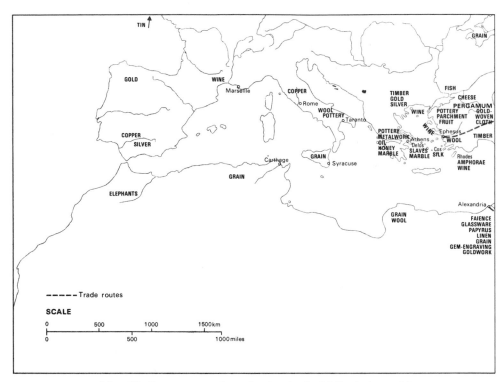

Map 22. Resources and production in the Hellenistic world.

the First Punic War Carthage applied to Ptolemy II for a loan of two thousand talents. The king, who was trying to keep on good terms with both Carthage and Rome—he had sent an embassy to Rome as early as 273, and established some sort of concordat (*homologia*)[57]—turned down the request with the diplomatic comment that it was not proper to help friends against friends; but that such an application could be made at all reveals the close relationship existing between the two countries.[58]

In the Seleucid empire we find a less efficiently organized bureaucracy, and a somewhat greater degree of acculturation to local *mores*, but behind it all the same principles at work:[59] a royal monopoly on minting in gold or silver,[60] an ingenious variety of taxes, *ad hoc* levies, tribute (*phoros*), excise and customs charges, tithes, sales taxes, a poll tax (possibly only in Jerusalem), taxes on salt and slaves, a sovereign's crown tax (*stephanētikos*), and the inevitable but tiresome obligation of billeting troops, plus that traditional practice—despite a reliable, and abundant, silver coinage—of storing wealth unproductively in the royal treasury (Jesus knew better: consider the parable of the talents), which had earlier marked the Persian empire, and remains a sure index of economic backwardness. No investment, that is, in any undertaking that would improve production. The Seleucids, like the Ptolemies, were immensely wealthy,[61] though in the last resort it was the obligated peasantry, the *laoi basilikoi*, rather than taxation, on whom that wealth depended; and when, from 166 onwards (below, p. 436), the Romans began to drain off this labor force via the slave

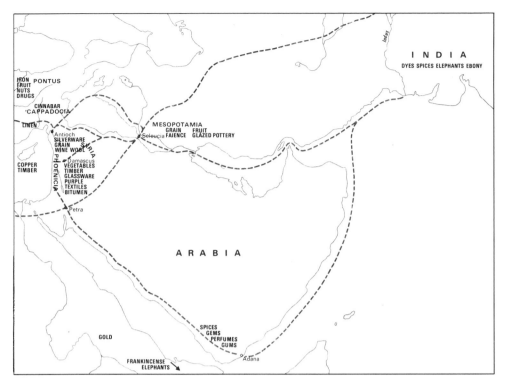

From *CAH, Plates to Volume VII Part I*, pp. 92–93.

marts, Seleucid resources were steadily eroded.[62] There was, and could be, nothing resembling the Ptolemaic planned economy in the widespread and administratively ill-organized Seleucid domains. Yet even allowing for incompetence, wastage, and dishonesty, the revenues from these various sources were enormous. After all, with an overall population estimated at thirty million inhabitants, however inefficient the tax collecting some kind of reasonable income must have been assured. Seleucus III's contribution to Rhodian relief after a devastating earthquake (below, p. 381) included a ten-vessel squadron, fully equipped, two hundred thousand *medimnoi* (= 300,000 bushels) of wheat, and vast quantities of timber.[63] War booty could be profitable (above, p. 362); it was only after Antiochus III tangled with Rome, however, that a habit arose of plundering the empire's temples, on the principle of *l'état c'est moi*.[64]

Once again, the guiding principle is political rather than economic. Under the Seleucids we see the old Achaemenid feudal system taken over virtually unaltered for exploitation by the new ruling class of Greeks and Macedonians. Grants of royal domain (*basilikē chōra*) continue, to temples, friends at court, or veterans, with the Greek *poleis* as the only new category of beneficiary, and the peasants (*laoi, paroikoi*) still working the land for this privileged minority.[65] Yet despite this continuity there were also profound changes taking place. The innumerable new foundations, both cities and colonies (*katoikiai*), the eastward drift of Greek businessmen, technicians, and professionals that inevitably followed, brought an unprecedentedly active element into this hitherto static—and theocratic—world. Demographic patterns changed, urbanization bred new syncretisms, exploitation wore an unfamiliar face.[66] As in Ptolemaic Egypt (above, p. 323), unrest and subversion drove the Seleucids to attempt some kind of *rapprochement* with the old indigenous ruling classes and priest-hoods,[67] both of which had an equal interest in maintaining the feudal, and exploitative, mode of production, however much they may have politically resented their new overlords. It is no coincidence that the more territory the Seleucids lost, the more concessions they made to cities and temples: a paradox in economic terms, this made good sense if looked at politically. What did more than any other single factor to disrupt the economy (and was a direct cause of the deeply resented despoliation of temples under Antiochus IV Epiphanes and his successors) was the huge war indemnity imposed by Rome, a matter of fifteen thousand talents (below, p. 421).

The case of Pergamon is akin to that of Ptolemaic Egypt in that it offers an example of both immense wealth, firmly in the hands of the ruling dynasty, and great natural resources, well exploited. If the wealth of the Attalids became proverbial, this was because, having started well with the nine thousand talents embezzled by Philetairos, they proceeded to impose a highly efficient system of tribute and taxes, both on their own population and on the *poleis* under their control. "The cities," as Esther Hansen reminds us, "were so heavily taxed by the kings that they were unable to increase their municipal taxes to cover the cost of their municipal administrations."[68] Duties on imported goods also proved immensely profitable, and at the same time the Pergamene kingdom was itself immensely rich and fertile: surplus produce included not only grain, grapes (and wine), olives (and oil), and livestock of every sort, but also—a key export—timber and pitch for shipbuilding. An abundance of excellent wool supported a flourishing textile industry; pottery clay was also first-class. Tight governmental controls combined with rich resources made Attalid Pergamon economically akin, on a smaller scale, to both the Ptolemaic and the Seleucid kingdoms: it seems clear that the Attalids consciously imitated the latter, in particular, when first establishing themselves. As for the cities of mainland Greece (for which our evidence is on the whole poor), though they continued to suffer, as they had always done, from the need to import basic raw materials—most notably grain and timber—they also seem to have benefited, until well into the third century, from the demand for Greek goods and expertise (especially in the building trade) in the new colonies abroad. Those, like Athens and Rhodes, with a strong maritime tradition also cashed in on the highly profitable Mediterranean carrying trade.

Thus despite the essentially political and social upheaval (with strong religious undertones) that followed the dismemberment of the Achaemenid empire by Alexander, commerce, as such, went on very much as before. Indeed, grain prices at Delos (for which we have good epigraphical evidence) fell steadily—seasonal fluctuations apart—from 270 onwards, "a fact which testifies both to the abundance of supply and to the sound state of the market":[69] famines became much less frequent. Trade in general was expanded enormously, and also simplified a good deal: the

Mediterranean world now had far fewer independent governments, and in consequence a great reduction in the number of competing coin standards.

Alexander had issued an imperial coinage on the Euboic-Attic standard, with a
seventeen-gram tetradrachm. The vast amount of specie he released also meant a
corresponding increase in the amount of currency actually circulating. To begin
with, all three Successor kingdoms coined on this standard. But the Ptolemies very
soon broke away from the Attic tetradrachm (ca. 310–300), gradually lightening the
weight of their issues to about thirteen or fifteen grams, probably because of the
silver shortage. The effect was to isolate Egypt commercially to some extent from
the rest of the Hellenistic world.[70] The new standard came closer to (but did not exactly match) those of Rhodes, Chios, and Phoenicia. (The Rhodian-Chian tetradrachm weighed 15.3 grams, and the Phoenician shekel 14.0.) It seems also to have
been aligned with that of Egypt's dependency Cyrene.[71] The actual minting was
done in the Phoenician cities under Ptolemaic control (e.g., Tyre and Sidon). We
have already noted the anomalous Ptolemaic copper coinage (p. 366), in part a
concession to the native Egyptians, who were suspicious of silver, and tended to
hoard it as bullion.[72] The Ptolemies also, unlike the other Successor kingdoms,
issued an extensive gold coinage: most notably a series of octadrachms known as
mnaieia (= 1 mina of silver in value), bearing posthumous portraits of various officially deified monarchs, from Soter to Philopator, and their consorts. These issues
seem to have been used mainly for foreign trade and political subsidies (e.g., those
made, at various times, to Sparta and the Achaean League), so that their minting
was, *inter alia*, a matter of dynastic propaganda, a calculated display of wealth and
magnificence. After the reign of Ptolemy V Epiphanes (204–180) this series, like all
Ptolemaic currency, shows a sharp decline in quality. (It is worth noting that the
Ptolemies' use of both gold and copper for currency, and their eventual abandonment of the silver standard, can be directly related to the availability of all three
metals within their own domains.) The Ptolemaic currency, like the Attalids' after
188 (p. 375),[73] was thus almost exclusively for internal use, operating within a closed
economy; from some point after 285 foreign coins were barred from circulation,
being melted down and reissued, with a tax on both the minting and the exchange.[74]

By these somewhat draconian methods the Ptolemies enforced a monopoly of
their own coinage throughout their domains. What was more, as Theocritus's enthusiastic testimony and the extraordinary public procession recorded by Callixeinos both make amply clear (pp. 146, 158 ff.), the system—at least down to the time
of Epiphanes—was a resounding success.[75] Later it was another matter. From the
mid-second century the cost of living regularly outstripped minimum wages, while
the copper currency had already been systematically debased (225–221), its ratio to
silver jumping from 1:60 to 1:455 after the year 200. By striking and circulating this
low-grade copper currency the Ptolemies became, as it were, self-licensed profiteers
on an enormous scale. They also, not surprisingly, faced, in the long run, quite appalling inflation. An *artaba* (slightly more than a *medimnos*) of wheat in the third century cost 75 copper drachmas; by the second, the price had risen to 350.[76] In Greece,

Euboea and the islands used the Rhodian or Phoenician standard, and the Peloponnese, independent as always, retained the old Aiginetan standard, with a five-gram drachma.

But just as Greek government made little difference to local methods of production, so Greek finance largely bypassed the local inhabitants, who had lived by barter before invasion, and continued to do so.[77] Thus in Ptolemaic Egypt, orthodox banking operated side by side with a warehousing system, based on a network of royal grain depositories, that took care of loans, credits, and tax payments in kind, as well as transactions more specifically limited to the freightage and delivery of wheat consignments.[78] The Ptolemies could, and did, turn the barter economy to their advantage. Salaries were normally paid part in cash, part in oil or wheat; but a proportion of the payment in kind tended to be commuted to cash, the rate being calculated so as to benefit the king, and keep real wages as low as possible. We hear of a soldier in 158 whose monthly pay was 150 copper drachmas plus three *artabai* of wheat: one *artaba* was paid in kind, but the other two were commuted at the rate of 100 copper drachmas per *artaba*, when the market rate was in fact between six and nine times that amount.[79] Thus the total real pay this unfortunate man drew can be calculated as between 2 and 2.5 silver drachmas, no more than the wage of an ordinary Egyptian laborer.

We should also note the development of banking practices among temple treasurers, who had long been in the habit of safeguarding deposits from individuals or government agencies, and now began to invest such deposits (with the depositor's consent, and subject to interest) in loans and other business ventures.[80] The best evidence for a more or less developed temple bank comes, again, from Delos, where Apollo, through his priesthood, ran a flourishing loan business, at 10 percent interest, to fund various civic projects such as wax for statues, gold wreaths for visiting dignitaries, the bulk purchase of wheat, and a lookout post against Etruscan pirates.[81] It is interesting that Plautus, who borrowed so heavily from Hellenistic Greek models, portrays soldiers of fortune as regular clients of the trapezitic banks, not least since in Egypt, as we have seen, the standard rate of interest was, from the early third century if not earlier, over double the going rate (10–12 percent) in the rest of the Hellenistic world. (The steadiness of these interest rates is significant: it was not till the Romans took a hand in the game that the market lost its basic stability.) This policy of dear credit may well, as Rostovtzeff argued, have been due in the first instance to a shortage of coined money, particularly silver;[82] it was also clearly designed not only to profit the bankers, but to discourage peasant or other "little man" investment.[83] Initiative of this sort was always regarded, in times of social unrest, as a potential source of trouble (cf. above, p. 369). After Raphia (217), with inflation rampant, the Ptolemies became peculiarly sensitive to the risks of social revolution, and a peasant with a stake in property was liable to be that much more independent, and hence more vocal, in demanding his rights. In the next chapter we shall examine the general consequences of these economic policies in human, social, even ideological terms: the deep and exacerbated divisions between rich and poor, rulers and ruled, leading at one level to dreams of utopia, and at another to revolutionary outbreaks against the suffocating *status quo*.

One of the few generally beneficial improvements that Greek settlers brought with them (at least south of a certain latitude) was viticulture; and in the north, around the Black Sea and the Danube regions, where the vine would not grow well, the itinerant wine merchant, with his cargo of pitch-sealed amphoras, came to be a familiar sight.[84] The best vintages were those from northern Syria (exported via Laodicea-on-Sea) and the Ionian coast and offshore islands.[85] Analogies from similar cultures would suggest a rise in alcoholism, especially among depressed peasants and *déraciné* intellectuals. The prevalence of Dionysiac motifs in Hellenistic art might serve as some confirmation of this. Greek olive oil, similarly, found a wide market.

Philanthrōpia was well aware of the need for bread and circuses: the Alexandrian mob could get ugly when aroused, as Ptolemy V and his ministers had been made uncomfortably aware (above, p. 304). Maritime loans apart, there was still—one of the most far-reaching economic differences between ancient society and our own— no scheme remotely comparable to the system of modern personal or industrial insurance,[86] which was replaced in part by patronage, in part by a formalized network of reciprocal family obligations. The normal cost of money, as we have seen, ranged (except in Egypt) between 10 and 12 percent: in special circumstances it might go as high as 18 percent. Loans on ships and cargoes, since they carried an added charge to cover what was in effect insurance, could rise as high as 22.5 or even 30 percent, depending on the sailing season, though lower rates are sometimes found, and no clear distinction was ever drawn between loan interest and high-risk insurance cover.[87] Banks also often put up the capital for that other notorious source of social inequity, the farming of taxes. With a 5 percent (later 10 percent) commission on top of the profit to be derived from speculation, this was a lucrative game, in which the only constant sufferers were the wretched populace. Along with the equally profitable business of marketing slaves (production energy, as it were, on the hoof: one more reason for the failure of science to achieve greater advances in technology), it was to be pursued most ruthlessly, from the mid-second century onwards, by the Romans.

The cities of Old Greece, as we have seen, were very much eclipsed by these new Hellenistic superpowers, with their vast resources of manpower and raw materials. For one thing, the development of the Hellenistic kingdoms' productivity severely limited the export markets available to the mainland *poleis*: trade shifted eastward, to Alexandria, Rhodes, Antioch, Pergamon, or Seleucia-on-Tigris. Pergamon and Rhodes in particular—to judge from the so-called cistophoric coinage, minted from about 170 on the Rhodian standard by various cities within the Attalid sphere of influence—seem to have benefited from this change. The case of Antigonid Macedonia, however, is in many ways the exception that proves the rule. Macedonian timber for shipbuilding was both plentiful and of the very highest quality; the country had grain and livestock in abundance, and the gold and silver mines, despite their decline, were still being profitably enough worked in the mid-second

Fig. 130. The so-called cistophoric, or "casket-bearing," coinage (so named from the
cista mystica, or ritual casket, with snake, on the obverse) was first minted in
Pergamon from ca. 170 B.C., and later, under the Romans, became standard currency
in western Asia Minor. The reverse of this specimen from Pergamon, minted ca.
150 B.C.(?), shows two serpents twined round a bow case.
British Museum, London.

century for the Romans to shut them down to keep them out of the exploitative
hands of the *publicani* (below, p. 430). Thus, unlike most of the Balkans, Macedonia
maintained a healthy import-export balance—something to which the stupendous
mass of rich loot displayed in Aemilius Paullus's triumph offers eloquent testimony
(below, p. 415).[88]

Second, even those still technically autonomous were often obligated, economically no less than politically, to some more powerful entity, league if not kingdom,[89]
with the inevitable result that their ingenuity in taxing their citizens soon came to
rival that of the Seleucids or Ptolemies.[90] Advances from individuals (*proeisphorai*),
sometimes repayable, sometimes not, with or without interest, were regarded as
preferable to formal loans, which were only contracted as a last resort.[91] Despite this,
the *poleis* frequently suffered the most frightful financial crises, with empty treasuries, unpaid troops, and no apparent resources to raise even modest sums: this was
true not only of small *poleis*, but also of large and apparently prosperous cities such
as Larissa, Olbia, even Miletus,[92] and led to an increasing reliance on voluntary contributions (*epidoseis*), in cash or kind, from individuals or private associations,[93] for
purposes (e.g., the building of granaries, city walls, a public library) that today
would probably be funded by municipal bond issues.[94] The number of *epidoseis* is
particularly striking for Rhodes. This may be no accident (see below).

The virtual disappearance of fine-quality pottery (which, in this more lavish
age, was largely replaced by silverware) removed one of the best sources of income
for Athens, though she continued to export Megarian-type bowls, and retained her
trade in fine-quality oil (some of which, despite the tariff, found its way to Egypt),

honey, figs, and, from the mid–second century, Pentelic marble.[95] At the same time, between 282 and the end of the century, the city's most essential import, wheat, after some fluctuations, rose from six or seven to between eight and ten drachmas per *medimnos*, while during a roughly similar period oil first dropped in price dramatically, from fifty-five to sixteen or eighteen drachmas per *metrētēs* (roughly 8.5 gallons), then remained stable till between 190 and 180, when it fell further, to between eleven and thirteen drachmas.[96] The cause of this disparity, in all likelihood, was the perennial preference, in a wholly unplanned economy, of landowners for the cultivation of vines and olives rather than cereals (since the former offered a more profitable cash crop), combined with a shortage of major wheat-growing regions. These were limited to Egypt, Sicily, southern Russia, North Africa, and the Po valley. Production of grain seldom reached glut level (the mid–third century seems to have been an exception), while prices were held artificially high by exporters who controlled a seller's market, and knew what they could get.[97] For Athens the result, in addition to her other troubles during the third century, was an adverse balance of trade, and recurrent crises over her grain supply.[98] It also looks as though mining for silver at Laurium was discontinued as unprofitable for a time after the Chremonidean War, but the evidence is uncertain.[99] The appearance of the so-called New Style Attic coins (ca. 165?), their flans stamped with wreaths on the reverse, and therefore known as "wreathbearers" (*stephanēphoroi*), suggests that silver was once more being extracted, at the latest, by the second quarter of the second century.[100] This resurgence is almost certainly to be connected with Athenian control of Delos.

Corinth continued to export high-quality bronzework, and the new demand for silk, as opposed to woolen, garments—another luxurious trend—created prosperity for the island of Cos: "Coan garments" were famous still in Augustan Rome.[101] But

Fig. 131. Athenian New Style coinage (also known, from the prominent wreath border, as *stephanēphoroi*). Silver tetradrachm minted ca. 165 B.C., with helmeted head of Athena Parthenos on the obverse and tutelary owl, with wreath, on the reverse. British Museum, London. Photo Hirmer.

in general both the carrying trade and commerce had shifted away from Greece proper to Asia Minor and Egypt, and, later, to the west. Miletus remained a busy center of the textile industry, but little more.[102] The one Greek power that preserved complete and genuine independence in Hellenistic times—at least until 168 (below, p. 431)—was the maritime republic of Rhodes.[103] Rhodian wealth came primarily from her extensive carrying trade; the island's location and two great harbors made it, like Piraeus, a natural transit center. Rhodes lay at the intersection of all the major Mediterranean shipping routes, from Egypt, Cyprus, and Phoenicia to the Aegean and the Black Sea, as well as Italy and North Africa. She was thus especially well placed to mediate between grain suppliers and their markets, and had ample capital for reinvestment in maritime undertakings. The Rhodian merchant marine was the largest in the Hellenistic world, and since the fourth century had been trading throughout the Mediterranean, particularly in wine and oil, as well as grain.[104]

As a result of this heavy and widespread maritime commerce, Rhodes also had a natural vested interest in the suppression of piracy; and when, from about the mid-third century, Ptolemaic Egypt could no longer ensure the safety of the seas (above, p. 150), it was the Rhodian squadrons that took over the task of policing them, a service that earned them considerable gratitude from the various Hellenistic powers.[105] The debt was compounded by a consistent Rhodian policy of selling grain cheap in emergencies, without the notorious price gouging that a famine normally produced.[106] No longer strictly democratic in government, Rhodes, with her benevolent naval aristocracy and her famous maritime laws,[107] nevertheless held out against the dominant pattern of Hellenistic kingship, and preserved much of the old classical Greek pride and civic intransigence. As early as 306 the Rhodians had made a treaty with Rome.[108] They defied Demetrius Poliorcetes and successfully withstood his siege (305–304: above, p. 33). Their bias in favor of the Ptolemies was probably due to the massive grain imports from Egypt on which they depended.[109] They forced their trade rival Byzantium to rescind her toll on the rich traffic through the Bosporus (220/19); they fought Eumenes II of Pergamon when he made a bid to shut off the Black Sea grain route (182–179); their squadrons kept the seas safe from piracy.[110]

Domestically, the Rhodians ran a kind of welfare program for their poorer citizens—"although their rule," says Strabo, with almost audible astonishment, "is not democratic"—which included a dole and a grain allowance, "so that the poor are fed, while the state has no lack of handy men, especially to serve in the fleet."[111] After Alexander's conquests, with easy commercial access now available to Egypt and Cyprus and the whole Phoenician coast, Rhodes became a logical entrepôt for the shipping of grain and other essential commodities between the Levant, the Mediterranean, and the Black Sea.[112] Her shipbuilding yards were off limits to all except those who worked there,[113] which suggests jealously guarded secrets of naval construction: we know that her vessels were universally admired, and the sophisticated ingenuity of her engineers became apparent during the great siege. Her port fulfilled the role that Piraeus had played in the days of Athenian power: "a centre of exchange

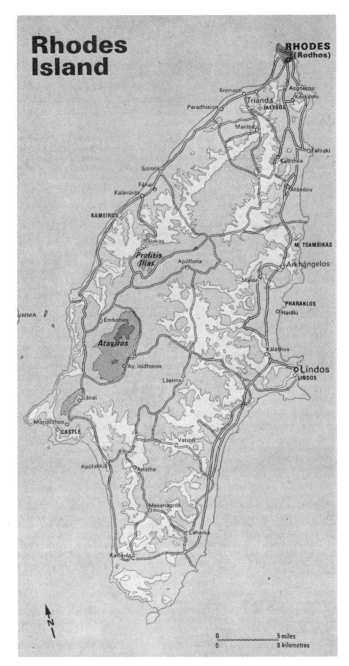

Map 23. Rhodes.
From the *Blue Guide* to Greece, ed. S. Rossiter, p. 682.

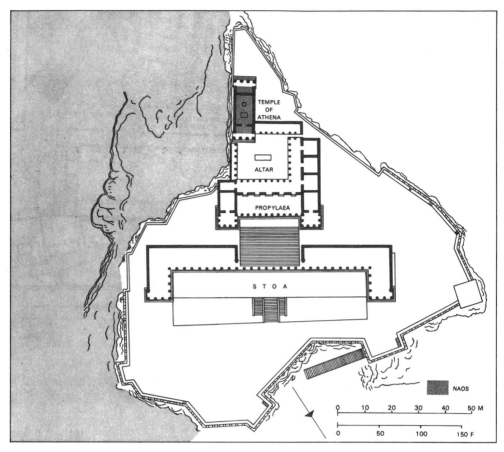

TEMPLE
OF
ATHENA

ALTAR

PROPYLAEA

S T O A

NAOS

0   10   20   30   40   50 M

0   50   100   150 F

Fig. 132. Plan of the acropolis of Lindos, Rhodes. From Charbonneaux, Martin, and
Villard, p. 362, fig. 419.

and capital and the enemy of piracy on the high seas."[114] Her large and powerful
fleet, manned by the poorer citizens (the exact equivalent of the Piraeus "naval
rabble"), and officered by sons of the island's most distinguished families, not only
guarded the sea lanes, but was the guarantee of Rhodian independence: it is significant that while everywhere else citizens had turned over military service to mercenaries, Rhodes—unlike Athens—could still furnish numerous proud citizen volunteers to fill her rowing benches. Their service was carefully recorded, and ex-service
associations of former ships' crews are known. The city's 2 percent customs duty
alone brought in a million drachmas annually, which implies a turnover of fifty million drachmas, or eighty-three hundred talents, in imports and exports.[115] Banking
and the carrying trade must have brought in much more. Commerce thus both
underwrote Rhodian security, and determined the island's prime objectives: the suppression of piracy and internecine warfare, the maintenance of a balance of power
between the great kingdoms. It also suited these kingdoms to have such an exchange

center available; at the same time Rhodes offered a haven from the long arm of Hellenistic authoritarianism—as Apollonius, for one, discovered to his gratitude (above, p. 203).

Just how highly valued Rhodes was for her various indispensable services we can judge from the general reaction to the city's virtual destruction in a great earthquake (228/7) that, *inter alia*, shook down the famous Colossus (p. 33).[116] Almost all the governments in the Mediterranean, from Hieron II of Syracuse to the Ptolemaic and Seleucid regimes, vied with each other in the munificence of their aid to ensure Rhodian recovery: seventy-five talents for a new gymnasium, customs immunity for Rhodian merchants, over a million *artabai* of grain (35,000 tons, the second-largest consignment recorded in the ancient world), three thousand talents for the repair of the Colossus (one of the most spectacular casualties, and it never was repaired, so one wonders where the money went), a hundred master builders with 350 workmen, and pay to support them, ten fully equipped quinqueremes, three thousand talents of iron, a thousand talents of pitch, timber and roofbeams galore.[117] One notable absentee from the list of contributors was Pergamon; but then her king Attalus I shortly afterwards backed Byzantium's attempt to levy tolls on Black Sea shipping (220/19), and sided with her against Rhodes in the commercial war that followed; so the relationship between the two powers was probably cool.

Once again we catch a fascinating glimpse of the moral astigmatism that was liable to afflict even the shrewdest of ancient commentators (and Polybius was nothing if not hardheaded) when it came to economic realities. Why this extraordinary generosity? Because, Polybius explains, "by exaggerating both the extent and the frightfulness of the calamity, and by conducting themselves, both on official embassies and in private discussions, with high solemnity and dignified aplomb, the Rhodians affected the cities, and the kings in particular, so much, that not only did they receive most lavish gifts, but the givers themelves felt that a favor was being bestowed on them."[118] Another triumph for *sophrosyne*, in fact (above, p. 365): once again the hard economic facts were politely ignored.[119] The Romans, impervious by nature to this kind of high-flown hogwash, knew just how to hit the Rhodians where it really hurt (below, p. 431). In 167, irritated by the ambiguity of Rhodes's allegiances during the Third Macedonian War, they opened up Delos as a free port in direct competition, and in very little time the Rhodians were complaining bitterly— if with some exaggeration—that their customs revenues had fallen from 1,000,000 to 150,000 drachmas per annum.[120] It was not on the battlefield alone that Rome took the measure of the Hellenistic world, and played a winning hand.

CHAPTER 22

THE INDIVIDUAL AND SOCIETY: SLAVERY, REVOLUTION, UTOPIAS

So far we have examined the evolution of the Hellenistic states in political and economic terms, with concomitant developments in art and literature. It remains now to consider the social consequences of those various fundamental changes that took place in the fourth and third centuries: the virtual disintegration (except in a narrow parochial sense) of effective *polis* society, the reversion to authoritarian government by royal fiat, the removal of real civic power (and, hence, civic involvement) from the ordinary citizen, the replacement of political ideals by commercial avarice, social ambition, or bookish introspection, the enlargement of physical and psychological horizons to embrace wide areas of the *oikoumenē*, an ever-increasing trend toward urbanization (however rudimentary in the modern sense), with the resultant split, not only between town and country, but also between a bourgeois elite that lived—and in many cases made its income—in nonagricultural areas, and the rural peasantry whose labor, and products, were increasingly exploited by government and private speculator alike.[1] This struck at the Greek concept of freedom in a very real sense, since the basic definition of a free man depended far less on the kind of work he did than on his doing it for himself, and not, under constraint, for others.[2]

Several interrelated phenomena emerge from a study of social trends in the Successor kingdoms. We find, predictably, an ever-increasing inequity in the distribution of wealth.[3] Though a great deal more capital was generated overall in the Hellenistic than in the classical period, the general standard of living actually fell: the wealthy minority became still richer, whereas those who had been poor before moved closer to the starvation line. This trend was only minimally offset by the eastward drift of emigration (above, p. 372). At the same time widespread warfare throughout the Mediterranean, culminating in the Roman conquests of the second and first centuries, while it drained the resources of the Greek economy, also made available—primarily, though not exclusively, in Italy and Sicily—a vastly increased number of slaves,[4] thus answering an obvious economic need, while at the same time offsetting the resultant short-term benefits by still further discouragement of technological progress. A basically preindustrial society still needs to generate power and labor, preferably minus those costly acknowledgments of human rights imposed by the employment of free citizens, while the spread of urbanization and commercialism (if not of industrialism in the modern sense) makes this need more acute.[5] "The first and most essential kind of capital possession," observes the Peripatetic author of the *Oeconomica*,[6] "is also the best and most economical: that is, a human being." Thus the kidnapping and sale of children was a perennial hazard in the eastern Mediterranean: exposed infants were commonly reared as slaves—to the enrichment of plots in New Comedy (above, p. 73)[7]—and though Alexander's immediate successors seem on the whole to have avoided mass enslavement of prisoners, by the late third century this practice had once more become common. Greek objections to it, as we have seen, normally applied (if at all) only when it was visited upon fellow Greeks: the Mantineans sold off by Antigonus Doson and the Achaean League in 223, the Thasians and others whom Philip V made a tidy profit on some twenty years later (203/2).[8]

Aristotle himself regarded slavery as both justified and essential for the running of a democratic *polis*:[9] in a famous definition he described the slave as an "animated tool" (*empsychon organon*).[10] Herodotus had earlier cited the popular view that the Greeks were naturally free, whereas *barbaroi*, in particular the Oriental variety, were natural slaves,[11] a theory Aristotle was to justify by the assertion that they lived exclusively by and for the senses,[12] and which was essential to the panhellenic program of Eastern conquest.[13] Officially, Greeks were debarred from enslaving other Greeks[14] (this is the attitude taken by Plato in the *Republic*),[15] but the harsh facts of life from the fourth century onwards soon diluted this principle to a simple maxim, applied as early as Xenophon's day,[16] of enslaving your enemy but not your friends— a flexible rule with which it would be hard for a Greek to find fault. (In retrospect it might be held to justify those notorious instances of mass enslavement in earlier periods, for example of the women and children on Melos during the Peloponnesian War.)[17] The Romans, brutal campaigners at the best of times, never had any such qualms when fighting on Greek soil, where their atrocities very soon got them a bad name (p. 300).

Moral objections to slavery as such were very rare indeed; the two instances known to us were uttered by a wandering sophist and a foreign playwright, men whose intellectual liberalism was least restrained by investment in the social, moral, or (above all) financial *status quo*.[18] It was Gorgias's student Alcidamas who declared that "God has left all men free; Nature has made no one a slave";[19] it was the Syracusan comic poet Philemon, long resident at Athens, who wrote:[20]

Servitude owns one flesh with other mortals:
No man was ever born a slave by nature,
But it was Fortune that enslaved his body.

Euripides' views are hard to assess, since we know only what he put in his characters' mouths, and this included much commonplace justification of slavery (not invariably by unsympathetic figures);[21] but even if no abolitionist, he certainly voiced frequent sympathy for the lot of slaves, and it is plain that the topic was a widely discussed one, at least from the closing decades of the fifth century.[22] Yet the distinction between objecting to slavery on principle and sympathizing with, or urging humane treatment for, the slaves of one's society remains crucial, and the first alternative is everywhere conspicuous by its absence. The second, often remarked at Athens, where slaves were protected by various regulations (though still required to give evidence only after torture),[23] was something quite different, and based, ultimately, on pragmatic considerations of advantage. If you treat a slave well, it was argued, you lessen his urge to rebel, and get better work out of him over a longer period.[24] In third-century Egypt it was illegal to beat slaves, tattoo them (done for purposes of identification), or sell them abroad—a nice mixture of concerns, with the ubiquitous royal control over exports well to the fore (above, p. 88).[25]

The argument is essentially the same as that presented by Diodotus, in Thucydides' account of the debate on how to deal with the rebellious citizens of Mytilene: not that kindness is morally preferable, but that it achieves better results for the ruling power.[26] We have to accept the fact that the vast majority of Greeks, whether they themselves owned slaves or not, took the practice for granted in every area of life, and that only poverty (though slaves were cheap enough) stopped any individual from taking advantage of its benefits. The paradox we have already studied in connection with Sparta (p. 250), of freedom and equality for an elite made possible by widespread servile labor, had more general application throughout the Greek world. "The cities in which individual freedom reached its highest expression—most obviously Athens—were cities in which chattel slavery flourished."[27] The Hellenistic period shows no fundamental change of heart in this respect. Thus we have to allow for an element of what Flaubert, in *Salammbô*, rightly perceived as, in modern terms, blank stony cruelty and indifference when assessing the ancient world's attitude to slavery as an institution. No one could even begin to conceive the world without it. This will very largely explain the general absence of slave revolts (fugitivism was another matter), and *a fortiori* of organized revolution in the sense in which we understand that term.

Yet during the late Hellenistic period we find clear evidence for the first, and, arguably, for the second as well. Why? And why, slightly earlier, in the third and second centuries, do we also meet with scattered, but recurrent, instances of utopian fantasies, possibly applied as blueprints to breakaway communal experiments, and in one case at least (it has been argued) the inspiration behind an actual revolt? The answer, clear but depressing, emerges from a study of the massive (and unique) slave revolts that took place in Sicily and Italy—with minor repercussions elsewhere—between 140 and 70, culminating in the famous rising led by Spartacus. Anarchic conditions and constant widespread warfare, from the third century onwards, had, as we have seen, brought about a vast increase in the turnover of slaves throughout the Mediterranean. After 167 Delos was being used as a central mart and distribution point, and Strabo alleges that "tens of thousands of slaves" changed hands there daily: a palpable exaggeration, but clearly based on knowledge of intense, and rapid, trading.[28] He quotes a popular saying from this period about Delos: "Merchant, put in, unload—all's sold."

We know where too many of these slaves went: on to the great cattle ranches (*latifundia*) and wheat farms of Sicily and southern Italy, to be housed in barracks (*ergastula*) and worked as chain gangs.[29] But where did they come from? During the wars of the Successors, and even more during Rome's expansionist activities in regions of the Mediterranean from Spain to Illyria, more and more slaves, far from being ignorant and genuinely barbarian tribesmen, were being drawn from areas that enjoyed a high level of (most often Greek-based) civilization. It follows that a high percentage of the vast numbers enslaved not only had been free men prior to capture, but were both intelligent and civilized. Such men, while by no means challenging slavery as an institution, objected violently to being enslaved themselves; they also had the brains and the organizational ability to make what were very often highly successful bids to break out of the trap in which they had been caught.[30] Paradoxically, far from wanting to change the class structure of their society, they merely aimed to correct what they saw as an improper skewing of the balance between natural free men and natural slaves. In their view they had been wrongly categorized.

Social and class convictions also explain why, as a group, these slaves got virtually no support from those whom one might have thought their natural allies: the poor free men, peasants for the most part, who had been reduced to near-starvation by systematic exploitation and crushing taxes under the Ptolemies, the Seleucids, and their lesser imitators.[31] However low they had fallen, the idea of joining a servile revolt (whatever the original status of the slaves) was anathema to them[32]—striking proof of class attitudes to the institution as an accepted feature of society—and in consequence Marxist theories of a natural "proletarian class" rising against capitalism make very little sense for the ancient world,[33] even though the distinction between free, bond, and slave was at times a very fine one, and the categories might actually overlap.[34] Finally, those who were incapable of action could at least dream: the utopias that gained currency now were a logical extension of that growing escapist literature, the roots of which we have traced back as far as the late fifth century. Such egalitarianism as does emerge from our sources belongs here, in the category of wishful thinking and compensation fantasy. The basic dichotomy between freedom and servitude proved a far stronger force than actual socioeconomic conditions.[35] Those conditions, in any case, were by no means so intolerable as they became after Rome's takeover in Greece and Asia Minor: Hellenistic Greek slavery was, relatively speaking, humane.[36] It is significant that the kind of eschatological revenge fantasy that visualizes the oppressors of the chosen people suffering the torments of the damned for all eternity, while the oppressed themselves enjoy not only the luxuries of paradise, but, even more, the thought (and sometimes the sight) of those torments, was largely elicited by Roman depredations: its absence from Hellenistic utopian literature is striking.

Thus we see that though the total wealth of the Hellenistic period was much greater than that previously in circulation (a conclusion reinforced by the surviving artifacts), and also distributed over a wider area, nevertheless an even larger proportion of it was monopolized by the very tip of the social and political pyramid, not least (appropriately enough) in Egypt: the monarchies, their courtiers, high officials of the bureaucracy, successful merchants, and, in the Greek *poleis*, enterprising urban oligarchs. Even the imposition of a Greek monetary system did little more than streamline the process of exploitation (above, p. 366). The failure to use capital as an instrument of improved productivity explains why prices generally, despite fluctuations, tended to remain high. To compound the problem, the use of slave rather than free labor (however cheap the latter might be) meant that wealth was not being redistributed in such a way as to create, much less enlarge, markets for goods and services. Apart from the royal establishments, those who did best out of the new regime were wholesalers, middlemen, loan sharks, carrying agents, while those hardest hit were small manufacturers—still in the vast majority: cottage industry remained almost universal—as well as wage earners and consumers generally.

Those extravagant displays of hoarded wealth in which Hellenistic monarchs took such pleasure must have caused increasing aggravation as time went on. When Ptolemy II in 275/4 organized that great public procession of his (above, p. 158),[37] with its dazzling accumulation of gold and other tangible wealth, the economy was still absorbing (along with temporary inflation) the direct benefits of Alexander's global essay in piracy, and such a display could indeed "be interpreted as an act of general benevolence towards the populace because of the free entertainment and food provided."[38] But by the time that Antiochus IV Epiphanes mounted a similar show in 167 (below, p. 432), to emulate the games given by Aemilius Paullus after Pydna,[39] or Ptolemy VIII Physcon paraded his treasures to impress a Roman embassy in 140,[40] the social situation had deterioriated sharply, with starvation, acute poverty, and actual or threatened revolt the rule rather than the exception. These conditions seemed all the more intolerable since they had developed in the midst of visible plenty. We have detailed evidence, from the papyri, of the estates, shipping, and workshops controlled by Ptolemy II's minister Apollonius, and there is no reason to suppose his case exceptional.[41] One of Antiochus III's ministers was able to bankroll an army out of his private funds.[42] On every side one could see luxurious houses and estates, costly furniture, fine clothes, exquisite gold ornaments, rare jewelry, embossed silver plate and vessels, a positively Edwardian indulgence in gourmet food and vintage wines.[43]

Nor was this ostentatious affluence restricted to the courts of the leading Hellenistic monarchs.[44] Commercial Greek *poleis* such as Rhodes or Miletus reveal identical trends. Ephesus, at the head of the Anatolian caravan route, had the same kind of showy monumental buildings going up as we find in Pergamon or Antioch. In mainland Greece, the Aetolians and Acarnanians who did well out of piracy and the slave trade (two closely linked activities) were likewise making their mark as *nouveaux riches*: one Aetolian entrepreneur had a fortune estimated at two hundred talents.[45] Dowries, trust funds, and public *philanthrōpia*, another ironic label, all went up among the fortunate, whose birth rate, in Greece at least, began to fall, since

those with wealth now wanted to enjoy their pleasures without the expensive encumbrance of offspring. Also, as Polybius remarked, apropos Boeotia and the Peloponnese, it was no longer just girls who were regularly exposed—by which he
probably meant sold into slavery *sub rosa*.[46] Putting money out at interest, in particular for maritime loans that the banks and temples regarded as too risky to fund
(above, p. 375), was a high gamble; but if the gamble came off, it brought enormous
profits, and was, in any case, far more attractive to Greeks now largely deprived of
political outlets for their ambitions than the selfless civic function of raising sons to
serve the state.

Some saw the dangers clearly: among them that fascinating character Cercidas
of Megalopolis (ca. 290–ca. 220), lawgiver, soldier, statesman, friend of Aratus, and
despite his aristocratic background a Cynic by conviction, who gave vent to his contempt for current social trends in meliambics, satirical poems written in lyric meters.[47] There is nothing particularly new about the fragments that survive except for
their peculiar vividness and virulence. The actual complaints voiced by Cercidas had
been commonplaces from Hesiod's day onwards,[48] and were also being made by
other third-century poets such as Phoenix of Colophon.[49] If Zeus was truly lord,
what had become of justice and equity? Why should it be the greedy spendthrifts
who got all the money? We find warnings against the sharp tongues and hairsplitting
quibbles of lawyers, the mischief making of Stoic activists such as Sphaerus (p. 252).
This is hardly radicalism. Passionate emotions, whether political or sexual, arouse
Cercidas's distrust; even music (especially that of the new Oriental modes) is associated with vice and luxurious self-indulgence. The tone is puritanical, almost ascetic.
War against gross flesh, Cercidas tells us, avoid grand passions, slake your desires on
Aphrodite-of-the-agora, steer your course with (what else?) *sōphrosynē*.

The no-saying of a puritan can sometimes wear what looks, coincidentally, like
a revolutionary air, but in fact is nothing of the sort. The *nouveaux riches* who, according to Phoenix, spent millions on palatial houses with colonnades were criticized for neglecting, not the proletariat, but their own intellectual and spiritual welfare.[50] A similar attack by Cercidas is strictly *ad hominem*: his real complaint about
Zeus favoring greedy cormorants such as Xenon is that the god's scales never incline
toward *him*. This may not be, as Tarn suggested, a conservative call to the aristocracy for reform from within; but neither is it ideological, much less utopian or revolutionary.[51] What Cercidas looked back on with pride in his old age was his pursuit
of the Muses rather than his political activities: for him literature came first.[52] This
offers a neat symbolic contrast to the spirit of Aeschylus, who in writing his own
epitaph mentioned his military service in defense of Athens, but said not a word
about the plays he had written.[53]

Whatever Cercidas may have been, he was no revolutionary, any more than Agis
IV or Cleomenes III of Sparta were revolutionaries in the modern sense. Indeed,
what is strikingly absent from all the social unrest and actual insurrections of this
period is any kind of genuine ideological motivation. No one wanted to change the
system (except a few eccentrics who had dropped out of it, and even in their case the
evidence is ambiguous): the prime aim, always, was to better one's own position

within the system as it stood. Even for rebels stability remained the basic ideal. What had been lost, irretrievably, in the rough transition from the classical to the Hellenistic era was the old sense of social fellowship (*koinōnia*) within a cohesive, self-determined group such as the free *polis* had provided. The Stoic notion of man as world citizen (*kosmopolitēs*), though it recognized this disorientation, was a poor and ultimately meaningless alternative. Local substitutes abounded—the gymnasium, various types of club and association (*eranos, thiasos*), all the trivia and trumpery honors of the *polis* in reduced circumstances—but none was altogether adequate. There remained a void at the heart of things, a rootlessness that was one of the Hellenistic age's most enduring and characteristic features.

Oddly, the one group to derive positive benefit from these developments was that of the classical era's silent half—women. Previously, real freedom had been restricted to the morally compromised *hetaira*, and carried severe disadvantages with it. But the swing away from public involvement, the all-masculine ideal, to more private and personal concerns—as we have seen in the visual arts, the plays of Menander, the delineation of Medea by Apollonius, the search for *ataraxia*—meant, inevitably, a higher value being placed on human relationships, on romantic affections, and, most important of all, on the institution of marriage, which came to be seen as something more than a mere family contract.[54] One inevitable side effect of all this was an upgrading of heterosexual passion and a consequent striking improvement in the status of respectable women. Menander's old men may still haggle over dowries, but his juveniles are besotted with love, and their love, now, frequently leads them into marriage. Bereaved husbands and wives, too, speak of their dead spouses in funerary epigrams that reveal real affection, personal grief:[55]

> Traveler, feel no regrets as you pass by my monument:
>   I've no cause for lamentation, even in death.
> I left children and grandchildren, grew old enjoyably
>   With the same dear wife; married off three sons,
> Rocked their babies asleep on my lap, so often,
>   And none of them got sick, none died: no grief.
> So now they in their turn have poured wine for my painless journey,
>   Sent me off to that sweet sleep among the holy dead.

It should not, however, be assumed from such evidence that a sudden wave of middle-class respectability had hit Greek society, the kind of cloying, all-pervasive familial sentiment that we find in Plutarch or, later, in Dickens and Coventry Patmore. The erotic in all its manifestations, in or out of wedlock, heterosexual or homosexual, was now at a premium: puritanism remained, as always, a minority option. Nothing so clearly symbolized the shift from public to private life, from civic involvement to personal self-absorption, from duty to hedonism, as the enhanced value placed, at all levels, on personal relationships. Those who had been *engagé* now got themselves engaged, while the best and most disinterested of a citizen's old political virtues were devoted to safeguarding the future for his wife and children.

Among the well-to-do classes, at any rate, girls were now given a better education—witness the women poets and artists who begin to appear in Hellenistic times[56]—while wives, if not daughters, were clearly far freer in their movements than those of the fifth and early fourth centuries: the smart middle-class ladies depicted by Herodas or Theocritus come and go as they please, to shops or concerts or temples (above, pp. 243 ff.). It has been suggested that the so-called inspectors of women (*gynaikonomoi*) who are found, for example, in the Athens ruled by Demetrius of Phaleron, represent a chauvinist male reaction against this new sexual liberty.[57] I think it far more likely that they were part of a general attempt to clamp down sumptuary restrictions on excessive luxury (highly visible in the form of silk dresses, jewelry, and other forms of feminine display), and that the mood they represent is rather the fundamentally conservative, anticonsumer, disciplinary revisionism that we can see in a poet such as Cercidas. How far women of all classes acquiesced in the established practice of exposing or selling off unwanted daughters at birth,[58] or the more radical methods of disposal that developed from the late third century onwards in Greece (above, p. 386), we cannot be certain. There are no known criticisms of such activities till well into the Roman imperial period, and then the most notable comes from a male Stoic ex-slave, Epictetus.[59] Nor can the motive have been a widespread fear of too many mouths to feed, since during the late Hellenistic period the birth rate in Greece seems to have fallen—certainly among the wealthier classes—and the Roman civil wars left much of Greece desolate and uninhabited. It looks very much as though Polybius, describing this situation in the mid-second century, may have been right when he attributed the apparent low birth rate (if not the depopulation of certain areas) to pure greed, irresponsibility, and the pursuit of affluence, which led a number of prosperous men either to avoid marriage altogether, or else to rear no more than one or two children, disposing of the rest for profit.[60]

The *oikoumenē* did break down the old ethnic barriers with progressive thoroughness as time went on: as Tarn says, "Juvenal's esurient Greekling had often little that was Greek about him but his name and speech," though this did nothing to remove his ethnic prejudices.[61] The old class distinctions were, more often than not, simply replaced by the yardstick of income. In cosmopolis who you were mattered much less than how much you made. The millionaire called the civic shots, most noticeably in the quasi-independent cities like Corinth or Athens, Ephesus or Miletus, where we find public-minded benefactors staving off famine with wheat consignments, issuing free passes to festivals, lending the city large sums interest-free, building gymnasia and temples, underwriting military expenses, providing banquets, serving without fee on embassies, sometimes even footing the bill for the commemorative statues voted in their honor by grateful fellow citizens.[62] Public finances, on the other hand, tended, as we have seen (above, p. 376), to be shaky, and to rely unduly on *epidoseis* from the private sector. It often looks very much as though most of these Hellenistic Greek communities—certainly those outside the major kingdoms—survived, hand to mouth, on the casual generosity of their wealthiest members, the aggregate of their private, wholly undirected, capital resources.[63] But whether in Alexandria or Antioch, Rhodes or Athens, the same overall impression predominates: a *laissez-faire* economy run by and for an elite, who kept the simmering pot of social unrest from boiling over by random handouts that had little to do with philanthropy in the modern sense of the word.[64]

Samos, about the mid-third century,[65] did establish relief funds earmarked for the purchase and distribution of emergency grain; but even this was largely supported and run by the same small group of plutocrats. In any case, *ad hoc* charity was only a palliative, not a cure. The sufferings of the labor force, which lay at the root of the problem, could only have been eradicated by a fundamental change in the whole economic and administrative system of the Hellenistic world; and for that there was neither the desire nor the theoretical knowledge. Instead, the old system was strained to breaking point by the Romans, who played Alexander's game of making people pay through the nose for the privilege of being conquered, and did it with such brutal and efficient cynicism that in little more than a century they virtually bankrupted the Greek world. There were riches galore for the taking, and generals from Sulla to Antony were not slow to skim the cream. What they left, the tax collectors (*publicani*) and provincial governors soon absorbed. But the system still had not changed.

Rising prices, low wages, and the competition of slave labor meant a perennially bleak outlook for the unskilled or semiskilled free worker. It is surprising, in fact, how few uprisings actually took place. (In Egypt, where conditions had always been depressed, the second century witnessed a series of rebellions by the native peasantry [above, p. 323], but this seems to have been at least as much a nationalistic as an economic phenomenon, directed against foreign rule as such.) Strikes of free laborers are known; but they were infrequent, and very hard to sustain—especially without substantial reserve funds—in the face of an autocratic government that could always replace the strikers with slaves. But even if social rebellion was in fact rare, the fear of it can be found in our sources—conservative almost to a man—from the fourth century onwards. We have already noted that both Alexander's and Demetrius Poliorcetes' treaties with the cities that formed the League of Corinth contained a specific clause calling upon Macedonia and League members to suppress any movement involving abolition of debt, redistribution of land, confiscation of personal property, or the freeing of slaves to promote revolution (above, p. 252).[66]

This is revealing. As a radical program it is, first and last, agricultural: it takes no account whatsoever of commercial developments or urbanization. It is also remarkably old-fashioned. There is nothing innovative about this manifesto; it could well have been put out in the archaic, let alone the classical, era. The first two items, indeed, had been hotly debated at Athens in Solon's day, over three hundred years earlier (594/3?), and the last two were equally familiar. Plato in both the *Republic* and the *Laws* was continually concerned with the agrarian problem of haves and have-nots, though he hardly dealt with it in a way calculated to soothe the latter group.[67] Isocrates in various treatises gives a graphic picture of *stasis*, pillaging, destitution,

and wandering desperadoes; but his all-purpose cure for such ills was a war of conquest against the barbarian, followed by mass emigration to alleviate land hunger,
and some of the things that we would regard as measures (however inadequate) to
deal with the situation—abolition of debts, redistribution of land, and revisions in
the constitution—Isocrates saw rather as antecedent causes of social anarchy.[68] In
short, we are concerned, essentially, with the same kind of agrarian economy still:
only the scale of operations has changed. The debts are those of peasants or smallholders; the land is land they have lost through pledging it after a succession of bad
harvests. Urban property does not enter into consideration here. Confiscation,
again, is clearly of the stock and buildings on rural estates. Similarly, the slaves to be
freed are country-estate workers, and not any kind of city proletariat (the first Sicilian rising of 139 offers good evidence for this).[69] Despite the growth of the economy, nothing could more plainly show how little the nature of that economy had
changed. Nor, indeed, had the exploitation that provoked unrest taken on a new
face: it too was the old system still, more effectively done, better organized, and
operated through a bureaucracy rather than by individual landowners.

It is, then, perhaps not altogether surprising that the actual risings we know
about are lacking in specific revolutionary content, and that several of them, indeed,
are not revolutionary at all.[70] One of the most interesting episodes took place on the
island of Chios, probably in the early third century,[71] and is reported by Nymphodorus of Syracuse.[72] Numerous slaves deserted and took to the hills under a slave
named Drimakos, who "led the fugitive slaves as a king leads an army." His military
organization proved highly successful: he staved off numerous attacks by the Chians,
and finally made a treaty with them, which allowed him and his band to live undisturbed in the mountains. As a *quid pro quo* he promised moderation in robbing
their storehouses(!), and a scrutiny of all slaves who in future applied to join him: he
would accept only those who had suffered "irreparable damage" from their masters,
and the rest would be sent back. He maintained strict discipline among his followers,
and survived to a ripe old age. He then told his boy lover to kill him, take his head to
the Chian authorities, and claim the price they had set on it. It is sadly ironic that his
advice to the boy as to what he should do with the money thus realized was, first and
foremost, to get himself a gentleman's education.[73] The sophists and Isocrates had
not labored in vain.

After Drimakos's death a hero's shrine was built in his honor, and myths began
to circulate about him: he was, for example, supposed to warn Chians in dreams of
plots being hatched by their slaves—hardly, one might have thought, a revolutionary characteristic. What it rather suggests is coexistence: by far the most interesting
feature of the Drimakos story, and something that recurs in both Sicilian slave wars,
is the attempt to form a permanent alternative society. It is, moreover, a society of
the Homeric sort, in that it survives by raiding the property of others. There is no
hint of any ideological opposition to the society from which the slaves have escaped,
no determination to tear it down and replace it with some brave new utopian ideal:
indeed, the coexistence implies a close symbiotic relationship. Without those store-
houses to raid, those sacrificial animals to steal, Drimakos and his men would have

to become farmers and herdsmen themselves, return to the old heartbreaking cycle on their own account. That they did not envisage such a course is both symptomatic and revealing.

What we glimpse here is yet another attempt to realize that perennial utopian fantasy of the Greek world, agricultural plenty minus the toil that goes with it. It is the memory of a lost Golden Age: probably, as Dicaearchus seems to have realized, folk recollection of the Stone Age hunting era, when the still-seminomadic population ate wild fruit, grains, and berries, free from the backbreaking cycle of cultivation.[74] Then, as Hesiod put it, men lived like gods, without toil or grief.[75] The fertile earth bore fruit for them in abundance. All men in the beginning had been equal ("When Adam delved and Eve span / Who was then the gentleman?": things had not changed much by Wat Tyler's rebellion of 1381). There were no slaves. The absence of toil was a regular feature of this myth, and—most interestingly for modern students—it was, from a very early period, closely linked with the idea of automation.[76] Not only did the earth then produce her bounty unaided; from Homer's day onwards servile work was regularly thought of as being done, in an ideal world, by machines, like those Hephaestus designed for household chores.[77] Better still was the idea of self-functioning pots, tables, cups, or (an interesting forecast) plumbing. "What was needed came of its own accord."[78] In the fifth century the comic poets regularly evoked a society in which rivers ran wine and gravy, fish obligingly baked themselves, trees bore roast birds that still managed to fly into the diner's mouth, kitchens did their own cooking, dishes were washed without human aid.[79] "If things were like that," one of the discussants in the *Deipnosophistae* very reasonably asks, "what need did we have of servants?"[80] Just so. The impulse may have been fantastic and escapist, but it nevertheless also got hold of a very sound social perception, which was given its most memorable early expression by Aristotle: that nothing but automation would ever abolish slavery.[81] Nearly two millennia later this insight was proved uncomfortably correct, since not until the Industrial Revolution brought automation within the realm of the practicable did Christian and other moralists suddenly discover that their consciences could no longer tolerate servitude.

The so-called proletarian revolt that took place at Cassandreia in 279, and was finally put down by Antigonus Gonatas, had nothing genuinely proletarian about it, but, as Diodorus makes clear, was an old-fashioned tyranny.[82] Its leader, Apollodorus, operating in time-honored style, seized power with the aid of Galatian mercenaries, and established himself by raising the *dēmos* against the oligarchs: nothing revolutionary there, unless every case of *stasis* is to be so described. Similarly, the evidence for fear of internal revolution sometimes adduced from Aeneas Tacticus's monograph on siege warfare in fact also deals with instances of traditional *stasis*, endemic to *polis* life from the archaic period onwards.[83] The activities of Agis IV and Cleomenes III at Sparta we have already examined: they too did not raise revolutions in the modern sense, but rather military coups that aimed to restore the power and authority of a ruling elite, the *homoioi* who monopolized any equality (*isotēs*) going. Nabis, who came to power in 207 (above, p. 301), might seem at first sight to have been more radical (he freed a number of helots, though he does not seem to have dealt with the problem of helotage as such); yet it is hard to believe that he was not making a bid to finish the work that Agis and Cleomenes had begun. In any case, the tradition concerning him is so violently hostile that to sift truth from propaganda in it is virtually impossible.[84] If he was not a mere run-of-the-mill tyrant, no more was he a Bolshevik born before his time.[85]

To terrorize your opponents by mass executions, to raise quick funds by despoliating men of property—these were well-tried devices throughout antiquity, without any basic ideological connotations. The cries of the threatened rich might seem to suggest otherwise; but any attack on the *status quo*, for whatever end, was liable to elicit the same anguished scream from those who had clawed their way to the top of the heap, or through birth or wealth had inherited a place in the sun. In this connection we should note that one slow but fundamental change in Greek society since the fifth century had been the completion of what Solon had begun, the shift of status from blood to capital, with a concomitant blurring of the class structure and a huge increase in upward mobility. When the haves are largely those who have made it by their own efforts, it becomes very hard for a have-not (who may yet do the same) to think ideologically in terms of a rigid class-bound society. What Nabis really appealed to (in addition to ambition) was a mixture of patriotism, nostalgia for the *ancien régime*, and the snobbery of belonging to an exclusive club: small wonder that he found support. His failure was largely due to a chronic shortage of funds, coupled with the severe decrease in population that Polybius noted for Greece (above, p. 389), which was particularly acute at Sparta.

Agrarian debt-encumbrance continued to cause trouble, prior to 200, in Thessaly and Boeotia and the Aetolian League; but this kind of problem had been endemic to the system since Solon's day, and hardly suggests a new ideology. The slave risings that broke out like an epidemic shortly before 130 were almost certainly encouraged by what took place in Sicily under the leadership of a miracle-working Syrian named Eunus;[86] and it is noteworthy that what Eunus aimed to set up was a replica, down to the last detail, of the royal Seleucid court—he even renamed himself Antiochus, and two of his henchmen similarly took the names of Antiochus III's ministers.[87] Again, the ultimate aim was an alternative society. On the other hand the revolts of slaves on Delos and, particularly, in the mining area of Attica, seem to have been nothing more than desperate protests against intolerable conditions. Once they had been put down there were no repetitions.[88]

The most interesting instance, and the one most touted by ideologists, is the rising at Pergamon led by Aristonicus, in 132.[89] Aristonicus aimed at creating a new "City of the Sun"; he was joined in this endeavor by the Stoic philosopher Blossius of Cumae, who had been tried for high treason after the death of his friend Tiberius Gracchus, but, luckily, acquitted. Now perhaps about 250 or 225 (the exact date remains uncertain) one Iambulus had written a utopian novel about an island on the equator, in the Indian Ocean, inhabited by sun worshippers: a communal paradise of tall sages with hairless skin and flexible bones, who lived in kinship groups of about four hundred persons, shared all property (women and children included: there was no marriage), and voluntarily committed suicide, by lying down on a lethally

soporific plant, at the age of 150, or sooner if crippled or diseased.[90] It has been argued that Aristonicus, with Blossius's advice, was trying to establish this odd Heliopolis on earth.[91] Now it is quite possible that Aristonicus knew Iambulus's fable,
even that he borrowed the idea of Sun Citizens (*Hēliopolitai*) from it.[92] But at the
same time we should take heed of Finley's salutary warning, for a society in which
literature was monopolized by the educated (i.e., upper) classes, "against seeking
some particular book behind every popular idea or popular action."[93] More important is the fact that Aristonicus was an illegitimate aspirant to the throne of Pergamon, and furious because Attalus III had, the year before, bequeathed his entire
kingdom to Rome (cf. below, p. 529). His appeal to the serfs on the great estates,
and the uncommitted smallholders of the interior (as opposed to the wealthy, who
were only too willing to truck with Rome, and, as usual, took fright at any threat to
redistribute wealth or land), sounds far more like personal and nationalist ambition.[94] That he held out promises of freedom and justice to his supporters is likely
enough, and this may well have involved the connection, common in Near Eastern
religious thought, between the divine sun and human justice.[95] But the motivation,
again, is hardly ideological.[96]

It is not easy to take any of the Hellenistic utopias seriously: they positively invited the unkind attention of a satirist such as Lucian, being "escapist, uncommitted,
and gelatinous."[97] Behind most of them lurks the ideal of *ataraxia*, escape from
stress: universal brotherhood expressed in terms of fugal myths glorifying the distant and exotic, the Noble Savage as Scyth, Indian, or Hyperborean, the rehashing
of sailors' yarns (above, p. 327), the self-tilling allegorical landscape of Theopompus, with its city called Pious (*Eusebēs*) enjoying perpetual peace and an absence of all
diseases, not to mention rivers called Pleasure (*Hēdonē*) and Grief (*Lypē*) a contrasting *polis* of warriors known as Warlike (*Machimos*), and a mysterious City of No
Return (*Anostos*) enveloped in "fog and fiery turbidity."[98] It is noteworthy that since
Plato's day the ideal of the *polis* has been largely abandoned, and that there is a more
flexible cooperation at least envisaged between social classes; the old sharp distinction between Greek and barbarian has likewise been greatly modified.[99] All this is
just what we would expect from the other evidence we have studied.

Nothing better demonstrates the well-articulated power of the social *status quo*
than the fact that only in dream and fantasy do we find such principles as the abolition of slavery, or communism, free love, social anarchy (no temples, law courts, or
gymnasia; even more important, no coinage), universal citizenship, the perfectibility
of man and nature, the outlawing of private property. These notions were not new;
Zeno and the Cynics toyed with them (below, p. 639); Aristophanes made several of
them the basis for some of his most hilarious comedies (*Lysistrata*, *Ecclesiazusae*) as
early as the fifth century. No accident that in the brave new feminist world of Prax-
agora the farm work, it turns out, will be done by the slaves;[100] but then, Mrs. Pank-
hurst never envisaged a world without maids. Nor are the schemes of Phaleas of
Chalcedon and Hippodamus of Miletus, examined by Aristotle in the *Politics*, any
more egalitarian, but closely modeled on the Spartan system.[101] Phaleas wanted
equality of land *klēroi* for an elite, while all artisans and craftsmen were to be reduced

to the status of public slaves; Hippodamus proposed a three-class system of warriors, farmers, and artisans, wherein the last-named, again, were set up as second-class citizens, having neither land nor the right to bear arms.

Besides Iambulus, Euhemerus (p. 55) also presented an ideal society, lodged, again, on an island (Panchaia), somewhere in the Indian Ocean, purged of nature's more savage elements, and functioning in a blissful void under the watchful solar eye of heaven[102]—but, we may note, like Hippodamus's model, firmly tied to a static three-class social tiering: priests and administrators first, then farmers, with soldiers and herdsmen at the bottom of the heap.[103] Hardly a communist paradise. With the possible exception of Aristonicus, no one, so far as we can tell, ever thought of actually putting these ideas into practice.[104] The one case we hear of is, as we might expect, a private venture on the part of an eccentric, with no revolutionary violence involved, an Epicurean-style withdrawal from society supported by ample private funds. Cassander's brother Alexarchus is said to have founded a city named Ouranopolis, "The City of Heaven," on the Athos peninsula: it would be nice to think that the monastic tradition there owed something, even if only indirectly, to his example. We should not attach too much significance to the fact that he took the radiant sun as a symbol on the coins he struck, since the sunburst, though used in Near Eastern sun cults, may also have served, at least since Philip II's day, as the emblem of the Macedonian Argead dynasty.[105] More interestingly, he was a linguist, who invented a language for his foundation: a specimen preserved by Athenaeus looks like the Greek equivalent of Anthony Burgess's Nadsat in *A Clockwork Orange*, foreign loan words oddly compounded.[106] It would be interesting to know if he actually got people to talk that way. But this dotty (and obviously financially secure) contracting-out has more in common with Coleridge's dream, in 1794, of Pantisocracy on the banks of the Susquehanna than with any kind of organic movement to change the fundamental structure of Hellenistic society. The notion of the alternative society, on the other hand, deserves more attention than it has hitherto received: at least it restated the popular urge to reject society as it stood in positive, constructive terms. All it needed—but failed to discover—was its America.

CHAPTER 23

RULER CULTS, TRADITIONAL RELIGION, AND THE AMBIVALENCE OF TYCHE

Belief—its presence or absence, and, where present, its nature—forms one of the most revealing guides to any culture. We have already noted, in passing, some of the more characteristic religious trends in the Hellenistic period: the steady erosion of the old Olympian pantheon (still accorded traditional public honors, but progressively more peripheral); a corresponding increased addiction to foreign, and particularly enthusiastic, cults; a preoccupation with Tyche (Fate, Fortune, Chance);[1] the practice of instituting ruler cults, at first of deceased monarchs, but soon of the throne's living occupant;[2] and, in Egypt at least, the deliberate fostering of official cults devoted to quasi-Hellenized and in part syncretic deities such as Sarapis and Isis. Striking developments in mathematics and astronomy were accompanied by the efflorescence of the latter's bastardized (and essentially deterministic) offshoot, astrology, which became as popular as the Tyche cult, and for very similar reasons (below, pp. 453 ff., 595). The papyri, the curse tablets (*defixionum tabellae*), and the literary sources also reveal a rapid growth in the practice of magic, which we may define, in this context, as a system of bypassing both natural law and the divine order to manipulate for one's own private benefit anything from the weather to erotic impulses.

How far can we relate these various phenomena, first, to each other, and second, to the sociopolitical patterns we have seen developing in the Successor kingdoms? The most striking, and obvious, characteristic we find here, overall, is a clear disillusionment with the efficacy or validity of traditional religion. The old gods—Zeus above all, but also Poseidon, Athena, and the rest—retain their official civic status: their worship and calendar were too deeply embedded in the structure of *polis* life; they were part of the obsolescent fabric to which Greek city dwellers obstinately clung. Zeus, who even in Aeschylus's day had been ripe for revamping as a universal divine power, was a special case. During the Hellenistic period he not only served the Stoics as a kind of holy holdall for anything from common custom (*koinos nomos*)

396

to right thinking (*orthos logos*), but at a popular level was, like Isis (below, p. 410), assimilated to a bewildering assortment of (mostly Oriental) deities—Ahura Mazda, Sabazios, Sarapis, Amon, even Yahweh[3]—in a process of mass syncretization known as *theokrasia*. In the Graeco-Roman period the titles accumulate and multiply: we find, in dedications and the papyri, such composite monsters as "Zeus Helios Mithras Sarapis Aniketos [= "Unconquered"; and with that lineup, why not?]."[4] The Seleucids offered special worship to Apollo:[5] the god, it was claimed, had sired Seleucus I, and left in his mother's bed a ring with an anchor device on the bezel. Legitimate descendants in the direct line were all said to have an anchor-shaped mark on their thigh.[6] The propaganda is palpable but significant.

The Attalids, similarly, instituted a special cult of Athena,[7] while in Egypt, Dionysus was held in high honor, especially by Ptolemy IV Philopator.[8] The citizens of Alexandria invoked, and took official oaths by, the trinity of Zeus, Hera, and Poseidon.[9] The Antigonids associated themselves with Heracles, the putative founder of the Argead dynasty.[10] Clearly, the prime motive activating all three major dynasties in such associative *pietas* was an urge for legitimization by divine pedigree. "The new kings who succeeded Alexander were all in a sense usurpers,"[11] and thus anxious to justify their rule: descent from a god was still regarded as the best royal qualification going. This did not mean that the gods themselves, in the business of everyday life, were always taken seriously. Ethical and scientific advances had robbed them of many of their original functions as anthropomorphized natural forces, and middle-class city dwellers had long looked askance at their indifference to civic morality. The polyphiloprogenitive habits of Zeus or Heracles, so uncomfortably reminiscent of primitive tribal chieftains, were a perennial embarrassment. Spiteful Olympian vendettas offered ample scope for Euripidean satire. Thunder, lightning, earthquakes, and eclipses, even the movements of the heavenly bodies, were all being shifted firmly out of the sacral domain.

The philosophers, too, were busy with religion, doing their best, in the spirit of Anaxagoras, to redesign the Father of Gods and Men as a power almost as abstract as Mind (*Nous*). This trend led later to wholesale allegorizing that was, arguably, even more embarrassing than the myths it tried to explain away: here the Stoics have a lot to answer for. Chrysippus interpreted Athena's title Tritogeneia ("Trito-born") as symbolizing the triple division of philosophy into logic, ethics, and physics. The same explanation was used, even more grotesquely, to account for the hellhound Cerberus's three heads. This *cocasserie* may possibly be traced back to Cleanthes, the religiose ex-boxer who succeeded Zeno of Citium as head of the Stoa (263–232), and anticipated the Holy Office by denouncing Aristarchus's heliocentric theory as impious atheism (p. 186).[12] Furthermore, the Olympian pantheon had been very much local, city-state deities in origin, and "the transplanting of city-gods to the East was a more delicate undertaking than Apollonius' experiments in the acclimatisation of fruit trees."[13] Like some wines, they did not travel too well. There were also, now, in this transformed world, too many emotional, intellectual, and ethical problems for which they offered no solution, too many aspects of their nature that could only be seen as, at best, archaic and irrelevant anachronisms.

The natural outcome of those scientific and exploratory trends that characterize the late archaic and classical periods was a far greater reliance by man on his own creative or analytical resources. The investigations of the sixth-century Milesian physicists, the New Learning propagated by the sophists of the Periclean era, all encouraged an anthropocentric attitude to life, summed up by Protagoras's famous tag, Man the measure of all things—not to mention his notorious claim to be able to make the weaker argument the stronger, and, even more notorious, his professed inability to know whether or not the gods existed.[14] Though for traditionalists his disclaimer smacked of atheism,[15] and his self-reliance of hybris and arrogance (we can catch echoes of the debate in Aeschylus's *Prometheus* and Sophocles' *Antigone* and *Oedipus*), the general attitude they embodied continued to gain ground in the fourth and third centuries. Man had moved boldly into more and more areas hitherto dominated by the old gods, and the gods had, when appealed to, offered unpredictable help, or, worse, no help at all. (It is significant that political, as opposed to ritual or private, consultations of the Delphic Oracle cease by the mid-fourth century.)[16] Besides, were not philosophers such as Aristotle now proclaiming that men should emulate gods? "We must not think only in mortal terms," he wrote in the *Nicomachean Ethics*[17]—thus deliberately challenging one traditional religious tenet, Think mortal—"but, as far as we can, make ourselves like immortals," an aim that was to be realized through the life of pure reason.

There was also the influential, and far from coincidental, theory of Euhemerus (which, as we have seen [p. 189], developed and spread precisely when ruler cults were coming into vogue), maintaining that the gods themselves had originally been great monarchs honored for their achievements on earth. In that case, if the gods were no more than powerful kings enjoying apotheosis, then their number could be added to from among suitable modern candidates. The way was open to recognize the great rulers (and some not so great) of the Hellenistic era as gods themselves. It is against this background that we should consider the famous, or notorious, Athenian hymn to Demetrius the Besieger that we glanced at earlier.[18] Demetrius was greeted as the son of Poseidon and Aphrodite; his wife Phila, as an avatar of Demeter. Then followed the claim that the other gods were deaf, or indifferent, or absent, whereas " *You* are here, and visible to us, / Not carved in wood or stone, but real, / So to you we pray." The prayer that follows is—like most Greek prayers—both specific and practical: bring peace, and rid us of those marauding Aetolians (here symbolized as a new, devouring Sphinx). The quotation breaks off before we learn what Athens will offer her refurbished human god in return for such favors. In 304/3 it had been the back chamber of the Parthenon as a residence, with Athena as his sister, an ace it would be hard to trump on the second round.[19]

If the flattery was palpable, it also hints at desperation; and by no means all Athenians endorsed it. The sycophantic excesses honoring Demetrius were violently attacked—after 301, it is true, when Demetrius was safely out of the way—by the comic playwright Philippides, a friend of Lysimachus, who in 285 received an honorific decree for his services to Athens.[20] Interestingly, the criticism is not directed at flattery *per se*, but takes a surprisingly old-fashioned religious tack, claiming that

Athenian misfortunes can be ascribed to the impiety that sanctioned such hybristic assumption of godhead by a mere mortal:[21]

> The man who chopped the year into a single month,
> Who made the Acropolis his common doss house,
> Bringing whores into the Virgin Goddess's shrine,
> Because of whom the frost burned up our vines,
> Through whose impiety the Robe was split asunder
> Because he took for men the gods' rights—*this*,
> Not comedy, is what destroys our people.

One clear implication is that those who vote such honors are at least as culpable as those who accept them;[22] but the passage as a whole should make us cautious about overestimating the degree of public cynicism we might infer from the hymn itself. Religious traditionalism, the fear of divine retribution, still had a strong grip on the majority of Athenians, and fostered, in an increasingly godless age, remarkable susceptibility to any exotic cult with emotional drawing power.

It was the thinking man, familiar with progressive ideas, who, as always, proved most susceptible to antireligious rationalism; and, again as always, it was the intellectuals, the philosophers and poets and playwrights, the articulate formulators of ideas, who both spearheaded the new trends and left us our only surviving records of them. The evidence thus tends to be misleading. We sometimes forget the stubborn, glacial resistance, at a lower level, to what must seem, in retrospect, a general collapse of faith. The hymn to Demetrius, in its pragmatic realism, is (as has often been remarked) a logical consequence of the sophistic movement; but what proportion of the population did that movement really affect, even in the third century? How far did such ideas effectively penetrate? The same question arises over the obvious Epicurean element in the hymn, the removal of the gods from the center of human affairs to some remote Elysium, where they command the occasional polite genuflection, for old time's sake, but play no vital part in men's daily lives. And how many people were ready to dismiss the gods' images as mere idols rather than finding them a comforting focal point for prayer?

There was, at the same time, an obvious attraction in the idea of the god manifest on earth, incarnate as the reigning monarch, and physically accessible to his petitioners. At such a level it is easy to see how the great Hellenistic dynasts could step into the shoes of the Olympians. Both politically and psychologically it was an easy transition. And among educated persons (which included most Epicureans, and just about everyone exposed to the sophists' persuasive syllogisms) it did indeed reflect a substantial decline in traditional religious belief as such. The only gods worth having, the argument ran, the only true potential benefactors, are here on earth: no wonder Euhemerus enjoyed such popularity. But not everyone was educated; and indeed not even all those whose intellect officially freed them from superstition could avoid an inarticulate sense of loss, of spiritual starvation. Their brains told them one thing; their emotions, quite another. Since anthropomorphism had become increasingly disreputable among the educated ever since Xenophanes took it apart in the sixth century (after all, men who had made themselves the measure of all things hardly needed the competition of gods, even gods created in their own image), these emotional needs tended to seek satisfaction in rather different fields.[23]

Hence, of course, the growing addiction to magic, a do-it-yourself power trip that enabled the adept to usurp controls hitherto reserved for nature or the gods. (The gods alone had had the privilege of reversing nature: this now emerged as a popular attribute of Hellenistic and Graeco-Roman witches.) Hence, too, the cult of Tyche—"Tyche, a tyrant over all the gods," wrote the fourth-century tragedian Chaeremon[24]—and the obsession with astrology: not only a bypassing, again, of actual deities (Antioch's anthropomorphized Tyche was no more than an allegory in human form), not just a weary shelving of human responsibility, but also a bid to deal with the tyrannous, if seemingly random,[25] unpredictabilities of existence.[26] The principle was much akin to that of the professional gambler with a system. If the universe operated on a deterministic basis, then it should not be beyond man's wit to figure out the pattern and live a life forewarned and forearmed. Hence astrology, which offered an elaborate mathematical pseudoscience of prediction based on the Stoic notion of cosmic order in the heavens. The Stoics in general, as we shall see, were profoundly antiscientific:[27] this did not stop Zeno's student Persaeus from arguing—with a characteristic string of negative epithets—that the wise man should remain undefeated, unenslaved, uncontaminated, and unaffected by Tyche.[28] Tyche as such was simply a recognition of this random factor in human affairs, stripped of divine motivation, and thus liable to veer between the unknowable (for which prayer to someone or something still seemed the only hope) and the merely inscrutable (which could, with luck, be rationalized into a pattern).[29] The bitter curses against Tyche on so many grave inscriptions show that, like Moira (Fate, Destiny), Tyche was often identified with the final, if unpredictable, inevitability of death.[30] The Alexandrians, with a nice blend of optimism and cynicism, maintained a cult of an anthropomorphic goddess called Agathe Tyche, "Good Fortune"—the scales, as it were, always weighted on the hopeful side.[31]

There is a detectable progression from specificity to abstraction, from individual deities to "the gods" in general, and then to phrases such as "the divine element" (*to theion, to daimonion*), when attributing ulterior responsibility for human affairs.[32] The development of Tyche fits in well with this wider shift of attitude. Etymologically *tychē* is cognate with the verb *tychein* or *tynchanein*: transitively, to hit the mark, attain one's goal; intransitively, to happen, and hence, on occasion, to happen *to* someone.[33] The verb occurs in Homer, primarily with the satisfied connotation of success; the noun does not. Homeric man may be subject to the gods and to *moira*, his allotted destiny; but by and large they do not stop him going for, and getting (*tychein*), what he wants. He is not pushed around by inexplicable happenstance. With Hesiod and the lyric poets, however, Tyche appears as an external, palpable, quasi-personified force,[34] distinct from Moira, sometimes neutral or even benevolent, more often malign: what happens *to* one, increasingly seen as happenstance rather than an act of God, the unwilled, unpredictable factor. As time goes on it becomes progressively wider in scope, more irresistible, more fatal in every sense. "How am I, a mortal, to fight against godlike Tyche?" asks one of Sophocles' characters, and the question is not rhetorical.[35] Critias, that aristocratic intellectual ultra, might claim that Tyche fought on the side of right-thinking people;[36] but this smacked of hybris, and Critias duly came to a bad end. In his *Cyclops* (424/3?) Euripides makes Odysseus argue that flagrant divine injustice necessitates "regarding Tyche as a divinity, and the attributes of divinity as less than Tyche."[37] Tyche undoubtedly benefited from the weakening of religious ties at the end of the fifth century. There is a semantic slide here, accentuated as time goes on, that suggests progressive loss of control over one's own destiny. The characteristic of malevolence or envy so often associated—surprisingly at first sight—with this nonsentient force, even by so intelligent a writer as Polybius, is generally ascribed to ingrained Greek anthropomorphism;[38] but it could also be produced by civilized discomfort at the *ad hominem* spitefulness of the archaic gods, and a strong desire to relocate so embarrassing an attitude elsewhere, in a nonanthropomorphic context.[39]

By the end of the fourth century this aspect of Tyche was well established.[40] Demetrius of Phaleron brooded on the ineluctable reversals of fortune that Tyche brought (above, p. 271). Philemon distinguished between Tyche and pure accident (*to automaton*),[41] probably following Aristotle, who devoted much thought to defining both—for him *to automaton* was any kind of accident, whereas *tychē* could be applied only to sentient beings capable of choice—and to estimating their validity in the chain of causation.[42] He admitted, in passing, that there were those who regarded *tychē* as "being in some sense divine,"[43] but he did not pursue the implications inherent in such a view.[44] It could, as we have seen in the case of Polybius (above, p. 273), lead to considerable intellectual confusion,[45] since, though he reserved it, in theory, for those aspects of human affairs that defied all rational explanation, we find him also treating it as a conscious and teleological force shaping the destiny of nations;[46] and it is not hard to see how the concept of an individual's personal Tyche, determined at his birth,[47] could be accommodated, as time went on, to the pseudorational mystique of casting his horoscope.

We will deal later with the magic, the astrology, the foreign and mystery cults, what might be termed the uncontrollable emotional component of Hellenistic religion (pp. 586 ff.). For the present, I want to concentrate on its more rational, secular, political manifestations: the enskyment—sometimes by literal assumption to heaven—of the monarch, the new official cults, and Tyche as a kind of ambivalent halfway house between nontheistic thinking and the old divinely ordered cosmos. In considering the nature of the various ruler cults that emerge during our period, we need to ask a number of careful questions about them. The first, often neglected, is: How did the Greeks and Macedonians themselves view such a cult? Did they, in any real sense, believe that the monarch in question had been deified, contained a genuine spark of divinity? Put in such terms, the answer is clearly no, they did not. Alexander's deeds outshone those of the gods, yet his demand to be worshipped as a god himself aroused ribald mockery and contempt.[48] Society had come a long way since the sacred god-kings of Ur and the Egyptian Old Kingdom. There is no record of a Hellenistic ruler cult that was set up in genuine religious belief.[49]

Indeed, if the cult now signified anything in purely religious terms, it was a rejection of belief, as the hymn addressed to Demetrius strongly suggests. Mere mortals, with Euhemerus to encourage them, were now to be raised to that pinnacle hitherto reserved for deities long remote, in nature and powers alike, from mankind. The mystery, and indeed the functions, of these archaic gods had been severely curtailed by two centuries of scientific inquiry. Zeus's mythic instinct for nailing Prometheus to that remote rock was, on his own terms, very sound: no god whose *numen* depends on human ignorance of the natural order can afford to leave freethinking investigators and inventors on the loose. If man is the measure, then, *per contra*, divinity gets short shrift. It is highly probable that in many, perhaps the majority, of cases the prime objective in the deification of these rulers was to offer them divine honors. Throughout Greek history, alongside moral warnings against hybristic, more-than-mortal aspirations, we also find the quasi-metaphorical definition of rare individuals as, in some sense, *theoi*, divine, at least in the speaker's estimate: a god *to him*,[50] *isotheos*, the gods' equal, whether in attributes or achievement. Much confusion has been caused by scholars who, having seen that certain humans were given honors that gods also received, drew the conclusion (by a famous logical fallacy) that these kings must have been deified, rather than simply sharing, as a high compliment, some of the gods' divine prerogatives. Sacrifices, sacred enclosures, tombs, statues, prostration (*proskynēsis*), hymns, altars, and other such divine appanages are all, as Aristotle specifically states,[51] simply marks of honor: the gesture itself, not its recipient (whether god or man), is the important thing.

Looked at in these terms actual divinization becomes something of a red herring. Special cases certainly existed, in the sense that some rulers—Alexander the Great almost certainly; Antiochus IV Epiphanes very possibly—became megalomaniac enough to believe in their own godhead, a condition that would make it prudent for others to announce a similar belief; but by and large what we are faced with here is a system of formalized honors that, because of the new political conditions prevailing, went more and more to human recipients. Kings, after all, were potentially helpful patrons: a petitioner knew what he had a reasonable chance of getting. The quasi-divine epithets attached to their names—Savior (*Sōtēr*), Benefactor (*Euergetēs*), God Manifest (*Epiphanēs*: "*You* are here, and visible to us"), Victor (*Nikatōr*)—are highly revealing. A commercial age wanted investments it could see and judge, with a fair chance of returns: this applied to its royal pantheon no less than to its buildings or estates. The Olympians had long paid poor and irregular dividends. Nor was there any check on their activities. Alexandria offers little evidence for the personal, as opposed to the formal and public, cult of the Olympians; more popular were those demotic deities of grain and grape, Demeter and Dionysus, together with that least anthropomorphic of all-purpose deities, the Good Spirit (*Agathos Daimōn*), which sometimes manifested itself as a house snake.[52]

Greek cities everywhere instituted individual cults of the great Hellenistic monarchs. Whatever the motive—gratitude for favors received; hope of favors to come—a sudden collective conversion to royal divinity seems implausible. Lysimachus, as a reward for his military aid to Priene against Magnesia, got an altar, a statue, and an annual procession of priests and magistrates, complete with gold crowns (287/6?).[53] Seleucus Nicator was similarly honored by Ilion with quadrennial games and a month named after him (281/0?).[54] Chalcis even instituted a cult of the Roman Flamininus (ca. 195), who was not, by any stretch of the imagination, divine material: again, thanks for benefits conferred seems the obvious motive.[55] From very soon after Alexander's death municipal cults to the various Successors began to appear in countless Greek cities. Antigonus One-Eye was so honored by Scepsis in 311,[56] and, together with his son Demetrius, at Athens and in the Cyclades a few years later. Ptolemy I received a cult in Rhodes in 304: it was the Rhodians, in fact, who first bestowed on him the title of Soter.[57] Demetrius, again, had an annual festival established in his honor—like a founder, says Diodorus, a telltale point[58]—by the citizens of Sicyon, in gratitude for their "liberation." Acknowledgment of such benefits was a regular motive for the bestowal of divine honorifics,[59] and some came fairly cheap: for reestablishing democracy in Miletus, Antiochus II was entitled to tack on the title God (*Theos*) to his name.[60]

We have already had occasion to notice the orgy of flattery that the Athenians lavished on Demetrius the Besieger and his father: their images woven into the Panathenaic robe, two new tribes bearing their names, and so on (above, p. 48). But such honors could be, and often were, very soon discontinued: the Sicyonians abolished their festival *in toto*; the Athenians, their Antigonid and Demetriad tribes. There are even cases where their names have been chiseled off monuments.[61] At a certain time, in a certain context, they had been the gods' equals, *isotheoi*, and honored accordingly. But that, it seems clear, was all. Such high achievers were *like* the gods—not least, as Aristotle observed, among their fellow men[62]—they deserved similar honors; but they were not, as yet, gods themselves in any meaningful sense. Though Lysimachus and Seleucus I Nicator similarly received statues, games, processions, even priests, there was no question of their divinity. Even Alexander himself, from whose cult so much of this Hellenistic personal enskyment ultimately derived, seems to have had his down-to-earth moments. When he received a slight wound in the ankle during his Indian campaign, a bystander quoted Homer—"Ichor, such as flows from the blessed gods"—to be cut short with the testy comment, "That's not ichor; that's *blood*."[63] It is also worth noting that some dynasties, for example the Attalids (below, p. 406), were less enamored of such recognition than others. Antigonus Gonatas, as we saw earlier (p. 143), regarded kingship rather as a "noble servitude," a phrase that glanced critically at the irresponsible absolutism of less conscientious Hellenistic monarchs.[64] It is sometimes argued that the Macedonians, who supported the only genuinely nationalistic monarchy of the period, would not have stood for such pretensions, and that may be true; but it is also true that both Philip II and Alexander made vigorous efforts—which drew only token opposition—to promote their own isotheism.

There is no evidence that the Greek cities were in any way coerced into their widespread cult of the kings, and much to suggest that such demonstrations were spontaneous, if not invariably sincere: the ratio of flattery to self-interest remains more or less constant. The psychology of heroization is complex, and the instinct for worship deep-rooted in human nature. The monarchs of the Successor kingdoms had come, in a very real sense, to replace the old gods. Their achievements were more tangible, and, at least in the case of Alexander, arguably superior. What, asked the flatterers, were the deeds of Heracles or Dionysus by comparison? And for once the question was not mere hyperbolic rhetoric. The Ptolemies and Seleucids in particular were fabulously wealthy, ruled vast tracts of territory, and had virtually limitless resources at their disposal. They ruled like gods on earth: why not honor them as such? What is more, they also ruled, as we have seen, as though their kingdoms were their personal patrimony: they held absolute sway over their subjects. They also professed *philanthrōpia*. Amid the pomp and ceremony it must sometimes have been hard to decide just where the dividing line was to be drawn between a petition and a prayer. Saviors and benefactors, hedged about with the radiate gold trappings of royalty, they must have offered comfort to many in this new, vast-horizoned world of huge impersonal cities and individual drift.

In Egypt especially, where the Ptolemies had consciously borrowed much from the pharaonic tradition (brother-sister marriage being only the most obvious item), there was a sense of depth and continuity lacking elsewhere. Yet the dynasty still rested on a solid Graeco-Macedonian base. More important than any Egyptian assimilation was the cult of Alexander the Great instituted by Ptolemy I Soter: in a very real sense Ptolemy owed his throne to Alexander, who was, besides, the founder of Alexandria. His legitimizing body remained on display, like Lenin's, in its mausoleum, known simply as "The Tomb" (*To Sēma*)—no need to ask whose—which formed a natural cult center.[65] Alexander's officers, as we have seen (above, p. 19), could successfully invoke the authority of his empty throne, his robe, and diadem:[66] how much more powerful, then, the effect of that gold coffin and its numinous occupant, preserved, seemingly for ever, by the embalmer's art! As Callisthenes said (and everyone agreed), Alexander's spirit did indeed have a super·man quality about it:[67] here was a case where divinization came easy, and was hard to refute. "From Zeus let us begin," Aratus wrote: every later Ptolemaic cult looks back to this one, and its very potency made crossing the invisible barrier to the deification of a living monarch a quick and easy matter.[68]

Arsinoë II, Ptolemy Philadelphos's wife, was granted divine honors in her own lifetime,[69] and thereafter the Alexandrian priesthood maintained a public cult of successive royal couples, known variously as Sibling Gods, Benefactor Gods, Savior Gods, Gods Manifest, and so on, with precedence established on a chronological basis: the older the cult, the higher its standing on the ladder.[70] This was an official dynastic cult, promoted by the kings themselves, and distinct from the *ad hoc* honors paid them by cities or individuals. It included the worship (in whatever sense) not only of the Ptolemies, but also of Alexander, with whom Ptolemy Soter, as part of his quest for legitimization, maintained a fictitious personal relationship: his propaganda suggested that he was a bastard son of Philip II, and thus Alexander's half-brother.[71] The practice originally looked back, again, to the Greek cities, which had long made a habit of paying such honors to athletes (e.g., Theagenes of Thasos) or successful conquerors (Lysander, Demetrius).[72]

Thus whatever the ruler cult's intended effect on the Egyptians—Alexander himself had undoubtedly been well aware of the monarch's cult role in the Eastern kingdoms—it was, in essence, a Greek phenomenon, designed to strengthen the Ptolemies' position in the eyes of the local Graeco-Macedonian community (which, for good reasons, remained remarkably loyal to the dynasty), and to enhance their prestige among other Greeks abroad. The same is true of public displays such as the great Dionysiac procession of Ptolemy II (above, p. 158), Greek in concept and designed, above all, to impress the Greek world with Ptolemaic magnificence and strength.[73] We should never forget the artificiality of Ptolemaic rule in Egypt; though it was quite willing to borrow pharaonic trappings of godhead (and though, indeed, each ruler, beginning with Ptolemy V, was enthroned as pharaoh at Memphis), it was still never seriously integrated with Egyptian culture, and remained to the end, despite superficial social and religious syncretization, an alien, largely detested imposition. The Greeks and Macedonians had originally imported their own deities, and built temples for them.[74] Dedications to Zeus Soter, Hera, Apollo, Artemis, and other gods are known. We should also note in this context the propaganda accompanying Ptolemy II's reclamation of the marshy Arsinoite nome, south of Memphis on the west bank of the Nile. This area, of about thirty by forty miles, was carefully and deliberately Hellenized, with a Greek center, the Hellenion, temples to Greek gods (including Tyche and Nemesis as well as more conventional deities), and towns—Philadelphia, Philoteris, Dionysias—that were named for the king's relatives, or, in the last-named case, his supposed divine ancestor.[75] The area was colonized by veteran soldiers and retired officials, who were allotted tracts of land to develop.[76]

The dynastic cult of the Ptolemies thus remained "a Greek cult, with a Greek hierarchy, and with worshippers (if that be the correct word) drawn from the Greek-speaking population of the country."[77] Borrowings from pharaonic cult practice made no fundamental difference to this basic fact.[78] The nearest the Ptolemies came to any kind of integration was the imposition of themselves, and their cult, for political ends, on the native theocracy. They came to treat the Egyptian priests with some munificence (above, p. 192), and in return they enjoyed pharaonic privileges and honors. Even so, it is clear that the priests—of Upper Egypt in particular—still regarded them, privately, as foreign interlopers, another Hyksos dynasty, to be expelled when the time was ripe. This was hardly surprising. Not content with being crowned at Memphis, the Ptolemies also insisted that individual royal recipients of cult honors (e.g., Arsinoë II) should be established in Egyptian temples as "gods sharing the same shrine" (*theoi synnaoi*).

The official ruler cult was established by Ptolemy II Philadelphos.[79] Interestingly, it included the idea of assumption into heaven. Theocritus and Callimachus, court poets both, treat this theme with apparent seriousness.[80] The first described how Aphrodite, to spare Berenice I the horrors of Acheron, bore her off to her own heavenly temple, where thenceforth she enjoyed divine honors, while her husband Ptolemy I occupied a golden throne (beside Alexander!) in the halls of Zeus; the second pictured the Dioscuri wafting Arsinoë II off to become a goddess, and was also responsible for the catasteristic conceit, better known to us through Catullus, of Berenice II's dedicated lock reappearing as a constellation (above, p. 174). At first Ptolemy I was omitted from the cult—perhaps at his own request, to avoid invidious competition with the deified Alexander: Theocritus's reference shows just how embarrassing this theme could be—but he was later instated by that *louche* hedonist Ptolemy IV, a ruler who needed all the retrospective legitimization he could get. More and more priests and cult titles were added as time went on. The collective functioning of the ruler cult, always linked to that of Alexander, was kept distinct from the various individual cults that it embodied: it seems always to have been the exclusive preserve of the royal family.[81] Just as the Ptolemies' political rule was in effect a family fief, so their official worship remained a family interest too.

Their practice was imitated by the Seleucids, as we know from an edict of Antiochus III dated 205, establishing a priesthood for his wife Laodice.[82] Again, this is quite distinct from external municipal honors paid to the royal house. The Attalids, though cultivated in this manner by various Greek cities[83]—and indeed by their own ministers, who offered a cult, and a most flattering eulogy, to Attalus I's wife, Apollonis, "on her removal to the gods"[84]—seem not to have instituted an official royal cult themselves till after 188, and even then deification remained strictly posthumous.[85] Attalus III came close to being worshipped in his own lifetime, but got no farther, after a military victory, than being made *synnaos* with Asclepius.[86] The later Antigonids, perhaps with Demetrius Poliorcetes in mind as an awful warning, steered clear of ruler cults altogether.[87] Isolated in an alien land, the Ptolemies were, in the end, more influenced by local *mores* than they ever fully understood. It was only Cleopatra VII who realized the extraordinary potential of this strange symbiosis (below, p. 678); and by then it was far too late.

This emerges with some clarity in the curious efforts of the first two Ptolemies to establish a syncretic, anthropomorphized, Graeco-Egyptian deity who could serve the needs of the polyglot non-Egyptian ruling community of Alexandria, Memphis, Ptolemaïs, and the other administrative and commercial centers of the country.[88] The deity was Sarapis, "Serapis" in Latin authors, originally (though this has been much debated) worshipped as Osor-Hapi, the dead and mummified Apis bull identified with Osiris, in the Sarapieion of Memphis.[89] Our evidence, especially for Ptolemy I, is sketchy, and from what we know it would seem that Sarapis was only one among many deities, both Greek and local, who received royal support during this period (a tradition inherited from Alexander, who propitiated a variety of deities wherever he went); but the case of Sarapis does seem to have had unique features. The metamorphosis and promotion of this deity as a prop of the royal cult were carried out, in the first instance, by Greek intellectuals (e.g., Demetrius of Phaleron) and Greek artists. Demetrius gave the god a splendid early boost in his *Paeans* by claiming a miracle: the god had restored his failing eyesight (cf. above, p. 48).[90] The miracles multiplied: as in other healing shrines, such as that of Epidaurus, the process known as sleeping-in (*enkoimēsis, incubatio*), spending the night in the god's precinct, produced some notable cures. Strabo gives a vivid picture of the Sarapieion at Canopus on the Nile, with its "very distinguished" patients, and the nightly crowd of licentious revelers aboard the riverboats.[91]

The Hellenized Egyptian priest Manetho was on hand to offer local technical advice; but it was the Greek court sculptor Bryaxis who designed the huge seated cult figure, bearded and benign, half Zeus, half Pluto, head crowned with the grain *modios* symbolic of fertility, establishing an iconography that was quintessentially Greek.[92] As usual, in religion as in other matters, Greeks remained cautiously conservative. Sarapis in general much resembled Zeus, with whom indeed he came to be syncretized in the Roman period, giving rise to the popular slogan "There is one Zeus Sarapis."[93] Onto this composite figure there were also grafted the healing attributes of Asclepius, and, later, Helios, the Sun, as well as the underworld connections of Osiris, though with Greek Cerberus rather than Egyptian Anubis seated at his feet.[94] The intention may have been to appeal to Egyptians as well as Greeks,[95] but we can also detect, in this heavily syncretized deity, a growing trend toward monotheism, a general assimilation of local or specialized cults, that, like the Stoic world soul, was a natural product of the *oikoumenē*, and would reach its logical climax

Fig. 133. Roman bust of Sarapis (ca. A.D. 100), with the characteristic *modios* (grain measure) headgear. British Museum, London.

under the early Roman empire. What we do not find is any true Greek interest in Egyptian cults as such.

Sarapis was also—reasonably enough as a creation of the establishment[96]—very soon accorded special respect by Ptolemaic bureaucrats as a god who could, if properly propitiated, boost their official reputations, or give them a leg up the promotional ladder. One letter to Ptolemy II's financial minister Apollonius reminds him pointedly that Sarapis could still further improve even his already exalted position in the king's eyes.[97] The implications of this kind of patronage for the nexus between monarch, priesthood, and civil service are fascinating. Soldiers, of course—another powerful lobby in Ptolemaic Egypt—would particularly appreciate the god's supposed ability to cure wounds and offer protection in battle. It was Ptolemy II's officers and civil servants, for the most part, who introduced the cult of Sarapis to Greece and the Aegean, and indeed throughout the *oikoumenē*. We have to make a clear distinction between the public, official, established creed—inevitably, a political phenomenon, which tended to fall off in the third century both abroad, after Ptolemaic loss of naval hegemony (above, p. 150),[98] and at home, with the native resurgence that followed Raphia[99]—and the considerable popularity enjoyed by this oddest of ancient deities from his launching in Alexandria until his final eclipse, and partial absorption, by Christianity.[100]

A cynic might argue that a god who promised his devotees both physical health and material riches[101] could hardly go wrong with Hellenistic devotees so long as he made good on even a small percentage of his promises; but there was more to it than this. Sarapis answered prayers, gave dreams and visions, "answered the need for intimate contact with divinity so common in the early Hellenistic age."[102] In some way his cult managed to assuage the crying need for immanent transcendence and mysticism, qualities notably absent both from the Olympian pantheon and from the lucubrations of the philosophers.[103] Children in all walks of life were named Sarapion after the god. Chance has preserved a late third-century aretalogy of Sarapis from Delos, which offers us a glimpse of a family priesthood there, the building of a shrine, prosecution of the priest by a group of xenophobic Delians on the excuse that he had failed to obtain a building permit, and his acquittal and triumph thanks to the *aretē* of the god, who regularly gave his acolyte instructions during nocturnal visitations.[104]

In Alexandria itself, on the other hand, the Sarapis cult was rather slow to catch on outside official circles (perhaps because of its very success within them), and when it did, this was due in great part to the accident of its association with the cult of Isis, well addressed as "Thou of Countless Names," the goddess who in the end indeed became all things to all men and all women—slaves included.[105] Isis, in Egyptian belief the wife of Osiris and the mother, via his revitalized corpse, of Horus (now Hellenized as Harpocrates), was now refurbished as Sarapis's official spouse, in which role she enjoyed an even greater and more widespread success. The balance in this new syncretic Isis between Greek and Egyptian elements is complex and perhaps ultimately impossible to determine, though her more Promethean qualities, associated with the discovery of a whole range of inventions, from writing to husbandry,

Fig. 134. Boat-shaped Isiac lamp from Puteoli, with multiple wick holes. In the upper relief panel, Sarapis being crowned by Isis; below, the Dioscuri. British Museum, London.

essential for civilized life, have a decidedly sophistic flavor, and her mysteries, similarly, suggest Eleusis rather than Memphis.[106]

The Isis cult began to spread through the Mediterranean world as early as the
fourth century, largely carried by Egyptian sailors:[107] an inscription of 333 records
the establishment of a temple of Isis in Piraeus.[108] The cult also acquired dynastic
currency, as it were, among the Egyptian Greeks through its adoption by Arsinoë II,
as part of the joint Sarapis-Isis promotion campaign, and because of her own subsequent assimilation, after death (270), to the goddess's persona or avatar. We find
dedications made in the name of Isis Arsinoë Philadelphos, and sacrificial vases inscribed with the same title, for the use of Alexandrian ladies who hoped for a share
of her beauty, intelligence, and success.[109] By Ptolemy III's day Isis and Sarapis were
included, together with the deified rulers, in the royal oath. By the Graeco-Roman
period Isis had become the most influential and emotionally potent deity known to
the ancient world. Statues, shrines, and *bondieuserie* of every sort associated with her
worship have been found throughout the length and breadth of the Roman empire.[110] Isis came to assimilate not only a wide assortment of goddesses (most notably
Demeter), but also a quite extraordinary range of functions, as is apparent from her
surviving aretalogies.[111] She is Queen of every land, the Goddess among women,
giver not only of fruitfulness but also of literacy, who came down to earth from
heaven, traced out the courses of the stars, taught men the ways of the sea (and thus
became the patron and protectress of sailors), revealed the holy mysteries:[112]

Fig. 135. An Isiac altar from Rome.
The carved figure is a devotee of the
goddess, with offerings. On either side,
a sacred ibis.
British Museum, London.

Fig. 136. Wall painting from Pompeii of an Isiac ceremony, with priests, acolytes,
altar, and double massed choirs.
Museo Nazionale, Naples. Photo Alinari.

I am the Lady of the Thunderbolt,
I calm and swell the sea,
I am in the rays of the sun,
I am the sun's attendant in his journeying,
That which I will finds fulfillment,
All things yield before me,
I free those in bonds,
I am Mistress of Seafaring. . . .
I raised up islands from the depths to the light,
I am the Lady of Rains,
I vanquish Destiny.

Fig. 137. Fine silver patera from the Boscoreale treasure (first century A.D.), showing the assimilation by Isis of characteristic features of Artemis (e.g., the bow and quiver, here visible behind the goddess's right shoulder).
Musée du Louvre, Paris. Photo Giraudon.

There are strong mystical undertones about Isis; as is clear from the famous description of her by Apuleius,[113] with her long, rippling hair and lunar aureole, she supplied the essential iconography, and perhaps also some of the early liturgical material, for the subsequent cult of the Blessed Virgin.

But to begin with, this was a wholly unforeseen development. The Hellenization of Isis and Sarapis offers us a vivid glimpse into a kind of spiritual black hole: Egypt's Graeco-Macedonian elite was suffering from something worse than cultural alienation. Materialism had bred its own too-human god-kings, while the Olympians, anthropomorphic tribal patriarchs that they were, had simply reverted to type, and left a void that neither affluence nor astrology could fill. Protagorean man had sickened of his own image, so that for many people the quasi-abstract Tyche, whether as inexorable fate or unpredictable accident, the incalculable flaw in any rational universe they could conceive, must have seemed a truer, perhaps even a more acceptable, symbolization of their spiritual dilemma.

CHAPTER 24

FROM CYNOSCEPHALAE TO PYDNA: THE DECLINE AND FALL OF MACEDONIA, 196–168

Only twenty-eight years separated Cynoscephalae from Pydna, yet in that time Rome advanced from a reluctantly self-assertive role in Balkan affairs to a position where—reluctant still—she was the absolute arbiter of nations throughout the eastern Mediterranean. Philip V, Antiochus III, and Perseus all tried conclusions with the legions on the battlefield, and all three went down in defeat. From the very beginning, while Greeks were talking airily about Roman barbarians, the Senate in Rome or the proconsul on the spot had displayed not only an irritated unconcern with Greek affairs, but, when pressed, an arrogant indifference to Greek sensibilities. Flamininus might proclaim Greek freedom and autonomy; but he and those like him were more than ready, as the occasion might require, to make and break alliances or rewrite frontiers, not only for the warring mainland states of Greece (e.g., Aetolia), but for the Attalids and Seleucids as well. Each victory accentuated their confidence: after Pydna in 168 Rome simply abolished the Antigonid monarchy altogether, and split Macedonia up into four small independent republics (below, p. 430).[1]

But, equally, Rome's prestige, her ultimate *de facto* authority, had been acknowledged very early on—if not in so many words—by the increasing recourse had to her as arbitrator by the eternally quarreling Greek powers. Envoys flocked to Rome from every minor capital to ensure their own loyal status and to lay long complaints about their rivals.[2] The Senate encouraged this tattling: divide and rule (*divide et impera*) was already a well-tried device of Roman diplomacy, and the more the Greek cities complained about the Successor monarchs, the easier it was to keep the latter in order, or at least to have a ready-made excuse for moving against them. What is significant is the fact that, from Cynoscephalae onwards, it was Rome to which these factions naturally turned. Just how sincere or cynical Flamininus was in his proclamation of freedom for the Greeks is impossible to determine; but using the principle of autonomy to break up hostile federations was already a time-honored

414

device, and there is no reason to suppose that Flamininus was not well aware of it.[3] Ironically enough, as a well-read *soi-disant* philhellene he probably picked it up while briefing himself on earlier Greek history: he would have found the Great King's peace of 387/6 particularly instructive.[4]

It was now, too, that the great senatorial families and equestrian businessmen began to realize the untapped potential for large-scale exploitation that lay in the East. If they had not understood this before, Aemilius Paullus's lavish triumph, in celebration of his victory over Perseus at Pydna, can have left them in no doubt. Romans stared, in wide-eyed amazement, at the fantastic treasures looted wholesale from the Macedonian palace at Pella: the gold, the tapestries, the slaves, the works of art. The conquering Roman general sailed up the Tiber to Rome in the royal Macedonian barge, and the last Antigonid king was paraded before him in his triumphal procession.[5] The keynote to this victory was loot on the grand scale, a foretaste of further depredations to come. The troops, who had seen too much hard fighting for too little return, grumbled: but the speculators and predators had smelled a richer scent than that of blood. The total value of *official* booty taken in Rome's eastern wars down to 167 (the gross total must have been many times greater) reached the staggering sum of seventy million denarii; and after Pydna alone, Plutarch tells us, such a vast quantity of money was turned in to the public treasury that it replaced all extraordinary taxes until the first conflict between Antony and Octavian (43 B.C.: in Cisalpine Gaul).[6]

Two or possibly five years later Perseus, like Demetrius the Besieger, died in captivity, at Alba Fucens (165/2). Apparently he starved himself to death. One of his sons, an expert in embossing and calligraphy, survived to become secretary to the magistrates in Rome. On a small scale he had learned the lesson propounded by Polybius: be realistic, learn the language, adapt yourself to the new regime. His father and brothers chose otherwise.[7]

But this is to anticipate. After Cynoscephalae Flamininus's behavior made it quite clear that the Greek liberation he proclaimed at the Isthmus was very much conditional upon Rome's convenience, and indeed that the arbitrator, though as yet unwilling to move in as more than a very temporary caretaker, was quite ready to rearrange the chessboard without consulting the supposedly free-to-move pieces, black or white. His public letter to the city of Chyretiae in Perrhaebia protests noble and honorable intentions a little too stridently, refers to slanders against him and Rome by less-than-scrupulous men unnamed, angrily denies charges of avarice. The implications of this text are revealing.[8] On the Senate's instructions Flamininus removed Demetrias, Acrocorinth, and Chalcis—the Fetters—from Philip's control, and garrisoned them with Roman troops:[9] those garrisons were withdrawn in 194, when Flamininus evacuated Greece,[10] but a point had been made. A chorus of complaints against Nabis of Sparta, who was steadily strengthening his position in the Peloponnese once more,[11] did get action of a kind out of Flamininus. Helped by fifteen hundred Macedonians from Philip, a contingent of Spartan exiles led by the Agiad Agesipolis, and the all-too-willing levies of Rhodes, Pergamon, Thessaly, Messenia, and the Achaean League,[12] he captured the port of Gytheion, drove Nabis

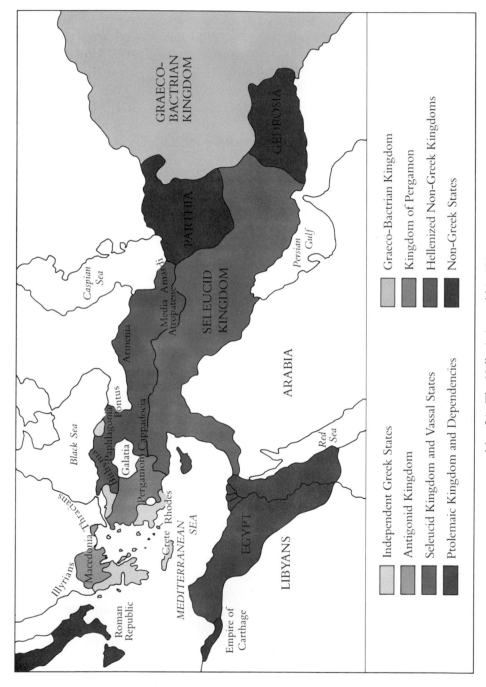

Map 24. The Hellenistic world in 185 B.C.
From Ferguson, *Heritage of Hellenism*, p. 155.

GRAECO-
BACTRIAN
KINGDOM

GEDROSIA

PARTHIA

Caspian
Sea

Media Atropatene
Media Amardi

SELEUCID
KINGDOM

Armenia

Persian
Gulf

Pontus
Paphlagonia
Bithynia
Cappadocia
Galatia
Pergamon
Black Sea
Thracians
Crete Rhodes

ARABIA

MEDITERRANEAN
SEA

Illyrians
Macedonia
Roman
Republic

Red
Sea

EGYPT

Empire of
Carthage

LIBYANS

Independent Greek States

Antigonid Kingdom

Seleucid Kingdom and Vassal States

Ptolemaic Kingdom and Dependencies

Graeco–Bactrian Kingdom

Kingdom of Pergamon

Hellenized Non-Greek Kingdoms

Non-Greek States

back to Sparta, and forced him to negotiate[13]—but then, instead of finishing the Spartan ruler off once and for all, he merely made him give up Argos, surrender his fleet, and pay an indemnity over the next eight years, probably calculating that Nabis was a useful counterweight to the Achaean League. He was also in a hurry, uneasily aware that to prolong the siege of Sparta might well mean surrendering credit for the campaign to some ambitious replacement from Rome.[14] It is noteworthy that he did not restore Agesipolis, as he so easily could have done.

In general, Flamininus treated his Greek allies with cavalier indifference. He did make some concessions to the Aetolians, returning Phocis and part of Thessaly to them, but not (in the Aetolians' view) nearly enough, a fact that dictated their subsequent actions.[15] Instead, with that arrogant Roman partiality for redrawing other men's maps, which also affected Aemilius Paullus, he created four artificial federal cantons from what remained of Thessaly, and set up the *poleis* of Euboea as an independent league. Like almost all proconsuls he tended to favor the local plutocrats— one more reason for doubting that Nabis was any kind of true revolutionary—and took steps to ensure that only men of means should be eligible for public office.

All this time Flamininus was dealing with (or, to be more accurate, rebuffing) embassies from Antiochus III, now campaigning aggressively in Asia Minor and showing an untoward interest in the Hellespont.[16] Eumenes II, since 197 king of Pergamon, was joined by representatives from the cities of Smyrna and Lampsacus in making loud complaints about Antiochus's activities. The diminished kingdom that Eumenes inherited had suffered a good deal from Antiochus's inordinate ambitions, and the new Pergamene monarch was not one to forget a grudge.[17] He spent much of his reign working to harness the power of Rome against his enemies (as his father, Attalus I, had done against Philip V), and with remarkable success. His propaganda was as unscrupulous as it was unrelenting: in a very real sense he was the nemesis both of Antiochus and, later, of Perseus (below, p. 427). In 193 we find him working tirelessly to present Antiochus as a dangerous and ambitious imperialist, against whom Rome's only safe course was a preemptive war.[18] He was also very busy behind the scenes, coaching other complainants from Asia Minor—with some skill— in how best to impress Roman officials.[19] Antiochus offered Eumenes marriage with one of his daughters: dynastic diplomacy was as endemic to the Seleucids as, later, to the Hapsburgs. Eumenes, however, refused the proffered *douceur*: he was playing for higher stakes.[20]

Flamininus, acting very much *de haut en bas*, had already (196/5) sent envoys to Antiochus at Lysimacheia, in Thrace, telling him to leave the newly autonomous Greek cities alone, to keep out of Europe, to give up the towns he had taken from Ptolemy. Antiochus, nothing fazed, pointed out, correctly, that Flamininus had no overriding authority to speak for the Greek *poleis*, reiterated his claim on the cities he held by right of prior conquest and possession—his argument throughout being that he was simply recovering his ancestral domains, even in Thrace—and announced his forthcoming (195) peace treaty with Ptolemy V, leaving the latter Cyprus, Thera, and a few towns in eastern Greece. Ptolemy may well have been only too glad to settle on these terms.[21] Antiochus was emboldened by his successes to square off for a showdown with Rome. He told Flamininus's envoys that it was solely due to his, Antiochus's, magnanimity, not to Rome, that the Greek cities enjoyed what liberty they had; he also snubbed the Romans when they attempted to arbitrate his differences with the cities of Smyrna and Lampsacus. At this point, says Polybius, they "broke up the conference, by no means pleased with each other."[22]

The Senate, understandably, feared that Antiochus meant to invade the Greek mainland. This fear was further exacerbated when, in the fall of 195, the exiled Hannibal found asylum with the Seleucid monarch at Ephesus, another former Ptolemaic possession.[23] Hannibal was said to be urging Antiochus to set his aim not on Greece but on Italy.[24] What effect this rumor had on senatorial policy is debatable. Scipio Africanus and a sizable senatorial group called for the retention of an occupation force in Greece, precisely because of Antiochus's unpredictable ambitions. But they were voted down, and the Senate recalled Flamininus: not even the Acrocorinth garrison was left behind.[25] The evacuation took place late in 194. The philhellene Flamininus carried off numerous works of Greek art and considerable treasure to adorn his triumph.[26] He also kept Armenes and Demetrius, the sons, respectively, of Nabis and Philip V, in his retinue as hostages. Obsequious Greeks, of the kind who could afford such gestures (and were thus likely to do well out of collaboration with Rome) dedicated cults and monuments to him. Antiochus, meanwhile, cemented his alliance with Ptolemy V by giving the young king of Egypt his daughter Cleopatra in marriage, an act with interesting consequences, since it later enabled Ptolemy VI's ministers to claim that Coele-Syria had been promised to Egypt as part of the queen mother's dowry.

Flamininus, before he pulled out, neither set up a general federal league of Greek states, nor arranged for any kind of Roman liaison team during the transition. The result was inevitable: the Greeks "celebrated their liberty by falling out with each other, and with their liberator."[27] The Aetolians, still smarting from what they regarded as their unjust deal at Flamininus's hands, went shopping round for supporters in a putative crusade against Rome (193). The excuse was ill timed and improbable: it is far more likely that with the Roman evacuation the Aetolians, opportunistic as always, sensed a chance for expansion in Greece. A meeting at Naupactus came up with the three obvious names to approach: Philip, Nabis, Antiochus.[28] Philip, who had been offered alliance by the Senate as a condition of retaining the throne from which the Aetolians (not unnaturally) wanted him removed, turned the latter's invitation down flat.[29] This was not surprising. Rome at this point had no wish to antagonize Philip, and was, indeed, encouraging him to retake, and keep, cities he had earlier lost to the Aetolians. So much, as Gruen says, for the "freedom of the Greeks and the sloganeering of the Second Macedonian War."[30]

Nabis of Sparta, on the other hand, who at this point would take any alliance he could get, and had not forgotten his charitable humiliation at Flamininus's hands, proved as enthusiastic as Philip was recalcitrant. Indeed, he promptly went off and got himself embroiled with Philopoemen and a Roman naval squadron while attacking some of the newly autonomous cities of Laconia:[31] defeated and put under siege yet again, he once more cut a deal with Flamininus, on the basis of their earlier treaty, that left him still in power at Sparta.[32] Even a Spartan king of his stamp was, clearly, preferable in Roman eyes to an Achaean monopoly of power in the Peloponnese. The Aetolians next applied to Antiochus, openly inviting him—only four years after Cynoscephalae!—to liberate Greece. Antiochus was in an ambivalent position. Despite the urgings of Hannibal, he clearly wanted to treat with Rome if he could.[33] Indeed, in 193 he had made another formal attempt to negotiate through Flamininus, now back in Rome.[34] Flamininus, speaking on behalf of the Senate, made him a very fair offer: he would be left at full liberty in Asia Minor if he abandoned his claim to Thrace, and conceded Rome's right to act as diplomatic arbiter in Europe. If, however, he insisted on maintaining dynastic claims beyond the Hellespont, then Rome would similarly maintain—indeed, increase—her alliances in Asia, with rights of patronage (*patrocinium*) over the Greek cities.

At this point Antiochus, through his representative, made the first of two fatal mistakes. He held out for Thrace. Why, it is hard to see, unless he was driven by an irrational and chauvinistic determination to recover every inch of territory ever held, however briefly, by Seleucus Nicator (and that may be no more than the simple truth). Thrace, beyond the Hellespont, could be nothing but a territorial liability to him. But he was intransigent, and the negotiations (the so-called Conference of Ephesus) broke down. Thus when the Aetolians, having severed their relationship with Rome,[35] applied to Antiochus, he was (they must have reasoned) in a potentially receptive mood. He was certainly ready enough to pose as the defender of Greek freedom, a preferable patron in that role to Rome.[36] But did this necessarily mean committing himself to a direct armed confrontation with Roman power? Not even the Aetolians seem to have wanted this at first. Besides officially inviting Antiochus to liberate Greece (which may have meant no more in fact than to support them in their own expansionist activities), they expressed a hope that he would arbitrate between them and Rome.[37] Yet Antiochus was still understandably cautious. It seems clear that he did not seek a confrontation with Rome; he certainly had no interest in Italy or the West. It took him until the autumn of 192 to make up his mind, and, by accepting the Aetolians' invitation, to commit his second fatal error.

The Aetolians had certainly shown willing. At Chalcis their surprise attack failed, but they had little trouble in winning control of Demetrias (summer 192),[38] which meant that Antiochus would have a good, safe base on arrival. They also descended on Nabis, who received them cheerfully as friends and allies; they then proceeded—pirates first and last—to have him assassinated during a parade, and to pillage the city of Sparta (fall 192).[39] Neither short nor long term did this do them much good. Far from welcoming them as tyrannicides, the Spartans, once over their surprise, proceeded to slaughter the looters. At this point Philopoemen and the Achaeans, seeing their chance, marched on Sparta and without much effort talked her now-leaderless citizens into joining the Achaean League, a move that marked the end of Sparta as an independent power.[40] Not long afterwards Messene and Elis, Aetolia's only remaining Peloponnesian allies, were also to be coerced into the Achaean camp, which would then, at last, control the whole of the Peloponnese (fall 191).

Thus when Antiochus landed at Demetrias in the fall of 192 he was putting his

trust in an isolated and dangerously weak ally.[41] What was worse, he himself brought
no more than ten thousand men—and only six of his famous elephants. The Aetolians, who had been touting him as the conqueror of the East, a second Alexander,
now found potential supporters reassessing the situation and giving Aetolian envoys
the polite brush-off. It is hard to decide where, if anywhere, Antiochus's real support
in Greece lay, beyond Aetolia. Livy identifies it as coming from the *Unterschicht* of
the population, the masses as opposed to the wealthier element, which was firmly
pro-Roman.[42] There may be some truth in this, though it would be unwise to press it
too far: Livy, notoriously, overschematizes the distinction,[43] and in any case Antiochus was not the man to make demagogic concessions even for short-term advantage.[44] If the anti-Roman sought a champion, this was not he. Antiochus's Aetolian
allies had an appalling reputation, and his campaign in Greece was clearly doomed
before it even began. The Achaean League joined Rome in declaring war on Antiochus; so did Rome's new ally Philip, little more than a decade after the treaty of
friendship he and Antiochus had signed (203); but in the world of Hellenistic politics
ten years was a very long time.[45]

Antiochus started well enough. He took Chalcis, and married a young Chalci-
dian girl on the strength of it; he renamed her "Euboea," a clear hint of his European
ambitions.[46] He got support from the Boeotians.[47] Then, however, the combined
forces of Philip and the Roman consul Manius Acilius Glabrio routed him, with severe losses, at Thermopylae, and he reembarked, in some ignominy, for Asia
Minor.[48] The Romans made a separate truce with the Aetolians in the fall of 191, and
in 190 set about running Antiochus down beyond the Hellespont:[49] the first time that
a Republican army had crossed into Asia, and a move that the Seleucid king did not
foresee.[50] Ptolemy V, realizing which way the wind was now blowing, twice sent
envoys to Rome offering help (of whatever sort might be needed) and, latterly, con-
gratulations. The Senate treated these turncoat overtures with understandable contempt; they could manage very well without Ptolemy's opportunistic support.[51]

By now Rome had, not surprisingly, the alliance of both Rhodes and Pergamon
(common commercial interests made this almost inevitable), and their combined
naval squadrons proved a formidable fighting force:[52] Rhodes had resurrected the
old Cycladic League of Islanders under her leadership, with its base on Tenos.[53] On
land, Antiochus scored some further successes, in particular against Eumenes, laying
siege to Pergamon and ravaging the king's territories with a horde of Galatian mercenaries—perhaps a deliberate affront to Attalus I's much-publicized victories (above,
p. 150). The arrival of the Roman and Rhodian fleets, however, combined with the
knowledge that a consular army was ready to cross the Hellespont from Macedonia,
led him to try for a peace settlement. Both the Roman and the Rhodian delegates
were ready to treat; only Eumenes, his royal capital blockaded, would have none of
it.[54] His obduracy paid off. The siege was raised with the help of a contingent from
the Achaean League; soon afterwards the Roman and Rhodian naval squadrons went
into action.[55] Antiochus's admiral was beaten by them off Cape Corycos; Antiochus
rebuilt his fleet, putting one squadron under Hannibal's command, only to be beaten
again, first off Side and then at Myonnesos (Aug.–Sept. 190), with the Rhodians
earning most of the credit for both victories.[56]

Meanwhile the Roman legions, led by Lucius Cornelius Scipio, with his more famous brother, Scipio Africanus, as legate, crossed the Hellespont into Asia Minor, aided by Philip, who, as a *quid pro quo*, had his war indemnity canceled, and also got back his son Demetrius, still a hostage in Rome.[57] The Scipios could muster no more than thirty thousand men against Antiochus's seventy-five thousand; but the Seleucid army was a mixed bag, and by now Antiochus knew the potential of a Roman legion. Once again he offered to negotiate: he would pay a partial war indemnity, and return a number of the towns, in Europe and Asia Minor, that he had occupied. But Scipio would have no truck with this. What he demanded was the complete evacuation of Asia Minor as far as the Taurus range, plus full indemnity for the campaign.[58] Antiochus (as Scipio no doubt had calculated) turned this proposal down: a battle he had a chance of winning, whereas this represented total surrender.

So once again in Hellenistic history a desperate commander staked everything on a set engagement. The battle took place at Magnesia-by-Sipylos, near the confluence of the Hermos and Phrygios rivers, late in 190 or early in 189.[59] Raphia, and the memory of Demetrius the Besieger at Ipsus, had taught Antiochus nothing. Once again a Seleucid monarch led a massive, and successful, cavalry charge by his right wing; once again he failed to disengage from pursuit in time. Despite a heroic stand by the phalanx of the center, Antiochus's forces were finally shattered while he was still occupied elsewhere. His elephants stampeded, and contributed materially to the rout. On the Roman side, a key role was played by Antiochus's enemy Eumenes II of Pergamon, who impacted the Seleucid left wing with a well-timed attack.[60] Once the phalanx broke, the Romans began their methodical butchery of the fugitives. It was the bloodiest slaughter since Rome's defeat at Cannae. When it was finally over, the Scipios marched east, and occupied Sardis.

The battle of Magnesia left no doubt in anyone's mind—certainly not among the Greek communities of Asia Minor—that from now on their survival or annihilation depended, *de facto* if not *de jure*, on Rome's fiat: this may well be why Ariarathes IV of Cappadocia now decided to make his peace with Eumenes and to bring his country into the Roman alliance.[61] By now the slogan of "freedom" had become a decidedly tarnished concept. Rome's leaders were in competition for rich pickings.[62] The Greek states that did best out of Magnesia, and indeed had fought Antiochus with just such a payoff in mind, were Rhodes and, in particular, Pergamon, with both of which, as we have seen, Rome had close commercial ties. After Magnesia (the preliminary agreement was made at Sardis, early in 189) Rome imposed by right of conquest the terms that Antiochus had earlier refused.[63] He was to pay a war indemnity of fifteen thousand talents (the highest that had ever been recorded), with a first immediate deposit of five hundred talents, and twenty-five hundred more on the ratification of the treaty in Rome, followed by twelve equal annual installments of a thousand talents each, plus ninety thousand *medimnoi* of wheat. He also had a sizable debt of four hundred silver talents to pay off to Eumenes.[64] In territorial terms, he was effectively barred from Greece and western Asia Minor, though he retained control of Cilicia, Coele-Syria, and Phoenicia.[65] He was to renounce all claims on Thrace, and evacuate Asia Minor as far as the Taurus Mountains and the Halys River. These territories were divided between the Rhodians and Eumenes II, along the line of the

Maeander, with Rhodes getting all Lycia and much of Caria, while Pergamon at one stroke acquired most of western Asia Minor, including Lydia and Hellespontine Phrygia.[66]

The two beneficiaries (who were not signatories to the peace) intrigued and fought over the wealthy cities of Ionia that Antiochus had controlled.[67] The Rhodians, mainly interested in trade, argued for their autonomy; Eumenes, who was empire-building, had other ideas. The Romans compromised. Any city that Antiochus had captured from Attalus became subject to Eumenes, who thus left the conference table the most powerful dynast in Asia Minor.[68] The rest were made autonomous. Antiochus was required, in addition, to surrender hostages—including his son the future Antiochus IV—together with Hannibal and his other anti-Roman advisers (Hannibal sought refuge with Prusias I of Bithynia, a move that staved off his fate for another six or seven years); to give up his elephants and his war fleet, except for ten vessels;[69] and to refrain from either recruiting or campaigning in Roman-controlled territory. The rich pickings that went to Eumenes and the Rhodians were perhaps more illusory than their recipients realized at the time. The weakening of Seleucid power meant that henceforth they were far more dependent on Rome's good will. We have already seen how Rome considered Greek freedom a *munus* (p. 311), a gift bestowed by a patron on a client: the same, it is clear, was true of the dispensations to Rhodes or Pergamon. These were gifts too, and could, at Rome's good pleasure, be revoked.[70] The Rhodians regarded them as absolute: that was their mistake.

In 189 Scipio's successor in Asia, Gnaeus Manlius Vulso, with the assistance of Eumenes' brother Attalus, conducted a successful (and immensely profitable) campaign against the Gauls, largely as a result of Eumenes' energetic representations to the Senate. Manlius got a cheap triumph, and Eumenes still further strengthened his kingdom: neither could complain.[71] Then, as they had done in Macedonia after Cynoscephalae, the Romans also withdrew their troops from Asia Minor, to demonstrate *inter alia* that they were not mere landgrabbing imperialists.[72] The terms of the peace were negotiated through the Senate in Rome, then ratified at Apamea (188). Though once again the Senate kept clear of direct permanent involvement in Asia Minor, leaving Pergamon and Rhodes to keep the peace as the price of their territorial gains,[73] it is symptomatic that ambitious Romans were now angling for an Asiatic command. The degree of competition can be gauged from the fact that Lucius Scipio, the victor of Magnesia, was prosecuted, for allegedly skimming off a portion of the public booty that should have found its way to the treasury.[74]

Seleucid domination in Anatolia had been to all intents and purposes obliterated by the treaty of Apamea, yet at the same time the heartland of the empire remained virtually intact. Syria was still prosperous: Antiochus still held the Fertile Crescent.[75] But the mines of Anatolia were lost, and the king was faced with a severe shortage of silver for minting currency.[76] Shaken, but gamely determined to recoup his fortunes (or at least pay off the indemnity) in the way he understood best, Antiochus first set up his son the future Seleucus IV as co-regent, and then set off east to plunder and pillage. While stripping a temple in Elam he was murdered (3 or 4 July 187).[77] Antiochus never quite achieved the greatness of his public title, and the title itself, as we have seen (above, p. 296), rested at least as much on skillful propaganda as on substantive emulation of Alexander's Eastern conquests. He was a man of energy and mercurial brilliance rather than solidity, and many of his troubles stemmed from his own erratic estimates of men and affairs. Yet he undoubtedly left his mark on the dynasty. The Seleucids were by no means finished yet, but never again did they come quite so close to recovering the lost glories of their founder as during the reign of Antiochus III.

The elimination of Antiochus apart, the treaty of Apamea changed very little— one reason why it caused so much resentment, not least in mainland Greece. The Aetolians, though granted a permanent alliance by Rome, were forced to renounce their claim to all cities captured by, or surrendered to, the Romans since 192.[78] Otherwise things went on much as before. The Romans were fundamentally uninterested in Peloponnesian politics, and the leaders of the Achaean League now deliberately exploited this unconcern to deal their old enemy Sparta a crippling blow. The Spartans, deprived of an outlet to the sea, with all their coastal cities under Achaean control and occupied by their own political exiles, were desperate: desperate enough to assault and capture (if only for a few hours) the little harbor town of Las (fall 189).[79] Philopoemen, the hawkish leader of the Achaean League, now in his sixth generalship, pounced on this excuse to destroy the threat of Sparta once at for all. He demanded the surrender of those responsible for the raid on Las; the Spartans not only refused, but instead made formal surrender of themselves (*deditio*) to the Romans.[80] The consul Marcus Fulvius Nobilior played safe by sending Achaean and Spartan missions to argue their case before the Senate.[81]

The Senate hedged, merely requiring that there should be no change in Spartan circumstances, a phrase capable of wide interpretation.[82] Philopoemen, who had already observed Rome's unwillingness to look after those who sought her protection empty-handed, read this ambiguous message well. In spring 188 he repatriated the Spartan exiles (a long-cherished project of his),[83] murdered or executed those responsible for the attack on Las, disenfranchised and banished the citizen helots (some of whom were sold into slavery) and the foreign mercenaries, tore down the new city walls, abolished Sparta's educational system, the famous *agōgē*, rewrote the ancient Lycurgan constitution to bring it into line with those of other members of the Achaean League, and stamped out the last vestiges of Nabis's supposedly revolutionary reforms.[84] The Senate expressed its disapproval of Philopoemen's extreme measures, but took no further action. Megalopolis, on the other hand, understandably voted him heroic honors.[85] Traditional Sparta was destroyed for ever. The return *en masse* of the exiles made the old property laws unworkable. A last attempt at social revolution quickly collapsed (181). The *agōgē* was only revived as part of the antiquarian tourist trade; the rebuilding of the walls came as an empty gesture, and changed nothing.[86] Philopoemen, with characteristic arrogance, claimed that the League was acting within its rights. More to the point was the fact that property owners in the Peloponnese had been, for whatever reason, united in their detestation of Nabis's activities; and since Rome tended to side with this class in its foreign dealings, the Senate may well have felt that the noninterventionist goals of "peace, stability, and the due recognition of *clientela*"[87] would be better achieved through the Achaean League than by the preservation of a volatile, unpredictable, and by now socially alarming Spartan regime. What Rome felt about the League's aggressively independent foreign policy at this time is another matter.[88]

The Romans also had to deal with numerous complaints about the behavior of Philip.[89] After 187, with the death of their bugbear Antiochus, they were more disposed to treat Philip as another potential danger. He had not evacuated the Thracian and Thessalian towns of Antiochus, though Rome had promised the former to Eumenes; nor did he do so when ordered to by a senatorial commission, led by Quintus Caecilius Metellus. (In Philip's favor it must be said that the commissioners seem to have stacked the deck against him ab initio.)[90] Further, he had occupied Aenus and Maroneia, left by the Romans as a neutral zone between him and Eumenes.[91] The Senate officially reasserted the freedom of both cities: Philip retorted by staging a pogrom in Maroneia (186/5).[92] More complaints poured in from interested parties. In 184 Philip sent his younger son, Demetrius, back to Rome to lobby for him: as a hostage the boy had been highly popular, and had made many useful friends.[93] He now worked patiently to bring senatorial opinion round. But Eumenes' ambassador was a stubborn diplomat, and in spring 183 another senatorial commission, led by Flamininus, forced Philip's evacuation of both Aenus and Maroneia, though Eumenes does not seem to have recovered them.[94]

The general view of Greece and the Near East at this point from Rome was by no means discouraging. Antiochus III was dead, and his son Seleucus IV—a less feeble monarch than is often supposed—was observing the terms of the treaty of Apamea with scrupulous correctness. In Egypt, after a period of rebellion and anarchy, Ptolemy's forces were beginning to restore law and order: 187 or 185 saw the recapture of Thebes, and the end of the great rebellion in the south.[95] While cynics doubtless argued that this relief of pressure would mean renewed trouble, sooner rather than later, in Coele-Syria, nevertheless Rome always welcomed the stabilization of an acceptable regime. The volatile king of Macedonia was beginning to look a little more like what Rome expected a subordinate ally to be. The problem of Sparta, it is true, produced a series of irritated missions and countermissions to Rome, and some very cool snubs to Roman legates who visited Achaea: both Philopoemen and Lycortas, Polybius's father, stressed the League's autonomy, while querying Rome's right to meddle in Peloponnesian affairs. A Roman commission of arbitration, led once again by Flamininus, worked out a compromise (184): Sparta's walls would be rebuilt, but the city would remain part of the League.[96]

In 183 the intractable Philopoemen—well characterized as a bourgeois reactionary, whose wealth made it easy for him to take an incorruptible stance[97]—was captured and forced to drink hemlock while trying to put down a Messenian revolt,[98] and though his party colleagues, such as Lycortas, continued influential, the pro-Roman group inevitably gained ground. In 180 the Achaean embassy to Rome was led by the latter's spokesman, Callicrates, whom Romans found more to their taste than his opponents (cf. above, p. 275). Narrow xenophobic nationalism of the kind that Philopoemen had represented (and which was shortly to create even more trouble in Judaea: below, p. 517) always left the Senate suspicious and uneasy. What Rome wanted was unstinted, preferably obsequious, collaboration, a proper sense of *clientela*. This Callicrates provided, even, as we have seen (p. 277), later supplying the Roman authorities with a list of likely deportees (167/6), which included both Polybius and his father, Lycortas.[99]

Eumenes II of Pergamon was now established as a close ally of Rome's, and attempts by his neighbors, such as Prusias I of Bithynia, to trim his expanding frontiers got short shrift in settlements approved by Rome[100]—though Eumenes was left to do his own fighting, on land as at sea, with the added hazard that Hannibal was now Prusias's military adviser. When the ingenious Carthaginian caused a panic rout of Eumenes' fleet by the *outré* device of lobbing jarfuls of poisonous snakes aboard his flagship,[101] a Roman delegation forcibly reconciled the two monarchs, and at the same time demanded the surrender of Hannibal (183). The Carthaginian, seeing the net closing on him, and too proud to grace a triumph in Rome, committed suicide that same year.[102] Eumenes' further triumphs over the Gauls, culminating in his acquisition of Galatia, were celebrated in 182 by the establishment of new games, the Nikephoria,[103] initial work on the Great Altar (above, p. 351), and the addition of the title *Sōtēr* ("Savior") to the monarch's name. The whole Greek world was invited to Pergamon to participate—and admire. Eumenes was equally successful in his efforts to stall Pharnaces of Pontus, who captured Sinope, on the southern shore of the Black Sea, after which he invaded Cappadocia, Paphlagonia, and (after breaking a truce) Galatia (183–179). Once again a Roman commission ruled in Eumenes' favor, though it was not concerned to enforce its findings, and returned home, leaving Eumenes to finish the war on his own—which he did, after an invasion of Pontus, in 179.[104] Ptolemy V, after finally putting down the last of the insurgents in the Delta (184–183), died in 181/0, while still only twenty-eight. There were, of course, rumors that he had been poisoned.[105] He left his wife, Cleopatra I, Antiochus's daughter, as regent for their young son: a stable but weak regime was exactly what pleased Rome best.

Unfortunately, the weaknesses—and this was true not only of Egypt—always tended to undermine the stability. Cleopatra, too, died prematurely (176), and the boy-king Ptolemy VI Philometor[106] was very much under the control, initially at least, of his guardians, Eulaeus and Lenaeus, a eunuch and a Syrian ex-slave,[107] who soon began to display territorial ambitions (below, p. 429). However, it was the situation (admittedly an unforeseeable one) of the Macedonian monarchy that now put fatal pressure on an always fragile balance of power. Briefly and disastrously, the Antigonid regime reverted to the kind of lurid, murderous intrigue that characterized the Argead dynasty of Philip II and Alexander at its worst. When Philip V's younger son, Demetrius, returned from Rome in 183, wearing well-deserved diplomatic laurels, he seems to have driven his elder half-brother, Perseus, into a frenzy of jealous paranoia. Demetrius's Roman associations, not least with Flamininus, encouraged fantasies—modern no less than ancient[108]—of senatorial efforts at king-making in Macedonia, of an aggressive Roman foreign policy aiming to place the complaisant Demetrius on the throne at the expense of the legitimate, but uncomfortably independent, heir.

This is highly improbable. While some Romans might well have preferred, other things being equal, to deal with Demetrius, whom they knew and liked, nevertheless "Roman policy towards Macedon in this period is remarkable not for its aggressiveness but its passivity."[109] That there was serious friction between the brothers seems certain:[110] Philip was much saddened by it, and at first refused to believe the charges Perseus brought against Demetrius.[111] Nor was the mudslinging entirely one-sided: as heir to the throne Perseus now (like Alexander, and with equally slight justification) had to face rumors of his illegitimacy, and was thus highly sensitive to any real or imagined threat of competition. Convinced, partly because of the Senate's attitude,[112] that Demetrius was plotting to oust him from the succession, but unable to prove his suspicions, Perseus finally confronted his father with an alleged letter from Flamininus (probably, as Livy claimed, a forgery)[113] that spelled out Demetrius's treasonable aspirations to the throne. Faced with this evidence, Philip had Demetrius executed (180). He then, when it was too late, became convinced that Perseus had fabricated his testimony.[114] Luckily for Perseus, Philip died (179)—of remorse, Livy suggests[115]—before he could execute a second son as a blood offering to the first. From now on it was Perseus with whom Rome had to deal.

The circumstances of Perseus's accession could hardly fail to make the Senate suspicious of him from the start, not least since Demetrius had enjoyed considerable popularity in Rome. The new king seems to have been regarded there as fully responsible for his brother's death—a charge supported, with lurid rhetorical detail, by Polybius and Livy. It is not surprising, then, if our ancient sources assume that Perseus inherited what is now known as the Third Macedonian War from his father.[116] Not surprising; but almost certainly, to judge from subsequent events, untrue. To begin with, Perseus lost no time in asking the Romans to ratify him as king, and to renew the friendship (*amicitia*) they had concluded with Philip.[117] Polybius offers a favorable sketch of him at this stage, and confirmation from the Senate, even if *faute de mieux*, was in fact forthcoming.[118] On the other hand it is also true that he soon began to show characteristics that—even if their effect on Rome has been much exaggerated[119]—were hardly calculated to reassure Roman businessmen on the spot, let alone natural enemies such as Eumenes or the ever-suspicious leaders of the Achaean League. (An attempt by Perseus at achieving reconciliation with the League soon broke down, in part as the result of Roman diplomacy.[120]) Perseus seemed to be planning wide-ranging alliances, what has been termed a "coalition of kings": he married (178/7?) Laodice, daughter of Antiochus the Great's successor Seleucus IV, while Prusias II of Bithynia in turn married Perseus's half-sister.[121] Though such intermarriages were standard Hellenistic practice, in the strained atmosphere then prevailing they could not fail to arouse misgivings.

Indeed, every act of Perseus was interpreted by Eumenes (in this case correctly) as anti-Pergamene, and also reported to Rome—for his own ends—as part of a calculated anti-Roman policy. This included Perseus's *rapprochement* with Delphi (174) and his strengthening of the northern Macedonian frontiers against tribal incursions (179/8), things that as evidence of anti-Roman feeling Rome was unlikely to take overseriously.[122] But Perseus was, also, disturbingly prone to the kind of pseudo-radical social measures that had got Agis and Cleomenes a bad name. He canceled debts, wrote off taxes, and amnestied exiles, all of which caused considerable public enthusiasm, though not in the right quarters.[123] When debtors in Aetolia became embroiled with the pro-Roman landowners, Perseus was blamed for the situation. A Roman embassy sent in 173 to check on his activities (including an alleged approach to Carthage) was refused a hearing, and reported back—mistakenly, but understandably—that Perseus was ready to go to war.[124] Eumenes, not now the most popular of monarchs in Greece, came to Rome in 172 to press these and other charges, with all the unscrupulous rhetoric at his command.[125] His senatorial audience was predisposed to believe him, and a few days later rejected out of hand the case presented to them by Perseus's envoys.[126] Livy says that in the Greek states "the multitude" was all for Perseus and Macedonia, whereas important citizens were split on the issue, but for the most part favored the prospect of control by Rome.[127] Polybius makes a similar claim for the period after war was declared.[128] The truth of this claim is at best dubious, though it may have been a belief (whether justified or not) in populist pro-Macedonian feeling that finally helped to nudge the Senate into a declaration of war.[129]

It was also disastrously true that the complex intrigues of the Greeks, and their even more complex partisan oratory, frequently baffled the self-styled plain, blunt men of Rome. As a result those in authority too often tended to go along with individuals they knew and therefore trusted—Eumenes, for example, or, on the other side of the fence, Philip's son Demetrius. But Demetrius was no longer around to argue his brother's case. The Senate decided to trust Eumenes' word. Just how uneasy Rome was about the justice of this war may be determined from a Delphic inscription listing Macedonia's alleged offenses.[130] This statement of charges, which seems to have been concocted for the Delphic Amphictyony by a Roman official, covers various putative improper acts of Perseus and possibly also—the inscription is badly mutilated—of his father, Philip, going back over a fifteen-year period. The seriousness of these may be gauged by the fact that Perseus was charged, *inter alia*, with planning to poison the Roman Senate, or, alternatively, the Roman commanders and envoys passing through Brundisium (mod. Brindisi) *en route* for Greece.[131] This was scraping the bottom of the barrel with a vengeance.

Rome's determination, moreover, was hardened by something that was, almost certainly, an accident. On his journey back to Pergamon from Rome, Eumenes was nearly killed by a rockslide near Delphi. He at once accused Perseus of trying to have him murdered:[132] if mass poisoning in Italy, why not well-aimed rocks in Greece? Polybius, uneasily, supported Eumenes' charge, while Livy presents a circumstantial account (presumably also derived, in the first instance, from Pergamene accusations) of the supposed assassination attempt.[133] It also figures in the Delphic inscription, which means that it was made an official issue. (The situation was given a comic twist by the prompt action of Eumenes' brother Attalus: on hearing of Eumenes' supposed death, he promptly declared himself king and married his brother's "widow"—a dynastically prudent act that must have caused, subsequently, a certain amount of familial embarrassment on its reversal.)

What were Eumenes' motives in bringing these persistent and far-fetched accusations,[134] not to mention his edgy reminders of Macedonia's vast resources, all now, as he insisted, being readied for an invasion of Italy? He felt threatened by Antiochus, perhaps with justice. But what was Perseus to him? Eumenes, more than most, seems to have been alarmed by Perseus's simultaneous *apertura* to Bithynia and the Seleucids, above all by his marriage to Laodice. A Macedonian-Seleucid alliance could be seen as a threat to Pergamon's new Rome-backed expansionism, and Eumenes' subsequent involvement (p. 429) in winning the throne for Antiochus Epiphanes (if not in the assassination of his predecessor Seleucus IV) makes it very clear that he wanted the Seleucid alliance for himself.[135] No single person worked harder to precipitate Rome's final conflict with Macedonia. Eumenes' remarkable unpopularity with the Greeks, despite a consistently liberal policy to the cities under his control,[136] was surely caused by his open commitment to Rome, at a time when the resurgent hope of Greek independence caused most states to pin their hopes on Perseus.[137]

The interesting thing about this situation is that Perseus himself had in fact done nothing except try to keep out of trouble, while at the same time securing his own position. The initiative lay elsewhere: in Pergamon, with the Achaean League, at Rome, and even so was far from decisive or clear-cut. For a long while the Senate delayed taking action, and it has been plausibly argued that there was a conflict between old arrogance and new unscrupulous ambitions, between the senatorial aristocracy, which wanted peace (Rome still being entangled in Spain), and the *noui homines*, who were hot for new action and the prospect of rich pickings.[138] It was not until the spring of 171, after the election of two plebeian consuls (18 Feb.), Publius Licinius Crassus and Gaius Cassius Longinus,[139] that a conditional declaration of war was made against Perseus,[140] and an expedition was mounted, while diplomatic negotiations for peace were still being conducted, in the clear expectation at Rome that Perseus, faced with a strong Graeco-Roman coalition, would capitulate. This was an error of judgment. Perseus's three embassies show he had no wish for war; but there were clear limits to the terms he would accept. Rome's self-exculpatory Delphic inscription (see above) was presented to the Greeks as a kind of manifesto. Perhaps the Senate felt it was now or never.[141] In the quarter-century since Cynoscephalae Macedonia had made good its manpower losses:[142] the official complaints about Perseus's aggressiveness stress, significantly, what he might do rather than what he had already done. There were signs that he was prepared to fight.[143] The war was thus seen as preemptive. The booty motive is suggested by the fact that the campaign lasted four years, with only one consul and a limited force taking part in it annually. It is also relevant, in assessing the Senate's reluctance to act, that the drawn-out war in Spain and Liguria had drained Rome's resources and exhausted her veterans.[144]

Not until June 171, after an unsatisfactory meeting with yet another Macedonian legation, did it become clear that Perseus had no intention of letting himself be either bullied or humiliated, and that nothing but force would shift him. Then, at long last, the expeditionary force that had been placed on standby was dispatched across the Adriatic, and the Third Macedonian War began. Rome had committed herself too far to back out at the eleventh hour. Yet even now for several years the war was limited to minor campaigns (171–168), while Perseus remained on the defensive and put out constant peace feelers. The Rhodians—snubbed by the Senate and alarmed at Eumenes' evident interest in controlling the Hellespont[145]—began to waver from their temporary support of Pergamon and Rome. Perseus, one eye on the Rhodian fleet, went out of his way to conciliate them; as a result, despite the lobbying of a group of pro-Roman pragmatists, the general mood was now strongly pro-Macedonian.[146] The pragmatists, who simply advocated joining the winning side, were, on their own terms, right: Rhodes's ambivalence during this Third Macedonian War cost her dearly when the war was over (cf. p. 431).

Eumenes himself, despite his energetic military commitment, seems to have lost some favor with the Romans: he may have fallen victim to the same sort of nasty innuendo with which he blackened his opponents, a case of poetic justice. He was, besides, too successful, too independent, too popular at home.[147] That he planned to switch sides and join Perseus, as several sources allege,[148] is ludicrous at this juncture; that he even hoped to make a killing as a mediator—Polybius's explanation[149]— seems highly implausible. Yet it remains true that from now on the Senate inclined rather toward his brother Attalus (who, with unusual loyalty, would have nothing to do with Rome's overtures). Rumors of conspiracy had made Eumenes suspect: no smoke without fire.[150] Among other improbable charges brought against Eumenes and Perseus was one of trying to raise a royal alliance against Rome that included the Seleucid Antiochus IV[151]—whom Eumenes and Attalus had helped to the throne in 175 after Seleucus IV's assassination by one of his ministers.[152] But Antiochus, a flamboyant and eccentric character (cf. below, p. 437),[153] who had spent time in Rome as a hostage,[154] was known to be pro-Roman: he had had a house built for him in Rome at public charge, and later expressed gratitude to the Senate for the kind treatment he had received.[155] It has even been suggested that Seleucus's murder was possibly engineered by Rome in order to get a safe man established in the Near East.[156] But if there was, in fact, an external finger in that particular pie (which is by no means certain) it belonged, almost certainly, to Eumenes.

In any case, Antiochus's overriding interest, like Perseus's, lay in stabilizing his own kingdom, and at this point he was too busy dealing with yet another confrontation over Coele-Syria (the Sixth Syrian War, 171/0–168) to commit himself in Europe. (He had already, in anticipation of just such a conflict, gone out of his way in 173 to ensure Rome's diplomatic support.)[157] The details of this war remain uncertain. Ptolemy VI Philometor was no more than sixteen when it broke out, and still very much in the hands of his advisers (above, p. 425). Diodorus blames them for forcing Ptolemy to fight;[158] Livy and others put the responsibility on Antiochus.[159] In fact the long history of this territorial quarrel suggests that both sides must, inevitably, share the blame. The claims and counterclaims went, as we might expect, to Rome, where the Senate, as usual in such cases, prevaricated.[160] Ptolemy sensibly proclaimed himself of age (170), thus obviating the need for a regency, married his sister, Cleopatra II, and took as their co-regent their young brother, Ptolemy VIII, not yet of the bulk that would later win him the nickname of *Physkōn* ("Potbelly," "Bladder").[161] While Rome was moving in on Perseus, Antiochus drove south against Ptolemy (spring 169).[162] He wiped out the Egyptian expeditionary force, captured Pelusium, and became virtual master of Egypt except for Alexandria. Ptolemy VI changed his advisers and decided to negotiate: Antiochus was, after all, his uncle. In Alexandria these events sparked off a revolution. Antiochus's troops had been looting temples; the Alexandrians decided to wash their hands of Ptolemy VI, and proclaimed Ptolemy VIII Euergetes joint ruler with his sister, Cleopatra. After a half-hearted attempt to besiege Alexandria Antiochus withdrew (169), and left the two rivals to fight it out on their own. This was arguably a mistake, since instead they patched up a reconciliation.[163] By 168 Antiochus, resigned now to the exercise of naked *Machtpolitik*, was back in Egypt, while his fleet invested the Ptolemaic stronghold of Cyprus, which soon fell to him.

Meanwhile, after more than three years of foot-dragging, the war in Macedonia was moving toward its climax. The consul assigned Greece in 168, Aemilius Paullus, having disembarked at Itea, the port of Delphi, marched directly north to confront Perseus. The final encounter took place on the coast of Macedonia at Pydna (22 June), after some casual skirmishing between outposts, and began with a massed advance by the Macedonian phalanx[164]—no longer Alexander's loose, flexible unit, but a spear-solid hedgehog formation designed to counter Roman legionary discipline.[165] Aemilius Paullus, a veteran commander, declared afterwards that this advance was the most terrifying thing he had ever witnessed. But the charge lost its impetus; the legionaries infiltrated gaps in the ranks, and—just as at Cynoscephalae—the Macedonians were finally slaughtered almost to a man. The legion had, once and for all, proved its superiority over the phalanx. It was the end of Macedonia as an independent nation.[166] The monarchy was abolished, the country split into cantons, and Perseus carried off (after an abortive attempt at flight) to adorn Paullus's treasure-rich triumph (above, p. 415). Before leaving Greece the Roman commander took a cultural tour of the country, picking up choice *objets d'art* here and there, and in Epirus collecting a little matter of 150,000 slaves after turning his men loose to rape and pillage. At Delphi, his statue was erected on a large base previously designed to accommodate the likeness of Perseus.[167] Greek talk about western barbarians was now proved something more than mere idle rhetoric.[168] He also lent the Aetolians five hundred troops to pay off a few old scores on their own account: the result was a particularly nasty episode. The gold and silver mines in the area of Mt. Pangaeum were closed, and coining in these metals ceased—a senatorial measure aimed, in part at least, at controlling the politically disruptive exactions of the tax farmers (*publicani*), and perhaps with an eye to underwriting monopolies elsewhere, for example in Spain.[169] Severe restrictions were placed on the trade in salt and naval timber, and about half of the old Macedonian royal tax money was now diverted to Rome. The staggering accumulation of Macedonian wealth revealed by Paullus's triumph was not to be allowed to recur.[170]

Rhodes was paid off for her lukewarm support during the war by the loss of Lycia and Caria,[171] and the establishment of Delos as an Athenian dependency and free port (Athens had supplied grain to the Romans in 171, and Athenians, anti-Macedonian to the end, not only fought at Pydna, but were specially honored by Council and Assembly for so doing).[172] In Greece there was some witch-hunting of pro-Macedonian notables, with the usual reprisals, and some suicides.[173] Polybius and his fellow Achaeans were deported to Rome (above, p. 276). Except for the northern frontier of Macedonia, the country was demilitarized. Once again, though, Roman troops did not remain. There was no army of occupation. As Claire Préaux wryly observes, destroying the country sufficed.[174] The four new Macedonian republics—in theory autonomous—were left, ungarrisoned, to get on as best they could without a king. Despite the optimism of Polybius, civil strife was soon rampant once more.[175]

With Pydna behind them, the Romans now turned their attention to Antiochus IV Epiphanes (168), who had been working hard, and with considerable success, to win friends and influence in Greece, the Aegean, and Asia Minor, and whose coinage, markedly improved in both quality and quantity, suggests a powerful resurgence in the Seleucid economy.[176] Clearly, though, from a Roman viewpoint the Seleucid had been overreaching himself while Rome was otherwise occupied, and seriously disturbing the balance of power in the process. An official order (*senatus consultum*) was sent to Antiochus to evacuate not only Egypt, but also Cyprus, where his troops were going on a rampage of looting and destruction.[177] The Roman envoy, Popillius Laenas, met the king in the Alexandrian suburb of Eleusis (July 168), and waited in silence while he read the Senate's message. When Antiochus asked for time to consider the request, Popillius simply drew a ring round the king with his stick in the dust, and told him peremptorily to answer yes or no before he stepped out of the circle.[178] Antiochus may have been nicknamed *Epimanēs* ("Mad-

Fig. 138. Antiochus IV Epiphanes. Gold stater minted at Antioch(?), probably either in 169 B.C. (when Antiochus, prior to his first Egyptian expedition, presented a gold stater to every citizen in Naucratis: Polyb. 28.17.10–11), or in 166 (to mark the ceremonies at Daphne; cf. p. 432). British Museum, London.

man") by his own people, a parody of what he called himself on his coins, *Theos Epiphanēs* ("God Manifest"),[179] but he could be discreet enough when he chose. He bowed to the inevitable, swallowed his pride, answered yes, and surrendered his winnings, well aware that Roman policy had no time for a revived Seleucid empire on the grand scale, that "mediation, reconciliation, and concord continued to be the aim." It has even been argued—and the argument has something to commend it— that he knew very well he could not win his Egyptian campaign and was only too glad of Popillius's gesture as an excuse for extricating himself from trouble. Yet the humiliation was real, and palpable.[180] Then, after what came to be known as the Day of Eleusis, he went back home, and got revenge of a kind by celebrating those famous games at Daphne that put Aemilius Paullus's triumph in the shade (cf. p. 438),[181] and also—despite his Egyptian setback—sent a message of strength and determination to Antiochus's rivals in the Greek world, just as Ptolemy Philadelphos's grand procession had done over a century before (above, p. 158). As a *réplique* it was quintessentially Hellenistic: it made a vast impression at the time, cost a great deal, and substantially altered nothing.

PART FOUR
THE BREAKING OF NATIONS
167–116 B.C.

CHAPTER 25

THE WILDERNESS AS PEACE, 167–146

The period between Rome's defeat of the last Macedonian king at Pydna (168) and the sack of Corinth by Mummius (146)—a lurid and notorious climax to the so-called Achaean War (*bellum Achaicum*)—has been stigmatized by modern historians for its incoherence, confusion, partisan anarchy, and lack of conscious purpose. Until the eleventh hour, we are told, Rome had no positive or consistent policy in Greece, Macedonia, or Asia Minor.[1] It was a world, says Edouard Will, "in the final stage of decomposition, only awaiting the *coup de grâce* and . . . the peace of the graveyard."[2] There is some truth in this; but the pattern is perhaps clearer, and Rome's long-term policy less shapeless, than such a verdict might suggest. Polybius at one point comments, shrewdly, on Rome's constant capacity to profit by the mistakes of others;[3] and whether or not she here applied her famous dictum of divide-and-rule with deliberate foresight, it remains undoubtedly true that everywhere she found division, and ended by ruling. Her generals and commissioners were confronted, again and again, with "conflicting parties whose one idea of political liberty was to fight each other."[4]

Roman political disclaimers of imperial or expansionist ambitions, genuine so far as they represented governmental thinking, were offset, and eventually denied, by the rapacity of her speculators and proconsuls. Senatorial noninterventionism (or inertia)[5] had to compete with the intrigues of businessmen, ambitious officials, and their backers, and was to some degree exacerbated by conflicting policies within the Senate itself.[6] If there was a consistent or dominant senatorial foreign policy during this period (which is debatable), it was to preserve a balance of power between stable, friendly, or neutral foreign states such as would, with minimal interference on Rome's part, effectively prevent a recurrence of the Carthaginian nightmare. The cynicism and self-interest that Polybius saw everywhere after Pydna indeed existed, and grew worse as time went on; but how far he was right to identify this mood as the motivating force behind senatorial policy is quite another matter. Our evidence suggests rather a radical split between traditional, that is, aristocratic, senatorial opinion, which was by instinct isolationist and, in the last resort, morally based, and the exploitative plans of the business community, joined very soon by on-the-spot officials, with the latter slowly but surely shifting the former toward more aggressive involvement. This process was hastened by Sulla's reform of the Senate: a flood of new entrants dependent on non-landed wealth rapidly eroded old principles and sharpened official greed.[7] The conflict of the censors with the tax farmers (*publicani*) in 169 shows, already, a surprisingly strong popular interest in the latter's contracts, as well as clear senatorial awareness of the dangers inherent in powerful business consortia.[8] The closing of the Macedonian mines two years later (above, p. 376), and their reopening in 158, reveals a similar conflict between the public and the private sector: Livy stingingly observes that the mines "were unworkable without a contractor, and the presence of a contractor meant the flouting of common law and the denial of freedom to the allies."[9]

Far from trade following the flag (or in this case the fasces), Rome's military machine and administrative authority—exercised increasingly as time went on by those with a large stake in overseas commercial exploitation themselves—were invoked, again and again, to protect or enhance her own vested interests. Trade went in first, and the flag followed. The Romans, moreover, did not regard warfare as an occupation for gentlemen: they expected to turn a profit on any campaign, and were not fussy about how they did it. The widespread massacre of Roman traders, tax collectors, bankers, and similar oppressive profiteers during Mithridates VI's "night of the long knives" in 88 (below, p. 561) both highlights the bitter resentment felt by the Greeks, and indicates very clearly what its specific occasion was—not senatorial policy, but uncontrolled (and to a great extent uncontrollable) free enterprise. This dichotomy is apparent, in increasingly acute form, from Pydna onwards, and exercises progressively greater, if often unacknowledged, control over military activity in the East.

Thus from the Third Macedonian War onwards "destruction of cities, enslavement of the population, requisitions, confiscations, were of constant occurrence."[10] Freedom for the Greeks had been all very well so long as they behaved themselves as good clients, eschewed imperial ambitions, and carried out Rome's wishes. This raises the intangible yet crucial problem of the psychological relationship subsisting between Rome and the Hellenistic states during this final period of the latter's titular independence. It has often been remarked (indeed, no student can avoid noticing the phenomenon) that interstate diplomacy consisted to a surprising degree of, on the one hand, embassies to Rome (from kings, or leagues, or individual cities), complaining about their rivals and seeking redress through arbitration; and, on the other, of commissions of inquiry sent out by the Roman Republic to settle the problems thus raised. These commissioners saw themselves as vested with absolute authority, subject only to senatorial approval, to settle Greek matters by fiat. At the same time Rome felt no obligation to enforce, by military or other means, the decisions thus reached. That was the responsibility of the interested parties.

It is sometimes surprising just how far this noninterventionism would go. Gnaeus Octavius, sent out east as head of a three-man delegation to check on Seleucid compliance with the terms of the treaty of Apamea, found—in contravention of what had been agreed[11]—a large fleet and numerous royal war elephants. Without more ado his men set about burning the ships and hamstringing the elephants. An enraged observer of this scene thereupon assassinated Octavius (163/2), and felt so confident in the justifiability of his act that he offered to come to Rome and defend himself before the Senate.[12] Lysias, regent for the young Antiochus V (p. 439), gave Octavius a ceremonial funeral and sent a mission to Rome disclaiming responsibility for the murder. The Senate made no comment one way or the other, though on the face of it they had every reason for moral outrage, if not for a declaration of war. From all this it seems clear that Octavius was a hard-liner who had considerably exceeded his official brief:[13] similarly, Popillius Laenas's offhand brusqueness with Antiochus IV (above, p. 431) was undoubtedly his own improvisation, not senatorial policy.

Such violent incidents, however, were rare. For the most part the relationship that now developed between Rome and the Greek kingdoms or cities was essentially parental in nature, with the Greeks playing the part of quarrelsome, feckless, undisciplined children, while Rome functioned as an increasingly stern *paterfamilias*. A situation of this sort is never altogether imposed by external action; nor is it exclusively one-sided. The game of unhappy families requires at least two players, and this remains as true at the political as at the personal level. If Rome from the beginning saw her role in Greece and Asia Minor as that of an authoritative arbiter (but one pleasantly free of any responsibility for enforcing her judgments),[14] the quarrelsome and increasingly fissile Greeks were, likewise, only too glad to find a higher authority to take the burden of ultimate decisions and responsibility off their shoulders. Neither side, perhaps, was ever fully conscious—at least till it was too late, and the course of events had become irreversible—of the part that circumstances had forced it to play.

After Pydna, with the elimination of Macedonia and—less often noticed—Illyria,[15] the Successor kingdoms were reduced to two. Of these the Seleucid, largely on account of the personality of Antiochus IV Epiphanes, seemed in 167 the stronger and more aggressive. We shall in due course see something of Antiochus in his dealings with the Jews, and understand why the Judaic tradition draws him as a monster of cruelty (pp. 513 ff.). To Polybius he was more of an eccentric.[16] Like Peter the Great, he was fond of hobnobbing with craftsmen and metalworkers—a sign of mental instability to the class-conscious Polybius. He would stroll through the streets of his capital, alone or with two or three attendants, distributing largesse—gold rings, pebbles, knucklebones—as the fancy took him. He liked *louche* parties and low drinking companions. Like Nero, he fancied himself as an actor. He frequented the public baths, where on one occasion he emptied a jar of expensive unguent over his fellow bathers, for the fun of seeing them all roll about the slippery floor to get a share of it. Wits in Antioch, as we have seen, changed his royal epithet of *Epiphanēs* ("Manifest," of a god) to *Epimanēs* ("Manic," "Crazy").

Yet his behavior as king, his official persona, shows a very different side to him. His royal title, and his identification on his coinage as Helios, the Divine Sun, were part of a careful campaign to legitimize his questionable accession. The first five years of his reign he had, technically, been regent for Seleucus IV's young son, whom he appears to have adopted,[17] and then, after the birth of his own son, the future Antiochus V, had put to death (170/69). This usurpatory move coincides with the first emission of the Helios-type coins.[18] The symbolism of the sun as first among all heavenly bodies, the all-powerful universal eye of the world, and hence, as Cleanthes said, its leading principle (*hēgemonikon*), is obvious.[19] No accident that Antiochus chose to emphasize his own divinely justified and absolute power at this precise point, or that we find him described in an inscription as "Savior of Asia."[20] Like his father, he worked to reconsolidate the empire's military strength and extend its frontiers. By the end of his comparatively short reign he was regarded as the most powerful Greek monarch of his time,[21] despite his failure to achieve much more than the maintenance of "a precarious *status quo.*"[22]

Antiochus's great forte was political propaganda, as his calculated use of the currency makes clear; he put himself forward as the patron and benefactor of the Greek cities, and a staunch defender (bearing in mind his own divine pretensions) of the traditional Greek gods. He sought dynastic prestige, and was, as even Mørkholm grudgingly admits, "a shrewd politician who may even deserve to be called a statesman."[23] In his dealings with Rome he was shrewd, cautious, and diplomatic: a buffoon or a megalomaniac would never have appreciated the significance of the circle that Popillius Laenas drew round him, much less have pulled out of Egypt as he did. He would have had the Roman's head off his shoulders, and committed himself to a war he could not hope (and knew he could not hope) to win. Antiochus had been humiliated by the Day of Eleusis. He had counted too much on Rome's support because of his long residence and personal connections there. He would not make that mistake again. The lesson that Antiochus III had learned, the hard way, at Magnesia-by-Sipylos had not been lost on him.

In this spirit he sent an envoy to Rome bearing the message that peace with the Roman people was preferable to any victory over Egypt. He also congratulated the Romans on their triumph at Pydna. The grateful envoys of the two Ptolemies, their uneasy joint rule one more testimonial to Roman diplomacy, reached Rome about the same time, and were well received. Antiochus returned home, and solaced his pride and reputation with extravagant ceremonial. But like the May Day parade in Moscow, the processions through Daphne (167/6) were also a demonstration of strength, and as such had an immediate end in view.[24] The king had assembled no less than fifty thousand men, not to mention a corps of elephants. The inevitable Roman commission appeared to find out what was going on. He wined and dined them all, and reassured them that he was planning neither a fresh attack on Egypt nor an alliance with Eumenes of Pergamon, now out of favor with Rome (p. 429),[25] but a new eastern anabasis to complete the work of restoration his father had begun. Since such a campaign would remove Antiochus from Mediterranean circulation for months and possibly years, Rome, having no stake in the eastern Seleucid empire, could scarcely raise any objections to it. The flouting of military restrictions as laid down in the treaty of Apamea (pp. 436–37) was, for the time being, ignored: Rome did not play this restrictive card until after Antiochus IV's death, and even then, as we have seen, with no great conviction.

From Antiochus's own viewpoint this new campaign was essential. Antiochus III had made treaties in the East, but done very little more (above, p. 295). Seleucus IV seems to have restricted his diplomacy to the West. The Bactrian king Euthydemus (p. 334) might have acknowledged Antiochus III as his titular overlord; but Euthydemus's son Demetrius, after the news of Magnesia reached him, seems to have launched a full-scale campaign of conquest and expansion in the great eastern satrapies.[26] It was to meet this menace, as well as to pick up loot with which to help pay off Rome's heavy indemnity, that Antiochus III had made his last, ill-fated expedition. The fact that Demetrius's descendant Agathocles in turn fell victim, about 170, to a newcomer, Eucratides I, did nothing to resolve the situation as far as the Seleucids were concerned. The Parthians, too, under an equally aggressive new monarch, Mithridates I Arsaces V (acceded 171?), were also threatening the stability of Antiochus's always insecure territories beyond the Tigris. Another anabasis was urgently needed.

In the midst of Antiochus's preparations came news of a major Jewish revolt (below, pp. 513 ff.). The king's tough response to this (167) must be assessed in the context of his forthcoming eastern campaign. Here was a fire that needed quick and effective dousing, since the last thing any eastern campaigner needed (as Alexander the Great well knew) was trouble in his rear. Thus it was not until 165 that Antiochus Epiphanes finally set out, leaving his nine-year-old son and designated heir,[27] the future Antiochus V, in the guardianship of his chief minister, Lysias. However, he got no farther than Persia, where he fell ill and died (164), still in his early forties.[28] Among his last alleged acts were an edict rescinding the decree of persecution against the Jews, and the dispatch of one Philip, at the head of an army corps, to replace Lysias as chief minister and take over the guardianship of young Antiochus.[29] What was the significance of these decisions?

Lysias, in Antiochus's absence, had suffered a humiliating series of defeats at the hands of the Jewish insurgents, culminating in one for which he was personally responsible. He therefore urged Antiochus to grant amnesty to all Jewish guerillas who returned to their homes. This, perhaps with some misgivings, Antiochus did (early 164). But he refused to deal with Judas Maccabaeus, the leader of the revolt, preferring instead to negotiate through Menelaus the High Priest and the Jewish Hellenizing party (below, p. 518). Thus Judas was faced with the choice of capitulation to Menelaus or fighting on: his decision was never in doubt. Though the Akra, the citadel, held out, Judas captured the rest of Jerusalem, and in December 164 purified the Temple—an act still commemorated by the feast of Hanukkah. Then, in 163, he launched an attack on the Akra itself.

Lysias dispatched a strong force to counter this attack, but when he was on the point of defeating Judas, he instead (as the representative of the boy-king Antiochus V) made peace with him: a peace that had senatorial approval.[30] Why did he do so? For one thing, he knew that Philip was coming back to replace him as regent and chief minister, but had no more idea than we do whether this appointment originated (as Philip claimed) with the dead king, or had been invented by Philip himself for his own benefit. Lysias was equally aware that the murder of Seleucus IV in 175 (above, p. 429) had left a rival claimant to the Syrian throne in the person of

Fig. 139. The boy-king Antiochus V
Eupator. Silver tetradrachm, mint
unknown (? Antioch ca. 164–162 B.C.).
British Museum, London.

Seleucus's son Demetrius, since 176/5 a hostage in Rome.[31] Lysias thus needed to get the Jewish question settled fast. In the name of Antiochus V a decree was promulgated admitting the incompatibility of the Mosaic Law and Hellenism, officially returning the Temple to Yahweh, and guaranteeing "ancestral traditions." Menelaus was executed, but the Akra retained its garrison, and another Hellenizer, Alkimos, became High Priest.[32] For the Jewish people, this was the first step toward true independence; for Lysias, it meant the defeat of Philip and the retention of the regency— for a while: in Seleucid politics nothing was ever certain for long.

The moment he heard of his uncle Antiochus IV's death, the young prince Demetrius in Rome went before the Senate with his claim to the throne. He was vigorous, intelligent, dynamic, good-looking, twenty-four years old, and Seleucus IV's legitimate son: in other words (says Polybius) as far as the Romans were concerned, a disruptive menace.[33] Far better a boy-king and a pliable regent: these the Senate knew how to handle. This sounds like mere Polybian disgruntlement. The obvious aim was to avoid further destabilization of the regime. As Polybius himself admits, those at the top in Syria did not want Demetrius's restoration, and sending him back would have provoked an inevitable civil war.[34] Demetrius's claim was turned down.[35] Clearly there existed a split in senatorial opinion over Syrian policy: it was now that a commission betook itself to Antioch and began checking on Seleucid military resources (163/2), with unfortunate results (above, p. 437).

Demetrius, after a second rebuff,[36] seeing he would get nowhere through official channels, enlisted the aid of sympathizers in Rome, Polybius among them, and contrived to escape.[37] (Polybius is unlikely to have acted without the connivance, if not the active support, of his powerful Scipionic patrons.) In 162/1 Demetrius disembarked at Tripolis in Phoenicia, and made straight for Antioch, where he received an enthusiastic public welcome as the legitimate heir to the throne (which, it could well be argued, he in fact was). Resistance quickly collapsed: Philippus's men at the top did not, it is clear, have the people behind them. Lysias and young Antiochus V were executed; several other would-be pretenders and supporters of the boy-king were dealt with in very short order. A Roman embassy under Tiberius Gracchus was sent out to observe and report. Demetrius duly flattered Tiberius, showed himself eager to collaborate, and was well reported on. He even sent Octavius's murderer to Rome, along with the usual honorific gold crown. The Senate accepted the crown, and released the murderer, who thus found his cheerful confidence well justified.[38] The motive, as Polybius saw it, was to hold charges in reserve against a more profitable occasion. Demetrius was recognized as king—conditional on his satisfactory conduct.[39] The Senate showed itself cool and cautious, but by no means overtly hostile.

It is true that in 161 Rome, on Judas Maccabaeus's initiative, made a treaty with Judaea:[40] since this was a mutual defense pact, it in effect recognized Judaea as an independent state, and one Jewish source alleges that the Senate wrote to Demetrius, threatening him with war if he continued his harassment of the Jews.[41] Is this letter mere fictional propaganda? Hard to decide, and in any case it does not matter, since Demetrius failed to take the slightest notice of it. He went ahead and crushed the rebellion regardless. Judas Maccabaeus died without either demanding or getting help from Rome, and the Senate took no retributive action. In the circumstances we may legitimately wonder just what this much discussed treaty was really worth. Once again Rome had obliged with the intangible seal of her *auctoritas,* but then re-

Fig. 140. Bronze portrait statue (mid to late second century B.C.), probably of a Hellenistic ruler—variously identified as Demetrius I Soter of Syria, Attalus II of Pergamon before accession, Philip V, Perseus, Antiochus II, and Alexander Balas (!)—but also claimed by some as a Roman *triumphator,* perhaps Flamininus.
Museo Nazionale, Rome. Photo Hirmer.

Fig. 141. Ptolemy VI Philometor.
Silver tetradrachm minted at Ptolemaïs-
Ake ca. 160–150 B.C.
Bibliothèque Nationale, Paris. Cabinet des
Médailles.

frained from action. "From the senate's vantage point, the Jews . . . could claim independent status. But the maintenance of their independence was not Rome's affair."[42]

In Egypt, the reconciliation of Ptolemy VI Philometor and his younger brother, Ptolemy VIII Euergetes II Physcon (above, p. 430), was proving predictably fragile.[43] Philometor's sister-wife, Cleopatra II, reigned as the third member of this odd triad. Alexandria seethed with palace intrigues: the mob was restless, the troops were mutinous, while the fellahin plotted insurrection, aided and encouraged by the native Egyptian priesthood.[44] When Popillius Laenas forced Antiochus Epiphanes to hold his hand at the very gates of Alexandria he must have wondered, in his heart of hearts, if Rome was not perhaps backing the wrong horse. But orders were orders: he hopefully urged the three co-regents to maintain brotherly (or sisterly) concord, and then removed himself before they could disregard his official advice. Like most compromises, this one made for trouble. Someone should have recalled Odysseus's shrewd saying: "Multiple rule is no good: let there be one king, one ruler."[45] The obvious candidate, for ability as well as on grounds of precedence, was Philometor. But lacking absolute authority and adequate backing, what could he do? He showed himself a clever, civilized,[46] and (for a Ptolemy) energetic ruler; but he could not fight everyone at once. In October 164 the machinations of his brother drove him from Alexandria to Rome, where he quietly took up residence in a working-class district, in ostentatious poverty, and waited for the authorities to discover his plight and come to him, in embarrassment and with largesse, which duly happened.[47]

However, as regards substantial political aid, Philometor's venture got him very little. He had not yet learned the simple lesson that in their dealings with foreign rulers the Romans much preferred winners to distressed suppliants. The Senate opted for the *status quo*, merely instructing a mission already on its way to Asia Minor to visit Alexandria and effect a reconciliation.[48] Philometor thereupon took off for Cyprus, to have some sort of base from which to operate.[49] Envoys from Alexandria, where Physcon's rule was proving intolerable, soon arrived begging

Philometor to come back. This change of heart in Alexandria may well have dictated what happened next. In May 163 the two brothers, with the approval of Rome's commissioners, agreed on a partition of the realm: Physcon would rule the western province of Cyrenaica, while Philometor was to reign in Egypt.[50] It was a makeshift solution, and one that—since Philometor did so well out of it, reducing Physcon to his more proper status of crown prince—in no way reduced, indeed exacerbated, the brothers' rivalry; but at least it gave the country a breathing space, and it held up, precariously, until Philometor's death in 145.

Even so, both brothers continued their *opéra bouffe* attacks on one another. Physcon, complaining that partition had been forced on him against his will (which was true enough), talked the Senate into backing his claim on Cyprus. Philometor ignored this ruling, and Physcon failed to reconquer the island.[51] As a result the Senate repudiated its alliance with Philometor, and sent his ambassadors home (161), a clear notice to Physcon that he had considerable latitude of action.[52] Perhaps in consequence of this Philometor tried, unsuccessfully, to have Physcon assassinated (156/5).[53] At this Physcon, still planning the recapture of Cyprus, announced that if he died childless he was bequeathing Cyrenaica to Rome.[54] (We have an inscription recording the will: no ancient literary source, interestingly, refers to it).[55] He then went back to Rome, showed (like Peisistratus) the scars of his attempted assassination, and finally got some token military support—five ships, Roman advisers, and the authorization to levy Greek troops at his own expense—for his Cyprus venture.[56] Why a majority in the Senate supported him is uncertain; Cato, for one, was against the idea, and spoke in favor of Philometor,[57] being old-fashioned enough to find Physcon not only politically opportunistic but morally offensive. It is tempting, though perhaps overspeculative, to see this vote as an index of the profound change in ethical values now taking place at Rome.

In any case the Cyprus expedition fizzled out ignominiously, and Physcon was captured by his brother. Philometor, with commendable patience (and perhaps a little uneasy about the line Rome might take over that provisional bequest of his vital western frontier province), not only spared Physcon's life, but offered him his own daughter Cleopatra Thea, Physcon's niece, in marriage.[58] For a family in which sibling incest had became almost *de rigueur*, this merely nepotic match was very small beer. Obviously Philometor was hoping that Physcon would sire a child in short order and nullify his bequest. He also, on Rome's insistence, sent his peccant brother back to Cyrene: the distributive *status quo* was to be preserved. He then appointed his own son, Ptolemy Eupator, governor of Cyprus, with royal prerogatives (Eupator died there, still very young, in 150).[59] From now (154) on Philometor's position was secure, his reputation at its height, his royal cult widespread. The Athenians, to whom he had presented a library and, possibly, a gymnasium, in gratitude erected a bronze equestrian statue of him on the Acropolis (ca. 150), and celebrated the so-called Ptolemaea with great lavishness.[60] Benefactions of this kind were common, and formed an integral part of Philometor's foreign policy, creating not only good will but also, he hoped, a network of accepted obligations. Thus, until Philometor's death on campaign in Coele-Syria (145), Physcon was stalemated. It·is too often assumed that this represented a setback for Roman policy in Egypt. In fact Rome endorsed, indeed insisted on, partition, and had everything to gain from the relatively stable decade that followed as a result, with Physcon well out of the way. To call Rome's dealings with Alexandria at this time "irrational" or "somewhat erratic,"[61] and then to argue that Philometor's activities subverted such preferred lunacies, is to stand logic doubly on its head. Like Eliot's women of Canterbury, the Senate did not want anything to happen; and in Ptolemaic Egypt, for a surprisingly long time, what they wanted was exactly what they got.

Demetrius I, meanwhile, was making powerful enemies in Syria. Despite his taste for hunting (which was how he came to meet Polybius) he had a sour, aloof manner: a solitary drinker and possible alcoholic,[62] he offered a striking contrast to the eccentric but extrovert Antiochus Epiphanes. He backed the wrong (suppositious) brother in a Cappadocian dynastic feud, and by so doing contrived to offend not only both Rome and Pergamon, but also his own unsuccessful candidate, Orophernes, who—accusing Demetrius of lukewarm support—raised the Antioch mob against him.[63] The rising was put down with violence: this did not make Demetrius any the more popular.[64] To add to his troubles, Attalus II of Pergamon—who had at last, aged over sixty, succeeded to the throne on the death of his brother Eumenes II (160/59), was on much better terms with Rome than Demetrius,[65] and in due course established himself as the leading dynast of Anatolia[66]—now produced a pretender to the Seleucid throne, a character called Balas,[67] who claimed to be the son of Antiochus IV (and is so presented by our Jewish sources), but was almost certainly an impostor.[68] Impostor or not, Attalus packed him off to Rome, where the Senate—still prevalently hostile to Demetrius, and now sensing his weakness—approved Balas's dubious credentials (153/2). To do so, as usual, committed them to nothing. Polybius's predictably tendentious account of the debate denigrates both the motives and the intelligence of those supporting Balas,[69] claiming that "bal-

Fig. 142. The pretender Alexander Balas. Phoenician silver tetradrachm struck at Sidon, 149/8 B.C. Photo Hirmer.

anced" senators saw through him.[70] In point of fact Balas probably seemed, at this juncture, the lesser of two evils, with a better chance of stabilizing the regime.[71]

Endorsement, of course, did not imply material aid. Rome, it should be remembered, was at war in Spain, and already contemplating a third round against Carthage: there were more pressing problems to settle than the endless squabbles of petty Hellenistic dynasts. Balas might have Rome's approval, but his real backing came from Attalus, Ptolemy VI (his eyes once more turned toward Coele-Syria), and Ariarathes V, the successful claimant in Cappadocia.[72] Now styling himself Alexander Balas, he landed at Ptolemaïs-Ake, near Mt. Carmel. Both he and Demetrius began bidding vigorously for the support of the Jewish guerilla commander Jonathan (152/1; cf. below, p. 523); Demetrius offered him, *inter alia*, the military command in Judaea, with the right to levy troops, while Balas countered with the post of High Priest.[73] Jonathan accepted both offers, but took Balas's side (Oct. 152). After a short campaign Demetrius died fighting (winter 151/0), and Balas, the impostor, became king.[74]

Ptolemy VI, shrewd and patient, saw at once that here was a simple adventurer, who relished the trappings and perquisites of power, but was otherwise lacking in both dynastic ambition and political *savoir-faire*. He therefore encouraged Balas (150/49) to marry his daughter Cleopatra Thea, briefly betrothed earlier to Physcon, who had other ideas in mind.[75] This time the wedding came off, and "one of the most energetic and murderous" Hellenistic queens,[76] strong-featured child of incest and ambition,[77] was duly launched on her lurid career. But all this lay in the future: for the moment the bride's father had his own reasons for the match. No Ptolemy would ever pass up the chance of becoming the power behind the Seleucid throne: certainly not while Coele-Syria was still potentially recoverable.

Ptolemy's chance soon came. Though Demetrius I had been killed, his sons had escaped, and now young Demetrius II returned to Syria with a force of Cretan mer-

Fig. 143. Alexander Balas and his wife, Cleopatra Thea, shown wearing veil and *kalathos* (ceremonial basket). Silver tetradrachm minted at Seleucia-in-Pieria ca. 150–146 B.C. British Museum, London.

cenaries. Ptolemy, as though going to his son-in-law's assistance, swept north into Palestine. Jonathan of Judaea, similarly on the lookout for gain, now occupied the ports of Joppa and Ascalon. Balas, who at least had the wit to see what Ptolemy was about, tried to procure his assassination. The attempt failed. Ptolemy pressed on north toward Antioch. His daughter Cleopatra Thea found her way back to him (having had the good sense to realize that Balas was finished), and Ptolemy, declaring her marriage void, coolly prepared to refurbish her as a bride for the young Demetrius: the price, it goes without saying, was Coele-Syria.[78] The volatile citizens of Antioch, having transferred their allegiance from Balas to Demetrius, now took even the intrigue-hardened Ptolemy by surprise: they acclaimed *him* as the new Seleucid monarch. Ptolemy—like his ancestor Soter in very similar circumstances (above, p. 14)—must have had a moment of quite appalling temptation.[79] The ultimate prize that had so bedazzled Ptolemy III had been tossed into his lap. But the prize had come too late, and Ptolemy knew it. This was 145: Carthage and Corinth had both fallen to Rome, and Philometor had not forgotten how Popillius Laenas treated Antiochus on the Day of Eleusis.[80] It has been argued that he was confident of being able to count on Rome's indifference.[81] This is the optimism of hindsight. Be that as it may, Philometor refused the offer, and persuaded the citizens of Antioch to stick with Demetrius—who promptly became his new son-in-law, and ascended the throne as Demetrius II Nicator Theos Philadelphos. Loss of Seleucid prestige and territory was compensated for, as time went on, by ever-more grandiloquent and lengthy titles. Balas was killed soon afterwards in northern Syria—by an Arab chieftain with whom he had sought refuge after suffering a crushing military defeat—and

Fig. 144. Demetrius II Nicator of Syria, during his first reign (145–140/39 B.C.). Silver tetradrachm minted at Seleucia-on-Tigris ca. 145–141 B.C. On the reverse, the seated figure of Tyche (Chance)—an appropriate emblem, given the vicissitudes of Demetrius's fortune.
Numismatic Fine Arts, Inc.

his head brought to Ptolemy. Unfortunately, Ptolemy himself was wounded in the same battle, and died two days later. The way was open for his still-resentful brother, Physcon, chafing in Cyrenaica, to stage a comeback—which in due course, as we shall see, he did.[82]

At this point we must backtrack a few years to follow events in Macedonia and the Aegean world. The frontier bickering between Pergamon and Bithynia (156–154) is of real interest only insofar as it involves more important protagonists:[83] for example, when Rome, still smarting at the part Pergamon had played at the time of Pydna, in 166 proclaimed the freedom of the Galatians, and publicly snubbed Eumenes II by passing a decree that placed Rome off limits for any king.[84] The partial eclipse of Rhodes by Delos had led directly to a recrudescence of piracy, since it had been the Rhodian squadrons that patrolled the sea lanes.[85] Once again Roman policy had been *ad hoc* and shortsighted: a century later it would take the Republic's full resources, under Pompey's direction, to clear the Mediterranean of this scourge (below, p. 657). Economic distress still further exacerbated the tensions between haves and have-nots; yet the crop of pretenders recorded during this period makes it all too clear that monarchy was still seen as the only feasible solution in political terms.

The most notable of these pretenders appeared in Macedonia.[86] His name was Andriscus, but he claimed in fact to be Philip, Perseus's son by Laodice (who of course was not only Seleucus IV's daughter, but also Demetrius I's sister).[87] Demetrius, who, as we have seen, had problems of his own, sent Andriscus to Rome (153/2). The Senate was not interested. Not, that is, until Andriscus—after conning travel funds, slaves, royal robes, and a diadem out of an ex-concubine of Perseus, royal recognition from Byzantium, and troops from various Thracian chieftains[88]—advanced from Thrace into Macedonia (like a bolt from the blue, Polybius says),[89] and won control of the country after two battles (149/8). Opposition came chiefly from the landed classes, as we might expect: Andriscus proscribed men of wealth and property, basing himself on popular support. This proved both widespread and enthusiastic: so much so that Andriscus extended his operations into Thessaly. It seems clear that Macedonians would rather have a king, any king, than be parceled out into faceless cantons and lose their much-treasured ethnic identity.[90] A hastily mustered Roman force was cut to pieces by the pretender; but two more legions, under Quintus Caecilius Metellus Macedonicus, soon put an end to Andriscus's career—with symbolic aptness, at Pydna (148).[91] Macedonia now lost its independence entirely, becoming, with Illyria, a Roman province. One of the first marks of permanent Roman occupation was the construction of that great trunk road the Via Egnatia, which ran from Epidamnus on the Adriatic to Thessalonike, where the governor now had his headquarters.[92] Its well-engineered linkage of the northern Balkans was a visible condemnation of separatism, and ushered in an era of pragmatic unification such as even Alexander had never dreamed of.

The gold and silver mines had already been reopened, in 158 (above, p. 436); Polybius, no Macedonian irredentist, remarks that Rome had proved Macedonia's benefactor by freeing her both from a tyrannical monarchy and from her internal dissensions.[93] Yet—perversely, viewed in Polybian terms—there were many, still, in the Greek states as well as in Macedonia, who preferred the freedom to pursue their own feuds and intrigues over the well-ordered tutelage of Rome. Andriscus was not the only leader who could count on the support of the dispossessed or politically alienated masses. Roman brutality and highhandedness after Aemilius Paullus's conquest in 168 had not been forgotten; nor had the collaborationist activities of pro-Roman oligarchs such as Callicrates (above, p. 425). The Achaean League had fought as Rome's ally in turn against Philip V, Antiochus III, and Perseus. It is a mark of how far public feeling had changed in a short time that by 146 the League's leaders were ready to engage in a desperate last-ditch war against Rome, which they must surely have known, in their innermost hearts, that they had no real chance of winning. Why was this? A class struggle has been suggested, with the Greek masses, whipped into action by Achaean demagogues, rising against Rome as the power behind their oppressive oligarchical regime.[94] Yet while it is true that Rome, notoriously, tended to back the wealthy upper classes in any country, she was also ready to accept, in a true pragmatic spirit, support from wherever it might be offered,[95] and this by no means always meant the propertied classes. *Per contra*, it was by no means only the dispossessed who nursed fierce dreams of independence.

Alternatively, the initiative has been attributed to Rome, anxious for an end to her complex and ultimately unsatisfactory policy of nonintervention in Greece, and thus implementing an administrative mopping-up operation to round off the provincialization of Macedonia.[96] Yet this too seems unlikely. For one thing, the Senate was preoccupied, to the exclusion of almost everything else, with tough campaigns against Carthage and the Spanish tribes. A simpler explanation suggests itself. Granted the conditions prevailing in Greece from 167 onwards, it was only a matter of time before the sullen and resentful subservience, the child–parent relationship symbolized by endless embassies and requests for Roman arbitration, the fear of random Roman cruelty and even more random favoritism, exploded in open, violent, hopeless, and hysterical revolt. Those who characterize the war as a patriotic and nationalistic uprising[97]—seldom the most rational of enterprises—seem to me to be on the right track.

Already the conflict between pro- and anti-Roman elements had led to a grisly series of reprisals, exiles, suicides, and condemnations,[98] sometimes involving torture or other atrocities.[99] Polybius was caught between his admiration for Rome and his innate Achaean patriotism. Once the war was lost, he personally argued the Achaean cause in an endeavor to mitigate Roman severity,[100] but his real anger, as countless passages demonstrate,[101] was reserved for the violent demagogues who led the Achaean League, hopelessly unprepared, into a war with Rome, which they stood no chance of winning.[102] The misfortune (*atychia*) that afflicted the Greeks at this time was, in Polybius's view, culpable. He even attributes Rome's success to Providence, to Tyche reversing the effects of *atychia*: "If we had not collapsed so quickly," he quotes people as saying, "we should have been utterly destroyed."[103] Not, be it noted, by the Romans (who in this context are made to look like saviors), but by the purges of their fellow citizens, the indiscriminate use of terrorism, which the Achaean populists in office were (or so Polybius claims) making a commonplace instrument of policy.[104] There speaks the collaborating liaison officer, Rome's agent of conformism, and his role explains why Polybius's villainous demagogues remain, in the end, mere sadistic bogeymen, devoid of rational motivation. He even at one point describes the whole country as "bewitched."[105] He attacks the arrogant, couldn't-care-less attitude of the freed slaves.[106] All this class-conscious social sniping distracts attention from the real, and obvious, driving force behind Achaea's ultimate defiance of Rome: patriotic nationalism, the will, against all odds, to fight for true freedom and independence. In his ambivalent position Polybius can only argue that to resist the inevitable is criminal stupidity,[107] a proposition that—fortunately for mankind—has seldom made much of an impression on committed freedom-fighters.[108]

During the decade prior to the Achaean War the differences between various Greek states—Athens and Oropus over violence and illegality in the collection of tolls;[109] Rhodes against Crete regarding Cretan piracy (155/4);[110] above all, Sparta's split from the Achaean League over a territorial claim disputed with Megalopolis[111]—had continued to force themselves on the Senate's attention, though the Romans still avoided direct intervention where possible, preferring to work through advisory commissions or neutral arbitration. (Since all these cases were rife with bribery and political intrigue, it is hard to blame them.) For example, when the Athenians took their case to Rome, the matter was turned over to Sicyon. Condemned by Sicyonian assessors to pay Oropus damages of five hundred talents, an exorbitant sum, the Athenians played on their city's intellectual prestige by sending their three leading philosophers (Carneades, head of the New Academy, Diogenes the Stoic, and Critolaus the Peripatetic) back to Rome to plead their cause (155).[112] The Romans, who admired Athenian culture but respected legal decisions, let the judgment stand; they did, however, cut the damages assessed by four-fifths. An Athenian garrison was placed in Oropus, and hostages taken.[113] Oropus subsequently appealed to the League (not, be it noted, to Rome) against alleged outrages by this garrison and their appeal was upheld—exactly as we might expect, since the Senate ruled that all cases except those of a capital nature should remain under the Achaean League's jurisdiction,[114] and the League had no great love for Athens.

This happened in a further development of Sparta's quarrel with the League over Megalopolis. The Spartan envoy to Rome challenged Achaean authority; Callicrates the Achaean as firmly defended it; Rome endorsed Callicrates and the League. The endorsement encouraged a highhanded attitude to Sparta on the part of the Achaean government, and the following year both sides once more had embassies in Rome (149/8). Callicrates, the original leader of the Achaean delegation, had died *en route*,[115] which meant that his role as spokesman went to the ranking member, Diaeus, a tough activist in the Philopoemen tradition. Diaeus was not only anti-Spartan, but shrewd enough to exploit Rome's reluctance to become embroiled in Greek domestic quarrels. A shouting match before the Senate between him and his Spartan opponent produced the promise of yet another on-the-spot Roman commission of inquiry to adjudicate rival claims. For whatever reason, it was a year and a half before it set out, during which time a great deal happened.

We need not (as has often been done) invoke reasons of *Machtpolitik* for this de-lay.[116] Ingrained and habitual senatorial procrastination seems a far likelier reason. It is also true that, with the pretender Andriscus still operating in Macedonia and Thessaly (149/8), the Roman authorities had more pressing business on hand. They were certainly not bothered at this stage by the League, which provided auxiliaries to help put down Andriscus. Polybius, recently returned from Italy to Achaea (150; see p. 278), was sent, at the consul's request, to conduct negotiations with Carthage.[117] "As late as the spring of 147 there is no sign of anti-Roman activity and no indication of an approaching conflict."[118] Diaeus, meanwhile, had reported that Rome opposed Spartan secession from the Achaean League; the Spartan envoys announced the opposite.[119] The Roman commission waited, in tactful indolence, perhaps until Andriscus was defeated, but more probably without a firm policy of any sort except to spin things out as long as possible, before finally landing in Greece (late spring 147). Then, however, their decisiveness made up for lost time. They announced not only that Sparta was indeed to be detached from the League, but that various other cities, including Corinth and Argos, were similarly to be "freed" and enjoy independence.

Here was a surprise, and no mistake. Polybius claims[120]—and he may well have been in a position to know—that the idea was simply to shock the League out of its stubborn intransigence by scare tactics.[121] Perhaps the threat was not meant seriously (there had been numerous precedents for such intimidatory bluster), but this time it was seen, understandably, as a blatant attempt to manipulate the League's internal affairs, and produced an explosion of resentful fury. The Achaeans had Sparta's dele-gates arrested (some of them actually in the houses occupied by the Roman commis-sioners), and the Romans themselves were roughly treated in the assembly. They returned to Rome at once.[122] Yet the Senate, far from taking a tough line, merely sent out a second mission to deliver a mild censure and with a request that the Achaeans themselves should discipline those responsible for the outbreak.[123] The League had already sent off its own official mission, led by Polybius's brother Thearidas, to apologize. The two parties met in mid-journey and got on very amicably. Achaea was simply admonished to avoid further attacks on Rome or Sparta. Though the measure was not officially rescinded, there was no more talk at this stage of forcibly removing cities from the League.[124]

Diaeus, Critolaus (the *stratēgos* for 147/6), and their backers may have inter-preted this as a sign of weakness.[125] Critolaus is, inevitably, pictured as a rabid war-monger by our ancient sources, presumably on a *post hoc, propter hoc* basis: the Achaean War was, after all, fought and lost during his generalship.[126] Yet it was Critolaus who now (autumn 147), at a meeting with Spartan and Roman delegates in Tegea, stalled action for another six months by claiming that only the Achaeans in full assembly could negotiate a settlement, and that their next official meeting (*synodos*) would not take place until the spring of 146.[127] This undoubtedly irritated Sextus Julius Caesar, the Roman commissioner, who returned to Rome fuming about Critolaus's procrastinating tactics; but was it the insult that made war inevitable?[128] Hardly, and certainly not with Thearidas and his conciliatory mission still *en route* for Rome. What is more, the Romans took no action till, precisely, the following spring—which makes it look as though they had acquiesced in the six-month postponement[129]—and, even then, when Caecilius Metellus sent yet another legation, it was as amicable as its predecessors.[130] It has been suggested that one reason for delay at the Roman end was that there was no qualified magistrate available in 147 to conduct the Achaean War;[131] but there is no substantial reason for believing that at this point Rome wanted a war at all. Even Harris, who never misses an opportunity to stress Rome's supposed aggressiveness and acquisitiveness, has to admit that "the League could cause the Roman Senate no more anxiety than a wasp on a warm afternoon."[132]

The situation in Achaea, however, had changed over the winter of 147/6. War fever had indeed swept the country, and Critolaus seems to have been largely responsible for it; but it was directed against Sparta rather than Rome, and the violent anti-Roman propaganda in our sources (which we need not doubt, once war with Rome was a fact) has been antedated by several months 'from the high summer of 146. It was then that Critolaus inveighed against Roman highhandedness,[133] then that Greeks were called to fight for freedom once more, to throw off the strangling yoke of Rome.[134] In any case the legation sent by Metellus from Macedonia found the Achaean assembly in a fine lather of nationalistic hysteria.[135] Their conciliatory words were shouted down, and they were hustled out of the meeting. With inflammatory talk of traitors and collaborators Critolaus persuaded the assembly to vote for war against Sparta[136] and to suspend debt payments for the duration of the conflict, a much-misunderstood measure.[137] He also declared his desire to remain on friendly terms with Rome, though not with despots, an ambiguous caveat. What he seems to be implying is that this was a private conflict between Greeks, and interference by outsiders was not welcome. Also, Rome—whether through indifference, or because she was preoccupied elsewhere—had let Achaea have a free hand with Sparta in the past; why should she not continue to do so now?[138]

But for once Critolaus had miscalculated, and badly. Rome's patience was at long last exhausted. Achaea's bellicose determination to settle the Spartan problem by force could not be ignored: the balance of power, as with Antiochus IV in Egypt, was being gravely threatened. When Critolaus marched north to discipline the apostate city of Heracleia he found himself, to his horror, confronted by a Roman army under the redoubtable Metellus (April 146). At Scarphaea, near Thermopylae, he was crushingly defeated, and may have committed suicide.[139] Reality had eclipsed rhetoric: the *bellum Achaicum* was now a fact. A kind of passionate last-ditch determination swept the country. Boeotia and Euboea, Phocis and Ozolian Locris joined the League's forces.[140] The mood resembled that of the American Old South in 1860, and the military preparations were no less inadequate. Nor, clearly, had a vigorous Roman offensive been foreseen. Through the fiery rhetoric we glimpse disorder, civilian panic, flight. Yet once committed, the cities of the League reveal an unshakeable determination to fight on, whatever the cost. A few prominent citizens, predictably, argued for capitulation: they were imprisoned or executed.[141] The vast majority of the population—not merely, as has been thought,[142] the lower classes—meant to see this crisis through to the bitter end.[143]

Diaeus manumitted, and enlisted, twelve thousand carefully chosen slaves,[144] called for the release of imprisoned debtors, levied a special war fund, and prepared to base his defense on Corinth.[145] Metellus's forces met those of Lucius Mummius, his consular successor for 146. Polybius paints a scene of panic and confusion sweeping the cities of Greece.[146] Diaeus refused to negotiate, and was defeated. Mummius settled down to besiege Corinth. Despite his fierce rhetoric, despite the fact that he had executed at least two subordinates who urged surrender on terms, Diaeus, instead of holding out, fled by night with the tattered remnants of the Achaean army, presumably judging his position hopeless (which indeed it had been from the beginning). He made for Megalopolis, where—like the Gaul commemorated by Attalus I's Pergamene sculptors (above, p. 340)—he first slew his wife to prevent her falling into Roman hands, then committed suicide.[147] The Achaean War was over, almost before it had begun. Mummius gave his troops *carte blanche* to loot and destroy Corinth: in this he was acting on specific senatorial instructions, though probably not (as was once thought) with the intention of eliminating a bothersome commercial rival. Women and children were sold into slavery; any men still in the city when it fell were slaughtered without mercy. This did not stop cities like Elis from honoring Mummius with lickspittle dedications praising his benevolence (*sic*) toward the Greeks.[148] Sparta, the accidental *casus belli*, never again played any active role in the affairs of Greece.

Corinth was still a heap of ruins when Cicero visited the site, at some point between 79 and 77;[149] it was not rebuilt till 44, and then only at Caesar's express command.[150] Polybius, returning to Greece from Carthage, describes the systematic plundering of works of art.[151] However unwillingly, the Senate had been led, step by step, after the annihilation of the Antigonid regime, into the dangerous but temptingly profitable labyrinth of a long-term Greek involvement. Like Alexander at Thebes, Rome had finally made clear to the Greeks, in a way that no rhetoric or diplomacy could conceal, just where the true power lay. The slogan of "freedom for the Greeks" had been buried at last in the smoking ruins of Corinth, and it was not to be truly revived until, almost two millennia later, on 25 March 1821, Bishop Germanos raised the banner of revolt against the Turks at the monastery of Aghia Lavra, below Kalávryta[152]—with symbolic aptness (though probably no one noticed this at the time) in the very heart of Achaean League territory.

CHAPTER 26

MATHEMATICS AND ASTRONOMY: THE ALTERNATIVE IMMORTALITY

In the course of this study we have had occasion to note a number of social, political, and religious characteristics that typify the Hellenistic period as a whole. These include a reversion to large-scale authoritarian government, the emergence of ruler cults, the increased availability of slave labor, a marked inclination toward superstition and astrology, the enskyment of Tyche (Chance, Fate, Providence), a decline in the respect paid to the Olympian gods, a corresponding enhancement of exotic foreign cults, the collapse of the inner spirit animating the *polis*, the loneliness of the individual adrift in the urban jungle, and, finally, the subsidization—meaning control—of scholarship and science by royal patronage. Since this is commonly portrayed (at least until the second century B.C.) as the great age of Greek scientific discovery, above all in mathematics and astronomy, we should, from a historical viewpoint, be concerned to see how far the science reflects, or indeed is conditioned by, new social or political conditions, how far it modifies those conditions, and how far (as an inherently elitist occupation) it operates independently of current trends—either unknown to, or rejected by, popular opinion.[1]

This is an immensely complex problem, without cut-and-dried answers. It has been suggested that the early scientific efflorescence that reached its apogee with Anaxagoras, Democritus, and the Hippocratic writers was cut short by the decline in political liberty, and replaced, from the fourth century, with more purely philosophical, religious-infiltrated, anti-empirical thinking.[2] The key justification for such a belief is Polybius's assertion that many Greek leaders turned to intellectual pursuits because they were now debarred from political or military careers.[3] This statement may well be factually correct, yet still, as a generalization, remain, at best, a dangerous half-truth. For one thing, high achievement in both literature and science tapers off sharply from the end of the third century, which makes it tempting to correlate this decline, too, with the advent of Rome. Nevertheless, the history of mathematics (to take one obvious example), from the Pythagoreans through Plato to Euclid and beyond, does strongly suggest that for some exceptionally talented men such a discipline offered a more attractive road to self-fulfillment than the fast-vanishing ideal of civic involvement. Political considerations continued to influence the development of science, but in more subtle and long-term ways. Just as there had been a close correlation, in the archaic period, between the development of general intellectual principles and the concept of democracy and justice for all through equality under the law (*isonomia*), so now royal patronage and the reversion to authoritarianism came, slowly, to determine, and limit, major areas of research.

Yet in the long run perhaps no single factor exerted so profound an influence on scientific thought as that all-pervasive monadism, that habit, common to Greeks throughout ancient history, of "viewing the cosmos as a living organism, a body that can be understood and comprehended *in its entirety*."[4] At the same time there was no lack of socially or politically related phenomena in the intellectual movements of the Hellenistic era. It is notable, for instance, that the Epicureans were left very much outside the new social establishment represented by the Greek world's largely depoliticized business plutocracy, in a way that none of the other major philosophical schools (with the exception of the Cynics, who were social pariahs anyway) seem to have been: why was this? The aversion of any well-heeled oligarch to the Cynic's antisocial anarchy is as understandable as his natural liking for Stoicism, which always catered to the authoritarian *status quo*; but what was it about the Epicureans that aroused such hostility and prejudice? Not, I think, so much the casual sidelining of the gods (though that must have given great offense to traditionalists) as the atomic theory of nature, the concept of a world formed from random atoms in the void, of material universes that came into being and passed away by a process of mechanistic causation, with no divine teleological principle behind them.

This kind of physical cosmology was indeed the exception rather than the rule. Plato, Aristotle, and the Stoics all posited a divine and mathematically ordered cosmos, revolving round earth—itself unmoving—as a central focal point: a theory that might have been designed to encourage hierarchical, fixed-order concepts, macrocosm and microcosm reflecting physical, theological, and political immutability (or, from a different viewpoint, stagnation), on earth as in heaven. The apparent uniformity of movement in the heavens gave rise to a complex, and ultimately lunatic, astral theology (p. 596), by which the stars and planets, sun and moon, were endowed not only with sentient life, but with the power to affect every detail of human life and society, through a process of cosmic correspondences. Hence the development of the misconceived pseudoscience of astrology. The divinity and life of the heavenly bodies, their supposedly regular, circular, uniform movement, the geocentric postulate that underlay almost all astronomical theory: these emerge as aspects of a *Weltanschauung* so deeply rooted in the Greek psyche that even seemingly contrary evidence could not eradicate it, and which led to quite extraordinarily ingenious theorizing—though not, it should be stressed, to consciously dishonest casuistry—in the process known to contemporary thinkers as "saving the appearances,"[5] a "wondrous problem"[6] that involved, first and foremost, explaining the seemingly irregular movements of the planets in terms that preserved overall circularity and regularity in the revolutions of the heavenly bodies as a whole.

The problem had already been touched on by Plato in his *Timaeus*:[7] behind it lay a fundamental terror of chaos that emerges clearly in thinkers from Hesiod onwards. Before the end of the fifth century this fear was compounded by an increasing political fragmentation, a polarization between extreme demagogues and ultras of the right, that is reflected in Plato's own life and work. His horrific personal experiences,[8] both with right-wing totalitarianism (the regime of the Thirty, who included a number of his own aristocratic relatives and friends), and with the increasingly volatile and unpredictable Athenian democracy, which in 399 executed his mentor, Socrates, drove him more and more to seek some eternal pattern, perfect and changeless (though still rooted in aristocratic elitism), behind the bewildering flux and corruption of the visible world. Hence that astonishing remark in the *Republic*, that "we shall approach astronomy, as we do geometry, by way of problems, *and ignore what's in the sky*, if we intend to get a real grasp of astronomy."[9] Hence the Theory of Forms, or Ideas, those perfect models of which all physical entities are no more than flawed copies. Hence the Platonic obsession with mathematics, and above all with geometry, as the one mode of learning supposedly subject to pure reason, demonstrable by proof, and universally consistent.[10] God, Plato is said to have declared, always geometrizes.[11]

There is rather more behind this last gnomic assertion than meets the eye. The discussion in Plutarch's *Symposiaka* ("Dinner-Table Discussions") is revealing. One speaker argues, as we might expect, that the words allude to geometry as the pursuit of eternal abstract truth, and another (Plutarch himself) that they symbolize the perfect, ideal monadism of matter and form established in the cosmos by the Demiurge; but the third contends that, whereas arithmetic is egalitarian and populist (for which reason Lycurgus is said to have banned "arithmetic proportion" from Sparta), geometry is ideal for a "prudent oligarchy" or "legitimate monarchy." How does he reach this striking conclusion? "The one distributes on a basis of quantitative equality, but the other on that of proportionate merit. . . . The equality that the many pursue—in fact the greatest of all *injustices*—God eradicates as far as possible, and preserves, by geometrical canons, the proportionate relation as the yardstick of legality."[12] It would be hard to find an analysis that better illustrated the all-pervasive Greek nexus between intellectual thought and authoritarian politics: Plato's statement could, in this context, be translated as "God always supports proper class distinctions."

Thus the pursuit of mathematics can be seen as one element in the complex movement that, from the fourth century onwards, placed increasing stress on *bien-pensant*, property-owning conservatism, with a correspondingly deep contempt (compounded of ignorance and snobbery) for the banausic activities of daily life, above all for manual labor and the skills of artisan or craftsman.[13] Social no less than intellectual exigence explains why a knowledge of geometry was the one great prerequisite for any student hoping to enter the Academy,[14] and just what Plato meant when he claimed that geometry—the instrument of class-conscious oligarchs eager for stability on their own terms—aspired upward toward pure thought, rejected mere materialism or gain: easy enough to be high-minded on a secure private income. It is remarkable (though perhaps not all that surprising) how far both Euclid and Plato managed to fog the political issue behind a smokescreen of moral uplift. Just as Euclid contemptuously ordered his slave to give a three-obol tip to the student who asked what he could gain out of learning geometry,[15] "since he's got to make a profit from what he learns," so Plato condemned mathematicians who tried to duplicate a cube mechanically, by means of instruments, precisely because this brought geometry down from the eternal and incorporeal to mere physical reproduction.[16] No aristocrat, least of all Plato, could bring himself to believe that true excellence, *virtù* (*aretē*), was teachable (least of all for a fee) rather than innate: hence much of the early, emotionally loaded, discussion in the *Meno* and elsewhere. What Plato aimed for was an elaborate intellectual, moral, and social elitism that transcended the existing political order by introducing rigorous thought into old aristocratic concepts.

Ironically we know today, too well, that the absolute trust placed by Plato in geometry was illusory: ever since Riemann, Bolyai, and Lobachevsky broke the Euclidean mold in the nineteenth century,[17] it has been clear that Euclid's basic postulates, far from being sacrosanct and self-evident verities, are simply the basis for a logico-deductive scheme where consequences are drawn systematically and rationally from whatever set of axioms we may choose.[18] What is more, it seems clear that Euclid himself (*fl.* ca. 300), who founded a school in Alexandria, was equally well aware of this. He may not have developed any alternative system, and indeed retained a good deal of traditional lumber, by then obsolete, from his predecessors, but at least he knew that his schema was hypothetical, in the sense that some of his postulates ran counter to what other early mathematicians believed: his work seems to have been followed by a period of assimilation.[19]

We have to make a clear distinction, throughout the Hellenistic period, between individual scientific discoveries, which range from Aristarchus's heliocentric theory to Hero's discovery of rotary steam propulsion, and the circumstances—immediate, gradual, or (in many cases) nonexistent—of their practical exploitation.[20] We also need to explore the various factors, social, economic, technical, religious, that kept a surprising number of these innovations from effective development. There are several cogent reasons for the notorious split between pure and applied science in the Greek world: chief among them the fact that, while Greek mathematicians, geographers, physicists, and astronomers made theoretical discoveries that would not be matched, let alone surpassed, till long after the Renaissance, there was virtually no development of technology, even though more technological expertise existed than is sometimes thought. One obvious reason for this is the intellectual elitism and acute social snobbery inherent in Greek society, which (for example) stultified the advance of scientific chemistry, since this not only called for accurate quantification, but was associated in the Greek mind with such banausic pursuits as dyeing, mining, and herbal medicine (hence, later, with the quackery of alchemical transmutations), all practiced in an *ad hoc* fashion by common artisans.[21]

Both Plato and Aristotle, as is well known, looked down on the mechanical aspects of production, not only exalting theory above practice (which is arguable), but also, Plato in particular, equating this with an ingrained contempt for experiment, by no means universally shared,[22] but widespread enough,[23] and setting against it a firm belief in the sovereign powers of unaided reason. Class prejudice (experiments were how mere craftsmen went about their business) was reinforced by a well-justified fear of inaccuracy and a lack of proper controls. Here, interestingly, they may well have used an analogy from the law courts,[24] where arguments "from probability" (*apo tōn eikotōn*) were habitually advanced in preference to the use of witnesses, on the grounds (too often well justified) that a witness would invariably lie his head off—fifteen witnesses once swore to the death of a slave girl who was subsequently produced alive in court[25]—or prove an untrustworthy observer even when he was trying to be honest. Logical reasoning (these logical minds held) was far more likely to arrive at a fair conclusion. A similar, though to us even more surprising, prejudice long existed against written texts, so easy for lazy or clever-stupid scribes (craftsmen again!) to garble, whereas verbal dialectic advanced on purely intellectual premises: here the Peripatetics and the Alexandrians, forced by an increasing flood of material to establish permanent records, did much to preserve not only literature, but advances in science as well.[26]

This brings us to another weakness that ancient scientist and ancient forensic specialists shared: the crippling lack of advanced technical instruments to aid direct observation. (For simpler devices such as celestial-sphere models and the *dioptra*, see below, p. 480.) Experimentation existed; but it was rudimentary, random, unsystematic, indifferent to statistics,[27] and, since it lacked adequate equipment or controls, appallingly inaccurate. (It has, for instance, been calculated that the best an ancient astronomer could do in the vital matter of timekeeping at night was a margin of roughly ten minutes.)[28] In physics it was sporadic (optics and hydrostatics did well), in astronomy impossible by definition, in biology handicapped by inadequate controls, in chemistry further held up by quackery, fraud, and guild secrecy. The Pythagorean discovery of arithmetical ratios in harmonious musical intervals may well have been due to pure luck. As has been well said, "there is no science at all without a society of scientifically interested and competent persons, making, checking, and recording; and their instruments for doing these things."[29] No telescopes, no microscopes, none of the apparatus we take for granted today (cf. p. 486): inaccurate azimuths and sundials, with true sophistication, as in the case of the astrolabe, restricted to pragmatic arts, such as navigation, which did not attract the attention of the major theorists.[30]

Thus the pressure, socially and politically, in a society that never lost its elitist assumptions—indeed, merely translated them from aristocratic into plutocratic terms—was all away from controlled observation, change, random factors, experiment, or (in any radical sense) revolution, what the Romans so revealingly termed *res nouae*, "new things," and toward universal abstract theories predicating a consistent, unchanging, cosmic pattern of existence, a sanctified *status quo* revolving eter-

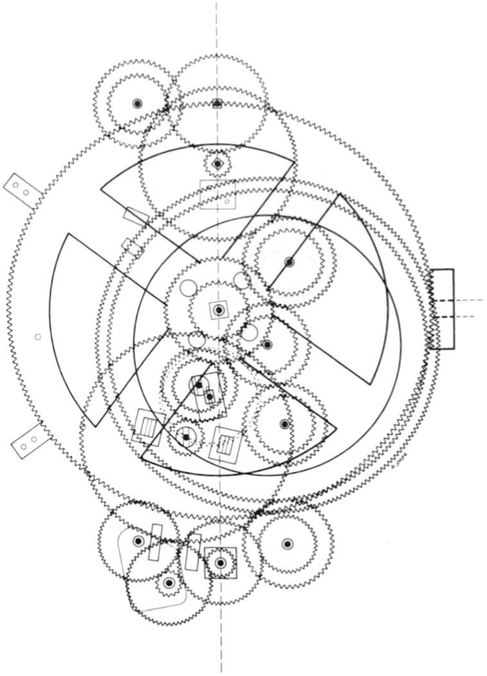

Fig. 145. The Antikythera astrolabe.
Reconstruction by Derek de Solla Price
of the gearing system of a calendar
computer (ca. 80 B.C.) containing over
thirty interdependent gear wheels.
From Derek de Solla Price, *Gears from the
Greeks* (New York, 1975), fig. 29.

nally on itself in perfect circularity. It is not that scientists were incapable of operating outside this pattern: the atomists and the great astronomer Aristarchus of Samos (*fl.* first half of 3d c. B.C.) both did so, with remarkable prescience and success. What they could not count on was any kind of general social acceptance. When the Athenian Cleanthes (p. 186) dismissed Aristarchus's heliocentric theory (which he combined with the already existing notion, duly refuted by Aristotle, that the earth rotated about its own axis)[31] as impious, on the grounds that "he was displacing the Heart of the Cosmos,"[32] he was giving voice to a mainstream opinion—and one in which by then an enormous amount of religious, scientific, and social capital had been invested.

Its survival, moreover, was virtually guaranteed, not only by public emotional support, but also by the refusal of those scientists who could have assaulted its underpinning to come down from their theoretical heights. Archimedes might have been conscripted to organize the defense of Syracuse with elaborate military gadgetry (213/2: cf. p. 227), but he still refused to write a handbook on engineering, because "he regarded the business of mechanics and every skill that grapples with men's daily needs as ignoble and vulgar, devoting himself exclusively to those pursuits in which beauty and subtlety were uncontaminated by mere need."[33] Cheap labor, the Egyptian fellahin, the slave as animated tool (p. 383)—these may well have discouraged technological advance, though less than has often been supposed; far more insidious was the ingrained Greek conservatism that never felt the world should be changed, merely analyzed and explained, with the social structure, like everything else, regarded as a fixed datum, part of a divinely ordered and immutable pattern. Small wonder that the slave revolts of the second century did not achieve more (p. 384): the miracle is that they ever got off the ground at all.

The mere existence of Aristarchus's heliocentric hypothesis, or of the Democritean atomic theory, testifies to the indomitable inventiveness and originality of Greek intellectual thought. Yet the arguments supporting heliocentrism were not, as yet, strong enough to dislodge the geocentric theory—Hipparchus and others dismissed them as conflicting with accepted astronomical observations[34]—and that society as a whole should prefer the latter is no more than we might expect; that Aristotle, with the enormous weight of his authority, had come out in support of a sentient, geocentric universe did more to hold up the progress of astronomy than any other single factor.[35] To keep the earth at the center of things flattered man's self-esteem and avoided psychic displacement; to make the whole intricate pattern of the heavens not only control man's destiny but also, as sailors and farmers knew well, serve his purposes—that, in a subtle way, offered not only spiritual comfort, but greater flattery still. The same stars that shaped men's lives enabled them to steer their ships and time their sowing or plowing.

The twinkling night sky was, moreover, a rich emotive pageant of theological belief, divine catasterisms, pregnant aetiologies: to study it was to become involved not only in scientific observation, but willy-nilly in a whole complex projected macrocosm, in mythological semiotics. The astronomer Claudius Ptolemy (*fl.* 2d c. A.D.) expressed something of this in a haunting epigram:[36]

> I know I am mortal, ephemeral; yet when I track the
>   Clustering spiral orbits of the stars
> My feet touch earth no longer: a heavenly nursling,
>   Ambrosia-filled, I company with God.

There is a real alternative immortality here; but it involves something over and beyond the joys of pure research. Mathematics and astronomy are, after all, sciences of the infinite. It is not in antiquity alone that we find a fruitful interplay—as with the Pythagoreans—between religion and mathematics. "All things began in order," wrote Sir Thomas Browne, "so shall they end, and so shall they begin again; according to the ordainer of order and mystical mathematics of the City of Heaven."[37] The perennial stress on universal order, with its political corollary of fixed degree, is highly significant. Behind it we can trace the belief, very much alive for Plato and by no means dead even today, least of all among professional mathematicians,[38] that mathematics offers the one true key to the unseen realities of the universe, and thus has a paramount claim to be, itself, regarded as a religion.

Whether Plato originated the cosmology on which Eudoxus of Cnidos (ca. 390–ca. 340), Apollonius of Perge (*fl.* latter half of 3d c.), and Hipparchus (190–126?) subsequently produced modifications is uncertain. In any case it was an enduring model that survived, little changed, in Stoic thought, a curious mixture of formalized pattern making and theological symbolism. In Plato's *Timaeus* we learn that the Demiurge created the universe in the form of a sphere, turning uniformly upon its axis:[39] thus it followed that "whatever the *apparent* movements of the heavenly bodies might be Plato was convinced on religious grounds"—a sphere being the most perfect figure—"that the *true* movements must be revolutions at uniform speed in perfect circles."[40] Thus the scientific problem, granted this axiom, was to explain the seeming irregularity of astral patterns of movement in terms of uniform revolutions.[41] But, as Plato well knew, the four seasons, which should theoretically have been identical in length, were not: what did this imply about the sun's supposed revolution from solstice to equinox? Above all, how were the wanderings of the planets (*planētai*, "wanderers") to be regularized?

The Greeks might not be able to perform strictly controlled laboratory experiments; but the eternal march of the celestial phenomena set up recurrent patterns, which they could not help but observe.[42] Eudoxus and Aristotle justified the geocentric model by assuming that the planets and fixed stars rotated in a complex series of concentric spheres: twenty-seven in Eudoxus's model, thirty-four in the revision by Callippus of Cyzicus (*fl.* ca. 330), no less than fifty-five by the time Aristotle had finished with the problem.[43] Yet all three were well aware of irregularities that rendered the theory suspect. Planets and stars do *not* maintain the same distance from the earth, as the variation in their brightness alone would suffice to make clear.[44] Annular and total eclipses tell a similar story, the former taking place when the moon is at too great a distance from earth to black out the sun completely. Variant observed speeds in the movements of heavenly bodies imply an eccentric (i.e., off-center) terrestrial observation point. Sosigenes (2d c. A.D.), drawing on Eudemus's history of mathematics (late 4th c. B.C.), states unequivocally that these facts were known; but they still made no headway against a system that set all the spheres concentrically about the center of the universe.[45]

An epistemological and psychological barrier existed here: the theoretical model exerted an irresistibly seductive lure.[46] Socioreligious conviction, in short, proved more potent—as at most periods of the world's history—than objective, empirical arguments based on scientific observation: indeed, it seems clear that in this case it genuinely blinded the scientists to what they had no wish to see.[47] We are used to thinking of Aristotle as a rational philosopher-scientist, "the master of them that know," as Dante called him, and outside the vexed area of the heavens this was very largely true. But for Aristotle, no less than for Plato, the earth, as the center of a rotating body, was at rest in mid-universe,[48] while "since the activity of God is eternal life, and since the heavens are divine, the motion of the heavens must be eternal, and therefore the heavens must be a rotating sphere."[49]

Thus Aristarchus and the atomists were, no less than Galileo (in ways perhaps more), guilty not of mere scientific error but, more important, of something more akin to theological heresy. As late as Lucretius's day, in the first century B.C., it was still necessary to reassure those who in this manner "with their reasoning shake the ramparts of the universe" that they were not liable to divine retribution for so monstrous a crime (*immani pro scelere*), that earth and heaven were *not* divine and eternal.[50]

Yet the concentric-sphere theory was being overtaken by ever more accurate observations at least as early as the second century B.C., and "saving the appearances" demanded not only increasingly ingenious theories, but a willingness (whether unconscious or not) to work against the natural grain of the evidence. A desire for
perfection in the ordering of the universe still countered apparent flaws with the
claim that these were ascribable to human error, partial understanding, mistaken
perceptions. Hence the "eccentric" theory, which preserved the sun's steady revolution by assuming that earth did not lie at the exact center of the solar orbit (in itself a
significant theological concession); and the theory of epicycles, which got round the
dangerous notion of an ellipse—something perfectly familiar *per se* to Greek astronomers and mathematicians, though whether any of them possessed the skills at Kepler's
disposal for calculating orbits seems doubtful—by positing additional revolutions of
the planets and fixed stars round points located on the sun's presumed trajectory
about the earth.[51]

The special pleading involved in this hypothesis should not blind us to its extreme mathematical ingenuity. As Geoffrey Lloyd points out, "by choosing suitable
parameters, the epicyclic model can indeed be made to yield any figure, curved or
straight, if the speeds with which the epicycle and the deferent [i.e., the main cycle]
revolve are allowed to vary."[52] For an elliptical orbit, indeed, not even a variation in
speed is required. What underlies all these theories is the paramount need to assume
regular and uniform motion, and the regularity itself is a necessary postulate of celestial divinity.[53] It may also be relevant, as Ritchie points out (with a legitimate
touch of cynicism), that the circle "is the only figure of uniform curvature with
which calculation is relatively easy."[54] It is no accident, either, that observational astronomy flourished in precisely those areas—for example, Hipparchus's surveying
of the fixed stars, or his discovery of the precession of the equinoxes—where theology had least at stake. Ideological considerations dictate similar selectivities today. It
is noteworthy, but not surprising, that Hellenistic research in general preferred topics devoid of political sensitivity and ideological dogma, with an emphasis either on
consolidation and cataloguing (textual criticism; Callimachus's *Pinakes*), or else on
pure science (e.g., Apollonius of Perge's investigation of conic sections).[55] Again,
modern parallels suggest themselves.

It is also noteworthy that the Greeks, having no sense, as we do, of mechanical
causation, regarded the fixed and repetitive movements of the heavens as evidence
for divinity, whereas we are far more likely to see analogies with the world of machines. The heliocentric theory seems to have originated, in some sense, with the
Pythagoreans, though it was Aristarchus who expressed it in its most uncompromising form. Heracleides Ponticus (4th-c. Academician) seems to have produced a
modified version whereby, first, Venus and Mercury, never being visible at an increased angular distance from the sun, revolved round the sun rather than the earth;
second, the appearance of a daily revolution of the heavens was to be explained by
the earth's daily rotation on its own axis; but, third, the sun and the other planets did
still circle the earth.[56] The geocentric format was, barely, preserved, but at the same

time this theory, like that of the epicycles, made perilous concessions to heliocentric displacement: the sun became a second center, while the earth, though central still, was no longer fixed.

However, the appearances had, with a considerable effort, been preserved. Heracleides and the Hipparchan epicycles between them ensured that the world would be left, for nearly two millennia, to enjoy the Stoic world soul, stellar determinism, the medieval ladder of being, and the fatalistic-predictive joys of astrology, disbelief in which was regarded by Stoics as tantamount to atheism.[57] We cannot properly assess the Hellenistic or the Graeco-Roman world unless we acknowledge the depth, persistence, and ubiquity of the belief in an organic, living cosmos, which directly affected the course of men's lives on earth: no mere popular superstition, either, but a theory to which some of the best brains of the age lent their support. Not only Plato, but even Aristotle, as we have seen, shared the animistic concept that the heavenly bodies were living, sentient creatures.[58]

It is, then, predictable that Greek mathematicians should have been most consistently successful when dealing with abstract problems that had no immediate social, or even practical, connotations. Indeed, if Archimedes is to be regarded as typical—and a great deal of evidence suggests that he had simply inherited the intellectual tradition of Plato and Aristotle—then it was almost a point of honor to avoid what had mere vulgar applicability to the problems of daily life, and to concentrate on pure theory, an educated gentleman's proper concern. This meant, first and foremost, geometry. Here an interesting problem arises. We are often reminded, correctly, that the Greeks, despite Pythagorean analyses of "side" and "diameter" numbers,[59] and the ease with which some Euclidean propositions can be converted into algebraic terms,[60] did not, in fact, acquire any true understanding of algebraic method, let alone an effective algebraic notation, until the time of Diophantus (*fl.* ca. A.D. 250).[61] Yet it has long been assumed by historians of mathematics that the Greek system has an underlying algebraic basis, and should be so interpreted. It is also taken as a virtual article of faith that "the thought processes of the Babylonians were chiefly algebraic,"[62] even though "the step to a consciously algebraic notation was never made,"[63] and the Babylonians, like the Greeks, were limited to arithmetical and geometrical expressions.

Obviously a modern mathematician can, without difficulty, and using the advantage of hindsight, reconstitute both Greek and Babylonian texts as algebraical functions, for example as quadratic equations. Yet a comparison of the processes in the actual texts with their modern interpretations reveals disquieting discrepancies,[64] including an occasional tendency to fill crucial gaps.[65] Mathematically, such a method can be, and has been, defended. But how far is it justifiable in historical terms? Recently it has been so challenged in a remarkable paper by Sabetai Unguru, who argues flatly that "no algebra exists in Babylonian and pre-Diophantian Greek mathematical sources,"[66] and that the "hidden algebraic structure" is "the intellectual product of foreigners . . . reading Greek mathematical texts in the light of their own idiosyncrasies."[67] The assertion has generated considerable academic debate;[68] but whatever its mathematical standing, historiographically Unguru's position remains impeccable. These specific numbers and spatial diagrams would, eventually, lead to algebra; they did not contain it.[69] The most we can say is that, like Molière's M. Jourdain speaking prose, both Greeks and Babylonians may have expressed themselves in potentially algebraic terms without knowing it; but the crucial point, precisely, is that they did not know, and that Diophantus did.[70]

It is also true that the two Greek numerical systems were neither of them easily adaptable to large-scale or complex computations, since they lacked a zero,[71] employed a cumbersome system of positionally nonvariable alphabetic notation—never adapted, as it so easily could have been, to algebra, thus getting the worst of both worlds—and, oddest of all to our way of thinking, treated the number one not so much as one integer among others, but as an indivisible unit, on the grounds, as Aristotle argued, that the measure, the One, is not the things measured, but the principle of number.[72] Archimedes (ca. 287–212), with characteristic ingenuity, solved the problem thus raised in his *Sand-Reckoner* (*Psammitēs*), using a system of verbal modifiers grouped by octads (10^8 . . . 10^{16} . . . 10^{24}, etc.) to express high-powered multiple numbers,[73] and to get around the intractable fact that each of the twenty-seven alphabetical signs had one value only, irrespective of position.[74] This *tour de force* solution never passed into general use. Instead, though the Greeks were perfectly competent to perform arithmetical functions—numerical computations in fact proliferated[75]—they developed an ingrained tendency to express them in geometrical terms, thus sidetracking the disadvantages of their numerical systems.[76]

The geometrical approach to number, though shared, up to a point, by both Egyptians and Babylonians,[77] was something characteristically Greek. This does not necessarily flatter Greek intellectualism, since modern mathematicians tend to assume that "historically and psychologically the intuitions of geometry are more primitive than those of arithmetic"[78]—perhaps one unacknowledged reason for the modern determination to credit the intellectually dazzling Greeks with an innate algebraic mode of thought. It can be seen as one more mark of the Epicureans' divergence from mainstream Greek thinking that they, like the Cynics and Skeptics, seem to have rejected geometry altogether,[79] mainly on the grounds of "the opposition between the fundamental hypotheses of mathematics and the data of sense. There are no such things, they said, as mathematical points, lines, etc. Even if points exist, you cannot make up a line out of points. It is absurd to define a line as that which, if it be turned about one of its extremities, will always touch a plane; a line being, say, length without breadth, and therefore an insubstantial thing, cannot be turned around at all."[80]

These objections may have been wrongheaded, but they did at least highlight the undoubted truth that mathematical language deals constantly in theoretical entities that can have no physical existence except as a loose approximation, if that. The relation of a straight line as drawn to the ideal straight line of geometry bears directly on Plato's Theory of Forms, and indeed suggests a possible source for that theory: the refinement of spatial experience into an idealized mathematical concept.[81] From the Pythagoreans onwards, there was always a standing temptation to connect number and quantity, to identify the arithmetical unit with the geometrical point, to see (for instance) fractions, which the Greeks did not express in arithmetical terms, as proportions between line segments, a development of Pythagorean harmonics. The Pythagoreans, indeed, convinced, to begin with, that mathematics demonstrated the innate harmony of the natural world, were horrified to discover (and did their best to hush up) the fact that numbers could be incommensurable, irrational: that, for example, "the lengths of the side of a square and its diagonals cannot be expressed as the ratio of two integers."[82] In other words, you cannot obtain an integral solution to $\sqrt{2}$. Theodorus of Cyrene, as early as the fifth century, further demonstrated the incommensurability of squares containing three, five, seven (and so on, up to seventeen) square feet;[83] Archimedes later worked out approximations for these surds by a complex—and to modern mathematicians naturally algebraic—formula expressed in geometrical terms.[84]

Euclid, Archimedes, and Apollonius of Perge were the three greatest mathematicians of the Hellenistic era. All were based in Alexandria, and all three benefited from the work of their predecessors—Hippocrates of Chios, Eudoxus of Cnidos, and the Pythagoreans.[85] Egyptian influence is more problematical. Earlier, it had been important; but by the Hellenistic period its lessons had long been assimilated.[86] Euclid's *Elements* is probably the most successful school textbook ever written[87]— from Archimedes' day on its author was known simply as "the *Elements* man"[88]— and certainly the longest-enduring. Euclid himself was an Athenian, one of only two distinguished Athenian intellectuals resident in Alexandria: the other was Demetrius of Phaleron (above, p. 48), and the two may well have arrived together, in the first wave of immigrant savants.

In an age of moral and political uncertainties there must have been something fundamentally comforting about Euclid's axioms and postulates: that a point is that which has position but no magnitude; that all right angles are equal to each other; that, "if a straight line falling on two straight lines makes the interior angles on the same side less than two right angles, the two straight lines, if produced indefinitely, meet on that side on which are the angles less than the two right angles"— something, incidentally, that may sound like a solemn enunciation of the obvious, but was furiously challenged by Proclus and others in antiquity: whole non-Euclidean geometries have been built on a denial of this famous Fifth Postulate.[89] In addition to plane geometry, Euclid also treated solid geometry—which later enabled the Neoplatonists to interpret geometry in cosmic theological terms[90]—and number theory.[91] In Book 10 he dealt with incommensurables, that is, straight lines "which are irrational in relation to any particular straight line assumed as rational."[92] His theorems and procedures established a methodological framework for all his successors. How far his work can be termed original in the strict sense, and how much of it was a systematization of discoveries made by his (now lost) predecessors, remains a hotly debated question. Yet simply to take hundreds of earlier geometrical theorems and derive them from no more than ten postulates was in itself a stunning achievement. It also reinforced that aura of absolute truth and universal validity surrounding geometry, which constituted perhaps the most crucial single influence on Plato and his successors.

Archimedes, in the mathematical field, is chiefly remembered for his elegant attempt to square the circle, that is, to ascertain its area by using infinitesimal approximations, sometimes known as the method of exhaustion (with its complement, the *reductio ad absurdum*);[93] but he also employed traditional methods to prove many theorems that would now be demonstrated by means of integral calculus (e.g., finding the area of a parabolic segment), and some of his discoveries, for example the approximation to π and the formula for the volume of a sphere, have become mathematical commonplaces.[94] In geometry he took up where Euclid left off in Book 13, doing highly original work on the quadrature and cubature of curved surfaces, paving the way for Kepler and his successors. His work in mechanics was fundamental, and he virtually invented the science of hydrostatics.[95] Heath did not exaggerate when he wrote: "This represents a sum of mathematical achievement unsurpassed by any one man in the world's history."[96] When Archimedes rejected, in effect, applied science, and concentrated on pure research, he knew very well what he was doing. The common world, consciously or not, got its revenge for this slight; not only was Archimedes murdered by a common soldier, but his tomb was soon forgotten, and rediscovered, and rescued from oblivion, only by Cicero in 75, when he was serving as quaestor in Sicily.[97]

Apollonius of Perge worked in Alexandria under Ptolemy III and his successor, but later changed his patron to Attalus I of Pergamon, the recipient of several of his dedicatory epistles. He extended the mathematical use of geometry to conic sections, in work (*Conics*, Bks. 5–7, surviving only in an Arabic translation) so abstruse—if traditional—that only professional mathematicians can fully appreciate it even today, and which earned him the title of "The Great Geometer." What Attalus I made of the work thus presented to him is not on record. Even the four introductory books, preserved in Greek and thought of by their author as elementary, offer a marvelous reordering of fundamental definitions and methodology, streamlining the latter by generating all functions from the common double oblique circular cone.[98] The Byzantine mathematical savant Leon (9th c. A.D.) wrote of this treatise:[99]

> Deep, friend, and exceedingly hard the nature
> Of those inner matters with which I, this book,
> Do travail: what's needed is a Delian diver.
> But if one such dive into my secret recesses
> And accurately fathom every depth,
> He'll win first prize among the geometricians
> And be reckoned, without cavil, a learned man.

With Archimedes and Apollonius Greek geometry not only attained its apogee, but in effect reached its technical limits: as in applied mechanics (below, p. 470), theory far outstripped the instruments available for its expression. As Heath correctly stresses, classical Greek geometry lacked an adequate system of coordinates, as well as the manipulative scope afforded by modern algebra. "All the solutions were *geometrical*; in other words, quantities could only be represented by lines, areas and volumes, or ratios between them."[100] There were no algebraic quantities, let alone a symbolic notation in which to express them. It is remarkable, in the circumstances, that so much, of such originality and lasting value, was nevertheless achieved.

The success—and seductiveness—of Euclid's method leaves us torn between admiration and unease. To bring the whole compass of geometry within a deductive process based on a limited group of axioms, definitions, and postulates was an extraordinary coup. It was also, not least when applied outside pure mathematics, by analogy, potentially dangerous. Intellectual hybris can be as insidious as any other kind. The ancient scientist, as Farrington remarked, "tended to regard as science whatever could be included as deductions from a few self-evident principles in a logically constructed system."[101] Challenging the axioms on the basis of systematic experiment or observation—not least when those axioms carried a heavy load of social or religious faith as underpinning—was discouraged by the built-in passion of the Greeks for pattern making, monadism, and logical consistency, which was at once their intellectual glory and their greatest handicap. Thus system building always tended to take precedence over observational research, and what could not be made to fit into the system was ignored or explained away. Are we so different today? The ghosts of Marx and Freud would return a dusty answer. There is no royal road to geometry, Euclid told Ptolemy I in Alexandria.[102] There, at least, is one axiom that no one would think of challenging.

CHAPTER 27

TECHNOLOGICAL DEVELOPMENTS: SCIENCE AS *PRAXIS*

Among the many social paradoxes we have noted during the Hellenistic age none, surely, is more striking or improbable to the modern mind than the wide gap between theoretical and applied science: the brilliance of intellectual achievement in areas such as pure mathematics, the limitations and poverty of technological development. Why should brains capable of conceiving a heliocentric universe, or of doing pioneer work on conic sections, so signally fail to tackle even the most elementary problems of productivity? In this context it should, I think, be borne in mind that, whereas technological development is, more often than not, socially, economically, or politically determined, original scientific or technological discoveries tend to be random, idiosyncratic, and unpredictable.[1] A good example is the famous story of Archimedes pondering the problem of specific gravity and displacement in his bath, seeing the bathwater slop over as he settled down in it, jumping out and rushing naked through the streets of Syracuse crying "Eureka!"[2] Experimentation and formal proof followed later. Nor is such a breakthrough invariably followed up for practical purposes: the early history of research in electricity and magnetism is a good case in point. Knowledge *per se* does not suffice. A pressing, but economically viable, public need is often essential to facilitate development, and even then it can often be frustrated by innate conservatism or social (most often religious) prejudice.[3]

Even though the sum of their technological progress is generally regarded as slight, Hellenistic scientists certainly cannot be said to have lacked inventive ingenuity. They developed cogged gears, the pulley system, the screw,[4] glassblowing,[5] hollow bronze casting,[6] surveying instruments,[7] the torsion catapult,[8] the screw press,[9] even an odometer and a pantograph, or copying instrument.[10] They produced experimental working models of the water clock[11] and the water organ,[12] the machine gun (to rapid-fire a succession of quarrels or arrows),[13] and the fire-engine pump.[14] It is often stated, incorrectly, that they discovered, though they did not develop, the steam engine. All they in fact did was to set up a simple model that generated rotary power by jet propulsion, with steam as the motive force (cf. below, p. 474).[15] Water-driven and rotary mills were probably in scattered use before the first century B.C., but their genesis is much debated.[16] One of the most ingenious inventors, Hero of Alexandria, known as "the Mechanician" (*fl.* 1st c. A.D.), and the author of several surviving treatises that embody earlier Hellenistic material, designed, *inter alia*, an automatic puppet theater, operated entirely by complex arrangements of wheels, drums, and strings, without any cogging or clockwork.[17] In similar vein was the odd passion for illusionist devices, more often than not designed to impress credulous temple worshippers: doors that seemingly opened of their own accord,[18] statues that made libations,[19] drinking vessels that poured both wine and water, never-empty mixing bowls replenished from invisible cisterns,[20] Archytas's mechanical wooden dove, which was made to fly by expelling a current of hot air.[21]

Nevertheless, "neither increased productivity nor economic rationalism (in Max Weber's sense) was ever achieved in any significant measure."[22] The list of Hellenistic inventions and achievements suggests one possible answer.[23] In no case, except possibly that of grain milling,[24] is there any attempt, predictably, to improve industrial efficiency: once again the *status quo* represents the goal, and change implies degeneration. Applied science is used, even by researchers working from the Museum in Alexandria, primarily to design efficient weapons of war and siege engines;[25] to streamline monumental building, by the improvement of pulleys, hoists, cranes, and modes of transport for heavy beams and columns;[26] to construct celestial spheres for

Fig. 146. Terra-cotta figurine of a slave using an Archimedean screw to press grapes (Alexandria, first century B.C. or first century A.D.).
British Museum, London.

the benefit of astronomers;[27] to raise water, for irrigation or from mine shafts, whether by Archimedean screw, bucket wheel, multiple water wheels, bucket chain, or piston-driven force pump (the most remarkable engineered water system was that constructed for Eumenes II of Pergamon);[28] and—seemingly a whole minor industry, to which repeated references are made—to turn out magicians' toys, mechanical or pneumatic or hydraulic conjuring tricks. Humankind, as Eliot said, cannot bear very much reality. No accident that the original meaning of the Greek word *mēchanē* was "trick," "ruse."[29]

Significantly, the hoists and the Archimedean screw for raising water both seem to have involved a considerable amount of manual labor. If we are looking for those characteristic features of modern applied science—labor-saving devices, servo mechanisms, inventions designed to promote increased efficiency or to streamline production—we will look in vain. The machinery, at least in its component parts, was all there; what no one ever developed was a practical alternative source of motive power to human or animal muscle, or a more efficient fuel than charcoal.[30] The dream cherished by the fifth-century comedians, of self-cooking food and automation in the kitchen (above, p. 392), has clearly been forgotten. What is even more interesting, there is strong evidence to show that when a potentially efficient or labor-saving device did appear, no one was in any great hurry to adopt it. The classic example is that of the water wheel, which, well known at least as early as the first century B.C., was not put into general use until about the third century A.D., the motive then being an increasing shortage of available manpower.[31]

Several conclusions can be drawn from this, which other evidence confirms. First, long-term capital investment in industry was not looked on with approval. Indeed, capital investment also struck agriculturalists as a ruinous waste, its avoidance as the best source of income. Intensive cultivation, with a few uncharacteristic exceptions, such as the experiments carried out on large estates in Ptolemaic Egypt, was equally abhorrent to them: better to acquire more land than to maximize the yield of what you already owned.[32] Surplus cash tended to go, as we have seen (above, p. 368), into civic benefactions or conspicuous consumption. Second, to any ancient businessman the natural source of power lay in dependent human labor or draft animals, and the prospect of shifting to some inanimate power source lacked appeal so long as muscle power remained cheap and plentiful. Why let workers or donkeys (even donkeys do not seem to have been used for milling till the first century B.C. at the earliest)[33] sit idle in order to squander more initial capital on a substitute for them? Third, the thought of an idle labor force terrified all upper-class intellectuals (and many others), since it was taken as axiomatic that unless such workers were kept occupied at menial tasks and, thus, in their proper fixed station, they would at once attempt, through revolt, the violent subversion of that divinely established order on which the world's harmony depended. It was not so much the availability of the "animated tool" that discouraged technical progress and labor-saving discoveries,[34] as the nightmare of what that tool might achieve if released, in large numbers, from lifelong servitude. Confirmation can be found in the fact that genuine labor-saving devices, such as Hero's boxed gear system (whereby a weight of a thousand talents could be lifted by a force of five),[35] never got beyond the drawing board or experimental stage, while those that were actually used—for example, the "hoisting machines" described by Vitruvius, or Strabo's irrigation screw pumps in Egypt: devices employing lever, pulleys, or water hoist[36]—required manpower on a large scale to provide their motive energy. As a result the true water wheel for long remained an expensive luxury,[37] while the windmill was only introduced by the Arabs.

We have already had occasion to note, in various contexts, the ingrained contempt of the Greek intellectual (who was also an upper-class, and more often than not oligarchic, elitist by instinct no less than tradition) for banausic or mechanical occupations,[38] which—for David Hume as for Socrates—"debase the minds of the common people, and render them unfit for any science or ingenious profession."[39] We have also seen his deep-rooted preference for theory over mere vulgar application. Herein lay one further reason for the ancient world's lack of technological development. In a revealing, and notorious, letter Seneca criticizes Poseidonius (below, pp. 643–44 ff.) and Democritus for attributing to intellectuals the various key discoveries of mankind.[40] Not only does he argue, with passion, that such inventions were beneath the contempt of thinking men (cf. the case of Archimedes, p. 458), and invariably the product of vulgar and pragmatic artisans; he also maintains that all devices designed to economize on labor or to promote human comfort were pernicious, since their inevitable consequence was the encouragement of luxury and self-indulgence. Nothing but the resultant corruption had made laws necessary: the ideal should be a return to the Golden Age of homespun high-mindedness. There is no reason to suppose that the millionaire Seneca had his tongue in his cheek when he penned this *simpliste* fantasy: in one way or another it had been an article of faith with most educated people at least since the fourth century B.C.

The Greeks had no word for "scientific researcher" in our sense of that term; a *physiologos* was rather a natural philosopher, and the development of scientific knowledge always remained subordinate to what was primarily philosophical speculation.[41] Quantitative methods, essential to true scientific progress, were conspicuous by their absence. Thus while the phenomena at times needed saving, and their causes always provoked more or less imaginative speculation and hypotheses, it was not felt necessary to describe them with any real precision—in this respect unlike a Hippocratic case history (p. 483), where correct diagnosis, and, very often, a patient's life, might depend on meticulously recorded observations. Since the philosophical outlook (with a strong moral component) predominated, evaluative judgments too often replaced mensuration, the qualitative took precedence over the quantitative, so that experiments, even where they existed, tended to be both inaccurate and unsystematic.[42]

This is a fundamentally aristocratic attitude, with strong sociopolitical overtones, and is by no means restricted to the ancient world. As Sir Desmond Lee sensibly asks, "At what time in the world's history has the attitude of the upper and controlling classes been different?"[43] It is based on social values that remain tied to the land, where the only recognized source of wealth (apart from the "heroic" alternative of plundering other men's property in time of war) is farming your own estate. No accident that rulers with a strong interest in technology, for example Dionysius I of Syracuse[44] or Antiochus IV Epiphanes (above, p. 437), were autocrats who could follow their unfashionable whims with impunity; even so, both acquired a reputation for suspect eccentricity, largely because of their ungentlemanly habit of keeping company with technicians and artisans. Landowner, warrior, farmer, priest: the legitimate occupations for a gentleman were few, his ideal state that of the leisured rentier. Later his permissible activities were extended to take in certain pursuits—e.g., philosophy, literature—that were not a source of income, and at least two, law and politics, that unofficially came to generate untold profit.

But to be a merchant, or to work for others, remained by and large anathema. This was certainly true of Homer's Phaeacians: when Euryalus wants to impugn Odysseus's honor and question his physical prowess, he compares him to a merchant-skipper, greedy for commercial gain rather than athletic achievement.[45] The Milesian philosophers, on the other hand, like Solon in sixth-century Athens, show a lively interest in commerce and the processes of industry, in fulling and potting and the smith's forge. It was a transitional age of opening horizons and new democratic formulations: the old rules were, for a while, relaxed. In the fifth century Herodotus can still exhibit an unself-conscious interest in the minutiae of foreign trade, and may well have traveled as a merchant himself.[46] We also find a keen sense of the importance of, in the widest sense, scientific inventiveness and progress: Aeschylus's Prometheus not only symbolizes this trend,[47] but stands in conscious opposition to religious authoritarianism, to all arbitrary theological taboos on the free exercise of human reason. For Sophocles (ca. 441) this attitude is beginning to cause alarm:[48] though intellectually admirable, it nevertheless tends to breed lawlessness and atheism, to subvert the established order.[49]

By Plato's day this reversion is complete. Elitism is resurgent, the getters and spenders have once more been relegated (by the elite, if by no one else) to a position of despised social inferiority: they are the faceless mass in the *Republic,* subordinated to moralizing but nonproductive administrators.[50] Socrates' joky references to cobblers and pack asses and similar mundane matters are seen as eccentric at best,[51] and in any case regrettably vulgar, even though his contempt for such people when it comes to the serious business of government is made very clear indeed. To study methods of acquisition for practical purposes Aristotle considered "in poor taste."[52] This attitude persisted, by and large, throughout the Hellenistic age and the Graeco-Roman period that followed it.[53] We have already seen its conscious formulation by Archimedes, the most brilliant and creative scientist known to us from antiquity. All Archimedes wanted to be remembered for was his theoretical discoveries; it took "the extraordinary and irresistible stimulus of the siege of his native Syracuse by the Romans" to make him apply his knowledge to problems of siege warfare.[54] When Syracuse fell, Archimedes was absorbed in a mathematical proposition, oblivious to the legionary who cut him down. He died as he would have wanted.[55]

When we add to this attitude our knowledge of Hellenistic royal government, especially in Ptolemaic Egypt, the exploited estate *par excellence* (above, pp. 187 ff.), it becomes easy enough to see how and why technology labored under the handicaps that it did, however brilliant the scientific discoveries of the age. The whole concept, further, of a fixed world order, embracing everything from the heavenly bodies to the social structure, virtually eliminated change—*res nouae* in any sense—as a desirable objective. This put stability and permanence at a premium, and created great suspicion of what the Milesians described, rather cumbersomely, as "coming to be" (*genesis*) and "passing away" (*phthora*).[56] Man, it was now felt, had no business tampering with nature,[57] which suggests one possible reason why the Greeks excelled in areas (e.g., hydrostatics) where movement was not in question, "whereas their ideas on dynamics and ballistics were surprisingly incomplete and inaccurate."[58] The framework of existence was immutable: scientists might interpret and explain it, but the impulse to transform the world (an impulse that lies at the heart of all modern, post-Copernican, postindustrial revolutions) was restricted to a small and powerless minority of philosophical dropouts.

Even the great slave revolts carried no ideological implications (p. 391): their leaders simply wanted room to establish a free alternative society, in which, no doubt, sooner rather than later they would have acquired their own slaves. Furthermore, animated labor, whether slave or free, animal or human, might be wasteful or inefficient (not so inefficient either: much slave labor in Hellenistic and Roman times was professional to a degree), but it came far cheaper, in the short term, than the bugbear of capital investment. It is not, then, surprising that though wind, hot air, and steam were recognized in antiquity as potential sources of energy, they were never exploited; that water power was not developed at all widely until the first century B.C.; and that from start to finish the scene was dominated by human and animal muscle power,[59] even if harnessed to capstan, plow, cart, or treadmill. The most *outré* device in this last category (outside our period, but too good to miss) is the fourth-century-A.D. revolving ship's capstan, geared to a transverse crown wheel and axle fitted with external paddle wheels, and propelled (as round a threshing floor) by several pairs of oxen yoked to the capstan bars.[60] This is the first time in history that we hear of an attempt to move a ship without oars or sails: the anonymous author also has a good claim to have invented the paddle wheel, perhaps on the analogy of the water mill.[61]

The main aim of wealthy landowners was not so much to make wealth as to spend it, on luxuries, political self-advancement, or warfare: capital investment conflicted directly with this goal. Similarly the new rich (whether they had been commercially successful, or had made their money through war or public affairs or tax farming) all acquired land as their first priority. Industrialization, in our sense of the word, remained minimal: factories never got beyond the cottage-industry level, while specialization was rudimentary. The economy, at base, stayed agricultural throughout, its units of production the peasant, the ox, the donkey. Thus all that the landed rentier could envisage, over and above the profit margin, was conspicuous consumption, just as the only known way to curb such spending was by clapping on sumptuary laws. The Ptolemies show us this mentality in a context of political isolation, immense resources, and a virtually limitless labor force: they are simply a case of Veblenism run mad.

Patronage, too, had its limitations no less than its advantages. One perennial hazard, as prevalent today as in antiquity, was the disinclination to invest in research that did not seem likely to produce quick or striking returns. The elder Pliny, writing in the first century A.D., complained bitterly about the lack—despite arbitrary imperial generosity—of original research, the inability of greedy and shortsighted businessmen to understand that increased knowledge meant increased profits.[62] We have no reason to suppose that a dissimilar situation prevailed in the funding of the Museum. This may help to explain why, when Alexandrian scientists were lured away from their abstract speculations, it was, more often than not, to help their patrons get an edge in their favorite occupation, namely, warfare, or else to keep the general populace quiet by catering to their seemingly insatiable appetite for miracles and thaumaturgy and magic.

Thus there was no cogent reason apparent to anyone for either labor saving or increased productivity. Both tied up capital that could be more enjoyably used, and the first in particular was feared as a potential cause of unemployment and slump, hence of social unrest. The Roman who invented unbreakable glass is said to have been executed, along with his secret, by Tiberius—to whom he had applied for a reward—on the grounds that, if the invention gained wide circulation, the bottom would drop out of the gold market![63] As Finley says, the really curious thing about this anecdote is that the inventor looked to the emperor for a reward, rather than trying to get backing to put his discovery into production. It is also possible—and in Ptolemaic Egypt a virtual certainty—that one further block to technological development in methods of production was occasioned by the incompetent, dishonest bureaucracy responsible for the running of commerce and agriculture (cf. above, p. 368).[64] These *petits fonctionnaires* need ensure only that an adequate profit margin was maintained, that output reached a reasonably acceptable level. Given the social conditions of the Hellenistic world, their only solution for any problem was liable to take the form of increasing, or replacing, the labor force. They had no incentive to do otherwise: as minor officials their sole aim (like that of so many other people in this static world) was to keep old wheels turning at traditional speed. Nor was there any real lack of capital; it was simply that the capital was channeled into anything—public works and military defense above all—rather than long-term production.

With such a gulf fixed between research scientist and practical craftsman, it should come as no surprise to find that many inventions failed to get off the ground through lack of technical expertise.[65] The Greeks (by which, in this context, we mean Greek doctors or physicists) may have used, and understood the effects of, a wide variety of chemical substances, but they remained notoriously deficient in any theoretical knowledge of chemistry, since in its practical application (e.g., metallurgy and the glazing of ceramics) it belonged to the despised banausic craftsmen (above, p. 456),[66] and was a world away from post-Empedoclean theories of matter and form.[67] Again and again an advanced concept failed to achieve practical implementation through a mixture of inadequate skills and insufficient motivation. Theophrastus's successor as head of the Peripatetic school (287/6–269/8), Strato of Lampsacus, clearly understood, and produced experiments to demonstrate, the nature of air compression and a vacuum.[68] Yet technical primitivism effectively prevented the exploitation of this discovery. Hero's steam jet was a mere toy.[69] The Greek inability, despite possessing all its separate parts, to develop an efficient steam engine (above, p. 467) was long ascribed to a lack of the technique that would enable them to precision-turn and cast close-fitting metal cylinders and pistons. This assumption may be wrong: four bronze-cast force pumps found in the wreck of a first-century-A.D. Roman merchantman were tooled to an all-round clearance between piston and cylinder of between 0.1 and 0.35 mm, and when greased could operate at over 95 percent efficiency[70]—which suggests, once again, a socioeconomic rather than a technological reason for lack of development in the crucial field of alternative sources of energy to human or animal muscle power.[71] Even the sophisticated paddle boat described earlier, a pioneering invention remarkable for its ingenuity, was dependent on oxen to keep it moving.

Iron smelting was another process that suffered from technical problems. Though it is now known that charcoal-fueled furnaces could reach temperatures of at least 1300° C rather than the 1150° C that was previously thought to be their maximum,[72] it is quite certain that they did not attain the 1540° C needed for the production of tempered steel: the best they could manage was wrought iron, by way of "a spongy bloom which needed frequent reheating and hammering to reduce it to serviceable metal."[73] Similarly, deficiencies in constructional techniques lay behind the nonproduction, on any scale, of the screw cutter and the repeating arrow firer (above, p. 467), which was hard to manufacture and, though accurate, had a short range compared with a normal ancient bow. Even the fairly complex gear systems devised by Hellenistic scientists often failed in practice: since the cogging was done individually and by hand, occasional deviations from accuracy were inevitable, and sufficed to confound even the most meticulous of theoretical calculations. Vitruvius, a practical Roman architect, knew very well that in his profession neither theory nor practical experience could survive without the other.[74] Regrettably few Hellenistic Greeks shared this sensible attitude.

Contempt for the banausic carries its own penalties, foremost among them an embarrassing inability to get things done in real life. Hellenistic education, consisting at the secondary level of little but literature, athletics, and, above all, rhetoric, did little to help here.[75] The Greek world, which knew all about the principles of lever and pulley, could not even dream up so simple a device as the wheelbarrow. Methods of human porterage were about as inefficient as the harness used on horses (in essence an ox harness), which was liable to slide up and choke a heavy-laden hard puller.[76] The reason in each case was the same: a massive indifference both to increased efficiency and to the well-being of the carrier.

Warfare elicited some of the most striking instances of applied science in the Hellenistic period, in particular as regards siege equipment: the tower, the ram, the flame thrower, above all the torsion catapult.[77] This last consisted of an arm that could be pulled round to stretch the springy braided rope through which it passed, and on release would snap back with tremendous force, activating a kind of large mechanical crossbow. When the fourth-century Spartan king Archidamus saw an early catapult imported from Sicily his comment was: "By Heracles, there's an end to manly valor!"[78] So must a medieval knight have felt when confronted with the first bombard. Xenophon, Plato, and (with reservations) Aristotle all similarly felt that skulking behind siege fortifications would sap the warrior's courage.[79] Such social and moral qualms were reinforced by the fact that the normal gentlemanly qualities of birth, wealth, and political or rhetorical accomplishment counted for nothing when it came to the business of military technology. What was needed there, as the anonymous author of the *De Rebus Bellicis* well knew,[80] was a good original scientific brain, and this (he admits) tended to appear without respect for social rank. In the Hellenistic age Ctesibius the Alexandrian barber's son (below) is a nice instance of such random selectivity. Though the *De Rebus Bellicis* was written in the mid-fourth century A.D., when the problem had become acute (and thus discussable), the assumptions behind it had existed at least since Aristotle's day.

Military necessity (like the life-and-death exigencies of medicine) put a premium on applied science at the expense of the fixed order: here the technicians came into their own. The Ptolemies financed the research of their military engineers, who found, for example, that the crucial element in constructing efficient artillery was the diameter of the holes in the frame through which the spring cord—a twisted skein of animal sinew or horsehair—was threaded, and by means of repeated experiment worked out a valid formula for its dimensions in each case:[81] "The weight of the stone to be hurled is the basis upon which the engine must be constructed. This

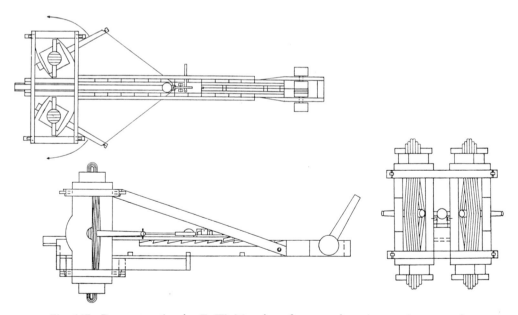

Fig. 147. Reconstruction by E. W. Marsden of a stone-throwing torsion catapult
introduced ca. 270 B.C., and described by Hero and Philo.
From E. W. Marsden, *Greek and Roman Artillery: Historical Development* (London, 1969).

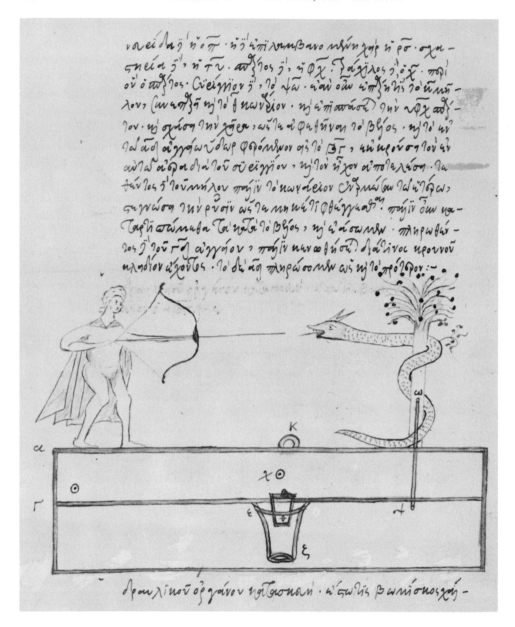

weight is first reduced to units, the cube root of this quantity extracted, a tenth of this root added to the root, and the result is the number of digits in the diameter of the opening that receives the skein."[82] This can be expressed as the formula $D = 11/10 \sqrt[3]{100\,M}$, where D = the diameter of the hole (in digits, or *daktyloi*) and M = the weight of the stone in Attic minas.[83]

Fraser hardly exaggerates when he says that "in the middle of the third century Alexandria was a leading centre of ballistics research."[84] The torsion catapult had a maximum effective range of about four hundred yards: various efforts were made,

Fig. 148. The device of Heracles and the snake (Hero, *Pneumatica* 1.41). When the
apple is lifted, Heracles draws his bow and shoots, while the snake hisses. As
Schmidt's illustration shows, the scribe of this manuscript failed
to understand the working of the device.
British Library, London.

by inventors such as Ctesibius (ca. 300–ca. 230), to improve on it. We have already
noted the machine gun, or repeater catapult, which fired a succession of arrows. We
also hear of catapults that worked on the compressed-air principle, or had metal (as
opposed to torsion) springs; but neither of these seems to have been a practicable
proposition.[85] (The air catapult had small bronze cylinders and pistons that were
compressed by the lowering of the bow to load it, and released by its firing.)[86] The
giant siege tower or "city taker" (*helepolis*) we know best through the one built by
Epimachus the Athenian for Demetrius Poliorcetes during the siege of Rhodes in 304

(above, p. 32).[87] Its given dimensions vary in our sources, but it seems probable that the tower was well over a hundred feet high, and half that size in the length of its square base: it was built in nine tapering stories, with stone throwers on its lower decks, light catapults on the upper levels, and a water tank at each stage in case of fire. It ran on swivel wheels, and needed several thousand men (musclepower again!) to maneuver it. Sometimes it carried a boarding bridge, in addition to its heavy swing-ram, to assault the wall against which it was set. Despite its iron plating and protective hides, it was easily set on fire or undermined, and its usefulness seems to have been debatable. On the other hand, as a characteristic essay in Hellenistic gigantism (above, pp. 95–96), it can be regarded in much the same light as Hieron's giant ship or the short-lived Colossus of Rhodes.

Ctesibius was undoubtedly a mechanical genius in his own way;[88] but it is odd how little practical effect most of his inventions seem to have had—except, perhaps, for purposes of prestige, always a prime consideration with Ptolemaic rulers. It is by no means certain that his fire engine[89] was ever used to put out real fires (such as those set, with depressing frequency, by the Alexandrian mob), though it was a genuine double-action force pump,[90] with valves and plungers, not unlike one found at Bolsena, in Etruria.[91] And did anyone, I cannot help wondering, ever really play his Heath Robinson water organ?[92] Not, I suspect, a serious musician, though it did possess a keyboard, and Drachmann makes out a plausible case for Ctesibius's having invented this *ex nihilo*.[93] His most useful discovery by far, however, was an accurate water clock, a great improvement on the existing sundial (useless at night or in cloudy weather) and clepsydra (not really a clock at all, but the ancient equivalent of an egg timer, using water instead of sand). This he achieved, in the first instance, by regularizing the water flow and making it constant.[94]

What we have here, by and large—even to a surprising extent in the military sphere—is a collection of elaborate mechanical toys, curiosities, the subsidized exotica of an authoritarian regime.[95] Even the illusionist devices employed in temples and elsewhere cannot have been taken overseriously as miraculous phenomena except by the excessively ignorant and naïve.[96] For one thing, their working was no secret, and is described, in detail, in surviving monographs—of which there must have been many more at the time. Philo's enclosed siphon[97] is for the most part applied to what Drachmann nicely describes as pneumatic parlor magic:[98] toys featuring such things as singing birds or drinking dragons.[99] Hero describes a mechanical model of an animal that can go on drinking after its neck is severed with a knife,[100] and shows how, when a fire is lit on a specially constructed altar, expansion of the air in a hidden chamber below forces water through a siphon into a bucket, which then sinks, opening the temple doors by mechanical means.[101] When the fire goes out and the air below cools, the siphon sucks back the water, the bucket is lifted against a counterweight, and the doors close once more. A similar mechanism, also powered by hot air,[102] presents two statues that are made to pour libations of real wine; in one version there is also a snake coiled round the altar, which hisses at the moment of libation, or, alternatively, a trumpet that sounds as the doors open.[103] Hero also demonstrates a magical jug that can, seemingly from the same source, pour either wine, water, or a mixture of the two,[104] and, fascinatingly, a coin-in-the-slot machine for obtaining holy water with which to asperge oneself.[105]

The average spectator must have enjoyed these opening doors and automatic libations in much the same spirit as the audience at a modern conjuring show; the same applies to Ctesibius's original water clock, which was clearly splendid entertainment:[106] puppets emerged, propelled by rack and pinion, black and white cones were turned to show the time, pebbles or balls were dropped into a bronze basin to count the hours, and at noon horns were blown by some kind of pneumatic device. Even more astonishing was the presentation, in Hero's automatic puppet theater, of the drama *Nauplius*,[107] with dolphins playing round a ship that sank in a storm, lured onto rocks by wreckers, leaving Ajax to swim ashore and be greeted by an epiphany of Athena amid thunder and lightning. Exhibitions of this sort were analogous to the great Ptolemaic processions in their blend of ostentation, entertainment value, and complete irrelevance (like most of the Ptolemies' subsidized amusements) to Egyptian society.

Perhaps the last word on this looking-glass world of lunar economics and scientific dilettantism should go to Hero of Alexandria, who begins the introduction to his *Belopoeica*, unexpectedly, with the words: "The largest and most essential part of philosophical study deals with absence of disturbance [*ataraxia*]."[108] Though the observation is, in itself, an unexceptionable Hellenistic truism (above, p. 55), we may legitimately wonder what it has to do with a technical treatise on arms manufacture. We soon learn. The search for *ataraxia*, Hero says, will never be fulfilled through philosophical debate, mere talk. But mechanics—or at least that branch dealing with the construction of effective artillery—"has outstripped mere verbal training in this matter and taught all men how to live a life devoid of worry."[109] A strong reserve of artillery will keep you safe from aggression, and ensure your superiority in a defensive war. As Vegetius put it in a famous (and generally misquoted) tag, those who want peace must put themselves on a war footing.[110] As a formula for *ataraxia* this smacks of special pleading; but the argument has an oddly modern ring to it.

CHAPTER 28

HELLENISTIC MEDICINE; OR, THE EYE HAS ITS LIMITATIONS

By now the complex revolutionary profile of Hellenistic scientific thought, and its close involvement with the social, political, and intellectual trends that developed in the Successor kingdoms or the semiautonomous *poleis*, should be tolerably clear. At one level, that of the actual problems we find being investigated, there is no real watershed between the classical and the Hellenistic eras.[1] Aristarchus's heliocentric theory, as we have seen (above, p. 461), picked up an idea that had earlier caught the attention of the Pythagoreans. Those anomalous planetary movements that so preoccupied Apollonius of Perge and Hipparchus (above, p. 460) had caused just as great concern to Plato.[2] The same was true of the conflicting dietetic theories held by various medical schools,[3] and still in competition as late as Tiberius's day.[4] Geographers such as Eratosthenes worked on cartography and refined their estimates of the world's circumference,[5] but these problems were already in vogue when Aristophanes wrote *The Clouds* (423), and Aristotle had also tackled them.[6] Tides presented a new phenomenon, though theories of subsidence in the Mediterranean sea level can, again, be traced back to the observation of marine fossils on land by Herodotus and, especially, the sixth-century thinker Xenophanes.[7] Euclid was to a great extent refining and reformulating propositions well known by his predecessors (above, p. 464).

Where, then, did the change lie? Progress of a sort did take place, but, as the last two chapters suggest, it is most notable in two disparate areas: pure mathematics (largely unencumbered by crippling apriorisms or socioreligious inhibitions), and technical aids to observation, devices occupying that gray, indeterminate area between genuine scientific research and applied mechanics. We have already noted Archimedes' system for expressing numbers up to virtually unlimited power (above, p. 463), and seen that this was probably no more than an intellectual *tour de force*; more characteristic were Ctesibius's improved water clock (above, pp. 478–79)— designed the first instance, like the new models of celestial spheres, to help astronomers in their computations[8]—and Archimedes' *dioptra*, improved by Hipparchus, with its movable plate and pinpoint aperture, which made possible the basic sighting and measuring of stars.[9] Astronomical mathematics, similarly, was greatly aided by

Apollonius's and Hipparchus's advances in trigonometry,[10] a branch of science that, like surveying generally, offered a nice blend of theoretical and practical mensuration.

Yet against these improvements we also find a dead-weight legacy from the past that in many ways made true progress virtually impossible. Most important, ultimately, was the slow but ineluctable shift away from the freethinking rationalism that had marked the late archaic and early classical periods (above, p. 399), the reversion to authoritarian modes of thought not in government alone, but in every socially conditioned aspect of Hellenistic culture. A tight nexus bound together phenomena often treated separately: technological primitivism; the deep, radical split in sensibility (and the consequent lack of communication) between theorist and craftsman; the resurgence of religious enthusiasm (in particular by way of magic and the more exotic foreign cults); the subordination of experimental science to philosophical system-building on a cosmic scale. Intellectual formulations seldom found their way into practice, and when they did it was more often than not—as in the case of Archimedes' inventions during the siege of Syracuse—the result of a pressing *ad hoc* emergency, a request by some all-powerful patron, who could not be refused.

The craftsman could and did work from tradition, on the basis of accumulated experience; but he still remained incapable of real innovation in the scientific sense, since his work depended on trial and error rather than implementing general principles. The theorist, on the other hand, could pioneer new concepts, but lacked the constructional precision and experimental control to carry them out. Since interchange of ideas between the two groups was virtually nonexistent, with the *physiologos*, moreover, holding the *banausos* in considerable contempt, intellectual no less than social,[11] progress was largely blocked. Though remarkable accuracy (considering the limitations involved) is often evident in such fields as architectural design and, intermittently, the tooling of simple mechanical equipment (above, p. 474), it remains noteworthy only insofar as it contrives to surmount its own inadequacies. No steam gauges, thermometers, microscopes, telescopes, fine-calibrated lathes: nothing, in short, to take science beyond the primitive frontiers of what could be done with the unaided human hand and eye.

Because of this failure—since, in effect, observation and experiment, even where they existed, could be neither adequately controlled nor guaranteed to give accurate results—there had developed what we may term the habit of theoretical tyranny (a comfortable companion to its political counterpart). It has often been remarked, as one of the odder features of Greek intellectual life, that science was, to a quite extraordinary degree, dominated by philosophy: a domination to which, until very recently, labels such as "natural philosophy" gave vivid expression. The reason is not far to seek. We know today, as the Greeks knew, that theoretical research is essential to the healthy growth of any scientific discipline. We also take it for granted that the progress of such research is by way of rigorously controlled experiment. For the Greeks it was different. Lacking the instruments or the laboratory conditions necessary to control experimentation, they argued, reasonably enough on their own terms, and with uncomfortable analogies from forensic practice (above, p. 457), that pure reason was a more trustworthy guide than the all-too-fallible senses. Though this did not—at least during the earlier, more creative years of the Hellenistic era—preclude some impressive, if random, experiments,[12] the result, inevitably, was a climate of opinion in which observation was at a heavy discount when faced with a comprehensive, internally consistent, and morally acceptable system. This trend culminated in the abandonment of true research, the reversion to uncontrolled (and thus increasingly fanciful) theorizing, and, finally, the adaptation of Stoicism as the intellectual ideology best suited to a ruling elite (below, pp. 631 ff.).

Man is, in any case, a natural pattern maker; and throughout our period—despite some sturdily dissentient minority voices—acceptance went, all along the line, not merely to the systematizers as such, but to those systematizers who were socially and psychologically acceptable to the majority. The Epicureans propounded their own atomic universe (below, pp. 621 ff.); but its bleak anti-eschatological premises could never compete with the divine cosmos and world soul touted by the Stoics. In other words, theory was only minimally affected by observation, and, for the rest, provided it touched the right inner nerves, could be (and more often than not was) a mishmash of mathematics, teleology, rehashed myth, and prescriptive moralizing. No clear line was drawn, or indeed conceived, between philosophical and experimental models. Research was hampered still further by a ubiquitous dead-weight conservatism (the obverse of Greek originality) that habitually sought precedent and authority in every area from religion to literary criticism, from ethics to politics. It was in this sense that Homer, even in the Graeco-Roman period, so often came to be used as a final arbiter, an irrefutable court of appeal. During the fourth and third centuries, when government was, increasingly, by royal or oligarchical fiat, such an instinct found its ideal climate. If the authority was distinguished enough, and propounded a view that people wanted to believe, that more than sufficed. Plato had spoken for concentric spheres; Aristotle had come out in favor of a geocentric universe with a fixed center. To save the appearances was also to save that static social order in which every upper-class Greek thinker had so large an intellectual and emotional stake.

The fixed world order of Hellenistic Stoicism had, again, been inherited from earlier thinkers, complete with the four elements (earth, air, fire, water) and their analogues, the four humors (below, p. 489), plus the interplay and tension of opposites (hot/cold, dry/moist, etc.), and, above all, the principle of sympathy linking all phenomena, microcosm and macrocosm, in a spherical, harmonious, evenly revolving universe (above, pp. 457–58). A better example of an arbitrary, teleological, and morally symbolic model for existence would be hard to conceive. It is also noteworthy how far the sympathetic principle, in particular, lay open to systematic abuse, especially at the hands of do-it-yourself individualists. Astrology, alchemy, and the practice of magic (erotic magic especially) are all based on a limited exercise of the sympathy principle—*pars pro toto* or *similia similibus*—removed from its universal function, and harnessed for private ends (below, pp. 595 ff.). The ever-increasing popularity of these fads in the Hellenistic age suggests one early solution to the perennial urge for special knowledge or instant gratification. Do not pray to the gods (the adept would argue) for an answer or, *a fortiori*, a favor, which is more than likely to be denied, if not ignored; instead, win control over an arcane power system to obtain all you want, fast, on your own behalf, and then if supernatural beings are involved, *they* will come under *your* control, rather than vice versa. At the worst, if Fate, the Stoic *heimarmenē*, is preordained, then human intelligence, working from the celestial analogue, can compute its pattern and apply it. What is fixed must be predictable.

It might have been thought that medicine, as a working discipline with a stake in human lives, would be comparatively free both from the split between theorists and practitioners, and from the excesses of philosophically grounded systematization. It was, after all, the most famous Hellenistic medical pioneer who declared: "If health be absent, intelligence cannot manifest itself, skill will languish unseen, strength for the struggle be lacking, wealth become useless, reason without power."[13] Yet nothing could be farther from the truth than such a supposition. What in fact is remarkable is the extent to which developments in medicine mirror those in the other sciences. Here too the great period of original research, detailed observation, and theorizing comparatively unencumbered with tyrannous apriorisms came in the fifth century, with the early Hippocratic movement.[14] The evolution of medicine from the fourth century onwards—insofar as this can be unraveled by an analysis of references in later sources: no firsthand Hellenistic literary evidence has survived[15]—reveals a flourishing competition in the form of temple healing and medical magic; a progressively greater subordination to philosophical theory (and, in consequence, to conflicting sectarian polemic); a steady decrease, even among the hopefully but misleadingly named Empiricists, in experimentation, which from the third century B.C. fell into almost total abeyance;[16] and a corresponding lack of contact between the medical theorists, on the one hand, and, on the other, the herbalists, midwives, and barber-surgeons, with their mixture of superstition and accumulated practical knowledge.[17]

The religious and political conservatism that played so prominent a part in shaping Hellenistic culture inevitably took its toll in the field of research. Significantly, what is almost universally agreed to have been the highest achievement of Hellenistic medicine[18]—that is, the advance in human anatomical knowledge associated with the names of Herophilus of Chalcedon (ca. 330?–ca. 255?) and his slightly younger contemporary Erasistratus of Ceos (ca. 325?–ca. 240?)—was due entirely to the arbitrary fiat of an absolute ruler, Ptolemy II Philadelphos,[19] who provided these researchers with a supply of convicts from his state prisons, for dissection and (it is to be feared) vivisection,[20] just as Mithridates VI Eupator (below, p. 558) and Attalus III of Pergamon (below, p. 530) later used to test out poison antidotes on condemned criminals.[21] There were other advances: it is characteristic of the period that increased attention should have been given to gynecology and children's diseases (cf. above, p. 345).[22] But it is, first and foremost, anatomical dissection for which the Alexandrian school is still remembered, and this proved a transient benefit: without royal support and patronage, dissection—indeed, experimentation generally—soon succumbed once more to public opprobrium and intellectual prejudice.

This, unfortunately, was all too typical of Greek medicine throughout its long history. Rationalism, despite the Hippocratic contempt—intermittent and partial at best—for superstition, went only skin-deep, and observation, lacking precision, was always outstripped by necessary theory, however *outré*, from the four humors to arterial *pneuma*, from cupping and trepanning to a system (methodism) that attributed all disease to improper constriction or relaxation of the pores. It is easy enough to see how some tenets of Hippocratic medicine were eventually adapted by the Stoics. In Plato's *Phaedrus* it is stated that Hippocrates held knowledge of soul and body to be attainable only in the context of knowledge of "the nature of the whole,"[23] a disputed phrase of which the likeliest meaning is that Hippocrates "assumed that man must be considered as under the influence of surrounding nature."[24] Such a view is obviously consonant with the principle of sympathy. Elsewhere Plato in the *Timaeus* shows how fatally easy it was—just as in Greek economics (above, p. 363)—to introduce an inappropriate *moral* element into problems of anatomy.[25] Discussing the physical location of the soul, he suggests that the midriff acts as a divider (like the wall between the men's and women's quarters in a house, he adds revealingly) to keep the mere appetites apart from the noble passions. The appetites are controlled by the liver, onto which the mind projects visible images, as on a mirror. The function of the spleen, therefore, is "to keep the liver bright and clean, like a duster kept handy to clean a mirror."[26]

Now even if Plato is having fun here (and he may be), the form the fun takes is significant. The instinct to moralize bodily functions is not only a sure mark of the philosophical domination over anatomy, but a clear reminder, amply confirmed by the passage as a whole, and other sections of the *Timaeus*, that in Plato's day very little was in fact known about the internal working of the human body. The notion that the head controls the body because of its roundness, that is, as a microcosmic equivalent of the spherical universe (cf. above, pp. 457–58), may, again, be a joke; but it is a joke with powerful associations.[27] And what about Plato's mind-bending account of the digestive and respiratory system, complete with extra pipes through which there circulate both air and fire, and in structure resembling a tall lobster pot or wicker fish trap?[28] Perhaps the best-known evidence for this kind of anatomical ignorance is the idea, so popular in antiquity, that the lungs regularly absorbed liquid,[29] a fallacy that (one might have supposed) the results of drinking a mouthful of water the wrong way would very quickly dispel.

Certainly until the fourth century, and in most areas for long after that, human bodies continued to be regarded throughout the Greek world as sacrosanct, through "the ancient and popular belief that the dead body still has some awareness of the things that happen to it, and therefore an absolute right to be buried intact and undisturbed."[30] It followed that all knowledge of the appearance, function, and interrelation of the internal organs was deduced either by analogy from the anatomy of animals (goats, sheep, pigs, and, latterly, monkeys), or else through scattered and surreptitious work on casual corpses (battlefield disembowelments, victims of wild beasts, etc.). There was also guesswork based on external palpation: athletic trainers will probably have helped here. In other words, once again we find theory operating without proper observation or controls.

This should be borne in mind when considering, say, the apparent paradox of Erasistratus's conflict with the Empiricists, since it was Erasistratus who argued that observation *per se* was not enough, that generic conclusions had to be drawn from individual cases or experiments concerning the aetiology of diseases (an impeccably scientific attitude), whereas the Empiricists depended on personal sense impressions, largely passive and piecemeal, reinforced by the comparable experiences of other witnesses (*historia*), and on simple analogies drawn from parallels with seemingly similar drugs, diseases, or parts of the body (*metabasis*).[31] This offers a remarkable testament to the strength of the reaction that developed against excessive and sterile intellectualism in medicine, since the Empiricist theory of no-theory—and indeed of no experiment, since experiments were held, reasonably, to be inseparable from aprioristic model building—held the field from soon after the deaths of Herophilus and Erasistratus until the late first century B.C.

In a sense, of course, the Empiricists were simply promoting as sectarian doctrine what many herbalists and wisewomen did as a matter of course: that is, establish medical treatment on a basis of repeated observation, without recourse to any generic aetiology at all. As their most perceptive critic points out, "they were not interested in non-apparent causes or invisible principles, they did not probe into anything that does not lie on the surface, they were not interested in the *physis*, *arche*, or *aitia* of anything."[32] In the name of pragmatic common sense, that favorite rallying cry of anti-intellectual reactionaries throughout history, they killed serious medical research stone dead for almost three centuries. There is piquant irony in the fact that it was they, as a sect (*hairesis*), who first appear to have stuck the exponents of the Hippocratic tradition with the pejorative label of "Dogmatists" (*dogmatikoi*) or "Verbalists" (*logikoi*) for adhering to principles at the alleged expense of practice.[33]

As a result of all these interlocking factors the Greek medical tradition came to embody an extraordinary mixture of practical know-how, superstitious nonsense, and theories—ranging from the brilliant to the lunatic—based on false if not irrational assumptions. The key, throughout, is what we might term the *visible function of causality*. How clear, in everyday observational terms, is the connection between cause and effect in terms of illness? In some cases the link is obvious, and the solution, by commonplace analogy, simple. What we now call orthopedic surgery (that is, the treatment of bone fractures) offers an excellent example. If a man falls down and breaks his leg, it is clear how the trouble came about, and easy enough to suggest a cure. A broken spear can be splinted and bound; fruit trees are grafted, and the graft takes. Experience shows that a leg can be dealt within the same way: the sympathetic principle has always encouraged such homely inferences. Complaint and treatment, from start to finish, are both comprehensible. Up to a point (i.e., short of bacterial infection) the same is true of wounds, especially those received in battle. The cause is known. The treatment suggests itself. What man has inflicted, man can, given luck and intelligence, put right. It is no coincidence at all that by far the most modern and effective treatises in the Hippocratic corpus are those dealing with wounds, joints, fractures, and their treatment.[34]

It is when the cause—and, thus, the cure—is unknown that other factors enter.

Without dissection (the exceptions—e.g., Alcmaeon of Croton excising the eye and learning its nervous connection with the brain in the sixth century B.C.[35]—remain exceptions, and nothing more), without microscopes, stethoscopes, clinical thermometers, and other such instruments, Greek doctors were in effect restricted to what they could see for themselves, externally, with the naked eye. This is why they never grasped, though they came very near (p. 493), the principle of the circulation of the blood; why they did not, and could not, have any concept of bacterial or viral disease. (Appallingly, the same word in Greek, *helkos*, means both "wound" and "purulent ulcer." The two invariably went together, and the erroneous notion of "laudable pus"—in fact no more than one symptom of a comparatively mild infection—persisted until Lister's day, in the nineteenth century.)[36] However much they stressed the need for precise clinical observation, for proper prognosis and diagnosis, however much they might attack false philosophical apriorisms in the practice of medicine (as the author of the Hippocratic treatise *On Ancient Medicine* does with some vigor),[37] the fact remains that these medical pioneers were condemned, like it or not, to generalize, always, from hopelessly insufficient evidence.

We often hear that the most important advance the Greeks made in medicine was to slough off the incubus of religious or magical superstition, especially as regards the assignation of antecedent causes. There is, obviously, some truth in this assumption, but it can be very misleading. A perverse rational hypothesis is no improvement on a religious one: what is the point of breaking away from superstition if you promptly become a slave to some arbitrary philosophical system? Besides, the religious hypothesis often possesses psychological value, and on occasion may have physical benefits too. A severe pain in head or tooth might (in default of other theories) be attributed to a demon having taken up residence there. The demon, then, had to be let, or driven, out. This led to the worldwide early practice of trepanning, or trephining, that is, cutting a circular hole in the skull.[38] Oddly enough, this alarming remedy not only, despite lack of anesthesia and acute bacterial infection,[39] in many cases failed to kill the patient, but sometimes, especially if the trouble was a depressed fracture, actually brought belief.

As for the psychological side, Homer was well acquainted with the psychosomatic interrelation of physical and emotional symptoms,[40] while the continuing success, throughout antiquity, of the cult of Asclepius shows very clearly that medicine was never fully divorced from its religious connections. Nor does there seem to have been anything but the friendliest of relationships between the Hippocratic practitioners (despite their much-vaunted rationalism) and the Asclepiad medical priests. Asclepius was, after all, still the patron deity of the Hippocratics. The author of *Regimen IV* offers an engaging, and probably characteristic, compromise: "Prayer is good, but while calling on the gods a man needs to lend a hand himself, too." The physician-as-philosopher may be, in Hippocratic terms, the equal of a god (*isotheos*)—a concept central to the Dogmatists' stress on theoretical systematization— but in *Regimen IV* the paramount role of divine power in medical treatment is also stressed: the gods are the true physicians. With so much unknown, so many complaints inexplicable and incurable, this was a wise attitude. Of the forty-two cases described in *Epidemics* 1 and 3, no less than twenty-five, that is, almost 60 percent, terminate fatally.[41] Secular physicians or surgeons will have been only too glad to turn over to the god cases seen to be beyond their own merely human competence.[42]

In such cases (and in many others, where no prior recourse was had to a non-Asclepiad doctor) the patient would spend a night in the god's precinct or temple, a process known as "sleeping in" (*enkoimesis, incubatio*), described, in graphic and skeptical detail, by Aristophanes.[43] The fashion seems not to have really caught on until the fourth century: it was then that the great healing center of Asclepius on Cos was established.[44] Thus we have rational and thaumaturgic medicine developing together through the Hellenistic period *pari passu*, rather in the manner of astronomy and astrology. Very often—not surprisingly—the sleeper would dream he was being cured: perhaps through being licked by serpents, or by means of an operation carried out by the god himself. The remarkable thing is the number of cases where a surviving *ex voto* inscription or temple record testifies to some kind of reality behind the dream.

Two large marble stelae (ca. 350 B.C.) found at Epidaurus contain a representative, and on occasion quite extraordinary, collection of such successes.[45] Typical in its dramatic symptoms and baffling yet incontestable resolution is the following:[46] "Gorgias of Heracleia: purulent. This man was wounded in the lung by an arrow during a battle, and for eighteen months suffered such chronic suppuration that he filled sixty-seven [*sic*] basins with pus. While sleeping in, he had a vision. It seemed to him that the god extracted the arrowhead from his lung. When day came, he walked out well, carrying the arrowhead in his hands." Sometimes—for example, in the rather charming case of the patient with "a stone in his private parts" (prostatic calculus?), who dreamed of a beautiful boy and voided his stone in a spontaneous ejaculation[47]—we can see how the cure worked. More often this remains quite uncertain: by no means every case can be explained in terms of hysteria or psychosomatic relief. Disabilities treated include blindness, lameness, consumption, paralysis, suppurating wounds, dumbness, dropsy (one female patient's mother dreamed that Asclepius cut off her daughter's head and hung her upside down to drain),[48] even baldness and nonterminating pregnancies.

The dream element is constant and therapeutic: the case of the boy who was cured of a growth on his neck by a temple dog licking him while he was awake is exceptional.[49] On the other hand we find the temple snakes actually credited with the healing of a poisoned toe (by licking it),[50] in a case where the patient dreamed that he was being treated with a salve by a handsome young man.[51] Some of the prescriptions are clearly derived from popular folk medicine,[52] while others have a Hippocratic flavor about them.[53] The Asclepiad shrines seem also, exceptionally in the ancient world, to have offered some sort of charitable aid to the poor,[54] and served as models for later Christian hospitals and poorhouses (which, naturally, did not deter Christian apologists from making unpleasant comments on their pagan shortcomings). Certainly the age-old tradition of the leech, of popular medicine, found its best continuity here.

By their very nature, however, neither the Asclepiad priest-doctors nor the

Fig. 149. Reconstruction of the Asclepieion (temple and healing center of Asclepius) on Cos, begun in the fourth century B.C. and continued throughout the Hellenistic period.
From P. Schazmann and R. Herzog, *Asklepion*, Kos I, 1932.

leeches and herbalists (three groups that between them constituted the majority of healers) could offer any sort of developing medical theory. They may have been the repositories of age-old tradition, but it was not their business, nor were they trained, to think for themselves. In this respect we are brought back to the medical schools of Cos, Cnidos, Croton, or Alexandria: the difference is at once apparent. Though they did, as their clinical records demonstrate, regularly treat patients, it would seem to have been very much in the spirit, and with the priorities, of a large modern teaching hospital.[55] Research and theory came first. The author of the famous Hippocratic treatise on the so-called sacred disease, that is, epilepsy, had very little time for magicians or quacks: these gentry, he records, "being at a loss, and having no treatment that would help . . . concealed and sheltered themselves behind superstition, and called this illness sacred, in order that their utter ignorance might not be manifest."[56] His introductory statement is often cited: "It is not, in my opinion, any more divine or more sacred than other diseases, but has a natural cause."[57]

This heartening broadside in favor of scientific rationalism is much better known—and with good reason—than the "natural cause" that follows, since the author goes on to assure us that what in fact causes the disease is the melting and dispersal of phlegm from the brain.[58] There could be no better simultaneous demonstration of the glories and shortcomings of Greek medicine. A lapidary principle is undercut and nullified by a false theory based on inadequate evidence and fanciful (not to say poetic) speculation. The phlegm in question forms part of an elaborate general doctrine, that of the four humors, which had a very long run for its money. Ultimately it was grounded in the Empedoclean principle of the four supposed elements: earth, air, fire, and water. On the principle of analogical sympathy, the four constituent elements, or humors, in man were identified (for reasons that will shortly become apparent) as phlegm, blood, yellow bile, and black bile, all of which had to be in the correct proportions to one another.[59] Metaphors based on mixing (krasis) and cooking (pepsis), and applied in particular to the digestive process, suggest homely parallels between a full stomach and a stewpot bubbling on the kitchen range.[60] The fourfold pattern was infinitely adaptable: to the seasons, the winds, the elements, even, in due course, the Evangelists. It offered a kind of universal holdall, in which tastes, temperaments, and a surprising number of diseases could find loose accommodation. Though virtually worthless as a theory, it remained the fundamental prop of European medicine for over two millennia, a chastening reflection.[61]

It is also fascinating to see how a superficial observation (e.g., the increase of phlegm, i.e., nasal mucus, in winter) was made grist for the mill of an aprioristic theory. The theory had respectable antecedents. A century before Thucydides, Alcmaeon of Croton, in southern Italy, formulated the notion of health as "a balance among the powers of the body, these powers being constituent fluids with definite qualities and causal properties."[62] When the fluids were in proper equilibrium, that was isonomia, equality under the law, whereas illness Alcmaeon defined as monarchia, the dominance of one. Here we can see both the balance of opposites and the golden mean in embryo; but even more interesting is the way in which medicine absorbed analogies from politics, from the sixth-century democratization of the city-state, it-

self influenced by the emergent rationalism and generalizing principles of the Milesian philosophers.[63]

What were the elements to be held in balance? Heat and cold, moisture and dry-
ness, sweet and bitter—all permanently inherent in the four humors, or fluids, that
supposedly rule the body. Again, observe how everyday life, as noted by the naked
eye, goes to build a theory round blood, phlegm, and two sorts of bile. When you
cut yourself, you bleed. When you catch a cold, you drip phlegm. When you vomit,
you throw up bile. "Black bile" is less straightforward: it may have been either the
clotted dark blood produced by an internal hemorrhage or the vomit characteristic
of remittent malaria:[64] in either case a fanciful guess at what was going on inside.
The two commonest diseases in ancient Greece were chest complaints and malaria,
both of which fit this picture rather well (cf. above, p. 123, for the hereditary *phthisis*
suffered by the Antigonids). An imbalance in the humors produced disease, it was
argued, and nature then attempted to put things right by *krasis* and *pepsis*, an internal
mixing and cooking of the elements until their proper proportions were restored.[65]
This theory was probably encouraged by the symptoms common in a high fever. At
some point a *krisis*, literally "a moment of decision," would be reached, when either
nature or the disease prevailed, and the patient either turned the corner toward recovery, or died. All the physician could do was give nature every chance to operate
beneficially.

There is something subtly seductive about the four humors: their widespread
and lasting impact on European thought has been out of all proportion to their
medical value. Even today, when we use the word "humor" as a synonym for
"mood," or describe a person's temperament as "sanguine" or "melancholy," "bil-
ious" or "atrabilious," we are upholding the old theory, since the four fluids were
held to condition innate character. Similarly, the word "crisis" still bears the special
medical meaning that the Hippocratic writers gave it. All this put a heavy brake on
the progress of physiological research, since there were few phenomena for which
the humors could not be made to yield some sort of easy explanation. It is greatly to
the credit of Erasistratus that he largely discarded the humoral theory; it is even
more significant that (so far as we know) no one else did, so that blood, phlegm, and
bile (whether yellow or black) survived into the Renaissance as the constituent elements of the human body. At least, unlike that other popular fantasy, phlogiston,
they actually did exist.

Our estimate of Hellenistic medicine, then, will be in direct proportion to the
degree in which it managed to break loose from, or succeed in spite of, this traditional and in essence philosophical straitjacket.[66] The key figures here are Erasistratus
and Herophilus, who worked in Alexandria under the first two Ptolemies. Their
own writings do not survive: they have to be reconstructed from quotations and references in later authors.[67] However, enough can be gathered from these sources to
form a fairly clear idea of their remarkable achievements. Erasistratus worked in
Antioch as well as Alexandria: he seems to have been instrumental in diagnosing the
semi-illicit passion of Seleucus Nicator's son Antiochus I Soter for his beautiful

young stepmother, Stratonice, and in persuading the politically astute Seleucus to surrender Stratonice to him (294/3?).[68] Clearly the support and patronage of Ptolemies or Seleucids provided enough freedom from some, at least, of the normal social and intellectual pressures prevalent elsewhere to encourage individualism. This becomes very clear when we compare Herophilus with his immediate predecessors, Diocles of Carystos, a student of Aristotle's,[69] and Praxagoras of Cos, Herophilus's own teacher.

Diocles, who worked in Athens and wrote in Attic[70]—"a factor," it has been alleged, "which may have made him more interesting to later medical men than he would otherwise have been"[71]—believed in the four humors; he also, like his master, Aristotle, accepted the heart as the seat of intelligence, and indeed employed much of Aristotle's general terminology. Tradition made him the next major Dogmatist after Hippocrates.[72] He was a great upholder, like the Stoics after him, of the notion that air, *pneuma*, was a vital spirit, alive, intelligent, divine, with cognizance of the Deity (a view already ridiculed in the fifth century by Aristophanes).[73] According to this theory *pneuma* was disseminated from the heart to the sense organs as a means of facilitating perception. When unbalanced humors blocked the "pores" (*kenōmata*) through which it passed, disease or death followed. Sperm, for Diocles, came from the brain and spinal marrow, so that excessive intercourse was held by him to affect the eyes and mind:[74] could this be a distant ancestor of the widespread Victorian belief that chronic masturbation led to blindness and insanity? Digestion, similarly, was a fermentation or putrefaction of food, together with its *pneuma*, in the stomach (a tantalizing near-miss solution), while indigestion resulted from an unbalanced proportion between these elements.

Diocles, seeing very clearly that the future for an ambitious doctor lay in royal patronage, wrote a pamphlet *Health Hints*, as a form of self-promotion, for Cassander's brother Pleistarchus, who ruled briefly in Cilicia after Ipsus (301), and a similar treatise, in the form of an open letter, addressed to Antigonus One-Eye (above, p. 8), who was urged to drink cabbage water with honey and salt for complaints of the gut, the penalty for ignoring symptoms in this region being, *inter alia*, diarrhea, gout, apoplexy, piles, and arthritis.[75] Apart from the kind of common-sense knowledge picked up in practice, it is clear that Diocles' medical lore was both derivative and, to a very large extent, purely theoretical: "hints and guesses, hints followed by guesses." The same is true of Praxagoras of Cos,[76] his slightly younger contemporary, whose main claim to fame (apart from having been Herophilus's teacher) was to have increased the number of humors from four to ten, thus at least indicating, like modifiers of the concentric-sphere theory, that he had observed phenomena hard to reconcile with the original model. His categories included the sweet, the uniformly mixed, the glassy, the acid, the nitrous, the salty, the bitter, the leek-green, the yolk-colored, the corrosive, and the clotting, an instructive mixture of incompatible genres.[77] He knew about the connection between the brain and the spinal cord, but still believed the arteries to contain *pneuma*, drawn in from the outside rather than innate.[78] He was regarded in antiquity as a notable dietician; he also

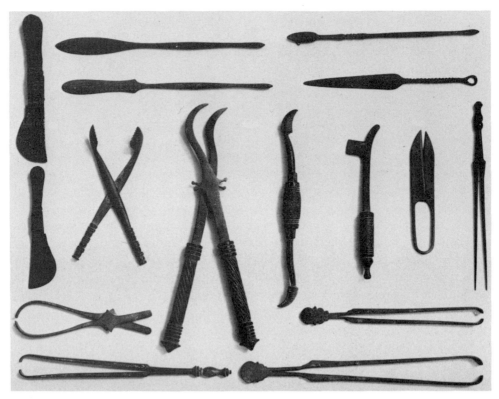

Fig. 150. A selection of bronze surgical instruments from Pompeii (first century
A.D.), including scalpels, various types of probes and forceps, and surgical scissors.
Museo Nazionale, Naples. Photo Alinari.

carried out fairly sophisticated operations, including one to remedy scrotal hernia.
He was, it has recently been claimed, "a bridge between the old and the new in
medicine." [79]

But the contrast between him, or any other pre-Alexandrian doctor, and Herophilus is instantly instructive. With the latter one is struck, again and again, by an
accuracy of observation that can only derive from autopsy, in every sense of that
word, whether Herophilus is examining brain or eye, liver or genitals, the nervous
or the vascular system. [80] He not only distinguished the cerebrum from the cerebel-
lum and traced the nervous system between brain and spinal cord, as Aristotle and
Praxagoras had successively done before him, [81] but made the crucial inference from
these findings that they had not, firmly locating the seat of intellect, not in the heart
(as both Stoics and Peripatetics held as an article of faith), but in the brain, in the
cavity of the fourth ventricle, still known today as *calamus scriptorius*, the Latinization
of what, with characteristic metaphorical aptness (cf. n. 60, p. 861), he termed the
"pen hollow" (*anaglyphē kalamou*), from its resemblance to the slot in an Alexandrian
writing pen. [82] It should come as no surprise that, despite Herophilus's irrefutable testimony to the primacy of the brain, Chrysippus—that passionate Stoic convert—

still obstinately defended the heart as the organ of reason, citing to that end the authority of Praxagoras from half a century before.[83]

Herophilus also dissected, and identified, the four membranes of the eye, investigated the pancreas,[84] did detailed work on the anatomy of the liver, distinguishing the bile ducts from the portal veins,[85] described (and named) the "twelve-finger outgrowth" (*dōdekadaktylos ekphysis*), still known, in its Latin translation, as the duodenum, and made a detailed study of the pulse, even designing a portable clepsydra to time it,[86] and working out a mathematical formula to express variations in its rate.[87] His perception that pulsation in the arteries derives from the heart brought him within a hair's breadth of anticipating Harvey's discovery of the circulation of the blood.[88] He may also have determined that the arteries contained blood rather than *pneuma*, but evidence for this is uncertain.[89] All in all, it is a stunning record.

In some ways, inevitably, Herophilus pursued the old beliefs: for example, he clung, in an extreme form,[90] to the humors as a base for the aetiology of disease, having no instruments capable of identifying bacteria (let alone viral bodies) and thus correcting such a view.[91] Despite his brilliant work on the nervous system, he still thought that the optic nerves conveyed "sensory *pneuma*."[92] He also placed great reliance on purges, not least hellebore "the supreme enema of antiquity,"[93] which he called "the bravest of captains," since "after stirring up all within, it sallies forth itself in the van."[94] Both black hellebore (*Helleborus niger*) and white hellebore (*Veratrum album*) are in fact lethally poisonous irritants, liable to induce symptoms ranging from vomiting and diarrhea to muscular spasms, asphyxia, and cardiac failure.[95] In this context it is perhaps unfortunate that he referred to drugs as "the hands of the gods." He was, we may assume, familiar with Book 9 of Theophrastus's *History of Plants*, which contains much useful pharmacological material.[96]

Thus it is clear that where Herophilus broke new ground, and achieved epoch-making results, was, precisely, in any area where he could make fresh direct observations as a result of the new availability of cadavers for dissection.[97] Both Plato and Aristotle, it has been argued, had prepared the climate of opinion here, by treating the soul as the paramount element in a human organism: it followed that the body was a mere discardable envelope, to be treated without regard for its supposed awareness or rights.[98] But even granted the existence of this attitude (which was, in fact, no more than a reversion to Heracleitus's sixth-century opinion that corpses should be thrown out like so much dung),[99] it cannot have been held by more than a small intellectual minority. Neither Plato nor Aristotle was any more popular, let alone populist, in his opinions than Heracleitus, and in fact, as we have seen, the only thing that made dissection or, *a fortiori*, vivisection possible in Alexandria, even for a short period, was the active support of the reigning monarch.

It should be noted that a fair proportion of Herophilus's pioneering work in human anatomy was gynecological, for example on the ovaries and the Fallopian tubes, which he discovered,[100] and it is improbable, to say the least, that such research was carried out at the expense of condemned criminals. Fraser argues that "his knowledge of the internal genital organs is much weaker,"[101] which, if true, might strengthen the case for his having enjoyed greater freedom to dissect, or vivisect, male bodies; but this judgment is by no means certain. Fraser also remarks that "Herophilus's erroneous statement that the ovarian arteries and veins are not present in all instances may be explained on the hypothesis that he had chanced to dissect elderly women, in whom those vessels are not easy to identify." The possibility that he was denied access to young female corpses has interesting implications, *inter alia* in connection with the much-debated possibility that he gleaned information from, and perhaps observed the techniques employed by, the Egyptian embalmers—though, as Von Staden reminds us, "the level of anatomical knowledge required by Egyptian methods of embalming is closer to that of a skilled butcher than of a Hellenistic physician."[102] Let Herophilus himself have the last word: his healthily pragmatic attitude is summed up in the pithy comment (today more often applied to politics) that medicine is, in effect, the art of the possible, and the best doctor is he who knows what is possible and what is not.[103]

Erasistratus, the son of a doctor, met Theophrastus and other Peripatetics during his medical studies in Athens, and became influenced by their ideas.[104] In 294/3, as we have seen (above, p. 491), he was in Antioch, and already an experienced enough physician to be consulted for a puzzling diagnosis, which suggests a birth date not later than 325; he was still alive in 258.[105] About 280 he visited Cos, where he met Ptolemy II's physician Chrysippus: it was probably Chrysippus who brought him to Alexandria. From Theophrastus and Strato of Lampsacus—Theophrastus's successor (ca. 287) as head of the Lyceum, and a former tutor of Ptolemy (above, p. 84)—he seems to have picked up the notion of what has been termed "disseminate void,"[106] that is, that matter consists of minute particles separated by equally small interstices, any larger void being instantly filled by surrounding matter on the principle of *horror vacui*. This theory has clear links with the principle of the vacuum as outlined in the preface to Hero's *Pneumatica*,[107] rather than (as used to be thought) with the somewhat different atomic theory propounded by Democritus. Erasistratus combined his corpuscular concept of matter with a belief in *pneuma*; his physiological researches into digestion rejected *pepsis* and *krasis*, positing instead a fundamentally mechanical and muscular (rather than a chemical, organic-transformational) process, whereby food was forced through infinitely fine pores in the walls of the stomach and gut. This and other dead-end theorizing did not prevent him from achieving a great deal—once again, via direct observation—in the fields of physiology and anatomy. His work on the heart and the vascular system was fundamental: discovery of the bicuspid and tricuspid valves led him to appreciate the heart in its function of double-action pump—even though he decided that its use was to force *pneuma* through ever-finer *kenōmata* to every part of the body,[108] a nice and characteristic blend of acuity and mistaken interpretation. Like Herophilus, he also worked on the brain, making a clear distinction between the sensory and motor nerves.

For both Herophilus and Erasistratus the great break with their predecessors lay, simply and solely, in the right to dissect: the difference in quality between the research they carried out on this basis and their more philosophical speculations is startling. Through their royal charter of privilege they had acquired a precious new observational facility in a discipline where observation was, as we have seen, strictly limited. When the privilege was again removed (in all likelihood long before Ptolemy VIII's expulsion of the intellectual community from Alexandria [below, p. 538]: mere lack of active support would, in this case, suffice), it was not long before Greek medicine relapsed into sterile theoretical feuding, between rival sects as opinionated as they were fanciful.[109] If folk medicine minus theory precluded real advance, theory without a true observational and experimental base was little more than a branch of philosophical (or, indeed, mythical) speculation.[110]

One more important point needs to be made in closing. The many inscriptions commemorating benefits conferred, by cities and individuals, on the public and private doctors of the Hellenistic era offer[111]—in a society not generally notable for its altruism or selflessness—a most moving record of service over and above the call of duty. Those early aspirations enshrined in the Hippocratic oath, or in treatises such as *On Ancient Medicine* or *Precepts*, have not been wholly forgotten in a more materialistic and less civic-minded age. Some physicians, it is clear, were primarily interested in their fees, and needed reminding that it was "better to reproach patients after recovery than to screw money out of them *in extremis*";[112] but when in history has this not been true? Nor did the Hellenistic medical fraternity, as liberal historians once hopefully argued on minimal evidence, ever include slaves, except in the subordinate roles of nurses, orderlies, or assistants:[113] indeed, the social conditions we have studied surely precluded the emergence of such *Sklavenärzte* almost by definition. An equally popular chimera is the belief that some at least of the cities that hired public physicians did so in order to provide their community with free, that is,

Fig. 151. Tombstone of Jason, an Athenian physician of the second century A.D. He is shown palpating a boy apparently suffering from consumption or the effects of malnutrition. Note the stylized and proportionately oversized cupping vessel in front of them.
British Museum, London.

socialized, medical care. This, again, would have run flat counter to the antipopulist hysteria of the day.[114] *Philanthrōpia* was the thing, and as we have seen (above, p. 386), all Hellenistic cities, through their wealthier members, practiced it as a matter of course. But free medical care as an institution would have meant conceding moral, if not legal, rights to the despised and feared lower orders, and this remained anathema. Andrew Carnegie's thesis of paternalistic charity exactly matches the attitude found among Hellenistic millionaires:[115] as Tarn pithily observed, "they would not pay, but they would give."[116]

It is, then, within this framework of formalized philanthropy, detached from any implication of political egalitarianism, that we must consider the numerous testimonials to Hellenistic physicians put on record by the grateful recipients of their professional care. That fact must illuminate, but should not be allowed to detract from, what remains, on any count, a most remarkable achievement. These men did, again and again, provide their services free of charge to the needy when they were under no obligation to do so, and this fact is commemorated with especial gratitude.[117] They also, in the best Hippocratic tradition, gave treatment, without distinction, to "all equally, poor and wealthy, slave and free."[118] They risked their own lives to save battle casualties; they worked through earthquakes; they coped with famines and lethal epidemics.[119] They gave long years of faithful service to their communities.[120] In an age that witnessed the increasingly bloody-minded pursuit, at all levels, of personal wealth and power, these men deserve the commemoration they got: they may serve to remind us that, amid all the political complexities of a new world, in which progress of any sort depended on patronage or charity, the basic human decencies were not entirely forgotten.

CHAPTER 29

HELLENISM AND THE JEWS: AN IDEOLOGICAL RESISTANCE MOVEMENT?

For reasons that have little to do with Hellenistic history, the part played by the Jews under Ptolemaic and Seleucid rule tends to get a closer, more detailed scrutiny than, say, the precisely comparable activities of the separatist movements in Bithynia or Commagene.[1] What marks off Judaism both in its own right and as the precursor, and seedbed, of Christianity is its ideological element (taking "ideological" as a religious no less than a political term). The fact of faith, as a datum, conflicts with normal historical criticism, presupposes what Eliot called "the intersection of the timeless with time." The historian, who is required to study the secular genesis of events rather than their divine revelation, cannot in any open sense work *sub specie aeternitatis*: though he must, and does, recognize the force of faith as a major historical determinant, he can only evaluate it in linear, temporal terms. If he accepts its presuppositions, he becomes, strictly speaking, a propagandist—which means that, for the highest of nonhistorical motives, he has betrayed his calling.

His perspective on events will also be drastically altered. For the clarification of Hellenistic history it should always be borne in mind that the Jewish problem, including the nationalist revolt under Judas Maccabaeus (below, pp. 518 ff.), was, from the viewpoint of Alexandria and, subsequently, Antioch, a comparatively minor affair, involving local tribal politics, and significant chiefly because of its strategic setting, between Idumaea and Samaria, on the marches of Coele-Syria.[2] It was also—as should by now be abundantly clear—a phenomenon by no means without precedent. Ethnic revolts within the Seleucid empire were nothing new. Nor, indeed, was the eager embracement of Greek public *mores* (the use of the gymnasium in particular) by an ambitious elite, coupled with an indigenous indifference to, or active rejection of, Greek religious beliefs and practices (cf. above, pp. 320 ff.). Jerusalem's Hellenizing upper-class minority can be matched throughout the *oikoumenē*, from Pontus to Bactria. The emergent Jewish state differed little, in broad political outline, from those of Parthia or Armenia. Even the monotheistic religious ideology

497

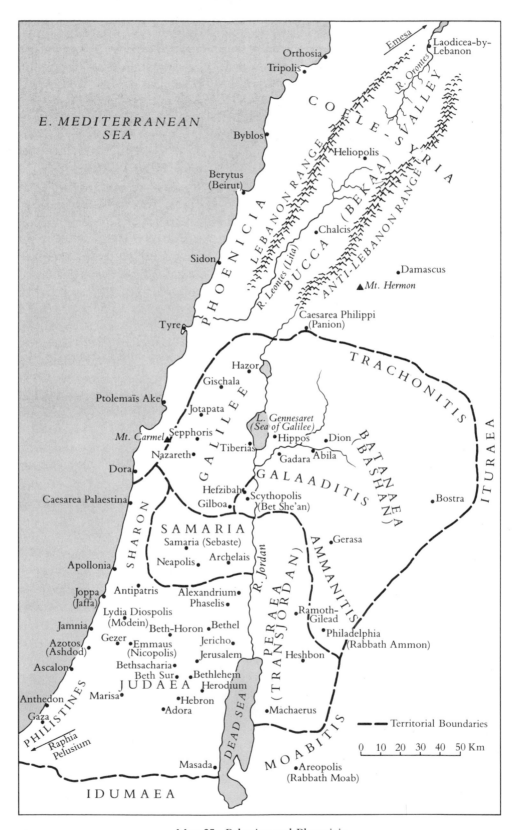

Map 25. Palestine and Phoenicia.

underpinning Judas Maccabaeus's resistance movement had a more or less exact precedent in the priestly opposition to Alexander the Great maintained by the Persian Magi, in the name of the One God Ahura Mazda.[3]

From the historical viewpoint, indeed, the relationship between Judaea and the great Hellenistic kingdoms offers, first and foremost, a model confirming those stress patterns we have noted in all areas where Seleucids or Ptolemies established their rule over a civilized indigenous population. For the Graeco-Macedonian conquerors there was nothing special, to begin with, about the Jews: they saw Jerusalem as one more *polis*, and Judaea as the area it controlled.[4] Alexander spent little time on Palestine, having other goals in mind, and late accounts (in particular that of Josephus), claiming that he made a special journey to Jerusalem, indeed offered sacrifice there, are mere *ex post facto* legends, put out by pious ideologues determined to show that the legendary world conqueror knew a true Holy City when he saw one.[5] To the Successors, Judaea—indeed, Palestine as a whole, of which Judaea formed the southern part—figured chiefly as territory adjacent to that ill-defined no-man's-land Coele-Syria,[6] fought over by successive Ptolemies and Seleucids in recurrent Syrian wars.

In the fourth century, it will be recalled (above, pp. 28 ff.), Syria and Palestine changed hands several times.[7] After Alexander's death Laomedon held the area till 320, when Ptolemy Soter annexed it.[8] In 315 Antigonus One-Eye stormed Joppa (Jaffa) and Gaza and occupied all Palestine;[9] Ptolemy in 312 wrested the area from Antigonus's son Demetrius;[10] in 311 Antigonus recaptured it.[11] Since Palestine was crucial territory in his conflict with Ptolemy he now almost certainly followed his normal practice of establishing Greek and Macedonian settlers there.[12] Thus Greek influence will have made itself felt early. After Ipsus (301) Seleucus, though never officially renouncing his claim,[13] in effect conceded control of Palestine to Ptolemy (above, p. 35);[14] even so, Demetrius for about another decade still retained control of the great ports of Tyre and Sidon.[15]

One inevitable result of this protracted tug of war was the emergence of pro-Ptolemaic and pro-Seleucid groups within Judaea itself.[16] Ptolemy I seems to have been more popular than Antigonus One-Eye, who had a well-deserved reputation for toughness: thus when Ptolemy pulled out in 311, some of his more committed Jewish supporters, including Hezekiah the High Priest, went with him rather than face Antigonus's wrath.[17] However, Ptolemy's civility was strictly relative. In 302/1 his return found him in an anything but mild mood. In collusion with his Jewish friends he entered Jerusalem during the Sabbath, and took advantage of the law prohibiting work or the bearing of arms, even for self-defense, on that day—as others were to do later, in the early stages of the Hasmonean revolt (below, p. 517)—to bring the city completely under his control.[18] He deported various opponents to Egypt, and when forced to evacuate the city, destroyed the walls so that Antigonus could not use it as a stronghold. But Antigonus's death at Ipsus brought Ptolemy back to Jerusalem for the fourth time (late 301): he and his heirs held Judaea during the next century, until Antiochus III's crushing victory at Panion (200: above, p. 304).[19]

Fig. 152. View of the desert between Jerusalem and Jericho, looking eastward across the Jordan valley to the mountains of Moab.
Photo Ronald Sheridan.

The political status of the Jewish people during this period is of interest. The classic evolution from kings to an aristocratic priesthood had already taken place.[20] Also, significantly, the local political representation (*prostasia*) with the ruling power—now the Ptolemies, as previously the Persian Achaemenids—was no longer vested in a satrap or the equivalent, but exercised by the High Priest, whose office was hereditary and (in theory at least) held for life. Thus what had been a purely cultural autonomy under the Persians was acquiring political characteristics and the potential for independence, and "the High Priest at the head of the people assumed the aspect of a petty monarch."[21] This sacerdotal authority, backed by a council of elders (*gerousia*) and centered on the Temple, must be clearly distinguished from that operating among the Jews of the Diaspora, for example in Babylonia or Alexandria, where a less rigid, and certainly less politicized, authority prevailed, associated with the synagogue, scribal exegesis, and the reading and exposition of the Torah.[22]

These dispersed communities were peculiarly exposed to Hellenistic influences; and since their members made pilgrimages when they could to Jerusalem (which was, in any case, by no means cut off from the outside world, especially the world of commerce), such influences, though resisted by strict upholders of the Mosaic Law, nevertheless infiltrated Jewish society at all levels. The Jews of Alexandria, though they lived in a separate community, mixed freely—at least until the late Ptolemaic period, when growing hostilities drove them to embrace the life of the ghetto[23]—with the Greek population: so much so, in fact, that most of them seem to have lost the use of Aramaic and Hebrew, a major factor governing the production of the Septuagint during the reign of Ptolemy Philadelphos (above, p. 317). The language of the Septuagint closely resembles that of the Graeco-Egyptian papyri, while its vocabulary has parallels in certain Alexandrian writers:[24] *inter alia* it hints, in its use of the terms *theos* and *kyrios* to convey Yahweh's synonyms, Elohim or Adonai, at the characteristic Greek abstracting tendency where divinity was concerned. The Diaspora produced the so-called liberal version of Judaism, which soft-pedaled, for the benefit of the *goyim*, those more exotic practices and taboos featured in Leviticus and Deuteronomy, while presenting Moses as a kind of enlightened philosopher, whose teachings were subsequently corrupted by bigotry, superstition, and obscurantism.[25]

This side of Judaism made a favorable impression on Hellenistic Greeks, who thought of the Jews as a race of philosophers (a view sustainable only by the failure to read anything they actually wrote: the same applies to the myth of Egyptian wisdom), and whose own increasing tendency, for example in the case of Isis (cf. p. 410), to universalize local deities and their attributes could quite easily embrace assertive monotheism, a process we can see beginning as early as Aeschylus's day. Yahweh, being known as the "All-Highest," *hypsistos* in Greek, was easily identified with Zeus, or, through his epithet *Sabaoth*, "Lord of Hosts," etymologically confused with Sabazios. Alexandria both encouraged Jewish proselytization and facilitated the penetration of Judaism by Greek philosophical concepts, even to the point of deriving Greek philosophy from the Mosaic Law and interpreting the Torah in Hellenic terms.[26]

In Judaea itself Greek influences can be detected, for example in the "sceptical, pessimistic rationalism"[27] of the Book of Qoheleth (Ecclesiastes),[28] the third-century author of which not only bears witness to the existence of a vast bureaucratic hierarchy (5.7), but also reveals, prior to his all-flesh-is-grass reversion (e.g., at 5.10 f.), a highly Hellenistic, not to say Veblenish, preoccupation with the wealthy oligarch's dream: the building of villas, the planting of vineyards and orchards, the acquisition of great parks and estates, the purchase of flocks and herds, the amassing of gold and silver via the exaction of revenue; casks of wine in the cellars, and a vast household of slaves, including singers, concubines, and catamites.[29] By way of reaction we find the civilized and meditative anti-Hellenism of Ben Sira,[30] whose *Wisdom* (more familiar to us by its apocryphal title, Ecclesiasticus) was composed between 200 and 180: about fifty years later his grandson translated it into Greek, which gave it a much wider circulation, above all in the Egyptian Diaspora.[31]

Joshua Ben Sira was no puritan by nature: he enjoyed good food and wine, was widely read and highly intelligent. Because of this he knew, all too well, the perils inherent in a free mind engaged upon intellectual inquiry, *historia*, and seeking answers to its questions by reason alone, unrestrained by taboo, dogma, or shibboleth. For him, a little wisdom with the fear of God was preferable to much wisdom without it (19.4), and his bitterest anger is reserved for those who cast aside the Mosaic Law in pursuit of ambition and undirected knowledge. Alien ways, he insisted, were dangerous for Judah: only under the Law of Yahweh could she triumph against her foes (47.4–7). The High Priest's duties were to teach the Torah, to offer sacrifice, to make atonement on behalf of his people; by eloquent omission we are made to feel the perils attendant upon the exercise of this office by a Hellenizer.[32] The materialistic lure of the Greek lifestyle is aptly summed up: "Feasts are held at will, and wine gladdens life, and money answers everything."[33] Ben Sira had traveled (51.13); he knew the wider world beyond the confines of Judaea. Despite this, he returned as orthodox as when he left: Greek culture was not for him. At the same time he understood, very well, the perilous chasm—in his own people as elsewhere—between rich and poor, though like so many other pious observers he took this to be immutable, and due to God's will. There is a curious flavor of Stoicism about his advice to the downtrodden, whom he exhorts to pursue self-knowledge and wisdom as an answer to their quest for freedom.[34] Rebellion and freedom fighting are not in his scheme of things, and we see, reading his work, why for so long Jewish nationalism lacked a revolutionary dimension.

Between 301 and 219 Palestine continued to be ruled by the Ptolemies in comparative peace (except for the capture of Samaria by Demetrius the Besieger in 296), since the various frontier wars did not penetrate that far south. From the Zenon papyri[35] it seems clear that the same complex economic forces, the same strangling bureaucracy, the same military occupation that cluttered people's lives in Egypt also operated here.[36] Defense is a prime concern: we hear of cleruchies and fortresses, garrisons, grants of land to veterans. In 261/0 Ptolemy II's officials organized the census, and taxation, of livestock in the area, and banned the acquisition of free Syrians or Phoenicians as slaves; it is further alleged that the king ordered the general manumission of all Syro-Phoenician and Jewish prisoners captured during his father's campaigns in the area, but this is highly debatable.[37] There is, however, no doubt that Jews found their way into the Ptolemaic administration, in both Egypt and Palestine.[38] The father of Joseph the tax collector (of whom more in a moment), a wealthy magnate named Tobiah,[39] held high rank in the Ptolemaic army: this is extremely significant, since in Egypt the Ptolemies shrank from giving any responsible office to native Egyptians, and the insurrections that followed their enrollment of Egyptian hoplites (above, p. 191), in an emergency, for the battle of Raphia (217) shows how sound this instinct was.

In Palestine, however, they needed indigenous support for their endless struggle with the Seleucids, and it was inevitable that the Jews themselves, certainly their leaders, should align themselves with one side or the other.[40] Tobiah, like other Palestinian sheiks, was a man worth cultivating: in fact both he and his son maintained a firm loyalty to the Ptolemies, probably as the ruling power rather than through any natural affinity. There is evidence that in 259/8, when Zenon toured Syria, Phoenicia, Judaea, and Transjordan on behalf of the *dioikētēs* Apollonius, efforts were being made to organize the same kind of all-embracing bureaucratic estate management here as in Egypt.[41] The larger the royal domains, the more authority had necessarily to be delegated; and despite the presence of resident Greek administrators, it was inevitable that Ptolemy, as absentee landlord (above, pp. 187 ff.), should entrust much of the day-to-day work to native officials. Local priests, aristocrats, or city magnates often acted as such liaison officers, remaining very much in *de facto* control.

Thus through the cleruchies and the Ptolemaic civil service the Jews came to acquire firsthand knowledge of Greek customs, proficiency in the Greek *koinē*, a taste for Hellenized names, even mixed marriages, and their initial approach to social Hellenization generally;[42] while at the same time Jewish leaders were not only left in possession of their holdings, but co-opted into roles of political and administrative authority. Inevitably, there developed an alignment between the Ptolemaic (and, later, the Seleucid) government and a Hellenizing, collaborationist elite among the Jews. The latter's political rivals thus tended to identify themselves, quite naturally, with a more strictly Judaic, anti-Hellenizing, noncollaborationist attitude: during the Seleucid regime they also sought, and obtained, aid from the Ptolemies, but largely in the traditional Jewish spirit of "My enemy's enemy is my friend." As Eddy says, "the history of the ruling circle was the aggrandisement of one noble or priestly faction at the expense of another,"[43] a dichotomy exacerbated by the long-simmering conflict over Coele-Syria. Thus at a deeper level the ground was being prepared for a nationalist reaction against both Hellenism and foreign rule as such, which were, with some justice, seen as indistinguishable.

From 219, as we have seen (above, p. 288), Antiochus III made vigorous efforts to recover Coele-Syria and advance his frontiers toward Egypt: the following year he invaded Galilee, crossed the Jordan, and entered Samaria, but his defeat at Raphia forced him to postpone his plans for almost two decades. Then, between 201 and 199/8, he systematically reduced all the strongholds of Coele-Syria,[44] and when the

Ptolemaic forces evacuated the area this time, it was for ever. Palestine now became a Seleucid fief. Jerusalem, which changed hands twice during the fighting,[45] finally expelled its Ptolemaic garrison in 198 and welcomed the new overlord, but not before it was clear beyond any doubt that Antiochus had in fact won.[46]

The events of these years suggest a sharp internal struggle between pro-Ptolemaic and pro-Seleucid factions in Judaea; Antiochus's victory saw many of Ptolemy's supporters (as had happened nearly a century before) beat a prudent retreat to Alexandria.[47] This division is reflected in the generous terms that Antiochus negotiated for the status of the Jewish *ethnos*. His letter of concession is addressed not to the Jewish people, but to the governor of Coele-Syria, and pointedly omits any reference to the High Priest *qua* Jewish leader.[48] This suggests that the latter was a Ptolemaic sympathizer, as indeed in terms of *Realpolitik* he would have to have been: changes of regime can be awkward for the functionaries of satellite nations.[49] Willing cooperation with Antiochus—a splendid reception, lavish gifts of provisions and elephants—paid off. Seleucid bureaucrats were said to be easygoing;[50] Jewish officials still untainted by Ptolemaic connections saw the glittering prizes of preferment within their reach.

Antiochus was certainly generous. Sacrificial animals, oil, wine, wheat, flour, salt, and incense, to the value of twenty-thousand silver drachmas annually, would be provided for Temple use. The Temple itself, damaged during the fighting, would be repaired, and all tolls waived on timber imported for it. These clauses perpetuated a long-standing tradition of subsidy by the ruler, going back as far as Darius (515) and Artaxerxes I (459).[51] Citizens driven out or enslaved in the course of the war were to be reinstated in their former positions, and their property restored to them. Priests, scribes, temple singers (cantors?), and members of the council of elders were to be exempt from personal taxes in perpetuity, and the city as a whole tax-exempt for three years, with a subsequent reduction of liability by one-third. Most important of all, the Jews were guaranteed the right to live under their own ancestral constitution, that is, by the Torah. In another edict Antiochus reinforced, by the imposition of punitive fines, various Mosaic religious laws, including the ban on foreigners entering the inner court of the Temple, and that on the importing of animals regarded as unclean.[52] Now it is unlikely that Antiochus knew, or indeed cared, about the Jewish way of life, being in this like most Greeks and Romans of all periods;[53] but he undoubtedly understood what made for a lasting political settlement, and even if he did no more than initial a bill of particulars presented by the Jewish *gerousia*, as a *quid pro quo* for willing collaboration, it remains true that "the foundation was laid for the peaceful existence of the Jewish people under Seleucid overlordship."[54]

The pro-Seleucid faction now came into its own. It has sometimes been alleged that this faction consisted *ab initio* of dedicated Hellenizers, who aligned themselves with a conscious policy of Greek cultural diffusion on the part of the Seleucids, but for neither of these suppositions is there any real evidence. The Seleucids were not proselytizers but exploitative imperialists (above, pp. 187 ff.), and their Jewish supporters in 198 were, as we might expect, acting from strictly political motives. The current High Priest, Simon the Just, seems to have led the pro-Seleucid group, and he could hardly be accused of Hellenizing tendencies. What he did do was rebuild the ruined city of Jerusalem, in accordance with Antiochus III's guarantees. His main supporters were drawn from the elite: the priests, the aristocrats, the wealthy, who saw (even before 200) that the Ptolemies were a lost cause. What Antiochus offered them was a ratification of titular autonomy, that favorite Hellenistic device, the right to live as a more or less self-governing political entity within the Seleucid empire. Far from attempting to dragoon these people into Hellenism, Antiochus left them alone, under the enhanced authority of their own priests and religious laws. What we now have to figure out is just how and why, only thirty years later, Antiochus IV Epiphanes came to attack the Jewish religion and the Mosaic Law with such furious violence, banning circumcision and the observance of the Sabbath, instituting the cult of "Olympian Zeus" (or rather, a semisyncretized version of Baal-Shamin) in the Holy of Holies of the Temple in Jerusalem—acts not only in complete violation of his father's policy, but also strikingly at odds with that general feeling for broad-minded tolerance in religious matters that is one of the Hellenistic age's most characteristic, and endearing, traits.[55] Universal syncretism is hardly a convincing basis for iconoclastic bigotry. What, then, had happened?

Most of the popular theories (popular either in antiquity or among modern scholars) can be dismissed out of hand. Antiochus IV was certainly an odd, and perhaps in ways an unbalanced, character, with some of the habits of the later Julio-Claudian emperors (above, p. 437),[56] but religious persecution *per se* had no charms for him. He was a professed Epicurean,[57] and though he cracked down on the Jews, he left their neighbors in peace. The favorite modern view is that he was "the Helleniser *par excellence*,"[58] using Hellenic culture to weld the heterogeneous mass of his empire into a cohesive whole, to eradicate superstition and promote Greek reason, and in the Jews alone found obstinate non-takers.[59] Antiochus was certainly pro-Greek, but he was also, perforce, pro-Roman. His Hellenism was on occasion a useful political instrument, but he had not the slightest interest, any more than his father had had, in stamping out local culture as such, let alone in acting as a proselytizer for Hellenism, a role that is very largely a modern invention (cf. above, p. 324). A third suggestion is that he was imposing political unity by way of a single prescribed religion, syncretistic in its manifestations. But this kind of "pagan monotheism" was unheard of in antiquity till the third century A.D.

Antiochus's coins suggest that he may have tried to organize his own worship in the avatar of Zeus or Helios (above, pp. 437–38), but that was nothing new; the only people liable to think of Antiochus's imposed cult of "Olympian Zeus" as prescriptive monotheism were the Jews, who, as dedicated monotheists themselves, "saw in every tendency to prefer one cult over another an attempt to set up a uniform religion with the aim of abolishing the rest."[60] An amalgam of the preceding theories might suggest that Antiochus was simply exploring every available method to shore up his crumbling empire; but that does not tackle the problem of selective religious enmity. One last theory, that of Elias Bickerman in *The God of the Maccabees*,[61] argues, correctly, that religious fanaticism of the kind displayed (or apparently displayed) by Antiochus was unparalleled in the ancient world,[62] and from this infers that the real instigators of the purge were the Hellenizing Jews, the High Priest Menelaus and his supporters (below, p. 513), anxious to break down Jewish exclusiveness, so barbarian in the eyes of the Hellenistic world. But there is no evidence to connect this group with Antiochus's decrees, nor indeed for their embracement of Greek philosophical ideas (as opposed to Greek social fashions: *cucullus non facit monachum*)—and if they *had* acquired them, why did they turn fanatic? They should have become tolerant liberals. Let us take a closer look at the background to the persecution.[63]

The Greek and Macedonian immigrants who had entered Palestine were not, for the most part, educated men, but rather—here as elsewhere—soldiers and settlers of relatively humble origin. Thus their intellectual impact on the area was small; what they brought with them were the externals of Greek city life, temples, gymnasia, the *koinē*, theaters—and, if theaters, then popular culture of a sort, probably enhanced by a smattering of the Greek poets taught in school (cf. above, pp. 319 ff.). But they were also quickly influenced by the indigenous population, and soon acquired what Greek purists referred to as a "mixobarbarian" culture, sacrificing to strange gods while building in Hellenic style: thinking Oriental, dressing Greek. What we have to explain is the fact that from the early second century a group of Hellenizers in Jerusalem not only achieved power, not only introduced Greek public *mores* (including the gymnasium and everything associated with it), but actually tolerated the influx of Greek cults into Judea, until the nationalists under Judas Maccabaeus reasserted the supremacy of the strict Mosaic Law.

In contrast to the Scribes, exegetes of the Torah, and closely associated with the strict sect of the Hasidim,[64] who achieved new authority and power about the time that Antiochus III confirmed the Jews in their autonomy, there were other figures, very different yet equally symptomatic, who breached the old exclusiveness of the priestly caste by a candid reliance on Mammon rather than God. Of these perhaps the most notable was Joseph, son of that Tobiah who held high rank in the Ptolemaic army (above, p. 503). Quite apart from being Ptolemy II's military representative in Transjordan, Tobiah had also hedged his sociopolitical bets by marrying the sister of the High Priest Onias II. He was, in addition, a business associate of Apollonius, Ptolemy's enormously influential finance minister (*dioikētēs*: above, p. 386). His correspondence reveals a significant degree of Hellenization. His son Joseph thus grew up in a cosmopolitan Greek atmosphere; but he was also nephew to the High Priest. As a Transjordanian—and, worse, one who had dealings with the hated Samaritans—he must have aroused suspicion: his entire career was predicated on a conscious opposition to the kind of narrow ethnic and religious loyalties that were *de rigueur* among Jewish traditionalists.

Joseph son of Tobiah was, in fact, the prototype of the international financier for whom neither frontiers nor restrictive ethical considerations exist: he has been described (without any irony, I think) as "the first great Jewish banker."[65] At some point in the 240s he obtained, from Ptolemy III Euergetes,[66] the office of *prostatēs*, which carried with it, *inter alia*, the responsibility for collecting taxes.[67] This duty had previously been reserved to the High Priest in Jerusalem, who was held personally responsible for paying a lump sum of twenty talents,[68] but lately had neglected to do so, an omission that made Ptolemy threaten to turn Judaea into military cleruchies, and look favorably on Joseph's bid for the revenue contract. The post he sought was based not on theocratic privilege but on secular competence; it could, moreover, be expanded beyond the frontiers of Judaea proper (i.e., the former kingdom of Judah, little more than the city of Jerusalem with its *chōra*)[69] to include the tax farming of all Coele-Syria, Phoenicia, Judaea, and Samaria.[70] Joseph, in short, was offering to take over the fiscal control of the entire Syrian province, with the guarantee of a far higher return on it. Ptolemy accepted his bid, appointed him as *prostatēs* (he seems to have retained the position till 218),[71] gave him a bodyguard, and backed him when, very early in his new career, he executed twenty recalcitrant officials in Ascalon who refused to pay taxes to this foreign interloper.[72]

Joseph cheerfully broke any Mosaic law in the line of duty: he dealt with Samaritans, he ate prohibited food at the king's table, he dallied with Greek dancing girls. He also, more significantly, maintained a permanent agency in Alexandria, where large sums were on deposit at interest.[73] The Hellenistic world beckoned alluringly, and he followed. Many of his more ambitious contemporaries got the message. To succeed as Joseph did meant, almost by definition, rejecting the narrow code of Judaism: there was no other way. And that, again almost by definition, meant embracing the *ēthos* of the conqueror. Here, in embryo, we can see the future ideology of the Jewish Hellenizing party: separatism had brought nothing but backwardness and trouble, whereas close cooperation, at every level, with the Gentiles would produce an economic and cultural boom.[74]

Joseph's son John Hyrcanus likewise secured the tax-collecting concession, but, fatally, lacked his father's diplomatic skills. He fought furiously with his brothers (ca. 200?), was forced back into Transjordan, chose the wrong side in the Seleucid-Ptolemaic conflict, and after some time as a petty desert chieftain, committed suicide rather than face Antiochus Epiphanes (ca. 175/0?).[75] To set up an independent kingdom was in the classic Hellenistic tradition; so were Hyrcanus's drinking parties, which recall those of Demetrius the Besieger (above, p. 50). Again, it was the trappings, rather than the essence, of Hellenism that most influenced both father and son: glittering social prizes for the upwardly mobile. Josephus—that wealthy Romanized Pharisee—claimed that Joseph brought the Jewish people from indigence to "a more splendid standard of living,"[76] but in fact the Jewish people as a whole got nothing from the deal: it was a model for rich and well-connected go-getters only. Hellenism in Judaea, as elsewhere (above, pp. 315 ff.), had very little to do with culture. It was far more a matter of using the social status, the *entrée*, conferred by Greek public *mores* to further a ravenous appetite for wealth and power. Hence the animadversions of Ben Sira on haves and have-nots (above, p. 502). Hellenistic Greek towns were all around;[77] the Greek *koinē* had become an indispensable *lingua franca*. From mint after local mint, good and abundant Greek coin issues testify to flourishing international trade.[78]

Joseph's sons—that is, the five of them who survived in Jerusalem—emerged as leading figures in the Hellenizing movement:[79] known collectively as the Tobiads, they later allied themselves with Menelaus, who succeeded Jason as High Priest under Antiochus Epiphanes (see below, p. 512), and his brothers, Simon and Lysimachus (the Hellenized names are characteristic).[80] The Tobiads were vastly wealthy, in part by inheritance, in part as the result of their own financial activities. *Inter alia* they seem to have had control of the Temple treasury, and to have developed a promising new line in loan investment.[81]

But this is to anticipate slightly. A struggle for control broke out after the death, in 175, of the High Priest Simon II—known as "the Just," and a powerful patron of the Tobiads—and the succession of his pro-Ptolemaic son, Onias III, a strict zealot.[82] This conflict was resolved in the (pro-Seleucid) Hellenizing party's favor as follows. Onias's brother, Jesus, better known by his Greek name of Jason, went and petitioned the king—that is, Antiochus IV, Seleucus IV having just been murdered as the result of a court intrigue (175)—for Onias's removal, well aware that this High Priest was already suspect in official circles (see below). By offering Antiochus no less than 140 talents over and above the prevailing tribute rate of 300 talents—in other words, by restoring the quota to its old Ptolemaic level—he in effect got the high priesthood by purchase, so that from now on the holder of that office became "a Seleucid royal official utterly dependent on the king's favour."[83] The ease with which this mercenary deal was clinched on both sides reminds us that the Seleucids, too, had their problems, many of which (a common feature of the second and first centuries B.C.) were occasioned by Rome.

By now Antiochus III's punitive indemnity after Magnesia (above, p. 421) had long been creating tensions in the increasingly unstable Seleucid empire, and it is interesting to observe the ways in which his heirs had gone about servicing the vast debt that they had inherited from him. The Temple in Jerusalem had already excited the cupidity of Seleucus IV, who, acting on information supplied by a disgruntled Jewish administrator,[84] sent his minister Heliodorus to expropriate its funds and abolish its financial autonomy; he may also have intended to discipline John Hyrcanus, who had substantial cash deposits there.[85] Heliodorus was refused access to the inner sanctum by the High Priest, Onias; Jewish tradition preserves an apocalyptic legend of his having been flogged senseless outside the treasury by a trio of handsome young angels in golden armor,[86] a theme that, understandably, excited derisive skepticism at the time, but was later to inspire Raphael and Delacroix. Heliodorus's empty-handed return angered Seleucus, and the king's subsequent assassination may have been, in part, due to this imbroglio, since Heliodorus, anxious to prevent his own dismissal, if not demise, was responsible for it. Seleucus also noted, for future reference, the obstructive attitude of the High Priest in refusing his minister's request, a lesson that was not lost on his successor. Antiochus IV therefore at first took the simple step of buying himself a more compliant High Priest; it was only later, under considerable stress (below, p. 513), that he turned to simple plunder and rapine.

What Jason also obtained at his famous interview with Antiochus, reportedly by the offer of yet another 150 talents, was the authority to build a gymnasium, to organize training for a corps of ephebes (*ephēbeia*)—both classic elements in Hellenistic

Fig. 153. Raphael's *Expulsion of Heliodorus from the Temple* (1512–14): Heliodorus is attacked by three angels, who were traditionally supposed to have frustrated his attempt at raiding the treasury of the Temple in Jerusalem.
Vatican Museums.

higher education, such as it was—and to "register the Antiochenes in Jerusalem," a phrase that has been interpreted in different ways.[87] From a careful reading of the main sources it becomes clear that the object of this move was systematic Hellenizing propaganda, sociocultural and antitheocratic in tendency, but limited to an elite group and thus civic only in a highly modified sense.[88] Whether the petitioner was Jason or, as Josephus suggests, Menelaus backed by the Tobiads, the privileges requested are for a special minority group. It is they, not the Jews as a whole (or even the citizens of Jerusalem), who express the desire "to abandon their country's laws and the *politeia* enjoined by these, and to follow the royal laws, and adopt the Greek *politeia*."[89] It is they, not the majority, who hope to be registered as "Antiochenes" (i.e., Hellenized inhabitants of a Hellenized and renamed—for them—"New Antioch"), to exercise *à la mode grecque*, to form a select club of progressive Hellenizers, to which their adolescent sons would be admitted only after passing through that rigorous two years' training, both military and athletic, provided by the ephebic system.

This point is worth stressing, since it has been forcefully argued,[90] and widely accepted, that what Jason asked for, and got, was the transformation of Jerusalem, by fiat, into a full-blown Greek *polis*, a thesis for which there is no compelling evidence. Indeed, it is hard to see how, in practical terms, so unprecedented a change could have been imposed, not least since Jerusalem remained under priestly rule throughout. There was not, as yet, any hint of interference with Jewish religious practices (except insofar as the sale of the high priesthood and the introduction of Greek fashions could be held, *per se*, to constitute offenses against the Jewish faith), and at the time of Antiochus IV's famous letter rescinding his religious persecution[91] the Jews were clearly still regarded as an autonomous, if tributary, *ethnos*.[92] At the very most, it seems clear, what Jason envisaged was a privileged enclave, a Greek-style *politeuma* within the Jewish theocracy; and probably no more, in fact, than the creation of a specially favored cosmopolitan class dedicated to social and political self-advancement via the promotion of Hellenism.[93]

In this latter aim, however, he enjoyed, for a year or two, a certain *succès de scandale*. Antiochus cheerfully authorized the "Antiochenes" to "perform the rites of the heathen."[94] The gymnasium was built on the Temple hill, below the fortress, and crowds of young men, wearing the broad-brimmed hat (*petasos*) of the ephebe, among them some priests who had abandoned their more decorous Temple duties for the lure of naked athletics (in particular discus throwing), now began to exercise with the enthusiasm of converts.[95] For many the urge to break away from the isolation imposed by strict Judaism had become very strong. However, these impassioned would-be Greeks had one embarrassing problem to overcome: the highly un-Greek fact of their circumcision. In one scholar's delicate phrase, they "employed artificial means to efface it."[96] Just how they "concealed" or even "removed" evidence of the *mohel*'s knife is not at all clear.[97] All we know is that a surprising number of people did so.[98] Yet there were some aspects of Hellenization that still caused qualms to Jews, however liberal in their beliefs and practices. When Jason sent a delegation of "Antiochenes" to Tyre, with a cash offering to Heracles-Melkart on the occasion of the quinquennial games instituted by Alexander,[99] the syncretistic gesture misfired: his emissaries, unable to stomach the idea of placating a heathen god against whom Elijah and Elisha had triumphed, arranged for the sum—three hundred silver drachmas—to be applied instead to the construction of triremes.[100]

Oddly enough, in all this there does not seem to have been any technical violation of the Mosaic Code.[101] Athletic games and physical training might not be in the spirit of the Torah, but Moses had never specifically banned them: neither Egypt nor the wilderness had forewarned him of this eighth plague. Nor at the time did conservative exegetes have the ingenuity of those Victorian nonconformists who quoted Psalm 147 ("The Lord sets no store by the strength of a horse, neither does he delight in a runner's legs") to get racing and football banned on Sundays. The rationale, the program of the Hellenizers is reported in these words: "Let us go and make a covenant with the heathen round about us; for ever since we separated from them, many evils have found us out."[102] What the "Antiochenes" sought was sociopolitical privilege and status, better cosmopolitan communications, above all with the Seleucid court. Antiochus, for his part, was by no means loath to have a friendly, obligated, influential elite in a city of this size and power, so strategically placed near the southern frontier of his empire. The concession for which he was asked cost him nothing, and nothing but good (he must have reasoned) would come of it.

So from 175/4 to 172/1 Jerusalem, though officially under sacerdotal rule, enjoyed—to the scandal of the pious and the great delight of her progressives—a brief

Fig. 154. The walls of the Old City, Jerusalem, showing David's Tower.
Photo Ronald Sheridan.

efflorescence of fashionable Hellenization, mainly restricted to the more obvious and external features associated with that phenomenon. However, its leader turned out to have, despite everything, the remnants of a Jewish theocratic conscience, and this proved his political undoing. Jesus might rename himself Jason, but he was still of the High Priest's line, and thus there were some things that he, unlike the Tobiads, could not quite bring himself to do: plundering the treasures of the Temple was one of them. When Antiochus, like Seleucus, demanded access to them (171), Jason proved as adamant as Onias. Perhaps he was banking on the credit he won by his splendid reception of the Seleucid monarch in 172, when Antiochus had come down from Joppa to be welcomed by cheering crowds and a great torchlit procession.[103] If so, he miscalculated badly. Antiochus needed that money; and the Tobiads, who were determined to keep in with the king, and had more realistic notions than did Jason of how this end could best be achieved, meant to see that he got it.

They therefore decided to get rid of Jason, and to replace him with their own candidate, another Hellenizer, who called himself Menelaus (his Jewish name is uncertain). Being from the tribe of Benjamin,[104] Menelaus was not of priestly descent, and might thus be expected to have more accommodating moral standards. He already enjoyed some kind of official position, since he was now sent by Jason on a mission to Antiochus; but the Tobiads had primed him well for his interview, at which he dealt with Jason precisely as Jason himself had dealt with Onias III. Knowing well that the king's shortage of funds was the crucial issue, Menelaus simply out-bid Jason by three hundred talents for the office of High Priest, and was appointed on the spot.[105] Jason refused to budge, and civil war broke out. Finally ejected, he sought refuge in Transjordan, and the pro-Seleucid extremists took over. The common people, acquiescent under Jason's moderate regime, very soon turned against Menelaus and his backers, who were imposing ever higher taxes to meet their expensive obligations. Genuine religious outrage also played its part. The last straw was when Menelaus, under pressure after failing to pay Antiochus the sums he had promised (the king was showing ominous signs of impatience),[106] embezzled gold vessels from the Temple in order to bribe high officials in Antioch, and, in desperation, also had the deposed Onias III assassinated (170).[107] So died the last legitimate Zadokite High Priest. Further sacrilegious pilfering took place. Fiery apocalyptic propaganda whipped up the Jerusalem mob: Menelaus's brother and deputy, Lysimachus, was killed, and his private army scattered, in a savage street battle. Menelaus somehow suppressed this popular uprising, bribed his way back into Antiochus's favor, and "as a great enemy of his countrymen" held on to the high priesthood.[108] It is against this lurid background that we must consider Antiochus's subsequent persecution of the Jews.[109]

The precise course of these events, in particular the chronology between 169 and 167, has been much debated.[110] How many times in that period did Antiochus Epiphanes enter Jerusalem? When, precisely, did Jason stage his counterattack from Transjordan? Do the accounts in 1 and 2 Maccabees duplicate incidents that in fact only happened once? Given the nature of our testimony it is unlikely that agreement will ever be reached on all these points, let alone on the motives of each protagonist in the drama. What follows is, like all previous versions, an attempt to reconstruct historical developments through a critical reexamination of admittedly recalcitrant evidence. Like them, too, it cannot claim to be more than a provisional hypothesis.

Late in 169, after his first expedition to Egypt (above, p. 430), Antiochus Epiphanes entered Jerusalem, with his army, on his way back north to Antioch. He was, as always, short of money, and the object of his visit was to raise some quick loot. The plundering of sanctuaries had become a common habit since Antiochus III had embarked on it (above, p. 422), and Epiphanes himself was no stranger to the practice: his death followed an abortive attempt to sack the same rich temple in Elymaïs (Elam).[111] He now improved on Menelaus's *ad hoc* pilfering by removing a substantial amount of treasure from the Temple; since he later returned to complete the job more thoroughly, there is a certain confusion in our sources between the two occasions.[112] There was no open uprising at the time, but Antiochus's actions left a legacy of deep hatred and resentment behind, and not only among strict traditionalists: what the king regarded as no more than catching up on arrears of tribute, and, thus, his royal prerogative, appeared in Jewish eyes as plain sacrilege.[113]

During Antiochus's second Egyptian campaign, in 168 (above, p. 430),[114] a false rumor that the king was dead reached Jerusalem, and encouraged Jason to launch an assault against the city from his base in Transjordan. At the head of a thousand men he broke through the defenses, forcing Menelaus to seek temporary refuge on the

Fig. 155. Bronze bust from
Herculaneum, possibly of Antiochus IV
Epiphanes.
Museo Nazionale, Naples. Photo Deutsches
Archäologisches Institut, Rome.

acropolis. Jason slaughtered large numbers of his opponents, which was probably a mistake, even though he seems to have had the anti-Hellenist majority of the population solidly behind him.[115] Menelaus and his supporters, the Tobiads prominent among them, fled from Jerusalem to Antiochus, with a convincing tale of pro-Ptolemaic insurrection[116]—convincing, because Alexandria was the natural place for any anti-Seleucid faction near Coele-Syria to turn to in search of backing. Indeed, when Antiochus afterwards sacked the city, he is said to have killed "a large body of Ptolemy's supporters."[117] This report of disaffection could hardly have reached the king at a worse time. After a successful Egyptian campaign he had been abruptly checkmated, and, worse, insulted, by Popillius Laenas, the autocratic Roman envoy (above, pp. 431–32): the notorious Day of Eleusis, the memory of that humiliating circle drawn round him in the dust, cannot have left him in anything but a mood of black fury and frustrated vengefulness. It hardly needed the urging of Menelaus or the Tobiads to make him take vigorous reprisals against the rebellious city.[118]

Whatever had happened during his earlier visit paled into insignificance beside the bloodbath that now took place. Jason, fearing to face a Seleucid army, prudently fled before Antiochus's arrival; but Ptolemy IV, who knew all about his pro-Seleucid past, refused him asylum, and he was forced to move from city to city, finally dying as an exile in, of all places, Sparta.[119] He was luckier, even so, than those who stayed to face the wrath of Antiochus Epiphanes. The king is said to have set out from Egypt "raging like a wild beast."[120] He took Jerusalem by storm, aided by the treachery of his Jewish supporters, who opened the gates to him.[121] His soldiers were given instructions to spare no one, young or old, man, woman, or child: they also had *carte blanche* to plunder the city.[122] The only figures at our disposal show a total of eighty thousand killed in three days, half of that number in hand-to-hand fighting, and as many more again sold into slavery.[123] Accompanied by his creature Menelaus,

Antiochus entered the Temple, and stripped it of all remaining sacred precious vessels and ornaments, including the golden candelabra and altar top. He took besides accumulated bullion to the value of eighteen hundred talents.[124] Then he returned to Antioch, leaving two overseers (*epistatai*), as well as Menelaus, in charge of the stricken city.[125]

There must have been continued rebellion despite these savage punitive measures, since in 167 Antiochus sent to Jerusalem a second expeditionary force, commanded by a Mysian officer named Apollonius. Though the atrocities attributed to Apollonius sound suspiciously like doublets of those committed by Antiochus's troops, he did (like Ptolemy I) occupy Jerusalem on the Sabbath, when the inhabitants were not bearing arms; he then proceeded to tear down the city walls, and to build, probably on a spur opposite Mt. Zion, south of the Temple, in the old city of David, an impregnable fortress known as the Akra, garrisoned with non-Jewish military settlers, a refuge for Hellenizers, and—despite all the successes of the Maccabaean faction (see below)—a safeguard of Seleucid rule for almost three decades, till Simon finally won control of it in 141 (p. 523).[126] It is worth noting that despite his military activities, Apollonius's official title was that of chief tax collector,[127] and

Fig. 156. The Citadel, Jerusalem, consisting to about half its height of blocks of
Herodian masonry from the late first century B.C.
Photo Ronald Sheridan.

thus we may assume (what all our other evidence confirms) Antiochus's concern
with Judaea to have been at least as much financial as strategic. Indeed, Antiochus
may well have introduced the new proportional land tax that replaced the old fixed-
tribute quota—another source of resentment, since by 153 the quotas seem to have
been one-third of the grain produced and no less than half the fruit.[128]

Antiochus's motivation at each stage, in fact, seems comparatively straightforward, and reveals throughout the usual Hellenistic ignorance of, or indifference
to, the powerful forces—isolation, monotheism, exclusionary pride in their history
and religious laws—that shaped and sustained the Jewish people. He badly needed
funds; he was anxious about the security of Coele-Syria. All his actions in Judaea to
achieve these ends ran into a very special kind of religious-inspired ethnic resistance.
Other victims of temple robbery merely grumbled (or, if they were desperate, killed
the robber); the Jews cried sacrilege and prepared to fight *en masse*, often vanishing
into the countryside for the purpose, a form of passive resistance known as *anachōrēsis*, which could easily be escalated into guerilla warfare, and also offered good
opportunities for avoiding taxation.[129] Seleucid divide-and-rule tactics might generate rivalry between Hellenizers and traditionalists, but in the last resort the latter
were stronger, and more numerous, and more passionate in their beliefs: they stood
firm in the face of odds, and were prepared to make sacrifices, indeed to die, for
what they held most dear. Even the most energetic and seductive Hellenizing propaganda failed to soften the vast majority of Jerusalem's religious fanatics, just as massacres, far from breaking their spirit, simply stiffened their will to fight.

Antiochus, who himself was by no means insensitive to the value of theocratic
self-promotion (above, p. 438), must very soon have perceived that his stumbling
block in Judaea, what nullified his efforts at every level, was, precisely, this Chosen
People's fierce and exclusive faith. How far active resistance had yet broken out is
uncertain,[130] though the garrisoning of the Akra must have done much to bring dis-
content to a head. At all events, during 167 Antiochus made every effort to crush
Jewish resistance by eradicating the Jewish faith. The method he chose, that of violent coercion, represented a more than usually gross error of judgment; but taking
into account his naturally autocratic temper, in conjunction with the exploitative atmosphere in which he had been raised, it is very hard to imagine him trying a more
conciliatory approach—not, that is, until he had finally learned, the hard way, that
coercion in this case was something worse than counterproductive, a lesson that
went against the grain of every Ptolemaic or Seleucid principle of government.

He was also, it is clear, strongly supported in the measures he now took by the
Hellenizing party under Menelaus and the Tobiads. Their antinomian position could
only be regularized by a complete jettisoning, indeed extirpation, of the old Law. It
has been argued that the initiative came from them in the first place (above, p. 506),
since, *inter alia*, the persecution was purely local, and did not apply to the Jews of the
Diaspora (who were, in any case, of a more liberal disposition).[131] This is mere
speculation. I am equally skeptical of the suggestion that what Menelaus and the
"sons of the Akra" hoped to enforce was a new, liberal tolerance on the part of the
unenlightened,[132] an early version of the principle *sois mon frère ou je te tue*. Both for

Antiochus and the "Antiochenes" the true issue at stake was that of economics combined with power politics: increase of revenues, defense of Seleucid frontier interests.[133] Religious syncretism had long been recognized as a useful instrument of political unification, and Antiochus's enhanced title "God Manifest, Bearer of Victory"
(*Theos Epiphanēs Nikēphoros*), duly inscribed on his coinage from 169/8,[134] bore witness to this, as did his marked interest in the cult of Olympian Zeus (or his local
avatars),[135] and his self-identification with Helios, the royal and all-seeing Sun (above,
pp. 437–38).[136] It is in this context that we must consider the king's edict, allegedly
promulgated throughout his kingdom, ordering that "all should abandon their local
customs and become one people."[137] Even if this report is true (which has been
doubted), the viewpoint of the reporting may well be local and Palestinian, and not
refer to the Seleucid empire as a whole. "All the heathen accepted the decree." *All?*
More interesting is the fact that "many from Israel" did so.[138]

But about the edict of religious persecution there can be no doubt: it was directly
aimed at Jerusalem and Judaea,[139] where it was hand-delivered in written form. The
neighboring Greek cities of the region were likewise required to enforce it, but this
would seem to have been the limit of its applicability.[140] The Jews of Samaria protested to the king that they really traced their origin from Sidon, and—a nice touch
of sardonic realism—that if they were left in peace they would find it easier to pay
their taxes. They also offered to dedicate their temple to Zeus. Antioch granted their
petition: this was the kind of reaction he was used to, the rationale behind the commands he now sent to Judaea and its environs.[141] All he aimed to achieve was the
elimination of a rebellious local group by abolishing the ideological code that sustained it. This was why, even within the Seleucid domains, the Jews of Babylonia
and northern Syria remained unaffected.

But in Judaea itself, under the king's further edict, all Jewish rites and observances, those of the Sabbath included, were to be done away with, as evidence not so
much of superstition (though this was alleged too) as of offensive separatism.[142] The
Books of the Law, the Torah, were to be torn up and burned. There were to be no
more sacrifices or burnt offerings or drink offerings in the Temple. The death penalty was decreed for a whole range of offenses: possession of the Jewish scriptures,
nonconformity with Greek customs,[143] observance of Jewish religious law, and, in
particular, the practice of circumcision. Mothers of circumcised male children were
thrown off the city walls with their babies strung round their necks; not only the
circumcisers, but their entire families were executed.[144] In addition to these negative
prohibitions came positive injunctions. The Jews were to set up Greek-style altars,
images, and sacred groves, to sacrifice pigs and ritually unclean cattle, to eat pork[145]—
a peculiarly vindictive requirement, since it was by no means the Jews alone who
regarded this animal as impure[146]—to worship Hellenic gods, to celebrate the king's
birthday with monthly offerings, to walk ivy-wreathed in procession during the
biennial festival of Dionysus. In December 167 the Temple was rededicated to
"Olympian Zeus," that is, the Syro-Phoenician Baal-Shamin,[147] whose Hebrew
name verbally echoes the "abomination of desolation" in the Book of Daniel.[148] The
placing of a small heathen altar of burnt offerings in the Holy of Holies, and the

slaughter on it, ten days later, of a pig, can be seen as a deliberate affront to Jewish religious separatism.[149]

Reaction was instant and violent. Though many complied under duress,[150] many more did not. One road to follow was that of conscious martyrdom, and some striking instances are on record.[151] Another was the withdrawal into the wilderness (*anachōrēsis*), leaving fields untilled and taxes unpaid, a passive resistance naturally treated as rebellion by the authorities. Such fugitives were hunted down and, where possible, killed, a task made easier by the fact that strictly orthodox Jews would still not raise a hand in their own defense on the Sabbath, and thus, if caught, could be slaughtered with impunity, like cattle.[152] In such circumstances of harsh repression, which struck at the deepest spiritual convictions of an entire people, it was inevitable that, sooner rather than later, a nationalist guerilla movement, of the type we have come to know so well today, should crystallize around some charismatic leader. All that had been won in centuries of Jewish history—and confirmed by the edicts of Antiochus III—was now at hazard. The aim of the Hellenizers, to bring Judaea out of political and cultural isolation into the mainstream of Near Eastern (which meant Seleucid) civilization, seemed a wholly inadequate return for the loss of monotheism in Yahweh and Yahweh's Law.[153] Better death in action than a shameful compliance.[154] Were not the Syrian and other foreign troops in Jerusalem making blasphemous sacrifices to Baal-Shamin, and filling the Temple courts with sacred (or not so sacred) prostitutes?[155] The time was ripe for action; and the time duly called forth the man.

The spark for insurrection was provided by the action of a priest, Mattathias, of the Hasmonean family,[156] in the village of Modein (el-Medieh), northwest of Jerusalem, near Lydda.[157] A royal officer, Apelles, arrived to supervise, and enforce, heathen sacrifice on the part of the villagers. He appealed to Mattathias, as a local leader, to set a good example that others would then follow. Mattathias refused, with a ringing reaffirmation of his faith,[158] and, when a less defiant Jew came forward to make the sacrifice, killed both him and Apelles, after which he overthrew the altar. "Let everyone," he cried, "who is zealous for the Law, and would maintain the covenant, follow me."[159] Then he and his five sons—John, Eleazar, Simon, Jonathan, and Judas, known as Maccabaeus (probably "the Hammer")[160]—took off into the Judaean hills. Here they heard of the deaths of a thousand fugitives who had refused to defend themselves on the Sabbath, and took the momentous decision that, in upholding the covenant that God had made with their forefathers, they were prepared to fight on all seven days of the week.[161] Reinforced by the strict and populist Hasidim, a sect that provided their movement with both the apocalyptic inspiration and the ideological purity that it needed,[162] Mattathias and his rapidly growing band of followers embarked on a kind of religious *razzia*, preaching open resistance, killing apostates, burning their towns and villages, tearing down non-Jewish altars, and forcibly circumcising all uncircumcised male children. In the matter of intolerance there was, clearly, very little to choose between them and their persecutors; at times one begins to feel a certain sympathy for the much-despised Hellenizers.

This vigorous program proved too much for the elderly Mattathias, who died that same year (166), full, if we can trust our sources, of edifying rhetoric to the last.[163] His importance in the rebellion has probably been exaggerated. With the assumption of military command by his son Judas Maccabaeus insurrection entered upon a new phase: it became a highly politicized revolutionary war, challenging the Seleucid regime and aiming, ultimately, at complete independence for the Jewish *ethnos*. Judas was a natural general, who welded a heterogeneous mass of untrained followers, in a remarkably brief space of time, into a formidable fighting force, over six thousand strong. He not only showed a flair for guerilla tactics, but proved himself capable of winning pitched battles. He fought Apollonius the tax collector (above, p. 514), now governor of Samaria and Judaea, defeated and killed him, and took his sword to use in all future engagements.[164] Another Syrian officer, Seron, was put to ignominious flight.[165] It was now that Antiochus Epiphanes, anxious to embark on his eastern campaign against the Parthians (165), set out from his capital, leaving his viceroy, Lysias, to deal with, among other things, the Jewish rising (above, p. 439).[166]

Lysias instructed the governor of Phoenicia and Coele-Syria, Ptolemy son of Dorymenes, and Philip, the royal *epistatēs* in Jerusalem (above, p. 440), to take appropriate military action. Their combined forces marched south, only to be outmaneuvered and defeated in the rugged hill country of Judaea.[167] At this point Lysias decided he had no alternative but to put down the rebels himself. In the autumn of 165 he brought Judas to battle near Beth-Zur, south of Jerusalem, and fared little better than his predecessors, being defeated (though not annihilated) and forced to retreat to Antioch in search of reinforcements.[168] Here, however, on reflection, he came to the conclusion that he would—for the present at least—get farther, and with less effort, by negotiation. He therefore sent a conciliatory dispatch to Judas, promising to use his best offices with Antiochus to obtain a just settlement.[169] Probably in November, a petition from Judas, embodying some of Lysias's suggestions, was forwarded to Antiochus in the east. It is noteworthy that the envoy who delivered it, and argued the Jewish case, was Menelaus, still officially High Priest and the representative of Seleucid authority in Jerusalem. Thus, in his dealings with Judas, Lysias was, as Marxists would say, involved in a contradiction. The conflict between Hellenizers and Jewish traditionalists was on hold for the moment—the edict of persecution had seen to that—but very far from resolved.

Early in 164, in response to this diplomatic *démarche*, a remarkable document from Antiochus reached the Jewish *gerousia*. It contained an amnesty for those guerillas who returned to their homes by a certain date, and a pledge that henceforth the Jews would be permitted to revert to their own laws and dietary code (or, perhaps, system of taxation).[170] Antiochus clearly had the good sense to realize when a policy was proving disastrous, and to reverse it; but his persistence in dealing only with Menelaus and the Hellenizers shows either that he still did not fully understand the Jewish problem,[171] or, more probably, that he understood it very well, and was playing a long-term game, making what were to him unimportant concessions, while at the same time not losing any substantial power. His letter made no mention of the high priesthood, no reference to control of the Akra. Perhaps his immediate aim was to put a stop to the fighting, in which Judas had been all too successful: to buy time.

Political realignments, if unavoidable, could come later. Lysias had, it is clear, presented forceful pragmatic arguments in favor of a change in policy, which Menelaus (with whatever private misgivings) duly conveyed to the king. It is no accident that for the rest of 164 there would seem to have been a complete cessation of hostilities in Judaea. The insurgents, whose long-term ambitions had been heightened, and politicized, by success, used this time to build up their reserves and, almost certainly, to restore the country's disrupted agricultural life.[172]

Judas Maccabaeus had won the first round, but much still remained to be done. Political ambition and religious zealotry fused in him to form an explosive driving force. From now on, two objectives were clear in his mind: the purification of the priesthood (or, put differently, the removal of the High Priest's office from the Hellenizing party), and the reestablishment of Judaea as an independent, sovereign state. These two goals were, of course, indissolubly linked. Hellenizing High Priests such as Menelaus not only represented the "sons of the Akra"; they were the appointed spokesmen and instruments of Seleucid policy. Similarly, to free Judaea from foreign overlordship meant, inevitably, a return to that strict separatism demanded by the Torah. But over and above these high motives we can also detect something more familiar, more mundane: the unmistakable appetite for power. The Hellenizers, as we have seen, enjoyed substantial support, by no means all of it from wealthy progressives or *collabos*. The smell of intellectual and cultural freedom can be intoxicating, especially to the young: our own age can provide parallels and to spare. Thus while the Hasmonean brothers were indeed fighting a religious war of liberation in 165, they were also—like Jason, like Menelaus—increasingly engaged, as time went on, in a fratricidal struggle for the high priesthood, and, thus, in a separatist theocratic state, for supreme political power.[173] All subsequent events—culminating in the establishment of the Hasmoneans as hereditary High Priests of Israel (below, p. 524)—must be scrutinized with this consideration in mind.

Judas's next move was a master stroke, combining impeccable piety with immensely potent symbolic propaganda. In October or November of 164 he and his troops marched into Jerusalem with one object in view:[174] the rebuilding, purification, and rededication of the Temple, according to strict Judaic law.[175] They found the gates burned, the sanctuary desolate, the altar profaned, weeds sprouting in the courts. Liberal polytheism had done its worst. Antiochus's letter had, wisely, not attempted to adjudicate between Jewish religious rivals; so while the work of reconstruction went on, Judas's guerillas stood guard to prevent any untoward interruptions by the Hellenizers' Syrian garrison in the Akra. The heathen altar was removed, its defiled base dismantled, a new one of uncut stones set in its place. New doors were fitted, new sacred vessels of gold consecrated. On 25 Kislev, in December 164, the lights were kindled, the shewbread set out, incense burned, sacrifice offered; for eight days of ceremonial rejoicing—still repeated annually as the feast of Hanukkah—the restoration of the Temple brought joy to the hearts of the faithful, emphasized (as nothing else could have done) the triumph of the Torah over liberalism, and associated that triumph indissolubly with the Hasmoneans. It was Judas Maccabaeus's finest hour, the high point of his achievement. Yet it also, inevitably,

Fig. 157. Scale-model reconstruction of the Temple, Jerusalem, as it was in the late
first century B.C. (beginning of the Second Temple period).
Photo Ronald Sheridan.

heralded his decline and fall. With the religious phase of the struggle accomplished,
Judas's role now became that of the politically ambitious rebel guerilla, lured on by
apparent weaknesses in the Seleucid military machine.[176] As he was soon to find, this
course had its moral no less than its physical hazards.

The first step he took after the purification of the Temple was to fortify Mt.
Zion and the southern border city of Beth-Zur, facing Idumaea.[177] In 163, with Antiochus IV dead, and Lysias holding an uncertain regency on behalf of the king's nine-
year-old son, Antiochus V Eupator (above, p. 439), Judas felt safe to go on the
offensive again: the Syrian government had more pressing concerns just then than
interstate feuding in Palestine. He spent the spring and summer in a series of vigorous local campaigns: how far these were provoked by harassment from the king's
garrison commanders, as our Jewish sources allege, is problematical.[178] Jewish minorities were successfully evacuated from Gilead and Galilee. Hebron was besieged
and destroyed. Judas invaded the land of the Philistines, justified his aggression by
much ostentatious destruction of altars and idols, and came back laden down with
valuable loot. The toll in lives, plunder, and ruined property was heavy. Judas's policy hardly increased the good will of neighboring states such as Idumaea toward Je-

rusalem, and his now-open defiance of Seleucid overlordship caused serious alarm in Antioch.[179] This situation was further exacerbated by the passionate anti-Seleucid propaganda that, inevitably, now began to circulate, the most notable example being the Book of Daniel.[180] In Sehürer's words, "it was quite clearly no longer a matter of protecting the Jewish faith but of consolidating and extending Jewish power."[181] The farther Judas moved in this direction, of course, the less likely any Seleucid ruler would be to reach an accommodation with him: he was rapidly taking on the lineaments of that perennial Hellenistic bogeyman, the nationalist troublemaker, the subverter of established law, order, and social privilege.

These new and alarming moves culminated in a direct assault against the Syrian garrison of the Akra, which Judas now placed under siege (163/2).[182] Some of the garrison escaped and, accompanied by Menelaus the High Priest, took their complaints to Lysias in Antioch. Lysias and the boy-king Antiochus V moved south with a powerful Syrian army: Judas suffered his first serious defeat, his brother Eleazar was killed on the battlefield, the fortress of Beth-Zur was stormed and taken, and Jerusalem itself placed under siege. Since it was a sabbatical year the defenders had inadequate rations, and it looked as though Lysias was on the point of scoring a major victory against the nationalists.[183] Unfortunately for him, it was at this precise moment (summer 162) that he found himself threatened with replacement by Antiochus IV's general Philip (above, p. 439), and was thus forced to raise the siege of Jerusalem with more haste than dignity. To save face he had Antiochus V sign a document that confirmed his father's concessions to the Jews, endorsed (after the event) the return of the sanctuary to its original state, and expressed a pious hope that "the kingdom's subjects should be undisturbed in the pursuit of their own affairs," a singularly mild admonition to Judas Maccabaeus concerning his new policy of military aggression.[184] The absence of political endorsement is predictable. On receipt of this document the defenders withdrew from Mt. Zion, and Lysias—in contravention of his oath—pulled down the fortifications before returning to Antioch, where, as we have seen (above, pp. 440–41), he and the boy-king Antiochus, after some initial successes, soon fell victims to Seleucus IV's son Demetrius.[185]

One positive, and somewhat unexpected, action Lysias had taken during this expedition was the execution of Menelaus, whom he had identified as "the cause of all the trouble,"[186] a view with which Judas would doubtless have agreed, but which suggests that what Lysias objected to in this oversubservient High Priest was not so much his strength as his fatal weakness. His removal did not imply a shift in policy, since Lysias at once replaced him with another Hellenizer, Yakim, or Jehoiakim, known by his Greek name of Alkimos.[187] This was only logical. So long as the Hellenizing party had the support of the Akra garrison, and enjoyed even a modicum of popular support,[188] no Seleucid minister in his right mind would abandon it in favor of a separatist state headed by a fighting zealot like Judas Maccabaeus. This should be remembered when we are tempted to criticize Antiochus IV and his successors for clinging to a policy that we, with the advantage conferred by hindsight, can see as doomed to failure from the start. Lysias had in fact chosen Alkimos with some care. There was nothing amiss with his priestly pedigree:[189] he could, indeed, claim descent from Aaron, and his legitimacy was at first recognized even by the Hasidic pietists.[190] Opposition, predictably, was limited to Judas and his adherents, who claimed that only they could guarantee true religious freedom.[191]

What followed was a naked power struggle of the kind in which Hellenistic history abounds: there is nothing specifically Jewish about it. The siege of the Akra might have failed, but Judas kept up a relentless pressure against his rivals. Alkimos and others of his party went up to Antioch, where they regaled the newly crowned Demetrius with lurid tales of Judas's pogroms against them.[192] Demetrius, in this if nothing else like Antiochus, had no taste for troublemakers. He not only confirmed Alkimos as High Priest, but sent an army under his lieutenant Bacchides to restore order, protect the Akra, and see Alkimos safely established in his priestly-*cum*-political office.[193] The result was more trouble. Despite their oily assurances that they came in peace (which were, at first, taken at face value, in view of Alkimos's priestly antecedents), Alkimos and his backers lost no time in arresting, and executing, sixty of the Hasidim who had assembled to "seek justice," that is, to put forward proposals for the new regime.[194] At first sight this seems incomprehensible: why alienate one's supporters? But by no means all the Hasidim did in fact back Alkimos—indeed, as we have seen (p. 517), they started out pro-Maccabaean—and later Alkimos himself identified them to Demetrius as active revolutionaries under Judas's leadership.[195] Josephus claims that these executions were a deliberate deterrent, to discourage desertions to Judas.[196] If so, they were predictably counterproductive. What is absolutely clear is that Bacchides and Alkimos were committed *ab initio* to the eradication by force of Judas and his supporters, and killed Maccabaeans without compunction wherever they found them.[197] Religious rights were one thing—the concessions made had come to stay—but an independent, and hostile, Jewish regime was quite another.

Judas, who had wisely refused to meet either Bacchides or Alkimos on their arrival, also contrived, despite Alkimos's Syrian army, to debar the new High Priest from setting foot in the Temple, a notable propaganda victory.[198] Open warfare now ensued between the rivals, with further appeals by Alkimos to Antioch for support (Bacchides had already returned there). A great victory by Judas in 161 was followed up by his petition to the Roman Senate for a treaty of alliance, this by now being the acceptable mark of international recognition: the treaty appears to have been secured (above, p. 441), though, as usual with Rome on such occasions, it was "a ceremonial convention, not a plan for military action."[199] A routine *pro forma* warning to Demetrius from the Romans to refrain from hostilities against Rome's allies, the Jews[200]—if in fact it was ever delivered—was anticipated by Demetrius himself, who followed up his defeat in Judaea with a vigorous campaign under Bacchides that destroyed Judas's army and left its famous leader dead on the battlefield (161/0).[201] For a while, at least, Hasmonean hopes lay shattered by the unpredictable exercise of Seleucid *force majeure*. The Jewish nationalists were in disarray, the "sons of the Akra" triumphant.

Bacchides, taking advantage of his victory, spent a year fortifying and garrisoning strategic towns, including Jericho and Emmaus, throughout Judaea. He also took a number of Jewish hostages, who were held in custody on the Akra.[202] Alkimos, now Judas was dead, had no trouble in entering the Temple sanctuary, where he ordered certain structural alterations, including the demolition of the wall of the inner court. Less than a year later he too died (159), apparently of a stroke, and zealots claimed that God had struck him down for laying blasphemous hands on the holy stones.[203] Demetrius, by now too well aware of the irreconcilable conflicts inherent in the High Priest's office, solved the problem by making no appointment at all.[204] The office remained vacant until 152, when it was renewed as one item in the competitive bribery between Demetrius and Alexander Balas (above, p. 445). The lucky recipient was Judas's brother Jonathan, whose roving guerilla bands had, since 160, defied all efforts by the Seleucid government to dislodge them, and virtually established an alternative, country-based, government to the increasingly unpopular Hellenizing junta in Jerusalem. For the protagonists in this new Syrian dynastic power struggle, the support of the Maccabees—despite their nationalist aspirations—was well worth having. Demetrius lavished military privileges on Jonathan; but Alexander Balas countered, as we have seen (above, p. 445), with the high priesthood.[205] By now it should by clear enough why it was Balas's offer that Jonathan accepted.[206]

The Hasmonean dream was moving toward its final fulfillment. Demetrius, in desperation, offered Jonathan every inducement he could think of, including the surrender of the Akra and the rebuilding of Jerusalem's city walls at Seleucid expense.[207] Jonathan shrewdly refused, figuring that if Demetrius lost to Balas his promises were useless, and if he won he would forget he had ever made them. When Balas in 150 defeated and slew Demetrius (above, p. 445), Jonathan was officially confirmed by the new king as civil and military governor of Judaea.[208] When Demetrius's son, Demetrius II, in turn replaced Balas as king (145; cf. p. 446), Jonathan, with cool effrontery, not only laid siege to the Akra, but then asked Demetrius for three provinces of Samaria and general tax exemption as the price for lifting the blockade. Demetrius II, a weaker man than some of his ancestors, and with problems of his own to solve, paid up.[209] Jonathan subsequently switched sides to support Diodotus Tryphon and Balas's son, Antiochus (below, p. 534), a move that in the end cost him his life as the result of Tryphon's treachery.[210] At an assembly in Jerusalem Jonathan's brother Simon—the last surviving son of Mattathias—was elected to succeed him as national leader.[211]

Tryphon's betrayal made a *rapprochement* with Demetrius II inevitable, and Simon was determined to exploit this alliance for all it was worth. The moment was propitious. Demetrius had to face not only Tryphon, but also a Parthian invasion of Babylonia (p. 533). Simon, with shrewd timing, petitioned him for exemption, in perpetuity, from all future tribute: in other words, for Judaea's independence. The petition was granted, and an alliance made (spring 142).[212] Nothing was said about the Akra; here Simon simply went ahead, enforced a blockade, and starved the Syrian garrison into surrender (June 141),[213] calculating, correctly, that Demetrius would be in no position to do anything about a *fait accompli*. He also conquered Gazara and secured the port of Joppa.[214] Then, in September 140, by unanimous vote of the Jewish priests, elders, and leaders in assembly, Simon was confirmed not only as military commander and ethnarch, but also as hereditary High Priest of Israel.[215]

So the Hasmonean family at last came into its inheritance, and fulfilled its long-standing ambition by succeeding to the defunct priestly house of Onias. The eulogistic paean to Simon in 1 Maccabees suggests the grounds for his popularity: he extended and safeguarded the frontiers, so that farming and herding could continue in peace ("Old men sat in the streets, all of them talking about the good times"); he fortified the cities, guaranteed the food supply, enforced the Torah, brought justice to the humble—"Everyone sat under his own vine and fig tree, and there was no one to terrify them. No one was left in the country to make war against them, and the kings were crushed in those days."[216] Propaganda perhaps; but one senses the very real relief that Simon undoubtedly brought to his war-torn people. It is worth recalling that in the two and a half centuries between Alexander's death and Pompey's capture of Jerusalem, more than two hundred campaigns were fought in or across Palestine.[217] For nearly a century—apart from one brief Seleucid resurgence (below, pp. 535–36)—Mattathias's line enjoyed absolute rule. It was not until 63 (below, p. 658), with the final Seleucid collapse, that the Romans, despite their *senatus consultum* of alliance with the new princely temple-state,[218] wrote finis to this dynasty, as they had done, and would do, to so many others.

CHAPTER 30

PTOLEMAIC AND SELEUCID DECADENCE AND THE RISE OF PARTHIA, 145–116

The last half of the second century B.C., following on Rome's destruction of Corinth (146), saw the virtual eclipse of independent history throughout mainland Greece, at least in any meaningful sense. The revolt under Mithridates in 88 can be seen as one last, hopeless act of rage against the dying light (below, pp. 561 ff.). Documents now begin to date in terms of an "Achaean era," thus implicitly conceding the existence of a watershed in Greek affairs, "after which the fortunes of Hellas could never be the same."[1] Macedonia was now a Roman province. The assemblies (*synedria*) of the Achaean League and other groups that had fought Rome were dissolved; Mummius introduced a limited franchise based on a property qualification. However, after a few years the old basis of government was restored (140), on the highly pragmatic grounds that the Romans wanted efficient administration, but still preferred not to supply it themselves.[2] The date suggests that this reversal of policy may have been due to Scipio Aemilianus and his traveling commission (cf. p. 539), which had as its object the regularization of government and administration throughout the *oikoumenē*.[3]

Those Greek cities that had been pro-Roman or neutral during the Achaean War were allowed to retain their titular autonomy from the start: they included Sparta, the members of the Aetolian League, and, above all, Athens,[4] which had been aligned with Rome ever since the Second Macedonian War—less out of positive conviction than through her traditional and long-standing antipathy to Macedonia.[5] Thus in 170 (above, p. 431), when most of the Greek states threw their support behind Perseus, sinking local differences in the face of this new common foe that was Rome, Athens had ended up in the western barbarians' camp, and got small thanks for her loyalty: the Roman commanders turned down (with what implied contempt we do not know) her offer of troops, and instead demanded—requisitioned—no less than a hundred thousand *medimnoi* of grain,[6] a severe imposition, met notwithstanding. The appearance in Rome of the three leading philosophers of Athens to defend

525

her actions against Oropus exposed the Romans to Greek thinking and oratory at their current best, and made a great impression (156/5; see p. 449): it is from now on that the reputation of Athens as a center of culture and the arts seems to have firmly established itself with them, and the notion of a year or two's higher education there to have become *de rigueur* among the Roman upper classes.

If it is true that from 200 on the Roman nobility "had eaten of the apple of knowledge and knew themselves to be culturally naked,"[7] it is equally true that many of the Greeks—though not those primarily responsible for this state of mind—had themselves grown increasingly addicted to commerce. Trade was flourishing, and the world of big business—not least through Athenian control of the free port of Delos—steadily encroached on old constitutional freedoms.[8] The Areopagus, that venerable and long-largely-decorative body of ex-archons, nonfunctional in any real sense since Ephialtes had clipped its powers in the mid-fifth century, now began to regain limited authority and prestige. Romans warmed to it; it was the nearest thing Athens had to the Roman Senate.[9] That the people's courts lost their judicial powers should not surprise us. Though Ferguson's theory of an "oligarchical revolution" around 103/2 cannot be sustained (cf. below, p. 562), there was now a definite conservative, commercial-slanted bias to Athenian government,[10] and this reflected, among other things, the determination of the business community to keep in well with Rome. Rhodes was there as a grim reminder of what was liable to happen to a flourishing maritime republic that ignored this simple precaution (above, pp. 378 ff.).

Visiting Romans—especially if they happened to be senators, or were otherwise well connected and influential—got preferential treatment: a special platform (*bēma*) from which to harangue the Athenian *dēmos*,[11] an escort of ephebes, their own residential club:[12] since 152 they had been classified *en bloc* as benefactors (*euergetai*), and were thus entitled to divine honors, while Rome, duly deified as an eponymous goddess, enjoyed her own special festival, the Romaea. The immanent cultural prestige of Athens—and, one suspects, the fact that she was now so clearly *hors de concours* in political terms—encouraged various Hellenistic rulers and home-grown *nouveaux riches* to win borrowed artistic luster by adding to the city's already cluttered monumental record, turning it still further into a commemorative museum. Eumenes II and Attalus II of Pergamon built huge stoas on the south and east sides of the Agora (it is Attalus's that has been rebuilt *in situ* by the American School).[13] Antiochus IV Epiphanes in 174 had work resumed on the huge temple of Olympian Zeus, begun by Peisistratus or his sons (530–515), and completed only by the emperor Hadrian (A.D. 131/2): the assertive gigantism of its ruins still reminds us that, from start to finish, only authoritarian rulers had any part in it.[14]

With the abolition of the old individual liturgies, the state had become responsible for public works; but millionaires eager for municipal office were still not slow to adorn the city with highly visible, and costly, embellishments. These offices in fact were largely honorific or ritual (the number of festivals multiplied, rather like Ptolemaic titles, as real Athenian power and influence diminished). They still, nevertheless, attracted fierce competition. Both the theater and athletics showed an ever-

Fig. 158. The temple of Olympian Zeus, Athens. Begun by the Peisistratids
ca. 530–515 B.C., and worked on by Antiochus IV Epiphanes ca. 174 B.C.,
it was completed ca. A.D. 125–32, seven centuries after its inception,
by the emperor Hadrian.

increasing trend toward professionalism: one more symptom of that move away
from all-round amateur involvement that had been the hallmark of the *polis* in its
classical heyday; one more similarity with our own age, a world of spectator sports,
or organized shows, of passive, nonparticipating audiences. Gigantism and ostentation were everywhere. The so-called Pythaïs, the sacred procession sent by the Athenians from Delos to Delphi to sacrifice to Pythian Apollo, and bring back fire from
the sacred hearth (abandoned during the Macedonian interregnum, renewed in
138/7, and staged thereafter at irregular intervals), was aggressively showy, if not
quite in the Ptolemaic class: led by the ephebes, one hundred strong, with every civic

bigwig, and the knights, and the light cavalry, and "a great chorus of flute-players, singers, poets, actors, and all the various gentry who belonged to the guild of Dionysiac artists."[15]

The Athenian *ephēbeia* went through its elaborate two-years' training still, but now no longer for the defense of the realm. The armed forces in general were minimal, and only kept up for ceremonial purposes. The *pax Romana* imposed a blanket peace on the Greek states; like most public activities in Athens, ephebic exhibitions of skill had become a nonfunctional exercise, a genuflection to ancient custom, a show to attract the tourists.[16] The year of the philosophers' visit to Rome was also that selected by the elder Pliny as the point from which Greek art began to recover itself after a century and a half's eclipse[17] (above, p. 336). What he in fact meant was that the conservative, academic, classicizing artists of Athens—who had gone on working in the realistic but restrained tradition of Praxiteles or Lysippus, avoiding the adventurous, baroque emotionalism that marked the Rhodian and Pergamene schools—now suddenly found themselves with a whole new, and virtually insatiable, clientele: the Romans (below, pp. 566 ff.). The plunder of Greek works of art, from Syracuse to Pella, by conquering Roman generals, had given well-heeled Romans a taste for more. Statues of contemporary notables, copies of famous Old Masters, paintings, bronzes, cameos, mosaics: the commissions never stopped, and Athenian ateliers expanded to meet the demand. The mood was eclectic, a sterile (and often mechanical) re-creation of the past.

The attitude of the Romans to Greek art is summed up to perfection by an anecdote told of Lucius Mummius. After the sack of Corinth, with priceless art treasures being piled up on the quayside for removal to Rome (Polybius says he saw soldiers playing draughts on stacks of classical paintings),[18] Mummius—who, as Strabo says with demure wit, was a generous patron rather than an art lover—apparently insisted on retaining one regular clause in his contract with the shipping agency: if any of these *objets-d'art* were lost or destroyed in transit, they were to be replaced by others of equal value.[19] This was an attitude that the businessmen of Piraeus, who were quite ready to honor Mummius when he turned up at Olympia or Delphi, and would not be sorry to get some of the trade that Corinth lost,[20] could understand very well; and it was they, now, who exercised the real power in Athens. Many of them, inevitably, also extended their operations to the great trading center, and slave mart, of Delos (cf. p. 384).[21]

One direct and far-reaching consequence of the anarchic, widespread warfare of the Mediterranean from the mid-third century onwards was, as we have seen (above, pp. 382–83), a glut of slaves: mostly prisoners of war, the majority of them from the East, but including Epirotes, Carthaginians, and many other formerly free men, whose built-in resistance to the servile condition would be in direct proportion to their previous independence, not to mention their degree of civilization and technical or other skills. With thousands of such newly enslaved prisoners thrown on the market, and bearing in mind the depressed economic conditions that Polybius describes,[22] it was inevitable that ambitious royal claimants such as Andriscus in Macedonia (p. 447) or Aristonicus in Pergamon should consider tapping this new source of resentful manpower.

Though in most of the revolts the immediate cause was gross ill treatment of individual slaves (especially in the mines, or on the great cattle ranches [*latifundia*] of Italy and Sicily),[23] and though the Pergamene rising, at least, seems to have had some kind of *ad hoc* programmatic backing, it remains clear that both Andriscus and Aristonicus simply exploited servile unrest (and a vastly increased pool of slaves) for their own ambitious ends,[24] while in the case of slave-led rebellions (Eunus-Antiochus and, later, Spartacus) the aim, as we have seen (p. 391), was pragmatic: to escape from servitude, if possible to create an alternative state, but not in any sense to abolish slavery as such or to attack it in principle. From this viewpoint the pseudo-Seleucid court of Eunus-Antiochus is highly suggestive.[25] Clearly by the mid-second century the Mediterranean world was swarming with unlucky war captives who had nothing against slavery provided it was not they themselves who were forced to wear the shackles. It is also of interest that though the risings were initially successful, and extremely hard to put down, once they had been crushed there was no recurrence. Apart from a second Sicilian insurrection (104), and the famous revolt under Spartacus (73–71), all these slave outbreaks took place in the decade between 140 and 130, and were in all likelihood interconnected.

Further, the whole free population (with few and doubtful exceptions) was against such movements: Andriscus or Andronicus may have used servile support in an emergency—just as Nabis, also in an emergency, freed the helots (above, p. 392)—but it was a dangerous precedent, with unpredictable consequences. It is, at the very least, highly improbable that Aristonicus, had he been successful, would actually have set up a classless Sun City (*Hēliopolis*) along Stoic lines,[26] rather than go the route of every other ambitious Hellenistic ruler actually in power—as even the slave-king Eunus-Antiochus clearly intended to do. It is worth noting that we hear nothing about Heliopolis until Aristonicus had suffered a severe naval defeat at the hands of the Ephesians and was forced back into the hinterland, where he rallied the landless and the slaves, as well as a cadre of anti-Roman Macedonians,[27] as a last desperate measure.[28] There is no reason to suppose that he began his revolt as anything but a blood claimant to the Pergamene throne, the bastard son of Eumenes II by an Ephesian concubine, who styled himself Eumenes III, issued his own coinage,[29] and was determined to frustrate his half-brother's legacy of the kingdom to Rome.[30]

In fact, Aristonicus's inflammatory propaganda, whatever its true purpose—his invocation of Helios may even have been royal self-promotion borrowed from Antiochus Epiphanes (above, p. 437)—played straight into Rome's hands.[31] Attalus III's much-debated bequest of Pergamon in 133[32]—by making Rome his legatee he seems to have been trying to forestall Aristonicus's royal ambitions[33]—came as something of an embarrassment, initially, to the Senate (how was it to be administered, or who was to get the benefit of it?),[34] and, by tempting the greed of the cash-hungry Gracchan reformers, was in part responsible for the conflict in which Tiberius Gracchus lost his life.[35] But Aristonicus's refusal to accept the terms of his eccentric and re-

Fig. 159. Second-century-B.C. marble head of a diademed ruler, from Pergamon, tentatively identified as Attalus III.
Ny Carlsberg Glyptotek, Copenhagen.

clusive half-brother's will,[36] his determination to win the throne and keep Pergamon out of Roman hands, his fomenting a rebellion that sounded like raw social revolution—all this made things much easier for Rome, and goes a long way to explain the zeal with which neighboring kingdoms such as Bithynia, Pontus, and Cappadocia fought to bring the Pergamene revolutionary down. It is generally asserted that their aid was co-opted by the Senate;[37] but none of our sources in fact says this,[38] and it seems far more likely that they converged on Pergamon of their own volition, in the spirit of vultures who scent a really juicy carcass. Though their unsolicited support may, to begin with, have been welcome—Rome had no adequate troops on the spot—there was always the obvious danger that these allies, not noted for altruism, would end by carving up the Attalid legacy for themselves.[39]

In the emergency, this prospect may have been regarded as the lesser of two potential evils. Aristonicus turned out to have an unexpectedly solid power base, which, after a typically sluggish Roman start, it took no less than three years to destroy:[40] years during which the countryside was continually ravaged and plundered by both sides,[41] and one Roman commander, Crassus Mucianus, was defeated and killed, his severed head being brought in triumph to Aristonicus.[42] The job was finally done by Marcus Perperna, consul for 130, fresh from his victory in Sicily over Eunus-Antiochus,[43] and thus presumably regarded as an expert in the breaking of slave rebellions.[44] Perperna died in Pergamon: this avoided an unpleasant confrontation with his successor, Manius Aquillius, equally anxious for a share of the glory.[45] Aristonicus was sent to Rome in chains, and there strangled by order of the Senate (128). Even after his removal the rebellion sputtered on until Aquillius, who had no gentlemanly qualms about poisoning local wells, finally stamped out all resistance, and then, aided by a ten-man senatorial commission, set about restoring law and order, Roman style.[46]

Once Aristonicus was out of the way (130), Pergamon could be policed as a protectorate, the original nucleus of what was to become—not earlier than 129, and perhaps not until 123—the vast and immensely profitable province of Asia.[47] Applying the Attalid legacy proved a hazardous and divisive business. Rome had never really trusted Pergamon, even though the Pergamene kings held their buffer state through Rome's good will. When Eumenes II defeated the Gauls in 166 (and, after all, keeping the Gauls of Galatia in order was, from Rome's viewpoint, one main reason for the Pergamene kingdom's existence), the Senate promptly declared them autonomous, presumably to stop Eumenes getting too big for his royal boots (cf. above, p. 429). Attalus II, writing about 159 to the priest-king Attis of Pessinus (a Gaul himself, but "a partisan of Pergamum and so of law and order"),[48] showed a clear understanding of the situation, in particular of Rome's juggling with the balance of power in Asia, remarking that he dared undertake no enterprise without Roman approval, because if he succeeded he would incur jealous enmity, while if he failed he could count on no help, but only on satisfaction at his failure.

Despite their ostentatious munificence, the Attalids were by no means popular with their fellow Greeks, either. In 172, probably through resentment of Eumenes' pro-Roman policies and his stand against Macedon (above, p. 427), the Greek cities of the Peloponnese decreed the destruction of all those "improper and illegal honors" previously granted him.[49] Thus Attalus III's decision to end the dynasty and turn its assets over to Rome (whether in self-defense against Aristonicus's ambitions or not) had a certain grim logic about it: it merely anticipated what was bound to happen sooner or later anyway, bequest or no.[50]

So Rome, reluctant as always, laid the foundations for her first province on Asiatic soil, with careful instructions to her generals and administrators to uphold all royal decrees and regulations of the Pergamene kings down to the death of Attalus III (thus excluding those of the *soi-disant* Eumenes III): the emphasis was on continuity rather than change, still—to borrow Badian's telling distinction—hegemonial rather than truly annexationist.[51] It may well be premature to speak, immediately, of provincialization, though the Attalid treasury and royal estates, being cash on the barrel, came as a welcome instant bonanza, and were, in all likelihood, responsible for the postponement of organized taxation until Gaius Gracchus (as Marcus Antonius later claimed)[52] in 123 used the *Lex Sempronia* to authorize state contracts for farming the Asiatic revenues, and thereby opened up one of the biggest gold mines in all Roman history.[53] Did the first post-Aristonican administrators—like the settlers of Chalcedon, who for years remained blind to the immense advantages of Byzantium across the straits—see none of this? It seems unlikely; and we may note that one of Manius Aquillius's first tasks after 129 was to repair, improve, and extend the road

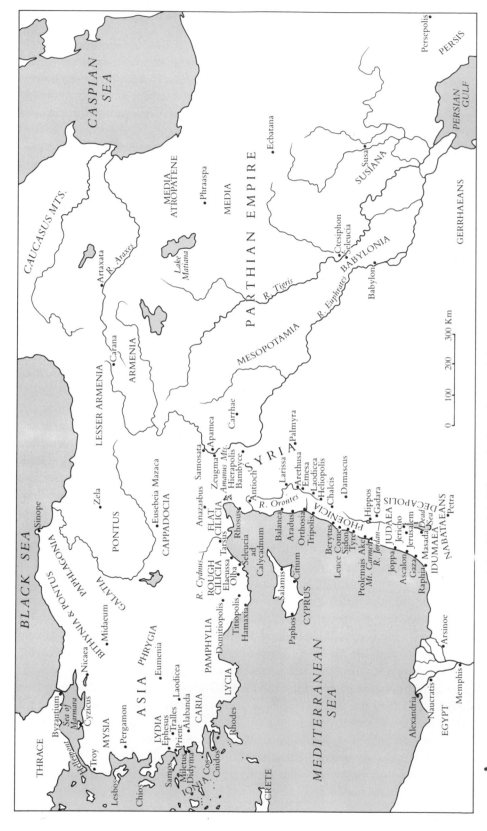

Map 26. Asia Minor, Syria, Judaea, and the East, c. 145 B.C.
From Grant, *Cleopatra*, pp. 136–37.

system: this is exactly comparable to the development of the Via Egnatia after the dismemberment of Macedonia (above, p. 447), and has far-reaching military, commercial, and administrative implications. Nothing, indeed, could have been more characteristic of a Roman provincial administrator.[54]

Aquillius stayed in Asia Minor for three years (eloquent testimony to the magnitude of his task), and was rewarded with a triumph (11 Nov. 126).[55] For whatever motive, a buffer state had been eliminated at the precise moment when the strife-torn and shrunken Seleucid realm was failing before vigorous pressure from Parthia.[56] How conscious a choice this was, and whether the Senate in Rome was aware of the inevitable need for Rome to annex more and more territory in Asia if she meant to stabilize the Eastern balance of power, must remain a matter for speculation. But within a century the whole of the Hellenistic East had passed under Rome's provincial administration:[57] the client-patron relationship, never formal in the Roman sense, had been abandoned for good.

In Parthia, that ill-defined and mountainous tribal region south and east of the Caspian, which had broken away from the Seleucids in the mid-third century (p. 293), Mithridates I Arsaces V, known as "the Great," had ascended the throne about 171;[58] about 148, after a protracted and sporadic war,[59] he had annexed Media, and by July 141 was in possession of Babylonia (including its capital, Seleucia-on-Tigris), and poised for further westward expansion.[60] Though Demetrius II Nicator had in 145 defeated Alexander Balas, with Ptolemy VI Philometor also dying of his wounds after the battle (above, p. 447), he was not destined, to put it mildly, for a quiet reign.[61] He bought off the Jewish leader Jonathan with yet more privileges and promises, so that when the Antioch mob rose against him, it was a Jewish army that put down the riot: not gently, since the Jews had old scores to settle.[62] The young son of Alexander Balas and Cleopatra Thea was set up as rival claimant to the throne by Diodotus, the military commander in Apamea, and proclaimed king as Antiochus

Fig. 160. Antiochus VI Epiphanes Dionysus (murdered by the usurper Diodotus Tryphon in 142/1 B.C.), wearing the radiate crown. Silver tetradrachm minted at Antioch, 144/3 B.C.
British Museum, London.

VI Epiphanes Dionysus, with Diodotus as his "tutor" (*epitropos*). Once again Antioch took to the streets for an enjoyable bout of king making, and Demetrius was forced to flee from the capital (summer 144). Since he reneged, perhaps involuntarily, on his promises to Jonathan, the Jewish leader changed sides and joined Diodotus, who, in the name of the boy-king Antiochus VI, confirmed him in all his previous honors, and made his brother Simon governor of all territory "from the Ladder of Tyre to the Egyptian frontier." [63]

Jonathan now set about consolidating his power (cf. above, p. 446). By a series of well-fought campaigns, from Gaza to Damascus, from Ascalon to the Sea of Galilee, he began to encroach on the sensitive frontier area of Coele-Syria. He built fortresses throughout Judaea, strengthened the defenses of Jerusalem, made diplomatic approaches to Rome, Sparta, and other foreign powers, and in general acted as an independent, not to say fiercely ambitious, ruler. [64] These moves, not unnaturally, alarmed both Demetrius and Diodotus, neither of whom had any room for local supporters who developed unseasonable dynastic urges of their own. While Demetrius moved troops against Jonathan, Diodotus, more brutal and pragmatic, lured him to Ptolemaïs-Ake, slaughtered his bodyguard, marched him around the country under close arrest, and finally, after botching a scheme to make the Jews pay ransom for his release, had him executed (143). [65] He then deposed and murdered the young Antiochus VI (142), putting it about that the boy had in fact died under the surgeon's knife, and proclaimed himself king, with the title of Tryphon ("the Magnificent"). [66] The rival dynasts split what was left of the Seleucid empire between them, Tryphon holding coastal Syria, while Demetrius retained Cilicia and the eastern satrapies toward Babylon. Demetrius, hard-pressed, now made the final deal with Jonathan's brother Simon that gave the Jews full independence (above, p. 523). The year 143/42 was subsequently established as the first year of the Hasmonean era, while Simon himself, as we have seen (p. 524), took office in 140 as the first priest-king.

Fig. 161. The usurper Diodotus
Tryphon. Silver tetradrachm minted at
Antioch ca. 140 B.C.
British Museum, London.

Demetrius was now free to deal with Tryphon; but before he could attend to his rival, the news from Babylonia made it clear that Mithridates of Parthia constituted a far greater threat, and would have to be neutralized first. So Demetrius, *faute de mieux*, left Tryphon to his own devices for the time being and marched east. He crossed the Euphrates and scored some initial successes;[67] but when he penetrated Iran he was defeated and captured by Mithridates (summer 139?), who then paraded him through the provinces he had been bent on recovering, a broad hint to Greeks and Macedonians that Parthian rule was not so easily shaken off.[68] Demetrius was kept in honorable captivity, and even married off to one of Mithridates' daughters, Rhodogune: as Tarn says, "it was convenient for Mithridates to have the legitimate king of Syria in his hands, as a piece to play, should occasion arise."[69] Mithridates himself died in 138/7, but the Parthian empire was now solidly established, a force to be reckoned with and still looking for further westward expansion.

If Tryphon was expecting, as a result of this *démarche*, to be left as sole ruler in Syria,[70] he had reckoned without the imprisoned Demetrius's younger brother, Antiochus, known from his childhood residence, Side, as Sidetes, resident in Rhodes, and now proclaimed king as Antiochus VII Euergetes.[71] When the news of Demetrius's capture reached him, he at once set out for Syria. In the spring of 138 he was about twenty-one. Demetrius's wife, Cleopatra Thea, holding out in Seleucia-in-Pieria,[72] appealed to this opportune brother-in-law for help. Antiochus not only rescued her, but, with something more than fraternal solicitude, became her third husband. He then hunted down Tryphon, captured him, and forced him to commit suicide.[73] This was late in 138. He also took a tougher line with the Jews, showing himself scrupulous over respecting their religion, but pressing for tribute, making territorial demands, and in general doing all he could to cut back their newly won political independence. In 131/0, after a long, tough siege, while Hyrcanus I was High Priest (appointed 134, after the assassination of his father, Simon),[74] Jerusalem

Fig. 162. Antiochus VII Euergetes (Sidetes). Silver tetradrachm minted at Antioch ca. 135–130 B.C. Private collection. Photo Hirmer.

fell to Antiochus—he had carefully sent animals into the beleaguered city so that the Jews could celebrate the Feast of Tabernacles (Sukkoth)—and though Hyrcanus retained the priesthood, the Jews, for a brief period, reverted to Seleucid rule.[75]

Having settled affairs at home, Antiochus, like his brother before him, set out to reconquer the East (130/29), at the head of a vast if heterogeneous army, including various Parthian allies and a Jewish brigade led by Hyrcanus in person.[76] At first he succeeded beyond all reasonable hope. Babylonia and Media fell to him; a little prematurely, he assumed the title of "the Great" that his great-grandfather Antiochus III had used.[77] This suggests that he, too, dreamed of winning back the whole of Seleucus Nicator's original empire. The new Parthian ruler, Mithridates' son Phraates II, was ready at this point to negotiate; but Antiochus, fatally, overplayed his hand. He demanded the release of Demetrius, who had already made several unsuccessful attempts to escape, and whom Antiochus had not the slightest intention of leaving behind to be used as a wild deuce against him;[78] the evacuation of all newly won Parthian territory, which would leave Phraates with only Hyrcania and his homeland of Parthyene; and the payment of tribute.[79] The Parthian king, not surprisingly, refused.

Cunningly, perceiving that Antiochus's solicitude for his brother concealed the determination to remove him as a rival,[80] Phraates now set Demetrius free and sent him back to Syria, in the hope of stirring up yet another dynastic quarrel;[81] and in anticipation of renewed conflict with Antiochus he also hired large numbers of wild "Scythian" (i.e., Saca or Tokharian) mercenaries from the steppes. It was a harsh winter, and the requisitions of Antiochus's army had not made him popular with the local inhabitants.[82] In the spring of 129 the Seleucid army was defeated, and Antiochus himself killed (the wily Hyrcanus survived to escape and fight another day in Judaea):[83] all temporary conquests made during the campaign now reverted to Parthia.[84] Phraates sent Antiochus's body back to Syria in a silver coffin, and established his young son Seleucus as a prince in his own court.[85] "Thus the last serious attempt by a Seleucid monarch to regain the lost eastern provinces ended in complete failure."[86] Hard-drinking,[87] ambitious, large of vision, Antiochus Sidetes was the last Seleucid to display the driving energy and courageous ambition that had distinguished his more famous ancestors.

For Phraates, however, this proved a Pyrrhic victory. Any westward advance he might have contemplated was aborted by his Tokharian mercenaries, who turned up too late for the battle, insisted on getting paid regardless, and, when Phraates refused, set about looting the countryside: Phraates, having defeated Antiochus, now met his own death trying to put down these rampaging barbarians he had conjured up. The remnants of Antiochus's army, forcibly conscripted by Phraates, changed sides during the battle and helped the Tokharians complete their work of destruction.[88]

Demetrius, meanwhile—unwanted, like the Devil at prayers—reappeared in Syria, to the irritation of everyone, not least of Cleopatra Thea, who had not survived her first and third husbands in order to welcome back the second. Besides, Demetrius had acquired, while in captivity, not only a beard and Parthian habits,

Fig. 163. Demetrius II Nicator of Syria, during his second reign (129–125 B.C.). Silver tetradrachm minted at Antioch ca. 129–125 B.C. Note the beard, grown during his Parthian captivity. Private collection. Photo Hirmer.

but, rather worse, a Parthian wife.[89] Cleopatra Thea hustled off her youngest son by Antiochus Sidetes to a safe retreat in Cyzicus, and prepared for war. In Judaea, Hyrcanus was busy restoring the Jewish freedoms that Antiochus had briefly snatched away,[90] and Demetrius, who lacked his brother's drive, did nothing to stop him, then or later. The cities of Syria, Antioch in particular, had no great enthusiasm for Demetrius. On the other hand, his Ptolemaic mother-in-law, Cleopatra II, saw him as the one possible solution to her many troubles, of which by no means the smallest was her gross brother, and wrote begging for his help. In return, he was offered nothing less than the throne of Egypt. What, we may well ask, had been going on in Alexandria since Ptolemy VI Philometor's death in 145?[91]

When Philometor died, his brother Physcon ("Potbelly," "Bladder"), still waiting in Cyrene like some vast malevolent spider (above, p. 447), saw his chance, and took it. Cleopatra II, Philometor's widow, had her son—now about sixteen years old, and already, earlier that year, appointed co-ruler by his father[92]—proclaimed king as Ptolemy VII Neos Philopator, under her regency. Physcon's agents in Alexandria whipped up the mob, which rioted, yelling for Physcon.[93] Cleopatra found her support largely restricted to the Museum intellectuals and the Alexandrian Jews, an inadequate power base, even if it did include her Jewish-officered palace guard.[94] The potbellied one duly arrived,[95] preceded by a general amnesty as earnest of his good intentions,[96] having traveled by way of Cyprus to secure himself a safe retreat at need. He could not get rid of Cleopatra directly, so he did the next-best thing and married her. The proposal was that he, she, and the young Ptolemy VII should rule conjointly—an uneasy compromise, as became clear when the hapless boy-king was assassinated during the wedding feast. Physcon does not come across, from our scanty evidence, as a man who believed in wasting either time or subtlety.[97] With the elimination of his nephew there remained no legitimate claimant to the throne but himself. For a quarter of a century Ptolemy VII suffered *damnatio memoriae*, was an unperson: not until 118 does his name reappear in the ruler-cult formulas.[98]

Physcon took the official title of Ptolemy VIII Euergetes II, the latter appellation deliberately recalling Ptolemy III, with reference to that monarch's territorial gains in Syria and Asia Minor during the Third Syrian War (above, p. 150). The irreverent Alexandrians soon converted *Euergetēs*, "Benefactor," into its antonym *Kakergetēs*, "Malefactor."[99] A year later the new king had himself enthroned as pharaoh at Memphis (144).[100] He also celebrated his return by mass purges and expulsions of those Alexandrians, most notably the Jews[101] and the intellectuals,[102] who had sided against him. He not only drove out the mercenary officers loyal to Philometor and Cleopatra, an obvious precaution,[103] but also executed, apparently in mere personal pique,[104] the Cyrenaeans who had followed him back to Egypt. Though not without intellectual pretensions himself—he wrote a critical study of Homer[105]—he was responsible, through executions and exile, for so emptying Alexandria of serious scholars and artists that the consequent intellectual impoverishment persisted for almost a century. Among those who fled the country were Aristarchus, then chief librarian, and Apollodorus the geographer. Things came to such a pass that Physcon was forced to replace Aristarchus with a nonentity named Cydas, described as "one of the spearmen."[106] Polybius, who probably visited the city in 140/39 with Scipio Aemilianus (see below), found the Greek and Jewish population of Alexandria "virtually wiped out." Among other horror stories, we hear of Physcon's mercenaries surrounding an ephebic gymnasium and massacring everyone inside it. Menecles of Barca reported that the vast diaspora of skilled professionals—artists, musicians, philosophers, mathematicians, doctors, philologists, among others—created a cultural renaissance (*ananeōsis paideias*) in the Aegean and mainland Greece.[107]

The reign that began in so grotesque and inauspicious a fashion turned out one of the longest, and by no means the least notable, of the Ptolemaic dynasty: Physcon survived until 116. Despite his obnoxious and obsessional character, he was no fool; but his undoubted intelligence was for too much of the time wasted on the pursuit of rancorous private intrigue, so much so that it is sometimes hard to see how the government of Egypt continued to function—just as we may wonder at the self-destructive rivalries, ambitions, and jealousies of a dynasty whose real power was so visibly crumbling around them. Everything wrong with the Ptolemies is summed up in the gross person of Physcon: the unswerving pursuit of sensual gratification (through food, drink, sex, or power), unhindered by any moral restraints, guilt, or fear of retribution; the acts of wanton, indeed sadistic, cruelty against his subjects;[108] the treatment of a whole country as the monarch's vast private estate, to be milked for personal profit; the inability to see beyond the cycle of self-perpetuating rule that these assumptions engendered. There is also, less often noted, a strong and obvious component of fantasy, of megalomaniac unreality, due to the accident of Egypt's secure frontiers and virtual immunity to external invasion.

On top of everything else, Physcon infuriated Cleopatra II (on whom in 144 he had sired a son)[109] by first seducing, then marrying his pubescent niece Cleopatra III, her daughter by Philometor (143): habitual incest seems to have brought out both the worst and the best in the Lagid genes.[110] This union not only exacerbated family tensions, but in a very real sense proved the beginning of the end for the Ptolemaic dynasty.[111] Cleopatra III is often referred to from now on in inscriptions as "Cleopatra the Wife," with Cleopatra II as "Cleopatra the Sister." It was this ill-assorted

Fig. 164. Black diorite portrait head of
Ptolemy VIII Euergetes II (Physcon),
wearing the double crown of Egypt
(date and provenience uncertain).
Musées Royaux d'Art et d'Histoire,
Brussels. Photo A.C.L.

triad that in 140/39 welcomed the peripatetic Roman commission headed by Scipio
Aemilianus.[112] Scipio compelled the bloat king to accompany him from his ship to
the royal palace on foot, through the crowded streets of Alexandria, carefully setting
a pace that made Physcon sweat, pant, and waddle in his billowing, semitransparent
chiffon robes. The bystanders got the point. "The Alexandrians owe me one thing,"
Scipio told Panaetius, his Stoic mentor; "they have seen their king walk!" The members of the commission, whose main task (like that of so many modern diplomats)
seems to have been the collection of intelligence, carefully noted the country's
wealth, resources, fertility, teeming fellahin (an ideal cheap labor pool), and advantageous terrain. It occurred to them, and they so reported,[113] that "a very great
power could be built there, if this kingdom should ever find rulers worthy of it."[114]

Weak or not, Physcon somehow clung to power: his more obnoxious qualities
hindered neither his capacity for survival nor his very considerable administrative

talents. For some years he and his incestuous consorts survived together, a triad of misrule, persecution, and bickering bloody-mindedness. But in 132/1, not surprisingly, there were riots again. The mob this time was on Cleopatra II's side, having had more than enough of Physcon's outrages, and, clearly with her connivance, set fire to the royal palace. Physcon, Cleopatra III, and their children left in a hurry for Cyprus. In places Cleopatra II seems to have been recognized, briefly, as sole sovereign.[115] However, the only possible male replacement for Physcon was his twelve-year-old son by Cleopatra II, Ptolemy Memphitis, so named because he was born at the time of Physcon's enthronement there. His mother duly had him acclaimed *in absentia* by the Alexandrian mob[116]—an unwise move when the boy was elsewhere, and there was a chance of her husband laying hands on him. Physcon, faced with this dynastic threat, indeed got hold of the unsuspecting boy (who either was in Cyrene, or else had been removed by Cleopatra II at the time of the royal flight), killed him, and sent his dismembered corpse back to Cleopatra the Sister as a birthday present.[117] At this the Alexandrian populace "went totally berserk with fury."

Nevertheless, by 130 Physcon was back in Egypt, and securely based at Memphis.[118] His previous cultivation of the native priesthood and the rural population now began to pay off: for one thing, it gave him a secure field of operations in the *chōra*. The Alexandrians of the capital, in particular the Jewish community and the more intelligent Greeks, were, as we have seen, supporting Cleopatra II. So it came about that, during the bloody civil war that followed, Cleopatra II, blockaded in Alexandria, offered her Seleucid son-in-law Demetrius II Nicator the throne of Egypt in return for his assistance against her hated brother-*cum*-husband.[119] Contemporary documents refer to the state of affairs in Egypt as *amixia*, nonintercourse, a proverbial confrontation of oil and water. It seems an accurate description.[120]

Demetrius took the bait, and also swallowed the hook. His attempt to relieve Alexandria got no farther than the frontier city of Pelusium, where his advance was blocked by Physcon's troops (who already controlled all Upper Egypt).[121] In any case, events in Syria soon forced him to march back north to protect his own interests (see below). Physcon then moved in on Alexandria, and at this point Cleopatra II judged it prudent to follow Demetrius to Syria, taking the royal treasure with her (127).[122] Alexandria in fact held out for another year, but by 126/5 Physcon was back in power, carrying out further atrocities against the Greek population, and cementing his counteralliance with the still-powerful Egyptian priesthood.[123]

In Syria, meanwhile, Demetrius was faced with mutiny and rebellion, almost certainly encouraged by his reluctant wife Cleopatra Thea, Cleopatra II's daughter. The rebels had applied to Physcon asking for a claimant, any claimant, to the Seleucid throne (129/8?). Physcon, with fine cynicism, and by no means averse to making trouble for the in-law who had so disobligingly tried to make trouble for him, sent them a pretender who pretended to be a pretender's son, an Egyptian passing himself off as the offspring of Alexander Balas.[124] The Antiochenes had no illusions about this character: they gave him the Aramaic nickname of Zabinas, "The Bought One."[125] On the other hand they figured that he was preferable to Demetrius: at least he had traits of generosity and kindliness, on account of which "he was much loved by the populace."[126] His coin portraits show a smiling, almost girlish face.[127] Alexander Zabinas's forces duly trounced Demetrius in Lebanon. When Demetrius fled to Ptolemaïs-Ake his ex-wife not only refused to give him shelter, but was probably responsible for his subsequent murder, after torture, in Tyre (126/5).[128]

What part, if any, Physcon and Cleopatra II played in these events we can only speculate;[129] but the surprising fact remains that early in 124 Cleopatra the Sister was back in Alexandria, reconciled—though for reasons of *Machtpolitik* rather than love, as one might expect[130]—not only with Physcon, but also with her daughter and rival consort, Cleopatra the Wife. Presumably she brought the treasure, in whole or part,

Fig. 165. The pretender Alexander Zabinas. Silver tetradrachm, mint unknown (Antioch?), ca. 128–123 B.C. British Museum, London.

Fig. 166. Cleopatra Thea. Silver tetradrachm minted at Ptolemaïs-Ake, 126/5 B.C. The reverse shows a double cornucopia, with the inscription *BASILISSĒS KLEOPATRAS THEAS EUETĒRIAS,* "of Queen Cleopatra Thea [the Goddess], Bringer of Plenty." British Museum, London.

back with her as a sweetener. With Demetrius dead, Physcon saw no point in continuing to support Zabinas rather than his own niece Cleopatra Thea, who did at least have a legitimate claim to represent the house of Seleucus; besides, the puppet Zabinas was showing an alarming degree of independence, popularity, and staying power.[131] From her various sons Cleopatra Thea—that enterprising matriarch—selected as her co-regent Antiochus, known as Grypos ("Hooknose"), educated in Athens and now about sixteen (125).[132] This honor was in the nature of a domestic siege perilous: Antiochus's elder brother, briefly elevated as Seleucus V (126/5), had been tried, found too independent, and murdered—a target, if we can believe Appian, for his mother's archery practice.[133]

In 124/3 Physcon sent off his second daughter by Cleopatra III (the Wife), Cleopatra Tryphaena ("Lady Magnificence"), to marry Antiochus Grypos,[134] now portrayed on coins[135]—behind his mother—as Antiochus VIII Philometor. Alexander Zabinas, hard-pressed by an opposition army now reinforced from Egypt, and short of cash for his own troops, followed the time-honored but hazardous Seleucid practice of raising funds in an emergency by robbing temples. This very soon dispelled his popularity with the Antiochenes, who were *louche* but superstitious. In 123 he was captured by Antiochus VIII, and put to death.[136] Success went to Grypos's head. He became progressively less amenable to domination by his terrible mother, and increasingly wary—with good reason—of her intentions toward him. Cleopatra Thea waited until 121/0, and then decided it was time to remove this insubordinate son as she had removed his brother. He came in one day hot from exercise, and she offered him a cup of poisoned wine. The solicitude was uncharacteristic, and in any case Antiochus had been tipped off as to her plans. He thereupon, with matricidal relish, forced her to drink off the cup herself.[137]

This sensible if unfilial act left Antiochus Grypos as sole ruler over the miserable Syrian remnants of the once-great Seleucid empire, and for a few years—at least un-

Fig. 167. Antiochus VIII Grypos ("Hooknose"). Silver tetradrachm minted at Antioch ca. 108–97 B.C. Private collection. Photo Hirmer.

til 114—he was left to enjoy his pleasures in peace. Like so many late Seleucids and Ptolemies, he was a self-indulgent fribble and dilettante. There were great feasts at Daphne, though the exchequer was perilously low. There were didactic verses to be written, in imitation of the third- or second-century poet Nicander, on the topic of poisonous snakes: a popular Hellenistic theme, and in Grypos's case of more than symbolic appropriateness. Grypos, in short, now enjoyed a brief Indian summer, a lull before the renewed domestic storm.[138]

The impact of these unedifying dynastic struggles on society at large is superbly evoked by Cavafy in his portrait of a penniless but ambitious Syrian Greek:[139]

> I'm reduced to near-poverty and homelessness.
> This fatal city, Antioch,
> Has swallowed up all my money,
> This fatal city with its extravagant lifestyle.
>
> Still, I'm young and in the very best of health,
> With a quite staggering mastery of Greek—
> I know Aristotle and Plato backwards,
> Poets, orators, anything, you name it;
> I've some notion of military affairs
> And close friends among the mercenary top brass.
> I also have an *entrée* to the world of government—
> Last year I spent six months in Alexandria,
> I know (now this is useful!) something of the scene there,
> The Malefactor's schemes, his low tricks, etcetera.
>
> So I figure I'm well and truly
> Marked out to serve this country,
> My beloved fatherland of Syria.
>
> Into whatever job they stick me I'll do my damnedest
> To be of use to the country. That's my intention.
> But if they obstruct me with their machinations—
> We know these fine fellows, a word's enough to the wise—
> If they obstruct me, I'm not to blame.
>
> I'll make my first approach to Zabinas,
> And if that clod doesn't appreciate me,
> I'll turn to his rival, Grypos.
> And if *that* idiot likewise fails to make me an offer,
> I'll go straight to Hyrcanus.
>
> One of the three is bound to want me, whatever.
> And my conscience is at rest

About not caring which of them I choose:
All three are equal disasters for Syria.

But I'm a ruined man, I'm not to blame—
Just a poor wretch trying to patch things up for himself.
The gods in their power should have taken the trouble
To fashion a fourth man, a good one.

I'd have been delighted to throw in my lot with *him*.

In Egypt, meanwhile, the formal reconciliation of 124 was followed in 118, after further domestic ructions,[140] by a detailed amnesty decree, proclaiming a series of benefactions (*philanthrōpa*) that made some concerted effort, by long-overdue concessions, to set the royal estate that was Egypt in order, and to strengthen its revenues.[141] The temple hierarchy, in accordance with Physcon's established policy (above, p. 540), was given substantial concessions. Arrears of taxes were written off, official abuses were condemned, various punitive penalties canceled. This occasion also saw the rehabilitation of the murdered Ptolemy VII (above, p. 537), presumably as a sop to Cleopatra the Sister, in which aim it proved, as events were to show, singularly unsuccessful. It was all too little, too late. As Austin rightly observes, "it goes without saying that the proclamations of 118 were no more effective than those which preceded them."[142] Physcon might legislate against officials arresting anyone "in pursuit of a private enmity," but who was to enforce the law? A corrupt bureaucracy is not so easily discouraged. Such superficial patching could neither cure the country's deep social ills, nor restore its ruined economy. All it did was enable Physcon to live out the rest of his self-indulgent life in relative peace. He died on 26 June 116, aged about sixty-five, "after thirteen years' unbroken possession of the desirable things for which he had intrigued and murdered,"[143] bequeathing his power to Cleopatra III, the Wife, and whichever of her sons she might prefer (a loaded clause, as we shall see). After his death the brief lull that had overtaken events in both Syria and Egypt was soon to be broken.

PART FIVE

ROME TRIUMPHANT
116–30 B.C.

CHAPTER 31

MITHRIDATES, SULLA, AND THE FREEDOM OF THE GREEKS, 116–80

The death in 116 of Ptolemy VIII Euergetes II Physcon heralded a fresh period of divisive and crippling royal intrigue, not only in Egypt, but also (by virtue of inter-marriage, if for no other reason) in what remained of Seleucid Syria. By some inexo-rable law of political degenerescence, the less power these Ptolemies or Seleucids had, and the narrower their frontiers became, the more ambitious the male heirs—and ruthless sister-queens[1]—they produced to fight, and kill, for the wretched heri-tage that remained.[2] Meanwhile city after city broke away from central bureaucratic control, while endless warfare and increasing piracy laid the countryside waste, dis-rupted legitimate trade, exacerbated still further the poverty of the peasantry and the urban poor (below, p. 555).[3] If Rome still hesitated to commit herself over the Successor kingdoms, that was due, in the last resort, neither to moral scrupulous-ness, now eroding with uncommon speed, nor to ignorance of the internal condi-tions, of which her statesmen had increasing daily evidence. A far more compelling factor was the serious crisis created by unending wars and internal dissensions at home, culminating in the final confrontation between Caesar and Pompey (below, pp. 664–65).

Meanwhile the moral gap between rapacious *publicani* and responsible procon-suls, between the new private and the old public sectors, narrowed daily. The wealth of Asia proved increasingly irresistible, to soldier, statesman, and civilian alike. Many made fabulous fortunes. Just how far this exploitative process had gone by 88 is made all too graphically clear by the massacre of Roman residents in Asia carried out during the Mithridatic rising (below, pp. 561 ff.). When the time did arrive for final, permanent intervention in the East, there was no hesitation; but until then the complex wrangling and intrigue, in Alexandria and Antioch alike, continued with unabated enthusiasm, and in an atmosphere of hothouse unreality. For the Ptolemies in particular, it was as though Egypt's physical isolation, combined with their own tradition of absolute and irresponsible power, had effectively neutralized any sense

547

of perspective they might once have maintained on world affairs as a whole. Cyprus, Cyrenaica, and the Egyptian *chōra* bounded their horizon; for the most part they saw no farther than the palace compound, the rivalries and gossip of malicious Greek administrators, their own violent, undisciplined appetites.

Cleopatra III, known to the Alexandrians as Kokke,[4] was a typically strong-minded queen mother. Seduced by her uncle Physcon while barely pubescent (above, p. 538), and then married to him while her mother was still his official wife, she had grown up match-tough, and now meant to make the most of her hard-earned royal legacy. She had borne Physcon two sons—Ptolemy IX Philometor[5]

Fig. 168. Clay sealing from Edfu (Apollonopolis Magna), now identified by H. Maehler as a portrait of Ptolemy IX Lathyros. (Cf. fig. 169.)
Royal Ontario Museum, Toronto.

Fig. 169. Clay sealings from Edfu (Apollonopolis Magna), now identified by H. Maehler as portraits of Ptolemy X Alexander I. Since these and fig. 168 certainly represented Ptolemy IX and X, Maehler correctly identified Ptolemy X by his known corpulence and his Alexander-style winged helmet, leaving fig. 168 by exclusion as the likeness of Lathyros. Note the radiate crown portrayed on the non-helmeted seal.
Royal Ontario Museum, Toronto.

Fig. 170. Antiochus IX Philopator
(Cyzicenus). Silver tetradrachm minted
at Ptolemaïs-Ake ca. 113–112 B.C.
Private collection. Photo Hirmer.

Soter II, known as Lathyros, "Chickpea" (the Greek equivalent of *Cicero*), born
142, and Ptolemy X Alexander I, who was about three years younger—as well as
three daughters, Cleopatra IV, Cleopatra Tryphaena, and Cleopatra Selene. There
was also in the running Physcon's bastard son by his mistress Eirene, Ptolemy
Apion, with some kind of a lien on Cyrenaica.[6] Physcon, in his will, had left the
succession to Cleopatra III and whichever son she preferred: a lethal parting shot,
redolent of *après moi le déluge*.[7] Cleopatra, as he well knew, hated Lathyros and doted
on her younger son, Alexander. The Alexandrians, on the other hand, were all for
Lathyros, then governor of Cyprus—a job he held, according to one's point of view,
either to prepare him for high office, or to keep him well out of the way while his
cadet ousted him.[8]

Predictably, Cleopatra III tried to run Alexander as king after Physcon's death;
but the Alexandrians would have none of him, and held out for Lathyros, who was
thereupon brought back from Cyprus, while Alexander was, tactfully, sent out to
replace him there. Equally predictably, the queen mother lost no time in launching a
campaign of attrition against her new co-ruler (115/4).[9] Her first move was to bully
him into repudiating his much-loved sister-wife, Cleopatra IV—a dangerously
strong-willed woman whose relations with her mother were far from cordial—and
replacing her with her sister Cleopatra Selene, who in the event proved even
tougher.[10] Cleopatra IV, thus discarded, took herself off, first to Cyprus, where she
raised an army but failed to marry Ptolemy Alexander,[11] and then—the dynastic
game being the only one she understood—to Syria, where she did contrive, using
her army as dowry, to marry Antiochus IX Cyzicenus, son of Antiochus Sidetes and
Cleopatra Thea (above, p. 537), an eccentric alcoholic whose main passions in life
were nocturnal hunting and the rather more recherché hobby of manipulating giant
puppets, a relief (one presumes) after live Seleucid courtiers.[12] She thus became involved, fatally, as things turned out, in the dynastic struggle between this Antiochus
and his cousin (and half-brother) Antiochus VIII Grypos, Demetrius II's son.

The Syrian conflict did not go unnoticed in Alexandria. Cleopatra III detested

Cyzicenus, and as a result favored Grypos and the Jews. Lathyros, whose sympathies lay in the opposite direction, infuriated his mother by covertly sending six thousand men to help Cyzicenus against the depredations of Hyrcanus (above, p. 537),[13] who was busy extending Jewish control into parts of Coele-Syria. To make matters worse, Grypos was married to Cleopatra IV's sister Cleopatra Tryphaena: no love lost there. When Cleopatra IV fell into Grypos's hands, in 112, Tryphaena had her executed as she clung to an altar: the wretched girl's wrists were hacked through to sever her sanctuary lifeline. (In this same year we find a Roman senator, Lucius Memmius, "a person held in high honor and esteem," visiting Egypt on a sightseeing tour: instructions for his official entertainment survive on papyrus, even down to the feeding of the sacred crocodiles, and reveal not only the V.I.P. treatment laid on for dignitaries of the new master race, but also how little these palace upheavals affected the Alexandrian bureaucracy.)[14] Shortly afterwards Antiochus IX Cyzicenus got his revenge by immolating Tryphaena as an expiatory offering to her sister's vengeful ghost (111).[15] Such domestic indulgences apart, by 108 Grypos was more or less in control of Syria, with Cyzicenus clinging to one or two coastal cities; not surprisingly, the coinage of both claimants deteriorated, and at times dried up altogether.[16]

Meanwhile in Egypt Cleopatra III, after one earlier botched attempt (110/9), in 107 finally succeeded in driving Lathyros out:[17] she accused him of trying to murder her, inflamed the Alexandrian mob, and left him no option but a quick retreat, leaving behind both his second sister-wife, Cleopatra Selene, and his two sons by her. Ptolemy X Alexander thereupon returned from Cyprus and assumed the crown. Lathyros, meanwhile, using Syria as a base, proceeded to establish himself in Cyprus, now vacated by Alexander: another royal round of Cox-and-Box was under way. An attempt by his mother to have Lathyros assassinated proved unsuccessful.[18] Thus for all practical purposes the Ptolemaic empire was now split up into three independent principalities: Cleopatra III and Alexander in Egypt, Lathyros in Cyprus, while Ptolemy Apion, Physcon's bastard, ruled over Cyrenaica. Both Cleopatra III and Lathyros spent 103/2 encouraging opposite sides in Syria, with Lathyros still backing Cyzicenus, while his mother favored Grypos;[19] the new Hasmonean priest-king, Alexander Jannaeus, played a double game with both, to his eventual undoing at Lathyros's hands.[20] That same year Cleopatra III decided that she had had enough of Alexander, too, so that he in his turn was forced to escape from Alexandria. In 101, however, he returned, on the pretense of a reconciliation, and assassinated his murderous mother. The historicity of this act has been doubted, but on no compelling grounds.[21]

This matricide of Alexander's, followed by his marriage to Lathyros's daughter, Cleopatra Berenice,[22] at least guaranteed him some years of uninterrupted power, during which he grew almost as monstrously fat as his father, Physcon.[23] His bastard half-brother, Apion, the ruler of Cyrene, did at his death in 96 what Physcon had once threatened to do: he bequeathed Cyrenaica to Rome. The Romans, however, having no wish to risk furnishing one of their number with so strong an overseas power base, were slow to pick up this rich legacy. They did not formally constitute

Fig. 171. Marble bust of a Hellenistic
queen wearing the *tainia*, or fillet
(Egypt; late second century B.C.?):
Cleopatra II and III have been suggested
as models. The latter seems a more
likely candidate.
Musée du Louvre, Paris. Photo Réunion des
Musées Nationaux.

the new province until 75/4, and only then at quaestorian level, as part of the drive against Mediterranean piracy.[24] Also in 96, Antiochus Grypos was assassinated, by one of his generals, in an abortive coup:[25] he left no less than five legitimate sons, a sure recipe for trouble.

Through this dynastic battlefield, picking the wrong side every time, moved Cleopatra Selene, who had first transferred herself (or been transferred by her imperious mother) from Lathyros to Grypos (ca. 102);[26] then, when Grypos was killed, to his still-eager would-be rival, Antiochus Cyzicenus; then, when Grypos's eldest son, Seleucus VI Epiphanes, finally defeated and killed Cyzicenus (95), to Cyzicenus's son, yet another Antiochus, known as "the Pious" (*Eusebēs*).[27] A game lady, one feels; neither age nor disappointment lessened her appetite for power one whit, though her judgment for recognizing where true power lay seems to have been, to say the least, defective. At all events, in 95 the self-proclaimed Antiochus X Eusebes Philopator took her over from his deceased father. Since her first marriage, to her brother Lathyros, had taken place in 116, she must by now have been at least in her mid-thirties, and we have by no means heard the last of her yet (below, p. 553).

Antiochus X lost no time in driving Seleucus VI out of Syria to Cilicia, where he soon died at the hands of a bloody-minded mob that roasted him in his own palace.[28] That left Seleucus's twin brothers, Philip I Epiphanes Philadelphos and Antiochus XI Epiphanes, plus yet another sibling, Demetrius III, known as "Lucky" (*Eukairos*), who established himself in Damascus, one eye on Coele-Syria. At this point, then, there were no less than four concurrent claimants for the Seleucid throne.[29]

Fig. 172. Seleucus VI Epiphanes Nicator. Silver tetradrachm, mint unknown (Antioch?) ca. 96–95 B.C. British Museum, London.

Fig. 173. Antiochus X Eusebes Philopator. Silver tetradrachm, mint unknown (Antioch?) ca. 94–93 B.C. British Museum, London.

Antiochus XI was drowned while fording the Orontes, but then the fifth and final brother, Antiochus XII Dionysus Epiphanes Philopator Kallinikos, appeared to contest the diminished Seleucid inheritance.[30] Philip fought Demetrius III (88), who had joined a Jewish movement against Alexander Jannaeus; blockaded by a force that included Arabs and Parthians, Demetrius, belying his nickname, was starved into surrender and ended his days in honorable captivity at the Parthian court.[31] His brother and successor, Antiochus XII Dionysus, held Damascus, but was later killed by the Arabs;[32] Philip based himself on Antioch. Fragmentation of command could scarcely go farther.

Though Antiochus X Eusebes had defeated Antiochus XI and Philip, he got no benefit from his victory: between 90 and 88 he was killed fighting the Parthians,[33] but not before he had sired on Cleopatra Selene at least one son, the future Antiochus XIII Dionysus Philopator Kallinikos, known as Asiaticus (below, p. 658).[34]

Shortly afterwards Ptolemy X Alexander was finally expelled from Egypt (spring 87), after selling off Alexander the Great's gold coffin to raise some quick cash.[35] Remembering what his bastard half-brother, Apion, had done with Cyrene, he then willed his kingdom to Rome. This was an ingenious move. While the testator remained alive, the legatee could not inherit; and meanwhile the will would offer a tempting security to Roman moneylenders.[36] Though it seems to have helped him to raise a loan and finance a fleet, as personal insurance it proved a flop. Alexander very soon lost his life in a naval battle off Cyprus,[37] and the patient Lathyros, now in his mid-fifties, was brought back and given the thankless task of trying to reunite the Ptolemaic empire.[38] As in the case of Cyrene, Rome showed no immediate haste to claim this new legacy; but the will was there, to be invoked at need, and was to have remarkable political repercussions a few years later (below, p. 554).

On Lathyros's return, Alexandrian wits at once tagged him with the nickname *Potheinos*, "The Much-Missed One:"[39] how sarcastic this was is hard to decide. In any case the Thebaid revolted against him almost immediately. Though his daughter Cleopatra Berenice,[40] who was also Ptolemy X Alexander's widow, came back to Egypt and was associated with him as joint ruler, her stepson—by Alexander's unidentified first wife—was in the hands of Mithridates VI of Pontus, along with two illegitimate sons of Lathyros himself, and thus a source of potential future trouble.[41] All three had been captured by Mithridates in 88, at the outset of his war with Rome (below, pp. 560 ff.). He picked them off the island of Cos, where their grandmother Cleopatra III had sent them, some years earlier, with much treasure, to be (ironically enough) out of harm's way.[42] Ptolemy Alexander's son, whom Mithridates brought up for a year or two as a young Hellenistic prince, then "escaped" to Sulla, the proconsul and future dictator, who—secure in his possession of Ptolemy Alexander's will—sent him on to Rome as a potential future card to play in the dynastic power-broking game. All this helps to explain why Lathyros, a year or so later (87/6), well aware of the will, and still unsure of his own throne, pleaded neutrality when the Roman Lucius Lucullus—emissary of a proconsul whose own status at this point was anything but clear[43]—came seeking a fleet for Sulla's campaign against Mithridates. He was also scared, and with good reason, of possible reprisals by the king of Pontus against his captive sons.[44]

If the situation in Egypt was uncertain, the Seleucid Near East presented a picture of anarchy and chaos. In 83 Armenian forces entered Syria. If Philip I had survived this long in Antioch (which is unlikely), he now vanished from the scene.[45] The long-suffering Antiochenes made up their minds that this suicidal internecine warfare between rival Seleucid claimants had lasted quite long enough. They therefore offered the throne to Tigranes of Armenia, who accepted it.[46] Even so, it took him until 69 to deal with Cleopatra Selene, still obstinately holding out in Ptolemaïs-Ake;[47] and when, that same year, he suffered a crushing defeat at the hands of the Romans, the resourceful Lucullus briefly resurrected a Seleucid ghost in the person of Antiochus XIII Asiaticus (below, p. 658).

Now, of all the Successor kingdoms, only Ptolemaic Egypt remained, in any effective sense; and even the Ptolemies owed their continued survival, for the next

fifty years or so, more to political rivalries in Rome than to any innate gifts of diplomacy or statesmanship. Lathyros died in 81/0, at the age of sixty-two. He had
reigned for thirty-seven years, no less than eighteen of which had been spent in
semi-exile on Cyprus. He left no legitimate male heir (both his sons by Cleopatra
Selene seem to have died young), and his daughter Cleopatra Berenice ruled alone
for a while. At this point, however, Sulla, now deciding foreign policy in semiretire-
ment,[48] came to the conclusion that the time was ripe for a safe pro-Roman puppet
on the throne of Egypt. To fill this role he sent out his waiting protégé, Ptolemy X
Alexander's son, with the title of Ptolemy XI Alexander II. Ptolemy Alexander's will
was produced in Rome to justify so flagrant a manipulation of Egyptian affairs. The
will's validity was challenged even in antiquity; but (leaving aside the moral issues
involved) it was probably genuine, and thus legally binding. It is also unlikely in the
extreme that the young boy-king would have been allowed to leave Rome for Alexandria without insurance of this sort for the ultimate benefit of his backers. Ptolemy
XI's mandate, besides, required him not only to wear the crown, but to marry his
middle-aged stepmother (or, possibly, his mother), Cleopatra Berenice. No one, at
this point, cared to argue with Sulla, and the marriage duly took place. Nineteen
days later young Ptolemy XI, driven by what motives, political or Freudian, it is
hard to decide, murdered his stepmotherly bride, and was thereupon lynched by the
furious city mob, with whom Cleopatra Berenice had been highly popular.[49]

It is significant that Sulla, once his candidate was dead, showed no eagerness
either to avenge the murder or to implement the will.[50] As so often, from the Roman
vantage point a waiting game seemed best, and annexation suspect. But if there was
to be no immediate annexation, where was Alexandria to find a sucessor to the
throne? The only possibility was the elder of Lathyros's two surviving illegitimate
sons, now in Syria under the tutelage of Mithridates. The king of Pontus, who saw
this as an opportunity to make trouble for Rome, was only too happy to release his
charges and, thus, prop up the Ptolemaic regime. The younger boy became governor of Cyprus; his brother was brought to Alexandria and duly proclaimed king that
year (80) as *Theos Philopatōr Philadelphos Neos Dionysos*, dropping his Ptolemaic nomenclature altogether. This grandiloquent title did not stop his subjects referring to
him, more commonly, as the Bastard or the Flute Player (*Aulētēs*): it is only in the
history books that he is labeled Ptolemy XII. Born at some point between 116 and
108, and not officially recognized by Rome—despite the application of considerable
largesse[51]—until 59, when Julius Caesar took a hand in the matter,[52] Ptolemy XII's
chief claim to fame, apart from a reputation for debauchery second only to that of
Physcon,[53] is the fact that he sired, on his sister-wife, Cleopatra V Tryphaena, a
daughter who, as Cleopatra VII, grew up to be the last, and the most famous, of all
the Ptolemies.

These extraordinary dynastic convulsions are, as Edouard Will observes, the
froth of history rather than its substance: symptoms of a deep and worsening malaise.[54] That this malaise was in some sense moral is, I think, impossible to deny. If
the word "degeneration" has any meaning at all, then the later Seleucids and Ptolemies were degenerate: selfish, greedy, murderous, weak, stupid, vicious, sensual,

vengeful, and, in the case of the Ptolemies, suffering from the effects of prolonged and repeated inbreeding. (The case of Cleopatra VII, however, suggests that habitual incest could still throw up a brilliant exception to the general rule: a refinement of genes rather than their dilution.) In both dynasties we also find the cumulative effect of centuries of ruthless exploitation: a foreign ruling elite, with no long-term economic insight, aiming at little more than immediate profits and dynastic self-perpetuation, backed (for their own ends) by shrewd local or foreign businessmen, and always able to count on a mercenary army when resentment reached boiling point.

Under this system, as we have seen, the gap between rich and poor grew steadily wider: if there was more real wealth available, there were also far more individuals, slave or free, whose lives had sunk to unending depressed poverty barely above starvation level. The intrusion of the Roman factor into such a situation merely made matters worse. Rome had never enjoyed anything remotely like the democratic experiments of the Greek *poleis*. Her representatives abroad, however upright and virtuous (which many of them to begin with were), inclined naturally toward the plutocrats, the oligarchs, the men of substance and *gravitas*, the authoritative and authoritarian upholders of privilege and order. When Cicero wants an equivalent Roman term for such people, he describes them, revealingly, as *optimates*,[55] a term that they themselves would accept as a fair translation of *kaloi k'agathoi*. The result, in the late Hellenistic period, was a progressive reinforcement of wealth (as opposed to family, political virtue, or even military success) as the dominant motivating force everywhere. This does not mean that the aristocracy, as has sometimes been supposed, was forced into opposition: far from it. In Athens, for which our evidence is most plentiful, it is clear that the nobility remained immensely influential in government, pursued plutocratic goals, and had nothing in common with the "debtor demos" that looked to Mithridates of Pontus for its salvation.[56]

It was, in every sense, a philistine age; and it was not made less philistine in any meaningful sense by the deliberate patronage extended to tame intellectuals in their gilded birdcages (cf. above, p. 87), most of whom had no intention of imperiling their own livelihood by radical criticisms of the regime: the purges of Ptolemy VIII were too recent and unpleasant a memory to allow luxuries of that sort (above, p. 538). There was, in the old-fashioned sense, a general breakdown of morality, to the point where naked power and sensual greed were (for the vast majority of those with any influence at all) the only serious driving forces in life. The malaise spread to Rome in the second century, and caught on there with uncommon speed: so fast, in fact, that old-fashioned moralists such as Cato the Censor (234–149) were still fulminating against latter-day degeneracy while their colleagues and agents were busy coining money through tax farming and other forms of colonial extortion. The trend culminated in figures such as Marcus Brutus, Caesar's assassin, whose high-minded philosophizing was underwritten by outrageous usury. Of his financial dealings on Cyprus it has been well remarked that he was a man of high principle, and even higher interest: 48 percent when 12 percent was the legal maximum.[57]

Such cases earned the Romans a reputation—undeserved at first—for money-grubbing hypocrisy. But nature abhors a vacuum, financial no less than territorial, and it rapidly became apparent, from the late second century onwards if not earlier, first to Rome's businessmen and investors, then to her soldiers, proconsuls, and administrators, and finally to anyone with eyes in his head, that the various areas in which Rome had, for the best and worst of mixed motives, become embroiled, from Spain to Asia—especially Spain; especially Asia—were sources of wealth undreamed of by their simpler forefathers. Volunteers for the Second Macedonian War against Philip V, and the campaign against Antiochus III that followed (cf. above, pp. 308, 420), were not all that easy to come by. But the loot they brought back made the recruiting of legionaries to fight Perseus, from 170 onwards, a simple matter. The triumph of Aemilius Paullus after Pydna paraded the wealth of the East for all to see (above, p. 415). The notion of Asia as El Dorado reached its stunning climax with Pompey's triumph in 61 (below, p. 661): on the proceeds of his campaigns he almost doubled the annual tributary revenue, from 200 million to 340 million sesterces, and after handing out 384 million sesterces to his troops, still had 480 million left over for the Roman treasury.[58]

During the period we are considering, the lure of the East in particular as a source of quick profit—and, scarcely less important, of cheap slaves—was constant: after the *Lex Sempronia* of 123 (above, p. 531) it snowballed. At times, predictably, the demands of the businessmen and entrepreneurs clashed with those of Rome's more conventional leaders in the Senate, who for long continued to think more in terms of national prestige and defense, even of morality. When this happened, it tended to be the financiers, ultimately, who won. There is a curious, and horrifying, illustration of this provided by the second servile insurrection in Sicily (104/3?). Unrest had, inevitably, been increasing as social conditions worsened, both in the slave gangs of the mines and plantations, and among the downtrodden free populace. In 116/5, for instance, at Dyme in Achaea, the mob rose against the propertied classes, burned the record office (presumably because of the mortgages and debt accounts stored there), and installed a new, democratic government, with the familiar call for a writing-off of debts. The Romans, predictably, intervened on the side of the old regime (probably one of the oligarchies set up by Mummius in 146), executed two of the revolutionary leaders, and took fierce repressive measures.[59]

The sheer availability of slaves was creating its own problems. In 104 a Roman *eques*, Titus Vettius, bought 500 suits of armor on credit, armed his slaves, and set himself up as a private condottiere and would-be king, complete with diadem, lictors, and purple cloak—within two hundred miles of Rome!—in order to avoid being brought to book for his overwhelming debts. He succumbed to a Roman army, but that he made the attempt at all was a sign of the times.[60] Yet who was going to control the supply of cheap slaves now flooding the market? Neither those who bought nor those who sold them had ever had it so good. The crunch came, finally, when Marius was trying to raise a contingent from Nicomedes of Bithynia, Rome's titular ally, to fight in the Cimbrian War (104/3), and Nicomedes objected that the bulk of his able-bodied men had been sold into slavery by Roman tax farmers.[61] The Senate, perturbed not only by the Cimbrian threat to northern Italy, but also by the rising problem of piracy (of which more in a moment), promptly "decreed that all enslaved allies of free birth should be set free in the provinces, and ordered governors to see that the decree was carried out"[62]—one of those famous orders more easily given than enforced, and, when enforced, liable to produce unforeseen and highly explosive results.

Nowhere was this more true than in Sicily. The governor, Publius Licinius Nerva, freed about eight hundred slaves; but then, so fierce was the resentment among the owners, he backed down, and the reversal of the original order at once produced a violent slave insurrection, under a leader named Salvius. Salvius, like the Seleucid pretender Diodotus (p. 534), took the title Tryphon, and kept royal court in true Hellenistic style: once again we find the mysterious link between Sicily and Antioch that marked the earlier rising under Eunus. It was not until 101 that Salvius and his fellow rebels finally succumbed to an experienced Roman commander, Manius Aquillius, son of the Asian proconsul (above, p. 531).[63] What the rebels wanted, and in the Mediterranean world as it then existed could not find, was that utopian chimera, an alternative society (cf. p. 391), a viable escape from their social and economic *huis clos*. If the social structure was immutable, then salvation must be sought elsewhere, a new society created over the horizon. This was as true of free men, below a certain level, as it was of the slaves, and some evidence suggests that there may have been more collaboration between them now. It also makes very clear just why both the Cilician pirates and—perhaps even more surprisingly—that thinly Hellenized Oriental monarch Mithridates of Pontus (below, p. 558) could command such remarkable allegiance from so wide a section of the Asiatic Greek population. Rome had not only endorsed the *status quo*, but brought exploitation to hitherto-unimagined levels.

Paradoxically, the Romans themselves, more than anyone, had been responsible for the immense growth of piracy in the second century. By crippling first the Seleucid and then the Rhodian fleet, without making any serious alternative arrangements for the policing of the Mediterranean, Rome was positively inviting corsairs and freebooters to establish themselves, with ever-increasing boldness, in the bays and inlets of Cilicia.[64] There is also evidence that piracy may, in fact, have been encouraged by Italian merchants, since one commodity that pirates were well equipped, by the nature of their calling, to provide was slaves, and it seems at least possible that a good percentage of the slave trade channeled through the great mart at Delos—since 167 under Athenian control, but always subject, in the last resort, to *de facto* Roman authority[65]—was carried out by a private working arrangement between dealers and pirates.[66] Mithridates, too, whose naval activities were very much dependent on the fleets of his maritime allies, had no scruples about using pirate squadrons for his own purposes.[67] By the turn of the century it seems clear that the supply of cheap slaves was creating problems for Rome—not yet fully recognized as such—that had begun to outweigh the advantages of the slaves themselves. The pirates, too, had become something of a nuisance (though not nearly so much of a menace as they got to be thirty-odd years later), and in 102 Marcus Antonius was sent out to deal with them.[68] Driven from Cilicia, where Antonius scored some successes against them, they regrouped on Crete.[69] In 100 a *Lex de piratis* banned them from every port in the Mediterranean. But Rome was not ready, yet, for the major concerted effort it would require to clear out this plague; besides, the pirates' continued ability, with no major wars going on in the Aegean or Asia Minor, to provide Italy with high-class slaves must have created a certain unwillingness (and not only in business circles) to disturb them.[70] In any case the Senate at this point was far more preoccupied with the expansionist activities of Mithridates.

Mithridates VI Eupator Dionysus[71] the Great[72] of Pontus (ca. 132–63)[73] is one of the oddities of history: the Oriental prince of a mountainous yet fertile country that derived its wealth from the iron it exported to the West,[74] a populous Black Sea empire poised perilously between two alien worlds; a Hellenized king who modeled himself on Alexander the Great in appearance,[75] if not as regards his own energetic heterosexual activities,[76] yet, fatally, lacked Alexander's strategic skill; a brilliant linguist who reputedly knew no less than twenty-two languages and dialects; a ruthless, abstemious, hard-riding, lion-hearted man, who absorbed Greek culture (music in particular) and united the Greeks of Asia as no man had done for centuries, yet never understood how to match himself with Rome; an indomitable fighter who did not know the meaning of the word defeat (like the snake, said one critic, that strikes with its tail when its head is crushed),[77] and ended his life—being immune to poison—by getting a mercenary to cut his throat.[78]

Mithridates' early career, insofar as it can be disentangled from legend (cf. pp. 501–2),[79] is a nice mixture of ruthlessness and cautious opportunism.[80] Co-opted as co-regent by his mother when twelve years old, after the murder in 120 of his father, Mithridates V Euergetes, he fled the court at Sinope for seven years—having from the start a healthy sense of self-preservation—to live in the hills as a voluntary exile, and (as subsequent events make clear) to prepare his own power base. In 112 he came back to Sinope, executed his brother, imprisoned (and later murdered) his mother, married his sister Laodice (whom he subsequently put to death for attempt-

Fig. 174. Mithridates VI Eupator of Pontus. Silver tetradrachm, mint unknown, 75 B.C. In sharp contrast to the brutal realism of portraiture affected by his ancestors, Mithridates VI presented himself, as here, even when advanced in age, as a romanticized reincarnation of Alexander the Great. British Museum, London.

ing to poison him),[81] and established himself as sole ruler of Pontus.[82] From then on he set himself, with energy and patience, to extend his realm: first along the southern shore of the Black Sea to Colchis, and north to the Crimea and its adjacent grain-fields (110–107);[83] next—after an incognito trip into Bithynia and the province of Asia, which opened his eyes to the degree of hatred engendered by Roman exploitation[84]—he turned his attention to the West. The timing was good. A disastrous series of military defeats, at the hands of the Thracians, Jugurtha, and the Cimbri in succession,[85] effectively prevented Rome from doing anything about Mithridates' activities until after Marius's decisive victory at Vercellae (101).

By means of a flexible, and often confusing, formula that mixed aggression, diplomatic alliances, dynastic marriages, and domestic murders in about equal proportions, he partitioned Paphlagonia and Galatia with Nicomedes III of Bithynia, but managed to finesse Cappadocia for his own son, Ariarathes, to Nicomedes' fury, blithely ignoring the warnings of Marius that unless he could make himself more powerful than the Romans, he would be well advised to obey them (99/8).[86] The good sense of this recommendation was demonstrated in 96 (or perhaps 92),[87] when Sulla, as propraetor of Cilicia, forced Mithridates to give up his territorial gains.[88] Unabashed, Mithridates married off a daughter to Tigranes of Armenia, and, with this new ally to support him, returned to the attack in Cappadocia, ousting the legitimate ruler, Ariobarzanes, who had been restored to his throne by Sulla in 92. Ariobarzanes and young Nicomedes IV (also run off his throne, on his father's death, by the indefatigable Mithridates) appeared in Rome, complaining loudly. The Senate, feeling that the king of Pontus had become a dangerous nuisance, ordered the two suppliant monarchs reinstated, and in 89 sent out Manius Aquillius to see that this was done. Though now a senior consular in high standing, Aquillius was a most impolitic choice: his father's record in Asia had not been forgotten (above, p. 531).[89] Perhaps Mithridates' opportunism, his willingness to back off, may have given the impression that he would be easy to handle—if so, another most grievous error of judgment.[90]

Thus we can see that at least from 103 Mithridates had been at odds with the Romans. What were his motives? His own personal and territorial ambitions, beyond a doubt; but we can also sense in him—perhaps engendered by that private fact-finding tour, and sharpened by the Hellenizing edge to his character—a sustained hatred and contempt for Rome and her ways. He had had, too, personal experience of Rome's Indian-giving. His father, who helped the Romans out during the revolt of Aristonicus (p. 530), was rewarded with the cession to Pontus of Greater Phrygia; but on his death the Senate, probably cashing in on the apparent weakness of the royal house,[91] reversed itself and annexed this territory to the province of Asia, an act that the young prince never forgot or forgave.[92] Nor had he any patience with the Roman habit of playing kingmaker in Anatolian countries. Besides, he had his own candidates, and they were not Rome's.

Mithridates' reactions, then, may well be imagined in 89, when not only were Rome's puppets, Ariobarzanes and Nicomedes IV, restored to the thrones of Cappadocia and Bithynia, but the Roman commissioner, Aquillius, further demanded that Mithridates pay an indemnity. When this was refused, Aquillius instructed his two client-kings to invade Pontus. Ariobarzanes, to his credit, did nothing; but Nicomedes was in the hands of Roman moneylenders, and had no choice.[93] Mithridates, very coolly, invited Rome to punish Nicomedes (or at least authorize him to do so), as though unaware that the Bithynian's move had Roman backing, indeed was made on Roman orders. He then threw Ariobarzanes out of Cappadocia for the third time, rejected Rome's ultimatum, and—the first Eastern ruler to dare it since Perseus in 170—went to war with the Republic (winter 89–88),[94] relying on his large, well-trained army and powerful fleet, the allies he had acquired, Rome's pre-occupation with the Social War in Italy,[95] and, last but not least, the violent anti-Roman feeling in Asia Minor.[96]

To begin with he was strikingly successful: a mark, it has been suggested, of Rome's negligence in the protection of her nationals and provincials,[97] but probably due primarily to *übermenschlich* overconfidence on the part of the colonial administrators. Who in Asia would dare to challenge the Senate and Roman People? Thus, to begin with, Mithridates enjoyed the advantage of surprise. All Asia Minor and Bithynia fell into his hands. Lucius Cassius Longinus, the provincial governor, fled the country. Aquillius tried to do the same, but fell ill and was captured in Mytilene.[98] The pirates, now in open alliance with Mithridates,[99] helped his squadrons to control the sea lanes. Mithridates was welcomed by the majority of the Greeks as a deliverer, as the New Dionysus.[100] What Roman rule, and Roman exploitation, had meant to them can best be judged by the intensity of their reaction. Once again, but now for the last time, they responded, with the hope born of a long despair, to the promise of freedom: freedom from the worst oppression they had known in their long and checkered history. The attraction of Mithridates for Greeks of all classes and conditions—including, sometimes, even members of the wealthy *Oberschicht*—lay, precisely, in the fact that he offered them their only chance to break loose from the hated domination of Rome. It is easy to be cynical about this: no doubt many people were at the time. Yet it is hard to imagine that even Mithridates—that ruthless, semi-Hellenized barbarian—could have offered them, in cold fact, anything that was not preferable to being ground down by the *publicani* and the *negotiatores*, with all the power of Rome's legions behind them. And Mithridates, barbarian or not, had at least the simple moral sense to know, and dramatize, just what was wrong with the Asian province. When Aquillius fell into his hands, he executed this Roman grandee by pouring molten gold down his throat[101]—a trick the Parthians later repeated when they captured Marcus Crassus after the disastrous battle of Carrhae (53).[102]

The *publicani* had been bleeding Asia white at least since 123; when a pair of honest administrators like Quintus Mucius Scaevola and Rutilius Rufus appeared, in 94/3, it was one of them who, in the end, fell victim to the financiers' supporters in Rome. Scaevola, as Pontifex Maximus, was probably felt to be too distinguished to attack. But Rufus was prosecuted for—of all things—extortion, convicted, and forced into exile: with mischievous relish, he chose an honorable retirement among the very people he was supposed to have plundered.[103] (He became a citizen of Smyrna, where Cicero afterwards met him.) Too many Roman business interests had heavy investments in Asia by now; too many cartels had paid out too much for the privilege of collecting taxes, and wanted a good return on their money. It was against this appalling regime of graft and extortion that Mithridates carried out the coup for which he is best remembered. In the summer of 88 secret orders went out to every town, every satrap, for a simultaneous pogrom, by night, of all Romans and Italians in the province. This "night of the long knives" is said to have claimed the lives of no less than eighty thousand traders, tax collectors, and other foreign residents, together with their families: even if that figure is exaggerated, we need not doubt that the slaughter was very large. Victims were torn from sanctuary and butchered, in scenes that recall the savagery of the *sans-culottes* in revolutionary Paris. What is astonishing is not so much the fact that some cities, such as Tralles, tried to minimize their complicity by hiring non-Greeks to do their killing for them, but rather the degree of collective unanimity behind this widespread act of violence.[104] It meant war to the death, and punitive reprisals in the event of failure: one obvious motive for Mithridates' action was to bind the Greek cities to the revolt by a kind of universal blood-guilt. Fear of Rome, clearly, was no deterrent. Compared to the exactions inflicted by Rome's agents, the chance of death was a more than acceptable risk—even though, ironically enough, the Pontic king turned out, later, almost as great a scourge to the Greeks of Asia as the Romans had been before him.

One of the most intriguing things about Mithridates is his highly skilled and adaptable propaganda.[105] By fastening on Rome as the great enemy, he could perform a remarkable balancing act between Greeks and Orientals, appealing to both without losing the appearance of sincerity. To the Greeks he represented himself as a latter-day Alexander,[106] the much-wronged standard-bearer of Greek culture with a sacred mission to expel the Romans from Asia, an impression reinforced by his superb coin portraits and his carefully cultivated reputation for liberality (*philanthrōpia*) and magnanimous compassion; he also hinted at redistribution of property and debt cancellation, though as we shall see, it was only as a last resort that he committed himself, too late, to any really radical measures.[107] His role as an avatar of Alexander must have awakened unpleasant memories among those non-Greeks who looked back to the lost glories of the Achaemenid empire (cf. above, p. 323), so to Iranians he stressed his descent from Achaemenid monarchs such as Cyrus and Darius.[108] He borrowed anti-Roman Greek propaganda from the time of the Third Macedonian War (above, p. 427); he even, with cool effrontery, revamped old anti-Macedonian oracles to predict the discomfiture of Rome (he seems, to judge from his coins, to have been planning war at least from 92),[109] and portrayed himself in them as the triumphant champion of Greeks and Orientals alike against the harsh rapacity of Roman fiscal exactions and commercial exploitation. The legends about the comets that supposedly marked his birth and accession,[110] his immunity to murderous attempts as a child, his ability to outrun and outfight wild beasts, may well all derive from this conscious self-projection as the invincible leader of a Graeco-Iranian apocalypse, in which "for all the wealth that Rome took from tribute-paying Asia, / Three times as much Asia shall take back from Rome; / And shall repay her for her deadly arrogance."[111]

Something of the excitement that Mithridates stirred up in Greece can be seen from the reaction in Athens. The Athenian government, for almost half a century now (cf. above, p. 525), had been in the hands of a mixed group, including aristocrats, wealthy businessmen, and others, united only in their commercialism, ambition, social elitism, and ultimate dependence on Rome.[112] Appointments on Delos, that hub of commerce, grew steadily in number and importance.[113] There is no need to posit an oligarchic takeover in 103/2 or any other year during the late second or early first century (above, p. 526): insofar as the term still had any substantive meaning, all Athenian ruling groups from the 130s until shortly before the Mithridatic revolt were *de facto* oligarchies.[114] Council and Assembly, to be sure, still passed decrees; the bureaucracy (e.g., the secretarial cycle) continued to function;[115] but by now it should be clear just how much, or how little, these traditional exercises had come to mean. Trouble seethed below the surface. Probably in 100/99[116] a serious slave revolt took place at the Laurium silver mines.[117] The slaves captured a fortress at Sunium, and for some while terrorized the Attic countryside. Economic disruption in the aftermath of this rising was exacerbated by the first signs of Delos's decline, as the island began to lose trade to Roman Puteoli.[118] Political resentments were met with increasingly repressive and authoritarian measures.

For the period 91/0 through 89/8 a junta led by a Piraeus millionaire, Medeius, who in 98/7 had been governor of Delos, monopolized power, with Medeius himself holding the eponymous archonship, illegally, for all three years in succession.[119] *Pace* Badian,[120] it seems clear that Medeius's government was pro-Roman, if for no other reason because of the Delian connection, and anti-Mithridatic, since it was frustrated democrats who, by and large, were now following where the king of Pontus led. Medeius and his followers banned public assemblies, closed the temples and gymnasia, suspended university lectures: the usual coercive measures, grimly familiar from every authoritarian regime down the ages.[121] The result was a popular coup that ousted Medeius from power.[122] Medeius had appealed for support to Rome; the new government looked in quite another direction. A certain Athenion was sent to approach Mithridates.[123] The Pontic king, who badly needed good harbors and naval squadrons, gave him every encouragement. He himself would land in Piraeus, Athens would have her democracy confirmed, debts would be canceled, there would be rich rewards: the days of Roman tyranny were over.[124]

Athenion, who came back to Athens decked out in purple and gold, living proof of Mithridates' lavish munificence, got a hysterically enthusiastic reception (slyly described by Poseidonius, nothing if not the class-conscious snob), was hailed as a savior, and elected hoplite general. Democratic institutions had already been restored;[125] eupatrid rule under Roman patronage was denounced as anarchy, and "a general exodus of the propertied classes began."[126] A reign of terror now took place against the old regime and its supporters.[127] A curfew was imposed, travel passes were required of all citizens, there were numerous arrests, torture and execution became commonplaces, confiscations yielded untold riches, fugitives were hunted down in the hills. Once again the parallel with revolutionary Paris suggests itself. Athenion's lieutenant Apellicon and a thousand men were ambushed by the Italians on Delos;[128] as a result Athenion was replaced by a Peripatetic philosopher named Aristion, who now found himself obliged, at short notice and with inadequate resources, to defend Athens against the vengeful wrath of the Romans. The democratic honeymoon— short, bloody, and woefully inept—was over.

Rome's supreme commander against Mithridates was Lucius Cornelius Sulla, her most formidable general, who had recently made history by marching on his own capital at the head of his legions, and was afterwards to earn further notoriety as dictator. At present his position was highly anomalous: to the government in Rome he was a rebel, and his survival (as he well knew) depended entirely on his success in the field. Mithridates could have had no more dangerous adversary. Sulla reached Greece, by way of Epirus, in the spring of 87, leading thirty thousand veterans of the Social War, and made straight for Athens and Piraeus. The Long Walls were in disrepair. Roman catapult balls reached the heart of the Agora. However, Mithridates' Greek general Archelaus conducted a spirited defense of Piraeus, burning the siege engines that Sulla had built *in situ* with timber provided by the wholesale felling of Attica's woods, including the trees in Plato's Academy and Aristotle's Lyceum. Athens, as so often in her history, starved: traitors in Piraeus enabled Sulla to intercept food convoys. The defenders boiled leather and ate it.[129] Finally, on 1 March 86, Sulla's troops scaled the walls and sacked the city. The Kerameikos ran red with blood: it was only through the entreaties of Medeius and other exiles in Sulla's retinue that the slaughter was finally stopped. A last stand was made on the Acropolis by Mithridates' supporters, including Aristion: Sulla left them to starve under blockade while he finally battered down the bastions of Piraeus.[130] He set the great port on fire, destroying Philo's famous arsenal (above, p. 52), and in general carrying out a peculiarly thorough, and brutal, demolition of all public facilities (later minimized in his memoirs). The cache of bronze statues found in Piraeus a few years ago was probably buried during the siege, and then forgotten.[131] After this Sulla moved on to defeat Archelaus at Chaeronea and Orchomenos in Boeotia (86/5), thus ending a campaign that had been marked, to a quite extraordinary degree, by looting, atrocities, savage slaughter, and wanton, wholesale destruction.[132] He was now free to deal with Mithridates.

As a result of Sulla's victories, Mithridates experienced a predictable backlash of local hostility against him in Asia Minor, and met it with crushing reprisals, on Chios and elsewhere. The self-styled apostle of freedom turned out (like all his predecessors in that role since Alexander the Great) to be as ruthless as any tyrant when crossed. This revelation was not forgotten. When Mithridates returned to the province of Asia twelve years later, he got a very different reception (below, p. 654).[133] In any case his resistance from now on was a forlorn gesture. In August 85, at Dardanus in the Troad, the chastened king of Pontus (who in desperation had been appealing to the slaves and landless men, like Aristonicus before him, and thereby forfeiting a good deal of his more solid support)[134] was compelled by treaty to surrender all the territory he had conquered. If Sulla's terms were—for a Roman—surprisingly mild, that is probably to be accounted for in part by his own most anomalous position, and in part by the fact that his opponent's fleet still controlled the Aegean. Still, for the moment—but only for the moment—Mithridates was beaten.[135]

In Greece, above all in Athens, Rome's victory marked an inevitable reversion to plutocracy. Though before the fall of Athens, in 87/6, a provisional government of businessmen had already been set up (everyone by now knew what kind of administrators Romans preferred to deal with), and was indeed afterwards confirmed in office, the city as a whole got harsh treatment. It lost all political privileges.[136] The Council and in particular the Areopagus were strengthened still further at the expense of the Assembly.[137] Sulla was in bad need of cash subsidies, and raided the treasures of the Acropolis without compunction. He is said to have appropriated forty pounds of gold and six hundred pounds of silver in this way for his personal use: by now it is unlikely that there was any more there.[138] Afterwards Athens was so poor that she was obliged to avoid insolvency by selling off the island of Salamis.[139] Sulla also—following what had become a tradition ever since the sack of Corinth—looted works of art and other valuables for dispatch to Rome, including, *inter alia*, columns from the temple of Olympian Zeus and the library of Apellicon of Teos, which contained copies of the works of Aristotle and Theophrastus. The neoclassicist sculptors' ateliers, not surprisingly, migrated to Rome about the same time.[140] Any men who had served in the pro-Mithridatic governments of Athenion or Aristion were executed; their supporters remained disfranchised, in their own city, for more than a decade.[141] "In less than two years the peace and prosperity of a century and a half had been annihilated."[142]

Still, Athenians could at least console themselves with the thought that their fate was mild compared with that reserved for the cities of Asia, on which Sulla imposed a collective indemnity of twenty thousand talents, the equivalent of five years' tribute plus the cost of the war.[143] The cost of maintaining the troops forcibly billeted on them has been calculated at as much again,[144] and raising this vast sum drove them into heavy debt, with widespread mortgaging of property, both public and private. Delos, on the other hand, briefly regained its independence, though the *negotiatores* and slave traders soon moved back there, and in 84 Rome returned the island to Athenian control.[145]

Sulla epitomized the triumph of everything the Greeks had fought to escape: elitism, authoritarianism, the rule of privilege, alien brutality and highhandedness. The sack of Athens, the burning of Piraeus (which, though restored, never fully recovered its old glory)[146]—not since the Persian Wars had such indignities been inflicted on the city of Cecrops—remained as a visible reminder of what Athens now was, what in bitter truth she had been since the Chremonidean War in the mid-third century (above, p. 147): a city overshadowed by its classical monuments, still busily cashing in on a long-overdrawn account stocked with past glories, still nursing an intellectual arrogance that, increasingly as time went on, lacked substantial means of support. As late as 211/0 pious hopes had still been recorded, on stone, that Athenians would soon see "the city restored to her original good fortune,"[147] but this could no longer be in the old Periclean way. Art, philosophy, literature, rather than political achievement or imperial domination, now offered the only road to supremacy. By a dilution of the Platonic ideal all this came to be subsumed under the loose heading of "beauty." A soft, retrospective, classicizing nostalgia prevailed: most strikingly in the art from the mid-second century onwards (below, pp. 568 ff.), but in fact permeating the entire fabric of society. It is entirely characteristic that one epigrammatist, praising the looks of his boy lover, should write: "Athens, his city, once mistress over land and waves, / Has now made all Greece a slave—to beauty."[148] Disaster drove the city of Cecrops back on "the great solace of her cultural superiority,"[149] with pedantic emphasis, now, on routine, form, traditional ceremonial, shadow rather than lost substance, and, in the second century, a shrill, nagging insistence that she had not only saved the sum of things at Marathon nearly four centuries before, but was responsible for just about every civilized invention and discovery in the world.[150] Cicero saw, too clearly, that the only real future for Athens was as the home of a distinguished university, a role that elevated the nostalgic enshrinement of past achievement as an Aristotelian function of unquestioned legitimacy.[151] To this we might add the city's second birth, apparent even then, as a perennial tourist center, the inhabitants of which were "a race no longer of heroes but of professors / And crooked businessmen and secretaries and clerks."[152] Yet Athens, Cicero was forced to admit, even so "enjoys such prestige that today the broken and debilitated name of Greece rests on this city's renown."[153] The extraordinary aura of what Pindar called "bulwark of Hellas, famous Athens, divine citadel" survived, and still survives, all time's vicissitudes.[154]

CHAPTER 32

LATE HELLENISTIC ART, 150–30: THE MASS MARKET IN NOSTALGIA

Mummius's sack of Corinth (146) and Attalus III's bequest of his kingdom to Rome (133) between them wrote finis to a long period of public, sponsored, monumental art: such creations as Ptolemy's gymnasium and the Middle Stoa in Athens, or the Great Altar of Pergamon. They also emphasized (if emphasis were needed) the paramount importance from now on, in artistic as in other matters, of Roman patronage and Roman taste. This did not, at least until the Augustan age, imply a Romanization of Greek canons in any creative sense: far from it. Captive Greece took her conqueror captive, and no aspect of contemporary culture demonstrates this more strikingly than the visual arts. Pliny's claim that art revived in 156/3 (above, p. 336: it was in 155, incidentally, that the leading philosophers of Athens visited Rome) commemorates the final Italian acceptance of Attic neoclassicism,[1] though the Pheidian gigantism of work by artists such as Damophon or Eubulides still had a strong element of baroque in it.[2] For Romans, Greek art was the best—which did not, naturally, stop them from displaying an invincible contempt for the artists who produced it[3]—and they were prepared to pay well for it (when, that is, they could not short-circuit normal channels by mass looting in the wake of a successful military campaign, a practice that aroused deep and lasting Greek resentment).[4]

But it had, obviously, to be the right art: ever since Syracuse (212), Tarentum (209), Cynoscephalae (197), and Magnesia (188), a steady flow of Old Masters to Italy had acclimatized Roman art fanciers to the archaic, the classical (epitomized by Pheidias and Polygnotus), and the best of the fourth-century sculptors, such as Lysippus or Praxiteles.[5] Aemilius Paullus toured Greece after his victory at Pydna (168), gazing with innocent yet acquisitive awe at the statuary littering the Acropolis, the gigantic Zeus of Olympia; afterwards he declared that only Pheidias had truly captured Homer's "Father of Gods and Men." Neoclassicist sculptors were quick to take the hint. The battle frieze he dedicated in Delphi is thoroughly traditional in design; it may even offer an updated version of the late fifth-century frieze on the Athena Nike temple. Interestingly, the battle it portrays is not mythical, but that of Pydna: one rider, indeed, has been plausibly identified as Aemilius Paullus himself.[6]

The victor also took back to Rome an Athena by Pheidias as a memento (an unfortunate but all too prevalent practice), and asked the Athenians to send him a painter to record his triumph, and a philosopher to educate his children. The Athenians, still bent on selling their city as the crucible of creative versatility, recommended a certain Metrodorus for both jobs.[7] He thus became one of the first Greek artists to settle in Rome and exploit this new expanding market.

The result of such infiltration was inevitable and predictable, and the Pergamene loot—including originals by Myron and Praxiteles—that found its way into Roman hands after 133 (above, p. 394) merely accelerated the process.[8] Copies of first-class classical works proved far more attractive than weak or obscure contemporary experiments. Once the mere ruthless plundering of the *oikoumenē* had been checked by strong opposition from civilized Romans, the first true art market in Europe now developed, complete with dealers, collectors, restorers, forgers, fashion chasers, copyists, and spiraling prices. As Pollitt says, "no aspect of late Republican Rome has a more modern feeling to it." Things have not changed all that much, say in Manchester or Dallas, today.[9] Here was a vast new market, its buyers endowed with more enthusiasm than taste, with more money than enthusiasm. Romans might officially despise painting and sculpture as the kind of contemptible frippery (along with athletics and oratory) in which Greeks were far too interested, "the delight and solace of their servitude,"[10] but nevertheless they continued to buy pictures and statues in unprecedented quantities. Living Attic sculptors, such as Timarchides, as well as painters and architects (Demetrius, Hermodorus), lost no time in visiting Rome and collecting commissions from the elite.[11] Timarchides' sons, Dionysius and Polycles, carried on what was clearly a lucrative business—one of them was employed by Caecilius Metellus Macedonicus—though they seem to have kept their atelier in Athens.

Nothing is more fascinating during this period than the ubiquitous and increasing passion, in Athens as in Rome, for putting up statues, of public figures, personal friends, or indeed of oneself, not least when we recall that the cost of such a gesture could run as high as the equivalent of ten years' average wages, that is, three thousand drachmas; though our evidence, such as it is, suggests that this was probably the conventional figure for top-quality work, and that the job could in fact be done a good deal cheaper.[12] The cult of the individual had replaced the collective ideal embodied in the *polis*, and was now seeking permanence in stone or metal, to counter the Hellenistic sense of personal impotence "by literally carving . . . a niche in history."[13] The prevalence of the habit may be judged from the fact that despite massive Roman depredations, cities such as Rhodes, Athens, Olympia, and Delphi still, in the first century A.D., possessed, according to Pliny, an average of three thousand statues each, on permanent public display.[14]

The disturbed economic and military conditions of the age had produced not only widespread poverty and hardship, but also a large enough class of wealthy (and increasingly often *parvenu*) entrepreneurs to sustain a flourishing art industry, primarily in statues and portrait busts, but also in mosaics, painting (murals as well as panelwork), embossed vessels of silver and gold (toreutics), and high-quality jewelry. Since the supply of work by certified top artists from the best periods was, as always, strictly limited, a secondary traffic developed in free, and, later, mechanical copies of such pieces.[15] This in turn could not fail to encourage the retrospective classicizing trend generally, and fostered a reversion to classical, or, sometimes, archaic, models even when direct imitation was avoided. This on occasion—witness the Aphrodite of Melos (Venus di Milo: below, p. 579)—could produce really memorable work; but such achievements were the exception rather than the rule. Neoclassicism, as we have seen, had always been a notable component of the Hellenistic mind: the sense of an unsurpassable canon to match or follow, the scholarly passion for analyzing, and building on, the sum of past achievement.

Thus Pheidias, Polycleitus, Praxiteles became a trinity of perfection, hard to emulate, impossible to eclipse, often copied. The Attalids and Antiochus Epiphanes, for example, both acquired reproductions of the Athena Parthenos, though these were adaptations rather than reproductions in the strict sense: techniques for accurate copying only appeared toward the very end of the second century (below, p. 574), and were given impetus by the extraordinary resurgence of classicism, above all in Athens, that got under way—by no coincidence—about the time of the Achaean War and Mummius's sack of Corinth. Over and above the stimulus provided by political annihilation, other causes suggest themselves. Most important, there was the popularity that classicism enjoyed with the Romans (and, now, with others, Syrians and Pergamenes included), which led, predictably, to a widespread, though never total, rejection of baroque. We may also note the increasing conventionality and conservatism of the ruling class—which, being also composed of the wealthiest citizens, had considerable influence, in a free market, on trends in artistic commissions—and, linked to this, from 166 the gross commercialism of the Athenian trading center on Delos,[16] restorer of the financial fortunes of Athens after a particularly low ebb,[17] playground of so many tough businessmen who did well out of Aegean trade while at the same time having very firm, not to say old-fashioned, ideas about just what representations of gods, kings, heroes, and modern dignitaries ought to look like. Fixated on the past, enjoying an inflated sense of the continuing role of Athens as guardian of Hellenic culture, they inevitably associated themselves with the classical, or classicizing, style, since this for them embodied all the ideal values (nostalgically, and without real risk) that they hoped to preserve for posterity.

Outside Attica the success of neoclassicism was more limited: total for the cult statue (a genre largely controlled by religious conservatism), intermittent as regards ruler portraits and architectural reliefs, largely absent in private commissions.[18] Even so, for art, literature, and philosophy Athens was still, rightly or wrongly, looked up to as the *fons et origo* of all creative virtues: the measure of her reputation can be gauged from those splendid monuments with which Ptolemaic and Pergamene monarchs endowed her, and, more revealingly, by the endless copies of earlier Greek masterpieces turned out for Roman clients by the flourishing Athenian workshops. In retrospect we can see that this was, in essence, a mistaken judgment: at the time men lived with a shorter perspective. Time has mercifully buried all but tattered shreds of the innumerable sub-Euripidean tragedies, and most of the synthetic post-

Theocritean urban pastoral. However, we know a good deal about what the philosophers were up to (cf. below, pp. 602 ff.), and in the visual arts also the record is clear enough: too clear, some might say.

Anecdotes enlighten. Attalus II had copies of Polygnotus's paintings at Delphi made for his own collection.[19] He was also in the market for originals. After the sack of Corinth, from which Pergamon was allotted a portion of the spoils, he put in a very high bid for one fourth-century painting, a Dionysus by the Theban artist Aristeides. (Acquisitiveness, or high-minded cultural salvage? Perhaps a little of both.) Mummius, thus alerted to the work's value, withdrew it from sale and himself dedicated it in the temple of Ceres in Rome (which probably, like so many temples at this time, had the secondary function of an art gallery: cf. above, p. 206).[20] As in our own day, art, through a series of sociopolitical accidents, was becoming very big business indeed. Gaius Verres, the notorious governor of Sicily (73–71) who was prosecuted by Cicero, seems to have been a near-professional antique dealer and art faker:[21] though he escaped into wealthy exile at Massilia (Marseilles), it is not unwelcome to hear that he was proscribed, a quarter of a century later, by Mark Antony—for the sake of his fabulous art collection, in particular his Corinthian bronzes, which enjoyed a special cachet among Roman connoisseurs.[22]

What sold best? Reassuringly old-fashioned stuff, it seems clear: decorative items for rich middle-class suburbanites, anxious to pep up house and garden long before *House and Garden*. The unpleasant realities of contemporary life could be sanitized and uplifted through the agency of archaizing figures from the heroic past.[23] Sulla, the Roman dictator, was by all accounts, despite his ruthlessness (above, p. 563), an intelligent, cultured man with an ironic sense of humor: the irony must have been well to the fore in the frieze he commissioned to celebrate his victory in Greece, which presented winged Victories (*Nikai*), decked out in chiton and himation, a nice advertisement for eclectic neo-Atticism, and in all likelihood executed by artists who emigrated in a hurry after the sack of Athens.[24] As always, the subject matter of ancient art is revealing. Cicero[25] makes it quite clear that an intelligent person was expected to choose his works of art "entirely for the associations aroused by their subject-matter:"[26] for a library he was happy to have herms with the heads of Athena or Heracles, but drew the line at Maenads, whom he considered "unsuitable."

However, as we might suspect from the hard-faced, unflattering portraits of those aggressive realists who were now the men with the money,[27] Cicero was in a minority. Dionysiac scenes were still extremely popular: beautiful silver cups, with repoussé work of flowers and tendrils, hint at luxury-loving symposiasts. Also, from the third century onwards (and indeed earlier) we find an ever-increasing number of terra cottas, gemstones, statuettes, bronzes (including mirror backs), and vase reliefs (all expensive items, and thus made for the luxury market) devoted to explicit representations of the sexual organs or sexual activity.[28] These are most often straight: copulation in a variety of positions, with nymphs occasionally being replaced by hermaphrodites, and at least once (for the benefit of Pan) by a she-goat, though homosexual scenes are comparatively rare, and certainly less common than in the classical period.[29] Occasionally, nevertheless, we encounter a mode that can only be de-

Fig. 175. Phallic tintinnabulum in bronze (Pompeii, first century A.D.). Apotropaic, kinky entertainment, or a little of each? The creation of small independent phallus-animals (here with phallus-tail, wings, and a phallus for the phallus) has a long history. British Museum, London.

scribed as kinky surrealist: the bronze tintinnabulum of a man attacking, with a knife, a rearing dog that is also his own gigantic penis;[30] two personified terra-cotta phalluses sawing an (evil?) eye in half;[31] the marble relief in which an old countryman is being ridden, succubus-style, by a winged Siren;[32] detached phalluses with human legs, or wings, and in one case a phallic tail and a mini-penis, a prick sporting a prick.[33]

Realism, which during the Pergamene ascendancy had been largely absorbed by baroque violence, began to reassert itself in different ways during the latter part of the second century, often at the expense of neoclassicism. What it now tended to concentrate on—a general predilection of which the sexually perverse formed one particular manifestation—was the ugly, the deformed, the grotesque, the odd: an elderly dwarf *danseuse*, a mongoloid removing a thorn from his foot, cripples and pariahs, the senile or alcoholic.[34] We have already encountered the post-Euripidean obsession with pathological conditions, and indeed the artistic interest in low life (above, p. 342); but now it has taken a rather unpleasant turn. Here we have the flotsam of the Hellenistic world's economic depression and war-torn anarchy, contemptuously immortalized to adorn a rich man's peristyle, to remind him that, in this cutthroat world, *he* has clawed his way out of the underworld; that like the visitor to a zoo, he is now a privileged spectator of the common scene.

Nowhere is the sense of wealthy self-indulgence more palpable than in the art and architecture of Delos—at least until, in 88, Mithridates' general Archelaus sacked the island. Though Delos recovered, this ruthless act of destruction had an irreversible social impact, crippling its art industry for ever.[35] The wealth of Delos rested on the slave trade. When we admire the superb mosaics of tiger or panther, the luxurious houses with their columned courtyards, we should pause once in a while and remind ourselves how they were paid for, in what dark ways the tiger was ridden. The reaction against neoclassicism is sharp and unmistakable, the break with Athenian portraiture decisive. The farthest outpost of Asiatic baroque? A haven of colonial eclecticism? In any case, since Delos was the commercial hub of the Aegean, with a large Italian colony and a constant flow of rich and influential Roman visitors, this trend is worth watching. The ingredients that went to make up late Republican portraiture were complex, and at times seemingly contradictory. The neoclassicist

Fig. 176. Bronze figurine of a male dancing dwarf (middle or late second century B.C.?), found in the Mahdia shipwreck of ca. 100 B.C. This cargo, consisting entirely of works of art, was formerly thought to be part of Sulla's spoils from the sack of Athens and Piraeus in 86 B.C., but the dating of the artifacts on board makes this unlikely, though not entirely impossible.
Bardo Museum, Tunisia.

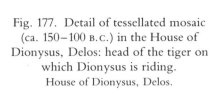

Fig. 177. Detail of tessellated mosaic (ca. 150–100 B.C.) in the House of Dionysus, Delos: head of the tiger on which Dionysus is riding.
House of Dionysus, Delos.

tradition seems to have been constantly modified by this Delian neorealism, till the disruption of 88 and the subsequent fragmentation of the Delian mode marked the end of a creative phase. But the influence had done its work regardless, and would remain as a permanent element in Graeco-Roman art.

We are confronted here with the energetic and, yes, eclectic self-expression of what has been well described as "a new class of nouveaux riches, grown fat on the business of Delos" and searching, with half its mind, for a new dynamic realism freed from the tired conformist stereotypes of tradition.[36] Of course, as always tends to happen with determined status seekers, these upwardly mobile merchants also, at the same time, yearned for acceptance by the existing elite, and thus ended up embracing many of the values, indeed the stereotypes, of the class to which they aspired.[37] This can be seen not only in their passion for portrait sculpture as such, but also in their unfortunate (and occasionally incongruous) weakness for the heroic, and colossal, nude athletic victor statue, an iconography not suited by design for the commemoration of underexercised businessmen.[38] With realists, a more prudent bourgeois mode prevailed. We know the names of an Athenian couple, Cleopatra and Dioscurides, who lived in the Theater Quarter of Delos and in 138/7 commissioned a pair of life-size his-and-hers statues, which both survive, tantalizingly, minus their heads.[39] Hers is revealing in more ways than one: we note the well-fed bulk, the modest pose (similar, appropriately enough, to that found in allegorical figures of Pudicitia), the suggestion of a transparent wrap, probably Coan silk, above heavy draperies, an odd blend—but one by no means unfamiliar today—of the stiflingly respectable and the erotic. The imitation of light material over heavy is ingenious; but there is something mechanical and mannered, almost rococo, in the folds of the drapery, and something decidedly Victorian about the concept: the physical woman is corseted almost to extinction.

What her husband might have looked like we can guess from a superb bronze head of almost exactly the same period: perhaps a decade or two later, the island's apogee.[40] (In 69, corsairs completed the destruction that Mithridates' forces had begun in 88: the island's support for Rome cost it dear, and it never fully recovered its former prosperity.)[41] It is generally agreed that the portrait is of a Greek, who has been variously, and implausibly, labeled an athlete, a general, or a prince. I doubt whether he was any of these: he looks far more like a rentier whose father made his millions in the slave trade, who was educated at the best philosophical schools in Athens, thus acquiring culture without a grain of originality: rather too fond of good

Fig. 178. Life-size marble statues, *in situ*, of an Athenian couple, Cleopatra and Dioscurides, who lived in the Theater Quarter of Delos (datable by the dedicatory inscription to 138/7 B.C.).
Photo Hirmer.

Fig. 179. Late second-century-B.C. bronze head from Delos.
National Museum, Athens.

food and drink, and suffering from the residual *Angst* and self-dramatizing guilt liable to beset those with more money than talent, who find time hanging heavy on their hands[42]—the epitome, in short, of agonized sensibility bankrolled by a large private income, and exploring the variations of sensuality with the wearily obsessional gourmandise of a Cavafy. It was for men of this stamp that erotic, mildly rococo groups such as the Aphrodite and Pan (ca. 100) were executed, with the goddess modestly (but invitingly) defending herself against the advances of the shaggy, and erect, goat god by placing one protective hand over her private parts, while with the other she wields a sandal (to smack or beckon?), and a small winged *putto* flutters, panderlike, above and between them, one arm extended to each (above, p. 346, fig. 116).[43] There must have been many men like these, on Delos and elsewhere, during the century that followed the sack of Corinth, and learning to cohabit with Roman rule was perhaps the least of their problems.

How far such Greek nabobs leavened Roman taste is another tantalizing question. The evidence is not encouraging. In art as in finance, Gresham's law seems to apply. Dorothy Thompson asks, rhetorically: "Did the appalling collapse of Athenian technique and taste . . . through the second century owe more to the degeneration of a weary spirit or to the debilitating effects of Roman reverence?"[44] The history of the period returns a dusty answer on both counts. About the year 100 a mechanical device for making exact copies of statues, by transferring points from a cast, was developed and came into general use;[45] casting itself was already common. Paintings, too, were regularly reproduced, often in the form of mosaics: witness the street scenes signed by Dioscorides of Samos, datable around 100 but reproducing third-century originals (above, p. 243), and the famous Alexander mosaic from the House of the Faun in Pompeii, which preserves a late fourth-century mural, probably by Philoxenus of Eretria. In sculpture and painting alike, not merely iconographic motifs, but also actual figures, were copied mechanically, as though from a pattern book, and sometimes placed in new contexts for which they were wholly inappropriate.[46] (Webster gives some fascinating instances of this process, e.g., a Dionysus in Maenadic procession who is having his shoe untied: odd, unless one knows that the figure was lifted from a different composition, where he was visiting a comic poet by way of inspiration, and took off his shoes before entering the house.)[47]

Most curious of all, statues now came equipped, regardless of suitability, with a variety of heads:[48] the bald and paunchy *negotiator* could thus, while remaining facially recognizable, assume the physical equipment appropriate for a Greek god. Headless torsos were mass-produced in a variety of flattering styles (not every businessman had the time, or indeed the inclination, for regular physical exercise, let alone a moderate diet), ready to accommodate any portrait. As Polybius noted,[49] the Romans were much attached (in the first instance perhaps through their use of funeral masks)[50] to good likenesses, and the increasing emphasis on objective accuracy in portraiture during the second and first centuries can confidently be ascribed, in large measure, to the requirements of Roman clients. The result was that blend of naturalism and classicizing noted by Christine Havelock.[51] As she says of the Delos bronze head, "the artist seems to mold rather than to carve, to think in terms of soft

Fig. 180. Roman patrician carrying two
portrait busts of his ancestors(?), the so-
called Barberini statue (marble, Rome,
late first century B.C.). The central
figure's head, though ancient, is a
substitute.
Capitoline Museum, Rome. Photo
Deutsches Archäologisches Institut, Rome.

clay or wax rather than hard stone": it is, in Rhys Carpenter's phrase, not so much "glyptic" as "plastic" art.[52] There is a certain vacuity about some of the predominantly classicizing portraits, where introspection is marked, and nostalgic escapism the most notable emotional component.

The new realism, on the other hand, is hard, tough, direct, and brutal. It extends, as we have seen (above, p. 350), to the coin portraits of the Asiatic and Bactrian kings, which similarly offer profiles that are harsher, more uncompromising, less traditionally idealized. It is also particularly associated, from about the mid-second century, with portrait busts (and some likenesses on coins and gems) of Romans. Such so-called Republican portraits, almost all of them executed by Greeks,[53] but very clearly not *of* Greeks, have been found not only in Italy, but also in Greece, the Aegean, and Asia Minor: Delos, not surprisingly, with its large Italian colony, has yielded an exceptionally rich hoard of them.[54] As Smith says, they "seem distinctly Roman and conform very satisfactorily to our idea of what tough Republican Romans ought to look like"; he argues, further, that the often unflattering realism was due not only to the needs of the sitters, who wanted their consular maturity and *auctoritas* emphasized, but also, rather more, to the covert dislike, resentment, and contempt felt by the artists for those who commissioned such portraits; that what we have here, in fact, is a subtle manifestation of an ingrained Greek anti-Romanism that, after the suppression of the Mithridatic revolt, was driven underground, and could only express itself indirectly.

Mithridates was by no means the only man in Anatolia who regarded the Romans as oppressive and arrogant predators, with the insatiable rapacity of the she-wolf that had suckled their founders;[55] but such open attacks were, perforce, abandoned when Rome finally set her seal on the Greek East. (The savage mock servility

Fig. 181. The Copenhagen bust of Pompey the Great (Roman, marble copy [reign of Claudius, 42–54 A.D.] of an original of ca. 50 B.C.). Ny Carlsberg Glyptotek, Copenhagen.

Fig. 182. Drunken old woman. Roman marble copy of an original from the late third or late second century B.C. (date disputed). Pollitt (*AHA* 143) draws attention to her dress, the *peronēma,* which indicates respectable social standing, and thus heightens the irony of her condition.

Staatliche Antikensammlungen und Glyptothek, Munich.

shown to Roman captives in the first century B.C. by Greek pirates is highly reveal-ing in this context.)[56] What remained was the opportunity for subtle denigration, for which the veristic demands of Roman portrait sitters provided an almost perfect opening. The Copenhagen head of Pompey, with its weak chin, piggy eyes, and self-satisfied smirk, is a fine (but by no means isolated) example of the result.[57] The Romans, as far as the Greeks were concerned, were not only foreigners, indeed bar-barians (and thus in line to be delineated on the same footing as dwarfs, Negroes, or elderly drunks), but, worse, "a group of foreigners whom in the second century BC the Greeks were finding increasingly unlikeable."[58] By now it should be very clear what occasioned that dislike. As has been well said, "it is not difficult to understand why the peoples of Asia massacred 80,000 Roman citizens in one day at the bidding of Mithridates Eupator; it is less clear why such horrors were not repeated."[59]

There were successful advances. In painting the combination of classicism and

Fig. 183. "Satyr and Maenad." Wall painting from the House of Epigrams, Pompeii, ca. A.D. 50.
Museo Nazionale, Naples.

the erotic baroque found its most effective expression in a florid, sensuous style not unlike that of Renoir (which it resembles both in palette and in brushwork),[60] and perhaps best expressed in a Pompeian wall painting, datable to about 30 B.C., the "Satyr and Maenad" from the House of the Epigrams.[61] Villard describes it as "a synthesis of all Hellenistic painting: the sense of space and light, the association of chiaroscuro with an impressionistic technique, the three-dimensional and fully expressive rendering of the human figure, the setting borrowed from nature."[62] Not fully baroque, in short, but well on the way. The trouble with most painting of this sort, as the famous group of the Three Graces from Stabiae makes clear,[63] is plain technical incompetence: the aim is clear (and derivative), the execution uncertain. When the execution is sure, the results, as in the so-called Primavera, which evokes Botticelli, can be memorable.[64]

The genre scenes, landscapes, and still lifes that, as we have seen (above, p. 118), were so abundant in Roman art must, it seems certain, have been derived from a Hellenistic tradition, and it is to them that a modern student perhaps finds it easiest to relate his or her own experience and taste, not least as regards the experimental attitude to space and perspective that marks the best of them (e.g., the great Esquiline wall paintings illustrating episodes from the *Odyssey*). Less easily appreciated today is the relentlessly literary attitude to art that hankered after famous scenes from drama, whether on drinking vessels, for example the splendid first-century kantharos decorated with scenes from an Iphigeneia tragedy,[65] or in the wall painting of the modish artist Timomachus of Byzantium (1st c. B.C.). Timomachus was as fashionable in his day as Frederick (later Lord) Leighton in late Victorian London, and for much the same reason, the ability to moralize a tragic dilemma in paint: Iphigeneia confronted with Orestes and Pylades, Medea brooding on the pros and cons of killing her children.[66] No accident that both paintings were the subject of numerous literary epigrams, laboring away at Timomachus's *ēthopoiia*, the tears showing through the threat, the rage in the pity, jealousy palpable through paint, the froth on the lips, the blood on the sword.[67]

Pliny's partiality for painters such as Timomachus is predictable: we know what he (or his source) thought about the emotional excesses of the Pergamene school (above, p. 336).[68] Contemporary Victorian critics said very much the same sort of thing about Leighton, and for very much the same reasons.[69] Julius Caesar bought two of Timomachus's pictures, the Medea and the Ajax, for the vast sum of eighty Attic talents, which perhaps tells us more about contemporary fashion than contemporary art.[70] Yet sometimes the classicizing trend forgot to be moral or literary, stopped fussing with heavy draperies (another weakness, incidentally, of Leighton's), and produced a sensuous masterpiece. It is easy to forget that the great Aphrodite of Melos (better known as the Venus di Milo) was created in the very middle of this late and depressed period, sometime between about 150 and 100 B.C.: a marvelous and dynamic variation, of true originality, on a theme by Lysippus (the Aphrodite of Capua), wholly human, the poised left knee giving the entire torso life and motion, the modeling of the marble fleshlike in its soft mass and warmth, the swelling hips in piquant—and symbolic—contrast to the cool, classical head.[71] The same artist, as Charbonneaux suggested, may well be responsible for the so-called Pseudo-Inopos

Fig. 184. Medea meditating the murder
of her children. Fragment of a wall
painting from Herculaneum, ca. A.D.
70, after an original of ca. A.D. 50.
Museo Nazionale, Naples.

Fig. 185. The Aphrodite of Melos,
more popularly known as the Venus di
Milo (marble, ca. 120–100 B.C.).
Musée du Louvre, Paris. Photo Hirmer.

in the Louvre:[72] this last, ironically enough, has been tentatively identified as a portrait of Mithridates Eupator, whose passion to present himself as the new Alexander is all too apparent from his coin portraits (above, p. 558).

We have already noted the Hellenistic preoccupation with the dynamics of space, with orchestrated architectural landscapes and complexes (above, pp. 168, 351). The economic boom generated by Delos not only resuscitated Piraeus as an international port, but also led to a flurry of repair work and new building in Athens itself, by various hands.[73] In 174 Antiochus Epiphanes, as we have seen (above, p. 526), caused work to be resumed on the gigantic unfinished temple of Olympian Zeus.[74] The Parthenon, ravaged by fire in the early second century, was restored to its pristine splendor, and a second statue of Athena erected in it. The financing of such work remained haphazard, and for the most part dependent on private initiative. Foreign munificence contributed substantially; in Athens itself recourse was

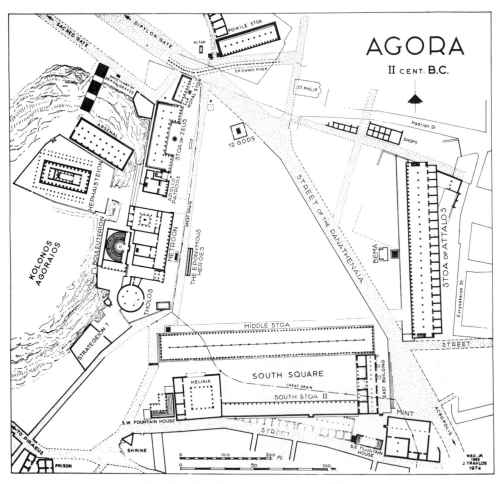

Map 27. The Athenian Agora, ca. 150 B.C.
From Camp, *The Athenian Agora*, p. 169.

Fig. 186. Scale model of the Athenian Agora, second to first century B.C., with the
Acropolis in the background.
Agora Excavations, American School of Classical Studies at Athens.

had to the *epidosis* (above, p. 376) and to *ad hoc* public subscriptions. Between about
150 and 125 improvements were carried out on the Acropolis, in Pericles' concert hall
(the Odeion), around the *temenos* of Dionysus, and elsewhere. Most important from
an architectural viewpoint was the reconstruction of the Agora, to accommodate
the South Stoa, the Stoa of Attalus II, the Hellenistic Metroön,[75] and the portico of
the second temple of Apollo Patroös. The Agora now takes on the appearance of a
wholly organic complex, like the acropolis of Pergamon (above, p. 168).

By the second century this attitude has been extended to private and domestic
building. Unlike classical or earlier Hellenistic houses, those on Delos now reveal
columnar symmetry in the planning of their central court, a pattern suggestive of the
Roman atrium.[76] Yet the Greeks never completely surrendered to Roman order, balance, and symmetry, as the enchantingly irregular Delian house plans make very clear:
"Roman architecture coerces the observer and compels him to follow a path laid out
by every detail of the design. Greek architecture entices the observer, offers him
choices, and finally allows him to remain spiritually free."[77] One fascinating example
of this principle in nonsecular architecture is the temple of Artemis Leukophryene
("White-Browed") at Magnesia-by-Maeander, built about 130. Hermogenes, who
designed it, was one of the greatest Hellenistic architects: his ideas have survived in

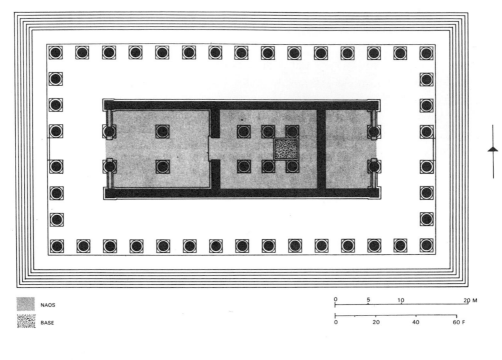

NAOS

BASE

| 0 | 5 | 10 | | 20 M |
| 0 | 20 | | 40 | 60 F |

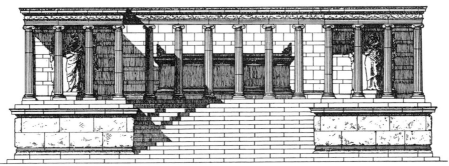

Fig. 187. Temple and altar of Artemis Leucophryene, Magnesia-by-Maeander, by
Hermogenes (early to mid second century B.C.). The elevation of the altar's facade is
seen from the west-southwest. From Charbonneaux, Martin, and Villard,
pp. 354–55, figs. 399 and 402.

part because of their discussion by the Roman writer Vitruvius (ironically enough,
Vitruvius himself was a pragmatist who took little interest in esthetic theory). In his
treatise on architecture Vitruvius noted that Hermogenes, for his temple of Artemis
as elsewhere, eliminated the inner row of columns, though leaving the other dimensions untouched, so that from the outside the temple appeared to be of the normal
dipteral type, with fifteen columns on each side to eight in the façade. But inside, in
fact, a dynamic increase in depth and space had been achieved, enhanced by the
mathematically subtle relationships of columns and intercolumnar spaces (the angle
columns, for instance, were enlarged by $\frac{1}{60}$th).[78]

The effect was a rational pattern ("like an abstract painting," Havelock claims),[79] a neat black-and-white chiaroscuro, a blending of the best in an overall Ionic design with Attic details. To Vitruvius, Hermogenes had been aiming to cut costs while preserving tradition, and in an inflationary age that might be partly true: just as it was also true that the impulse to dedicate such monuments to the old Olympians had sadly diminished. Hermogenes was among the last of a vanishing breed. He had also, said Vitruvius, been opening up a wider cloister for visitors to stroll in, or to use as a shelter in case of rain. Perhaps that is true. But the pure genius is there too, and visible: this temple of Artemis must stand, with the Aphrodite of Melos, as almost the last undeniable achievement of the pure Greek spirit before the advent of that transmuted hybrid, Graeco-Roman civilization. It is only when one looks at the classicizing frieze above the architrave (an echo of the Erechtheion),[80] with its modish, "endlessly monotonous" battle between Greeks and Amazons,[81] that one realizes how much has changed, and how subtly, since those proud young Athenian cavalrymen were set up to caracole on the great frieze of the Parthenon, three hundred years before. In 54 B.C. a Roman, Appius Claudius Pulcher (another great abstracter of Greek *objets-d'art*),[82] vowed a new propylaea to the precinct of Demeter at Eleusis, to mark his consulship. Like the designer of the frieze for the temple of Artemis at Magnesia, he (or his architect) sought inspiration from the fifth-century Erechtheion, which also had a porch with Ionic columns, frieze, and caryatids. Yet the overall design, with its excess of floral ornamentation, could never be mistaken for what it set out to evoke.[83]

What we see, then, to sum up, is a strong neoclassicist trend in all the visual arts, stimulated by Roman patronage, delimited by a persistent respect for Athens, yet at the same time offset by an element of baroque realism that manifested itself particularly in the erotic, the pathological, the grotesque. While the public image remained pompous, traditional, and self-assertive, the private art patron glutted himself on *Angst*, narcissism, and *nostalgie de la boue*; there is a certain delectable irony about rudely realistic portrait heads being clapped on mass-produced athletic torsos. Self-indulgent entrepreneurism and a nostalgic yearning for Old Masters between them set up some very curious tensions; yet the artistic trend they embodied—very much alive and, in cases like the Aphrodite of Melos, capable of producing an indubitable masterpiece—had a quality all its own, instantly recognizable, the forerunner of syncretic Augustanism.

All, all, of a piece throughout, as Dryden wrote in his *Secular Masque*: the most famous verse of that famous chorus could almost serve as an epitaph on the Hellenistic age. The chase had a beast in view indeed; the wars, for the most part, brought nothing about; and the lovers were untrue, many notoriously so. *'Tis well an Old Age is out, and time to begin a New*. Long before Actium, long before Caesar first set eyes on Cleopatra, Rome had set that new world in motion, and thereby given the old one its quietus.

CHAPTER 33

FOREIGN AND MYSTERY CULTS, ORACLES, ASTROLOGY, MAGIC

We have seen the public, official side of belief develop through the Hellenistic period; time, now, to look at the private scene, that curious underworld of exotic cults and associations, often foreign in origin; of curse tablets, spiked wax dolls, and formulas guaranteed to induce passion or dispose of enemies; of a proliferating variety of demons, friendly or malevolent; of mystery cults, syncretic distillations of Pythagoreanism and Orphism, oracles, miraculous cures, and, above all, astrology. Though the contrast with the ruler cults is apparent (above, p. 396: there is not only the political polarity, between conformism and individualism, but also a psychological, almost a theological split, of dark versus light), nevertheless both phenomena share some kind of common impulse: the urge to retreat from self-determination, to seek authority outside the self, to abandon the confidently rational approach to life and the universe that had defined all intellectual pioneers of the archaic or classical periods. Once again, we find the world of belief and ideas adjusting itself to patterns established by new forms of earthly government, the microcosm projecting its own macrocosm.

E. R. Dodds struck to the heart of the matter with brutally accurate concision when he insisted that anyone "who treats another human being as divine thereby assigns to himself the relative status of a child or an animal."[1] The Athenian hymn to Demetrius (above, p. 398), the divine honors voted to various Hellenistic monarchs, even the cult of Tyche, all imply a kind of personal surrender, a helpless dependence on some external force or object—even if, in the case of Tyche, that object merely crystallizes the negative, unknown, random, and, thus, arguably unpredictable element of existence. But against unpredictability was ranged something far worse, the other face of the same coin: a deterministic fate (*heimarmenē*) that, like most Hellenistic governments, made a macabre mockery of the principle of free will, of self-determination. Thus to manipulate, even to control, this fate for personal ends became an increasingly attractive compensation fantasy for the individual as political and economic conditions deteriorated.

The antisocial challenge could be either positive or negative, though in both cases it depended, to a greater or lesser degree, on the abrogation of the thorough-going rationalism that had underpinned all classical progress. In positive terms, it could range from a binding-spell to a full-scale slave revolt, neither being a phenom-enon primarily governed by reason. The negative alternative is well symbolized by the declared goal of the Hellenistic philosophers (cf. above, p. 55): absence of pain, grief, or disturbing emotions of any sort, the condition of being left alone by the world, a string of abstract nouns all beginning with the alpha privative, which, like a minus sign, negates what follows. (The peace that passes all understanding is less a paradox than we sometimes suppose: understanding, reason, has no part in it.) In all cases, positive and negative alike, men turned their backs on, and often worked ac-tively to subvert, not only the sociopolitical structure of their society, but, in a very real sense, the natural order as they perceived it. Neither offered them hope; self-realization would be sought, if at all, through alternative means. To hang one's fu-ture on the whim of a divinized king, a demon, a magical aphrodisiac, or the va-garies of Tyche (whether or not the individual flattered himself that he was actually able to control, or even influence, any of these erratic forces) was thus merely a matter of personal choice: the principle remained the same.

What was more, the rising ground-swell of old popular superstitions (none of these fads was new) began to acquire a supposititious basis of intellectual respec-tability. Astrology, for instance, had the support of Stoicism[2]—was, indeed, a natu-ral upshot of the Stoic world view—while Cynicism, by in effect proclaiming itself a counterculture (cf. p. 613), opened the way, as other countercultures have done, to an uncritical acceptance of some very odd principles simply because they were anti-establishment. Generalizations about the *Zeitgeist* are always dangerous, and it is probably safe to say—indeed, private inscriptions and papyri tend to confirm—that throughout the three centuries we are investigating the average individual got on with his or her everyday life very much as always, no more lonely or alienated, inso-far as we can judge, than at any other period of history. Yet the signs of spiritual malaise, of inner drift, are also unmistakably present: perhaps more noticeable (again as always) among intellectuals, for whom our literary evidence is more plentiful. In the Hellenistic era itself, indeed, this kind of private distress was not, for the most part, openly recognized (however clearly philosophy, art, and literature might reflect it), since as far as externals went little had changed: city-states still existed, local councils still went through the motions of democratic government, only the central spirit of the old system had died. Were not the Olympian deities still officially wor-shipped? Did not every *polis* retain its traditional divine patron? All true; and yet the image had grown dead and hollow, eaten away at the heart by the boreworms of political impotence, creeping secularism, social fragmentation, loss of cohesive iden-tity. Cities and empires had become too vast and heterogeneous to give adequate psychological support to inheritors of the old, local *polis* tradition: their society was no longer either integrated or manageable. The individual was thrown back on him-self; and though that, precisely, had been the criterion of judgment demanded by all Greek intellectuals, the loss of the *polis*'s tightly structured support system made such an isolated position hard to maintain.[3]

It was even harder when Hellenistic thinkers were stubbornly refusing to admit the passions as an operative factor of the human condition. Plato and Aristotle had both known better: they might want to curb the irrational element in man, by legislative control if need be, but they never (perhaps on that account) underrated its power. By the end of the fifth century this particular fallacy had been corrected the hard way, as we can see by reading, first, Thucydides on the Peloponnesian War, and then Euripides' *Bacchae*. By the third century, however, the philosophers were once again proclaiming that the ideal wise man attained his goal simply by taking thought, through the instrument of sovereign reason, and that the "so-called passions were merely errors of judgment, or morbid disturbances resulting from errors of judgment."[4] This attitude was, it goes without saying, an instinctive counterreaction to the widespread abrogation of reason we have been discussing; yet in attempting to disarm unreason simply by ignoring the passions, it not only failed to confront the problem, but in a sense compounded it. The objectives to be attained were altruism of action and judgment, plus personal inner detachment, ideals that, whatever their intrinsic merits, can be seen as fundamentally asocial. Detachment is the polar opposite of involvement, and what these contractors-out ended by doing (like Jonah taking ship for Tarshish) was running away from the dilemmas of their age rather than facing, let alone solving them.

A. N. Whitehead once wrote that "religion is what the individual does with his own solitariness," and for the Hellenistic centuries this apothegm offers an increasingly accurate picture as time goes by.[5] Much of what the man in the street did in such a context was old-fashioned in the extreme. This should not surprise us. Throughout Greek history there is a constant tension between intellectual advance (which came early and moved fast, the true "Greek miracle") and the conservative, socially binding forces of traditional belief and custom. Greek head was always at odds with Greek heart; old tribal shibboleths contested new civic statutes: Antigone and Creon, honest extremists both, could find no common ground on which to argue. Irrational beliefs, often archetypal, die hard, and frequently do not die at all: J. C. Lawson's *Modern Greek Folklore and Ancient Greek Religion* (1910) gives a startling account of the degree to which pre-Christian superstitions (concerning the Olympian deities, Charon, Nereids, Gorgons, centaurs, and much else that raised derisive snickers among ancient intellectuals) persisted into the twentieth century.[6] It had been the error of the fifth-century Protagorean movement, as it was later of the Stoics and Epicureans, to ignore this ineradicable element in human nature.

Further, what most often survives is the tangible ritual or taboo, long after any understanding of its significance has passed away. To quote Dodds again (by far the most perceptive analyst of this trend), "for the *vis inertiae* that keeps this sort of thing going—what Matthew Arnold once called 'the extreme slowness of things'—no rationalist ever makes sufficient allowance."[7] We have already seen middle-class Hellenistic women visiting the healing shrine of Asclepius, and attending a concert—sponsored by Queen Arsinoë, in the royal palace at Alexandria—to celebrate the festival of Adonis (above, pp. 243 ff.), and though both occasions are in the nature of social outings, they reveal a world as solidly predicated on religious obser-

Fig. 188. Nereid riding the sea monster
Ketos. Silver-gilt relief (ca. 130 B.C.) on
the lid of a pyxis found at Canosa, near
Taranto.
Museo Nazionale, Taranto. Photo Leonard
von Matt.

vance as that of Orthodox Greece today. We also find a proliferation of private religious clubs, whose members called themselves Apolloniasts or Sarapiasts, Her-
maists or Iobacchi.[8] Again, one senses a desperate reaching-out after identity and
community: those who can no longer be meaningfully involved with their society
can at least strive for oneness with God. The ties of the *polis* had broken down, and
these clubs enabled persons isolated in the new urban solitude of megalopolis to
reach out, through formal worship and shared banquets, not only to a communal
deity, but also to one another. At the same time we should not underestimate (however hard it may be to document) the more positive appeal that much of this new
religious efflorescence implies: to do so would be, in a sense, to compound the nega-
tivism of the philosophers. The essence of *enthousiasmos* is, precisely, enthusiasm;
and the devotees of Sabazios or Isis, the adepts of eschatological Orphism, the ecstatic firewalkers and casters of magical spells, the Trophonian initiates with their
visions of eternity (below, p. 594) all, whatever their prior motives, had acquired the
entrée to a new, rich, and immensely exhilarating world beyond that of their mundane diurnal existence.

For those—and there were many of them—in Antioch or Alexandria, even in
Athens, who found scant comfort from the old Greek pantheon, foreign cults, particularly those with a strong emotional and enthusiastic content, or the various mystery religions offering salvation in the afterlife by way of compensation for misery
on earth, proved immensely attractive.[9] Strabo, indeed, reports that the Athenians
"welcomed so many of the foreign cults that they were lampooned by their comic
playwrights for it."[10] This trend provided the leaven that slowly expanded the old
local cults into something more syncretic and universal. It is to be observed that the
traffic is virtually all one way, with the Greeks absorbing indigenous gods for their
own purposes (cf. above, p. 396): we find few, if any, cases of the native population
taking over a Greek deity. The Egyptians, as we have seen (p. 406), remained impervious to the attractions of the syncretized Ptolemaic Sarapis, whose worshippers

were, if not exclusively Greek, at least members of the bureaucratic or commercial elite. Isis of the Thousand Names (scarcely an exaggeration, as the Delian inscriptions testify)[11] was adapted for Greek worshippers, for example on Rhodes, in avatars that her pharaonic priests would hardly have recognized, even though she did bring a good deal of home-grown ritual with her: the black robes adopted by certain priestly brotherhoods on Delos are a case in point.[12] The so-called Isis aretalogies (above, p. 410), litanies of praise to the goddess, stress her universalism and multiple powers: she is Queen of Heaven, Mistress of Fate, inventor of all mankind's arts, and, later, the syncretic embodiment of every goddess from Leto to Demeter, from Hera to Aphrodite.

Her cult was akin to that of the Anatolian Great Mother, Ma or Cybele, with her youthful consort (Attis, Adonis, etc.).[13] The essential difference lay in the ecstatic element that formed so important a part of the Anatolian cult, and which produced not only the ability to prophesy, but also (like some modern ecstatic cults, including, in Greece itself, that of the Anastenarides, or Thracian firewalkers)[14] insensitivity to physical pain. The priests who served Cybele, like Attis himself in the original legend, were eunuchs who had castrated themselves in a climactic ritual act of devotion.[15] Cybele was a fertility goddess, mistress of beasts (she is regularly portrayed with attendant lions),[16] deity of the wild hills, of nature in the raw. Her worship was introduced into Greece during the fifth century: late at Athens, where it met with some resistance,[17] and seems to have been assimilated to that of Demeter.[18] More oddly, the cult of Cybele—centered upon a black baetylic stone from Pessinus in Phrygia—was officially imported to Rome in 205/4,[19] a strange by-product of the Hannibalic wars, which apparently witnessed a great increase of *superstitio* throughout the Republic.[20] Though Cybele's worship was for long restricted to the goddess's temple on the Palatine, and maintained only by native (i.e., non-Roman) priests, in a kind of ritual quarantine, the interesting thing is that she was admitted at all. In the end, under the empire, her worship became universal:[21] it would be hard to find any serious Roman art collection that does not possess some artifact or image associated with her.

Other similar Anatolian deities—the Thraco-Phrygian Bendis and Sabazios, Atargatis the Syrian fish goddess—had long been acclimatized throughout the Greek world by traveling sailors and merchants, and had acquired a growing band of devotees. Bendis was established in Piraeus as early as 430/29,[22] and a century later, to the year (330), we find Demosthenes ridiculing Aeschines for his participation in the rites of Sabazios,[23] while the cult of Atargatis was known in mainland Greece from the third century, and in 128/7 found a home on Delos.[24] This island in particular seems to have become a center, from the second century on, for foreign cults of every description:[25] hardly surprising when we recall its function as a great international clearinghouse (above, p. 384). Many of these religions were mystery cults: they required initiation, demanded secrecy of the initiates, promised salvation (*sōtēria*) in the afterlife, and sometimes offered visions or epiphanies here on earth. Olympianism had been strongly bound up with family and *polis*, but now the individual was adrift in an indifferent world and free to choose his own gods. Not sur-

Fig. 189. Bronze group of Cybele, the Great Mother Goddess (Magna Mater),
enthroned on a chariot drawn by lions.
Metropolitan Museum of Art, New York. Gift of Henry G. Marquand, 1897.

prisingly, he tended to pick those that could best replace the emotional and cultural support structure that he had lost.

It is thus no accident if the old cults that survived most strongly were those of Eleusinian Demeter, and of Dionysus,[26] a god from whom, as we have seen, the Ptolemies claimed descent. The mysteries of Dionysus, with their background of frenetic mountain climbing (*oreibasia*) followed by the dismemberment (*sparagmos*) and eating raw (*ōmophagia*) of wild animals—an ecstatic cult if ever there was one— were restricted to women. To judge from Euripides' *Bacchae*, they may well have been causing alarm in the *polis* by the close of the fifth century; they were undoubtedly flourishing two hundred years or so later.[27] Their Latin equivalent, the Bacchanalia, had to be forcibly controlled by senatorial decree in 186[28]—a decade after Flamininus had proclaimed Greek freedom (p. 311), and no more than twenty years after the sacred black stone of the Great Mother had been brought to Rome from Pessinus. Indeed, the second century (for reasons that by now should be clear enough) seems to have ushered in a general wave of religious emotionalism throughout the Mediterranean; if *bien-pensant* conservatives expressed shock, the poor, the desperate, and the dispossessed were (in every sense of the word) ecstatic.[29]

Initiatory rites for Isis, Mithras, and Cybele all seem to have been developed during the late Hellenistic period,[30] at a time when, for an ever-increasing proportion of the populace, bleak prospects on this earth made the promise of salvation in the hereafter look peculiarly attractive: it was a great age for demotic eschatology. The Cabiri, Phrygian deities who had a cult on the island of Samothrace, patrons and protectors of sailors, and specially favored by Ptolemy II's queen, Arsinoë (above, p. 145),[31] were similarly associated with mysteries: it was as initiates of the Cabirian cult that Philip II of Macedon and his future wife, the Epirot princess Olympias, traditionally first met.[32]

Most interesting of all is the development of Orphism during this period. Plato, who was strongly influenced by Orphic doctrines,[33] both in his myths and as regards his advice to "care for the soul,"[34] did as much as anyone to give the movement intellectual respectability. Orphics believed that the Titans had devoured Zagreus, the Divine Child, whose heart, saved by Athena, was used by Zeus to form a new child, Dionysus.[35] Zeus blasted the Titans to ashes, and from those ashes man was created, containing thus elements both of the divine, and of the evil nature of the Titans. The latter was associated with the physical body (*sōma*), the former with the soul or spirit, of which the body was regarded as a prison or tomb (*sēma*): hence the popular saying *sōma sēma*, "The body is a tomb," since it imprisoned the divine spark.[36] Physical abstinence—from killing animals or eating flesh, and from sexual indulgence—was perhaps the best-known tenet of Orphism. Through vegetarianism, chastity, offerings, and initiation Orphic devotees were promised purification from guilt, and freedom from punishment in the afterlife, a happy existence among the fellowship of the righteous; while non-initiates, who had failed to go through the steps of purification in this world, were doomed to stew for ever in the filth and mud of the underworld.[37]

This eschatological scenario, besides casting its shadow ahead to the familiar Christian version of heaven and hell, also hints strongly at the filling of a real, and growing, psychological need.[38] We noted earlier the fading of belief in a traditional Hades, the anxiety evident in epitaphs from the close of the classical era (pp. 175–76). Orphism offered a new spiritual topography of the afterworld for its elect, with detailed and specific instructions as to how the initiate should behave on arrival. A series of inscriptions on gold leaf from tombs in southern Italy and Crete give us a rare glimpse into this initiates' heaven.[39] The following text was composed in hexameters:[40]

> You will find, on the left of the House of Hades, a wellspring,
> And standing beside it a white cypress.
> Do not go anywhere near that wellspring;
> But you will find another beyond the Lake of Memory,
> Cold water flowing forth, and in front there are guardians.
> Say: "I am a child of earth and starry heaven,
> But my race is heavenly. This you know yourselves.
> I am parched with thirst and I perish. Give me quickly

Cold water flowing forth from the Lake of Memory."
Then they will give you to drink from that sacred wellspring,
And thereafter you shall lord it with the other heroes.

Other, more fragmentary passages contain tantalizing phrases such as "I have flown out of the sorrowful weary circle," or "A kid I have fallen into milk."[41]

It is all a world away from the civic cults of the Olympians, and indeed to begin with, certainly in the late fifth and early fourth centuries, seems, as we might expect, to have aroused considerable social prejudice. Orphism was associated in the vulgar mind (not always unfairly) with magic. The satyrs in Euripides' *Cyclops* claim to know "a real good incantation of Orpheus, that will make the stake go into his skull by itself."[42] In the *Hippolytus* (428), Theseus, convinced that Hippolytus has seduced Phaedra, attacks his chastity, vegetarianism, and devotion to Orphic texts as a hypocritical sham,[43] a cover for rampant lechery.[44] By the late Hellenistic period, with the bonds of the *polis* broken and spiritual solipsism the norm, Orphism, or something like it, had become much more a commonplace, less the socially suspect anomaly.[45]

A deteriorating economy may well have helped: with more and more people living on the edge of starvation, and subject to absolute arbitrary government in this life, the hope of paradise in the next one—or even of the existence of an afterlife at all[46]—must have seemed increasingly attractive. There was also that other comfort available to the downtrodden initiate, the fantasy of future punishment and hellfire for those powerful enemies who flourished in authority like the proverbial green bay tree here on earth, but yet might, granted cosmic justice, pay for their sins with interest in the unknown hereafter. Adeimantus, in Plato's *Republic*,[47] delivers a stinging attack on those itinerant magicians who, in the name of Orpheus, offer to relieve the wealthy of their sins,[48] or indeed to work mischief against their enemies, by means of sacrifices and spells, to smooth their passage to the (by now decidedly alarming) afterlife, to bend the very gods to their will. There is an oddly modern flavor about this scenario, standard among ancient critics of Orphism and its initiatory rites: their denunciation of the whole thing as an elaborate, and blasphemous, confidence trick, falsely promising absolution (not to mention eternal drunkenness in the hereafter),[49] sounds exactly like a fundamentalist attack on Catholicism. It is interesting, too, to find what we might call eschatological class warfare in full swing as early as the fourth century. The have-nots were, clearly, predicting the pre-Christian equivalent of Dante's Inferno for the haves; and the haves, in alarm, fell easy victims (as they have done throughout history) to the panaceas of spiritual mountebanks.

An odd resemblance can be traced between the vision revealed by these Orphic tablets and that associated with the oracular shrine of Trophonius,[50] at Lebadeia, near Mt. Helicon.[51] As we might expect, many local oracles took on a new lease of life in the Hellenistic period:[52] Branchidae, Claros, Didyma, Dodona, Corope in Thessaly, Argos, Ephyre (site of an ominously named "Oracle of the Dead").[53] Delphi, after falling into the hands of the Aetolians, became politically suspect abroad, and since the mid-fourth century the shrines no longer, in a more skeptical age, got their earlier volume of official diplomatic inquiries. But the private consultations, no less predictably, skyrocketed. In Egypt there were even manuals produced for the guidance of inquirers, with lists of stock questions, which offer a bizarre glimpse into prevalent obsessions and anxieties: "Am I to be divorced from my wife? Have I been poisoned? Shall I get my property?"[54] In an uncertain world, where men were increasingly loath to be responsible for their own decisions, and indeed often felt themselves mere puppets, jerked from point to point by the requirements of a Fate as inscrutable as it was inflexible, divine oracular fiat was one way of having the future mapped out on the individual's behalf. What was fixed by Fate could, given especial skills or insights, be predicted. It might not be what one wanted to hear; but forewarned at least was forearmed.

The appeal of Trophonius was doubly strong, because devotees got not only, or not primarily, an oracle in the strict sense of that term, but also a mystery cult that provided the initiate with a very literal *rite de passage*.[55] Pausanias, writing from his own personal experience, has left us a detailed description of this: "our only fully circumstantial narrative of the procedure of an oracle recorded by an actual enquirer."[56] The consultant had first to spend some days in a building sacred to Tyche and the Good Spirit (*Agathos Daimōn*), preparing himself and observing a regimen of abstinence. When he was ready he was taken by night, after the sacrifice of a ram, to two adjacent springs, of Forgetfulness and Memory. The water of Forgetfulness (*Lēthē*) was to clear his mind of all previous impressions; that of Memory (*Mnēmosynē*) to ensure that he recalled what he saw during his descent (*katabasis*). The link with Orphism is clear; but at Lebadeia it was the living initiate who had a vision of the afterworld. As Jane Harrison said, "Man makes the next world in the image of this present."[57]

The shrine itself was set on the mountainside, above a grove (its exact site remains in dispute). A white marble wall, about the size of a small circular threshing floor, and something over two feet high, enclosed a vertical shaft down into the earth, some twelve feet deep and six in diameter, and shaped like "a pot for baking bread in." The consultant was sent down this on a light portable ladder. At the bottom he found a small opening in the wall, flush with the floor, eighteen inches wide by nine high. He lay down on his back and put his feet, then his knees, through the hole, clutching a pair of sacrificial barley cakes kneaded with honey, a placatory offering to the sacred snakes he would encounter.[58] At this point he was sucked clean through the hole by some tremendous (and unexplained) force, "just as a man might be dragged down by the swirl of a strong and swift river," as Pausanias puts it, and the central part of his revelatory experience began.

The future was apparently revealed to initiates in different ways: some had visions, others heard voices. The only description of such a vision we have is that of one Timarchus, recounted by Plutarch[59]—Pausanias, tantalizingly, says not a word about what *he* heard or saw—and is generally dismissed as an elaborate fiction. But since all those who went through this strange experience (emerging feet first the way they had come) were required to write an account of what they had been shown or told, and to dedicate in the precinct the tablet on which they wrote it, we may assume that the general pattern of the ordeal was well known, and Plutarch is not likely to have diverged far from it. His initiate has the trancelike sensation of the sutures in his head parting and releasing his soul, which "spread out like a sail." He also had something that sounds oddly like a mescaline-induced vision: "When he looked up . . . he saw islands lit up by one another with soft fire, assuming first one color, then another, like a dye, as the light kept changing with their mutations." He also heard cries and lamentations coming from a great abyss, that (as he was told) of Hades, and was given answers to his questions concerning the underworld and the afterlife by a disembodied voice from the darkness. How these various effects were produced we can only surmise. What is of rather more interest is the fact that such an elaborately traumatic enactment of rebirth should have found so ready a market. The age was hungry for visions, for miracles, for knowledge of what lay beyond the boundaries of nature and reason: Plutarch's Timarchus was told he would die in three months, and did.

Another route into the unknown, this time at a truly cosmic level, was through the newly popular pseudoscience of astrology. I say "newly popular," because astrology was in fact very old. It seems to have been invented in Babylonia,[60] where it was elaborated from about 600 onwards in a rigid and complex series of sidereal computations.[61] Thence it spread to Egypt, where it picked up a good deal of local material,[62] and acquired real popularity in Greece only from the third century onwards, though both Herodotus and Plato show signs of acquaintance with its principles,[63] and Theophrastus is reported to have admired it as an exotic foreign art.[64] The Hellenized Babylonian priest Berossos, working for the Seleucid court (ca. 280: above, p. 190), did much to spread its tenets.[65] At first many intellectuals, including Eudoxus and Epicurus,[66] still strong in the tradition of classical rationalism, had been properly skeptical of its supposed ability to predict, in detail, the course of individual lives; on the other hand, it clearly influenced the thinking of Zeno of Citium, an accident with momentous consequences.[67] As time went on it gained more and more ground, till by the mid-second century it had won a commanding position among thinking men. Paradoxically, its technical and theoretical basis[68]—not for nothing were astrologers known in Rome as *mathematici*—ensured (contrary to what we might expect) that though it quickly caught on at the top, it only later spread down, in vulgarized form, to the masses. The earliest datable Greek horoscope belongs to the year 62 B.C., and this is the period when popular astrology first begins to establish itself.

The Stoics in particular, as we might expect, found the principles behind astrology eminently compatible with their view of the world.[69] Just as in physics the notion of inherent "natures" (*physeis*), or "properties," "powers" (*dynameis*), and, above all, "affinities" (*sympatheiai*) was grafted onto the Aristotelian concept of the unity of matter and the activization of bodies (*energeia*) to produce the bastard science of alchemy (the alchemist began by applying affinities and antipathies to lead), so in astrology we find the same premise—that the *dynameis* in one substance can affect those in another by natural sympathy—extended to include the heavenly bodies. Since fixed laws governed the motions of the planets and stars, a doctrine of analogous correspondence between heavenly and terrestrial bodies meant that men's actions and movements likewise followed fixed and predictable paths, determinable by computation. The fate that ruled the heavens shaped all mortal lives; monarchy on earth reflected astral dispensations. This was the enskyment of Tyche with a vengeance, and it is not hard to see how the Hellenistic age came to accept it. The introduction of Babylon, after Alexander's conquests, into the orbit of Hellenism had indeed proved to be "a conjunction that affected both cultures."[70]

The paradox of the matter is that while astrologers were busy setting up fixed correspondences between the macrocosm and the microcosm, a preparation, at several removes, for the medieval Ladder of Being, simultaneously the true science of astronomy was taking vast strides forward (above, pp. 453 ff.), and it is very often a hard business disentangling the two. The commonly made claim that astrology entirely eclipsed its legitimate sister science is at best a misleading half-truth.[71] Certainly in the second century the exact sciences declined (above, p. 453), but astronomical research never seems to have been entirely abandoned. Like nettles and dock leaves, astronomy and astrology for long flourished together,[72] and scientific originality was no inoculation against a belief in astral influences: not only Pythagoras and Hipparchus, but Kepler, Newton, and Tycho Brahe all subscribed in some way to such convictions. The treatise (late second century?) supposedly written by a (mythical) Egyptian king Nechepso and his priest Petosiris[73]—an air of hoary antiquity would, of course, make it sound more authentic—became the basis for the development and refinement of astrology throughout the *oikoumenē*, reaching a high peak of popularity under the Roman empire.

The Stoics, who held a similarly deterministic view of fate (*heimarmenē*), and also believed that the universe was an organic whole structured and held together by affinitive sympathies, above all that the motions of the heavenly bodies directly affected mankind,[74] took up the burden of this rigid rubbish, this ineluctable wheel of fate (no wonder Orphic initiates were glad to escape from it) with antiscientific enthusiasm. On the frieze of the Great Altar at Pergamon (and, thus, before the mid-second century B.C.) a variety of astral figures—Orion and Boötes, the Sun and Moon, Night, Dawn, and the Four Winds—are found, unlikely support troops for reason, fighting alongside the gods against the forces of darkness (see p. 356). Astrology, in short, was proving quite appallingly popular, and more ineradicable than even its most ardent advocates could have imagined early in the Hellenistic era. Rational men like Panaetius and Cicero, or, later, Plotinus, fulminated against it; their arguments proved hopeless when faced with the stubborn mindless glacis of public faith.[75] People wanted to believe in the stars; they still do.[76] Perhaps the greatest boost to this credo in antiquity was provided by Panaetius's student Poseidonius of Apamea (135–50), a Stoic philosopher and polymath who believed in the cosmos as a sentient, living entity,[77] was convinced that fate governed all human actions,[78] accepted the concept of universal *sympatheia*,[79] and had the reputation of himself being a leading astrologer.[80] Poseidonius is also notable, or notorious, for his application of the concept of *sympatheia* to the heliocentric theory, which resulted in something very like a solar theology; this approach he seems to have inherited from Cleanthes (cf. p. 458), and its effect, for example the parallel between human guiding reason (*hēgemonikon*) and the sun's rule over the universe, had already become widespread enough to provide both Antiochus Epiphanes and Aristonicus of Pergamon with a recognizable, universal, and highly potent symbol for their theories of government (above, pp. 394, 437).[81]

As Tarn pointed out, "the English language is full of the terminology of this outworn creed; men are still jovial, mercurial, or saturnine, talk of fortunate conjunctions of events, believe in unlucky numbers, and thank their stars."[82] The supposed importance of sidereal conjunctions at the day and hour of one's birth (or, alternatively, one's conception, harder to fix with precision, but astrologically more potent),[83] the belief underlying the whole notion of a personal horoscope, had a long history: in Greece it went back at least as far as Philochorus of Athens (340–263), the early Hellenistic historian who also, in 306, held the office of "seer and inspector of sacred victims" (*mantis kai hieroskopos*).[84] Too few people, even today, appreciate the inherent cosmic lunacy of disproportion in the thought that our daily relationships and fortunes are dictated by astral motions: "And I gaze at the planets in wonder / At the signs and the portents they send / All to warn me to be careful / In dealings concerning a friend."[85] The mathematical element, with its spurious air of scientific objectivity, proved, and still proves, irresistible. No less a scholar than Otto Neugebauer is on record as saying that "compared with the background of religion, magic and mysticism, the fundamental doctrines of astrology are pure science."[86] That the axioms on which it rested were mistaken is less important, Neugebauer seems to suggest, than the attitude of mind that promoted astrology as a serious discipline; and historiographically speaking this may well be true. After all, if the moon had the power to move the sea, why not to control human lives?[87] As Neugebauer shrewdly concludes, "the ease of such a transformation from science to humbug is not difficult to exemplify in our modern world." It is interesting to note that astrology even drove out, to a great extent, older methods of Greek and Roman divination. While intellectuals opted for an impersonal, abstract *heimarmenē*, popular astrology reverted to a kind of substitute Olympian formula, treating the heavenly bodies as anthropomorphized gods, who "could be pleased or offended and so were suitable objects of prayer and cult."[88] Once the sentient life of the cosmos had been conceded, this was an inevitable development.

The principle of affinity also applied, *a fortiori*, to the less intellectual, more arbitrary practice of magic, which could be carried out either by professionals (i.e., witches or magicians) or else by enthusiastic amateurs, more often than not those suffering from hopeless or unrequited passions. We have already seen how Simaetha, the middle-class lady in Theocritus's *Idyll* 2, living with a single maid in genteel poverty, no *hetaira* but a betrayed lover, and clearly not so young as she was,[89] in some desperation goes about exploiting the principle of sympathy for her own ends (above, p. 243). While the maid, Thestylis, strews barley on the fire, she is to say "I strew the bones of Delphis" (18 ff.). Simaetha herself makes the formulaic pronouncement "As the bay crackles loud when it catches fire, / And suddenly flares up, and we see it no more, not even its ash, / So may the flesh of Delphis waste in the flame" (24–26). Torn between desire and hatred, she ranges through a corresponding variety of spells: her faithless lover's flesh and bones are to be wasted, but it is far from certain whether the impulse behind this direction is erotic or murderous.[90] Indeed, she finally admits that if her love philters fail, she has "evil *pharmaka*" (drugs or spells, or both) that will leave him knocking at hell's gate (159–62).

Behind the assumption of enforcement through *sympatheia*—like to like (*similia similibus*), the part for the whole (*pars pro toto*), a belief that explains the abstraction of hair or nail clippings from ancient barbershops—we can glimpse a whole range of grim magical practices: not least the wax doll pierced with needles and melted, the chill lead tablet scrawled with curses and transfixed, those *katadesmoi* or *defixiones* of which increasing numbers are found in the Hellenistic and Graeco-Roman world from the fourth century onwards.[91] One lead tablet shows us a certain Antigone (whose position seems to have been very similar to Simaetha's) going on public record with a denial that she ever tried to poison Asclepiades (probably her husband), or to encompass his death through others, and invoking condign punishment on herself at the hands of Demeter if she should be forsworn.[92] This is one of a group of tablets found in the sanctuary of Demeter at Cnidos; others invoke conditional curses upon any who may try to alienate the affections of the dedicator's husband, or who falsely accuse her of working spells against him, or those who, even more specifically, came and beat her up.[93] These, however, are exceptional; most often the curse tablet relies on its own inherent power rather than appealing to a deity.

The relation between such Hellenistic phenomena and the later Graeco-Egyptian magical papyri (none prior to the second century A.D., though clearly embodying older material)[94] is very close,[95] but also shows changes inseparable from the spread and consolidation of Roman imperial rule.[96] The papyri, even more than the curse tablets, are cosmopolitan to a remarkable degree. They abound in Egyptian, Babylonian, Iranian, Jewish, and, later, Coptic divine names, whether of spirits, demons, angels, or deities.[97] By a nice extension of imperial court procedures, techniques are prescribed for acquiring a spirit as coadjutor or mentor (*paredros*),[98] for obtaining an introduction or commendation (*systasis*) to the sun god, for exploiting the hieratic order of divine precedence by using a senior demon to threaten, or countermand the orders of, a junior one. The magical practice known as "traducement" (*diabolē*), which consisted of informing on one's rival magician to the moon (e.g., in respect of inadequate sacrifices or alleged slanderous statements),[99] bears more than a passing resemblance to the unpleasant practice of denunciation (*delatio*) by professional imperial informers. The invocations, conjurations, and formal acts of flattery recall, with their neat asyndetic rhetoric, not only the aretalogies of Isis (pp. 410–11), but also much imperial encomiastic literature. The cosmic universality of *sympatheia* so dear to Stoic thinkers here acquires paradoxical confirmation. As human institutions change, so changes the spirit world: man once again can be observed creating God (or rather, in this case, a whole gallery of demons) in his own image. To read the magical papyri sometimes suggests, uncomfortably, what life must have been like for a backstairs intriguer at the Roman court; they contain, encapsulated and transmuted, the "dreams of grandeur of small men."[100]

Fig. 190. Two specimens of magical
papyri, taken from texts of the fourth
century A.D. (provenience uncertain).
Musée du Louvre, Paris. Photo Réunion des
Musées Nationaux; British Library, London.

What links these later spell books with the more universal and perennial types of love magic, *envoûtement*, or incantations known to us from the Hellenistic period is the furious faith they all reveal in the capacity of individuals, once they have mastered the secret formulas and collected the proper *materia magica*, to draw on the sympathetic connections inherent in the universe to achieve any desired end, from the inducement of erotic desire to the disabling of a racehorse.[101] Most of the love charms are a startling mixture of the pathetic and the nasty. They must often be worked in places where gladiatorial or other violent deaths have taken place,[102] and tend to combine invocatory gibberish with ingredients as disgusting as they are exotic. One spell requires the figurine of a dog (modeled from dough or wax) to be fitted with real eyes gouged from a bat, which is then released alive: the effect of the spell is to produce insomnia.[103] Another "infallible draw-charm [*agōgē*], guaranteed to work the same day," must be written in blood from the womb of a sheatfish mixed with the juice of the Sarapis herb, and the spirit Sisioth, who is required to deliver the reluctant lover, must be adjured with the formula "chuchachamer merouth chmeminouth thionthonth phiophao belechas aaa eee ēēē l s ss n n."[104] This whole inscribed package must then be placed, with vetch, in the mouth of a dead dog, "and it will bring her within the hour."[105]

The aim, in any case, was always strictly pragmatic. As Nock pointed out, where the Gnostics, say, "were passionately eager to know how the wheels went round, the authors and readers of the magical papyri desired simply to be able to make them turn."[106] Some spells, indeed, are all-purpose. "This is an inhibitory formula for every matter," one begins, "which also works on chariots. Moreover, it is also a formula for separation, and a spell for striking with disease, for destruction, for murder, and for the overturning of a chariot, for whatever you desire."[107] In the ever more popular practice of magic we see a sad compensatory attempt to control (by means of elaborate verbal abracadabra, recherché physical nastiness, and counter-scientific principles of affective action) a world that had grown dizzyingly impervious to individual reason. The more tongue-twisting the spell, and the odder the ingredients, the better: it was a regular rule in magic that the least variation on formula or prescription invalidated the whole attempt, and this let-out clause must have given great comfort to those who went through the motions but still got nowhere. Men who lived in terror of human autocrats dreamed of forcing demons to do their bidding. It must have been a comfort to drunken and penniless old crones to know they were thought to call down the moon, turn into bats after dark, reverse the flow of rivers, burst snakes. Perhaps they even believed it themselves.

It is here that the alternative societies fought for by slaves and dispossessed men (above, pp. 391–92), the utopias of the desperate, find their last pathetic apotheosis, when armed insurrection has failed, when all the frontiers are closed, when all roads lead to Rome: in synthetic power fantasies that overturn the laws of nature and by-pass all human institutions. Reason and philosophy are everywhere going down before the dogmatic (and, too often, hermetic) pronouncements of revelation.[108] Here, too, are the shortcuts to instant gratification ("Now, now, quickly, quickly" is a regular concluding formula in the papyri), the scraps of paper inscribed with secret nonsense and guaranteed to do anything (mostly things for which doctors had no answer, and no merely human counsel could ensure), from curing migraines or scorpion bites[109] to putting out fires, sending the right dreams, and ensuring fidelity in lovers.[110] There is even a Headless God, most suitable, one might suppose, as a *paredros* for mindless adepts.[111] Greed, hatred, concupiscence meet us on every page: as Gow says, even the most casual reader of papyri or curse tablets "must be struck by the passion exhaling from these scrappy and frequently illiterate texts."[112] What we glimpse here, in crude yet unforgettable form, is the dark side of the Graeco-Roman moon, the censored dreams of Endymion.

CHAPTER 34
ACADEMICS, SKEPTICS, PERIPATETICS, CYNICS

Throughout our investigation of Hellenistic history and culture we have, time and again, come up against the fundamental concepts that gave this culture shape, and which in turn were often dictated by changing stresses and pressures within the Mediterranean *oikoumenē*: elements and humors, concentric spheres, the world soul, gods as deified monarchs (and vice versa), the random dance of atoms, the challenge to the senses, the earth as the still center of a turning universe. We should now be in a more advantageous position to examine the ideas of the various philosophical schools, briefly, in the context of their historical perspective. One odd effect of the trend away from *polis* unity and toward individualism was a marked increase in functional specialization, in all areas and at all levels: astronomy and mathematics, literary criticism and philology, politics and the art of war, philosophy. In philosophy especially, "the systems that survived and flourished were those which could offer a single ethical goal towards which all other permitted areas of enquiry might be geared—a goal which sought to encapsulate man's correct stance in relation to the world."[1] The degree of their popular dissemination, and lasting effect (at however low or debased a level), may be judged by their impact on common speech. Like medicine (p. 490), like astrology (p. 597), they bequeathed to European culture a whole vocabulary of human characteristics: we still speak of people as stoical or epicurean, discuss academic questions, are properly skeptical, improperly cynical, or unreliably peripatetic. When we accept a decision "philosophically," the ghost of Stoicism's universal nature, the subordination of the part to the whole, still lingers on somewhere in the word's packed semantics.[2]

Two systems, the Platonic and the Aristotelian (if we can call Platonism a system, which is doubtful), were inherited from the classical era. These retained their intellectual force, but only for a highly educated minority: prior to its late revival in the Graeco-Roman world, Platonism, the Academy, came to be chiefly identified with the critical, and essentially negative, movement of the Skeptics, while Aristotle's Lyceum went through a somewhat barren period in the late third and second centuries, when its typologizing activities were concentrated on the rather shady area of biographical ethics. The reaction against theologically based cosmologies, in favor of what might be termed an austerely sensuous humanism, was picked up by the followers of Epicurus, although even they were not above saving the appearances in morally sensitive areas: well organized and anything but revolutionary, they still smacked of the nonintegrated commune, and thus could not reach those who obstinately persisted in valuing social involvement above their own independence. More extreme than the Epicurean movement was that of the Cynics: as has often been said, a way of life rather than a coherent body of doctrine,[3] a conscious challenge to established values, an anarchic assault on the entrenched and solid sociopolitical conservatism that pervaded the Hellenistic world at all levels—a counterculture, a generalized protest against the gods of the copybook headings, things-as-they-were, the inflexible code of a stonily ruthless plutocracy. Lastly, there was Stoicism: the most adaptable (hence, in part, the most successful) of the new systems, eclectic, psychologically in tune with the *Zeitgeist*, quick to reconcile the prickly individual conscience with a pseudoscientific religious universalism, to replace old, lost city-state loyalties with allegiances of a wider, indeed a more cosmic, nature, to admit at least the possibility of the "good man" engaging in public life—a let-out clause that the Romans, later, exploited to the full.

The one thing all these systems had in common was their ultimate goal, the achievement of *apatheia* or *ataraxia*, freedom from worry or suffering, the Hellenistic age's characteristically negative ideal (the modern pejorative sense inherent in our word "apathy" reveals a reversionary shift of opinion); where they differed was in the way they defined the condition, and the steps they took to attain it. While it is true, as Long rightly insists, that Hellenistic philosophy did not restrict itself entirely to ethics,[4] nevertheless the pursuit of happiness remained, in one form or another, fundamental; and if (to take one obvious example) happiness required a proper understanding of, and relation to, the universe, then cosmology would be stressed. Similarly with problems of language and logic: all were directed, increasingly as time went on, to this specific end. Xenocrates, who succeeded Plato's nephew Speusippus as scholarch, or head, of the Academy (339–314), put it this way: "The reason for discovering philosophy is to allay that which causes disturbance in life."[5]

Both the Academy and the Lyceum suffered, though in different ways, from the dominant, and decidedly idiosyncratic, personalities of their founders. That Plato ever intended his constantly fluid and evolving speculation to be frozen into a doctrinal system after his death seems unlikely, even though in the *Laws*, probably his final work, there is a far greater sense of prescriptive and formalistic rigidity than in the earlier dialogues. Aristotle and Xenocrates often betray uncertainty as to the meaning or precise interpretation of his theories, and it seems unlikely that this would have been the case had Plato himself worked to establish a consistent and systematic philosophy during his lifetime.[6] In any case, the attitude of those who followed him was palpably ambivalent. The first casualty was the famous Theory of Forms, or Ideas, which Speusippus, scholarch from Plato's death in 347 until 339, simply jettisoned, refusing to identify the Forms (*eidē*) with the mathematical numbers that he extrapolated from a transcendent One beyond Being. This resistance to the Forms was widespread and immediate: Aristotle, Eudoxus, and Xenocrates all shared it.

Nevertheless Xenocrates, for one, seems to have attempted a stereotyped formalization of Platonic thought (in this revealing himself a typical product of his age), while both he and Speusippus upheld Plato's reliance upon dialectic as an "autonomous and absolute route to knowledge,"[7] and also retained the emphasis on mathematics that had characterized Platonism *ab initio*. Aristotle—who took Speusippus seriously enough to buy his collected works for a very large sum of money[8]—characterized their treatment of mathematics and metaphysics alike as "Pythagorean."[9] Plato had in fact adopted his search for the elements of numbers (not to mention his ideas on the immortality of the soul)[10] from the Pythagoreans, and Speusippus here followed him.[11] A strong ethical component had always been present in Plato's thinking, and this—not surprisingly, when we recall the sociopolitical scene—grew considerably in importance after his death. Speusippus asserted that in no circumstances could pleasure be good, perhaps a reaction to the hedonism of Aristippus;[12] and with Polemo's appointment as scholarch in 314 mathematics and dialectic were largely abandoned, to be replaced by an obsessive concentration on ethical issues.

This, again, is just what we might expect. The vast majority of mankind dislikes thinking for itself, and much prefers to be told, acceptably but authoritatively, how it should act, what is proper for it to believe. In a transitional age of social and political confusion, such as that ushered in by the Macedonian victory at Crannon (322: above, p. 11), moral guidelines become imperative, and thinkers who fail to supply them will very soon find themselves sidelined in favor of those who do. A certain down-to-earth pragmatism does not come amiss either. Polemo was fond of saying that one should exercise one's wits on practical affairs, and not merely in abstract dialectical speculation.[13] The apothegm would have pleased Isocrates, as it was later to please Polybius; it must have made Plato turn in his grave. Yet during the late fourth century a number of professed Platonists, most notably the conservative and *bien-pensant* politician Phocion (above, p. 40), did, exceptionally, engage in public affairs; while somewhat later Philopoemen's Academic teachers, Ecdemus and Demophanes, emerged as backers of Aratus, campaigned against local *tyrannoi* in the Peloponnese, and helped to rewrite the constitution of Cyrene.[14]

If the bias in such cases was against tyranny (which was liable to lead to social upheaval), it was also, of course, against radical democracy. Here was an area where Academics and Peripatetics were in basic agreement. Characteristic of this prevalent intellectual attitude (which by now, hopefully, should come as no surprise to the reader) is the anonymous treatise, usually attributed to Anaximenes of Lampsacus,[15] the *Rhetorica ad Alexandrum*. The author is discussing rule-of-thumb arguments appropriate for a speaker called upon to advise on governmental procedures, whether democratic or oligarchic. His points are revealing. In a democracy, why should minor offices be appointed by lot? To prevent *stasis*. What should be the main function of law? To deter the populace from plotting against property owners, while encouraging the wealthy to spend money on public services (cf. above, p. 386)—a perfect encapsulation of the "fixed order" mentality, charitable but class-bound. What should be the proper attitude to the poor? The peasantry and sailors should be encouraged, but the city rabble needs keeping in its place: thus industriousness will be put at a premium, and freeloading discouraged. What about public lands? Stringent laws should be enacted to prohibit their redistribution. In an oligarchy (here treated as a viable, indeed commonplace, alternative form of government) the mob (*ochlos*) should never be brought into the city from the countryside, because such gatherings produce unity among peasants and proletariat, and thus facilitate the overthrow of the ruling order. Laws to prevent governmental abuse of individuals are, similarly, designed with a view to maintaining the *status quo*.[16] A further intellectual sign of the times is that kingship has come to be accepted; kings are the natural lawgivers, and if the king is a good king, which Speusippus seems to have regarded as axiomatic, then monarchy is eminently desirable.[17]

There is a sense here of some new Academics trying to reach out to a wider audience, against the strong, and more characteristic, countertrend of withdrawal from public life into the contemplative existence (*bios theōrētikos*).[18] By the end of the fourth century, with the wars of the Successors in full swing, every serious thinker was trying to produce a satisfactory answer to the question "What is happiness or well-being and how does a man achieve it?"[19] The interesting aspect of this phenomenon lies not so much in the answers given, revealing though these can be, as in the framing of the question itself. As the *polis* was eclipsed by the new monarchies, and slowly loosened its hold on the Greek psyche, men were driven, more and more, if they could not be masters of their fate, at least to remain captains of their souls, and for the most part without reference to the old familiar public support structures. Those whom Pericles had contemptuously dismissed as do-nothings (*apragmones*)[20] now established a new ideal that was private to the point of solipsism: the avoidance of all disturbance (*ataraxia*), escape from the violence, chaos, and anarchy of the world around them.

Neither Xenocrates nor Polemo seems to have shown much originality; but then in the circumstances originality was liable to produce more alarm than comfort. The nostalgic systematization of previous knowledge, that widespread and ultracharacteristic habit of the age, had its roots in the late fifth century, and seems to have taken hold early in the Academy. Xenocrates' one attempt to propound a mathematical proof, for the theory of indivisible lines, was destroyed in short order by Aristotle.[21] Polemo was a reformed alcoholic;[22] both he and Xenocrates—who also cultivated the shady side of Platonism by trying to fit gods and *daimones* into a celestial universe[23]—were primarily concerned with practical morality, propagating a kind of reach-me-down salvationism that inevitably bred its own reaction. There are also the external social and political pressures to bear in mind. Xenocrates, who had not lost the old ingrained sense of public duty, served as ambassador both to Philip II (who claimed that he was the only unbribable diplomat he had ever met), and to Antipater in 322, after the Athenian defeat at Crannon.[24] He also composed a protreptic treatise on kingship addressed to Alexander the Great.[25] In all this he makes an interesting contrast with Polemo, who already exhibits the more typically Hellenistic penchant for withdrawal from society into an ivory-tower existence.[26]

It is, I think, no accident that the Academy's celebrated shift to Skepticism, with
its denial of certainty and habit of suspending judgment—a change associated with
Arcesilaus of Pitane (316/5–242/1), who became scholarch about 260—was also precisely contemporaneous with the disastrous loss of Athenian political independence
after the Chremonidean War (above, p. 147). Skepticism had already been developed
independently, in the first instance as a way of life (agōgē), a philosophical training
for practical existence, by Pyrrho of Elis (ca. 365/60–275/70). Pyrrho, an ex-painter
who worked a small farm with his midwife sister,[27] approached ataraxia by denying
that positive knowledge (especially through sense perceptions) was attainable: live
provisionally by the appearances, he counseled, but don't commit yourself to their
ultimate truth—a comforting precept for troubled times. The road to equanimity,
his thesis held, can only be traveled with a constant abstention (epochē) from definite
judgments: all positive statements should be avoided. It is the civil servant's ideal;
but then Pyrrho was born into a bureaucratic age.[28] Not that the philosophic concept
was in itself new: Xenophanes, Democritus, Heracleitus, and other pre-Socratics
had all in one way or another challenged the validity of sense data;[29] Plato looked
constantly to the Forms (eidē) behind the phenomena.

Yet, oddly, Pyrrho and his successors, Arcesilaus included, went at the problem
as though Plato had never written a word. What is new is Pyrrho's ethical goal, his
pursuit of ataraxia: no one had previously suggested that "scepticism might be made
the basis of a moral theory."[30] Pyrrho had traveled to India with Anaxarchus in the
entourage of Alexander the Great; inevitably, it was afterwards claimed that he
picked up some of his ideas (including the need to live in solitude, withdrawn from
the world) during discussions with Indian "magi" (i.e., ascetics),[31] even though
he had an obvious model far closer to home in the Cynics. Timon of Phlius (ca. 325–
235), the one-eyed ex-dancer who was his student, publicist, and successor—best
remembered today for his deadly phrase about the "Muses' birdcage" in Alexandria
(above, p. 87)—argued that Pyrrho's approach to truth enabled him to cut free
from trendy fashion and current cant, and to go through life in the spirit (as we
might put it) of the young lady from Deal, who said, "I dislike what I fancy I feel."[32]
This implied, inter alia, conformism in practical life, combined with complete personal indifference, not only to political activism, but to human society as a whole.[33]
Epicurus, another propertied contractor-out (below, pp. 618 ff.), attacked Cynics as
"the enemies of Greece":[34] not surprisingly, since they directly threatened that status
quo on which Epicureans, after withdrawing from the world, still depended for their
equilibrium. Those who sidestep reality seldom put themselves at risk by trying to
change it.

Pyrrho seems to have written nothing; it is often claimed, on little or no evidence, that he modeled himself on Socrates and Democritus. He died at the age of
ninety,[35] and it seems clear that Arcesilaus, though a very different kind of person, "a
figure," as Long says, "of the Athenian philosophical establishment,"[36] was to some
extent influenced by him, though just how far remains debatable.[37] Basically, how

ever, "the Academic philosophy is not a continuation or elaboration of Pyrrho's views so much as a second version of Skepticism,"[38] which its proponents regarded as the logical development of the tradition they had inherited from Plato. To challenge the senses had good Platonic precedent, and there is evidence that Arcesilaus, in his running battle with the Stoics, believed he was getting back to Plato's own position: dialectical scrutiny free of aprioristic dogma. (In fact what he really seems to have resuscitated was not so much Platonic philosophy as the Socratic method.)[39] Epistemologically, he denied the Stoic concept of "true and certain perception" to which the reasoning mind could give assent (*synkatathesis*). Assent could, and should, be withheld (*epechein, epochē*); the correct intellectual position was that of agnosticism or absence of sure perception (*akatalēpsia*, yet another alpha-privative ideal).[40] There was no epistemological certainty,[41] only reasonable (*eulogos*) likelihood, to be calculated by the intellect (*phronēsis*) while performing the duties that prudence dictated (*katorthōmata*), but not on that account endowed with any kind of absolute truth, or even to be treated as persuasive (*pithanon*).[42]

True to his own logic, Arcesilaus maintained suspense of judgment by never writing a book, thus joining a select short list that included Socrates and Pyrrho.[43] Nor did he need to consider the more mundane things of life: he was well off, unmarried, childless, a *bon vivant* who eventually died from drinking unmixed wine, a bisexual enthusiast.[44] Diogenes Laertius preserves anecdotes illustrating his charity: he subsidized Ctesibius the inventor (above, p. 477) when the latter was sick, a nice instance of the theoretical coming to the rescue of the practical.[45] On the whole he kept aloof from politics (carefully avoiding efforts made to introduce him to Antigonus Gonatas), though he seems to have been on intimate terms with Eumenes I of Pergamon. Like so many Greek philosophers in these times, he did once serve on an embassy; he failed in his mission, but at least the logic of such appointments was unimpeachable. Arcesilaus had the reputation, not entirely undeserved, of an unoriginal and indecisive eclectic. One critic, in a neat Homeric parody,[46] described him as a chimera, "Plato in front, Pyrrho behind, in the middle Diodorus."[47]

A century or so later (156/5) we find another scholarch of the Academy, Carneades (214/3–129/8),[48] serving, together with the leaders of the Stoic and Peripatetic schools, as the representatives of Athens before the Senate in Rome (above, p. 449).[49] Carneades, a most formidable disputant,[50] yet at the same time an absent-minded philosopher so absorbed by ideas that he forgot, or never bothered, to trim either his nails or his hair,[51] was still carrying on the Academy's battle with the Stoics, above all with Chrysippus (p. 638),[52] over the nature of truth, the gods,[53] reality, and perception. In the Pyrrhonist tradition, he too never committed his ideas to writing: luckily for us, his student and successor, Cleitomachus, was a prolix philosophical blabbermouth who published over four hundred monographs,[54] many of them devoted to Carneades' doctrines, and later utilized by Cicero.[55] Cleitomachus praised his master for his "Herculean labor in ridding our minds of rash and hasty thinking,"[56] but also admitted that he hedged his judgments to a point where it was sometimes virtually impossible to figure out just what he did or did not believe.[57] No proposition, he argued, could finally be established as true or false; no cognitive im-

Fig. 191. Carneades. Roman copy of a
second-century-B.C. original, perhaps
the likeness commissioned for the
Athenian Agora.
Antikenmuseum Basel und Sammlung
Ludwig.

pression (*katalēptikē phantasia*) could guarantee its individual congruence with the truth.[58] All one could hope for was to establish the relative probability of each individual instance, and on this, waiving the suspension of judgment,[59] base a provisional hypothesis of existence—a small, but distinct, advance on the position taken up by Arcesilaus.

In Rome, with bitter skill, and in the powerful, ringing voice for which he was famous,[60] Carneades made eristic declamations before an audience that included Cato the Censor, praising justice one day and destroying its premises the next, a regular practice of his "in order that he might refute those with any positive opinion."[61] Small wonder: during the preceding centuries positive opinions had had their chance, and had killed more than the plague. Like Plato, Carneades was impatient with sophistic notions of justice; but he was also ready, within limits, to work with the world as he perceived it.[62] His arguments, a decade or so after Pydna, also had a decidedly contemporary application. Yes, he said, Rome too had her laws and constitutional safeguards, but they worked to the advantage of Rome and against non-Romans: this was self-interest rather than justice. "What are the advantages of one's native land, save the disadvantages of another state or nation? That is, to increase one's territory by property violently seized from others."[63] Carneades then backed up this argument with a down-to-earth example taken from daily life. If a man sells a runaway slave or a plague-infected house, should he reveal such faults to the buyer? Morality says yes; prudent self-interest, no. *Caveat emptor.* Again, the common-sense definition of self-interest might have made a rival philosopher balk, but would at once have been accepted by the Athenian man in the street—and, *a fortiori*, by a Roman *publicanus.* Cato's advice (Carneades' eristic ambivalence had shocked him profoundly) was to wind up these envoys' business and get them on their way again as soon as possible. Unscrupulous Roman businessmen were causing the Senate enough problems already (above, p. 436), without the sophistries of clever Greek amoralists to help them rationalize their conduct.

Carneades, who had learned, the hard way, those nice epistemological distinctions between certitude and probability, necessity and contingency, on which his reputation rests, was the last great Academic of the Hellenistic era.[64] With Antiochus of Ascalon (ca. 130/20–68?), who became scholarch in 79/8, taught Cicero in Athens, and was a friend of Sulla's lieutenant Lucius Lucullus,[65] critical Skepticism was virtually abandoned about the same time as the pro-Roman stance was embraced, and the essential unity of Academic, Peripatetic, and Stoic thought proclaimed.[66] Like so many other systems of the day, religious or secular, Platonism in the first century B.C. ended as just one more syncretic mishmash, sifted through the ever-widening mesh of Roman imperialism. Uniformity of government, especially when that government is in essence authoritarian, will always tend, in the long run, to produce a dull uniformity of conformist belief, even if the uniformity is achieved by a synthesis of innumerable diverse elements, worldwide. In the cosmopolis of the *oikoumenē, nomos,* local custom, though dethroned from the supremacy that Pindar and Herodotus had long before acknowledged,[67] still kept its harmless place. The cry of MacNeice's Libertine—*O leave me easy, leave me alone*—exactly catches the prevalent intellectual mood in a world where *ataraxia* offered the only coherent formula, outside the mystery religions, for individual salvation.

If Antiochus's belief that the intellect has an innate ability to distinguish truth from falsehood harked back to Plato,[68] his blunt assertion that happiness (*eudaimonia*), while identifiable with a life of virtue, cannot be separated from practical concerns[69] sounds distinctly Aristotelian, as Cicero himself admits.[70] The intellectual tradition of Aristotle's Lyceum was at once better defined and more wide-ranging. Throughout the earlier Hellenistic period, including the years of Strato's directorship (287–269: below, p. 611), the Peripatetics preserved Aristotle's own pioneering patterns of research: broad-based field work and sampling, which in turn led to the construction of typologies, whether in biology, botany, literature, or any other discipline. However, from the late third century the Lyceum seems to have gone through an uninspired period, during which its members fribbled their time away on nonscientific (if trendy) moralizing and gossipy trivialities. The story, told in detail by Strabo,[71] of how Aristotle's library was bequeathed by Theophrastus to Neleus of Scepsis, and kept locked in a damp cellar by his descendants until Apellicon of Teos rescued it about the time of the Mithridatic Wars, was clearly used to explain this falling-off in the post-Theophrastean period, by arguing that the Peripatetics then had no books available (except for a few popular treatises), "and thus were quite unable to philoso-phize in a substantial manner, but could only mouth out commonplaces."[72] Quite apart from the acid gibe at the group's derivativeness and total lack of originality (which clearly marks the anecdote as hostile propaganda), could it be true, even allowing for professional secrecy, that there was only one copy of Aristotle's works in Athens, so soon after his death?

It seems far more likely that the Academic shift in the direction of popular ethics (above, p. 604) was mirrored, for identical sociopolitical reasons, among Peripatetic thinkers, and that the legacy of Aristotelian science was not so much lost during the second century as ignored, in favor of loose ethical psychologizing based on an even looser quasi-metaphorical adaptation of the master's principles—yet another uncom-fortably modern phenomenon.[73] The *Characters* of Theophrastus, Menander's recur-rent dramatic types—the braggart soldier, the aphorizing cook—show the influence of such methods, together with that of the cognate humors predicated by Hippo-cratic medicine (above, pp. 489 ff.). The ethical bias apparent in Hellenistic biogra-phy, with *ēthos* dominant over *praxis* (inevitably, in an age and place where *praxis* got increasingly little scope for achievement), is apparent in the so-called Peripatetic tradition, heavily infected with moralizing and propaganda, that meets us at every turn from the age of Alexander onwards.

Travelers' tales (above, pp. 327 ff.), some more fanciful than others, but of slowly increasing sobriety as the horizons of the *oikoumenē* expanded, were amassed for various purposes, "cut to Peripatetic specifications or to provide grist for the rapidly turning mills of religious syncretism."[74] The best instance was perhaps Megasthenes' report on his mission (302–291) to the Indian king Chandragupta for Seleucus I, a geographical and ethnological survey conducted very much in accor-dance with Aristotle's principles (above, p. 327). This work, 'the *Indica*, based on careful autopsy, formed the basis for generations of subsequent writing on the Indian subcontinent.[75] Travel and exploration were one way, other doors being closed to the ambitious, to achieve the *bios praktikos*, always a closer concern of Aristotelians than of Platonists. Dicaearchus of Messene (*fl.* ca. 326–296), another philosophizing geographer, strove to avoid the temptations of *ataraxia*: like many, he still yearned for political independence, but he also (in sharp contrast to most Hellenistic thinkers) set high value on the notion of a political career. This gave his works, especially his universal history of Greek culture, considerable popularity when they began to cir-culate in Rome. A versatile scholar, Dicaearchus also wrote lives of Plato and other philosophers, works of literary criticism, and a skeptical account of the oracle of Trophonius (above, p. 593). In his political philosophy he seems to have come nearer to Plato's *Laws* than to Aristotle.[76]

Others, such as Theophrastus of Eresos (371/0–288/5), Aristotle's successor from 322 as director of the Lyceum, and a scholar almost as wide-ranging and pro-lific as the master himself, preferred the *bios theōrētikos*. The Lyceum, like all good research establishments and Walt Whitman, contradicted itself and contained mul-titudes. But there was less and less original research done after Aristotle's death;

Theophrastus, "a determined empiricist but an even more determined disciple," took his predecessor's theoretical structure as it stood and simply expanded it to include further subdisciplines.[77] His work on botany is a good case in point. Theophrastus turned botany into a science, but a science set up by analogy from the Aristotelian zoological model. He was a great collector of facts, an indefatigable compiler and orderer of other men's ideas. His *Doctrines of Natural Philosophers* (*Physikōn Doxai*) and *Laws* (*Nomoi*), both lost except for fragments, collected and systematized, respectively, the major philosophical and scientific theories prior to his day, and the various laws and customs of the Greek *poleis*.

Perhaps his most useful treatise (certainly his most modern) is that *On Stones*, where in his petrological analysis he notes such qualities as combustibility, is fully cognizant—a most unusual trait—of industrial processes, and (unlike his predecessors) has virtually no truck with the supposed magical or therapeutic properties of the stones he describes.[78] It was this sturdy streak of empirical rationalism that took him farthest from Aristotle, paradoxical though that may seem: in his *Metaphysics* he severely criticized and modified Aristotle's doctrine of final causes, with its essentially Platonic theology, steering a middle course between this and the antiteleological naturalism espoused by scholars such as Dicaearchus and the musicologist Aristoxenus (b. ca. 365). Theophrastus himself was no atheist, and never wholly freed himself from teleological explanations. Some of his most original ideas have to do with the concept of space, which he saw less as an entity in itself than as something to be defined by the relations and positioning of known bodies, a notion that had considerable impact upon Hellenistic architecture.[79] Nevertheless it has always, significantly, been his *Characters* (above, pp. 68 ff.) for which he is best remembered.

With Theophrastus's successor, however, Strato of Lampsacus, who became director of the Lyceum in 287, and died in 269, we are in a world that functions entirely through natural causes. Cicero was to criticize him for ignoring moral issues in favor of scientific investigation.[80] Not for nothing was he known as "the Natural Scientist" (*Physikos*).[81] Strato dispensed entirely with the Aristotelian divine unmoved mover, predicated the existence of void in the cosmos, and (like Carneades after him) was highly scornful of the Stoic tendency, when at a loss for an explanation, to invoke some deity; though sometimes the physical forces (*dynameis*) that he himself posited as a substitute can seem at least as arbitrary. This, of course, shows exactly why Stoicism caught on so widely, while Aristotelianism, until given the backing of an alien theological system, remained intellectual caviar. From 300 until his appointment to the Lyceum, moreover, we should not forget that Strato lived and worked in Alexandria, as tutor to the young Ptolemy II Philadelphos (above, p. 84), and adviser to his father, Ptolemy I Soter.[82] Despite his scientific bent, he also wrote works on kingship and the nature of justice; while he and that other Peripatetic, Demetrius of Phaleron (above, p. 48), may well have played a leading role in the establishment of Alexandria's civil code.[83] It was almost certainly through his urging that the Museum developed so strong a line of research in the natural sciences.[84] It was he, too, who used his position as head of the Lyceum to emphasize naturalism, to downplay, for a while, the epidemic obsession with ethics. Indeed he was, as Furley insists, "the last Head of the Peripatetic School to do important original work," and we may legitimately ask ourselves how this came about.[85]

The tendency to systematize the past rather than probe the future, to analyze rather than create— *These fragments I have shored against my ruins*—is one that we have met in every branch of Hellenistic science and literature. Dodds's "flight from reason" may play some part in this phenomenon;[86] there does seem to have been a failure of nerve, the sense that some dazzling peak of human achievement had been lost, that man's only task, now, was laboriously to recover, as far as possible, the fragments of that vanished dream. The mood was nostalgic and synthetic. A class-bound society that stigmatized political revolution simply as "novelty" (*neōtera, res nouae*) was not likely to foster originality in other socially related areas such as art and literature: as always under such conditions, what benefited most was science. Strato did useful research (appropriately enough) on air and the void—on the existence, in fact, of the vacuum that Aristotle had categorically rejected.[87] Hero of Alexandria records the simple experiments Strato employed to prove his thesis. The work he did provided, as we have seen, useful material for Erasistratus in physiology (above, p. 494), and for Hero himself—not to mention the technological illusionists—through a series of pneumatically controlled conjuring tricks (pp. 476 ff.). There is fine poetic justice about the void at the heart of things being set to work to simulate false miracles for the edification of the masses. Critias's cynical fifth-century thesis, that religious belief was "a deliberate imposture by government to ensure an ultimate and universal sanction for the good behavior of its subjects" now found an apotheosis such as even he could hardly have foreseen.[88] Theophrastus's relative concept of space had been made absolute. Yet neither Theophrastus nor Strato, nor indeed any of the Platonists, was to advance a general reinterpretation of the physical universe: the shadows of the two great founders lay athwart all such endeavors, with a decidedly inhibiting effect.[89] It was left to the Stoa and the followers of Epicurus to fill this need; and meanwhile there was another movement developing—predictable, if unprecedented—which aimed to explode, and dispense with, the entire social structure, sclerotic, immobile and class-ridden, that had persisted, with ever-increasing tenacity, from the classical into the Hellenistic world, and that still confronts us, virtually unchanged, throughout Rome's domination of the *oikoumenē*.

Antisocial tendencies, in particular protests against plutocratic-oligarchic rule that took the form of rejection of material wealth, were nothing new in the Greek world. Socrates himself might be regarded as an embodiment of the trend; even though he remained scrupulously careful to pay his dues to the *polis* and its beliefs in full, the unease he aroused is all too understandable. Antisthenes (ca. 445–ca. 360), one of his most devoted followers,[90] exhibited similar habits, and thus came (wrongly, as Dudley would argue), to be regarded as the founder of the Cynics,[91] though what we know of his philosophy sounds rather like a mildly puritanical mixed mash borrowed indiscriminately from Socrates and the sophists: he stressed semantics,[92] believed that a knowledge of virtue (*aretē*)—which he held to be teachable, thus annoying the *kaloi k'agathoi*[93]—entailed its inevitable pursuit, distrusted wealth while praising the simple life,[94] rejected all pleasures except those won through toil (*ponos*), revered Heracles as the embodiment of that toil and the virtue that accompanied it,[95] and seems (despite his reputation as an Attic prose stylist) to have had a gift for platitudinous aphorisms.[96] Theopompus claimed that Plato plagiarized his ideas.[97] Antisthenes in turn twitted Plato as a conceited horse fancier.[98] Cicero called him "sharp rather than learned,"[99] and Aristotle regarded him with frank contempt.[100]

Antisthenes' partiality for Heracles was certainly shared by the Cynics: we may perhaps attribute it in large part to Heracles' portrayal as a benevolent but at the same time massively antisocial loner, with appetites and habits (violence, rape, inordinate gluttony) that would be frowned on in all respectable circles. This is significant. We have no difficulty in listing the *habits* of a Cynic: ostentatious poverty, sexual license, the lifestyle of an itinerant beggar and preacher, a conscious rejection of common social norms and restraints (e.g., by public defecation and masturbation),[101] not to mention the responsibilities of citizenship. He boasted of being a "citizen of the world," which meant in effect enjoying universal patronage in every city he visited without giving anything in return except hot air.[102] The Elizabethans described such transients as "sturdy beggars," and clapped them in the stocks. It is amusing, in the circumstances, that the arch-Cynic Diogenes should, nevertheless, have regarded law as essential to civic life, indeed as the basis of civilization:[103] the suspicion forms that his main reason for so doing, despite an otherwise anarchic program, was to ensure that the society he was attacking continued to afford him and those like him an adequate degree of protection.

We know, too, all too well, what a Cynic was against: polite conventions, vulgar superstition, property and capital, the fixed class system, censorship, aristocratic breeding, and most intellectual pursuits (e.g., music, geometry, and astronomy, dismissed as "useless and unnecessary").[104] Some of these pet hates evoke more sympathy than others, but they leave an overwhelmingly negative impression. Even Cynical allegorizing tended toward ridicule, for example the rationalizing of Medea by Diogenes as a kind of masseuse who "rejuvenated" flabby old men by steam baths and exercise programs: so much for tragedy.[105] But what did a Cynic stand *for*? What did he envisage beyond mere protest?[106] To what was the lifestyle leading? True happiness, we are told. How was this happiness to be attained? By satisfying one's natural needs only in the cheapest and simplest ways. What is natural cannot be either dishonorable or indecent, and therefore both can and should be done in public. Any *nomos* to the contrary is unnatural, and therefore to be rejected. The ideal is thus self-sufficiency and independence (*autarkeia*), implemented through exercise and training (*askēsis*), and backed by lack of false shame (*anaideia*). Hence, of course, the nickname "Dog," with which the sect's true founder, Diogenes of Sinope (ca. 400–ca. 325), was tagged:[107] for the Greeks the dog, which both defecates and copulates in public—thus showing a total lack of social conscience—was the shameless creature *par excellence*.

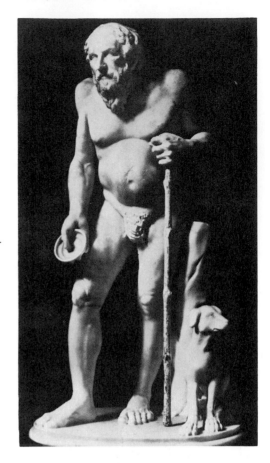

Fig. 192. Diogenes the Cynic, with stick, begging bowl, and dog. Roman copy of a third-century B.C.(?) original. Villa Albani, Rome.

There is something very odd about this program, even though (at least in the third century) it was capable of attracting a philosophical gadfly such as Bion of Borysthenes (above, p. 142),[108] or an odd but talented literary outsider like Leonidas of Taras (above, p. 175), who wrote supertramp poetry that can be construed as an embodiment of the Cynic ideal. Quite apart from the question-begging use of loaded words like "natural" and "unnatural," the argument is circular: the lifestyle is strictly self-promoting; it has no real ulterior end in view. We adopt the lifestyle to be happy. Happiness is defined through the lifestyle, which becomes an end in itself. The manipulation of these social concepts, the "natural" and the "shameless," simply gives the Cynic an excuse to thumb his nose at the society he is busy rejecting. Again, the act of rejection is its own reward; there is nothing positive offered as an alternative. Worst of all, the so-called self-sufficiency is a patent sham. The Cynic, in the last resort, exists as a tolerated parasite on the society that he condemns. Even Diogenes' famous phrase about "adulterating the currency," as a metaphor for social action, is revealing in this respect: unlike those, including the Sicilian slave rebels,[109] who chose to strike their own coinage, Diogenes only wishes to debase what is already there.[110] As Aalders well observes, "Cynics can live and preach in the Cynic fashion only because the loathed establishment continues to exist, and only by the grace of the liberal attitude of the Greek *poleis* which they detest."[111] The situation is not unfamiliar today.

"The Athenians," Diogenes once remarked, as he dossed down in some public colonnade, or his famous tub in the public record office (Metroön), "have provided me with places to live in."[112] They also provided the charity that gave him his daily bread: he was, in short, a panhandler, and the only return he gave for his keep was a series of what came to be known as *diatribai*, moral discourses, the ancestor of the nonconformist sermon. In these he preached, among other things,[113] the community of wives and children,[114] the legitimacy of incest (dogs do it, birds do it, the Persians do it),[115] cannibalism (an early *Modest Proposal?*), or robbing temples (since all property should be held in common, "all elements are contained in all things," and all things belonged to the gods anyway), the idiocy of supposing that initiation conferred privilege in the hereafter (was Epaminondas to stew in eternal mud while some sanctified nonentity enjoyed eternal bliss?), the uselessness of birth, fame, and fortune, the fatuity of scholars in researching Odysseus's faults while in ignorance of their own.[116] His ideal was the random indifference to the future that he professed to see in the behavior of a mouse. Theophrastus or Aristotle could have put him right here; but then he had dismissed science as a waste of time.[117]

There is a streak of pure arbitrary exhibitionism that shows through the anecdotes preserved about Diogenes: the legend may eclipse the reality, but it is also an index of that reality.[118] He attacks dream interpreters, but also astronomers; he approves of doctors, and in the same breath of ships' steersmen.[119] He dislikes rentiers (though if the definition of a rentier is someone who lives off unearned income, then he qualifies, on a modest scale, as a rentier himself), and at the same time seems to have had no more notion than the society he condemns of what constitutes a productive economy. His approval of Spartan toughness lacks any feeling for the social discipline and elitism that made it possible.[120] Plato is said to have described Diogenes as Socrates gone mad, and one can see why.[121]

The real trouble with Cynicism was that it consisted of little more than a stream of insecurely based moral obloquy directed against a faulty but stable social system. The Cynics offered no concrete alternative to that system, for the excellent reason that they depended on its continued existence to support their anarchic attitudinizing. Worst of all, they wholly lacked an economic sense. Cynics did no productive work themselves, nor did they pick out those who did for praise. Thus once again, as so often in this period, the revolutionary element in a movement turns out, on analysis, to be intellectual moonshine. One would expect the Cynics to command a dedicated minority following as long as they did not get entangled with politics: once that happened, disenchantment was bound to be swift. The historical record presents just such a case.

"In the life and literature of the third century," Dudley writes, "the Cynics had played a prominent part, but after about 200 B.C. strangely little is heard of them."[122] Why was this? One ancillary reason may have been the highly un-Cynical behavior of the Cynic poet-statesman from Megalopolis, Cercidas, whose violent attacks on wealth, privilege, and usury (above, p. 387) did not stop him from acting as the special ambassador of Aratus to Antigonus Doson of Macedonia when the latter was brought in to deal with Cleomenes III of Sparta in 225/4.[123] After Cleomenes fled into Egyptian exile, Cercidas played a major role in the rebuilding of Megalopolis: as Dudley says, "there had been nothing of the Cynic cosmopolitanism about Cercidas' conduct in standing so resolutely by his country in her misfortunes, and in being so concerned about the right ordering of her political affairs."[124] Worse, he had trucked with Macedonia, and shown himself, in a crisis, just one more parish-pump politician, whose horizons, far from reaching out to embrace the cosmos, extended no farther than the Peloponnese. It was the one occasion when a professed Cynic got publicity in an official role, and as far as his ideology went, it could hardly have been more disastrous.

But of course what really wound up the game of Cynicism in Greece after 200, and put paid to this thumbing of dissident noses, anarchic or intellectual, at the bourgeois establishment, was the disruption, and subsequent takeover, of that establishment by an alien external power. After Cynoscephalae (197) the edge must have been taken off the joke. After Pydna (168) no one was laughing at all; and after the sack of Corinth (146) these rebels against authority had nothing left to take a stand

Fig. 193. Crates and Hipparchia(?). Wall painting, Rome, second century B.C.
Museo Nazionale, Rome. Photo Alinari.

against except the monolithic power of Rome, an option of which they noticeably failed to avail themselves. When Cynicism reappears in the late first century B.C., at Rome, significantly, among other places, it has become a sanitized literary movement affected by wealthy young puritans and virtuous exhibitionists, who enjoyed annoying their contemporaries with homespun virtues, a meatless diet, and ostentatiously threadbare clothes, stage props that included the dirt-encrusted cloak, the wallet, the beggar's staff.[125] "Strip off all this gear," wrote one irritated critic; "it doesn't belong to you: lions are one thing, bearded goats quite another."[126] The uniform of protest, for what it was worth, had in the end become a mere costume for the pleasures of the idle rentier: as always, only the rich can afford to play at being poor.

Cynicism, in fact, offers a classic example of the protest movement, the counter-culture, that is overtaken by history. The most pleasant character it has to show us, amid much tedious posturing, is Crates of Thebes (*fl.* 328/5), a rich hunchback with a talent for parody,[127] who put his land out for sheep-grazing, threw his money into the sea,[128] "spent his entire life joking and laughing, as though on endless holiday,"[129] arbitrated family disputes and quarrels, and married, for love, the sister of one of his students,[130] a girl named Hipparchia, a philosopher in her own right, who lived with Crates on terms of absolute equality, in what they laughingly called their "dog marriage" (*kynogamia*), and, as astonished Greek critics noted, actually went out to dinner with him—something not even Pericles and Aspasia had done.[131] Amid all those indiscriminate sighting-shots that the Cynics fired at the structure of their society, it may at least be noted, to one Cynic's credit, that he struck a personal blow for the equality of the sexes.

CHAPTER 35

THE GARDEN OF EPICURUS

When Epicurus, having already established the principles for which he is best known,[1] finally made his home in Athens (spring 306),[2] it was in the wake of the famous law-suit that had, against strong opposition, upheld the right of free association, if not necessarily of free speech, for all *bona fide* religious and philosophical groups (above, p. 61).[3] Just over a decade later the volatile Athenian *dēmos* was to hail Demetrius Poliorcetes as a god-king (294), dismissing the other gods as remote, indifferent to human affairs, or even nonexistent (above, p. 55). What effect this politicized mis-representation of his creed had on Epicurus is unknown; but it does suggest that in twelve years some at least of his leading aphorisms had become popular common-places. *Nescit uox missa reuerti.* Nor was Athens the ideal setting for a withdrawal from the world. During the siege that preceded Demetrius's triumphal entry (296–294), wheat sold at three hundred drachmas the *medimnos*, a father and son fought for possession of a dead mouse, and Epicurus rationed his disciples to a handful of beans each a day.[4] By the time of his death (271/0) Athens was in effect subject to Antigonus Gonatas, and the Chremonidean War was only five years off. Epicurus, more than most men, was well aware of the instability of power.

Yet this wandering philosopher was also, we should never forget, a well-connected Athenian citizen, whose much-touted poverty (only true, one suspects, during his early days) did not stop him owning a town house in Melite, to which he and his supporters retreated during the siege, and a number of slaves, some of whom he manumitted at his death.[5] He paid eighty minas, or eight thousand drachmas, a very considerable sum, for the house and famous Garden (above, p. 60) outside the Dipylon Gate:[6] the natural inference, confirmed by independent testimony (below, p. 627), is that, like so many cult leaders, he was well supported by the faithful. Thus in troubled times, in or out of seclusion, he still enjoyed all of an upper-class Athe-nian citizen's rights and privileges. Despite his early wanderings abroad—during which, again, he suffered from political change, his cleruch father being forced, as we have seen (p. 58), to leave Samos for Colophon[7]—he was, in essence, as Athe-nian as Socrates. If he contracted out of political involvement, it was as a citizen, not, like Zeno of Citium, as a resident alien. This is worth bearing in mind when we examine the nature of his alienation. Like Socrates or Diogenes, too, he attracted anecdotes. People felt strongly about him, pro or con, and this intensity of reaction is reflected in the long account of him preserved by Diogenes Laertius.[8]

We are told that he first took up philosophy at the age of fourteen, in disgust at schoolmasters who could not explain the meaning of "chaos" in Hesiod.[9] It was also claimed that his mother had been a village healer or wisewoman, who made him go the rounds with her and read out spells (*katharmoi*): an interesting allegation, in the light of his subsequent passionate determination to rid mankind of superstition.[10] *Ad hominem* motivation can, similarly, be read into his curious reduction of all sensible pleasure to that of the belly,[11] since he suffered from chronic intestinal complaints, and died, finally, in great pain, of strangury and renal calculus.[12] Among the accusations that he attracted from his enemies—unacknowledged plagiarism, for example of Democritus and Aristippus;[13] the cultivation of courtesans; flattery of politicians, for example, Lysimachus's Syrian minister Mithres;[14] gross gourmandizing; violent and intemperate abuse of his political opponents[15]—more often than not we find at least a grain of truth. Only the gourmandizing, it is generally held, must be dismissed as a total fiction. Yet even here doubt obtrudes. Epicurus does indeed seem to have led an extremely abstemious life, regarding a pot of cheese or watered wine as high luxuries in comparison with his normal diet.[16] On the other hand one of his former students claimed that he vomited twice daily. Indulgence (as the student, Timocrates, alleged),[17] or illness? Or perhaps both? It sounds as though Epicurus may have suffered from that variation of anorexia nervosa known as bulimia, a self-induced cycle of gorging and vomiting, by no means inconsistent with what else is known of his character and lifestyle.

His interest in women seems to have been strong, if tangential, and kept up (if we can trust Alciphron)[18] into extreme old age. Though his professed attitude to sex might be described as one of distrustful functionalism (see below, p. 624), the Garden abounded in stimulating female company, of which he clearly approved. Apart from conventional tributes to the beauty of his young student Pythocles ("I shall sit down and await your lovely and godlike entry")[19] there is, unusually, even among the attacks of his enemies, no suggestion that he was pederastic by inclination. Epictetus, to be sure, among other insults, calls him a "retailer of effeminacies" (*kinaidologos*), but how specific a charge this is must remain open to doubt.[20] It may in fact refer to Epicurus's own use of violent and offensive polemic, something for which he was notorious, ripe examples being carefully preserved for posterity. His former teacher Nausiphanes, for instance, he dismissed as "a jellyfish, an illiterate, a fake, a whore." Plato, Aristotle ("a spendthrift reduced to drug peddling"),[21] Democritus, and the Cynics fared no better.[22] Yet this was the same man, as Diogenes Laertius himself points out, indignantly, whose kindness, generosity, and benevolence were legendary.[23] It should not, today, be necessary to point out that these varying characteristics are by no means irreconcilable.

Perhaps the most important thing to realize about Epicurus is that he was, in fact, the founder of a quasi-religious sect (a familiar paradox where crusaders are concerned: witness the habits of Marxists and professional atheists). His philosophy was long on dogma, short on free debate: rival creeds, clearly, were anathema, to be damned rather than refuted.[24] It is highly significant that later Epicureans made virtually no changes or modifications to his *oeuvre*, treating it in effect as holy writ. Indeed, Epicurean communes were obliged to take an oath, not only to obey the founder, but also to accept his doctrines.[25] He was known as "The Leader" (*Hēgemōn*), and flattered like a god.[26] His forty Principal Doctrines (*Kyriai Doxai*) formed a basic catechism not unlike the Thirty-Nine Articles;[27] his doctrinal letters, to Herodotus (not, of course, the historian), Pythocles, and Menoeceus,[28] are oddly reminiscent of the Pauline Epistles in tone, if not in content. All these are preserved in full. Like St. Paul, too, Epicurus used such letters to keep in touch with the various centers in Greece and Asia Minor. His followers formed not so much a philosophical school as a community, of which the modern analogue "is not a college or research institution but a society of friends living according to common principles, in retreat from civic life."[29] There was, it seems, despite the occasional lecture, no formal curriculum of study, though the Leader gave instruction to neophytes.

Socially, the group was egalitarian, admitting both women and slaves. The women ranged from courtesans to married ladies: the latter were not necessarily given preferential treatment, to the great scandal of outside observers. Whether, as has been argued, "philosophical ability was the basis of seniority" seems at least open to question.[30] Though the Epicureans found sex unprofitable and illusory (below, p. 624), they did not on that account ban it, and "there is no need to assume that the relations between the male and female members of the school were platonic."[31] The Leader seems to have enjoyed *droit de seigneur* with several of his followers' wives and mistresses;[32] his attitude may have been further influenced by his chronic intestinal illness, since he insisted that one should "use" (*chrēnai*) sex only when there was no risk of its upsetting the digestion.[33] Since his authority was absolute, the presence of slaves in the commune posed no problem: the Garden had its own rules and standards, by which all were bound, and thus those who were slaves outside could stand on an equal footing with free members of the sect. To this extent Epicurus was, in fact, creating an alternative society, though in ways it remained uncomfortably like the one he had abandoned (cf. below, p. 630).

Like Havelock Ellis, Epicurus seems to have enjoyed playing the patriarch with his disciples, and one may surmise that he was indeed gentle and benevolent as long as he commanded agreement and fidelity among them. The insults, as so often, were reserved for deviants and heretics. "Act always," he told his followers, "as though Epicurus is watching"; and though Long, for one, indignantly rejects the obvious Orwellian Big Brother parallel, in a subtle sense I suspect that it remains all too apposite.[34] We read a good deal today about the psychological profiles of cult leaders, and many traits recorded of Epicurus raise disquietingly familiar associations. The tone of his *Letter to Pythocles* veers from the self-complacent ("you continue to be kindly disposed toward me—very properly, in view of my zeal on your behalf") to the snide ("you claim that what we have written on this subject in other treatises is difficult to remember, even though—or so you say—you have my books constantly in your hands"),[35] and reveals a nagging tendency, evident elsewhere in his surviving *obiter dicta*, to let brute dogmatic assertion do the work of reasoned argument. He was not, clearly, immune from the cult of personality, besides revealing that highly characteristic trick of the charismatic preacher, a tendency to disown later in life those from whom he had learned most: Nausiphanes, Democritus, Leucippus.

He is also, as Lloyd has pointed out, fundamentally antiscientific, in that his only concern with the interpretation of celestial phenomena is to kill superstition and thereby attain inner *ataraxia*.[36] No need, he insists, to study physics or astronomy any further than is necessary to discount supernatural or divine intervention, and to quieten the irrational fears that arise from such beliefs. Epicurus has no intrinsic interest in science at all; it is simply grist for his ethical mill. If it were not for our delusions about the natural order and its mythical interpretations, he wrote, we would have no need of natural science (*physiologia*); but as things are, "without science it is impossible to attain unalloyed pleasure."[37] In his *Letter to Menoeceus* he even argues that "it would be better to go along with the myths about the gods than become enslaved by the fixed fate [*heimarmenē*] of the natural philosophers [*physikoi*]," since the gods might conceivably be appeased by worship, whereas this (Stoic) fate "implies an implacable necessity."[38] He thus rejects the whole notion of prophecy, a stance, again, not liable to win favor among traditionalists.[39] For him Tyche is no god; man's will is free, and can decide, for better or worse. "Better to reason well and fail than to succeed in unreason";[40] the trouble is that too often he manages neither. The road to his particular hell is paved with good ethical intentions (his robust defiance of Tyche is as admirable as it is muddleheaded), but potholed with faulty, and sometimes dishonest, logic, the dogma of the sage surrounded by yes-men.

For Epicurus "research is futile if it does not contribute to peace of mind."[41] Worse: if peace of mind is disturbed by anything in a physical theory, Epicurus is more than ready to manipulate the theory for the sake of *ataraxia*. His fiercely anti-teleological opposition to the notion of a divinely regulated world led him to pick up Democritus's old atomic theory; but it very soon became clear to him that, were nothing to disturb the regular and predictable fall of the atoms, his account of the soul (itself made up of superfine atoms) and, hence, his moral philosophy, would be snagged in a deterministic *huis clos*. He therefore posited a slight swerve (*parenklisis*, *clinamen*) in the atomic trajectory to set the creative process off.[42] In other words, he was stacking his physical theory for ethical purposes. It is interesting that in the process he came to see the world as analogous to the human individual, in that it too was created (from a fortuitous concourse of atoms), and in due course would also age and die, as Lucretius makes clear:[43] not a prospect naturally conducive to *ataraxia*, and thus subject to the same kind of rallying propaganda as that designed to fortify the good Epicurean against any lingering fear of death (below, pp. 625–26).

Epicurus's determination to jettison all mythical or fatalistic explanations, to observe the phenomena, to interpret the unknown accordingly,[44] does not stop him, throughout the cosmological and meteorological discussion that fills the *Letter to Pythocles*, from advancing (though here he was in good company) the wildest pseudo-scientific explanations, for example that eclipses may be due to the light in sun or moon temporarily going out, or that clouds are formed from the entangling of atoms, or that thunder is caused by "the friction and splitting-up of clouds when they have become as firm as ice."[45] We may reflect, once more, that there can be scientific no less than religious myths—as that odd Hippocratic treatise *On the Sacred Disease* earlier made all too clear (cf. above, p. 489)—and that Epicurus might have done better, in this case, to pay more attention to the natural scientists, in particular the astronomers, whom he so despised.[46] He has sometimes been described as an empiricist, but in fact such approaches are the very antithesis of genuine empirical research. Rather, he had a dogma to propagandize (the material basis of the universe, and the necessary removal of superstitious fear that this implied), for which he would use any tool that came to hand. Nothing better reminds us that Greek scientists were hopelessly hampered by being restricted to what they could see with the naked eye, and deduce intellectually *ex cathedra*, than this Epicurean swerve, an appearance-saving invention the sole purpose of which was to bolster the cause of rational causality and human free will.

One of the most intriguing things about Epicurus's system is the violent and passionate opposition it aroused. Why was this? At first sight it might seem anything but inflammatory: a society of friends anxious to escape from the political stresses of a changing world (not so far in that from the monastic ideal), an epistemology based on sense perceptions and quite ready to accommodate the gods,[47] an austere pursuit of pleasure through the removal of pain. There were, however, four crucial factors that made for opposition.

First, for most people, merely to admit the *existence* of gods was not enough. Gods had to control, not only the heavens but also mankind's destiny, whereas the Epicureans had left them, in their perfection, to occupy the remote Elysium of outer space, the void between the worlds, the *intermundia* described (though, oddly, never named as such) by Lucretius, neither affecting men nor approachable by them.[48] The gods had not made the world, nor did they judge human conduct: so much for divine providence, a dismissal that outraged religious opinion.[49] Content to relax in their own blissful immortality, they saw no good reason to involve themselves with human affairs, which, being both messy and anarchic, would inevitably disrupt the tranquil perfection they enjoyed.[50] Further, since Epicurean theology could be seen as an irreverent, not to say parodic, version of Homer's Olympians at their most solipsistic and irresponsible, it caused peculiar annoyance at all levels. One obvious characteristic that the Epicurean gods shared with their Homeric models was a marked anthropomorphism, an all-too-human psychology. Epicurus (perhaps influenced more by Euhemerus than he realized) clearly hoped to present them as ideal, immortal exponents of what he took to be perfect happiness: "in short . . . a society of Epicurean philosophers, who have everything that they can desire—everlasting life, no care, and perpetual opportunities of sweet converse."[51] Epicurus was accused, understandably, of being a crypto-atheist, despite the fact that (like Socrates) he believed in performing public religious duties as a civic obligation, and was even an initiate of the Eleusinian Mysteries.[52] In fact, to do him justice, he was simply following his cognitive theory of sense impressions to its logical conclusion. Men saw the gods, or at least had visions of them; *ergo*, they were real, and, if divine, then perfect, taking no account of human frailties.[53]

Second, there was the Epicurean withdrawal from public and political life, which, however much it might reflect the realities of a new age—the huge authoritarian kingdoms with their centralized bureaucracies, the illusive simulacrum of autonomy left to the *poleis*—nevertheless struck hard at a fundamental instinct of the Greek at all times: to act as a "*polis*-dwelling animal," in the famous Aristotelian phrase,[54] to have a voice in the affairs, and the decisions, of government. To be rendered politically impotent by external conquerors was one thing; to turn one's back on political involvement as a matter of principle was quite another. The first condition was, hopefully, transient, whereas the second implied a freely chosen act of abnegation. The Epicurean *sophos* would "pay court to a king at the right moment,"[55] while at the same time turning up his nose at political involvement:[56] he was thus both a *collabo* and a *fainéant*, a combination that did not make for popularity.

Third, as a corollary to the Epicureans' withdrawal, we may consider their deliberate rejection of generally accepted social and cosmological tenets, a self-absorbed and (in the eighteenth-century sense) Whiggish individualism, modified only by the creed of communal friendship among the chosen. To deny at one stroke providence, immortality, and any direct interrelationship between man and the heavens (now robbed of all sentient force and reduced to a mere dance of atoms)—this might be touted, by Lucretius and his predecessors, as grounds for relief from the tyranny of superstition, but to most people in the Hellenistic age it brought sheer terror and despair, soon converted to aggressively incredulous rejection.

Last, it was, however, the apparent hedonism of the Epicureans (even though modified in practice by the most stringent ascetic ideals) that aroused opposition of a peculiarly hysterical sort—in writers as diverse as Cicero and Plutarch—and led directly to the propaganda that portrayed Epicureans as gluttonous and voluptuous pigs, mere slaves to sensual self-indulgence. "We say that pleasure is the beginning and end of living happily," Epicurus declared in his *Letter to Menoeceus*, a statement almost always cited out of context.[57] It all depends, of course, on what you mean by pleasure, and here Epicurus equates it, as usual, with that which removes pain. He and his followers distinguished with great care between types and levels of satisfaction; but always they aroused in their opponents the deep (and not wholly unjustified) fear that, once the pleasure principle was accepted, personal asceticism and integrity would be no guarantee against its systematic abuse. This criticism provoked a whole series of Epicurean aphorisms on the general theme Enough Is Enough— "It is not, as popular opinion has it, the belly that is insatiable, but the false belief that to fill the belly demands an unlimited amount"[58]—but these clearly failed to appease suspicion.

Hedonism, of however rarified a sort, was an unfortunate criterion for the thinking man to adopt at a time when Demetrius Poliorcetes' orgies in the opisthodomos of the Parthenon were still a bad memory for most Athenians (above, p. 50); it would look even worse in the heyday of Antiochus IV Epiphanes or Ptolemy VIII Physcon. Hence, of course, the endless lubricious stories about the courtesans who were members of the Garden community (and with whom Epicurus maintained a brisk intellectual correspondence, not what one normally does with geishas), or the daily mina (100 drachmas) that was spent on catering (but how many disciples and servants did his household contain?).[59] Yet Epicurus's own statements could sometimes be less than helpful. In one treatise, *On the End*, he declared: "Personally, I cannot visualize the Good if I omit pleasures to be got from taste, sex, sound, or the movements of an attractive figure."[60] He also wrote: "The beginning and root of all good is the pleasure of the belly, and everything wise or exquisite must be referred back to this criterion," and again, more concisely, "I spit on the Good . . . when it produces no pleasure."[61] All justifiable statements, but all potentially, to say the least, misleading. Anyone (for instance) who joined the Epicurean movement expecting a nonstop sexual free-for-all was liable to be disappointed. "No pleasure is a bad thing in itself," Epicurus pronounced, "but the means of achieving certain pleasures bring also disturbances many times greater than the pleasures."[62] That sex was one of the main offenders he made very clear: it "never profited a man, and he whom it never hurt is lucky."[63] "The Epicureans," Diogenes Laertius reports (apparently from the same source: he goes on to cite the same aphorism), "do not approve of intelligent men falling in love . . . nor do they regard love as heaven-sent."[64]

Nor, indeed, was the "intelligent man" (*sophos*) expected to marry or to raise children, except in very special circumstances.[65] He was allowed, grudgingly, to "indulge your urge, so long as you break no law, offend against no well-established custom, annoy none of your neighbors, cause yourself no bodily harm, and spend nothing earmarked for necessities."[66] There is no puritan like a humanist busy getting rid of religious morality in the name of the pleasure principle. In any case, Epicurus made it clear that for him the highest good, the definition of pleasure, was *ataraxia* interpreted as the absence of pain and fear—a proposition not entirely to be explained (though it was undoubtedly enhanced) by the fact that Epicurus himself was an invalid who suffered from excruciating internal discomfort for a great deal of his life (constant vomiting alone would have damaged his digestive system irreparably).[67] The Hellenistic negative ideal, what we might call the alpha-privative syndrome, was far too widespread to be explained in terms of one man's personal problems: Epicurus was, rather, a more than usually striking symptom of his age. We are left, in the end, with the grim suspicion that the best *anyone* felt able to hope for, spiritually or politically, was some limited relief from suffering.

Epicureanism has been called, with some justice, "the only missionary philosophy produced by the Greeks," and that in itself makes it a more than usually interesting phenomenon.[68] After Epicurus's death in 271/0 the Garden continued as a commune, with regular feasts held in memory of the founder, who was not only praised for his *philanthrōpia* but addressed as "Savior" (*Sōtēr*), all under the watchful eye of his portrait.[69] The act of salvation he had performed was to rescue mankind from superstition; the irony of that being expressed in religious terms seems to have eluded his followers. It is no hyperbole to speak of the "Epicurean gospel," which spread to Antioch and Alexandria, and later throughout Italy and Gaul.[70] Since the definition of pleasure (and indeed that of the absence of pain, with which it was equated) could vary, without open conflict, from person to person, it is easy to see how a wide variety of individuals could be attracted by such a creed (or anticreed);

yet by its very nature it could never hope to win widespread social acceptance, since its efficacy rested, as we have seen, on a way of life that was in itself a withdrawal from society as constituted, a retreat to privacy (as, later, to the wilderness). It offered nothing to the ambitious, the public-minded, the conformist, the *engagés* of this world: austere itself in practice, it offended puritans, deists, and idealists in about equal measure. It appealed, in short, to the kind of thinking person who would consider joining a commune in any age.

Thus we are brought back, again, to the problem of Epicureanism's attraction. Just what was it, in the third century B.C., that drew so many adherents to a dogmatic creed of this sort? Its writings, as Furley rightly insists, are "needlessly difficult, clumsy, ambiguous, badly organised, and full of jargon," a weakness to which ideologues, like social scientists, seem more prone than most.[71] More attractive was the stress on personal relationships. Though Epicureanism found sexual passion a disruptive phenomenon, to be tolerated but kept within bounds, its chief message was a paean to private friendship, *philia* rather than *erōs*, expressed in hyperbolic terms—"Friendship dances round the whole world [*oikoumenē*], proclaiming to us all that we should rouse ourselves to give thanks for happiness"[72]—and coupled with a call to withdraw from public or competitive life: "We must free ourselves from the prison of affairs and politics."[73] There was a stronger element of Epicureanism in the Bloomsbury mystique than is generally recognized; Epicurus's followers, like E. M. Forster, would also have felt, if it came to the crunch, that it was preferable to betray your country than betray your friend.

The key slogan here was "Live unnoticed": unnoticed by whom? one asks oneself.[74] Presumably the outside world, from which the commune is to separate itself.[75] Again, this is the ideal of the fugitive, the escaped criminal, the political dropout: as a general injunction it goes against the grain. Worse still, Epicureans were called upon to reject not just the divinely ordered cosmos, but the prospect of immortality itself. Here lay a great hazard. As the founder's favorite disciple wrote, "where death is concerned, all of us human beings inhabit an unwalled city."[76] It was, therefore, essential that the way of life taught should guarantee the ability to face death (that one irrefutable necessity) and, more important, oblivion, with serene indifference. "Death," Epicurus insisted, "is nothing to us, for matter dissolved lacks sensation, and what lacks sensation is nothing to us."[77] In the *Letter to Menoeceus* he put it even more strikingly: "Thus that most fearful of evils, death, is nothing to us, since when we are, death is not present, and when death is present, we are not."[78]

Lucretius developed this notion in a famous and sustained stretch of poetic rhetoric, the shrill reiterations of which betray an unacknowledged horror at the prospect of that inevitable fate to which the poet meant to reconcile his readers: "An end stands fixed for mortals' lives, / And death cannot be avoided, but meet it we must."[79] Attacks on this attitude—Plutarch's is typical[80]—largely restricted themselves to complaints that Epicurus was robbing human souls of all the hopes and joys and pleasures they looked forward to in the hereafter, an argument more notable for its emotional content than its rational cogency. But it was, of course, emotional comfort of which the average mortal stood most in need. Epicurus shut the door, without compunction, not only on immortality but also on metempsychosis: "We are born once; to be born twice is impossible; we must cease to be for all eternity";[81] and how many people would be satisfied with the Cavafy-like dictum "So long as we are on the road, we must try to make the latter end better than the beginning; but when we reach terminus, we must be cheerfully content"?[82]

There is a flavor about such statements very much in accord with those modern existential writers who have attacked the same problem. The knowledge of death as a cutoff point, of this life as a unique and unrepeatable experience, goes a long way toward explaining Epicurus's emphasis on pleasure and sensation. However much elevated by high principle, what he propounded was still the *carpe diem* solution: *Gather ye rosebuds while ye may*. In that sense his critics had a point. A more telling objection might be that to do nothing in this once-only existence except stay out of trouble is hardly an inspiring creed. Here the existentialists do rather better. "The vitality of death," Peter Koestenbaum writes, "leads one to adopt an ideal or a goal, a noble life, or a major achievement as the purpose of existence."[83] Doubtless Epicurus (like Plato or Aristotle, to whom he had so many unacknowledged debts) felt that the contemplative life was far preferable to that of action, that public *praxis* could not compare with *theōria* as cultivated in the Garden. Yet the existentialist has a positive quality that the negation-haunted Epicurean lacked. Whether *ataraxia* could be described as an ideal or a noble goal is debatable: a Buddhist is more likely to assent to the proposition than a Western humanist. Epicurus certainly believed it was. But a major achievement? There is (one wants to protest) more to life than conquering the fears and superstitions associated with death, the jealousies and failures inherent in ambition. What Epicurus offered was mere quietism, near-total negation, a wholesale repudiation of Hellenistic life, politics, society, eschatology. With no afterlife to look forward to, the best that Epicurus could still do with this present existence was to sit still and try to achieve a state of negative harmony, untroubled by the demons of unreason or power, and, like Gerard Manley Hopkins' nun, "out of the swing of the sea."[84]

Epicureanism was, in the last resort, the brainchild of an antisocial and anti-intellectual dogmatist, with a bee in his bonnet about providential gods, and more than a passing urge (perhaps not consciously realized) to replace the deity himself. It might be argued that his communes, doctrinal propaganda, and paradoxically religious-style ritual offered just the alternative society that all Hellenistic rebels and dropouts sought.[85] If there is any truth in this claim, its application remains highly restricted. To begin with, the Epicurean commune, even more than the Cynics (above, p. 614), remained parasitical upon—indeed, systematically invested in—the society it had rejected. Like them, but with more at stake, it required a strong framework of law and political rule to guarantee security and freedom from anarchy.[86] In other words, it used the existing order as its base. "Epicurean political quietism," says Aalders, "is *de facto* concomitant with a conventional and conformist attitude in political and social respects, with a kind of indifferent conservatism."[87]

One thing strikingly, but not surprisingly, absent from all the stories about Epicurus's Garden is even a hint of anyone actually working: this was very much (despite those women and slaves) an Athenian upper-class establishment, its ideal the perpetuation of endowed leisure. Now clearly the commune had to pay its way, and the obvious answer is that it was a rentier foundation. We saw earlier that Epicurus himself suffered poverty and hardship at the beginning of his career (above, pp. 58 ff.). He nevertheless ended it, a point less often stressed, in very considerable affluence, as his will makes clear.[88] The contributions of the faithful, as with so many cults, had left the founder very comfortable. It has been suggested that "the communities outside Athens may have paid some kind of dues to the central organisation,"[89] and this seems to be confirmed by fragmentary letters that mention annual contributions of 120 drachmas, and gifts of five and seven minas.[90] The return was the instruction that Epicurus gave.[91] We find Epicurus writing to his disciple Idomeneus, "So send us, for the care of our holy body, first fruits on behalf of yourself and your children."[92] This is very close to an assumption of divinity.

On the other hand, neither wealth nor (possibly) godhead had filled the founder with the more cooperative virtues. He did not believe in Pythagoras's dictum that the property of friends should be held in common: his trust funds and other dispositions make it clear that the finances of the Garden, and the property it occupied, were in his name alone.[93] His excuse for not sharing it was the lame one that such a practice implied mistrust, though precisely the opposite could in fact be argued: one senses the well-born Athenian landowner's instinct at work here. His provisions are generous, but hint at absolute control during his lifetime. He gave four of his favorite slaves their freedom, but the way that clause is phrased in the Greek suggests that he owned many more.[94] The philosophical community, however homespun its tastes, had ample, and very businesslike, support.

Epicurus was also, we should not forget, a prolific writer (he is credited with over three hundred rolls, chief among them the treatise *On Nature*, in thirty-seven volumes),[95] and the Garden's staff will undoubtedly have included copyists to facilitate publication. Once again the rigid structuring of Hellenistic society obtrudes itself, even in this off-center group. What in effect Epicurus had done was to set up a charitable foundation dependent on contributions, or, after a while, on the interest of accumulated investments. The Garden was thus, in economic terms at least, no more than a subbranch of the commercial society from which Epicurus and his friends professed to have withdrawn. To that extent there is a fundamentally unreal quality about Epicureanism as an alternative lifestyle: unlike Cynicism, it was designed in the first instance for those with private incomes. Now it is true that their contributions also supported members, including slaves, who might otherwise never have been able to join the group, but this was a normal manifestation of *philanthrōpia* (above, p. 386). To assert, as De Witt does, that the bulk of Epicureans came from the middle or lower classes is to miss one essential fact about the Garden.[96] It may be true that the price Epicurus paid for it (80 minas) was less than Gorgias had charged for one course of lectures;[97] but even allowing for fourth-century inflation, it still represented well over five years' wages for the average worker (cf. p. 374).

The house and garden, as Cicero noted, were small, and the commune always overcrowded.[98] But we need not doubt that the pleasantly named *hetairai* who formed a prominent part of the group—Mammarion, Leontion, Hedeia, Erotion, and the rest[99]—could pay their way. The enclave, and the peace of mind that went with it, still depended on commerce as well as contributions: no institution in the Hellenistic age that rejected the banausic and the practical life could afford to do otherwise, unless it took the Cynics' road; and even the Cynics were not quite so independent as they sometimes liked to pretend (above, p. 614). Epicurus remarked that the life of freedom cannot be lived if one acquires *great* riches, because to get them normally means making yourself a slave, to the mob or to a king. But "a life of freedom has everything in continual abundance, and if by chance it should happen on great wealth, it is easy, by distributing this, to win the good will of one's neighbors."[100] The financial attitude is indistinguishable from that of any respectable pillar of *polis* society (above, p. 386), not least in the immediate assumption that the most acceptable disposal of a cash surplus is in charity (above, p. 157).

What, one wonders, did members of the commune do with their time once they had memorized the forty Principal Doctrines and mastered the quasi-atomic physics,[101] together with the *Canon* (a work now lost, which taught initiates how to distinguish true from false sense impressions)?[102] Epicurean philosophy, as we have seen, did not evolve, had no real dialectic—a practice abhorrent to its begetter, who much preferred dogmatic pronouncement, with no unseemly contradictions—and thus hardly offered food for intellectual growth. There is, indeed, an anti-intellectual, anticultural element in Epicureanism ("Hoist sail and steer clear of all education, dear boy," the Leader once wrote to Pythocles),[103] which is precisely what we might expect from its sectarian, not to say missionary, antecedents. Students were not required to undergo any preliminary educational training, while such disciplines as rhetoric, philology, and mathematics were dismissed as valueless.[104] Again, it looks very much as though Epicurus may have been compensating for his own well-known lack of early instruction; besides, it meant that the neophytes were less likely to argue with what they were told. In any case this stance gave hostile critics a field-day when attacking Epicurus's logical deficiencies.[105]

What one visualizes is a group of friends enjoying a life of what might be described as secular monasticism (but with the hard work done by slaves), endorsing the founder's dogma, and reassuring each other at intervals that death was nothing. It sounds pleasant, but bland. Yet nearly three centuries later Lucretius was inspired by Epicureanism to write that most passionate of all didactic poems, the *De Rerum Natura* ("On the Nature of Things"). The creed had something: it made converts everywhere. What was more, however much it might incur charges of atheism, its religious atmosphere was all-pervasive. Its gods might live in remote and uninvolved bliss (an ideal for commune members to emulate), but they must surely have approved the atmosphere that it created. Epicurus himself was called Savior: Lucretius, in the emotional proem to his fifth book, describes him, without any apparent sense of irony, as a god.[106] Nor was identification with godhead restricted to the founder. The true Epicurean was told that he "would live as a god among men; for the man who lives among immortal blessings is in no way like a mortal."[107] At one end of the scale this recalls the Orphic initiate (above, p. 592), and, even more strikingly, the shamanism of that early fifth-century guru Empedocles ("An immortal god, mortal no longer, honored by all I go among you");[108] at the other, the current fashion for king-worship and Euhemerism. Epicurus was, to put it mildly, tapping a potent source.

His own position, similarly, carries odd echoes of ruler-cult practices, a significant phenomenon. His disciples put his image on their rings and drinking cups, or on small ikons and busts with which they adorned their homes[109]—one hint of a distinction between commune members and nonenclosed followers. Epicurus was indeed watching them, wherever they went. After his death they circulated hagiolatric lives of him along with his own doctrinal letters and sayings. They rejected conventional teaching, and founded their own schools, based on this literature. They celebrated love feasts at regular intervals, on the twentieth of each month (a sacred day in the Greek calendar), which earned them the nickname of *Eikadistai*, "Twentyers."[110] They carried out religious rituals in memory of the founder. As De Witt says, "the first missionary philosophy was a natural preparation for the first missionary religion. . . . It would have been singularly easy for an Epicurean to become a Christian."[111]

It was also true that Epicurus had put his finger on a deep malaise of his age. "At a time of political instability and private disillusionment, Epicurus saw that people like atoms are individuals and many of them wander in the void."[112] He also believed that "the whole world lives in pain; it is for pain that it has most capacity";[113] and though it is clear that his own physical suffering must have shaped the aphorism (as

Fig. 194. Sealings from Epicurean seal rings of the Roman period, confirming
Cicero's statement that Epicurus's followers had signets engraved with
the master's portrait.
British Museum, London.

it did his whole gastroenteric obsession with pleasure as relief from agony), never-theless when we look back over the Successor kingdoms and their societies, who in good conscience could argue with such a judgment? To kill fear, to pursue happiness and friendship, in a world where the former was considerably more widespread than the latter, was an objective as praiseworthy as it was elusive. There is a ringing de-fiance about the "fourfold remedy," the *tetrapharmakos*: "The gods are not to be feared, there is no risk to run in death, the good is easy to get, the bad easily borne with courage."[114] A hint of Nirvana here, though no Greek would ever tolerate that kind of voluntary self-eclipse. There is more to life, in the end, than *ataraxia*.

The saddest thing, in the last resort, about Epicureanism is its failure to get away from the dominant modes, political and economic no less than social, of the age. Just as the slave leaders, a Eunus or a Salvius, consciously aped the pomp, government, court protocol, and nomenclature of the Seleucid monarchy in their striving for an alternative society (above, p. 393), so Epicurus, in turning his back on the Hellenistic world (and even so not severing his economic ties to it), merely set up another Suc-cessor kingdom in miniature, with the Sage ruling in absolute power over his ob-sequious courtiers, a god-king manifest, the philosophical analogue to Antiochus Epiphanes. The true tyranny of this world was embodied in the predestinate natural order, which offered no possibility of change, nothing to offset authoritarian rule. Though Epicurus was ready to challenge the cosmic manifestations of this order, denying both the compulsion of Fate (*heimarmenē*) and the teleological providence supposedly immanent in the heavens, when it came to social planning he could see no farther than the world around him. Under that sun there could be nothing new: even the rebel framed his revolt in the terms of what he strove to reject.

CHAPTER 36

STOICISM:
THE WIDE AND SHELTERING PORCH

Popular philosophies—and Stoicism must be accounted one of the most popular ever[1]—almost always tend to have an intellectually suspect quality about them. They are popular, in the last resort, because they tell a wide range of people what they want to hear, and encourage them to believe what they believe already. Sometimes, though not often, such a message may also coincide with the rigorous pursuit of truth, the laborious exercise of reason. In the common way of things, however, such a philosophy is far more liable to be shaped by historical and social circumstance rather than to reshape old ways of thinking: its appeal is epidemic rather than intellectual; it strokes the emotions, not the brain.

Too many aspects of Stoicism fit this definition with uncomfortable accuracy. Despite its materialist explanation of reality,[2] it offered a traditional religious believer everything, except permanent and guaranteed immortality,[3] that he could possibly want: a geocentric universe, Zeus as universal prime mover, a cosmological system that, in a very real sense, made the whole world kin. It gave intellectual backing, of a very sophisticated sort, not only to divination and astrology, but also to the belief in demons.[4] Its promotion of natural law (that notorious holdall) encouraged authoritarian figures of every sort, from Roman jurists to the Church Fathers, in the exploitation of this concept "simply as a term of approval for whatever idea they wanted to recommend at any particular time."[5] What it could not swallow as fact it happily allegorized. Above all, as Aalders demurely observes, in its later phases "it displayed a remarkable adaptability to practical needs and to established structures and situations."[6] By favoring kingship or oligarchy it endorsed the political *status quo*; by conceding a level of conduct compatible with public service it got round the awkward hurdle of withdrawal from the world; its notion of the cosmopolis was easily adaptable to the spread of Roman *imperium*. For those, like Marcus Brutus or the younger Seneca, with a schizoid urge not to let their morals get in the way of their political and financial dealings, it was the ideal creed. No wonder, either, that it caught on so well with the ruling classes. A system that bound the ordering of this world in a close nexus with the movements of the heavens could hardly fail to give comfort to those in power: as the one was a symbol of unchanging governance, so must the other be.

To understand what Stoicism was, it may help to begin by reminding ourselves what it was not. Cicero observed, shrewdly, that hedonism as a creed could hardly be advocated with any success in the Senate or law courts, on active service, or before the censors.[7] There were many possible reactions to the new realities of the postclassical era, and a deliberate rejection of public life in favor of private quietism was a logically defensible choice; but it offered nothing to the patriotic, the politically minded, the ambitious, those endowed with the Aristotelian qualities of magnificence (*megaloprepeia*) or greatness of spirit (*megalopsychia*).[8] An Epicurean might well retort that *megalopsychia* was in fact a mere euphemism for arrogance, and better discarded; but it would be hard to argue that the world as it was could be run from the Garden, or its equivalent. The Epicurean, as we have seen, consciously turned his back on the world, and on several of the world's most cherished beliefs at the same time: a providential universe, the concept of man as a *politikon zōon*, a belief in duty above pleasure (however sternly that pleasure might be defined). Intellectually, Epicurus's doctrines offered room for debate; but no one could deny that they ran flat counter to almost every comforting article of social or eschatological faith that humankind had evolved over the millennia.

Thus, to the traditionalist, Epicureanism must have seemed both emotionally bleak and morally offensive. Yet the sociohistorical crisis of the later Hellenistic period was all too real: political institutions had lost their stability, if not their titular autonomy; private disillusionment and disorientation were rampant; *physis* as might-is-right had, to all appearances, triumphed over reason and *nomos*; the individual, his old support system undermined, was adrift in a terrifying spiritual void. Euhemerus's claim looked incontrovertible: gods had been kings, and now kings were gods. Idealism and principle were being swept away with all the other outmoded public detritus of the *polis*. Democracy, once taken for granted as an inalienable civic right (and yet always rare, exceptional, the maverick among Near Eastern systems), now seemed little more than a quaint historical memory amid the universal bureaucratic rule of autocratic monarch, oligarchic group, or business consortium. We have seen how a series of despairing attempts to throw off this yoke—at Crannon, in the Chremonidean War, under Mithridates VI of Pontus—were all crushed. The Ptolemaic concept of the realm as royal estate seemed set, with variations, for ever: the advent of Roman power in the Greek world merely streamlined and professionalized the systematic process of extortion. Men who had cursed the Seleucids or the Ptolemies found the *publicani* a worse scourge yet. *Machtpolitik* reigned supreme; greed, lust, and ambition more and more came to dominate public life. Protests were reduced to mere hopeless explosions of impotent fury: the slave revolts, the risings of the fellahin in Egypt, the radical (but far from egalitarian) activities of a Cleomenes or a Nabis in Sparta.

Increasingly as time went on, there were only two choices open to an intelligent citizen of the Greek *oikoumenē*. He could do what the Epicureans and Cynics did, and turn his back on the whole poisonous mess: in the case of the Epicureans this involved an economic compromise with the rejected system (above, p. 627), while for most people the more radical solution of the Cynics, though logically consistent, was too extreme. To be a total dropout calls for a degree of individualism and considerable stamina; worse, it still involves a certain degree of parasitism. Zeno of Citium, who to begin with was strongly influenced by the Cynics, in his first work, *The Republic* (*Politeia*), argued, as we saw earlier (above, pp. 63–64), for the abolition of temples, law courts, gymnasia, everything that made for the cohesion of the *polis* as men knew it;[9] but he very soon seems to have modified this extreme position, and his successors were at some pains to tone down aspects of his early doctrine (e.g., the community of wives) that caused particular social offense.[10] They were moving, perhaps in conscious opposition to Epicureanism, toward the obvious alternative approach: that is, the attempt to work out a creed that would enable men to come to terms with the world as it was, to operate successfully in it while at the same time retaining some kind of spiritual balance and moral self-respect. This, in the long run, was where Stoicism achieved its greatest and most lasting success.

It would, indeed, be hard to find a system more diametrically opposed to the tenets of Epicureanism at every point. As Long says, "the coherence of Stoicism is based upon the belief that natural events are so causally related to one another that on them a set of propositions can be supported which will enable a man to plan a life wholly at one with Nature or God."[11] This universality interpenetrated every aspect of Stoicism, predicating a cosmos in which macrocosm and microcosm achieved perfect mutual harmony, a rationally organized structure subject to *logos*, reason, and *physis*, nature.[12] Chrysippus (ca. 280–207), who succeeded Cleanthes as head of the Stoa, is quoted as saying that "no particular object, not even the most minute, can come into being otherwise than in accordance with common nature and its own rational mode [*logos*]."[13] Thus for a Stoic there was no real distinction between the existence of God and the divinity of nature, and much effort was devoted to proving the existence of an all-encompassing divine providence. Cleanthes employed four main arguments to this end: men's foreknowledge of future events; the benefits they derive from the earth in a temperate and fertile zone; the awe inspired by physical manifestations such as lightning, comets, and earthquakes; above all, the ordered beauty and uniform movement of the heavenly bodies.[14]

This last was a popular (because visibly demonstrable) thesis, and largely accounts for the extraordinary success of a work such as Aratus of Soli's *Phaenomena* (cf. above, p. 184): the court of Antigonus Gonatas was, as we have seen, actively interested in Stoicism, and Zeno's disciple Persaeus lost his life in Antigonus's service (p. 142)—thus reminding us that a Stoic, in sharp contradistinction to an Epicurean, could reconcile his ethical beliefs with a public career, one major key to the system's peculiar success in Rome. As Chrysippus, again, argued, "the heavenly bodies, and all those that possess some sempiternal regularity, cannot be fashioned by man; therefore that by which they are fashioned is better than man; but what would you call this, if not God?"[15] The argument from design led some Stoics into a kind of aggressive and uncompromising meliorism, arguing that "this is the best of all possible worlds with divine purpose immanent in it and working for the benefit of rational beings."[16] The Stoic cosmos, then, is not only intelligible but intelligent: as Lloyd stresses, "the universe is not simply like a living creature, it *is* one."[17] The idea was not entirely new: Anaxagoras of Clazomenae had long before posited Mind (*Nous*) as the prime mover and substance.[18] Like Diogenes of Apollonia, too,[19] the Stoics conceived a universal substance, the *pneuma* (air plus fire: cf. above, p. 491), as their active principle (*hēgemonikon*), "an all-pervasive intelligent material which is identical to God and accounts for differences in particular things by differentiations of itself."[20] In other words, we have here an early version of the world-as-continuum theory.[21]

Again, the contrast with Epicureanism is striking, since early atomism foreshadows the main alternative theory of matter, that based on material particles. Yet it also seems clear that the Stoics—in this at least like the Epicureans, and (if it comes to that) most Greek thinkers—were only interested in physics, or indeed in scientific theory generally, insofar as the findings of science could be used, from Zeno's day onwards, to demonstrate or confirm their preferred system of ethics.[22] The adumbration of what sound, in many respects, like modern theories of matter and energy had importance for them only as a means to a moral end: economics was by no means the only discipline that in this period suffered from a teleological cuckoo in the nest (above, p. 363). For the Stoics, universal causality—the so-called causal nexus—was fundamental, and human happiness wholly dependent on finding one's correct relationship with nature or God, or both. Possessions or achievements were unimportant in comparison with maintaining the proper attitude to such things. "The external world should not be a matter of indifference to [the Stoic], and he is bound to recognise differences of value in it, but they are not values that contribute to his excellence and his happiness, of which he is the sole arbiter."[23] The advantages of this specious argument are considerable, since it will not only help the unfortunate to face their lot without complaining, but also provide a device whereby the wealthy and powerful can reconcile their status (and, more important, their actions) with moral peace of mind. Those Chrysippan paradoxes about the wealth (in virtue, understood) of the wise man,[24] or the role of the *sophos* as king, lawgiver, general,[25] however ironic, cannot have failed to reconcile many rich rulers, never slow to appreciate their own wisdom, to the greatness that they had achieved, or to which they had—in accordance with the dictates of an inscrutable universal providence—been born.

Stoic theology was, basically, pantheistic (another plus for Romans, capable of seeing divinities everywhere, even in a door hinge); and though a consistent, logical, all-embracing pattern to creation inevitably reinforced the concept of Fate, at least it put paid to the random and the irrational. "If there could be any mortal whose mind grasped the connection of all causes," it was argued, "nothing would ever deceive him. For he who grasps the causes of future events must needs grasp all that lies in the future."[26] Chance, Tyche, became no more than a label for yet-undiscovered causes.[27] There is something immensely comforting about a closed universal system of this sort, and not merely for the feebleminded, as both Catholics and Marxists will be well aware. Its initial premises once accepted, it can then supply answers to any problem under the sun, or, if it comes to that, about the sun; and the Stoics were nothing if not systematic, ranging from physics to semantics, from metaphysics to a highly sophisticated epistemology, from ethics to something uncommonly like transactional grammar, but always with the same ultimate end in view—that is, the rationalizing of man's place in, and relation to, a supremely logical cosmos.

There were interesting consequences to this. If all future events were theoretically predictable, then divination and "scientific" astrology could be, and were, appealed to, by a familiar circular argument, as evidence for universal causality: as so often happened with Stoicism, a powerful lobby for the *status quo* (in this case of priests and professional seers) was placated in the process. We should not regard this as a case of cynical manipulation; it was, rather, a natural by-product of the system. Sandbach correctly notes that "the belief that the world was entirely ruled by Providence would have an appeal to the ruling class of a ruling people."[28] What Stoicism offered, in fact, was a built-in justification—moral, theological, semantic—for the social and political fixed order: it was the most powerful and subtle instrument of self-perpetuation that the Hellenistic ruling class ever conceived. The mere fact of anything happening meant that it had been fated to happen; and since nature was providentially disposed toward mankind, what was fated could not fail to be all for the best. This interesting version of determinism is most often presented as a source of comfort when things seemingly went wrong; but of course, as I have suggested, it would be of even greater benefit to those who were anxious to have some moral principles to offer the world in justification of ruthless self-interest. If it was bound to happen, it had to be right.

I am putting the case in an extreme form, but even so it is hardly an exaggeration: small wonder that the Stoics had, notoriously, a great deal of trouble in coming to terms with the problem of evil. They tended to approach it by means of what I would term the "long perspective" gambit, arguing that, despite seeming local faults and imperfections, nature contrives, ultimately, to harmonize the greater whole. Individual sufferings or excesses can then be subsumed to some vast universal scheme of nature or the Demiurge, an argument that has had a remarkably long life since the Stoics first formulated it. "Nothing," wrote Marcus Aurelius, "is harmful to the part that is advantageous to the whole."[29] Then what about natural disasters? These, according to Chrysippus, possess their own *logos* "in accordance, somehow, with the *logos* of nature."[30] Without the bad, there could be no definition of good. It was a weak argument, and Chrysippus knew it was. It suffers, moreover, from the incurably meliorist belief (shared by Socrates) that all human evil springs from lack of knowledge, ignorance, misapprehension: there is no real place in this system for plain, conscious, innate wickedness, irrespective of intellectual perception. The irrational element in the human psyche is, and has to be, ignored, because in the Stoic world view everything, from the celestial bodies to individual human motivation, is dictated by reason. The cosmic pattern is universal. Local complaints of disease and poverty are, in every sense of the word, partial: they must be viewed in the overall context of the whole, a perspective that will reveal even such phenomena as "not unnatural, because all natural events contribute to the universal well-being"[31]—a

Fig. 195. Roman bronze statuette from
Brindisi (second century A.D.),
plausibly identified as a portrait of
Cleanthes.
British Museum, London.

theological gambit to set beside the one-rotten-apple-in-the-barrel escape clause commemorated by Hesiod.

The Stoics had to admit (indeed, some insisted) that bad actions, namely, those contrary to nature, did exist, and that nature did not will them; however, nature would always so adjust the universal harmony as to make allowances for these aberrations. As Cleanthes declared in his famous *Hymn to Zeus*,[32]

> No action takes place on earth apart from you, O Deity,
> Nor in the airy divine firmament nor on the sea,
> Except what bad men do through their own follies;
> But you know how to make the odd even,
> And to harmonize the dissonant; to you what's alien is your own,
> For thus you have melded together all things good and bad into one.

Obviously, in a system that laid such stress on ethics, the individual will had to remain free in some real sense, despite universal law; so the determinism was modified by individual character, itself diversified through the effects of heredity and environment. But the problem of evil was never satisfactorily resolved.

This moral incoherence at the heart of Stoicism (despite its remarkable intellectual achievements in a diversity of fields, most notably logic) was almost certainly responsible for the double standard of conduct notoriously practiced by such men as Brutus or Seneca. The system of moral casuistry worked out by Panaetius's disciple Hecaton (2d–1st c. B.C.), and dedicated to Quintus Aelius Tubero, an earnest Roman student of Stoicism who figures as a character in Cicero's *De Republica*, showed how the virtuous man would deal with apparent conflicts of interest.[33] It was designed, like Stoicism's second-rank precepts for those who did not aspire to the perfection of the sage, to keep statesmen and businessmen happy.[34] Wealth (despite the Stoic paradox of riches not being a good) Hecaton justified by the intent to use it well, a crucial matter for Romans, who set great store by the maintenance of family property (*res familiaris*). Were provisions dear? Then economize on your slaves. Did shipwreck threaten? The Stoic had a moral duty to look after himself first. No wonder Hecaton was popular in Rome. Intellectuals have always been adept at rationalizing their own hypocrisies, so that Brutus saw no inconsistency between his Stoic ideals (which were quite genuine) and his financial extortions on Cyprus (above, p. 555), while Nero's tutor and minister Seneca was quite happy, while extolling poverty, to reap the rich rewards of corrupt imperial patronage for as long as favor continued to come his way.[35]

It could almost be said that one purpose of Stoicism—certainly of Roman Stoicism—was, precisely, to enable such men to live with their own consciences, and to have a consistent moral front to present to the world. The fact that Stoicism also provided moral and intellectual backing for would-be Republican opponents of the Julio-Claudian emperors is in no way contradicted by this. A universal system has something for everyone, and can be interpreted in many ways. Scaevola and Rutilius Rufus found in it arguments against robbing their province;[36] Brutus, clearly, took a different view. It is, indeed, arguable that the close association of Stoicism with Roman Republicanism was purely fortuitous, being occasioned in part by a vague similarity of moral attitude, but more by the roll call of distinguished Roman figures, from Scipio Aemilianus onwards, who had (often because of that similarity) taken an active interest in Stoic ethics prior to the fall of the Republic.[37] Indeed, it is often hard to tell where the *mos maiorum* ends and Stoicism begins. Both Quintus Mucius Scaevola and Rutilius Rufus (like Cato of Utica in a later generation) conducted their public lives with a rigorous honesty, moderation, and regard for justice that was taken at the time, by some, as an index of Stoic principles;[38] but the Stoics had no monopoly of integrity, and our evidence suggests that both these men, Rutilius Rufus in particular, may have been at least as strongly influenced by their own traditional stern Roman code.

Stoicism may be conveniently divided into three main periods, with only two of which are we directly concerned here. The Early Stoa[39] (3d–2d c.) witnessed the pioneering work of the founder, Zeno of Citium (335/4–263/2), breakaway movements by Ariston and Herillus (interesting chiefly in that they were treated as heretics by the apostolic succession),[40] and the systematized development of Zeno's teaching by two successive heads of the Stoa: Cleanthes, who succeeded Zeno in 263/2, and, above all, Chrysippus (*prostatēs* from 232 until his death in 207), with follow-up work done by their disciples, continuing unbroken at least through the tenure of Antipater of Tarsus (ca. 150–129), though the last-named heralded change by making modifications (not always sensible ones) to Stoic ethical theory in response to Academic criticism.[41]

Fig. 196. Composite portrait of
Chrysippus (marble torso in the
Louvre, plus a cast of a head in the
British Museum). Roman copies from a
late third-century-B.C. Greek original.
Musée du Louvre, Paris. Photo Giraudon.

That criticism was, as we have seen (above, p. 607), itself occasioned by the
wide-ranging, often brilliant work of Chrysippus. "Without Chrysippus," it was
said, "there would have been no Stoa," but the precise nature of his achievement has
been much debated.[42] That he systematized and strengthened Stoic doctrine against
attacks by Skeptics and Academics is certain.[43] "Give me your doctrines," he told
Cleanthes, very much in character, "and I will find the proofs for them."[44] But how
original was he? He wrote an enormous amount (705 books, according to one estimate), setting himself to turn out five hundred lines a day without fail; but much of
this seems to have been padded out with citations from other authors, not at first
sight an encouraging sign.[45] On the other hand his reputation for dialectic stood very
high: if the gods took it up, the saying went, Chrysippus would be their model.[46]
The best modern investigation, that by Josiah Gould, confirms his ancient reputation, and emphasizes the original elements in his thought: in particular his novel "development of a logic of propositions in the context of dialectic, conceived as the
search for truth by means of argument" (though here surely Plato had blazed the
trail?),[47] his systematic defense of providential determinism, his stress on sound
logic, his ethical radicalism, the cumulative impact his work had on subsequent gen-

erations. He anticipated Poseidonius in working out a theory of universal *sympatheia*; his main weakness was an understandable desire to reconcile the principle of determinism with a belief in the individual's accountability for his conduct. Arrogant and caustic, a former long-distance runner, this short, slight man[48] comes across, in the few anecdotes we have of him, with extraordinary vividness and power.

Chrysippus never dedicated any of his innumerable volumes to a king; and this was not, I think, because some king (unnamed, but probably Ptolemy II or Antiochus I)[49] confiscated his father's Cilician estate when he was a boy. Criticized for not going along "with everyone" to hear Ariston lecture, he retorted: "If I went along with everyone, I wouldn't be into philosophy." Asked by a father to suggest the best mentor for his son, Chrysippus named himself: "If I thought there was anyone better around, I'd be studying with him."[50] He also mocked the new genteel puritanism, not only by repeating those old Cynical clichés designed to *épater les bourgeois*, endorsements of cannibalism and incest (above, p. 615), but also by including, in a treatise *On the Ancient Natural Philosophers*, an "extraordinarily indecent" version of "the Zeus and Hera story," including details and words "that no one would soil his lips by repeating."[51] He sounds a delightful person. And who could resist his acerbic comments on several of the more popular ways ("ridiculous," he calls them, and not without reason) in which Hellenistic intellectuals made a living? Don't accept royal patronage, he says: you have to go along with your patron. Don't cadge off your friends: that turns friendship into a commercial transaction. In fact, don't live by your wits, since that means your wits are for hire.[52] Prosy and pretentious Chrysippus may have been on occasion; but in this world of tired rhetoric, venal ambitions, and endemic hypocrisy he comes across like a fresh wind off the sea.

By the time of the Middle Stoa (late 2d–1st c.) Stoicism had spread from Athens to various other parts of the Mediterranean, including Rome. The Middle Stoa was chiefly remarkable for revisionist work—in part at least stimulated by the attacks of Carneades—carried out by the Rhodian Panaetius (ca. 185–109), who succeeded Antipater of Tarsus in 129, and the cosmopolitan Syrian Greek Poseidonius of Apamea (135–ca. 45), who taught in Rhodes, where Cicero met him (79–77).[53] Panaetius—followed in some areas by Poseidonius, rejected in others—set about purging Stoicism of its more embarrassing early tenets (e.g., the Cynic belief in the abolition of temples, marriages, and coinage; the justification, in certain circumstances, of incest—a bow to the Ptolemies?—and cannibalism; the odd concept of *ekpyrōsis*, a recurrent world conflagration);[54] revamped its physics to bring them more into line with current advances in astronomy and mathematics; rejected, as a corollary, the practice of astrology, while casting serious doubts on divination (both were soon back again: their removal put too much strain on the doctrine of *sympatheia*);[55] and, perhaps most important in the long run, diluted Stoicism's ethical stringency to provide a moral package deal with attractive features for generals, statesmen, and financiers. They were, in fact, unconsciously preparing the Stoa, in those crucial years between Pydna (168) and Sulla's sack of Athens (86), for a pragmatic takeover by Rome.

Many principles and beliefs of Stoic philosophy sorted well, as we have seen, with the early Republican ethical tradition: in particular the emphasis on plain simple thought, and a plain simple manner of speaking in which to express it. Perhaps more important was the "Stoic insistence on *humanitas*, man's moral obligation to consider the interests of other members of his species,"[56] though the way in which this tenet was interpreted on occasion (by Stoics as by others: not everyone could be a Scaevola) must have brought wry smiles to the lips of, say, the Asiatic Greeks. All this led, eventually, to the third and final phase of Stoicism, under the Roman empire, which in Seneca, Epictetus, and the emperor Marcus Aurelius—an oddly assorted trio— produced the only Stoics whose work survives today other than in quotations and fragments.[57] Their value is thus immeasurable: not so much doctrinally, since here they have little new to offer, but in the emotional quality of their committal, some- thing we miss in earlier fragments—though here, as in other matters, Seneca presents something of a special case.[58] By their day both doctrine and universe had, so to speak, congealed; and "what matters above all to Epictetus and Marcus Aurelius in the sec- ond century AD is moral exhortation within the framework of the Stoic universe."[59] The tone is the same in each case: urgent, passionate, hortatory. Emperor and ex-slave speak with the same moral fervor. To read them is a haunting experience.

Zeno's death occurred within the period 263–261: he was awarded a gold crown, a tomb at public expense in the Kerameikos, and funerary reliefs in the Academy and the Lyceum.[60] He had been a friend of Antigonus Gonatas, against whom Athens had joined that desperate Peloponnesian coalition to fight the ill-starred Chremoni- dean War (above, p. 147). On the other hand he had rebuffed approaches from Ptolemy III Euergetes, who supported Athens (for his own purposes, and with no great vigor) against Antigonus.[61] Despite these alignments, the citizens of Athens could still, in defeat, the prospect of freedom gone, do honor to the memory of this resident alien who had refused their citizenship, because (as they put on the citation) he "had turned the younger generation toward virtue and *sōphrosynē*, and had exem- plified in his own life the virtues that he taught." They may have been obliging An- tigonus—it was his agent, we are told, who requested a Kerameikos burial for Zeno[62]—but I think there was more to it than mere political subservience. That dark and enigmatic figure in the Painted Stoa,[63] with his diet of bread and honey, and his modest cup of good wine, had become, like Socrates before him, an institution. More important still, the vision of universal harmony that he proclaimed must have sustained and comforted many in those dark days, when a Macedonian garrison was quartered on the Hill of the Muses, and the democratic leaders of Athens were either dead or (like Chremonides himself) in the service of Ptolemy. Antigonus was gener- ous to Athens: as early as 256/5 he pulled out his garrison and left the city to manage its own internal affairs (above, p. 147).[64] But everyone knew, too well, where the real power lay now, and just how much freedom to manage the city's affairs was worth.

This historical background should never be forgotten when we are examining Stoic doctrine.[65] At the time even the assumption of a new universe, arising from the fiery ashes of its predecessor, might well have had a certain *Götterdämmerung*-like attraction, while faith in a fundamentally providential universe, with reason and na- ture achieving perfect concord, offered a powerful temptation to belief. To live in harmony with reason was to live in harmony with nature; to live in harmony with nature was to live in harmony with God, and this harmonious relationship was itself the definition of virtue based on true knowledge, which for Zeno formed the only good. It was charged against the Stoics, very early on, that they set up a goal beyond human achievement, since the Stoic sage—absolutely wise, brave, continent, and just in his knowledge of truth, indifference to fortune, and freedom from prejudice—was an ideal (to put it mildly) more easily defined than attained. Such ideals, however, in a world of crumbling assurances, have a sustaining value irrelevant to their practicability.

A more telling criticism would be that Stoicism failed to satisfy everyday religious needs: its adherents were, paradoxically, less tolerant of traditional observances and popular (as opposed to intellectual) superstitions than the Epicureans. To find room for the other Olympians—Zeus, of course, was a special case—only as personified natural phenomena (e.g., Hephaestus as fire, Hera as air) shows the bleak side of that celestial cosmos, with its unrelenting universal rationalism. Nor was there any place in this creed for mysticism, since mysticism, again, defied the canons of reason. This may well be what prompted a resurgence, in the first century B.C., of—of all things—Pythagoreanism, not to mention the steady and progressive increase of interest in magic, ecstatic cults, and the like (cf. above, pp. 586 ff.). The only logical outlet of this sort that Stoicism could provide was by way of divination and mathematical astrology.[66]

On the other hand, increasing commercialism, and the vast new potential clientele represented by Rome's administrative and business world, made it inevitable that the moral rigidity of early Stoicism should be progressively relaxed under the Middle Stoa. Once Panaetius had rejected the stern dictum that only the wise man could be virtuous, the rest followed easily enough.[67] Virtue, of a middling sort, could now be conceded to those who were "progressing" (*prokoptontes*) toward its acquisition. It was no longer essential to aspire to absolute wisdom. Cicero's *De Officiis* gives a fascinating account of this "second-level," practical moralizing in action.[68]

It is tempting, but probably useless, to speculate how far, and in what ways, the ethics of the Middle Stoa may have influenced individual Roman statesmen; to what extent the latter were forced, by the demands of Roman politics, to compromise their Stoic principles; or, indeed, the degree to which the principles themselves may have been modified as a result of exposure to Roman pragmatism. By the nature of the case, evidence is lacking: private (as opposed to declared) motivation is, by its very genesis, almost impossible to document. It could be argued that men like Scipio Aemilianus and Rutilius Rufus, however much they might amuse themselves by taking up Stoicism as an intellectual pastime, had the aristocratic *mos maiorum* to guide them, and were well able to make difficult moral decisions, in their public no less than their private lives, without any recourse to theoretical rules of conduct drawn up by Greek philosophers. At the same time there can be no doubt that Panaetius, Poseidonius, and Hecaton went to great pains to work out a code of ethics tailor-made for men of action, and their careers suggest with some force that it was a

Roman audience that they primarily had in mind. To work in active cooperation with the world order would not be too hard when that order was being more closely identified, as time went on, with Roman *imperium* itself. It looks very much as though Hecaton's moral casuistry in particular was designed to cater for Rome's new politicians, whose moral sensibilities were a good deal more accommodating than Cato's, and who were naturally eager to acquire intellectual justification for their ambitious (but less than scrupulous) enterprises.

Though Panaetius clung to the providential framework (and even served on Rhodes as a priest of Poseidon),[69] he was quite ready, as we have seen, to reject astrology and divination, and indeed to play down the cosmic aspects of Stoicism generally in favor of practical ethics. (As Rist says, "it is clear that Panaetius's formulation of the end for man is this-worldly.")[70] Virtue is all very well, but health, strength, and capital are all prime desiderata.[71] Act in consonance with human nature as a whole, and your own nature in particular: the *De Officiis* may not have been written as a handbook for self-deceivers (any more than Panaetius's lost work *On Duty*, which formed its source), but on occasion it reads remarkably like it.

Lesky claims that Panaetius wrote his tract "with one eye on Rome," and that about sums it up.[72] Von Fritz takes a similar line: "He tried to adapt Stoic ethics to the requirements of the life of the Roman *grands seigneurs* with whom he associated, by putting into the foreground the more active and brilliant virtues of magnanimity, benevolence, and liberality."[73] This was a natural attitude for him to assume. He was aristocratic and paternalist in outlook, property-conscious, closely associating generosity (i.e., charity) with the concept of justice.[74] In Rome as a young Rhodian nobleman he had been admitted to the circle of Scipio and Laelius (ca. 144),[75] and saw how Stoic doctrine could be modified to win a socially prestigious following from this new world. Head of the Stoa from 129 until his death, he divided not only his time but also his moral protreptics between the needs of Athens and of Rome.

Poseidonius—his student in Athens, and perhaps the most elusive figure in Stoicism (ca. 135–ca. 45)[76]—was a widely traveled polymath, familiar with North Africa and the western Mediterranean,[77] who not only dabbled (though without much originality) in every subject from oceanography to mathematics, but also wrote history (starting in 146, where Polybius left off)[78] as a vindication of Roman imperialism, especially in the East. He was, not surprisingly, strongly biased in favor of the *nobilitas*, and thus came out against the Gracchi, the *equites*, and, indeed, the "independent" Greeks who had, so fatally for themselves, supported Mithridates.[79] Pompey, not surprisingly, treated him with considerable respect: the respect seems to have been mutual. Before setting out on his campaigns against the pirates, Mithridates, and the Parthians (68/7: below, pp. 657–58 ff.), the Roman general attended a lecture by the Stoic philosopher, who sent him on his way with an encouraging tag from Homer.[80] On his triumphant return in 62, Pompey once more visited Rhodes, where he heard Poseidonius, along with other orators, deliver a polemical display speech (each of them got a talent for his pains: the victor was in a generous, Alexander-like mood). He also paid a personal call on the old philosopher at home, leaving his lictors outside as a mark of respect. Poseidonius, though laid low by a painful, and

Fig. 197. Poseidonius. Roman copy of
an early first-century-B.C. original.
Museo Nazionale, Naples. Photo Alinari.

symbolically opportune, attack of arthritis, insisted on giving Pompey a long private
lecture from his sickbed, on the theme "Only the honorable is good," punctuated by
cries of agony that also let him stress his refusal to admit pain as an evil.[81] Seldom in
the ancient world can we so clearly observe two publicity-hungry V.I.P.'s putting
on an act for each other. No accident that Poseidonius—playing Callisthenes to
Pompey's Alexander—afterwards wrote an account of The Great One's eastern
campaigns.

Poseidonius, rationalizing a *fait accompli* to the best of his considerable abilities,
"aimed at showing that the Roman empire, embracing as it did all the peoples of the
world, embodied the commonwealth of mankind and reflected the commonwealth
of God, to which deserving statesmen and philosophers were to be admitted after
the fulfilment of their earthly task."[82] Rome, in short, was now being incorporated
into the cosmic order, just as her emperors would, in due course, be assimilated to
the heavenly pantheon. Poseidonius attacked Chrysippus for denying the existence
of an irrational element in the soul (this inferior element was the cause of human
passion, i.e.—an interesting equation—of moral evil, and had to be subordinated to
reason: again, a highly Platonic concept),[83] though whether he was ready to concede
a matching irrationality in the cosmos is not at all clear. He also credited early *sophoi*
with technological inventions, for example husbandry, metalworking, house construction: a standard notion, one might have thought, and straight from Aeschylus's
Prometheus,[84] but it shocked Seneca, who reports it, as being irredeemably banausic:[85]

no sage—declares that wealthy rentier—ever troubled his head with such mundane matters.

It has been argued that Poseidonius was, *inter alia*, determined to bring Stoicism back to the empirical sciences, to cut it free from overdoctrinaire scholasticism, and in a restricted sense this is true;[86] but it only takes Seneca's comment to remind us of just what such an effort was up against: the whole cultural dead weight of the Graeco-Roman class structure, the deep prejudice against applied science of any sort, the mingled fear of, and contempt for, the artisanate. In any case, despite his own practical skills (mapmaking, construction of spheres, measuring the earth's circumference), Poseidonius was still very much in thrall to traditional Stoic dogma. His research still aimed to demonstrate an essential harmony between the divine and the mundane worlds: not for nothing did he posit a class of heroes and *daimones* as intermediaries between mankind and the prime mover (an archaic reversion that would have won Pindar's approval). He may have investigated causation, but if so he was on his own: most Stoics were only interested in causes as an aspect of personal responsibility. Poseidonius could not reverse this trend singlehanded, and indeed seems to have capitulated to it.[87] Worse, he lost no time in restoring divination and astrology (so recently outlawed by Panaetius) to their old place of honor in Stoic physics,[88] and, if Rist is right, his rejection of other traditional Stoic views on physics and the soul was directly responsible for the subsequent degeneration of Stoicism generally into mere tired moralizing.[89]

What he ended by doing, in effect, was writing ethical guidelines for Roman businessmen and provincial governors; and just how morally effective his exhortations were we may judge from Cicero's prosecution of Gaius Verres, or the extortion and chicanery that led to Mithridates' mass slaughter of Roman businessmen and officials in Asia. He and Panaetius between them had introduced Stoicism to Rome; once that was done, the restless, questing intellectual energy that had, to begin with, characterized the Middle Stoa became a liability rather than an asset, and duly gave way to safe systematizing, the rationalization of self-advancement (though only in the *Überschicht*), and legalistic arguments for a general law of nature, to which all human laws—not to mention the lower orders—must inevitably conform. For the Romans, philosophy was, at best, a moral instrument for the reinforcement of practical objectives, and, in the last resort, cultural top-dressing rather than an integral part of human existence. Pohlenz's bitter assault on the pragmatic, antispeculative nature of the Roman mind went too far,[90] and a case could be made for Roman Stoics choosing to concern themselves with day-to-day ethics rather than "the niceties of cosmological speculation about a mentally constructed universe."[91] But it is hard to deny what has been called "the monumental moralising dullness" of Roman Stoicism,[92] and in the concept of natural law (see below) it left a dangerous legacy to the Renaissance. Cicero summed up the Roman attitude to perfection: "One should know what philosophy teaches, but live like a gentleman."[93]

As Long stresses, it was exceptional men like Cato who managed, by sheer dint of moral example, to make Stoicism a workable Roman ideal.[94] It was also such men (and, on occasion, women) who gave considerable publicity to what has always been one of the most ethically ambiguous of Stoic precepts: that suicide, in appropriate circumstances—if found "naturally advantageous," for example during a painful terminal illness, or under intolerable political oppression—is not only logical, but commendable.[95] Socrates, for instance, was held to have died voluntarily, when a more tactful defense (or a privately arranged escape from prison) could have saved him,[96] and Plato seems to allow an exception here (as he also does in cases of prohibitive suffering or shame) to his general condemnation of taking one's own life. That Seneca, of all people, should have been obsessed by the idea of suicide as the key to freedom is ironic;[97] but the principle of "reasonable departure" (*eulogos exagōgē, rationalis e uita excessus*), though treated to begin with, in a mood of very un-Senecan indifference, as simply one more option open to the wise man, went back at least as far as Chrysippus.[98] It was probably even older, since both Zeno and Cleanthes are reported to have put an end to their own lives (the first by holding his breath after breaking a toe, the second by starving himself while suffering from inflammation of the gums).[99] It is, of course, possible that what we have here are late *ex post facto* fables designed to make a neat point (and to give a more recent concept the founder's *imprimatur*); it could also be that Zeno and Cleanthes, both of whom died at an advanced age, simply took a symptom—the broken toe, the inflamed gums—as a sign that their time had come.

Now the Cynics, including Diogenes and Crates, had casually recommended suicide as "the remedy for any kind of failure to live a rational life,"[100] and this may have been one of the notions that Zeno took over from them in his early formative period. As we might expect, what most interested the Stoics was when it could be regarded as reasonable (*eulogon*) to kill yourself: appropriate intention was all. A wide gap, both in time and attitude, separated this coolly rational vindication of free will from the virtual suicide cult that afterwards developed among Republican-minded Roman intellectuals under the Julio-Claudian emperors. Yet we should also note that acceptance of the political motive for suicide began early: if Plato means what he says, with Socrates. What later came to be known, somewhat pretentiously, as the "gateway to freedom"[101] took the notion of contracting out of society (which Epicureans had only played at) to a theoretical extreme as grim as it was irrefutable, and offers eloquent testimony to the mounting strains and pressures of the Hellenistic age.[102]

The Stoic attitude to suicide is only one of many paradoxes engendered by a system that attempted to reconcile free will and moral responsibility with a deterministic and materialistic world ruled immutably by fate and providence.[103] The will *was* free, and, thus, morally responsible, but should ideally be subsumed to living in harmony with nature (*physis*); and nature, through that *sympatheia* binding microcosm and macrocosm, moved with the eternal regular order of the heavens. Thus the Stoic always trod a thin line between brilliant intuitions and theoretical nonsense, between continuum physics and astrology.[104] His ethics, to begin with, were no better nor worse than those of any other Greek philosophical movement: the pursuit of happiness (*eudaimonia*) as the prime good, the identification of happiness with virtue, and of virtue with knowledge—none of this was new, and much of it had been more forcefully propounded by Plato. But the notion that what mattered was a right attitude to the things of this world, most of which were morally neutral or indifferent (*adiaphora*), had, as we have seen, a most interesting consequence: it allowed anyone to square the vicious circle of his conscience by professing a set of moral beliefs, without detriment to his worldly circumstances. As a device for serving both God and Mammon this was unbeatable.

More important still, the idea of natural law could be exploited to provide backing, justification, and stability for authoritarian government. Order and hierarchy were all: the stable *status quo* must be preserved for ever. Just how all-pervasive this concept could be becomes clear when we compare late Hellenistic society with post-Reformation Tudor England. Hooker's *Laws of Ecclesiastical Polity* (1593), Sir Thomas Elyot's *Boke Named the Governour* (1531; 10th ed. 1600), and Shakespeare's *Troilus and Cressida* (1603?) all speak with the same voice, which by now the reader should have no difficulty in recognizing: "The heavens themselves, the planets and this centre / Observe degree, priority and place . . / . . Take but degree away, untune that string, / And hark, what discord follows!" Like Hellenistic rulers, too, Tudor sovereigns "regarded rebellion as the greatest danger to society as well as to their dynasty, whether it was provoked by 'over mighty subjects' or fermented by discontented rural labourers."[105] It is odd to reflect that Charles I may have lost his head because of a long-delayed and violent reaction against theories first propounded by Zeno, Chrysippus, and their successors; odd, and also sobering, since it reminds us that the most powerful and persistent ideas are not always those dictated by reason or common sense. We have to face the fact that "for the Stoics cosmology was an integral part of philosophy, and inextricably connected with their ethics":[106] hence the world as a providentially planned work of the divine mover, with which human reason must coincide; hence the necessary acceptance of fate, of the fixed order. The political and social implications of such a system need no further emphasis. What is perhaps less obvious, yet even more deleterious in its long-term effects, is the all-too-characteristic confusion of physical and ethical determinants that flaws the Stoic model of the universe.

CHAPTER 37

CAESAR, POMPEY, AND THE LAST OF THE PTOLEMIES, 80–30

One of the more tempting excuses for Rome's progressively more radical, steadily less reluctant policy of intervention and eventual takeover in the eastern Mediterranean was, beyond any doubt, the patent inability of the rulers *in situ* to manage their own affairs. This not only encouraged what Rome, and conservatives generally, saw as dangerous sociopolitical trends—mass movements by the dispossessed, encroachment by non-Mediterranean tribal elements—but, worse, proved disastrous for trade, a fault that Roman administrative paternalism could seldom resist the temptation to correct. In addition to the rampant scourge of piracy—for which, as we have seen (above, p. 557), Roman policy itself was at least in part responsible—a general condition of acute economic and, intermittently, political anarchy now afflicted both Syria and Egypt. Cities, local chieftains, and individuals all broke away when they could from a now highly inefficient (though no less captious and oppressive) system of central bureaucracy. Endless internecine dynastic conflicts, combined with relentless extortion (to pay for these and other excesses), had all but destroyed the countryside.

Since both Syria and Egypt were potentially the most fertile and productive areas imaginable, this represented a more than usually monumental feat of short-sighted stupidity—and indeed one is constantly amazed at just how much, even *in extremis*, could still be extracted from the inhabitants to meet yet another crisis. Alexandria, of course, had the advantage, in addition, of still-substantial royal treasures. In 59 Ptolemy XII Auletes raised almost six thousand talents,[1] perhaps a year's revenue, perhaps less, to bribe Caesar, now consul, into successfully upholding his claim to recognition by the Senate,[2] which thus showed itself prepared, once again, to forget the terms of Ptolemy X's will (above, p. 553). Though some of this money was raised through a loan, or loans, from the Roman banker Gaius Rabirius Postumus,[3] the rest came from Ptolemy's own resources, while the loans were recouped by extorting extra funds from his long-suffering subjects. His annual revenues, in-

647

deed, were variously estimated at between six and twelve and a half thousand talents.[4] Even so, the Egyptian *chōra* was in a desperate state. Too many peasants had either been sold off into slavery, or else driven by despair to quit their holdings and join the ubiquitous bands of brigand mercenaries that had come, together with the pirates,[5] to form a virtual *tiers état*, an unacknowledged countersociety preying on the system it had abandoned.

This was a situation that positively invited Rome's attention. Unfortunately, as we have seen, the profit principle proved no less irresistible to Roman administrators, businessmen, and, all too soon, senators than it had done to the Macedonians. The tradition, after all, was well established. It had been what panhellenism was all about, as early as the fourth century: a united ethnic crusade against the East, with wealth and power as its objectives, cultural superiority (and Xerxes' long-past invasion) as its justification. That had been the whole moral basis of Alexander's expedition, of the sharing of the spoils by his successors. Material greed and racial contempt had been the fuel that maintained Macedonians in power, from the Nile to the Euphrates, for three centuries—while their own *mores* steadily degenerated, and, more subtly, were infiltrated by the culture of those whose capital they stole, whose languages they ignored. Now, with the Romans—whom Alexander's descendants, prematurely, also dismissed as mere barbarians (above, p. 318)—the situation was abruptly reversed: it was Rome that very soon began to display contempt for these effete and fractious dynasts.

Examples abound. We recall the circle that an impatient commissioner drew in the dust round Antiochus Epiphanes on the Day of Eleusis (above, p. 431), or the way in which Scipio Aemilianus led the unwieldy Ptolemy Physcon, at a cracking pace, on foot, through the streets of Alexandria (above, p. 539). For indecision or excess a well-brought-up Roman had nothing but contempt. When Ptolemy XII Auletes, *en route* for Rome, visited Cato of Utica in Rhodes, after being driven out of Alexandria (59/8)—his six-thousand-talent bribe might have bought him Rome's recognition, but the extortions employed to pay it off did not endear him to his subjects[6]—Cato, who had a touch of the coarse Cynic about him to offset his Stoicism, received his visitor while suffering from acute dysentery, and lectured him, in vain, on the disadvantages of dealing with Rome's corrupt leaders.[7] Had the Romans brought to Asia a reasonable moderation to temper their administrative efficiency, they would have been welcomed everywhere with open arms. Unhappily, the basic attitude of almost every Republican proconsul or praetor was precisely that of his Macedonian predecessors: here was an unbelievably rich Oriental milch cow, to be squeezed for all it would yield, a handy source for paying off campaign debts or funding grandiose Campanian building projects. The principle of exploitative foreign domination was upheld: the Romans, as should by now be clear, simply organized the extraction with greater ruthlessness and finesse.

The provincials did not fail to take note of the fate (in this case a rigged trial and exile) that befell an administrator, like Rutilius Rufus, who tried to give them equitable treatment.[8] The inevitable result was Mithridates' massacre of Roman and Italian citizens, followed by a major uprising. Yet the lesson was not learned even then.

In 68 the effective political destruction of Lucullus,[9] despite his formidable successes against Mithridates (below, p. 656), showed just what lay in store for any Roman consul or general, however well placed, who incurred the wrath of the tax farmers and *negotiatores* by showing himself too lenient (in their view) toward provincials. It took Octavian's cool and long-term cynicism to realize that better results could be obtained by clipping the herd rather than fleecing it, and his immense *auctoritas* to deal with the financiers effectively. With the empire came some sort of equity, provincial justice, and sensible capital investment. Under the dying Republic it was, rather, a case of one corrupt foreign administration stepping in to replace another when it destroyed itself.

Behind the last convulsive struggles of Seleucids and Ptolemies Roman policy— or, worse, free enterprise minus a policy—can always be sensed in the background. Worse still, from the viewpoint of the Greeks in particular, was the imposition of rival foreign warlords—Caesar and Pompey, Octavian and Antony—who not only fought out their own dynastic struggles on Greek soil and in Greek waters, but bled the inhabitants white for supplies, from grain to warships, and had an unnerving habit of executing those who chose the wrong (i.e., the unsuccessful) side. Roman egotism was matched, as so often, by Greek cynicism: survival became the prime objective, and Cavafy catches the mood to perfection in a poem about the news of Actium, a naval battle that Octavian (against Greek hopes and expectations) won, reaching Asia Minor. A local official, responsible for the organization of an honorific decree lauding the victor, reflects: "But there's no need for us to draft a new text. / Only the name needs changing."[10] The "parody of a Caesar," the "ruinous" figure from whom Greece has been rescued, is now, like one of those mass-produced statues with interchangeable heads (above, p. 574), ANTONIOS rather than, as originally planned, OKTABIOS: the same number of letters, a snug fit for a *stoichēdon* inscription, with its crosswordlike regularity of horizontal and vertical spacings.

If Ptolemy Auletes—the self-styled *Theos Philopatōr Philadelphos Neos Dionysos*, but known in Alexandria, more accurately on several counts, as "the Bastard" (above, p. 554)—enjoyed a relatively undisturbed reign of almost thirty years (80– 59/8, 55–51) in which to indulge his passion for flute playing (*Aulētēs* means "Piper") and other, less mentionable, habits, that was no tribute to his strength of character.[11] "He was not a man," says Athenaeus, contemptuously, "but a flute blower, a trickster."[12] On an inscription from the temple of Isis at Philae one of the king's Greek votaries proudly describes himself as "Tryphon, Catamite of the Young Dionysus":[13] he was perhaps a member of one of those Dionysiac guilds of actors and musicians that supported the Ptolemaic ruler cult.[14] There were, in fact, two good reasons why Ptolemy Auletes, and his kingdom, survived as long as they did. To begin with, he had no serious rivals for the throne. This did not mean he was popular—far from it—but it did set his enemies a problem when it came to replacing him. At the time of his enforced exile in 59/8, while this new *socius atque amicus populi Romani*, based, with his retinue, on Pompey's Alban estate, was shopping round Rome for further political backing (and, more important, for further massive loans to service his existing debts), the Alexandrians—who had thrown him out, in

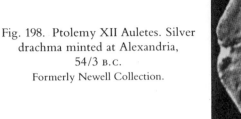

Fig. 198. Ptolemy XII Auletes. Silver
drachma minted at Alexandria,
54/3 B.C.
Formerly Newell Collection.

the first instance, partly for his tame acquiescence in Rome's absorption of Cyprus (below, p. 652), partly on account of the extortionate way he went about recouping the bribes he had disbursed,[15] and in general showed remarkable unanimity in their opposition to his Roman subservience[16]—scraped the very bottom of the dynastic barrel trying to find any acceptable substitute for him.[17]

After a little-known son of Cleopatra Selene had died on them during negotiations, and a grandson of Antiochus VIII Grypos had been vetoed by Aulus Gabinius, Pompey's henchman and now governor of Syria (who was by this time in receipt of bribes from Auletes), in desperation they picked on an alleged royal claimant whose chief title to consideration was the name of Seleucus.[18] His appearance, and oafish manners, got him the nickname in Alexandria of *Kybiosaktēs*, "the Salt-Fish Hawker." The ulterior purpose of this frantic search was to find a male consort for Auletes' daughter Berenice, who had been proclaimed queen in her father's absence, perhaps at first as a temporary measure. The evidence is patchy, and in places contradictory,[19] but sense can be—indeed, has been[20]—made of it. Auletes left behind, as co-regents in his absence, his wife (and sister) Cleopatra V Tryphaena, together with their eldest daughter, Berenice IV.[21] Two other daughters, Arsinoë and Cleopatra VII, the future queen, were barely adolescent, while the boys, Ptolemy XIII and Ptolemy XIV, were still infants. Cleopatra Tryphaena's regency was terminated after about a year, in 57, by her death. At this point it was considered vital that Berenice IV, now sole regent, should marry, and Seleucus Kybiosaktes was picked, *faute de mieux*, as consort. Berenice and her backers were now clearly aiming at permanent usurpation.

After a few days of marital intimacy, however, Berenice came to the conclusion that there were some humiliations not even political ambition could sweeten, and had her new husband strangled. To replace him *en secondes noces* she chose one Archelaus, who claimed Mithridates as his father (and had been making overtures to Aulus Gabinius on that basis), but was in fact the son of Sulla's old opponent of that name (above, p. 563). A little plebeian blood, it might be thought, would not come amiss in the Ptolemaic pedigree. Not that this alliance did her much good either: in due course her father, Auletes, having laid out the vast sum of ten thousand talents for that privilege,[22] was brought back to Egypt, in anything but a loving paternal mood. Aulus Gabinius—hand in glove with the king's backers, led by Rabirius Postumus (see below)—invaded Egypt, defeated Archelaus's lackluster army, and, on Pompey's advice, returned Auletes to his throne (55), where one of the restored monarch's first acts, predictably enough, was to execute the overambitious Berenice.[23] Gabinius's cavalry commander during this expedition was the young Mark Antony,[24] who (as at least one ancient source, almost inevitably, alleges)[25] found himself much attracted by another of the king's daughters, the fourteen-year-old

Fig. 199. The Ptolemaic temple of Horus at Edfu (Apollonopolis Magna). The great pylon shown here was begun in 116 B.C. and completed only in 57 B.C. Ptolemy XII Auletes is portrayed both making offerings to the gods and smiting his enemies in traditional style.
Photo Roger-Viollet.

Cleopatra, now left, in terms of age, as next in line for the throne. Nothing came of this attraction at the time, if it ever existed: Cleopatra always went for top people, and Antony still had his way to make.

Despite his spendthrift ways and dissolute character, Auletes, once restored, held on to the throne of Egypt until his death. Cyrenaica had been finally taken over by Rome in 74 (above, p. 551); Cyprus, too, as we have seen, in 58 became part of the province of Cilicia,[26] so that Ptolemy was now left with Egypt alone as his fief— a situation that his daughter Cleopatra, in due course, would go to great lengths to reverse. Even here, however, he was encumbered by maladministration and bad debts. As a desperate measure, and under heavy pressure from Gabinius, he invited his main Roman creditor, the banker Gaius Rabirius Postumus, to become his finance minister (*dioikētēs*). Better, from Rome's viewpoint, to let the local bureaucracy collect what was owing, under Roman supervision, than turn the country over to the doubtful mercies of an overindependent tax-gathering consortium.[27] The financial activities of Rabirius are graphically described by Cicero in a speech for his defense: we hear of his wide-ranging contracts, his involvement in state enterprises, his provincial investments and vast foreign loans, to governments and kings.[28] We know such men well: today their credit is similarly overextended abroad, and they suffer very similar embarrassments in consequence.

Rabirius, though a little unhappy (like many Romans of his sort, he was thoroughly xenophobic) at the thought of abandoning his toga and going Greek, nevertheless saw this appointment as a godsend. He had an enormous amount at stake, and what better way was there to enforce the payment of the king's debt, with interest, than to preside over the royal exchequer?[29] In other words, as *dioikētēs* he would be using the available Ptolemaic system to guarantee Roman interests. He set about this task with such uncommon dedication that before a year was out he had to leave Egypt in a hurry (54/3): Ptolemy's "imprisonment" of him—a restriction from which he seems to have escaped without trouble—was in fact almost certainly a protective measure designed to shield this exploitative Roman *dioikētēs* from the fury of the Alexandrians. Rabirius's enemies in Rome prosecuted him for accepting tainted money from Gabinius; Cicero made the speech in his defense.[30] The case was abandoned on a technicality. Aulus Gabinius himself had not been so lucky. His restoration of Ptolemy and his alienation of the *publicani* (again, it was suggested, through lenience to the provincials)[31] exposed him to no less than three prosecutions, for treason, bribery and extortion, and corrupt practices, respectively. The first charge—for having left his province to conduct a campaign in Egypt—ended in an acquittal, and the third was dropped; but they nailed him on the second (extortion in his province, taking bribes from Ptolemy). Cicero spoke for the defense, even though he had, shortly before, described the treason acquittal as an "impurity law," and indeed had assured his brother that he would never touch the case.[32] Despite his efforts Gabinius was found guilty, and fined ten thousand talents: by no coincidence, the precise sum that Ptolemy was said to have disbursed. This meant, in effect, a sentence of exile.

Behind this flurry of litigation in Rome we glimpse the jealous infighting of rival magnates, of Populares and Optimates; and herein, of course, lay the second reason for Ptolemy's long survival. The idea of annexing Egypt had been in the air for some time, at least since Scipio Aemilianus and his mission had come to spy out the country's resources (140/39: above, p. 539). Ptolemy X Alexander's will bequeathing Egypt to Rome of course added a new dimension to this proposition (above, p. 553). Crassus, as censor, spoke out strongly in favor of annexation (65).[33] It is no accident that the will, and the political exploitation surrounding it, first surface in a speech of Cicero's, the *De Lege Agraria*, delivered two years later, during his consulship. There were, in fact, powerful objections to annexation. A strong proconsul in Egypt, to begin with, would have an almost perfect launching pad to supreme power: all political groups in Rome were anxious, and with good reason, to keep their opponents from securing such a plum. A second, perhaps even more cogent reason was the lack of that independent municipal self-government essential to mediate between Rome and the royal fiscal bureaucracy.[34] No senatorial proconsul could find his way through *that* maze; far better to retain the monarchy, which at least could operate its own system, and then collect from the top. Thus a weak Ptolemaic ruler was the perfect compromise solution, and the Flute Player survived until his natural death in 51 through the mutual suspicions, hostilities, and calculations of his ambitious Roman patrons. No accident that when Egypt was finally, and inevitably, annexed, Augustus—in this like any Ptolemy before him—kept the country as his personal fief, entrusted it only to prefects of equestrian rank, created a professional Roman bureaucracy to administer it, and would not let a senator so much as set foot on its soil without personal authorization.

While Ptolemaic Egypt ran down slowly on borrowed time, Seleucid Syria— and Asia Minor generally—foundered in a series of almost nonstop wars. The treaty of Dardanus, imposed by Sulla on Mithridates in 85,[35] proved singularly ineffectual: it was verbal only, it lacked ratification by the Senate, and it lost all effective force with Sulla's death (78).[36] Mithridates, in fact, had received no more than a temporary setback. He had never surrendered all Cappadocia to Ariobarzanes, and as early as 83 was busy preparing a large expeditionary force to recover the Greek settlements of the Cimmerian Bosporus. On the excuse that this force constituted a threat to Rome, Sulla's governor Licinius Murena, ignoring the treaty, went to war again, and got beaten for his pains. Mithridates found this an excellent opportunity (since he could complain, justifiably, of bad faith) to expel all Roman garrisons from Cappadocia.[37] He also showed alarming signs of once more offering a focal point for all anti-Roman rebels and counterculturalists. He offered slaves their freedom, he was hand in glove with the Cilician pirates,[38] and—worst of all—in 76 or 75, seeing that another confrontation with Rome was inevitable, he made a deal with the Roman rebel general Sertorius in Spain. The political impact of this move was on a par with Philip V's Carthaginian treaty in 215 (above, p. 297).

Mithridates offered Sertorius forty ships and three thousand talents, a very sizable subvention; in return he got a military mission to reorganize his own army along Roman lines.[39] In the expectation that Sertorius would, ultimately, win his war and then, like Sulla, impose his will on Rome, Mithridates sought recognition from him of Pontic rule in Asia Minor. Sertorius, ever anxious to publicize his own Republican *bona fides*, rebel or no, conceded Mithridates' right to occupy Cappadocia and Bithynia, "nations ruled by kings and of no concern to the Romans,"[40] but

roundly condemned any attempt to recover the province of Asia, which was, he asserted, legitimately Rome's.[41] Mithridates' final objective, it seems clear, was Roman
recognition for an Anatolian empire that would, in effect, replace the crumbling Seleucid regime.[42]

The support of Sertorius was probably the decisive factor that led, almost immediately, to another Mithridatic war against Rome.[43] This time the king of Pontus,
stung by senatorial bad faith, and seeing clearly that there were many more ambitious men like Murena, only too eager to renew a, hopefully, profitable war, took
the initiative in 74 by invading Bithynia, possibly already annexed as a Roman province.[44] It is a mark of what he was up against that the situation, on the face of it, was a
good deal less encouraging than it had been in 89/8. There were, for instance, no less
than four legions now stationed in Asia Minor: a regular army of occupation. On the
other hand Mithridates had strengthened his navy, was reorganizing his army along
Roman lines, could count on the Cilician pirates as firm allies,[45] and had already
scored a more than psychological success by his defeat of Murena. The Romans,
too, were obliged to deal with Sertorius in Spain, and this reduced the forces they
could spare for an eastern campaign. But Mithridates was taking no chances. He
spent the summer and winter of 74/3 making energetic preparations for war—felling timber, building more ships, manufacturing arms, stockpiling grain, and conducting a vigorous recruiting campaign.[46] He was, as Velleius justly observed, "the
last, bar the Parthians, of the autonomous kings,"[47] independent, no puppet of
Rome—and meant to stay that way.

When Rome mobilized, late in 74, both consuls—Lucius Licinius Lucullus and
Marcus Aurelius Cotta—were commissioned to defend the East, a remarkable compliment to Mithridates' reputation: neither Philip V nor Perseus had rated this peculiar mark of respect.[48] Cotta, a breathtakingly incompetent political appointee,[49] was
to take the fleet to Bithynia (which he did, and promptly lost it); Lucullus, with all
his invaluable experience as Sulla's lieutenant, would have command of the legions in
Asia and Cilicia—a force, be it noted, less than one-quarter the size of his opponent's—and go in pursuit of Mithridates (spring 73).[50] It is interesting, and significant, that Cilicia was envisaged as the likeliest theater of operations, since this was
where the pirates conducted their business, and they, too, were very much in the
Senate's mind during 74. It was now that a special maritime command, an *imperium
infinitum*, was set up to enable a competent commander to tackle the problem of
Mediterranean piracy without being restricted to any one province.[51]

The problem had indeed become critical.[52] As early as the time of Diodotus
Tryphon in the mid-second century (above, p. 557),[53] rival rulers and rebels had encouraged the organization of piracy on a hitherto-unprecedented scale.[54] The most
profitable attraction for these corsairs, as Strabo makes clear,[55] was the slave trade, in
which the pirates for a long while got considerable covert support from Roman
businessmen.[56] But it was the backing of various governments, above all that of
Mithridates, that really encouraged what has been well described as "the biggest
growth-industry and protection-racket in the ancient world."[57] It was the growing
success of the enterprise that finally turned even Roman slave dealers against it: the

legitimate trade of the entire Mediterranean was being crippled. Piracy ruled the seas from Sicily to Crete,[58] from Crete to the Cilician coast.[59] The straits between Crete and the southern Peloponnese yielded such rich booty that the pirates referred to this stretch of water as the Golden Sea. Corsairs now ventured ashore, attacked towns and fortresses, raided temples and shrines for their valuables, even sailed into the harbor at Ostia, the port of Rome, burning and pillaging:[60] to such an extent did they disrupt commerce that the grain supply to the capital was seriously threatened.[61] Coastal areas round Brundisium and in Etruria were regularly raided: well-connected women travelers, even two praetors, despite their official insignia, had been carried off.[62]

But there was another, more socially threatening, side to the pirates' activities. They now operated with over a thousand large ships, "scorned the title of corsairs," and "likened themselves to kings, tyrants, great armies, believing that if they united, they would be invincible."[63] They are reported to have been among the first to practice Mithraism, as a secret and binding cult. They also took particular pleasure in viciously mocking Roman power and authority when a captive of rank fell into their hands.[64] Once again the lure of the alternative society can be glimpsed in this cutthroat world of rapine and revolt: not for the last time, antipopulist rhetoric about piracy and brigandage hints at a violent, desperate, but unacknowledged social conflict.[65] It was this combination of economic disruption and political radicalism that now made firm action by Rome inevitable. Short-term profiteers who had made their fortune through dealing with the pirates now were the first to demand protection against the hideous specter they had raised. There had been previous reprisals against the pirates: by Marcus Antonius in 102/1 (above, p. 557),[66] and, more recently, by Publius Servilius Vatia between 79 and 75.[67] Though more or less successful at the time, these efforts had done nothing to eradicate the plague on a permanent basis: like pitchforked Nature, the pirates always returned.

Now, at least, the problem rated an *imperium infinitum*, probably with proconsular authority—dangerous power for one man, though as Velleius cynically remarked, concern was considerably modified by the recipient, and intrigue in Rome guaranteed that competence was the one quality the first holder of the command lacked.[68] Marcus Antonius was presumably appointed in 74 because he was his father's son, and his father had dealt with the pirates a quarter of a century earlier (see above); but this talent was clearly not hereditary. What Antonius did understand, however—not surprisingly in the circumstances—was extortion: indeed, he got a reputation for causing worse depredations than the pirates themselves.[69] On the other hand, when he tried to settle accounts with the Cretans at sea, he suffered a humiliating defeat: many of his ships were cut off, and their occupants (including his quaestor) were strung up from their own yardarms in the chains they had brought with them.[70] Antonius had no option but to patch up a humiliating peace with the pirates (71):[71] his title, "Creticus," seems to have been bestowed on him as a kind of derisive joke, and he died soon afterwards.[72] Curiously, his main claim to fame is the fact that he was the father of Mark Antony, a very different character. When he returned to Rome, the Senate, perhaps emboldened by the recent death of Sertorius

(72) and Crassus's savage annihilation of the great slave revolt led by Spartacus (71)—
social revolution was now everywhere in retreat—decided to ignore his reluctant
treaty. Instead, they sent out to Crete a strong, efficient, and brutal commander,
Quintus Caecilius Metellus, who not only "laid waste the whole island with fire and
sword,"[73] but subsequently, when the Cretans, their cities now besieged by his land
forces, attempted to surrender to Pompey (see below), flatly refused to acknowledge
Pompey's *maius imperium*, thus precipitating an unpleasant diplomatic incident.[74] He,
too, though for rather different reasons, "got nothing out of his striking victory
apart from the title Creticus":[75] at this stage Pompey was riding very high. Even so,
the quarrel had come within appreciable distance of escalating into "a minor civil
war."[76]

Despite Metellus's depredations, the pirates generally were bolder than ever; and
now they once more had Mithridates in the field to support them. His initial successes caused great alarm, and with good reason, in Rome. That Asia Minor was not
lost to the Romans at this point was entirely due to the efforts of that extraordinary
individual Lucullus, an often scandalously underrated soldier and statesman,[77] who
in three short years (73–70) raised the siege of Cyzicus, pursued Mithridates
through Bithynia into Pontus, rescued his wretched colleague Cotta (who had been
blockaded in Chalcedon and lost sixty-four ships there), raised a new fleet with
which he regained supremacy at sea, took Mithridates' capital cities of Sinope and
Amaseia; then shook the brief Armenian empire of Tigranes to pieces (69/8), and, in
short, did all the hard fighting for which Pompey, a year or two later, got the credit,
besides making an equitable financial settlement in Asia—something, as we have
seen (above, p. 649), that was his ultimate undoing.[78] Plutarch gives a graphic, and
unpleasantly plausible, account of the outrageous abuses by Roman *publicani* and
moneylenders that Lucullus summarily terminated.[79] Sulla's indemnity of 20,000 talents had already been paid off twice over; yet (like a modern house mortgage) the
total, by the accruing of interest, had been brought up to the staggering figure of
120,000 talents, so that cities, no less than individuals, were desperately in debt, with
public property mortgaged to the hilt,[80] and many free citizens reduced to serf status.
Lucullus cut the annual interest rate to 12 percent maximum, abolished all interest in
excess of the principal, set a ceiling of one-fourth of any debtor's income on the
amount payable to a creditor, and penalized any moneylender who added interest to
principal by mulcting him of the entire sum due. As a result, all debts were paid off,
and all liens and mortgages canceled, within four years. But, hardly less important,
Lucullus acquired a group of deadly and implacable enemies in Rome. Since the financial lobby, as a matter of policy, had lent large sums, on nominal security, to
many of the leading politicians, it could always count on raising a powerful pressure
group at need, operating, more often than not, through venal tribunes of the people.

Lucullus's veterans—probably with encouragement and disinformation from
interested parties—came near to mutinying: it is true that his discipline was tough,
but it had been singularly effective, and in the ordinary course of events it takes more
than strictness in the field to rouse experienced troops against so fair and successful a
commander. They grumbled at inaction, at not pursuing Mithridates *à outrance*; but

the canny Lucullus knew better than to let himself be lured into a disastrous wild-goose chase among the remote mountains of eastern Anatolia. In Pontus he would stay: let Mithridates commit himself. This strategy did not make Lucullus popular; and meanwhile his powers were being skillfully cut from under him in Rome. Pompey (who knew how to get on with the business community) obtained a special command to clean up the mess. The *Lex Gabinia* of 67 invested him with sweeping powers; Lucullus was eased out of office and left to enjoy a leisured, luxurious retire-ment, a wealthy Epicurean whose pleasures were by no means all philosophical, an intellectual *bon vivant* and man of action whose most lasting legacy to Italy and the West was the Pontic cherry tree.[81] Pompey proceeded to steal his glory—Lucullus got a grudging triumph, for which he had to wait till 63, but small thanks other-wise[82]—and made a showy end to the work that his predecessor had all but completed.

First, however, he had to deal with the pirates. Under the piracy law proposed by Aulus Gabinius, a consular—carefully left unnamed—would be given a three-year *imperium*, covering the entire Mediterranean, with the right to levy troops and to raise funds (the latter not only from the Roman treasury, but also from officials abroad). He would have a fleet of two hundred fighting vessels, and be entitled to appoint fifteen *legati* at praetorian level. His authority would cover all islands, and extend fifty miles inland.[83] After violent senatorial opposition (but with the help of Caesar and his friends) the bill was finally passed, and a further law was then tacked on, appointing Pompey to the command, and increasing the forces at his disposal: five hundred ships, 120,000 infantry, five thousand cavalry, twenty-four *legati* in-stead of the original fifteen, with a couple of quaestors thrown in.[84] With this vast, indeed excessive, force at his disposal, Pompey divided the Mediterranean into thir-teen separate subcommands, with a *legatus* in charge of each.[85] The aim was to sweep the seas in an easterly direction, thus reopening Rome's supply lines from Sicily, Sar-dinia, and North Africa as quickly as possible. In a mere forty days this task had been accomplished, and the pirates were forced to regroup along the Cilician coast.[86] Even now Pompey still faced such implacable opposition in Rome as necessitated his re-turn to the capital in mid-campaign.[87] But on his return to Cilicia he wound up the operation with speed and vigor. Every ruler in Asia Minor was obliged to supply troops or cash for the war effort.[88] Within three months (rather than the three years envisaged by his commission) Pompey had stormed the pirates' last stronghold, and the campaign was over.[89] The menace of piracy, despite some flattering claims to the contrary,[90] had not been entirely eradicated; nothing, granted the social conditions of the age, could do that. But it had been dealt a crippling blow.

Pompey had, it must be admitted, done a brilliant job; but there does seem to have been something suspiciously easy about it. Between the pirate leaders and the Roman *imperator* backed by the *publicani* (and, thus, violently opposed, even at the height of his success, by conservatives such as Piso, who sneered at him as a "new Romulus")[91] some kind of deal could well have been worked out in advance: Pompey's agents were everywhere long before his official arrival. There is a most uncharacteristic lenience in the treatment of these defeated sea rovers (who, among their other crimes, had sheltered runaway slaves, kidnapped high Roman officials, and fought for Mithridates): not only a mass amnesty, but something very like an environmental rehabilitation program. Normally a captured pirate could expect the worst, as Cicero, not a vindictive man by nature, emphasizes with some relish.[92] Pompey's prisoners, on the other hand, were treated as victims of circumstance, which indeed most of them were; they were encouraged to take up farming, and settled in abandoned cities on the Cilician plain and elsewhere.[93] Virgil's old bee-keeper in the *Georgics*, it has been suggested, was one such resettled corsair.[94] It does seem as though Pompey had perceived, and attempted to deal with, some of the grim endemic problems that lay behind the social scourge of piracy; at least he had the common sense to realize that out-of-work pirates needed an alternative way of making a living.

Nothing, of course, succeeds like success, and in 66 Pompey was given—by the *Lex Manilia*, and with the support, this time, of *bien-pensants* such as Cicero and Servilius Vatia as well as that of Caesar and the financiers[95]—an extended command to deal with those two elderly bogeys, Mithridates and Tigranes, both of whom had already had the heart knocked out of them by Lucullus.[96] Adding insult to injury, Pompey met Lucullus and stripped him of his troops, calling him a Xerxes in a toga; Lucullus, with waspish venom, retorted that Pompey was a vulture, never killing its own prey, but always feasting on the carrion that other beasts had killed.[97] Pompey then, insisting on unconditional surrender in order to avoid an overeasy victory,[98] drove Mithridates back through Cappadocia and Pontus, shut all doors of retreat on him, and forced his lukewarm son-in-law Tigranes (who was left his throne, but little else) to deny him even his indirect support. Finally, in 63, the old Pontic lion chose death rather than keep up his now-hopeless struggle, getting a Gaulish officer to dispatch him when he found himself immune to even the strongest poisons, embarrassed, at the last, by his lifelong instinct for self-preservation.[99]

Meanwhile, in the late summer of 64, Pompey had moved down into Syria. Here, at Antioch, he was confronted, perhaps to his surprise, with the pathetic figure of Antiochus XIII Asiaticus (above, p. 553), still hopefully chasing that will-o'-the-wisp, the Seleucid crown, just as a decade earlier he had gone to Rome to seek the throne of Egypt. He had, indeed, already had a heady taste of glory. When Tigranes evacuated Syria in 69, the Antiochenes had hailed Antiochus XIII as their rightful king.[100] Lucullus approved the appointment, and Antiochus was duly crowned as the heir of the Seleucids.[101] Since then another claimant, his third cousin Philip II, had appeared. They had the backing (indeed, were the creatures) of two powerful rival Arab emirs.[102] When Pompey scornfully turned down Antiochus's plea for confirmation, with the scathing comment that the man who had yielded Syria to Tigranes was not likely to save it from Arabs and Jews[103]—indeed, he might have added, was only too likely to make a present of it to his Arab patron—Antiochus had no option but to go back to that patron, Sampsiceramus (Shemash-geram). The Arab, not being a man to throw good money after bad, lost no time in murdering him. If Philip II was, in fact, that grandson of Antiochus VIII Grypos

Fig. 200. Antiochus XIII Dionysus Philopator Kallinikos (Asiaticus). Silver tetradrachm, mint unknown (Antioch?), ca. 69–65 B.C. Numismatists have labeled his expression "foolish" and "utterly vacuous," but I suspect such verdicts were elicited by a knowledge of the sitter's identity.
British Museum, London.

whom Aulus Gabinius refused to allow into Egypt (56/5: above, p. 650), he survived a little longer, but after 63 we hear no more of his claims to kingship.[104]

So, ingloriously and amid greater issues, died the last obscure claimants to the empire that Seleucus Nicator had founded, which at its apogee had stretched east to the Land of the Five Rivers, westward as far as the Hellespont, and south to the very gates of Egypt. Much ink has been spilled on the problem of just why Pompey reversed Lucullus's policy and abolished the Seleucid dynasty: to have a Roman bastion against the Parthians, to police Syria properly, to prevent the revival of piracy, or simply because any decision of Lucullus's was better reversed (the theory of inevitable imperial expansion scarcely merits discussion). The true answer is surely simpler and more pragmatic: Pompey did away with the Seleucids because they were now too weak to be any conceivable use to Rome as a client kingdom, and through their weakness would be a continual focal point for instability and insurrection.[105] The time had come for tidy, effective government, the imposition of the *pax Romana*: indeed, it is arguable that Pompey had regarded Syria as Roman property ever since the surrender of Tigranes in 69.[106] This kind of arrangement was something that Pompey understood and in which he believed: vain, venal, and pliable in his political dealings, he was a first-class administrator of the Roman *status quo*.

His settlement of the East is not strictly relevant to this story in detail, but one or two general observations on it may be worth making.[107] First, it was unique in being, for the first time, executed by one man with supreme powers, on the spot, and responsible to no senatorial commission. Thus it paved the way for the very similar authority late exercised by Augustus. Second, it was immensely profitable, on a scale not seen since Alexander handed out largesse after his Eastern conquests.[108] The client-kings, for instance, paid tribute, and this line item formed a substantial element from now on in the imperial budget.[109] More graphically put, in terms of per-

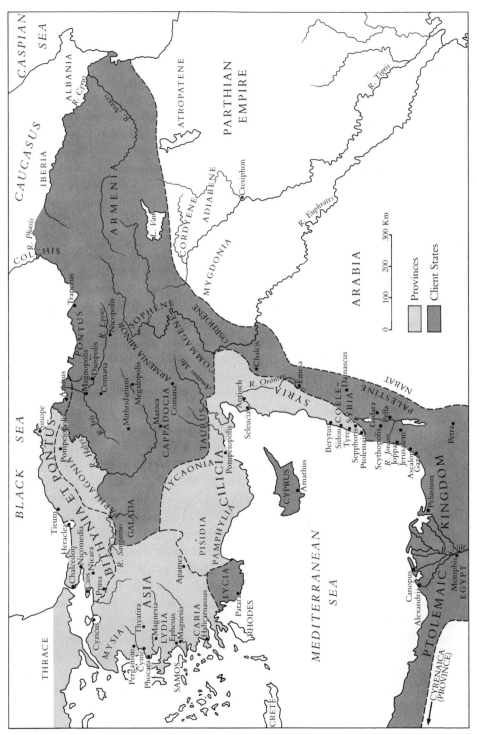

Map 28. Pompey's settlement of the East, 63 B.C.
From *CAH*, vol. IX, *The Roman Republic, 133–44 B.C.*, p. 397.

sonal wealth Pompey "could have bought Crassus out without feeling the pinch"—
and Crassus was the man who said that no one could call himself rich unless he was
in a position to support a legion out of income.[110] Large loans, to cities or individuals, ensured political subservience. Pompey came home a multimillionaire, almost
literally holding the gorgeous East in fee. Third, his settlement reinforced the tradition of imperial foreign government that, as we have seen, was the mainstay of the
Successors. With a fine-tuned sense of relative xenophobia, Rome henceforth administered the civilized, that is, Hellenized, areas of the *oikoumenē* directly, while
turning over the nonassimilated fringe to the mercies of client-kings with grotesque
non-Mediterranean names. Pompey observed that he had found Asia a frontier
province, but left it at the heart of the empire;[111] beyond the new provinces of Pontus
and Bithynia, Syria and Cilicia, there now lay a whole string of dependent kingdoms—Colchis, Paphlagonia, Commagene, Judaea, Armenia, among others.

Finally, after learning one or two lessons the hard way, Roman administrators
were, for some centuries, to make a success of the job—something their Greek or
Macedonian predecessors had never quite got the hang of. The *laissez-faire* excesses
of the *publicani* were brought into line, local leaders were tempted with the offer of
Roman honors and appointments. Nothing had changed in principle; the Romans—
with that coarse psychological pragmatism that was at once their curse and their
greatest blessing—simply made the system work. In 60 B.C. Diodorus Siculus saw
a Roman lynched in Egypt for killing a cat;[112] Romans were no less contemptuous
of foreign ways by Juvenal's day, over half a century later,[113] but at least they had
learned better tact and public manners. The disastrous bellicosity and even more disastrous greed of a governor such as Lucius Calpurnius Piso Caesoninus showed
himself in Macedonia (57–56) became less common as time went on:[114] in other
words, Roman imperialism depended for its effectiveness on its officials' sense of law
and decorum. It is a tribute to Roman *mores* that this foundation proved as strong as
it did; but ultimately it became exposed to the same weaknesses as had assailed the
Ptolemies and Seleucids. It is, as we are often reminded, no answer to the problem of
slavery to be consistently kind to one's slaves.

If the Seleucids fizzled obscurely, the Ptolemies went out in a blaze of glory that
has inspired great poetry down the ages. In the spring of 51 Ptolemy Auletes died,
leaving the kingdom in his will, jointly, to his eighteen-year-old daughter Cleopatra,
and her younger brother Ptolemy XIII, then about twelve.[115] In Cleopatra the tradition of brilliant, strong-willed Macedonian queens reached its apotheosis. With
Cyprus, Coele-Syria, and Cyrenaica gone, with the world her ancestors had known
crumbling about her, with famine at home and anarchy abroad, this astonishing
woman not only dreamed of greater world empire than Alexander had known, but
came within an iota of winning it. Tarn, with romantic hyperbole, claimed that
Rome had feared two people only, Hannibal and Cleopatra.[116] That is to be taken in
by the propaganda mills presenting her as an Oriental ogre, a drunken hypnotic
Circe of all the passions, to distract Roman attention from the fact that what Octavian was really fighting was a desperate civil war against his own former comrade.
But no one could fail to take her seriously. How far her sexual allure was exercised

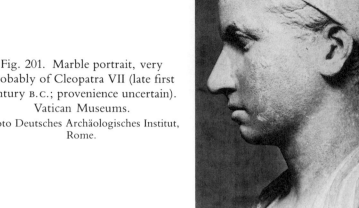

Fig. 201. Marble portrait, very probably of Cleopatra VII (late first century B.C.; provenience uncertain). Vatican Museums.
Photo Deutsches Archäologisches Institut, Rome.

for its own sake, and how far in pursuit of power, we shall never know for certain. But there are one or two pointers. Like many Hellenistic queens, she was passionate, but never promiscuous. Caesar and Antony apart, we hear of no other lovers, and a prurient tradition could hardly have failed to commemorate them had they existed.[117] The wretched surviving iconography—a far from flattering series of coin portraits, the uncertainly ascribed Cherchell bust[118]—suggests neither a raving beauty nor a voluptuary. Pascal's remark about the world being changed if Cleopatra's nose had been shorter is singularly unfortunate,[119] since if her portraits show her as she was, it could hardly have been longer.[120] She appears to have inherited this physiognomy from her father, Auletes.[121] There is also her choice of lovers to consider. Anyone who so consistently aimed for the top is unlikely to have been motivated by nothing apart from sheer unbridled passion.

The irresistible conclusion is that if Pompey rather than Caesar had come calling in Alexandria after the battle of Pharsalus in 48, the result would have been precisely the same: Pompey was no less conceited than Caesar, and at least as ambitious. Indeed, when in 49 Pompey's son came to Alexandria looking for men and ships and cash, it was suggested that he may have obtained the queen's favors as well, as a gesture of good will and support.[122] If we can believe our sources (and they are all, for this period, heavily, and inevitably, tinged with propaganda or corrective hindsight, or both), Cleopatra even, at the age of thirty-nine, with Antony's corpse scarcely cold, made a desperate pass at the young Octavian after Actium.[123] On her record it could well be true; and whatever that record suggests, it is not nymphomania. The contrast between her handling of Caesar and the way she treated Antony is also highly instructive. In neither case, Shakespeare notwithstanding, does the evidence suggest a *grande passion*. What it does indicate is that while Cleopatra—brilliant, quick-witted, fluent in nine languages (which did not, interestingly, include Latin),[124] a mathematician and shrewd businesswoman[125]—had a genuine respect and admiration for Caesar, Antony's emotional vacillations, intellectual shallowness, and coarse excesses nearly drove her insane. She had to deal with Antony, so she made the best of him; but we do not hear of her laying on those endless stupefying entertainments for the abstemious Caesar, whose wit and brilliance matched her own. To Caesar she was delivered at night, by a Sicilian merchant, concealed in a carpet or bedroll, a through-the-enemy-lines joke that he appreciated, as she well knew he would;[126] it was for Antony that she devised that vast and overornate parade down the river Cydnus to Tarsus, immortalized by Shakespeare and thus not always seen for what it was: a vulgar bait to catch a vulgar man, a conscious parody of those processions that earlier Ptolemaic monarchs had laid on for the delectation of the Alexandrian mob, and as a self-promoting gimmick abroad (above, pp. 158 ff.).[127] She fought for her country, and her country—the Egyptian *chōra* rather than Alexandria—responded by offering to rise for her when all was lost, and treating her as a still-living legend for years after she was dead. She spoke Egyptian; she was the New Isis;[128] from the very beginning of her reign she participated in Egyptian religious festivals;

Fig. 202. Roman ceramic lamp of the first century A.D., portraying part of the city of Alexandria, including the royal necropolis.
Muzeum Narodowe, Poznan.

her portraits and hieratic cartouches adorned the temples of the old gods.[129] She was, in short, a charismatic personality of the first order, a born leader and vaultingly ambitious monarch, who deserved a better fate than suicide with that *louche* lump of a self-indulgent Roman, with his bull neck, Herculean vulgarities, and fits of mindless introspection.[130]

The times, however, were hard, and she was forced to make of them what she could—which was a great deal. The civil wars in Italy broke out in 49, two years after she came to the throne. She made her independent spirit clear from the start. By August 51 she had already dropped her young brother's name from official documents, despite traditional Ptolemaic insistence on titular male precedence among co-rulers.[131] (Throughout her reign, independent or not, Cleopatra was always forced to accept either a brother or a son, however underage or otherwise ineffectual, as obligatory consort: there were some traditions not even she could ignore.) She also, exceptionally, put her own portrait and name on her coinage, again ignoring those of her brother. This, not surprisingly, alarmed the more powerful court officials in Alexandria. Moreover, when her Gabinian mercenaries killed the Roman governor of Syria's sons, who had come to require their presence to help their father against the Parthians, she at once, on her own initiative, sent the ringleaders to Syria in chains.[132] Such behavior very soon brought opposition to a head. Certainly by 48, and in all likelihood two years earlier, a palace cabal, led by Theodotus, the eunuch Pothinus, and a half-Greek general, Achillas, ousted Cleopatra in favor of her more pliable younger brother, with themselves as a council of regency.[133]

Between 51 and 49 Egypt was also suffering from drought, inadequate Nile floods, and the inevitable consequence: bad harvests and famine. A royal decree of 27 October 50—with Ptolemy XIII's name on it—banned the shipping of grain to any destination except Alexandria. It has been plausibly argued that Cleopatra had already been driven out, probably to the Thebaid, and that the decree sought, *inter alia*, to deprive her and her supporters of supplies.[134] In any case she soon set about raising an army among the Arab tribes east of Pelusium, much as Cleopatra IV had done in not-dissimilar circumstances (above, p. 549). At some point she and her sister Arsinoë moved to Syria,[135] and it seems likely that they went there from Upper Egypt, returning subsequently by way of Ascalon—which may have temporarily served as Cleopatra's base[136]—and the eastern marches of Egypt beyond Pelusium.[137]

Meanwhile Pompey, defeated at Pharsalus (Aug. 48), took ship for Alexandria. He was relying, unwisely, on his position as backer, indeed as Senate-appointed guardian, of young Ptolemy XIII;[138] the Egyptian alliance, as we have seen, had sent him men and ships. He seems not to have realized, till it was too late, just how far Pharsalus had destroyed his international reputation and credit. Achillas and his fellow regents were already working out their best approach to Caesar; in their eyes Pompey was nothing but a dangerous embarrassment. They had him murdered as he stepped ashore (28 Sept. 48), an object lesson for the precocious boy king, who watched this scene from the dockside, arrayed in his diadem and purple robes. Pompey's severed head was pickled, and afterwards presented, as an earnest of good will, to his conqueror, who at least had the grace to shed tears at the sight.[139] Caesar

Fig. 203. Marble portrait bust of Julius
Caesar (mid-first century B.C.,
Tusculum).
Castello Ducale di Agliè.

may have been only too glad to have Pompey thus providentially put out of the way, but the circumstances of his death were appalling, and Caesar himself knew this better than anyone. At the same time the episode encouraged him in what was to prove a near-fatal Egyptian adventure.[140] When he came ashore himself at Alexandria four days later (2 Oct.), he was in a mood of careless and arrogant confidence, with an escort of no more than thirty-two hundred legionaries and eight hundred cavalry. His public reception was anything but ecstatic: he had been accompanied ashore by twelve lictors carrying the fasces, a clear hint of his intentions. Riots followed.[141]

Ptolemy XIII was away at Pelusium, ready to defend the frontier against his elder sister.[142] Caesar coolly installed himself in the royal palace and began issuing orders. Pothinus the eunuch, determined not to meet the Roman's exorbitant financial and other demands (including the discharge of vast debts still owing to Rabirius Postumus, which Caesar, for his own purposes, had underwritten),[143] brought Ptolemy back to court, but took no steps to disband his army. At this point Cleopatra, anxious not to be left out of any deal being cut, had herself smuggled through these hostile lines, like contraband, and turned up in her carpet. Both she and her brother were invited to appear before Caesar's *ad hoc* judgment seat the following morning; but by then Caesar, who was instantly captivated by Cleopatra's insistent charms, had already made her his lover, as she doubtless intended he should.[144] Young Ptolemy instantly grasped the situation (hardly difficult, in the circumstances), and rushed out in a fury, screaming that he had been betrayed, to rouse the Alexandrian mob.[145] The general belief, fomented by Pothinus, that Caesar indeed planned to make Cleopatra sole ruler, as a puppet of Rome, had generated a highly inflammatory mood in the city. Ptolemy, however, was quickly brought back by Caesar's guards, while Caesar himself went out and made a conciliatory speech. Highhandedness had perforce, for a while at least, to be abandoned.

The danger of Caesar's position was such that he provisionally recognized the two co-regents' younger brother and sister, Ptolemy XIV and Arsinoë, as joint rulers of Cyprus,[146] even though Cyprus had been officially annexed by Rome a decade before (above, p. 650), and exploited with vigor by Caesar's future assassin Brutus (above, p. 555), who did very well out of loans on which he charged 48 percent annual interest.[147] (Once Caesar got back in control of the situation, however, he rapidly reneged on this concession; Arsinoë, to her great annoyance, far from descending on Cyprus *en grande dame*, was kept under virtual house arrest in the royal palace, a decision with embarrassing consequences, as we shall see.)[148] There followed a series of lavish Alexandrian parties. But Pothinus had not played his last card: in November he summoned Ptolemy XIII's veterans from Pelusium, and Caesar suddenly found himself blockaded in Alexandria by an army twenty thousand strong.[149]

The so-called Alexandrian War, which followed, though in many ways pure *opéra bouffe*, came as near to destroying Caesar himself, let alone his reputation, as any campaign, military or political, that he ever fought. Once he had to swim from

Fig. 204. Aerial view of modern Alexandria, from the west. On the left, the Mediterranean; on the right, the Western Harbor. The Eastern Harbor appears at the top of the photograph, with the link to the mainland at the top right. Note how, as in the parallel case of Tyre, the original mole (Heptastadion) linking the city with Pharos Island (top left-hand corner) has silted up into a broad isthmus.

Photo Hulton Picture Company.

the mole to save his life, leaving his purple general's cloak behind as a trophy for the enemy (Feb. 47).[150] The warehouses and some part of the great Alexandrian Library went up in flames.[151] Caesar managed to capture the Pharos lighthouse (above, p. 158), which safeguarded his control of the harbor.[152] Arsinoë, meanwhile, contrived to escape from the palace, fled to Achillas, and was promptly proclaimed queen by the army and the Macedonian mob, an act for which her sister never forgave her.[153] All through that winter fighting and intrigue sputtered on. Arsinoë's eunuch, Ganymede, murdered Achillas; Caesar meanwhile executed Pothinus. In February 47, at some cost to himself, he extended his control to Pharos Island and the Heptastadion mole (this was the occasion on which he lost his cloak), and also turned Ptolemy XIII over to the Egyptian opposition as a good-will gesture, probably in the covert hope of stirring up trouble between his advisers and those of Arsinoë.[154] In any case, Caesar's intelligence officers reported that relief was at hand. At the eleventh hour he and his beleaguered legionaries were rescued by a mixed force under Mithridates of Pergamon (26 Mar. 47).[155] Ptolemy XIII fled and was drowned in the Nile.[156] Thus Cleopatra, whom Caesar had restored, officially, to joint occupancy of the throne of Egypt, now, in effect, indeed became sole ruler—although as a sop to tradition she was duly married off to her younger brother Ptolemy XIV, now aged eleven.

Caesar is more likely to have got himself into his dangerous and demeaning scrape out of careless arrogance and a determination to lay hands on Egypt's still-vast accumulated resources rather than through a simple infatuation for Egypt's queen. At the same time the personal advantages of this stylish and intelligent young lady, not to mention those of the system she had inherited, were clearly not lost on him. For one thing, he had lost no time in getting her pregnant, a move that we can safely attribute to dynastic policy, not mere carelessness. Rather than make Egypt a province, with all the senatorial intrigue and rivalry that this was bound to entail, Caesar had every intention of shoring up the Ptolemaic regime, on his own terms. To have a son in line for the throne would by no means come amiss, whatever the status of consort and heir in Rome. Meanwhile, to placate the Alexandrians and the Egyptian priesthood, Cleopatra obligingly wed her sibling co-regent, while her younger sister, Arsinoë, languished under arrest with a charge of high treason pending against her. By way of compensation for all she had been through, Caesar now took his ripening *inamorata* on a prolonged pleasure trip up the Nile,[157] and only left to attend to more pressing business in Syria a few weeks before the birth of her, and his, son Ptolemy Caesar, known as Caesarion, on 23 June 47.[158]

In July 46, after his successful African campaign, Caesar returned to Rome, to be showered with unprecedented honors, including four successive triumphs and a ten-year dictatorship. During these celebrations (Sept.–Oct.) he brought over Cleopatra and her entourage, establishing them in his own town house, a return of hospitality that caused considerable offense among conservative Republicans, and was not made easier by the queen's *de haut en bas* social manners.[159] By then he was mulling over ideas about deification and world empire that seemed, or were thought, to include the establishment of Alexandria as a second capital, and of Cleopatra herself as some kind of bigamous queen-goddess,[160] the New Isis, as she styled herself. Rome buzzed with gossip. Everyone, whatever they said about her in private, paid visits to

Fig. 205. Nilotic river scene. Mosaic from the sanctuary of Fortuna, Praeneste, ca.
A.D. 80.
Museo Nazionale, Rome.

Cleopatra in Caesar's villa across the Tiber—even Cicero, whom she snubbed, and who professed to find her both odious and arrogant.[161] Her underage brother-*cum*-husband also accompanied her: it was all very un-Roman.[162] Perhaps on her insistence, her sister Arsinoë, chained, was led in Caesar's triumph (46), to the evident disgust of the crowd. Caesar, always alert to public opinion, released Arsinoë,[163] whose ambition—as one might expect in a Ptolemaic princess—was no whit dampened by the experience. Cleopatra herself lived in luxurious style, with a huge retinue. Caesar erected a golden statue of her in the temple of Venus Genetrix (where else?), and claimed paternity of Caesarion, something Republicans found alarming, since it suggested that he planned to marry Cleopatra, despite the laws against bigamy and unions with foreigners.[164] On the other hand, they could thank the Alexandrian astronomer Sosigenes—basing himself on the work of Callippus in the fourth century (above, p. 460)—for Caesar's introduction of a rational solar calendar, a welcome reformation, since the civic year had got no less than three months ahead of the solar one.[165] His irrigation schemes and establishment of public libraries also betray obvious Alexandrian influence: the Egyptian interlude had clearly not been a total waste of time.

But the Ides of March 44 put an end to all these grandiose dreams. Two weeks after Caesar's assassination, when the will was known and Caesarion, inevitably, had no place in it, Cleopatra, with more speed than dignity, and perhaps in real danger of her life, left Rome and returned to Alexandria. "The queen's flight does not worry *me*," Cicero wrote to Atticus, with relish.[166] On her arrival Cleopatra lost no time in having her sibling consort, Ptolemy XIV, assassinated, and Caesarion established, at the tender age of four, as her new co-regent.[167] She found Egypt suffering from both famine and plague, due in part to the neglect of the Nile canals during her absence: inundations were still low, and bad harvests continued from 43 until 41, with consequent social unrest.[168] The last thing Cleopatra needed at this stage was another palace revolution. While civil war raged between Caesarians and Republicans, she secured recognition for Caesarion from Caesar's former lieutenant Dolabella by sending him the four legions Caesar had left in Egypt:[169] this also provided her with a good excuse to get them out of the country. They were, in any case, captured or taken over by Cassius, and Dolabella committed suicide at Laodicea (summer 43).[170] She stalled demands by Cassius himself for ships by pleading impoverishment through famine and plague,[171] but was, clearly, acting on behalf of the Caesarian cause. After Dolabella's defeat and death, only a violent storm prevented her from joining Antony and Octavian with a large fleet.[172]

In 44 Antony, during his brief period of supreme power, had set up Arsinoë as ruler of Cyprus (thus implementing Caesar's unfulfilled promise),[173] and also, in all likelihood, as a potential counterweight to Cleopatra: at this stage he still believed in hedging his bets. During the fraught years that followed, Cleopatra seems to have regained Cyprus from her sister, who fled to Ephesus (43?).[174] In any case, after the two battles of Philippi (42), which saw the deaths of Brutus and Cassius, and the triumvirs Antony, Octavian, and Lepidus triumphant, it became quite clear to Cleopatra with whom she would have to deal. Octavian went back to Italy so ill that his life was despaired of: Antony was the man to watch. Meanwhile she got an unex-

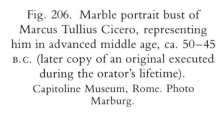

Fig. 206. Marble portrait bust of
Marcus Tullius Cicero, representing
him in advanced middle age, ca. 50–45
B.C. (later copy of an original executed
during the orator's lifetime).
Capitoline Museum, Rome. Photo
Marburg.

pected bonus: on 1 January 42 Caesar's official divinization was announced in Rome,
and though its main object was the promotion of Octavian, who now proclaimed
himself "Son of Divine Julius" on his coins, a deified father—even on the wrong
side of the blanket—would not come amiss for Caesarion, either,[175] not least since
the triumvirs, in recognition of her aid to Dolabella, had granted her son the right to
the title of king.[176]

By the time that Antony summoned her to that fateful meeting at Tarsus, in 41,
she already knew more than enough about him: his limited tactical and strategic
abilities, his great popularity with his troops; his blue blood, which was so embar-
rassingly offset by financial impoverishment; the drinking, the philoprogenitive
womanizing, the superficial philhellenism, the Herculean vulgarity, the physical ex-
uberance and brutal ambition, the Dionysiac pretensions to godhead.[177] Rural Egypt
might be on the verge of economic collapse, but the queen—who had still further
debased Auletes' already poor silver coinage, cutting the proportion of actual silver
from 33 to 25 percent[178]—put on a show that Ptolemy Philadelphos could not have
outdone:[179] the gilded poop, the silver oars, the purple sails, the Erotes fanning her,
the Nereid handmaids steering and reefing. All this made an immense impression at
the time, and (via North's *Plutarch*) provided Shakespeare with one of his most famous bravura descriptive passages.

Antony was tickled by the idea of having a blue-blooded Ptolemy (his previous
mistresses, not to mention his present wife, Fulvia, a powerful termagant, all seem
to have been shrewishly middle-class),[180] and by the coarse implications of all this
royal finery: eight or nine years later we find him writing to Octavian, asking him
why he has changed so much, turned so hostile—"Is it because I get into the

queen?"[181] He spent the winter of 41/0 with Cleopatra in Alexandria, emphasizing his private status on arrival: Caesar's gaffe had not been lost on him. Our sources outdo each other in proclaiming his subservience to the queen, the life of dissolute luxury they led together.[182] One hears the grinding, *ex post facto*, of Augustan axes here. Cleopatra, they insist, could get whatever she wanted out of him—including the execution of Arsinoë (never forgiven for her brief fling as titular queen in 48–47) who, for obvious reasons, now fancied the Republican cause. Now it is quite true that Antony executed Arsinoë in 41;[183] but this was done at least as much out of political calculation as in a state of besotted subservience to a lover. Tarsus, too, had been the scene of "a good deal of unromantic negotiation."[184] Arsinoë had revealed herself as an ambitious and unscrupulous enemy: the volatile Alexandrians had already recognized her claim to the throne once, and might well do so again. Antony's decision to eliminate her needs no other explanation. What was more, he showed himself equally firm with Cleopatra herself at this stage. The evidence suggests that Cyprus was removed from her control: despite all the romantic publicity surrounding her first encounter with Antony, he seems to have been a good deal less pliable than propaganda would suggest.[185] Indeed, to some extent it may well have been Cleopatra who was exploited. The triumviral finances badly needed reinforcement, and Cleopatra could be generous enough in the pursuit of her own ends. Like Cae-

Fig. 207. Marble portrait bust of Mark Antony (late first century B.C., Narbonne).
Musée Archéologique Municipal, Narbonne.

sar, Antony found Egypt full of attractions, not all of them sexual or antiquarian. Logistics, too, played their part.

Both Cleopatra and Antony, then, had highly practical ulterior reasons for cultivating one another; how much personal chemistry helped the equation is hard to tell. Nor can anyone be certain how soon Antony planned to return when he left Cleopatra in the early spring of 40, or what he told her—not necessarily the same thing. Her magnetism was by no means irresistible, since in the event he did not see her for another four years. His wife, Fulvia, who had become involved in a serious breakaway movement against Octavian over land allotments for veterans, fled to Greece, where, after a bitter confrontation with Antony, she fell ill and died—a fortuitous accident that, again, did Cleopatra less immediate good than she had hoped or expected.[186] Public considerations once more came first. That same autumn Antony made his peace with Octavian at Brundisium (Brindisi), cemented the alliance by marrying his fellow triumvir's sister, Octavia—a beautiful and high-minded

Fig. 208. Fulvia, first wife of Antony. Gold quinarius struck in 43/2 B.C. by Antony as proconsul of Gallia Cis- and Transalpina.
Staatliche Museen zu Berlin.

Fig. 209. Octavia, second wife of Antony and sister of Augustus. Gold aureus, with Antony's likeness on the reverse, and thus almost certainly struck in 40 B.C. to commemorate their marriage.
Staatliche Museen zu Berlin.

Fig. 210. Pompey's son Sextus
Pompeius. Gold aureus struck in Sicily
ca. 42–38 B.C.
Staatliche Museen zu Berlin.

young intellectual, recently widowed, and with three children from her first marriage, to Gaius Claudius Marcellus—and became officially responsible for the
East.[187] The civil wars at last seemed at an end; this was the period in which Virgil,
during the pregnancies of Octavia and Octavian's wife, Scribonia, wrote his famous,
and famously ambiguous, fourth *Eclogue*, prophesying the approach of a new
Golden Age with the birth of an (unnamed) child—a gift, later, for Christian
propagandists. Meanwhile in Alexandria Cleopatra, never one to do things by
halves, bore Antony twins, a boy and a girl. His first child by Octavia, a girl, was
born in 38.

Just what Antony thought he was doing at this point is not wholly clear. He
may have been playing the Roman card; he may have thought he could finesse
Cleopatra against Octavia, in whose company, during the winter of 38–37, he
played the dutiful intellectual in Athens, attending lectures and going the rounds of
the philosophical schools. At all events, a fresh Parthian invasion of Syria, led by the
Roman turncoat Labienus,[188] kept his uneasy relationship with Octavian going until
37, when it took another meeting and treaty, signed at Tarentum (Taranto) and
largely achieved through Octavia's tireless personal diplomacy, to patch up the
shaky alliance.[189] Subsequent events suggest that Antony felt, from now on, that a
power play was developing against him in Italy. This, of course, was true: at Tarentum, for instance, he had left two squadrons (120 vessels) of his fleet for Octavian to
use against Sextus Pompeius's quasi-piratical forces in Sicily, against a promise of
four legions that, for one reason or another, failed to materialize, an omission that
may well have tipped the scales in his final choice between Octavia and Cleopatra.[190]
Octavian's growing enmity also must have turned him back toward the idea of playing winner-take-all, with Alexandria as his base. If Octavia had borne him a son,
things might have been different; but she had not, and Cleopatra had. Cleopatra also
held the still-impressive accumulated treasure of the Ptolemies, something that Octavian, too, kept very much in mind, and with good reason: when he finally laid

hands on it, and this became known in Rome, the standard interest rate at once fell from 12 to 4 percent.[191]

So Antony left Italy and went east, with the Senate's authority to reallocate client kingdoms—a commission that, as we shall see, he proceeded to interpret in a more than liberal fashion—and to deal with the Parthians. By now his mind must have been made up. Octavia, whose second child by him—another daughter—had just been born, accompanied him as far as Corcyra, apparently in a poor state of health; Antony then sent her back home, on the excuse, *prima facie* reasonable enough, that he was about to embark on the Parthian campaign, and did not want to have her exposed to the rigors and dangers that a life in the field would entail. Besides, she would be of more use to him in Rome, keeping the peace with her unpredictable brother and looking after her five children.[192] All plausible enough; and yet the first thing that Antony did, on reaching Antioch, was to send for Cleopatra. After their long separation it was now that his, or their, schemes for what Will calls a "Romano-Hellenistic Orient" began to take shape.[193]

Antony proceeded to lavish on the queen not only Cyprus, which he had so unceremoniously removed from her control at Tarsus in 41, but also the cedar-clad Cilician coast, so ideal for shipbuilding, not to mention Phoenicia, Coele-Syria, and the richest spice-bearing regions of Judaea and Arabia, dispositions that not unnaturally caused vast offense in Rome,[194] and not only because of Cleopatra's personal unpopularity there: these provincial areas were in fact not in his authority to dispose of, and the obvious purpose of their allocation to Cleopatra, Egypt itself being virtually without timber, was to provide lumber and shipyards for the creation of a large Egyptian fleet.[195] The twin children were also now acknowledged by Antony, and officially named Alexander Helios and Cleopatra Selene, titles powerfully evocative of Hellenistic dynastic ambition.[196] This is confirmed by the fact that Cleopatra now inaugurated a new era of her reign (37/6), probably to celebrate these new territorial acquisitions.[197] Whatever ultimate plans Antony may have had, however, the plain fact of the matter was that he needed Cleopatra's support for his forthcoming Parthian campaign. This proved a disastrous fiasco (36), and Antony in defeat became more obligated to Cleopatra than ever. She had just borne him a third child. Now she met him and his ragtag army, two-fifths of which had been lost, on their return to Syria, bringing food, clothing, and cash subsidies with her. In early 35 Antony returned with her to Egypt.[198]

Octavia, in Athens, also with supplies and reinforcements, wife and mistress in nurturing competition, received a curt letter from her husband forbidding her to come farther.[199] Octavian had released no more than two thousand troops, together with seventy of Antony's own ships: it is more than possible that he meant to provoke Antony into a showdown. The future Augustus could now invoke this calculated insult to his sister (whether sexually or politically motivated made little odds) when the need for a *casus belli* arose. War between him and Antony was now more or less inevitable. Even when Antony had the fugitive Sextus Pompeius executed,[200] Octavian, while publicly congratulating him, also contrived to make capital out of the incident by contrasting it with his own lenient treatment of Marcus Lepidus, the

Fig. 211. Mark Antony and Cleopatra VII. Phoenician silver tetradrachm, mint uncertain, ca. 34 B.C.
Fitzwilliam Museum, Cambridge.

ineffectual ex-triumvir whom he had allowed to retire into private life. Had Antony gone to Rome in 35 himself, he might have patched things up, both with Octavian and with his wife; but he did not, and it seems safe to assume that Cleopatra at this stage used all her influence to keep him in Alexandria. Octavia, whatever the truth concerning what Shakespeare called her "cold and holy disposition," and despite Antony's snubs and infidelities, remained unswervingly devoted to him through thick and thin, even looking after his children by Cleopatra when the queen was dead;[201] this does not sound like a mere Roman sense of duty, and Cleopatra was surely well advised to keep Antony away from her at all costs.

So it came about that in 34 Antony committed himself still further to his independent Graeco-Roman dream. After a successful—and financially rewarding—Armenian campaign he celebrated a triumphal parade through Alexandria, playing the role of the New Dionysus, while Cleopatra, enthroned as the New Isis, presided over the ceremony.[202] (Inevitably, when the news reached Rome, this occasion was misinterpreted as an unauthorized and improper Roman triumph.) Only a few days later a yet more explicit political ceremony took place.[203] In the great Gymnasium of Alexandria, with Cleopatra once more robed as Isis, and Antony enthroned by her side, titles were bestowed upon the royal children. Ptolemy XV Caesar (Caesarion)—though carefully subordinated to the royal pair—was made joint ruler of Egypt with his mother and proclaimed King of Kings (she became Queen of Kings, a higher honor still). Alexander Helios, robed like an Achaemenid monarch, was declared Great King of what had been the Seleucid empire at its zenith, Parthia included. His sister, Cleopatra Selene, was instated as Queen of Cyrenaica and Crete. The youngest son of Antony and Cleopatra, Ptolemy Philadelphos—his name a deliberate evocation of past glories—was proclaimed, at the age of two, King of Syria and Asia Minor: he was also dressed in Macedonian royal robes.

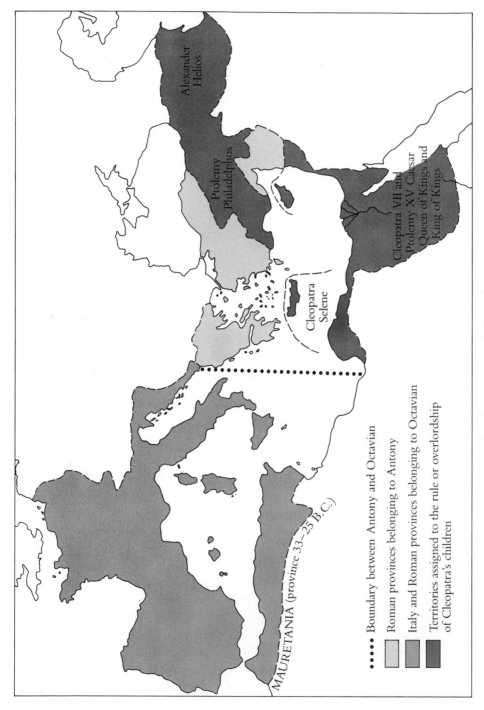

Map 29. The donations of Alexandria, 34 B.C.
From Grant, *Cleopatra*, p. 167.

MAURETANIA (province 33–25 B.C.)

Alexander
Helios

Ptolemy
Philadelphos

Cleopatra VII and
Ptolemy XV Caesar
Queen of Kings and
King of Kings

Cleopatra
Selene

••••• Boundary between Antony and Octavian

Roman provinces belonging to Antony

Italy and Roman provinces belonging to Octavian

Territories assigned to the rule or overlordship
of Cleopatra's children

Fig. 212. Cleopatra VII and the baby Caesarion. Bronze issue struck ca. 47/6 B.C., probably on Cyprus. She wears the royal diadem and coronet (*stephanē*), and carries a scepter.
British Museum, London.

Fig. 213. Marble portrait bust, very probably of Ptolemy XV Caesar (Caesarion). A likely date for its execution is 34 B.C., when Caesarion was declared Caesar's legitimate heir and "King of Kings" at the Donations of Alexandria, then being thirteen years old.
Nasjonalgalleriet, Oslo.

Fig. 214. Cleopatra Selene, daughter of Antony and Cleopatra, married to King Juba II of Mauretania (r. 29 B.C.–A.D. 5/6). Silver tetradrachm, mint and date unknown.
Private collection.

Cavafy, in one of his most brilliant poems, "Alexandrian Kings," comments: "The Alexandrians realized, to be sure, / That all this was mere words, theatricality."[204] True enough in the strict sense: the titles bestowed, like certain modern Catholic sees, did not correspond with political realities—("What hollow words these kingdoms were!").[205] Young Ptolemy Philadelphos had in effect been given the Parthian empire, while Cleopatra Selene "ruled" over a Roman province. However, as a program of intentions these so-called Donations of Alexandria were disquieting: they served clear notice of Antony's far-reaching ambitions, as indeed did Cleopatra's role as the New Isis, his as the New Dionysus; they also stressed the dynastic form that he had chosen to implement them.[206] Though Roman generals in the East since before Pompey's day had been making and unmaking client-kings,[207] this situation was different. True, Antony sought senatorial approval for the Donations after the event; but he can hardly have believed that it was wholly through Octavian's obstructionism that his request was refused.[208] The Donations not only laid improper claim to territories that were either outside Rome's control or, worse, already under Roman administration; they also made it only too clear that Cleopatra and the formidable resources of Egypt were backing Antony's dreams. Once again the irresistible lure of world empire was in the air: the grim lessons of the past three centuries had been quickly forgotten.

Oracles foretold a coming of true harmony between East and West, between Greek and Roman, under Antony and Cleopatra's biracial New Order.[209] Coins issued in 34/3 to celebrate the Donations bore the legend *Basilissa Cleopatra Thea Neōtera* ("Queen Cleopatra, the Younger Goddess"), and were minted in Antioch, thus emphasizing the queen's, and her consort's, determination to amalgamate the Ptolemaic and Seleucid royal houses. In addition, the last three words of the inscription were superbly ambiguous, since they could also mean "the New Cleopatra Thea"—and in such a context what better model to adopt than the formidable queen who, a century before, had married three Seleucid kings, outlived them all, and issued coins stamped with her own title and portrait (cf. above, pp. 445, 541)?[210] Ten years after Caesar's assassination Cleopatra once again, as Bevan says, "saw herself within measurable distance of becoming Empress of the world."[211] Her favorite oath was now "As surely as I shall yet dispense justice on the Roman Capitol."[212]

In 32/1 Antony formally divorced Octavia, thus forcing the West to recognize his relationship with Cleopatra; he had already, unprecedentedly, put the Egyptian queen's head and name on his official Roman coinage, the silver denarii that enjoyed an enormously wide circulation throughout the eastern Mediterranean.[213] These acts also terminated even the pretense of his Roman allegiance, and Octavian proceeded to publish those clauses in Antony's will that reproduced the Donations of Alexandria, forcibly removing the will from the custody of the Vestal Virgins in order to do so.[214] He then formally declared war on Cleopatra, and on her alone; no mention was made of Antony.[215] The whipped-up hysterical xenophobia current in Rome at the time can be sensed from the (largely factitious) propaganda of such Augustan poets as Virgil and Propertius.[216] Cleopatra was the drunken lascivious Oriental, worked over by her own house slaves (*famulos inter femina trita suos*), whoring after strange gods and foreign ways. Horace describes her brain as "soused in Mareotic booze,"[217] while for Propertius her tongue had been "submerged by endless tippling,"[218] and Strabo claims that Octavian "stopped Egypt from being abused with drunken violence."[219] Inevitably, she was also portrayed as an indiscriminately sensual harlot,[220] a charge that, as we have seen, was almost certainly false, though she did (it was claimed) derive a "really sensuous pleasure" from literature.[221]

Antony became the target of more serious, and better founded, political accusations, for example that he had misused troops, acted without senatorial authorization, and given away territories that belonged to Rome,[222] yet a serious statesman of Messalla's caliber still thought it worthwhile to charge him with using a golden chamberpot in Alexandria, "an outrage at which even Cleopatra would have blenched,"[223] and which certainly shocked the elder Pliny, who reports it, adding that for such an offense Antony "should have been proscribed—by Spartacus" (the context makes it clear that this was not an ironic joke, and in any case Pliny's sense of humor was vestigial). The mixture of coarseness and sensibility in Roman *mores* is fascinating: one can never be certain just which improbable peccadillo will next call down the full force of some weighty gentleman's rhetorical disapproval.[224]

The exaggerated charges against Cleopatra also reveal fear; and though today the outcome may seem inevitable—it is true that Antony's Roman support had begun to crumble long before his actual defeat—at the time many must have believed that the New Isis would triumph, that Antony would indeed launch a dazzling new career of world conquest and imperial co-partnership from Alexandria. *Dis aliter uisum*: Jove and the future Augustus decided otherwise, and the dream of universal empire took a different form. Octavian's crushing naval victory at Actium, on 2 September 31[225]—planned and won for him by his admiral Agrippa—finally put paid to Antony's ambitions. Less than a year later, after a halfhearted defense of Alexandria against Octavian's advancing army, Antony committed suicide. Cleopatra soon followed his example,[226] perhaps with Octavian's covert encouragement: if she was too proud to adorn a triumph in chains, like Arsinoë, her conqueror had not forgotten how the crowd warmed to that spirited captive. How much more sympathy, then, might not go out to his own adoptive father's former lover? Better, as for Caesar after Pompey's defeat, to be presented with a convenient, and dramatic, *fait accompli*. So Cleopatra's prospective role in Octavian's triumph was carefully explained to her, and she duly found her own solution—as her handmaid Charmian said, one fitting for a queen descended from so many kings.[227] Once she was safely dead, admiring tributes to her noble end could be entertained without risk,[228] while her heir Caesarion was butchered without compunction.[229]

On 29 August, 30 B.C., Octavian officially declared the Ptolemaic dynasty at an end, thus writing finis—as we can see now—to the whole Hellenistic era of the Successors. In due course Hellenistic art and literature, sanitized and Romanized, were used, first, to kill off the old vigorous, and too independent, Republican literary tradition, and second, to promote the *pax Augusta*. By Ovid's day this imperial-

Map 30. The battle of Actium, 31 B.C.
From Grant, *Cleopatra,* p. 210.

Fig. 215. Gold aureus minted at Rome, 27 B.C., to celebrate the fall of the Ptolemaic dynasty, symbolized by the chained crocodile on the reverse, with the legend *AEGYPT. CAPTA,* "For the capture of Egypt." On the obverse, head of Octavian, with the legend *CAESAR. DIVI F. COS. VII,* "Son of the Deified Caesar, in his seventh consulship."
British Museum, London.

Fig. 216. Marble portrait bust of Octavian shortly after his annexation of Egypt in 30 B.C. (from Arsinoë, in the Fayyûm). The rarity of busts of Cleopatra VII is due to the fact that throughout Egypt they were destroyed and replaced by the likeness of her conqueror.
Ny Carlsberg Glyptotek, Copenhagen.

Fig. 217. Gold Hellenistic snake-
bracelet from Eretria (third
century B.C.).
Schmuckmuseum, Pforzheim.

encomiastic literature was parodying itself, and after Juvenal the Roman literary tradition guttered out altogether: quite an achievement in two short centuries. The
Successors' territories, meanwhile, were absorbed into the administrative efficiency
of a semi-Stoicized universal empire. No room, there, for the New Isis. Yet Cleopatra achieved her dying wish. Unlike her forebears, she knew the country she
ruled; and when she had the famous asp—in fact an Egyptian cobra[230]—smuggled to
her in a basket of figs, it was in the belief that, as Egyptian religion declared, death
from snakebite would, the uraeus or cobra being sacred, confer immortality.[231] She
was not mistaken. Only Alexander—another Macedonian—could eclipse the mes-
meric fascination that she exercised down the centuries, and still exercises, upon the
European imagination: the perennial symbol of what, had Actium gone the other
way, might have been a profoundly different world. We end, as we began, with a
legend.

CHRONOLOGY

684

320/19	Alexander hunting group at Delphi (Leochares, Lysippus), Metroön at Olympia, monument of Nicias? Pyrrho (Skeptic) *fl.* in Elis Birth of Asclepiades of Samos? Antipater in Macedonia	Seleucus enters Babylon (Nov.?) Eumenes and Antigonus (?) in Cappadocia	Antipater regent of empire Ptolemy I annexes Syria and Palestine	Agathocles, backed by Carthage, captures Syracuse, elected *stratēgos*
319	Execution of Demades by Cassander Birth of Pyrrhus I Death of Antipater (fall); Polyperchon appointed regent Cassander leaves Macedonia Choragic monuments of Lysicrates and Thrasyllus in Athens	Antigonus defeats Eumenes in Cappadocia (spring) Eumenes besieged in Nora (June) Antigonus campaigns in Pisidia	Ptolemy annexes Syro-Phoenicia	
319/8	Cassander joins Antigonus	Antigonus winters in Celaenae?		
318	Phocion negotiates with Nicanor over Piraeus Polyperchon's "Freedom Decree" Democratic revolution in Athens (early fall?–May 317)	Philip Arrhidaios attacks Cyzicus (spring) Eumenes is released from Nora by Antigonus (summer), then accepts alliance with Polyperchon Antigonus campaigns in eastern Aegean against Ephesus, Cyme (summer)		Agathocles driven into exile by oligarchs Roman prefects sent to Capua and Cumae; two tribes created in northern Campania
318/7		Eumenes in Cilicia and Phoenicia Antigonus begins campaign against Eumenes (–316/5)		
317	Phocion executed (April) Cassander arrives in Athens (spring) Demetrius of Phaleron chosen *epimelētēs* (governor) of Athens (July) Polyperchon fails to capture Piraeus, campaigns in Peloponnese Eurydice declares for Cassander Cassander invades Macedonia (fall), has Nicanor assassinated, takes charge of Roxane and Alexander IV	Nicanor and Antigonus's naval victory over Cleitus at the Bosporus (summer) Antigonus in Cilicia (fall)	Hecataeus of Abdera writing in Egypt?	Agathocles returns to Syracuse from exile in Morgantina

DATE	GREECE AND THE AEGEAN	ASIA MINOR AND THE EAST	EGYPT, AFRICA, EASTERN MEDITERRANEAN	ROME, ITALY, SICILY, SPAIN
317	Philip Arrhidaios murdered by Olympias; Eurydice forced to commit suicide (Oct.)		Berenice I becomes Ptolemy I's mistress	
317/6	Cassander in Peloponnese?	Antigonus in Mesopotamia; Eumenes in Babylon		Second Samnite War renewed Agathocles *stratēgos autokratōr* in Syracuse (−289)
316	Menander's victory with *Dyskolos* (Jan.) Cassander invades Macedonia (spring?), defeats Polyperchon	Antigonus moves to Susa (spring) Eumenes' victory at Coprates River in Susiana (July) Battle of Paraetacene (fall)		
316/5	Siege of Pydna Birth of Arcesilaus of Pitane Demetrius of Phaleron imposes sumptuary laws on Athens	Eumenes defeated at Fabiene, executed by Antigonus Hieronymus of Cardia transfers allegiance to Antigonus	Seleucus joins Ptolemy in Egypt (Sept.?)	
315	Fall of Pydna; death of Olympias (spring) Cassander marries Thessalonike, founds Cassandreia South Stoa of Corinthian Agora Extension of Theater of Dionysus in Athens Death of Aeschines Formal burial of Philip Arrhidaios and Eurydice at Aigai Cassander in Peloponnese (fall), refounds Thebes	Antigonus controls Alexander's Asian conquests, reorganizes upper satrapies Coalition of satraps against Antigonus (−311) Seleucus, threatened by Antigonus, leaves Babylon (late summer) Antigonus returns to Cilicia (Nov./Dec.)	Birth of Aratus of Soli? Antigonus occupies Palestine	Capua rebels, joins Samnites Exiles in Sicily fight Agathocles
315/4	Cassander returns to Macedonia Polyperchon's son Alexander deserts to Cassander		Antigonus marches on Syria, rejects demands of Ptolemy, Lysimachus, Cassander	
314	Antigonus sends Aristodemus to Peloponnese? Antigonus's lieutenant Dioscurides organizes League of Islanders; Lemnos, Imbros, Delos break with Athens Death of Xenocrates, succeeded as scholarch of Academy by Polemo Seleucus operates in the Aegean		Antigonus occupies Syria, begins siege of Tyre (Mar./Apr.?) Antigonus captures Joppa, Gaza The "Old Tyre Manifesto" (fall)	Roman victory at Tarracina; Capua reduced

Year				
313	Cassander in Nemea (summer) Polyperchon joins Cassander? Aristodemus persuades Aetolians to join Antigonus (Sept.?), campaigns in Peloponnese Cassander sends troops to Caria, fleet to Lemnos (ca. Oct.)		Tyre falls to Antigonus (ca. June) Ptolemy crushes revolt in Cyprus, moves capital from Memphis to Alexandria, meets Antigonus in Egypt, issues "Freedom Decree"	Latin colonies at Suessa Auruncula, etc.
313/2		Antigonus at Celaenae	Demetrius Poliorcetes in Syria	
312	Zeno of Citium arrives in Athens? Timaeus of Tauromenium in Athens, begins his history of Sicily	Antigonus meets Cassander at Hellespont Seleucus regains Babylon, Susiana, Media; first regnal year of Seleucid dynasty	Ptolemy restores order in Cyrene, ravages Cilicia from Cyprus Ptolemy defeats Demetrius Poliorcetes at Gaza (fall?)	Agathocles exiles Timaeus of Tauromenium Censorship of Appius Claudius Via Appia and Aqua Appia begun
311	Period of the Great Tomb at Lefkadia (Macedonia)? Epicurus on Lesbos (~310) Euhemerus of Messene in Cassander's entourage (~298)	Seleucia-on-Tigris capital of Seleucid empire (~301) Satrapal coalition makes peace with Antigonus (late summer?): Seleucus excluded All Greek cities obtain "freedom and autonomy"	Antigonus recaptures Coele-Syria; Ptolemy withdraws ?Ptolemy now marries Berenice	Carthaginian invasion of Sicily Agathocles defeated by Carthaginians, retains only Syracuse *Duoviri navales* appointed in Rome
310	Cassander executes Alexander IV and Roxane: end of Argead dynasty	War breaks out again (spring) Antigonus campaigns in Babylonia Portrait of Seleucus by Bryaxis? Epicurus moves to Lampsacus	Ptolemy puts Cyprus under direct Lagid control (Menelaus) Agathocles invades Africa (August), captures Tunis; forms alliance with Ophellas	Roman advance into Etruria (via Ciminian Forest) Amazon Sarcophagus, Tarquinia Birth of Theocritus in Sicily (?–300)
309	Polyperchon executes Heracles, is confirmed as *stratēgos* in Peloponnese Lysimachus founds Lysimacheia Demetrius of Phaleron "elected" archon in Athens Areus I king of Sparta (~265/4)		Birth of Ptolemy II Philadelphos	
309/8		Seleucus victorious over Nicanor in the East; Antigonus abandons Iran Execution of Alexander's sister Cleopatra in Sardis	Agathocles murders Ophellas, takes over his army	

DATE	GREECE AND THE AEGEAN	ASIA MINOR AND THE EAST	EGYPT, AFRICA, EASTERN MEDITERRANEAN	ROME, ITALY, SICILY, SPAIN
308	Polyperchon in Macedonia, reconciliates with Cassander / Ptolemy sails to Greece, "liberates" Corinth and Sicyon (temporary standoff with Antigonus)	Ptolemy's generals occupy coast of Pamphylia, Lycia / Seleucus begins reconquest of eastern provinces, in conflict with Chandragupta (–303)	Ptolemy makes peace with Cassander, secures Cyrene after death of Ophellas / Defeat of Agathocles (Oct./Nov.)	Roman alliance with Tarquinii renewed for 40 years / Agathocles returns to Sicily
307	"Four-year war" (–304) begins between Demetrius Poliorcetes and Cassander / Demetrius "liberates" Athens (June), exiles Demetrius of Phaleron, marries Ophellas's widow Eurydice / Honors in Athens for Antigonus and Demetrius / Cassander loses Epirus, campaigns against Ptolemy / Law passed in Athens against schools of philosophy; Theophrastus and others leave Athens	Foundation of Antigoneia	Euclid(?) and Demetrius of Phaleron in Alexandria	Peace between Syracuse and Carthage
306	Demetrius Poliorcetes recalled to Asia Minor / Law against philosophy schools in Athens rescinded / Theophrastus recalled; Epicurus returns to Athens, opens Garden (spring)	Antigonus and Demetrius assume title of joint kings (new dynasty) / Rhodian treaty with Rome	Demetrius Poliorcetes' naval victory over Ptolemy; capture of Cyprus / Antigonus's abortive campaign in Egypt / Agathocles evacuates North Africa	"Philinus" treaty between Rome and Carthage / Birth of Hieron II / Agathocles returns to Syracuse
305/4	Athenian ephebic service no longer compulsory			
305	Olympiodorus defeats Cassander at Elatea / Mosaics by Gnosis at Pella (–301)	Lysimachus, Seleucus, Ptolemy, Cassander all assume kingship	Demetrius Poliorcetes besieges Rhodes (–304) / Birth of Callimachus in Cyrene?	Agathocles defeats exiles
304	Cassander's successes in Greece reversed by Demetrius Poliorcetes / Fl. Philoxenos of Eretria (painter) / Macedonian garrison installed on Acrocorinth	Spartocus III king of Cimmerian Bosporus	Demetrius raises siege of Rhodes / Chares commissioned to design Colossus	Agathocles assumes title of king in Syracuse / End of Second Samnite War / Repeal of Appius Claudius's reforms / Roman alliance with Marsi, etc.

304/3	Demetrius Poliorcetes and his mistresses occupying Parthenon			Cleonymus at Taras
303	Demetrius Poliorcetes scores successes against Cassander	Renewed coalition against Antigonus / Seleucus's pact with Chandragupta (Gandhara, eastern Arachosia, Gedrosia ceded)		
302	Demetrius Poliorcetes resuscitates League of Corinth / Demetrius Poliorcetes' truce with Cassander / New League of Corinth nominates Demetrius commander-in-chief / Demetrius admitted (illegally) to Eleusinian Mysteries / Demetrius recalled to Asia by Antigonus	Lysimachus deposits 9,000 talents at Pergamon, marries Amastris of Heracleia / Teos conquered for Cassander / Antigonus executes Mithridates of Cius / Mithridates I Ktistes founds kingdom of Pontus (−266/5) / Megasthenes' expedition to India (−291)	Ptolemy attacks Jerusalem	Agathocles in southern Italy (−293)
301	League of Corinth dissolved / "Center-party" government at Athens under Phaedrus / Demetrius retreats to Corinth	Battle of Ipsus: death of Antigonus / Partition of Antigonus's kingdom by victorious opponents	Ptolemy regains Judaea (−200), occupies Coele-Syria	
300	(Ca.) Derveni krater, early Tanagra figurines / Statue of Menander by Cephisodotos and Timarchus / Decline of Pangaeum mines begins	Demetrius Poliorcetes resumes war against Lysimachus / Lysimachus marries Arsinoë II / Seleucus I sends Megasthenes to India / Fl. Duris of Samos (historian), Praxagoras of Cos (physician) / Seleucus I initiates new Temple of Apollo at Didyma	Abdalonymus commissions Alexander Sarcophagus / Eutychides' Tyche of Antioch? / Strato of Lampsacus tutor to Ptolemy II / Foundation of Seleucia-in-Pieria, Antioch / Seleucus acquires N. Syria / Pleistarchus in Cilicia	Magas governor of Cyrene / Agathocles captures Corcyra (or 298?), marries Theoxene daughter of Ptolemy / Ficorini cistus; later Gnathia vases
299	Warrior tomb at Vergina?	Alliances of Ptolemy and Lysimachus, Seleucus and Demetrius / Demetrius Poliorcetes betrothed to Ptolemy's daughter Ptolemaïs	Poetic revival (Philetas, Asclepiades) / Ptolemy's daughter Lysandra marries Alexander V / Pyrrhus I is sent to Alexandria as envoy-hostage, marries Berenice's daughter Antigone	Latin colony at Narnia / Agathocles besieges Croton?
298	Lachares seizes Athens?	Demetrius Poliorcetes and Seleucus occupy southern Anatolia		
298/7	Death of Cassander			

DATE	GREECE AND THE AEGEAN	ASIA MINOR AND THE EAST	EGYPT, AFRICA, EASTERN MEDITERRANEAN	ROME, ITALY, SICILY, SPAIN
297	Death of Cassander's son Philip IV / Division of Macedonia between Cassander's younger sons / Pyrrhus I returns to Epirus	Zipoëtes king of Bithynia (−279) / Beginning of Ponto–Bithynian era	Foundation of Museum and Library, Alexandria, appointment of Zenodotus as Chief Librarian?	
296	Siege of Athens by Demetrius Poliorcetes (−295)	Coalition against Demetrius	Demetrius's forces capture Samaria / Birth of Apollonius Rhodius? / Eutychides' Tyche of Antioch (?−293)	
295	Athens starved into surrender (spring) / "Freedom" restored in Athens / Macedonian garrison in Piraeus / (Ca.) Portico of Echo, Olympia; Kazanlak tomb paintings	Seleucus I acquires Cilicia / Lysimachus acquires Ionia	Ptolemy recovers Cyprus, sends fleet to relieve Athens, without success	Agathocles seizes Hipponium (?); his daughter Lanassa marries Pyrrhus I / Roman victory at Sentinum over Etruscans
294	Demetrius Poliorcetes acclaimed king of Macedonia (autumn) and a god in Athens / Oligarchic regime in Athens		Antiochus I marries stepmother Stratonice, is raised to co-kingship with Seleucus I	Pliny claims that "art stopped at this point" (−156/3)
293	Foundation of Demetrias / End of "center party" in Athens; Phaedrus joins Demetrius Poliorcetes / Demetrius reconquers Thessaly, founds Demetrias (Volos)		Erasistratus in Antioch	
292	Demetrius orders restoration of exiled Athenian oligarchs / Death of Menander (drowned off Piraeus?) / Aetolia and Boeotia rise against Demetrius Poliorcetes / Demetrius reduces Thebes		Philetas of Cos tutor to Ptolemy II / Ptolemy's protectorate over Aegean islands	Latin colonies at Venusia, Hadria, etc.
291	Demetrius Poliorcetes retakes Thebes (after second revolt), invades Thrace, wars with Aetolia and Pyrrhus I			

Year				
290	Demetrius Poliorcetes returns to Athens with Lanassa, is hymned as god, stages Games; Teisicrates' statue of Demetrius; Birth of Cercidas of Megalopolis?; Aetolians seize Phocis, ban Demetrius and allies from Games at Delphi	Temple of Athena, Pergamon; *Fl.* Chares of Lindos; rise of Rhodian school of sculpture	Herophilus of Chalcedon in Alexandria	End of Samnite Wars; Rome annexes Sabines as *cives sine suffragio*; Agathocles breaks with Pyrrhus, allies himself with Demetrius Poliorcetes; Demetrius Poliorcetes marries Lanassa, daughter of Agathocles: Corcyra as dowry
289	Demetrius Poliorcetes invades Epirus, prepares to invade Asia			Death of Agathocles; Syracuse liberated; warfare in Sicily
289/8	Pyrrhus I abrogates treaty with Demetrius Poliorcetes			
288	Coalition against Demetrius Poliorcetes (spring); Pyrrhus I and Lysimachus invade and partition Macedonia; Nationalist government in Athens (July); Fall of Demetrius (Sept.?); he flees to Cassandreia; suicide of Phila			Hicetas in Syracuse (−278); Birth of Archimedes?
288/7	Demetrius returns to Peloponnese			
287	Athenian democratic rebellion against Demetrius (April/May); Demetrius besieges Athens (May/June); Athens freed by treaty, Demetrius keeps Piraeus (July); Pyrrhus visits Athens	Demetrius Poliorcetes crosses into Asia Minor (fall?)	Ptolemy repudiates Eurydice and Keraunos	Hortensian Laws at Rome
287/6	Strato of Lampsacus succeeds Theophrastus (d. 288/5) as head of Lyceum in Athens			
286	Demetrius Poliorcetes' son Antigonus Gonatas assumes title of king; Abortive Athenian attempt to recover Piraeus	Demetrius captures Sardis, marries Ptolemaïs (spring?); Demetrius campaigning in Anatolia and Cilicia	Ptolemy wins Tyre, Sidon from Demetrius	

DATE	GREECE AND THE AEGEAN	ASIA MINOR AND THE EAST	EGYPT, AFRICA, EASTERN MEDITERRANEAN	ROME, ITALY, SICILY, SPAIN
285	Lysimachus king of Macedonia (−281), seizes Thessaly / Pyrrhus I makes secret treaty with Antigonus Gonatas, returns to Epirus / Philippides (comic poet) honored for services to Athens / Large houses being built in Pella	Demetrius Poliorcetes captured by Seleucus (spring)	Ptolemy II made joint king, marries Arsinoë I / Lighthouse of Alexandria built by Sostratos of Cnidos	Thurii honors Roman tribune? / *Fl.* Leonidas of Taras
284	Lysimachus conquers Paeonia / Pyrrhus recovers Corcyra?	Philetairos switches allegiance from Lysimachus to Seleucus I / Patroclus explores central Asia and Caspian		Manius Curius defeats Senones
283	Antigonus Gonatas succeeds to throne of Macedonia	Death of Demetrius Poliorcetes in captivity (spring)	Lycophron of Chalcis *fl.* in Alexandria; Tragic Pleiad / Ptolemy II becomes sole king (−246) on death of Ptolemy I	Defeat of Boii and Etruscans at Lake Vadimo
283/2		Lysimachus executes his son Agathocles		
282		Agathocles' widow Lysandra and Ptolemy Keraunos flee to Seleucus I / Philetairos of Pergamon defects to Seleucus I, with 9,000 talents of Lysimachus's / Seleucus invades Asia Minor		Roman squadron in Gulf of Tarentum (Taras)
281	Antigonus Gonatas captures Athens, but is defeated by Ptolemy Keraunos / Ptolemy Keraunos murders Seleucus I (Sept.)	Lysimachus defeated and killed at Corupedion (Feb.) / Arsinoë II escapes to Macedonia / Antiochus I succeeds Seleucus I as sole king (−261)		Tarentine appeal to Pyrrhus I
280	Gauls invade Thrace / Achaean League refounded (or 282?) / Areus introduces coinage at Sparta? / Gauls invade Illyria / Polyeuctus's statue of Demosthenes / Palace of Palatitsa (Macedonia) / Temple of Mesa, Lesbos / Birth of Chrysippus	Nicomedes I accedes in Bithynia (− ca. 250) / Berossos writing history of Babylonia in Greek for Antiochus I	*Fl.* Theocritus, Herodas, Callimachus? / Hedylos of Samos in Alexandria / Death of Demetrius of Phaleron? / Syrian war of succession (−276) between Antiochus I and Ptolemy II / Erasistratus comes to Alexandria? / *Fl.* Aristarchus of Samos	Sicilian cities threatened by Carthage / Pyrrhus I lands in Italy (May) / Pyrrhus defeats Romans at Heracleia, campaigns in Italy, Sicily (−275)

280/79	Rome rejects Pyrrhus I's peace offer (spring) / Roman defeat at Asculum	Ptolemaieia celebrated in Alexandria		Ptolemy Keraunos king of Macedonia, marries Arsinoë II
279				Gauls invade Macedonia (Feb.) / Death in battle of Ptolemy Keraunos / Gauls desecrate royal Macedonian tombs / Antipater "Etesias" king for 45 days; rule of Meleager / Revolt at Cassandreia / Gauls invade Greece, are driven out by Aetolians
279/8		Arsinoë II returns to Egypt	Ptolemy II establishes bridgehead at Miletus	
278	Carthage blockades Syracuse / Pyrrhus I crosses to Sicily (fall) / Pyrrhus relieves Syracuse, drives out Carthaginians (except from Messina and Lilybaeum) / Rome negotiates with Pyrrhus / Pyrrhus refuses Carthaginian peace offer, fails to capture Lilybaeum		Gauls cross to Asia Minor with connivance of Nicomedes I of Bithynia / Treaty between Antigonus Gonatas and Antiochus I on Europe/Asia basis (fall)	Expansion of Aetolian League begins
278/7				Sosthenes (Macedonian general) dies fighting the Gauls
277			Gauls spread terror in Asia Minor, occupy Galatia in eastern Phrygia	Anarchy in Macedonia / Aetolians win control of Delphic Amphictyony / Antigonus Gonatas defeats Gauls at Lysimacheia (early summer) / Antigonus wins back Thessaly, storms Cassandreia
276	Pyrrhus I returns to Italy (fall), spends winter in Taras / Birth of Eratosthenes of Cyrene?	Ptolemy II defeated by Antiochus I in Syria / Ptolemy II marries Arsinoë II? (before 274/3)	Philetairos of Pergamon and Asian cities resist Gauls	Antigonus Gonatas reestablished as king of Macedonia (−239) / Aratus of Soli and Zeno of Citium at Antigonus's court / Antigonus marries Phila, daughter of Seleucus I / Antigonus repairs desecration of royal tombs at Aigai; builds great Vergina tumulus? / Aetolians seize Dolopia

DATE	GREECE AND THE AEGEAN	ASIA MINOR AND THE EAST	EGYPT, AFRICA, EASTERN MEDITERRANEAN	ROME, ITALY, SICILY, SPAIN
275	Pyrrhus I returns to Epirus (fall) Death of Pyrrho of Elis Birth of Demetrius II, son of Antigonus Gonatas	End of Babylon Antigonus I defeats Gauls, drives them into Phrygia Philetairos strikes first coins in Pergamon	Great Portico of the agora, Cyrene Apollonius leaves Alexandria, revises *Argonautica* on Rhodes? Magas of Cyrene attacks Egypt? Theocritus makes bid for Hieron II's patronage (Id. 16)	Pyrrhus I defeated by Romans at Beneventum (summer), leaves Italy
275/4			Grand Procession of Ptolemy II	Hieron II commands Syracusan forces
274	Pyrrhus I invades Macedonia and Thessaly; Antigonus Gonatas flees	Conquests by Ptolemy II in Asia Minor	First Syrian War (Antiochus I vs. Ptolemy II, –271) Aratus of Soli in Antioch (–272)	Pyrrhus I withdraws bulk of forces from Italy
274/3	Athens honors Pyrrhus I		Arsinoë as queen on Pithom stele	Hieron II fights Carthaginians of western Sicily?
273	Pyrrhus I briefly reasserts claim to Macedonian throne		Exchange of ambassadors between Ptolemy II and Rome: *amicitia* agreement	Latin colonies at Paestum, Cosa
272	Pyrrhus I invades Peloponnese Antigonus Gonatas recaptures most of Macedonia, marches on Argos Death of Pyrrhus in Argos (fall) Aratus of Soli returns to Pella	Victories by Ptolemy II in southern Anatolia		Livius Andronicus comes to Rome Anio Vetus aqueduct
272/1			Ptolemy II wins back coastal Syria	
271	Antigonus Gonatas permanently reestablished as king of Macedonia Pro-Macedonian tyrannies in Peloponnese Beginning of Phylarchus's *History* (–220) Athenian decree honoring Demochares? Death (and portrait) of Epicurus		End of First Syrian War Ptolemy II's victory celebrations in Alexandria Ptolemy and Arsinoë II receive divine honors ?Theocritus writes *Encomium of Ptolemy* (Id. 17)	Rome conquers Taras (Tarentum)
270	Antigonus Gonatas annexes Euboea? Revolt of slaves on Chios (–260) Arrival of Sarapis in Piraeus? Grain prices falling on Delos	Victory of Antiochus I, with elephants, over Gauls in Asia Minor Second period of building at Ai Khanum	Apollonius Rhodius returns to Alexandria?	Rome captures Rhegium (Reggio)
269	Athenian decree for Callias of Sphettos	Birth of Attalus I of Pergamon	?Herodas's *mimiamboi*	First silver coinage minted by Rome

694

	Greece and Macedonia	Asia	Egypt and culture	Rome and the West
268	Death of Strato of Lampsacus, succeeded as head of Middle Academy (–241) by Arcesilaus; Coalition of Athens, Sparta, Egypt against Antigonus Gonatas (fall), leading to the Chremonidean War (–263/2?)	Antiochus I's imperial edict; Accession of Asoka in India?	Death and deification of Arsinoë II (1 or 2 July)	Hieron II king of Syracuse (–215); Hieron makes treaty of alliance with Carthage; Latin colony at Beneventum
267	Antigonus Gonatas in Attica			Rome captures Brundisium (Brindisi)
266	Spartan force stopped at Isthmus; Antigonus Gonatas holds Corinth	Antiochus II Theos made co-regent on execution of his elder brother Seleucus		Apulia and Messapia join Roman alliance; Roman rule covers all Magna Graecia
265	Antigonus Gonatas defeats Spartans near Corinth: Areus II killed fighting; Antigonus puts Athens under siege (–262); Birth of Cleomenes III of Sparta?	Nicomedes I of Bithynia founds Nicomedia? (or 260); Cult statue of Zeus Stratios by Doedalses at Nicomedia	Apollonius Rhodius appointed chief librarian in Alexandria?	
264	End of Parian Marble chronology		*Fl.* Callimachus of Cyrene	First Punic War begins (–241); First gladiatorial show in Rome; Roman army to Sicily
263	Death of Zeno of Citium, succeeded in Stoa by Cleanthes of Assos	Death of Philetairos of Pergamon; accession of Eumenes I (–241), who declares independence		Hieron II of Syracuse becomes ally of Rome, repudiates Carthaginian alliance
262	Besieged Athens capitulates to Antigonus Gonatas; Spartans defeated by Aristodemus, tyrant of Megalopolis	Antiochus I defeated by Eumenes I of Pergamon near Sardis (or 261)		Romans capture Agrigentum (Sicily); sea battle off Mylae
262/1		Ephesus controlled by Ptolemy II		
261	Antigonus Gonatas defeats Ptolemaic fleet off Cos?; Alexander of Epirus invades Macedonia; End of *Atthis* of Philochorus, last of the local historians of Attica; Acrotatus of Sparta killed	Death of Antiochus I (June); accession of Antiochus II Theos; Antiochus Gonatas attacks Miletus; Birth of Apollonius of Perge, mathematician (–190)	Peace between Ptolemy II and Antiochus I; Ptolemy II organizes census; Apollonius *dioiketes* (finance minister; – ca. 242)	Romans build fleet

DATE	GREECE AND THE AEGEAN	ASIA MINOR AND THE EAST	EGYPT, AFRICA, EASTERN MEDITERRANEAN	ROME, ITALY, SICILY, SPAIN
260	Arcesilaus of Pitane appointed scholarch of Academy Painted stelae at Demetrias	Ariobarzanes king of Pontus? (−250?) Hellenistic fortifications of Doura-Europos Edict of Asoka in Greek and Aramaic at Kandahar	Death of Theocritus?	Hieron II's great altar in Syracuse
259	Macedonian–Seleucid alliance		Second Syrian War (−253) between Ptolemy II and Antiochus II Revenue laws in Egypt	Romans occupy Corsica
259/8			Zenon touring Syria and Phoenicia for Apollonius the *dioikētēs*	
258		Antiochus II recovers Ephesus, "liberates" Miletus		
257	Demetrius II co-regent with Antigonus Gonatas	Beginning of Parthian breakaway from Seleucid empire?		
256	Antigonus Gonatas restores autonomy to Athens (−253/2?)	Diodotus I independent ruler in Bactria? (−248?)		Hieron II's scene-building for the-ater in Syracuse
255	Antigonus Gonatas secures Island League (*Nēsiōtēs*) Argos independent of Macedonia	Ariarathes III king of Cappadocia (−220)	Truce between Ptolemy II and Antigonus Gonatas Death of Herophilus?	Regulus lands in Africa, is defeated
254		Ziaēlas gains control of Bithynia		
253		Peace between Antiochus II and Ptolemy II: end of Second Syrian War	Ptolemy II recognizes independence of Corinth	Roman fleet wrecked off Cape Palinurus
253/2	Macedonian restrictions reimposed on Athens Antigonus Gonatas's nephew Alexander revolts in Corinth, declares himself king? (or 249)			
252	Death of Aristodemus of Megalopolis, city freed?	Berenice daughter of Ptolemy II marries Antiochus II, who repudiates Laodice to do so (see 246 for "Laodicean" War)		

251	Aratus frees Sicyon (May), brings it into Achaean League		Aratus of Sicyon visits Egypt: Ptolemaic subsidy for Achaean League	Roman siege of Lilybaeum
250	*Sōtēria* festival at Delphi made panhellenic Peak period of Ptolemy II's Aegean power New Cynosarges gymnasium in Athens Aristomachus I tyrant of Argos (−248) Aratus fights Alexander of Corinth (−248) *Fl.* Cercidas of Megalopolis (poet and Cynic)	Embassy of Asoka to the West? Final breakaway by Bactria and Sogdiana from Seleucid empire?	*Fl.* Philinus of Cos (physician) Translation of Bible (LXX) into Greek begun Ptolemaic exploration of eastern Africa for elephants	*Fl.* Archimedes (287–212) in Syracuse Birth of Plautus Death of Magas of Cyrene(?); Demetrius the Fair sent by Antigonus Gonatas to take over
249	Second Ptolemeaea founded on Delos			Roman naval defeat at Drepana: fleet wrecked
248		Invasion of Parthia by Parsa tribes under Arsaces Accession of Diodotus II of Bactria? (−235)		Demetrius the Fair murdered at instance of Berenice II, daughter of Magas?
247	Athens temporarily freed of Macedonian restrictions (−245)	Arsaces I king of Parthia? (−230/27?) Beginning of "Parthian era"		Carthaginian offensive against Sicily Rome renews alliance with Hieron II of Syracuse
246	Antigonus Gonatas recovers Corinth	Death of Antiochus II; accession of Seleucus II (−226)	Death of Ptolemy II; accession of Ptolemy III Euergetes (29 Jan., −222) Third Syrian ("Laodicean") War between Ptolemy III and Seleucus II (−241) Revolt in Egypt Callimachus's *Lock of Berenice*	Egypt recovers Cyrene?
246/5	Death of Alexander of Corinth? Seleucus II wins naval victory off Andros?		Eratosthenes succeeds Apollonius Rhodius as head of Alexandrian Library (−205/1)	
245	Aratus's first command as *stratēgos* of Achaean League (May) Aetolian League defeats Boeotians at Chaeronea (fall) Aratus recovers Acrocorinth (winter)	Ptolemy III moves from Ephesus to the Euphrates Mithridates IV king of Pontus? (−220) Antiochus Hierax rules Asia Minor	Ptolemy III wins back Antioch (−244) and Seleucia-in-Pieria (−219)	Development of Hellenistic Acragas (Agrigentum)

DATE	GREECE AND THE AEGEAN	ASIA MINOR AND THE EAST	EGYPT, AFRICA, EASTERN MEDITERRANEAN	ROME, ITALY, SICILY, SPAIN
244	Lydiades tyrant at Megalopolis	Ptolemy's forces fighting in south-western Anatolia (−241)	Apollonius retires to Rhodes Birth of Ptolemy IV?	Latin colony at Brundisium (Brindisi)
244/3	Agis IV king of Sparta (−241)			
243	Persaeus of Citium (Stoic) in Corinth Aratus's second *stratēgia*; he recaptures Acrocorinth from Macedonians, expels garrison (summer) Megara and Argos join Achaean League		Joseph son of Tobias made *prostatēs* in Judaea by Ptolemy III? (−218)	New Roman fleet built from voluntary loans
243/2	Social reforms in Sparta Antigonus Gonatas and Alexander II of Epirus allied with Aetolians			
242	Cancellation of mortgages in Sparta Achaean–Spartan alliance Aratus attacks Attica Achaean-Macedonian armistice	Antiochus Hierax co-ruler with Seleucus II, confirmed in lands west of Taurus Mts.	Ptolemy III appointed honorary admiral of Achaean League Birth of Antiochus III?	*Praetor peregrinus* established
241	Execution of Agis IV of Sparta Aratus drives Aetolians from Peloponnese Death of Arcesilaus; Lacydes succeeds him as scholarch of Academy	Peace between Seleucus II and Ptolemy III: end of Third Syrian War Death of Eumenes I of Pergamon; accession of Attalus I (−197)	Ptolemy confirmed in possession of Ephesus and Seleucia-in-Pieria	End of First Punic War Roman occupation of Sicily Revolt of mercenaries against Carthage (−238/7)
241/0	Antigonus Gonatas makes peace with Achaean League			
240	Death of Alexander II of Epirus? Aratus begins attacks on Athens, raids Argos Work begun on Asclepieion of Cos	Development of Greek architecture in Bactria	Ptolemy III's pylon at Karnak Foundation plaques of Alexandrian Sarapieion Death of Callimachus?	First presentation of Greek tragedy and comedy in Latin translation by Livius Andronicus
240/39	Death of Aratus? Macedonia and Aetolia allied against Achaean League			
239	Death of Antigonus II Gonatas; accession of Demetrius II (−229) Demetrius II marries Phthia of Epirus	"War of the Brothers" between Seleucus II and Antiochus Hierax (−236) Seleucus is defeated by Hierax, retreats to Cilicia		Birth of Ennius

	Greece and Macedonia	Asia Minor and the East	Egypt	Rome and the West
239/8	Aetolia attacks Epirot Acarnania; "War of Demetrius" between Macedonia and the Achaean and Aetolian Leagues (−229)		Canopus Decree (March)	Romans seize Sardinia, occupy and reduce it (−225) and Corsica
238	Birth of Philip V of Macedon	Attalus I of Pergamon fights Antiochus Hierax		
238/7	Aratus's fifth *stratēgia*			
237		Attalus I defeats Gauls on Caicos River, proclaims himself king(?), plans major sculptural dedications	Ptolemy III lays foundation stone of Horus Temple at Edfu (August)	Hamilcar of Carthage in Spain; revival of Carthaginian empire there (−206)
236		Seleucus II makes peace with Antiochus Hierax, cedes him territories north of Taurus Mts.		First play of Naevius
235	Aratus's sixth *stratēgia*; he attacks Argos Cleomenes III king of Sparta (−222) Megalopolis joins Achaean League Anti-Macedonian Greek coalition Sphaerus (Stoic) in Sparta Death of Timon of Phlius?	Euthydemus I king of Bactria (−200?) Campaigns by Attalus I against Antiochus Hierax (−228)		Temple of Janus closed Carthaginian conquests in Spain
234	Lydiades' first *stratēgia* in Achaean League			Birth of Cato the Censor
233	Seventh *stratēgia* of Aratus; he attacks Athens, reaches Academy Battle of Phylacia: Aratus defeated			
232	Death of Cleanthes of Assos, succeeded as head of Stoa by Chrysippus			
231	Eighth *stratēgia* of Aratus (May) Illyrian forces defeat Aetolians in Acarnania	Seleucus II's expedition against the Parthians Attalus I's campaign against Antiochus Hierax (−229?)		Roman embassy to Hamilcar in Spain
230	End of Epirot royal house (or 233?); attacks by Illyrians under Teuta Corcyra appeals to Achaea and Aetolia	Ziaëlas of Bithynia killed by Galatians, succeeded by Prusias I (−182?) Portico of Attalus in Athena's sanctuary, Pergamon		Death of Hamilcar, replaced by Hasdrubal in Spain

DATE	GREECE AND THE AEGEAN	ASIA MINOR AND THE EAST	EGYPT, AFRICA, EASTERN MEDITERRANEAN	ROME, ITALY, SICILY, SPAIN
229	Macedonian garrison removed from Piraeus Roman legate assassinated in Illyria; so-called First Illyrian War (−228) Death of Demetrius II, succeeded by Antigonus III Doson (−221), guardian of Philip V (minor) Argos joins Achaean League Cleomenes III attacks Megalopolis Teuta attacking Illyrian coast, Corcyra (First Illyrian War)			Foundation of New Carthage in Spain
229/8	Thessaly revolts from Macedonia Aratus's ninth *stratēgia*; he frees Athens from Macedonian garrison	Attalus I's final defeat of Antiochus Hierax near Pergamon		
228	Beginning of Cleomenes III's war against the Achaean League Illyrians defeated by Rome; recapture of Corcyra Romans admitted to Isthmian Games (spring); envoys in Athens and Corinth Aristomachus *stratēgos* of Achaean League	Expansion by Attalus I of Pergamon over Seleucid Asia Minor (−223) Seleucus II drives Antiochus Hierax out of Babylonia		
227	Cleomenes III's return to Sparta; his brother Archidamus assassinated Antigonus III Doson's expedition to Caria Antiochus Hierax murdered by Gauls in Thrace Aratus takes Mantinea, is defeated at Megalopolis	Antiochus Hierax surrenders to Ptolemy III at Ephesus, escapes to Thrace Pergamene sculptures marking Attalus I's Galatian victories? (or ca. 230?) Earthquake in Rhodes shakes down Colossus		Sicily a Roman province Four praetors established in Rome
227/6	Cleomenes III's reforms in Sparta Achaean diplomatic contact with Macedonia	Contributions to recovery of Rhodes		

700

	Greece and Macedonia	Seleucid kingdom	Egypt	Rome and the West
226	Aetolians dominate Delphic Amphictyony Achaean success at Orchomenos (Jan./Feb.) Spartan successes against Achaea (–224)	Death of Seleucus II; accession of Seleucus III (–223)	Ptolemy III switches his support from Achaean League to Cleomenes III	Invading Gauls defeated at Telemon
226/5	Cleomenes captures Argos, Corinth, Mantinea			
225	Aratus elected *stratēgos* of League Argos and Corinth join Cleomenes Cercidas goes as envoy to Macedonia Aratus and Antigonus III Doson allied against Cleomenes		Debasement of Ptolemaic copper coinage	
224	Formation of Hellenic League (symmachy) against Cleomenes and Sparta Antigonus III Doson in Peloponnese, takes Argos, is appointed commander-in-chief of allied forces Aratus *stratēgos* with emergency powers			
223	Antigonus III Doson and Aratus destroy Mantinea, sell inhabitants into slavery Cleomenes captures Megalopolis (July)	Seleucus III murdered; accession of Antiochus III the Great (–187)		Flamininus defeats Insubres
222	Cleomenes III defeated at Sellasia (July) by Antigonus III Doson, who takes Sparta; Cleomenes escapes to Egypt	Revolt of Molon against Antiochus III; he assumes royal title Achaeus recovers Asia Minor	Death of Ptolemy III (Feb.)	
222/1			Accession of Ptolemy IV Philopator (winter 222/1 – Summer 204)	
221	Death of Antigonus III Doson (summer); accession of Philip V (–179)	Antiochus III marries Laodice daughter of Mithridates II of Pontus		Death of Hasdrubal, replaced in Spain by Hannibal

DATE	GREECE AND THE AEGEAN	ASIA MINOR AND THE EAST	EGYPT, AFRICA, EASTERN MEDITERRANEAN	ROME, ITALY, SICILY, SPAIN
221	Aetolian aggression against Epirus and Messenia War of the Allies (Social War) begun against Aetolia (–217)	Antiochus puts down Molon's revolt; Molon commits suicide	Rhodian war with Byzantium over tolls *Fl.* Euphorion of Chalcis	Via Flaminia begun Starting point of Polybius's *History*
220	Ariston Aetolian general Aetolian invasion of Messenia Aratus defeated at Caphyae (May) Philip V allied with Scerdilaidas of Illyria Massacre of Macedonian party in Sparta Hypostyle Hall on Delos Death of Cercidas of Megalopolis?	Revolt of Achaeus, who is proclaimed king in Phrygia and usurps the throne (–213) Antiochus III suppresses revolts in Media, Persis, Babylon		
219	Second Illyrian War (against Demetrius of Pharos) Lycurgus king of Sparta (–211), allied with Aetolia Rising in Messenia (expulsion of oligarchs) Lycurgus invades Argolid, declares war on Achaea Philip V invades Aetolia and Acarnania Demetrius of Pharos joins Philip Dardanian invasion of Macedonia: Philip recalled to deal with it		Fourth Syrian War (–217) between Antiochus III and Ptolemy IV Death of Cleomenes III in Egypt during abortive Alexandrian revolt Antiochus III takes Seleucia-in-Pieria, Ptolemaïs, Tyre	Roman envoys in Carthage Hannibal begins siege of Saguntum (spring) Fall of Saguntum (Nov.)
218	Philip V's invasion of Aetolia and Laconia Sack of Thermon Aetolians attack Messenia and Thessaly	Attalus I and Prusias of Bithynia fight Achaeus Attalus captures cities in northern Ionia and the Troad	Brief truce between Antiochus III and Ptolemy IV (winter 219/8) Antiochus moves south into Coele-Syria	Second Punic War declared between Rome and Carthage (–202) Hannibal leaves Spain for Italy, crosses Alps Hannibal wins battles of Trebbia (Dec.) and Ticinus
217	News of Trasimene reaches Greece (June) Peace of Naupactus (Aug./Sept.) Scerdilaidas of Illyria breaks with Philip V		Ptolemy IV wins battle of Raphia (22 June) against Antiochus III Coele-Syria returned to Ptolemaic control Ptolemy IV marries his sister Arsinoë III (Oct.) Synod at Memphis (Nov.); Pithom stele	Hannibal's victory at Lake Trasimene (spring) Fabius Maximus Cunctator dictator Roman naval victory off the Ebro

	Greece and Macedonia	Asia	Egypt	The West
216	Philip V in western Greece, drives out Scerdilaïdas Philippeia founded on Delos	Antiochus III and Attalus I fight Achaeus	Native risings in Upper Egypt	Roman defeat by Hannibal at Cannae Revolts in central Italy (Capua)
215	Treaty between Philip V and Carthage Philip in Peloponnese Civil *stasis* in Messene Demetrius of Pharos killed in assault on Ithome First Macedonian War (−205)	Achaeus besieged in Sardis		Death of Hieron II of Syracuse The Scipios launch successful campaign in Spain (−212) Hannibal in southern Italy
214	Laevinus off Illyria with fleet Philip V retreats overland from Aoös in western Greece (late summer)			Marcellus sent to Sicily
214/13	Birth of Carneades (New Academy) Roman squadron stationed off Illyria			
213	Philip V ravages Messenia, captures Lissos Death of Aratus Birth of Perseus, elder son of Philip	Achaeus captured and executed by Antiochus III		Hannibal occupies Tarentum (except the acropolis) Sack of Leontini Roman siege of Syracuse begins
212	Philip V campaigns in Illyria	Beginning of Antiochus III's eastern anabasis (−205); he regains control of Armenia		Siege of Capua Fall of Syracuse to Marcellus; death of Archimedes
212/11	Roman–Aetolian alliance			
211	Death of Lycurgus king of Sparta, succeeded by his son Pelops (minor) Aetolian attack on Thessaly, Acarnania Philip V garrisons Tempe	Attalus I joins Roman–Aetolian pact Antiochus III at Ecbatana, assembling army		Introduction of denarius in Rome Hannibal's march on Rome Fall of Capua Defeat and death of Scipios in Spain
210	Philip V returns to Pella Sulpicius takes Aegina, gives it to Aetolians Portrait of Chrysippus by Eubulides?	Lindos acropolis in progress	Birth of Ptolemy V (Oct.?) Ptolemaic Egypt abandons silver as standard currency	Fall of Agrigentum

DATE	GREECE AND THE AEGEAN	ASIA MINOR AND THE EAST	EGYPT, AFRICA, EASTERN MEDITERRANEAN	ROME, ITALY, SICILY, SPAIN
209	Achaea appeals to Philip V Philip campaigns in Peloponnese Punic fleet off Corcyra Romans off Naupactus Attalus I of Pergamon Aetolian *stratēgos*	Antiochus III campaigns in Parthyene		Recapture of Tarentum Scipio Africanus wins New Carthage
208	Philip V recalled by barbarian invasion Attalus returns to Pergamon Aetolians fortify Thermopylae Philip campaigns in central Greece Philopoemen Achaean *stratēgos*: raises army of 20,000 men	Antiochus III attacks Bactria, besieges Zariaspa (−206)		Hasdrubal leaves Spain for Italy Death of Marcellus
207	Philip V recovers Zakynthos Philopoemen defeats Machanidas at Mantinea Nabis in power at Sparta Philip invades Aetolia	Attalus I attacked by Prusias I of Bithynia, retreats to Pergamon	Spread of insurrection in Thebaid	Hymn composed by Livius Andronicus Rome defeats Hasdrubal at the Metaurus
206	Death of Chrysippus?	Antiochus III makes peace with Euthydemus I of Bactria		Final reduction of Spain by Scipio Africanus; Carthaginians evicted
206/5	Aetolians make independent peace with Philip V			
205	Publius Sempronius reaches Illyria (Epidamnus) Peace between Rome and Philip V agreed at Phoenice (summer)	Antiochus III in Arabia Antiochus III returns to Seleucia-on-Tigris, assumes title of Great King	Upper Egypt under independent kings (Harmachis, Ankmachis; −185)	Scipio in Sicily
204	Philip V's expedition against Illyria and Thrace Dicaearchus's corsair activities in Cyclades Nabis of Sparta begins war against Megalopolis	Antiochus III moves on Hellespont from Asia Minor	Death of Ptolemy IV (summer; death not announced till Nov.) Regency of Agathocles for Ptolemy V Agathocles makes contact with Rome	Scipio Africanus lands in Africa Ennius brought to Rome by Cato Cult stone of Mother Goddess (Cybele) brought from Pessinus in Phrygia to Rome (April) Death of Livius Andronicus
203	Philip V builds fleet Marriage proposed between daughter of Philip and Ptolemy V Epiphanes	Antiochus III and Philip V form secret coalition against Ptolemaic Egypt(?)	Agathocles lynched by Alexandrian mob	Hannibal recalled to Carthage

Year				
203/2	Philip V seizes Thasos and Lysimacheia, sells Thasians into slavery			
202	Aetolian appeal to Rome rejected	Rhodes declares war on Philip	Antiochus III invades Coele-Syria, beginning of Fifth Syrian War (–195)	Scipio Africanus's victory over Hannibal at Zama (North Africa) First prose history of Rome (in Greek) by Fabius Pictor
201	Philip V in Cyclades with new fleet, seizes Samos Philopoemen halts Nabis's attack on Messene	Battle of Lade (May): Philip defeats Rhodians, is joined by Miletus Attalus I and Rhodes appeal to Rome (late summer) Allied fleet defeats Philip off Chios (fall) Philip retreats to Miletus, is blockaded in Bargylia (winter)	Antiochus III in Coele-Syria, captures Gaza	Peace between Rome and Carthage; Carthage becomes client state
200	Attalus I's state visit to Athens Senatorial commission to Greece Athens declares war on Philip V, rescinds his previous honors Philip attacks Athens, ravages Attica Achaean League fights Sparta Roman fleet and army reach Illyria Philip's portico on Delos	Philip breaks blockade, returns to Europe Philip takes Abydos Roman envoys warn Philip (summer) Demetrius I king of Bactria and India (– ca. 190)	Antiochus III defeats Ptolemy V at Panion Roman envoys warn Antiochus Fl. Philo of Byzantium Antiochus captures Sidon *Oracle of the Potter* produced in upper Egypt?	Sulpicius consul with Macedonia as province War motion rejected by *comitia centuriata* in Rome War declared on Macedonia (Second Macedonian War, –197)
199	Aetolians invade Thessaly as Rome's allies Mutiny among Roman troops Philopoemen in Crete as mercenary Nabis besieges Megalopolis	Antiochus III in Asia Minor		Death of Naevius?
198	Titus Quinctius Flamininus takes command of Roman force in Greece Flamininus wins battle of Aoös Pass (25 June); Roman troops on Corinthian Gulf Conference of Sicyon: Achaea joins Rome		Antiochus III completes subjugation of Coele-Syria	Praetors increased to six in number Revolt in Spain
197	Battle of Cynoscephalae (June): Philip V defeated Conference of Gonnus: peace concluded between Macedonia and Rome (winter)	Death of Attalus I; accession of Eumenes II in Pergamon (–160/59)		

DATE	GREECE AND THE AEGEAN	ASIA MINOR AND THE EAST	EGYPT, AFRICA, EASTERN MEDITERRANEAN	ROME, ITALY, SICILY, SPAIN
196/6	Antiochus III occupies Ephesus, invades Pergamene territory			
196	Council of Corinth Philip V evacuates "Fetters of Greece" Flamininus proclaims "Freedom of the Greeks" at Isthmian Games (June) Antiochus III rebuilds Lysimacheia Roman envoys warn Antiochus at Lysimacheia	Antiochus III crosses Hellespont Smyrna and Lampsacus appeal to Rome Foundation of Pergamene Academy? Pergamene school of sculpture	Rosetta Stone decree (27 March) in Memphis Consecration of Ptolemy V in Memphis (Nov.) Death of Eratosthenes, succeeded as head of Alexandrian Library by Aristophanes of Byzantium	Hannibal suffete in Carthage, begins democratic reforms Roman embassy to Carthage Hannibal goes into exile (summer)
196/5				
195	War against Nabis of Sparta: he submits to Flamininus Chalcis institutes cult of Flamininus	Antiochus III and Ptolemy V ratify peace treaty Hannibal joins Antiochus at Ephesus (fall)	Peace between Antiochus III and Ptolemy V	
194	Roman evacuation of Greece (fall); Flamininus returns to Italy with numerous works of art	Antiochus III reopens negotiations with Rome		Roman colonies at Volturnum, Puteoli, etc. Birth of Terence (Publius Terentius Afer) War with Lusitani (Spain)
194/3			Ptolemy V marries Cleopatra I at Raphia (winter; with Coele-Syria as dowry?)	
193	Aetolians offer support to Antiochus III Nabis attacks Achaean League	Eumenes II of Pergamon working to influence Rome against Philip V	Roman embassy to Antiochus III Rupture between Antiochus and Rome	
192	Defeat and death of Nabis: Sparta forced by Philopoemen to join Achaean League Aetolians secure Demetrias Antiochus III lands in Greece (Oct.)			Rome declares war on Antiochus III (Oct./Nov., –188)

191	Acilius Glabrio lands in Greece (Feb.) / Antiochus III defeated at Thermopylae, flees to Ephesus (April) / Factional trouble at Sparta	Pergamon and Rhodes join Rome / Livius brings Roman fleet to Asia Minor / Antiochus III's fleet defeated off Cape Corycos	Composition of Ben Sira's *Wisdom* (Ecclesiasticus)?	Carthage offers to pay off war indemnity *in toto*; Rome refuses
190	Rome makes armistice with Aetolia / Philip V's portico at Megalopolis?	Scipionic forces land in Asia Minor from Greece, campaign against Antiochus III / Antiochus's fleet defeated at Side and Myonnesos (Aug./Sept.) / Eumenes II blockaded in Pergamon / Antimachus I king of Bactria (–175?)	Ptolemy V's offer of support rejected by Rome / Winged Victory of Samothrace?	
189	Fall of Ambracia to Marcus Fulvius Nobilior / Sparta secedes from Achaean League, makes *deditio* to Rome / Final peace between Rome and Aetolia, which loses control of Delphic Amphictyony	Antiochus III defeated at Magnesia-by-Sipylos (Jan.?); Romans occupy Sardis, begin discussion of peace terms / Gnaeus Manlius Vulso raids Galatia / Antiochus III's son Antiochus (IV) held hostage in Rome		Campanians enrolled as *cives* / Latin colony at Bologna / Freedmen enrolled in rural tribes
188	Achaean war with Sparta / Philopoemen and Achaeans force submission of Sparta (early summer) / Spartan exiles brought home	Treaty of Apamea: settlement of Asia / Eumenes II and Rhodians share Seleucid spoils		Lucius Scipio brings back 134 statues from Asia / Citizenship granted to Arpinum, Formiae, Fundi
187	Second Roman evacuation of Greece?	Death of Antiochus III in Elam (July); accession of Seleucus IV		Marcus Fulvius Nobilior brings back 285 bronze, 230 marble figures from Ambracia / Rome liquidates war debt / Building of Via Aemilia
186	Roman envoys at Philip V's court (winter)	Prusias I of Bithynia campaigning against Pergamon (–183)	Recapture of Thebes, end of secession in Upper Egypt?	Noncitizens expelled from Rome / Senatorial decree suppresses Bacchanalia
186/5	Beginning of Macedonian recovery / Philip V's massacre in Maroneia			
185		Pharnaces I king of Pontus (–170)		
184	Philip V sends his son Demetrius to Rome	Birth of Panaetius?		Death of Plautus / Cato's censorship

DATE	GREECE AND THE AEGEAN	ASIA MINOR AND THE EAST	EGYPT, AFRICA, EASTERN MEDITERRANEAN	ROME, ITALY, SICILY, SPAIN
184	Appius Claudius Pulcher lets Spartans send envoys to Senate as compromise solution			Rome's drainage modernized Citizen colonies at Parma and Mutina Death of Scipio Africanus (winter)
183	Philip V forced by Rome to evacuate Aenus and Maroneia in Thrace (spring) Return of Demetrius from Rome to Macedonia Messenian revolt against Achaeans	Pharnaces I campaigning in Sinope and Cappadocia War between Pontus and Pergamon (–180)		
183/2	Death of Philopoemen	Death of Hannibal in Bithynia		
182		Death of Prusias I of Bithynia; accession of Prusias II (–149) Rhodes fights Pergamon (–179) Eumenes II establishes Nikephoria		
182/1			Ptolemy V revives alliance with Achaean League?	
181	Philip V's Balkan expedition	Sosus of Pergamon (mosaicist) active		Rebellion in Corsica and Sardinia Roman campaign against Celtiberians in Spain
181/0	Polybius on embassy to Ptolemy V		Death of Ptolemy V Epiphanes; Cleopatra I becomes regent for Ptolemy VI Philometor	
180	End of Achaeo-Spartan quarrel Philip executes his son Demetrius Achaean embassy to Rome under Callicrates		Death of Aristophanes of Byzantium(?), succeeded by Aristarchus of Byzantium as head of Alexandrian Library	Birth of Lucilius
179	Death of Philip V; accession of Perseus	End of Pontus–Pergamon war Great Altar of Pergamon? Roman intervention in Asia Minor	Farnese Cup made in Alexandria? Decline in quality of Ptolemaic coinage	Wars in Spain wound up
179/8	Stratēgia of Callicrates (or 180/79?) Perseus strengthening Macedonia's northern frontiers			
178	Agora and gymnasium complex at Sicyon?	Perseus marries Laodice daughter of Seleucus IV Prusias II of Bithynia marries Perseus's half-sister	Seleucus IV's minister Heliodorus fails in attempt to expropriate Temple funds in Jerusalem	

Year	Greece / Macedonia	Seleucid & East	Egypt & Judaea	Rome / Italy
177				Gracchus reduces Sardinia Latins expelled from Rome Demetrius I replaces Antiochus IV as hostage in Rome (−162/1)
176			Death of Cleopatra I (spring); accession of Ptolemy VI Philometor as minor Death of High Priest Simon ("the Just") in Judaea, succeeded by Onias III	Sardinia reduced by Rome
176/5				Demetrius son of Seleucus IV a hostage in Rome
175		Seleucus IV assassinated by Heliodorus (3 Sept.); Antiochus IV regent for Seleucus IV's son (−170) Civil war in Bactria (Eucratides vs. rivals)	Jason's petition to Antiochus IV for "Antiochenes" in Jerusalem (or 174?) "Hellenization" period in Jerusalem (−172/1)	
174	Work resumed on temple of Olympian Zeus, Athens, by Antiochus IV			
173	Perseus refuses to hear Roman embassy	Antiochus IV renews alliance with Rome	Maccabean revolt in Judaea (−164)	Latins struck off citizen rolls Two Epicurean philosophers expelled from Rome
172	Roman mission in Greece Peloponnesian cities rescind honors to Eumenes II War between Rome and Perseus (Third Macedonian War, −168/7)		Roman embassy to Antioch Antiochus IV visits Jerusalem	Eumenes II in Rome, denounces Perseus
171		Eumenes II joins Rome against Perseus	Antiochus IV in Tyre, prepares war against Egypt	Rome dispatches expeditionary force across Adriatic
171/0		Eucratides I king of Bactria (−155) Mithridates I Arsaces V king of Parthia (−138/7)	Sixth Syrian War (Antiochus IV vs. Ptolemy VI, −168)	
170	Perseus reoccupies northern Thessaly Polybius hipparchos in Achaean League	Mithridates IV king of Pontus (−150) Indo-Bactrian expansion under Demetrius and Eucratides I	Ptolemy VI marries Cleopatra II Ptolemy VIII Euergetes II (Physcon) co-regent (joint rule −164) Seleucus IV's son murdered	Birth of Accius

DATE	GREECE AND THE AEGEAN	ASIA MINOR AND THE EAST	EGYPT, AFRICA, EASTERN MEDITERRANEAN	ROME, ITALY, SICILY, SPAIN
170	Athens supports Rome Eumenes II's portico below Athenian Acropolis?	Temple of Dionysus at Teos (Hermogenes)	Antiochus IV king (–164) Menelaus obtains office of High Priest in Jerusalem by bribery	
170/69				
169	Quintus Marcius Philippus marches into Macedonia	Ambivalent stalling by Rhodes	Antiochus IV's drive through Coele–Syria to Egypt (spring) Antiochus IV withdraws to Antioch from before Alexandria, raids Jerusalem Temple *en route*	Death of Ennius
168	Defeat of Perseus at Pydna by Aemilius Paullus (June) Macedonian monarchy abolished, replaced by four republics Aemilius Paullus tours Rome		Antiochus IV launches fresh attack on Egypt, withdraws on receiving Roman ultimatum ("Day of Eleusis") (July)	Crates of Mallos Eumenes II's ambassador in Rome
167	Romans plunder and enslave Epirus Deportation to Rome of Polybius and 1,000 other Achaeans Delos made free port under Athenian control Pangaeum mines closed	Pergamon and Rhodes weakened by Rome	Antiochus IV's bloodbath in Jerusalem in suppression of Jewish revolt Jerusalem Temple rededicated to "Olympian Zeus" (Dec.) Conflict between Ptolemy VI and Ptolemy VIII (–152) Establishment of Akra in Jerusalem	Aemilius Paullus's triumph (including 250 cartloads of works of art) Library of Perseus brought to Rome
167/6			Maccabaean revolt under Mattathias (d. 166) and his son Judas Antiochus IV's festival at Daphne	
166		Freedom of Galatians proclaimed by Rome after Eumenes II's victory over them		Rome declared off-limits for kings Terence's first play (*Andria*) produced
165	New Style Attic coinage (*stephanēphoroi*)?		Antiochus IV sets out for the East Antiochus V under Lysias's guardianship Judas Maccabaeus defeats Lysias at Beth–Zur (fall)	Perseus's death in captivity (or 162?)
164			Antiochus IV rescinds edict of Jewish persecution, offers amnesty (spring?)	Demetrius I (son of Seleucus IV) appeals to Roman Senate to back his claim to Seleucid throne

Year				
163	Demetrius I escapes from Rome with Polybius's aid	Ptolemy VI flees to Rome from Alexandria Rededication by Judas Maccabaeus of Temple in Jerusalem (= Hanukkah; Dec.) Death of Antiochus IV in Media Accession of Antiochus V Eupator (as minor under Lysias's regency) Ptolemy VI returns to Alexandria Partition of Ptolemaic realm (May) Ptolemy VIII to Cyrene; Ptolemy VI keeps him from Cyprus Antiochus V restores Temple and Mosaic Law in Jerusalem Demetrius I Soter and Alexander Balas claim Syrian throne	Ariarathes V king of Cappadocia (–130)	
163/2		Judas Maccabaeus attacks Akra in Jerusalem		
162		Gnaeus Octavius destroys Seleucid ships, elephants; is murdered		
162/1		Demetrius I lands in Phoenicia, reaches Antioch		
161	Greek teachers and philosophers expelled from Rome Rome repudiates alliance with Ptolemy VI Philometor	Demetrius I Soter becomes king, executes Lysias and Antiochus V Rome repudiates treaty with Ptolemy VI Roman treaty with Judaea		Hipparchus (astronomer) observing heavens on Rhodes
160	Rome finally recognizes Demetrius I Soter	Demetrius I's general Bacchides defeats and kills Judas Maccabaeus Jonathan takes over as leader of Jewish resistance movement	Death of Eumenes II of Pergamon (or 159); accession of Attalus II Philadelphos (–138) Accession of Indo-Bactrian king Menander? (–130?)	
159	Death of Terence	Death of High Priest Alkimos in Jerusalem; office vacant till 152		
158				Macedonian mines reopened (after 168/7 closure by Romans)

DATE	GREECE AND THE AEGEAN	ASIA MINOR AND THE EAST	EGYPT, AFRICA, EASTERN MEDITERRANEAN	ROME, ITALY, SICILY, SPAIN
157	Roman campaign in Dalmatia			
156		War between Attalus II of Pergamon and Prusias II of Bithynia (–154)		According to Pliny, art begins to "recover"
156/5			Ptolemy VI tries to have Ptolemy VIII assassinated Ptolemy VIII threatens to will Cyrene to Rome	
155	Athenian "philosopher embassy" to Rome (Carneades, Critolaus, Diogenes) over Oropus dispute		Leak publication of Ptolemy VIII's supposed will bequeathing Cyrene to Rome Ptolemy Eupator governor of Cyprus (d. 150)	
154		Rhodes embroiled with Crete over piracy	Ptolemy VI captures Ptolemy VIII in Cyprus, returns him to Cyrene	Roman war in Lusitania (–138)
153		Attalus II supports Alexander Balas against Demetrius I Soter		Consuls enter office on kalends of January Roman war against Celtiberians (–151)
153/2	Andriscus, Macedonian pretender, sent to Rome			Alexander Balas approved by Rome as legitimate claimant (i.e., as son of Antiochus IV)
152	Panaetius of Rhodes student in Athens Romans visiting Athens now classified as "benefactors"		Alexander Balas and Demetrius I Soter competing for support of Jonathan Jonathan joins Balas as High Priest (Oct.)	Masinissa raiding Carthage
151				Carthage declares war on Masinissa
151/0			Death of Demetrius I Soter fighting Alexander Balas (winter) Alexander Balas becomes king	
150	Return to Greece from Rome of surviving Achaean exiles (including Polybius) Antipater of Tarsus head of Stoa		Ptolemy Eupator dies on Cyprus	Roman decision to intervene in North Africa

712

Year					
150/49	Athenian bronze statue of Ptolemy VI on Acropolis Attalus II's portico in Athenian Agora?		Alexander Balas marries Cleopatra Thea.		*Fl.* of Moschus of Syracuse
149	Fourth Macedonian War: Andriscus invades Macedonia, attacks Thessaly, defeats Roman force Sparta secedes from Achaean League; both sides send embassies to Rome	Nicomedes II king of Bithynia (–95)		Death of Cato the Censor Roman force lands in Africa: siege of Carthage begins (Third Punic War, –146) Permanent extortion court established in Rome (*Lex Calpurnia de repetundis*) Cato's *Origines* published Polybius accompanies Scipio to Spain and North Africa	
149/8	Andriscus in control of Macedonia				
148	Andriscus defeated at Pydna by Quintus Caecilius Metellus Macedonia becomes Roman province under praetor	Mithridates I Arsaces V of Parthia annexes Media		Via Postumia to Genoa Roman campaign at Carthage meets setbacks	
147	Roman embassy in Greece recommends separation of Sparta from Achaean League (spring); Achaean resentment, compromise Critolaus stalls diplomatic action *in re* Sparta for six months (fall)		Ptolemy VI backs Demetrius II for Seleucid throne Cleopatra Thea repudiates Alexander Balas, marries Demetrius II Polybius on exploratory voyage round coast of Northwest Africa?	Viriathus wins successes against Romans in Spain (–138) Via Egnatia begun Scipio Aemilianus continues siege of Carthage	
146	War between Rome and the Achaean League Corinth sacked and destroyed by Mummius (spring) Collapse of Achaean resistance; Diaeus commits suicide at Megalopolis			Sack and destruction of Carthage (spring) Roman province of Africa created Polybius in North Africa with Scipio	
146/5	Polybius returns to Greece from Carthage				

DATE	GREECE AND THE AEGEAN	ASIA MINOR AND THE EAST	EGYPT, AFRICA, EASTERN MEDITERRANEAN	ROME, ITALY, SICILY, SPAIN
145			Ptolemy VI intervenes in Syria, but refuses offer of Seleucid throne against Demetrius II and Ptolemy VI (also killed) at Oenoparas in Coele-Syria Accession of Demetrius II (−140/39, 129−125) War between Demetrius II and Alexander Balas's son Antiochus VI (supported by Diodotus) Return of Ptolemy VIII Euergetes II (Physcon) to Alexandria, joint rule with Cleopatra II and Ptolemy VII	
145/4			Ptolemy VII Neos Philopator murdered by Ptolemy VIII	
144			Ptolemy VIII enthroned as pharaoh at Memphis Demetrius II flees from Antioch (summer) Purge of Alexandrian intellectuals	Panaetius admitted to Scipionic circle in Rome Aqua Marcia aqueduct
143			Diodotus executes Jonathan, who is succeeded as High Priest by his brother Simon Ptolemy VIII marries Cleopatra III?	Numantine War (−133)
142			Simon wins tribute exemption (= independence) for Judaea from Demetrius II (spring) Birth of Ptolemy IX Lathyros?	Censorship of Scipio Aemilianus First stone bridge over the Tiber
142/1			Diodotus murders Antiochus VI, ascends throne as Diodotus Tryphon (−138), fights Demetrius II in Galilee	
141		Mithridates I Arsaces V of Parthia annexes Babylonia	Simon Maccabaeus regains control of Akra in Jerusalem, wins concessions from Demetrius II	

Year				
140	Restoration of Achaean League government	Defeat of Heliocles I by Saca tribes	Birth of Ptolemy X Alexander I? Simon Maccabaeus first Hasmonean priest-king (Sept.) Third Sibylline Oracle produced by Jewish zealots	*Lex Gabinia* prescribes balloting for elections in Rome Death of Spanish rebel Viriathus
140/39			Scipio Aemilianus heads Roman mission to Alexandria	
139		Defeat and capture of Demetrius II by Parthians	Birth of Ptolemy X Alexander?	
138		Death of Attalus II of Pergamon, succeeded by Attalus III	Antiochus Sidetes (2d son of Demetrius I) proclaimed king as Antiochus VII Antiochus VII defeats Diodotus Tryphon, who commits suicide	
138/7	Restoration of Athenian Pythaïs to Delphi from Delos Cleopatra and Dioscurides statues on Delos	Death of Mithridates I Arsaces V of Parthia		
137				*Lex Cassia* introduces ballot in Roman law courts Decius Brutus campaigning in Lusitania
136	Carneades resigns as head of the Academy, succeeded by Crates of Tarsus(?)			
135			Birth of Poseidonius	Outbreak of First Sicilian Slave War (–132) Panaetius teaching in Rome
134	Slave revolts on Delos and in Laurium mines		Seleucid power restored in Judaea by Antiochus VII Sidetes Death of Simon Maccabaeus, succeeded as High Priest by John Hyrcanus	Slave risings in Italy Tiberius Gracchus tribune (10 Dec.) Scipio Aemilianus in Spain
133		Death of Attalus III of Pergamon, who bequeaths his kingdom to Rome		Tiberius Gracchus's land bill passes Gracchus proposes dealing with Attalus's bequest by popular vote Death of Gracchus Fall of Numantia; Scipio pacifies Spain

DATE	GREECE AND THE AEGEAN	ASIA MINOR AND THE EAST	EGYPT, AFRICA, EASTERN MEDITERRANEAN	ROME, ITALY, SICILY, SPAIN
132		Revolt of Aristonicus (Eumenes III?) in Pergamon (–130) Birth of Mithridates VI Eupator of Pontus?	Cleopatra II raises revolt in Alexandria against Ptolemy VIII, who retires to Cyprus	Publius Rupilius puts down Sicilian slave revolt, organizes Sicily (*Lex Rupilia*) Anti-Gracchan court set up in Rome
132/1			Murder of Ptolemy Memphitis	
131		Demetrius II released, returns to Syria	Cleopatra II sole ruler in Alexandria Antiochus VII takes Jerusalem, recovers Babylonia, Media (–130)	*Lex Papiria* extends ballot to legislation
130		Marcus Perperna defeats Aristonicus of Pergamon: end of revolt Temple of Artemis Leukophryene at Magnesia-by-Maeander	Antiochus VII Sidetes embarks on campaign against Parthia (spring) Ptolemy VIII returns to Egypt (Memphis): civil war between him and Cleopatra II Birth of Antiochus of Ascalon?	
129	Death of Carneades: Cleitomachus returns to Academy Panaetius head of the Stoa	Marcus Perperna and Manius Aquillius organize Asia Minor; grant of Phrygia to Mithridates V of Pontus	Demetrius II fails to relieve Cleopatra II in Alexandria Antiochus VII defeated and killed by Phraates II of Parthia	Death of Scipio Aemilianus Senate refuses to confirm grant of Phrygia to Mithridates V of Pontus Aristonicus of Pergamon executed in Rome
128	Cult of Atargatis established on Delos			
127			Ptolemy VIII sets up Alexander Zabinas as Seleucid pretender Cleopatra II flees from Alexandria to Syria	
126			Alexander Zabinas drives Demetrius II out of Antioch Ptolemy VIII reestablished as sole ruler in Alexandria	Rising in Sardinia *Lex Iunia de peregrinis* bans foreigners from Rome Manius Aquillius's triumph (Nov.)
125			Demetrius II captured, put to death in Tyre (or 125) Seleucus V murdered Cleopatra Thea associates her son Antiochus VIII (Grypos) with her in power	Proposal to enfranchise Latins quashed by Senate Revolt and destruction of Fregellae

124	First tribunate of Gaius Gracchus (10 Dec.)	First official reconciliation of Ptolemy VIII with his queens; general amnesty in Egypt Cleopatra Tryphaena marries Antiochus VIII Grypos	Mithridates II of Parthia beats off nomad invasions?	
123	*Lex Sempronia de prouincia Asia* marks first establishment of Asia as a province? Gaius Gracchus reelected tribune for 122	Alexander Zabinas defeated by Antiochus VIII, executed Junonia founded on site of Carthage (*Lex Rubria*)		
122	Conquest of Balearic Islands Opposition by Marcus Livius Drusus; Gaius Gracchus fails to win reelection			
121	Death of Gaius Gracchus; first use of *Senatus Consultum Ultimum* Gracchans executed by Opimius Via Domitia built	Cleopatra Thea forced to commit suicide by Antiochus VIII Grypos		
120	Trial and acquittal of Opimius		Mithridates V of Pontus assassinated; Mithridates VI Eupator co-opted as co-regent by his mother, flees the country	
119	Gaius Marius tribune, legislates against improper pressure on voters Abolition of Gracchan land commission			
118		Second official reconciliation between Prolemy VIII, Cleopatra II, and Cleopatra III; general amnesty reiterated in Egypt Jugurtha joint ruler of Numidia		Death of Polybius?
117		Dynastic struggle between Antiochus VIII Grypos and Antiochus IX Cyzicenus; Antiochus VIII driven out of Antioch Discovery of monsoon route from Egypt to India		

DATE	GREECE AND THE AEGEAN	ASIA MINOR AND THE EAST	EGYPT, AFRICA, EASTERN MEDITERRANEAN	ROME, ITALY, SICILY, SPAIN
116	Revolt against landowners at Dyme in Achaea suppressed by Rome		Senatorial commission sent to Numidia Death of Ptolemy VIII Physcon (26 June) Cleopatra III and Ptolemy IX Lathyros joint rulers Ptolemy X Alexander I governor of Cyprus Ptolemy Apion governor of Cyrene	Birth of Marcus Terentius Varro
115				Marcus Aemilius Scaurus consul
115/4			Ptolemy IX repudiates his wife Cleopatra IV, marries Cleopatra Selene	
114				Gaius Marius serves in Spain
113			Cleopatra IV marries Antiochus IX Cyzicenus	Beginning of southward migration of Cimbri and Teutones
112		Mithridates VI returns to Sinope, executes brother, marries sister, establishes self as sole ruler of Pontus	Antiochus VIII defeats Antiochus IX; Cleopatra Tryphaena has Cleopatra IV killed Rome declares war on Jugurtha after his sack of Cirta	
111			Antiochus IX executes Cleopatra Tryphaena Rome makes provisional deal with Jugurtha	
110	Death of Panaetius? (or 109)	Expansion of Mithridates VI's territories (–107)	Ptolemy X Alexander I recalled to Alexandria, made "king" of Cyprus War renewed against Jugurtha	
109			Quintus Caecilius Metellus campaigns against Jugurtha	Birth of Titus Pomponius Atticus
108			Antiochus VIII Grypos controls most of Syria; Antiochus IX Cyzicenus holds a few coastal cities	

107	Marius (cos. 1) enlists volunteers and *proletarii*	Cleopatra III forces Ptolemy IX Lathyros out of Egypt to Cyprus; Ptolemy X Alexander I returns to Alexandria, assumes crown; Ptolemy IX driven from Cyprus to Syria, reconquers Cyprus		
106	Birth of Cicero and Pompey	Marius in Numidia: surrender of Jugurtha		
105	Two consular armies destroyed by Cimbri and Teutoni at Arausio in Gaul			
104	Outbreak of Second Sicilian Slave War (−100); Armed revolt of Titus Vettius in Campania; Cimbrian threat to northern Italy; Marius (cos. 2) reorganizes Roman army			
103	Marius (cos. 3) trains army in Cisalpine Gaul	Alexander Jannaeus priest-king in Judaea (−76); Cleopatra III evicts Ptolemy X from Alexandria (or 102)	Mithridates VI of Pontus and Nicomedes II of Bithynia partition Paphlagonia, occupy Galatia	
102	Marius (cos. 4) defeats Teutoni at Aquae Sextiae; Death of Lucilius	Antiochus VIII Grypos marries Cleopatra Selene	Rome at war with pirates: Marcus Antonius sent to Cilicia	
101	Marius (cos. 5) and Catulus defeat Cimbri at Vercellae	Ptolemy X returns to Alexandria, murders Cleopatra III, marries Cleopatra Berenice		
100	Marius (cos. 6) restores order in riot-torn Rome by invoking *Senatus Consultum Ultimum*; Manius Aquillius puts down Second Sicilian Slave War; Birth of Julius Caesar; *Lex de piratis*	*Fl.* of Meleager of Gadara	Mithridates VI of Pontus occupies Cappadocia; Reduction of Aï Khanum by Kushana tribes	Slave revolt in Laurium mines (Attica) (−49); Campaigns of Titus Didius in northern Macedonia
99/8			Mithridates VI partitions eastern Anatolia with Nicomedes III of Bithynia	

DATE	GREECE AND THE AEGEAN	ASIA MINOR AND THE EAST	EGYPT, AFRICA, EASTERN MEDITERRANEAN	ROME, ITALY, SICILY, SPAIN
98	Medeius governor of Delos	Marius arrives in Asia Minor from Rome		Revolt in Lusitania (Spain)
97				Sulla praetor (or 93?)
96		Sulla propraetor of Cilicia: commissioned to restore Ariobarzanes to throne of Cappadocia, he forces Mithridates VI to surrender territorial gains (or 92?)	Death of Ptolemy Apion: bequest of Cyrene to Rome (cf. 75) Assassination of Antiochus VIII Grypos Cleopatra Selene marries Antiochus IX Cyzicenus	Birth of Lucretius?
95		Tigranes king of Armenia; Ariobarzanes restored in Cappadocia	Antiochus IX killed by Seleucus VI Cleopatra Selene marries Antiochus X Eusebes Philopator Death of Antiochus XI Demetrius III in Damascus, Philip I in Antioch	Quintus Mucius Scaevola consul *Lex Licinia Mucia* expels *socii* from Rome
94		Quintus Mucius Scaevola and Publius Rutilius Rufus in Asia Minor Death of Nicomedes III of Bithynia Nicomedes IV expelled from Bithynia by Mithridates VI		
93		Tigranes marries daughter of Mithridates VI, drives Ariobarzanes out of Cappadocia	Civil war in Judaea	
92		Sulla restores Ariobarzanes and Nicomedes IV		Condemnation of Rutilius Rufus on extortion charge Censors suppress Latin *rhetores*
91	Oligarchic authoritarian government under Medeius tightens hold in Athens (−89/8)			Tribunate of Marcus Livius Drusus; failure of his reform schemes, followed by his murder Outbreak of Social War Massacre of Romans at Asculum
90	Poseidonius of Apamea lectures in Rhodes?		Cleopatra Selene bears Antiochus X a son, Antiochus XIII Asiaticus	Roman setbacks in Social War All non-revolting communities are offered citizenship (*Lex Iulia*)

89	Victories of Sulla in Social War Pasiteles (sculptor, writer on art) comes to Rome		Manius Aquillius supports Nicomedes IV of Bithynia against Mithridates VI Mithridates VI goes to war with Rome (winter) Antiochus X killed fighting Parthians (ca. 90/88)	
88	Sulla's march on Rome; escape of Marius Defeat of last resisters (Samnites) in Social War	Philip I fighting Demetrius III	Mithridates VI orders general massacre of Romans and Italians in Asia (80,000 killed) Demetrius III of Syria exiled to Parthia	Athens, under restored democracy, joins Mithridates against Rome Mithridates' troops capture Ptolemy IX's two illegitimate sons on Cos Mithridates' unsuccessful siege of Rhodes
87	Cinna (*cos.* −84) and Marius in command in Rome; massacre of pro-Sullans Birth of Catullus	Ptolemy X Alexander I expelled from Alexandria (spring) Ptolemy IX Lathyros recovers throne; Cleopatra Berenice returns from exile as joint ruler after Ptolemy X's death in naval battle off Cyprus Revolt of the Thebaid (−86)		Sulla lands in Greece, blockades Athens and Piraeus
86	Death of Marius (Jan.) Birth of Sallust	Antiochus XII in Damascus	Flaccus and Fimbria sent to Asia Minor	Athens and Piraeus fall to Sulla (March); Piraeus burned Sulla wins battles of Chaeronea and Orchomenos against Mithridates' general Archelaus
85			Mithridates VI makes treaty of Dardanus (Troad) with Sulla (Aug.), cedes all conquered territory Nicomedes IV and Ariobarzanes restored to their thrones	Athens stripped of all political privileges
84	Cinna murdered by mutineers New citizens allotted to all 35 tribes	Antiochus XII dies on expedition against Nabataean Arabs		Athens resumes control of Delos Sulla visits Athens and Delos
83	Sulla lands in Italy, gains Pompey's support, wins battle of Colline Gate		Murena begins second campaign against Mithridates VI Mithridates expels all Roman garrisons from Cappadocia Tigranes of Armenia accepts offer of Seleucid throne	Sulla removes library from Athens containing works of Aristotle and Theophrastus

DATE	ROME, ITALY, SICILY, SPAIN	EGYPT, AFRICA, EASTERN MEDITERRANEAN	ASIA MINOR AND THE EAST	GREECE AND THE AEGEAN
82	Civil war in Italy won by Sulla; Pompey crushes anti-Sullans in Sicily; Sertorius leaves Italy, establishes independent base in Spain; The Sullan proscriptions		Murena driven out of Cappadocia; Sulla orders termination of hostilities	
81	Sulla dictator: his constitutional settlement; Sertorius driven out of Spain	Death of Ptolemy IX Lathyros (or 80); Cleopatra Berenice sole ruler in Alexandria; Pompey campaigns in Africa		
80	Sertorius back in Spain, leads revolt of Lusitani, organizes army	Ptolemy XI Alexander II proclaimed king of Egypt on Sulla's nomination: he marries Cleopatra Berenice, kills her, is lynched by Alexandrian mob; Ptolemy IX's illegitimate son seizes throne as Ptolemy XII, known as Auletes; Ptolemy XII marries his sister Cleopatra V Tryphaena		Antikythera astrolabe lost in wreck off southern coast of Greece?
79	Sulla relinquishes his dictatorship; Sertorius defeats Metellus Pius			Cicero in Athens and Rhodes; Antiochus of Ascalon scholarch of the Academy
78	Death of Sulla in Campania; Marcus Aemilius Lepidus attempts to overthrow Sullan constitution	Publius Servilius Vatia campaigns against pirates in eastern Mediterranean (−75)		
77	Defeat and death of Marcus Aemilius Lepidus; Marcus Perperna joins Sertorius in Spain; Pompey assigned command in Spain			
76	Sertorius wins successes against Metellus and Pompey, makes treaty with Mithridates VI	Death of Alexander Jannaeus in Judaea	Mithridates VI's treaty with Sertorius	

75	Cicero visits ruins of Corinth	Mithridates VI declares war on Rome (Third Mithridatic War, –67) Death of Nicomedes IV of Bithynia; his kingdom bequeathed to Rome	Sons of Antiochus X and Cleopatra Selene (including Antiochus XIII Asiaticus) seek refuge in Rome Cyrene made a Roman province (or 74?)	Both consuls ordered to defend the East Reinforcements sent to Spain *Imperium infinitum* set up to deal with Mediterranean piracy
74		Lucius Lucullus gets command against Mithridates VI Expedition of Marcus Antonius (with *imperium infinitum*) against Cilician pirates (–71) Mithridates invades Bithynia, defeats Murena		
73		Lucius Lucullus relieves Cyzicus, defeats Mithridates VI		Slave revolt of Spartacus begins at Capua (–71) *Lex Terentia Cassia* on grain supply
72	Marcus Antonius defeated by pirates off Crete	Lucius Lucullus scores victories over Mithridates VI in Pontus Marcus Lucullus, governor of Macedonia, pushes eastward to the Black Sea		Perperna murders Sertorius in Spain, is defeated by Pompey: settlement of revolt Successful campaign by Spartacus
71		Mithridates VI defeated by Lucius Lucullus, takes refuge with Tigranes in Armenia Lucullus reduces last Pontic strongholds, winters in Asia, checks extortion Marcus Antonius forced to make peace with pirates	Return of Antiochus XIII Asiaticus (recognized by Rome)	Crassus defeats Spartacus, crucifies 20,000 slaves along Via Appia from Capua to Rome
70	Quintus Caecilius Metellus ravages Crete, pirate bases	Tigranes refuses to extradite Mithridates VI to Rome		First consulship of Pompey and Crassus Restoration of full tribunician powers Cicero prosecutes Gaius Verres, governor of Sicily *Lex Aurelia* reconstitutes *iudicia publica* Birth of Virgil

Year				
62	Defeat and death of Catiline at Pistoia (Jan.) Clodius profanes Bona Dea festival Concordia Ordinum Pompey returns to Italy, disbands his army (Dec.)	Syria organized as Roman province John Hyrcanus High Priest in Jerusalem	Bithynia and Cilicia organized as Roman provinces Pompey sets up client-kings (e.g., in Commagene)	Pompey visits Poseidonius on Rhodes First datable Greek horoscope Rome annexes Crete
61	Caesar governor of a Farther Spain Clodius tried, acquitted Pompey's settlement opposed in Senate; his triumph (28 Sept.) Unrest in Gaul			
60	Caesar returns from Spain: formation of the First Triumvirate (Caesar, Pompey, Crassus)	Diodorus Siculus sees Roman lynched in Egypt for killing a cat		
59	Caesar consul, persuades Senate to recognize Ptolemy XII Auletes Pompey marries Julia daughter of Caesar *Lex Vatinia* gives Caesar Gallic command	Ptolemy XII Auletes driven out of Alexandria		
59/8			Ptolemy XII Auletes visits Cato on Rhodes *en route* for Rome	
58	Ptolemy XII Auletes seeks refuge in Rome Cicero exiled Clodius tribune, backs First Triumvirate Caesar campaigns in Gaul (–51)	Annexation of Cyprus to province of Cilicia by Cato (*Lex Clodia*) Berenice IV ascends throne, marries (i) Seleucus Kybiosaktes, whom she murders, (ii) Archelaus		
57	Ptolemy XII Auletes in Rome: problem of Egypt once more under discussion Street fighting between gangs of Clodius and Milo Return of Cicero (Sept.) Pompey secures Rome's grain supply Caesar defeats Nervii in Gaul	Death of Cleopatra V Tryphaena	Civil war in Parthia: Mithridates III vs. Orodes II Catullus on Memmius's staff in Bithynia	Lucius Calpurnius Piso (governor) plunders Macedonia

DATE	GREECE AND THE AEGEAN	ASIA MINOR AND THE EAST	EGYPT, AFRICA, EASTERN MEDITERRANEAN	ROME, ITALY, SICILY, SPAIN
56			Cato leaves Cyprus for Rome	First Triumvirate under strain: conference of Luca (April)
55		Defeat of last Indo-Greek king, Hermaeus	Aulus Gabinius governor of Syria, restores Ptolemy XII Auletes to throne in Alexandria	Crassus and Pompey (*coss.* 2) carry out reforms Pompey dedicates first stone theater in Rome Caesar bridges Rhine, invades Britain
54		Mithridates III executed by Orodes II (winter)	Crassus in Syria mounting Parthian campaign Gaius Rabirius Postumus in Alexandria as Ptolemy's finance minister (*dioikētēs*) Aulus Gabinius recalled to Rome	Pompey governs Spain from Rome through *legati* Consular elections prevented by rioting Death of Pompey's wife Julia (Sept.) Revolt in Gaul; Caesar's second invasion of Britain Death of Catullus? Aulus Gabinius prosecuted for taking bribes from Ptolemy XII Auletes, is fined 10,000 talents
53		Crassus defeated and killed by Parthians at Carrhae (May)	Gaius Rabirius Postumus forced to leave Egypt because of extortionate practices	Consular elections postponed till July by continued rioting Caesar puts down Gallic revolt; second bridging of Rhine Gaius Rabirius Postumus prosecuted: case dropped
52				Murder of Clodius (Jan.) Pompey sole consul till August Revolt of Vercingetorix in central Gaul Death of Lucretius?
51		Cicero governor of Cilicia	Death of Ptolemy XII Auletes: Ptolemy XIII marries his sister Cleopatra VII; they become joint rulers Drought in Egypt (–49) Parthian invasion of Syria	Optimate attacks on Caesar Gallic rebellion continues
50			Cleopatra VII at war with Ptolemy XIII	Caesar comes down from Gaul to northern Italy

Year				
49	Pompey arrives in Greece (Feb.)	Curio defeated and killed in North Africa	Ban on shipping of grain in Egypt except to Alexandria (27 Oct.) Cleopatra VII and Arsinoë leave Alexandria for Thebaid and Syria	Pompey ill (summer) / Curio's proposal for both Caesar and Pompey to lay down arms passes, but is vetoed by Marcellus (*cos.*) / Marcellus calls on Pompey to "save the state" (Nov.): tribunes leave Rome / Caesar crosses Rubicon / Civil war: Caesar dictator (1), passes emergency legislation / Caesar defeats Pompeian forces in Spain; surrender of Massilia
48	Campaign of Dyrrhachium in western Greece / Caesar defeats Pompey at Pharsalus (6 June) / Pompey flees to Lesbos, then to Egypt	Pharnaces of Bosporus (son of Mithridates VI) defeats Domitius Calvinus in Pontus	Pompey reaches Alexandria: Ptolemy XIII's ministers have him assassinated (28 Sept.) / Arrival in Egypt of Caesar (2 Oct.): the Alexandrian War	Caesar consul (2) / Disturbances in Italy: death of Milo
47	Caesar defeats Pharnaces at Zela (spring; occasion of *Veni, vidi, vici*) / Caesar settles affairs in Asia Minor		Caesar rescued by Mithridates of Pergamon (March) / Death of Ptolemy XIII: Cleopatra VII and Ptolemy XIV set up by Caesar as joint rulers (March) / Caesar settles affairs in Syria (early summer) / Birth of Caesarion (Ptolemy Caesar) to Cleopatra (June)	Caesar appointed dictator (2) *in absentia*, with Marcus Antonius (Mark Antony) as his Master of Horse / Antony tries to maintain order in Italy / Caesar returns to Italy (July), puts down mutiny in Campania / Caesar arrives in Rome (Oct.) / Caesar resigns dictatorship, leaves for North Africa (Dec.) / Birth of Propertius
46		Caesar campaigns in Africa / Victory of Thapsus (April); Cato's suicide / Roman province of Africa Nova ("New Africa") established		Caesar returns to Rome (25 July): consul (3), dictator (3), ten-year dictatorship, extraordinary honors including four triumphs (Sept.–Oct.) / Cleopatra and entourage arrive in Rome (–44) / Caesar leaves for Spain (Nov.) after instigating reform of calendar

DATE	GREECE AND THE AEGEAN	ASIA MINOR AND THE EAST	EGYPT, AFRICA, EASTERN MEDITERRANEAN	ROME, ITALY, SICILY, SPAIN
45	Death of Poseidonius?			Caesar dictator (4), consul (4): wins victory over Pompeians at Munda (17 March), returns to Rome (Oct.), celebrates triumph
44	Corinth rebuilt at Caesar's orders		Arsinoë appointed ruler of Cyprus by Antony Cleopatra returns to Alexandria from Rome after Caesar's death Cleopatra has Ptolemy XIV assassinated, makes Caesarion her consort	Caesar dictator for life, consul (5), is offered divine honors; refuses crown at Lupercalia (15 Feb.) Assassination of Caesar on Ides of March Return of Octavian to Rome Antony obtains five-year command in Gaul Cicero's *Philippics* 1–3 (Sept.–Dec.)
43			Cleopatra sends Dolabella four legions from Egypt: these are captured by Cassius Dolabella commits suicide at Laodicea (summer) Cleopatra recovers Cyprus: Arsinoë flees to Ephesus Famine and plague in Egypt	Hirtius and Pansa (*coss.*) killed at Mutina Octavian's first consulship (Aug.) Birth of Ovid (Mar.) Second Triumvirate (Antony, Octavian, Lepidus) formed (Nov.) Proscriptions: execution of Cicero
42	Battles of Philippi (Oct.): suicides of Brutus and Cassius	Accession of Ariarathes X in Cappadocia Antony rules eastern Roman provinces		Deification of Caesar (1 Jan.) Sextus Pompeius holds Sicily Birth of Tiberius
41	Nicias, with Antony's support, becomes tyrant of Cos (–33)	Parthians raid Asia Minor (–38)	Antony meets Cleopatra at Tarsus, has Arsinoë executed, removes Cyprus from Cleopatra's control Antony winters in Alexandria with Cleopatra (–40)	Perusine War in Italy
40	Antony in Greece Invading Illyrian tribesmen driven back from Macedonia	Death of Deiotarus, king of Galatia	Parthian invasion of Syria Herod nominated as king of Judaea by Roman Senate Cleopatra bears Antony twins	Perusia surrenders to Octavian Treaty of Brundisium (Oct.) divides up Roman world Death of Fulvia; Antony marries Octavia Virgil's *Eclogue* 4
39			Ventidius defeats the Parthians	Concordat of Misenum between Antony, Octavian, Sextus Pompeius (spring) Agrippa campaigns in Gaul

Year				
38	Octavian marries Livia (Jan.) Sextus Pompeius wins successes against Octavian in Straits of Messina Octavia bears Antony a daughter	Second victory of Ventidius over the Parthians: death of Parthian Pacorus Antony captures Samosata		Antony and Octavia winter in Athens (−37)
37	Pact of Tarentum (spring): renewal of Second Triumvirate(?) Varro's *De Re Rustica*	Antony marries Cleopatra in Antioch: bestows Cyprus and Cilicia on her, acknowledges children: the "New Era" Herod and Sosius capture Jerusalem (July)	Ariarathes executed, replaced by Archelaus in Cappadocia Amyntas king of Galatia Polemo king of Pontus	
36	Lepidus dropped from Second Triumvirate Octavian takes over Sicily from Lepidus, suffers defeat (Aug.) Sextus Pompeius defeated off Naulochus in northern Sicily (Sept.) Octavian receives tribunician sacrosanctity	Cleopatra bears Antony their third child, meets and subsidizes his army	Antony suffers setback at Phraspa in Parthia, retreats through Armenia	
35	Death of Sallust	Antony and Cleopatra in Egypt	Sextus Pompeius executed in Asia by Marcus Titius	Octavia in Athens
34		Antony's "triumph" in Egypt: the Donations of Alexandria	Antony reinvades Armenia, captures Artasvasdes	Octavian in Dalmatia
33	Octavian consul (2)	Death of King Bocchus II: Mauretania ceded to Rome Antony and Cleopatra winter in Ephesus (−32)	Antony in Armenia (spring), leaves legions there till fall	
32	Octavian's defense before the Senate Octavia divorced by Antony Octavian publishes Antony's will in Rome Restoration of Pompey's theater			Antony and Cleopatra winter in Greece (−31)
31	Octavian consul (3, and thenceforward annually till 23 B.C.)	Antony and Cleopatra retreat to Alexandria	Octavian in Asia Minor (−30)	Agrippa takes Methone in the Peloponnese Octavian lands in Epirus Battle of Actium (Sept.); defeat of Antony and Cleopatra
30	Tribunician power conferred on Octavian for life	Suicide of Antony in Alexandria Octavian enters Alexandria: suicide of Cleopatra Ptolemaic empire declared at an end (29 Aug.)	Phraates captures Media, restores Artaxes to throne of Armenia	Crassus campaigns in Balkans (−28)

GENEALOGICAL TABLES

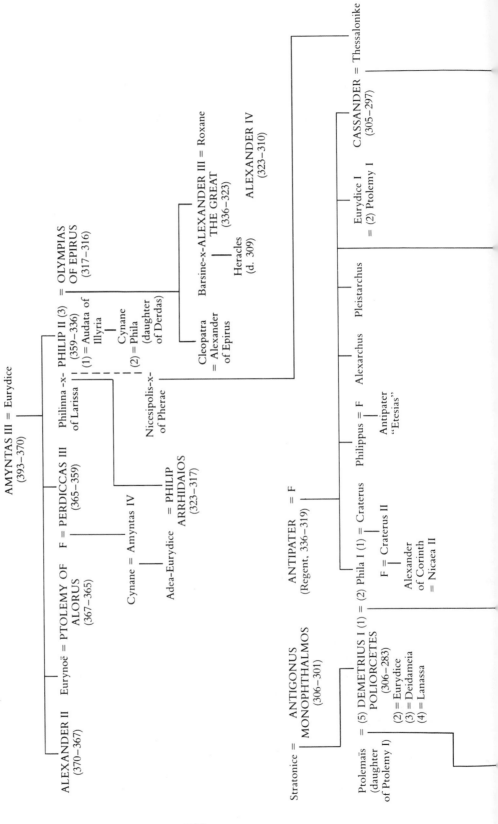

Genealogy 1.

THE MACEDONIAN AND THRACIAN DYNASTIES

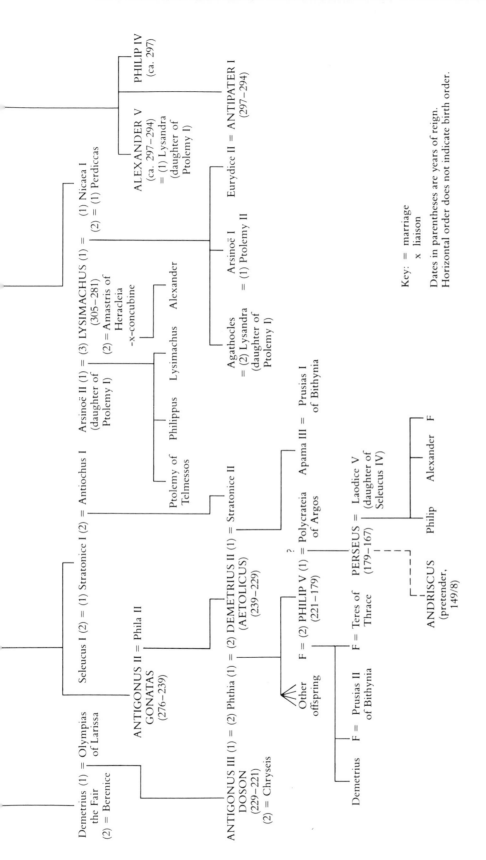

Demetrius (1) = Olympias
the Fair   of Larissa
(2) = Berenice

Seleucus I (2) = (1) Stratonice I (2) = Antiochus I

ANTIGONUS II = Phila II
GONATAS
(276–239)

Arsinoë II (1) = (3) LYSIMACHUS (1) = (1) Nicaea I
(daughter of   (305–281)   (2) = (1) Perdiccas
Ptolemy I)
                   (2) = Amastris of
                         Heraclea
                       -x-concubine

PHILIP IV
(ca. 297)

ALEXANDER V
(ca. 297–294)
= (1) Lysandra
(daughter of
Ptolemy I)

Eurydice II = ANTIPATER I
(297–294)

Ptolemy of   Philippus   Lysimachus   Alexander
Telmessos

Arsinoë I
= (1) Ptolemy II

Agathocles
= (2) Lysandra
(daughter of
Ptolemy I)

ANTIGONUS III (1) = (2) Phthia (1) = (2) DEMETRIUS II = Stratonice II
DOSON   (AETOLICUS)
(229–221)   (239–229)
(2) = Chryseis

Apama III = Prusias I
of Bithynia

F = (2) PHILIP V (1) = Polycrateia
(221–179)   of Argos

?

PERSEUS = Laodice V
(179–167)   (daughter of
            Seleucus IV)

Philip   Alexander   F

F = Teres of
Thrace

ANDRISCUS
(pretender,
149/8)

Other
offspring

F = Prusias II
of Bithynia

Demetrius

Key: = marriage
      x liaison

Dates in parentheses are years of reign.
Horizontal order does not indicate birth order.

733

Genealogy 2.
THE SELEUCIDS

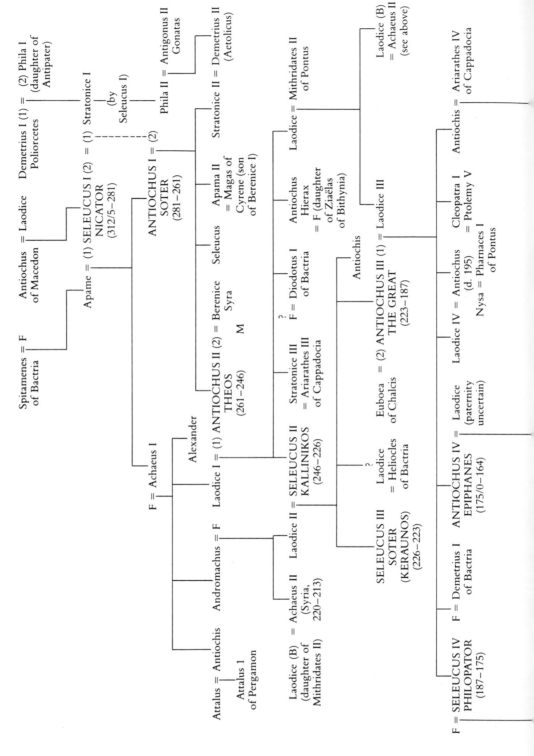

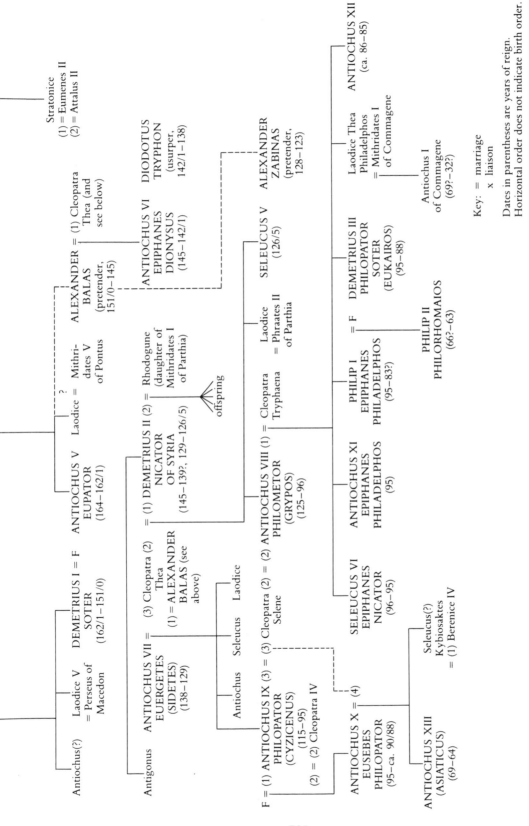

Genealogy 3.
THE PTOLEMIES

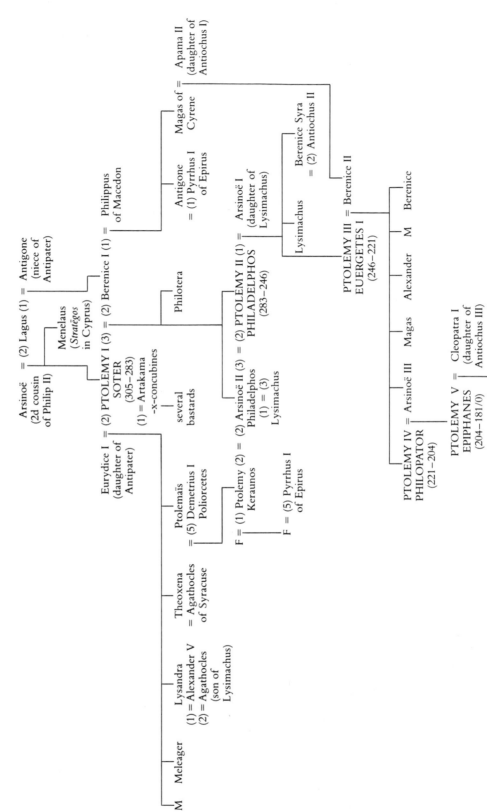

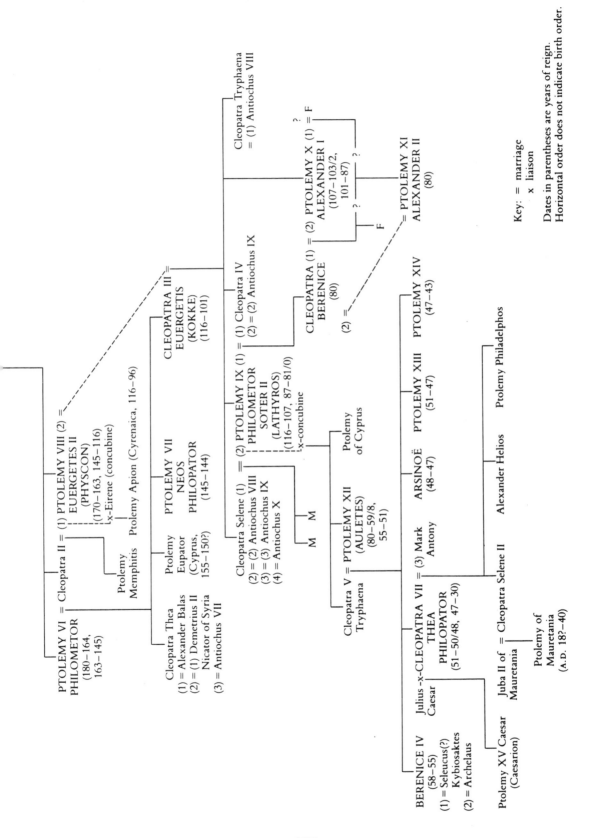

Genealogy 4.
THE ATTALIDS

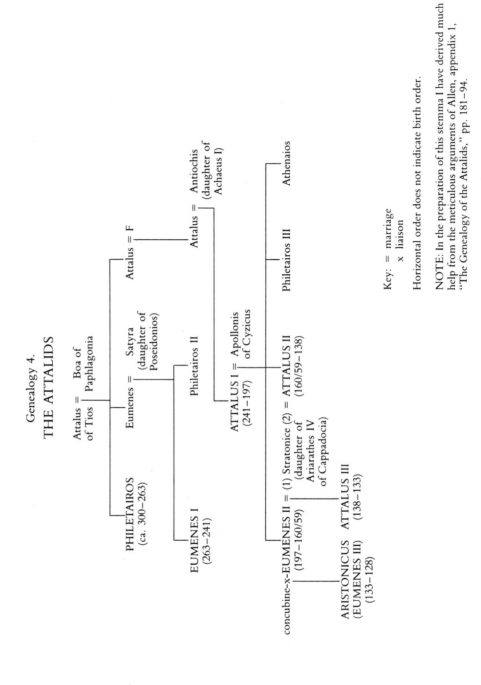

Key: = marriage
x liaison

Horizontal order does not indicate birth order.

NOTE: In the preparation of this stemma I have derived much help from the meticulous arguments of Allen, appendix 1, "The Genealogy of the Attalids," pp. 181–94.

Genealogy 5.
THE GREEK INDO-BACTRIAN KINGS

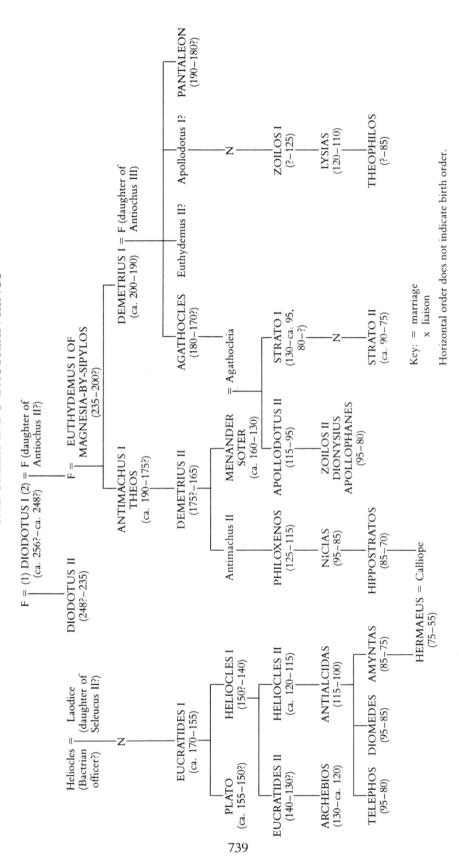

Key: = marriage
x liaison

Horizontal order does not indicate birth order.

NOTE: Though I have, I hope, taken all relevant recent scholarship into account when compiling this stemma, readers should be warned that the evidence is highly debatable, and much of the reconstruction is hypothetical.

NOTES

For full information on authors and titles cited in short forms in these notes, see the Select Bibliography, pp. 909–28. Abbreviated names and titles of ancient authors, standard modern works of reference, and scholarly journals are given in general in the forms listed in the front matter of H. G. Liddell and R. Scott, eds., *A Greek–English Lexicon*, 9th ed., rev. H. Stuart Jones (Oxford, 1968; abbreviated herein as LSJ); of N. G. L. Hammond and H. H. Scullard, eds., *The Oxford Classical Dictionary*, 2d ed. (Oxford, 1970; abbreviated as *OCD*²); of P. G. W. Glare et al., eds., *The Oxford Latin Dictionary* (Oxford, 1982); and of the annual issues of *L'Année Philologique*. Other abbreviations used in this volume are as follows:

Bouché-Leclercq, *HL*	A. Bouché-Leclercq, *Histoire des Lagides*
Bouché-Leclercq, *HS*	A. Bouché-Leclercq, *Histoire des Séleucides*
Ferguson, *HA*	W. S. Ferguson, *Hellenistic Athens*
Gruen, *HW*	E. S. Gruen, *The Hellenistic World and the Coming of Rome*
Pollitt, *AHA*	J. J. Pollitt, *Art in the Hellenistic Age*
Rostovtzeff, *SEH*	M. Rostovtzeff, *The Social and Economic History of the Hellenistic World*
Walbank, *HC*	F. W. Walbank, *A Historical Commentary on Polybius*
Will, *HP*²	E. Will, *Histoire politique du monde hellénistique*, 2d ed.

PART ONE. ALEXANDER'S FUNERAL GAMES, 323–276 B.C.

Chapter 1. Perdiccas, Eumenes, Cassander, 323–316

1. Perdiccas's rank while Alexander still lived was that of chiliarch, literally "commander of a thousand," and thus the rough equivalent of colonel or brigadier, in either the cavalry or the infantry: in Perdiccas's case, commander of the Royal Bodyguard, a Persian-derived and highly honorific post (Arr. *Succ.* 1.3A, Dexippus *FGrH* 100 F 8.4), to which Alexander had appointed him when it fell vacant on the death of the king's favorite, Hephaestion. He "thus controlled the apparatus of empire": Badian, "Treaty" 381.

2. DS 18.2.4, cf. Just. 13.4.5.

3. The question whether Perdiccas or Craterus was made regent at Babylon I, like Badian, *Gnomon* 34 (1962) 383, am tempted to regard as an unproblem created by Beloch's perverse ingenuity; however, for a judicious discussion of what Badian terms "one of the most vexed questions of Hellenistic scholarship," see Bosworth, esp. 129–34, who comes down, decisively and irrefutably, in favor of Perdiccas.

4. Arr. *Anab.* 7.26.3; DS 17.117.4, cf. 18.1.4; QC 10.5.5; Just. 12.15.8.

5. DS 17.117.4. If Alexander in fact died without naming a successor, as is often held—

see, e.g., Hammond and Walbank 100—then the likelihood of Perdiccas's having manufactured both these famous apothegms becomes a near-certainty.

6. Arr. *Anab.* 7.4.4–8; DS 17.107.6; Plut. *Alex.* 70, *Mor.* 329D–E; Just. 12.10.9–10; Chares of Mytilene *ap.* Athen. 12.538b–539a; cf. Green, *Alexander* 447–48.

7. QC 10.6.13. The same objection applied to Heracles, Alexander's bastard by Memnon's widow, Barsine: cf. p. 28.

8. Satyrus *ap.* Athen. 13.557d, Plut. *Alex.* 77, DS 18.2.2. A useful survey of what is known or can reasonably be deduced about Arrhidaios's general background and mental condition is provided by W. Greenwalt, "The Search for Arrhidaeus," *AncW* 10 (1984) 69–77.

9. Badian, "Treaty" 382, sums up the case against Arrhidaios well: "Not only was A. the only male Argead left alive by Alexander (which is strong evidence), but we always find him, in his brief reign, in someone else's power. He never acts independently of a noble or of his own ambitious wife; in fact, someone is always in charge of him."

10. Will, *HP*[2] 1.27–28, repeated in *CAH* VII[2].1 29.

11. Hornblower 158. For the age and status of these veterans, see DS 19.28.1, 30.5–6, 41.2; Plut. *Eum.* 16; cf. Hammond, "Alexander's Veterans," 51 ff.

12. Plut. *Eum.* 18.

13. QC 10.6.9, 16–18, 21 ff.

14. QC 10.6.10–12.

15. The proverbial saying "All Cretans are liars" was attributed to Epimenides, and cited by Callimachus, *Hymn* 1.7–8, and St. Paul, Titus 1.12. A somewhat fanciful explanation of the proverb by Athenodorus of Eretria (preserved by Photius, p. 150 Bekker) is that Idomeneus of Crete, called upon to adjudicate between Thetis and Medea in the matter of beauty, favored Thetis—whereupon Medea, the enchantress, laid a curse on all Cretans, so that they could never tell the truth.

16. QC 10.6.16–18, Just. 13.2.13. On the essential distinction between the old Macedonian concept of monarchy and the new Hellenistic absolutism, see Leon Mooren, "The Nature of the Hellenistic Monarchy," in Van't Dack et al. 205 ff., esp. 231–32.

17. QC 10.7.2 ff.; Arr. *Succ.* 1.1A, B; Just. 13.3.1–2; DS 18.2.2. I am suspicious of analogies alleged by some modern scholars in Curtius from early Roman imperial history, and supposedly designed to minimize such competence as Arrhidaios is here credited with: see Bosworth 128 and other reff. there cited. Curtius, here and later (10.8.2, 6, 8, 15–22), represents Arrhidaios as both moderate and decisive, Meleager as the infantry's spokesman *ab initio*, in contrast to both Diodorus and Justin.

18. QC 10.7.4–10; Just. 13.2.8, 3.1; Arr. *Succ.* 1.1; cf. DS 18.2.4.

19. QC 10.7.16–21, 8.1–23; Just. 13.3.5–7, 4.1–3; Arr. *Succ.* 1.1.

20. Arr. *Succ.* 1.4A, Just. 13.4.7–8, QC 10.6–10 *passim* (elephants, 10.9.11–19); cf. DS 18.4.7.

21. QC 10.9.19–21.

22. Not surprisingly, our sources tend to equivocate over the precise nature of Perdiccas's office: QC 10.10.1, 4 leaves it open, as does Just. 13.4.5; Arrian and Dexippus (above, n. 1) claim that he was still chiliarch; only DS 18.2.4, probably based on Hieronymus of Cardia, identifies his title as ἐπιμελητὴς τῆς βασιλείας. That this is correct we can at once deduce from DS 18.48.4–5, where the relative status of the two offices is made all too clear. Antipater, on his deathbed, appointed his son Cassander chiliarch, but Polyperchon ἐπιμελητής, which Cassander found so great an insult (DS 18.49 *passim*) that he at once raised a revolt (see pp. 8 ff., 70).

23. DS 18.3 *passim*, Arr. *Succ.* 1.5–8, QC 10.10.1–6. Just. 13.4.9–25 is so garbled as to be virtually useless here.

24. Cf. Green, *Alexander* 459 ff.

25. Arr. *Anab.* 7.12.3–4, DS 18.4.1.

26. Arr. *Anab.* 1.29.1–4, QC 3.1.1–13.

27. Plut. *Demetr.* 2, 3, 18, 19; *Eum.* 10, 15.

28. Arr. *Succ.* 1.3A, B; cf. 1.7–8A (where the office is to be shared with Craterus; see n. 31 below), and DS 18.3.2, 4.1 ff.

29. Arr. *Succ.* 1.3–4B, Dexippus *FGrH* 100 F 8.8.

30. Bosworth, 133, doubts this appointment, but it could well have been made, for its propaganda effect and to play for time, while Craterus was still in Cilicia.

31. Badian, "Treaty" 384, cites with approval Schwahn's theory that Perdiccas may well have let Alexander's appointment of Craterus stand (cf. Arr. *Succ.* 1.7–8A), leaving him and Antipater to argue things out in far-off Macedonia. But not even Perdiccas, though he lacked finesse as a conspirator, would have failed to appreciate the obvious danger inherent in such a move, i.e., that Antipater and Craterus might well form common cause against *him*—as indeed happened all too soon (see p. 13).

32. DS 18.3.1, Arr. *Succ.* 1.6, QC 10.10.2, App. *Syr.* 53.1–2. Paus. 1.6.2 attributes the main initiative in this division of the satrapies to Ptolemy; but though he may well have pressed his own claims to Egypt, it seems clear that the prime mover throughout was Perdiccas.

33. Walbank, *CR* 26 (1976) 93; cf. Engel 5 ff.

34. DS 18.4.1–6 *passim*.

35. Arr. *Succ.* 1.5A.

36. DS 18.7 *passim*.

37. DS 18.8.1; cf. Berthold, *Rhodes* 36–37 with n. 58.

38. DS 17.111.1–3, 18.8.6–7, 9.1; Hypereid. *Epitaph.* 10–23; Arr. *Succ.* 1.9, 12–15, 17, 22–23; Plut. *Phoc.* 23 ff. Spartan neutrality: DS 18.11.2, Paus. 1.25.4. Will, *CAH* VII².1 30, argues inconsistency in Diodorus's explanations of the Lamian War; but the availability of mercenaries and the fury generated by the Exiles Decree are not mutually exclusive. Rather they form complementary elements in a general impulse to rebellion stimulated by Alexander's death. The impulse had in fact been there for some time, arguably since before the arrival of Harpalus in 324: see N. G. Ashton, "The Lamian War: A False Start?" *Antichthon* 17 (1983) 47–63.

39. Lepore, 161 ff., sees two distinct sources, and two motives for war, in DS 17.111.1–4 and 18.8–9, one a nationalist war of liberation, the other a mere venture by freebooters. That nationalism played a powerful role should be clear from the alternative title, the "Hellenic War," as it was officially known in Athens: see N. G. Ashton, "The Lamian War—*stat magni nominis umbra*," *JHS* 104 (1984) 152–57. But what, surely, we have here is rather a case of historical serendipity: an ill-prepared but financially secure Athens was eager to strike a blow for freedom, and could pay others to fight for her, while at the same time large numbers of professional mercenaries were easily available, and, because of Alexander's death, out of a job. For a well-documented narrative of the war see Hammond and Walbank 107–17.

40. DS 17.111, 18.9–17 *passim*; Plut. *Phoc.* 23 ff.; Paus. 1.25.4–5; cf. Ferguson, *HA* 14 ff., with further testimonia, and, on Leosthenes, Lepore 178 ff. For his death, see *Suda* s.v. Λε- ωσθένης, and Just. 13.5.12.

41. Plut. *Eum.* 3.

42. DS 18.15.1–4, Just. 13.5.14, Plut. *Phoc.* 25.

43. Ashton 1–11. Will, *CAH* VII².1 32, writes: "Salamis had laid the foundation of Athenian naval power, which now sank for ever in the waters of Amorgos."

44. DS 18.16.4–17.5, Plut. *Phoc.* 26. Will, *CAH* VII².1 32, correctly emphasizes the policy (borrowed from Philip II) by which Antipater and Craterus refused to deal with their enemies *en bloc*, thus provoking further defections.

45. *SIG*³ 317, esp. 15–23.

46. Ste Croix 301, 609–10; cf. *SIG*³ 317.10.

47. DS 18.48.2; cf. Errington, "From Babylon" 62.

48. DS 18.18.1–6.

49. Lepore 183–84, with testimonia there cited.

50. For the campaign, see DS 18.24–25 *passim.*

51. Plut. *Eum.* 3.

52. DS 20.37.3–6.

53. DS 18.16.1–3, 23.1–3. Just. 13.6.4–7 suggests that Perdiccas kept both women in play and finally married neither of them. Arr. *Succ.* fr. 25 Roos §§8–12, 16–18, is too fragmentary to be of real help. Cf. Plut. *Eum.* 3–4, App. *Mithr.* 8.

54. DS 18.8.7, Paus. 1.6.8, App. *Syr.* 62; cf. Seibert, *Historische Beiträge* 12–13, 16.

55. DS 18.23.3.

56. Arr. *Succ.* 1.22, 23 Roos; DS 19.52.5; Polyaen. 8.60.

57. DS 18.16.1–3; Plut. *Eum.* 3, 6; Just. 13.6.1–3.

58. DS 18.23.3–4, 25.3–4.

59. Arr. *Succ.* fr. 25 Roos §§2–8; cf. Hauben, "First War" 91–93.

60. DS 18.25.6, 29.1–3; Arr. *Succ.* 1.26, cf. fr. 25 Roos §§10–18.

61. Arr. *Succ.* fr. 26 Roos; cf. Hauben, "First War" 107–8. Hornblower 161–62 toys with the idea that Eumenes may have been involved with Cleopatra himself, and "played Tristan to Perdiccas' King Mark."

62. DS 18.29.1, 33.1.

63. Arr. *Succ.* frr. 17, 18 Roos; DS 18.19–21 *passim;* cf. Seibert, *Untersuchungen* 91–95. For Ptolemy's constitution for Cyrene (of uncertain date), see *SEG* 9 (1944) 1.1–46, pp. 1–3; corr. ibid. 18 (1962) 726, pp. 228–29 = Harding 126, pp. 159–61.

64. QC 10.5.4.

65. DS 18.26.3, 28.2–4, Paus. 1.6.3, Strabo 17.1.8 (C.794); Ael. *VH* 12.64, cf. Fraser 1.15–16 and n. 79 (2.31–32); Hammond and Walbank 120. The coffin was probably the same anthropoid Egyptian-style gold shell described by Diodorus. For the Orientalization of Greek art in Alexander's funeral cortege, see Pollitt, *AHA* 19.

66. Arr. *Succ.* 1.28.

67. On Cleomenes, see Seibert, *Untersuchungen* 39–51, who, however, whitewashes him beyond what either our sources or human probability allow; for a less favorable estimate, see Green, *Alexander* 278–79, 440, 466.

68. Ps.-Arist. *Oecon.* 1352^a–53^b.

69. Plut. *Eum.* 5, DS 18.29.2–4.

70. Errington, "From Babylon" 65, citing DS 18.33.2 f. and Arr. *Succ.* fr. 28 Roos.

71. DS 18.33.5–36.5; Arr. *Succ.* 1.29; Just. 13.6.18–19, 8.1–2, 10; Plut. *Eum.* 5–7. For a close analysis of this episode, see Seibert, *Untersuchungen* 122–26.

72. Hauben, "First War" 86–87.

73. DS 18.36.6, Arr. *Succ.* fr. 29 Roos; cf. Just. 13.6.20; Seibert, *Untersuchungen* 126–28.

74. DS 18.36.6–7, Arr. *Succ.* 1.28–30.

75. Plut. *Eum.* 5–7 *passim,* DS 18.29–32 *passim,* Nep. *Eum.* 4.

76. DS 18.37.1; cf. Plut. *Eum.* 8.

77. Plut. *Eum.* 8, DS 18.37.2; cf. Errington, "From Babylon" 67.

78. Arr. *Succ.* 1.30–38 *passim,* DS 18.39.1. The exact location of Triparadeisos remains uncertain: it may have been somewhere in the fertile Beqaa plain, between Lebanon and Anti-Lebanon; cf. Schlumberger, *BMB* 22 (1969) 147–49.

79. DS 18.39.2.

80. DS 18.39.5–7, Arr. *Succ.* 34 ff.; cf. Engel 16–28.

81. DS 18.39.5.

82. DS 18.37.3–4; cf. Niese 1.225–26.

83. DS 18.39.7, 40.1.

84. Plut. *Demetr.* 14, DS 19.59.3–6; Errington, "From Babylon" 71; Seibert, *Historische Beiträge* 12–13.

85. DS 18.39.7; cf. Hauben, "First War" 118–19.

86. Plut. *Eum.* 11.

87. Hornblower 154 ff.

88. Westlake, "Eumenes" 322–23 and n. 41, with reff.; Anson, "Discrimination" 55–59.

89. Plut. *Eum.* 3. Cf. p. 11.

90. E.g., Anson, "Eumenes" *passim.*

91. Plut. *Eum.* 1.

92. Plut. *Eum.* 9, 14; DS 18.40 *passim*; Just. 14.2.1–3.

93. Arr. *Succ.* 1.39–41, DS 18.41.1–3, Plut. *Eum.* 9–11 *passim*, Nep. *Eum.* 5.3–7, Just. 14.2.4.

94. Arr. *Succ.* 1.39; DS 18.44.2–45, 50.1.

95. DS 18.49.4. The dying Antipater had warned him against just this move: DS 19.11.9.

96. DS 18.48.4–5.

97. DS 18.49 *passim.*

98. DS 18.41.6–7, 42.1; Plut. *Eum.* 10.

99. DS 18.53.5, 54.3; cf. 18.44.2, 50.1–2; Anson, "Siege" 251–56.

100. DS 18.57.3–4, 58.1–4, 59.1; cf. Hornblower 161. In Plutarch's account of this episode, *Eum.* 12, echoed by Nepos, *Eum.* 5.7, Eumenes cunningly changes the terms of the oath he had to take at Nora, so that he swears allegiance, not to Antigonus alone, but also to the kings, and to Olympias as dowager queen. The local Macedonian commander sanctions this (to him) harmless and pious(?!) addition, and releases Eumenes, who is safely away by the time Antigonus finds out what has happened. Anson, "Siege" 251–56, argues convincingly that Plutarch probably got this version of events from Duris of Samos, who in turn may have used self-exculpatory propaganda put out by Eumenes himself, in his anxiety to avoid the stigma of being a turncoat, and stressing his overriding loyalty to the kings (cf. DS 18.58.4). After all, if Eumenes took what amounted to a simultaneous oath of loyalty to both sides, what did it matter which side he finally chose to serve?

101. DS 18.58.1, 59.3; Plut. *Eum.* 13.

102. DS 18.56; cf. Bengtson, *Strategie* 1.84 ff.; Hammond and Walbank 133–34.

103. DS 18.56.1; cf. Heuss, "Antigonos" 143 ff. Cf. also Will, *CAH* VII².1 42–43: Polyperchon's "proclamation was an amnesty, which reminded the Greeks of their fault only to pardon it."

104. QC 10.6.4 (Perdiccas); DS 18.60 *passim*, 19.15.3–4; Plut. *Eum.* 13; Nep. *Eum.* 7.2–3; Polyaen. 4.8.2.

105. DS 18.72 *passim.*

106. DS 18.49.4, 57.2, 58.2–4, 19.11 *passim.*

107. Duris *ap.* Athen. 13.560f. Cassander's regency: Just. 14.5.1–3.

108. DS 19.11.8; cf. Plut. *Alex.* 77. The propaganda could cut both ways. After Alexander's death the Athenian orator Hypereides moved a decree—perhaps ironically, perhaps not—to honor Iolaus as his murderer. Antipater did not forget or forgive this gesture. When the Lamian War was over, Hypereides either bit his tongue off, or had it cut out, before execution (probably in Corinth, though both Macedonia and Cleonae are recorded as variants), and his body was not returned to Athens for burial: Ps.-Plut. *Vit. X Orat.* 849B–C; cf. Plut. *Dem.* 28, Bosworth 113.

109. DS 18.74–75 *passim*; cf. Niese 1.247.

110. DS 19.35–36 *passim*, 49–51 *passim*; Paus. 1.25.6; Just. 14.6.1–12.

111. DS 19.11.1–9, 52.5, 53.2, 54.1; Diyllus *ap.* Athen. 4.155a; Just. 14.5.1–6. Thessalonike was the daughter of a Thessalian, Nicesipolis, who may herself have been the niece of Jason of Pherae, ruler of Thessaly ca. 385–370.

112. Cf. Bengtson, *Strategie* 1.109–10, and, for the campaign in general, Niese 1.258 ff.

113. DS 18.57.3–63 *passim*, 73, 19.12–34 *passim*, 37–44.2; Plut. *Eum.* 12–19 *passim*; Just. 14.2–4. Hammond, "Alexander's Veterans," argues that the Silver Shields "regarded Eumenes now as a false Alexander; for the great Alexander had not only brought them victory but had safeguarded their possessions" (p. 61).

Chapter 2. Antigonus One-Eye's Bid for Empire, 316–301

1. DS 19.46.1–5; cf. 18.7.4.

2. DS 19.48.5–6.

3. DS 19.46.6, 48.7–8.

4. Plut. *Eum.* 19, DS 19.48.3–4, Just. 14.4.20. Cf. Hammond, "Alexander's Veterans" 61 with n. 31.

5. DS 19.55.2–9. Will, *CAH* VII².1 46, writes of a "surprise attack on Babylonia" by Antigonus, but this seems to be a fiction, with no basis in Diodorus's text.

6. DS 19.56 *passim.*

7. DS 19.48.1, 57.1; cf. 56.5; Bengtson, *Strategie* 1.111; Niese 1.273–74.

8. DS 19.57.1, 85.3; Just. 15.1.2. Wesseling at DS 19.57.1 reads Ἀσάνδρῳ rather than Κασάνδρῳ.

9. DS 19.58–59 *passim.*

10. DS 19.58.5; cf. Berthold, *Rhodes* 61.

11. DS 19.59.1, cf. 79.5; Arr. *Succ.* fr. 24 Roos §§15–19.

12. DS 19.60.1.

13. E. Will, "Monde hellénistique" (1975) 356, says that by so doing Antigonus "affirma des prétentions européennes," surely an overstatement.

14. DS 19.57.5.

15. DS 19.61.1–4; cf. Just. 15.1.3; Austin 29, pp. 54–56; Manni, *Demetrio* 99–106.

16. DS 19.53.2, 52.2; Paus. 9.7.4; *IG* VII 2419 (donations for the rebuilding of Thebes in 316) = Harding 131, pp. 164–65.

17. Austin, pp. 54–55, states the problem with great succinctness. Cf. Heuss, "Antigonos" 146–52; Simpson, "Antigonus the One-Eyed" 389 ff.

18. Polyb. 18.46.5.

19. Cf. Simpson, "Antigonus the One-Eyed" 385; also Mastrocinque, *Caria* 206: "La *polis* si avvia a diventare *municipium*; le libertà contano ancora, ma solo perché significano esenzioni, soprattutto delle tasse; non più perché permettono al *demos* di far politica." This is an unfashionable view today; characteristic is Hornblower's review of Mastrocinque, *JHS* 101 (1981) 202–3, which extols "a more interesting approach, which takes the Hellenistic period to be the time when the *polis* triumphed as a form of social life," citing, among other scholars, Claire Préaux, *Monde* 2.401, who I suspect would have been surprised to hear this view attributed to her. A cynic might perhaps argue that Hornblower is actually saying the same thing as Mastrocinque, Simpson, and myself, but views the emasculation of political life in the *polis* as a blessing rather than a disaster.

20. DS 19.62.1.

21. Will, *HP²* 1.56–57; Simpson, "Antigonus the One-Eyed" 390.

22. Simpson, ibid. 391.

23. Evidence for the League of Islanders, τὸ κοινὸν τῶν Νησιωτῶν, is exclusively epigraphical: see, e.g., *SIG³* 390 = Austin 218, pp. 359–60. See also Merker, "Ptolemaic Officials" 141–42, 156–58, with further refs.; and Simpson, "Antigonus the One-Eyed" 395. According to Merker (p. 158), "most if not all of the islands of the Cyclades" belonged. Cf. *IG* XI 4.1036 (= Harding 136, pp. 170–71) for the League's establishment of the Demetrieia festival on Delos, ca. 306/5.

24. DS 19.61.5.

25. DS 19.79.1–3; cf. Will, *HP²* 1.60.

26. DS 19.59.3–6. Demetrius was also very partial to pretty boys: Plutarch, *Demetr.* 19, tells a nice story of how his father, visiting him when he was supposed to be sick, met one such young beauty just coming out of the bedroom. Antigonus went in and took his son's pulse. "The fever's gone now," Demetrius said, defensively—to which Antigonus retorted, "Yes, I just met it outside."

27. L. C. Smith, *AJPh* 82 (1961) 288 with n. 18; cf. Hauben, "On the Chronology" 257.

28. DS 19.80.3–86.5, App. *Syr.* 54; cf. Seibert, *Untersuchungen* 164–75. Paus. 1.6.5 and Just. 15.1.6 add little of value. As Seibert says, "beruht jede Darstellung allein auf der kritischen Auseinandersetzung mit Diodor," and his discussion largely vindicates the Diodoran account.

29. DS 19.91–92, Plut. *Demetr.* 7, App. *Syr.* 54; cf. Marinoni 579–631.

30. DS 19.105.1; cf. Austin 30, pp. 56–57; Wehrli, *Antigone* 52 ff.; and Simpson, "Historical Circumstances." As Niese remarks (1.303), "Der Vertrag war im wesentlichen eine Anerkennung des damaligen Zustandes." See also Will, *CAH* VII².1 50–52.

31. The Greek verb is ἀφηγεῖσθαι, which basically means "to be in front" or "to lead the way": where it implies actual leadership, it is seldom political or military in the strict sense; the examples cited by LSJ s.v. include a colony, an embassy, a school, and a herd of cattle.

32. Simpson, "Historical Circumstances" 30–31.

33. *OGIS* 5; Welles, *Royal Correspondence* 1; Schmitt, *Staatsverträge* 428, pp. 40–44 = Austin 31, pp. 57–59; Bagnall and Derow 6, pp. 11–13; Harding 132, pp. 165–67. As Harding says, it is unlikely that Scepsis, an unimportant town, was the only recipient of this exercise in propaganda.

34. *OGIS* 6 = Austin 32, pp. 59–60. These and similar surviving inscriptions, no less surely than the Linear B tablets from the Mycenaean era, show us something about which our literary sources remain silent: the ubiquitous bureaucratic infrastructure that accompanied even the most convulsive political upheavals in the Greek world.

35. Will, *HP²* 1.62.

36. DS 20.19.3–4.

37. DS 19.105.2; cf. DS 19.52.4, Paus. 9.7.2, Just. 15.2.3–5. Cf. Gruen, "Coronation" 253–54. Egyptian records and Assyrian cuneiform tablets maintain the fiction of a living Alexander IV until 305/4—i.e., until fresh dynasties were established to replace that of the Argeads. It is not necessary to explain the hiatus by the assertion that the boy-king in fact survived another five or six years after 310, as is argued by B. Z. Wacholder, "The Beginning of the Seleucid Era and the Chronology of the Diadochoi," in F. E. Greenspann et al., eds., *Nourished with Peace: Studies in Hellenistic Judaism in Memory of Samuel Sandmel* (Chico, Calif., 1984) 183–211 and supported by Hammond and Walbank 162–68 on the basis of a late execution combined with efficient concealment of the deed.

38. DS 19.105.3–4. Cassander's Macedonian balancing act is an interesting one. He was working toward a Macedonian policy in deliberate opposition to Alexander *qua* world conqueror—his restoration of Thebes (DS 19.53.2 ff.) was a calculated affront to Alexander's memory—yet at the same time consciously nationalistic and dynastic in its emphasis on local *pietas*, as his marriage to Philip II's daughter Thessalonike, and the honorable burials he had given Philip Arrhidaios, Eurydice, and Cynane, all demonstrate; cf. Errington, "Alexander" 151–52. It is as though he were attempting to cash in on Argead sympathies without reference to the dynasty's most famous member; and since Alexander, in his new role as Lord of Asia, had in fact shifted his center of power from Macedonian Pella to Babylon, Cassander's policy was not so paradoxical as it might at first sight appear. His actions could well appeal to that fundamental irredentism that remains a major factor throughout Macedonian history.

39. Cf. Brunt 22–34.

40. DS 20.20.1–4, 28.1–4; Just. 15.2.3.

41. DS 20.37.3–6. Though now in her mid-forties, Cleopatra had been making a hopeful play for Ptolemy. Antigonus, we are told, "took care that she got a royal funeral."

42. DS 19.92, App. *Syr.* 55; cf. Will, *HP²* 1.66–67.

43. Bevan, *House of Seleucus* 1.52; cf. Will, *HP²* 1.67.

44. Strabo 15.2.9 (C.724), Just. 15.4.12–21; cf. Will, *HP²* 1.264–66; Musti, "Stato" 87–88; Narain 8; Woodcock 47 ff. For Seleucus's eastern campaigns, and his conscious *aemulatio* of Alexander as conqueror, see Holt, *Alexander* 99–103.

45. Arr. *Ind.* 43.4; cf. Bouché-Leclercq, *HL* 1.55–56; Niese 1.311.

46. DS 19.58.2–5.

47. DS 20.37.1–2; *Suda* s.v. Δημήτριος; Schmitt, *Staatsverträge* 433, pp. 49–50 = Harding 133, pp. 167–68. Cf. Will, *HP²* 1.69–71; Bengtson, *Strategie* 1.142–43.

48. Ferguson, *HA* chap. 3 *passim*; cf. Mossé, *Athens* 108–14. The main sources are DS 20.45–46.5, Plut. *Demetr*. 8–14 *passim*, *Suda* s.v. Δημήτριος. For the stockpiling of artillery on the Acropolis (307–6), see *IG* II² 1487 fr. A = Harding 135, pp. 169–70.

49. DS 20.46.5, cf. 46.2; Plut. *Demetr*. 10 ff.; Ferguson, *HA* 108–9; Simpson, "Antigonus the One-Eyed" 402; Meiggs 364, citing *IG* II² 1492.

50. DS 20.47–52 *passim*, Plut. *Demetr*. 15–16, Just. 15.2.6, Polyaen. 4.76; cf. Seibert, *Untersuchungen* 190–206, and, on the fleet strength of each side, Hauben, "Fleet Strength" 1–5.

51. DS 20.73–76 *passim*, Plut. *Demetr*. 19, Paus. 1.6.6; cf. Seibert, *Untersuchungen* 207–24, who rightly stresses (222) "der ganze defensive Charakter der Aussenpolitik des Lagiden." Hauben, "Antigonos' Invasion Plan," while acknowledging the strategical excellence of Antigonus's plan, gives Ptolemy credit for well-concerted defense measures. In fact, opportune storms and the Nile flood also contributed.

52. DS 20.76.7.

53. Jenkins 536, 537, pp. 224–25; cf. Kraay and Davis 146.

54. DS 20.53.2–4, Plut. *Demetr*. 17–18, Just. 15.2.10, App. *Syr*. 54; cf. Austin 36, pp. 65–67; Bengtson, *Strategie* 1.119, Hammond and Walbank 172–75. For an excellent analysis of the Macedonian kingship and its fundamental difference from these new dynasties, see L. Mooren, "The Nature of the Hellenistic Monarchy," in Van't Dack et al. 205 ff., esp. 231–32.

55. Argued by Mueller 87 ff.; challenged by Errington, *JSH* 95 (1975) 250. Will, *CAH* VII².1 57, 63, endorses Mueller with some confidence; but the problem remains elusive. At the time perhaps even Antigonus himself did not see his role with complete clarity.

56. Funck, 505–20, argues that Seleucus's dynastic ambitions long antedated his official declaration of kingship; this is probably true of all the Successors. Cf. Just. 15.3.10–12. Gruen, "Coronation" 257–58 with n. 37 (p. 267), suggests that Ptolemy may not have assumed the diadem till well on in 304, and then as a celebration of his support for Rhodes against Demetrius Poliorcetes. I do not find this convincing. The tradition that Ptolemy assumed the diadem before his rivals (Plut. *Demetr*. 18, App. *Syr*. 54) is not to be impugned without solid evidence; and as Gruen admits (n. 39, with evidence), Seleucus became king in April 304 (cf. Gruen, pp. 258–59 with n. 41).

57. Plut. *Demetr*. 18. Cf. Gruen, "Coronation" 259 with nn. 42, 43.

58. Seltman 218–19 and pl. L.3; Gruen, "Coronation" n. 43 (p. 268). A. Pandermalis's *Dion* (Thessalonike, n.d.), a guidebook to the site, reproduces the (dedicatory) inscription in full: ΒΑΣΙΛΕΥΣ ΚΑΣΣΑΝΔΡΟΣ ΜΑΚΕΔΟΝΩΝ ΑΝΤΙΠΑΤΡΟΥ ΔΙΙ ΟΛΥΜΠΙΩΙ. I owe this reference to Professor E. N. Borza. Cf. *SIG*³ 332.

59. Plut. *Demetr*. 25 (Demetrius mocked the other Successors' pretensions by allotting them subordinate titles: e.g., Seleucus he referred to as the master of elephants, Ptolemy as admiral, and Lysimachus as treasurer [γαζοφύλαξ], a jibe that cut Lysimachus to the quick, since the office was normally held by a eunuch). On the Argead claim, see C. F. Edson, *HSCPh* 45 (1934) 213–46; cf. Austin p. 66.

60. On this, see the sensible remarks of Cohen, "Diadochoi" 177–79. The rivalry in prestige with Antigonus is clear from DS 20.53.4 and Plut. *Demetr*. 18.

61. See the shrewd comments of Bouché-Leclercq, *HL* 1.71: "Pour apprécier la portée de la royauté par des parvenus, il faut tenir compte de la magie des mots. Sans le titre de roi, on pouvait commander; on n'avait pas le droit, un droit inhérent à la personne et inaliénable, d'exiger l'obéissance."

62. *Suda* s.v. βασιλεία, tr. Austin 37, p. 67 (cf. p. 66), and Samuel, *Ptolemaic Chronology* 4–11. For Antiochus IV's attitude to territorial conquest as the best justification of sovereignty, see Polyb. 28.1.6, cited by Walbank, *CAH* VII².1 66.

63. *SIG*³ 332: βασιλεὺς Μακεδόνων. Cf. above, n. 58.

64. DS 20.81.2. See Berthold, *Rhodes* 38–58, esp. 56 ff.

65. The assertion that Alexander had shown Rhodes especial favor, and had even deposited his will there, seems to be a fictional interpolation in an otherwise reliable passage (DS 20.81.3); cf. Hauben, "Rhodes" 318–19; and Berthold, *Rhodes* 37 n. 58, who argues that the Rhodians, at some uncertain point, themselves created (or at least embellished) the forgery.

66. DS 20.46.6.

67. DS 19.57.4, 58.5, 61.5, 62.7, 64.5, 77.3; cf. Hauben, "Rhodes" 322 ff.

68. See Berthold, *Rhodes* chap. 3, "The Diadochoi and the Great Siege," *passim*; cf. Niese 1.324 ff., Hauben, "Rhodes" 317 ff.

69. Vitruv. 10.16.4; cf. DS 20.91.2.

70. DS 20.81–88, 91–100 *passim*; Plut. *Demetr.* 21–22; cf. Marsden, *Greek and Roman Artillery: Historical* 105–8; Meiggs 165–69.

71. DS 20.88.9, 96.1–3, 98.1, 100.3–4; Paus. 1.8.6; Athen. 15.696f–697a (Gorgon of Rhodes).

72. Strabo 14.2.5 (C.652); Plin. *HN* 34.41; Plut. *Demetr.* 20, *Mor.* 183B; Vitruv. 10.16.8; cf. Berthold, *Rhodes* 80 with n. 42. A head of Helios now in the Rhodes Archaeological Museum (Pollitt, *AHA* fig. 48) may have been modeled on the Colossus. Its appearance is otherwise unknown.

73. Bouché-Leclercq, *HL* 1.79–80. For an interesting Athenian inscription recording details of this campaign, see Moretti, *Iscrizioni* 1.5, pp. 8–10 = Harding 137, pp. 171–72.

74. DS 20.100.5–7, 102–3; Plut. *Demetr.* 23–27; Moretti, *Iscrizioni* 1.12–15.

75. *SIG*³ 344; Welles, *Royal Correspondence* 3–4, pp. 15–32 = Austin 40, pp. 70–75 = Bagnall and Derow 7, pp. 13–17; cf. DS 20.107.5.

76. Schmitt, *Staatsverträge* 446, pp. 63–80; Moretti, *Iscrizioni* 44, 1.105–18; Plut. *Demetr.* 25; Austin 42, pp. 76–78; Bagnall and Derow 8, pp. 17–20; Harding 138, pp. 172–74. Cf. Will, *CAH* VII².1 58–59 = Will, *HP²* 1.77–79.

77. DS 20.102.1; cf. Will, *HP²* 1.77–79; Simpson, "Antigonus the One-Eyed" 397.

78. Préaux, *Monde* 1.134.

79. DS 20.106.

80. Schmitt, *Staatsverträge* 447, pp. 80–81, with reff.; DS 20.106.1–5; cf. Seibert, *Untersuchungen* 231 ff.

81. DS 20.113; cf. Seibert, *Untersuchungen* 231–33, esp. 232: "Der Lagide trieb sein eigenes Spiel, während seine Verbündeten das Risiko einer Niederlage gegen Antigonos trugen."

82. DS 20.107–9, 21.1.2–4b, Just. 15.4.22, Plut. *Demetr.* 28–29, Polyaen. 4.7.4, Lucian, *Macrob.* 11 (Hieronymus of Cardia, *FGrH* 154 F 8).

83. Scullard 97–98.

84. Plut. *Demetr.* 30; cf. Will, *HP²* 1.80–83.

85. DS 21.1.5, a crucial passage often neglected.

86. Most recently by Edouard Will; see *HP²* 1.80: "En un certain sens, la disparition d'Antigone le Borgne marque le fin d'une époque. . . . nulle politique désormais ne tentera plus sérieusement . . . de ressusciter l'empire d'Alexandre." Cf. *CAH* VII².1 61.

Chapter 3. Demetrius of Phaleron: The Philosopher-King in Action

1. Plut. *Dem.* 28, Ps.-Plut. *Vit. X Orat.* 849B–C.

2. Cf. Mossé, *Tyrannie* 157, 166.

3. Plut. *Demetr.* 23, 24, 26.

4. See Agora Inv. I 6524; Thompson and Wycherley 61 n. 173 with pl. 53a.

5. See Plut. *Cim.* 14 for his construction of the southern retaining wall of the Acropolis, and the various parks he built in Athens.

6. *IG* II² 417, cited by Mackendrick 30.

7. R. H. S. Crossman, *Plato Today* (Oxford, 1959) 367 ff. For Aristotle's obviously *ad hominem* defense of monarchy, see below, p. 779; and for the association of the Lyceum

under Aristotle and Theophrastus with oligarchy and pro-Macedonianism, cf. Ferguson, *HA* 104–5.

8. Ps.-Plut. *Vit. X Orat.* 841D, *IG* II² 351; cf. Ferguson, *HA* 8; Romano 442 ff.; Camp 154–59.

9. Arist. *Ath. Pol.* 42.3–5, with Rhodes, *Commentary* 493 ff.

10. Ferguson, *HA* 9.

11. O. W. Reinmuth, *The Ephebic Inscriptions of the Fourth Century B.C.* (Leiden, 1971) 133 ff.; cf. Rhodes, *Commentary* 494–95.

12. Arnott, *Menander* (Loeb) xiv–xv.

13. Diog. Laert. 5.79.

14. Isagoras and Cleisthenes: Hdt. 5.66, 69; Arist. *Ath. Pol.* 20.1–4, 21.1–4, *Pol.* 1275ᵇ 34–38. The Mytilene revolt and debate: Thuc. 3.36–50 *passim*. The Arginusae episode: Xen. *Hell.* 1.7 *passim*.

15. E.g., Lys. 22; Dem. 34, 37, 38. On deme activity, see David Whitehead, *The Demes of Attica, 508/7–ca. 250 B.C.* (Princeton, 1986) 358–60.

16. Ste Croix 609 n. 2.

17. Plut. *Phoc.* 25.

18. Ibid. 23 *passim*.

19. Ibid. 34–36 *passim*. L. A. Tritle's biography of this odd political figure, *Phocion the Good* (London, 1988), fills a long-standing gap, but somewhat overvalues him on the basis of Platonic δικαιοσύνη, a good excuse for authoritarianism in any age.

20. Quintil. 2.17.12, *Suda* s.v. Δημάδης.

21. Demetr. *De Eloc.* §283, Plut. *Phoc.* 22.

22. Bribes: Davies 100. Fine: Athen. 6.251b, Ael. *VH* 5.12.

23. DS 17.62.6–63.4, QC 6.1, Just. 12.1.6–11; cf. Badian, *Hermes* 95 (1967) 178–81.

24. DS 18.18.1–2, Paus. 7.10.1.

25. Plut. *Phoc.* 1.

26. Plut. *Dem.* 28.

27. Plut. *Phoc.* 30.

28. DS 18.48.1–4; Arr. *Succ.* 1.14–15; Plut. *Phoc.* 30, *Dem.* 31.

29. Ste Croix 300 and elsewhere.

30. See *Pol.* 1261ᵃ 5 ff., 1264ᵃ 11 ff., and elsewhere.

31. DS 18.18.4–5, 66.5; Plut. *Phoc.* 27–28.

32. Plut. *Phoc.* 28; DS 18.18.5 reads 22,000, probably a textual error, since it seems likely that the figure of 12,000 was obtained "by subtracting the 9000 registered citizens from the total of 21,000 ascertained at the census of Demetrius of Phalerum" (Ferguson, *HA* 22 n. 3).

33. DS 18.18.4.

34. DS 20.40.6–7.

35. Plut. *Phoc.* 28: οἵ τε μένοντες ἐδόκουν σχέτλια καὶ ἄτιμα πάσχειν, a phrase often mistranslated: see, e.g., the Loeb version, "appeared to be suffering grievous and undeserved wrongs." I am grateful to Prof. F. W. Walbank for discussion of this phrase.

36. *Suda* s.v. Δημάδης; cf. Ferguson, *HA* 23.

37. DS 18.18.5.

38. *SIG*³ 317 = Austin 26, pp. 48–50: the key phrase in Greek is οἱ ἐν τεῖ ὀλι[γ]αρχίαι πολιτευόμενοι.

39. Plut. *Phoc.* 27, 30.

40. DS 18.56 *passim*; cf. Plut. *Phoc.* 32.

41. Plut. *Phoc.* 31.

42. DS 18.64–65, esp. 65.6; Plut. *Phoc.* 31–38 *passim*; Nep. *Phoc.* 3–4.

43. Cleisthenes, similarly, was accused by his political enemies of enrolling slaves and foreigners in the new tribes: Arist. *Pol.* 1275ᵇ37.

44. Plut. *Phoc.* 34–37 *passim*; DS 18.66.3–67.6.

45. DS 18.67.3–5.

46. DS 18.67.6, Plut. *Phoc.* 36; *Nepos, Phoc.* 3–4. The executioner underestimated the amount of hemlock needed, and (with Phocion still to drink) refused to prepare more unless he first got the price of it, 12 drachmas. In the end Phocion asked one of his friends for the money, complaining that in Athens it was impossible even to die unless you paid for the privilege.

47. DS 18.68.1.

48. DS 18.74 *passim*; cf. Strabo 9.1.20 (C.398). Nicanor himself did not long survive the surrender: Cassander, suspicious of his growing arrogance and ambition, had him assassinated (DS 18.75.1).

49. Ferguson, *HA* 36.

50. Diog. Laert. 5.80–81 lists nearly fifty titles by him, on subjects ranging from Homer through marriage to the Athenian legislation.

51. Mackendrick 31–34; Mossé, *Tyrannie* chap. 2, pp. 155–66; Ferguson, *HA* chap. 2, pp. 38–94; *RE* 4 (1901) cols. 2817–41, s.v. "Demetrios" (85). I have not seen E. Bayer, *Demetrios Phalereus der Athener* (Stuttgart and Berlin, 1942).

52. Athen. 14.620b.

53. DS 18.74.3: ἕως ἂν διαπολεμήσῃ πρὸς τοὺς βασιλεῖς. Mossé, *Tyrannie* 161–62; *RE* 4 (1901) col. 2827.

54. Cf. Arist. *Pol.* 1295ᵃ25 ff. For a typically sedulous vote of honors to Demetrius (by the deme of Aixone, soon after his installation), see *IG* II² 1201+ (= Harding 129, pp. 163–64).

55. DS 20.27.1.

56. Ctesicles *ap.* Athen. 6.272b.

57. See, e.g., Finley, ed., *Slavery* 57–60, citing Lauffer.

58. Ferguson, *HA* 40 ff. For a good legislator Demetrius seems to have been oddly cavalier about his own title. ἐπιμελητής is the best and most formally attested: DS 18.74.3, 20.45.2; Paus. 1.25.6; Plut. *Demetr.* 8. But Strabo (9.1.20, [C.398]), and Diodorus elsewhere (20.45.5), imply that his title was ἐπιστάτης, "overseer," "governor"; and Polybius called him προστάτης, "champion" (20.13.9), though it is not clear just whom the historian took him to be championing. But since his power ultimately derived from Cassander, and everyone knew this, it could be argued that the label he wore was of relative unimportance.

59. Duris *ap.* Athen. 12.542b–e; Carystius of Pergamon ibid. 542e–543a.

60. Duris ibid. 542c.

61. Philochorus *ap.* Athen. 6.245c.

62. Demochares *ap.* Polyb. 12.13.9–11.

63. Diog. Laert. 5.75.

64. DS 19.54.1–3.

65. Ferguson, *HA* 49–51; Will, *HP²* 1.56–58.

66. DS 20.45–46.5, Plut. *Demetr.* 8–14 *passim*, *Suda* s.v. Δημήτριος.

67. Plut. *Demetr.* 10. Thus was ushered in a period of considerable instability: between 307 and 261 there were seven changes of government.

68. DS 20.45.4–5, Diog. Laert. 5.77–78, Strabo 9.1.20 (C.398).

69. Favorinus *ap.* Diog. Laert. 5.77, DS 20.46.1–2, Plut. *Demetr.* 11; cf. W. S. Ferguson, *HA* 101 ff., cf. "Demetrius" 114. Remains of a gilded bronze equestrian statue of Demetrius have been found in a well down which they were thrown in 200 B.C.: see Camp 164–65 with fig. 138, and Chap. 18, p. 307.

70. Thus, as Hypereides observed, *Epitaph.* 21 f., doing of their own free will what they had done for Alexander by coercion.

71. DS 20.46.2–4. Since Imbros had broken away from Athens precisely in the hope of a return to a more democratic regime, this was a cheap concession. Cf. Camp 163–64: as he points out, the creation of two new tribes "meant an increase in the Boule to 600 members and a reassigning of demes among twelve rather than ten tribes."

72. Ferguson, *HA* 101.

73. Cf. Will, *HP²* 1.69: "L'oligarchie patronnée par Cassandre cédait la place à la démocratie restaurée—mais patronnée par les Antigonides."

74. DS 20.46.5, 50.3, Plut. *Demetr.* 15.

75. Pollux 9.42, Diog. Laert. 5.38, Athen. 13.610f.

76. Text *ap.* Athen. 13.610e = Kock 2.327. The name of the play is uncertain: it may have been *The Horseman,* or *The Knight* (*Hippeus*).

77. The best account of this complex episode is still that of Ferguson, *HA* 103–7, which I largely follow.

78. Demochares *ap.* Athen. 11.508f–509b, cf. 610e; Diog. Laert. 5.38; cf. Ferguson, *HA* 106–7.

79. Diog. Laert. 5.38, 10.2.

80. DS 18.67.6, Nep. *Phoc.* 4.4, Ps.-Plut. *Vit. X Orat.* 850B.

81. Plut. *Demetr.* 23, Polyaen. 4.11.1, Paus. 1.35.2; cf. Ferguson, *HA* 115–17.

82. Plut. *Demetr.* 23–24, 26 *passim*; DS 20.100.5–6.

83. Cf. Head et al. 54, with pl. 29 nos. 8–10.

84. Plut. *Demetr.* 25; cf. W. S. Ferguson, "Demetrius" 122.

85. Ferguson, *HA* 131 with n. 3.

Chapter 4. Zeno, Diogenes, Epicurus, and Political Disenchantment

1. See Plut. *Mor.* 841B–D for Lycurgus's public-works schemes: Plutarch reports that he "carried out renovation work all over the city." See also Paus. 1.3.4, and cf. Thompson and Wycherley 21–23; Travlos, *Pictorial Dictionary* 96, 537–38; Wycherley, *Stones* 66–67, 210–11. On Lycurgus's benefactions to Athens in general see F. W. Mitchel, "Lykourgan Athens 338–322," *University of Cincinnati Classical Studies* 2 (1973) 163–214. Romano 441 ff. suggests, very convincingly, that the Lycurgan theater and Panathenaic stadium did not underlie the later Roman stadium, but were associated with the Pnyx.

2. *IG* II² 2318, 2320; cf. A. W. Pickard-Cambridge, *The Dramatic Festivals of Athens,* 2d ed. (Oxford, 1968), 99–101.

3. Ps.-Plut. *Vit. X Orat.* 841F.

4. *Poetics* 1452ª24 ff., and elsewhere.

5. Thompson and Wycherley 21.

6. See my *Essays in Antiquity* (London, 1960) 87; the phrase is Edwyn Bevan's.

7. Sandbach 23; Welles, "Alexander's Historical Achievement" 227.

8. Paus. 1.29.1; cf. Edwards, *Hesperia* 26 (1957) 320–49.

9. Hesiod, *WD* 176–292.

10. Cited by Polyb. 29.21.1–9; cf. Ferguson, *HA* 87 and n. 3.

11. Fr. 2 Nauck, *TGF*² p. 782: τύχη τὰ θνητῶν πράγματ᾽, οὐκ εὐβουλία. Cf. Plut. *Mor.* 104D: ἄσκοπος γὰρ ἡ τύχη, φησὶν ὁ Θεόφραστος.

12. *Hypobolimaios* fr. 417 Sandback = fr. 482 Kock.

13. Festugière, *Epicurus* 13.

14. Athen. 6.253b–f; cf. Austin 35, pp. 64–65.

15. DS 6.1.2–10, Euseb. *Praep. Evang.* 2.2, Sext. Emp. *Adv. Math.* 9.17; cf. Fraser 1.289 ff., Nilsson 283–89. It is amusing, and instructive, to note how critics in antiquity took Euhemerus's fable *au pied de la lettre*, and then attacked him for presenting such patently invented travels as truthful autobiography: see, e.g., Polyb. 34.5.8–9; Strabo 1.3.1 (C.47), 2.3.5 (C.102), 7.3.6 (C.299).

16. Cicero, *ND* 1.42, Varro, *RR* 1.48.

17. Aristoph. *Kn.* 261; Thuc. 6.18, cf. 2.40; Plat. *Rep.* 620C; Hdt. 1.59; Andoc. 1.84.

18. Eur. *Hipp.* 732–51; Aristoph. *Birds* 27 ff.; Eupolis frr. 90, 94, 96, 100, 116, 117 Kock.

19. K. J. Dover, *Aristophanic Comedy* (Berkeley and Los Angeles, 1972) 202.

20. Plato, *Ep.* 7.324B–326B (ed. Souilhé); relevant passages translated by H. D. P. Lee in his introduction to the Penguin Classics *Republic,* 2d ed. (Harmondsworth, 1974), 14.

21. Diog. Laert. 6.23 (cf. Sen. *Ep.* 99), 38 (cf. Plut. *Alex.* 14), 41, 54; Ael. *VH* 14.33.

22. Rankin 229, 232; Diog. Laert. 6.20–81 *passim*.
23. Diog. Laert. 6.63, 69; Pollitt, *AHA* 10–11.
24. *The Arbitration* (*Epitrepontes*) 1084–91 (ed. Sandbach).
25. Metrodorus *ap.* Diog. Laert. 10.1; Kirchner 4855. On Epicurus's life in general, see Rist, *Epicurus* chap. 1, pp. 1–13; Sedley 121 ff.; De Witt chaps. 2–4, pp. 36–105; Festugière, *Epicurus* 19–26.
26. Cf. *SIG*³ 312, recording the return to Samos of certain Samian refugees (321/0), and Diog. Laert. 10.1.
27. Hesiod, *Theog.* 116. The anecdote is related by Diog. Laert. 10.2 (citing the *Life of Epicurus* by Apollodorus) and Sext. Emp. *Adv. Math.* 10.18.
28. Diog. Laert. 5.5.
29. Plut. *Mor.* 1095C, where he is cited as feeling sickened by the prospect of studying Theophrastus on musical theory; cf. De Witt 50–51; Rist, *Epicurus* 2–3.
30. Demetr. Magnes. *ap.* Diog. Laert. 10.13.
31. Plut. *Mor.* 1128B–1130E. Plutarch entitled this essay "Is *Lathe Biōsas* Proper Advice?" (Εἰ Καλῶς Εἴρηται τὸ Λάθε Βιώσας), and concluded that it was not, completely misrepresenting Epicurus's intentions in the process. Cf. De Witt 188. The aphorism, not found in Epicurus's surviving fragments, is listed as fr. 551 Usener.
32. See Harding 128, pp. 162–63, and further evidence there cited.
33. Though perhaps not so sharp as hostile propagandists alleged: see Sedley 122 ff., who, however, cannot (and does not) make Timarchus the exclusive villain in this matter. Enough evidence remains to suggest that Epicurus was at least as talented a polemicist as St. Thomas More.
34. Diog. Laert. 5.38, 10.2; cf. Ferguson, *HA* 106–7.
35. Diog. Laert. 7.1 ff. *passim*; cf. Long, *Hellenistic Philosophy* 109–13; Sandbach 20–27; and esp. von Fritz, "Zenon (2) von Kition," *RE* 10A (1972) cols. 83–88, who discusses (cols. 83–85) the vexed problem of Zeno's chronology. I accept 262/1 as the date of his death (Hieron. *Chron.* Ol. 129.1, corrected by *PHerc.* 339 col. iv 9–14 = *SVF* 1.36a), 334/3 as the year of his birth, and 312/1 as the year of his arrival in Athens (Persaeus *ap.* Diog. Laert. 7.28). Evidence against this—e.g., his claim to have been eighty at the time Antigonus Gonatas invited him to Pella (Diog. Laert. 7.8–9), or Apollonius of Tyre's statement (Diog. Laert. 7.28) that he presided over his school for fifty-eight years, and died aged ninety-eight (cf. Lucian, *Macrob.* 19)—I take to have been manufactured to fit in with the assumption that he founded his school at his canonical ἀκμή, i.e., when aged forty. Von Fritz points out that other conflicting figures, e.g., that Zeno arrived in Athens *aet.* 30, and studied in Athens for ten years prior to setting up his pitch in the Stoa Poikile, are suspiciously rounded to decades (Diog. Laert. 7.2; at 7.4 it is also claimed that his period of apprenticeship lasted 20 years). The invitation from Antigonus Gonatas is almost certainly historical, and Zeno may well have given age as an excuse for refusing it; it is therefore logically to be dated after Antigonus's final acknowledgment as king (276), or even after the defeat of Pyrrhus (272; see p. 144).
36. Diog. Laert. 7.1–3, Demetr. Magnes. *ap.* Diog. Laert. 7.31. Pohlenz, 1.164 ff., is one of the most recent scholars to argue for Eastern/Semitic influences on Zeno's thought.
37. Diog. Laert. 7.26–27.
38. Diog. Laert. 7.5, 13, 15, 19, 22, 25. Sen. *De Tranq. Anim.* 14, and Plut. *Mor.* 87A, as well as an alternative version of the story recorded (and clearly not believed) in Diog. Laert. 7.5, claim that he lost everything at the time of his shipwreck, and that this turned him to philosophy; Diog. Laert. clearly prefers the more prosaic, but less romantic, variant, according to which "he first disposed of his cargo in Athens, and by this means was able to devote himself to philosophy" (ibid.). On balance this seems to me by far the likelier account.
39. Diog. Laert. 7.6–9, 13–15. The exchange of letters between Zeno and Antigonus, cited by Diog. Laert. from Apollonius of Tyre, is clearly a late rhetorical exercise (cf. above, n. 35), though the central fact it enshrines—that Antigonus invited Zeno to his court, and that Zeno refused, but sent two of his disciples instead—is probably true.

40. Diog. Laert. 7.6.

41. Diog. Laert. 7.12, Plut. *Mor.* 1034A; cf. Burstein, *Translated Documents* 59, pp. 81–82.

42. *OCD*² 1145b.

43. Diog. Laert. 7.32–34, 121, 129, 131; cf. Plut. *Mor.* 653E for Zeno's use in his *Republic* of the graphic term διαμηρισμός, "thigh spreading."

44. For an excellent analysis of the testimonia citing or referring to this remarkable work, see H. C. Baldry, "Zeno's Ideal State," *JHS* 79 (1959) 3–15.

45. Diog. Laert. 7.4.

46. Baldry (above, n. 44) 14. Cf. Plut. *Mor.* 329A.

47. Diog. Laert. 7.10. The Greek, much debated in translation, is ἀρετὴν καὶ σωφροσύνην.

Chapter 5. Theophrastus, Menander, and the Transformation of Attic Comedy

1. Cf., e.g., *Poetics* 1447ᵃ16, 19, 28; 1448ᵃ1, 20–24; 1448ᵇ7, 22; 1449ᵇ24–28; 1451ᵃ30; Plato, *Rep.* 595A ff., etc.; and see also the sensible remarks of F. L. Lucas in his edition of the *Poetics* (Oxford, 1968), app. 1, 258–72. Early references to μίμησις are, as he says (p. 268), rare, and well into the classical era realism of depiction was not the artist's prime concern (see below, p. 108).

2. Fraser 1.619–20 with reff.

3. See B. Snell, *Tragicorum Graecorum Fragmenta* vol. 1 (Göttingen, 1971) 189–312 *passim*, and the conspectus of names listed on pp. vi–viii.

4. Arist. *Rhet.* 1413ᵇ13.

5. Plut. *Mor.* 674B–C. A very similar story is told of the Victorian actor-manager Sir Henry Irving, who during a rehearsal upbraided his props manager for not producing sufficiently realistic thunder to accompany a storm scene. "But Sir Henry," protested the props manager, "that's a *real* thunderstorm, outside." "No matter: the Almighty's thunder is not necessarily good enough for the Lyceum."

6. The best-known example is Menander's reworking, in the *Sikyonioi*, of Euripides' *Orestes* 868 ff. Cf. Arnott, *Menander* (Loeb) xli–xlii with further reff.

7. E. Segal 129–36, where it is pointed out, correctly, that a concern with private, as opposed to public, solutions can be traced back at least as far as Aristophanes' *Acharnians* and *Knights*.

8. Cf. Treu, "Menanders Menschen" 213: "es ist bei M. immer noch sehr wichtig, ob jemand Polisbürger ist oder nicht. Wie er sich aber als Polisbürger im einzelnen betätigt und bewährt, interessiert sehr viel weniger."

9. Handley 3.

10. Arist. *Eth. Nic.* 1128ᵃ.

11. Webster, *Introduction* 94–99.

12. Nor do they always have quite the meaning popularly ascribed to them: take, e.g., the most famous of them all, "Whom the gods love die young." As Arnott, *Menander* (Loeb) 169–70, points out, Byron quietly changed the original singular to a generic plural (*Don Juan*, canto 4.12); in the *Dis Exapatōn* (*Double Crook*) of Menander (fr. 4 Arnott = 125 Kock) the line, "far from being a sentimental sigh about the Schuberts of this world," formed part of a slave's acid comment to an old man on his gullibility.

13. Quintil. 10.1.69, 71; Plut. *Mor.* 854B–D; Aristoph. Byz. *ap.* Syrianus on Hermogenes 2.23 Rabe = Körte and Thierfelder testim. 32.

14. Körte and Thierfelder testim. 49, 61, 41 (= Plut. *Mor.* 854D).

15. Cf. J. D. Denniston's edition of the *Electra* (Oxford, 1939), pp. xi–xii.

16. Körte and Thierfelder testim. 51, 55 = Euseb. *Praep. Evang.* 10.3.12.

17. Diog. Laert. 5.37–38, Strabo 13.2.4 (C.618), *Suda* s.v. Θεόφραστος.

18. Hermippus *ap.* Athen. 1.21a–b.

19. Diog. Laert. 5.42–50 *passim*, fr. 114 Wimmer; Hieron. *Adv. Jovin.* 1.47.

20. Diog. Laert. 5.39, 51–58 *passim*; Cic. *Tusc. Disp.* 5.9.

21. Diog. Laert. 5.38.

22. Ussher, *Characters* 12–14.

23. See ibid. 5–12 for a conspectus of theories.

24. Jebb 16–17.

25. Polycles, the dedicatee, may have been the adviser of that name in the entourage of Philip Arrhidaios's wife, Eurydice (DS 19.11.3); but the whole introduction is, in any case, almost certainly a spurious late addition, and valueless as evidence.

26. Jebb 58; Ussher, *Characters* 13, citing Cichorius.

27. Cf. Sandbach, *Gnomon* 39 (1967) 240, who emphasizes the undoubted truth that "by relieving the rich of liturgies and abolishing general payments from state funds, Demetrius must have fostered the growth of wealth and worsened the lot of the poor."

28. Ussher, *Characters* 5.

29. Ussher, ibid. 23–27, gives a useful breakdown of topics treated or referred to.

30. Soph. *ap*. Arist. *Poetics* 1460^{b}35.

31. Soph. *Ant.* 361–73.

32. Diog. Laert. 5.36.

33. Barigazzi 13; cf. Pollitt, *AHA* 4 ff.

34. Körte and Thierfelder testim. 2 [= Anon. *De Com.* §§15, 17], 3 [= *IG* XIV 1184], 4 [= *IG*² II 1926.19]; *Suda* s.v. Μένανδρος.

35. Körte and Thierfelder testim. 23a–c; for the problems regarding the date see Arnott, *Menander* (Loeb) xiv–xv: the most plausible date for the *Orgē*, on the evidence at our disposal, is 322/1, in the archonship of Philocles. Cf. Barigazzi 19, with n. 1.

36. E.g., frr. 116, 178, 179, 201, 202 Kock.

37. E.g., frr. 146, 216, 219, 228 Kock.

38. Frr. 65–67 Kock.

39. Fr. 90 Kock. For Alexis's grittily derisive attitude toward sophists, Pythagoreans, and Platonists, see frr. 1, 25, 220, 221 Kock. Cf. below, n. 84.

40. *Suda* s.v. Μένανδρος; Körte and Thierfelder testim. 2 (= Anon. *De Com.* §17); Aul. Gell. 17.4.4, citing Apollodorus.

41. Körte and Thierfelder testim. 15a–c; Aul. Gell. 17.21, 42; Schol. Ovid *Ibis* 591–92; Mart. 5.10.9; Paus. 1.2.2.

42. Richter, *Portraits* 2.224 ff. with figs. 1514–1643.

43. *Suda* s.v. Μένανδρος; for an excellent reproduction, in color, of the Mytilene mosaic, see L. Kahil, in S. Charitonidis, L. Kahil, and R. Ginouvès, *Les mosaïques de la Maison du Ménandre à Mytilène*, Antike Kunst, Beiheft 6 (Bern, 1970), 27 ff. with pl. ii; and for another likeness of Menander, a miniature bronze bust, which also shows a squint, see Ashmole, *AJA* 77 (1973) 61 with pls. xi–xii. Cf. Arnott, *Menander* (Loeb) xviii–xix with n. 1.

44. Körte and Thierfelder testim. 9 (= Phaedrus 5.1); cf. Diog. Laert. 5.36, 79. The Phaedrus fable is very seldom quoted, and Körte for one (ibid.; cf. *RE* 15 [1932] col. 709, s.v. "Menandros [9]") has no time for it at all, arguing that "im J. 317 war M. noch nicht *nobilis comoediis*, und die beiden kannten sich zweifellos längst aus dem Peripatos." But by 317 Menander had at least two victories to his name, including, most recently, the *Dyskolos* (unless we are to place this audience very early indeed); and if Theophrastus's lecture audience ran into the thousands, it is more than likely that Menander and Demetrius had not yet met.

45. *Suda* s.v. Μένανδρος: ὀξὺς δὲ τὸν νοῦν καὶ περὶ γυναῖκας ἐμμανέστατος.

46. Diog. Laert. 5.79. Menander had trouble later (301/0) with Lachares, who stopped his play *The Imbrians* from being put on, presumably on political grounds: Körte and Thierfelder testim. 28; cf. p. 124.

47. Sandbach, *Gnomon* 39 (1967) 239.

48. Cf. Arnott, "Moral Values" 215–17.

49. Cf. Plut. *Alcib.* 23.

50. The similarity has often been remarked; cf., e.g., Arnott, "Young Lovers" 2–4, 11.

51. Welles, *Alexander* 203.

52. Handley 123–24 with testimonia.

53. Arnott, "Moral Values" 215.

54. Handley 4 and n. 1, with reff.; cf. E. Segal 129 ff.

55. *Sikyon*. 150–57 Sandbach, where the speakers are tentatively identified as Smikrines and Blepes.

56. Cf. Goldberg 45–46.

57. Handley 13. For the unpleasant reality of itinerant mercenaries, see Ferguson, *HA* 74–75.

58. Webster, *Introduction* 15–18.

59. Treu, "Menanders Menschen" 213, who observes that "der Bürger ist in Geschäften unterwegs, geht in die Stadt, über Land, reist ins Ausland, ohne dass die Art der Unternehmungen gewöhnlich näher bestimmt wird."

60. For the constant operation of Tyche in the *Dyskolos*, see Casertano 258 ff.; Pollitt, *AHA* 5–6; and for Tyche in the *Aspis*, both as prologue speaker (*qua* post-Euripidean goddess), and as a plot device, to control action throughout (to the detriment of any character development), cf. Konet 90–92. Fr. 355 Kock (cited by Pollitt, *AHA* 2) is typical: "Fortune observes no rule by which she decides human affairs. Nor is it possible, while still alive, to say, 'I will not suffer this fate.'"

61. G. Lefebvre, *Fragments d'un manuscrit de Ménandre* (Cairo, 1907); cf. *Papyrus de Ménandre* (Cairo, 1911).

62. This to-and-fro vernacular chattiness makes it almost impossible to excerpt significant quotations from Menander, and I have not attempted to do so.

63. Webster, *Birth* 3.

64. R. Kassel and C. Austin, *Papyrus Bodmer XXV, XXVI* (Geneva, 1969).

65. *Menandri Reliquiae Selectae*, ed. F. H. Sandbach (Oxford, 1972).

66. Cnemon may rail (743–45) against the evils—war, imprisonment, lawsuits— brought about by greed (cf. Handley 7–8), but this fine old bromide is hardly specific in its application.

67. Dicaearchus *ap.* Soph. *OT* arg. §5.

68. Sandbach *ap.* Turner, ed., *Ménandre* 116; cf. Webster, *Introduction* 105.

69. Cnemon's animadversions (447–53) on worshippers who guzzle all the sacred meat except what is completely inedible are a stock topos of comedy (cf. Handley 214–15), and should not be taken as a veiled contemporary allusion to the new Athenian sumptuary laws (as, e.g., by Arnott, *Menander* (Loeb) 255 n. 2). If there is any kind of reference, which remains dubious, it is more likely to be to Theophrastus's treatise *On Piety*: see Webster, *Introduction* 45–46.

70. Handley (13) finds it "striking" that this speech parades ethical principles but "leaves the old man's emotions almost entirely to the audience's imagination." "Striking" is not the epithet that occurs to me.

71. Webster, *Birth* 13.

72. Clifton Fadiman, *Party of One* (New York, 1955) 98–125.

73. Tarn and Griffith 273.

74. C. Préaux, "Ménandre et la société athénienne," *CE* 32 (1957) 84–100.

75. Jaekel 257–65.

76. Turner, "Menander" 106–26, a direct counterattack on Tarn.

77. Goldberg 121.

78. Arnott, *Menander* (Loeb) xxx–xlv.

79. Arnott, "Moral Values" 215–16.

80. Arnott, "Young Lovers" 2. Cf. nn. 78 and 79 above.

81. *Aspis* 79–83, stressed by Arnott, "Young Lovers" 17–18.

82. Cf. Theophr. *Char.* 2.12.

83. Goldberg 3–4.

84. See, e.g., his blistering account of the tricks of dress and makeup that prostitutes employ to turn themselves out to best advantage (*ap.* Athen. 568a–d = fr. 98 Kock), a forerunner of the advice in Ovid, *AA* 3.135 ff., 261 ff., and 771 ff. The following lines are particularly striking:

> If her teeth are really pretty, then of course she has to laugh,
> So the company can notice what a fine old mouth she's got;
> But if laughing's not her forte, then she spends the whole day through
> Shut indoors, just like those goats' heads on display in butchers' shops,
> Mouth held open by a wooden sliver jammed between her lips,
> Till in course of time her grin is, willy-nilly, fixed for good.

85. Plut. *Mor.* 347E.

86. Arist. *Poetics* 1450ᵃ38.

87. See, e.g., Handley 10 ff., Goldberg 44 ff.

88. Cf. *Aspis* 404–18.

89. Cf. M. Poole, "Menander's Comic Use of Euripides' Tragedies," *CB* 54 (1977/78) 56–62.

Chapter 6. The Politics of Royal Patronage: Early Ptolemaic Alexandria

1. Cf., e.g., *Alcib. I* 127B, *Protag.* 313A, *Phaedr.* 247A, *Polit.* 307E, *Rep.* 433D.

2. *Odes* 3.29.12: "fumum et opes strepitumque Romae."

3. Cf. Plut. *Alex.* 26, DS 17.52.4, Polyb. 39.14, Dio Chrysost. *Orat.* 32.35–36. A useful general survey is Heinz Heinen's "Alexandrien—Weltstadt und Residenz," in Hinske 3–12. For the general Nilotic background during our period, see Bowman, chap. 1, "The Gift of the Nile," pp. 12–20; and Lewis, chap. 1, "The Background: Eldorado on the Nile," pp. 8–36. For Alexandria, see Bowman 204 ff.

4. Strabo 17.1.8 (C.794).

5. Fraser 1.687–90 with reff.; Pfeiffer, *History* 99–102.

6. Dio Cass. 42.38.2, Aul. Gell. 7.17.3, Sen. *De Tranq. Anim.* 9.5, Plut. *Ant.* 58; cf. the excellent discussion by Fraser 1.334–35, 2.493–94. See also below, Chap. 37, n. 151.

7. "In an Asia Minor Municipality": Cavafy, Ποιήματα Β΄ 50 = 2.264–65.

8. Forster 49–50; Rostovtzeff, *Encyclopaedia Britannica*¹⁴ (rev. 1965) 1.584, s.v. "Alexandria."

9. Plut. *Mor.* 11A, Hegesander *ap.* Athen. 14.620f–621a. Sotades is also reported to have attacked Lysimachus. The line quoted is even more effective in Greek: εἰς οὐχ ὁσίην τρυμαλίην τὸ κέντρον ὠθεῖς.

10. Herodian 4.9, Dio Cass. 77.22, Spartian. *Caracalla* 6.

11. Forster 52–54.

12. Rostovtzeff (above, n. 8) 1.584–85. For the later history of Alexandria, see P. M. Fraser, "Alexandria from Mohammed Ali to Gamal Abdul Nasser," in Hinske 63–74.

13. Cf. Fraser 1.8–11, 2.18–25.

14. DS 17.52.1–7; Arr. *Anab.* 3.1.5–2.2; Plut. *Alex.* 26; Strabo 17.1.6–10 (C.791–95); QC 4.8.1–2, 5–6; Just. 11.11.13; Val. Max. 1.4.7 ext. §1; Plin. *HN* 5.11.62–63. Cf. my *Alexander* 269–71, 275–76 with reff.; and see Pollitt, *AHA* app. 3, 275–77.

15. Strabo 17.1.7 (C.793).

16. Martin 116–17.

17. For tributes to Alexandria's size, favorable climate, beauty, and commercial prosperity, see, e.g., Strabo 17.1.7 (C.792–93), 17.1.13 (C.798); DS 17.52.5; Dio Chrysost. *Orat.* 32.35–36.

18. Diog. Laert. 1.53, schol. Aristeid. p. 323 Dindorf, Cic. *De Orat.* 3.34, Ael. *VH* 13.14, Paus. 7.26.14.

19. Ael. *VH* 2.21, 13.24, 14.17; schol. Aristoph. *Frogs* 85; Arist. *Rhet.* 139ᵃ8.

20. Fraser 1.305.

21. See R. B. Lewis, "Lifelong Learning as an Ideal in Fourth-Century Greece," (diss., Univ. of Toledo, 1980), and the abstract in *DA* 41 (1980) 1469A, from which my citation is taken.

22. Fraser 1.312 ff.

23. Diog. Laert. 5.37.

24. Ael. *VH* 3.17.

25. Fraser 1.306.

26. See my *Alexander* 54–62, with reff.

27. Diog. Laert. 5.58.

28. Fraser 1.322–23, with reff.

29. Strabo 14.2.19 (C.657): ποιητὴς ἅμα καὶ κριτικός. It should be emphasized that much of what follows is necessarily speculative: not only is virtually all Philetas's poetry lost, but it did not even survive into Roman times. Bracketed with Callimachus as one of the two canonical elegists from the Hellenistic period, Philetas remains one of those legendary and seminal figures whose influence has to be taken entirely on trust.

30. Pfeiffer, *History* 88.

31. Athen. 2.72a.

32. Hermesianax fr. 7.75–78 Powell (*Coll. Alex.* p. 100). The glossary: Athen. 9.383a–b.

33. Plut. *Mor.* 1095D, Strabo 17.1.8 (C.793–94).

34. Pfeiffer *History* 97. He asserts, oddly, that there were no philosophers: this is directly contradicted by Athen. 1.22d, and in any case the distinction between categories of research was not as precise then as it is today. If Strabo's φιλολόγων ἀνδρῶν can include scientists (Fraser 1.317–18), there is no reason why Athenaeus's φιλοσόφους, "maintained" (τρεφομέ-νους) in the Museum, should not refer to any kind of intellectual.

35. Fr. 191 Pfeiffer, *dieg.* 6.2 ff.

36. *Ap.* Diog. Laert. 9.6, = fr. 43 Diels.

37. *Ap.* Athen. 1.22d = fr. 12 Diels.

38. W. J. Slater, "Aristophanes of Byzantium and Problem-Solving in the Museum," *CQ*, n.s., 32 (1982) 346–49.

39. Diog. Laert. 5.78–79.

40. Plut. *Mor.* 189D; cf. Fraser 1.485.

41. Fraser 1.93 ff.; cf. Rostovtzeff, *SEH* 261–67, 1079–81.

42. Fraser 1.108, 134–35, 141–42, 150; Rostovtzeff, *SEH* 313, 389, 392, 926, 928.

43. Fraser 1.133 ff.

44. Diog. Laert. 5.58.

45. Though still not nearly as much as we would like: see Strabo 17.1.8 (C.793–94), and cf. Vitruv. 5.11.2, *Suda* s.v. ἐξέδρα, with the discussion by Fraser, 1.315 ff. What does seem clear is that the Museum was indeed planned in the direct Peripatetic tradition.

46. The figure is given by Tzetzes, probably derived from Callimachus's *Pinakes*: texts in Kaibel, *CGF* 17–33; cf. Fraser 1.320 f.f (esp. 328–29), 2.474, 484–85; Pfeiffer, *History* 98 ff.

47. Evidence well analyzed by Pfeiffer, *History* 99–104; cf. *Suda* s.v. Ζηνόδοτος. Wilamowitz's claim (*Hellenistische Dichtung* 1.22) that Demetrius was the first librarian may have been a mere slip, since later in the same work (1.165) he correctly identifies Zenodotus as the original holder of the office.

48. See L. D. Reynolds and N. G. Wilson, *Scribes and Scholars: A Guide to the Transmission of Greek and Latin Literature*, 2d ed. (Oxford, 1974), in particular chaps. 2 and 3, pp. 38 ff.

49. Plato, *Apol.* 26D6–9; cf. Eupolis fr. 304 Kock.

50. Diog. Laert. 9.6.

51. Cf. Athen. 1.3b.

52. Galen 15.105.

53. Known as "the salvaged material" (τὰ σῳζόμενα). Galen, *Comm. in Hipp. Epid.* 3, remarks that the rolls were not delivered directly to the libraries, but consigned in the first instance to warehouses, where they were stored "in heaps" (σωρηδόν), a description that should be instantly recognizable to anyone who has examined, say, the accessions basement of the Humanities Research Center in the University of Texas at Austin.

54. Galen 17(1).607.

55. Galen, *Comm. in Hipp. Epidem.* 3, reprinted *in extenso* by Fraser, 2.480–81, cf. 1.325.

56. See Reynolds and Wilson (above, n. 48) 7–15; Pfeiffer, *History* chap. 2, pp. 105 ff.; Fraser 1.320–35; and in particular E. G. Turner, *Greek Papyri: An Introduction* (Oxford, 1968) 100 ff.

57. Pfeiffer, *History* 24 ff., 103.

58. A. Carlini, in Bianchi Bandinelli 5.9.341. contrasts the fourth-century papyrus of Timotheus's *Persians* ("una scrittura rigida, con lettere angolari ancora strettamente legate a modelli epigrafici") with the third-century Flinders Petrie fragments of Plato's *Laches* and *Phaedo*, which "rivelano ormai l'affermazione di una scrittura libraria sciolta ed elegante."

59. See the excellent and sympathetic summary in Pollitt, *AHA* 13–14.

Chapter 7. Early Hellenistic Art and Its Antecedents, 380–270: Space, Pathos, Realism; or, The Horse as Critic

1. M. Robertson 292–94. Aristotle had apparently advised Apelles to commemorate the deeds of Alexander because of their *aeternitatem*: Plin. *HN* 35.106.

2. Plin. *HN* 35.90, Quintil. 2.13.12.

3. Ael. *VH* 2.3; Plin. *Nat. Hist.* 35.85–86, 92, 95. Alexander, still unsatisfied, had himself painted instead as Zeus, complete with thunderbolt.

4. See, e.g., Plato, *Soph.* 235E ff.; Arist. *Pol.* 1281[b]10; Cic. *Inv. Rhet.* 2.1.2–3; Vitruv. 7.5.4–7; other testimonia collected by Pollitt, *Ancient View* 170 ff.

5. Plin. *HN* 35.65–66.

6. See, e.g., the Boscoreale wall painting reproduced in Charbonneaux et al. as fig. 170, with Villard's comments *ad loc.* (pp. 166–67). For the general obsession with theatricality, see Pollitt, *AHA* 5–7.

7. Strabo 14.2.5 (C.652).

8. Protzmann 186: "Die Perspektive verbindet illusionär Bildwelt und Realraum."

9. Plato, *Soph.* 234B–236A, 268C–D; cf. Pollitt, *Ancient View* 46–47.

10. Cf. Plato, *Theaet.* 156A–157C.

11. Plin. *HN* 34.65, "ab illis factos quales essent homines, a se quales uiderentur esse," a distinction that has caused considerable scholarly debate; cf. Pollitt, *Ancient View* 180–82.

12. Cf. Protzmann 169: "Schien es stets klar zu sein, dass auch der Formenwandel in der Kunst als Ausdruck der gesellschaftlichen Krise, als Verfallssymptom der Poliskultur zu gelten habe." I am well aware of the baffling chronological problems confronting historians of Hellenistic art, in the history of sculpture especially: see Pollitt, *AHA* app. 1, 265–71. Dating on stylistic grounds is peculiarly hazardous: "what seems pathetic or realistic to one person may seem comic or rococo to another" (ibid. 270).

13. Pollitt, *Art* 136.

14. Brown, *Anticlassicism* chap. 5, "*Polis* and People," 44–63. Coming across this work only when my own book was in draft, I was encouraged to find so many of my own hypotheses confirmed by it.

15. Dem. 20.70, Paus. 1.24.3.

16. Plut. *Lys.* 18, Paus. 6.3.14–15, Duris *ap.* Athen. 15.696e, Hesych. s.v. Λυσάνδρια.

17. Ferguson, *HA* 8–9.

18. Dinsmoor 233, 240, 244.

19. Ibid. 246–49. Dr. Paul Cartledge reminds me that the height of the water table and consequent flooding are also relevant to the height of the base.

20. Dinsmoor (247) observes, "Comfort was slightly increased by hollowing the face of the seat by 3½ inches to permit the feet to be withdrawn as others passed by, and also by depressing the back half of each seat by 1½ inches for the feet of the occupant above; but even so it must have been necessary to bring cushions." Experience in the theater of Herodes Atticus in Athens, and in the theater at Epidaurus, suggests that this is, if anything, an understatement.

21. Ibid. 240–41.

22. Travlos, *Pictorial Dictionary* 348–51, 562–65; Dinsmoor 236–40 with pls. lix–lx and fig. 87.

23. Dinsmoor 239–40.

24. Ibid. 236 with fig. 86.

25. Dem. 3.29, Paus. 5.20.9; cf. Brown, *Anticlassicism* 52–53.

26. Dinsmoor 251.

27. Ibid. 241–42.

28. See D. J. Blackman in J. S. Morrison and R. T. Williams, *Greek Oared Ships 900–322 B.C.* (Cambridge, 1968) chap. 8, pp. 181–92.

29. Martin, in Charbonneaux et al. 4. There is no denying the vigor, or, indeed, the innovations. Winter, *CAH* VII².1 383, asserts that "probably no other period, either of Greek or of Roman architecture, can advance as impressive a claim to originality as the centuries from *c.* 350 to 100."

30. Vitruv. 7 *praef.* 12, 1.1.12.

31. Dinsmoor 221–23, D. S. Robertson 147–49.

32. Dinsmoor 223–29.

33. Strabo 17.1.43 (C.814), Dinsmoor 229–33.

34. Travlos, *Pictorial Dictionary* 402–11.

35. Finn and Houser 58–69 with the relevant (unnumbered) plates, by far the best color reproductions of these bronzes available.

36. Plin. *HN* 36.20–22, cf. Lucian, *Amor.* 13–14; Bieber 18–19; Pollitt, *Art* 157 and n. 9.

37. R. A. Higgins, *Greek and Roman Jewellery* (London and Berkeley, 1961) 155: the whole chapter on Hellenistic jewelry (chap. 15, 154–70) is of the greatest interest and value.

38. Bieber 124–25, 133, 146–47; Havelock 123, no. 89, which reproduces the late, predominantly feminine, reclining type. See Marie Delcourt, *Hermaphrodite: Mythes et rites de la bisexualité dans l'antiquité classique* (Paris, 1958) 86–103, for an analysis of the surviving representations. Cf. F. R. Walton, *OCD*² 502: a cult of Hermaphroditus existed in Attica in the fourth century. It is just as we would expect that "fourth-century art portrayed Hermaphroditus as a beautiful youth with developed breasts; later art as an Aphrodite with male genitals." The Stockholm and Paris statues portray Demeter-like matrons proudly lifting their peplos to reveal an erect penis (Delcourt 99), a development that should appeal to Freudians. Perhaps this was what Martin Nilsson had in mind when he asserted (1.491 n. 2), "Der Hermaphroditismus ist den ursprünglichen griechischen Vorstellungen so fremd, dass es nicht nötig ist, hier darauf einzugehen." His aversion proved to be so great that he found it "nicht nötig" in vol. 2 as well, where the omission is far less excusable. For a still useful survey of the hermaphrodite in ancient art, cf. P. Herrmann in Roscher's *Lexikon*, 1.2319–40, s.v. "Hermaphroditos."

39. Finn and Houser 92–133 *passim.*

40. Bieber 16–17, figs. 11–12; M. Robertson 386 ff., pl. 125b. As Prof. A. F. Stewart reminds me, "opinion now inclines to a Hellenistic date for the Hermes," though he adds that such a copy (if copy it be) is "probably *after* a Praxitelean bronze(?) of c. 330."

41. M. Robertson 466.

42. If this head is, in fact, by Silanion: Paus. 6.4.5 says that he made a portrait of Satyros,

a five-time Olympic boxing champion; the head is very much in his style, and it is very tempting to identify it as Satyros, but certainty is impossible. Cf. Caroline Houser's sensible remarks in Finn and Houser 36–37.

43. Charbonneaux, in Charbonneaux et al. 212.

44. Plin. *HN* 34.65.

45. Havelock 119; cf. Pollitt, *Art* 174–76, *Ancient View* 14–22; M. Robertson 464.

46. A much-debated work: see Protzmann 182 for conflicting judgments. Cf. Pollitt, *AHA* 47–48.

47. Protzmann 202.

48. Paus. 1.43.6, Plin. *HN* 36.25, Bieber 26 with n. 118.

49. See, e.g., M. Robertson 277 with pl. 60b (Corinthian terra-cotta sculpture), and, for a thorough discussion, H. Sichtermann, *Ganymed: Mythos und Gestalt in der Antiken Kunst* (Berlin, n.d.) 39–52.

50. Mus. Berl. (W)7928, well reproduced in J. Marcadé, *Eros Kalos* (Geneva, 1965) 15. With this compare the very different (and much less erotic) sculpture selected by Bieber, 62–63 and pl. 198. Pliny, *HN* 34.79, describes the eagle in Leochares' work as "conscious of what he was carrying off in Ganymede, and to whom he was taking it, and going easy on the lad with his talons, even through his clothes," which suits the mirror relief peculiarly well.

51. See, e.g., Marcadé (above, n. 50) 13–14, 16–17; Johns 107–9 with color pl. 21.

52. Roman copy in the Capitoline Museum, excellently illustrated in J. Boardman et al., *Art and Architecture of Ancient Greece* (London, 1967) pl. 246.

53. Paus. 1.8.2, 9.16.1–2, cf. Plin. *HN* 34.50, 87; Bieber 14–15; M. Robertson 384–85 with pl. 125a.

54. Bieber 125–26 with nn. 13–16, Charbonneaux et al. 287–88 with pl. 311. M. Robertson 535–36 is hesitant both about the ascription and in ascribing any social significance to changes in the iconography: "This is the grandest of Greek victories, and reminds one of the rashness of such generalisations as that the old themes had lost their power in the new age; but it is true that Victory is always well thought of, certainly not least at this epoch." Unexceptionable in itself, this statement seems to me to sidestep the crucial considerations of context, provenance, and special circumstance.

55. Plin. *HN* 34.58.

56. Protzmann 178–79.

57. Xen. *Mem.* 3.10.1–8.

58. Pollitt, *Art* 143 ff.

59. Webster, *Art* 41 ff., esp. pls. 47, 52, 63.

60. Havelock 19; cf. M. Robertson 504–7.

61. Thuc. 1.132, Hdt. 8.82, Nep. *Paus.* 1, Ps.-Dem. 59.97–98, Plut. *Mor.* 873C–D, *Suda* s.v. Παυσανίας; cf. Meiggs and Lewis no. 27, pp. 57–60.

62. Stewart 121–26.

63. Lullies and Hirmer 58 with pls. 24–25. The name of the dedicator, partially lost, was probably Rhombos.

64. Plin. *HN* 34.83.

65. Ibid. 36.11–12, *Suda* s.v. Ἱππῶναξ.

66. Richter, *Portraits* 1.97–99, 102–4, with figs. 405–8, 429–41; M. Robertson 187 ff., 335 ff., pl. 62d. For a general, and generally judicious, introduction to Greek portraiture, see Pollitt, *AHA* 59 ff. His notion of early portraits as generic "role-model" evocations is plausible, but debatable.

67. Plin. *HN* 34.76, Lucian, *Philops.* 18–20; cf. M. Robertson 504–5, 712 nn. 4–5.

68. Protzmann 177; Pollitt, *Art* 166–68.

69. E.g., by Seltman 221–22, Jenkins 218–21. Cf. R. R. R. Smith, *Hellenistic Royal Portraits* 12–14.

70. Kraay and Hirmer figs. 562, 563, 568 (Philip II), fig. 560 (Amyntas), pl. XVIII (Alexander), fig. 559 (Archelaus), fig. 561 (Perdiccas III); and cf. pp. 348–52. See also Pollitt, *AHA* 25–26.

71. DS 16.92.5.

72. Adams and Borza 119–20, 132, 149–50, 165 ff., with reff. to earlier literature. For Leochares' group in the Philippeion (338/7?), see Paus. 5.20.9.

73. A convenient conspectus is provided by M. Bieber, *Alexander the Great in Greek and Roman Art* (Chicago, 1964): cf. in particular pls. 2.3, 3.5, 6.6–7, 8.13–16, 9.17, 11.19, 15.26–27, 16.28, 17.31, 18.34a–b and 35, 22.43, 29.57, 36.71, 38.114, 42.83–85, 46.92. For the generic "Lysippan" portrait, see Plut. *Alex.* 4, cf. Plin. *HN* 7.125; other sources in F. P. Johnson, *Lysippos* (Durham, N.C., 1927) 301–6. Cf. Pollitt, *AHA* 20–22.

74. Our iconography of the whole Ptolemaic dynasty is, indeed, restricted for the most part to realistic, and often unflattering, coin portraits: once the Successors had established their own royal dynasties, the prejudice against self-representation in most (though not all) cases soon vanished. Ptolemy, Seleucus, and Demetrius Poliorcetes all availed themselves of this excellent medium for self-advertisement. Portrait busts, on the other hand, are rare: for possible exceptions see M. Robertson 515, 523; and I. Jucker, "Ein Bildnis der Arsinoë III Philopator," *HASB* 5 (1979) 5–9 (a bust of Arsinoë III dating from ca. 200).

75. M. Robertson 510–11.

76. Pollitt, *Art* 183. The original Demosthenes was by Polyeuktos; the Aristotle *may* be Lysippan. Pollitt, *AHA* 63, argues on the basis of these two examples that "psychological portraiture" probably originated in Athens.

77. M. Robertson 497. See Quintil. 12.10.6.

78. This assessment of red-figure I owe very largely to correspondence with Prof. A. F. Stewart.

79. Including by Andronikos himself: see *The Search for Alexander: An Exhibition* (Boston, 1980) 30–31.

80. A useful general survey of these Macedonian tombs is provided by Stella G. Miller, "Macedonian Tombs: Their Architecture and Architectural Decoration," in B. Barr-Sharrar and E. N. Borza, eds., *Macedonia and Greece in Late Classical and Early Hellenistic Times*, Studies in the History of Art, vol. 10, (Washington, D.C., 1982) 153–71: see in particular pp. 164–66 for the connection of illusionist architectural painting with the Roman Second Style. On the Great Tomb of Lefkadia, see the fundamental publication by its excavator, Ph. M. Petsas, Ὁ Τάφος τῶν Λευκαδίων (Athens, 1966), and the discussions by M. Robertson 568–72, with further reff., and V. J. Bruno, *Form and Colour in Greek Painting* (London, 1977) 23–30 with pls. 5b–9. The Tomb of the Palmettes is referred to briefly by M. Robertson 571, but the only full discussion remains the original publication by K. Rhomaiopoulou, "A New Monumental Chamber Tomb with Paintings of the Hellenistic Period Near Lefkadia (West Macedonia)," *AAA* 6 (1973) 87–92 with color pl. 1. She remarks of the painting on the roof of the antechamber that the "huge polychrome anthemia among other water flowers and plant motifs on a faded water-like blue ground show a remarkable command of the principles of perspective and the use of transitional tones of colours." On the Vergina tombs, all earlier studies and photographs have been superseded by Manolis Andronikos's sumptuous Βεργίνα: Οἱ Βασιλικοὶ Τάφοι καὶ οἱ ἄλλες Ἀρχαιότητες (Athens, 1984). For the paintings in the main tombs, see pp. 86–95, 100–117, with pls. 46–54, 57–71. For the 1981 excavation and tomb paintings, see pp. 22–24, 35–37, with pls. 12–16 (pl. 16 in particular is an excellent reproduction of the young dead warrior from the second tomb, in a perennial heroic pose, one arm supporting a vertical spear, the other akimbo).

81. Havelock 242–44 pls. VI–VII; Webster, *Art* 23, 66, 89, and pl. 19; M. Robertson 486–89.

82. P. Ducrey and I. R. Metzger, "La maison aux mosaïques à Érétrie," *AK* 22 (1979) 3–21, cf. *Arch.* 32 (1979) 34–42; D. M. Robinson et al., *Excavations at Olynthus*, vol. 8, *The Hellenic House* (Baltimore, 1938) *passim*; M. Robertson, *JHS* 85 (1965) 73 ff., 83 f., with pl. 18.

83. K. Dunbabin, "Technique and Materials of Hellenistic Mosaics," *AJA* 83 (1979) 265–77; Pollitt, *AHA* 21–12.

84. Webster, *Art* 38, 41, pls. 9–10, app. pl. 26; Havelock 191–92 with pls. 150–52; M. Robertson 481 ff. with pls. 151a–c.

85. J. J. Coulton, "Hellenistic Royal Architecture," *PCA* 77 (1980) 21–22.

86. Various attributes of Aphrodite, e.g., passion (ἔρως), desire or yearning (πόθος), longing (ἵμερος), had been represented on Greek vases from the late fifth century; see Brown, *Anticlassicism* 58 with n. 200.

87. See, e.g., the quotations, from Cleidemus and others, gathered by Athenaeus, 14.660d–62d.

88. E.g., by Praxiteles (Plin. *HN* 34.69) and Pausias (Paus. 2.27.3), who portrayed Methe sipping in style from her crystal goblet.

89. Quintil. 12.10.4.

90. Plin. *HN* 35.67–69; cf. Pollitt, *Ancient View* 30–31.

91. M. Robertson 414.

92. Vitruv. 7.5.2–3.

93. "Nature Morte," *Collected Poems* (London, 1966) 21.

94. All three of my chapters on Hellenistic art were written before Pollitt's *AHA* became accessible to me. I was therefore encouraged by the degree to which our conclusions coincided. In particular, Pollitt's tripartite division of the period (p. 17), into the Age of the Diadochoi (ca. 323–275), the Age of the Hellenistic Kingdoms (ca. 275–150), and the Graeco-Roman Phase (ca. 150–31), agrees almost exactly with my own.

Chapter 8. The Division of the Spoils, 301–276

1. Seibert, *Historische Beiträge* 72, argues that Ptolemy was the first Hellenistic ruler who consciously exercised a policy of solidifying alliances through well-placed marriages. In one sense royal incest might be regarded as this policy carried to its logical extreme.

2. Bouché-Leclercq, *HL* 1.101; cf. Joseph. *AJ* 12.2.

3. A good, if in places dated, account of her is provided by Macurdy 104–9. Schol. Theocr. 17.61 Wessner is crucial for establishing her genealogy.

4. Not his first, however: Ptolemy had played his part in the Susa mass marriages of 324 by taking to wife Artabazus's daughter Artacama (Arr. 7.4.6), only to repudiate her soon after Alexander's death. He married Eurydice in 321, in the wake of the Triparadeisos settlement: cf. Seibert, *Historische Beiträge* 16 ff., 72.

5. Theocr. 17.38–40.

6. Longega *passim*; Macurdy 111–30; Burstein, "Arsinoe" 197 ff.

7. Seibert, *Historische Beiträge* 74.

8. Plut. *Demetr.* 30, DS 21.1.4; cf. Manni, *Demetrio* 42 ff. Will, *CAH* VII².1 101, stresses (perhaps overstresses) the total dependence of Demetrius on his father's cool-headed strategy and long-term planning.

9. Shear 72.

10. Demetrius's marital record is interesting. His first wife, who remained loyal through all her husband's political vicissitudes (not to mention his various polygamous and extra-marital excesses), only to kill herself in despair after the retreat to Cassandreia (see p. 127), was Antipater's daughter Phila, fifteen years Demetrius's senior, and the widow of Craterus: Plut. *Demetr.* 14; cf. Wehrli, "Phila" 140 ff. She clearly loved this beautiful and narcissistic young man a good deal more than he did her, since his father, old Antigonus, had to push him into the match with a quotation from Euripides' *Phoenician Women* (396): "Where gain lies, wed one must, against the grain." Subsequent wives included the Athenian Eurydice, Ophellas of Cyrene's widow and a Philaid aristocrat (307), who was clearly linked with Demetrius's ambitions in Greece, and, if Seibert, *Historische Beiträge* 28, is right, in North Africa too; Deidameia, the sister of Pyrrhus (303: Plut. *Demetr.* 25, *Pyrrh.* 4; cf. Lévêque, *Pyrrhos* 104), whose

value lay in her connection with Alexander the Great's line, and who died in 298, in Cilicia; and Lanassa (see p. 126), Agathocles of Sicily's daughter and the ex-wife of Pyrrhus, who brought her husbands the key islands of Corcyra and Leucas as a much-coveted dowry. Demetrius also planned to marry Ptolemaïs, Ptolemy I's daughter by Eurydice, but political circumstances changed too fast, and he broke with Ptolemy (p. 122) before the wedding could take place. This was in 299. However, in 287, Demetrius, who was clearly not the man to forget unfinished business, married Ptolemaïs after all, in curious circumstances (p. 129). Seibert, *Historische Beiträge* 31–33, comments shrewdly on the *ad hoc*, improvisational quality of Demetrius's political marriages, contrasting them with those of Pyrrhus, who practiced a genuine *Heiratspolitik*.

11. Plut. *Demetr.* 31.

12. The number of nubile daughters that these rulers, Antipater in particular, had permanently available for such contingencies never ceases to amaze one. Whoever else might expose unwanted female infants in the ancient world (Pomeroy, *Goddesses* 68 ff., 127), the Successors most assuredly did not.

13. Seibert, *Historische Beiträge* 93–95; Burstein, *Outpost* 82–85; after her repudiation Amastris continued to rule Heracleia in her own right, as well as setting up an independent fief in Paphlagonia; a few years later she was drowned, perhaps on her son's orders (284).

14. Seibert, *Historische Beiträge* 74.

15. Just. 15.4.23 ff.; Plut. *Demetr.* 31–32; Paus. 1.9.6, 10.3; Memnon *FGrH* 434 F 9.

16. *OGIS* 10.

17. Lévêque, *Pyrrhos* 107; cf. n. 10 above.

18. Ibid. 94–105.

19. DS 19.88 ff.; Paus. 1.11.5; Plut. *Pyrrh.* 4, *Demetr.* 31.

20. Lévêque, *Pyrrhos* 107: he "se méfiait de la versatilité bien connue déjà de Démétrios."

21. Plut. *Demetr.* 6.

22. Jacoby, *RE* 10 (1917) col. 2312, s.v. "Kassandros (2)"; Will, *HP*² 1.93.

23. Plut. *Demetr.* 5; Paus. 1.6.8, 11.5; cf. Niese 1.361–62.

24. Plut. *Pyrrh.* 6.

25. Plut. *Demetr.* 36; Just. 15.4.24; Euseb. *Chron.* 1.231 Schoene, whose version of Cassander's death *tabido morbo* (line 16) is more convincing than Pausanias's tale of dropsy and phthiriasis (9.7.2–3, a fate clearly seen, if not invented, as a just retribution from heaven for his alleged hatred of Alexander), especially since Pausanias himself admits consumption (νόσος φθινώδης) as the cause of Philip IV's demise, and the complaint seems to have been hereditary.

26. Plut. *Demetr.* 36, *Pyrrh.* 6; Just. 16.1.1–9; DS 21.7; Paus. 9.7.3.

27. Justin's comment (16.1.3) is revealing: this crime was found all the more abhorrent, he alleges, "because there was no evidence of deception on the mother's part" (*quod nullum maternae fraudis vestigium fuit*): a little *fraus*, one feels, would have been felt to go a long way toward justifying matricide.

28. The parallel is true in more ways than one: *SIG*³ 362 and 374 suggest, despite the polite disclaimers, discreet politicking by the Athenians with Demetrius's opponents, in particular Cassander and Lysimachus.

29. *POxy.* 17.2082 = *FGrH* 257a F. Translation in Burstein, *Translated Documents* no. 5, pp. 5–6. The papyrus, of the second century A.D., has been identified tentatively as an Olympiad chronicle by Phlegon of Tralles.

30. Paus. 1.25.7.

31. Paus. 1.25.7, cf. 29.10; Plut. *Demetr.* 33; Polyaen. 4.7.5, cf. 3.7.

32. Ferguson, *CPh* 24 (1929) 1–20; others listed by Shear 52–53 n. 144.

33. Shear 52 ff.; Habicht, *Untersuchungen* 1–33.

34. *POxy.* 17.2082, combined with Paus. 1.25.7; cf. M. J. Osborne, *JHS* 102 (1982) 273.

35. *POxy.* 10.1235 lines 105–12 = Körte and Thierfelder testim. 28. Ferguson, *CPh* 24

(1929) 12–14, argues convincingly for dating this production to 301/0. Habicht's efforts (*Untersuchungen* 16–21) to downdate as far as 295 are ingenious to a degree, but seem dictated by his main thesis: I do not find them convincing.

36. Plut. *Demetr.* 33: during the siege of Messene he got a crossbow bolt through his jaw.

37. Habicht, *Untersuchungen* 2–13, would postdate all these events by a year, placing Lachares' coup in the spring of 295, and Demetrius's entry into Athens in the spring of 294. I am not persuaded that what Demetrius at first imposed, whatever he may have done later (see p. 126), was the oligarchy referred to in *IG* II² 646, on which Habicht (pp. 5–8) relies for a firm date in Elaphebolion (roughly, March) 294.

38. Cf. Habicht, *Untersuchungen* 66.

39. His subsequent fate is uncertain: according to Pausanias (1.25.7) he was soon murdered for his ill-gotten gains, but Polyaenus (3.7.1–3, 6.7.2) has him alive as late as 279, when we find him being expelled from Cassandreia after an unsuccessful attempt to betray the city to Antiochus I.

40. Plut. *Demetr.* 34.

41. DS 21.9.

42. Plut. *Demetr.* 34, Paus. 1.25.8; cf. Habicht, *Untersuchungen* 103–4 with n. 51.

43. E.g., Shear 53 ff.; Habicht, *Untersuchungen* 22 ff.

44. Shear 53 ff., and Habicht, *Untersuchungen* 4 ff., discussing *IG* II² 643, 646, 647. It hardly needs pointing out that the decree honoring Herodorus (of Cyzicus or Lampsacus) for his part in the negotiated peace is not necessarily (as Habicht seems to assume) coterminous with the peace itself; indeed, it may well have postdated it by months: compare, say, the English Honours List. Thus there is no reason to suppose that *IG* II² 646 of Elaphebolion 294 could not refer to a peace made in 295; indeed, the likelihood lies in that direction.

45. Plut. *Demetr.* 34: κατέστησεν ἀρχὰς αἳ μάλιστα τῷ δήμῳ προσφιλεῖς ἦσαν.

46. *IG* II² 644, 645, 682.21–23; cf. Habicht, *Untersuchungen* 3 ff.

47. Plut. *Pyrrh.* 5; cf. Vartsos, "Ἀκμή" 93 ff.

48. Plut. *Demetr.* 35, cf. 38; *SIG*³ 368.1–9; cf. Will, *HP*² 1.92, who also points out (*CAH* VII².1 108) that Ptolemy—a point seemingly lost on Demetrius—had no intention of resting content with Cyprus, and indeed, at some point between 291 and 287(?), gained control of the League of Islanders.

49. Plut. *Pyrrh.* 6.

50. Paus. 2.10.1–2; Plut. *Demetr.* 36, *Pyrrh.* 6. Cf. Hammond and Walbank 214–15.

51. Plut. *Demetr.* 35, Polyaen. 4.7.9–10, Paus. 1.13.6; cf. Piper 14.

52. Just. 16.1.7–8; Plut. *Demetr.* 36–37, cf. *Pyrrh.* 5.

53. Just. 16.1.10–17.

54. Plut. *Demetr.* 37: βελτίονος δὲ ἀπορεῖν.

55. Plut. *Demetr.* 41–42, *Pyrrh.* 7; cf. Wehrli, "Phila" 144.

56. Plut. *Demetr.* 41; cf. Newell *passim*. On Demetrius's Hellenistic theatricality, see the excellent analysis by Pollitt, *AHA* 6–7; for his probably having been the first ruler to portray himself on his coinage, see Seltman 222.

57. Plut. *Demetr.* 39, Strabo 9.5.15 (C.436).

58. Plut. *Demetr.* 39–41.

59. DS 21.14.1–2, Plut. *Demetr.* 40.

60. Plut. *Demetr.* 43, *Pyrrh.* 7, 10, with Lévêque, *Pyrrhos* 142 ff. See also Schmitt, *Staatsverträge* no. 463, pp. 96–99, for an Aetolian-Boeotian alliance which *may* belong to this period, but could also possibly fit in the context of 301/299, after Ipsus.

61. Plut. *Pyrrh.* 10, cf. 9; Lévêque, *Pyrrhos* 139–42.

62. Macurdy 66–67, and see above, p. 763 n. 10.

63. Plut. *Demetr.* 40.

64. Shear 53–55; Habicht, *Untersuchungen* 28–30.

65. Dion. Hal. *Deinarch.* 3 = *FGrH* 328 F 67.

66. Habicht, *Untersuchungen* 29, analyzes this situation with great percipience: "Auch danach [i.e., after the recall of the oligarchs in 292] war Athen nicht eigentlich ein oligarchisches Staatswesen, aber es gab doch genügend Erscheinungen in diesem Staat, die so bezeichnet werden konnten. Von Demochares und Laches ist ja auch nicht die Terminologie von Verfassungsrechtlern zu erwarten; sie formulierten und schrieben in der politischen Sprache der radikalen Demokraten, und von ihrem Standpunkt aus hatten sie durchaus Grund, die Jahre zwischen 294 und 287 als eine Periode der Oligarchie zu bezeichnen."

67. Demochares *ap.* Athen. 6.253c–d.

68. Cited by Duris of Samos, ibid. 253d–f. = *FGrH* 76 F 13. Translation, with further refs., in Burstein, *Translated Documents* no. 7, pp. 8–9.

69. Cf. DS 21.9.

70. Mossé, *Athens* 124.

71. Plut. *Demetr.* 43. Plutarch's claim that Demetrius was planning a large-scale invasion of Asia is not perhaps so fanciful as some scholars have assumed. Cf. Walbank, *CAH* VII². 1 108 with n. 26; and Hammond and Walbank 226–27, with a percipient analysis of the numismatic evidence.

72. Plut. *Demetr.* 44; Just. 16.2.1–2, cf. Plut. *Pyrrh.* 11.

73. Will, *HP*² 1.94–96; Shear 78 with n. 217.

74. Plut. *Pyrrh.* 11–12, *Demetr.* 44, Paus. 1.10.2, Just. 16.3.1–2. Oros. 3.23.54–55; Cic. *De Offic.* 2.26. The date is disputed. Hammond and Walbank 229 n. 1 argue for an invasion in 287 rather than 288. But the earlier date is supported by the narrative of Plut. *Demetr.* 45–46; and Habicht's argument, *Untersuchungen* 60 n. 63, that Athens could not have delayed nine months after Demetrius's defeat before revolting (the date of the revolt is independently secure at June 287) I find less than convincing. The Athenians at this point were quite capable of such nervous wait-and-see procrastination.

75. Plut. *Demetr.* 42: there is a telling anecdote here of his collecting written petitions from his subjects, only to dump them contemptuously in the Axius River as he crossed it.

76. Plut. *Demetr.* 44–45, *Pyrrh.* 11; cf. Cavafy, Ποιήματα Αʹ 27 = *Collected Poems* 40–41: "Behaving like an actor / Who, the show once over, / Changes his clothes and leaves."

77. Plut. *Demetr.* 45; cf. Agora Inv. I 7295 (the Callias Decree) lines 16–18, with Shear 16 and n. 25. For the Callias Decree in general, see Burstein, *Translated Documents* no. 55, pp. 74–76.

78. Plut. *Pyrrh.* 12, Paus. 1.10.2.

79. Plut. *Demetr.* 46; Paus. 1.26.1–3; *IG* II² 666, 667; the Callias Decree (above, n. 77), esp. lines 11–15; cf. Shear 14 ff., 19 ff., and chaps. 3–5, pp. 61–86; Habicht, *Untersuchungen* chap. 4, pp. 45–62.

80. Habicht, *Untersuchungen* 51–60, against Shear 52 ff. and chap. 3, arguing for 286.

81. Callias Decree (above, n. 77) lines 24–27, *IG* II² 682 lines 35–36; cf. Habicht, *Untersuchungen* 52.

82. *IG* II² 682 lines 32–35; περιστάντων τεῖ πόλει καιρῶν δυσκόλων. . . .

83. Plut. *Demetr.* 46; cf. Shear 54 with nn. 150–53.

84. Paus. 1.26.1–3, cf. 29.13; *IG* II² 666 lines 9–15, cf. Shear 15. Pausanias's reference to Olympiodorus recovering Piraeus and Munychia is clearly separate from this account, and must refer to a different occasion: Habicht, *Untersuchungen* 102–7, plausibly assigns it to an occasion in the Four Years' War (307–304). Cf. Ferguson, *HA* 144–45.

85. Cf. *IG* II² 650.

86. Plut. *Demetr.* 46; cf. *Pyrrh.* 12.

87. Callias Decree (above, n. 77) line 30.

88. Shear 75.

89. Callias Decree (above, n. 77) lines 34–37, *IG* II² 682 lines 36 ff.

90. *IG* II² 682 lines 21–22. Note that his appointment, even under Lachares, involved him in being ὑπὸ τοῦ δήμου χειροτονηθείς, a patent rubber-stamp formality that tends to support those (e.g., Shear 70 with n. 199; Tarn, *Antigonus* 46; Mackendrick 39) who take a

cynical view of the realities behind such democratic phraseology under a restrictive regime. *Contra*, Habicht, *Untersuchungen* 55 ff.

91. Habicht, *Untersuchungen* 58–60, with a highly convincing supplement of the erased matter; and *Studien* 147–50, relating this act to the general *damnatio memoriae* of Philip V and his ancestors described by Livy, 31.44.1–9. Cf. above, p. 309.

92. Ibid. 62 ff., against Shear, chap. 4, pp. 74 ff., who regards it rather (cf. below) as a quadripartite agreement between Seleucus, Ptolemy, Lysimachus, and Pyrrhus.

93. Shear 76–78.

94. Plut. *Mor.* 851E.

95. Demetrius, perhaps as part of the agreement, did nevertheless retain his naval base at Miletus: Plut. *Demetr.* 48; cf. Shear 78.

96. Shear 78 with n. 217.

97. Plut. *Pyrrh.* 12.

98. Plut. *Demetr.* 46 ff.

99. This identification, however, is highly speculative. The figures have also been identified as, e.g., Phila and Antigonus Gonatas (Villard, in Charbonneaux et al. 134–35): the sex of the left-hand figure is ambiguous. M. Robertson, 572–73, thinks rather in terms of allegorical figures.

100. So Ferguson, *HA* 151; Tarn, *Antigonus* 100 with n. 21; and others; *contra*, Shear 86 with n. 235, whose dating of the Athens revolt in 286 necessitates a wholesale revision of the chronology relevant to Demetrius's final campaign and end.

101. Plut. *Demetr.* 50: μιαρὸν . . . καὶ βάρβαρον.

102. Ibid. 52. As Will says (*HP²* 1.95), "Plutarque ne manque pas de philosopher sur cette triste fin."

103. Cf. the summing-up by Manni, *Demetrio* 61 ff., who observes: "ardito e audace, non sempre seppe misurare le proprie possibilità." A similar estimate by Will, *CAH* VII².1 101–3, 108–9.

104. Plut. *Dem. Ant. Comp.* 6. Cf. Will, *CAH* VII².1 109.

105. Ps.-Plut. *Vit. X Orat.* 851E; *IG* II² 650, 651, 653, 654, 655, 662, 663; cf. Habicht, *Untersuchungen* 51–52, Shear 79–82. Ferguson, *HA* 146–47, though outdated in some respects, is still useful: see, e.g., 147 n. 4 for the interesting suggestion that gifts sent by Demetrius of Phaleron from Alexandria to Athens (Plut. *Mor.* 601F) belong to this period.

106. Polyaen. 5.17.1, Paus. 1.29.10; cf. Shear 82–83.

107. *IG* II² add. 5227a, lines 5–6.

108. Plut. *Pyrrh.* 12, Paus. 1.10.2, Just. 16.3.1–2, Polyaen. 4.12.3, *SIG³* 361; cf. Lévêque, *Pyrrhos* 164 ff.

109. Paus. 1.12.1, Just. 25.4.8.

110. Lévêque, *Pyrrhos* 178 ff.

111. Just. 16.2.4–5; cf. Shear 82 n. 225.

112. Tarn, *Antigonus* 113–14 with n. 4.

113. Ael. *VH* 12.25; cf. Tarn, *Antigonus* 34–36.

114. Will, *HP²* 1.96–97.

115. Plut. *Demetr.* 52–53.

116. Just. 17.1.3–6, Memnon *FGrH* 434 F 5–6, Paus. 1.10.3–4, Strabo 13.4.1 (C.623); cf. Longega 44–54, who regards Memnon as the most reliable of our sources; Macurdy 55–58, 113–14; and Heinen, *Untersuchungen* 7 ff.

117. *CAH* VII 97; cf. *Antigonus* 123.

118. Paus. 1.10.3, citing various (unnamed) writers for his information (ἤδη δὲ ἔγραψαν, etc.).

119. Memnon *FGrH* 434 F 5–6; cf. Tarn, *Antigonus* 125. App. *Syr.* 62 does not, as is sometimes claimed (e.g., by Macurdy 57 with n. 145), mean that Keraunos accompanied his sister to Seleucus, in the circumstances a wholly illogical step for him.

120. Just. 17.1.7–12, 2.1; App. *Syr.* 62, 64; Memnon *FGrH* 434 F 5.7; Paus. 1.10.5. For the date, see Will, *HP²* 1.103.

121. Paus. 1.10.5.

122. Polyaen. 8.57; cf. Macurdy 114.

123. App. *Syr.* 62.

124. Tarn, *Antigonus* 129 with n. 39. The murder was widely recorded in antiquity; see, e.g., Memnon *FGrH* 434 F 8.3; App. *Syr.* 62; Strabo 13.4.1 (C.623); Paus. 1.16.2, 10.19.7. Cf. Hammond and Walbank 243 with n. 4.

125. Just. 17.2.4–8, 24.2–3.

126. Trog. *prol.* 24.5.

127. Tarn, *Antigonus* 131–33.

128. Ibid. 139 ff.; Will, *HP*[2] 1.105–7, and see *CAH* VII[2].1 114–15. For the Gauls' crossing into Asia, cf. Memnon *FGrH* 434 F 11.1–7 = Burstein, *Translated Documents* no. 16, pp. 21–22. Honors to a citizen of Priene for mobilizing defenses against the Gauls' depredations: *OGIS* 765 = Burstein, *Translated Documents* no. 17, pp. 22–24.

129. Just. 24.5.1–7, DS 22.3.4, Paus. 10.19.7.

130. Tarn, *Antigonus* 147; cf. above, p. 134; Heinen, *Untersuchungen* 58 with no. 217.

131. Paus. 1.4, 10.19–23; Polyb. 4.46; Memnon *FGrH* 434 F 8, 11; cf. Tarn, *Antigonus* 155–59. See also DS 22.3–4, 9; Just. 25.1–2.

132. Just. 24.1.2, 7; Plut. *Mor.* 850F. On Areus's activities, see Piper 15; Hammond and Walbank 249–50, with reff.

133. Tarn, *Antigonus* 161. Antiochus I's anti-Macedonian stance won him instant popularity among the Greek cities of Asia Minor: see, e.g., the honorific decree of Ilion, shortly after his accession, *OGIS* 219 = Burstein, *Translated Documents* no. 15, pp. 20–21; *OGIS* 223 = Burstein, *Translated Documents* no. 23, pp. 30–31, an acknowledgment by Antiochus I (or II) of honors paid him by Erythrae.

134. Euseb. *Chron.* 1.235–36 Schoene, Just. 24.5.12–14, DS 22.4. Cf. Hammond and Walbank 254–55, and for the date of Sosthenes' death, app. 2, 580–81.

135. Polyaen. 2.29.1, Front. *Strat.* 3.6.7.

136. Just. 25.1.2–10, 2.1–7; Diog. Laert. 2.141; cf. Tarn, *Antigonus* 165.

137. Will, *HP*[2] 1.110 with reff.

138. Tarn, *Antigonus* 137 ff.

139. Merker, "Silver Coinage" 39 ff.; Tarn, *Antigonus* 174 and n. 20.

PART TWO. THE ZENITH CENTURY, 276–222 B.C.

Chapter 9. Ptolemy Philadelphos and Antigonus Gonatas, 276–239

1. See, e.g., Tarn, *Antigonus* 412 ff.; Préaux, *Monde* 1.88–89; Bengtson, *Griechische Geschichte* 399–400. A judicious general survey of sources is now offered by Walbank, *CAH* VII[2].1 chap. 1, pp. 1–22. As he says, "only the literary sources can furnish a consecutive narrative," adding, "but this is often flat and jejune." *Verb. sap.*

2. Paus. 1.9.8, 13.9; cf. Hornblower, chap. 5, pp. 180–233.

3. Africa, *Phylarchus* chap. 1, pp. 1–13; cf. Tarn, *Antigonus* 413–14; E. Gabba, "Studi su Filarco: Le biographie plutarchee di Agide e di Cleomene," *Athenaeum*, n.s., 35 (1957) 3–55, 193–239.

4. Polyb. 2.56–63 *passim*; cf. 2.40.4 for his defense of Aratus.

5. Plut. *Dem.* 3, *Demetr.* 18, *Cleom.* 13, 16; cf. Austin 3.

6. Cf. A. E. Wardman, *Plutarch's Lives* (London, 1974) 194.

7. E.g., Strabo 8.7.3 (C.385) on the Achaean League; Paus. 2.9.1–3, 8.49.4–6 on Cleomenes III.

8. Polyb. 2.37–71 *passim*.

9. Most useful general collections: *SIG*[3] and *OGIS*; Hunt and Edgar, vols. 1, 2; Page; Welles, *Royal Correspondence*; Schmitt, *Staatsverträge*; Moretti, *Iscrizioni*; and, in translation, with a valuable up-to-date commentary, Austin. Turner, *CAH* VII[2].1 118–19, rightly stresses

the patchiness of the papyri, their local limitations, and the fact that a great deal of what has been found still remains unpublished.

10. Préaux, *Monde* 1.106–10; Davis and Kraay *passim*; Jenkins 211 ff.; Hadley 50–65; Newell *passim*. Specialist studies are innumerable. For the Indo-Bactrian literature see p. 818.

11. Welles, *Alexander* 75.

12. Will, *HP²* 1.135 ff. For a revealing treaty between Antiochus I (or perhaps II) and the strategic city of Lysimacheia in Thrace, see Burstein, *Translated Documents* no. 22, pp. 29–30, with further documentation. Satraps in the east had been showing signs of independence ever since Eumenes' defeat in 316: see Holt, *Alexander* 96 ff., for local coinage issues minted by, and in the names of, the satraps themselves.

13. Bouché-Leclercq, *HL* 1.141 ff.; Bevan, *House of Ptolemy* chap. 3, pp. 56 ff. Both these accounts are obsolete in many respects, but have yet to be superseded as overviews of Philadelphos's reign.

14. Jaehne, "Syrische Frage" 501 ff.: "Der eigentliche Konfliktstoff der 'syrischen Frage' lag im Bereich des Ökonomischen."

15. Larsen, *Greek Federal States* 80, 196.

16. Memnon *FGrH* 434 F 7; App. *Mithr.* 9; DS 20.111.4; Rostovtzeff, *SEH* 1.26–27, 566 ff., 571 ff., 585 ff.; Magie 1.177 ff., 302 ff.

17. Livy 38.16, Strabo 12.5.1 (C.566–67), Paus. 10.23.14, Just. 25.2.8–11; cf. Will, *HP²* 1.143–44, for epigraphic evidence and the copious modern scholarship; also *CAH* VII p. 702.

18. Tarn, *Antigonus* 144–46.

19. For Antigonus's appearance, and the meaning of the epithet "Gonatas," see Sen. *De Ira* 3.22.4; cf. C. Edson, *CPh* 29 (1934) 254–55, *CAH* VII p. 94, and E. L. Brown in *Arktouros* (Berlin and New York, 1979) 299–307, esp. 304 ff. For the connection with Pan, in particular on Antigonus's coinage, see Merker, "Silver Coinage" 39–52; Tarn, *Antigonus* 174 with nn. 19–20; Theocr. 7.111–12; and above, p. 141.

20. Just. 25.1.1; cf. *OGIS* 219 lines 13 ff.; Tarn, *Antigonus* 168; Will, *HP²* 1.143. Phila was also Antigonus's niece, since his sister, Stratonice, Antiochus's wife, was formerly married— one more family complication—to Antiochus's father, Seleucus Nicator.

21. Tarn, *Antigonus* 175–76.

22. Ibid. chap. 8, pp. 223 ff.; cf. *CAH* VII 203 ff.

23. Diog. Laert. 7.6–9: though the exchange of letters between king and philosopher is clearly a late rhetorical forgery, there is no reason to doubt that the invitation was in fact issued and refused. See also Chrysippus *ap.* Plut. *Mor.* 1043C.

24. Paus. 2.8.4, 7.8.3. An alternative version of events has him escape: Hermippus *ap.* Athen. 4.162d.; cf. Polyaen. 6.5, followed by Tarn, *Antigonus* 398 n. 9.

25. Ael. *VH* 2.20; cf. Tarn, *Antigonus* 254–56 with n. 122; and Béranger 3–16, who suggests that this concept also reflects the vicissitudes suffered by city-state rulers determined (in however limited a form) to preserve their freedom in the new world of the Macedonian conquistadors.

26. Stob. *Flor.* 7.20, 49.20; cf. Plut. *Mor.* 360C.

27. Diog. Laert. 2.141–42.

28. Cf. Hornblower chap. 1, pp. 5–17; chap. 3, pp. 76 ff.; chap. 5, pp. 180 ff.

29. Diog. Laert. 4.46–57 *passim*; cf. Tarn, *Antigonus* 234–39; Dudley, *History* 62–69, 89–92. Bion, who made sharp comments on Pyrrhus *qua* tomb robber, was not above jeering at Gonatas's flight on that occasion: a more than usually privileged court jester, it would seem. See Teles' diatribe on poverty, cited by Walbank *CAH* VII².1 224.

30. Quoted by Cicero, *Tusc. Disp.* 3.26. Bion's homely bromides (e.g., "Don't blame fate, blame yourself," the direct ancestor of "The fault, dear Brutus, is not in our stars / But in ourselves") inevitably gave rise to the charge that he was a mere charlatan, peddling platitude as diatribe; much of this animus seems to have come, as we might expect, from the pretentious intellectuals whom he ridiculed: cf. Dudley, *History* 91–92.

31. DS 16.92.5; cf. p. 403.

32. *Suda* s.v. Ἀντίπατρος.

33. Plut. *Pyrrh*. 26, Paus. 1.13.2, Just. 25.3.1–5; cf. Niese 2.54 ff.; Tarn, *Antigonus* 259 ff.; Lévêque, *Pyrrhos* 557 ff.

34. Just. 25.3.7–8.

35. DS 11.2.12; Plut. *Pyrrh*. 26; cf. Lévêque, *Pyrrhos* 508–9, Hammond and Walbank 262.

36. Just. 25.4.4–10, Plut. *Pyrrh*. 26.

37. Just. 25.4.4.

38. Plut. *Pyrrh*. 26–30, Paus. 1.13.6–7, Just. 25.4.6–10, Polyaen. 8.49; cf. Lévêque, *Pyrrhos* 592 ff.

39. Paus. 1.13.7; cf. Tarn, *Antigonus* 271 ff.; Lévêque, *Pyrrhos* 606–8.

40. Plut. *Pyrrh*. 30, Polyaen. 8.68, Just. 25.5.1.

41. Plut. *Pyrrh*. 32, Polyaen. 8.68. The evidence for these events is highly confused and contradictory; the best analysis is still that of Lévêque, *Pyrrhos* 613 ff.

42. Plut. *Pyrrh*. 32–34, Paus. 1.13.8, Polyaen. 8.68, Just. 25.5.1–2; cf. Lévêque, *Pyrrhos* 622 ff. The incident may also have created a topos. Hornblower 104 observes that "the victor weeping over the vanquished is a motif of Hellenistic historiography of which this is apparently the first instance," and cites later parallels: Antiochus and Achaeus, Scipio at the burning of Carthage, Octavian lamenting Antony, Aemilius Paullus moralizing over the downfall of Perseus, etc. (Polyb. 8.20.10, 29.20.1–4, 38.20.1, 21.1–3, 22; Plut. *Ant*. 78).

43. Tarn, *Antigonus* 277.

44. *IG* II² 683, 677 (= *SIG*³ 401). For the date (in Hieron's archonship) see Habicht, *Studien* 70; for the erection of stelai I accept A. N. Kontoleon's supplement [στήλ]ας replacing Lolling's [γράφ]ας. Cf. Habicht, *Untersuchungen* 71 with n. 18.

45. Cf. Habicht, *Untersuchungen* 68, 108.

46. Grimal 133.

47. Longega 71 ff.; Burstein, "Arsinoë" 200 ff.; cf. Just. 24.1.3, Paus. 1.7.1. Good reproductions of the coins in Jenkins nos. 558, 564; and in Davis and Kraay nos. 15, 18, 20, 21, 22.

48. Fraser 2.367 n. 228; cf. Burstein, "Arsinoë" 202 n. 27.

49. Theocr. 17.128–30; cf. Koenen, in Van't Dack et al. 157–58.

50. For a sensible modification of the extreme views taken, e.g., by Macurdy 118–19, Bevan, *House of Ptolemy* 60–61, Tarn, *Antigonus* 262–63 (cf. Tarn and Griffith 16–17), and Longega *passim*, see Burstein, "Arsinoë" 203 ff., and Pomeroy, *Women* 17–18, who, while confirming Burstein's assessment of the evidence, reminds us that "older siblings often maintain their authority over younger ones, even if the older one is female and the younger one male." For a renewed (but not generally convincing) vindication of Arsinoë's supposed influence on foreign policy (itself here excellently analyzed for the period of Ptolemy II's reign), see Hans Hauben, "Arsinoé II et la politique extérieure de l'Égypte," in Van't Dack et al. 99–127.

51. Paus. 1.7.3; F. Koepp, "Über die syrischen Kriege der ersten Ptolemäer," *RhM* 39 (1884) 209–30, followed by Bouché-Leclercq, *HL* 1.171 ff., and Jaehne "Syrische Frage" 501 ff.; cf. Heinen, *CAH* VII².1 416–17. His argument that the great procession described by Callixeinos (Chap. 10, pp. 158–60) was to celebrate the successful conclusion of the First Syrian War has been disproved by Foertmeyer (see below, Chap. 10, n. 19).

52. Will, *HP*² 1.139–42.

53. He may already have had control of Miletus at the time of Demetrius Poliorcetes' move there from Athens (above, Chap. 8, with n. 98). In the confused circumstances of 262, with Antigonus Gonatas operating in the Aegean, we find Ptolemy at some pains to reward, and prolong, the loyalty of key ports such as Miletus: see Welles, *Royal Correspondence* no. 14 = Burstein, *Translated Documents* 95, pp. 120–21.

54. Paus. 1.7.2, Polyaen. 2.28.

55. Theocr. 17.85–94.

56. *CAH* VII 653, 823.

57. Will, *HP*² 1.220–21.

58. While economic considerations may have had some weight in bringing about the Chremonidean War—so, e.g., Rostovtzeff, *SEH* 1.215 ff; Tarn, *Antigonus* 219 ff.: Ptolemy wanted to make Piraeus "his main clearing-house," while the Athenians were anxious to safeguard their grain imports—it seems clear that the immediate motivation, on all sides, was political and diplomatic: cf. Will, *HP*² 1.219 ff., esp. 222. But both on economic and on political grounds, Macedonian control of Piraeus, then as always, was a standing invitation to direct intervention. See Habicht, *Untersuchungen* 108–9.

59. In 282/1 an honorific decree referred, hopefully, to a time when "Piraeus and City shall be one again": Moretti, *Iscrizioni* 1.14, p. 28; cf. Meritt, *Hesperia* 7 (1938) 100–102, no. 18, lines 28–31; and Habicht, *Untersuchungen* 99.

60. Cf. Hegesander *ap*. Athen. 6.250f.

61. Heinen, *Untersuchungen* 97–100; Walbank, *CAH* VII².1 236 ff.; Hammond and Walbank 276–89. Main sources: Paus. 3.6.4–6; Just. 26.2.1–8.

62. *IG* II² 686–87 = *SIG*³ 434–45; Schmitt, *Staatsverträge* 476, pp. 129–33; Austin 49, pp. 95–97; Bagnall and Derow 19, pp. 39–41; Paus. 3.6.4–8. See also Burstein, *Translated Documents* no. 56, pp. 77–80.

63. Mossé, *Athens* 127.

64. Tarn, *JHS* 54 (1934) 37, cited by Habicht, *Untersuchungen* 112. On the war in general, see Heinen, *Untersuchungen* 97–202; and Will, *HP*² 1.219–28.

65. Burstein, "Arsinoë" 208; Rostovtzeff, *SEH* 1.215 ff.; Walbank, *CAH* VII².1 237–38.

66. Plut. *Agis* 3; cf. Paus. 3.6.6.

67. Plut. *Mor*. 183C, 545C; Mosch. *ap*. Athen. 5.209e. For the date, cf. Walbank, *CAH* VII².1 239–40. Hammond and Walbank 291, and app. 4, "The Battles of Cos and Andros" 587–600, esp. 595 ff., now suggest 255 as an alternate date, but their arguments are not conclusive. Gonatas is said to have asked, on learning that Ptolemy's fleet outnumbered his own, "How many ships is my presence worth?" The Ptolemaic capture of Ephesus (lost again ca. 258): Orth 130 ff.; cf. Heinen, *CAH* VII².1 418.

68. Similarly Stalin, with equal lack of compunction, let the Greek Communists go to their doom in 1949. For such help as Ptolemy offered Athens (mainly through the agency of his admiral Patroclus), see Walbank, *CAH* VII².1 238–39.

69. Paus. 3.6.6; Apollod. *FGrH* 244 F 44. For the date of surrender "in the archonship of Antipater," see Walbank, *CAH* VII².1 238 and n. 32. Cf. Burstein, *Translated Documents* no. 58 (pp. 80–81).

70. Will, *HP*² 1.228–31, with further literature; Habicht, *Studien* 55–59.

71. Habicht, *Studien* 34–47, who argues strongly that Athens retained the right to mint her own coins; Hammond and Walbank 286–87. The quotation is from Louis MacNeice, "Autumn Journal," in *Collected Poems* (London, 1966) 118.

72. Rostovtzeff, *SEH* 1.37.

73. The Borsippa inscription, in cuneiform, on a cylinder seal: translated by L. Oppenheim in J. B. Pritchard's *Ancient Near Eastern Texts*, 2d ed. (Princeton, 1955), 317. It is noteworthy that Seleucus had never styled himself "Great King." Cf. Musti, "Stato" 100.

74. Strabo 13.4.1 (C.623; cf. Paus. 1.8.1) claims that Philetairos, as a baby, was so crushed in a crowd while being carried by his nurse as to be maimed or castrated (πηρωθῆναι), a peculiarly implausible story, in all likelihood no more trustworthy than Carystius's claim (*ap*. Athen. 13.577b) that he was the son of a prostitute. He was eighty at the time of his death: Lucian, *Macrob*. 12.

75. Strabo 13.4.1–2 (C.624); cf. Hansen 21–22.

76. Euseb. *Chron*. 1.249 Schoene.

77. Bouché-Leclercq, *HS* 1.72–73; Bevan, *House of Seleucus* 1.169.

78. Phylarchus *ap*. Athen. 10.438c, Ael. *VH* 2.41.

79. Tarn, *Antigonus* 315–17.

80. Will, *HP*² 1.234–39; Préaux, *Monde* 1.141–42, with further literature; Jaehne, "Syrische Frage" 506. See also Heinen, *CAH* VII².1 418–19.

81. Tarn, *Antigonus* 364 ff.

82. Trog. *prol.* 26; *Suda* s.v. Ἐυφορίων; cf. Will, *HP*² 1.316–17. On the disputed date, see Walbank, *CAH* VII².1 247, with n. 69 and further literature there cited, esp. Urban, *Wachstum* 14 ff.

83. *OGIS* 226, App. *Syr.* 65.

84. Hieron. *In Dan.* 11.6; cf. Will, *HP*² 1.239–42.

85. *OGIS* 225 = Welles, *Royal Correspondence* 18–20; Burstein, *Translated Documents* no. 24, pp. 31–32; Austin 185, pp. 305–7; Bagnall and Derow 25, pp. 48–49.

86. App. *Syr.* 65, Phylarchus *ap.* Athen. 13.593c–d.

87. Jaehne, "Syrische Frage" 508. On the Third Syrian (or Laodicean) War, see Heinen, *CAH* VII².1 420–21.

88. Just. 27.1.7; Polyaen. 8.50; *FGrH* 160 = Austin 220, pp. 363–64; Bagnall and Derow 27, pp. 50–52.

89. Just. 27.2.1, Euseb. *Chron.* 1.251 Schoene.

90. *OGIS* 54 = Austin 221, pp. 365–66; Bagnall and Derow 27, pp. 50–52; Hieron. *In Dan.* 11.7–9. See also Burstein, *Translated Documents* no. 98, pp. 123–25; no. 99, pp. 125–26.

91. Jaehne, "Syrische Frage" 507; Will, *HP*² 1.235–38. The sources are Trog. *prol.* 27 and Plut. *Pelop.* 2, neither of which permits us to date this naval battle with precision. Other suggestions (see Will ibid.) range from 259/8 (Momigliano) to Manni's theory that there were two battles of Andros, the second during the reign of Antigonus Doson. Walbank, *CAH* VII².1 248–49, adds nothing new to the debate. On the insurrections and financial problems of the 240s in Egypt, see Turner, *CAH* VII².1 158–59.

92. Polyb. 5.58.10 ff. The strategic and commercial value of Seleucia-in-Pieria was enormous: Jaehne, "Syrische Frage" 509 ff. It had, indeed, originally been Seleucus's capital: Musti, "Stato" 106.

93. Will, *HP*² 1.294–95.

94. Hansen 28. For Eumenes I's support of the Platonic Academy and the Peripatetics in Athens see Diog. Laert. 4.38, 5.67; cf. Pollitt, *AHA* 79.

95. Diog. Laert. 4.38, 5.67; cf. Pollitt, *AHA* 79.

96. Livy 38.16, Polyb. 18.41.7–8, Strabo 13.4.2 (C.624).

97. Plut. *Pelop.* 2.

98. Plut. *Arat.* 17, Polyaen. 4.6.1; cf. Walbank, *Aratus* 42–43; Tarn, *Antigonus* 372–73. Gonatas arranged a marriage between Alexander's widow, Nicaea, now threatened by the Aetolians, and his son, Demetrius. While the festivities, attended by most of the garrison troops from the fortress, were at their height, he slipped away, strode up to the top of Acrocorinth (no mean feat for a knock-kneed septuagenarian, as anyone who has done the climb can testify), banged on the gates, and was admitted by the bemused guards, so that the almost impregnable fortress fell into Macedonian hands once more. The citadel once secured, Gonatas went back down into town, understandably cheerful, and joined in the celebrations with some abandon, shaking hands and drinking toasts all round.

99. Plut. *Arat.* 9, Polyb. 2.43.3; cf. Tarn, *Antigonus* 362–63; Walbank, *Aratus* 32 ff., 176–77. For the League's earlier history, cf. the useful summary by Walbank, *CAH* VII².1 243 ff. A full account, somewhat marred by excessive skepticism as regards the admittedly sparse evidence, is provided by R. Urban, *Wachstum und Krise des achäischen Bundes: Quellenstudien zur Entwicklung des Bundes von 280 bis 222 v.Chr.* (Wiesbaden, 1979). See the review by Briscoe, *CR*, n.s., 31 (1981) 89–90.

100. Plut. *Arat.* 16, 18–24; Polyaen. 6.5; cf. Tarn, *Antigonus* 396 ff.; Walbank, *Aratus* 45 ff., and *CAH* VII².1 251, where he observes, correctly, that "at one blow Aratus had thus wholly reversed the balance of power in southern Greece."

101. Larsen, *Greek Federal States* 215–40, 305 ff.; cf. Polyb. 2.43.4–6.

102. Plut. *Arat.* 15. Ptolemy's arrangements to establish himself as Aratus's paymaster are

described ibid. 13: 40 talents down, a further 110 by installments. Cf. Walbank, *CAH* VII².1 246–47.

103. Will, *HP²* 1.325–28.

104. Polyb. 2.43.10, 9.34.6, and esp. 18.4.8–5.2.

105. Polyb. 2.45.1; 9.34.7, 38.9. On the falsity of this claim see Urban, *Wachstum* 97 ff.

106. Plut. *Arat.* 24.

107. Tarn, *Antigonus* 403–4; Plut. *Arat.* 31–32, *Agis* 14–15.

108. Tarn, *Antigonus* 403–4.

109. Plut. *Arat.* 25.

110. Ibid. 33: τοὺς . . . ᾿Αθηναίους σπουδάζων ἐλευθερῶσαι.

111. Ibid.: ὥσπερ οἱ δυσέρωτες.

112. On the period before Agis's accession, see Plut. *Agis* 3; cf. Piper 23 ff. For Agis's reign: Plut. *Agis* 13–21 *passim*; cf. Shimron, *Late Sparta* 14–27; Fuks, "Spartan Citizen-Body" 244 ff.; Walbank, *CAH* VII².1 252 ff., who makes the realistic assessment that "Agis' primary aim was probably to win power for Sparta and glory for himself." The best account of these events is now that by Piper, chap. 2, pp. 25–41, with full documentation: note in particular her judgment on Agis (pp. 40–41), that his experiment was "a revolution from the top," and that he "was no more a socialist than Lycurgus."

Chapter 10. The New Urban Culture: Alexandria, Antioch, Pergamon

1. Giuliano, *Urbanistica* 129. The available evidence for study of such conurbations in antiquity covers a wide field, ranging through on-site topographical and archaeological exploration (including aerial photography) to inscriptions, coins, and literary references, both contemporary and late-antiquarian (in the latter category notably Strabo and Pausanias).

2. Rostovtzeff, *CAH* VIII 600–601.

3. Daphitas, a third-century satirist, described the Attalids (probably in the person of Attalus I) as "purple clots, filed scraps from Lysimachus's treasure," a clear reference to Philetairos's embezzlement of 9,000 talents entrusted to his care (p. 132): he was crucified for his pains. See Strabo 14.1.39 (C.647), and, for a variant version of the incident, *Suda* s.v. Δαφίτας.

4. See, e.g., André Parrot, *Nineveh and Babylon* (London, 1961) 170 ff.; and esp. A. L. Oppenheim, *Ancient Mesopotamia* (Chicago, 1964) chap. 2, pp. 74–142.

5. J. Boardman, *The Greeks Overseas*, 3d ed. (London, 1980), 38–54, 130–31, 165–66; *CAH* II³.2, chap. 21(b), pp. 130 ff.

6. E.g., Hdt. 1.45–56 *passim*; 6.37, 125.

7. Canonized by Philo of Byzantium in his *De Septem Mundi Miraculis* (ed. Hercher: Paris, 1858).

8. Giuliano, *Urbanistica* 131–32.

9. Herodas, *Mim.* 1.26–35.

10. Theocr. 17.13 ff., 77 ff., 106 ff.

11. A. T. Olmstead, *A History of the Persian Empire* (Chicago, 1948) 297–99.

12. Theocr. 17.116–17: τί δὲ κάλλιον ἀνδρί κεν εἴη / ὀλβίῳ ἢ κλέος ἐσθλὸν ἐν ἀνθρώποισιν ἀρέσθαι;

13. In a mosaic signed by the late third-century artist Sophilos: J. Ferguson, *Heritage* 29 with fig. 16; Villard, in Charbonneaux et al. 159–60 with fig. 162; Pollitt, *AHA* 222.

14. Theocr. 17.125: πάντεσσιν ἐπιχθονίοισιν ἀρωγούς.

15. Nilsson 689 ff.; A. D. Nock, *Conversion* (Oxford, 1933) 204 ff.

16. H. Thiersch, *Pharos, Antike Islam und Occident* (Leipzig and Berlin, 1909) 7–34, gives the ancient testimonia; cf. Fraser 1.17–20, with further literature.

17. Strabo 17.1.8 (C.793).

18. Fraser 1.147.

19. Callixeinos *ap.* Athen. 196a–203b *passim*. See also Rice, *Grand Procession*; Pollitt, *AHA* 280–81. The date has been accurately calculated, on astronomical grounds, by Victoria Foertmeyer, "The Dating of the Pompe of Ptolemy II Philadelphus," *Historia* 37 (1988) 90–104; see esp. p. 103.

20. Pollitt, *AHA* 255, 280–81.

21. Ibid. 281.

22. He might have taken some slight comfort from the fact that the greatest piece of gigantism conceived in this period, the twenty-bank vessel *Lady of Alexandria* (Athen. 5.206–9 *passim*) was a present from Hieron of Syracuse rather than a home-grown monster; even so, Ptolemy IV Philopator soon outdid Hieron, with a *forty*-bank flagship 420 feet long (Callixeinos *ap.* Athen. 5.203e–204d; cf. Meiggs 138–39). Turner, *CAH* VII².1 139, nicely remarks that the procession described by Callixeinos "could be illustrated only by combining elements out of the Parthenon frieze with frescoes in the tombs of the Nobles of the New Kingdom."

23. Wycherley, *How the Greeks Built* 35.

24. And not only in Asia: for the use of the grid by Cassander in Thessalonike (316), see M. Vickers, *JHS* 92 (1972) 156 ff., with figs. 3 and 4.

25. Downey, *History* 15–23, *Ancient Antioch* 11–20.

26. Downey, *History* 62–64.

27. "Greek from the Year Dot," Cavafy, Ποιήματα Β' 60 = *Collected Poems* 282–83; Downey, *History* 50–51.

28. Arr. *Anab.* 2.13.7–14.1.

29. Liban. *Orat.* 11 (*Antioch.*) 72–77, 87, 250.

30. DS 20.47.5.

31. Wehrli, *Antigone* 79–93, has an excellent general discussion of Antigonus's foundations.

32. Downey, *History* 63–64.

33. Cohen, *Seleucid Colonies* 16–17; Downey, *History* 54. See also Pollitt, *AHA* app. 3, p. 277.

34. Downey, *History* 67 ff.

35. Arr. *Anab.* 3.2.1–2, Plut. *Alex.* 26, QC 4.8.6, Liban. *Orat.* 11 (*Antioch.*) 90.

36. DS 17.52.2, Liban. *Orat.* 11 (*Antioch.*) 222–26, Vitruv. 1.6.12; cf. Downey, *History* 70–71.

37. Downey, *History* 73–75, *Ancient Antioch* 35 ff.; Havelock 133–34 with pl. 117; Charbonneaux et al. fig. 251. Praxiteles executed a statue of Tyche for Megara (Paus. 1.43.6), but it was from Eutychides' figure that a standard format for images of Tyche was derived (Pollitt, *AHA* 3).

38. Downey, *Ancient Antioch* 36.

39. Malalas 201.18–202.6, Liban. *Orat.* 11 (*Antioch.*) 92; cf. DS 20.47; Downey, *History* 79–80.

40. Downey, *History* 85 with n. 142; Plin. *HN* 34.73.

41. Phylarchus *ap.* Athen. 6.254f–255a, App. *Syr.* 63; cf. Bikerman chap. 7, esp. p. 248.

42. Habicht, *Gottmenschentum* 164 ff., 171.

43. Bikerman 157.

44. Downey, *History* 112–13.

45. Knaack, *RE* 2 (1896) cols. 392–93, s.v. "Aratos (6)."

46. For the transfer, see Downey, *History* 87: from 280 onwards there is a significant rise in activity of the Antioch mint, matched by a corresponding decline in that of Seleucia-in-Pieria.

47. Downey, *History* 89–90.

48. Strabo 16.2.4 (C.750).

49. Polyb. 30.25 ff.

50. Cf. Martin 127–28, which I can confirm from personal inspection of the terrain.

51. Hansen 1–4.

52. Xen. *Anab.* 7.7.57, 7.8.8 ff.; cf. Hansen 8–10.

53. Hansen 12 with reff.; cf. above, p. 28.

54. For a portrait of him on a tetradrachm, minted by Eumenes I, see Jenkins no. 557, p. 242.

55. Strabo 13.4.1 (C.623).

56. *OGIS* no. 748; cf. Hansen 18–19 with n. 26.

57. Hansen 17, 216 ff.

58. Davis and Kraay 250–52, with figs. 50, 51, 53.

59. Hansen 203 ff.

60. Varro *ap.* Plin. *HN* 13.70; cf. N. Lewis, *Papyrus in Classical Antiquity* (Oxford, 1974) 9.

61. Eur. fr. 627 Nauck², Hdt. 5.58.3, Ctesias *ap.* DS 2.32.4; cf. G. R. Driver, *The Judaean Scrolls* (Oxford, 1965) 407–8, cited by Lewis, *loc. cit.* (above, n. 60).

62. Hansen chap. 7, pp. 234 ff.; Martin chap. 3, pp. 127 ff.

63. *SIG*³ 666; cf. Hansen 396.

64. Hansen 253–59.

65. Hansen 433.

66. Ibid.

67. M. Collignon and E. Pontrémoli, *Pergame* (Paris, 1898) 229.

68. Theocr. 15.44 ff.

Chapter 11. The Critic as Poet: Callimachus, Aratus of Soli, Lycophron

1. On Kazantzakis's *Odyssey*, see my *Essays in Antiquity* (London, 1960) 44–51.

2. Callim. *Epigr.* 28 Pfeiffer = Gow and Page 2, p. 57. It is characteristic of Callimachus that an epigram leading off with a rejection of epic and common literary cliche, an assertion of discriminating taste, should wind up as a reproach to a promiscuous boy lover, the prostitution-of-art metaphor in reverse:

> I hate the cyclic poem, no path gives me any pleasure
> That's trodden by many, to and fro—
> I loathe, too, a gadabout lover; not from the common fountain
> Do *I* drink: I abhor all public things.
> You're lovely, lover, yes, lovely; but quicker than Echo,
> "He's another's lover," someone says.

The last two lines, it has been suggested (Gow and Page 2.156–57), may be a later addition. I doubt it. The bittersweet twist is entirely appropriate, not only for Callimachus, but for Hellenistic love epigrams as a whole: cf. Garrison 66, and Ireland in *G&R* 26 (1979) 196. See also pp. 175 ff.

3. Callim. *Hymn* 2.108–9.

4. Juv. *Sat.* 3.61 ff.: "Iam pridem Syrus in Tiberim defluxit Orontes / et linguam et mores . . . / . . . secum / vexit."

5. "Poeta Fit, Non Nascitur," *The Collected Verse of Lewis Carroll* (London, 1932) 202–5. For the Alexandrian aetiologizing passion, see Zanker 131 ff.

6. Cf. Sale 163.

7. Callim. *Aet.* 4 fr. 110 Pfeiffer (pp. 112 ff. = Trypanis 80 ff.). Cf. Zanker 129 ff.

8. Cf. J. S. L. Tarán, *The Art of Variation in the Hellenistic Epigram* (Leiden, 1979), with the reviews by Arnott, *G&R* 28 (1981) 94–95; Cunningham, *JHS* 101 (1981) 173–74; and Schmiel, *Phoenix* 35 (1981) 170–72. Cf. Hutchinson 20–24.

9. Epigrams in Gow and Page 1.44–56; commentary 2.114–51; cf. Wilamowitz 1.146 ff.; Garrison chap. 4, pp. 48–61; Fraser 1.560 ff.; Hutchinson 264–76. Lesky 739 with old-world charm describes his work as *risqué* but acquits him of prurience.

10. Epigrams in Gow and Page 1.107–39; commentary 2.307–98; cf. Wilamowitz 1.139

ff.; Webster, *Hellenistic Poetry* 217–21; C. M. Dawson, "Some Epigrams by Leonidas of Tarentum," *AJPh* 71 (1950) 271–84. Wilamowitz's harsh judgment ("Er aber war nur ein formales Talent, spielte mit alten Motiven und hat die Nachfolger in diese Bahnen getrieben") completely misses his black humor and striking originality.

11. Gow and Page 93 = *AP* 7.715:

> Far from Italy I lie and my homeland of Taras: this is
> 　More bitter to me than death.
> Such is a wanderer's life, no life: yet the Muses loved me;
> 　No sorrows now are mine, but honey sweet,
> For the name of Leonidas is not forgotten, the Muses' bounty
> 　Trumpets my name to every sun.

12. Gow and Page 23 (= *AP* 12.162) 22 (= *AP* 12.105); cf. Garrison 54–56.

13. Bieber 38 with figs. 87–89.

14. Charbonneaux et al. figs. 272, 273, 353.

15. See, e.g., Gow and Page A 1 = *AP* 5.168.

16. Gow and Page 19 (= *AP* 12.153), 42 (= *AP* 5.188).

17. Garrison 57.

18. Gow and Page 4 (= *AP* 5.157), 7 (= *AP* 5.206).

19. Fraser 1.588.

20. Gow and Page 15 = *AP* 12.46.

21. Cf., e.g., Diog. Laert. 5.11 (Aristotle), 5.51 (Theophrastus): ἐὰν δέ τι συμβαίνῃ, συμβῇ.

22. Gow and Page 87 (= *AP* 6.226), 50 (= *AP* 6.296), 36 (= *AP* 6.300), 37 (= *AP* 6.302), 39 (= *AP* 6.355).

23. Gow and Page 77 = *AP* 7.472.

24. Gow and Page 31 = *AP* 16 (= *Anth. Planud.*) 306. Cf. Paus. 1.25.1 for a statue of Anacreon on the Athenian Acropolis that fits Leonidas's description.

25. Gow and Page 5 = *AP* 9.326. Cf. Zanker 128 for other examples.

26. Gow and Page 31 = *AP* 7.524.

27. The Greek is αἱ δ' ἄνοδοι τί; which does not, *pace* Paton and others, simply mean "the upward way": the plural implies those ascents from Hades accomplished, e.g., by Heracles and Persephone. Cf. Gow and Page 2.189.

28. Juv. *Sat.* 2.149–52.

29. Louis MacNeice, *Collected Poems* (London, 1966) 530. Cf. above, Chap. 3 n. 46 (p. 751).

30. See K. Ziegler, *RE* 13 (1927) cols. 2316–81, s.v. "Lykophron (8)"; S. Josifovič, *RE* Suppl. 11 (1968) cols. 888–930 (downdating the *Alexandra*, not in my opinion convincingly, to 197: see cols. 925–29); G. W. Mooney, *Lycophron: The Alexandra* (London, 1921); Mair and Mair 477 ff.; Wilamowitz 2.143 ff.

31. Pfeiffer, *History* 119–20, and Fraser, 1.449, 2.649, give the essential testimonia: cf. Athen. 4.140a.*

32. *Suda* s.v. Λυκόφρων; for other reff., cf. Mair and Mair 480.

33. *Suda* ibid.: τὸ σκοτεινὸν ποίημα. Analysis in Hutchinson, 257–64, who, oddly, compares Lycophron to Lucan.

34. Unless Josifovič is right in dating the poem to 197 (above, n. 30), in which case Rome's intervention in the Balkans was already a *fait accompli* (see Chap. 18, pp. 299 ff.). Stephanie West's ingenious article "Lycophron Italicised," *JHS* 104 (1984) 127–51, posits an interpolator, a "deutero-Lycophron," for the Roman passages: I find her arguments stimulating, but remain unconvinced.

35. Wilamowitz, 2.148–49, argues that "es ist auch sprachlich und metrisch die Form keineswegs tragisch," mainly on the ground that Lycophron does not employ the resolutions available to fifth-century dramatists; Wilamowitz prefers to regard the poem as oracular literature in iambic form ("wichtig, dass es auch iambische Orakelsprüche gab").

36. E. A. Barber, *OCD*² 628a, s.v. "Lycophron."

37. Ciani, "Scritto con mistero" 132–48.

38. George Orwell, "Benefit of Clergy: Some Notes on Salvador Dali," *Collected Essays* (New York, 1968) 3.156–65.

39. Cedric H. Whitman, *Aristophanes and the Comic Hero* (Cambridge, Mass., 1964), chap. 5, "The Anatomy of Nothingness," pp. 167–99.

40. Cf. Clem. Alex. *Strom.* 5.8.50 = Pfeiffer, ed., *Callimachus*, testim. 26, p. xcix.

41. Pfeiffer's great edition of 1949 has been reprinted (Arno: New York, 1979); it also forms the basis for the excellent Loeb volume by C. A. Trypanis (Cambridge, Mass., 1978). The bibliography on Callimachus is enormous. I list here only one or two recent studies that I have found of particular use. Some of the most intelligent discussions will be found in P. M. Fraser's *Ptolemaic Alexandria*: see in particular chap. 11, "The Horizon of Callimachus," pp. 717–93, and, for other references, his general index, pp. 17 ff. Cf. also Wilamowitz 1.169 ff., 2.1–161; C. M. Dawson, *YClS* 11 (1950) 1–168 (on the *Iambi*); Pfeiffer, *History* chap. 3, pp. 123 ff.; Webster, *Hellenistic Poetry* chap. 5, pp. 98 ff.; Meillier, *Callimaque*, *passim*; and, for general up-to-date reference, H. Herter, *RE* Suppl. 13 (1973) cols. 184–266, s.v. "Kallimachos (6) aus Kyrene." A useful introduction, more sympathetic than the assessment here, and seeking to isolate Callimachus's "elegant vitality" in the widest sense, has been written by Hutchinson, pp. 26–84. Equally enthusiastic is Bulloch's survey in Easterling and Knox, eds., 549–70. Pedantry is justified by a comparison with Dante: the *Aitia* has a "polychromatic surface" (p. 43); *Hymn* 1 reveals "the lurking scholar" (p. 65). The judgments are enjoyable—at times perversely so—and intermittently persuasive.

42. Mart. 10.4.11–12.

43. *Suda* s.v. Καλλίμαχος.

44. Pfeiffer, ed., *Callimachus*, testim. 14c, p. xcvii.

45. See, e.g., Lesky 702.

46. Frr. 392, 228, 110 Pfeiffer (pp. 322, 218 ff., 112 ff.) = Trypanis pp. 242–43, 163 ff., 80 ff.

47. Fr. 191 Pfeiffer (pp. 161 ff.) = Trypanis 105 ff.

48. This project must, among other results, have vastly increased Callimachus's already encyclopedic knowledge in every area: it has, for instance, recently been shown that his description of Leto's birthing position (*Hymn* 4.205–11), which significantly changes (by 180°!) that in the *Homeric Hymn to Delian Apollo* (3.117), reveals knowledge of the theories of Herophilus (see p. 209): G. W. Most, "Callimachus and Herophilus," *Hermes* 119 (1981) 188–96.

49. Including one epigram (Pfeiffer 8, p. 83) in which his urge for concision finds witty and paradoxical expression in a final six-syllable word: βραχυσυλλαβίη.

50. *Hymn* 2.113.

51. Text in Pfeiffer, ed., *Callimachus* 1.1–160 = Trypanis pp. 2–99.

52. Klein, "Role" 217 ff.

53. Xenophanes fr. 169 Kirk and Raven = Sext. Emp. *Adv. Math.* 9.193. Cf. Guthrie, *History* 1.370–73, and, for a late fifth-century concern with the same problem, Eur. *HF* 1341 ff.

54. Fr. 178 Pfeiffer, lines 13 ff. (pp. 150 ff.) = Trypanis pp. 94–97.

55. His name for them is Τελχῖνες: aptly enough, since the Telchines in legend were a group of chthonian dwarves, skilled in metalworking, and somewhat akin to Teutonic Kobolds, with equally maleficent habits: DS 5.55, Strabo 14.2.7 (C.654); Callim. *Ait.* 1 fr. 1 Pfeiffer, with schol. Flor. *ad loc.* (= Pfeiffer, ed., *Callimachus* p. 3; cf. Trypanis pp. 4 ff.).

56. Frr. 230–377 Pfeiffer (pp. 226–303) = Trypanis pp. 176–225.

57. G. Zanker, "Callimachus's Hecale: A New Kind of Epic Hero?" *Antichthon* 11 (1977) 68–77.

58. Schol. Callim. *Hymn* 2.106.

59. Cf. Plut. *Thes.* 14, with Trypanis p. 176.

60. *Hymn* 1.78 ff.

61. Fr. 384 Pfeiffer (pp. 311 ff.) = Trypanis pp. 232 ff.; cf. Meillier, *Callimaque* 225 ff.; Wilamowitz 2.87 ff.

62. Polyb. 5.34–39, 15.24–25, 34; Plut. *Cleom.* 33–35.

63. Fr. 384.54–55 Pfeiffer.

64. Lloyd-Jones 67.

65. The wit, too, can be problematical. McKay, *Erysichthon*, assumes that in *Hymn* 6, to Demeter, lines 24–115, Callimachus is exercising mischievous and double-edged humor. The story of Erysichthon certainly lends itself to such a supposition. According to the myth, Erysichthon cut down a poplar in Demeter's grove to roof a banquet hall, and was afflicted by the vengeful goddess with an appalling and insatiable hunger that, far from increasing his weight, left him mere skin and bone, so that when he had eaten his family out of house and home, he was reduced to begging for crusts at the crossroads. There are certainly flashes of black humor in Callimachus's account, not least the bright social excuses by which Erysichthon's parents explain his absence from other people's dinners (lines 66–86: since it took twenty cooks and twelve wine waiters to satisfy him, he might have proved an embarrassing guest); but this is the old Euripidean trick of highlighting archaic primitivism by setting it without comment in an up-to-date social context. As an example of Demeter's divine wrath (cf. lines 116–17) the anecdote is horrific, and nicely illustrates the ambivalence of Callimachus's attitude to myth: civilized mockery will keep breaking in, but the search for roots is strong too, despite the embarrassment at primitivism and amorality that such archaic material so often produces. Fraser, in a different context (1.592), isolates as one of Callimachus's "fundamental literary habits . . . the combination of deep feeling and frivolity in one and the same context." Reading Callimachus's levels of irony and wit is, clearly, a chancy business: reviews of McKay ranged from delighted panegyrics—Waters, *Phoenix* 18 (1964) 88–89; Parker, *CW* 57 (1964) 358—to the hysterical and furious assault by Brooks Otis, *AJPh* 85 (1964) 423–26, and Levin's more moderate comment, *CPh* 59 (1964) 296–98, that while "subtle erudition and highly charged emotion need not be mutually exclusive," there is by the end reason to suspect that "the real purveyor of 'mischief' is not the subtle and erudite author of the *Hymns*, but his even more subtle and erudite latter-day explicator." Cf. Lloyd-Jones 67–68.

66. Cf. Fraser 1.790.

67. See, e.g., Plato, *Charm.* 154A–155E, *Phaedr.* 256A, *Symp.* 180D–184A; cf. Dover, *Greek Homosexuality* 5–9, 153–67; T. Africa, "Homosexuals in Greek History," *Journal of Psychohistory* 9 (1982) 401–20, esp. 404–14.

68. *Epigr.* 28, *Iamb.* 4, 5; cf. Fraser 1.739–40, 741 ff., 790–91.

69. Aeschin. 1 (*In Timarch.*), esp. 160 ff.; and cf. Dover, *Greek Homosexuality*, chap. 2, pp. 19 ff.

70. Biographical testimonia assembled in Maass, *Commentariorum . . . Reliquiae* 76–79, 146–51, 323–26; cf. *Suda* s.v. Ἄρατος; Mair and Mair 359–63; Wilamowitz 2.274 ff. Hutchinson's evaluation of Aratus (pp. 214–36), though enthusiastic, tends—an endemic fault of Hellenistic literary criticism—to lose itself in detailed exegesis; and it is remarkable, though symptomatic, that he manages to complete his analysis without once mentioning Stoicism.

71. Gow and Page 56 = *AP* 9.507: Callimachus praises the Hesiodic qualities of the *Phaenomena*, which, again, suggests a reaching-back to older patterns of thought and belief. Cf. Sale's penetrating comment (p. 163): "When he calls the Bear fearful and Cassiopeia hapless and Cetus a great terror, he is filling the sky not just with life, but with gigantic men, and violent and frightening animals. There is a poetic vision here intermingled with the scientific vision, a poetic vision recalling a time more naive, when men might actually believe that the sky contained such life as this." Aratus was also praised by Leonidas of Taras (see pp. 175–76): Gow and Page 101 = *AP* 9.25.

72. This ascription was challenged by Erren 192 ff., but his arguments were refuted by Pingree, *Gnomon* 43 (1971) 347–50.

73. *Vit.* 1 Maass, 77–78.

74. Maass, *Commentariorum . . . Reliquiae* 3–24, 143, 149–50.

75. Cic. *De Orat.* 1.69, *De Re Publ.* 1.(14)22.

76. Damagetos, Gow and Page 9 (= *AP* 7.497), cf. 10 (= *AP* 7.735); Hegesippus, Gow and Page 7 (= *AP* 7.276); Leonidas of Taras, Gow and Page 60 (= *AP* 7.264); Phaidimos, Gow and Page 4 (= *AP* 7.739); Phanias, Gow and Page 5 (= *AP* 7.282); and, for later epitaphs of shipwreck, *AP* 7.263–79, 282–94.

77. As Wilamowitz says (1.201), "Astronomie zu lehren, wie sie etwa in Platons Schule getrieben ward, war Arat nicht imstande."

78. Hesiod, *WD* 105–200.

79. Gow and Page 56 = *AP* 9.507: but this was pot calling kettle black, since Callimachus himself elsewhere claimed, in true Hesiodic style, to have been given the *Aitia* by the Muses on Mt. Helicon (*Ait.* 1 fr. 2 Pfeiffer, with schol. *ad loc.*, pp. 9–11).

80. Hesiod, *WD* 256.

81. Webster, *Hellenistic Poetry* 38; Wilamowitz 2.265.

82. Webster, *Hellenistic Poetry* 34.

83. Clem. Alex. *Strom.* 5.3.17 = *SVF* no. 559, 1.127–28: οὐ γὰρ πλῆθος ἔχει συνετὴν κρίσιν . . . ὀλίγοις δὲ παρ' ἀνδράσι τοῦτό κεν εὕροις.

84. Plut. *Mor.* 923A, Archimed. *Sand-Reckoner* 4–5.

Chapter 12. Kingship and Bureaucracy: The Government of the Successor Kingdoms

1. δορίκτητος χώρα: cf. Rostovtzeff, *SEH* 1.267, *CAH* VII 113; and particularly A. Mehl, "Δορίκτητος χώρα: Kritische Bemerkungen zum 'Speererwerb' in Politik und Völkerrecht der hellenistischen Epoche," *AncSoc* 11/12 (1980–81) 173–212. The existence of private land in no way invalidates the general principle of crown ownership. Cf. Turner, *CAH* VII².1 148–49; and Davies, *CAH* VII².1 296 ff.

2. Green, *Alexander* 156, 530 n. 7.

3. The fullest and most detailed account of the postclassical destruction of Greek freedom by the Greek propertied classes is that of Ste Croix 300 ff. Here the author's doctrinaire preconceptions do less harm to his remarkable historical erudition than in other parts of this brilliant yet infuriating work. Cf. my review, *TLS* 4167, 11 Feb. 1983, 125–26.

4. Goodenough 55 ff., collects most of the key testimonia. Cf. also Préaux, *Monde* 1.183; Rostovtzeff, *CAH* VII 114.

5. E.g., by Cleanthes, Persaeus, and Euphantus of Olynthos: Diog. Laert. 7.174, 7.37, 2.110.

6. See in particular Isocr. 5 (*Philip*) 113–16; 2 (*Ad Nicocl.*) 5, 18, 29, 31, 35; 1 (*Ad Demon.*) 36.

7. *Pol.* 3.9.1284ᵇ35–1288ᵇ7. Note in particular 1287ᵇ38 ff., where a defense is made of kingship on the grounds of exceptional excellence, something that finds a precedent in the famous Persian defense of monarchy advanced in the pages of Herodotus (3.82), and later in Plato's claims for the ruler as a being superior to ordinary law: *Polit.* 293C–E, 294A, 296E ff. (cf. 300C); *Laws* 711E–712A, 875C. Elsewhere (*Pol.* 1310ᵇ9 ff.) Aristotle gives the game away by defining kingship as the defense of the elite against the common people, whereas tyranny is the people's protection against the elite.

8. Cic. *Ad Att.* 12.40, 13.28.

9. Plut. *Mor.* 189D, Stob. *Flor.* 4.7.27; cf. p. 88. The need for such advice is highlighted by the disillusioned comment of Polybius (15.24.4), who observes of kings that they begin with talk of freedom, but once in control treat even their loyal supporters as slaves.

10. Goodenough 59–61.

11. Aelian *VH* 2.20. Walbank, *CAH* VII².1 77, is perhaps too dismissive in his claim that "it is hard to detect any practical application of Stoic precepts in the realities of Antigonus' government."

12. App. *Syr.* 61: the speech is often said to be spurious (cf. Rostovtzeff, *SEH* 1.430–31, 434), but nevertheless, as Rostovtzeff says, it "goes back to an early Hellenistic source and accurately represents the ideas of the time."

13. Préaux, *Monde* 1.181 ff.; cf. Rostovtzeff, *CAH* VII 162.

14. Préaux, *Monde* 1.183 ff.

15. Ibid. 1.202–9: she remarks that "la notion de *philanthropia* fut tellement galvaudée que l'index des OGIS renonce à en dénombrer les mentions" (p. 207). On the royal Friends, see now the excellent account by Walbank, *CAH* VII².1 68 ff.; and see ibid. 81–84 for an analysis of the qualities attributed to the ideal Hellenistic monarch: courage, justice, generosity, and, supporting all these, wealth.

16. Plut. *Demetr.* 42.

17. Fraser 1.505–10; Préaux, *Monde* 1.236.

18. The Hellenizing-mission argument was first given wide currency by Plutarch, in one of his rhetorical treatises, *De Alexandri Magni Fortuna aut Virtute* (*Mor.* 328E). For a penetrating study of this ideological confrontation in Asia see Eddy, *The King Is Dead*. Few things, also, are more remarkable than the near-total lack of interpenetration between Greek and Egyptian culture, literature above all, during the three centuries of Ptolemaic rule. In the introduction to vol. 3 of her remarkable series of annotated texts in translation, *Ancient Egyptian Literature* (Berkeley and Los Angeles, 1980), Miriam Lichtheim claims that Egyptian civilization "continued to endure" (p. 4), which is true, but that it also "absorbed with surprising elasticity elements of Greek culture in art and literature." The art is debatable (and much-debated); but as regards the literature, one need only examine the texts she prints to see how profoundly alien they are from anything that Alexandria would recognize. No accident that the Egyptians, yearning for a new σωτηρία, and oppressed by Roman exploitation, should have so readily, and violently, embraced Christianity.

19. Bagnall 235, Bowman 56 ff.; cf. Rostovtzeff, *CAH* VII 125. See also Koenen, in Van't Dack et al. 149 ff.

20. Rostovtzeff, *SEH* 272–73. For the dating systems, see Turner, *CAH* VII².1 146.

21. H. Kees, *Ancient Egypt: A Cultural Topography* (London, 1961; repr.: 1977), chap. 2, pp. 52–61; J. E. Manchip White, *Ancient Egypt: Its Culture and History* (New York, 1970), chap. 1, pp. 1–7. Evidence on tenders for repairing the Nile embankments: Hunt and Edgar 2.346, pp. 406–9, dated to 257.

22. Rostovtzeff, *SEH* 1.386 ff.

23. C. H. V. Sutherland, *Gold: Its Beauty, Power and Allure*, 3d ed. (London, 1969), 74.

24. Rostovtzeff, *CAH* VII 116–18. On the crucial role of the Friends, see Walbank, *CAH* VII².1 70. Turner, *CAH* VII².1 123, stresses the reliance on foreign mercenaries. For a vivid glimpse of the life led by a cavalry officer stationed near Thebes in Upper Egypt, see Lewis, chap. 6, pp. 88–103.

25. For Alexander's enthronement as pharaoh at Memphis see Ps.-Callisth. 1.34.1–2. Ptolemy III's pharaonic status is clearly implied in *OGIS* 56.1–20 = Austin 222, p. 366. Cf. Préaux, *Monde* 1.259–60.

26. See, e.g., *OGIS* 56.8–12; and, for temple building under Ptolemy IV, Bevan, *House of Ptolemy* 238. The Rosetta Stone (*OGIS* 90) offers a detailed account of the kind of benefits for which the Egyptian priesthood was prepared to go along with, and honor, the Ptolemies: see Burstein, *Translated Documents* no. 103, pp. 131–36.

27. Bevan, *House of Ptolemy* 239; cf. Polyb. 14.12.3–4.

28. Rostovtzeff, *CAH* VII 112.

29. Sir Alan Gardiner, *Egypt of the Pharaohs* (Oxford, 1961) 147–72; William C. Hayes, *CAH* II³.1 (1973) 54 ff. The domination of the Hyksos in Egypt lasted from ca. 1720 to 1567 B.C.

30. *Uatch-ur*: see E. A. Wallis Budge, *An Egyptian Hieroglyphic Dictionary* (London, 1920; repr.: 1978) 1.151a.

31. Hunt and Edgar 2.203, pp. 10–35 = Austin 236, pp. 400–407; Bagnall and Derow 95, pp. 153–60; cf. Préaux, *Économie* 65 ff., Rostovtzeff, *SEH* 1.302–5.

32. Austin p. 401. Efficient exploitation was, clearly, the object of an amazingly compre-

hensive land survey and census ordered by Ptolemy II in 258 for all Egypt: Turner, *CAH* VII².1 135–36: Burstein, *Translated Documents* no. 97, pp. 122–23.

33. Fraser, chap. 3, 1.93 ff.

34. Bagnall 238. The visit of a royal finance officer and his retinue seems (like all such peregrinations throughout history) to have been vastly expensive to those visited in the matter of entertainment and transport: for such a visit in 224(?), see Hunt and Edgar 2.414, pp. 562–63.

35. Bagnall 240.

36. Ibid. 213 ff., 251.

37. Ibid. 73.

38. Ibid. 236 with n. 38.

39. Ibid. 210–12.

40. Green, *Alexander* 268–70.

41. Rostovtzeff, *CAH* VII 181. For a grant of royal land to a citizen of Assos by Antiochus I, see *OGIS* = Burstein, *Translated Documents* no. 21, pp. 26–28.

42. Tarn and Griffith 130, 243–44; cf. Rostovtzeff, *CAH* VII 174–75; Bevan, *House of Seleucus* 1.164 ff.; Musti, *CAH* VII².1 184.

43. Habicht, "Herrschende Gesellschaft" 6 ff.; Heuss, *Stadt*, rev. ed., 294; Orth 181.

44. Cohen, *Seleucid Colonies* 87–88; Bar-Kochva 25 ff., esp. 37–39; S. M. Sherwin-White, *JHS* 100 (1980) 260; Musti, *CAH* VII².1 189–90.

45. Bagnall 248–51; Musti, *CAH* VII².1 185.

46. E.g., in the case of Mazaeus at Babylon: see Green, *Alexander* 304.

47. Bikerman, chap. 2, pp. 31 ff.; Musti, *CAH* VII².1 186 ff.

48. Bar-Kochva 39 ff.

49. Bar-Kochva 67 ff.; Rostovtzeff, *CAH* VII 169.

50. Strabo 16.2.10 (C.752); cf. Bar-Kochva 75–83; Scullard 121, 189.

51. Bikerman 250–53; Rostovtzeff, *SEH* 1.431; Musti "Stato" 95–98.

52. *OGIS* 212.

53. Bikerman 243–45.

54. Antiochus IV, for example, collected titles of deification piecemeal, after his victory over Ptolemy VI (p. 430) and his triumphal celebration at Daphne in 166 (Bikerman 239); he finally came to be known as "King Antiochus, God Manifest, Victorious" (Βασιλεὺς Ἀντίοχος θεὸς Ἐπιφανὴς Νικηφόρος), and it is significant that his godhead, as so often with Hellenistic rulers, was acquired in the first instance as a result of military merit.

55. Cf. Polyb. 15.2.4; Préaux, *Monde* 1.194: "Le roi défend les villes des attaques de ses ennemis. Il les 'libère,' ce qui veut dire qu'il les arrache à ses concurrents." On the problem of the king's relations with the *poleis* see Musti, *CAH* VII².1 204 ff. It should be apparent from my interpretation that I have very little sympathy with the *Idealtypus* of Greek *polis* independence promoted by Heuss, *Stadt*, in Weberian terms, as a kind of romantic wish fulfillment; the realism of Bikerman and Orth (above, p. 197) is considerably more to my taste, and, I believe, nearer to the truth.

56. DS 5.42.5; cf. Aalders 66–69.

57. Mastrocinque, "Eleutheria" 1–23; cf. Musti, *CAH* VII².1 207–9.

58. Badian, "Alexander" 37 ff., esp. 38.

59. Cf. A. H. M. Jones, *Greek City* 157–58.

60. Cf. Orth 179–80: "So gross die Bedeutung des Autonomie-Begriffes in der politischen Diskussion der Zeit sicher gewesen ist, so wenig wurde die politische Wirklichkeit von ihm geprägt." E. Will, "Monde hellénistique" (1975) 456–57, similarly observes that "dans les choses grecques, il n'est pas plus recommandable de pousser le juridisme à l'excès que d'en faire litière. Or il est patent que les relations entre les vieilles cités et les souverains ont été essentiellement des relations de force et que le droit, qui n'a jamais été perdu de vue, s'est constamment plié aux faits."

61. A. H. M. Jones, *Greek City* 95.

62. E. Will, "Monde hellénistique" (1975) 457.

63. G. Herman, "The 'Friends' of the Early Hellenistic Rulers: Servants or Officials?" *Talanta* 12/13 (1980/81) 103–49, a penetrating and original examination of the available evidence, which nevertheless underemphasizes the degree of readiness shown by Athenian officials to perform such duties.

64. I am reliably informed that in the American South the euphemism "visiting" serves an almost identical purpose.

65. Orth 53–55, 111–16; cf. ibid. 180 for Ilion's "sklavischer Unterwürfigkeit" (*OGIS* 219).

66. E. Badian, "Hegemony and Independence: Prolegomena to a Study of the Relations of Rome and the Hellenistic States in the Second Century B.C.," *Actes du VIIᵉ Congrès de la F.I.E.C. (Aug. 1979)* (Budapest, 1984) 1.399–414. The quotation is from p. 403. R. M. Errington, *JHS* 95 (1975) 251–52, takes Orth to task in his review for not clearly distinguishing between *Völkerrecht* and *Machtpolitik*; but—except in the most pallid academic sense, never put into common practice—what *was* there, in effect, to distinguish them, throughout the Hellenistic period, throughout the Successor kingdoms? The first only existed on sufferance from the second; it could be, and was, regularly superseded—or, worse, exploited—in the interests of power politics.

67. W. W. Tarn, *Alexander the Great* (Cambridge, 1948) 2.370 ff., well refuted by J. P. V. D. Balsdon, *Historia* 1 (1950) 386–87: "If the Greeks said, 'But you are not empowered to command the recall of the exiles,' he [*sc.* Alexander] would be able to say, 'Ah, you ought to have thought of that before you voted me a god.' Is this really the kind of behaviour which fits at all with Tarn's, or indeed with any historian's, picture of Alexander?"

68. Cf. Orth 178 ff.; Musti, *CAH* VII².1 206 ff.

69. A. H. M. Jones, *Anatolian Studies Presented to W. H. Buckler* (Manchester, 1939) 103 ff.; cf. Préaux, 1.409–10.

70. Cf. A. H. M. Jones, *Greek City* 98.

71. Ibid. 270; Ste Croix 302–3.

72. Errington (above, n. 66), 251–52. Cf. Davies, *CAH* VII².1 304–15, in a section characteristically entitled "The Polis Transformed and Revitalised."

73. Atkinson 32 ff.; cf. Musti, "Stato" 145 ff. Musti notes the tendency to favor "moderate democracies," and a generally tolerant attitude to "le libertà cittadine, pur non immune da atteggiamenti autoritari" (p. 145).

74. Rostovtzeff, *SEH* 250.

75. Green, *Alexander* 47, 117, 159.

76. Cary 253.

77. Tarn, *CAH* VII 200 ff.

78. DS 16.8.6–7; App. *BC* 4.106; Strabo 2.7.4 (C.323), 7 fr. 34 Jones.

79. Plut. *Aem. Paull.* 28.

80. See the long fragment of Hippolochus preserved in Athen. 4.128a–130d for a graphic description of the kind of conspicuous consumption (confirmed now by the splendid artifacts: cf. *Macedonia and Greece in Late Classical and Early Hellenistic Times*, ed. B. Barr-Sharrar and E. N. Borza [Washington, D.C., 1982]) indulged in by Macedonians of the late fourth and the third century.

81. Davis and Kraay 223–25 with pls. 119, 120, 122; Jenkins pl. 539.

82. Rostovtzeff, *SEH* 1.253–55.

83. See N. G. L. Hammond and G. T. Griffith, *A History of Macedonia*, vol. 2 (Oxford, 1979), chap. 11, pp. 383 ff.; cf. Cary 249.

84. Archytas of Taras, cited by Goodenough 59 ff.; cf. Diotog. *ap*. Stob. *Flor*. 4.7.61.

85. Plut. *Mor.* 360D; cf. 182C.

86. Suet. *Div. Vesp.* 23.4: "Uae, puto, deus fio." For a similarly ironic comment on his own supposed godhead by Alexander, see p. 403.

Chapter 13. Armchair Epic: Apollonius Rhodius and the Voyage of *Argo*

1. I am suspicious of recent fashionable attempts to dismiss this famous quarrel as mere aetiologizing, or scandalmongering, on the part of bored, ill-informed, and depressingly literal-minded scholiasts, who raided the protagonists' own works for promising titbits, historicizing the most casual or literary fancy into pseudobiographical pabulum. Most of this antibiographical movement rests on an *argumentum ex silentio*: the (probably nonsignificant) absence of Apollonius's name from among the "Telchines" referred to in the scholion on Callimachus's prologue to his *Aitia* (p. 180). See, e.g., Lefkowitz 1–19, esp. 13 (Apollonius was *born* a Rhodian!), or J. Smolarczyk-Rostropowicz, "Comments on the Controversy between Apollonius Rhodius and Callimachus," *Eos* 67 (1979) 75–79 (no personal feud, and Apollonius's choice over Callimachus as chief librarian was due to his Egyptianizing bent, which promised better implementation of an integrationist policy!), and Lloyd-Jones 58–60. Bundy, 39 ff., goes to great lengths to show that the epilogue to Callimachus's *Hymn to Apollo* (2.105–13) is, though discontinuous, quite normal literary practice, a correct conclusion that nevertheless does not, *per se*, cast any doubts on the historicity of the quarrel. Hutchinson, pp. 86–87, is equally skeptical. His general survey of the poem (pp. 85–142) contains much valuable material, but is chiefly noteworthy for achieving the almost impossible result of making Apollonius sound dull.

2. Useful surveys of the evidence in Fraser 1.636 ff., 749 ff.; Pfeiffer, *History* 140–44; cf. Klein "Callimachus" 16 ff.; Lefkowitz 1 ff.

3. The authorship has been doubted, most recently by Lloyd-Jones 59, and is not accepted by Gow and Page (though Page included it in his posthumous *Further Greek Epigrams* [Cambridge, 1981] 53–54); but in the *Palatine Anthology* the epigram is attributed to Apollonius "the scholar" (γραμματικός), while the lemmatist specifically identifies him as "the Rhodian." This may not be the best of evidence (Pfeiffer, *History* 143), but it is not necessarily on that account to be rejected. Here, it seems to me, the onus is on the disprover: what other Apollonius would be more likely, and for what reason, to produce an occasional squib of this sort?

4. *AP* 11.275 = Pfeiffer, ed., *Callimachus*, testim. 25; cf. A. Croiset, *Histoire de la littérature grecque*, 4th ed. (Paris, 1899), 5.211 n. 5.

5. *Suda* s.v. Καλλίμαχος; Ovid, *Ibis* 55–60; cf. R. Ellis, *P. Ovidii Nasonis Ibis* (Oxford, 1881) xxxi–xxxv.

6. Aristotle (*HA* 9.617ᵇ29), Herodotus (2.75), Strabo (17.2.4 [C.823]), and Aelian (*NA* 10.29) all describe the ibis, and its habits, in some detail: as we might expect, Aristotle's account is the most accurate, Aelian's the most fanciful (though not on that account the least useful in the present context, since he embodies beliefs that, though fictional, were widely held). Cf. Schol. Ovid *Ibis* 3(C₁) La Penna.

7. Thoth, the god of the scribes, was ibis-headed; and Jaroslav Černý, in *Ancient Egyptian Religion* (London, 1952) 144, remarks that "the outstanding characteristic of the late Egyptian religion is the revival and extensive growth of the worship of animals," due in great measure to "the endeavour of the priests and theologians to revert to the archaic state of the Egyptian way of life and thought." There is an interesting analogy here to the Alexandrian passion for resuscitating ancient myth.

8. Aelian *NA* 2.35, cf. 10.29; Plin. *HN* 8.97.

9. Strabo 17.2.4 (C.823). Aelian's description (10.29) is worth recording verbatim: πανταχοῦ δὲ καθιεῖσα ἶβις τὸ ῥάμφος, τῶν ῥυπαρῶν καταφρονοῦσα καὶ ἐμβαίνουσα αὐτοῖς ὑπὲρ τοῦ καὶ ἐκεῖθέν τι ἀνιχνεῦσαι, ὅμως δ' οὖν ἐς κοῖτον τρεπομένη λούει τε πρότερον ἑαυτὴν καὶ ἐκκαθαίρει.

10. Arist. *Poet.* 1459ᵃ3 (the translation is S. H. Butcher's). Cf. Pfeiffer, *History* 143. The exact figures are: Bk. 1, 1,362 lines; Bk. 2, 1,285 lines; Bk. 3, 1,407 lines; Bk. 4 (the repository for much peripheral matter), 1,781 lines. The normal session in the Theater of Dionysus consisted of four dramas: three tragedies followed by a satyr play.

11. Callim. fr. 398 Pfeiffer; cf. Pfeiffer, *History* 146.

12. Callim. fr. 359 Pfeiffer = Athen. 3.72a; cf. Klein, "Callimachus" 21–23; K. Ziegler, *Das Hellenistische Epos*, 2d ed. (Leipzig, 1966), cited by Lloyd-Jones 58, with further confirmatory material.

13. The classic example in Theocritus is the rape of Hylas, briefly sketched in *Id.* 13, and developed, at greater length and subtlety, with graphic erotic detail absent in the Theocritean version, by Apollonius (1.1207–72), who fashions a consistent and credible narrative (so, rightly, Zanker 130–31 with nn. 20–22) out of "bewilderingly divergent traditions about Hylas' fate"; cf. also the boxing match between Polydeuces and Amycus (Theocr. 22.27–134, Apollon. 2.1–97). If the essence of Hellenistic *imitatio* is to embellish, improve, expand (even this is arguable), then a good case can be made for the Theocritean versions having been earlier: well argued by Koehnken; see esp. pp. 17–25 ("Die Form der Kios-Episode"), 82; cf. Pfeiffer, ed., *Callimachus* 2.xlii, for the chronological difficulties involved in dating any poem of Theocritus later than 270.

14. Fraser 1.636–40. Though I basically agree with Fraser, Koehnken, and Pfeiffer against those—e.g., G. Serrao, "Problemi di poesia alessandrina, II," *Helikon* 5 (1965) 541–65—who give chronological priority to Apollonius, I would readily concede that the final judgment must rest on circumstantial probabilities and *a priori* esthetic assumptions, so that (Beye 30) "nothing substantial can be proved or demonstrated." On Callimachean echoes in Apollonius, see Lloyd-Jones 58.

15. Callim. frr. 7–21 Pfeiffer; Apollon. 4.1711–30. Cf. Fraser 1.722, with 2.1008–9 nn. 27–30.

16. Apollon. 3.927–37; Fraser 1.639 with n. 162.

17. For the testimonia see Vian and Delage 1.viii–xxv; cf. Lefkowitz 1–4, 12–16. See also *Suda* s.v. Ἀπολλώνιος and the two tantalizing *vitae* (1 and 2) printed on pp. 1–2 of Wendel.

18. Pfeiffer, ed., *Callimachus*, testim. 11a–19a.

19. Fraser, 1.330–32, argues that Apollonius became librarian at Alexandria *before* his departure for Rhodes (in F.'s view ca. 245), and never returned; but this involves too ruthless a discarding of such evidence as we have, on no very convincing grounds. I prefer the theory of Grenfell and Hunt, *Oxy. Pap.* vol. 14 pp. 100–101, which accepts the early rebuff and Rhodian sojourn; though I would, with Fraser, nevertheless place the date of Apollonius's appointment as librarian ca. 270–265 rather than (as Grenfell and Hunt do) in 246/5, a date that probably in fact marks the appointment of Eratosthenes, by Ptolemy Euergetes III. Cf. Pfeiffer, *History* 124, 141.

20. The existence of an early draft (προέκδοσις) of the *Argonautica* is proved by the scholia to the poem, which note variant readings in the two editions. It is noteworthy that while there are six such instances in Book 1 (at lines 284, 515, 542, 725, 788, and 800), there is only one in Book 2 (963), and none at all in Books 3 and 4: see Mooney, app. 1, "The Double Recension of the *Argonautica*," pp. 403–11; cf. Pfeiffer, *History* 141. This obviously does not *prove* that Apollonius in these latter books ceased to borrow from Callimachus, or indeed that Books 3 and 4 did not figure in the early draft (the former supposition, at least, is demonstrably untrue: see Fraser 2.1056 n. 272, and 1.638 ff.); but it does at least reveal a suggestive pattern. My own hunch (I would hardly call it more) is that a rough draft of Books 1, 2, and 4 existed from a very early period, perhaps including some matter now in Book 3, but that the working-up of Medea's passionate committal to Jason, together with what one might call a general "Callimachizing" of the treatment to bring it into line with current literary fashion, constituted the main addition to the final revised version. It is interesting, and perhaps significant, that the invocation to Book 4 (1–5) balks at trying to describe Medea's emotional state ("the mind within me flounders about in speechlessness") and asks the goddess to help out, whereas in fact Book 3 has handled this precise problem with subtlety and aplomb.

21. Tarn and Griffith 176 and n. 3. Berthold, *Rhodes* 48 n. 36, observes that "there is no direct evidence on a Rhodian maritime code, but later Roman sources indicate that Mediterranean sea-law was commonly known as 'Rhodian.'"

22. Book 4, which contains the most geographical and exploratory matter, is significantly longer than the other three books (in fact, 374 lines longer than Book 3, the next-longest). If this was the result, as it may have been, of revision and expansion, there can be no doubt that the context was a congenial one for the form that that expansion took.

23. *Vita* 2; *POxy.* 10.1241, ii.1; *Suda* s.v. Ἀπολλώνιος (though by a characteristic confusion this entry makes Apollonius succeed, rather than precede, Eratosthenes).

24. Pfeiffer, *History* 141; Fraser 1.452 with n. 38, citing schol. Ven. A on Hom. *Il.* 13.657.

25. Pfeiffer, *History* 140–42; Fraser 1.330–32. The reader should be warned that the dates, and sequence, of the first three librarians are still highly controversial, as is most of the evidence for Apollonius's career, in particular that regarding the chronology of his withdrawal or withdrawals to Rhodes: see, e.g., Lefkowitz 1–2; and Pfeiffer, *History* 141, who writes despairingly of the testimonia: "This is a labyrinth of self-contradictory statements, and no thread of Ariadne leads out of the darkness."

26. *POxy.* 10.1241, ii.

27. "Some maintain . . ." (*Vita* 2).

28. Fraser 1.625.

29. See, e.g., Fraser 1.626–34.

30. Carspecken 107; Lawall, "Apollonius' Argonautica" 119 ff. This, as Klein, "Callimachus" 22 with n. 16, points out, is no new perception, but goes back at least as far as A. Gercke's "Alexandrinische Studien," *RhM* 42 (1889) 247; see also M. Hadas, "The Tradition of the Feeble Jason," *CPh* 31 (1936) 166–69.

31. Fraser 1.627 ff.; Van der Valk 1.202–302.

32. Hurst 11 ff.

33. See E. Phinney, "Hellenistic Painting and the Poetic Style of Apollonius," *CJ* 62 (1967) 147–49.

34. Apollon. 1.519–58.

35. Webster, *Hellenistic Poetry* 30.

36. Ibid. 80.

37. H. A. Shapiro, "Jason's Cloak," *TAPhA* 110 (1980) 268–86, though he goes too far in asserting that this passage is the *only* instance of true *ekphrasis* in the *Argonautica*. On pictorial realism in Apollonius, and the "use of aetiology designed to link mythological past and contemporary experience," see Zanker 125–45, esp. 126–28.

38. Theocr. 15.78–86.

39. Herodas, *Mim.* 4.20–38, 56–76.

40. Hurst 21.

41. Cf. ibid.; Jenkins pls. 557, 558.

42. See, for an excellent example, his thumbnail sketch of the wretched Phineus (2.197–205), amid the stinking mess left by the Harpies (originally, I suspect, kites or vultures, which—as I have seen in India—have a knack of dive-bombing any exposed food with the speed and accuracy of a Stuka, snatching it on the wing as they go):

> He struggled up from his bed, dreamlike, spiritless,
> And tapped his way to the door on bony feet,
> Huddling over a stick, feeling the walls, joints shaking
> From weakness and age: his parchment flesh was cured
> With dirt, only the skin cobbled his bones together.
> Out of the house he came, knees buckling, and collapsed
> On the courtyard threshold. Blood rushed to his head, the ground
> Seemed to swim under his feet. He lay there speechless,
> Unconscious, unstrung.

43. E.g., Hom. *Il.* 12.243, "One omen is best, to fight for your fatherland," very popular among those who habitually paid mercenaries to fight for them.

44. Webster, *Hellenistic Poetry* 76; cf. Beye 152.

45. Apollon. 3.109–10.

46. Heracleitus *ap.* Hippolytus, *Ref.* 10.9.6 = fr. 242 Kirk and Raven.

47. Hom. *Il.* 24.129–31; cf. Beye 4–5, and Van der Valk, vol. 2 *passim*, which is, as Beye says (p. 179 n. 2), "a treasure house of examples of the execution of the theory of propriety by the Hellenistic textual critics of Homer."

48. Lesky 734.

49. See, e.g., Ciani, "Apollonio" 80–81; Pfeiffer, *History* 105 ff.; Fraser 1.463 ff.

50. Carspecken 131; cf. Apollon. 2.541–46.

51. Ciani, "Apollonio" 82, sees this very clearly: "Nell' ambiente culturale contemporaneo, se l'omerismo poteva esser fatto rivivere nella lingua e nelle forme esteriori, mancavano i presupposti fondamentali per la rinascita del genere epico, e cioé: il senso del grandioso, del meraviglioso, il senso del miracolo, del mito, la fede negli dèi, tutto il patrimonio di un' epoca primitiva che non poteva più rivivere genuinamente al tempo in cui viveva Apollonio."

52. Cf. R. Wyss, *Die Komposition von Apollonios' Argonautika* (Zurich, 1931) 41, and Carspecken 110 ff.; see also Klein, "Apollonius' Jason" 117 ff. I cannot take overseriously H. Fränkel's attempt to meliorize Jason's ἀμηχανία as "reflectiveness" or "prudence": see *MH* 17 (1960) 1–20, and Lloyd-Jones 70–71—or, indeed, Klein's efforts (ibid.) to interpret Jason in existentialist or structuralist terms, or both; though Alexandrian pedantry would surely have rejoiced in such splendid claptrap as (p. 124) "an avalance [*sic*] of binary algorithms, paradigmatic oppositions, operating within the symbolic code but hopelessly unmediated," etc. All of which seems to boil down to the not very extraordinary claim that Jason has elements in him of both hero and villain.

53. Ciani, "Apollonio" 84–85.

54. See J. R. Bacon, *The Voyage of the Argonauts* (London, 1925) chap. 9, "The Homeward Routes," pp. 107–24, esp. 118 ff.

55. Callim. *Hymn* 1.4–9; cf. Hurst 32.

56. Aristarchus *ap.* Athen. epit. 1.12c–f; cf. Pfeiffer, *History* 112; Beye 5.

57. Apollon. 1.774 ff. The scholiast on 1.721–22 comments on Jason's being presented in a cloak rather than armor because he is "unwarlike" (ἀπόλεμος), a quality also attributed to Paris (another erotic achiever) by Homer: cf. *Il.* 3.369–454. On Jason's sexual component as a distinctively Hellenistic trait see Beye, *GRByS* 10 (1969) 49–54.

58. As the magic practiced by Simaetha in Theocr. *Id.* 2 (and an increasingly common phenomenon as the Hellenistic age proceeds) makes all too clear. Cf. pp. 597 ff.

59. For a good recent analysis see J. H. Barkhuizen, "The Psychological Characterisation of Medea in Apollonius Rhodius *Argonautica* 3.744–824," *AClass* 22 (1979) 33–48, comparing Apollonius's interpretation with that of Euripides in his *Medea* and Pindar's in his fourth *Pythian Ode*.

60. Cf. also the account of Mopsus's death from snakebite (4.1518–25), and Phineus's fainting fit (above, n. 42), with Fraser's comments (1.634). See also Zanker, 131–32, who connects the passage with Herophilus's researches on the *medulla oblongata* (cf. p. 492).

61. G. Zanker's thesis in "The Love Theme in Apollonius Rhodius's *Argonautica*," *WS*, n. F., 13 (1979) 52–75, that love forms the main theme of the whole epic, not merely of Book 3, can only be sustained by a carefully selective reading.

62. Cf. Apollon. 4.419–20: "Kill Apsyrtos, if you like," Medea says, in effect; "I don't care": οὔτι μεγαίρω, "I don't grudge it one whit."

63. Schol. Apollon. 4.223–30; cf. Apollod. 1.9.24.

64. Apollon. 3.968–70.

65. Ibid. 4.693 ff.

66. Yet the charge is brought against him rather less often than one might suppose from Hadas's remarks; cf. *CW* 26 (1932) 44, *CPh* 31 (1936) 167, and his *History of Greek Literature* (New York, 1950) 203; echoed by Carspecken 101–2: eight times in all, counting every cognate form of the term, as pointed out by John Collins, "Studies in Book One of the *Ar-*

gonautica of Apollonius Rhodius" (diss., Columbia Univ., 1967) pp. 43–45. It is also used to characterize the Argonauts generally, and even Medea herself (3.772, 951, 1157; 4.107, 1049). Yet its application to Jason is peculiarly apposite on each occasion, and lingers in the memory: see 1.460; 2.410, 623, 885; 3.336(?), 423, 432; 4.1318. Cf. also Klein, "Apollonius' Jason" 116 ff. with n. 3.

67. Apollon. 4.1141–43.

68. Ibid. 1381–92. Zanker, 132 ff., stresses Apollonius's emphasis on surviving ancient landmarks to endorse the historical validity of myth: "The poet is nailing down the tradition with a vengeance."

69. Apollon. 1.888–909.

70. Ibid. 1207–10, 1221–39, 1324 ff.

71. Ibid. 2.194–269, 293 ff., 317–23, 549–602.

72. *Argo* passes through an invented river or canal directly linking the Po to the Rhône: Apollon. 4.625–29; cf. Eur. *ap.* Plin. *HN* 37.32. There are further odd divagations at 4.634–44 (cf. p. 327). Zanker, 135 n. 41, argues that such errors are due to Apollonius's reliance on trusted scholars to give him an authoritative account.

73. C. Day Lewis, *Collected Poems 1929–1936* (London, 1954) 149.

74. Cavafy, Ποιήματα A′ 23–24 = *Collected Poems* 66–69. "Always have Ithaca in your mind: / Arrival there is your destined goal / —But don't hurry the journey at all . . . / Ithaca gave you the marvelous journey. / Without her you'd never have set foot on the road."

75. Apollon. 2.516–27, 4.1641–88, 4.597–611, 620–26, 2.946–54.

76. Sirius, Apollon. 3.957–59, Hom. *Il.* 22.26–31; fleeing doves, Apollon. 1.1049–50, Hom. *Il.* 22.139–42; oxen, Apollon. 2.662–67, Hom. *Il.* 13.703–7; bees, Apollon. 1.879–82, Hom. *Il.* 2.87–90; boy in river, Apollon. 4.460–61, Hom. *Il.* 21.282–83. Cf. Carspecken 68 for other examples; and for an exhaustive compilation of all echoes from early epic, see M. Campbell, *Echoes and Imitations of Early Epic in Apollonius Rhodius* (Leiden, 1981).

77. Carspecken 70.

78. Callim. fr. 260 Pfeiffer, lines 64 ff. The final line is highly conjectural.

79. Apollon. 3.1020–21, Hom. *Il.* 23.598–99. Recent appreciations of Apollonius include A. W. Bulloch, in Easterling and Knox, eds., 586–98, and Hutchinson 85–142. For Bulloch, Jason is sinister rather than vacillating; what interests Hutchinson (in an otherwise plodding exposition) is the bizarre quality of Apollonius's wit. *Quot capita, tot sententiae.*

Chapter 14. Events in the West: Sicily, Magna Graecia, Rome

1. Cf. Just. 4.2.3: "No land was richer in tyrants."

2. DS 20.54.1; cf. 21 fr. 2.1 Walton: his assumption of the crown is here backdated to 307, during his African campaign. See also Just. 22.6.2.

3. Plut. *Tim.* 34; cf. Clearchus *ap.* Athen. 12.541d–e.

4. DS 16.65.1, Plut. *Tim.* 1.

5. Plut. *Tim.* 1, Just. 21.3.9–10.

6. Plut. *Tim.* 8–13, 20–21; DS 16.65 *passim*, 68.10–11, 69.3–6, 70.4–6; Nep. *Tim.* 2.1, 3.3.

7. Plut. *Tim.* 14–15, Just. 21.5 *passim*, Aelian *VH* 6.12, Clearchus *ap.* Athen. 12.541e, Cic. *Tusc. Disp.* 3.12.

8. Plut. *Tim.* 25–29 *passim*, DS 16.79–81, Nep. *Tim.* 2.4; cf. Freeman 4.324–30, Niese 1.422, Holm 2.208–10. The last-named remarks, probably correctly, that even if the river Halycus formed the boundary, "jedoch griechische Gemeinden, wenn auch westlich von ihm gelegen, frei waren." For the site of the battle, see Holm 2.208, 470; Talbert 69–74.

9. Lévêque, "De Timoléon" 138–39 with n. 15.

10. Plut. *Tim.* 35.

11. Talbert 163–66; cf. Dem. 32 *passim*, 56.9–10; Theophr. *HP* 8.4.5.

12. DS 16.82.6; cf. Talbert 133; Lévêque, "De Timoléon" 137.

13. Finley, *History* 97.

14. Westlake, *Timoleon* chap. 1 and pp. 55 ff.

15. Plut. *Tim.* 36; cf. Westlake, *Timoleon* 4, 56; Lévêque, "De Timoléon" 139–40.

16. Cf. Holm 2.217, who still manages to overrate his virtues (as opposed to his virtuosity), comparing him to, of all people, Garibaldi.

17. Polyb. 12.23.4–7.

18. Cic. *Ad Fam.* 5.12.7, Marcell. *Vit. Thuc.* 27, *Suda* s.v. Τίμαιος; cf. Westlake, *Timoleon* 2.

19. DS 16.69.5, 82.6; Plut. *Tim.* 22; Nep. *Tim.* 3.3.

20. DS 16.70.5, Plut. *Tim.* 22, 35.

21. Plut. *Tim.* 36–39, DS 16.90.1, Nep. *Tim.* 4–5.

22. Plut. *Tim.* 39; DS 16.90, cf. 83.

23. For the much-debated question of whether Timoleon set up this council, only to have it change its political tune after his death (the likeliest explanation, adopted here), or, alternatively, did not set it up, the council as described in our sources being a revolutionary group that only seized power when he was gone (cf. Berve, *Herrschaft* 23–24 n. 17), or, again, *did* set it up, his own council thereafter being disbanded and replaced by a new group of the type Berve envisions, see the judicious discussion by Talbert, 139–43, and cf. DS 19.4.3, 5.6, 6.4.

24. DS 19.6.4; cf. 5.6.

25. Cf. the special issue of *Kokalos*, vol. 4 (1958), devoted entirely to the impact of Timoleon on Greek Sicily, and Lévêque, "De Timoléon" 138–39.

26. DS 16.83.1–2; cf. Nep. *Tim.* 3.1–2.

27. For the huge influx of Corinthian silver into Sicily under Timoleon, see Talbert 161 ff.

28. See H. J. W. Tillyard, *Agathocles* (Cambridge, 1908); Berve, *Herrschaft*, and *Tyrannis* 1.441–57, 2.728 ff.; Mossé, *Tyrannie* chap. 3, pp. 167–77; Cary, *CAH* VII chap. 19, pp. 617–37. For Agathocles' coup, cf. Consolo Langher, "Agatocle" 382 ff.; and Lévêque, "De Timoléon" 141 ff., with bibliography there cited. See also K. Meister, *CAH* VII².1 chap. 10, "Agathocles," 384 ff.

29. Polyb. 12.15; cf. DS 19.2.1–7.

30. DS 21.17.1–3, Polyb. 12.15. Cf. Meister, *CAH* VII².1 384 n. Among other slurs, Timaeus described the young Agathocles as "a common whore" (*FGrH* 566 F 124b).

31. DS 21.17.1, Marcell. *Vit. Thuc.* 46. The value, and sources, of Diodorus's account (19.1.5–9.7, 65.1–6, 70.1–72.2, 102.1–104.4, 106.1–110.5; 20.3.1–18.3, 29.2–34.7, 38.1–40.1, 42.3–44.7, 54.1–57.3, 61.5–72.1, 77.1–79.5, 89.1–90.2, 101.1–4; 21.2–4, 8, 15–17.3) are much debated: see, e.g., Consolo Langher, "Strategato" 168 ff. Diodorus himself, though he severely censures Timaeus for a sustained campaign of lying vilification against Agathocles in Books 34–38 of his *History* (21.17.1–3; cf. 13.90 and Polyb. 12.25), nevertheless seems to share much of his bias. Since his other main source (apart from Duris of Samos?) was Callias of Syracuse, whom he also criticizes (21.17.4; but for precisely the opposite reason, i.e., that he was bribed by Agathocles into betraying the truthful function of history and "heaping continual unmerited praise on his paymaster"), it seems likely that he did little more than conflate the two accounts, using the one to trim the excesses of the other (e.g., over the matter of Agathocles' personal courage, 21.17.2–3). Timaeus is elsewhere praised by Polybius for careful and honest historiography (12.10.4); it seems likely that his treatment of Agathocles was a special case. Agathocles' supposed populist leanings (see p. 222) would automatically have ensured him a bad press with most contemporary historians.

32. Polyb. 15.35.1–6; cf. 9.23.2 and DS 20.63.

33. DS 19.1.7.

34. Just. 22.1.1–5, 12–14; DS 19.2, 3.1–2; Polyb. 12.15.2.

35. Just. 22.1.3–5: "forma et corporis pulchritudine egregius, diu vitam stupri patientia exhibuit. Annos deinde pubertatis egressus, libidinem a viris ad feminas transtulit. Post haec, apud utrumque sexum famosus, vitam latrociniis mutavit."

36. E.g., Mossé, *Tyrannie* 167.

37. DS 19.8.1.

38. DS 19.4.3–9.7 *passim*, Just. 22.2.1–12. For the Acragas-based opposition, under Cleomenes II's son Acrotatus, who proved himself a worse tyrant than most Sicilians, see DS 19.70.2–8, 71.1–5.

39. DS 19.5.5.

40. DS 19.5.6; cf. Just. 22.2.11.

41. DS 19.9.5–7.

42. Consolo Langher, "Politica" 29 ff., "Strategato" 117.

43. DS 19.106–10, 20.3–18, 29.2–34, 38–44.7, 54–70; Just. 22.4–7; cf. Niese 1.437–62; Will, *HP*² 1.114–18 (with exhaustive documentation).

44. DS 20.5.1–4 describes how he took advantage of the Carthaginians' preoccupation with an approaching grain convoy to get his squadron through the besiegers' lines; then, when the Carthaginian fleet decided to pursue him, the grain ships slipped into the Great Harbor and relieved the beleaguered city.

45. Finley, *History* 104.

46. Lévêque, "De Timoléon" 143.

47. Niese 1.457–59; Manni, "Agatocle" 156.

48. Schmitt, *Staatsverträge* no. 437, pp. 52–53; cf. Lévêque, "De Timoléon" 143 with n. 38.

49. DS 20.71–72, 77–79, 80–90.2; Just. 22.8.

50. Will, *HP*² 1.118–20.

51. Berve, *Herrschaft* 62–68, *Tyrannis* 2.730.

52. Manni, "Agatocle" 161. G. Marasco, "Agatocle e la politica siracusana agli inizi del III secolo a.C.," *Prometheus* 10 (1984) 97–113, has some interesting observations on Agathocles' anti-Carthaginian foreign policy, but exaggerates his influence in Magna Graecia and with the new dynasties of the Diadochoi.

53. Just. 23.2.6; cf. Will, *HP*² 1.120.

54. DS 20.104–5, 21.2; cf. Piper 12–13.

55. DS 21.4, Plut. *Pyrrh.* 9.

56. Plut. *Pyrrh.* 10, DS 21.15.

57. DS 21.16.1–5, Just. 23.2.3–12 (more reliable for the events surrounding Agathocles' death); cf. Niese 1.485–89. After he was dead his property was confiscated, his statues were pulled down, and by then, as seems clear, his popularity, even with the common people, had suffered considerable erosion: DS 21.18.1; cf. Meister, *CAH* VII².1 410.

58. Cary, *CAH* VII 636.

59. C. A. Gianelli, "Gli interventi di Cleonimo e di Agatocle in Magna Grecia," *CS* 11 (1974) 353–80. Cf. the evaluation by Meister, *CAH* VII².1 409–11.

60. Polyb. 15.35.6; cf. Manni, "Agatocle" 162: "Della grecità egli è quasi l'ultimo rappresentante, di Roma fu uno dei modelli più celebrati." Cf. Meister (above, n. 59) 411.

61. DS 21.16.1.

62. Plut. *Pyrrh.* 14: this all sounds remarkably like a reprise of the Athenian attitude to Sicily in 416: see Plut. *Nic.* 12, *Alcib.* 17; Thuc. 6.15.2, 90.2–4; cf. Kagan, *The Peace of Nicias and the Sicilian Expedition* (Ithaca, N.Y., 1981) 169 ff., and my *Armada from Athens* (London, 1970) chap. 3, pp. 37 ff.

63. Testimonia in Berve, *Tyrannis* 2.733–34: see esp. DS 22.13.1 ff., Polyb. 1.8.2–9.8, Just. 23.4.1–2.

64. Polyb. 1.11.7, DS 22.13.9.

65. Berve, *König Hieron* 70–71 with testimonia.

66. Athen. 5.206e, DS 16.83.2, Cic. *II Verr.* 4.53.118; cf. Finley, *History* 119–21; Berve, *König Hieron* 71; Pollitt, *AHA* 281.

67. Polyb. 1.62.8.

68. Kraay and Hirmer figs. 140–42.

69. Polyb. 7.8.1–8.

70. Cic. *II Verr.* 2.13.32, 26.63, 60.147; 3.6.14–15; 5.21.53, and elsewhere.

71. Livy 21.49–51, 22.37, 23.21.

72. Lucian, *Macrob.* 10; Polyb. 7.8.7; Livy 24.4.

73. Berve, *König Hieron* chap. 5, pp. 86 ff.

74. Livy 24.4–7; Polyb. 7.2.1–5.8, 7.1–8.

75. Berve (*loc. cit.* n. 73) writes, apropos Livy 24.27.1 ff., of "den Zwiespalt zwischen römerfreundlichen Oligarchen und karthagerfreundlichen Demos," which is perhaps too neatly symmetrical a division.

76. Livy 24.21 ff. *passim*; cf. Berve, *König Hieron* 95 ff.

77. Livy 24.29.4 ff.

78. Livy 24.30–34, Plut. *Marcell.* 14–19, DS 16.18–20.

79. Cited by Finley, *History* 122.

80. Arist. fr. 614 Rose, Just. 12.2.1–11, Livy 8.24, QC 8.1.37, Plut. *Mor.* 326B.

81. Plut. *Pyrrh.* 13–15; Just. 17.3.22, 18.1.1–3; Paus. 1.12.1–2; Zonar. 8.2.

82. Will, *HP*[2] 1.99, is worth quoting on this move: "P. retournait mettre son ardeur et ses talents au service de ses États héréditaires, en attendant que vînt l'en tirer sa grande tentation occidentale."

83. There seems little doubt that his plans in the West always involved the idea of conquest and empire: see Plut. *Pyrrh.* 14; cf. Lévêque, *Pyrrhos* 262 ff.; and above, p. 228.

84. Plut. *Pyrrh.* 13–15; Paus. 1.12.1–2; Just. 17.3.22, 18.1.1–2; cf. Will, *HP*[2] 1.122.

85. Will, *HP*[2] 1.130, citing the conclusions reached by Lévêque, *Pyrrhos* chap. 4, pp. 245–84.

86. Will, *HP*[2] 1.122.

87. 20,000 infantry, 3,000 cavalry, 2,000 archers, 500 slingers, and 20 (or perhaps 50) elephants: Plut. *Pyrrh.* 15, Just. 18.1.3, Zonar. 8.2.12.

88. Bengtson, *Griechische Geschichte* 395: he points out that it had more momentous consequences still: "entzündet hat sich der Konflikt zwischen Osten und Westen, zwischen Rom und Pyrrhos, an dem tarentinischen Kriege."

89. Zonar. 8.2–5; cf. Will, *HP*[2] 1.122–26, with full documentation; Grimal 302.

90. App. *Samn.* 10.1; cf. Lévêque, *Pyrrhos* 345–50.

91. Plut. *Pyrrh.* 22.

92. Polyb. 3.25.1–5; cf. Lévêque, *Pyrrhos* 416 ff.

93. DS 11.10.5–7, Plut. *Pyrrh.* 23; cf. Vartsos, "Osservazioni" 95–97.

94. Plut. *Pyrrh.* 22–24; Just. 23.3.1–10; DS 22.8, 10; Paus. 1.12.5.

95. The debate over whether Pyrrhus was, in any juridical or substantial sense, king of Sicily at this time (see Will, *HP*[2] 1.129) seems to me a wholly unreal academic exercise. Who made the rules? Pyrrhus's status was whatever he was capable, at any given point, of imposing by right of conquest, or eliciting by willing consensus.

96. Plut. *Pyrrh.* 25 ff.; cf. Lévêque, *Pyrrhos* 516 ff., with further testimonia.

97. Plut. *Pyrrh.* 26, Zonar. 8.6; cf. Will, *HP*[2] 1.131; and above, p. 144.

98. Zonar. 8.6.13.

99. Livy, *per.* 14; Dion. Hal. 20.14; Dio Cass. 10, fr. 41 Cary (cf. Zonar. 8.6); Just. 18.2.9; Val. Max. 4.3.9; cf. Holleaux, *CAH* VII 823.

Chapter 15. Urbanized Pastoralism, or Vice Versa: The *Idylls* of Theocritus, the *Mimes* of Herodas

1. Virg. *Ecl.* 4.58–59; 7.4, 26; 10.26, 31–33; cf. Rosenmeyer 232 with n. 2.

2. F. Brommer, *RE* Suppl. 8 (1956) s.v. "Pan," cols. 949 ff.; Rosenmeyer 239 ff. Pan was originally a local Arcadian deity; he only seems to have acquired more general currency in literature and art after 490, when he reputedly helped the Athenians at Marathon.

3. Hecataeus *ap.* Athen. 4.148e; Theopompus, *Philippika* 46 = Athen. 4.149d (both cited by Rosenmeyer 234).

4. Rosenmeyer 236.

5. Theocr. 1.1–2.

6. The point was made with telling force by Edward Abbey in his novel *The Brave Cowboy* (repr.: New York, 1977), and faithfully preserved in the film (retitled *Lonely Are the Brave*), with the eponymous hero, having rejected modern mechanized society, battling an *ēthos* that in the end destroys him.

7. Hesiod, *WD* 100 ff., 176 ff., 289 ff.

8. The classic work is J. K. Campbell's *Honour, Family and Patronage* (Oxford, 1964), which studies the Sarakatsani: see esp. chap. 2, "Of Sheep and Shepherds," pp. 19 ff., and appendixes 1 and 2, pp. 357 ff.

9. Theocr. 5.39–43, 87.

10. Theocr. 1.15; cf. Wernicke in Roscher's *Lexikon* 3.1 (1897–1902) cols. 1397–1400, and R. Blum and E. Blum, *The Dangerous Hour: The Lore of Crisis and Mystery in Rural Greece* (London, 1970) 329–32.

11. Wernicke (above, n. 10) cols. 1396–97. Dio Chrysostom (*Orat.* 6.17–20) cites Diogenes the Cynic as saying that Hermes took pity on Pan when the latter was roaming through woods and fields in hopeless ithyphallic passion for Echo, and taught him the art of masturbation, which Pan then passed on to all goatherds (a proverbially lecherous group: cf. schol. Theocr. 1.86a Wendel, λαγνότατοι οἱ αἰπόλοι).

12. Holden 27.

13. Van Sickle 18 with n. 1.

14. Dover, *Theocritus* lxi ff.

15. Ibid. lxii.

16. Dover, ibid., cites Gavin Maxwell, *The Ten Pains of Death* (London, 1959) 49 f., for a modern Sicilian parallel, the *botta e risposta*, which is "fiercely abusive and obscene."

17. Dover, *Theocritus* lxix.

18. Van Sickle 20. Hutchinson offers a competent, if unadventurous, literary survey of the poems (chap. 4, pp. 143–213). It is amusing that he, like some of the ancient critics, should be disconcerted by the "bizarreness" of Theocritus's "extreme rusticity" (p. 208). See also Bulloch in Easterling and Knox, eds., 570–86.

19. Halperin 237.

20. Theocr. 14.34–35.

21. Ibid. 7.78.

22. Aristoph. *Ach.* 994 ff.

23. Cf. Victor Ehrenberg, *The People of Aristophanes* (Oxford, 2nd ed. 1951, repr. with add. 1962) 319–21, with reff. there cited.

24. This is very much the view taken by Aristotle's student Dicaearchus of Messene (frs. 48–51 Wehrli; cf. Varro, *RR* 1.2.15, 2.1.3): he posits a sequence beginning with an underpopulated world of vegetarians, living off wild fruits and cereals, free from war and epidemics (the true utopian phase), and then moving on, via nomadism, the acquisition of property, stockbreeding, and population growth to the life of the settled farmer. Cf. below, p. 239; and Rosenmeyer 74 ff.

25. I remember once asking a classically educated farmer his opinion of the famous passage in the *Georgics* beginning *O fortunatos nimium, sua si bona norint, / agricolas* (2.458 ff.), and getting the diplomatic answer, "Well, I suppose it's all right as *poetry*."

26. Hesiod, *WD* 504 ff.

27. Arist. *Pol.* 1256ª29 ff.

28. Peters 202.

29. In *Modern Painters* (London, 1856) 3.157–72.

30. See, e.g., Dick 27 ff., and, for a more balanced view, Buller 35 ff., Rosenmeyer 248 ff.

31. Text in A. S. F. Gow, *Bucolici Graeci* (Oxford, 1952) 140–45.

32. Text ibid. 153 ff.

33. Lines 31–38; cf. Buller 36.

34. Theocr. 1.71–75, 7.74–77; Bion, *Lam. Adon.* 18; cf. Rosenmeyer 249.

35. On the ἀδύνατον in pastoral, see Rosenmeyer 264 ff.

36. Theocr. 7.131–38.

37. Rosenmeyer 248.

38. N. K. Sandars, *The Epic of Gilgamesh*, rev. ed. (Harmondsworth, 1972), 91–92; cf. Dick 27–28.

39. Hom. *Il.* 21.200–382.

40. Ibid. 14.346–51.

41. Ps.-Mosch. *Lam. Bion* 102–4; cf. Nilsson 204, 278; and p. 586.

42. Cf. Buller 47–48; "Nature must have harmony with man in order to be concerned about him; each man must be mortal in order to give nature an occasion for her grief."

43. Holden 13.

44. See J. Horowski, "Le folklore dans les idylles de Théocrite," *Eos* 61 (1973) 187–212; and cf. pp. 597 ff.

45. Rosenmeyer, chap. 4, 65–97 (quotation from 67–68); cf. Edquist, "Aspects of Theocritean Otium," in Boyle 19–32.

46. Rosenmeyer 42; cf. p. 243.

47. Rosenmeyer 77.

48. Aristoph. *Clouds* 46–50.

49. Rosenmeyer 71–72.

50. J. Ferguson, *Heritage* 83.

51. Testimonia and discussion in A. S. F. Gow 1.xv–xxii.

52. His *floruit* is variously placed in the 124th Olympiad (284–281: schol. Theocr. pp. 1, 135 Wendel = A. S. F. Gow 1.xv–xvi), or under Ptolemy I and Ptolemy II, which suggests a date around 280. Very little can be deduced from schol. Ovid *Ibis* 549, who claims that Hieron II had Theocritus strangled for lampooning his son and heir: the claim is almost certainly untrue, and is in any case no help in determining the date of death, except that it would create a *terminus post quem* of ca. 265 to allow the son, Gelon, to reach maturity.

53. Theocr. 11.7, 47 ff.; 28.16 ff.; *Suda* s.v. Θεόκριτος; cf. Dover, *Theocritus* xix.

54. Dover, *Theocritus* xix–xx.

55. Schol. Theocr. p. 1 Wendel = A. S. F. Gow 1.xv.

56. Lawall, *Theocritus' Coan Pastorals*, esp. 3 ff., 74 ff.

57. A. S. F. Gow 1.xxv.

58. Dover, *Theocritus* lvi.

59. Polyb. 1.8.3–5, Just. 23.4.1–2, Zonar. 8.6, Paus. 6.12.2.

60. A. S. F. Gow 1.xvii, 2.305–7; Dover, *Theocritus* xxi–xxii.

61. The chronology here is difficult. I am assuming that immediately after Hieron became στρατηγός in succession to Pyrrhus (275/4: Paus. 6.12.2, Polyb. 1.8.3–5, Just. 23.4.1) he was placed in command of a campaign against the Carthaginians of western Sicily (274/3?: Just. 23.4.2), in which he was victorious (Just. 23.4.12). His subsequent defeat of the Mamertines at the Longanus River (Polyb. 1.9.3–8) was followed by his elevation to the kingship in 269 (Polyb. ibid., cf. 7.8.4; DS 22.4) and his treaty of alliance with Carthage (Zonar. 8.6); that treaty he was later to repudiate when he entered into a permanent relationship with Rome (263: see p. 224).

62. Cf. Theocr. 15 *passim*, 7.91–93.

63. Theocritus opens with the same invocation as Aratus in the *Phaenomena*: "From Zeus let us begin" (ἐκ Διὸς ἀρχώμεσθα)—though it is uncertain, as between two roughly contemporary writers, who was quoting whom, or whether both of them were availing themselves of a familiar formulaic tag.

64. A. S. F. Gow 2.325.

65. For other examples of court flattery see 7.93; 15.46 ff., 94 f. Arsinoë is clearly described as sponsoring the entertainment (23–24: ἀκούω χρῆμα καλόν τι κοσμεῖν τὰν βασίλισσαν) and we know that she was alive at the time of writing: her death is now securely dated to 1 or 2 July 268; see E. Grzybek, *Du calendrier macédonien au calendrier ptolémζique* (Basel

1990) 103–12. I owe this reference to Prof. Christian Habicht. This gives *Id.* 15 a *terminus ante quem* of July 270. As we have seen (p. 240), though it is possible in this way to date one or two poems *before* 270, no work can positively be assigned to a later period (which of course does not rule out the possibility), and if Theocritus's 280± *floruit* is correct, the bulk of his *oeuvre* was indeed probably completed during Arsinoë's lifetime. It might help if we could date each version of Apollonius's *Argonautica* more closely, bearing in mind that Apollonius seems to have reworked Theocritus's treatment of at least two mythical themes (see Chap. 13 n. 13, p. 784); but the possible dates cover about two decades (ca. 285–ca. 265), and thus cannot be of significant use in this context.

66. See A. S. F. Gow 1.xxii–xxv. Lloyd-Jones, 66, remarks shrewdly that "English readers who can see little in Callimachus, Aratus or Apollonius frequently surrender to Theocritus, sometimes without realising that his aims and methods are a good deal more similar to those of his contemporaries than the bucolic poet's affectation of simplicity allows the unsophisticated reader to perceive."

67. Dover, *Theocritus* xviii–xix, lists *Id.* 8, 9, 19–21, 23, 25, 27, and *Epigrams* 23–27.

68. See, e.g., Theocr. 5.45 ff.

69. See Halperin, chap. 9, pp. 161 ff.; and the extensive literature there cited.

70. Athen. 11.476f–478e.

71. Homer, *Od.* 9.345–46; Athen. 11.481e; cf. Callim. *ap.* Athen. 11.477c = fr. 178.11–14 Pfeiffer.

72. Halperin 173.

73. Homer, *Il.* 18.483–603; Ps.-Hes. *Scut.* 139–317.

74. Webster, *Hellenistic Poetry* 160–61.

75. See, e.g., Charbonneaux et al. figs. 168, 273, 353.

76. Ibid. figs. 169, 171, 173, 174, 176, 178.

77. E.g., *Epigrams* 1–5, 8, 9, 17, 18, 21, 22.

78. Cf. Swigart 160: "The timelessness of the 'purest' pastorals is that of noon . . . a time when the world is drowsy with the humming of bees. This moment is extended for ever, and all the herdsmen of Theocritus are young."

79. G. B. Miles, "Characterisation and the Ideal of Innocence in Theocritus's Idylls," *Ramus* 6 (1977) 139–64.

80. Webster, *Hellenistic Poetry* 83.

81. Villard, in Charbonneaux et al. 140–41, with figs. 139, 140.

82. Theocr. 1.151, 4.46; cf. schol. 1.151d Wendel.

83. C. Segal, *Poetry* 83.

84. The wit and irony of Theocritus's treatment are well analyzed by Axel E.-A. Horstmann, *Ironie und Humor bei Theokrit* (Meisenheim, 1976) chap. 2, pp. 19–57.

85. Schol. Theocr. 15 arg. 8, p. 305 Wendel; cf. schol. Theocr. 2 arg. a, b, pp. 269–70 Wendel; cf. Van Sickle 30.

86. Plut. *Mor.* 712E (= *Quaest. Conviv.* 7.8.4).

87. Ibid. 712C (= *Quaest. Conviv.* 7.8.3).

88. Schol. Theocr. 2, arg. a, b, pp. 269–70 Wendel.

89. Page no. 73, pp. 328–31.

90. *Mim.* 8.77–79; the fragments of Hipponax are collected in M. L. West, *Iambi et Elegi Graeci* (Oxford, 1971) 109–71; cf. Knox 2–65 (somewhat outdated) for an eccentric but handy translation.

91. Ussher, "Mimiamboi" 65, 73–74.

92. Collected in G. Manteuffel, *De Opusculis Graecis Aegypti e Papyris, Ostracis, Lapidibusque Collectis* (Warsaw, 1930); many more easily accessible in Page 328 ff. Cf. Cunningham 7 ff.

93. *Suda* s.v. Σώφρων, Duris *ap.* Athen. 11.504b, Diog. Laert. 3.18, Quintil. 1.10.17.

94. Cf. Cunningham 8–9.

95. This is probably the correct form of the name: other variants known in antiquity were "Herondas" and "Herodes." See Ussher, "Mimiamboi" 65 and n. 1, with further reff.

96. When modern scholars are not huffing about his "kitchen sink" morality, they tend to overblow his literary skills (presumably in justification of the time and ingenuity they bring to his text): F. Will in his *Herondas* makes some inflated, not to say portentous, judgments on his work, e.g., (p. 52): "far from reproducing contemporary 'reality' Herondas pushes constantly towards a highly aesthetic strategy of historical reference, linguistic artifact-making, and general artistic distancing," etc. This is ingenious: at one stroke it promotes artistic subtlety and sanitizes the alleged moral reek of the gutter. There is similar symbolic overkill in J. Stern, "Herodas' *Mimiamb 6*," *GRByS* 20 (1979) 247–54. The attitude of Zanker 128 is far preferable: "slices from the lives of ordinary housewives, brutal schoolmasters, brothel-keepers, dildo-stitchers and go-betweens." Hutchinson's literary survey (pp. 236–57) adds little of substance, and at times betrays a rather charmingly donnish prissiness of the old school (e.g., p. 243, "a certain shoemaker's skill in making leather substitutes for the virile organ").

97. Cunningham 10, 66, 84, 117–18; cf. also Ussher, "Mimiamboi" 67 and nn. 10, 15; Mastromarco, *Public* 2–5.

98. Plin. *Ep*. 4.3.4.

99. Cf. Fraser 2.878 n. 30.

100. Cf. Arnott, "Herodas" 122.

101. Mogensen 395 ff.

102. Lawall, "Herodas" 165 ff., against Cunningham 174; cf. Veneroni 319 ff., and Cunningham's exposition in *CQ*, n.s., 14 (1964) 32–35.

103. Page no. 77, pp. 350–61; cf. Cunningham 8–9.

104. See Mastromarco, *Public*, for a summary of previous discussions and the latest restatement of what is now, in effect, the standard view: Herodas "designed his mimiambi for the social and cultural élite of the [*sic*] Hellenistic society" (p. 95).

105. In his review of Mastromarco, *Pubblico*, in *JHS* 101 (1981) 162.

Chapter 16. The Road to Sellasia, 239–222

1. Plut. *Arat*. 29: one is reminded of Admiral Lord Nelson's recurrent bouts of sea-sickness.

2. Polyb. 2.43.4; Plut. *Arat*. 16, 18–24; cf. above, p. 151, and Polyaen. 4.3.6.

3. Polyb. 2.43.5–6.

4. Plut. *Arat*. 16, Polyb. 20.4.5–6.

5. Plut. *Arat*. 31–32, *Agis* 13–15.

6. Larsen, "Aetolian-Achaean Alliance" 171; Marasco, "Politica" 113. Larsen's optimism perhaps does not take sufficient account of the unsavory reputation the Aetolians had as free-booters: in most of their alliances they were sought out, whether openly or covertly, as mercenaries.

7. Tarn, *Antigonus* 404.

8. Plut. *Arat*. 25–29, 33.

9. Cary 147 ff.

10. Arnold Toynbee, *The Greeks and Their Heritages* (Oxford, 1981) vii–viii, 65–72.

11. Cf. Pozzi 388–90, Piper 32–41.

12. Plut. *Agis* 12, *Cleom*. 10.

13. Plut. *Cleom*. 5, Polyb. 5.37.5; cf. Shimron, *Late Sparta* 36. On the demographic problems involved, see Davies, *CAH* VII².1 269. Polybius, whose prejudices on occasion get the better of his common sense, claims that it was *Cleomenes* who had Archidamus killed! Cf. Piper 51–52.

14. Shimron, *Late Sparta* 27: "In its first stage the Spartan movement would have looked askance at a general revolution in Greece or even in the Peloponnese; its aim was to rule over the other Greeks, and the Spartan tradition was one of support for the ruling classes." Cf. Oliva 179–80; Walbank, *CAH* VII².1 252 (on Agis's motivation).

15. Cf. Fuks, "Spartan Citizen-Body" 244 ff.

16. Plut. *Agis* 5; cf. Ollier 537; Fuks, "Spartan Citizen-Body" 254.

17. Rostovtzeff, *SEH* 1.191–211.

18. Cf. Ollier 536.

19. Shimron, "Polybius and the Reforms" 151, with further reff. Cf. Piper 33–34.

20. Plut. *Lycurg.* 31; cf. Diog. Laert. 7.172, Athen. 15.681c.

21. Ollier 548–50.

22. Plut. *Cleom.* 10. He specifically advised τῶν ξένων κρίσιν ποιεῖν καὶ δοκιμασίαν, ὅπως οἱ κράτιστοι γενόμενοι Σπαρτιᾶται σώζωσι τὴν πόλιν τοῖς ὅπλοις. Cf. below, n. 77.

23. Ollier 552.

24. Ollier, 538 (cf. 552–53), insists that "il y eut dans une telle entreprise une parte d'idéologie qui paraît incontestable," a view caustically challenged by Africa, *Phylarchus* 17.

25. Just. 28.1.2; cf. Dell 98. Hammond and Walbank 317–18 argue persuasively in favor of Demetrius's co-regency, but the motive alleged for his marriage to Phthia (the Aetolian *rapprochement* with Achaea) is less plausible.

26. Debate has centered on the possibility that the mother of Philip V was not Phthia, but the shadowy Chryseis—possibly a concubine, perhaps no more than a title of Phthia's (though why one indissolubly associated with Agamemnon's captive?)—who afterwards is said to have married Antigonus Doson. Historians are divided on this issue. Some identify Chryseis with Phthia; others see Chryseis as the mother (e.g., Will, *HP*[2] 1.360). S. Le Bohec, "Phthia, mère de Philippe V: Examen critique des sources," *REG* 94 (1981) 34–46, has persuasively demonstrated that Antigonus Doson first married Demetrius II's widow, Phthia, thus becoming the young Philip's stepfather, and then, when Phthia died, married Chryseis, who gave up her own children in order to rear the heir apparent.

27. Polyb. 2.44.1, 46.1, 49.7; Plut. *Arat.* 33.

28. Plut. *Arat.* 30, Polyb. 2.44.5, Polyaen. 2.36.

29. Plut. *Cleom.* 4.

30. Plut. *Agis* 13–15, *Arat.* 31.

31. Gruen, "Aratus" 613–14; cf. Plut. *Arat.* 35, with 25; Polyb. 2.44.6, 60.5. A useful survey of the Achaean League's position during this period is provided by P. Oliva, "Der achäische Bund zwischen Makedonien und Sparta," *Eirene* 21 (1984) 5–16.

32. Polyb. 2.43.7.

33. Plut. *Arat.* 34; Polyb. 20.5.3; *IG* II[2] 808; cf. Ferguson, *HA* 201 with further reff., Hammond and Walbank 331 with nn. 4–6, and M. J. Osborne, *Nationalization in Athens* (4 vols. Brussels 1981–83) 1.185–87, no. D 87; 2.172–77. *Contra,* Alan Henry, "Bithys son of Kleon of Lysimacheia", *Owls to Athens,* ed. E. Craik (Oxford 1990) 179–89, with a summary of earlier scholarship, identifies Bithys as a courtier of Lysimachus in the 280s.

34. Just. 28.3.4–8, Paus. 4.35.3, Polyaen. 8.52.

35. Hammond, *Epirus* 648 ff.; Will, *HP*[2] 1.349–51.

36. Polyb. 2.2.4–4.5.

37. Ibid. 2.4.6–9, 5 *passim*.

38. Ibid. 2.6.1–10, 8.4–5.

39. Gruen, *HW* 363–64.

40. Polyb. 2.6.7–8. Harris, 65, 195–97, overstresses the degree to which concern for Italian traders may have dictated Rome's reactions to Teuta. Gruen, "Material Rewards" 69, is more to the point: though the Senate was well aware of the commercial importance of the Adriatic, intervention by Rome was in response to claims by her allies and *amici* rather than on behalf of Roman or Italian mercantile interests.

41. Polyb. 2.9.1–7, 9; 2.10.1–9.

42. Gruen, *HW* 366.

43. Most notably by Maurice Holleaux: see *CAH* VII 828–33, 837–47.

44. Cf. Dell 99 ff.

45. Polyb. 2.11.1, 7: the figures reported are 200 ships, 20,000 infantry, and 2,000 cavalry.

46. Polyb. 2.11.4–12.13, App. *Illyr.* 7–8. Cf. Hammond and Walbank 334–35. The Illyrians were forbidden to sail south of Lissos.

47. Polyb. 2.2.1–2, cf. 2.12.7: Walbank, *HC* 1.153 merely remarks that "this war is important to P.'s main theme . . . as it first brought the Romans east of the Adriatic."

48. Livy 31.28; Trog. *prol.* 28; Just. 28.3.9, 14; Polyb. 4.5.3, cf. 2.44.2. Hammond and Walbank 335 seems to doubt that Demetrius died in battle, but Trogus clearly implies this.

49. Phylarchus *ap.* Athen. 6.251d; Livy 40.54.5.

50. Just. 28.3.11–16. He was also appointed *strategos*, military commander: Polyb. 20.5.7, Plut. *Aem. Paull.* 8.

51. Cf. Plut. *Cleom.* 16: ὑπὸ φθόης κατασηπόμενον.

52. Ferguson, *HA* 204–6.

53. Euseb. *Chron.* 2.120 Schoene, for the relaxation in 256; *IG* II² 775A 26, G. Dontas, *Hesperia* 52 (1983) 52–53, 57, *IG* II² 791.27, 788.29–30, for other fluctuations in strictness, based on the distinction between one comptroller or several (τὸν or τοὺς ἐπὶ τῆι διοικήσει), though study of the general phraseology in the various inscriptions (e.g., the use of the term κυρία ἐκκλησία with a single comptroller, and honorific references to Macedonian royalty with a plurality) suggests strongly that the distinctions, like most local privileges in this period, were merely titular and cosmetic.

54. Plut. *Arat.* 34, Paus. 2.8.6.

55. Polyb. 5.106.6, Plut. *Arat.* 41.

56. Patsch, *RE* 4 (1901) col. 2156, s.v. "Dardani," cites the proverb τρὶς τοῦ βίου λέλουται ὥσπερ Δαρδανεύς. Cf. Tarn, *CAH* VII 747.

57. Just. 28.3.14, Trog. *prol.* 28.

58. For the dates, see Lenschau, *RE* 11.1 (1921) col. 702, s.v. "Kleomenes (6)." Phylarchus, "romanesque et spartophile," perhaps a Stoic himself (Ollier 540) was Cleomenes' advocate (Polyb. 2.56, 63; Plut. *Arat.* 38, cf. *Them.* 32), Aratus his opponent: material from both sources has found its way into Plutarch and Polybius. Pausanias (2.9.1–2, 7.7.4, 8.27.15–16) seems to have drawn exclusively on Aratus. See also the judicious assessment by Piper, chaps. 3, 4, pp. 43–74.

59. Plut. *Cleom.* 1 *passim.*

60. Ibid.; Paus. 2.9.1; cf. 3.10.5. On Leonidas as the culprit, see A. Solari, *Ricerche spartani* (Leghorn, 1907) 69, cited by Shimron, *Late Sparta* 28.

61. Shimron, *Late Sparta* 36 n. 66. We do not need to waste time over Gabba's improbable theory, developed in *Athenaeum*, n.s., 35 (1957) 41 ff., and given a new lease of life by Shimron (ibid.), that Agis's son was eliminated, at the age of thirteen or so, by the ephors, at the time of Archidamus's recall.

62. Plut. *Cleom.* 2–4.

63. Marasco, "Polibio" 165 ff.

64. Polyb. 2.46 *passim*, Plut. *Cleom.* 6.

65. Polyb. 2.46.5–7; cf. Gruen, "Aratus" 614–15; Pozzi 390–91.

66. Plut. *Arat.* 35, *Cleom.* 4.

67. Plut. *Cleom.* 3.

68. Plut. *Arat.* 37, *Cleom.* 6; cf. Polyb. 2.51.3.

69. Polyb. 2.47.8–48.1, 48.5–7, 50.2.

70. Ibid. 2.50.10–51.1; cf. the excellent analyses by Gruen, "Aratus" 616; and Piper 59 ff.

71. Africa, *Phylarchus* 14 ff.; Ollier 548.

72. Will, *HP²* 1.371–72, puts it succinctly: "Cléomène III, ce 'révolutionnaire,' regardait en réalité vers le passé." Cf. Walbank, *CAH* VII².1 459, who describes Cleomenes' aims as being "practical and straightforward—to reimpose the ancient Spartan hegemony on Southern Greece."

73. Plut. *Cleom.* 13.

74. Polyb. 2.47.3; Plut. *Cleom.* 7–8, 10–11; Paus. 2.9.1; for the large modern literature (which adds surprisingly little), see Will, *HP²* 1.375; Shimron, *Late Sparta* v–xiii. Forrest, *A History of Sparta*, 2d ed. (London, 1980), 144, regards it as an "unanswerable question" whether the "social programme" of Agis and Cleomenes was "devised by them for the greater good of the world at large, of Spartans, of Sparta, or of themselves." This seems to me

unduly pessimistic. Even those, like Fuks, who are prepared to take the propaganda about equality ($\grave{\iota}\sigma\acute{o}\tau\eta\varsigma$) at its face value have to concede that it only applied to the Spartan citizen body. See Fuks, "Agis" 165.

75. Paus. 2.9.1, *IG* V.1 48 (and elsewhere), Plut. *Mor.* 795F. Cf. Pozzi 401 n. 144; P. Cartledge, A. Spawforth, *Hellenistic and Roman Sparta* (London and New York 1989) 51–52.

76. Plut. *Cleom.* 10–11. An admirable gesture, and first-class propaganda: however, it is by no means impossible that it enabled Cleomenes actually to *increase* his supporters' holdings, if not his own.

77. Plut. *Cleom.* 10, 11: the key terms are οἱ κράτιστοι and τοῖς χαριεστάτοις. The former has a range of meanings from "strongest," "most excellent" (LSJ s.v.), to a regular sense, in the plural, of "the aristocracy" (Xen. *Hell.* 7.1.42, etc.). The latter, more significantly, has a prime meaning of "graceful," or "beautiful," and in the plural comes to mean "men of elegance" (or of taste, or accomplishment): cf. Isoc. 12.8, Arist. *Metaph.* 1060^{a}25, Plat. *Rep.* 605B. The plural usage is contrasted by Aristotle to οἱ πολλοὶ καὶ φορτικώτατοι, which would seem to clinch the matter (*Eth. Nic.* 1095^{b}22; cf. *Pol.* 1267^{a}1).

78. Polyb. 2.47.3: τό τε πάτριον πολίτευμα καταλύσαντος καὶ τὴν ἔννομον βασιλείαν εἰς τυραννίδα μεταστήσαντος. Cf. Walbank, *Aratus* 84–86 and 165–66, and *HC* 1.245–46, where it is pointed out that Plutarch's version reflects that Phylarchan tradition (*Cleom.* 7), whereas Polybius was drawing on Aratus. This does not in any way invalidate the truth of Polybius's statement, as Walbank himself realizes (*HC* 245): "Behind all this was the ambition to establish a Spartan hegemony in Greece." Even Plutarch criticizes the killing of the ephors (*Cleom.* 9–10).

79. Paus. 3.7.1; cf. Marasco, "Storia" 7 ff.

80. Marasco, "Cleomene" 45 ff.

81. Plut. *Cleom.* 11.

82. Plut. *Agis* 8, *Cleom.* 11, *Arat.* 38.

83. Plut. *Cleom.* 17; cf. *Arat.* 39.

84. Dudley, *History* 74 ff.

85. Cf. Oliva 180: "Nun konnte er zur Verwirklichung seines wichtigsten Zweckes schreiten, nämlich für Sparta sein altes Ansehen zurückzugewinnen und es zur entscheidenden Macht auf dem Peloponnes zu machen," etc. Cf. Walbank, *CAH* VII².1 459.

86. Polyb. 2.51.1–2, Plut. *Cleom.* 22. Whether, as Polybius supposes, Ptolemy had been supporting Cleomenes from the beginning of the war (thus driving Aratus and the League to treat with Antigonus), or, alternatively, was only induced to do so by the Macedonian-Achaean *entente*, or, again, whether neither of these allegations is true, remains a problem on which much ingenuity has been expended and no final certainty is possible; it is also of relatively marginal importance. See Oliva 182–83 with n. 11 and bibliography there cited. Aratus had received an annual six talents since 251, when Ptolemy II visited Egypt and made the arrangement: Plut. *Arat.* 12, 41; *Cleom.* 19; Cic. *De Offic.* 2.82. Presumably Cleomenes now was allotted a similar amount. Cf. Walbank, *HC* 1.245–46, 250.

87. Plut. *Cleom.* 22.

88. "In Sparta" and "Come, O King of the Lacedaemonians": Cavafy, Ποιήματα Β΄ 64, 80 = *Collected Poems* 290–91, 314–15. The first of these poems concludes with the following splendid stanza:

> As for the humiliation, she couldn't care less.
> The Spartan spirit, of course, was something
> No *parvenu* Lagid had the wit to understand,
> So Ptolemy's demand could not,
> In fact, humiliate a manifest
> Lady like herself, a Spartan prince's mother.

89. Plut. *Cleom.* 11, 14, *Arat.* 39; Polyb. 2.51.3, 58.4; Paus. 2.9.2, 7.7.3.

90. J. V. A. Fine, *AJPh* 61 (1940) 140; E. Bikermann, *REG* 56 (1943) 295, 303.

91. Polyb. 2.51.4–7; cf. Gruen, "Aratus" 623–24, who argues, rightly in my opinion, that this move was not a piece of secret diplomacy on the part of Aratus, and that the presence

of his son on the embassy was an attempt to block any really exorbitant demands on Antigonus's part.

92. Plut. *Cleom.* 15, *Arat.* 39. Cleomenes "vomited a great deal of blood and lost the power of speech."

93. Plut. *Cleom.* 15, based on Phylarchus, stresses Cleomenes' dominance; *Arat.* 38–39 undercuts Phylarchus for gross prejudice in Cleomenes' favor, gives Aratus the key role in blocking negotiations, and offers some interesting details about the personal feud between the two leaders. Piper 61 surprisingly characterizes Cleomenes' demands as "moderate."

94. Plut. *Arat.* 39–40, *Cleom.* 17–19; cf. Polyb. 2.52.1–3.

95. Plut. *Cleom.* 19, *Arat.* 41.

96. Both passages of Plutarch (ibid.) assert that Cleomenes offered Aratus, specifically, "double the contribution he was getting from King Ptolemy," i.e., twelve talents. It would be unwise to take this anecdote as sure evidence that as late as 225 Aratus was still *necessarily* on Ptolemy's payroll (though he may have been: Ptolemy could well have decided to hedge his bets for a while). What makes it peculiarly implausible is the unlikelihood of Cleomenes at any time disposing of sufficient funds to spare twelve talents as a bribe. Indeed, it is very unlikely (see n. 86, above) that his entire subvention from Ptolemy exceeded that originally bestowed on Aratus, and he had far more pressing uses for this (not least the payment of the mercenaries on whom he depended) than squandering it as a *douceur*, without any guarantee that this would have the desired effect. If Cleomenes made the offer at all, it could well have been with the object of making Aratus suspect to other League members. This would also explain his careful refusal to touch Aratus's property in Corinth (Plut. *Arat.* 41; cf. *Per.* 33). That he had such a sum available is improbable; that he would actually have spent it in this way is incredible.

97. Plut. *Cleom.* 16: τὸ δεινότατον ὧν κατηγόρει Κλεομένους, ἀναίρεσιν πλούτου καὶ πενίας ἐπανόρθωσιν.

98. Plut. *Arat.* 39, 44, *Cleom.* 17–19, Polyb. 2.52.1–2. Piper 63 rightly stresses the prestige accruing to Cleomenes for his unprecedented success with Argos.

99. Plut. *Cleom.* 19, *Arat.* 41.

100. Polyb. 2.52.3–4; Plut. *loc. cit.* (n. 99). Cf. Hammond and Walbank 348–49: the terms of the agreement with Antigonus are in many respects demeaning to the Achaean League and indicate with some clarity just how desperate Aratus and his supporters had become.

101. Plut. *Arat.* 38.

102. Polyb. 2.47.4 ff., Plut. *Arat.* 38. By far the best analysis of these tangled events is that of Gruen, "Aratus" 609 ff., to which, as will be apparent, I am heavily indebted.

103. Plut. *Cleom.* 16, *Arat.* 38.

104. Gruen, "Aratus" 618–19; cf. Plut. *Arat.* 38.

105. The League: Polyb. 2.38.6, 42.3. The Aetolians: 2.45.1–4, 46.1–3. Antigonus Doson: 2.47.5, 64.6, 68.1–2, 70.1.

106. Plut. *Cleom.* 16, 18; *Arat.* 39.

107. Plut. *Arat.* 43–45, *Cleom.* 20–27.

108. Polyb. 2.52.2, 53.2 ff.; Plut. *Cleom.* 17–18, 20; cf. Oliva 184–85; Shimron, *Late Sparta* 46.

109. Plut. *Cleom.* 20. This argues against the otherwise sensible-sounding thesis of Urban, *Wachstum* 207 ff., that such alignments were more dependent upon traditional support for Sparta or Aetolia. Cf. Piper 65–66.

110. Will, *HP*[2] 1.400; cf. Plut. *Cleom.* 22. Phylarchus, in a passage rightly castigated by Polybius (2.63.1), but accepted by Walbank (*CAH* VII[2].1 471), dramatizes the cutoff by placing it only ten days before Sellasia, a characteristic Phylarchan embellishment.

111. Plut. *Cleom.* 23; cf. Macrob. 1.11.34; I. Didu, "Cleomene III e la liberazione degli iloti," *AFLC*, n.s., 1 (1976/77) 5–39; Fuks, "Agis" 165–66 with n. 40; Africa, *Phylarchus* 65. The theory advanced by Daubies, *Historia* 20 (1971) 665–96, that *no* helots fought at Sellasia,

has (rightly) found few takers: see the criticisms of Urban, "Heer" 95 ff.; Marasco, "Cleomene" 46 with n. 7. See also Piper, 71–72, who sees no problem in helots finding the sum of five minas "now that Laconian economy was based on money," a not altogether convincing assertion. It is hard to estimate what this meant in terms of real money—perhaps between one and two years' wages for the average working man: a plasterer on Delos, for example, now made 1½ drs. a day. See G. Glotz, *Ancient Greece at Work*, tr. M. R. Dobie (London, 1926), 359–61.

112. Schmitt, *Staatsverträge* no. 507, pp. 212–17, with full bibliography (= *SIG*³ 1.518); cf. Polyb. 4.54.3. See also Niese 2.335 ff.; Will, *HP*² 1.389–94; Larsen, *Greek Federal States* 324 ff.

113. Larsen, *Greek Federal States* 325.

114. Plut. *Arat.* 45.

115. Polyb. 5.39.6; 9.23.3, 29.10; 18.36.3; cf. Marasco, "Storia" 27.

116. Polyb. 2.37–71 *passim*, esp. 2.40.4; but cf. 2.47.11.

117. Paus. 2.9.1–2, 7.7.4, 8.27.15–16; cf. Ollier 539; Pozzi 388.

118. Plut. *Cleom.* 23–25, *Philop.* 5; Polyb. 2.55.1–7, 62.9–10.

119. Polyb. 2.65–69 *passim*; Plut. *Cleom.* 27–28, *Philop.* 6, *Arat.* 46; cf. Tarn, *CAH* VII 758–62; Hammond and Walbank 354–61 with fig. 11; and, for the site, W. K. Pritchett, "The Battle of Sellasia in 222 B.C.," *Studies in Ancient Greek Topography*, part 1 (Berkeley and Los Angeles, 1965) 59–70; *contra*, J. D. Morgan, *AJA* 85 (1981) 328–30. Bearing in mind Polybius's well-known insistence on autopsy of sites and, in general, personal experience (αὐτοπάθεια: Polyb. 12.25ʰ4–6 Paton; cf. Paus. 8.30.8), it is reassuring to examine the vindication of Polybius's account of Sellasia that Pritchett (that peerless and highly critical topographer) provides, against much previous disbelief. He finds no error in P.'s version (p. 69); indeed, he concludes, "I know of no other ancient battle in which the account and the topography seem to accord so easily."

120. Plut. *Cleom.* 29.31–32, Polyb. 2.69.10–11.

121. A friend—clearly acting on Stoic principles—is said to have counseled him to prefer suicide to Ptolemy's patronage; but Cleomenes refused, on the grounds that all was not yet lost, and they should not give up hope: Plut. *Cleom.* 31.

122. For an anecdote of Sphaerus at the court of Philopator, showing the barely veiled contempt with which he was treated there, see Athen. 8.354e, Diog. Laert. 7.177; cf. Ollier 544–45.

123. Africa, *Phylarchus* 59, with testimonia; Piper 80–81.

124. Plut. *Cleom.* 36–37, Polyb. 5.39, Just. 28.4.10–11.

125. Plut. *Cleom.* 30; Polyb. 2.67.4–8, cf. 68.1–2. For the "Alexandrizing" of Doson's fortunes, see Athen. 251d; and for his dedication of spoils to Apollo after Sellasia, *SIG*³ 518 = Burstein, *Translated Documents* no. 63, p. 86.

126. Polyb. 2.70.1; Paus. 2.9.1–3, 4.22.4; Plut. *Cleom.* 30; cf. A. H. M. Jones, *Sparta* 157; Shimron, "Polybius and the Reforms" 149–50, and *Late Sparta* 60–61.

127. Polyb. 4.6.4–7.

128. Polyb. 4.9.6, 15.4–6, 16.5, 19.1, 24.6. Cf. Shimron, *Late Sparta* 67–68. Piper 74 states, bleakly: "With the defeat of Cleomenes, Spartan history ceases to be a chronicle of greatness and declines into a story of petty tyrannies."

129. Walbank, *Aratus* 112.

130. Ibid. 201. It is one of fate's ironies that (Plut. *Cleom.* 27), had Cleomenes held off only another two days or so before giving battle, the news from Macedonia would have made it clear that Doson must evacuate the Peloponnese at once, and Sellasia need never have been fought. The situation is reminiscent of Perdiccas in Egypt, succumbing only a day or two before the news of Eumenes' great victory would have secured his position beyond immediate challenge. See above, p. 14 with n. 76.

131. Plut. *Cleom.* 30, *Arat.* 46–47; Polyb. 2.70.4–7. See Walbank, *CAH* VII².1 473, for a balanced assessment of Doson's achievements in stabilizing the Macedonian regime and restoring its dominance in central Greece and the Peloponnese. Cf. also Hammond and Walbank 362–64.

132. Polyb. 2.63.1; cf. Will, *HP*² 1.400.

133. Polyb. 5.34.6–9, a thumbnail sketch of the generally vigorous foreign policy of the first three Ptolemies (in pointed contrast to that of Ptolemy IV Philopator).

134. *OGIS* 56, pp. 93 ff. = Austin 222 (with omissions), pp. 366–68; cf. Bouché-Leclercq, *HL* 1.266 ff. On Berenice II, note the sensible remarks of Pomeroy, *Women* 20–23.

135. In the next year (23 Aug. 237) Ptolemy III laid the foundation stone of the colossal Horus temple at Edfu (Apollinopolis Magna), which was only completed nearly two centuries later by Cleopatra VII's father, Ptolemy XII Auletes.

136. Polyb. 5.58.10 f.; cf. Will, *HP*² 1.255–59.

137. Tarn, *CAH* VII 720; questioned by Will, *HP*² 1.296.

138. Just. 27.2.6–11, Trog. *prol.* 27; cf. Will, *HP*² 1.295.

139. Testimonia conveniently assembled in Will, *HP*² 1.296–301; cf. Hansen 34–35. The date of Attalus's assumption of the title of βασιλεύς is disputed: some (e.g., most recently Pollitt, *AHA* 81) postpone it until the defeat of Hierax; but the evidence, though sketchy, seems to me to indicate an earlier period.

140. Hansen 36–37.

141. Alcman 1.16–17 Page.

142. Bouché-Leclercq, *HL* 1.274–76.

143. Ibid. 277–78.

144. Tarn, *CAH* VII 722–23; Bevan, *House of Seleucus* 1.202–3.

145. Bevan, *House of Seleucus* 1.203–5, assembles the sketchy and scattered evidence for his career; further details in Will, *HP*² 1.313–14.

146. Polyb. 4.48.6–13.

147. The exact date, because of conflicting theories concerning Egypt's two calendars, is uncertain: estimates vary from Oct.–Dec. 222 to Feb. 221. See Will, *HP*² 2.28, who also correctly observes (p. 27) that Ptolemy IV "fut à coup sûr le premier souverain médiocre de la dynastie et . . . c'est sous son règne que l'Égypte commence à connaître les difficultés internes qui vont ruiner irrémédiablement sa puissance."

PART THREE. PHALANX AND LEGION, 221–168 B.C.

Chapter 17. Polybius and the New Era

1. For the concept of συμπλοκή, the interconnection of events, in Polybius's opinion, from the time of the Naupactus conference (217) to Pydna (168), which marked the beginning of full Roman domination, see Walbank "*Symploke*" 197 ff. = *Selected Papers* 313–24.

2. Polyb. 1.3.1.

3. Polyb. 5.33.1–2, 15.36.8–9; cf. Sacks 214–17. Polybius claimed, mistakenly, that Ephorus had attempted something of the sort in the fourth century.

4. Polyb. 1.1.5, cf. 3.1.4–5; Eisen 13.

5. Polyb. 3.4–5 *passim*, esp. 3.4.1–2, 7–8; Shimron, "Polybius on Rome" 99 ff.

6. Ziegler cols. 1482–83.

7. See, e.g., Musti, "Polibio negli studi" 1116–17; Walbank, *HC* 1.292 ff., *Selected Papers* 280–82.

8. Walbank, *HC* 1.299 ff., *Selected Papers* 325 ff.

9. Walbank, *HC* 1.296, lists some of the apparent additions, including 3.32.2, 37.11, 39.6–8, 59.4, 61.11, 86.2; 12.3.1–6(?), 27 ff.

10. Eisen 31 with n. 37, Ziegler col. 1487.41; cf. Polyb. 3.5.7–8 and (for what is, in effect, a redactor's obituary note) 39.5. The way in which the whole paragraph is cast suggests that there may well have been considerable spackling of historical gaps by an editor who was quite ready to assume, as Polybius himself did on occasion, first-person narrative. Indeed, the smoothness of integration here makes any second-guessing of other such patches the merest

speculation: who would have suspected an editor's intrusion here had reference to the author's death not revealed it?

11. The uncompromisingly unitarian thesis of H. Erbse, "Zur Entstehung des poly-bianischen Geschichtswerkes," *RhM* 94 (1951) 157–79, according to which the whole of the *Histories* was composed after 146, is hard to accept. Cf. other reff. in Musti, "Polibio negli studi" 1118; *contra*, Brink and Walbank, *CQ*, n.s., 4 (1954) 97–122.

12. Roveri 55.

13. Cf. G. Nenci, "Il motivo dell' autopsia nella storiografia greca," *SCO* 3 (1955) 14–46, esp. 38–40.

14. See Musti, "Polibio negli studi" 1122–24, for a useful breakdown of scholarship on these terms, and in particular Walbank, *Polybius* chaps. 2–3 *passim*.

15. Polyb. 1.14.6, 12.12.3; cf. 34.4.

16. Walbank, *HC* 1.16–26, *Polybius* 58–65; Ziegler col. 1532.

17. Polyb. 29.21.3–7.

18. Walbank, *Polybius* 68 (cf. 58–65), makes the perceptive comment: "*Tyche* and Poly-bius are shown as being in a sense complementary to each other: each is a creative artist in the relevant field, the one producing the *oecumene*, the other its counterpart in the unified work of history. . . . *Tyche* stands in an absolutely fundamental relationship to his whole conception—without her, the pattern collapses." Cf. Polyb. 29.22.2–3.

19. Polyb. 36.17.1–2, 15, cf. 18.28.4–5; Roveri, "Tyche in Polibio," *Convivium* 24 (1956) 275–93; Lesky 777.

20. Scholars on the whole concede Polybius's basic rationalism in his handling of Tyche, "pur nella varietà delle sfumature nei giudizi dei vari studiosi" (Musti, "Polibio negli studi" 1126–27). Lesky, 777, observes that "in Polybius we find the multiplicity of notions which in the Hellenistic age had collected as the flotsam of religious thought."

21. Polyb. 1.4.1–2.

22. Polyb. 1.4.5.

23. Polyb. 1.35.6.

24. Polyb. 2.35.4–6; 11.5.8, 6.5–7; 29.19.1–2.

25. Polyb. 16.12.3–11.

26. Pédech, "Idées" 35 ff., cf. *Méthode* 397 n. 296, tries to demonstrate that Polybius's religious beliefs were (though he does not put it quite that way) as systematic and coherent as those of a French Catholic intellectual; the attempt is not convincing, and has been effectively demolished by A. J. L. van Hooff, "Polybius' Reason and Religion," *Klio* 59 (1977) 101–28, though the latter goes too far the other way in making Polybius an equally systematic Marxist atheist.

27. Polyb. 6.56.6–12.

28. Polyb. 16.12.9.

29. Fr. 25 Battegazzore and Untersteiner (*I sofisti*, vol. 4 [Florence, 1962], 304–15) = 88 B 25 D-K; cf. Walbank, *HC* 1.741–42.

30. M. Dubuisson, "Sur la mort de Polybe," *REG* 93 (1980) 72–82, following Pédech, *LEC* 29 (1961) 145–56, repeated in *Méthode* 518 ff., argues for 208; but this conflicts with the very specific evidence of Lucian (*Macrob.* 23) that Polybius was 82 at the time of his death, if we also take into account Polybius's own reference (3.39.8) to the Via Domitia, only con-structed 120–118. This gives us a *terminus post quem* for his death, making 200 the earliest pos-sible date for his birth, and agrees well with his still being a "boy" (παῖς) in 182 (Plut. *Philop.* 21). Attempts to treat Lucian's figure as calculated merely on the basis of Polybius's ἀκμή are, as Ziegler says (col. 1445), "Hyperkritik."

31. The name and relationship are confirmed by an inscription of thanksgiving from the men of Elis: *SIG*³ 686; cf. Polyb. 22.3.6; Paus. 8.9.1, 30.8, 37.2, 48.8; *Suda* s.v. Πολύβιος.

32. Livy 38.33–34, Plut. *Philop.* 16.

33. Cf. Gruen, *HW* chap. 14, 481 ff., esp. 496–505.

34. Polyb. 31.14.3, 29.8.

35. Polyb. 22.19. The exact date is uncertain: it may have been either 187 or 184; cf. Ziegler col. 1446.45–46.

36. Polyb. 24.11–13; Plut. *Mor.* 790F; Walbank, in Gabba 7, and *HC* 3.264–65; Lehmann 240 ff.; Errington, *Philopoemen* 218 ff.; Gruen, *HW* 482–83.

37. Polyb. 22.7.7, 24.13.8–9; cf. Gruen, 482–83 with nn. 7–11.

38. Gruen, *HW* 500 with n. 85.

39. Plut. *Philop.* 21.

40. Polyb. 10.21, Ziegler col. 1472.

41. Polyb. 29.24.6.

42. Walbank, *HC* 3.258.

43. Polyb. 22.9.1–12; cf. 22.1.5–7, 3.5–9, 7.1–2.

44. But see Polyb. 12.25^{g}1–2 Paton for a withering criticism of historians who presume to write about battles without the benefit of personal military experience.

45. Polyb. 28.6.9.

46. Ziegler col. 1448.

47. Polyb. 28.6–7.

48. Polyb. 28.13.1.

49. Polyb. 28.3 *passim.*

50. Polyb. 28.6 *passim.*

51. Polyb. 24.8.8–10.15 *passim.*

52. Polyb. 24.9.3–7, 10.14.

53. Gruen, *HW* 497 n. 70, and "Class Conflict" 50 n. 24, gives a representative selection. Gruen's analysis of this vexed episode in the *Histories* is the most persuasive known to me, and my own account is heavily indebted to it.

54. Polyb. 24.8.6.

55. Polybius is reduced to arguing that Callicrates was supposed to present a different brief, but ignored his instructions (24.8.7–9)—and this in the presence of two fellow envoys! It has been left for Lehmann (287 n. 303) to get round this difficulty by suggesting that Callicrates *spoke in Latin,* which neither of the other two understood.

56. Polyb. 24.8.1.

57. Gruen, *HW* 498.

58. Polyb. 24.9.11–14.

59. Callicrates' στρατηγία is generally dated to 180/79—e.g., by Walbank, *HC* 3.19, cf. 264—but 179/8 is also a possibility (Errington, *Philopoemen* 263 ff.; cf. Gruen, *HW* 499 with n. 80), and this would imply the customary alternation of parties in the Achaean leadership. In any case it is highly unlikely that Callicrates' election was the direct result of his ambassadorial activities.

60. Gruen, *HW* 500 with n. 85; cf. "Class Conflict" 33 with n. 35.

61. P. S. Derow, "Polybios and the Embassy of Kallikrates," *Essays Presented to C. M. Bowra* (Oxford, 1970) 12–23. On the restoration of the exiles, see Polyb. 24.8–10; *SIG*³ 634.

62. Polyb. 28.3.8–10.

63. Polyb. 28.6 *passim.*

64. Polyb. 28.3.6.

65. Polyb. 28.12.1–6, 13.1–6.

66. Polyb. 28.13.7–14.

67. Paus. 7.10.11, Livy 45.31.9; cf. Polyb. 30.13.

68. He did not, as has been argued from his assertion (29.21.8) that he personally witnessed the end of the Macedonian monarchy, ἅτε γεγονὼς αὐτόπτης τῆς πράξεως, himself take part in the battle of Pydna. On this theory Ziegler (col. 1450.28–32) had the last word: "Teilnahme auf römischer Seite wäre ein so grosses Verdienst, auf makedonischer Seite eine so schwere Verfehlung gegen die Römer gewesen, dass beides mit dem späteren Schicksal P.'s unvereinbar ist."

69. Polyb. 3.4.2–3.

70. Polyb. 24.10.8, 13–15; cf. Shimron, "Polybius on Rome" 97–98; Marcellinus, *Vit. Thuc.* 46.

71. Polyb. 31.23.3–5. As Ziegler (col. 1451 n. 1) pertinently asks, "Wer lieh wem Bücher?" He concludes that it was Polybius who did the lending, and infers from this that he had been allowed to ship his books and papers from Megalopolis to Rome.

72. Polyb. 31.23 ff.; DS 31.26.5; Vell. Pat. 1.13.3; Plut. *Mor.* 659F, cf. 199F.

73. Livy 45.28, Polyb. 31.24.9; cf. Walbank, in Gabba 9.

74. Ziegler col. 1470; cf. Momigliano, "Polibio" 185; Walbank, *Selected Papers* 157–58.

75. Polyb. 31.11–15 *passim*.

76. Polyb. 31.25.5; cf. 31.25–29 *passim*. Shimron, "Polybius on Rome" 102–3, points out, acutely, that Polybius restricts his praise of Scipio to personal qualities, and is very careful to avoid all comment on him as politician or general. The clear implication is that there were elements in Roman policy of which Polybius did not approve, but which he knew better than to criticize directly (see p. 279).

77. Usher 121.

78. Polyb. 1.14.4–8, 8.10 *passim*, 29.12.3, and 16.14.6, where he remarks, with some equivocation, "I would concede that writers must be biased in favor of their own country, but not that they should make statements about it that are contrary to the facts."

79. Walbank, *HC* 1.6–16 *passim*, *Polybius* 6 (the passage cited).

80. Walbank, *Polybius* 9.

81. Momigliano, *Alien Wisdom* 26 ff., *Essays* 74.

82. Momigliano, *Alien Wisdom* 26 ff., a brilliant analysis.

83. Polyb. 31.25.5; 35.6; 36.14; 39.1; Plin. *HN* 7.100; Plut. *Cat. Maj.* 15.

84. Polyb. 30.32.9. Attempts to get the detainees released were made in 164, 159, 155, and 153: see Polyb. 30.32 *passim*, 32.3.14–17, 33.1.3–8.3, and 33.14; cf. Walbank, *HC* 1.4 n. 11, and Ziegler cols. 1452–53.

85. Polyb. 35.6 = Plut. *Cat. Maj.* 9; Paus. 7.10.12 (and cf. 7–11 for a detailed account of Callicrates' involvement in this unsavory episode, probably derived from Polybius).

86. Polyb. 36.11.2.

87. Shimron, "Polybius on Rome" 99.

88. Ziegler col. 1454 n. 1; Polyb. 9.25.1–4, cf. 3.59.7–8.

89. Plin. *HN* 5.9; cf. Carpenter 102, who argues that, like Hanno the Carthaginian, he sailed as far as the Senegal estuary.

90. Polyb. 36.11.1–2.

91. Polyb. 38.19–22 *passim*; DS 32.23–24; App. *Lib.* 132, 628–30; cf. Momigliano, *Alien Wisdom* 22–23.

92. Polyb. 38.1, 9–18, 19–22; DS 32.26–27; Paus. 7.14.5–16.8.

93. Polyb. 39.2 = Strabo 8.6.2 (C.381).

94. Polyb. 39.5 *passim*; cf. Paus. 7.16.9 ff., 8.30.9.

95. Cf. the shrewd comments of Musti, *Polibio* 145: "quando ci si trova di fronte a un documento così ampio e complesso come le *Storie* di Polibio, concepito in una condizione personale e generale così sfavorevole all' espressione di una protesta o di una rivolta, anche *les nuances* (se afferrabili, se ricorrenti) contano."

96. Polyb. 3.4.4–6, 36.9 *passim* (the most crucial passage), 38.19–22; cf. Momigliano, *Alien Wisdom* 29–30, *Essays* 74.

97. Polyb. 5.11.4–6; cf. Walbank, *HC* 1.549.

98. Polyb. 3.4.3; cf. Musti, *Polibio* 141.

99. Polyb. 39.3.11, 4.2; Paus. 8.30.8–9, 37.2.

100. Polyb. 38.3.10, 13; cf. Shimron, "Polybius on Rome" 108. Polybius is equally scathing about Hasdrubal's self-indulgent obstinacy during the siege of Carthage: Polyb. 38.7.1, 8.7. On the Achaean War, cf. Polyb. 38.9.7, 10.8 ff.

101. Polyb. 34.14.1–6 = Strabo 17.1.12 (C.797).

102. Doubted by Walbank, *HC* 1.6, but by no means impossible: see Ziegler col. 1458, with reff. there cited.

103. Polyb. 3.48.12, 12.5.1–3.

104. Lucian, *Macrob.* 23.

105. Grant, *Ancient Historians* 156.

106. Walbank, *OCD*[2] 854.1, s.v. "Polybius."

107. Walbank, in Gabba 27.

108. Polyb. 31.24.11, a revealing autobiographical fragment.

109. Ste Croix 307 ff.; Momigliano, *Alien Wisdom* 29–31; and esp. Shimron, "Polybius on Rome" 94–96, a particularly percipient discussion. Cf. also Walbank, in Gabba 3–38. Gruen, "Class Conflict" 29 ff., issues a salutary warning, backed up by close scrutiny of the evidence pertaining to the Third Macedonian War, against the practice of assuming that "aristocratic elements sided with Rome, the masses looked to Perseus." For the lineup in this particular conflict he amply proves his point: as he says (p. 48), "security and survival were the dominant motives, not class consciousness." But it is a long (and in my view unjustifiable) step from this conclusion to the further general rebuttal of the widely, and I think rightly, held opinion that "Rome put her weight behind the upper classes in Greece, the wealthy and the noble who would run their states in conformity with the social order in Italy." For a recent survey of evidence supporting this claim see Ste Croix 307 ff.

110. Shimron, "Polybius on Rome" 96.

111. Momigliano, *Alien Wisdom* 30.

112. Grant, *Ancient Historians* 153–54. Polybius's concern for Roman readers: Polyb. 6.11.3–8.

113. Cic. *De Rep.* 1.34.

114. Polyb. 6.11.11–12.

115. Walbank, *HC* 1.643–48, "Polybius and the Roman State" 239–60.

116. Walbank, *Polybius* 137 ff.

117. *Römische Geschichte*, 7th ed. (Berlin, 1908), 2.452.

118. Pédech, "Polybe" 195, notes the increasing power of the senatorial oligarchy, the impoverishment of the middle classes, the influx of slave labor and real wealth, with a consequent lowering of moral standards among the elite, and a simultaneous upsurge of demagoguery and electoral corruption.

119. J. S. Richardson, "Polybius's View of the Roman Empire," *PBSR* 47 (1979) 1–11; cf. Roveri 143–62.

120. Walbank, *Polybius* 8.

121. Shimron, "Polybius on Rome" 115 with n. 97.

122. Polyb. 6.2.9 f.; cf. Eisen 24: "Mit dieser Erklärung eines historischen Phänomens durch die Verfassung stellt sich Polybios in eine Reihe mit Herodot V,78 und Thukydides II,36,3." See also Gelzer, *Über die Arbeitsweise* 25.

123. Polyb. 2.37.9–11, 38.6 f., 43.7; cf. Musti, "Polibio negli studi" 1120 with further reff.; Walbank, *Selected Papers* 296–97.

124. Polyb. 12.25[b]1–2 Paton.

125. Tapp 33 ff.

126. Polyb. 2.56.10.

127. Polyb. 1.35.1, 11.2.11.

128. Polyb. 22.19, and above, p. 274.

129. Polyb. 2.49.4–5.

130. Polyb. 31.24.9–10.

131. Polyb. 10.21.8.

132. Polyb. 6.57.4–10.

133. On Polyb. 12.25[j]5 Paton, see Walbank, *HC* 1.14 n. 2; cf. Polyb. 36.1.6–7. *Contra*, Ziegler col. 1527. Further reff. in Musti, "Polibio negli studi" 1125.

134. Polyb. 12.28.1–5.

135. He discovered a bronze dedication tablet set up by Hannibal on the Lacinian promontory, in southern Italy, which listed the Carthaginian's battle units: 3.33.17–18, 56.1–4.

136. Polyb. 12.6.7–15.12; 12.23–28ª Paton *passim*.

137. Polyb. 6.27–42; cf. Momigliano, *Alien Wisdom* 25–26, with further instances, and the interesting comments of Margherita Isnardi, *SCO* 3 (1955) 102–10.

138. A. Momigliano, *RSI* 71 (1959) 544 ff.

139. Polyb. 2.56 *passim*, esp. §7.

140. Polyb. 15.25–33 *passim*, esp. 31 ff. (with a pious complaint at 34.1 about other authors who, in treating these events, "introduce sensationalism and various devices to amaze their readers"!); 38.20 *passim*; 38.1–3 (followed by an apologia at 38.4.1 for abandoning the style proper to historiography and launching into a "more ambitious and declamatory recital"); 38.15.8–16.10. See Walbank's penetrating essay "Polemic in Polybius," *JRS* 52 (1962) 1 ff. = *Selected Papers* 262–79. His final verdict strikes me as eminently just: "Nearly always Polybius' motives are mixed; and his attitude towards earlier historians can usually be seen to reflect personal or political considerations no less than those of literary and historical merit."

141. *De Comp. Verb.* 4.

Chapter 18. Antiochus III, Philip V, and the Roman Factor, 221–196

1. Polyb. 5.101.3–10, 102.1–2; cf. Hammond and Walbank 387–88.

2. Gruen, *HW* 369–73.

3. For a detailed account of it, with full testimonia, see Walbank, *Philip V* chap. 2, 24–67, not rendered entirely obsolete by his more recent version in *CAH* VII².1 473 ff.; see also Piper 76 ff. For the declarations of Philip and his allies with regard to cities under Aetolian control, see Polyb. 4.25.6–8; cf. Gruen, *HW* 141.

4. Polyb. 7.10.1 (= *Suda* s.v. ἰσηγορεῖ); cf. Mendels, "Messene" 246 ff.; Piper 76 ff.

5. See the remarkable, though fragmentary, inscription on this topic: Moretti, *Iscrizioni* 114, 2.108 ff. = Austin 74, pp. 136–38; and cf. Walbank, *Philip V* 289 ff.

6. Walbank, *Philip V* 45 ff., 54 ff., 63, 259; Hammond and Walbank 371–77.

7. Polyb. 4.4–37 *passim*, 57–97; 5.1–30.7, 91, 100.8.

8. Polyb. 5.10.10; Livy 27.30.9, 32.22.11.

9. Polyb. 4.87.8, 5.26–28.8 *passim*; Errington, "Philip V" 19 ff., esp. 31–35.

10. Polyb. 7.12.9; Plut. *Arat.* 49, 50, 51.

11. Polyb. 7.11.8.

12. Polyb. 5.100.9–105.2.

13. Polyb. 5.102.1 and elsewhere: e.g., 5.105.1, 5; 5.108.4–7. Cf. Walbank, *Philip V* 65.

14. Polyb. 4.16.6–21.12; Walbank, *Philip V* 28–29.

15. Polyb. 5.104.7, 10–11.

16. A good case has been made for treating it as a Polybian fiction, designed to confirm his thesis of "interweaving" (συμπλοκή) in Mediterranean affairs: see Mørkholm, "The Speech of Agelaus" 240ff., esp. 245, 251–53, and Walbank, *HC* 1.629–30, both of whom point out that neither the islanders nor the Greek cities of Asia Minor made any kind of appeal to Rome until 201 (if we reject the inclusion of Ilion in the treaty of Phoenice in 205: see p. 300). Hammond (Hammond and Walbank 390 with nn. 2–3) agrees: the cloud was a literary cliché. *Contra*, Deininger 26 ff., who argues for the speech's authenticity "in ihrem wesentlichen Inhalt" if not "in ihrem Wortlaut"; and Walbank, *Selected Papers* 153, who regards the vivid metaphor of "the cloud in the west" as evidence for an actual turn of phrase that was long remembered.

17. Tarn, *CQ* 18 (1924) 17–23; Walbank, *Philip V* 258 with n. 1.

18. Gruen, *HW* 374.

19. Livy 23.33.1–4.

20. Badian, *Foreign Clientelae* 75.

21. Gruen, *HW* 440: full discussion 377–81.

22. Polyb. 5.41–42, 45.5–7, 49.1–7, 50 *passim*, 51.4, 53.6, 54.10–12, and, for Hermeias's assassination, 56 *passim*: after his death his wife and children were stoned to death in Apamea. Cf. Schmitt, *Untersuchungen* 150–58, 175 ff., who argues (p. 156) that "er hatte sicher Fehler, wohl auch Verbrechen begangen, aber Verrat war ihm anscheinend nicht nachzuweisen."

23. Polyb. 4.48.5–13, 5.40.5–7.

24. Polyb. 5.40.5–54 *passim*; cf. Schmitt, *Untersuchungen* 116 ff.

25. Polyb. 5.42.9, 45.5–46.5, 67.5–8. Cf. Huss, *Untersuchungen* 20 ff.

26. Polyb. 5.58–61.2. For a detailed account of the Fourth Syrian War prior to Raphia, see Huss, *Untersuchungen* 26–55; cf. also H. Heinen, *CAH* VII².1, chap. 11 §5, 433 ff.

27. Polyb. 5.62.7–8.

28. Polyb. 5.61–62 *passim*.

29. Polyb. 5.63.1–7, 66–67 *passim*; cf. Schmitt, *Staatsverträge* 447, pp. 80–81.

30. Polyb. 5.63.8–65.11.

31. A much put-upon lady, as Polybius, who talks of "the insults and contumely she had to bear all her life" (15.25.9), makes clear. She seems to have been personally fastidious (Eratosthenes *ap*. Athen. 7.276b)—not a helpful characteristic, one might have thought, in Philopator's court. For a recently discovered near-contemporary bust of her, see I. Jucker, "Ein Bildnis der Arsinoë III Philopator," *HASB* 5 (1979) 5–9; and in general Macurdy 136–41. Cf. Pollitt, *AHA* 9–10.

32. Detailed studies by E. Galili, "Raphia, 217 B.C.E., Revisited," *SCI* 3 (1976/77) 52–126; and Huss, *Untersuchungen* 55–68. Cf. Bar-Kochva 128 ff. on Antiochus's army.

33. Polyb. 5.84.

34. Polyb. 5.79–87 *passim*, Just. 30.1.6.

35. Jaehne, "Politische Aktivität" 406, observes aphoristically that "Raphia war nicht Ausdruck der Stärke, sondern Zeichen der Schwäche . . . eines ganzen gesellschaftlichen Organismus."

36. E.g., by Huss, *Untersuchungen*, who tries to elevate overseas contacts into a coherent, dynamic foreign policy. On this, see Errington, *JHS* 99 (1979) 196–97; and Sherwin-White, *CR* 28 (1978) 308–10, who writes: "The force of Polybius's criticism seems to be the lack of Ptolemy's will to act, not his lack of power. In fact the results of Huss's enquiry do not disprove Polybius's underlying criticism, that the king abandoned policy-making to Sosibius and his other ministers; there is no new, or real, evidence to do so."

37. Polyb. 5.34, 62.7–8.

38. Polyb. 5.62–63 *passim*.

39. Polyb. 5.87.3, cf. 14.12.3; Plut. *Cleom.* 33, 34; Strabo 17.1.11 (C.796); and, for Ptolemy's three-month stay in Coele-Syria and Phoenicia, Polyb. 5.87.6.

40. Polyb. 5.34.1, 36.1–2; 15.25.1–2; Plut. *Cleom.* 33; Just. 29.1.5, 30.1.2.

41. Bevan, *House of Ptolemy* 230–31.

42. Polyb. 5.107.1–3; cf. 14.12.3–4.

43. Préaux, "Sur les causes" 475 ff., "Polybe" 364–65, 374–75; Reekmans, "The Ptolemaic Copper Inflation," in E. Van't Dack and T. Reekmans, *Ptolemaica* (Louvain, 1951) 61–118; Jenkins 245–46; further bibliography in Will, *HP²* 2.107–8. The year 210 was also when a senatorial delegation visited Alexandria, bringing gifts, renewing Rome's friendship (*amicitia*) with Ptolemy, and urgently seeking supplies of grain, during a great Italian shortage, from Egypt, the one country (Polybius says) not then ravaged by war: Polyb. 9.11ª1–2, Livy 27.4.10. It is noteworthy that Alexandria's grain trade could not, apparently, ensure her an adequate reserve of silver. Cf. Fraser 1.150 ff.

44. See, e.g., Will, *HP²* 2.34–37, for a survey of conflicting views.

45. Polyb. 5.107.1–3; cf. 14.12.4.

46. Cf. Will, *HP²* 2.105–8.

47. Peremans 398.

48. *OGIS* 56, 90 = Austin 222, 227, pp. 366–68, 374–78; cf. C. Onasch, "Zur Königs-ideologie der Ptolemäer in den Dekreten von Kanopus und Memphis (Rosettana)," *APF* 24/25 (1976) 137–55.

49. Rostovtzeff, *SEH* 2.707–12.

50. Polyb. 4.51.4, 8.20.11: he was the son of Andromachus (whose sister, Laodice, married Antiochus's father, Seleucus Kallinikos), and was thus a Seleucid both by marriage and by birth, in direct line of descent from Seleucus I and Apama.

51. Polyb. 5.57–58.1; cf. 4.48.9–13.

52. Badian, *Gnomon* 38 (1966) 714.

53. Polyb. 5.72–78 *passim*, 107.4, 7, 15–18; 8.15–23 *passim*; cf. B. A. van Prosdij, "De Morte Achaei," *Hermes* 69 (1934) 347–50.

54. Schmitt, *Untersuchungen* 87, sees this clearly: "von nun an lässt sich nicht verkennen, dass der König sich ein grosses Programm gesetzt hatte," etc.

55. Cf. Will, *HP*² 2.51–54.

56. Rostovtzeff, *SEH* 1.447, 546; cf. Tarn, *Greeks* 104 ff.

57. Schmitt, *Untersuchungen* 85 ff., and cf. chap. 2, part 1, "Das Territorialbestand des Seleukidenreichs," pp. 32 ff., for a detailed survey of Seleucid territories at the time of Antiochus III's accession.

58. Polyb. 8.23, Strabo 11.14.15 (C.531).

59. Polyb. 5.55; cf. Schmitt, *Untersuchungen* 148–50.

60. Polyb. 10.27.

61. Polyb. 10.28–31 *passim*, Just. 41.5.7.

62. Polyb. 10.49, 11.34.1–10. *Inter alia*, a daughter of Antiochus married Euthydemus's son Demetrius I, thus reinforcing the Seleucid genes in this Indo-Bactrian dynasty (see genealogical table, p. 739).

63. Rostovtzeff, *SEH* 1.459.

64. Polyb. 11.34.11–12, 13 ff.

65. Polyb. 13.9.

66. Polyb. 11.34.13–16.

67. Will, *HP*² 2.66–68 with further literature. As Will points out, the title does not figure in official royal documents, or on coins, but solely in honorific decrees and private dedications. Cf. Schmitt, *Untersuchungen* 92–95.

68. Polyb. 2.10.8, 11.17, 12.13; App. *Illyr.* 7–8; cf. Gruen, *HW* 367 with n. 41. The actual extent of his territorial acquisitions is uncertain.

69. Polyb. 2.65.4, 3.16.3.

70. Polyb. 5.12.5–7, 101.7–8, 105.1, 108.5–8; 7.9.14, 13.3–8.

71. Polyb. 4.19.8.

72. Eutrop. 3.7.1.

73. Polyb. 4.29.1–7; 5.4.3, 95.1, 108.1–2, cf. 101.1–3; Ormerod 176 ff.

74. Polyb. 3.16.2 ff., 3.18–19 *passim*. Polybius argues that Demetrius, though technically Rome's ally, was being punished for ingratitude and the abuse of friendship: the simple truth seems to have been that he was an unmitigated nuisance.

75. Polyb. 5.101.7–10.

76. Polyb. 5.101.8, 108.5–7.

77. Polyb. 5.109.1–4, 110; cf. Gruen, *HW* 375, who cites Livy 23.33.6–8 to show that "many Romans even in 215 were prepared to believe that Philip would make alliance with them," and E. Will, "Monde hellénistique" (1975) 398. Hammond and Walbank 393 stresses Polybius's prejudice against Philip over this episode.

78. Cf. Gruen, *HW* 375–76, with testimonia.

79. Cary 182.

80. Polyb. 7.9 *passim*; Livy 23.33.9, cf. 38.4, with Walbank, *HC* 2.42–56. Cf. Schmitt, *Staatsverträge* 528, pp. 245–50 (with full conspectus of testimonia) = Austin 61, pp. 119–21.

The Roman version of this treaty (Livy *ut supr.*, App. *Mac.* 1, Zonar. 9.4.3) has been generally rejected by modern scholars: see Will, *HP*² 2.84 ("unanimement et avec raison rejetée . . . ne mérite pas de discussion particulière"). Useful background material in A.-H. Chroust, *C&M* 15 (1954) 60–107; Walbank, *Philip V* 71–72; Hammond and Walbank 393–95.

81. Cf. Walbank, *HC* 2.44.

82. Polyb. 8.13–14 *passim*.

83. Gruen, *HW* 377, citing Livy 23.38.4–11.

84. Livy 24.40, Plut. *Arat.* 51, Zonar. 9.4.

85. Livy 24.40.17, Polyb. 8.1.6.

86. Moretti *Iscrizioni* 2.114, pp. 108–14 = Austin 74, pp. 136–38; cf. Walbank, *Philip V* 289 ff. This fragmentary inscription gives us a fascinating glimpse of Macedonian army regulations and discipline: the duties of patrols, the rules for surrendering booty, details of camp building, penalties for offenses ranging from losing equipment to sleeping on guard duty (a one-drachma fine, surprisingly lenient). Cf. Burstein, *Translated Documents* no. 66, pp. 88–90.

87. Livy 22.33.3. The historicity of the request has been doubted (cf. Gruen, *HW* 373–74 with n. 83), but on insufficient grounds.

88. Plut. *Arat.* 49.

89. Polyb. 7.12, Plut. *Arat.* 50.

90. But not, as is so often assumed, through a massacre conducted by Philip and Demetrius themselves: see, e.g., Errington, "Philip V" 36; and Walbank, *Philip V* 73, who further asserts that Philip *seized* Ithome instead of being allowed to sacrifice there under safe-conduct, as the Polybian tradition specifically states (Polyb. 7.12.1). The evidence of Pausanias, 4.29.1–5, 32.2, clearly refers to the subsequent attack on Ithome by Demetrius.

91. Polyb. 8.8.1, cf. 12.1; Plut. *Arat.* 51.

92. Polyb. 3.19.11; Paus. 4.29.1–5, cf. 32.2.

93. Polyb. 7.11.8.

94. Polyb. 7.11.10–12, 13.6–8, 14 *passim*; Plut. *Arat.* 49, 51; cf. Hammond and Walbank 397. We do not need to subscribe to Polybius's psychological theory of μεταβολή in order to credit the picture of an ambitious and powerful Macedonian king giving rein to his latent savagery and turning, like so many of his predecessors, into a classic overreacher. At the same time he was still capable (in 215 or 214) of taking a personal interest in apparently unjustly disfranchised Thessalian citizens: *IG* IX.2 517; *SIG*³ 543.26–39 = Burstein, *Translated Documents* no. 65, pp. 87–88.

95. Polyb. 8.12.1–5, Plut. *Arat.* 52. Piper 88 appears, surprisingly, to believe this canard.

96. Livy 26.24.16; cf. Walbank, *Philip V* 80.

97. Livy 27.30.13; 29.12.3, 12–13; Polyb. 8.38. The capture of Lissos: Polyb. 8.13–14 *passim*, cf. Hammond and Walbank 398–99.

98. Livy 24.13.5; cf. Just. 29.4.4 for Tarentum as a possible bridgehead: accepted by Niese 2.475, and Holleaux, *Rome* 199–200, *CAH* VIII 123; *contra*, Walbank, *Philip V* 81–82.

99. Gruen, *HW* 377–78.

100. Schmitt, *Staatsverträge* 536, pp. 258–66; Moretti, *Iscrizioni* 2.87, pp. 45–48 = Austin 62, pp. 121–22, Bagnall and Derow 32, p. 65; also Livy 26.24.7–15 for what purports to be a somewhat fuller version, and 25.23.9, 26.24.1–8 for preceding negotiations. Translation and recent documentation in Sherk, *Translated Documents* 2, pp. 1–2, who stresses that the phraseology reflects a fairly literal translation of the original Latin text. See Hammond and Walbank 400–401, where it is well described as "a treaty of expediency between unscrupulous partners."

101. Livy 26.24.1.

102. Polyb. 9.39.3; cf. Oost 39.

103. *SIG*³ 543; *IG* IX.2 517 = Austin 60, pp. 117–19.

104. Livy 27.29.

105. Polyb. 28.8, Livy 43.19.12–20.4 *passim*. For Mantinea, see Plut. *Philop.* 10, Polyb. 11.13–14.

106. App. *Mac.* 3.1.7; Polyb. 9.42.5–8, 11.5.6–8; Livy 28.7.4, 32.22.10.

107. The evidence for this period is scattered and confusing: well analyzed by Will, *HP*² 2.89–94. Cf. Holleaux, *Rome* 213–57, and *CAH* VIII 125–35; Walbank, *Philip V* 84–107; Hansen 46–48; Errington, *Philopoemen* 49 ff.; and, on Philopoemen's army reforms, J. K. Anderson, *CPh* 62 (1967) 104 ff.

108. Polyb. 11.4–6, Livy 29.1.2; cf. Holleaux, *CAH* VIII 134–35, *Rome* 255 ff.

109. Polyb. 5.9; 9.30; 11.7.2–3.

110. Livy 29.12.1–4.

111. Livy 29.12 *passim*, cf. 31.18.4; Polyb. 16.34.7; Appl *Mac.* 3.2; Just. 29.4.11; Zonar. 9.11.7; cf. Schmitt, *Staatsverträge* 543, pp. 281–84; Badian, *Foreign Clientelae* 58–61.

112. Gruen, *HW* 381 with n. 130. Hammond and Walbank 409–10, 463 ff., argues for Philip's retention of Lissos on the basis of numismatic evidence (Macedonian emblems on coins of the Selcë hoard), but the dating of these coins remains problematical.

113. Gruen's reminder, *HW* 534, is salutary: "What matters is that rivalry and warfare, alignment and realignment among the Hellenistic powers proceeded almost without interruption after the peace of Phoenice; that western Asia Minor and the eastern and northern Aegean supplied deadly battlefields to settle or aggravate disputes; that cities and territory exchanged suzerains at an accelerated pace; that Philip, Rhodes, Pergamum, Prusias, and, to a lesser extent, Antiochus and Ptolemy embroiled themselves in dizzying quarrels. All this before anyone undertook to solicit the intervention of Rome." The only exception known to me is the case of Scerdilaidas (see p. 296); and that was local and strategic rather than political in the larger sense.

114. See Shimron, *Late Sparta* 80–83; Piper 95 ff., 115–16; and cf. *IG* V.1 885, *SIG*³ 584. The literary sources all, almost certainly, derive from Polybius (see Polyb. 13.6–8; 16.13, 16.1–3, 17.1–3; Livy 29.12, 31–35 *passim*, esp. 34.3; Paus. 4.29.10–11; 7.8.4–5, 9.2; 8.50.5–51.2; Plut. *Philop.* 13–15, *Flam.* 13), and Polybius was flatly hostile to Nabis, whom he saw as the typical τύραννος. Modern writers, as Shimron points out, are almost all strongly partisan, either accepting the Polybian tradition, e.g., Aymard, *Premiers rapports* 33 ff., or else vindicating Nabis as an idealizing reformer, victim of unscrupulous propaganda: see J. Mundt, *Nabis, König von Sparta* (Münster, 1903), and Hadas, "Social Revolution" 65–68, 73–76, esp. 74 ff. For a more balanced view, see Texier, *Nabis* 103–5; and Piper 115–16. See also DS 27.1, 28.13. Evaluation of sources: Texier, *Nabis* 14–15, 19–20.

115. Texier, *Nabis* 17, who argues that he must have gone into exile with Cleomenes after Sellasia, and that it was only in Alexandria that he could have come into close contact with a Jewish intellectual community. Cf. Fraser 1.53–58, 84–86, 283–85, 805.

116. Homolle's thesis, based on *SIG*³ 584 (see *BCH* 20 [1896] 504 ff., and Hdt. 6.67–70), has been widely, and I think rightly, accepted: see, e.g., Mossé, *Tyrannie* 183–84; Shimron, *Late Sparta* 83 n. 13 with further reff.; Texier, *Nabis* 16; Aymard, *Premiers rapports* 33 with n. 12; Piper 95 with n. 3.

117. Kraay and Hirmer no. 522, pl. 161. Nabis's age is also determined by the fact that in 197 he had sons of marriageable age: Piper 95.

118. Polyb. 13.6.4.

119. DS 27.1, Polyb. 13.6–8, Livy 34.36.3, Paus. 4.29.10. Cf. Shimron, *Late Sparta* 73 ff.; and Texier, *Nabis* 19: "Sans doute Nabis procéda-t-il à son arrivée sur le trône à certaines épurations et fut-il obligé, sous peine d'être lui-même éliminé, de pratiquer une répression parfois brutale." See also Aymard, *Premiers rapports* 36 n. 33, who points out that, for whatever reason, Nabis took no action against the exiled king Agesipolis (Livy 34.26.14).

120. Polyb. 13.6.3, 7.3–11; 16.13.1; Livy 34.26.12–13, 27.3–8, 32.12; cf. Aymard, *Premiers rapports* 34–35.

121. Livy 34.29.2–3, 35.5, 9, 36.3; 35.12.7; Polyb. 13.8.2. Nabis also made a treaty with Crete, thus winning ports of refuge on the island: Piper 99 with n. 28.

122. Polyb. 5.22.11, 23.10; Livy 34.34.2–4, 38.2; Paus. 1.13.6, 7.8.4–5, 9.5; cf. Shimron, *Late Sparta* 90–91 with n. 30.

123. Texier, *Nabis* 27.

124. Polyb. 21.9.1.

125. *SIG*[3] 584. Cf. Homolle (n. 116 above).

126. Polyb. 16.13.1; Livy 34.31.11, 14; 32.9; 35.4; 36.6; 38.34.2; Piper 96–98; Aymard, *Premiers rapports* 35 with n. 25; cf. DS 27.1. As Piper pertinently asks (p. 98) "How many [helots] were freed and what was their status?" The answers seem to be: far from all of them, and highly dubious. The helot system in fact survived until Roman times.

127. Polyb. 13.8.2: Nabis apparently took a cut of their plunder. He also (Polyb. 13.6.6 f.) employed them to carry out assassinations of exiled Spartans on his behalf; cf. Polyb. 13.6.4, 8.2; DS 27.1; Livy 34.35.6. Doubts have been cast by scholars on the validity of this evidence; but since the activities attributed to Nabis are commonplaces today—and indeed on ideological grounds—among a number of theoretically civilized countries, I see no reason to question our ancient testimony.

128. Polyb. 13.6–8, Plut. *Philop.* 12. Both Aymard, *Premiers rapports* 36–37 n. 33, and Texier, *Nabis* 19, reject the iron maiden out of hand, even though Aymard, for one, is well aware of "la fertilité d'invention humaine en matière de tortures," which he characterizes, correctly, as "illimitée." For Apia, cf. Walbank, *HC* 1.265.

129. Polyb. 16.13.3; Livy 34.32.16, 35.6; Plut. *Philop.* 12; Paus. 4.29.10, 8.50.5; cf. Errington, *Philopoemen* 80–81; Mundt (above, n. 114) 33; Niese 2.566; Piper 99–100.

130. Polyb. 16.36–37 *passim*; cf. Aymard, *Premiers rapports* 43 ff.

131. Plut. *Philop.* 13, Paus. 8.50.6.

132. Polyb. 16.36–37 *passim*; Paus. 4.29.10, 8.50.5.

133. The inhabitants are said to have run so short of food that they were reduced to growing wheat in the streets: Plut. *Philop.* 13.

134. Livy 34.40–43 *passim*.

135. Polyb. 13.8.2, Livy 34.32.18–36.3.

136. Activities of Antiochus are now attested both in Caria and at Teos: Polyb. 15.35.13; cf. Welles, *Royal Correspondence* no. 38, pp. 165–69 = Burstein, *Translated Documents* no. 33, pp. 43–44; Austin no. 151, pp. 253–54. It may have been about this time, too, that he proposed the peremptory removal of 2,000 Jewish families from Babylonia to Lydia and Phrygia (which had been in revolt) as a stabilizing influence: Joseph. *AJ* 12.148–53.

137. The discrepancy of a year between the date given by the Egyptian records (204) and the literary sources (all derived from Polybius?: 203) has provoked much discussion: for a summary see Will, *HP*[2] 2.108–11. In particular it has been suggested, on the evidence of the power struggle after Ptolemy IV's death, that any announcement of that death was suppressed for a considerable time: see, e.g., Briscoe *Commentary* (1973) 36, and in *CR*, n.s., 16 (1966) 98–100, dating the death to 28 Nov. 205 and its announcement to 8 Sept. 203. Fullest and most convincing discussion in Schmitt, *Untersuchungen* chap. 4, 189–237 (summary of conclusions, p. 236), who places both Ptolemy IV's death and Ptolemy V's succession in the summer of 204. Cf. Walbank, *Selected Papers* 38–55, with the updated bibliography of n. 125.

138. Jaehne, "Politische Aktivität" 416 ff.

139. Ibid. 419 ff.

140. Polyb. 15.25–36 *passim*; cf. Just. 30.2.7–8.

141. Cf. Jaehne, "Politische Aktivität" 417 with reff.

142. Polyb. 15.25.13–15.

143. Schmitt, *Staatsverträge* 547, pp. 288–91; cf. Austin 152, pp. 254–55; Polyb. 3.2.8, 15.20.2–6, 16.1.8; Livy 31.14.5; Trog. *Prol.* 30; Just. 30.2.8; App. *Mac.* 4 (though he gets the wrong Ptolemy!).

144. Polyb. 15.20.6.

145. Polyb. 16.18–19 (largely devoted to a refutation of the historian Zeno of Rhodes), Just. 31.1.1–2, Joseph. *AJ* 12.130 ff.

146. The notion that Rome ca. 200 acquired some kind of tutelary control over Egypt's

young Ptolemy V through M. Aemilius Lepidus is an anachronistic fiction unknown to Polybius or Livy: see Just. 30.2.8, 3.1, 4; 31.1.2; Val. Max. 6.6.1; cf. Gruen, *HW* 680–82. See also Sherk, *Translated Documents* 3, pp. 2–3, who further cites the evidence of a denarius, minted in 61 B.C. by M. Aemilius Lepidus, the future triumvir, and describing his ancestor as "guardian of the king." Even if the title was ever bestowed, its effective force must have been dubious, and in fact it is far more likely to have originated in subsequent retrospective propaganda.

147. Polyb. 16.27.5; App. *Mac.* 4; Just. 30.3.3–4, 31.1.2.

148. Livy 33.19.8 (Coele-Syria), 32.19.8–11 (coastal raiding), 32.8.9–16 (invasion of Pergamene territory); cf. Mastrocinque, "Osservazioni" 307 ff., esp. 322. Handouts (via Laodice III) to Iasos: Burstein, *Translated Documents* no. 36, pp. 47–48, with further reff.

149. Polyb. 18.47.1–4, Livy 33.34.1–4. The rebuilding of Lysimacheia: Polyb. 18.51.8; Livy 33.41.4, 36.7.15. Its use as a military base: Livy 36.33.6, App. *Syr.* 21.

150. Cf. Will, *HP²* 2.190–92.

151. Livy 35.13.4.

152. So Polyb. 28.20.9; cf. App. *Syr.* 5, but also Polyb. 28.1.2–3.

153. Errington, *Dawn* 160.

154. Polyb. 18.49–52 *passim*, Livy 33.39–41 *passim*.

155. The construction of such a fleet was in his mind as early as 207, when Livy (28.8.14), retailing an admitted rumor, reports that he was said then to be laying down a hundred warships in the naval dockyards at Cassandreia. However, there is no sign of their completion at that time. Cf. Holleaux, *Rome* 246 with n. 2.

156. See Polyb. 16.2.9 for the figures given for Philip's fleet at the battle of Chios: 53 decked warships, 150 cutters (λέμβοι), and an indeterminate number of other fighting vessels. Walbank, *HC* 2.505, argues, on the basis of 16.6.4, 7.2, that his fleet "consisted mainly no doubt of quinqueremes and quadriremes," which seems dubious. For Philip's naval offensive in general see Hammond and Walbank 412–16.

157. DS 28.1; cf. Walbank, *Philip V* chap. 4, 108 ff., "Sea-Power" 228–33, Hammond and Walbank 411.

158. Polyb. 13.3–5, 18.54.8; DS 28.1–2; Polyaen. 5.17; cf. Errington, *Philopoemen* 34 ff.

159. Livy 31.15.8, Polyb. 18.54.8.

160. Polyb. 18.54.7–11.

161. Cf. Holleaux, *Rome* 284–85 with n. 5.

162. Polyb. 15.24.1–6; Livy 33.30.3; cf. Hammond and Walbank 413.

163. Polyb. 15.21–23 *passim*; 18.2.4, 3.11–12, 4.7, 5.4; Livy 32.33.15, 34.6; Strabo 12.4.3 (C.564).

164. Walbank, "Sea-Power" 229–30.

165. Polyb. 16.2.4, 9; Livy 31.31.4; App. *Mac.* 4.

166. Polyb. 16.10.1, 14.5–15.8; Walbank, *HC* 2.497–98, following Holleaux, *Études* 4.211 ff., and reversing his previous, more sensible judgment in *Philip V* 118–24, 307–8, places Lade *after* the battle of Chios. I am not convinced by their circumstantial arguments. Philip's activities make far better strategic sense if the victory off Lade and the attack on Pergamene territory precede his crushing defeat off Chios: so, rightly, Berthold, "Lade."

167. Polyb. 16.1, DS 28.5.

168. Polyb. 15.20.3, 22.3; 16.1.1–6, 24.4; and elsewhere.

169. See, e.g., Kraay and Hirmer no. 577, pl. 175; Head et al. V.B.5, p. 62 and pl. 35.

170. Cf. Cary 187.

171. Polyb. 16.2–8 *passim*; cf. 16.7.1–2, 8.6.

172. Polyb. 16.15.6, 24.9; cf. Walbank *HC* 2.512, 519.

173. Polyb. 16.24.1–8.

174. Polyb. 16.24.3, Livy 31.2.1–2, Just. 30.3.5; cf. Will, *HP²* 2.128–30. Berthold, *Rhodes* 126, remarks that "with Rhodes and Pergamum as allies the Romans could face Philip under a philhellenic banner, something all but impossible had they been allied with the Aetolians alone." But how far would this have weighed with the Senate?

175. Polyaen. 4.18.12: he sent an Egyptian deserter to tell Attalus and the Rhodians that he was planning an attack for the following day, and then slipped out at night, leaving numerous campfires burning while his opponents were busily preparing their ships for battle, and to this end had called in the vessels guarding the harbor mouth.

176. Livy 31.14.9–10.

177. Livy 31.15.5, Polyb. 16.26.9–10.

178. Polyb. 16.25.9.

179. Polyb. 16.25.4 ff., 26.5 ff.; Livy 31.15.3–5.

180. Livy 31.15.8, Polyb. 16.26.10.

181. Livy 31.45.1–8.

182. Polyb. 16.27.1–5.

183. Livy 36.16.1–2.

184. Livy 31.16.4–6, 29.3.

185. Livy 31.16.6–17.11, 18.6–8; cf. 16.30–33 *passim*, 34.7–12.

186. Polyb. 16.34.1–7, Livy 31.18.1–5; cf. Gruen, *HW* 393 with n. 198.

187. Polyb. 16.34.7–12.

188. Livy 31.6.1–8.4.

189. Livy 31.18.9, 22.4.

190. Livy 31.18.9.

191. Badian, *Foreign Clientelae* 69.

192. Holleaux, *Rome* 306 ff.; cf. Gruen, *HW* 387 n. 162, for a list of further adherents to this thesis. Hammond and Walbank 419 is sensibly skeptical.

193. Polyb. 15.20.6.

194. For a cogent analysis of these and other theories, see Gruen, *HW* 382–98.

195. Livy 31.3.4–6 suggests this.

196. Walbank, *Philip V* 131–32.

197. Badian, *Foreign Clientelae* 66 ff.

198. Gruen, *HW* 397.

199. Badian, *Foreign Clientelae* 63–69.

200. Cf. Cary 189.

201. Polyb. 16.35.

202. Plut. *Philop.* 12, Just. 29.4.11, Paus. 8.50.4; cf. Deininger 42 ff.

203. Livy 32.19.2.

204. Livy 32.32.1–33.2, Polyb. 16.35; cf. Aymard, *Premiers rapports* 66–69, 78–102.

205. Livy 31.25.3–11, 32.19.6; cf. Gruen, *HW* 446.

206. Livy 31.32.5, 40.9–41.1. On Philip's (understandable) upbraiding of the Achaean deserters to Rome for gross ingratitude and abuse of εὐεργεσίαι, see Polyb. 18.6.5–7.

207. Livy 31.44.2–9; cf. Briscoe, *Commentary* (1973) 150 ff.; and, for archaeological evidence of these activities (e.g., the chiseling-off of names from inscriptions, and the destruction of statues: cf. above, pp. 48–49) Camp 167–68.

208. E.g., by Cary 190.

209. Polyb. 10.26.1–2; cf. Briscoe, "Rome" 3; Mendels, "Polybius" 55 ff.; Green, *Alexander* 17.

210. Livy 31.24.4–18, 26 *passim*.

211. Livy 31.22–46 *passim*, 32.3–6; cf. Walbank, *Philip V* 138–51.

212. Will, *HP*² 2.153.

213. Badian, *Titus*, an incisive and cogent dismissal of much romantic flimflam built up round the figure of Flamininus: see esp. 53 ff.

214. Livy 32.10.1–8, DS 28.11, App. *Mac.* 5, Plut. *Flam.* 3; cf. Hammond and Walbank 424.

215. Cf. Seager, "Freedom" 108.

216. Polyb. 18.9.1; cf. Badian, *Foreign Clientelae* 71–72.

217. Plut. *Flam.* 5, Livy 32.14.5–8. This was policy pure and simple: Flamininus could be brutal enough when it suited him.

218. Polyb. 18.1–12 *passim*, Livy 32.32.5–37 *passim*, Plut. *Flam.* 5–7.

219. Livy 32.37 *passim*, App. *Mac.* 8.

220. Livy 32.38.2–39.10 *passim*. As Shimron, *Late Sparta* 91, says, "one can hardly absolve Nabis of the charge of duplicity; even if he estimated Philip's chances correctly, he acted treacherously." See also Gruen, *HW* 446–47; Aymard, *Premiers rapports* 132 ff.; Piper 102–4; and esp. Texier, *Nabis* chap. 2, 45–66. It is interesting that Philip made no objection to the Roman demand that he abandon Argos (Polyb. 18.6.8): they can hardly have foreseen his giving the city away to Nabis. Clearly he wanted, at all costs, to keep it out of the hands of the Achaean League. Texier's thesis (pp. 53 ff.) that Nabis was bent on exporting the Spartiate revolution to Argos is hard to sustain in detail. His main concern in Argos was not so much ideological as financial: what he needed was hard cash, and he relied on the propertied classes to supply it. Those who paid up avoided maltreatment, but (Livy 32.38.8; cf. 40.10–11) "quos occulere aut retrahere aliquid suspicio fuit, in seruilem modum lacerati atque extorti."

221. Livy 32.33.1–2, Polyb. 18.42.6–7. As Gruen, *HW* 443, says, "the *patres* had no intention of binding their hands for the future."

222. Polyb. 18.31.9–12.

223. Polyb. 18.18–27, 28–32 (tactical disquisition on legion vs. phalanx; cf. M. M. Markle, *AJA* 81 [1977] 323–39); Livy 33.3–10; Plut. *Flam.* 7–8. The irresistibility of the phalanx charge: Polyb. 18.29.1, 30.11; Plut. *Aem. Paull.* 20; Livy 44.41.6–7. For the topography of Cynoscephalae, see W. K. Pritchett, "The Battle of Kynoskephalai in 197 B.C.," *Studies in Ancient Greek Topography*, part 2, *Battlefields* (Berkeley and Los Angeles, 1969), 133–44. The campaign and battle: Hammond and Walbank 432–43, with figs. 14 and 15.

224. Polyb. 18.33.

225. As early as 198 Antiochus had been encroaching on the territory of Pergamon (above, p. 304): Livy 32.8.9–16, 27.1; cf. Gruen, *HW* 538–39 with n. 43, who rightly stresses the authenticity of this episode.

226. Will, *HP²* 2.161–64 with full testimonia; cf. Errington, *Philopoemen* 70 ff. See in particular Polyb. 18.33–34, 44, and Livy 33.11–13, 24, 30, for the rhetoric of the occasion.

227. Seager, "Freedom" 109.

228. Polyb. 18.46.5. For examples of individual decrees, see, e.g., *SIG³* 612, 618 = Sherk, *Translated Documents* 14–15, pp. 13–15.

229. Sherk, *Roman Documents* 33, pp. 199, 211–13; Badian, *Titus* 54 ff.

230. Polyb. 18.46–47; Livy 33.32–34; App. *Mac.* 9; Plut. *Flam.* 10, 16–17. For a representative selection of honors to Flamininus, see Sherk, *Translated Documents* 6, pp. 6–7, citing instances from Chalcis, Corinth, Gytheion, Eretria, Delphi, Argos, and Thessaly (Scotoussa) in the form of commemorative inscriptions. Cf. Gruen, *HW* 167.

231. Livy 34.49.11 ff.; cf. Préaux, "Alexandrie" 1.158–59; Badian, *Foreign Clientelae* 73–74; Gruen, *HW* 172–73.

232. Polyb. 18.45.

233. Attalus's death: Livy 33.1–2 *passim*, 21.1–5; Plut. *Flam.* 6; Zonar. 9.16; cf. Hansen 67. The succession: Polyb. 32.8.3.

Chapter 19. The Spread of Hellenism: Exploration, Assimilation, Colonialism; or, The Dog That Barked in the Night

1. The first coherent statement of Droysen's thesis appeared in the preface to the first edition of his *Geschichte der Diadochen* (Gotha, 1836), and was not reprinted, either in the revised *Geschichte des Hellenismus* (Gotha, 1877) or later. See A. Bouché-Leclercq's remarks in the introduction (pp. vii ff.) to his translation of the 1877 work (Paris, 1883); and, on Droysen and Hellenism in general, B. Bravo, *Philologie, histoire, philosophie de l'histoire: Étude sur J. G.*

Droysen, historien de l'antiquité (Wroclaw, Warsaw, and Krakow, 1968), esp. 338–49. A convenient summary in Préaux, *Monde* 1.7 ff.

2. Diog. Laert. 6.63, 72; cf. Democr. fr. 68[55] B 247 D-K.

3. The later Stoics tried to get round this inherent contradiction by arguing that *any* good man, whatever his ethnic affiliation, was a citizen of the human world community, a dilution so vast that it became virtually meaningless, like Caracalla's extension of Roman citizenship throughout the empire. Cf. Cic. *De Div.* 3.19.64 = *SVF* 3.333: "Mundum autem censent . . . ease quasi communem urbem et ciuitatem hominum et deorum." See also Clem. Alex. *Strom.* 4.26 = *SVF* 3.327; and Philo, *SVF* 3.323: ἡ μὲν γὰρ μεγαλόπολις ὅδε ὁ κόσμος ἐστί.

4. Préaux, *Monde* 2.555–56; Launey 1.362 (only six known Macedonian terms, and five of them military!).

5. Avi-Yonah 138. See, e.g., Hdt. 1.60.3; and cf. R. Müller, *Klio* 60 (1978) 183 ff.

6. R. R. R. Smith, "Greeks, Foreigners" 24–25.

7. Arist. *Eth. Nic.* 1145ᵃ30, 1149ᵃ10; *Pol.* 1252ᵇ8, 1327ᵇ23 ff; fr. 658 Rose.

8. Aristoph. *Ach.* 100 ff., *Thesm.* 1001 ff.; Eur. *Orest.* 1369 ff.

9. *Orat.* 4 (*Panegyr.*) 50; cf. 9 (*Evag.*) 47 ff.

10. Bikerman 97; Mørkholm, *Antiochus IV* 128; Avi-Yonah 182.

11. Meleager, *AP* 7.417.5–6, 419.7–8. For an excellent analysis of the complex problems inherent in the Hellenization of Syria, see Fergus Millar, in Kuhrt and Sherwin-White, chap. 5, pp. 110–33.

12. *PZenCol.* 66 = Austin 245, p. 418; Peremans, in Reverdin 138.

13. *PYale* 46, col. 1.13; cf. Rostovtzeff, *SEH* 3.1644.

14. Polyb. 5.83.7; cf. Préaux, *Monde* 2.559; Avi-Yonah 160; Walbank, *CAH* VII².1 70. There are endless Egyptian texts extolling the scribe's life as a refuge from hardship: see, e.g., Miriam Lichtheim, *Ancient Egyptian Literature*, vol. 2, *The New Kingdom* (Berkeley and Los Angeles, 1976), pt. 5, pp. 167 ff.; *CAH* II³.2, chap. 25, §4. On marriage customs and citizenship, see Fraser 1.52 ff., 65 ff., 71 ff., 2.155 n. 239; Zanker 137–38, with nn. 48, 50, and further literature there cited. For an exhaustive survey of the evidence (such as it is) for bilingualism in Ptolemaic Egypt, see W. Peremans, "Le bilinguisme dans les relations Gréco-Égyptiennes sous les Lagides," in Van't Dack et al. 253–80; and, for the survival of pharaonic methods under the Ptolemies, L. Koenen, ibid. 149 ff. For a thorough refutation of the supposed early "Egyptianizing" policy of Ptolemy I as satrap, see Turner, *CAH* VII².1 125–27.

15. See, e.g., Fraser 1.70–85.

16. For a stimulating and informative introduction to this aspect of ancient music, which does its best with such evidence, direct or comparative, as is available, see H. Husmann, *Grundlagen der antiken und orientalischen Musikkultur* (Berlin, 1961).

17. Ptol. *Georg.* 6.12.6 Nobbe; Bernard, "Aï Khanum" 92, now confirmed by further excavation: see Leriche 252 ff. (*terminus ante quem* of 329), and Bernard, "Campagne" (1971) 452 (1975) 195 ff.

18. Bernard, "Aï Khanum" 71; Arr. *Anab.* 4.22.3.

19. Hdt. 2.50; Plato, *Tim.* 21E–23C; Arist. *Pol.* 1329ᵇ.

20. Eddy p. vii and *passim*; Treloar 87; Ruben 1087: "Ihr kultureller Einfluss auf Indien war gering."

21. Habicht, "Herrschende Gesellschaft" 1–16. A somewhat more optimistic picture is drawn by Samuel, *From Athens* 110–17.

22. This habit, so totally alien to Oriental feelings for physical *pudeur*, extended even to the Hellenizing Jews: see below, pp. 508–10.

23. Macedonian resentment at Alexander's Orientalizing policy and personal behavior (Green, *Alexander* 333 ff.) was very far from being an isolated instance: see Plato, *Laws* 3.693A, Strabo 17.1.12 (C.797; = Polyb. 34.14.1–5), Livy 38.17.9–13, Athen. 4.131b–c (Anaxandrides satirizing Iphicrates' marriage to the king of Thrace's "savage" daughter). Good case

histories of upward mobility among Egyptians in the civil service and armed forces are documented by Lewis, chaps. 7 and 8, pp. 104–52.

24. Strabo 1.4.9 (C.797); cf. Baldry, in Reverdin 191–92.

25. Even in this area we find ethnic prejudices. The author of the pseudo-Platonic dialogue *Epinomis*, though well aware (987A–C) of the debt Greek astronomy owed to Egypt and Babylon, nevertheless asserts (987D–E; cf. Plato, *Tim.* 24C) not only that the Greek physical environment is most propitious "for excellence" ($\pi\rho\grave{o}\varsigma$ $\mathring{a}\rho\epsilon\tau\acute{\eta}\nu$), but that "whatever Greeks take over from barbarians, they finally make over into something better" ($\mathring{o}$ $\tau\acute{\iota}$ $\pi\epsilon\rho$ $\mathring{a}\nu$ $\mathring{E}\lambda\lambda\eta\nu\epsilon\varsigma$ $\beta\alpha\rho\beta\acute{\alpha}\rho\omega\nu$ $\pi\alpha\rho\alpha\lambda\acute{\alpha}\beta\omega\sigma\iota$, $\kappa\acute{\alpha}\lambda\lambda\iota o\nu$ $\tau o\hat{\upsilon}\tau o$ $\epsilon\mathring{\iota}\varsigma$ $\tau\acute{\epsilon}\lambda o\varsigma$ $\mathring{a}\pi\epsilon\rho\gamma\acute{\alpha}\zeta o\nu\tau\alpha\iota$).

26. Préaux, *Monde* 2.562–65.

27. Cf. ibid. 2.550 ff.

28. Tcherikover 56 ff.; Fraser 1.57, 2.141 n. 162.

29. Fraser 1.283–84, 298.

30. Fraser 1.687–90: at least the Law and the Pentateuch will have been available, in Greek, for synagogue use, by the mid-third century. For an excellent English version of, and commentary on, the so-called *Letter of Aristeas* (mid-2d c. B.C.?) purporting to describe the genesis of these translations, see Bartlett 11–34.

31. Fraser (2.1000–1002 n. 255) can produce only one even remotely cogent echo, that between Callim. *Ep.* 55 (56) = *AP* 6.148, and Isaiah 14.12 on the fall of Hesperus (Lucifer), the Morning Star: $\mathring{E}\sigma\pi\epsilon\rho\epsilon$, $\pi\hat{\omega}\varsigma$ $\mathring{\epsilon}\pi\epsilon\sigma\epsilon\varsigma$ = $\pi\hat{\omega}\varsigma$ $\mathring{\epsilon}\xi\acute{\epsilon}\pi\epsilon\sigma\epsilon\nu$ $\mathring{\epsilon}\kappa$ $\tau o\hat{\upsilon}$ $o\mathring{\upsilon}\rho\alpha\nu o\hat{\upsilon}$ $\mathring{o}$ $\mathring{E}\omega\sigma\phi\acute{o}\rho o\varsigma$. He argues that Callimachus may, in the course of his duties in the Library, have read a translation of Isaiah, which is possible. But the influence still remains minimal. It is also worth noting that the epigram concerns the dedication of a lamp to the "god of Canopus," i.e., Sarapis (Paus. 2.4.6), a Graeco-Egyptian deity (cf. p. 406); so that Callimachus may be in fact making a sly syncretic joke at the expense of the notoriously separatist Jews. Koenen's efforts, in Van't Dack et al. 174 ff., to link Callimachus's *Hymn to Delian Apollo* with the *Oracle of the Potter* (see p. 323) seems to me speculative at best.

32. Fraser 1.707–8, 2.987 n. 203; text in J. Wieneke, "Ezechielis Iudaei Poetae Alexandrini Fabulae Quae Inscribitur $\mathring{E}\xi\alpha\gamma\omega\gamma\acute{\eta}$ Fragmenta" (diss., Münster, 1931). See also *The Exagoge of Ezekiel*, ed. and tr. H. Jacobson (Cambridge, 1983). For Philo and Theodotus, see Lloyd-Jones and Parsons 688, 757–64; cf. Lloyd-Jones 61–62, who rightly describes Philo's style as "involved and pretentious." On the lack of cross-fertilization in literary matters between Greeks and Egyptians, see Samuel, *From Athens* 71 ff., who points out, *inter alia*, that, on the evidence of the papyri, Greeks in Ptolemaic Egypt not only ignored Egyptian literature, but took very little heed of contemporary Greek writing either, preferring to concentrate on the established classics, from Homer through the fifth century B.C. (pp. 67 ff.)— "another aspect of the aversion to change and lack of any interest in growth." Ludwig Koenen's recent attempt to prove substantial cross-cultural influence (in Van't Dack et al. 145–49) is a rather desperate exercise in barrel scraping. He throws in Manetho (see above, p. 190), the Isis aretalogies, Hermetic as well as Judaeo-Christian literature, and a far-fetched attempt to correlate the so-called Petubastis Cycle with Homeric epic. Most of this material is late; none of it affects my main point. Koenen's claim (p. 151) that "die Griechen . . . bemühten sich . . . ägyptische Traditionen zu verstehen; dabei knüpften sie an Kunst, Literatur und Vorstellungen der Ägypter an und verglichen sie mit eigenen Traditionen" is, as a generalization, simply not supported by the evidence.

33. Hor. *Epist.* 2.1.156–57: the passage that follows testifies eloquently to the prevalent sense of inferiority among Romans confronted with Greek literature.

34. R. E. Smith, *The Failure of the Roman Republic* (Cambridge, 1955) 12.

35. Cato *ap.* Plin. *HN* 29.14, cf. 8.82, 21.178, 28.112, 29.11; Cic. *Tusc. Disp.* 2.60, *De Rep.* 1.5, *Pro Flac.* 16, 19, 24; and the famous tirade by Juvenal, *Sat.* 3.58–83; cf. Wardman 6–13.

36. Polyb. 31.25.4, 6–7; cf. 39.1.10; also, e.g., 39.1.1–4; and see Cic. *Tusc. Disp.* 2.27.

37. Cf. above, p. 309, with chap. 18 n. 207.

38. Livy 31.34.8, Pliny *HN* 29.14, Aul. Gell. *NA* 13.9.4. The Greeks also sometimes referred to the Romans as Ὀπικοί, i.e., Oscans, with the implication of uncouthness.

39. Cic. *Tusc. Disp.* 1.1: "meum semper iudicium fuit omnia nostros aut inuenisse per se sapientius quam Graecos aut accepta ab illis fecisse meliora—quae quidem digna statuissent in quibus elaborarent."

40. Livy 38.17.11. The epithet μιξοβάρβαρος, known from the fifth century onwards (cf. Eur. *Phoen.* 138; Xen. *Hell.* 2.1.15; Plato, *Menex.* 245D), always recognized the possibility of assimilation, though it leaves a certain semantic ambivalence between the notions of a Greek going native and a Hellenizing barbarian. Cf. the corresponding epithet μιξέλλην (Polyb. 1.67.7).

41. Juv. *Sat.* 3.58–125.

42. Kreissig, "Landed Property" 5–26; Schiffmann 203 ff., esp. 209–10.

43. Fraser 1.54, 107–8; Zanker 139–40.

44. Arr. *Anab.* 7.4.4–8; cf. App. *Syr.* 5; Plut. *Alex.* 70, *Mor.* 329D–E; Just. 12.10.9–10; Chares of Mytilene *ap.* Athen. 12.538b–539a; DS 17.107.6.

45. Cf. Briant, "Colonisation" 91–92, analyzing "tout un processus qui tendait à fermer la communauté et à exclure les indigènes." Sherwin-White (in Kuhrt and Sherwin-White, p. 30), while arguing that "there is more evidence of Seleucid promotion of Greek culture . . . in non-Greek contexts than is at present admitted," nevertheless then goes on to speak of "the Seleucids' *imposition* of specifically Greek cultural traditions to create a recognisably Greek cultural activity *for Greek and hellenised inhabitants of their empire*" (Italics mine).

46. Avi-Yonah 125.

47. Citizenship, in Alexandria and elsewhere, to avoid ethnic dilution was frequently restricted to the offspring of two full citizens (Avi-Yonah 131), and in any case was hedged about with checks and provisos, more often than not including a formal assembly vote (Avi-Yonah 132–33). Hence in part the prevalence of resident aliens (μέτοικοι, metics). Cf. also Bell, *Egypt* 71; Fraser 1.77, 2.160 n. 281.

48. Avi-Yonah 126–28. In Memphis, that ancient, multiracial city (Strabo 17.1.32 [C.8077]), the former pharaonic capital, integration seems to have come much more easily: see D. J. Thompson, *Memphis* chap. 3, pp. 82 ff.

49. See *SEG* 7 (1934) 38, 39, for "Aristeas, also Ardybelteios" (= "the minister Belit"), who served in this capacity at Babylon in 109.

50. Avi-Yonah 129. For Diotimus, see Burstein, *Translated Documents* no. 34, pp. 45–46, and J. K. Davies, *CAH* VII².1 258, who seriously overestimates the significance of non-Greek athletic victors in Greece.

51. Tac. *Ann.* 6.42: "Seleucenses . . . ciuitas potens . . . neque in barbarum corrupta sed conditoris Seleuci retinens." Cf. Avi-Yonah 130.

52. Cavafy, Ποιήματα Α' 37 = *Collected Poems* 72–73 ("Philhellene").

53. Avi-Yonah 178.

54. *OGIS* 352, *IG* IV² 591.

55. Sedlar 66.

56. Narain 96 with reff.

57. As suggested by the *Questions of King Milinda*, ca. 150–100 ("Milinda" was the name by which Menander passed into Indian tradition); cf. Sedlar 64.

58. Narain 97–100; Woodcock, chap. 6, 94 ff.; Wheeler 163.

59. Cf. F. Maraini, *Where Four Worlds Meet* (London, 1964) 71, with pls. 4–5 between pp. 72 and 73.

60. Narain 11. Baldry, in Reverdin 184 ff., argues for the possibility that this general process of absorption, especially on the outer fringes of the Seleucid empire and in Alexandria, is reflected in the increasing popularity of "cosmopolitanism" in Greek thought (cf. p. 388), the idea of a morality transcending narrow ethnic boundaries; but since such symptoms began to appear much earlier, I suspect that the phenomenon, if not a case of cart before horse, may at least have been far more symbiotic than Baldry supposes.

61. Above, p. 312, with n. 1.

62. Eddy 328.

63. Eddy 307, 309–10, 315–16; Bowman 30–31. Text in L. Koenen, *ZPE* 2 (1968) 178–209 with pls. 3–6 = Burstein, *Translated Documents* no. 106, pp. 136–39. Cf. Koenen, in Van't Dack et al. 174–89. For arguments in favor of a later date, see Koenen, ibid. 148 with n. 18.

64. Polyb. 34.14.1–6 = Strabo 17.1.12 (C.797) characterizes the Alexandrians as "not clearly *polis*-minded" in the mid-second century—even if preferable, on balance, to the natives and mercenaries—"but nevertheless, though a mixed lot, still Greek by origin, and mindful of the customs common to the Greeks." His claim that Ptolemy VIII Physcon purged this group (ca. 145/4; cf. p. 538) indicates that what he had in mind was the top intellectual layer, since we know that these formed Physcon's chief target (cf. Menecles of Barca *ap.* Athen. 4.184b–c = *FGrH* 270 F 9). Afterwards, he says, things got worse; and Strabo (17.1.13 [c.798]) confirms this for the Augustan period.

65. Fraser 1.71, 509, 683–84, 716; cf. Peremans, in Reverdin 137–42, 151. On the *Sibylline Oracles*, see Bartlett 35–55, esp. 38–39, 42 ff., discussing Bk. 3.

66. Eddy 335.

67. Eddy 59, 324.

68. Eddy 112–13.

69. Eddy 12–19; cf. in particular *Oracula Sibyllina* 3.388 ff., cited by Eddy, p. 12 n. 17.

70. Plut. *Mor.* 328E, in a fulsome essay "The Fortune or Virtue of Alexander."

71. See chap. 4, "Barbarian Receptivity," pp. 30–44 *passim*: the giveaway remark about the "upper classes" comes on p. 30. A similar admission is made by E. Will, "Monde hellénistique" (1975) 508, even for "l'Asie méditerranéenne urbanisée"; and cf. Préaux, *Monde* 2.250.

72. Cf. Avi-Yonah 157.

73. Cavafy, "A Prince from Western Libya" (Ποιήματα Β' 68) and "Returning from Greece," *Collected Poems* 298–99, 368–69.

74. Hadas, *Hellenistic Culture* 45; cf. Avi-Yonah 181.

75. Cf. the interesting comments of Eddy, p. 334: "The serious struggle in the East was the fight against the Makedonian kings, and against their economic and military agents." I am not so sure as he is, however, that "everywhere parts of Greek culture, economic innovations, bureaucratic organisations, the methods and styles of artists, even certain religious ideas, were borrowed by the Orient and made a part of its various cultures." That this process on occasion took place is certain; that it was as pandemic as Eddy suggests I very much doubt. The *aperçu* about Arabs and Jews I owe (among many other substantial debts) to a percipient comment by Dr. August Frugé.

76. Peremans, in Reverdin 137.

77. Ibid. 135.

78. See Kuhrt, in Kuhrt and Sherwin-White 56. Greek texts of Manetho (no. 609) and Berossos (no. 680) in *FGrH* IIIC, pp. 5–112, 364–97; Manetho is also available in a Loeb edition (Cambridge, Mass., and London, 1940), translated by W. G. Waddell.

79. Cf. Peremans, in Reverdin 138 ff.; Rostovtzeff, *SEH* 2.1096.

80. Ants: Hdt. 3.102–5. Hyperboreans: Pind. *Ol.* 3.14, 8.47, *Pyth.* 10.31, *Isthm.* 5.22; Hdt. 4.13; schol. Ap. Rhod. 4.28.6. Skiapods: Aristoph. *Birds* 1553 and schol. RV *ad loc.*; *Suda* and Steph. Byz. s.v. Σκίαποδες; cf. Plin. *HN* 7.23. Long penis: Ctes. *Ind.* 24 (ed. Henry). In general see Cary and Warmington, chap. 10 "Imaginary Discoveries," pp. 194 ff.

81. Strabo 2.1.9 (C.70); cf. 15.1.36 (C.702).

82. Hdt. 4.42; cf. Cary and Warmington 87–95; Carpenter 71–74, 103–5. For Eudoxus of Cyzicus, see Strabo 2.3.4 (C.98–100); he had been commissioned to explore the Indian trade route by Ptolemy VIII Physcon.

83. Arr. *Anab.* 5.26.1–2.

84. DS 5.21–23 *passim*. On Pytheas in general see Carpenter, chap. 5, 143–98, and especially, on the problem of his date, pp. 145–51: Carpenter argues for 240, but does not dispose satisfactorily of all the evidence suggesting an earlier period.

85. Strabo 2.4.1 (C.104). On ice-sludge, see the report of Fridtjof-Nansen, cited by Carpenter, 179–80.

86. *Ap.* Strabo 2.4.2 (C.104).

87. Cary and Warmington 33. Carpenter, who believes Pytheas was sent to reopen Greek commerce in the Atlantic after Rome's removal of the Carthaginian threat, is forced to ignore the evidence of Dicaearchus (cf. n. 86 above).

88. Pliny *HN* 6.100–106 *passim.* For Ptolemy VIII's investigation of the eastern sea routes, see above, n. 82. Hippalos: Carpenter 242–44. Trade with India: Cary and Warmington 81. Periodicity of the monsoons: Fraser 1.181–84.

89. Tarn and Griffith 243 ff. give an excellent brief survey.

90. *OGIS* 86 = Austin 279, p. 459; cf. Scullard 123 ff. Fraser (1.175 ff., 2.299 ff.) and Scullard (126–37, with nn. 69–79) discuss the Ptolemies' elephant hunting and conveniently tabulate the scattered evidence.

91. Polyb. 5.84.5.

92. J. O. Thomson, *A History of Ancient Geography* (Cambridge, 1948) 159–62; Tarn and Griffith 302. See also Dilke 31–35 with fig. 4.

93. Casson, *Travel* 117; cf. Samuel, *From Athens* 101 ff., confirming the Greek base of this "international" tradition. Examples of Egyptianizing of Greek art cited by Koenen in Van't Dack et al. 144–45. Of such *Vermischung* he tells us "Sollen hier nur einige Beispiele aufgezählt werden": the suspicion arises that this is because no other ones exist.

94. See, e.g., Will, *HP*² 2.350–52 for a fairly up-to-date summary; the most important theories will be found in Tarn, *Greeks* 82 ff.; Narain 21 ff.; Simonetta 154 ff.; Mørkholm, *Antiochus IV* 172 ff.; and, most recently, Holt, "Euthydemid Coinage" 19 ff., 31 ff., who revives (in my opinion with considerable plausibility) the currently unpopular theory that Diodotus I minted in Antiochus II's name, whereas his son, Diodotus II, abandoned all pretense of Seleucid vassalage: cf. Tarn, *Greeks* 72. The parallel with Philetairos and his successors in Pergamon scarcely needs stressing. Holt, "Discovering the Lost History" 3–28, provides both an excellent survey of the scholarship and a very comprehensive bibliography. Particularly useful is the section on coins (including forgeries) and inscriptions (pp. 7–9). See now Pollitt, *AHA,* app. 4, 284–89.

95. Hdt. 4.204, 6.9; Strabo 11.11.4 (C.518), 14.1.5 (C.634); Plut. *Mor.* 557B; QC 7.5.28–35; cf. Narain 2 ff.

96. Tarn, *Greeks* 119–20.

97. DS 17.99.5–6, QC 9.7.1–11. See Holt, *Alexander* 82–86. The rebels actually seized the satrapal capital of Bactra.

98. DS 18.4.8, 7.1–9. As Holt, *Alexander* 85, stresses, "these events make it certain that Bactria-Sogdiana, indeed much of the east, was in turmoil by the time of Alexander's death." His excellent account of the 323 campaign (pp. 88–91) supersedes all others.

99. DS 18.39.6, 19.48.1; Just. 41.4.1; cf. Bevan, *House of Seleucus* 1.277–78.

100. Just. 15.4.11: "auctis ex uictoria uiribus Bactrianos expugnauit."

101. Tarn, *Greeks* 72.

102. Just. 41.4.5, Strabo 11.9.2–3 (C.515), Trog. *prol.* 41.

103. Narain 11 in rebuttal of Tarn, *Greeks* xx. See also Holt, "Discovering the Lost History" 4, broadly in agreement with the view argued here.

104. Bernard, "Aï Khanum" 74.

105. Bernard, "Quatrième campagne" 354.

106. Bernard, "Aï Khanum" 89. See also the useful general summary by Bernard, "An Ancient Greek City in Central Asia," *Scientific American* 247 (Jan. 1982) 148–59. For recent archaeological work at Samarkand, Old Kandahar, etc., see Holt, "Discovering the Lost History" 6–7. Text of the Delphic maxims translated in Burstein, *Translated Documents* no. 49, p. 67.

107. Polyb. 10.49.1; cf. Tarn, *Greeks* 82, 102, 124; Holt, "Euthydemid Coinage" 35.

108. Bernard, "Campagne" (1972) 608–25.

109. Bernard, "Fouilles" 285 ff.; cf. Bikerman 177–81; Briant, *Actes du Colloque sur l'esclavage, Besançon 10–11 Mai 1971* (Paris, 1972) 93–133.

110. Bernard, "Campagne" (1975) 189 ff.

111. Bernard, "Campagne" (1976) 307 ff., figs. 14–18; cf. P. Leriche and J. Thoraval, *Syria* 56 (1979) 171–205.

112. Bernard, "Campagne" (1980) 435 ff.

113. Bernard, "Campagne" (1976) 314 ff., (1978) 421 ff.

114. Plut. *Mor.* 328D.

115. Bernard, "Campagne" (1978) 456 ff.; cf. Arist. *Phys.* 224–226^b.

116. Bernard, "Campagne" (1976) 299–302 with fig. 10; cf. Vitruv. 9.8.1; Plut. *Mor.* 410E.

117. Cf. Leriche, "Aï Khanoum: Un rempart hellénistique en Asie centrale," *RA* (1974) 231–70.

118. Bernard, "Campagne" (1975) 175 ff.

119. Seltman 201–2 with pl. 47 nos. 8, 9; cf. B. Ployart, *Choix de monnaies gauloises* (Paris, 1980) *passim*, esp. pl. 1 fig. 10; pl. 2 figs. 19, 28; pl. 3 figs. 38, 42; pl. 4 fig. 55. I owe this reference to my colleague Professor J. H. Kroll.

120. Bernard, "Traditions" 245 ff.

121. Bernard, "Campagne" (1976) 303 ff.

122. Bernard, "Quatrième campagne" 339 ff. with pl. 31. For a thorough and perceptive analysis of this difficult but fascinating topic, see Malcolm Colledge, in Kuhrt and Sherwin-White, chap 6, "Greek and Non-Greek Interaction in the Art and Architecture of the Hellenistic East," 134–62.

123. Narain 17.

124. Polyb. 11.39.1–2.

125. Strabo 11.11.1 (C.517), Polyb. 11.39.8–9.

126. Tarn, *Greeks* chap. 4, 129 ff., doubted by Narain 28 ff.

127. Davis and Kraay 243.

128. Plut. *Mor.* 821D–E. For the legend that developed concerning Menander, see Tarn, *Greeks* 264–68, 414–15, 432–36.

Chapter 20. Middle-Period Hellenistic Art, 270–150: *Si Monumentum Requiris . . .*

1. Stewart 3 with nn. 1–9 and further reff. there cited.

2. Plin. *HN* 34.51–52. Stewart 3 translates *cessauit* as "languished," an unjustified softening of Pliny's blunt assertion. Pliny lists, *honoris causa*, in the 121st Olympiad Eutychides, Euthycrates, Daippos, Cephisodotos, Timarchos, and Phyromachos; then comes the gap; and in the 156th Olympiad the art "revived again" (*rursus . . . reuixit*), though with exponents "far inferior to those already mentioned" (*longe quidem infra praedictos*). On neoclassicism in general, see Pollitt, *AHA* 164–75.

3. Havelock 151; Pollitt, *AHA* 163, *Ancient View* 78–79.

4. Stewart 4–5, with his appendix, pp. 157 ff. Of the Attic sculptors in his periods I (330–266) and II (266–210) he remarks: "Almost all are recorded to have made portraits, and many are known for nothing else." The statement is hardly less true for his period III (210–160). Portraiture was, after all, the studio photography of the ancient world. It had other functions, but this was its chief one.

5. Stewart 6; cf. Ferguson, *HA* 176–85, 212–13, 230; Rostovtzeff, *SEH* 1.215–18.

6. Datable to 228/3, the early period of Attalid expansion in Asia, and apparently under the direction of a native Pergamene sculptor, Epigonos: Stewart 19, with nn. 77–79 and further reff. there cited; M. Robertson 528 ff., with pls. 167–68, 170. On the Pergamene team of sculptors, see Pollitt, *AHA* 84–85.

7. Will, *HP*² 1.296–97; Hansen 28–33; Allen 29–34 (good discussion of the chronology: he places the Caicos victory "within the period 238–235"), cf. 136–41 and appendix 2, pp. 195 ff.; cf. Livy 38.16.14; Polyb. 18.41.7–8; Strabo 13.4.2 (C.624).

8. Charbonneaux, in Charbonneaux et al. 259 ff., with figs. 281, 282, 285; Havelock nos. 140–42, pp. 145 ff.; M. Robertson 529 ff., with pls. 167b, c, cf. 170b, c; Webster, *Art* 92–96, *Hellenistic Poetry* 185–86; Bieber 107–10; cf. Onians 81 ff. For a matching description of the Gauls' most characteristic physical features, see DS 5.28.1–3, cited by Pollitt, *AHA* 86.

9. Epigraphical evidence conveniently collected by Allen, 195 ff.; literary sources as in n. 7 above, with the addition of Paus. 1.25.2. The best general description is that of Pollitt, *AHA* 85. Thorough discussions in E. Kuenzel, *Die Kelten des Epigonos von Pergamon* (Würzburg, 1971); R. Wenning, *Die Galateranatheme Attalos I: Eine Untersuchung zum Bestand zur Nachwirkung pergamenischer Skulptur* (Berlin, 1978). I am grateful to Prof. A. F. Stewart for drawing my attention to these two monographs.

10. *OGIS* 277; cf. Allen 35–36.

11. Perhaps the work of the Athenian baroque sculptor Phyromachos: Plin. *HN* 34.84; cf. Stewart 9, 19–23.

12. Paus. 1.25.2, *OGIS* 271–72. Hansen 309–14 and Bieber 109–10 both, rightly, reject the theory that Attalus II is referred to here. See also Pollitt, *AHA* 90–91.

13. A. Schober, *MDAI(R)* 51 (1936) 104–24. For the main arguments against his reconstruction, see Pollitt, *AHA* 89–90.

14. Similarly in our own day A. E. Housman—another scholar-poet—created a mythic pastoral landscape out of the Shropshire he had never explored in sober fact.

15. Well reproduced in Charbonneaux et al. fig. 169; cf. Villard, ibid. 164.

16. Dinsmoor 298 ff. It is noteworthy that in Athens, where classical tragedy was still regularly revived, the proscenium had to be a removable wooden structure to enable both types of play to be staged. It was not till about 150—the time of the Roman conquest—that Athens, last among Greek cities, introduced a permanent stone proscenium.

17. Bernard, "Campagne" (1976) 307 ff.

18. Plin. *HN* 35.112.

19. Villard, in Charbonneaux et al. 140 ff., with figs. 139, 140, 156, 158.

20. M. Robertson 570 ff.

21. Havelock 252 with pl. XI; Plin. *HN* 35.110.

22. Dinsmoor 320–21.

23. Charbonneaux, in Charbonneaux et al. CMV 248.

24. Herod. *Mim.* 4.20–78; see esp. lines 25 ff. For a discussion of the boy-strangles-goose piece (by Boethus of Chalcedon?: cf. Plin. *HN* 34.84) and of so-called Hellenistic rococo in general, see Pollitt, *AHA* 128 ff.

25. Havelock, p. 238 and pl. IV; Charbonneaux, in Charbonneaux et al. 308–10, with fig. 336, repeating the theory elaborated in *MMAI* 50 (1958) 80–103, which I follow here: Havelock's arguments for downdating the cameo to the late second century do not seem to me compelling. The date and interpretation have both been much disputed: periods from the third to the first century have been suggested, while Bastet, *BAB* 37 (1962) 1–24, sees the mother-and-son pair as Cleopatra III and Ptolemy XI, ca. 100 B.C., with the allegorized monarch as a (miraculously slimmed and revivified) Ptolemy VIII Physcon. Pollitt, *AHA* 257–59, with fig. 279, tentatively supports a date for the cameo ca. 100–50 B.C. Koenen, in Van't Dack et al. 171–73, takes this downdating process one step farther. Basing himself on Dorothy B. Thompson's thesis, first published in *Das ptolemäische Ägypten* (Mainz, 1978: the proceedings of an international symposium held in Berlin, 27–29 Sept. 1976) 113 ff., with figs. 97–109, he argues that the Farnese Cup was created after Actium, as a piece of allegorical propaganda on behalf of C. Cornelius Gallus. *Credat Iudaeus Apella, non ego.* Charbonneaux's conclusions still seem to me on all counts the most consistent and by far the most plausible. For Cleopatra I's death in spring 176, rather than three or four years later, see F. Uebel, *APF* 19 (1969) 75 ff.

26. The pose, interestingly, was a popular Hellenistic motif: cf. Havelock fig. 177.

27. Villard, in Charbonneaux et al. 159 with fig. 162; J. Ferguson, *Heritage* fig. 16. Daszewski 146–60 identifies the figure as Berenice II, but his arguments remain inconclusive.

28. Kraay and Hirmer nos. 747, 746, pl. 205; Charbonneaux, in Charbonneaux et al. 296–97 with fig. 321; Havelock no. 10, p. 31; Jenkins nos. 523, 575; Richter, *Portraits* figs. 875–79 with pp. 270 ff.; Seltman pl. 53 nos. 1, 3.

29. Havelock no. 9 and p. 30; cf. Richter, *Portraits* fig. 1915 and pp. 273–74.

30. Richter, *Portraits* figs. 1910–14, p. 273; Kraay and Hirmer nos. 737–39, pl. 203; Head et al. pl. 32 no. 4; Jenkins no. 577; Charbonneaux et al. fig. 368.

31. Jenkins no. 569; Davis and Kraay nos. 29, 33; Richter, *Portraits* fig. 1827; cf. the bust also identified by her as Ptolemy IV (figs. 1829–30), and p. 264.

32. Cf. Jenkins nos. 566, 570.

33. Kraay and Hirmer nos. 802, 804, 805, pls. XX, 219; Jenkins nos. 567, 568; Davis and Kraay nos. 20, 21, 25, 28, 31, 34.

34. Charbonneaux et al. nos. 340–41, p. 312.

35. Kraay and Hirmer no. 578, pl. 175; Jenkins no. 543; Havelock no. 11 with pp. 31–32; Davis and Kraay nos. 125, 128; Richter, *Portraits* fig. 1749.

36. Kraay and Hirmer no. 579, pl. 175; Seltman pl. 1, no. 12; Richter, *Portraits* fig. 1761, who comments (p. 259) on his "strikingly Greek appearance"; and cf. the interesting marble portrait bust from Delphi sometimes identified as Flamininus, Charbonneaux et al. fig. 319, p. 294.

37. Kraay and Hirmer nos. 764–65, pl. 209; Davis and Kraay no. 191; Richter, *Portraits* fig. 1922.

38. Kraay and Hirmer nos. 770–72, pl. 210; Davis and Kraay nos. 203, 206.

39. R. R. R. Smith, "Greeks, Foreigners" 26 ff.

40. Davis and Kraay no. 133.

41. Richter, *Portraits* figs. 1970–71, cf. p. 278; Havelock no. 12 with p. 32; Davis and Kraay no. 613.

42. Kraay and Hirmer no. 778, Jenkins no. 616, Davis and Kraay no. 143.

43. Jenkins no. 615; Richter, *Portraits* fig. 1977.

44. Richter, *Portraits* fig. 1986; Davis and Kraay no. 148.

45. Richter, *Portraits* fig. 1993; Jenkins no. 622; Davis and Kraay nos. 162, 164, 166, 167.

46. Cf. Plin. *HN* 34.84.

47. Martin chap. 3, 127 ff.

48. Walbank, *Philip V* 269.

49. Stewart 23–25. The most recent general survey is that by Pollitt, *AHA* 97–110: a judicious text with well-chosen illustrations.

50. Dux Schneider, *The Traveller's Guide to Turkey* (London, 1975) 324–25.

51. M. Robertson 538.

52. Allen chap. 4, 76 ff.; M. Robertson 538.

53. Charbonneaux, in Charbonneaux et al. 265–66.

54. Allen 123–29, 133–34; Hansen 448 ff.; *SIG*³ 629, 630; Welles, *Royal Correspondence* nos. 49, 50.

55. Apollod. 2.7.4, 3.9.1; DS 4.33.7–12; Strabo 13.1.69 (C.615); Paus. 8.4.9, 47.4, 54.6; 10.28.8.

56. Hansen 272–73; 355–56.

57. M. Robertson 539–40, Onians 84–88.

58. Pollitt, *AHA* 102.

59. Charbonneaux, in Charbonneaux et al. 270, remarks: "The way these gods brandish their weapons suggests the implacable ferocity of a squaring of dynastic and familial accounts." Pollitt, *AHA* 105, stresses, *per contra*, the Olympians' divine serenity in the face of violence. Both can offer partial evidence in support of their views. Between them they convey, perhaps unintentionally, the striking emotional range and variety of the frieze.

60. Schol. Aristoph. *Thesm.* 1059.

61. Charbonneaux, in Charbonneaux et al. 292 with pl. 317; M. Robertson 562–64 with pl. 172c; Bieber 127–28 with figs. 497, 404 (close-up of Ptolemy IV and Arsinoë III); Havelock no. 170, pp. 200–201. Most recent discussion by Pollitt, *AHA* 15–16: he favors the earlier date (ca. 225–200) suggested by Fraser and Guarduca. However, in my opinion Schede's arguments for 125± remain more convincing. For reff., see Pollitt, *AHA* 304 n. 26.

62. Athen. 8.347e; the same passage quotes a statement by Aeschylus to the effect that his tragedies were dedicated to Time, and he knew he would get his fitting reward. Archelaus of Priene presumably had this prediction in mind when he created his relief. For Galaton's picture see Ael. *VH* 13.22, and cf. Fraser 2.862–63. I suspect another round in the Callimachus vs. Apollonius battle here. "Not from the common fountain do *I* drink," Callimachus had said (above, p. 171); "I abhor all public things." But arguably a vigorous flow is preferable to a restrained trickle: many thought so at the time. Perhaps both sides might have done better to heed Aristotle's warning in the *Poetics* (1450^b35–1451^a6) against creating works that are either too long *or* too short, on the grounds that the minuscule eludes our vision, whereas the gigantic we cannot comprehend as a unity.

63. Vitruv. 7 *praef.* 5–7.

64. Hor. *AP* 268–69.

65. Ibid. 1–13.

66. Cf. Green, *Essays in Antiquity* (London, 1960) 163 ff., and *ClAnt* 1 (1982) 202 ff.

67. Cf. the statues of Ptolemy VII, Antiochus VIII Grypos, and Demetrius I of Syria: Charbonneaux et al. figs 344, 328, 323.

68. Pollitt, *AHA* 69 and fig. 67.

69. Villard, in Charbonneaux et al. 156 with fig. 156; Plin. *HN* 36.184. See also Pollitt, *AHA* 221–22 with fig. 233.

70. M. Robertson 541 ff. with pl. 170a; Havelock no. 146 with pp. 149–50; Bieber 134–35 with figs. 530–33; Charbonneaux, in Charbonneaux et al. 333–34 with pl. 362 (excellent photograph); cf. Plin. *HN* 36.37. I need not enter here into the vexed questions of the group's stylistic relation to the recently discovered sculptures from Sperlonga, or discuss the possibility that we may have to do with an original two-figure Pergamene group of the second century, redone in the first century A.D. (with the addition of an extra, classicizing, figure) by the three Rhodian sculptors—Hagesander, Athenodorus, Polydorus—whom Pliny names as the Laocoön group's creators. See, for a persuasive presentation of this theory, Peter von Blanckenhagen, "Laokoon, Sperlonga und Vergil," *AA* (1969) 256–75 with figs. 1–16. Further arguments (leaning toward a first-century-A.D. date) in Pollitt, *AHA* 120–26.

71. Cf. R. Jenkyns, *The Victorians and Ancient Greece* (London, 1980) 13. I am not convinced by Onians' theory (pp. 91 ff.) that explains the obsession with pain and suffering as Stoic-inspired instances of morally justified punishment for sensual transgression. The early Stoics (as Onians himself admits, p. 94) took little interest in art, and certainly were in no position to use such costly works as the Marsyas or the Laocoön as vehicles for propaganda. And for what sensuality was the Dying Gaul being punished?

Chapter 21. Production, Trade, Finance

1. As E. Will remarks, "Monde hellénistique" (1975) 524–25, "il suffit de soupeser les trois volumes du *magnum opus* de Rostovtzeff et de mesurer la bibliographie qui s'y est ajoutée depuis 1941 pour comprendre qu'il ne saurait être question ici d'entrer dans le détail de problèmes aussi vastes et controversés que ceux que pose l'économie du monde hellénistique." Amen to that. Throughout this chapter, even more than elsewhere in the present work, I am acutely conscious that what I have written is an *essay*: personal, selective, aimed at disengaging certain dominant assumptions and practices, and with no pretense whatsoever of having covered, or even touched on, every important topic and problem.

2. See, e.g., M. I. Finley, *The World of Odysseus*, 3d ed. (New York, 1978), 27–29, 61–62, 64–66, 95–98, 120–23.

3. Arist. *Pol.* 1256ᵇ23 ff.: καὶ ἡ πολεμικὴ φύσει κτητική πως ἔσται.

4. Davies, *CAH* VII².1 276 ff.; Goukowsky, in E. Will et al. 316 ff.; Will, "Monde hellén-istique" (1975) 548–49; Green, *Alexander* 316 with n. 11; R. D. Milns, *Alexander the Great* (London, 1968) 137; C. H. V. Sutherland, *Gold: Its Beauty, Power and Allure*, 2d ed. (London, 1960), 74.

5. Préaux, *Monde* 1.367, with testimonia and further examples.

6. Ormerod 67 ff.

7. Hom. *Od.* 8.159–64.

8. E.g., Arist. *Pol.* 1337ᵇ4–22, *Eth. Nic.* 1123ᵃ19; Plato, [*Epin.*] 976B, *Ep.* 7.334B, *Laws* 1.644A, cf. 5.741E.

9. See, e.g., Davisson and Harper 152; Cary 294; Walbank, *Hellenistic World* 159.

10. Samuel, *From Athens* 33 ff., esp. 37–38.

11. Isocr. 8.117–19. On change and stability in general, see the acute discussion by Samuel, *From Athens* chap. 1, 1–38 *passim*. The basic point he is making was adumbrated long ago by R. W. Macan, *Herodotus: The Fourth, Fifth and Sixth Books* (London, 1895) 1.320: "Ancient civilisations, based on war, slavery, blood and religion, tended to stereotype classes, to give fixity to status, to limit contract, to eliminate individualism and competition."

12. Xen. *Mem.* 2.7.6; cf. Aristoph. *Ach.* 519, *Peace* 1002. Xenophon remarks that in order to facilitate the manufacture of ἐξωμίδες, peasants' working tunics, the Megarians are in a position to purchase foreign slaves and set them to work: the clear implication here is that such work is fit only for slaves, since a contrast is then emphasized between the Megarians and Aristarchus, whose household is limited to "free persons and relatives."

13. Arist. *Pol.* 1278ᵃ25, 1321ᵃ28; cf. Préaux, *Monde* 1.362.

14. Ps.-Arist. *Oecon.* 2.1.8, 1346ᵃ–25 ff.; Davisson and Harper 159.

15. Arr. *Anab.* 3.5.1–5, cf. 7.23.6 ff.; QC 4.8.4–6; Ps.-Arist. *Oecon.* 1352ᵃ–1353ᵇ; Dem. 56.7–10, 16–17; Xen. *Oecon.* 20.27–28; Lys. 22.5–10, 12–16; cf. Green, *Alexander* 278–79.

16. Ps.-Arist. *Oecon.* 2.2.13, 1348ᵃ15 ff.

17. DS 3.12.1–14.6.

18. Moretti, in Bianchi Bandinelli 4.8.333. "Everyone's scared of the customs inspectors," says a character in one of Herodas's *Mimes* (4.64).

19. *PZenCol.* 83; cf. Préaux, *Monde* 1.377; Fraser 1.134–35.

20. The actual price of a papyrus roll at any given period has been the subject of much argument. See N. Lewis, *Papyrus in Classical Antiquity* (Oxford, 1974) 129–34, for the most recent, and most sensible, discussion. Such figures as we have are often puzzling. At Athens in 407 a roll cost 1 dr. 2 ob. (*IG* I² 374); on Delos between 279 and 179 the price varied from 1 dr. 3 ob. to 2 dr. 1 ob. In Egypt itself, ca. 259–257, the figure is 3½–4 ob. (*PCairZen.* 59010, 59687, 59688 + *PZenCol.* 4), which might suggest the imposition of a high foreign tariff; but by 251/0 this has abruptly risen to 1 dr. 1 ob. As Lewis warns us (p. 132), there are always two unknown factors: the length of the roll and the quality of the papyrus.

21. Préaux, *Économie* 276.

22. Achaemenid fiscal policy: A. T. Olmstead, *A History of the Persian Empire* (Chicago, 1948) 297–99. Alexander: DS 17.64.3, 66.1, 71.1, 80.3 (180,000 talents); Just. 11.14.9–10, 12.1.3 (190,000 talents); Strabo 15.3.9, C.731 (180,000 talents). Cf. Avi-Yonah 26–27.

23. Heichelheim, *Wirtschaftliche Schwankungen* 40–41, 55–56; Larsen, "Roman Greece" 380; Day 4 with n. 19, 7–8.

24. For an excellent analysis of Greek banking in this period, see Bogaert, *Banques, passim*, and in particular chaps. 1 (terminology), 2 (Attica), pp. 37 ff., and 3.A.1 (Delos), pp. 126 ff. Ptolemaic banking has been the subject of much controversy: see also Bogaert, "Statut" 86 ff. Bogaert identifies three types of bank: private enterprises, which were the first to import banking techniques into Egypt; the royal banks established by Ptolemy II Philadelphos, not

later than 265, which combined the functions of bank proper and treasury suboffice; and, not later than 259, banks run by public lessees on contract from the crown (δημόσιαι τράπεζαι), with a monopoly of the right to exchange, "ce qui a dû provoquer la disparition des banques privées, car sans droit de change, une banque ne peut pratiquement pas faire d'opérations dans l'antiquité" (p. 99). There were thus not many of these banks in comparison with the royal banks proper. Here as in other fields, the Ptolemies disliked competition, and exercised stringent control over their privileges. For earlier views see Préaux, *Économie* 280 ff., "De la Grèce" 243 ff.; Rostovtzeff, *SEH* 1.404 ff., 2.1282 ff. For Ptolemaic banks deriving from Athenian models, see Bogaert, in Van't Dack et al. 15–29.

25. Cf. S. C. Humphreys, *JHS* 90 (1970) 253, and, for the complex problems involved in the interpretation of διαγράφειν, Bogaert, *Banques* 50–55.

26. Selective survey in White, *Greek and Roman Technology* chap. 4, 27–48. Due attention should be paid, at the same time, to his salutary reminder (p. 14) that the history of technology is *not* identical with the history of inventions, and that the scarcity of inventions in classical times should not be overstressed, since "some of the most significant advances in man's control of his environment have come about, not as a result of an invention, but via one of its applications." Yet even in this latter area, as White himself admits, there were many inhibiting factors, economic and social no less than technical.

27. A good description of the *shaduf* (still frequently employed in Egypt and the Near East) is given by Landels, 58–59. Basically it consists of a long pole balanced on a crutch, with a well bucket at one end and a sliding counterweight at the other. As Landels says, "using one of these machines is not much less laborious than using a bucket on a rope." Cf. Menander, *Dysk.* 533–38, for a vivid metaphorical transference of the rigid up-and-down movement of the *shaduf* to Sostratos toiling with his mattock, back muscles all locked solid from shoulders to hips. The Roman name for it was *ciconia* ("stork").

28. White, *Greek and Roman Technology* 30, 63–67.

29. Ibid. 31–32.

30. Vitruv. 10.2.1–10; cf. Landels 84 ff.; White, *Greek and Roman Technology* 14–15. The pulley first appears on an Assyrian bas-relief of the eighth century B.C., some two millennia later than the wheel.

31. Lloyd, *Greek Science* 99–100.

32. Healy, 95–96; Landels 59 ff.; White, *Greek and Roman Technology* 32.

33. Hero, *Pneum.* 1.28; Vitruv. 10.7; Plin. *HN* 19.60. For the working of this pump, see Landels 75 ff. The identification of Pliny's *organum pneumaticum* with the pump invented by Ctesibius is made, very convincingly, by White, *Greek and Roman Technology* 17; cf. 32–34.

34. Casson, *Ships* 243 ff., 277.

35. Callixeinos of Rhodes *ap.* Plut. *Demetr.* 45: apparently this monster never even left its moorings, let alone went into action. Cf. Landels 152–53; Samuel, *From Athens* 53–54.

36. Finley, "Technological Innovation" 29 ff. = *Economy* 176 ff. On the shortage of agricultural technology in Egypt, see Samuel, *From Athens* 47 ff.

37. Walbank, *Hellenistic World* 160, citing *PCairZen.* 59155, which, as Samuel, *From Athens* 47, observes, is the text regularly adduced to demonstrate intensification of agriculture. On fallow land, cf. Préaux, *Monde* 2.478 with n. 1 for further reff.

38. Davisson and Harper, 155.

39. Bogaert, *Banques* 336, 368–70.

40. Finley, *Ancient Economy* 141.

41. Ibid.; Bogaert, *Banques* 355–57, "Banquiers" 140 ff.

42. Finley, *Ancient Economy* 141.

43. Avi-Yonah 223.

44. See Walbank, *CAH* VII².1 64 ff.

45. Petron. *Sat.* 54.3; cf. Finley, *Ancient Economy* 115–16.

46. Heichelheim, *Ancient Economic History* 191 ff.

47. Rostovtzeff, *SEH* 1.385, 2.1094. For a fascinating instance of Ptolemy II intervening

personally to choke off advocates who were "intervening in fiscal cases to the detriment of the revenues," see Burstein, *Translated Documents* no. 96, pp. 121–22, with further reff. there cited.

48. Rostovtzeff, *SEH* 1.274 ff.; Avi-Yonah 204 ff. We possess (*PTeb.* 703) a memorandum of instructions from a διοικητής to a local inspector, which goes into mind-numbing detail on everything from weaving sheds to grain taxes: see Burstein, *Translated Documents* no. 101, pp. 128–30.

49. Avi-Yonah 212–16.

50. I fail to understand Avi-Yonah's assertion (p. 205) that "profit-making for its own sake, the alpha and omega of capitalism, was not [the Ptolemies'] dominant motive," especially when he proceeds to define their chief objective as being "to harness in the most efficient manner the resources of a whole society *for purposes basically not its own*," i.e., theirs (italics mine).

51. Fraser, 1.132–88 *passim.* Cf. the useful general account given by Bowman, 90 ff.

52. For a vivid account of Apollonius the chief financial officer (διοικητής) of Ptolemy II, and his subordinate Zenon, see Rostovtzeff, *Large Estate* 28 ff.; cf. *SEH*, index s.vv. "Apollonius *dioicetes* of Philadelphus," "Zenon, steward of the *dioicetes* Apollonius," and "Zenon's correspondence." As Samuel, *From Athens* 123, stresses, "in culture as in business, in everyday life as in the theories of the philosophers, stability was the good, and stability reigned."

53. Rostovtzeff, *SEH* 1.381 ff.

54. Theophr. *HP* 4.2, Pliny *HN* 13.56–67; cf. Meiggs 57–62.

55. *PCairZen.* 59157, 59233; cf. Avi-Yonah 197; Cary 293 with n. 2.

56. E. Will, "Monde hellénistique" (1975) 528–29; Cary 293; Avi-Yonah 199.

57. Holleaux, *CAH* VII 823.

58. App. *Sic.* 1; Rostovtzeff, *SEH* 1.394–97; Huss, "Beziehungen" 119 ff., cf. B. H. Warmington, *Carthage*, 2d rev. ed. (London, 1969), 62. Huss argues that despite cultural interpenetration "auf künstlerischen und religiösen Gebiet," and the fact that relations in general "weit intensiver gewesen sind, als es zunächst erscheinen mag" (p. 136), nevertheless trade remained limited.

59. Bikerman, chaps. 4, 5, pp. 106 ff.; Rostovtzeff, *SEH* 1.429 ff. (including a detailed analysis of Ps.-Arist. *Oecon.* Bk. 2); Préaux, *Monde* 1.384 ff.

60. Rostovtzeff, *SEH* 1.447: as he says, the few concessions in this respect to Greek cities only serve to confirm the rule.

61. Plut. *Agis* 7, Livy 35.48.7; cf. Bikerman 126 ff. For the range of taxes, see Musti, *CAH* VII².1 193. Problems of billeting troops: Hunt and Edgar vol. 2 no. 413, pp. 561–63.

62. Musti, *Economia* 149–50.

63. Polyb. 5.89.9; for similar munificence by Demetrius (Poliorcetes?), cf. DS 31.36 (200,000 μέδιμνοι of wheat, 100,000 of barley).

64. Bikerman 121–22.

65. Kreissig, "Landed Property" 5–26, *Wirtschaft*, esp. 124–25: a sensible analysis, though non-Marxists may take some of his remarks about *die altorientalische Produktionsweise* with a pinch of bourgeois salt.

66. Bikerman 38 ff., 83 ff.; Musti, "Stato" 90 ff.; Cohen *passim.*

67. Eddy 130 ff.

68. Hansen 205–6.

69. Rostovtzeff, *SEH* 1.393; breakdown of prices in Heichelheim, *Wirtschaftliche Schwankungen* 51 ff.; cf. Jardé 167 ff.; Larsen, "Roman Greece" 383 ff.

70. Rostovtzeff, *SEH* 1.399.

71. Seltman 240–41.

72. Rostovtzeff, *SEH* 1.400.

73. Allen 109–14.

74. Jenkins 235 ff.; Préaux, *Économie* 271 ff.; Rostovtzeff, *SEH* 3.1416–18; cf. 1.401; Walbank, *Hellenistic World* 104–5. Cf. the remarkable letter (*PCairZen.* 59021) of 258, to

Ptolemy II's financial director (διοικητής) Apollonius (Hunt and Edgar vol. 2 no. 409, pp. 548–51) from Demetrius, a mint official, giving a vivid picture both of the turnover in reminting (a recent batch totaled 57,000 gold pieces) and of the foreign traders and merchants and middlemen whose coin was, for various bureaucratic reasons, refused, much to their fury.

75. Cf. Rostovtzeff, *SEH* 1.407 ff.

76. Avi-Yonah 209–10.

77. Rostovtzeff, *SEH* 1.403–4.

78. Ibid. 1.406–7; Préaux, *Économie* 142.

79. Avi-Yonah 209, with reff. there cited.

80. Rostovtzeff, *SEH* 2.1278.

81. Bogaert, *Banques* chap. 3.A.1, pp. 126 ff.; Larsen, "Roman Greece" 337–48.

82. Rostovtzeff, *SEH* 1.404.

83. Préaux, *Monde* 1.377.

84. Rostovtzeff, *SEH* 2.1253.

85. Tarn and Griffith 255.

86. Rostovtzeff, *SEH*, significantly, contains no entry (in an otherwise very comprehensive index) headed "Insurance."

87. Dem. 50.17 refers to a maritime loan at 12.5 percent, which is unusually low. At 56.17 he carefully distinguishes "maritime interest" (ναυτικοὺς τόκους) from the ordinary sort, and at 34.23 he cites a bottomry loan on which 30 percent interest was charged.

88. Tarn, *CAH* VII 212. On the cistophoric coinage, see Davies, *CAH* VII².1 278 and n. 121, with further reff. For the economic resources of Antigonid Macedonia, see Borza 2–16; Rostovtzeff, *SEH* 1.251–53; Jardé 203; Hammond and Griffith 68 ff.; Meiggs 123 ff., 144–46, 432–33, 444.

89. See Polyb. 4.60.4 for the εἰσφορά paid by member cities of the Achaean League.

90. Moretti, in Bianchi Bandinelli 4.8.340 ff.

91. Ibid. 370–74.

92. Moretti, *Iscrizioni* 2.102 (pp. 76–79); *SIG*³ 495; Moretti, in Bianchi Bandinelli 4.8.366 ff. The crisis in Larissa is datable to 200, that in Miletus to 205/4.

93. E.g., Eurycleides of Cephisia: see Ferguson, *HA* 205. As ἀγωνοθέτης of the Dionysia he spent no less than 7 talents: *IG* II/III² 834.4–5.

94. For an instance of ἐπίδοσις at Athens (245/4: archonship of Diomedon; cf. Meritt 84, 95) in the interests of national defense (εἰς τὴν σωτηρίαν τῆς πόλεως καὶ τὴν φυλακὴν τῆς χώρας), with contributions set at a minimum of 50 and a maximum of 200 dr., see *SIG*³ 491, and cf. Day 11–12, 36.

95. Tarn and Griffith 257; Ferguson, *HA* 376; Day 21–22. See Polyb. 4.38.5, Athen. 10.432c.

96. Heichelheim, *Wirtschaftliche Schwankungen* 51–52; Larsen, "Roman Greece" 384–85; Jardé 182–83; Day 7–8, 47.

97. Larsen, "Roman Greece" 386. Those who doubt the ancient evidence (which is considerable) for price gouging, profiteering, and political manipulation of the grain supply (cf. above, p. 366 and n. 15) should study Dan Morgan's remarkable monograph on contemporary grain cartels, *Merchants of Grain* (New York, 1979), in particular chaps. 7, 11, pp. 220 ff., 334 ff.

98. Day 21 with nn. 116–18.

99. Seltman 259–60; Day 4–6 with n. 31; E. Ardaillon, *Les mines de Laurion dans l'antiquité* (Paris, 1897) 160–63.

100. Kraay and Hirmer 325 with nos. 364–65, pl. 120; Day 31–33. On the (much-debated) date of the appearance of the στεφανηφόροι, see Gruen, *HW* 312 with n. 125, who gives a useful survey of recent numismatic scholarship.

101. Tarn and Griffith 256–57.

102. Plin. *HN* 8.190, Theocr. 15.126, Athen. 12.540d; cf. Tarn and Griffith 256.

103. Fraser 1.164–72; Rostovtzeff, *SEH* 2.676–93, *CAH* VIII 619 ff.; Préaux, *Monde*

2.489 ff.; Berthold, *Rhodes*, esp. chap. 2, 38 ff.; J. H. Michel, "Rhodes ou le dynamisme de l'état-cité à l'époque hellénistique," *CE* 60 (1985) 204–13.

104. Polyb. 30.31; Dem. 56.3–5, 10; Strabo 14.2.9 (C.654); cf. Casson, "Grain Trade" 168 ff.; Fraser 1.164. Strabo compares the axial-grid plan of the city of Rhodes to that of Piraeus. See also Berthold, *Rhodes* 53 ff.

105. Ormerod 132 ff.; Préaux, *Monde* 2.490–91.

106. *SIG*³ 354 = Austin 112, pp. 193–94: Ephesus as beneficiary, ca. 300. *SIG*³ 493 = Austin 115, pp. 197–98: Histiaea as beneficiary, ca. 230–220.

107. Strabo 14.2.5 (C.652–53); Préaux, *Monde* 2.495; Rostovtzeff, *CAH* VIII 636–67; Davies *CAH* VII².1 284 with n. 167 for further literature.

108. Polyb. 30.5.6.

109. Fraser 1.164–65; he suggests, ingeniously (p. 168), that they paid for their grain very largely with empty amphoras.

110. Polyb. 4.47.1–3, 52.1–5 *passim*; 27.7.5–6. Cf. Berthold, *Rhodes* 94 ff.; Davies, *CAH* VII².1 273.

111. Strabo 14.2.5 (C.653).

112. Casson, "Grain Trade" 168 ff. For an excellent account of the purchase, marketing, and storing of grain in the Greek *poleis*, see Moretti, in Bianchi Bandinelli 4.8.354 ff.

113. Strabo, *loc. cit.* (n. 111); cf. Rostovtzeff, *CAH* VIII 635.

114. G. T. Griffith, *OCD*² 923. Cf. the detailed account of Berthold, *Rhodes* 42 ff. In this connection it may be worth quoting the following observations by John Stuart Mill: "War is an ugly thing, but not the ugliest of things: the decayed and degraded state of moral and patriotic feeling which thinks nothing *worth* a war, is worse. . . . A man who has nothing which he is willing to fight for, nothing which he cares about more than he does about his own personal safety, is a miserable creature who has no chance of being free" ("The Contest in America" [1862], reprinted in *Essays on Equality, Law and Education*, vol. 21 of *The Collected Works of John Stuart Mill* [Toronto and London, 1984], 141–42). Such sentiments are not popular today, among historians or the public at large; but we should be wary of retrojecting our postnuclear assumptions into eras where they do not apply.

115. Polyb. 30.31.10–12.

116. Polyb. 5.88–90 *passim*, DS 26.8.1, Plin. *HN* 34.41; cf. Strabo 14.2.5 (C.652); Casson, "Grain Trade" 171–72; Berthold, *Rhodes* 92–93.

117. For other examples from this period of such unofficial insurance payments, see, e.g., Polyb. 5.88, 31.31; DS 20.46.4, 31.32, cf. 36; App. *Syr.* 47; Plut. *Demetr.* 10; Ps.-Plut. *Vit. X Orat.* 1037D; *IG* II/III² 1492; *OGIS* 748; cf. Moretti, in Bianchi Bandinelli 4.8.335–36.

118. Polyb. 5.88.4.

119. As Casson, "Grain Trade" 171–72, rightly says of the Ptolemaic grain donation (30,000 tons), "A gift of these proportions from a member of the hardest-fisted, most businesslike family known to the history of the ancient world" is by itself "ample evidence of Rhodes' commercial importance."

120. Polyb. 30.31.9–12; Rostovtzeff, *SEH* 2.771–72. Berthold, *Rhodes* 205 ff., points out that Rhodes kept her lucrative grain trade (for which the harbors of Delos were unsuitable) and in fact remained comparatively affluent long after Delos was ruined. The benefits to Delos (and indeed to Athens and Rome) of free-port status have been exaggerated; it has, indeed, been argued that the chief advantage was the lack of interest in, or control over, the antecedents of goods passing through: the proceeds of piracy and slaving were what kept Delos in profitable business. See D. V. Sippel, "A Reward for Athens, a Punishment for Rhodes?" *AncW* 12 (1985) 97–104.

Chapter 22. The Individual and Society: Slavery, Revolution, Utopias

1. Ste Croix 298 ff.

2. Arist. *Rhet.* 1367ᵃ32; cf. Finley, "Was Greek Civilisation Based on Slave Labour?" and

Economy 99. The much-debated question of how far agricultural labor was in the hands of slaves, as opposed to a free but obligated peasantry (more so in Greece, I would argue, than in the Seleucid or the Ptolemaic domains, where the indigenous population became generally subject to foreign overlordship), does not affect this fundamental issue, since in neither case could a worker consider himself "free" as the Greeks understood that term.

3. Cf. Fuks, "Patterns" 56.

4. In 167 alone, 150,000 Epirotes were enslaved, by order of the Senate: Polyb. 30.15, Livy 45.34.5–6; cf. App. *Illyr.* 2.9, and p. 430. The total number of prisoners taken by the Romans between 200 and 150 has been estimated, conservatively, at close to 250,000 (Frank 1.188). During the first Sicilian slave war alone at least 70,000, and possibly 200,000, slaves rebelled: DS 34/35.2.18, Livy, *per.* 56, Oros. 5.6.1–6. Mass enslavements in Italy had begun as early as the Third Samnite War of 296, during which at least 40,000 captives suffered this fate: cf. Finley, *Ancient Slavery* 83. For the westward traffic in Oriental slaves, see DS 36.3, with Westermann 29, 34, 57ff.

5. Westermann 34 argues for an overall *decline* in slave ownership during the Hellenistic period, but the evidence he adduces (e.g., that of the Delphic manumissions) need not be construed in this sense.

6. Ps.-Arist. *Oecon.* 1.5.1, 1344^{a}24.

7. Westermann 28–30. For the fiction of exposure as a means of avoiding the laws that prohibited selling free children into slavery, see I. Biezunska-Malowist, "Die Expositio von Kindern als Quelle der Sklavenbeschaffung im griechisch-römischen Aegypten," *JWG* 2 (1971) 129–33.

8. Polyb. 2.56.7, 58.12; 15.23.9, 24.1–3; Plut. *Arat.* 45. In the same way, it was illegal for Alexandrians to enslave fellow citizens: a very necessary social precaution in that melting pot of a city, and one quite compatible with enthusiasm for slavery as such. See Westermann 30 with n. 37.

9. *Pol.* 1.2 *passim*, esp. 1254^{a}5–15, 22–24; 1254^{b}15–30; 1255^a–1255^{b}40.

10. *Eth. Nic.* 8.11.6–7, 1161^{b}4–5; cf. *Pol.* 1.2.4, 1253^{b}30 ff.

11. Hdt. 7.135.

12. *Eth. Eudem.* 1215^{b}35.

13. Cf. Isocr. 4 (*Panegyr.*) 181; καὶ γὰρ αἰσχρὸν ἰδίᾳ μὲν τοῖς βαρβάροις οἰκέταις ἀξιοῦν χρῆσθαι, δημοσίᾳ δὲ τοσούτους τῶν συμμάχων περιορᾶν αὐτοῖς δουλεύοντας, etc.

14. Westermann's denial of this principle (p. 44) is far too sweeping and emphatic: though the taboo was frequently disregarded, it existed, and to claim that "with no consideration even of fellow-citizenship in the same polity, but with ruthless logic, they [the Greeks] 'denationalised' the idea of slavery" gives a thoroughly misleading impression.

15. *Rep.* 5.469B–C; cf. Xen. *Hell.* 1.6.14.

16. Xen. *Mem.* 2.2.2.

17. Thuc. 5.116.4.

18. Aristotle, *Pol.* 1.2.3, 1253^{b}20 ff., recognizes the existence of a theory arguing that slavery was "contrary to nature," being justified solely by custom and imposed by force; but we have no means of knowing how widely held this view was. The absence of corroborative evidence suggests strongly that it was promulgated by a small minority only.

19. Schol. Arist. *Rhet.* 1373^b.

20. Philemon fr. 95 Kock; cf. fr. 22.

21. Eur. *IA* 1400–1401, frr. 48, 49, 50, 51, 86 Nauck^2.

22. Cf. the evidence collected by Schlaifer, in Finley, ed., *Slavery* 199–200; and Guthrie, *History* 3.157–59.

23. Ps.-Xen. *Ath. Pol.* 1.10–12, Hypereides *ap.* Athen. 6.266f.–267a.

24. Xen. *Oecon.* 9.5, 13.9–12, *Mem.* 2.10.1; Arist. *Pol.* 7.9.9, 1330^{a}26 ff. (on which passage Heinen, "Zur Sklaverei" 132, rightly observes: "Daraus spricht weder besondere Humanität noch klassenkämpferische Schärfe, sondern ganz einfach nüchterne Berechnung"); Dem. 21.47; Ps.-Arist. *Oecon.* 1.5.1–6, 1344^{a}23–1344^{b}22 *passim* (stressing both stick and car-

rot); Ps.-Phocyl. 223–27 Young. At the same time there is all-too-plentiful evidence suggesting that the only way of making a slave see reason is by brute force (e.g., Lys. 4.12–17, Isocr. 12 [*Panath.*] 181, Xen. *Mem.* 2.1.15–17), and the callousness later exemplified by Cato, who recommended selling off old worn-out tools, harness, and slaves in the same breath, is notorious: Cato, *De Agric.* 2.7; cf. Plut. *Cat.* 4, 5, 21. Beloch, *Griech. Gesch.* III² 1.322, uses the graphic phrase "mit Hunger und Peitsche" to describe ancient methods of stimulating servile production.

25. P. Jouguet, *Papyrus de Lille* vol. 1 (Paris, 1912) no. 29.9–12, cited by Westermann 52 n. 46.

26. Thuc. 3.44–48 *passim.*

27. Finley, "Was Greek Civilisation Based on Slave Labour?" and *Economy* 114.

28. Strabo 14.5.2 (C.668): μυριάδας ἀνδραπόδων.

29. Florus 3.19: "hic ad cultum agri frequentia ergastula catenatique cultores materiam bello praebuere." Cf. Green, "First Sicilian Slave War" 10.

30. Vogt chap. 3, esp. pp. 44–46; Green, "First Sicilian Slave War" 24, 28 n. 120 (with further reff.); Finley, "Utopianism" 184–85.

31. As we have seen, in both Egypt and the Seleucid domains the land was worked, in the first instance, not by slave labor, but by a technically free, though heavily obligated, quasi-serf peasantry: thus in these areas the servile population consisted chiefly of domestic servants and skilled specialists, in workshops of various sorts. Cf. Westermann 47 ff.

32. Cf. Finley, "Was Greek Civilisation Based on Slave Labour?" and *Economy* 107.

33. Vogt 89.

34. The best discussion of this complex—and not always juridical—problem is that by Finley, "Between Slavery and Freedom," "Servile Statuses," and "Debt-Bondage," conveniently reprinted as chaps. 7–9 of *Economy,* pp. 116–66; cf. also, for the confusion of status in Syro-Phoenicia, Levi 25–65.

35. E. Will, "Monde hellénistique" (1975) 563.

36. Cf. Westermann 40 ff.

37. Rice, 186–87, suggests that the πεντετηρίς of Callixeinos is that of 279–275; but this coincides with setbacks in the First Syrian War, and is at odds with the astronomical evidence: see Chap. 10, n. 19, p. 774.

38. Ibid. 190.

39. Polyb. 30.25.

40. DS 33.28b.1.

41. Rostovtzeff, *Large Estate.* Cf. *SEH* 1.226–29, 352, 389, 419; 2.1252–54, 1270.

42. Polyb. 5.50.1–2. The minister concerned was Hermeias (cf. p. 289).

43. For the elaborate and pretentious mystique of Hellenistic chefs, see the long passage of Damoxenos's *Fosterlings* (*Syntrophoi*) cited by Athenaeus, 3.101f–103b = Kock 3.349.

44. See, e.g., the sources cited by Athenaeus, 12.549d–550b.

45. Polyb. 21.26.14; cf. Thuc. 1.5.3 for earlier evidence of traditional piracy in this area, and see also Ormerod 139 ff.

46. Polyb. 20.6.5–6, 36.17.5–8. See D. Engels, "The Use of Historical Demography in Ancient History," *CQ,* n.s., 34 (1984) 386–93, esp. 391–92. Why, as he asks, expose infants when there was a good profit to be made by selling them in a high-demand market? See below, n. 60.

47. A useful general account in Dudley, *History* 74–84.

48. Powell, *Coll. Alex.* 201 ff.; Knox 190 ff.; Diehl, *Anth. Lyr.* vol. 3 (Leipzig, 1923) 305 ff.; cf., e.g., Hesiod, *WD* 248–73.

49. Powell, ibid. 231–36; Knox 242 ff.; Diehl, ibid. 290 ff.

50. Phoenix fr. 6 Powell = Diehl, ibid. 290–93; Knox 248–50.

51. Tarn, *CAH* VII 755. Finley, "Utopianism" 178–79, goes so far as to compare Cercidas's grumbling to those lead curse tablets (*tabellae defixionum,* καταδεσμοί) so popular among the superstitious from the fourth century onwards (see p. 598).

52. Cercidas frr. 4.3–6, 4.29–33, 7.6–10 Powell = Knox 194–95, 206–7.

53. Paus. 1.14.5, Athen. 14.627e–628d, *Vit. Aesch.* 120 Westermann; cf. Plut. *Mor.* 604F. Cavafy wrote a sharp-edged poem stressing the irritation of later *littérateurs* at Aeschylus's (to them) perverse scale of values: Cavafy, Ποιήματα Β' 16 = *Collected Poems* 196–97 ("Young Men of Sidon, A.D. 400").

54. See, e.g., the tradition enshrined in Plut. *Mor.* 769A–770A.

55. Carphyllides, *AP* 7.260.

56. Pomeroy, *Goddesses* chap. 7, 136–39.

57. E. Will, "Monde hellénistique" (1975) 522.

58. A useful assembly of testimonia in Tarn and Griffith 100–102; but note the caveats of Engels (above, n. 46).

59. Epict. *Diss.* 1.23.

60. Polyb. 36.17.5–7. The whole passage is of great significance and interest. "During our own lifetime all Greece has been afflicted by a shortage of children and general depopulation, on account of which cities have been deserted, and the land bears no crops, though there have been neither continuous wars nor visitations of plague. . . . Men had become so pretentious, idle, and money-mad that they had no wish to marry, or, if they did marry, to rear the resultant children, or, at most, one or two, so that they could leave them in affluence and bring them up to be spendthrifts. As a result of this, the evil spread rapidly and insensibly; for in a family of one or two children it often happens that one will die in war and the other succumb to disease, and where this happened the homes had to be left unoccupied, and as in the case of swarms of bees, so, little by little, the cities became weak and defenseless." Davies, *CAH* VII².1 268, correctly remarks that "the pattern of behavior he describes is a class phenomenon, not a demographic phenomenon," and argues (less convincingly) that "regional population densities need not have changed appreciably."

61. Tarn and Griffith 103.

62. Ibid. 108–9.

63. Cf. E. Will, "Monde hellénistique" (1975) 558–59.

64. See Hands 39 ff., and chap. 7, 89 ff.

65. *SIG*³ 976 = Austin 116 (pp. 198–201), Hands 178–80 (no. D.6), a decree now shown by S. V. Tracy, "The date of the Grain Decree from Samos: the prosopographical indicators," *Chiron* 20 (1990) 98–100 (cf. also 59–96), to be dated c. 260, gives detailed evidence of how a civic fund was established for the purchase and gratis distribution of grain in Samos (to be paid for with the interest accruing from loans). Similar provisions are recorded for 246/3: see *SEG* 1.366 (1923), lines 36 ff., = Austin 113 (pp. 194–96), Hands 176 (no. D.3).

66. See Ps.-Dem. 17.15, echoed by *SEG* 1 (1923) 75, p. 14, col. 1.28.

67. See Fuks, "Patterns" 64 n. 15, for an exhaustive conspectus of relevant passages in both the *Republic* and the *Laws*.

68. See Fuks, "Isokrates" 17–44.

69. Green, "First Sicilian Slave War" 15; Vogt 43 ff.

70. Fuks, "Patterns" 51, argues that "in the course of over two centuries *dozens of attempts* were made in Greece to change the social-economic position by way of revolution" (italics mine), a thoroughly misleading statement, but not unexpected to those familiar with the general thrust of this scholar's work.

71. Chios, with its large slave population, had a history of servile risings going back at least to 412, when runaways helped the Athenians ravage the countryside: Thuc. 8.40.2; cf. Fuks, "Slave War" 108–9 with n. 12.

72. Nymphodorus *ap.* Athen. 6.265d–266e; cf. Wallon 1.318–20; Fuks, "Slave War" 102–11 (a useful collection of material but highly suspect in its conclusions); Vogt 79 ff.

73. Nymphodorus *ap.* Athen. 266b–d. Fuks, "Slave War" 110 with n. 19, rejects the account of Drimakos's death as "a Hellenistic love-story"; I find its circumstantiality very convincing. On the other hand I agree with Fuks (ibid.) that if anyone broke the armistice, it was the Chians, since for them the "existence of an enclave of 'free slaves' in Chios was a crying

anomaly, and an utter impossibility . . . in the long run." What we have here is an excellent parallel to the eighteenth-century phenomenon of *marronage*: cf. K. R. Bradley, "Slave Kingdoms and Slave Rebellions in Ancient Sicily," *Historical Reflections / Réflexions historiques* 10 (1983) 435–51, esp. 446 ff., though Bradley does not in fact utilize the case of Drimakos to support his thesis.

74. Dicaearchus *ap.* Porph. *De Abst.* 4.1.2 = Müller, *FHG* 2.233–34.

75. Hesiod, *WD* 118 ff.

76. Vogt 28 ff.

77. Hom. *Il.* 18.373 ff.

78. Telecleides *ap.* Athen. 6.268b: αὐτόματ᾽ ἦν τὰ δέοντα.

79. The *locus classicus* is Athen. 6.267e–270a, including generous extracts from Crates' *Wild Beasts* (= Kock 1.133), Telecleides' *Amphictyons* (= Kock 1.209), Pherecrates' *Miners* (= Kock 1.174) and *Persians* (= Kock 1.182), and the *Thurio-Persians* of Metagenes (= Kock 1.706).

80. Athen. 6.268d.

81. Arist. *Pol.* 1253^{b}33 ff. I am not (at this point) directly concerned with the much-debated converse problem of whether the existence of slavery in antiquity was in any sense responsible for the lack of technological development: see pp. 366 ff. Briefly, my own conviction (*pace* Westermann 120; Africa, *Science* 95; C. G. Starr, *Journal of Economic History* 18 [1958] 29, and others) is that, inevitably, it had to be: for a useful survey of recent views, see Kiechle, 1–11, who cites Farrington's claim (with which I am in substantial agreement) that "ancient society had set in a mould which precluded the possibility of an effective search for power other than the muscles of slaves." For the low technological level achieved in the ancient world, see p. 367, and cf. L. White, *Speculum* 15 (1940) 141–59.

82. DS 22.5 *passim*, Polyaen. 6.7 *passim*, Plut. *Mor.* 555B; cf. Tarn and Griffith 122–23; Fuks, "Patterns" 61.

83. Ed. L. W. Hunter (Oxford, 1927): see esp. 1.3.6–8; 2.1.7–8; 3.3–7 *passim*; 5.1–2; 10.3–26 *passim*. Other reff. collected by Fuks, "Patterns" 65–66 n. 16. On this matter of στάσις in general, see the excellent monograph by Andrew Lintott, *Violence, Civil Strife and Revolution in the Classical City 750–330 B.C.* (London, 1982).

84. This is true both of Polybius (Bks. 13–18) and Livy (Bks. 31–35), the second being largely derived from the first: see Texier, *Nabis* 105, who attributes Polybius's hostility to "amour-propre achéen," "rancune familiale," and "intérêt de caste," and that of Livy to "amour-propre romain."

85. For the first view, see, e.g., Passerini, "I moti politici-sociali della Grecia e i Romani," *Athenaeum*, n.s., 11 (1933) 316; for the second, Holleaux, *CAH* VIII 147, 189.

86. DS 34/35.2.19, Oros. 5.9.4–8; cf. Ferguson, *Klio* 7 (1907) 238; Green, "First Sicilian Slave War" 17.

87. Green, ibid. 20, 27 n. 93.

89. Vogt chap. 4, 93–102.

88. Vogt 39, 75, 84–88.

90. DS 2.55–60 *passim*.

91. On the basis of Strabo 14.1.38 (C.646) combined with DS 2.59.7: see Tarn and Griffith 125. More circumspect is Dudley, "Blossius."

92. J. Ferguson, *Utopias* 143–44.

93. Finley, "Utopianism" 180, 183–85; cf. Africa, "Aristonicus" 110; Will, *HP*² 2.419–23; Vogt 37 with further reff.

94. Africa, "Aristonicus" 122–23, sees this very clearly.

95. Finley, "Utopianism" 184.

96. Vogt 69 ff.

97. Manuel 82. The sages in Iambulus's island utopia had double tongues: this made them not only great mimics (of animals as well as of other people) but also capable of holding more than one conversation at the same time. Slavery seems to have been nonexistent, since all essential work was distributed between citizens by rota, and the abolition of private property led—in theory—to a life without wealth, ambition, or poverty, a life of concord (ὁμό-

νοια) untroubled by στάσις. Leadership was on the gerontocratic principle; both the island and its inhabitants were named after the sun. There may be, along with much fantasy, some garbled knowledge of Ceylon (Sri Lanka) in this account. Its continued stress on education suggests Stoic or Platonic influence. It is also the last recorded Hellenistic utopia: Rome had a genius for killing off fantasies.

98. Cf. Ael. *VH* 3.18 = *FGrH* IIB 115, 75c (pp. 551–52); Müller, *FHG* 1.76 (pp. 289–90); Manuel 84 with n. 27; J. Ferguson, *Utopias* 122–23.

99. Cf. L. Giangrande 17–33.

100. Aristoph. *Eccles*. 651–52.

101. *Pol*. 2.4.1.–5.14 *passim*, 1266ᵃ–1269ᵃ28.

102. Callimachus in his *Iambi* (1.9–11, fr. 191 Pfeiffer) talks of Euhemerus as an old man (ca. 270 ?) "babbling and scribbling his impious books" in a shrine of Sarapis outside the walls of Alexandria. For the remains of Euhemerus's work, see *FGrH* 63 (pp. 300–13), and G. Vallauri, *Evemero di Messene: Testimonianze e frammenti* (Turin, 1956); cf. also H. Braunert, *RhM* 108 (1965) 255–68.

103. DS 5.42.4–46.6.2. As Finley, "Utopianism" 187, rightly observes, "in antiquity it is hard to find any utopian thinking which is not hierarchical."

104. The story told by Diodorus (5.9) about common holding of land in the Lipari Islands during the sixth century merely records a quite exceptional emergency: half the labor force farmed while the rest fought off, or competed with, Etruscan pirates.

105. The identity of the sunburst emblem is much less securely attributed than one might assume from, say, the confident pronouncements of Prof. Andronikos, followed by J. R. Ellis in "The Unification of Macedonia," *Philip of Macedon*, ed. M. B. Hatzopoulos and L. D. Loukopoulos (Athens and New Rochelle, N.Y., 1980), 38, with pl. 21. Two recent articles have gone into the problem in some detail. E. N. Borza, "The Macedonian Royal Tombs at Vergina: Some Cautionary Notes," *ArchN* 10 (1981) 81–82, 87 n. 59, both queries the evidence for the sunburst as a dynastic badge, and stresses the ambiguities inherent in any interpretation of it in nationalistic terms: how would any fourth-century Macedonian define the dividing line between the ethnic and the dynastic? J. P. Adams, "The *larnakes* from Tomb II at Vergina," *ArchN* 12 (1983) 1–7, investigates the emblem's varied provenience (which includes Panathenaic vases possibly, but not necessarily, representing Macedonians), and concludes not only that the sunburst could be religious rather than political in meaning, but also that it, like so many symbols, "can embody simultaneously several different, even contradictory, ideas." It may have been, *inter alia*, a royal badge—Herodotus's story (8.137–40) about the encircled shaft of sunlight taken as a symbolic fee by the early Argead Perdiccas is, for me, very persuasive—but a *non liquet* verdict is probably unavoidable.

106. Athen. 3.98d–e; cf. Tarn, *Alexander the Great* (Cambridge, 1948) 2.429 ff.; Vogt 70.

Chapter 23. Ruler Cults, Traditional Religion, and the Ambivalence of Tyche

1. One interesting, and seldom-noticed, literary offshoot of Tyche, something that first appears toward the end of the Hellenistic period, is the prose romance or novel: throughout its history this genre has always relied heavily on fate, accident, and coincidence to keep its fictional characters busy and its plots moving. Cf. Herzog-Hauser 1670–73 for the incidence of Tyche in "Roman und Märchen."

2. I should emphasize that I am not including in this generalization the unsolicited honors—altars, priests, processions, feast days, etc.—offered to distinguished leaders, from Lysander onwards, by the Greek *poleis*, since in such cases the recipient was normally regarded as ἰσόθεος (like or equal to a god in achievement and generosity, rather than divine); but rather I mean to describe the dynastic cults instituted by the rulers themselves. For a convenient summary of, in particular, the physical evidence for ruler cults, see Pollitt, *AHA*, app. 2, "The Ruler Cult and Its Imagery," 271–75.

3. Cf. Origen, *Cont. Cels*. 5.41.

4. Beare 97 ff.

5. Bikerman 253.

6. *OGIS* 212 (pp. 319–21), Just. 15.4.1–9, App. *Syr.* 56–57.

7. Allen 121–29, Hansen 447 ff.

8. Fraser 1.197, 201–7, 211–12; cf. 43–45 for Ptolemy IV. The great procession of Ptolemy II (above, pp. 158–60) was in honor of Dionysus: Rice *passim*, Fraser 1.231–32.

9. Fraser 1.194.

10. Walbank, *Philip V* 258–59 with n. 3; cf. 243–44.

11. Walbank, *Hellenistic World* 210.

12. Tritogeneia: Chrysippus *ap.* Philod. *De Piet.* 16 = *SVF* 2.258, no. 514. Cerberus: Heracleitus, *Hom. Alleg.*, ed. Buffière (Paris, 1962), 33.9. The attribution to Cleanthes of the Cerberus allegory is often assumed (see, e.g., Cary 362) but in fact unproved. Heracleitus (not he of Ephesus, but an Augustan academic) has an allegorizing chapter on the Labors, in which (33.1) he cites "the most reputable Stoics" for the allegorizing of Heracles (cf. Epictetus, *Encheir.* 3.24.13). Cornutus (*Ep.* 31 = *SVF* 1.115–16, no. 514) informs us that Cleanthes treated the Labors allegorically. The assumption that Heracleitus drew on Cleanthes is thus plausible, but far from certain. For Cleanthes' attack on Aristarchus, see Plut. *Mor.* 923A = *SVF* 1.112, no. 500.

13. Cary 366.

14. Protag. frr. 80 B 1, 4 D-K; Arist. *Rhet.* 1402ᵃ23 ff.; cf. Guthrie, *History* 3.181 ff. (especially useful for variant interpretations of Protagoras's man-the-measure aphorism); J. Barnes, *The Presocratic Philosophers*, rev. ed. (London, 1982), 448–49, 541–42.

15. Cf. Diogenes of Oenoanda's comment (80 A 23 D-K): "He said he did not know if there are any gods, and that is the same as to say he knew that there are no gods" (tr. Barnes, *op. cit.* [n. 14] 449, who very properly castigates the faulty logic of this stance; but I suspect it was widely held at the time).

16. See J. Fontenrose, *The Delphic Oracle* (Berkeley and Los Angeles, 1978) 244–67.

17. Arist. *Eth. Nic.* 1177ᵇ–1178ᵈ.

18. Above, Chap. 4, p. 55 and n. 14: Duris *ap.* Athen. 6.253d–f; cf. Taeger 1.271–3.

19. Plut. *Demetr.* 23.

20. Philipp. fr. 25 Kock, *SIG*³ 374; cf. Taeger 1.269.

21. For Demetrius's manipulation of the Athenian calendar, and the other enormities that were thought to have produced signs of ill omen—frostbitten vines, a tear in the sacred Panathenaic robe as it bellied in the wind, saillike, during its procession to the Acropolis—see Plut. *Demetr.* 10, 12, 23, 26, 27. Cf. above, p. 399.

22. For a sustained attack on Athenian habits of flattery, with ample contemporary documentation, cf. Athen. 6.254a–255c.

23. See Xenoph. frr. 169–72 Kirk, Raven, and Schofield, pp. 168–69, for Xenophanes' argument that Homer and Hesiod attribute every kind of immorality to the gods, and, more important, that every local tribe makes its gods in its own ethnic image, so that (fr. 169) "if oxen and horses or lions . . . could draw like men, they would draw gods with bodies precisely like their own."

24. Chaeremon *ap.* Stob. *Flor.* 1.6.16.

25. For the power, blindness, and irresistibility of Tyche, see the testimonia collected by Herzog-Hauser, 1667–68.

26. Many, of course, tried to have it both ways by associating a semipersonalized avatar of Tyche with city, god, or ruler: Antioch, again, is the obvious example. Cf. Herzog-Hauser 1665–66.

27. Nilsson 258–62.

28. *SVF* 1.99, fr. 449: ὁ σοφὸς ὑπὸ τῆς τύχης ἀήττητός ἐστι καὶ ἀδούλωτος καὶ ἀκέραιος καὶ ἀπαθής.

29. The *Suda* definition sums it up well: Τύχη παρ᾽Ἕλλησιν ἀπρονόητος κόσμου διοίκησις ἢ φορὰ ἐξ ἀδήλων εἰς ἄδηλον καὶ αὐτόματον.

30. Herzog-Hauser, 1676–77, collects some interesting examples.

31. Fraser 1.241–43, Herzog-Hauser 1685–86.

32. Nilsson 200.

33. Useful discussions, in this context, in Herter 76 ff., Herzog-Hauser 1643–46.

34. Cf. Hesiod, *Theog.* 360, and in particular Archil. fr. 16 West = Stob. *Flor.* 1.6.3: πάντα Τύχη καὶ Μοῖρα, Περίκλεες, ἀνδρὶ δίδωσιν.

35. Soph. fr. 196 Pearson.

36. In his *Pirithoös*, fr. 21 Untersteiner: ὡς τοῖσιν εὖ φρονοῦσι συμμαχεῖ Τύχη.

37. Eur. *Cycl.* 606–7.

38. Polyb. 39.8.2.

39. For the increasing disinclination, as time went on, to attribute divine "envy" (φθόνος) to individual deities, or even to the gods as such, see Aalders 4 ff., though he draws no significant conclusions from his remarkable findings.

40. Cf. Chaeremon, frr. 2, 19 Nauck[3]: "All things Chance vanquishes and turns around"; "Chance, not good counsel, rules the affairs of mortals."

41. Philemon, fr. 137 Kock.

42. Arist. *Phys.* 2.4–6 *passim*, 195[b]30–198[a]13.

43. Ibid. 196[b]6: θεῖόν τι οὖσα καὶ δαιμονιώτερον.

44. Cf. Herzog-Hauser 1659–61 for the invocation of Tyche by the orators, Demosthenes included, who (1661.64–67) "neben den Göttern noch eine unpersönliche, mehr oder weniger unberechenbare und unzugängliche Schicksalsmacht wirksam glaubt."

45. Cf. Polyb. 36.17 *passim* for his own views; cf. 2.4.3; 5.26.12; 8.4.3, 22.10; 15.6.8; 29.5.3, 6[c]; 30.10.1.

46. Walbank, *Polybius* 60–65, with further reff.

47. Nilsson 210.

48. Green, *Alexander* 451 ff.

49. Taeger 1.285.

50. Nock, *Essays* 1.145.

51. Arist. *Rhet.* 1361[a].

52. Fraser 1.193–210.

53. *OGIS* 11, pp. 33–35.

54. *OGIS* 212, pp. 319–21: for cults in honor of later Seleucids, see Bikerman 243 ff. It is perhaps worth drawing an analogy here with the Catholic festivals in honor of saints; popular Protestant misconceptions to the contrary, neither a saint nor his or her image is worshipped, or regarded as divine, but rather is honored for holiness and invoked for intercession on a petitioner's behalf in Heaven. The parallel seems to me remarkably exact, the only substantial difference being that no saint, by definition, could be so honored in his own lifetime.

55. Plut. *Flam.* 16 *passim*.

56. *OGIS* 6, pp. 19–21 = Austin 32, pp. 59–60.

57. DS 20.100, Paus. 1.8.6.

58. DS 20.102.2–3: "They called the city Demetrias, and voted him sacrifices and festivals and the annual celebration of games, and to bestow upon him all the other honors of a founder."

59. Cf. Arist. *Rhet.* 1361[a].

60. App. *Syr.* 65.

61. Plut. *Demetr.* 46, DS 20.102.3; cf. Préaux, *Monde* 1.246–47. The Romans, who were intensely suspicious of kings as such, made a point (as we shall see) of cutting the Hellenistic monarchs they encountered down to size. Cf. Walbank, *CAH* VII[2].1 99–100.

62. Arist. *Pol.* 1284[a]11.

63. Plut. *Alex.* 28, *Mor.* 180E, 341B; Aristobulus *ap.* Athen. 251a; Hom. *Il.* 5.340.

64. See Volkmann, "Basileia" 155 ff., who appositely cites Soph. fr. 464 Nauck[3] on the servitude of herdsmen to the flocks they control: the key concept is dutiful responsibility, which in the "nonaccountable rule" (ἀρχὴ ἀνυπεύθυνος) of an autocrat remains dangerously absent.

65. Fraser 1.215 ff., Nilsson 154–56.

66. Cf. Plut. *Eum*. 13, DS 18.60–61.

67. Callisthenes *ap*. Polyb. 12.23.5.

68. Préaux, *Monde* 1.256–57. For Hellenistic dynastic cults, see also Walbank, *CAH* VII².1 96–99.

69. Fraser 1.216–17 with n. 208 (2.364–65), Avi-Yonah 64–65.

70. Avi-Yonah 62–63.

71. QC 9.8.22, Paus. 1.6.2.

72. Paus. 6.11.8–9, Plut. *Lys*. 18.

73. Rice 190.

74. Arr. *Anab*. 3.1.5; cf. Fraser 1.193 ff.

75. For the connection with Dionysus, especially in respect of Ptolemy IV, cf. Plut. *Cleom*. 34; cf. also Brady 25 with further reff.

76. Brady 14.

77. Fraser 1.214.

78. For Egyptian influence, see Koenen, in Van't Dack et al. 152 ff. For the well-documented collaboration between the Ptolemies and the priests of Ptah in Memphis, see D. J. Thompson, *Memphis* 125 ff.

79. Nock, *Essays* 1.204 ff.

80. Theocr. 17.16–19, 46–50; Callim. *dieg*. 10.10, fr. 110 Pfeiffer; cf. Catull. 66 *passim* on the Lock of Berenice.

81. So, rightly, Fraser 1.226.

82. Welles, *Royal Correspondence* 36–37, pp. 156–65: improved text in L. Robert, *Hellenica* 7 (1949) 5–22 = Austin 158, pp. 262–63; cf. Bikerman 247.

83. Often not even as a *quid pro quo* for specific favors received, but simply as a gesture of gratitude for peace, freedom, and equitable government: cf. Habicht, *Gottmenschentum* 241.

84. *OGIS* 308–9, pp. 477–80); cf. Polyb. 22.20 for a similar address in her honor. She was associated with Aphrodite, in her temple at Teos, as "the goddess Apollonis the Pious."

85. Allen chap. 6, 145–58; Hansen 453–70.

86. *OGIS* 332 (pp. 513–19), esp. line 9; Allen 156–57; Hansen 467.

87. Cf. Nock, *Essays* 1.250, and esp. Habicht, *Gottmenschentum* 79–81, who can find only a few scattered and dubious cases of divine honors voted to Antigonus Gonatas by the Greek states; it would not be surprising, given his known views, if he actively discouraged such compliments.

88. The origin of the cult is clearly assigned to the reign of Ptolemy I by both Tacitus, *Hist*. 4.83–84, and Plutarch, *Mor*. 361F–362B, cf. Clem. Alex. *Protrept*. 4.48: the king is supposed to have seen in a dream a statue that was identified as one in Sinope on the Black Sea, and when this had been brought to Alexandria Manetho and his associates convinced Ptolemy that it represented Sarapis, here equated with Pluto. See Samuel, *From Athens* 82 ff., for a balanced assessment of Ptolemy I Soter's promotion of Sarapis and other deities.

89. Préaux, *Monde* 2.649–55, offers a brief but up-to-date survey; cf. Fraser 1.116–18, 246–59, 273–74; Stambaugh *passim*; Brady, 9–41; Engelmann *passim*; Nilsson 156 ff.

90. Diog. Laert. 5.76.

91. Strabo 17.1.17 (C.801).

92. Probably the grandson of the Bryaxis who worked on the Mausoleum: see Bieber 83–84 with figs. 296–97 and n. 45; Clem. Alex. *Protrept*. 4.48. Cf. Havelock 107 (with pp. 130–31), who, however, attributes the Sarapis, wrongly, to the elder Bryaxis, as does the glossary-index of Charbonneaux et al. (p. 460). Clement describes how the image was covered with an odd mixture of gold, silver, bronze, iron, and lead filings, mixed up with powdered gems (sapphire, topaz, emerald, hematite), and colored dark blue. As Havelock says, "it must have been a weird but dazzling statue."

93. Stambaugh 83–84.

94. Ibid. chap. 8, 75 ff.; chap. 9, 79 ff.

95. Ibid. chap. 4, 36 ff.

96. It was, however, always stressed in official circles that Sarapis was a venerable god of long-standing fame who had simply been rescued from undeserved oblivion and restored to his proper place.

97. *PCairZen* 59034.

98. Brady 23; P. M. Fraser, *OAth* 3 (1960) 1–54, esp. 17. For a record of the establishment of the Sarapis cult on Delos, ca. 200, see *SIG*³ 663 = Burstein, *Translated Documents* no. 102, pp. 130–31.

99. Stambaugh 96–97, Brady 24 ff.

100. Sarapis's temples had groups of resident devotees kown as κάτοχοι, "novices," or perhaps "recluses": the precise terms of their residence, and release from the god's service, remain uncertain. See Wilcken, *Urkunden* 1.52–77; Avi-Yonah 46; Préaux, *Monde* 2.654. They seem to have been, in some sense, the rough equivalent of the medieval mendicant friars: looked on with suspicion both by Egyptians and by respectable Greeks, prickly, often quarrelsome, another side of that ill-documented counterculture better known to us through the Cynics. The cult of Sarapis at Memphis in the mid-second century B.C. is vividly illustrated by the documents relating to the family of a recluse domiciled in the shrine, Ptolemaios son of Glaucias. These testimonia, superbly edited in Wilcken, *Urkunden* vol. 1, can best be studied by English-speaking non-specialists in Lewis, chap. 5, pp. 69–87; and in D. J. Thompson, *Memphis* chap. 7, pp. 212–65 (the best and most recent treatment).

101. As specifically stated by Aristeides, 45.18–20 Keil.

102. Stambaugh 101.

103. Cf. Cyril Bailey, *Phases in the Religion of Ancient Rome* (Berkeley, 1932) 224–25, 242–45.

104. Engelmann *passim*.

105. Cf. *SIG*³ 1130 ff.

106. Préaux, *Monde* 2.657 ff., gives a succinct report on recent scholarship in this field.

107. R. E. Witt, *Isis in the Graeco-Roman World* (London, 1971), esp. chap. 4, 46 ff.; F. Solmsen, *Isis among the Greeks and Romans* (Cambridge, Mass., 1979), esp. chap. 1, 1–25; Dunand 1.27 ff.

108. *IG* II.1 337.42–45; cf. Dunand 2.4 ff. For the arrival of Sarapis in Piraeus ca. 270, see Ferguson, *HA* 171.

109. *OGIS* 30–33, pp. 57–59; Preisigike, *Sammelb.* nos. 601–2; cf. Brady 13.

110. Dunand, vols. 2 and 3 *passim*. For the worship of Isis at Philae in 32 B.C. by a Roman officer, with his family and friends, see *OGIS* 196 = Sherk, *Translated Documents* 90, p. 112.

111. For a convenient conspectus, see Grandjean 8–11, and app. 3, 122 ff., for the Greek text of the only complete aretalogy to survive, an inscription from Cyme in the Aeolid; cf. also DS 1.27.3–5. See Burstein, *Translated Documents* no. 112, pp. 146–48, for an English version of this remarkable text. For the assimilation of Demeter, see Solmsen (above, n. 107) 9–11.

112. Translated from the Greek text of Grandjean, 123–24.

113. Apul. *Met.* 11.3–4.

Chapter 24. From Cynoscephalae to Pydna: The Decline and Fall of Macedonia, 196–168

1. Livy 45.17.1–3, 18.6–8, 29.1–10, 32.1–2; DS 31.8.1, 6–9.

2. Polyb. 23.1 *passim*; cf. Livy 39.46.6. Even so, as Gruen, *HW* 107 ff., points out, the Romans preferred to delegate such matters to neutral Greek arbitration whenever possible. A long inscription of 196/5 from Lampsacus, honoring the Lampsacene Hegesias for his devoted representations on the city's behalf to Flamininus, offers a vivid and revealing glimpse of this process in action. See *SIG*³ 591; translation and notes in Sherk, *Translated Documents* 5, pp. 4–7.

3. Badian, *Titus* 53–57; Will, *HP*² 2.172–74.

4. Cf. C. D. Hamilton, *Sparta's Bitter Victories* (Ithaca, N.Y., 1979) 306–25.

5. Livy 45.33.1–7, 35.1–4, 40 *passim*; DS 31.13; Plut. *Aem. Paull.* 30–35 *passim*.

6. Plut. *Aem. Paull.* 38; Badian, *Publicans* 30. But as Gruen observes, "Material Rewards" 63, "politics rather than economics took central place": the Senate would cheerfully reduce, or even cancel, an indemnity in the right circumstances.

7. Plut. *Aem. Paull.* 37, DS 31.9.7, Porph. *FGrH* 260 F 3(18).

8. Cf. Livy 31.41.5, 32.33–34 *passim*. The letter to Chyretiae: *SIG*³ 593; translation in Sherk, *Translated Documents* 4, p. 5. See also D. Armstrong and J. J. Walsh, "*SIG*³ 593: The Letter of Flamininus to Chyretiae," *CPh* 81 (1986) 32–46. This article rightly stresses the thoroughness of Flamininus's settlement in Greece, but (I think) gives him too much personal credit for what was almost certainly the work of Greek bureaucrats. The expertise in constitutional law, the mastery of the *koiné* evinced in the text—such things are by no means necessary proof of Flamininus's own philhellenism, merely of an efficient local administrative liaison group.

9. Polyb. 18.45.4–6, 11–12; note especially the Aetolians' claim that "all this made it easy for anyone to see that the Fetters of Greece were simply being transferred from Philip to the Romans, and that what was happening was not the freeing of the Greeks, but a mere change of masters." Such changes, Polybius says, were repeated *ad nauseam* (κατακόρως).

10. Livy 34.43.48–52 *passim*; DS 28.12, Plut. *Flam.* 13, Just. 31.3.2.

11. Livy 33.44.8; cf. 34.32.18 for charges of piracy against Nabis, and in general Texier, *Nabis* 70–71.

12. Livy 34.25.3 (Achaean League: a total of 11,000 troops in the field from the League's resources); 34.26.10 (Macedonians, Thessaly); 34.26.11, 29.4–5, 30.7, 35.2 (Rhodes and Pergamon); 34.38.3 (Spartan exiles); Polyb. 24.5 (Messenia). It should be noted that the war was officially declared, and conducted, by the Hellenic League, with Flamininus acting as the League's agent. This was not, in the strict sense, a Roman war: Livy 34.24.6–7. For a self-promoting dedication of spoils after the campaign by Eumenes of Pergamon, see *SIG*³ 595A–B; translation in Sherk, *Translated Documents* 7, pp. 8–9.

13. For this campaign, see Livy 34.28–29 *passim*. Nabis refused to concede defeat: Livy 34.31.1.

14. Livy 34.31–34 *passim*, Plut. *Flam.* 13. On the uncertainty of prorogation in command, even for a seasoned and successful general such as Flamininus, see Gruen, *HW* 216–17.

15. Polyb. 18.45.1–7, 46.5–6, 47.6–10, 48.5–10; cf. Livy 33.34.

16. Polyb. 18.47.1–4.

17. Polyb. 18.44.4, Livy 33.30.3.

18. Livy 35.13.6–10; cf. 34.57.2.

19. Livy 35.17.1.

20. App. *Syr.* 5, Polyb. 21.20.8–9, Livy 37.53.13–14.

21. From the Rosetta Stone of 196—*OGIS* 90 = Austin 227, pp. 374–78; Bagnall and Derow 196, pp. 226–30—we learn of the concessions he had been making to the Egyptian priests to keep their support during a long period of internal στάσις, and it is at this point that Egypt begins to show severe depreciation of the currency (see p. 366).

22. Polyb. 18.49–52 *passim*; cf. Errington, *Dawn* 156 ff.

23. Livy 33.45–49 *passim*; App. *Syr.* 15; Will, *HP*² 2.194–95.

24. Livy 34.60.3–4.

25. Livy 34.43.3–9, 48.2–52 *passim*.

26. Livy 34.52.4–8, Plut. *Flam.* 14.

27. Cary 194.

28. Livy 35.12; cf. Larsen, *Greek Federal States* 407–8.

29. Livy 36.7–8, App. *Syr.* 16.

30. Gruen, *HW* 400.

31. Or, if we are to believe Aymard, *Premiers rapports* 297 n. 18, rescuing them from

Achaean domination; cf. Texier, *Nabis* 95–96. Both these scholars are anxious to interpret Nabis's actions in as good, i.e., as revolutionary-populist, a light as possible.

32. Livy 35.12.1–2, 27–30 *passim*; Plut. *Flam.* 18; Paus. 8.50.6–10.

33. Livy 35.12–20 *passim*.

34. Will, *HP²* 2.196–203, offers an excellent analysis of our confused and in places suspect sources, mainly Livy 34.57–59; cf. Briscoe, *Commentary* (1981) 137 ff., and the same scholar's remarks in *Latomus* 31 (1972) 34–36.

35. Livy 34.60–62.

36. Livy 35.32.2–4, 8–11, 33.8, 38.9, 44.6, 46.6; 36.9.4; Polyb. 3.7.3. For the Roman use of the "freedom" slogan against Antiochus, see, e.g., Livy 35.31.8–10.

37. Livy 35.33.8. For a shrewd analysis of Antiochus's position, cf. Gruen, *HW* 635–36, who suggests, *inter alia*, that "in the end, Rome and Antiochus were driven to war by the logic of their own propaganda," a persuasive—and eerily modern—thesis.

38. Livy 35.34.6–11.

39. Plut. *Philop.* 15, Livy 35.35–36 *passim*, Paus. 8.50.10. What prompted the Aetolians to this action? It has been variously suggested that they wanted to impress Antiochus with military successes, that they hoped to cash in on Nabis's unpopularity to make territorial gains in the Peloponnese, that they were trying to restore democracy (!) in Sparta, that they were after Nabis's treasury: see Shimron, *Late Sparta* 100, for an analysis of these theories, none of which (except perhaps the last) is even remotely plausible. The Aetolians' mentality much resembled that of Scerdilaidas of Illyria (above, p. 296): raiding and looting were the things they really understood. They may not have read *The New Yorker*, and their trust in God was patchy; but they certainly took short views.

40. Polyb. 20.12, 21.3.4, 23.17.6–18.2; Livy 35.35–36 *passim*, 37.1–3; Plut. *Philop.* 15; Paus. 8.51.1–2. After Nabis's murder the Spartans are said to have elected a boy-king named Lacon, but nothing further is heard of him: Livy 35.36.8. Cf. Piper 114–16.

41. A good account in Badian, "Rome and Antiochus" 122 ff.

42. Livy 35.33.1, 34.3; cf. Deininger 72–73.

43. On this point, see Derow's excellent review of Deininger, *Phoenix* 26 (1972) 303–11, esp. 307–9; and Gruen, "Class Conflict" 31.

44. Cf. Mendels, "Attitude" 27 ff.

45. Livy 35.56.2, App. *Mac.* 9.5.

46. Polyb. 20.8 (= Athen. 10.439e–f), Plut. *Flam.* 16, Livy 36.11.1–4, DS 29.2, App. *Syr.* 16.

47. Polyb. 20.7.3–5.

48. Livy 36.13–21 *passim*, App. *Syr.* 17–20, Just. 31.6.4–5. For the topography of the 191 B.C. battle of Thermopylae, see W. K. Pritchett, *Studies in Ancient Greek Topography*, part 1 (Berkeley and Los Angeles, 1965), chap. 5, 71–82.

49. Livy 36.27–30, App. *Syr.* 21, Polyb. 21.8.

50. Livy 36.41.1.

51. Livy 36.4.1–4, 37.3.9–11.

52. Berthold, *Rhodes* 151–52.

53. Ibid. 142.

54. Polyb. 21.8, 10, Livy 37.18–19.6; cf. Hansen 84–85; Gruen, *HW* 546.

55. Livy 37.20–22, App. *Syr.* 26.

56. Livy 37.23–24, 27–32; Polyb. 21.13; DS 29.5; App. *Syr.* 27–28; Just. 31.7.1–2; cf. Berthold, *Rhodes* 156 ff.

57. Livy 37.1–7; Polyb. 21.2–4; App. *Mac.* 9.5, *Syr.* 20; Plut. *Flam.* 14; Just. 31.7.1–2. The cancellation of Philip's indemnity: Polyb. 21.3.3, 11.9; Livy 37.25.12; App. *Mac.* 9.5, *Syr.* 23; Plut. *Flam.* 14. It is interesting to find the Delians, a year or two earlier, bestowing formal honors upon Scipio Africanus (193?): *IG* XI.4 712; translation in Sherk, *Translated Documents* 9, p. 10.

58. Livy 37.33–36, Polyb. 21.13–15, DS 29.7, App. *Syr.* 29, Just. 31.7.3–9.

59. Livy 37.37–44 *passim*, App. *Syr.* 30–36, Just. 31.8.1–8; cf. Bar-Kochva chap. 14, 163–73.

60. Hansen 86–87 suspects "the hand of a Pergamene historian" here, and consequent exaggeration of the role played in the battle by Eumenes and his brother Attalus. The Achaeans (who also fought at Magnesia) afterwards dedicated a statue of Attalus, commemorating their alliance and participation in the fighting, and Attalus's noteworthy courage: *SIG*[3] 606; translation in Sherk, *Translated Documents* 13, pp. 12–13.

61. Polyb. 21.40, 44; Livy 38.37.5–6, 39.6.

62. Livy 36.1.6.

63. Polyb. 21.16–17 (esp. 17.3–8); Livy 37.45.4–21 *passim* (esp. 11–18), 55.4–7, 56; DS 29.10; App. *Syr.* 38–39; cf. Gruen, *HW* 640–43; Mørkholm, *Antiochus IV* 22 ff. Sherwin-White 23 regards the treaty of Apamea as, *inter alia*, "an arbitrary act of power," to be associated with the idea of spear-won territory. This seems to me the correct explanation.

64. Polyb. 21.43.20–21, Livy 38.38.14.

65. See A. Giovannini, "La clause territoriale de la paix d'Apamée," *Athenaeum*, n.s., 60 (1982) 224–36.

66. For the division, see Polyb. 21.24.7–8, 46.8; Livy 37.55.5, 56.5–6; App. *Syr.* 44; DS 29.11; cf. Berthold, *Rhodes* 162–65, 167–68.

67. Polyb. 21.18–24, Livy 37.52–56.

68. Hansen 94, Sherwin-White 21.

69. App. *Syr.* 38–39, DS 29.10: this clause seems to have been laxly enforced, since later Antiochus IV disposed of both elephants and a fleet. Testimonia in Mørkholm, *Antiochus IV* 27 with n. 28.

70. Préaux, *Monde* 1.162; Sherwin-White 23–24.

71. Livy 37.60.2, 38.12–15, 18–27, 37.1–5, 40.1–3, 48.7–8; Polyb. 21.33–41, 45; DS 29.12, 13; cf. Hansen 88–92; Gruen, *HW* 549.

72. Polyb. 21.47, Livy 38.40–41.

73. So, rightly, Gruen, *HW* 550.

74. Livy 38.50.4–60, esp. 55.5–13.

75. Rostovtzeff, *SEH* 2.696; Mørkholm, *Antiochus IV* 30–31.

76. Mørkholm, ibid. 32: "At some time after 188, the royal treasury remedied an acute shortage of silver coins in Syria by circulating large quantities of silver tetradrachms from Asia Minor, counterstamped with the Seleucid anchor to transform them into local coins."

77. DS 29.15, Just. 32.2.1–2.

78. Polyb. 21.32.2–4, 13; Livy 38.11.2–3, 9; Gruen, *HW* 26.

79. Livy 38.30.6–9, 31; cf. Piper 122–23.

80. Livy 38.31.2–6.

81. Livy 38.32.4.

82. Livy 38.32.9; cf. Gruen, *HW* 474. Piper, 123, puts it in a nutshell: "The Achaeans naturally took this to mean that they had full authority to deal with Sparta, while the Spartans believed that their independence had been approved."

83. Livy 38.31.4.

84. Livy 38.33–34, 39.37.1–8; Polyb. 21.32c.3, 22.11.7; Plut. *Philop.* 16, 17; cf. Piper 124–25.

85. Polyb. 22.7.6, cf. 22.3.3; DS 29.17; Errington, *Philopoemen* 151–52; Shimron, *Late Sparta* 105 ff. Philopoemen's heroic honors: *SIG*[3] 624 = Burstein, *Translated Documents* no. 73, pp. 98–99.

86. Livy 45.28.4; Paus. 7.14.2, cf. 7.9.4; Plut. *Philop.* 16; Shimron, *Late Sparta* 112–17. For Chaeron's abortive attempt at revolt, see Polyb. 24.7; cf. Niese 2.57–58, Piper 131–32.

87. Errington, *Philopoemen* 152.

88. Cf. Gruen, *HW* 483–84.

89. Polyb. 23.1 *passim*, Livy 39.23–24. Philip had previously been at some pains, as his changes in coin iconography suggest (thunderbolts replaced by ploughs, etc.) to convince

Rome of his peaceful intentions: Hammond and Walbank 455. But this seems to have been tongue-in-cheek propaganda.

90. Polyb. 22.6, 11.1–4, 13–14; 23.1–3, 8; Livy 39.24–29, 33–35, 46–48, 53. For the prejudicial behavior of the commission see Hammond and Walbank 456.

91. Livy 39.27.10; cf. Walbank, *Philip V* 216, 223.

92. Polyb. 22.13.

93. Polyb. 23.1–2, Livy 39.47.

94. Polyb. 23.8.1–2, Livy 39.53; further testimonia in Will, *HP*² 2.250–52, and cf. Gruen, "Last Years" 226 ff.

95. Polyb. 22.17.1–5; cf. Bevan, *House of Ptolemy* 274; Will, *HP*² 2.302; Walbank, *HC* 3.203–5; P. W. Restman, *CE* 40 (1965) 157–70.

96. Polyb. 22.12.2–10, 23.4.1–9; Livy 39.33.6, 36–37, 48.4; Paus. 7.9.4–5. The exiles of 188 were also recalled; capital offenses were removed from the League's jurisdiction and turned over to outside arbitration. The problem of property ownership, not surprisingly, proved intractable: cf. p. 251.

97. R. Renaud, "Philopoimen," *LEC* 39 (1971) 437–74, esp. 472: "Philopoimen est sans conteste intègre; ses successeurs, qui vont précipiter la ruine de sa patrie, sont corrompus, véreux, indignes. Il est désintéressé; mais qu'est-ce qu'il lui en coûte, puisqu'il est riche?"

98. Polyb. 23.12.16, Livy 39.49–50, Plut. *Philop.* 16.

99. Will, *HP*² 2.245, argues that "le malheur de Callicratès fut de n'avoir pas en assez d'influence pour empêcher les 'patriotes' de conduire leur patrie à la catastrophe finale": it depends which way you look at it! Cf., however, Polyb. 24.8.6–7 for his declared belief that "neither law nor the text of a treaty should be more binding than this"—i.e., a request on the part of Rome.

100. Hansen 99–100; Gruen, *HW* 552.

101. Nep. *Hann.* 10–11, Just. 32.4.2–8. Unlike many scholars, I see no *a priori* reason to disbelieve this anecdote. Pollitt, indeed (*AHA* 82), suggests that "this snake-attack so impressed itself upon the conciousness of the Pergamenes that there is an indirect allusion to it in the snake-infested quality that pervades the Gigantomachy frieze on the Altar of Zeus. . . . If so, it was Hannibal's last and most lasting contribution to the history of his time."

102. Livy 39.50, Nep. *Hann.* 13.2.

103. Hansen 448 ff., cf. 104–5; Allen 123 ff. Cf. also Burstein, *Translated Documents* no. 87, pp. 110–111.

104. Polyb. 23.9.1–3, 24.1.1–3; Livy 40.2.6–8; Hansen 101–4; Gruen, *HW* 553–54.

105. DS 29.29.

106. "Motherlover," a title that has been held to emphasize his mother's Syrian connections, and his own territorial expectations in that area: see Gruen, *HW* 687.

107. DS 30.15.

108. Gruen, "Last Years" 234 with nn. 43, 44, collects a representative sample of modern scholarship taking this line.

109. Ibid. 245.

110. See, e.g., Polyb. 23.10.3.

111. Polyb. 23.11; Livy 40.8, 16.1–3.

112. Walbank, *Philip V* 239–41.

113. Livy 40.23.6–9.

114. Polyb. 22.6, 11, 13–14, 18; 23.1–3, 7–11; Livy 39.23–29, 33–35, 46–48, 53.1–9; 40.2–16.3, 20–24, 54–56; DS 29.16, 25; Plut. *Aem. Paull.* 8, *Arat.* 54; Just. 32.2.5–3.4; cf. Meloni 55 ff.; Adams, "Perseus" 242 ff.

115. Walbank, *Philip V* 274–75, argues that Philip's place in world history is "solely as the unwitting instrument that enabled the culture of Greece to spread along the paths of the legions to Rome, and so to the western civilisation that grew up after her"; but the cumulative impact of his own excellent biography suggests a more generous verdict: Philip was at least as

great a patriot as Philopoemen, and despite his many flaws—that feral temper, those unmanly passions—a king in the old nationalist tradition of the Argead dynasty. Amid the relentless *Machtpolitik* of his rivals Philip's energetic and simple Macedonianism comes as a breath of fresh air by comparison. The summing-up in Hammond and Walbank 472–87 is enthusiastic: a brilliant commander, a flexible statesman, an efficient organizer and administrator.

116. Polyb. 22.18.10; Livy 42.5.1, cf. 40.52.3, 57; App. *Mac.* 11.1; Just. 32.3.5. On Polybius and Livy as sources for the reign of Perseus see Hammond and Walbank 488–90, stressing the hostile propaganda that these texts embody.

117. Livy 40.58.8, 41.24.6, 45.9.3; Polyb. 25.3.1; DS 29.30. Livy's assumption that Perseus made this move only to stall Rome *dum firmaret res* is pure speculation, and in the light of his subsequent reluctance for war very unlikely.

118. Polyb. 25.3.4–8.

119. Gruen, *HW* 404 with n. 31.

120. Livy 42.5.7–6.4, 41.22–23 *passim*, 24.20.

121. Coalition: Adams, "Perseus" 246. Marriages: Polyb. 25.4.8–10; Livy 42.12.3–4; App. *Mithr.* 2, *Mac.* 11.2. It is interesting that since Perseus had no fleet, while the Seleucid navy was forbidden, by the terms of the treaty of Apamea, to enter the Aegean, Laodice was conveyed to Macedonia by a Rhodian squadron, Rhodes enjoying friendly commercial relations with both powers. The service was also well rewarded, with a grant of shipbuilding timber and gold crowns for members of the flagship's crew.

122. *Rapprochement* with Delphi: Livy 41.22.5–8, 23.13–16; 42.42.1–3. Frontier defense: Polyb. 22.18.2–3, Livy 42.41.10–12.

123. Polyb. 25.3.1–4, with Walbank, *HC* 3.274 ff.; and Gruen, *HW* 403–6.

124. Livy 42.2.1–3.

125. Livy 42.6.3–5, 11.1, 5–9, 12–13; App. *Mac.* 11.1–2; cf. Meloni 150 ff.

126. Livy 42.14.2–4; cf. App. *Mac.* 11.3.

127. Livy 42.30 *passim*.

128. Polyb. 27.9.1, 10.1, 4.

129. See Gruen, "Class Conflict" 30 ff. Meloni 158 comments on "la sostanziale differenza fra il vero profondo motivo del dissidio romano-macedone [fear at Rome of a serious disturbance in the Eastern balance of power], che solo con la sconfitta definitiva della Macedonia poteva essere sanato, ed il contenuto giuridico, molto povero in verità, che si diede alle accuse specifiche." Cf. App. *Mac.* 11.3.

130. *SIG*³ 643 = Austin 76 (pp. 140–41); Sherk, *Roman Documents* 40A (pp. 234 ff.); *Translated Documents* 19 (pp. 18–20).

131. Poisoning the Senate: App. *Mac.* 11.7 (incorporated as a supplement at *SIG*³ 643.19–20). Poisoning Roman generals or ambassadors at Brundisium: Livy 42.17.3–9.

132. Livy 42.15–16, 18, 40; cf. App. *Mac.* 11.4; *SIG*³ 642.29 ff. = Sherk, *Translated Documents* 19, p. 19, for the Delphic inscription's reference to these events. The specificity of the charges (the main boulder-roller was identified as a Cretan mercenary, one Evander) does not *per se* validate them: Hammond and Walbank 499–501.

133. Polyb. 22.18.5–8, Livy 42.15.4–16.5.

134. Livy 42.11–13 *passim*.

135. This is clearly understood by Hansen, 106 ff. I cannot see the logic of Allen's claim that "Eumenes was only vaguely interested in the Roman war with Perseus" (p. 80). On the part played by Eumenes and his brother in helping Antiochus IV to the throne, see *OGIS* 248 = Burstein, *Translated Documents* no. 38, pp. 51–52.

136. Hansen 109 with n. 126, citing *SEG* 2 (1924) 663.

137. Cf. Livy 42.5.1–3, who observes that this resentment of Eumenes existed despite the fact that (because?) almost every city was under some sort of obligation to Pergamon. He also suggests the desire for revolutionary change and Greek contempt for a *parvenu* state as possible alternative or supplementary motives.

138. Senatorial delay: cf. Gruen, *HW* 410 ff. Conflict: Préaux, *Monde* 1.164; cf. Adams, "Perseus" 249–50.

139. Livy 42.28.4–5.

140. Livy 42.30.8–11: the campaign would get under way only "nisi de iis rebus [*sc.* Perseus] satisfecisset."

141. Roman envoys in 172 found considerable enthusiasm in both Antioch and Alexandria—not surprisingly—for a war against Perseus (Livy 42.26.7–8, App. *Mac.* 11.4), confirmed by Ptolemaic and Seleucid missions to Rome the following year (Livy 42.29.6–7). Despite such protestations of support, however, both kings were, in the event, too taken up with their own private quarrel to provide substantial support. Cf. Gruen, *HW* 651–52.

142. Livy 42.51–52.

143. Livy 42.30.11. See Hammond and Walbank 503–4 for an analysis of Philip's changes in the coinage at this time, reducing the weight of his tetradrachms (and thus devaluing them) as an economy measure—which would, *inter alia*, mean considerable savings in the payment of mercenaries.

144. Livy 42.33.4; cf. 34 *passim*.

145. Polyb. 25.4.1–5, 27.7.4–8; Livy 41.6.8–12, 42.67.4; App. *Mithr.* 62. The Rhodians were particularly annoyed at Roman tergiversation over Lycia (on this episode, see Berthold, *Rhodes* chap. 8, 167 ff.), where in 178 Rhodes had put down a revolt, only to be informed by the Senate that Lycia was not (as they had previously been given to understand) a Rhodian possession, but an independent friend and ally, to be treated with respect. For this startling reinterpretation of the treaty of Apamea they blamed (probably with justice) the machinations of Eumenes. For Rome's attitude to benefactions conferred upon Rhodes and Pergamon as *munera* that a *patronus* could withdraw at will, see p. 422.

146. Polybius (27.7.12, 30.7.9–9.21) claims that the pro-Macedonian Rhodians were bribed by Perseus, a wholly unnecessary assumption. Gruen, *HW* 335, suggests that Perseus picked up support from Greeks who were irritated by Rome's unpredictable switch from indifference to massive intervention.

147. For a good critical discussion of the evidence, see Gruen, *HW* 558–63. Polybius (32.8.2–7) pays Eumenes some very solid compliments in summing up his career. For honors bestowed upon him by cities of the Ionian League (and his complacent reaction to them), cf. *OGIS* 763 = Burstein, *Translated Documents* no. 88, pp. 111–13.

148. Polyb. 29.4.8–10, 6.1–2, 7.8, 8.3–9; Livy 44.13.9, 24.1–10, 25.5–12; App. *Mac.* 18.1.

149. Polyb. 29.7.4–8.

150. Polyb. 29.6.2–5.

151. Livy 44.24–25 *passim*; Polyb. 29.4.8–10, 8.3–9.

152. App. *Syr.* 45; *OGIS* 248 (esp. lines 10–13) = Austin 162, pp. 268–69; Burstein, *Translated Documents* no. 38, pp. 51–52; cf. Mørkholm, *Antiochus IV* 38 ff.

153. Polyb. 26.1 *passim*, DS 29.32, Livy 41.20.1.

154. App. *Syr.* 39; cf. p. 422. He had been exchanged, after ten years' detention in Rome, for another hostage, Seleucus IV's son (and his nephew) Demetrius several years previously: App. *Syr.* 45; cf. Mørkholm, *Antiochus IV* 35–36.

155. Ascon. *Comm. in Pis.* 12, Livy 42.6.9.

156. Will, *HP*² 2.306–8, with something less than his usual skeptical caution: probably following the theory of Bouché-Leclercq, *HS* 1.241. The theory has won tentative approval from Walbank, *HC* 3.285.

157. Gruen, *HW* 648–50.

158. DS 30.15–17.

159. Livy 42.29.5, Just. 34.2.7, App. *Syr.* 66, 1 Macc. 1.16, Joseph. *AJ* 12.242.

160. Polyb. 28.1 *passim*.

161. Polyb. 28.12 *passim*; *PRyl.* 583; Préaux, *Monde* 1.169.

162. DS 30.14–18; Polyb. 28.18, 21.1–5; cf. Walbank, *HC* 3.321 ff.

163. Polyb. 28.22.1, 29.23.4; Livy 44.19.6–9, 45.11.2–7; Joseph. *AJ* 12.243; DS 31.1; Porph. *FGrH* 260 F 49; Dan. 11.21–24; 1 Macc. 1.20; cf. Gruen, *HW* 653–54, for the best recent analysis of these tangled events. Translation of Porphyry and the text of Daniel, with a useful commentary, in Burstein, *Translated Documents* n. 39, pp. 52–54.

164. Livy 44.17–18, 20–21, 28, 32–46 *passim*, 45.4–8; Plut. *Aem. Paull.* 10–27 *passim*; cf. Meloni, chap. 6, 349–440, for the most thorough and detailed discussion of the battle; and W. K. Pritchett, *Studies in Ancient Greek Topography*, part 2 (Berkeley and Los Angeles, 1969), chap. 12, 145–76, on the site. The Polybian fragments: Walbank, *HC* 3.378–91. See also the general reassessment by N. G. L. Hammond, "The Battle of Pydna," *JHS* 104 (1984) 31–47, and Hammond and Walbank 547–57, with fig. 18, justly defending the Macedonians' decision to fight, however irrationally and against impossible odds, for liberty as they understood it.

165. Welles, *Alexander* 110.

166. Will, *HP*² 2.279–85, assembles and discusses the scattered testimonia with judicious skill.

167. *SIG*³ 652a; cf. Sherk, *Translated Documents* 24, p. 25, with further reff.; Pollitt, *AHA* 155–58.

168. Mørkholm, *Antiochus IV* 190, remarks, with justice: "The naked brutality of Roman politics after 168 must have been a shock to the Greek states, which up to this date had harboured some illusions as to the possibility of establishing a decent *modus vivendi* with the great power in the West."

169. Livy 45.18.3, 29.11; DS 31.8.7; cf. Gruen, *HW* 426–27. By 158 the mines were open and working again. That the action was directed against the *publicani* is clear from Livy 45.18.4; cf. Badian, *Publicans* 40–41, who points out that the deprivation of income implied by the closure of the mines was somewhere between one and two *million* denarii per annum.

170. Livy 45.18.7, 29.4, 11, 14; DS 31.8.7; Plut. *Aem. Paull.* 32–33.

171. Polyb. 30.5.11–15, Livy 45.25.11–13, Strabo 14.2.3 (C.625). See Berthold, *Rhodes* 195 ff.; Gruen, *HW* 571–72. The damage suffered by Rhodian trade as a result of this settlement has been exaggerated: Berthold, *Rhodes* 205 ff.; cf. Sherwin-White 30–36, who remarks that what *was* crippled was Rhodes's ability to wage war by land.

172. Polyb. 30.19.17–20.9, 31.10; cf. Berthold, *Rhodes* 202 ff. For the honoring of Athenian combatants at Pydna, see Moretti, *Iscrizioni* 1.35 = *SEG* 25 (1971) 118; translation in Sherk, *Translated Documents* 23, pp. 23–24.

173. Polyb. 30.6–9, Livy 45.31.

174. Préaux, *Monde* 1.166.

175. Polyb. 36.17.3; cf. Gruen, *HW* 425 with n. 154.

176. Mørkholm, *Antiochus IV* 51–63; Walbank, *HC* 3.287–88; C. Boehringer, *Zur Chronologie mittelhellenistischer Münzserien, 22–160 v. Chr.* (Berlin, 1972) 86. I owe this last reference to Gruen, *HW* 647, who also points out the relevance to Antiochus's economic revival of Polyb. 26.1.10.

177. Polyb. 29.27, Livy 45.12–13.

178. Polyb. 29.27.1–10, Livy 45.12.3–8, DS 31.2, App. *Syr.* 66, Just. 34.3.1–4, Vell. Pat. 1.10.1; cf. Mørkholm, *Antiochus IV* 94 ff. Sherwin-White 36 sees "a touch of megalomania and resentment" both in this gesture and in Rome's treatment of Rhodes (see p. 431 and n. 171 above).

179. Mørkholm, *Antiochus IV* 132 ff.

180. Gruen, *HW* 659. For Antiochus as knowing he could not win the war, and therefore welcoming the Day of Eleusis, see Tarn, *The Greeks in Bactria and India* 192, and M. Gwyn Morgan, "The Perils of Schematism: Polybius, Antiochus Epiphanes, and the 'Day of Eleusis,'" *Hist.* 39 (1990) 37–76. I am grateful to Prof. Morgan for letting me see this article in advance of publication.

181. Polyb. 30.25–26, DS 31.16, Athen. 195a–b; cf. Walbank, *HC* 3.448 ff.; Bunge, "Feiern" 53 ff., esp. 67 ff., where the propagandistic aspects of the Daphne celebration are analyzed; Mørkholm, *Antiochus IV* 97–101; Pollitt, *AHA* 283–84.

PART FOUR. THE BREAKING OF NATIONS, 167–116 B.C.

Chapter 25. The Wilderness as Peace, 167–146

1. Gruen, *HW*, is the latest and most thorough exponent of this view: his key terms for the attitude of the Senate to Eastern affairs are "lethargy," "apathy," "inertia," and "indifference."

2. Will, *HP*² 2.385; cf. 359.

3. Polyb. 31.10.7.

4. P. V. M. Benecke, *CAH* VIII 292.

5. Gruen, "Rome and the Seleucids" 94–95, and frequently elsewhere, e.g., *HW* 663 ff.

6. Cf. Briscoe, "Eastern Policy" 60 ff.

7. Badian, *Publicans* 98–99, and for the sense of rectitude engendered in the landowning class, 52–53. H. Hill, *The Roman Middle Class in the Republican Period* (Oxford, 1952), chap. 4, 87 ff., collects some interesting evidence on the ways in which commercial and financial interests attempted to influence senatorial policy. These attempts, to begin with, were for the most part unsuccessful: Gruen, *HW* 306.

8. Livy 43.16.2–16, 44.16.8; Val. Max. 6.5.3; Badian, *Publicans* 38–40; Gruen, *HW* 306. The tax farmers were the individuals or, more often, the consortia that bid for the privilege of collecting taxes on behalf of the Roman government, contracted to deliver a fixed sum, and made their profit from what they could extract over and above this, a process that inevitably led to gross extortion.

9. Livy 45.18.3–4, 29.11; DS 31.8.6; useful discussion in Gruen, "Macedonia" 262–64, with further bibliography.

10. Rostovtzeff, *SEH* 2.739.

11. App. *Syr.* 46, Zonar. 9.25, Polyb. 21.43.12–13, Livy 38.38.8.

12. Polyb. 31.2.7–11, App. *Syr.* 46, Plin. *HN* 34.24; cf. Broughton, *Magistrates* 441, 443. See also Polyb. 31.11.1–3, 32.2.4–3.4. Octavius had been by no means universally unpopular among the Greeks: an Argive inscription of 170 survives conferring προξενία and other honors on him for his services to the Achaean League. See Moretti, *Iscrizioni* 1.42; translation in Sherk, *Translated Documents* 22, pp. 22–23. Cf. Polyb. 28.3–5, Livy 43.17.2–10.

13. Polyb. 31.2.7–11, followed by App. *Syr.* 46, attributes the orders for the destruction of ships and elephants to the Senate; but then his object is to prove that Rome wanted a weak Syrian government, and thus explain why his friend Demetrius was refused recognition as king (p. 277). Yet there had been no prior clampdown, e.g., after Daphne, where Antiochus IV gave an open display of military power (p. 432); while Zonaras claims, convincingly in this instance (9.25), that Octavius's decision was taken on the spot. Cf. Gruen, "Rome and the Seleucids" 81–84, *HW* 127–28.

14. For the Roman habit, in many cases, of delegating arbitration to Greek tribunals, and the independent persistence of (largely honorific and formal) interstate Hellenistic diplomacy, cf. Gruen, *HW* 519, with nn. 188–90.

15. Illyria was, very similarly to Macedonia, split up into three independent cantons and compelled to pay Rome half the tribute that had previously gone to the kings: only those settlements that had seceded to Rome were exempt: Livy 45.17.1–4, 18.1.7, 26.13–15; DS 31.8.3–6.

16. Polyb. 26.1, 1a *passim*, cf. Livy 41.20.1–4, DS 29.32, 31.16.

17. Mørkholm, *Antiochus IV* 44–50; cf. Bunge, "Theos Epiphanes" 57 ff.; Bevan, *CAH* VIII 713–14. The name of Seleucus IV's son also seems to have been Antiochus.

18. Bunge, "Antiochos" 168 ff. Since Seleucus IV's second son, Demetrius, was still a

hostage in Rome, Antiochus clearly (and rightly) figured on getting himself well established on the throne without any immediate interference from that quarter.

19. Nilsson 274.

20. *OGIS* 253; cf. Bunge, "Antiochos" 171 ff., esp. 174: "Ebenso wie Helios als unbestrittener Herrscher über den Gestirnen stand, war nun auch Antiochos unbestrittener Alleinherrscher seines Reiches."

21. DS 31.17a; cf. Bunge, "Antiochos" 188.

22. Mørkholm, *Antiochus IV* 187.

23. Ibid.

24. Polyb. 30.25–26 (= Athen. 5.194c, 10.439b); DS 31.16.

25. Cf. Will, *HP*[2] 2.346.

26. The history of this period in the Indo-Bactrian East is much debated, and rests on hopelessly patchy evidence. For varying interpretations, and a conspectus of the testimonia, such as they are, see Tarn, *Greeks* 82 ff.; Narain 21 ff.; Will, *HP*[2] 2.348–52.

27. 2 Macc. 9.23–27.

28. DS 31.17a, 18a; Polyb. 31.9.1–4; App. *Syr.* 46, 66; Joseph. *AJ* 12.354–59; 1 Macc. 6.1–16; 2 Macc. 1.13–17, 9.2–29; Porph. *FGrH* 260 F53, 56.

29. 1 Macc. 6.14–15, 55; Joseph. *AJ* 12.360.

30. 2 Macc. 11.13–38.

31. Will, *HP*[2] 2.365, argues that nothing did more to precipitate the collapse of the Seleucid empire and dynasty than this rancorous and long-enduring dynastic quarrel. The premature death of Demetrius's elder brother Antiochus left him with a clear claim to the throne: see L. Santi Amantini, "Il misterioso fratello di Demetrio I di Siria nella testimonianza di Giustino (XXXIV.3.5–7)," *MGR* 9 (1984) 105–16.

32. 1 Macc. 2–6; 2 Macc. 8–13 (dubious); Joseph. *AJ* 12.265–385 *passim*, *BJ* 1.36–40; Will, *HP*[2] 2.341–44.

33. Polyb. 31.2.7; cf. 31.11.11.

34. Polyb. 31.2.10.

35. Polyb. 31.2, 8, 11–15; App. *Syr.* 46–47; Livy, *per.* 46.

36. Polyb. 31.11.10, App. *Syr.* 46.

37. For a useful account of this episode, see Bevan, *House of Seleucus* 2.188–93, based on the account in Polyb. 31.2.1–8, 11–15.

38. Polyb. 31.33.5, 32.2.1–3.12; DS 31.28–29; App. *Syr.* 46–47; Just. 34.3.6–9; Joseph. *AJ* 12.389–90.

39. Polyb. 32.3.13.

40. 1 Macc. 8.23–30; cf. Joseph. *AJ* 12.414–19; cf. D. Timpe, "Der römische Vertrag mit der Juden von 161 v.Chr.," *Chiron* 4 (1974) 138–52.

41. 1 Macc. 8.31–32.

42. Gruen, "Rome and the Seleucids" 86–87. Cf. 1 Macc. 9.1–27, Joseph. *AJ* 12.420–34.

43. Cf. Gruen, *HW* 692.

44. Cf. Fraser 1.119–21.

45. Hom. *Il.* 2.204.

46. Polyb. 39.7.3–4.

47. DS 31.18; Livy, *per.* 46; Porph. *FGrH* 260 F 2; Val. Max. 5.1.1–2.

48. Polyb. 31.2.14.

49. Will, *HP*[2] 2.360.

50. DS 31.17c; Polyb. 31.10.1–4; Livy, *per.* 46–47; Porph. *FGrH* 260 F 2.7.

51. Polyb. 31.10, 17–19, 39.7; cf. *OGIS* 116.

52. Polyb. 31.20.3; cf. Briscoe, "Eastern Policy" 50–51 with n. 10; Gruen, *HW* 701 n. 141.

53. Polyb. 33.11.1–3.

54. Not, as Seibert, *Historische Beiträge* 85 remarks, very likely, since he was only thirty

at the time, and the chances of his dying without issue (given his age and personal habits) were clearly slim.

55. *SEG* 9 (1938) 7, pp. 10–11 = Austin 230, pp. 381–82; Bagnall and Derow 43, pp. 79–80. See also Sherk, *Translated Documents* 31, pp. 31–32, with useful bibliography and notes in addition to his translation. Physcon's motivation was both political and opportunistic: Winkler 47 ff.; Gruen, *HW* 193, 700–702.

56. Polyb. 31.2.10, 17–20; 33.11; DS 31.23, 33.

57. Gruen, *HW* 707–8.

58. Polyb. 39.7.6–7, DS 31.33.

59. *OGIS* 125–27.

60. See M. Thompson, "Ptolemy Philometor and Athens," *ANSMusN* 11 (1964) 119–29. For arguments attributing the gymnasium to Ptolemy III see Habicht, *Studien,* 112–17.

61. E.g., Will, *HP²* 2.363: "plutôt velléitaire."

62. Polyb. 31.13.8; cf. 33.19.

63. For a good, clear account of this confusing episode, with full documentation, see Gruen, "Rome and the Seleucids" 88–90.

64. DS 31.19.7–8, 21–22, 28, 32, 34, 40a; Polyb. 3.5.2; 31.3.1–2, 7–8, 32; 32.1.1–4, 10–12; 33.6; App. *Syr.* 47–48; Livy, *per.* 44, 45, 47; Just. 35.1.1–5, 36.1.1.

65. Though surprisingly independent of Rome in his foreign policy, and very far from maintaining the obsequious subservience once attributed to him: see Hopp chap. 4, 59 ff.

66. Hopp 102 ff.; Gruen, *HW* 591.

67. The best modern account is that of Hopp, 79–85; cf. Gruen, *HW* 585–86.

68. App. *Syr.* 67, Just. 35.1.6.

69. Polyb. 33.18.6–13; cf. 33.15.1–2, 18.1–5.

70. It is hard not to agree with Briscoe, "Rome" 61, and Volkmann, *Klio* 19 (1925) 385–86, that this refers to the Scipionic group, in particular to the family of Aemilius Paullus, with which Polybius had close connections, and who almost certainly were behind Demetrius's escape from Rome (p. 440).

71. Cf. Hopp 85.

72. Polyb. 3.5.3, App. *Syr.* 67, Just. 35.1.6–9.

73. 1 Macc. 10.14–21.

74. Polyb. 33.15.1–2, 17, 18.5 ff.; DS 31.32a; App. *Syr.* 67; Joseph. *AJ* 13.35–61, 116–19; Just. 35.1.5–11, 2.3–4; Strabo 13.4.2 (C.624); 1 Macc. 10.22–50, 11.14–19.

75. 1 Macc. 10.51–58, Joseph. *AJ* 13.80–83; cf. Will, *HP²* 2.377; Macurdy 93 ff.

76. Macurdy 93.

77. Macurdy figs. 3, 5a; Richter, *Portraits* 3.267 with figs. 1850–52 (attribution in all cases uncertain, but plausible).

78. 1 Macc. 11.1–13; DS 32.27.9c; Livy, *per.* 52; Joseph. *AJ* 13.103–15.

79. Joseph. *AJ* 13.113, DS 32.27.9c; 1 Macc. 11.13 suggests, wrongly, that he did in fact succumb, while Polyb. 39.7.1 describes him as "king of Syria," but at best this can be construed as *de facto* rather than *de jure* recognition.

80. Will, *HP²* 2.378 correctly stresses this correlation.

81. Gruen, "Rome and the Seleucids" 94. Josephus, *AJ* 13.114, claims that he declined the throne to avoid giving offense to the Romans: an overstatement in view of his previous record, but he may have thought it more diplomatic to exercise his influence through the young and pliable Demetrius II. Cf. also Gruen, *HW* 711.

82. DS 32.27.9c–d, 33.3; Livy, *per.* 52; Joseph. *AJ* 13.116–19; App. *Syr.* 67; Just. 35.2 *passim*; Strabo 16.2.8 (C.751); 1 Macc. 11.14–19.

83. Hopp 74–79.

84. Polyb. 29.6.4, 30.19, 28; Livy, *per.* 46.

85. Cf. Berthold, *Rhodes* 227–28.

86. Cf. Hopp 93–96; Gruen, *HW* 431–32.

87. Livy, *per.* 48–49; DS 31.40a, 32.15.1; Zonar. 9.28.

88. DS 32.15 *passim*.

89. Polyb. 36.10.2: πάρεστί τις ἐπὶ τὴν Μακεδονίαν ἀεροπετὴς Φίλιππος, καταφρονήσας οὐ μόνον Μακεδόνων ἀλλὰ καὶ Ῥωμαίων.

90. Cf. Flor. 1.30.3, well cited by Gruen, *HW* 432.

91. Polyb. 36.10 *passim*, 17.13–15; DS 32.27.9a–b, 15; Livy, *per.* 49–50; Paus. 7.13.1; cf. Morgan 423 ff.

92. Strabo 7.7.4 (C.322–23); cf. Larsen, "Roman Greece" 303; J. P. Adams, "Polybius, Pliny and the Via Egnatia," in Adams and Borza 269–302. Walbank, *Selected Papers* 193–209, charts the progressive stages (148–101 B.C.) of Roman expansion eastward from Macedonia.

93. Polyb. 36.17.13.

94. Most recently by Ste Croix 524–25, who also, predictably, challenges the downplaying of social conflict by Gruen, "Class Conflict" 29 ff., for the Third Macedonian War. Cf. Deininger 217–19, 226–38; Larsen, *Greek Federal States* 489–90; further bibliography in Fuks, "Bellum Achaicum" 78, and Gruen, "Origins" 46 nn. 1, 2.

95. Briscoe, "Rome" 3–20.

96. Most recently by Will, *HP*[2] 2.391; cf. Fuks, "Bellum Achaicum" 78–79, 86–87; Schwertfeger 10–12, 16–17; for further bibliography, see Gruen, "Origins" 46 n. 4.

97. See in particular Fuks, "Bellum Achaicum" 79, 84–89, following Gaetano De Sanctis, *Storia dei Romani* (Florence, 1964) 4.3.144–46, 151–54.

98. Correctly noted by Briscoe, "Rome" 3–20, esp. 15–19, but not in itself, as he seems to suppose, an adequate motive for the Achaean War.

99. Polyb. 38.1, 3; DS 32.26–27.

100. Polyb. 38.4.7.

101. Polyb. 38.3.13, 9.4–5, 10.8, 10.12–13, 11.6–11, 12.5–10, 13.6–8, 15.8, 16.1–10, 17.9–10; cf. Paus. 7.14.4–6, 15.2, 7, 16.6.

102. Main sources for the Bellum Achaicum: Polyb. 38.9–18 *passim*; Paus. 7.14–16; cf. Fuks, "Bellum Achaicum" 78 n. 9, for other testimonia. Niese's narrative (3.337–52) is still of considerable value.

103. Polyb. 38.18.12; cf. 13.7 on the acquisition of absolute power by the στρατηγοί, and, for the general atmosphere of terror, delation, and indiscriminate arrests, 16.5–6. The apothegm that Polybius quotes is a proverb; he suggests that it was being widely cited at the time.

104. Polyb. 38.18.1–6.

105. Polyb. 38.16.7.

106. Polyb. 38.15.10: τὴν δὲ τῶν οἰκετῶν ἀνάτασιν καὶ τὸν ἐπισυρμὸν βαρέως ἔφερον.

107. E.g., Polyb. 3.4.3.

108. Fuks, "Bellum Achaicum" 88–89, understands this very well; Gruen, "Origins" 46, here as elsewhere, tends to underestimate the immense and irrational force of ethnic pride and independence—a force that, to take one striking modern example, enabled Great Britain to hold out against the Third Reich after Dunkirk, at a time when too many French intellectuals had argued, with compelling logic, for the inevitability of surrender.

109. Paus. 7.11.4–8, 12.1–3; cf. Polyb. 32.11.5–6; *SIG*[3] 675.

110. Polyb. 33.4.1–4, 15.3–4, 16.1–8, 17.1–5; DS 31.37–38, 43, 45; cf. Berthold, *Rhodes* 223–24.

111. Polyb. 31.1.6–7; cf. Paus. 7.11.1–2, 12. It is hard not to sympathize with Gruen's observation, *HW* 520, that "two decades after Pydna and a half-century after Cynoscephalae one finds a stunning sameness in the issues that beset the Peloponnese and the actions taken to resolve them, most particularly in the conflict between Achaea and Sparta." The perspective remained inherently local, and any interference by powerful outside parties (however much they might be courted for immediate advantage) could, in the long run, cause nothing but hatred and resentment.

112. Paus. 7.11.4–7; Polyb. 33.2 = Aul. Gell. *NA* 6.14.8–10; Plut. *Cat. Maj.* 22; Cic. *Acad.* 2.137, *De Rep.* 3.9; cf. Ferguson, *HA* 324–28. Carneades was from Cyrene, Diogenes

from Seleucia-on-Tigris, and Critolaus from Phaselis: Davies, *CAH* VII².1 309, argues that before 300 such ethnically diverse representation would have been "inconceivable."

113. Paus. 7.11.5.

114. Paus. 7.12.4.

115. Paus. 7.12.8.

116. Will, *HP*² 2.391, for instance, assumes that Diaeus's intransigent performance in Rome determined the Senate to stamp out the Achaean League, "dernière 'puissance' grecque et source d'éternelles complications," but that this decision was kept secret for the time being in order to avoid a linkup between the League and Andriscus(!).

117. Livy, *per.* 50; cf. Polyb. 36.10.5, 11.

118. Gruen, "Origins" 57.

119. Paus. 7.12.9.

120. Polyb. 38.9.6.

121. Gruen, "Origins" 60, believes Polybius: the idea has had few other takers, but strikes me as inherently plausible.

122. Paus. 7.14.1–3, Polyb. 38.9.1–2; cf. Just. 34.1.5, Flor. 1.32.2, DS 21.72.1.

123. Polyb. 38.9.3–5.

124. Polyb. 38.10.1–5, Paus. 7.14.4.

125. Polybius attacks not only their politics but their social origins, and claims that they were appealing to the debtor class for support: 38.2.8, 11.7–11; DS 32.26.3. Once again Polybius seems to be using the red herring of populism to obscure the nature of a national uprising.

126. See, e.g., Polyb. 13.10.12–13, 38.11.6–11; Paus. 7.14.4.

127. Polyb. 38.10.8–11.6, Paus. 7.14.4–5.

128. So Larsen, *Greek Federal States* 493.

129. Gruen, "Origins" 62–65.

130. Polyb. 38.12.1–3, Paus. 7.15.1.

131. Morgan 440.

132. Harris 243.

133. Polyb. 38.12–13, DS 32.26.4–5.

134. Paus. 7.14.5–6.

135. Polyb. 38.12–13 *passim*.

136. Polyb. 38.13.6: λόγῳ μὲν τὸν πρὸς Λακεδαιμονίους πόλεμον, ἔργῳ δὲ τὸν πρὸς Ῥωμαίους, says the historian, but this is merely the benefit of *parti pris* hindsight; cf. DS 32.26.5. Paus. 7.14.5 characteristically makes it a declaration of war on Rome *tout court*.

137. Polyb. 38.11.10; cf. Fuks, "Bellum Achaicum" 79–81.

138. Polyb. 38.12.8, DS 32.26.4; cf. Gruen, *HW* 336, 521.

139. Paus. 7.15.3–5; cf. Livy, *per.* 52; Flor. 1.32.3. See also Deininger 234–35.

140. Polyb. 38.3.8.

141. Polyb. 38.17.1–18.6.

142. Deininger 220 ff.

143. So, rightly, Fuks, "Bellum Achaicum" 86: "The Bellum Achaicum was a national war, a war of the Achaean people, not a class movement."

144. Like the temporary suspension of debt payments, this was an emergency rather than a revolutionary measure: Fuks, "Bellum Achaicum" 82.

145. Polyb. 38.15.1–7, Paus. 7.15.7–8; cf. Fuks, "Bellum Achaicum" 81 ff.

146. Polyb. 38.15.8–16 *passim*.

147. Paus. 7.16.7–8; DS 32.27.1; Polyb. 39.2–6; Dio Cass. 21.72; Livy, *per.* 51, 52. Cf. Sherk, *Translated Documents* 35, pp. 35–36.

148. The Eleian dedication: *SIG*³ 676 = Burstein, *Translated Documents* no. 78, p. 102.

149. Cic. *Tusc. Disp.* 3.53.

150. DS 32.27.1–3.

151. Polyb. 39.2 = Strabo 8.6.23 (C.381); cf. Vell. Pat. 1.13.4.

152. R. Clogg, *A Short History of Modern Greece* (Cambridge, 1979) 53. One possible earlier attempt is the widespread rising organized by Mithridates VI Eupator of Pontus (88–86: below, pp. 561 ff.); but there are features about this movement that put it in a special class of its own.

Chapter 26. Mathematics and Astronomy: The Alternative Immortality

1. Ste Croix (*ap.* Crombie 81) in 1961 deplored the fact that "most historians of ancient science should make no attempt, or only the most perfunctory attempts, to relate the evolution of ancient scientific thought to the development of political institutions." Since then things have improved: see, e.g., J.-P. Vernant, *Mythe et pensée chez les Grecs* (Paris, 1965) 145–68 (on the symbolic relationship of the circle and the democratic assembly), and the same author's review essay on *Clisthène l'athénien* (Paris, 1964), by P. Lévêque and P. Vidal-Naquet, ibid. 159–61.

2. Ste Croix, *ap.* Crombie 81.

3. Polyb. 3.59.3–5; cf. Africa, *Science* 47.

4. Sambursky, *Physical World* 241. Cf. below, p. 634.

5. In Greek, σῴζειν τὰ φαινόμενα, on which see Simplicius's *Commentary* on the *De Caelo* of Aristotle, ed. I. L. Heiberg, *Commentaria in Aristotelem Graeca* (Berlin, 1894) 7.422; cf. 488, 492–93. The best analysis known to me is that of Lloyd, "Saving the Appearances" 202–22, a salutary corrective to the still enormously influential view presented by P. Duhem in *Le système du monde*, 2d ed., vol. 2 (Paris, 1954), esp. 114–15, that Greek astronomers were fundamentally indifferent to the actual truth of their hypotheses; that the theory was more precious than the facts, which could be, and were, consciously manipulated to fit aprioristic patterns or systems; that the running battle throughout the history of science was between such "theorists" (e.g., Ptolemy, Proclus, Maimonides, Aquinas, Bellarmin) and "realists" (e.g., the Averroists, Kepler, Galileo). Again, there is a kernel of truth in all this; unfortunately Duhem not only overschematized his thesis but elevated the espousal of "realism" into no less rigid a schema than what he was opposing.

6. Simplicius (above, n. 5) 422.13.

7. Plato, *Tim.* 38C–39E and elsewhere.

8. Plato, *Ep.* 7.324B–D.

9. Plato, *Rep.* 7.530B–C.

10. Ritchie 16 (cf. also 52–53) is worth quoting at length in this context: "By a lucky accident, or error, the Greeks turned from arithmetic in order to study geometry. Starting with an idea that numbers are units, and in some sense spatial, they tried to develop an arithmetical geometry: that is to say to treat geometry as a *species* of the *genus* arithmetic. At an early stage they came across incommensurables, by finding that some lengths could not be equated with numbers if certain others were so equated. They then decided there was something fishy about numbers, changed their tactics and treated arithmetic as a *species* of the *genus* geometry. Under the circumstances of the 6th and 5th centuries BC this was a far more fruitful method."

11. Plut. *Mor.* 718B–720C (= *Quaest. Conviv.* 8.2.1–4); cf. Farrington, *Science* 26–32. The actual statement ὁ θεὸς ἀεὶ γεωμετρεῖ occurs nowhere in Plato's own surviving work, but we have no reason to doubt Plutarch's specific attribution: it is highly characteristic.

12. Plut. *Mor.* 719B–C: ἡ μὲν γὰρ ἀριθμῷ τὸ ἴσον ἡ δὲ λόγῳ τὸ κατ᾽ ἀξίαν ἀπονέμει . . . ἣν γὰρ οἱ πολλοὶ διώκουσιν ἰσότητα, πασῶν ἀδικιῶν οὖσαν μεγίστην, ὁ θεὸς ἐξαιρῶν, ὡς ἀνυστόν ἐστι, τὸ κατ᾽ ἀξίαν διαφυλάττει, γεωμετρικῶς τῷ κατὰ λόγον τὸ κατὰ νόμον ὁριζόμενος.

13. Arist. *Pol.* 1278ᵃ; cf. 1258ᵃ22 for the landed ideal and 1326ᵇ for the notion of privileged autarky; cf. J.-P. Vernant's essay "Aspects psychologiques du travail dans la Grèce ancienne," *op. cit.* (above, n. 1) 219–25.

14. Tzetzes, *Chiliad.* 8.972: ἀγεωμέτρητος μηδεὶς εἰσίτω, ran the inscription over the Academy's entrance, "Let no one without knowledge of geometry enter."

15. Stob. *Flor.* 4.205: τί δέ μοι πλέον ἔσται ταῦτα μανθάνοντι; The anecdote forms the epigraph to James Gow's *Short History of Greek Mathematics*, which tells us at least as much about Gow as it does about Euclid.

16. Plut. *Mor.* 718F.

17. Sarton 41.

18. See Davis and Hersh 217: "Such a logico-deductive scheme may be compared to a game and the axioms of the scheme to the rules of the game. Anyone who plays games knows that one can invent variations on given games and the consequences will be different. A non-Euclidean geometry is a geometry that is played with axioms that are different from those of Euclid." At the same time, speaking as a non-mathematician, I must confess to an obstinate affection for the Euclidean postulates, which seem to me not at all arbitrary (let alone game counters of *homo ludens*), but a serious and largely successful attempt to codify self-evident, if nonprovable, base data. In 1931 Kurt Gödel proved that there will *always* be mathematical truths that cannot be proved by logic; this would not have surprised Euclid. Cf. M. Guillen, *Bridges to Infinity* (Los Angeles, 1983) 117 ff.

19. Heath, *History* 1.356; Lloyd, *Greek Science* 39; Fraser 1.396.

20. Cf. White, *Greek and Roman Technology* 14 ff.

21. Arist. *Pol.* 1337[b].

22. See Lloyd, "Experiment" 50 ff., esp. 70–71.

23. See, e.g., Plato, *Rep.* 529A ff., 531A ff.

24. Cf. Plato, *Phaedr.* 266E3, 273B3, *Gorg.* 471D–472C; Arist. *Rhet.* 1376[a]19 ff., 1402[a] 17 ff., *Anal. Prior.* 70[a]2 ff.; cf. G. Kennedy, *The Art of Persuasion in Greece* (Princeton, 1963) 30–31, 89–90, 100.

25. Isocrates 18 (*Against Callimachus*) 53–54.

26. Ritchie 20.

27. White, "Some Thoughts" 29 ff.

28. Lloyd, "Observational Error" 143 with n. 36 and further reff.; cf. Préaux, "Sur la stagnation" 250, on chemical measurement; and Lee 187.

29. Ritchie 20.

30. That practical devices of high technological sophistication existed in the Hellenistic period has been strikingly demonstrated by the discovery, in an Antikythera shipwreck of ca. 80 B.C., of "an astronomical or calendrical calculating device involving a very sophisticated arrangement of more than thirty gear-wheels": Derek de Solla Price, *Gears from the Greeks: The Antikythera Mechanism, A Calendar Computer from ca. 80 B.C.* (New York, 1975) 5. Price compares the Tower of the Winds in Athens (1st c. B.C.) in this context, which he describes as "a sort of Zeiss planetarium of the classical world" (p. 51), and associates both with those products of high technology "that are in some ways intimately associated with the sciences, drawing on them for theories, giving to them the instruments and the techniques that enable men to observe and experiment and increase both knowledge and technical competence," identifying as practitioners in this context "the instrument makers, the teachers of navigation and surveying, the writers of hack books on the useful scientific crafts" (p. 52). Samuel, *From Athens* 60, argues, on the evidence of the Antikythera mechanism, that "there probably was a great deal more realization in technology of the physical and astronomical achievements of Hellenistic science."

31. Advanced, e.g., by Philolaus (Diog. Laert. 8.85) and other contemporaries of Aristotle and Theophrastus: testimonia in Préaux, "Sur la stagnation" 244; refuted by Aristotle in the *De Caelo*, 2.14, 296[a] (he does not, however, seem to have been familiar with the heliocentric theory).

32. See Heath, *History* 2.2–3, 81; Plut. *Mor.* 922F–923A; Diog. Laert. 7.174; Archimedes, *Sand-Reckoner*, quoted by Heath, ibid.; cf. Fraser 1.397 with further reff.

33. Plut. *Marcell.* 17, cf. 14: unnecessarily queried by Lloyd, *CAH* VII[2].1 337, since the

purported attitude is consonant with all we know—which is a good deal—of the Greek intellectual tradition. Dijksterhuis, 13–14, reports this attitude, but has no comment on it.

34. T. L. Heath, *Aristarchus of Samos* (Oxford, 1913) 308; cf. Préaux, "Sur la stagnation" 245–46. A useful rundown of the arguments, pro and con, is now provided by Lloyd, *CAH* VII².1 339–41.

35. So, rightly, Préaux, "Sur la stagnation" 245–46.

36. *AP* 9.577.

37. Sir Thomas Browne, *The Garden of Cyrus* (London, 1658) chap. 5.

38. Cf. the remarkable section devoted to this topic by Davis and Hersh, 108–12.

39. Plato, *Tim.* 34A.

40. Farrington, *Greek Science* 216.

41. Cf. Wasserstein 52 ff.

42. Cf. Ritchie 17.

43. A useful account in Lloyd, *Early Greek Science* chap. 7, 82–98.

44. Cf. Préaux, "Sur la stagnation" 238.

45. Cited by Simplicius in his *Commentary* on Aristotle's *De Caelo* (above, n. 5) 492.31–493.4 Heiberg, cf. 488.21 ff.; cf. also Préaux, "Sur la stagnation" 237–39.

46. Préaux, ibid. 238–39, summarizing the arguments of Gaston Bachelard, writes: "C'est que la séduction du schéma des sphères homocentriques est d'autant plus forte et l'arbitraire condition imposée à l'explication d'autant plus impérieuse que ce schéma ordonné et rassurant est préféré pour les connexions qu'il entretient avec le goût des morales de l'ordre, avec les spéculations mystiques sur le cercle, avec l'émerveillement que suscitent les propriétés du mouvement circulaire, sans commencement ni fin, avec le caractère rassurant enfin qu'aurait un monde si aisément explicable, si exempt d'exception."

47. Lloyd, "Saving the Appearances" 219 ff.: he emphasizes, wisely, that in many cases we simply do not possess the evidence to reconstruct their views.

48. Arist. *De Caelo* 269ª20–270ᵇ; cf. *Met.* 12.8.4–14, 1073ª–1074ª.

49. Farrington, *Greek Science* 227.

50. Lucret. 5.110–25.

51. Cf. Lloyd, *Early Greek Science* 94–97, *Greek Science* 61–67, 72–74, 119–127. The key text is Simplicius's *Commentary* on Aristotle's *Physics* 193ᵇ, ed. H. Diels (Berlin, 1882) p. 292. See also Préaux, "Sur la stagnation" 240, and Duhem (above, n. 5) vol. 1, 440 (cf. 434–41 generally), for the familiarity of Apollonius of Perge (below, p. 465) with these theories.

52. Lloyd, *Greek Science* 74.

53. Arist. *De Caelo* 269ᵇ; cf. Lloyd, *Greek Science* 72.

54. Ritchie 68.

55. Cf. Préaux, "Sur la stagnation" 247.

56. Farrington, *Greek Science* 218–19; Lloyd, *Greek Science* 53–54. Testimonia in F. Wehrli, *Herakleides Pontikos* (Basel, 1953): see esp. Diog. Laert. 5.86–93, and cf. O. Voss, *De Heraclidis Pontici Vita et Scriptis* (Rostock, 1896).

57. Cic. *De Div.* 1.6; cf. Africa, *Science* 65, and the elder Pliny's encomium, *HN* 2.95, of Hipparchus, "numquam satis laudatus, ut quo nemo magis adprobauerit cognationem cum homine siderum animasque nostras partem esse caeli."

58. Arist. *De Caelo* 2.12, 291ᵇ–292ª, *Met.* 12.8, 1074ᵇ; cf. Lee 186.

59. Heath, *History* 1.91–97, 150–54; Thomas, 1.186–215, gives a full selection of this so-called geometrical algebra of the Pythagoreans, including geometrical solutions to quadratic equations.

60. Sir Thomas Heath, *History* 1.379 ff., *Manual* 220, long ago noted that the first ten propositions of Bk. 2 in Euclid's *Elements* are easily transposable into algebraic equations: e.g., prop. 3 comes out as $(a + b)a = ab + a^2$, and prop. 4 as $(a + b)^2 = a^2 + 2ab + b^2$.

61. Heath, *History* chap. 20, 2.440 ff.

62. Van der Waerden 72; more cautiously, Neugebauer, *Exact Sciences* 40 ff.

63. Neugebauer, ibid. 44.

64. On the Babylonian texts in particular, see Van der Waerden 63 ff., and R. Taton, ed., *Ancient and Mediaeval Science* (London, 1963), 95 ff. Van der Waerden constantly is obliged to make statements such as "We can therefore safely put the problem in the form of 2 algebraic equations," or "Through the geometric exterior the algebraic kernel is always visible," and of course for a contemporary mathematician this is true.

65. See, e.g., Van der Waerden 74, who has to admit that "the words in parentheses do not occur in the text; Neugebauer and Thureau-Dangin have added them in order to obtain the correct formula." Again (p. 67), apropos a problem in which the size of two fields is to be calculated in terms of their yield, Van der Waerden rightly, if apologetically, offers the kind of painstaking *arithmetic* solution that can be extrapolated from the text (which he likens to the manner in which "an elementary school teacher might explain the procedure to the children"), and concedes that such a method better approximates to Babylonian thought processes than does Neugebauer's "elaborate algebraic transformation."

66. One strong confirmation of this argument is the late arrival of algebraic methodology and notation: had the Babylonians in fact been algebraically conscious, it is almost inconceivable that, with their astronomical and other records available to Greek researchers, at least from the time of Alexander's conquest, if not earlier, algebra as a method should still have failed to penetrate Greek thought till the period of the later Roman empire.

67. Unguru 557, 564.

68. See Unguru's original article, "On the Need to Rewrite the History of Greek Mathematics," *AHES* 15 (1975) 67–114, with Van der Waerden's rebuttal, ibid. 199–210, and H. Freudenthal, "What Is Algebra and What Has It Been in History?" ibid. 16 (1977) 189–200.

69. Unguru 559.

70. Cf. Ritchie 45: "The use of substitute symbols (algebraic equations) in place of representative symbols (actual drawn figures) does not fundamentally alter what is done, but does call for an imaginative jump and new operational rules or conventions for using the new symbols."

71. Neugebauer, *Exact Sciences* 13, claims to have found the zero sign in papyri of the "Ptolemaic period." Though he correctly defines the latter (ibid. n. 2) as "the dynasty of the Ptolemies who ruled over Egypt during the last three centuries before our era," he then proceeds to cite as his source a papyrus of the second century A.D.

72. *Met.* $1092^b 10$; cf. Heath, *History* 1.69, with further reff.

73. The first order includes all numbers up to 10^8, which is formed from the available alphabetic notation by taking the highest unit, 10,000 (M), and squaring it, = 100,000,000, i.e., 10^8. This then in turn forms the unit of the second order, up to $100,000,000^2$, i.e., 10^{16}, and so on. The system, as Heath remarks, *History* 1.41, was infinitely extendible, but "has nothing to do with the ordinary Greek numerical notation." It might, Ritchie 83 remarks, be taken as a mathematical joke.

74. Heath, *History* 1.40–41, cf. 2.81–85; Lloyd, *Greek Science* 41–43; Fraser 1.406–7. For a masterly technical analysis, see Dijksterhuis 360–73.

75. Neugebauer, *Exact Sciences* 13–14.

76. The older of these, known chiefly from Attica, and perhaps dating back to the seventh century B.C., is the acrophonic (sometimes known as the "Herodian" system, through being recorded in a fragment of the 2d-c. A.D. grammarian Aelius Herodianus: see Stephanus, *TLG*, ed. Hase et al. [Paris, 1829], vol. 8, app. col. 345, cf. 346–51), which uses the initial letters of the words expressing numbers as symbols. The more common alphabetic system, a simpler method employing twenty-seven signs, equated the first nine letters of the alphabet (including digamma) with 1–9, the next nine (including koppa) with 10–90, and the remainder with 100–800, 900 being represented by an odd symbol called sampi. The thousands started from the beginning again, but with an accent mark or preceding stroke to distinguish them. For 10,000 and its multiples, acrophonic M ($\mu\acute{\upsilon}\rho\iota\omicron\iota$) was retained, with a small superscribed letter to indicate the multiplier: e.g., $\overset{\beta}{M}$ = 20,000. On both systems, see Heath, *History*

1.29–41, and, in particular, A. G. Woodhead, *The Study of Greek Inscriptions*, 2d ed. (Cambridge, 1981) , 108–12, a model of concision and clarity.

77. Van der Waerden 15–36; J. Gow, *Short History* 15 ff., 126 ff.

78. Davis and Hersh 158.

79. See Epicurus's letter to Herodotus, *ap.* Diog. Laert. 10.56–59; for an excellent recent discussion, cf. I. Mueller, "Geometry and Scepticism," in Barnes et al., chap. 3, 69–95, esp. 89–92.

80. Heath, *Manual* 206.

81. Cf. Arist. *Met.* 1060ᵃ28–1061ᵇ31.

82. Sambursky, *Physical World* 34.

83. Plato, *Theaet.* 147D.

84. Heath, *Manual* 309–10.

85. Reymond, *Histoire* 79; analysis of testimonia in Fraser 1.376 ff. (see esp. 383 ff.).

86. Reymond, *History* 2 ff.; J. Gow, *Short History* chap. 2, 15 ff.; Van der Waerden 15–36; Fraser 1.377.

87. Heath, *History* chap. 11, 1.354 ff.; J. Gow, *Short History* chap. 7, 195–221. For the European (and Arabic) line of transmission, cf. Sarton 47–52; J. Gow, *Short History* 203–9.

88. In Greek, ὁ στοιχειώτης. Cf. Heath, *History* 1.357; J. Gow, *Short History* 196–97.

89. Cf. Heath, *History* 1.358; M. Guillen, *Bridges to Infinity* (Los Angeles, 1983), 105–8.

90. Sarton 38.

91. E.g., Bk. 9, prop. 20, which in effect demonstrates that the number of prime numbers is infinite: J. Gow, *Short History* 76–78. For a stimulating discussion of this topic, cf. Davis and Hersh 210 ff.

92. Heath, *Manual* 241. For a judicious, but generous, estimate of Euclid's own contribution to mathematics, see Lloyd, *CAH* VII².1 331–32.

93. Others, particularly Hippocrates of Chios (ca. 470 – ca. 400), had attempted this geometrically insoluble task, which in Hippocrates' case led to some interesting incidental discoveries about the proportions of the lunes of a circle in relation to a right-angled triangle, inscribed within that circle with its hypotenuse forming the diameter: Reymond, *History* 69 = *Histoire* 58. For the best technical analysis of Archimedes' measurement of the circle, see Dijksterhuis, chap. 6, 222–40.

94. G. J. Toomer, *OCD²* 655, s.v. "Mathematics." On the volume of the sphere, see Dijksterhuis 169–82.

95. Ritchie 86 ff.

96. Heath, *History* 2.19–20; cf. Ritchie 83 ff., Fraser 1.399.

97. Cic. *Tusc. Disp.* 5.23. For variant details on Archimedes' death, see Plut. *Marcell.* 19, Livy 25.31, Val. Max. 8.7.7; the best modern account (which has Archimedes, correctly, working indoors on an abacus at the time rather than scratching in the sand *al fresco*) is that given by Dijksterhuis, 30–32.

98. Heath, *History* 2.133 ff.; Sarton 88 ff.

99. *AP* 9.578.

100. Heath, *History* 2.197.

101. Farrington, *Greek Science* 213.

102. Proclus, *On Euclid* p. 68 lines 10 ff. = Heath, *History* 1.154–56. Cf. Fraser 1.386–87, 2.563–64.

Chapter 27. Technological Developments: Science as *Praxis*

1. This point is well made by Lee, 65 ff.

2. Vitruv. 9 *praef.* 9–12. It is less often appreciated that the occasion of this famous discovery was a commission from Hieron II of Syracuse (p. 224) to prove that he had been cheated in the matter of a gold crown by the craftsman who made it, substituting silver for a proportion of the gold supplied to him: thus the experimentation to discover the comparative

specific gravity of gold and silver "ex eo inuentionis ingressu," i.e., the development of Archimedes' insight to the point that could provide formal proof (see Cohen and Drabkin 237–38 for a convenient summary of his propositions 3–7 on hydrostatics), might indeed be said to be socially, if not economically, dictated. Dijksterhuis 18–21 points out, what is seldom noted, that the anecdote as told does not in fact depend on the famous law of hydrostatics, but rather on the volumetric principle.

3. See the penetrating discussion in White, *Greek and Roman Technology* 20–21. He also appositely cites (p. 27) the remark of C. S. Smith, "Technology in History," *Minerva* 8 (1970) 470: "Every invention is born into an uncongenial society, has few friends and many enemies, and only the hardiest and luckiest survive."

4. On the "five simple machines"—which are really rather "tools or mechanical aids" (Lee 183)—i.e., wheel and axle, lever, pulley system, wedge, and endless screw, see Hero, *Mech.* 2.1–6 (Schmidt and Nix 2.94 ff.) = Cohen and Drabkin 224 ff.

5. Athen. 11.784c; cf. Avi-Yonah 236.

6. Neuburger 54–61.

7. Hero, *Dioptra* 3–5, 8, 14, 15 (190 ff. Schoene) = Cohen and Drabkin 336 ff.; cf. Lloyd *Greek Science* 67–69.

8. Marsden, *Greek and Roman Artillery: Historical* 56 ff.

9. Drachmann, *Ancient Oil-Mills, passim*; White, *Greek and Roman Technology* 31–32, 66 ff.

10. Hero, *Dioptra* 34 (292 ff. Schoene) = Cohen and Drabkin 342 ff.; *Mech.* 1.15 (Schmidt and Nix 2.30 ff.); cf. Drachmann, *Mechanical Technology* 33–37, 159 ff.

11. Vitruv. 9.8.4 ff.; cf. Drachmann, *Ktesibios* 16 ff.

12. Hero, *Pneum.* 1.42 (Schmidt 1.192 ff.) = Cohen and Drabkin 331 ff.; cf. Drachmann, *Ktesibios* 7 ff.

13. Philo, *Belop.* 73–77 (= Marsden, *Greek and Roman Artillery: Technical* 146–53 with fig. 9, *Greek and Roman Artillery: Historical* 94); cf. Landels 123 ff. with fig. 44.

14. Hero, *Pneum.* 1.28 (Schmidt 1.130 ff. with fig. 39) = Cohen and Drabkin 329 ff.; cf. Drachmann, *Ktesibios* 4 ff.

15. Hero, *Pneum.* 2.11 (Schmidt 1.228 ff. with fig. 55) = Cohen and Drabkin 254–55 (they correctly call the model "A Ball Rotated by Steam": it was J. G. Greenwood, the translator of the *Pneumatics*, who entitled this section "The Steam-Engine"). Cf. Landels 28–31 (his working model achieved a speed of 1,500 rpm); White, *Greek and Roman Technology* 57, app. 4, 195.

16. See White, ibid. 64–66, 162–69, and esp. app. 6, 196 ff., for a judicious summing-up of the available evidence; cf. Landels 15–25.

17. Hero's *De Automatis* is edited by Schmidt, 1.338–453, with figs. 82–109; cf. Drachmann, *Mechanical Technology* 197.

18. Hero, *Pneum.* 1.38 (Schmidt 1.174 ff. with fig. 39) = Cohen and Drabkin 328 ff.

19. Hero, *Pneum.* 1.12 (Schmidt 1.80 ff.) = Cohen and Drabkin 327–28.

20. Philo, *De Ingen. Spirit.* 10, 12–14 (Schmidt 1.480–86 with figs. 117–21).

21. Aul. Gell. *NA* 10.12.8, citing Favorinus; = Cohen and Drabkin 335–36.

22. Finley, "Technological Innovation" 30 = *Economy* 177 (with the caveat added, "so far as we can tell").

23. Confirmed by later literary sources, e.g., Pappus and Proclus: cf. Lloyd, *Greek Science* 91–93.

24. Cf. White, *Greek and Roman Technology* 64 ff.

25. Cf. Pappus, *Math. Coll.* 8.1 ff. (Hultsch 3.1022 ff. = Cohen and Drabkin 183 ff.).

26. Landels chap. 4, 84 ff.; White, *Greek and Roman Technology* 78 ff.

27. Archimedes and Poseidonius are both credited with the construction of such spheres (planetaria): Cic. *De Rep.* 1.22, *Tusc. Disp.* 1.63, *ND* 2.88 = Cohen and Drabkin 142–43.

28. White, *Greek and Roman Technology* 32–34; Landels 47–48; cf. Schneider 2.392.

29. Often associated with Odysseus: see, e.g., Hom. *Od.* 5.203, 10.488, and cf. De Gandt, in Barnes et al. 97 with n. 1.

30. Cf. Avi-Yonah 235.

31. Cf. White, *Greek and Roman Technology* 198–99. While it is true that parts of the Mediterranean world (notably mainland Greece) were lacking in those fast, constant streams that actively encouraged the development of water wheels in northwestern Europe, this was far from being a universal drawback (as the case of Italy makes clear), and cannot be adduced as a general explanation for the entrenched reluctance to exploit this and other inanimate sources of motive power.

32. The evidence is largely Roman, e.g., Columella, *RR* 3.3, and Pliny, *HN* 18.36, 38, 43, cited by Pleket, "Technology" 19, but equally applicable to the Hellenistic period.

33. Landels 15.

34. The slave as "animated tool": Arist. *Eth. Nic.* 1161^{b}4. No real distinction was made between free and servile labor in this context: cf. Kiechle 170, Ste Croix 133 ff. On the other hand, with regard to this lack of innovation it must be noted that Aristotle, *Pol.* 1253^{b}33–1254^a 1, argues the only alternative to slavery is complete automation; cf. Crates *ap.* Athen. 6.267e–268a. It is tempting to link some of the comic poets' automation fantasies with the mass desertion of slaves that took place during the Peloponnesian War (cf. Thuc. 7.27.5, who puts the figure at "over 20,000"), even though the passage from Crates cited here shows that such notions had gained currency earlier.

35. Hero, *Mech.* 1.1 (Schmidt and Nix 2.2 ff.; cf. Hultsch 3.1060 ff.); cf. Drachmann, *Mechanical Technology* 22–32.

36. Vitruv. 10.2 ff., Strabo 17.1.30 (C.807); the former were powered by treadmills, while the latter called for no less than 150 prisoners of war to keep them running. Cf. Pleket, "Technology" 9–11.

37. Cf. *AP* 9.418, by Antipater of Thessalonike (*fl.* 1st c. B.C. – 1st c. A.D.), in which a water mill is praised for giving women relief from the backbreaking task of hand-grinding grain: the clear implication is that water power has only lately been adopted. Cf. White, *Greek and Roman Technology* 198. However, the last two lines—"We taste once more the pleasures of archaic life, / Learning to feast on Demeter's works without labor"—smell of literary pastoralism, and suggest a court conceit akin to Marie Antoinette's mummery as a shepherdess; the acclimatization of such a trope probably took time, and it is possible, therefore, that the actual introduction of the water mill came a little earlier than is generally supposed.

38. Shared, to a surprising degree, by modern scholars who have worked on such authors as Ctesibius or Philo, and profess shock at the taste they (and Hero) show for "conjurors' apparatus": ancient authors are expected to be serious and high-minded. See the salutary comments by Drachmann, *Ktesibios* 3, 45–46.

39. David Hume, *Essays and Treatises* (Edinburgh, 1825) 195, cited by Guthrie, *History* 3.128, 410–11; Xen. *Mem.* 3.7.6 puts into Socrates' mouth a searing indictment of those who make up the Athenian Assembly: "the witless, the weaklings—fullers, cobblers, builders, smiths, farm workers, merchants, the market traders whose sole interest is buying cheap and selling dear" and "who have never bothered their heads with public affairs." Cf. *Mem.* 1.2.9.

40. Sen. *Ep. Mor.* 90.

41. Pleket, "Technology" 2; White, *Greek and Roman Technology* 12.

42. Cf. W. J. Verdenius, "Science grecque et science moderne," *RPhilos.* 152 (1962) 319 ff.

43. Lee 70–71.

44. DS 14.41–42 *passim.*

45. Hom. *Od.* 8.158 ff.

46. See, e.g., W. W. How and J. Wells, *A Commentary on Herodotus* (Oxford, 1912) 1.16 ff.

47. See Aesch. *PV* 447 ff. for the list of benefits bestowed by Prometheus on mankind, ranging from astronomy, mathematics, and literacy to house building, navigation, and the domestication of animals for plowing and transport.

48. Soph. *Ant.* 332 ff., esp. 361–72.

49. I find it remarkable that Lee, 70, "cannot . . . see any obstacle to the development of science or technology in ancient religion": how would he explain the fifth-century impiety

trials and the ban on the teaching of astronomy, or the attitude of Cleanthes to the heliocentric theory (p. 186)?

50. E.g., Plato, *Rep.* 425B–427B.

51. Cf. Plato, *Symp.* 221E5.

52. Arist. *Pol.* 1258[b]33 ff.

53. The "mechanicals of Hero's school," who embraced both theory and practice, were an exception; yet even they largely restricted themselves to the better development of civil and military gadgets. Cf. Cohen and Drabkin 183–84; text in Hultsch 3.1022 (= *Math. Coll.* 8.1): τῆς δὲ μηχανικῆς τὸ μὲν εἶναι λογικὸν τὸ δὲ χειρουργικὸν οἱ περὶ τὸν Ἥρωνα μηχανικοὶ λέγουσι.

54. Finley, "Technological Innovation" 33 = *Economy* 181; Plut. *Marcell.* 14.

55. Archimedes' tomb, in accordance with his own wishes, carried a representation of a sphere circumscribed by a cylinder, with the 3:2 ratio between them that he had been the first to work out: Plut. *Marcell.* 17, Cic. *Tusc. Disp.* 5.64–66.

56. How far Milesian thought was genuinely scientific, in the sense that we would understand that term, is highly debatable: see the sensible caveats of Lee, 66 ff., 180–81.

57. Verdenius (above, n. 42) 330. The Milesian attitude had probably always been that of a minority. Herodotus, 1.174, tells the story of how the Cnidians wanted to cut a canal through their peninsula, and sought the Delphic Oracle's approval for such an undertaking. But the Oracle replied: "Neither wall your isthmus nor ditch it; Zeus, had he been so minded, would have made it an island." No less significant than the Oracle's reply is the fact that the Cnidians felt obliged to consult it in the first place.

58. Landels 186.

59. Landels chap. 1, 9–33; White, *Greek and Roman Technology* 49 ff.

60. Anon. *De Rebus Bellicis* 17.1–3 = E. A. Thompson, *Roman Reformer* 102, cf. 50–54; Landels 15–16.

61. Landels, 16, finds the device impractical, observing that to give the oxen free room to move would require a vessel at least 13 ft. in the beam and 43 ft. overall. "Communication between the 'bridge' and the 'engine-room' might also be a trifle difficult." But E. A. Thompson, *Roman Reformer* 54, cites an almost exact parallel from Yarmouth in 1818: a "horse packet" 60 ft. overall, with an 18-ft. beam, worked in precisely the same way by four horses driving a pair of 7-ft. paddle wheels, and capable of maintaining a speed of about 6 knots.

62. Plin. *HN* 2.117–18: "nec reputat caeca mens et tantum auaritiae intenta id ipsum scientia posse tutius fieri." Cf. White, *Greek and Roman Technology* 13; Kiechle 173–74.

63. Plin. *HN* 36.195, Petron. *Sat.* 51, Dio Cass. 57.21.7; cf. Finley, "Technological Innovation" 41 = *Economy* 189–90.

64. Cf. Hodges 179.

65. At the same time, as Lee remarks (77–78), the Industrial Revolution was given its impetus by the discoveries of men (such as Abraham Darby, the ironmaster who developed the production of coke) who were τεχνῖται rather than scientists; so the question of technical incompetence in antiquity remains open.

66. Arist. *Pol.* 1337[b]; cf. Préaux, "Sur la stagnation" 250.

67. Cf. Landels 197–98.

68. Strato *ap.* Hero, *Pneum.*, proem. (Schmidt 1.4 ff. = Cohen and Drabkin 249 ff.); cf. Lloyd, *Greek Science* 17 ff.; Furley, *OCD*[2] 1018, s.v. "Straton (1)," with further reff.; Pleket, "Technology" 3.

69. Drachmann, *Ktesibios* 128; Lloyd, *Greek Science* 104–6.

70. Landels 81–83; White, *Greek and Roman Technology* 17 with nn. 36, 70; but see, *contra*, Landels' remarks elsewhere (p. 129) on the experimental pneumatic piston-and-cylinder catapult: "To bore the cylinder and turn the piston (a piston without rings, and with no gland on its driving-rod) with sufficient accuracy was beyond the technology of the time."

71. Landels 28–31: he also points out that Hero's large-scale model steam jet would have had a vast fuel consumption and very low efficiency. But—leaving aside the unresolved prob-

lem of technical ability—the fact remains that neither Hero nor anyone else in antiquity thought of combining the essential elements, *all known*, of boiler, valves, cylinders, and pistons to form a steam engine in the modern sense, i.e., as an effective alternative source of motive power. Why not? Could it have been through fear of doing anything liable to throw the labor force out of work and, hence, to foster revolution?

72. Landels 31.

73. Lee 76; White, *Greek and Roman Technology* 10, 36, 125–26; Healy 182 ff. On the spongy quality of the bloom, see Plin. *HN* 34.146: "mirumque, cum excoquatur uena, aquae modo liquari ferrum, postea in spongeas frangi." Cf. DS 5.13.1–2.

74. Vitruv. 1.1.1–2: "Itaque architecti, qui sine litteris contenderant, ut manibus essent exercitati, non potuerunt efficere, ut haberent pro laboribus auctoritatem; qui autem ratiocinationibus et litteris solis confisi fuerunt, umbram non rem persecuti uidentur."

75. Avi-Yonah 248 ff.; cf. in general H. I. Marrou, *Histoire de l'éducation dans l'antiquité*, 6th ed. (Paris, 1965), part 2, "Tableau de l'éducation classique à l'époque hellénistique," 151 ff., which makes peculiarly depressing reading. Marrou notes both the lack of technical training (pp. 287–88) and the progressive drying-up of scientific studies generally (pp. 274–77).

76. Lee 73 with further reff.

77. On siege equipment in general, see Garlan, *Recherches* part 4B, "Les machines de siège," 212 ff. For the torsion catapult cf. Marsden, *Greek and Roman Artillery: Historical* 56 ff.; Landels 106 ff., with figs. 35–37.

78. Plut. *Mor.* 219A.

79. Xen. *Oecon.* 6.6–7; Plato, *Laws* 6.778D; Arist. *Pol.* 1330^b–1331^a.

80. Anon. *De Rebus Bellicis*, *praef.* 4 (= E. A. Thompson *Roman Reformer* 91): "Constat enim apud omnes quod nec summa nobilitas nec opum affluentia aut subnixae tribunalibus potestates aut eloquentia litteris acquisita consecuta est utilitates artium in quibus etiam armorum continetur inuentio: sed ingenii tantummodo magnitudo, quae uirtutum omnium mater est, naturae felicitate subnixa: quod quidem sine personarum electione uidemus accidere." Pleket, "Technology" 18, observes correctly that "thanks to the literary-rhetorical, semi-philosophical pattern of education, the ruling classes were not in the least interested in the Anonymous' labour-saving, 'mechanising' inventions."

81. Philo, *Belop.* 51 = Marsden, *Greek and Roman Artillery: Technical* 108–9; cf. Landels 120–23.

82. I have here used the translation of Cohen and Drabkin, 319, in preference to that in Marsden, *Greek and Roman Artillery: Technical* 109, which is closer to the Greek in literal expression, but less easily grasped.

83. Marsden, ibid. 157–58; Landels 120; Cohen and Drabkin 319 n. 1.

84. Fraser 1.429.

85. Philo, *Belop* 56–57, 70–72, 77–78 (= Marsden, *Greek and Roman Artillery: Technical* 116–19, 138–43, 152–55); cf. Marsden, *Greek and Roman Artillery: Historical* 5 ff., 41–42, 168; Landels 127–30.

86. Cf. above, n. 70, and Landels 129.

87. Plut. *Demetr.* 21.1–2, DS 20.91.2–8. For an account of the similar devices employed at the siege of Syracuse in 213–212, see Polyb. 8.4–6 *passim*, Plut. *Marcell.* 17.

88. Main sources for Ctesibius's life and work: Vitruv. 9.8.2–7, 10.7–8; Athen. 4.174b–e, 11.497b–e; cf. Drachmann, *Ktesibios* 1–3, 184.

89. Vitruv. 10.7.1–3.

90. Hero, *Pneum.* 1.28 = Schmidt 1.130 ff. with fig. 29 (p. 133); cf. Drachmann, *Ktesibios* 4–7.

91. Schmidt 1.xxxiii–xxxv with figs. 29a, b; Cohen and Drabkin 331.

92. Vitruv. 10.8.1–6; he concludes, somewhat despairingly, with this *cri de coeur*: "Quantum potui niti, ut obscura res per scripturam dilucide pronuntiaretur, contendi, sed haec non est facilis ratio neque omnibus expedita ad intellegendum praeter eos, qui in his generibus habent exercitationem." Anyone who has ever tried to make practical sense of the description

preceding this disclaimer will surely sympathize. Cf. Hero, *Pneum.* 1.42 = Schmidt 1.192 ff. with figs. 43, 43b; cf. also Philo, *Belop.* 77.26–28 = Marsden, *Greek and Roman Artillery: Technical* 153; Cohen and Drabkin 331–33; Drachmann, *Ktesibios* 7–16 with figs. 1a, 1b.

93. Drachmann, *Ktesibios* 16.

94. Vitruv. 9.8.4–7; cf. Drachmann, *Ktesibios* 16 ff.

95. Vitruv. 10.7.4–5 is very scathing about such things as blackbird calls and mobile drinking figurines, devices that "non sunt ad necessitatem sed ad deliciarum uoluntatem": moral utilitarianism has a long history. Drachmann, *Ktesibios* 3, comments pungently: "I fail to see that it was better to invent catapults—which never came into practical use—than singing blackbirds which led to the invention of the organ, and of which we still find a descendant in the cuckoo-clock."

96. Perhaps this is overoptimistic. I have in mind the alarming readiness of many otherwise intelligent people—but not, of course, professional conjurors—to believe, literally, in the spoon bending and other parlor tricks of Uri Geller.

97. Philo, *Pneum.* 10 = Schmidt 1.480–81.

98. Drachmann, *Ktesibios* 46–47.

99. Philo, *Pneum.* 59–61, cf. Hero, *Pneum.* 1.16 = Schmidt 1.90 ff.; Drachmann, *Ktesibios* 115 ff.

100. Hero, *Pneum.* 2.36 = Schmidt 1.322 ff. with figs. 80, 80a, b, c.

101. Hero, *Pneum.* 1.38–39 = Schmidt 1.174 ff. with figs. 39–40; cf. Drachmann, *Ktesibios* 127.

102. Hero, *Pneum.* 1.12, 2.21 = Schmidt 1.82–83, 262–65, with figs. 13, 65; cf. Drachmann, *Ktesibios* 129–30.

103. Hero, *Pneum.* 1.17 = Schmidt 1.98–99 with fig. 18.

104. Hero, *Pneum.* 1.9 = Schmidt 1.64 ff. with figs. 10a, b (cf. also 1.18, 1.22, 1.33, 2.20, 2.28); Drachmann, *Ktesibios* 132–40.

105. Hero, *Pneum.* 1.21 = Schmidt 1.110–13 with fig. 22: a five-drachma coin is dropped into the neck of a jar and hits a plate that keeps the valve to an exit spout closed (on the same principle as the valve in a lavatory cistern); the weight of the coin opens the valve, and lets water flow out; the coin then slides off the tilted plate, which closes the valve once more.

106. Cf. Drachmann, *Mechanical Technology* 192, *Ktesibios* 19–21.

107. Hero, *De Autom.* 24–30 *passim* = Schmidt 1.423 ff.

108. Hero, *Belop.* 71 = Marsden, *Greek and Roman Artillery: Technical* 19; cf. Pleket, "Technology" 4: τῆς ἐν φιλοσοφίᾳ διατριβῆς τὸ μέγιστον καὶ ἀναγκαιότατον μέρος ὑπάρχει τὸ περὶ ἀταραξίας.

109. Hero, *Belop.* 72.

110. Veget. *De Re Mil.* 3 *proem.*: "Qui desiderat pacem, praeparet bellum." This most often appears as "Si vis pacem, para bellum."

Chapter 28. Hellenistic Medicine; or, The Eye Has Its Limitations

1. See, e.g., Préaux, *Monde* 2.623 ff.

2. Plato, *Laws* 7.822A, *Rep.* 7.530B.

3. Plato, *Tim.* 80D–81B.

4. Celsus, *De Med.*, proem. 9 ff.

5. A useful conspectus of testimonia in Cohen and Drabkin 149–53.

6. Aristoph. *Clouds* 201–5, Arist. *De Caelo* 298ª.

7. Strabo 1.3.4–20 (C.49–60), Xenoph. fr. 187 Kirk and Raven (pp. 176–77), Hdt. 2.12.

8. Vitruv. 9.8.2 ff.

9. Lloyd, *Greek Science* 67–69.

10. Heath, *History* 2.198, 257 ff.

11. E.g., Arist. *Pol.* 1337ᵇ; cf. Plut. *Per.* 1; Préaux, *Monde* 2.633.

12. Von Staden, "Experiment and Experience" 179 ff., analyzes five cases that meet most normal conditions set for qualification as a scientific experiment: the controlled weighing of an unfed cage bird, and its droppings, over a period to demonstrate loss of body substance through "emanations" or "evaporation" without external cause; the killing of a pig, while drinking specially dyed water, to prove that liquid lubricates the windpipe and enters the lungs (cf. below, p. 484); a test to determine whether the arteries contain $\pi\nu\epsilon\hat{\upsilon}\mu\alpha$ (vital spirit) or blood; an investigation of the function of the semilunar cardiac valves; and the Erasistratean tests on the human nervous system. Yet he finds (185) that these experiments are, nevertheless, "occasional" and often inconclusive or fallacious: "Some of them exhibit excessive confidence in an insidious method of analogy, some are prone to the fallacy of affirming the consequent; at times they lead to erroneous conclusions without becoming self-corrective; the use of quan-·titative methods is, in fact, minimal and inchoate."

13. Herophilus, *Dietetics*, *ap.* Sext. Emp. *Adv. Math.* 11.50 (text cited by Fraser 2.524 n. 144): Ἡρόφιλος δὲ ἐν τῷ διαιτητικῷ καὶ σοφίαν φησὶν ἀνεπίδεικτον καὶ τέχνην ἄδηλον καὶ ἰσχὺν ἀναγώνιστον καὶ πλοῦτον ἀχρεῖον καὶ λόγον ἀδύνατον, ὑγιείας ἀπούσης.

14. Though controversy still rages round the precise nature of Hippocrates' medical θεωρία, and the possible attribution to Hippocrates himself of any individual work in the Hippocratic corpus, so much seems clear: see, e.g., Edelstein's summary, *OCD*[2] 518–19 and further reff. there cited; Lyons and Petrucelli 209–17; and, for a brilliant analysis of the *parti pris* views taken of Hippocratic medicine in later antiquity, W. D. Smith, *Hippocratic Tradition* 179 ff.

15. We are dependent on writers such as Rufus of Ephesus, the gynecologist Soranus, the Roman encyclopedist Cornelius Celsus, and the author known as the *Anonymus Londinensis*— all of the first century A.D., but all, equally, embodying earlier material (bibliographical details in Longrigg 156 with nn. 10–14)—and, above all, on Galen (2d c. A.D.), whose voluminous writings are still most conveniently consulted, despite the *Corpus Medicorum Graecorum* edition, as yet incomplete, in the 20 vols. of C. G. Kühn, *Claudii Galeni Opera Omnia* (Leipzig, 1821–33). There exists no full scholarly collection of the fragments surviving from Alexandrian medical literature; but a notable step toward that goal has been achieved by Heinrich von Staden with his magisterial *Herophilus: The Art of Medicine in Early Alexandria* (Cambridge, 1989).

16. Von Staden 179, 185 ff.

17. Temkin 214 ff.

18. E.g., Von Staden, "Experiment and Experience" 179; Longrigg 162 (cf. 156) calls it "the most striking advance in knowledge of human anatomy the world has ever known—or was to know—until the seventeenth century AD." Cf. also Fraser 1.341.

19. It is argued, e.g., by Fraser 1.349–50 and Edelstein, "History" 287 ff., cf. Longrigg 162–63, that the breakthrough in dissection was achieved as a result of a change in the philosophical climate, which became progressively less concerned with the fate of the body after death. This is an intrinsically implausible argument. Philosophers as early as Heracleitus (fr. 96 Kirk and Raven) had shown contempt for the sacrosanctity of dead bodies without having any noticeable impact on public opinion; and dissection very soon ceased again, philosophical climate notwithstanding, without a powerful backer indifferent to popular prejudice. Intellectuals, alas, always tend to overestimate the influence of intellectual ideas.

20. There had been earlier instances of dissection, by Aristotle among others: see Lloyd, *Magic* 156–65. But these were crude and sporadic efforts, which did little to improve the still very limited medical familiarity with internal anatomy.

21. The key text is Celsus, *De Med.*, *proem.* 23: "Necessarium esse incidere corpora mortuorum eorumque uiscera atque intestina scrutari; longeque optime fecisse Herophilum et Erasistratum, qui nocentes homines a regibus ex carcere acceptos uiuos inciderint considerarintque, etiamnum spiritu remanente, ea quae natura ante clausisset." Cf. Tertull. *De Anim.* 10.4, 15.3, 5; other testimonia assembled by Von Staden, "Experiment and Experience" 196 n. 43. Needless to say, scholars have always been found who are ready to discard this clear

evidence and argue that two such great Greek scholars could not possibly have engaged in vivisection: for some instances see Longrigg 160–62 with nn. 45–57 *passim*. For a more balanced evaluation, see G. E. R. Lloyd's inaugural lecture, "Science and Morality in Greco-Roman Antiquity" (Cambridge, 1985), 5–10, and above all Von Staden, *Herophilus* ch. 6, 138–53, a dispassionate and thorough investigation that virtually clinches the matter. On the experiments of Mithridates VI and Attalus III, cf. Galen 14.2 Kühn.

22. Schneider 2.422, 429–31; Phillips 142–43 (Herophilus); Lloyd, *Science* 105 ff. Schneider observes, correctly (429) that "der Aufschwung der Gynäkologie und Pädiatrie entsprach dem hellenistischen Drang nach Leben und der Verehrung des Kindes."

23. Plato, *Phaedr.* 270C. The Greek is τῆς τοῦ ὅλου φύσεως.

24. Temkin 216, with a judicious discussion. Alternatively, the sense has been taken as "the nature even of the body can only be understood as a whole" (Jowett).

25. Plato, *Tim.* 69E–73A.

26. Ibid. 72B. I use the appealing translation of Sir Desmond Lee, *Plato: Timaeus and Critias* (Harmondsworth, 1971) 98.

27. Plato, *Tim.* 44D: σφαιροειδὲς σῶμα . . . ὃ νῦν κεφαλὴν ἐπονομάζομεν, ὃ θειότατόν τ' ἐστὶ καὶ τῶν ἐν ἡμῖν πάντων δεσποτοῦν.

28. Plato, *Tim.* 78A–79A; cf. Lee (above, n. 26) p. 105 with figs. 6, 7.

29. Plato believed this: cf. *Tim.* 70C–D, 91A; Aristotle (*Part. Anim.* 664[b]3–36) to his credit did not. Plutarch (*Mor.* 1047C–D) lists other authors, including Alcaeus, Euripides, and Eupolis, who apparently subscribed to the theory, as did some Hippocratics; others "disproved" it by erroneous facts (Hippocr. 7.604–8 Littré; cf. Von Staden, "Experiment and Experience" 194 n. 18), while the author of the Hippocratic treatise on the heart (9.80–82 Littré) confirmed it by means of an experiment that in fact was no confirmation at all (cf. Von Staden, "Experiment and Experience" 181).

30. Phillips 140.

31. Von Staden, "Experiment and Experience" 187 ff.

32. Ibid. 192.

33. W. D. Smith, *Hippocratic Tradition* 182; cf. Galen 14.683 Kühn.

34. See Withington 3.84 ff.

35. Chalcidius, *Commentarius in Platonis Timaeum* 246 = fr. 24 A 10 D-K; cf. Guthrie, *History* 1.349, and, for a salutary note of caution, Lloyd, *Magic* 156 with nn. 159–60.

36. Cf. Majno 183.

37. Hippocr. *Vet. Med.* 1–2 *passim* = W. H. S. Jones 1.12–17.

38. Hippocr. *Vuln. Cap.* 21 *passim* = Withington, 3.47–49; cf. Majno 24–28, 166–69, 196–97; Phillips 105–6.

39. Hippocr. *Epidem.* 5.16 = 5.217 Littré; 7.35 = 5.403 Littré; *Vuln. Cap.* 20 = Withington 3.45–47.

40. See R. B. Onians, *The Origins of European Thought*, 2d ed. (Cambridge, 1954), chaps. 1–3 *passim*.

41. Hippocr. *Reg.* 4.87 = 6.643 Littré, W. H. S. Jones 4.423: καὶ τὸ μὲν εὔχεσθαι ἀγαθόν· δεῖ δὲ καὶ αὐτὸν συλλαμβάνοντα τοὺς θεοὺς ἐπικαλεῖσθαι; cf. *Reg.* 4.89 *passim*, 90 *fin.*, 93 *fin.* Hippocr. *Decent.* 5 = Jones 2.286: ἰητρὸς γὰρ φιλόσοφος ἰσόθεος; cf. ibid. 6 = Jones 2.288 (a fascinating passage, but in places hopelessly corrupt). On the mortality figures in *Epidemics* 1 and 3, see Jones 1.144 and 2.ix–xiii. If the increased individualism of the Hellenistic age put an added premium on good health, thus heightening the public faith in, and gratitude to, physicians (cf. p. 495, and see Schneider 2.403: "Grenzenlos war das Vertrauen, das die Ärzte genossen, grenzenlos auch die Dankbarkeit, die man ihnen entgegenbrachte"), there were also perennial jokes, and far from kind ones, about the doctor's role as privileged murderer, seducer of female patients, fee-hungry con man, and pretentious quack: *AP* 11.112–26 offers a characteristic collection of antimedical epigrams. In an age with no proper licensing system for medical practice (Cohn-Haft 17–18; Jones 2.xxxvii–xl, 257–61) this was inevitable. To keep the quacks or incompetents out was impossible.

42. Edelstein and Edelstein 2.169.

43. Aristoph. *Plut.* 400–414, 633–747 = Edelstein and Edelstein 1.212–20. The *Plutus* was Aristophanes' last play (produced in 388), and it seems legitimate to assume that he was satirizing a new, or newly popular, fashion.

44. Phillips 198.

45. *IG* IV².1 121–22 = Edelstein and Edelstein 1.221 ff., no. 423.

46. Edelstein and Edelstein 1.226–27, no. 423 (xxx).

47. Ibid. 1.224, no. 423 (xiv). I owe the suggestion of prostatic calculus to Mr. Paul Psoinos.

48. Ibid. 1.225, no. 423 (xxi).

49. Ibid. 1.226, no. 423 (xxvi).

50. Majno, 203, identifies these as *Elaphe longissima longissima*, Europe's only constrictor, which grows up to five feet in length but is harmless to man.

51. Edelstein and Edelstein 1.224, no. 423 (xvii).

52. Lloyd, *Science* 202, observes that "a very considerable body of evidence can be assembled to show how much of Greek science consists in the rationalisation of popular belief," and his monograph is a fascinating demonstration of this contention. It is, for obvious reasons, more true in the case of medicine than that of, say, mathematics, and remains easily compatible with the sociointellectual split between φυσιολόγοι and βάναυσοι, given the addiction of the former for picking examples and analogies from everyday life.

53. Edelstein and Edelstein 2.112 n. 4; Lloyd, *Magic* 40 ff.

54. Edelstein and Edelstein 2.175 ff., Cohn-Haft 27–30; a more guarded evaluation in Hands 132 with n. 156 (p. 172).

55. Nor, despite the high ideals proclaimed in such tracts as *Precepts* or *On Ancient Medicine*, were their records always by any means impeccable: cf. Lloyd, *Science* 206.

56. Hippocr *Morb. Sacr.* 2.1–9 = W. H. S. Jones 2.140 (I use his translation here).

57. Ibid. 1.1 ff. = W. H. S. Jones 2.139.

58. Ibid. 6–10 *passim* = W. H. S. Jones 2.152 ff.

59. Cf. W. H. S. Jones 1.xlvi ff., Phillips 48–52.

60. W. H. S. Jones 1.li–lii. Herophilus's work on the pulse similarly induced a slew of metaphors, borrowed in this case from the musical theory of Aristoxenus of Taras (Longrigg 174). Herophilus was, indeed, the great medical metaphorist of antiquity, coining a whole series of physiological images, many of which are still in common use today: the "tunics" (membranes) of the outer eye, the "ravine" of the portal hepatic fissure, the *calamus scriptorius*, the *torcular Herophili*. See Longrigg 166, 176–77; Fraser 1.354–55. Herophilus likened the *os uteri* after parturition to the head of a cuttlefish and the posterior surface of the iris to a grape skin; he wrote of the pulse that bounded like a gazelle (δορκαδίζων) or fluttered like a trail of ants (μυρμηκίζων) beneath the physician's finger. An interesting literary study remains to be written on this topic.

61. Cf. Majno 178.

62. Phillips 20–21, citing Aëtius Amid. *Plac.* 5.30.1 = fr. 24 B 4 D-K; cf. Guthrie, *History* 1.346.

63. On the interaction of politics and science, see Lloyd, *Magic* 246 ff.; cf. Phillips 20–21.

64. Cf. Phillips 48–49, W. H. S. Jones 1.xlviii.

65. Hence, of course, the stress placed by Greek physicians on dietetics, "the great dynamic element within Greek medicine," as it has been called (Temkin 221). This does not of itself ensure that the diets recommended were healthy ones. Indeed, in the words of a distinguished surgeon (Majno 189), "whatever diet they prescribed was unwholesome even for the healthy, and would, if followed, have soon resulted in severe vitamin deficiencies, since they were suspicious of most vegetables, and even more so of fruit, concentrating for the most part on meat and cereals." See, e.g., Hippocr. *Vet. Med.* 8 = W. H. S. Jones 3.24–26.

66. I am not primarily concerned in this chapter with the maintenance of public health, important though that was: our best evidence suggests commonsensical care—at least in a

wealthy city such as Pergamon—over matters such as covered drains, efficient sewage disposal, and a clean water supply, as well as the regular hiring of public physicians, paid out of a special municipal tax fund, to ensure the availability of medical treatment, since doctors always tended to be in short supply. See *OGIS* 483 = Austin 216 (pp. 352–56), with Cohn-Haft 22–23, for the regulations in force at Pergamon, and *SEG* 2.2 (1925) 597.11–12 (pp. 108–9) = Austin 99 (pp. 176–77) for the medical tax fund (at Teos).

67. Erasistratus wrote a *General Treatise*; a work on anatomical dissection in two books; studies on fevers and the motion of the blood; a three-book monograph on diseases of the intestines; and several other minor works. Testimonia in Wellmann, *RE* 6 (1907) col. 350, s.v. "Erasistratos (2)"; cf. Phillips 145–46 with n. 400. Herophilus is credited with eleven volumes, at least seven of them genuine, including an anatomical treatise (three books), one-book studies of ophthalmology, midwifery, and dietetics, a monograph on the pulse (two books), and a polemic entitled *Against Common Opinions* (Πρὸς τὰς κοίνας δόξας). Cf. Gossen, *RE* 8 (1913) col. 1110, s.v. "Herophilos (4)"; Phillips 141 with n. 377, and—superseding all previous scholarship—Von Staden, *Herophilus*, esp. ch. 3, "Writings," 67–88.

68. App. *Syr.* 59–61 *passim*, Galen 14.630 Kühn, Plut. *Demetr.* 38, and elsewhere. Fraser 1.347, basing himself on an earlier article, "The Career of Erasistratus of Ceos," *RIL* 103 (1969) 518–37, has argued that Erasistratus and his followers never worked in Alexandria at all, a view endorsed by W. D. Smith, *Hippocratic Tradition* 189–90 with n. 15, 195, but well refuted by Lloyd, *JHS* 95 (1975) 172–75, and Longrigg 158 ff., among others.

69. Plin. *HN* 26.6. For Diocles' *floruit* (middle to late 4th century: contra Jaeger [below, n. 70], who places him 340–260) see Von Staden, *Herophilus* 44–46.

70. Useful accounts of Diocles in W. D. Smith, *Hippocratic Tradition* 181 ff., and Phillips 128 ff.; W. Jaeger's *Diokles von Karystos* (Berlin, 1938) is full but suffers from dubious chronological theorizing and a predictable overemphasis on the influence of Aristotle.

71. W. D. Smith, *Hippocratic Tradition* 181.

72. Plin. *HN* 26.10; Galen 6.455, 14.683 Kühn.

73. Aristoph. *Clouds* 225–36, 828–30, 930–31.

74. M. Wellmann, *Die Fragmente der sikelischen Ärzte Akron, Philistion und des Diokles von Karystos* (Berlin, 1901) fr. 141.

75. Treatise for Pleistarchus: Galen 6.455 Kühn; cf. Athen. 7.316c (where he repeats the old bromide, or rather in this case antibromide, about the aphrodisiac properties of shellfish). The *Letter to Antigonus* (Διοκλῆς Ἐπιστολὴ Προφυλακτική), preserved by Paul of Aigina (*Pragm.* 1.100), is printed by Jaeger (above, n. 70), pp. 75–78; cf. Phillips 132–33.

76. K. Bardong, *RE* 22 (1954) cols. 1735–43, s.v. "Praxagoras (1)"; F. Steckerl, *The Fragments of Praxagoras of Cos and His School* (Leiden, 1958); cf. Phillips 135 ff.; W. D. Smith, *Hippocratic Tradition* 188–89. Praxagoras's date is disputed: see Von Staden, *Herophilus* 43–44. A *floruit* of ca. 325 seems likeliest.

77. Phillips 136.

78. Steckerl (above, n. 76) 9 ff., 17 ff.

79. Fraser 1.346.

80. Excellent, and up-to-date, general accounts of Herophilus are to be found in Longrigg 165 ff.; W. D. Smith, *Hippocratic Tradition* 189 ff.; and especially in Fraser 1.348–57, with an exceptionally full range of testimonia, 2.503 ff. Until very recently there was no modern book-length study in existence: Von Staden's *Herophilus* has now filled that gap at ample length and with impeccable scholarship, both assembling the fragments of Herophilus and his successors and filling in the background with a series of essays on early Alexandrian medicine.

81. Arist. *Hist. Anim.* 495ª10 ff.; cf. Longrigg 191 n. 76. Texts in Von Staden, *Herophilus* 195–99 (T76–78).

82. Testimonia collected by Longrigg 191 n. 77. Cf. now Von Staden, *Herophilus* 155–61.

83. Cf. F. Solmsen, "Greek Philosophy and the Discovery of the Nerves," *MH* 18 (1961) 169 ff., esp. 194–95.

84. Galen 2.780, 4.646, 8.396 Kühn. See now Von Staden, *Herophilus* 160–61, 252–55, T84–89 (eyes), 164–65, 195 (pancreas).

85. Galen 2.570 Kühn. See now Von Staden, *Herophilus* 162 ff., 180–81, with Fr. 60a–b (pp. 182–83).

86. Testimonia conveniently assembled by Fraser, 2.518 n. 113. See now Von Staden, *Herophilus* 154, 165, T98a (duodenum), 262 ff. (pulse), 282–83 (clepsydra).

87. Galen 5.149–80 Kühn; other testimonia in Fraser 2.514 n. 101.

88. Galen 8.703 Kühn.

89. Longrigg 170–73 gives an excellent account of this still-unsettled debate, with full testimonia. See now Von Staden, *Herophilus* 265–67.

90. Celsus, *De Med.*, *proem.* 15.

91. The lesson here, as Fraser remarks (1.354), is that "medicine, like other sciences, moves fitfully to its goal."

92. Galen 3.813, 7.89 Kühn.

93. Fraser 1.353.

94. Plin. *HN* 25.58, cf. 15: "concitatis enim intus omnibus ipsum in primis exire." See also Galen 12.966 Kühn.

95. Majno 189, who points out that for Greek physicians to employ this killer primarily for its minor aperient side effects was wholly irrational: "One might as well shoot a gun blindly in order to enjoy the noise and the smell."

96. Cf. Scarborough, "Theophrastus" 353 ff.

97. Cf. Galen 2.895 Kühn.

98. Edelstein, "History" 275 ff.; Phillips 140.

99. Heracleitus fr. 96 Kirk and Raven.

100. Fraser 2.511 n. 94. Von Staden, *Herophilus* 167–69, points out how much Herophilus's gynecological theorizing seems to have depended, by analogy, on his knowledge of male dissection.

101. Fraser 1.351.

102. Von Staden, *Herophilus* 29. Hdt. 2.89 is instructive in this context.

103. Stob. *Flor.* 4.38.9.

104. Diog. Laert. 5.57; Galen 2.88, 4.729 Kühn.

105. Euseb. *Chron.* 2.121 Schoene. For his date see Von Staden, *Herophilus* 47, who argues persuasively in favor of ca. 330–255/250.

106. A useful summing-up by D. J. Furley, *OCD*² 1018, s.v. "Straton (1)."

107. Hero, *Pneum.* 1 *proem.* = Schmidt 1.4 ff, esp. 24 ff.; cf. Longrigg 178, Furley (above, n. 106).

108. Longrigg 180.

109. Celsus, *De Med.*, *proem.* 12 ff., 62–67; cf. Lloyd, *Magic* 86 ff.

110. Lyons and Petrucelli, 229, offer a salutary comment on this situation: "In retrospect we can see that many of these acid controversies were based principally on theoretical concepts. Time has wiped out their foundations. The teachers propounded, the followers disputed, the practitioners wrangled, and the sick hoped. To the extent that the physician's treatment was based on unprejudiced observations of the patient's condition, honest evaluation of past results, and sincere concern for the welfare of the ill person, the patient received benefit no matter which theory, sect, or doctrine was espoused." As Lloyd points out, *Science* 217, though "there was no Copernican revolution in the life sciences, no major paradigm shift," a great deal of value did, in fact, get done.

111. Conveniently listed by Cohn-Haft in an appendix, 76–85.

112. Hippocr. *Praec.* 4.12–14: κρέσσον οὖν σῳζομένοις ὀνειδίζειν ἢ ὀλεθρίως ἔχοντας προμύσσειν.

113. Kudlien, *Sklaven* chap. 4, 39 ff., esp. 41–42: the *seruus medicus* was an essentially Roman phenomenon.

114. See Cohn-Haft 32 ff. for a convincing refutation of this theory, and cf. Austin 217–18.

115. Cohn-Haft 40–41 n. 37 cites Andrew Carnegie's *Gospel of Wealth* (1899, reprinted 1933) to telling effect in this context.

116. Tarn and Griffith 108–9.

117. See Cohn-Haft 34–35 with n. 11 for an interesting collection of instances. For a decree of Ilion honoring Antiochus I's physician Metrodorus, see *OGIS* 220 = Burstein, *Translated Documents* n. 20, p. 26.

118. *IG* V.1 1145, lines 19–20: εἰς τὸ πᾶσιν ἴσος εἶναι κα[ὶ πένησι καὶ] πλουσίοις καὶ δούλοις καὶ ἐλευθέροις, cited by Cohn-Haft 37 n. 20 and Kudlien, *Sklaven* 40; the date is ca. 70 B.C., and refers to a Lacedaemonian doctor working in the Laconian port of Gytheion. Cf., for similar sentiments, *IG* XII.1 1032, a second-century B.C. inscription from Carpathos.

119. *SIG*³ 528 = Austin 124, p. 125; C. Habicht, *MDAI(A)* 72 (1957) 233–34 = Austin 125, pp. 217–18.

120. Menocritus of Samos, in the second century B.C., was public physician on the island of Carpathos for over twenty years: *IG* XII.1 1032; cf. Kudlien, *Sklaven* 39. Cf. also the third- or second-century decree honoring a public physician on Cos: *SEG* 27 (1977) 513 = Burstein, *Translated Documents* no. 27, p. 35.

Chapter 29. Hellenism and the Jews: An Ideological Resistance Movement?

1. Eddy 183 reminds us that "the study of Hellenistic Judaism is virtually a separate field in itself": a notable understatement. Few would claim—I most certainly do not—to have mastered all the ramifying (and often contentious) literature this topic has generated. That task would require several normal lifetimes. But I have paid careful attention to the original sources, and I hope I have familiarized myself with, and profited by, at least the more outstanding scholarly contributions, most notably those of Bickerman, Bringmann, Bunge, Hengel, Momigliano, Niese, Schürer (in the revised edition of Vermes, Millar, and Black [Edinburgh, 1979]), and Tcherikover.

2. Cf. Niese 3.220–22.

3. Cf. Eddy chaps. 2–3, 37–80.

4. Niese 3.224 with n. 3.

5. Joseph. *AJ* 11.304 ff., esp. 326–36; cf. Tcherikover 42 ff.; Marcus et al. 6.512 ff. (app. C, "Alexander the Great and the Jews"); Hengel, *Jews* 6 ff.; Schürer 1.138 n. 1, with further bibliography.

6. In the third century the border seems to have run from the small coastal stream of Eleutheros (Nahr-al-Kabir), situated north of Tripolis, southeast through the Beqaa valley—hence the name Coele ("Hollow") Syria—by Heliopolis (Baalbek) to Damascus. Damascus was disputed territory: in 259 part of the Ptolemaic empire (Polyaen. 4.15, *PCairZen.* 59006; cf. Hengel, *Jews* 22–23 with n. 12), but lost again to Seleucus II Kallinikos in the 240s; cf. Strabo 16.2.14 (C.754); Hengel, *Jews* 29. Batanaea and Trachonitis, the modern Transjordan, south of Damascus, were under Lagid rule. The Arabian desert formed a natural eastern boundary: a chain of defensive forts was built along it. Cf. Hengel, *Judaism* 1.7, 2.4 (n. 12), *Jews* 21.

7. Cf. in general Hengel, *Jews* chap. 2, 13–20.

8. DS 18.3, 39.6; QC 10.10.2; Just. 13.4.12.

9. DS 19.59.2.

10. DS 19.80–86 *passim*.

11. DS 19.93.4–7.

12. Tcherikover 52.

13. DS 21.1, fr. 5 Walton; Polyb. 5.67.4–10; cf. Hengel, *Judaism* 2.3 n. 1.

14. DS 21.1.5; cf. Tcherikover 53.

15. Will, *HP*² 1.134, well describes the third-century relationship between the Seleucid and Ptolemaic empires as "l'impossible stabilité."

16. Polybius (5.86.10) claimed that by and large the inhabitants of Coele-Syria always preferred Ptolemaic to Seleucid overlordship, but this seems a highly debatable assertion: for one thing, the Seleucid bureaucracy was known to be less strict (cf. p. 503). As Niese points out (3.224), despite Polybius "doch scheinen die Juden von ihnen [*sc.* the Seleucids] ungewöhnliche Bedrückung nicht erlitten zu haben."

17. Hecataeus *ap.* Joseph. *Cont. Ap.* 1.186–89.

18. DS 18.43; App. *Syr.* 50.52; Agatharchides of Cnidos *ap.* Joseph. *AJ* 12.3–6, *Cont. Ap.* 1.209–11.

19. Cf. Hengel, *Jews* chap. 3, 21–32.

20. Hecataeus of Abdera *ap.* DS 40.3.4–6; Joseph. *Cont. Ap.* 1.183 ff.

21. Tcherikover 59.

22. E. Will, "Monde hellénistique" (1975) 623.

23. Strabo *ap.* Joseph. *AJ* 14.117; cf. Fraser 1.54–55, 88 with n. 337.

24. Fraser 2.956 n. 71, with further bibliography; cf. esp. Bickerman, *Proceedings of the American Society for Jewish Research* 28 (1959) 11–13.

25. Strabo 16.2.35–37 (C.761); cf. E. Will, "Monde hellénistique" (1975) 625.

26. This seems to have been the aim of that curious Hellenized Jewish writer Aristobulus (*fl.* ca. 160), who dedicated his work *Explanations of the Book of Moses* to Ptolemy VI Philometor: the key excerpt is preserved in Euseb. *Praep. Ev.* 13.12, 663d–668b = Fraser 2.966 n. 110, cf. 1.694–96. Cf. also E. Will, "Monde hellénistique" (1975) 625. He is also the first writer to support the tradition that the initiative for the LXX came from Ptolemy Philadelphos and Demetrius of Phaleron: cf. Momigliano, *Alien Wisdom* 115–16.

27. E. Will, "Monde hellénistique" (1975) 626.

28. See in general Hengel, *Judaism* 1.115 ff.

29. Eccles. 2.4–10; cf. Applebaum 159–60.

30. Cf. Hengel, *Judaism* 1.31 ff., *Jews* 121–23.

31. Cf. Eddy 203 with further literature.

32. Cf. Momigliano, *Alien Wisdom* 95.

33. Ecclus. 10.19, cited in the translation of Hengel, *Jews* 113.

34. Ecclus. 2.10, 4.1–10, 5.4, 7.10, 20, 32, 11.21–28, 13.18–19, 14.6–16, 28.10, 29.1–14, 31.1–5, 33.24–31, 35.12–22.

35. Cf. Tcherikover 60 ff.

36. Cf. *Corpus Papyrorum Judaicarum* 1.115–46; cf. Abel, *Histoire* 60–71.

37. See *PErzRainer* 24552 = Préaux, *Monde* 2.568; what purports to be the decree of manumission is given by Joseph. *AJ* 12.28–32; cf. the so-called *Letter of Aristeas* 22–25. But a flourishing slave trade between Palestine and Alexandria is revealed by the Zenon papyri (cf. *PCairZen.* 59003, 59018): of the four slaves Tobiah sent to Ptolemy's minister Apollonius as a *douceur*, two were circumcised (*PCairZen.* 59075–76). Cf. Préaux, *Monde* 2.569.

38. In general see Hengel, *Judaism* 1.18–29.

39. Tcherikover 63–65.

40. Cf. Niese 3.225–26.

41. Cf. Hengel, *Jews* 24–25 with further reff.

42. Hengel, *Judaism* 58 ff., *Jews* 113 ff.; Préaux, *Monde* 2.570–71.

43. Eddy 201.

44. Polyb. 16.18–19, 39; Joseph. *AJ* 12.129–37; cf. Niese 2.577 ff.

45. Joseph. *AJ* 12.135–36.

46. Ibid. 12.138.

47. Hieron. *In Dan.* 11.14, cited by Tcherikover 76 with nn. 103–4.

48. Recorded by Joseph. *AJ* 12.138–44: the authenticity of this document, argued by Bickerman in *REJ* 197/8 (1935) 4–35, is now generally accepted. Cf. Burstein, *Translated Documents* no. 35, pp. 46–47, with further reff.

49. Cf. Will, *HP²* 2.119.

50. Eddy 200.

51. Ezra 6.9, 7.21–22; cf. Momigliano, *Alien Wisdom* 98.

52. Joseph. *AJ* 12.145–46.

53. Cf. Bartlett 4. He may, however, have learned something through the Babylonian Jews of the Diaspora: cf. Tarn and Griffith 219, 224–25.

54. Mørkholm, *Antiochus IV* 135–36.

55. Cf. Momigliano, *Alien Wisdom* 100: "Such direct interference in the ancestral cults of a nation was unheard-of in the Greek-speaking world from immemorial times."

56. The *locus classicus* is Polyb. 26.1.1–14.

57. This would not have made him popular in later rabbinical circles, where the term *apikoros*, a corruption of "Epicurean," came to be used as a synonym for "nonbeliever": see De Witt 335–36. However, whether it was Epicureanism as such, or the fact that it was the chosen creed of the hated Antiochus IV, that earned it its later reputation among Jews must remain a moot point. De Witt (ibid.) sees Epicurean influence in Ecclesiastes, but this is highly speculative.

58. Tcherikover 178: for a cogent rebuttal, see Mørkholm, *Antiochus IV* 138.

59. The key text here is Tac. *Hist.* 5.8: "rex Antiochus demere superstitionem et mores Graecorum dare adnisus, quominus taeterrimam gentem in melius mutaret, Parthorum bello prohibitus est." Modern supporters of this theory include Bevan, *House of Seleucus* 2.162–74, and Rostovtzeff, *SEH* 2.703–5. Other ancient texts: 1 Macc. 1.41; 2 Macc. 6.9, 11.24; Joseph. *AJ* 12.263.

60. Tcherikover 182.

61. Bickerman chap. 5, 76 ff.

62. Cf. above, n. 55.

63. One initial caveat must be made: our evidence is almost all from the Jewish side: the accounts of Polybius and Poseidonius covering the Hasmonean revolt are lost, so that "we are left with no genuine account of the wars between Seleucids and Jews from the Greek point of view": Momigliano, *Alien Wisdom* 102 ff. What follows should always be read with this in mind—though it is remarkable how much can be extracted from a close scrutiny of the *parti pris* narratives offered by 1 and 2 Maccabees and Josephus (a kind of second-rate Polybius, a Romanized Jewish Pharisee with the *collabo*'s distaste for nationalistic extremism, who saved his skin during the Jewish revolt of A.D. 66–70 by an inspired prediction of Vespasian's rise to the purple). For Josephus, see the shrewd analysis by Bartlett, 72 ff.

64. 1 Macc. 2.42, 7.13; cf. Tcherikover 124 ff.

65. Hengel, *Jews* 30.

66. Joseph. *AJ* 12.154–55, 158, in combination. The chronology and details are debatable, the main outline reasonably clear. See Tcherikover 129–30, Schürer 1.140 with n. 4, Marcus et al. 7.80–81. Josephus seems to confuse this occasion with the later (193) marriage of Ptolemy V Epiphanes to Antiochus III's daughter Cleopatra, and, in particular, with the latter's much-debated dowry (cf. p. 418), held to include the revenues of Coele-Syria (cf. Polyb. 28.20.9, App. *Syr.* 5) and, in Josephus's account (*AJ* 12.154), those of Samaria, Judaea, and Phoenicia besides. Josephus, having picked the wrong Ptolemy, resorts to the dowry to explain why, after the conquest of Coele-Syria by Antiochus III in 200, tribute is still being paid to Alexandria.

67. Joseph. *AJ* 12.160 ff.

68. Ibid. 12.158: the payment was made ἐκ τῶν ἰδίων.

69. Momigliano, *Alien Wisdom* 88.

70. Joseph. *AJ* 12.175–78.

71. Ibid. 12.224; cf. Rostovtzeff, *SEH* 1.349, 2.1400 n. 132; Tcherikover 130 ff.; Hengel, *Judaism* 1.27–28, 268 ff., *Jews* 30 with n. 49; Schürer 1.140 n. 4, 149–50 n. 30.

72. Joseph. *AJ* 12.180–84.

73. Ibid. 12.187, 198–201, cf. 176.

74. 1 Macc. 1.11, Joseph. *AJ* 12.224; cf. Hengel, *Jews* 31.

75. Joseph. *AJ* 12.222, 228–36; cf. 2 Macc. 3.11 ff. On the vexed chronology of Joseph and John Hyrcanus, see Tcherikover 128 ff.

76. Joseph. *AJ* 12.224: τὸν τοῦ Ἰουδαίων λαὸν ἐκ πτωχείας καὶ πραγμάτων ἀσθενῶν εἰς λαμπροτέρας ἀφορμὰς καταστήσας.

77. 2 Macc. 6.8.

78. Schürer 1.144; cf. Tcherikover 140.

79. Cf. Niese 3.226.

80. Joseph. *AJ* 12.239.

81. Tcherikover 152–56 with further reff.

82. 2 Macc. 4.2.

83. Tcherikover 161. For Jason's dealings with Antiochus, see 2 Macc. 4.8.

84. 2 Macc. 3.4–7. It has sometimes been asserted, on the basis of Livy 42.6.6–7, that the Roman indemnity was paid off *in toto* by 173; but—apart from the inherent unlikeliness of this—the passage in question clearly refers only to the payment *for that year*, brought personally, in one lump sum, by Antiochus's ambassador, as a token of apology for its lateness.

85. Eddy 205–6.

86. 2 Macc. 3 *passim*; cf. Bickerman 42–43, Eddy 205–6.

87. 2 Macc. 4.9: τοὺς ἐν Ἱεροσολύμοις Ἀντιοχεῖς ἀναγράψαι. The translation given in the text seems to me a far more natural way to treat the Greek than to take Ἀντιοχεῖς predicatively and translate (cf. Schürer 1.148) "to register the inhabitants of Jerusalem *as Antiochenes*." It also makes a clear distinction between these "Antiochenes" and the population as a whole.

88. 2 Macc. 4.7–15, 1 Macc. 1.11–15, Joseph. *AJ* 12.239–41 (who attributes these attempts at Hellenization to Menelaus and the Tobiads rather than to Jason, a variant that in essence makes little difference to the case).

89. Joseph. *AJ* 12.240: βούλονται τοὺς πατρίους νόμους καταλιπόντες καὶ τὴν κατ' αὐτοὺς πολιτείαν ἔπεσθαι τοῖς βασιλικοῖς καὶ τὴν Ἑλληνικὴν πολιτείαν ἔχειν. Cf. 2 Macc. 4.10–11.

90. Primarily by Tcherikover, 161 ff.; cf. Hengel, *Judaism* 1.277 ff., and the somewhat more cautious position of Schürer, 1.148.

91. 2 Macc. 11.27–33.

92. Bringmann 188–89 with n. 59; cf. Abel, *Livres* 332. This point clearly bothered Tcherikover, since he concedes (161) that not all the citizens of Jerusalem, in particular the "hewers of wood and drawers of water," became "Antiochenes." That point once admitted, the choice lies between a limited franchise of the kind employed by the Spartans (cf. p. 257) and membership in an elite club. Between these two alternatives the difference is only one of degree, not of kind.

93. This is essentially the view taken by Bickerman, chap. 3 §3, 38 ff., a work that I read only after I had, independently, reached an identical conclusion.

94. 1 Macc. 1.13.

95. 2 Macc. 4.7–10, 1 Macc. 1.11–15, Joseph. *AJ* 12.240–41.

96. Tcherikover 163.

97. Joseph. *AJ* 12.241, 1 Macc. 1.15. "They made themselves foreskins," the latter source asserts; but how? Perhaps by traction (epispasm) of the surviving skinfold with weights: cf. Schürer 1.148–49 with n. 28.

98. Hengel, *Judaism* 1.289, citing *Jubilees* 15.33 ff.

99. Arr. *Anab.* 2.24.6.

100. 2 Macc. 4.18–20.

101. Tcherikover 166.

102. 1 Macc. 1.11.

103. 2 Macc. 4.21–22.

104. 2 Macc. 4.23, cf. 3.4; Mørkholm, *Antiochus IV* 140 with n. 19.

105. 2 Macc. 4.24–26; Joseph. *AJ* 12.229, 240–41.

106. 2 Macc. 4.27–29.

107. 2 Macc. 4.26, 33–37.

108. 2 Macc. 4.27–50; cf. Tcherikover 170–74; Eddy 210–11. As Bickerman (43) says, Menelaus's "alliance with the government rested upon the solid basis of a common financial interest." Many in his party were conspicuously and, to a traditionalist, offensively, wealthy. Cf. Eddy 209.

109. Imperfectly understood by Josephus, *BJ* 1.31.

110. See in particular Niese 3.229–33 (still one of the most judicious accounts); Abel, *Histoire* 118 ff.; Bickerman 43 ff.; Will, *HP*² 2.334–41 (good on setting the revolt in its wider context); Schürer 1.150 ff. (esp. 152 n. 37); Tcherikover chap. 5, 175 ff. (attractive, in ways brilliant, but overbold in its theorizing); Hengel, *Judaism* 280 ff.; Mørkholm, *Antiochus IV* 142 ff. Antiochus's financial concerns: Bringmann 176 ff., and the same author's *Hellenistische Reform und Religionsverfolgung in Judäa* (Göttingen 1983) 111–40.

111. Polyb. 31.9 *passim*; DS 31.18a; App. *Syr.* 66 (where it is claimed that he succeeded in plundering the shrine); Joseph. *AJ* 12.354–59; Porph. *FGrH* 260 F 53, 56; cf. Mørkholm, *Antiochus IV* 170–71. Cf. above, pp. 422, 439.

112. 1 Macc. 1.20–28, which in detail clearly refers to the second, more punitive expedition of 168; cf. Dan. 11.28, 2 Macc. 5.21, Joseph. *AJ* 12.247. For the date of the earlier visit cf. 1 Macc. 1.16–20, where it is located in Seleucid year 143, i.e., between spring 169 and spring 168 (Schürer 1.153). Impecuniosity as a motive for raiding the Temple: Joseph. *Cont. Ap.* 2.83, 84 (citing Polybius and Strabo in passages now lost). Antiochus IV's habit of desecrating shrines (perhaps referring specifically to Egypt): Polyb. 30.26.9.

113. Cf. Mørkholm, *Antiochus IV* 143.

114. 2 Macc. 5.1 refers quite specifically to τὴν δευτέραν ἔφοδον. I am suspicious of attempts, for whatever motive, to force this clear statement into a description of two putative phases in the first Egyptian campaign: cf. Schürer 1.128–9, 153.

115. 2 Macc. 1.8, 5.5–6; Joseph. *AJ* 12.239.

116. Joseph. *AJ* 12.240, *BJ* 1.31–32.

117. Joseph. *BJ* 1.32: πολὺ πλῆθος τῶν Πτολεμαίῳ προσεχόντων ἀναιρεῖ. Cf. Polyb. 5.86.10, Hieron. *In Dan.* 11.14, Bickerman 44.

118. Joseph. *BJ* 1.32, *AJ* 12.240.

119. 2 Macc. 5.7–10; cf. Niese 3.231 n. 3. There was an alleged tradition (1 Macc. 12.71) that Spartans and Jews shared a common ancestry. For the antecedents of this belief, cf. Momigliano, *Alien Wisdom* 113–14, and Hengel, *Jews* 116–17, who suggests that such ancestral myths "served as an ideological preparation for the transformation of Jerusalem into a Greek *polis* after 175 BC." One does not need to subscribe to the modern myth of Jerusalem-as-*polis* to see the value of a connection with the most notoriously intransigent, individualistic, anti-League and anti-Successor state in Greece.

120. 2 Macc. 5.11: τεθηριωμένος.

121. Joseph. *AJ* 12.246.

122. 2 Macc. 5.12–13, Joseph. *BJ* 1.32; Dan. 11.29–30.

123. 2 Macc. 5.14.

124. 2 Macc. 5.15–16, 21; Joseph. *AJ* 12.247, cf. 249–50 (wrongly assigned to Apollonius's actions in 167), *BJ* 1.32.

125. 2 Macc. 5.22–23.

126. 1 Macc. 1.29–30, 34, 38, cf. 6.26, 9.53, 15.28; 2 Macc. 23–26 *passim*; Joseph. *AJ* 12.251, cf. Dan. 11.39; Schürer 1.154; Hengel, *Judaism* 1.281.

127. 1 Macc. 1.29: ἄρχοντα φορολογίας.

128. Mørkholm, *Antiochus IV* 146. The Jews certainly assumed that Antiochus's aims were financial: see, e.g., Joseph. *AJ* 12.237, 248–50, *Cont. Ap.* 2.83–84; 1 Macc. 3.27, 2 Macc. 4.1–9.

129. Cf. Hengel, *Judaism* 281–82.

130. Tcherikover, 191, argues that "it was not the revolt which came as a response to persecution, but the persecution which came as a response to the revolt": there may be something in this, but it remains at best a half-truth; and Tcherikover's thesis of an organized ethnic insurrection *before* Antiochus's sacking of Jerusalem, and largely organized by the Hasidim, lacks any real support in the evidence.

131. See in particular Bickerman 83 ff., and Hengel, *Judaism* 1.286 ff.; cf. Joseph. *AJ* 12.252.

132. Bickerman 88.

133. Bringmann, 184, sees this very clearly: "Die Politik des Königs folgte pragmatischen, nicht ideologischen Zielen." He also associates it with increase of tribute and loyalty to the king's interests. Cf. Joseph. *AJ* 12.261; 2 Macc. 11.19, cf. 4.2, 8.8; 1 Macc. 3.29–31.

134. Cf. Hengel, *Judaism* 1.285. For a fine specimen of this issue, see the gold stater published by Kraay and Hirmer, no. 749, pl. 206 (cf. p. 374).

135. Hengel, *Judaism* 1.285, with full testimonia.

136. Bunge, "Antiochos" 164 ff.

137. 1 Macc. 1.41–42: καὶ ἔγραψεν ὁ βασιλεὺς πάσῃ τῇ βασιλείᾳ αὐτοῦ εἶναι πάντας εἰς λαὸν ἕνα καὶ ἐγκαταλιπεῖν ἕκαστον τὰ νόμιμα αὐτοῦ.

138. 1 Macc. 1.43, 52–53.

139. 1 Macc. 1.44–64; 2 Macc. 6.1–11; Joseph. *AJ* 12.253–54; Dan. 7.25, 8.11 ff., 11.31 ff., 12.11.

140. 2 Macc. 6.8–9.

141. Joseph. *AJ* 12.257–64; cf. Mørkholm, *Antiochus IV* 147–48; Momigliano, *Alien Wisdom* 108 ff.; Eddy 213. Cf. Burstein, *Translated Documents* no. 42, pp. 55–57.

142. Cf. Bickerman 88 ff., chap. 5 §4, "The Ideology of Persecution."

143. 2 Macc. 6.9: τοὺς δὲ μὴ προαιρουμένους μεταβαίνειν ἐπὶ τὰ Ἑλληνικὰ κατασφάζειν.

144. 1 Macc. 1.60–61, 2 Macc. 6.10, Joseph. *AJ* 12.256.

145. 1 Macc. 1.47; 2 Macc. 6.21, 7.1.

146. Cf. Bickerman 88, who reminds us that not only did the taboo extend to Syrians, Phoenicians, and Arabs, but that even "among the Greeks, as a rule, the pig was customary only for sacrifices that were considered unfit for human consumption."

147. Cf. Bickerman 73.

148. Dan. 11.31; cf. Hengel, *Judaism* 1.296–97. LXX Hellenizes this phrase as βδέλυγμα τῆς ἐρημώσεως.

149. 1 Macc. 1.54, 59; Joseph. *AJ* 12.253–54.

150. 1 Macc. 2.16, 23, 6.21; Dan. 9.27.

151. 1 Macc. 1.62–63, 2 Macc. 6.18–7.42 *passim*; cf. Schürer 1.155–56.

152. 1 Macc. 2.29–38, 2 Macc. 6.11, Joseph. *AJ* 12.272–75; cf. Mørkholm, *Antiochus IV* 148.

153. Cf. Bickerman 91.

154. Joseph. *AJ* 12.267.

155. 2 Macc. 6.4–5; cf. Tcherikover 195.

156. "Der Ursprung der Familie," Niese (3.234) points out, "ist dunkel." He argues, plausibly, that it was both aristocratic and, more interestingly, not wholly untouched by Hellenizing influences, a fact that would illuminate the family's later history. Note the appearance of Greek names—Eupolemos, Dositheos, Sosipatros—among its early adherents: 1 Macc. 8.17; 2 Macc. 4.11, 12.19.

157. Narrative in 1 Macc. 2 *passim*, 2 Macc. 8.1, Joseph. *AJ* 12.265–85; cf. Abel, *Histoire* 132 ff.; Schürer 1.156 ff.; Mørkholm, *Antiochus IV* 148 ff.; Tcherikover, chap. 6, 204 ff. (with reservations); Russell, chap. 4, 43 ff.

158. 1 Macc. 2.19–22; cf. Joseph. *AJ* 12.269.

159. 1 Macc. 2.27.

160. Cf. Schürer 1.158 with n. 49.

161. 1 Macc. 2.41.

162. Cf. Hengel, *Judaism* 1.175 ff., *Jews* 123 ff.; Eddy 217–18.

163. 1 Macc. 2.49–70 *passim*, Joseph. *AJ* 12.279–84.

164. 1 Macc. 3.10–12, Joseph. *AJ* 12.287.

165. 1 Macc. 3.13–24, Joseph. *AJ* 12.288–92 (Josephus claims that Seron, too, was killed).

166. Joseph. *AJ* 12.295–96, 2 Macc. 11.1.

167. 1 Macc. 3.38–4.25 *passim*; 2 Macc. 8.8–29, 34–36; Joseph. *AJ* 12.298–312.

168. 1 Macc. 4.28–35, Joseph. *AJ* 12.313–15. It has been suggested, wrongly in my opinion, that this battle was a fabrication: see Mørkholm, *Antiochus IV* 152–54, and, for a brief but cogent refutation, Schürer 1.160 n. 69.

169. 2 Macc. 11.15.

170. 2 Macc. 11.15–21, 27–33. The term δαπανήμασιν (2 Macc. 11.31) is ambiguous: see Mørkholm, *Antiochus IV* 156 and n. 63, who translates it as "expenditures," against Bickerman's rendering, "food-laws" (p. 79). The supposed letter to the γερουσία from a Roman commission on this occasion (2 Macc. 11.34–38) may well be fictitious, and, even if genuine, should be taken as nothing more than the usual polite endorsement: cf. the sharp analysis by Gruen, *HW* 745–47, app. 2, "The First Encounter of Rome and the Jews." See also Burstein, *Translated Documents* no. 43, pp. 57–58. The supposed effusion of Antiochus to the Jews recorded at 2 Macc. 9.18–27 is also (like most of that chapter) a pious fiction. See C. Habicht, "Royal Documents in Maccabees II, *HSCP* 80 (1976) 1–18 (though I do not accept all his conclusions on the other events described here).

171. So Will, *HP*² 2.342.

172. Cf. McCullough 118, though this crucial problem, so central to any country that has been ravaged by civil war of a guerilla nature, is only mentioned in passing.

173. Eddy, 217, is the only modern scholar known to me who shows clear awareness of the implications of this conclusion.

174. Not, as has been suggested (e.g., by Eddy 218–19), on hearing the news of Antiochus's death, since this took place at the very earliest shortly before 20 November, and may have fallen several weeks later: cf. Mørkholm, *Antiochus IV* 171 with n. 19 and further bibliography.

175. 1 Macc. 4.36–59, 2 Macc. 10.1–8, Joseph. *AJ* 12.316–26.

176. Cf. McCullough 119.

177. 1 Macc. 4.60–61, Joseph. *AJ* 12.326.

178. 2 Macc. 12.2 ff., 1 Macc. 5.9 ff.; cf. Niese 3.239.

179. 1 Macc. 5. *passim*, Joseph. *AJ* 12.327–53, 2 Macc. 12.10–31; cf. Schürer 1.164–65; Eddy 218–19; McCullough 119–20.

180. Well discussed by Eddy, 219 ff.

181. Schürer 1.165.

182. 1 Macc. 6.18–27, Joseph. *AJ* 12.364–66.

183. 1 Macc. 6.28–54; 2 Macc. 13.1–22; Joseph. *AJ* 12.369–78, *BJ* 1.41–46.

184. 2 Macc. 11.22–26.

185. 1 Macc. 6.63, 7.1–4; 2 Macc. 14.1–2; Joseph. *AJ* 12.386–90; Livy, *per.* 46; App. *Syr.* 47; Just. 34.3.9.

186. 2 Macc. 13.4.

187. Joseph. *AJ* 12.385.

188. Cf. McCullough 123–24 with testimonia there cited.

189. Josephus's claim (*AJ* 12.387, cf. 20.235) that Lysias deliberately chose a non-Oniad

High Priest in Alkimos is probably false: see 2 Macc. 14.7, where Alkimos views the office as a προγονικὴ δόξα.

190. On Alkimos's appointment Onias IV gave up hope of succeeding to the office himself, and went instead to Egypt, where Ptolemy VI gave him a grant of land, on which he built a Jewish temple: Joseph. *AJ* 12.387–88, 13.62–73.

191. 1 Macc. 7.10–15, Joseph. *AJ* 12.395–96; cf. Schürer 1.169.

192. 1 Macc. 7.5.

193. 1 Macc. 7.6–9, 2 Macc. 14.3–10, Joseph. *AJ* 12.391–93.

194. 1 Macc. 7.10–18, Joseph. *AJ* 12.394–96.

195. 2 Macc. 14.6: οἱ λεγόμενοι τῶν Ἰουδαίων Ἀσιδαῖοι, ὧν ἀφηγεῖται Ἰούδας ὁ Μακκαβαῖος, πολεμοτροφοῦσιν καὶ στασιάζουν οὐκ ἐῶντες τὴν βασιλείαν εὐσταθείας τυχεῖν.

196. Joseph. *AJ* 12.396.

197. 1 Macc. 7.19–22, Joseph. *AJ* 12.397–400.

198. 2 Macc. 14.3, 7.13; 1 Macc. 7.11–12; Joseph. *AJ* 12.393–94.

199. Gruen, *HW* 42–46, 748 ff. On 1 Macc. 8.22–32, see Burstein, *Translated Documents* no. 44, pp. 58–59. For Judas's envoy, the writer Eupolemos, see Bartlett 56–71.

200. 1 Macc. 8.31–32.

201. 1 Macc. 9.6–21, Joseph. *AJ* 12.422–34.

202. 1 Macc. 9.50–53, Joseph. *AJ* 13.15–17.

203. 1 Macc. 9.54–56, Joseph. *AJ* 12.413.

204. Josephus (*AJ* 12.414) claims that Judas Maccabaeus became High Priest on Alkimos's death; but, apart from the chronological problem involved (Judas almost certainly died before Alkimos), 1 Maccabees makes no mention of his having held this office, and Josephus himself elsewhere (*AJ* 20.237) states that after Alkimos's death there was no High Priest in Jerusalem for seven years, i.e., until Jonathan's appointment in 152 (cf. p. 523). An early rabbinical tradition asserted that *all* Mattathias's sons had been High Priest in turn (cf. Marcus et al. 7.216, note *a*), which probably explains the error: this was the only available point at which Judas's high priesthood could be inserted.

205. 1 Macc. 10.22–45, Joseph. *AJ* 13.47–57.

206. 1 Macc. 10.15–21, Joseph. *AJ* 13.43–46.

207. 1 Macc. 10.22–45; cf. Schürer 1.178–79 with n. 14.

208. 1 Macc. 10.51–66, Joseph. *AJ* 13.80–85.

209. 1 Macc. 11.20–37, Joseph. *AJ* 13.120–28.

210. 1 Macc. 12.41–53, 13.1–24; Joseph. *AJ* 13.196–212.

211. 1 Macc. 13.1–9, Joseph. *AJ* 13.197–200.

212. 1 Macc. 13.34–42, Joseph. *AJ* 13.214.

213. 1 Macc. 13.49–52, 14.37; Joseph. *AJ* 13.215–17 (the statement that Simon leveled the Akra rather than refortifying and regarrisoning it is erroneous: Josephus may here be confusing Simon with John Hyrcanus; cf. *BJ* 5.139).

214. 1 Macc. 13.43–48, 14.5.

215. 1 Macc. 14.41–46.

216. 1 Macc. 14.6–15.

217. Morton Smith, *Palestinian Parties and Politics That Shaped the Old Testament* (New York, 1971) 64, 231–32 n. 57.

218. Joseph. *AJ* 14.145–48.

Chapter 30. Ptolemaic and Seleucid Decadence and the Rise of Parthia, 145–116

1. Gruen, *HW* 527 with n. 230; cf. Accame 11–14.

2. Paus. 7.16.9–10; cf. Polyb. 39.3.9–5.3. *SIG*³ 684 = Sherk, *Roman Documents* no. 43, pp. 246 ff., lines 9–10, confirms the existence of an Achaean πολιτεία in 115 (and perhaps as early as 144/3). An enormous amount of legalistic ink has been spilled over the academic question of Greece's administrative status between 146 and the Augustan settlement of 27: see, e.g.,

Accame chap. 1, 1 ff., with earlier bibliography; Schwertfeger chap. 3, 19 ff.; Gruen, *HW* 523 ff. The general consensus has been that some *poleis* were placed under the governor of Macedonia, others left free. But in what did this theoretical "freedom" consist (cf. *SIG*³ 684, lines 15–16), and how much substantive meaning did it possess? As Gruen, *HW* 527, says, "the emasculation of Greece, for all practical purposes, was complete."

3. Polyb. fr. 166 Hultsch = Athen. 6.273a; DS 33.28b.4. I owe this interpretation to some sensible remarks of Walbank in his review of Schwertfeger, *CR* 26 (1976) 238.

4. Accame 163 ff.; cf. Ferguson, *HA* chap. 8, 312 ff.; Mossé, *Athens* 138 ff.

5. Ferguson, *HA* 367, claims that "Athens was never so devoted to Rome as during the sixties, fifties and forties of the second century." Devoted? The epithet he is looking for is "subservient."

6. Livy 43.6.1–3.

7. R. E. Smith, *The Failure of the Roman Republic* (Cambridge, 1955) 12.

8. Accame 164; Tracy 231: "In the years after the acquisition of Delos in 167/6 the Athenians pursued vigorously and successfully a course of commercial leadership, based ultimately, however, on Rome's good will."

9. Cf. Ferguson, *HA* 420; Tracy 227–29.

10. For a concise demolition of Ferguson's theory, first proposed in *Klio* 4 (1904) 1–17, and further developed in *HA* 425–37, see Badian, "Rome, Athens, and Mithridates" 105–6.

11. Athen. 5.212f.

12. Ferguson, *HA* 366–67, 417–18; Mossé, *Athens* 142–43.

13. Hansen 295–98, Travlos, *Pictorial Dictionary* 505–35.

14. Travlos, ibid. 402–11; R. E. Wycherley, "The Olympieion at Athens," *GRByS* 5 (1964) 161–79.

15. Ferguson, *HA* 372–73; cf. Accame 165.

16. Ferguson, *HA* 377–78.

17. Plin. *HN* 34.52.

18. Polyb. 39.2.2 = Strabo 8.6.23 (C.381): the pictures included (almost too aptly) one of Heracles in agony, wearing the shirt of Nessus.

19. Vell. Pat. 1.13.4.

20. Will, *HP*² 2.394, correctly stresses the *political* motives behind Rome's decision to authorize the destruction of Corinth: "la destruction de Corinthe est . . . un 'exemple' destiné à terroriser la Grèce et à en finir une fois pour toutes avec l'agitation et les intrigues des politiciens du Péloponnèse et de Grèce centrale." The parallel with Alexander's sack of Thebes in 335 is inescapable. At the same time it remains true that, even if direct economic calculations did not dictate this punitive act (cf. above, p. 452, and, for a discussion of the theories, Will, ibid. 2.395–96), Roman and other businessmen must have done very well out of Corinth's elimination as an Aegean entrepôt. "Thou shalt not kill, yet need'st not strive, officiously, to keep alive."

21. Cf. Ferguson, *HA* 354 ff.

22. Polyb. 36.17.5 ff.

23. It hardly needs saying that the nationalist-religious insurrection led by the Maccabees falls into a quite different category, as Rostovtzeff (despite his obsession with a bourgeois-proletarian dichotomy) was well aware: see Rostovtzeff, *SEH* 2.805 ff., and (though here he hedges his bets) 2.705. McShane 194–95 is not so cautious.

24. There has, predictably, been a movement (which I find in essence unconvincing) to interpret Aristonicus as a utopian social reformer or advocate of slave emancipation: see, e.g., Rostovtzeff, *SEH* 2.807 ff.; Vogt 93 ff.; Vavřínek 203 ff. (more fully in "La révolte d'Aristonicos," *Rozpravy Československa Ved.* 67 [Prague, 1957] 1–69, not available to me); Delplace 33 ff.; Mossé, *Tyrannie* chap. 5, 193–201. *Contra*, Carrata Thomes 55 ff., Hopp 135 ff. The peculiar dearth of radical ideologizing in the ancient world means that any seeming exception tends to get promoted well beyond its merits.

25. Cf. Green, "First Sicilian Slave War" 20.

26. Dumont 195 suggests, cynically, that what Aristonicus in fact had in mind with his

Heliopolis was a regular military colony in which all slaves and other "éléments socialement dangereux" could be sequestered after victory, thus minimizing the risk of subsequent insurrection. Its creation, he argues, "aurait peut-être procédé d'un esprit plus conservateur que révolutionnaire." The only thing wrong with this ingenious and delightful notion is that it does not have one shred of evidence to support it.

27. Collins 83 ff.

28. Strabo 14.1.38 (C.646).

29. Allen 112; Gruen, *HW* 595 with n. 101.

30. Eutrop. 4.20.1, Plut. *Flam.* 21, Just. 36.4.6. Africa, "Aristonicus" 113, correctly defines the Pergamene rebellion as "a royalist *Jacquerie* rather than a Spartacus revolt." Cf. Allen 85. Since writing this chapter I have read two articles that independently confirm my interpretation of Aristonicus's motives: J. R. Martínez, "La rebelión de Aristónico: Un movimiento utópico antiguo?" *Anuario de Historia*, México Facultad de Filosofia y Letras, 11 (1983) 31–39; and C. Mileta, "Der Aristonikosaufstand," *Altertum* 31 (1985) 119–23.

31. It has also had its effect on conservative scholars: Magie, 1.31–32, 151, described Aristonicus as "a foe to Hellenic civilization" who "was wholly unfitted to be king of Pergamum" even though he was (148) "a man of boldness and ability." Cf. Rostovtzeff, *SEH* 1.756 ff., 806 ff.

32. For a convenient conspectus of numerous uniformly implausible theories as to Attalus's motives, see Gruen, *HW* 593–96 with n. 94.

33. Gruen, ibid. with n. 102.

34. Plut. *Ti. Gracch.* 14; Strabo 13.4.2 (C.624); Livy, *per.* 58, 59; App. *Mithr.* 62; Plin. *HN* 33.148; Vell. Pat. 2.4.1; Just. 36.45; *OGIS* 338, translation in Sherk, *Translated Documents* 39, pp. 39–40; cf. Larsen, in Frank 4.505 n. 1; Will, *HP*² 2.416–19; Gruen, *HW* 592 ff.

35. Africa, "Aristonicus" 111; cf. Badian, *Foreign Clientelae* 173–74, *Roman Imperialism* 21–22, 48–50; Gruen, *HW* 599–600. I prefer not to add to the more or less wild ideological speculation on just why, after the death of Tiberius Gracchus, the Stoic Blossius of Cumae sought refuge with Aristonicus, and committed suicide when the insurrection failed. Sensible comments in Dudley, "Blossius" 94 ff., esp. 98–99, and Carrata Thomes 59–60 with n. 45. His motives were almost certainly political rather than doctrinal. As Carrata Thomes says, "dopo l'uccisione di Ti. Gracco, è abbastanza naturale che Blossio cerchi scampo fuori d'Italia e possibilmente presso un nemico di Roma."

36. Just. 36.4.1–5, DS 34/35.3.

37. E.g., by Magie, 1.150, and Carrata Thomes, 49.

38. Strabo 14.1.38 (C.646), Oros. 5.10.2, Eutrop. 4.20.1.

39. So Gruen, *HW* 601–2.

40. Strabo 14.1.38 (C.646), Just. 37.1.2, Eutrop. 4.20.1–2, Oros. 5.10.2. We should take particular note in this context of *OGIS* 338 (pp. 533 ff.) = Austin 211 (pp. 343–45), also translated by Africa, "Aristonicus" 113–14, a Pergamene decree the liberality of which (citizenship to resident aliens, etc.) is best explained (so Africa and others; most lately Gruen, *HW* 596) as an emergency response to the rebellion then in progress, and an index of the alarm it was causing among the bourgeoisie. A rather different explanation in Delplace 21 ff.

41. Strabo, *loc. cit.* (n. 40); Just. 36.4.6–12; DS 34/35.2.26; cf. Larsen, in Frank 4.505–7 with nn. 4–22; Vogt 54 ff., 69 ff., 93–102.

42. Broughton, *Magistrates* 1.503. Gruen, *HW* 602, comments: "not the last Crassus whose head would become the sport of an eastern potentate." Cf. below, p. 560.

43. DS 34/35.2.21–22; Livy, *per.* 59, Flor. 2.7.8–9; cf. Oros. 5.8.6–8.

44. Eutrop. 4.20.2.

45. Just. 36.4.9–11, Strabo 14.1.38 (C.646), Vell. Pat. 2.4.1, Flor. 1.35.6–7, Val. Max. 3.4.5; cf. Hansen 155 ff.; Magie 1.147 ff.

46. Cf. Carrata Thomes 62–63 with nn. 55–56. We possess a somewhat cringing inscription of ca. 129, proclaiming Pergamon's alliance and friendship with Rome: *SIG*³ 694, translated in Sherk, *Translated Documents* 44, pp. 45–46. More realistic is the senatorial decree of the same year, dealing with boundary and territorial arrangements (Sherk, ibid., pp. 47–48).

47. On the vexed problem of annexation, see Rigsby 39 ff., and Gruen, *HW* 603 ff.

48. Welles, *Royal Correspondence* 246. The letter is edited by Welles, ibid. (no. 61), 245–46, 252–53; translation in Sherk, *Translated Documents* 29, pp. 28–29. It was only engraved (presumably from the archives) more than a century later; perhaps the priests then wished to recall that "their predecessors had corresponded with kings" (Welles 247).

49. Polyb. 28.7.9, Livy 42.5.1–3; cf. Hansen 108–9.

50. Cf. G. Cardinali, "La morte di Attalo III e la rivolta d'Aristonico," *Saggi di storia antica e di archeologia offerti a G. Beloch* (Rome, 1910) 269–320, esp. 278–80, though Cardinali is surely wrong in making this the *motive* for Attalus's bequest rather than leaving it as a probable future development.

51. Badian, *Roman Imperialism* 4. For the instructions given to Asiatic officials, see *OGIS* 435 (2.1–3) = Austin 214 (pp. 347–48), Sherk, *Roman Documents* 11 (pp. 59 ff.) and *Translated Documents* 40 (pp. 40–41). The decree should be dated in 129: so, convincingly, Gruen, *HW* 603–5; cf. Magie 2.1033–34 n. 1. *Contra*, Broughton, *Magistrates* 1.496–97 no. 1 (133); Badian, *JRS* 70 (1980) 202, who opts for 132; Sherk, *Translated Documents* ibid. (133).

52. App. *BC* 5.4 ff., discussed by Sherk, *Roman Documents* 67 ff., and Mattingly (below) 412 ff. One piece of evidence regularly adduced—cf. Gruen, *HW* 606 n. 140—in favor of activity by the *publicani* in Asia Minor as early as 129 is the *senatus consultum de agro Pergameno*: best edition and commentary by Sherk, ibid. no. 12, pp. 63–73, supplemented by the same author's revisions in *GRByS* 7 (1966) 361 ff., but not, surprisingly, included in Austin's selection. However, Magie 2.1045–47 nn. 34–36, and in particular 1055–56 n. 25, argued for a 101 date, the consulship (with C. Marius) of the younger M'. Aquillius. This thesis is supported by Gruen, *HW* 606–7, and, despite the objections lodged against it (see, e.g., Sherk p. 72), seems to me entirely plausible. As Magie says, *inter alia* (p. 1055), "it is hard to believe that a controversy between the *publicani* and the Pergamenes could have arisen as early as 129, when the revolt of Aristonicus had scarcely been quelled." Cf. Gruen, ibid. n. 146, and H. B. Mattingly, "The Date of the *Senatus Consultum De Agro Pergameno*," *AJPh* 93 (1972) 412–23.

53. Cf. Badian, *Roman Imperialism* 47–48, *Publicans* 63–64.

54. Magie 1.157–58, 2.1048–49 (nn. 39–40); Gruen, *HW* 605–6. For Aquillius's milestones, see Sherk, *Translated Documents* 42, p. 43, and the testimonia there assembled.

55. Magie 1.158.

56. Cf. Gruen, *HW* 601, who rightly characterizes the Attalid dynasty as "the bulwark of stability in Asia Minor."

57. Cf. Will, *HP*² 2.422.

58. Debevoise 19.

59. Just. 41.6.7; cf. Debevoise 21.

60. The scattered and ambiguous testimonia are well analyzed by Will, *HP*² 2.349–50, 400–403, 407–8; cf. Debevoise 22 ff.

61. Joseph. *AJ* 13.131–70, 174–224, *BJ* 1.48–50; 1 Macc. 11.39–15.39 *passim*; App. *Syr.* 68; DS 33.4a; Livy, *per.* 52, 55; Strabo 16.2.10 (C.752); further testimonia collected by Fischer, "Zu Tryphon" 201 n. 2, and evaluated in Fischer, *Untersuchungen* 5–25.

62. 1 Macc. 11.41–51, Joseph. *AJ* 13.133–42, DS 33.4.2–3.

63. 1 Macc. 11.30–59, esp. 54 ff.; Joseph. *AJ* 13.145–47; DS 33.4a; App. *Syr.* 68.

64. 1 Macc. 12.1–38, Joseph. *AJ* 13.148–86.

65. 1 Macc. 12.39–53, 13.1–24; Joseph. *AJ* 13.187–212.

66. 1 Macc. 13.31 ff., Joseph. *AJ* 13.218 ff., Strabo 16.2.10 (C.752); DS 33.28–28a, App. *Syr.* 68, Just. 36.1.7.

67. Just. 36.1.2–4.

68. Just. 36.1.2–7, 38.9.2–3; Joseph. *AJ* 13.184–86; App. *Syr.* 67; 1 Macc. 14.1–3; cf. Will, *HP*² 2.407; Debevoise 25.

69. Tarn, *CAH* VIII 528; cf. Will, *HP*² 2.408: "comptant évidemment le jeter dans les jambes de tout Séleucide, vrai ou faux, qui tenterait de relancer l'aventure."

70. Cf. Just. 38.9.3, Joseph. *AJ* 13.221–22.

71. 1 Macc. 15.1 ff., Joseph. *AJ* 13.222 ff., App. *Syr.* 68.

72. 1 Macc. 15.10, Joseph. *AJ* 13.222, Athen. 8.333b–d, DS 33.28.

73. 1 Macc. 15.1–39; Joseph. *AJ* 13.220–24, *BJ* 1.50; Strabo 14.5.2 (C.668); Just. 36.1.8; App. *Syr.* 68; Front. *Strat.* 2.13.2; cf. Fischer, "Zu Tryphon" 213 with n. 54, for the date of Tryphon's death.

74. 1 Macc. 16.11–17, Joseph. *AJ* 13.228–30.

75. See in general Joseph. *AJ* 13.219–48, *BJ* 1.50–61; App. *Syr.* 68; DS 24.1; Strabo 14.5.2 (C.668).

76. Just. 38.10.2–5, DS 34.17.1, Joseph. *AJ* 13.251–52. The numbers given are clearly much exaggerated.

77. Just. 38.10.5–6; DS 34.15–17, 19; Joseph. *AJ* 13.251; App. *Syr.* 68.

78. Just. 38.9.2–10.

79. Just. 38.10.7, DS 34.15.

80. So, rightly, Debevoise 31.

81. Just. 38.10.7.

82. Just. 38.10.8, DS 34.17.2.

83. Joseph. *AJ* 13.249–53.

84. Just. 38.10.10; cf. DS 34.16–17.

85. Just. ibid. and 39.1.6, App. *Syr.* 68.

86. Debevoise 35.

87. Athen. 10.439e.

88. Just. 38.10.9–11, 42.1 *passim*; DS 34.15–19 *passim*; Joseph. *AJ* 13.249–53; App. *Syr.* 68; cf. Debevoise 35 ff.

89. Just. 38.9.2–10, 39.1.3; App. *Syr.* 68; cf. Bouché-Leclercq, *HL* 2.76 n. 2.

90. Joseph. *AJ* 13.254–58; cf. *BJ* 1.62–63.

91. Just. 39.1.2; cf. 38.9.1. For the complex domestic intrigues and upheavals of the Alexandrian court during the reigns of Ptolemy VIII Physcon and Ptolemy IX Lathyros the detailed study of Otto and Bengtson still remains indispensable. Those familiar with this magisterial, if opinionated, work will recognize its influence throughout what follows, even where it is not directly cited.

92. Otto and Bengtson 25–26 with n. 2.

93. Otto and Bengtson, 26, theorize that L. Minucius Felix, the Roman ambassador, took a hand in this business on Physcon's behalf. All in fact we know is that he was in Alexandria at the time (Joseph. *Cont. Ap.* 2.50), and without further positive evidence such meddling strikes me as improbable in the extreme.

94. Cf. Fraser 1.121, with reff. 2.214 ff. See esp. Joseph. *Cont. Ap.* 2.49–50, 52.

95. Cf. Poseidonius *ap.* Athen. 12.549c.

96. For the text of the amnesty, see *SEG* 12 (1955) 548 (p. 143: much restored). Otto and Bengtson, 26, observe that he was, for propaganda purposes, making a particular effort "sich als gnädigen Herrscher zu erweisen und so das Land auf seine Seit zu bringen."

97. Just. 38.8.2–4, Oros. 5.10.6–7; cf. Joseph. *Cont. Ap.* 2.51; Otto and Bengtson 28–29.

98. *PBerl.* 3101; cf. Otto and Bengtson 29.

99. Cf. Otto and Bengtson 51 ff.

100. DS 33.13.

101. For Physcon's hostility to the Jews, see, e.g., Joseph. *Cont. Ap.* 2.51–55.

102. The Greek literary world, Athens in particular, got its revenge on Physcon by systematically blackening his name for all time as a monster of depravity, so that some of the more lurid anecdotes in the tradition may need to be taken with a grain of Attic salt; but the course of events suggests that the gossipmongers had more than enough genuine material to work with. Even so, the Ptolemaea, the lavish festival associated with the Lagids' ruler cult, was not discontinued: see, e.g., IG II² 963.3 for its celebration c. 140. I owe this reference to Prof. C. Habicht.

103. See DS 33.20, 22, for his expulsion of Galaestes, and the latter's activities in Cleopatra II's service, well analyzed by Otto and Bengtson, 36 ff.

104. DS 33.13: the charge, as reported, was that they had openly criticized Ptolemy's favorite concubine.

105. Cf. Fraser 1.311, with reff. 2.466.

106. Fraser 1.86, 121, 332–33, 462, 467–68, 538–39; *POxy.* 10.1241, col. 2, lines 16–17.

107. Polyb. 34.14.1–7 = Strabo 17.1.12 (C.797); Val. Max. 9.2.5; Menecles *FGrH* 270 F 9 = *FHG* 4.451 (Athen. 4.184b–c); Just. 38.8.6–7; DS 33.6, 6a, 12.

108. See, e.g., Just. 38.8.5; DS 33.6, 6a, 12.

109. DS 33.13, 34/35.14; Just. 38.8.11.

110. Cf. Volkmann, *RE* 23.2 (1959) cols. 1727–29, s.v. "Ptolemaios (27)."

111. Otto and Bengtson 35.

112. DS 33.28b.1–3, Athen. 549d–e, Just. 38.8.8–10, Plut. *Mor.* 200F–201A, cf. 777A. On Cleopatra II's dating and titulature in the papyri, see Samuel, *Ptolemaic Chronology* 145 ff.; Pomeroy, *Women* 23–24.

113. DS 33.28b.1–3, Athen. 6.273a.

114. Correct insofar as it went, this judgment should not be interpreted as an official recommendation either to annex or to ensure a weak Ptolemaic regime (cf. Gruen, *HW* 714–15): the first had, as yet, no appeal in Rome, while the second could safely be left to take care of itself.

115. Livy, *per.* 59; Just. 38.8.11, cf. DS 33.6, 6a; Otto and Bengtson 47 ff.

116. "Die wankelmütigen Massen der Hauptstadt," as Otto and Bengtson, 57, justifiably describe them—but also, shrewdly (p. 58), as "das wenig erfreuliche 'Ersatzgebilde' für die alte makedonische Heeresversammlung"; cf. n. 3, pp. 58–59.

117. Just. 38.8.13–14, DS 34.14, Livy, *per.* 59.

118. Otto and Bengtson 70.

119. Ibid. 97 ff.

120. Just. 38.9.1, 39.1.2; *PTeb.* 1.72 line 45, cited by Otto and Bengtson 65; cf. Bouché-Leclercq, *HL* 4.323.

121. Otto and Bengtson 94.

122. Just. 39.1.4.

123. Cf. Will, *HP²* 2.432–34, with his analysis of the sources.

124. Euseb. *Chron.* 1.257–58 Schoene; Just. 39.1.4–5 makes him an adopted son of Antiochus VII Sidetes. Perhaps he told both stories at different times.

125. Cf. Bevan, *House of Seleucus* 2.249 n. 3.

126. DS 34/35.22.

127. Jenkins n. 531, p. 220, cf. p. 271: a rare gold stater, probably minted from the melted-down Nike of Antiochus Epiphanes (cf. n. 136 below).

128. Joseph. *AJ* 13.267–69; App. *Syr.* 68–69; Livy, *per.* 60; Just. 39.1.7–9; cf. Bevan, *House of Seleucus* 2.248–50.

129. So, rightly, Will, *HP²* 2.435.

130. Otto and Bengtson, 104, rule out the possibility of a genuine *Versöhnung*: "Die beiden Partner haben sich allein aus nüchternen staatspolitischen Erwägungen wieder zusammengefunden, wobei sehr wohl ein gewisser äusserer Zwang mitgewirkt haben kann." In any case the "reconciliation" very soon began to show signs of strain. Cf. Just. 39.2.1–2.

131. Cf. Otto and Bengtson 104: "Jedenfalls hat Euergetes in Alexander Zabinas schliesslich einen nicht ungefährlichen Gegner gesehen."

132. Joseph. *AJ* 13.365.

133. App. *Syr.* 68–69; Just. 39.1.9; Livy, *per.* 60. Seleucus V's fault, it seems, was that of Prince Hal: an unseemly haste to assume the royal diadem.

134. Just. 39.2.1–3.

135. Cf. Davis and Kraay nos. 110, 115.

136. Just. 39.2.4–6, DS 34/35.28, App. *Syr.* 68–69; cf. Niese 3.307 ff.; Otto and Bengtson

104. Justin reports that Zabinas, after looting Antiochus Epiphanes' large gold statue of Nike from the temple of Zeus, joked that Jupiter had lent him Victory ("Uictoriam commodatam sibi ab Iove esse").

137. Just. 39.2.7–9, App. *Syr.* 69; cf. A. R. Bellinger, "The End of the Seleucids," *Transactions of the Connecticut Academy of Arts and Sciences* 38 (1949) 51–102.

138. Poseidonius *ap.* Athen. 5.210e, 12.540a–b; Galen 14.185 Kühn; cf. Bevan, *House of Seleucus* 2.252–53.

139. The poem is entitled "They Should Have Taken the Trouble . . ." (Ἄς φρόντιζαν . . .): Cavafy, Ποιήματα Β' 85–86 = *Collected Poems* 322–25. For "the Malefactor," cf. above, p. 538.

140. Otto and Bengtson 107.

141. Hunt and Edgar 2.210, pp. 58–75 = Austin 231, pp. 382–88; cf. Rostovtzeff, *SEH* 2.713–36, 870–914, esp. 878 ff.; Otto and Bengtson 109 ff. See also Turner, *CAH* VII².1 159 ff.; Burstein, *Translated Documents* no. 107, pp. 139–41.

142. Austin p. 382.

143. Bevan, *House of Ptolemy* 325; cf. Will, *HP²* 2.440.

PART FIVE. ROME TRIUMPHANT, 116–30 B.C.

Chapter 31. Mithridates, Sulla, and the Freedom of the Greeks, 116–80

1. The dominant strain in these formidable women is attributed by Diodorus (1.27.2), not altogether convincingly, to Egyptian tradition prescribing that καταδειχθῆναι μείζονος ἐξουσίας καὶ τιμῆς τυγχάνειν τὴν βασίλισσαν τοῦ βασιλέως, καὶ παρὰ τοῖς ἰδιώταις κυριεύειν τὴν γυναῖκα τἀνδρός. For a similar, earlier notion, cf. Soph. *OC* 337 ff.

2. Cf. Will, *HP²* 2.441.

3. Strabo 14.5.2 (C.668–69).

4. Strabo 17.1.8 (C.797), *Chron. Pasch.* p. 347 Bonn. ὁ κόκκης, said of Ptolemy X Alexander, is clearly a possessive, i.e., "son of Kokke." Bouché-Leclercq, *HL* 2.95, connects the word with its color sense of "scarlet" and speaks of "le digne fils de la vieille 'Bourgeon-née,'" as though Cleopatra III were some Hogarthian toper, while Bevan, *House of Seleucus* 326 n. 2, asserts that "it is idle to conjecture" the meaning. This may perhaps be because Hesychius gives the slang meaning of κόκκος as "vagina," which suggests that the queen may have been known to her irreverent subjects in Alexandria as Cleopatra the Cunt, with ὁ κόκκης, in Ptolemy X's case, conveying the equivalent of "son of a bitch."

5. Pausanias (1.9.1) remarks that this title was given to him in mocking irony (ἐπὶ χλευασμῷ) "since we know of none of these kings who was so detested by his mother."

6. Just. 39.5.2.

7. Cic. *Leg. Agr.* 1.1.1, 2.16.41–17.44. Bouché-Leclercq, *HL* 2.89–90, argues that the provision was made at Cleopatra III's urging, to enable her to set aside the law of primogeniture.

8. Will, *HP²* 2.440, suggests that Physcon's will may have guaranteed the Cyprus στρατηγία to whichever son did not ascend the throne in Alexandria.

9. Paus. 1.9.1–2.

10. Just. 39.3.1–2, 4.1; Paus. 1.9.1.

11. Cf. Bouché-Leclercq, *HL* 2.92.

12. Just. 39.3.3, DS 34/35.34.

13. Joseph. *AJ* 13.276–78: she came within an ace of expelling Lathyros from Egypt over this affair, ὅσον οὔπω τῆς ἀρχῆς αὐτὸν ἐκβεβληκυίας.

14. *PTeb.* 33 = Hunt and Edgar 2.416, pp. 566–67.

15. Just. 39.3.4–12; cf. Macurdy 164–65.

16. Will, *HP²* 2.440–48, assembles the scattered testimonia of this period: for the complexities, see, e.g., Joseph. *AJ* 13.365–71.

17. Just. 39.4.1–2, Paus. 1.9.2.

18. Just. 39.4.2, DS 34/35.39a.

19. Just. 39.4.4; cf. Macurdy 164–67.

20. Joseph. *AJ* 13.334–47.

21. Paus. 1.9.3, Just. 39.4.5, Poseidon. *ap.* Athen. 12.550a; cf. Bouché-Leclercq, *HL* 2.104–6.

22. Cf. Bouché-Leclercq, *HL* 2.105 with n. 1.

23. Poseidon. *ap.* Athen. 12.550b.

24. Will, *HP*² 2.520; Badian, *Roman Imperialism* 29–30, 35–37; Gruen, *HW* 716.

25. Euseb. *Chron.* 1.259 Schoene, Joseph. *AJ* 13.365, Trog. *prol.* 39.

26. Just. 39.4.4.

27. Another joke: App. *Syr.* 69 informs us that he got the title of "Pious" through marrying his stepmother, the ex-wife of both his father and his uncle, and, thus, "honoring" (i.e., endorsing) their choice. He also escaped a plot laid by his cousin Seleucus through the good offices of a prostitute who had fallen for his good looks.

28. App. *Syr.* 69, Joseph. *AJ* 13.368.

29. As Bouché-Leclercq, *HL* 2.108, remarks in this context, "il est relativement facile de suivre les desseins des grands politiques; il l'est moins de deviner les caprices des esprits faibles et des volontés changeantes."

30. I have a great sympathy with the comment of Will, *HP*² 2.445: "Il n'est d'autre moyen de suivre ces querelles que d'avoir sous les yeux un tableau généalogique."

31. Joseph. *AJ* 13.385–86.

32. Ibid. 387–91.

33. Ibid. 370–71; other sources (App. *Syr.* 49, 70; Porph. *ap.* Euseb. *Chron.* 1.261 Schoene) indicate that he was either driven out of Syria by Tigranes or else fled to the Parthian court to join Demetrius III.

34. App. *Syr.* 49, 70; Just. 40.2.2.

35. Strabo 17.1.8 (C.794). He replaced the gold coffin with one of alabaster.

36. Badian, "Testament" 184–85, 187, arguing cogently against the earlier assumption that the testator was Ptolemy XI Alexander II; cf. Harris 155.

37. Porph. *FGrH* 260 F 2, 8.

38. Just. 39.5.1.

39. Cf. Bouché-Leclercq, *HL* 2.111. For the Thebaid revolt, see Hunt and Edgar 2.417–18, pp. 568–70.

40. Paus. 1.9.3.

41. App. *Mithr.* 23 *ad fin.*

42. Cf. Bevan, *House of Ptolemy* 344–45.

43. Badian, "Testament" 188.

44. Plut. *Luc.* 2–3, App. *Mithr.* 33; cf. Reinach 199.

45. Cf. Bevan, *House of Seleucus* 2.263.

46. App. *Syr.* 48, Just. 40.1.3; cf. Koehler 10 ff.

47. Strabo 16.2.3 (C.749), Joseph. *AJ* 13.420.

48. In 80 Sulla was still consul, though probably by then no longer dictator; in any case his *auctoritas* remained immense. Cf. Badian, "Testament" 181, with n. 13.

49. App. *BC* 1.102, Euseb. *Chron.* 1.165 f. Schoene.

50. So, acutely, Badian, "Testament" 189 ff.

51. App. *Mithr.* 114, Suet. *Div. Jul.* 54, Dio Cass. 39.12.1, Joseph. *AJ* 14.35.

52. Caes. *BC* 3.107, Cic. *Att.* 2.16.2.

53. Strabo 17.1.11 (C.796).

54. Will, *HP*² 2.447.

55. E.g., Cic. *Brut.* 306: "cum princeps Academiae Philo cum Atheniensium optimatibus Mithridatico bello domo profugisset."

56. Cf. McKendrick 59 ff.

57. Cic. *Att.* 5.21; 6.1, 2; cf. B. Baldwin, *The Roman Emperors* (Montreal, 1980) 1.

58. Cary, *CAH* IX 396.

59. *SIG*³ 684; cf. Rostovtzeff, *SEH* 2.757; Ste Croix 307; and for a general recent survey of "private gain and public interest" among Romans, Gruen, *HW* 299 ff. For instances of senatorial self-restraint in financial matters during the second century, cf. Harris 74 ff.

60. DS 36.2.2–6, 2a.

61. DS 36.3.1–2.

62. Ormerod, *CAH* IX 351; DS 36.3.2.

63. DS 36.3.3–6, 4–10; cf. Vogt 56–59.

64. Strabo 14.5.2 (C.668–69), Flor. 1.41.1–3; cf. Ormerod 190 ff., esp. 207 for the link between piracy and the slave trade; Will, *HP*² 2.464–48; Brulé 61 ff.

65. Tracy 214, 231; Nicolet 783–84; cf. Day 50 ff.

66. Garlan, "Signification" 1–16, analyzes the various aspects of piracy in the ancient world with some acumen, isolating four main types: (1) *ad hoc*, local, individual, and unorganized; (2) organized and mercantile, conducted for long-term profit by large groups; (3) covertly organized by the state for its own advantage (cf. Elizabeth I and Sir Francis Drake); (4) social, an aspect of resistance to invasion or oppression. We are chiefly concerned in the Hellenistic period with (2), but on occasion also with (3) and (4). On the employment by Hellenistic rulers of corsairs as mercenary entrepreneurs see J. J. Gabbert, *Greece and Rome* 33 (1986) 156–63.

67. App. *Mithr.* 92–93, Dio Cass. 36.20–23, Plut. *Pomp.* 24.

68. Livy, *per.* 68; Jul. Obs. 44. Piracy laws from this period recorded at Delphi and Cnidos are full of grandiloquent, not to say bureaucratic, pronouncements, but do not suggest effective concerted action. See Sherk, *Translated Documents* 55, pp. 58–66.

69. Will, *HP*² 2.467; Nicolet 780.

70. Garlan, "Signification" 6, discussing Strabo *loc. cit.* (n. 64).

71. Cic. *Pro Flac.* 60; App. *Mithr.* 10, 113; Plut. *Mor.* 624A–B; Athen. 5.212d; *OGIS* 370.

72. Suet. *Div. Jul.* 35, Eutrop. 6.22.2.

73. See Reinach, *passim*: superseded in some respects, but still, as Will, *HP*² 2.470, rightly stresses, indispensable. Our main sources on Mithridates—Appian, Plutarch—are both late and in a pro-Roman tradition: caution is needed in evaluating them. Memnon, *FGrH* 434 F 22.1–10, supplies a useful summary of Mithridates' rise, and his wars against the Romans. See Sherk, *Translated Documents* 56, pp. 66–67, for a translation of this passage.

74. Reinach 10.

75. Nicolet 790 with further bibliography.

76. For characteristic coin portraits, see Kraay and Hirmer nos. 773–75, pl. 211; Jenkins no. 679, p. 278; and Davis and Kraay nos. 207–9. It is interesting, and significant, that the most striking of these, which portrays the king as a young and Dionysiac figure (Rolling Stones fans will notice an eerie profile resemblance to Mick Jagger) can be dated, precisely, to 75, when he was in fact almost sixty. Cf. Pollitt, *AHA* 35–37.

77. Flor. 1.40.24.

78. App. *Mithr.* 111, and the interesting summary of his career in 112; Dio Cass. 37.14; Plin. *HN* 25.5.

79. Bunbury's comment, in Sir William Smith's *Dictionary of Greek and Roman Biography and Mythology* (London, 1854) 2.1096, that "much of what has been transmitted to us wears a very suspicious if not fabulous aspect," still applies. Cf. pp. 561–62.

80. So, rightly, Glew, "Mithridates" 381, discounting Justin's argument (37.4.5) that Mithridates was, *ab initio*, an empire builder who regarded himself as more than a match for the Romans. Justin has found many takers: see, e.g., Magie 1.195.

81. Just. 37.3.6–8.

82. App. *Mithr.* 112; Just. 37.2.4–9 (with reservations); Plin. *HN* 25.5–7; Strabo 10.4.10 (C.478), 12.3.11 (C.545); Memnon, *FGrH* 434 F 1 (22) (30); Val. Max. 8.7.16.

83. Strabo 7.3.17 (C.306), 7.3.18 (C.307), 7.4.3 (C.308–9), 7.4.4 (C.310), 7.4.6 (C.311), 7.4.7 (C.312), 11.2.18 (C.499), 12.3.1 (C.540–41), 12.3.28 (C.555); App. *Mithr.* 15; Memnon *loc. cit.* (n. 82); Just. 37.3.1–12; *SIG*³ 709.

84. Just. 37.3.4–5.

85. Cf. Glew, "Mithridates" 386, with full testimonia; Magie 1.197.

86. Plut. *Mar.* 31.

87. Badian, "Sulla's Cilician Command" 157 ff. The later date (once popular, but put out of favor by Badian) has recently been reargued, most convincingly, by Dr. Pierre Cagniart, in a Ph.D. dissertation on Sulla presented to the Department of Classics in the University of Texas at Austin.

88. Just. 38.1–2 *passim.*

89. Glew, "Mithridates" 394.

90. Ibid. 390, 403–4.

91. Ibid. 386.

92. Just. 38.5.3, cf. 37.1.2; App. *Mithr.* 57.

93. App. *Mithr.* 11 ff.; Just. 38.3.4; Livy, *per.* 74; Eutrop. 5.5.1; Oros. 6.2.1; Dio Cass. fr. 99.2 Melber.

94. Good accounts by Will, *HP*² 2.473 ff., with a useful analysis of the (highly inadequate) sources, and by Rostovtzeff, *CAH* IX 234 ff. Sherwin-White's downdating of the chronology (pp. 121 ff.) ignores Sulla's presence in Italy in the spring of 88, and ultimately founders on a misapprehension of the Latin system of time computation.

95. DS 37.2.11.

96. Cf. Glew, "Mithridates" 397–98.

97. So Broughton, "Roman Asia" 512.

98. App. *Mithr.* 16–21 *passim;* cf. Magie 1.210 ff. with notes.

99. App. *Mithr.* 92.

100. DS 37.26, Cic. *Pro Flac.* 60, App. *Mithr.* 10.

101. App. *Mithr.* 21.

102. Dio Cass. 40.27, Flor. 1.46.10. In Crassus's case, as Plutarch also makes clear, *Crass.* 31–33, this indignity was visited on the victim's already dead and severed head.

103. Livy, *per.* 70; Vell. Pat. 2.13.2; Val. Max. 2.10.5; Cic. *Brut.* 22, 30; Sen. De Benef. 6.37. Cf. DS 36.3.1, and see Badian, *Publicans* 89–92.

104. Strabo 13.1.66 (C.614), App. *Mithr.* 22–23, Dio Cass. fr. 101 Melber, Val. Max. 9.2.3, Plut. *Sull.* 24; cf. Magie 1.216–17, 2.1103 nn. 36–37. On the date, see Cic. *De Imp. Pomp.* 7, cited by Sherwin-White 124–25 with n. 101. Sarikakis, "Vêpres" 253 ff., distinguishes between Mithridates' obvious supporters—the intellectuals, the patriotic Greek nationalists, the debt-ridden lower orders—and the wealthy aristocracy and bourgeoisie that would naturally, for self-advancement and profit, cooperate with the Romans. There is, obviously, some truth in this, but to overschematize it as a regular dichotomy would be misleading. Not all men of property opposed Mithridates, just as by no means all dispossessed minorities supported him.

105. Cf. in general Salomone Gaggero 89–123.

106. Glew, "Selling" 254–55 with further bibliography. Cf. Pollitt, *AHA* 36–37, for the possible interpretation of a group of statuettes from the Athena sanctuary at Pergamon as "an allegory in which Mithridates frees the old Hellenistic world from torturous oppression by the Romans."

107. Poseidon. *ap.* Athen. 5.212a = *FGrH* IIA 87 F 36; App. *Mithr.* 22.47.

108. Just. 38.7.1.

109. See M. J. Price, "Mithridates VI Eupator, Dionysus, and the Coinages of the Black Sea," *NC* 8 (1968), 1–12.

110. Just. 37.2.1 ff.

111. *Oracula Sibyllina* 3.350 ff. (tr. S. K. Eddy). Eddy's whole discussion (178–82) has contributed greatly to the present evaluation of Mithridates' propaganda.

112. Cf. Tracy 213 ff.; McKendrick 58 ff.; Badian, "Rome, Athens" 106–8.

113. Tracy 215 ff.

114. McKendrick 58–59; cf. above, p. 526.

115. Badian, "Rome, Athens" 106 with nn. 6–7 and literature there cited.

116. So, persuasively, Tracy 232–35, against the usual estimate of 104/3.

117. Poseidon. *ap.* Athen. 6.272e–f.

118. It is, however, unlikely that the mines were a large factor here, since they were already reaching exhaustion point, and by the end of the first century B.C.—according to Strabo 9.1.23 (C.99)—had been worked out.

119. *IG* II² 1713, lines 9–11; cf. Tracy 218, 222–23, 227; Ferguson, *HA* 440. Medeius's colleague, and possible kinsman by marriage, Sarapion of Melite, had also been ἐπιμελητής of Delos, in 100/99. Cf. *IDel.* 1757, 2364.

120. Badian, "Rome, Athens" 107. Nor do I see why, as Badian seems to suggest (ibid.), democratic anti-Romanism in Athens had to wait for the Social War in Italy; such sentiments had more combustible fuel a good deal nearer home, not least in the "Delian junta" as such, whose members were pro-Roman almost by definition.

121. Poseidon *ap.* Athen. 5.214d–215b.

122. So, rightly, Badian, "Rome, Athens" 110 ff., who points out that Athenion was *elected* (χειροτονηθείς) by the Assembly for his mission to Mithridates. This also explains the statement in *IG* II² 1713 = *SIG*³ 733 that in 88/7 there was ἀναρχία in Athens (here surely the deletion rather than the nonelection of an archon), which can be attributed to the post-Sullan government's objection to commemorating a "revolutionary" or "demagogic" eponymous archon elected by Athenion's government. Cf. Habicht, "Zur Geschichte" 128 ff.

123. Mossé, *Athens* 165 n. 27, like some earlier scholars, is of the opinion that Athenion and Aristion were in fact one and the same man. The critical habit, popular among ancient historians, of seeking out real or suspected doublets, and then reducing them by removing one term of the equation, has been considerably overdone: history *does* repeat itself, in incidents as in nomenclature. Badian, "Rome, Athens" 114–15, concludes that both men existed, and I concur.

124. Poseidon. *ap.* Athen. 5.212a ff. Cf. Badian, "Rome, Athens" 110–11. Ferguson, *HA* 442–43, gives a very sprightly translation of Athenion's address.

125. Badian, "Rome, Athens" 116–17.

126. Ferguson, *HA* 444.

127. Poseidon, *ap.* Athen. 5.214a–c.

128. Ibid. 214d–215b.

129. For a graphic description of the siege, with full documentation, see Ferguson, *HA* 448 ff.

130. Plut. *Sull.* 13 ff.

131. Memoirs: Plut. *Luc.* 19. For the Piraeus bronzes, see Robert Garland, *The Piraeus from the Fifth to the First Century B.C.* (Ithaca, N.Y., 1987) 56, 190.

132. App. *Mithr.* 30–50, 55, *BC* 1.76; Plut. *Sull.* 11–22; Vell. Pat. 2.23.3–5; Paus. 1.20.6.

133. As Magie 1.231 reminds us, "the last great anti-Roman and nationalist movement in Asia Minor was a total failure. . . . The provincials had found that a native monarch might be more tyrannous even than the foreigner and that, moreover, he could not fulfil his promise of deliverance."

134. App. *Mithr.* 48; cf. Plut. *Sull.* 18.

135. App. *Mithr.* 51–60; Plut. *Sull.* 22–25, *Luc.* 2–4; Vell. Pat. 2.23.6–24.1. Cf. Sherwin-White 143–46.

136. App. *Mithr.* 38.

137. Accame 171 ff.; cf. Ferguson, *HA* 455.

138. App. *Mithr.* 39; cf. Nicolet 801.

139. P. Graindor, *Athènes sous Auguste* (Cairo, 1927) 933.

140. Plin. *HN* 36.4; Plut. *Sull.* 36; Paus. 10.21.6; Lucian, *Zeux.* 3; cf. Pollitt, *AHA* 174–75.

141. App. *Mithr.* 39, Strabo 9.1.20 (C.399).

142. McKendrick 62.

143. Cic. *Pro Flac.* 32, Just. 38.3.9, Plut. *Sull.* 25, App. *Mithr.* 62.

144. Broughton, "Roman Asia" 517–18; App. *Mithr.* 61.

145. Ferguson, *HA* 452–53.

146. Strabo 9.1.15 (C.395).

147. *IG* II² 1304.7–8 (211/0?): ὅπως . . . ἡ πόλις ἀποκατασταθεῖ εἰς τὴν ἐξ ἀρχῆς εὐδαιμονίαν.

148. *AP* 12.55 (sometimes ascribed to Artemon): ἡ δ' ἀνὰ κῦμ' ἄρξασα καὶ ἐν χθονὶ πατρὶς Ἀθήνη / νῦν κάλλει δούλην Ἑλλάδ' ὑπηγάγετο.

149. Ferguson, *HA* 308.

150. Stewart 34 ff. (a highly percipient analysis); Ferguson, *HA* 307–11, citing (309) an Amphictyonic decree of ca. 117, one of many such cataloguing Athenian achievements, the claims of which were widely accepted in the late Hellenistic period: cf. DS 13.26–27; Cic. *Pro Flac.* 26, 62, *De Orat.* 1.4.13; Ael. *VH* 3.38.

151. Cic. *De Orat.* 3.43; cf. Ferguson, *HA* 458.

152. Louis MacNeice, "Autumn Journal," *Collected Poems* (London, 1966) 118.

153. Cic. *Pro Flac.* 62: "auctoritate autem tanta est ut iam fractum prope ac debilitatum Graeciae nomen huius urbis laude nitatur."

154. Pindar fr. 64 Bowra: Ἑλλάδος ἔρεισμα, κλειναὶ Ἀθᾶναι, δαιμόνιον πτολίεθρον.

Chapter 32. Late Hellenistic Art, 150–30: The Mass Market in Nostalgia

1. So, rightly, Stewart 46. Hanfmann, 80, emphasizes that the statement is applicable to painting no less than to sculpture: cf. Quintil. 12.10.2–6; Cic. *Brut.* 18, 70.

2. Bieber 158–59.

3. Cf. L. Friedländer, *Roman Life and Manners under the Early Empire* (London, 1913) 2.320 ff.; Richter, *Three Critical Periods* 39–41.

4. Polyb. 9.10 *passim*, 39.2, cf. 3.9–11; Livy 31.30; Cic. *II Verr.* 4.59.132 f.; cf. R. R. R. Smith, "Greeks, Foreigners" 36.

5. Statistics assembled by Richter, *Three Critical Periods* 38: L. Scipio brought back 134 statues from Asia in 188; M. Fulvius Nobilior acquired 285 bronze and 230 marble figures from Ambracia a year later; in his triumphal procession (167) Aemilius Paullus had 250 carts crammed with statues, paintings, and embossed vases. Mummius is said to have "filled all Rome with sculptures" in 146 (Richter, ibid.). At the sack of Tarentum in 209, Livy asserts (27.16.17), the Romans carried off, *inter alia*, no less than 83,000 pounds of gold. On Syracuse, cf. Plut. *Marc.* 21.

6. Pollitt, *AHA* 154–58 with figs. 162–64.

7. Livy 45.27.11, 28.5; Polyb. 30.10.5–6; Plut. *Aem. Paull.* 28; Plin. *HN* 34.54, 35.135. Cf. Pollitt, *AHA* 155.

8. Cf. Plin. *HN* 33.148–49; Pollitt, *AHA* 166–67.

9. Pollitt, *AHA* 160; cf. Bieber 167. Prices could be astronomical: 100,000 sesterces for some cups by a well-known classical-period engraver; 144,000 for a fourth-century work by a not-overdistinguished painter, Kydios (Plin. *HN* 33.147, 35.130). Demand far outran supply.

10. Cic. *II Verr.* 4.59.132–60.134 ("haec oblectamenta et solacia seruitutis").

11. Plin. *HN* 36.35, DS 31.18, Vitruv. 3.2.5, Cic. *De Orat.* 1.62, Val. Max. 5.1.1; cf. Stewart 42–44, 65 ff.; Richter, *Three Critical Periods* 39; Bieber 160. Pollitt, *AHA* 162, suggests that Timarchides and his sons both took part in a "Pheidian revival," and in some sense helped to pioneer the copying industry.

12. The figure of 3,000 drachmas for an honorific statue depends on a remark attributed to Diogenes (Diog. Laert. 6.35), and thus refers to the age of Alexander the Great. Cf. Stewart 120 with n. 37, who equates 3,000 drs. with $80,000 at the time of writing (1979) in terms of purchasing power. Prof. Stewart informs me that he has since found further inscriptions from Cnidos and Priene extending the (surely conventional) price of 3,000 drs. to the first century B.C. The question of wages in the Hellenistic period is bedeviled by lack of hard evidence, but

Larsen, "Roman Greece" 408 ff., suggests that 300 drs. per annum would indeed be something very close to an average annual wage, bearing in mind the increasingly depressed standard of living in the third and second centuries (Day 9 ff.; and cf. above, p. 374). To fix a dollar ratio for this amount, however, is much harder than might at first sight appear: cf. David C. Young, *The Olympic Myth of Greek Amateur Athletics* (Chicago, 1984) 116–27. It seems likely that in any case the figure of 3,000 drs. represents the cost of a bronze statue, the ultimate accolade, and infinitely more expensive than its equivalent in marble, which was far more common. Prof. Stewart writes (pers. comm. 1986): "I now reckon that with the halving of the gold/silver ratio after 330, the *bronzista* would net about 2000 drachmas, out of which he would have to pay his apprentices, keep his slaves, and buy charcoal." We may also note that by the first century A.D. prices had fallen considerably: see Friedländer (above, n. 3) app. 54, 4.287 ff., who observes that "the great difference between these prices and that mentioned by Diogenes is no doubt to be explained not by a rise in the value of money, but chiefly by the mechanical execution of the ordinary decorative and honorary statues turned out under the empire." Stewart's estimate, in other words, can be misleading, and should be used with some caution. See further R. Duncan-Jones, "An Epigraphic Survey of Costs in Roman Italy," *PBSR* 33 (1965) 189–306. My thanks to Prof. John H. Kroll for some useful suggestions on this topic.

13. Stewart 125.

14. Plin. *HN* 34.37: the consular date he gives is A.D. 70. Cf. Richter, *Three Critical Periods* 39, who, however, by an oversight prints the figure for each city as 73,000!

15. Richter, ibid. 37–38.

16. Stewart 35–38. As stimulus to the neoclassical mode he cites "the final consummation of Athens' own reactionary-cum-revanchist hopes and plans in her acquisition of a miniature maritime empire in 166" (repeated almost verbatim p. 48), which, as a description of the Delian concession, seems to me to be pitching it a bit strong.

17. Ferguson, *HA* 230, 237; Day 14–15, 90, noting the huge circulation of New Style drachmas during this period.

18. Stewart 38.

19. *SIG*³ 682; cf. Hansen 368 with n. 392; Webster, *Hellenistic Poetry* 186.

20. Plin. *HN* 35.24, cf. 7.126; Strabo 8.6.23 (C.381); Vell. Pat. 1.13.4; Hansen 139, 367–68. The allocation of spoils from Corinth to Pergamon: Paus. 7.16.8. On Attalus II's motives, cf. Pollitt, *AHA* 83.

21. Webster, *Hellenistic Poetry* 299–300, cf. *Art* 199–200, discussing Cic. *II Verr.* 4.24.54.

22. Plin. *HN* 34.6, Cic. *II Ver.* 5.17.44, Lactant. *Inst. Div.* 2.4.33–36; cf. Habermehl, *RE* 8A.2 (1958) cols. 1630–31, s.v. "C. Verres (1)." Pliny's acid remarks about *soi-disant* art experts remain as pertinent today as when they were first written.

23. Cf. Hanfmann 93: "Hellenistic art is a world of realistic unrealities—its major concerns are the defiant heroism of mythical and semi-mythical supermen," etc.

24. Webster, *Art* 166–68.

25. Cic. *Brut.* 24, 70 ff.; *De Orat.* 3.7.26; *Tusc. Disp.* 1.15.34; *Att.* 1.8.2, 4.10.

26. Webster, *Art* 201, cf. *Hellenistic Poetry* 302–3.

27. See, e.g., R. R. R. Smith, "Greeks, Foreigners" figs. 18a–25e.

28. See Boardman 146 ff.; and Johns, figs. 1, 4, 7, 8, 9, 11, 14, 16, 25, 30, 51, 84, 85, 87, 98, 101, 102, with accompanying discussion.

29. But see Johns, figs. 84 (p. 103), 25 (opp. p. 112).

30. Johns, fig. 14 (opp. p. 65).

31. Johns, fig. 51 (p. 68).

32. Boardman 158–59; Johns, fig. 87 (p. 106).

33. Johns, fig. 52 (p. 69); cf. Hanfmann 84.

34. See, e.g., Havelock nos. 83, 105, 136; R. R. R. Smith, "Greeks, Foreigners" 24–25; Pollitt, *AHA* 142–43 with figs. 152–54. I have not had access to W. E. Stevenson's "The Pathological Grotesque Representation in Greek and Roman Art" (diss. Univ. Pennsylvania,

1975). The Negroid type clearly fascinated Hellenistic artists, though, again, primarily as a study in barbarian exotica: see F. M. Snowden, *Blacks in Antiquity* (Cambridge, Mass., 1970) figs. 40, 42–49.

35. Stewart chap. 3, 65 ff. On the Delos mosaics, see Pollitt, *AHA* 215–18 with figs. 227–31.

36. Stewart 142. Though he still believes in the nonexistent oligarchic coup of 103/2 (above, p. 526), this does not invalidate his main point, taken from Kavolis 197, that with its removal from new social realities "an institutionalised style is transformed into a museum style."

37. Stewart 144, with reference (n. 58) to Veblen and to Vance Packard's *The Status Seekers*.

38. One such statue Stewart dismisses (ibid.) as "a pastiche, a piece of pure kitsch, a monster of inauthenticity": this was the monument put up (ca. 110?) to C. Ofellius Ferus by the Italian community (A. 4340, *IDel.* 1688; cf. Bieber 172).

39. Charbonneaux, in Charbonneaux et al. 290 with figs. 312–13; Bieber 131, 133, 175 with fig. 511.

40. Bieber, 164, places it ca. 100. For an excellent color reproduction, see Charbonneaux et al. fig. 326 (p. 300); cf. Havelock no. 20 (p. 37).

41. Stewart 65–67.

42. Biers 304: "The despairing expression has a typically Hellenistic theatricality."

43. Charbonneaux et al. fig. 353 (p. 321); Bieber 147–48 with figs. 629–30. Reactions to, and interpretations of, this group differ sharply. Biers 302 talks of "playful eroticism" that is "distasteful to many scholars" (though he does not name them). M. Robertson 1.556 suggests, ingeniously, that we have here an iconographic reference to the fact that prostitutes had the word "follow [me]" inscribed on the soles of their sandals as a signal (though no such inscription appears here). Bieber (147) thinks Aphrodite is using the sandal to ward off Pan's attack, and sees Eros as pushing Pan away. Charbonneaux (in Charbonneaux et al. 316) finds nothing erotic at all in the group, and speaks of "the timid advances of a shaggy Pan, whose importunity suggests, more than anything else, an over-enthusiastic dog." *Quot capita, tot sententiae.* Art critics, it would seem, are ill qualified to analyze erotic intentions.

44. *Hesperia* 34 (1965) 69, in an article entitled "Three Centuries of Hellenistic Terracottas."

45. Richter, *Three Critical Periods* 42 ff., with further literature there cited.

46. Copyists signed their own names to a reproduction rather than indicating the original artist. For instances of this practice (including a life-size copy of Pheidias's Athena Parthenos, proudly signed by one Antiochus of Athens), see Richter, ibid. 45–46. She cites only one known case where the original is acknowledged: Ἀπὸ τῆς ἐν Τρωάδι Ἀφροδίτης Μηνόφαντος ἐποίει.

47. Webster, *Art* 169–70, *Hellenistic Poetry* 297.

48. Richter, *Three Critical Periods* 59–60; cf. Cic. *Att.* 6.1.26; Paus. 1.2.4, 18.3; Plin. *HN* 35.4, and in general H. Blanck, *Wiederverwendung alter Statuen als Ehrendenkmäler bei Griechen und Römern* (Rome, 1969); Green, *AJAH* 3 (1978) 24–25 n. 146.

49. Polyb. 6.53.5 ff.; cf. Webster, *Art* 183–84.

50. This notion is critically examined, with several caveats, by R. R. R. Smith, 31–32, but I think there is a good deal to be said for it: cf. Richter, *Three Critical Periods* 61. For the use of funeral masks in the second century B.C., cf. Polyb. 6.53.

51. Havelock 22–23.

52. Rhys Carpenter, *Greek Sculpture* (Chicago, 1960) chap. 9, 228 ff.

53. Richter, *Three Critical Periods* 53 ff., followed by R. R. R. Smith, "Greeks, Foreigners" 28 ff.

54. R. R. R. Smith, "Greeks, Foreigners" 26 ff.; cf. Stewart figs. 18a–20d, 22a–b, and p. 72: "these heads surely represent an accommodation to . . . a bourgeois clientele dominated by non-Greeks, especially Italians." Cf. Pollitt, *AHA* 73–75 with figs. 75–78.

55. Just. 38.6.7–8; cf. *Oracula Sibyllina* 3.469.

56. Plut. *Pomp.* 24, appositely cited by R. R. R. Smith, "Greeks, Foreigners" 36.

57. Cf. Bieber 173.

58. R. R. R. Smith, "Greeks, Foreigners" 35. He also deals very sensibly (33 ff.) with the popular theory (which seems to me to have less than nothing to commend it) that Roman aristocrats went in for having themselves portrayed as Hellenistic kings, a profound misunderstanding (to look no farther) of the Roman ruling-class mentality.

59. G. Bowersock, *Augustus and the Greek World* (Oxford, 1965) 1.

60. Interestingly, Hellenistic painting of the third and second centuries, whatever its intrinsic qualities (for which we have far too little material to judge: we have to rely almost entirely on literary reportage and analogies drawn from later work), is seldom mentioned by ancient authors, who much prefer work of the high classical period and the fourth century. See Hanfmann 80, citing a seminar paper by J. H. Kroll, which established a statistical citation index of artists.

61. Excellent color reproduction in Johns, fig. 7 (between pp. 48 and 49).

62. In Charbonneaux et al. 198.

63. Havelock 268–69 with pl. XIX; Charbonneaux et al. fig. 154 (p. 154).

64. A. Maiuri, *Roman Painting* (Geneva, 1953) 83.

65. Webster, *Art* 190–91 with pls. 53, 54.

66. Both scenes are represented by copies from Pompeii and Herculaneum: cf. Havelock pl. XX (pp. 270–71), Charbonneaux et al. fig. 204 (p. 195), M. Robertson 1.589–90.

67. See *AP* 16 (= *Anth. Planud.*) 128 (Iphigeneia), 135–43 (Medea).

68. Villard, in Charbonneaux et al. 195, attributes to Pliny the statement that Timomachus "had restored its ancient dignity to the art of painting," but this phrase occurs nowhere, to the best of my knowledge, in the *Natural History*, and is certainly not said of Timomachus.

69. R. Jenkyns, *The Victorians and Ancient Greece* (Cambridge, Mass., 1980) 305 ff.

70. Plin. *HN* 7.126; 35.26, 136, 145.

71. Bieber 159.

72. Charbonneaux, in Charbonneaux et al. 324.

73. Rostovtzeff *SEH* 2.742–44, 755; Day 14–15, 77–90; cf. Ferguson, *HA* 375–76; Stewart 48–49.

74. Vitruv. 7.15.7, *IG* II² 4099; cf. Travlos, *Pictorial Dictionary* 402 ff.

75. Erected ca. 150–125; cf. Travlos, ibid. 352 ff. See also the admirable account in Camp 172–80, with figs. 141–51.

76. Dinsmoor 323–24 with fig. 118.

77. Havelock 70.

78. Vitruv. 3.2.6, 3.3.8–9, 7 *praef.* 12; cf. Martin, in Charbonneaux et al. 33 ff.; Havelock nos. 69–70, with p. 84; Dinsmoor 274–76.

79. Havelock 84.

80. Bieber 164–65.

81. Dinsmoor 275.

82. Cic. *Orat. de Dom.* 43.

83. Webster, *Art* 178–80 with fig. 49.

Chapter 33. Foreign and Mystery Cults, Oracles, Astrology, Magic

1. Dodds 242.

2. *SVF* 2.1191–95, 1210; Cic. *De Div.* 1.125; Diog. Laert. 7.149; cf. Nilsson 278.

3. Cf. Dodds chap. 8, 236 ff., "The Fear of Freedom."

4. Dodds 239; cf. *SVF* 1.199, 205; 2.823; 3.444, 456, 461.

5. A. N. Whitehead, *Religion in the Making* (Cambridge, 1926) 6, cited by Dodds 243.

6. Cf. also such works as Richard and Eva Blum, *The Dangerous Hour: The Lore of Crisis and Mystery in Rural Greece* (London, 1970); S. G. Paraskevaïdes, Ἐπιβίωσις τοῦ ἀρχαίου Ἑλληνικοῦ βίου ἐν Λέσβῳ (Mytilene, 1956), or Margaret Alexiou's *The Ritual Lament in Greek Tradition* (Cambridge, 1974).

7. Dodds 243, 260 n. 46. The Arnold quotation is from a letter to Grant Duff, 22 August 1879.

8. Nilsson 124, 358; Dodds 260 n. 41 with further literature.

9. For a good account, see Nilsson, 119 ff., "Die fremden Kulte in den altgriechischen Ländern." For the growing emphasis on salvation (σωτηρία), see Davies, *CAH* VII².1 315.

10. Strabo 10.3.18 (C.471).

11. Cf. Nilsson 131.

12. Nilsson 124.

13. See in general Graillot 1–107; Showerman 221–68; Vermaseren, *Cybele*; G. Sanders, "Kybele und Attis," in M. J. Vermaseren, ed., *Die orientalischen Religionen im Römerreich* (Leiden, 1981) 264–97. I have not seen Giulia Sfameni Gasparro's *Soteriologia e aspetti mistici nel culto di Cibele e Attis* (Palermo, 1979). By far the larger part of modern research has concentrated on Cybele's cult in the Roman empire.

14. On the Anastenarides, see K. J. Kakouri, *Dionysiaka: Aspects of the Popular Thracian Religion of Today* (Athens, 1965) 7–32. Cf. Loring M. Danforth, "The Ideological Context of the Search for Continuities in Greek Culture," *Journal of Modern Greek Studies* 2 (1984) 68 ff.

15. Vermaseren, *Cybele* 96 ff.; Graillot 11, 12, 20, 22, 75, 98, 115, 128–29; Showerman 236–37.

16. Graillot 18, 34, 73, 109, 135, 141, 148, 151–52, 190, 196, 198, etc.; Showerman 235; Vermaseren, *Cybele* 14–15, 18, 43, 84 with pls. 1, 3, 4, 25, 26, 74. Cf. Soph. *Phil.* 395; *AP* 6.51, 94.

17. Showerman 249–51; Vermaseren, *Cybele* 32–37, 71 ff.

18. H. A. Thompson, "Buildings on the West Side of the Agora," *Hesperia* 6 (1937) 206–7 (discussing the Metroön); cf. Vermaseren, *Cybele* 71.

19. Graillot 25–69; Vermaseren, *Cybele* 38 ff.; T. Köves, "Zum Empfang der Magna Mater in Rom," *Historia* 12 (1963) 321–47. The main source is Livy, 29.10.4–8, 11.1–8, 14.5–14; a more fanciful account in Ovid, *Fast.* 4.247–348.

20. Livy 25.1.6 ff.

21. Vermaseren, *Cybele* chap. 6, 126 ff.

22. Plato, *Rep.* 327A, 354A; Strabo 10.3.18 (C.471); cf. above, p. 589.

23. Dem. 18 (*De Corona*) 259–60.

24. Nilsson 123; Walton, *OCD*² 136, s.v. "Atargatis."

25. P. Roussel, *Délos colonie athénienne* (Paris, 1916) esp. 252 ff.

26. Cf. Nock, *Essays* 2.796 ff.; Bell, *Cults* 17–19.

27. Cf. the gravestone from Miletus (3d/2d c. B.C.) commemorating a priestess who led the faithful "to the mountain": W. Peek, *Griechische Grabgedichte* (Berlin, 1960) no. 178; cf. Schneider 2.880.

28. *CIL* I 196, Livy 39.8–18; cf. A. Dihle, *Hermes* 90 (1962) 376 ff.

29. Cf. Bell, *Cults* 18–19.

30. Nock, *Essays* 2.797 ff.

31. E.g., *PCairZen.* 2.59296.32; cf. Schneider 2.884.

32. Plut. *Alex.* 2.

33. Guthrie, *Orpheus*² 156 ff., 243 ff.

34. Plato, *Phaed.* 114D, cf. 69C.

35. DS 3.62.8; Paus. 8.37.5 = fr. 194 Kern; cf. Guthrie, *Orpheus*² 107 ff.

36. Plato, *Laws* 701C, *Crat.* 400C; Plut. *Mor.* 996C; cf. Guthrie, *Orpheus*² 156 ff.

37. Plato, *Phaed.* 69C, *Rep.* 364B.

38. Cf. Guthrie, *Orpheus*² chap. 5, 148 ff.

39. Text in Diels-Kranz[10] (Bonn, 1961) 1.15 ff. (nos. 17–21); cf. also G. Murray, "Critical Appendix on the Orphic Tablets," in J. E. Harrison, *Prolegomena to the Study of Greek Religion*, 2d ed. (Cambridge, 1908), 659–73; and Guthrie, *Orpheus*[2] 172–82.

40. The so-called Petelia tablet, named after its place of discovery in southern Italy: no. 17 Diels-Kranz (p. 15); Murray (above, n. 39) no. 1, pp. 659–60.

41. Nos. 18.13, 18; 20.4 Diels-Kranz.

42. Eur. *Cycl.* 646–48; cf. *Alc.* 966 ff.

43. Eur. *Hipp.* 948–57.

44. A few centuries later Juvenal (*Sat.* 2.1–20) was making precisely the same charge against *soi-disant* philosophers.

45. Bell, *Cults* 8, argues that the Orphics "were never more than a comparatively small minority, but their influence on later Greek paganism was powerful": this is probably an accurate assessment.

46. Plato, *Meno* 80E.

47. Plato, *Rep.* 364B–365A.

48. Cf. Aristoph. *Frogs* 1032–33.

49. Plut. *Comp. Cim. Luc.* 1.

50. Nilsson 469–70; Parke 126–29; P. Philippson, *Griechische Gottheiten in ihren Landschaften* (Oslo, 1939) 11 ff.; J. G. Frazer, *Pausanias's Description of Greece* (London, 1913) 5.196 ff.

51. Paus. 9.39.2.

52. Parke 121 ff.

53. S. Dakaris, "The Oracle of the Dead on the Acheron," in E. Melas, ed., *Temples and Sanctuaries of Ancient Greece* (London, 1973) 139–49. Secret passages and the remains of geared mechanical contrivances for lifting heavy weights (including sacrificial cauldrons) suggest that the priests of the sanctuary staged the appearance and disappearance of "apparitions" of the dead. For similar mechanical devices to impress the superstitious see above, pp. 477 ff.

54. *POxy.* 12.1477, cited by Bell, *Cults* 69.

55. Famous consultants included Croesus, Epaminondas, Amyntas III and Philip II of Macedon, and the Roman general Aemilius Paullus: Hdt. 1.46, Paus. 4.32.5–6, *GDI* no. 143, Polyaen. 2.3.8, Ael. *VH* 3.45, Livy 45.27.8.

56. Parke 126, discussing Paus. 9.39.5–14. I see no justification for Nilsson's confident claim (p. 470) "dass Pausanias Umgestaltungen und Ausdeutungen vorliegen, welche der Mentalität der Kaiserzeit besser als der der hellenistischen Zeit entsprechen." In such matters we simply do not have enough clearly distinguishing evidence to judge. A somewhat scoffing account of the *rite de passage* by Dicaearchus is referred to, and briefly quoted, in Athen. 13.594e–f; cf. 14.641e–f. Other references to the process of consultation in Strabo 9.2.38 (C.414); Philostr. *Vit. Apoll. Tyan.* 8.19; Lucian, *Dial. Mort.* 3.2; schol. Aristoph. *Clouds* 508; *GDI* no. 143; *Suda* s.v. Τροφωνίου κατὰ γῆς παίγνια.

57. Harrison (above, n. 39) 578.

58. *Suda*, *loc. cit.* (above, n. 56).

59. Plut. *Mor.* 589F–592F.

60. Eudoxus *ap.* Cic. *De Div.* 2.87.

61. For the date, see A. Sachs, "Babylonian Horoscopes," *Journal of Cuneiform Studies* 6 (1952) 49 ff. The evidence nevertheless remains scanty: Neugebauer, *Exact Sciences* 187.

62. Fraser 1.436–39; Nock, *Essays* 1.497 ff.

63. Hdt. 2.82.1; Plato, *Tim.* 40C–D, *Phaedr.* 247A, 252C–D. Nilsson 268 remarks: "Das waren die bescheidenen Anfänge einer Lehre, die zwei Jahrtausende hindurch die Menschheit beherrschen sollte."

64. Theophr. *ap.* Proclus *In Tim.* 3.151.1 ff. Diehl.

65. Joseph. *Cont. Ap.* 1.129; Vitruv. 9.6.2, cf. 9.2.1, 9.8.1; Bouché-Leclercq, *Astrologie* 36 ff.; Fraser 2.728 n. 96.

66. Epicur. *Ep.* 1.76–82, 2.85–88, cf. Festugière, *Epicurus* chap. 5, 73 ff., esp. 77–80.

Epicurus, however, is not primarily attacking the idea of determinism; as De Witt puts it (p. 176), "what chiefly outraged his feelings was the idea that august beings should be thought to assume the form of balls of fire and of their own choice go hurtling through circles for ever."

67. Nilsson 259, 268.

68. Cf. J. Beaujeu, "L'astrologie dans l'antiquité: Science ou charlatanisme?" *CEA* 4 (1974) 5–36.

69. The following account owes much to Peters 434 ff.

70. Peters 437.

71. Cf., e.g., Tarn and Griffith 346.

72. They still do, even in an academic context: for example, the University of Texas at Austin possesses an astronomy department ranked among the finest in the United States, while at the same time one of my professional colleagues, a not noticeably frivolous person, is in steady demand as an astrological consultant.

73. Nilsson 275–76; Festugière, *Astrologie* 76 ff.; Fraser 1.436–37, 2.630–31 (nn. 489–92).

74. For a crisp summing-up of the cardinal Stoic beliefs in this area, see Schneider 2.908. On the astrological implications of the Pergamon frieze, see Davies, *CAH* VII².1 318.

75. Panaet. fr. 74 Straaten, cf. frr. 68, 70, 71, 73; Cic. *De Div.* 1.12, 2.87–99; Plotin. *Enn.* 2.3, 2.9.13.

76. As a Capricorn I need only open my daily paper to find my future—and that of all other Capricorns—confidently predicted. Though, as it happens, the department in which I work contains not one but two Capricorns who are also left-handed, Cambridge-educated, and classicists, such stellar uniformity is not encouraging. At a slightly more refined level, the casting of individual horoscopes remains a major industry. It has been argued (Dodds 246) that the increasing popularity of astrological prediction from the late third century onwards was due to a combination of alarm at the notion of intellectual freedom—"better the rigid determinism of the astrological Fate than that terrifying burden of daily responsibility"—and a desperate need, in chaotic times, to know what the future held. *Plus ça change.*

77. Diog. Laert. 7.142–43 = fr. 99a Edelstein and Kidd, F 304 Theiler.

78. Diog. Laert. 7.149; cf. Cic. *De Div.* 1.125–28.

79. Cic. *De Div.* 2.33–35 = fr. 106 Edelstein and Kidd, F 379 Theiler.

80. August. *Civ. Dei* 5.2.5 = fr. 111 Edelstein and Kidd (cf. 112), F 384 Theiler (cf. 383).

81. Cleanthes: *SVF* 1.499–504, pp. 111–13; Poseidonius: F 344 ff. Theiler; cf. Peters 442 ff.; and, for much arcane detail, Nock, *Essays* 2.853 ff.

82. Tarn and Griffith 347.

83. Cf. Bouché-Leclercq, *Astrologie* 373 ff.

84. Philoch. *FGrH* IIIB 328 F 85–88; cf. Cic. *De Div.* 2.91.

85. Michael Flanders and Donald Swann, "Horoscope," from the intimate revue *At the Drop of Another Hat* (1963–64), Angel S.36388.

86. Neugebauer, *Exact Sciences* 171.

87. Cf. Schneider 2.909.

88. Peters 440.

89. Theocr. *Id.* 2.92.

90. Cf. Nilsson 221: "Das Schillern zwischen Liebes- und Schadenzauber spiegelt die zerrissene, zwischen Liebe und Hass schwankende Stimmung der verschmähten Frau wider."

91. A wide collection of such curse tablets is to be found in A. Audollent, *Defixionum Tabellae* (Paris, 1904); cf. also R. Wünsch, *Defixionum Tabellae Atticarum* (Berlin, 1897).

92. *GDI* no. 3536; cf. Nilsson 221–22.

93. *GDI* nos. 3540, 3542, 3545, 3548.

94. Nock, *Essays* 1.176–77.

95. Though it seems clear that such collections did not exist in early Ptolemaic times, nevertheless, "their numerous points of agreement with Theocritus . . . show that much of

the material which they systematise is far older than themselves, and some of it must be of immemorial antiquity" (A. S. F. Gow 2.35–36; cf. Nock, *Essays* 1.184).

96. Nock, *Essays* 1.185 ff.

97. E.g., *PMag.* I.296 ff. (Preisendanz 1.17), which ranges in its invocation from Apollo to Abrasax, from Gabriel to Adonai, Elohim, and Pakerbeth, the last a title of the Egyptian Seth-Typhon. Cf. Bell, *Cults* 72–73.

98. LSJ s.v. πάρεδρος, III.1, obscures the bureaucratic metaphor by translating "assistant divinity, familiar spirit."

99. *PMag.* IV.2441 ff., 2622 ff. (Preisendanz 1.148 ff., 154 ff.): Διαβολὴ πρὸς Σελήνην ποιοῦσα πρὸς πάντα καὶ πρὸς πᾶσαν πρᾶξιν. See also, e.g. III.494–611 (Preisendanz 1.52–59), VI.1–47 (1.198–200: approaches to the sun god), and LXXXIX.1–27 (Betz p. 300: demonic compulsion).

100. Nock, *Essays* 1.495.

101. Ibid. 1.184–85.

102. See, e.g., *PMag.* IV.1390 (Preisendanz 2.175).

103. *PMag.* IV.2943 ff. (Preisendanz 1.166).

104. *PMag.* XXXVI.361–71 (Preisendanz 2.175).

105. Moke, 197–204, offers a detailed analysis of the erotic συμπάθεια inherent in every item (blood, skin, vetch, etc.) of this spell: "a beautiful web-like weaving of an erotic context in which the factors are coherently intertwined from beginning to end" is his description. *Caveat emptor.*

106. Nock, *Essays* 1.193.

107. *PMag.* VII.429 ff. (Preisendanz 2.19–20), tr. Moke 366.

108. Cf. Bell, *Cults* 70.

109. *PMag.* VII.193–95, 200–203 (Preisendanz 2.8–9).

110. *PMag.* XIII.298 ff., 309 ff., 321 ff. (Preisendanz 2.102–4).

111. *PMag.* VIII.85 ff. (Preisendanz 2.49 ff.); cf. II.11 (1.20–21), V.145 ff (1.186–87), VII.233 ff. (2.10–11).

112. A. S. F. Gow 2.35.

Chapter 34. Academics, Skeptics, Peripatetics, Cynics

1. David Sedley, in Schofield et al. 3. Sedley goes on: "It has always been tempting to see this last development as a deliberate response to a cry for help—an attempt to restore moral purpose to life in an age when dynastic rule had stifled the old type of participatory city-state and was depriving the Greek citizen of a role in the politics of his own city." I would argue, at this stage in the present work, that it is not only tempting, but quite certainly correct. Sedley stresses that "this claim has not yet been substantiated" and goes on: "Any defence of it would probably require fuller knowledge than we possess of the social and political backgrounds from which the various adherents of the Hellenistic schools emerged." A sound caveat, but perhaps excessively pessimistic: what I suspect we glimpse here is a fundamental difference in the historian's and the philosopher's approach to evidence. In the nature of things substantiation of such a thesis is possible in historical terms; but it can only be advanced by the slow accumulation of a congeries of circumstantial evidence, varied in nature and drawn from widely different areas, yet all pointing in the same direction. Such evidence I have attempted to present during the course of this investigation. Sedley argues that part of the new emphasis is due to philosophy, now, having become "an entirely autonomous discipline and one which had to justify itself, often in direct competition, with other branches of learning." But this is a case of *post hoc, propter hoc*: what really challenges one's historical sense is the antecedent reason for that autonomy.

2. Cf. Long 179 ff.

3. Cf. in particular Dudley, *History* chap. 3, 59 ff.

4. Long 6.

5. Xenocr. fr. 4 Heinze.

6. Peters 350 ff.

7. Ibid.

8. Diog. Laert. 4.5, Aul. Gell. *NA* 3.17.3.

9. Arist. *Met.* 1072^{b}30, *Eth. Nic.* 1096^{b}6 (1.6.7).

10. J. E. Raven, *Plato's Thought in the Making* (Cambridge, 1965) 66 ff.

11. Owen, *OCD*^{2} 1009, s.v. "Speusippus," citing Plato Latinus 3.40.1–5.

12. Arist. *Eth. Nic.* 1152^{b}7 ff., 1153^{b}5 ff. (7.11.3, 13.1), 1172^{b}36–73^{a}12 (10.2.4–5).

13. Diog. Laert. 4.18.

14. Polyb. 10.22.2–3, Plut. *Philop.* 1, Paus. 8.49.2; cf. Aalders 12.

15. On the somewhat dubious basis of Quintil. 3.4.9.

16. *Rhet. ad Alex.* 1424^{a}13–^{b}15; cf. Aalders 9–11.

17. Ps.-Plato, *Minos* 318A, cf. 317A; Speusippus *ap.* Clem. Alex. *Strom.* 2.19.3; cf. Aalders 15, 17 ff.

18. Ps.-Plato, *Epin.* 992B–C; cf. Aalders 12; M. Isnardi, "Teoria e prassi nel pensiero dell' Accademia antica," *PP* 11 (1956) 401–33, esp. 431 ff. Note that Plato himself kept out of politics in Athens because bitter experience had suggested to him that this particular *polis* was past curing: *Ep.* 7.325B ff., cf. 322B.

19. Long 6.

20. Thuc. 2.40.2.

21. Arist. *De Cael.* 469^{b}14 with schol. *ad loc.*; cf. Heath, *History* 1.181.

22. Diog. Laert. 4.16, Lucian, *Bis Accus.* 16.

23. See, e.g., Plut. *Mor.* 416C, 419A, cf. 360D, 361A; Cic. *ND* 1.13. Xenocrates believed that happiness, εὐδαιμονία, was the indwelling of a good δαίμων.

24. Diog. Laert. 4.8–9; Plut. *Phoc.* 27, 29.

25. Diog. Laert. 4.14, Plut. *Mor.* 1126D.

26. Diog. Laert. 4.19.

27. Ibid. 9.62, 66; cf. Brochard 51 ff., 69 ff.

28. Diog. Laert. 9.61 ff.

29. Cf. ibid. 9.72–73.

30. Long 79.

31. Diog. Laert. 9.61, 63, 64–65.

32. *Ap.* Diog. Laert. 9.65.

33. Aalders 51 with n. 35: note in particular Diog. Laert. 9.61–62, 105; cf. Stough 30.

34. Diog. Laert. 10.8.

35. Ibid. 9.62.

36. Long 88.

37. Cf. Diog. Laert. 4.32–33.

38. Stough 6.

39. Long 89.

40. Cf. Cic. *Att.* 13.19.3, *Acad.* 2.18, 77; Sext. Emp. *Adv. Math.* 7.150–57.

41. Cf. Striker, in Schofield et al. 68–69.

42. Sext. Emp. *Adv. Math.* 7.158; cf. Brochard 110.

43. Diog. Laert. 4.32.

44. Ibid. 4.40, 43.

45. Ibid. 4.37–39.

46. Ariston *ap.* Diog. Laert. 4.33, parodying Hom. *Il.* 6.181. I do not see why Brochard (p. 117) should deduce from this that such ancient critics took Arcesilaus's Platonism to be mere top-dressing to an underlying alignment with Pyrrhonism.

47. Diodorus Cronus of Iasos (*fl.* ca. 300), fourth head of the Megarian school of philosophy, and a famous master of dialectic, who counted Arcesilaus among his students. Cf. Diog. Laert. 2.111; Strabo 14.2.21 (C.658), 17.3.22 (C.838); Plin. *HN* 7.180. While at the court of

Ptolemy I he is said to have died of shame and vexation after failing to solve a dialectical problem put to him by Stilpo during dinner with the king.

48. Based on Apollodorus *ap*. Diog. Laert. 4.65 and Lucian, *Macrob*. 20, which place his death in 129 at the age of 85; however, Cic. *Acad*. 2.16 and Val. Max. 8.7.5 make him 90 at the time of his death, so unless we opt to treat this latter figure as a mere rounding-off to the full decade, 219/8 is also possible as his date of birth.

49. Cf. Long 104–6.

50. Brochard, 126, collects the ancient testimony to his powers as a thinker and debater.

51. Diog. Laert. 4.62.

52. Carneades recognized the importance of Chrysippus in the history of Stoicism—Chrysippus was, indeed, said to have saved the Stoa from the attacks of the Academy (Plut. *Mor*. 1059A–C)—and the greatest compliment Carneades paid him was the time and energy he devoted to combating his ideas. There was a popular tag, preserved by Diog. Laert. 7.183: εἰ μὴ γὰρ ἦν Χρύσιππος, οὐκ ἂν ἦν Στοά ("Without Chrysippus, no Stoa"), which Carneades slily amended by changing the last word to ἐγώ ("Without Chrysippus, no me": Diog. Laert. 4.62).

53. Carneades, in this like the Epicureans, held that the gods were unconcerned with human affairs: Cic. *ND* 3.79 ff.; cf. Brochard 138 ff.

54. Diog. Laert. 4.67.

55. See, e.g., Cic. *Acad*. 2.98 ff.

56. Cic. *Acad*. 2.108, cited by Long 106.

57. Cf. Cic. *Acad*. 2.139.

58. Cf. Long 95.

59. Brochard 133 ff., citing Metrodorus and Philo *ap*. Cic. *Acad*. 2.78.

60. Diog. Laert. 4.63.

61. Cic. *De Rep*. 3.9; cf. Lactant. *Inst. Div*. 5.14.3–5.

62. As Long points out (p. 96), "by considering the conditions of sense-perception, Carneades arrived at a theory of knowledge which anticipates in many ways modern types of empiricism."

63. Cic. *De Rep*. 3.29, cited (and translated) by Long 105.

64. Cf. Brochard 181: "Dans tout l'enseignement de Carnéade, la partie maîtresse est la théorie de la connaissance."

65. Plut. *Cic*. 4, *Luc*. 42; Ael. *VH* 12.25; Cic. *Fam*. 9.8, *Acad*. 2.56 ff., 113, *Brut*. 315, *De Fin*. 5.1–8 (a vivid description of the impression made on educated Roman visitors by the antiquities and intellectual life of Athens); cf. Brochard chap. 6, 209 ff.

66. Cf. Long 222 ff.

67. Hdt. 3.38.4 = Pindar fr. 152 Bowra (more fully in Plato, *Gorg*. 484B; cf. schol. Pindar *Nem*. 9.35); well discussed by Dodds, *Plato: Gorgias* (Oxford, 1959) 270–72.

68. Cic. *Acad*. 2.56–61.

69. Cic. *Acad*. 2.131, *De Fin*. 5.24 ff., *Tusc. Disp*. 5.21–23.

70. Cf. Arist. *Eth. Nic*. 1098^{a}7–20 (1.7.14–16).

71. Strabo 13.1.54 (C.608–9).

72. Ibid. The idiomatic pithiness of the Greek renders it almost untranslatable and is certainly worth recording: μηδὲν ἔχειν φιλοσοφεῖν πραγματικῶς, ἀλλὰ θέσεις ληκυθίζειν. *Pace* LSJ, which connects ληκυθίζειν with the notion of a hollow or booming voice, i.e., the voice supposedly produced by speaking into a lekythos, it seems to me that the metaphor, since a lekythos (normally quite small) was an oil flask or unguent jar, probably has something to do with an oily delivery or well-oiled platitudes. In any case, if either Liddell or Scott ever contrived to boom by declaiming into the average-sized lekythos, with its long narrow body and even narrower neck, they must have been remarkably clever. My own efforts produced nothing more than the proverbial "soft oleaginous mutter."

73. Cf. F. A. Hayek, *The Counter-Revolution of Science* (London, 1955) 13 ff., 73 ff., 105–16.

74. Peters 111.

75. Strabo 2.1.9 (C.70), 15.1.36 (C.702); cf. Cary and Warmington 152–53. Megasthenes was not, however, immune to the usual anthropological fantasizing: e.g., his reports of tribes with no mouths, or living on scented air, or "with feet back to front and eight-toed" (*ap.* Plin. *HN* 7.22–23, 25). But then even Aristotle is not above this kind of thing, crediting the Machlyes not only with generalized androgyny, but also with having a man's left breast and a woman's right: cited *ap.* Plin. *HN* 7.15.

76. Aalders 6.

77. Peters 109.

78. Lloyd, *Greek Science* 11–12.

79. Theophrast. fr. 22 Wimmer.

80. Cic. *De Fin.* 5.13, *Acad.* 1.34.

81. Diog. Laert. 5.58–60 lists Strato's wide-ranging publications, not only on physics (or natural science generally), but also on logic, cosmology, ethics, psychology and zoology, starvation and dizziness (he had what sound like the symptoms of anorexia nervosa), mining machinery, and stockbreeding.

82. Diog. Laert. 5.58.

83. Fraser 1.114; cf. Diog. Laert. 5.59.

84. Fraser 1.427–28 with reff.

85. D. J. Furley, *OCD*² 1018, s.v. "Straton (1) of Lampsacus."

86. Dodds chap. 8, 236 ff.

87. Fraser 1.428, 2.619 n. 419; cf. Furley, *OCD*² 1018.

88. Guthrie, *History* 3.243, discussing Critias fr. 25 Battegazzore and Untersteiner 9 ff., pp. 308–10:

> Then, since the laws prevented men committing
> Acts of open violence, yet they still
> Committed them in secret, then, I believe,
> Some man of shrewd and subtle mind invented
> Fear of the gods for men, something to scare
> Those evildoers, even if they acted—
> Or spoke, or thought—in utter secrecy.

89. When a Peripatetic revival did take place, in the first century B.C., under Andronicus of Rhodes, it consisted in the first instance (as we might expect) of editing, commenting on, and establishing the order of Aristotle's works. How much this retrospective renewal of interest was stimulated (as has been argued) by Sulla's acquisition, and removal to Rome (whence it passed into Andronicus's hands), of the collection of manuscripts recovered through the efforts of Apellicon of Teos (Strabo 13.1.54 [C.609], Plut. *Sull.* 26) seems to me a point of purely academic interest. Cf. above, p. 609. What matters far more is the form that the revival took.

90. Xen. *Mem.* 3.11.17, *Symp.* 8.4; Diog. Laert. 6.2; cf. Rankin chap. 12, 219 ff.; Dudley, *History* chap. 1, 1–16.

91. Diog. Laert. 1.15, 6.2, 13.

92. Ibid. 6.3.

93. Ibid. 6.10: worse, he argued that only the virtuous are well bred!

94. Xen. *Symp.* 4.34–44.

95. Diog. Laert. 6.2.

96. Ibid. 6.3–9, 12–13.

97. *Ap.* Athen. 11.508c.

98. Diog. Laert. 6.7.

99. Cic. *Att.* 12.38: "homo acutus magis quam eruditus."

100. Arist. *Met.* 1024ᵇ27 ff., 1043ᵇ18.

101. Diog. Laert. 6.46, 69.

102. Ibid. 6.72; cf. 6.63, 93, 98.

103. Ibid. 6.72.

104. Ibid. 6.73.

105. Stob. *Flor.* 29.92.

106. Cf. Finley, "Diogenes" 89 ff.

107. Dudley, *History* chap. 2, 17 ff.; Rankin chap. 13, 229 ff.; Aalders 53 ff.

108. Dudley, *History* 62 ff.; Rankin 240–42.

109. E. S. Robinson, "Antiochus King of the Slaves," *NC* 20 (1920) 175 ff.

110. Diog. Laert. 6.20–21; cf. Dudley, *History* 20–23. The Greek is παραχαράττειν τὸ νόμισμα. Aalders (pp. 55–56) is thus wrong to equate the phrase with "a radical *remoulding* of morals and customs" (italics mine).

111. Aalders 63.

112. Diog. Laert. 6.22.

113. Ibid. 6.72–73 *passim.*

114. Ibid. 6.72; cf. Aalders 58.

115. Cf. Finley, "Diogenes" 93; Dudley, *History* 30.

116. Diog. Laert. 6.27.

117. Ibid. 6.22.

118. Finley, "Diogenes" 89; Rankin 229.

119. Diog. Laert. 6.24.

120. Ibid. 6.27, 59.

121. Ibid. 6.54, Ael. *VH* 14.33.

122. Dudley, *History* 117.

123. Cf. ibid. 74–84, and above, pp. 259 ff.

124. Dudley, *History* 78.

125. Cf. ibid. 122 ff.

126. Antipater of Thessalonike, *AP* 11.158.

127. Diog. Laert. 6.85–86 cites his witty utopian revamping of Hom. *Od.* 19.172 ff., and his thumbnail evaluation of current standards, quantified in terms of relative payments:

> Put down for the chef a thousand drachmas, for the doctor one,
> For the flatterer five talents, for the counselor smoke,
> For the whore a talent, for the philosopher three obols.

128. Diog. Laert. 6.87.

129. Plut. *Mor.* 226E.

130. Diog. Laert. 6.94.

131. Texts in Dudley, *History* app. 3, p. 221: Menander, *Didymi* fr. 117 Kock; *AP* 7.143, Epict. 3.22.76; add Diog. Laert. 6.96–98.

Chapter 35. The Garden of Epicurus

1. Rist, *Epicurus* 8.

2. For Epicurus's earlier career, see above, pp. 58 ff.

3. Pollux 9.42; Diog. Laert. 5.38, 10.2; Athen. 13.610e–f; cf. Ferguson, *HA* 104–7.

4. Plut. *Demetr.* 33–34.

5. Diog. Laert. 10.17, 21.

6. Ibid. 10.10–11.

7. Ibid. 10.1.

8. Ibid. 10 *passim*, esp. 1–22.

9. Apollodorus *ap.* Diog. Laert. 10.2, Sext. Emp. *Adv. Math.* 10.18.

10. Diotimus and others *ap.* Diog. Laert. 10.4.

11. Fr. 59 Bailey: Ἀρχὴ καὶ ῥίζα παντὸς ἀγαθοῦ ἡ τῆς γαστρὸς ἡδονή· καὶ τὰ σοφὰ καὶ τὰ περιττὰ ἐπὶ ταύτην ἔχει τὴν ἀναφοράν.

12. Diog. Laert. 10.15, 22 (quoting his last letter verbatim).

13. Ibid. 10.4, Plut. *Mor.* 1100A.

14. Diog. Laert. 10.11.

15. See, e.g., Diog. Laert. 10.4–7 *passim*.

16. Ibid. 10.11.

17. Timocrates *ap.* Diog. Laert. 10.6.

18. Alciphr. *Ep.* 4.17 (2.2), esp. paras. 1–2.

19. Fr. 34 Bailey: in any case his chief admiration seems to have been for Pythocles' intelligence, as Plut. *Mor.* 1124C = fr. 118 Arrighetti[2] makes abundantly clear.

20. Epict. *ap.* Diog. Laert. 10.6.

21. See Jannone, in Association G. Budé, *Actes* 342 ff.; and in general Bignone, *Aristotele* chap. 4, 1.273 ff.

22. Diog. Laert. 10.7–8.

23. Ibid. 10.9 ff.

24. Cf. Cic. *ND* 2.73, 93.

25. Philodemus, Περὶ παρρησίας p. 45.8–11 Olivieri.

26. Diog. Laert. 10.20; Cic. *Tusc. Disp.* 3.37; Plut. *Mor.* 1100A, 1117B–C.

27. Text: Usener 68–81; Arrighetti[2] 120–37 (with Italian tr.); Hicks 2.662–77, Bailey, *Epicurus* 94–105 (with English tr.); Bollack 209–407 (with an extensive French commentary and tr.). Arrighetti[2] and Bailey also provide commentaries. Translations without text: Geer 60–65, Strodach 196–203 (English); Bignone, *Epicuro* 55–69 (Italian).

28. *Ap.* Diog. Laert. 10.29 ff.; separate text in Usener 1–66; Arrighetti[2] 34–117 (with Italian tr.); Hicks 2.564–643, 648–59, Bailey, *Epicurus* 18–93 (with English tr.); Bollack et al. 67–165 (Herodotus letter only; French tr.); Bollack 51–85 (Menoeceus letter only; French tr.). Translations without text: Strodach 113–95, Geer 8–59 (English); Bignone, *Epicuro* 71–143 (Italian).

29. Long 15.

30. Rist, *Epicurus* 11.

31. Ibid. 10.

32. Plut. *Mor.* 1098B, 1129B.

33. Ibid. 653E–654F.

34. Epicur. *ap.* Sen. *Ep. Mor.* 25.5; Long 15.

35. *Ep. Pyth.* 84.

36. Lloyd, *Greek Science* 21 ff.

37. *Kyr. Dox.* XI–XII.

38. *Ep. Men.* 134.

39. Fr. 15 Arrighetti[2], p. 168.

40. *Ep. Men.* 135. Cf. *Kyr. Dox.* XVI, *Gnom. Vat.* XLVII.

41. Lloyd, *Greek Science* 24.

42. Cf. Lucret. 2.216–93; Cic. *De Fin.* 1.18, *ND* 1.70; further reff. in Usener 199 ff. (fr. 281). The belief that the *clinamen* was a late addition to Epicurean doctrine—see, e.g., Bignone, *A&R* 8 (1940) 159–98—has been well disposed of by Moutsopoulos, in Association G. Budé, *Actes* 175–82, who detects the presence of the concept in the *Letter to Herodotus*.

43. Lucret. 5.443–48 (concourse of atoms), 5.495–508 (creation of the world), cf. 1.1021–37; 2.1116–17, 1131–32, 1144–45, 1153–56, 1173–74 (decaying and end of the world).

44. *Ep. Pyth.* 104: μόνον ὁ μῦθος ἀπέστω· ἀπέσται δέ, ἐάν τις καλῶς τοῖς φαινομένοις ἀκολουθῶν περὶ τῶν ἀφανῶν σημειῶται, etc.

45. *Ep. Pyth.* 96, 99, 100.

46. *Ep. Pyth.* 93: μὴ φοβούμενος τὰς ἀνδραποδώδεις ἀστρολόγων τεχνιτείας; cf. Arrighetti[2] 528, "un piú che probabile accenno alla polemica contro gli ὄργανα astronomici."

47. See Taylor, in Schofield et al. 105 ff.

48. *Kyr. Dox.* I.139, Cic. *ND* 1.18, Lucret. 3.18–24; cf. Bailey, *Greek Atomists* 467 ff.; Rist, *Epicurus* 140 ff.

49. See frr. 367–69 Usener, pp. 245 ff.

50. Rist, *Epicurus* 148.

51. Zeller 405–8.

52. Rist, *Epicurus* 156–57.

53. *Ep. Men.* 123–24, Cic. *ND* 1.43–45.

54. Arist. *Pol.* 1253ᵃ3.

55. Diog. Laert. 10.120: μόναρχον ἐν καιρῷ θεραπεύσειν.

56. Aalders 40–41, with testimonia.

57. *Ep. Men.* 128.

58. *Gnom. Vat.* LIX: ἄπληστον οὐ γαστήρ, ὥσπερ οἱ πολλοί φασιν, ἀλλὰ δόξα ψευδὴς ὑπὲρ τοῦ γαστρὸς ἀορίστου πληρώματος. Cf. also *Gnom. Vat.* LXIII, LXVIII, LXIX; fr. 74 Bailey.

59. Diog. Laert. 10.4–7 *passim*.

60. Diog. Laert. 10.6 = Athen. 12.546e, with slight textual variants.

61. Athen. 12.546f, 547a = frr. 409, 315 Usener.

62. *Kyr. Dox.* VIII.

63. *Gnom. Vat.* LI: ἀφροδίσια γὰρ οὐδέποτε ὤνησαν· ἀγαπητὸν δὲ εἰ μὴ ἔβλαψαν. Arrighetti², p. 151, attributes this passage to Metrodorus rather than Epicurus.

64. Diog. Laert. 10.11 f.; cf. *Gnom. Vat.* LI.

65. Diog. Laert. 10.119, citing Epicurus's *Problems* (Διαπορίαι) and *On Nature* (Περὶ φύσεως); cf. Epict. *Diss.* 1.23.3.

66. *Gnom. Vat.* LI: the Greek has a contemptuous edge to it that cannot be caught in translation: σὺ δὲ ὅταν μήτε τοὺς νόμους καταλύῃς μήτε τὰ καλῶς ἔθη κείμενα κινῇς μήτε τῶν πλησίον τινα λυπῇς μήτε τὴν σάρκα καταξαίνῃς μήτε τὰ ἀναγκαῖα καταναλίσκῃς, χρῶ ὡς βούλει τῇ σεαυτοῦ προαιρέσει.

67. *Ep. Men.* 128: τούτου γὰρ χάριν πάντα πράττομεν, ὅπως μήτε ἀλγῶμεν μήτε ταρβῶμεν.

68. De Witt 329.

69. Diog. Laert. 10.18; cf. Festugière, *Epicurus* 22–26; De Witt 104–5.

70. E.g., Long 17; De Witt chap. 15, 328 ff.

71. Furley, *OCD*² 391, s.v. "Epicurus"; cf. Zeller 408 with n. 3.

72. *Gnom. Vat.* LII; cf. *Kyr. Dox.* XXVII, which rates friendship as the *summum bonum* of the complete life.

73. *Gnom. Vat.* LVIII.

74. Fr. 551 Usener = fr. 86 Bailey: λάθε βιώσας.

75. Cf. *Kyr. Dox.* XL.

76. Metrodorus *ap. Gnom. Vat.* XXXI.

77. *Kyr. Dox.* II.

78. *Ep. Men.* 125.

79. Lucret. 3.830–1094 *passim*; the lines quoted are 1078–79: "certa quidem finis uitae mortalibus adstat / nec deuitari letum pote quin obeamus."

80. Plut. *Mor.* 1107B–C: τοιαύτην χώραν ἡδονῶν τοσούτων Ἐπίκουρος ἐκτέμνεται. The image is surgical, perhaps even with a hint of gelding about it.

81. *Gnom. Vat.* XIV.

82. *Gnom. Vat.* XLVIII.

83. Peter Koestenbaum, *The Vitality of Death* (New York, 1971) 28.

84. The sea, perhaps not coincidentally, provides one of Lucretius's best-remembered images for just this condition (*DRN* 2.1–4): "Sweet, when over a great expanse of sea the winds are whipping up the wavetops, / To observe, from dry land, another's great tribulation: / Not because it is an enjoyable pleasure to watch anyone suffer, / But because it is sweet to perceive what ills you yourself are free from." The mixture of faint social guilt and overwhelming smug satisfaction is not attractive.

85. Cf. Bailey, *Greek Atomists* 218 ff.

86. Colotes *ap.* Plut. *Mor.* 1124D.

87. Aalders 43.

88. Preserved verbatim, Diog. Laert. 10.16–21 *passim*.

89. Rist, *Epicurus* 12.

90. Philodemus, *Pragm.* 19, 30 Diano = frr. 120–21 Arrighetti[2].

91. Fr. 42 Bailey.

92. *Ap.* Plut. *Mor.* 1117D–E = fr. 130 Usener.

93. Diog. Laert. 10.11.

94. Ibid. 10.21.

95. Diog. Laert. 10.26–28 lists a representative selection. Perhaps it was because of the accusations of plagiarism that Diogenes Laertius goes out of his way to say, of Epicurus's collected works, that "no external testimony is written into them: they contain Epicurus's own words throughout."

96. De Witt 337.

97. Cost of Garden: Apollodorus *ap.* Diog. Laert. 10.10. Price of Gorgias's lectures: DS 12.53.2.

98. Cic. *De Fin.* 1.65. In Cicero's day the house was in ruins, and both it and the Garden were owned by a wealthy Roman, C. Memmius, who was, ironically enough, Lucretius's patron and the dedicatee of that great Epicurean poem the *De Rerum Natura*. Memmius left the house as it was, but refused to give the Garden back.

99. Diog. Laert. 10.7.

100. *Gnom. Vat.* LXVII.

101. Cic. *De Fin.* 2.20, Diog. Laert. 10.12.

102. Evidence collected by Usener, pp. 104–6, no. 29: see in particular Diog. Laert. 10.30–31; Cic. *De Fin.* 1.63, *ND* 1.43; Plut. *Mor.* 1118A.

103. Diog. Laert. 10.6 = fr. 33 Bailey.

104. Diog. Laert. 10.6; Plut. *Mor.* 1093C–D, 1094–95 *passim*.

105. Sext. Emp. *Adv. Math.* 1.1, ἐν πολλοῖς γὰρ ἀμαθὴς Ἐπίκουρος ἐλέγχεται; Cic. *De Fin.* 1.22, 26; Diog. Laert. 10.31; Athen. 13.588a; Aul. Gell. *NA* 2.8.1–8, 9 *passim* (defense of Epicurus against Plutarch's criticisms); cf. Zeller 420 ff.; Rist, *Epicurus* 14.

106. Lucret. 5.8–10: "deus ille fuit, deus, inclyte Memmi, / qui princeps uitae rationem inuenit eam quae / nunc appellatur sapientia."

107. *Ep. Men.* 135: ζήσεις δὲ ὡς θεὸς ἐν ἀνθρώποις. οὐθὲν γὰρ ἔοικε θνητῷ ζῴῳ ζῶν ἄνθρωπος ἐν ἀθανάτοις ἀγάθοις. Cf. the letter to Colotes (Plut. *Mor.* 1117B = fr. 141 Usener, fr. 65 Arrighetti[2]).

108. Diog. Laert. 8.62; Clem. Alex. *Strom.* 6.30 = fr. 399 Kirk, Raven, and Schofield, pp. 313–14.

109. Cic. *De Fin.* 5.3, Plin. *HN* 35.5; cf. De Witt 100–101.

110. De Witt 104–5.

111. Ibid. 31–32.

112. Long 72.

113. C. Jensen, *Ein neuer Brief Epikurs* (Berlin, 1933) fr. 1.

114. *PHerc.* 1005 col. 4.10 Sbordone = fr. 196 Arrighetti[2], p. 548; cf. Festugière, *Epicurus* 32 with n. 30, p. 44; Diog. Laert. 10.133–34.

Chapter 36. Stoicism: The Wide and Sheltering Porch

1. For an excellent account of Stoicism's survivals and transmutations from the Middle Ages to the twentieth century, see Spanneut chaps. 6–8, pp. 179–382.

2. See, e.g., H. A. K. Hunt 17 ff., Watson 9 ff.

3. Diog. Laert. 7.156 = *SVF* 2.774, p. 217; Cic. *Tusc. Disp.* 1.77 = *SVF* 2.822, p. 225; cf. Hoven 44 ff.

4. Zeller 351 ff.

5. G. Watson, "The Natural Law and Stoicism," in Long, ed., *Problems* chap. 10, 235.

6. Aalders 75.

7. Cic. *Tusc. Disp.* 3.51.

8. Arist. *Eth. Nic.* 2.1107^{b}17–22.

9. *SVF* 1.222, 248, 252, 259–70 (pp. 54, 59–62).

10. There were exceptions; for the (perhaps joking) shock tactics employed by Chrysippus, see p. 639.

11. Long 108.

12. Cf. Sambursky, *Physical World* chap. 4, 81 ff., "The Whole and Its Parts."

13. *Ap.* Plut. *Mor.* 1050b = *SVF* 2.937, p. 269: οὐθὲν γὰρ ἔστιν ἄλλως τῶν κατὰ μέρος γενέσθαι οὐδὲ τοὐλάχιστον, ἢ κατὰ τὴν κοινὴν φύσιν καὶ κατὰ τὸν ἐκείνης λόγον.

14. Cic. *ND* 2.13–15; cf. Long 149.

15. Chrysippus *ap.* Cic. *ND* 2.16: "atqui res caelestes omnesque eae quarum est ordo sempiternus ab homine confici non possunt; est igitur id quo illa conficiuntur homine melius; id autem quid potius dixeris quam deum?"

16. Long 149.

17. Lloyd, *Greek Science* 29; cf. Moreau 166 ff.; H. A. K. Hunt chap. 2, 17 ff.; Hahm chap. 5, 166 ff. See *SVF* 1.97–114 (pp. 27–33), 2.633–45 (pp. 191–94).

18. See frr. 476–80 Kirk, Raven, and Schofield; Diog. Laert. 2.6; cf. Guthrie, *History* 3.272 ff.

19. See frr. 601 ff. Kirk, Raven and Schofield; cf. Guthrie, *History* 3.364 ff.

20. Long 150; cf. Rist, *Stoic Philosophy* 86–87.

21. Sambursky, *Physical World* 44: "The Stoic doctrine of pneuma was the first consistent and elaborate continuum theory of matter." Sambursky's entire monograph is of great importance for a proper appreciation of Stoic physics and cosmology, though he is perhaps a little overprone to stress parallels (sometimes more apparent than real) with modern scientific thought.

22. Cf. Sandbach 14 ff.

23. Ibid. 29–30.

24. Sext. Emp. *Adv. Math.* 11.170 = *SVF* 3.598, p. 156.

25. Clem. Alex. *Strom.* 2.420 = *SVF* 3.332, p. 81.

26. Cic. *De Div.* 1.127 = *SVF* 2.944, p. 272.

27. *SVF* 2.967, p. 281.

28. Sandbach 16.

29. Marc. Aurel. *Med.* 10.6; cf. 4.23, 5.8, 8.46, and elsewhere.

30. Chrysippus *ap.* Plut. *Mor.* 1050F: ἡ δὲ κακία πρὸς τὰ δεινὰ συμπτώματα ἴδιόν τινα ἔχει λόγον· γίνεται μὲν γὰρ καὶ αὐτή πως κατὰ τὸν τῆς φύσεως λόγον, καὶ . . . οὐκ ἀχρήστως γίνεται πρὸς τὰ ὅλα. Cf. *Mor.* 1065B, D, 1066D = *SVF* 2.1181, p. 339–40.

31. Long 180.

32. Preserved *ap.* Stob. *Flor.* 1.1.12 = *SVF* 1.537, pp. 121–23; lines 11 ff. are cited in the text. There is a complete translation in Sandbach 110–11.

33. For Tubero, see Klebs, *RE* 1 (1894) s.v. "Aelius (155)," cols. 535–37. Cicero elsewhere (*Brut.* 117), while conceding his virtue, describes him as "ut uita sic oratione durus, incultus, horridus."

34. See, e.g., Diog. Laert. 7.128; Cic. *De Offic.* 3.63, 89–90.

35. See, e.g., Sen. *Ep. Mor.* 17.3, *Dial.* 9.8.1.

36. Cic. *De Orat.* 1.228–29; cf. *De Offic.* 3.10, *Brut.* 113–15; Sen. *Dial.* 1.3.4, 7.

37. For a list of known Stoics at Rome under the Republic, with testimonia, see Reesor 5–6 with nn. 22–34. They included, among others, P. Mucius Scaevola (cos. 133), his son Quintus (cos. 95), P. Rutilius Rufus, and M. Porcius Cato Uticensis.

38. E.g., Cic. *Pro Mur.* 62.

39. As Rist, *Stoic Philosophy* 173, reminds us, these terms—unlike, say, the Middle Academy—were not known in antiquity; but I retain them as useful shorthand labels.

40. Cf. Arnold 81–83.

41. Cf. Long 114, 196.

42. Diog. Laert. 7.183; cf. above, pp. 638–39.

43. See, e.g., Pearson 48, Arnold 91–92.

44. Diog. Laert. 7.179.

45. Ibid. 180–81.

46. Dion. Hal. *De Comp. Verb.* 30 = *SVF* 2.28, p. 11; Diog. Laert. 7.180.

47. Gould 206.

48. Diog. Laert. 7.182. His statue in the Kerameikos was almost hidden by an equestrian group, and Carneades, in consequence, referred to him as Crypsippos ("Horse-Hidden") rather than Chrysippos ("Golden Horse").

49. Diog. Laert. 7.181, 185: the conflict between Ptolemy II and Antiochus I on the Cilician coast in the mid-270s would be the natural occasion for such a confiscation. Cf. Bevan, *House of Seleucus* 1.147 ff.

50. Diog. Laert. 7.182–83.

51. Ibid. 7.187–88. For the increase in middle-class puritanism during the postclassical period, cf. Green, "Sex and Classical Literature," in A. Bold, ed., *The Sexual Dimension in Literature* (London, 1983) 32 ff., 40 ff.

52. Diog. Laert. 7.32–34, 187–88.

53. Laffranque 46–48, 50–52; Plut *Cic.* 4–5, cf. Laffranque 93–94.

54. ἐκπύρωσις is outlined in frr. 64–69 Van Straaten: see esp. Cic. *ND* 2.118; Stob. *Flor.* 1.20; cf. Van Straaten, *Panétius* 64 ff.; Rist, *Stoic Philosophy* 175–76.

55. Cic. *De Div.* 2.87–97 = fr. 74 Van Straaten, cf. frr. 68, 70–71, 73; Rist, *Stoic Philosophy* 177–78. Panaetius's reasons for rejecting astrology are of interest: (1) events taking place so far away in the heavens cannot affect what happens on earth; (2) since the position of each star constantly varies in relation to different parts of the earth, it could not, in any case, produce uniform results. On the other hand Panaetius wrote a work *On Providence* (Cic. *Att.* 13.8 = fr. 33 Van Straaten), and probably aimed to modify, rather than abolish, the theory of cosmic sympathy and the practice of divination that went with it.

56. Reesor 4.

57. Cf. Sandbach 18: "A difficulty faces anyone who writes about the Stoics: not a single work remains extant that was written by any one of them during the first three hundred years after the foundation of the school." The Alexander historian, who has to deal with an identical problem, can only sympathize.

58. Seneca's style, now in rhetorical fashion again, was decried in antiquity (not without reason) as vulgar, hyperbolic, and ignorant: Aul. Gell. *NA* 12.2.1, Quintil. 10.1.125 ff. These criticisms still have some force; and just how firm Seneca was in his Stoic convictions is also open to doubt: cf. Arnold 114 ff. But the problem, fortunately, lies beyond the scope of the present work.

59. Long 115.

60. Diog. Laert. 7.6, 10–12; cf. Tarn, *Antigonus* 309 with n. 106.

61. Diog. Laert. 7.24.

62. Ibid. 7.15.

63. For Zeno's early career, see above, pp. 61 ff.

64. That concession had been procured through the representations of the tyrant of Argos, Aristodamus; Arcesilaus, then head of the Academy, had, for reasons best known to himself, refused to intervene. Cf. Ferguson, *HA* 191.

65. As Long says (p. 117), the state of our evidence is such that much of the time, particularly for the Early Stoa, it is hard to attribute ideas to specific individuals.

66. Cf. Dodds 245 ff. For Poseidonius's interest in astrology, see A. A. Long, in Barnes et al. 170–71.

67. Cf. Rist, *Stoic Philosophy* 197–98.

68. See, e.g., 1.15–17, 18–19, 20, 66–67, 93–101 = frr. 103–7 Van Straaten.

69. *SIG*³ 2.725a = fr. 4a Van Straaten.

70. Rist, *Stoic Philosophy* 189.

71. Diog. Laert. 7.128 = fr. 110 Van Straaten; cf. Rist, *Stoic Philosophy* 7–10.

72. Lesky 678.

73. Von Fritz, *OCD*² 774, s.v. "Panaetius"; cf. Aalders 100.

74. Cic. *De Offic.* 1.20 = fr. 105 Van Straaten.

75. *Suda* s.v. Παναίτιος; Cic. *De Fin.* 4.23, *Att.* 12.2; Plut. *Mor.* 814C–D.

76. Laffranque 1–44; Long 216–22; Rist, *Stoic Philosophy* 201 ff.; Sandbach 129–39.

77. Cf. T 14–26 Edelstein and Kidd. Laffranque, 66 ff., advances good arguments for placing Poseidonius's travels for the most part in the period between 101 and 91.

78. *FGrH* IIA 87, pp. 225–317; cf. Laffranque, chap. 4, 109 ff.

79. *FGrH* IIA 87 F 109–10, 111b, 112; cf. Treves, *OCD*² 868, s.v. "Posidonius."

80. Strabo 11.1.6 (C.492). The Homeric tag was the instruction given to Glaucus by his father, Hippolochus, when setting out for Troy (Hom. *Il.* 6.208), "ever to fight bravely and to be superior to others."

81. Cic. *Tusc. Disp.* 2.61 professes to render Poseidonius's apostrophe to his suffering verbatim: "Nihil agis, dolor! quamuis sis molestus, nunquam te esse confitebor malum." Further testimonia in Plut. *Pomp.* 42, Plin. *HN* 7.112. Of the meeting Laffranque shrewdly observes (pp. 94–95): "Hommage et coquetterie réciproques, apparamment."

82. Treves, *OCD*² 868.

83. Cf. Rist, *Stoic Philosophy* 212–13, who remarks that the "parallelism between man and the world-soul has begun to break down in Panaetius, and does not exist in Posidonius."

84. Aesch. *PV* 442–68.

85. Sen. *Ep. Mor.* 90.7 ff.

86. Long 218.

87. M. Frede, in Schofield et al. 225.

88. Diog. Laert. 7.149, Cic. *De Div.* 1.125 (= frr. 27, 107 Edelstein and Kidd; cf. frr. 108–113b).

89. Rist, *Stoic Philosophy* 217–18.

90. Pohlenz 1.257: "Spekulatives Denken und die hellenische Freude an der θεωρία, an der Schau und Erkenntnis um ihrer selbst willen, waren ihnen fremd," etc. Cf. Watson, 87–88: "Any philosophy fell into bad company in going to Rome; the very translation into Latin seems to degrade the thought and make it insincere and rhetorical. . . . The function philosophy acquired under the Empire was like that of court spirituality, the providing of a retreat from the harsh realities and decisions of everyday life."

91. Lapidge, "Stoic Cosmology," in Rist, ed., *Stoics* chap. 7, 184.

92. Watson 87; cf. Spanneut 214 ff.

93. Cic. *Ep.* fr. 8.4 Purser: "Philosophiae quidem praecepta noscenda, uiuendum autem ciuiliter."

94. Long 216; cf. 233.

95. Cf. Sandbach 48 ff.

96. Cf. Plato, *Phaed.* 62C6–8, cf. *Laws* 873C–D; Xen. *Mem.* 4.4.4; Rist, *Stoic Philosophy* 234–35; Arnold 310.

97. Cf. Rist, *Stoic Philosophy* 246 ff.

98. Plut. *Mor.* 1042D = *SVF* 3.759, p. 188; cf. nos. 757–68 *passim*.

99. Diog. Laert. 7.28, 176.

100. Rist, *Stoic Philosophy* 237, discussing Diog. Laert. 6.24, 86.

101. Sen. *Ep. Mor.* 12.10. Rist, *Stoic Philosophy* 247–48, deflates the Senecan exaltation of suicide with an attractive blend of logical rigor and historical insight.

102. In general the discussion by Rist, *Stoic Philosophy* chap. 13, "Suicide," 233 ff., is both thorough and penetrating; I am much indebted to it for what appears here.

103. Cf. Stough, "Stoic Determinism and Moral Responsibility," in Rist, ed., *Stoics*

chap. 9, 203–31; Long, "Freedom and Determinism in the Stoic Theory of Human Action," in Long, ed., *Problems* chap. 8, 173–99. Both agree on the validity of free moral choice for a Stoic, i.e., whether to live in harmony with nature or not. Over the causal nexus, Long concedes (pp. 193–94) that "the Stoics were too ready to keep their cake and eat it," and adds—a remark I heartily endorse—that "the demands of teleology and providence, combined with pantheism, impose an undeniable strain on the credibility of their ethics."

104. Sandbach 71; Sambursky, *Physical World*, esp. chap. 1.
105. Asa Briggs, *A Social History of England* (New York, 1983) 106.
106. Sandbach 69.

Chapter 37. Caesar, Pompey, and the Last of the Ptolemies, 80–30

1. The nomenclature and numeration of the Ptolemies, the latter in particular, have always caused problems. Ptolemy Auletes, at the time of writing, is labeled, variously, X (Sherwin-White 265), XI (Huzar 188, reviving an old tradition), XII (Will, HP² 2.519 ff.; Greenhalgh, *Pompey: The Roman Alexander* 141 ff.; Gelzer, *Caesar* 76, etc., Gruen, *HW* 167 n. 59; and others), and XIII (Seager, *Pompey* 115 ff., etc.). Since these rival computations are due merely to the inclusion or omission of various minor or illegitimate Ptolemies in the royal canon—e.g., Ptolemy Apion, or Auletes' younger brother, who ruled solely in Cyprus—they cause unnecessary confusion, without adding anything to our enlightenment except, perhaps, a suspicion of affectation in the historian. I am sticking to XII because, having by far the widest support, it remains the most easily recognized. Similarly, though Cleopatra VII should really be Cleopatra VI (below, n. 21), I have adhered to the more commonly accepted title.

2. Caes. *Bell. Civ.* 3.107; Cic. *Att.* 2.16.2, *Pro Rab. Post.* 3.
3. Von der Mühll, *RE* 1A (1914) cols. 25–28, s.v. "Rabirius (6)."
4. The bribe to Caesar: Suet. *Div. Jul.* 54.3. Loans (amount unspecified) from Rabirius: Cic. *Pro Rab. Post.* 4–6; cf. Dio Cass. 39.12.1. This passage of Dio also states that Ptolemy raised his bribes to "certain of the Romans" τὰ μὲν οἴκοθεν τὰ δὲ καὶ δανεισάμενος (Badian, *Roman Imperialism* 73, is therefore wrong to claim that the entire sum was obtained from "some equestrian circles"), and adds that Ptolemy was "forcibly recouping this money from the Egyptians." Estimates of Ptolemaic revenues in Auletes' time: DS 17.52.6 (over 6,000 talents); Cic. *ap.* Strabo 17.1.13, C.798 (12,500 talents). Cicero may well have been exaggerating for his own purposes.

5. App. *Mithr.* 63.
6. Dio Cass. 39.12.1–2.
7. Plut. *Cat. Min.* 35.
8. Cic. *Brut.* 30; Vell. Pat. 2.13.2; Val. Max. 2.10.5; Livy, *per.* 70.
9. Van Ooteghem 139 ff.; Greenhalgh, *Pompey: The Roman Alexander* 79–80, 88–89, 105–8.
10. "In an Asia Minor Municipality": Cavafy, Ποιήματα Β´ 50 = *Collected Poems* 264–65; quoted at greater length on p. 82 above.
11. Strabo 17.1.11 (C.796).
12. Athen. 5.206d: οὐκ ἀνδρὸς γενομένου ἀλλ᾽ αὐλητοῦ καὶ μάγου.
13. *CIG* III 29.4926: Τρύφων Διονύσου τοῦ Νέου Κίναιδος.
14. *OGIS* 50–51.
15. Dio Cass. 39.12.1–2.
16. Cf. Fraser 1.794–95.
17. For these negotiations, and their consequences, see Strabo 17.1.11 (C.796); cf. Dio Cass. 39.57.1–2; Livy, *per.* 105; Plut. *Ant.* 3.
18. H. Heinen, "Séleucus Cybiosactès et le problème de son identité," in *Antidorum W. Peremans* (Louvain, 1968) 105 ff., argues that Kybiosaktes was, in fact, a brother of Antiochus XIII, but the evidence is highly dubious.

19. Dio Cass. 39.13.1, 57.1; Strabo *loc. cit.* (above, n. 17); Porph. *ap.* Euseb. *Chron.* 1.167–68 Schoene.

20. See Bouché-Leclercq, *HL* 2.144 ff.; Macurdy 175 ff.

21. Though Cleopatra V Tryphaena, for whatever reason, is not mentioned in the surviving papyri after 69/8, she nevertheless appears in a temple inscription at Edfu of 5 December 57: a necessary corollary of this, accepted by Bouché-Leclercq (above, n. 20) but denied by many, is that all five of Auletes' known children—Berenice IV, Cleopatra VII, Arsinoë, Ptolemy XIII, and Ptolemy XIV—were his legitimate offspring, and Cleopatra Tryphaena their mother. Porphyry (*loc. cit.*, n. 19) mistakenly identifies her as Auletes' daughter rather than his sister-wife, a venial and easy error for anyone not closely familiar with the complex Ptolemaic genealogy, in which identical names endlessly repeat themselves. Scholarly acceptance of this fictitious "Cleopatra VI Tryphaena" (most recently by Pomeroy, *Women* 24) has merely added to the confusion. Similarly, far too much has been made of Strabo's statement (*loc. cit.*, n. 17) that of Auletes' three daughters, Berenice, Cleopatra, and Arsinoë (no room for an extra Cleopatra Tryphaena there), only the eldest, i.e., Berenice, was legitimate. Strabo here has clearly confused Berenice IV, Auletes' daughter, with his half-sister, Cleopatra Berenice, who indeed (after the elimination of two sons by Cleopatra Selene) *was* the only legitimate surviving issue of Ptolemy IX Lathyros (cf. Paus. 1.9.3), and who reigned alone for some months in 80 before her stepson (or, possibly, son) and husband, Ptolemy XI Alexander II, was associated with her (above, p. 554).

22. Cic. *Pro Rab. Post.* 20–21, 30, 36; Plut. *Pomp.* 45. Badian, *Roman Imperialism* 74, puts this figure in perspective by pointing out that it was "600 times the 'equestrian census' and more than the total of Roman revenues from the provinces before Pompey's eastern conquests."

23. Cic. *In Pison.* 48–50, Plut. *Ant.* 3, Strabo 12.3.34 (C.558), Dio Cass. 39.57.2–58.3, App. *Bell. Civ.* 5.8.

24. One interesting consequence of Gabinius's Egyptian campaign was that large numbers of his troops, attracted by the fleshpots of Alexandria, stayed on there as Ptolemaic mercenaries, and in that capacity later gave Caesar considerable trouble (cf. pp. 664–67): cf. *Bell. Alex.*, *passim*, Caes. *Bell. Civ.* 3.110.

25. App. *Bell. Civ.* 5.8 *ad fin.*

26. The annexation of Cyprus was achieved through the *Lex Clodia* of 59/8, against the vigorous opposition of Caesar's enemies (Clodius being his lieutenant), chief among them Cato, who, by a nice irony, was sent out to implement the decree he had fought. Ptolemy XII's younger brother, the ruler of Cyprus, committed suicide rather than go into "retirement" as a local priest: App. *Bell. Civ.* 2.23; Dio Cass. 38.30.5, 39.22.2–4; Cic. *Pro Sest.* 57, 59; Strabo 14.6.6 (C.684); Plut. *Cat. Min.* 34–38; Vell. Pat. 2.38.6, 45.5; Livy, *per.* 104.

27. Sherwin-White 266–68.

28. Cic. *Pro Rab. Post.* 4.

29. Ibid. 29.

30. Ibid. *passim*, esp. 4–8, 21–28, 39–40.

31. Cic. *De Prov. Cons.* 10.

32. Cic. *Ad Q. Fratr.* 3.1.5.

33. Plut. *Crass.* 13, Suet. *Div. Jul.* 11.

34. Sherwin-White 267–68.

35. App. *Mithr.* 54–58, Plut. *Sull.* 24; cf. Will, *HP*² 2.485.

36. App. *Mithr.* 67.

37. Ibid. 64–66.

38. Plut. *Pomp.* 24; App. *Mithr.* 63, 119; Flor. 1.41.2.

39. Plut. *Sert.* 23–24; App. *Mithr.* 68–70, 87, cf. Plut. *Luc.* 7; Cic. *De Imp. Pomp.* 9, *Pro Mur.* 32; Oros. 6.2.12; Sallust, *Hist.* Bk. 2, frr. 78–79 Maurenbrecher; Flor 2.10.4.

40. Plut. *Sert.* 23. We may note that very soon afterwards Nicomedes IV of Bithynia,

like Attalus III of Pergamon, left his kingdom to Rome, and it was thereafter turned into a province (74): Livy, *per.* 93; App. *Mithr.* 71, *Bell. Civ.* 1.111. Whether Sertorius's declaration affected this decision we have no means of knowing. For Mithridates' negotiations with Sertorius, cf. Magie 1.322–23, 2.1203.

41. Plut. *Sert.* 23. App. *Mithr.* 68 claims that Sertorius conceded Asia too; but the reservation Plutarch describes is absolutely in character and carries instant conviction. Cf. Sherwin-White 161 with n. 11; Philip O. Spann, *Quintus Sertorius and the Legacy of Sulla* (Fayetteville 1987) 89, 99–103.

42. Cf. Sherwin-White 161.

43. Technically, the third: the trouble with Murena in 83–81, which Sulla, through his agent Aulus Gabinius, finally stopped, reconciling Mithridates and Ariobarzanes (for the moment) through the marriage of the former's four-year-old daughter to the latter's son, was dignified with the name "Second Mithridatic War": App. *Mithr.* 64, 66; cf. Sherwin-White 149–52.

44. App. *Mithr.* 68–71; Livy, *per.* 93; Sallust, *Hist.* Bk. 4, fr. 69.13 Maurenbrecher; Cic. *De Imp. Pomp.* 9.24–25.

45. App. *Mithr.* 78, Plut. *Luc.* 23.

46. App. *Mithr.* 69.

47. Vell. Pat. 2.40.1.

48. Cf. Sherwin-White 163.

49. Cf. App. *Mithr.* 71, where he is described as ἀσθενὴς τὰ πολέμια πάμπαν.

50. Plut. *Luc.* 5–6, *Pomp.* 20; Vell. Pat. 2.33.1; Cic. *Pro Mur.* 33. On the chronology, see Sherwin-White 165 with n. 25.

51. Vell. Pat. 2.31.3; Livy, *per.* 97; Cic. *II Verr.* 2.3.8, 3.91.213.

52. Cf. Ormerod 227 ff., and in *CAH* IX 372–75; Garlan, "Signification"; Brulé 117 ff. (Crete); M. Clavel-Lévêque, "Brigandage et piraterie: Représentations idéologiques et pratiques impérialistes au dernier siècle de la République," *DHA* 4 (1978) 17–31.

53. Strabo 14.5.2 (C.668).

54. Cf. Garlan, "Signification": we have here a combination of his categories (3) and (4), state-organized piracy, and "social brigandage" as part of a resistance movement.

55. Strabo 14.5.2 (C.668).

56. App. *Mithr.* 70.

57. Greenhalgh, *Pompey: The Roman Alexander* 77, who also points out—an apt comparison—that Mithridates "took the pirates into his service in much the same way that the Ottoman sultans were to make use of the Barbary corsairs in the sixteenth century AD." Queen Elizabeth I's dealings with Sir Francis Drake also come to mind.

58. Cic. *II Verr.* 3.37.85, 80.186; 4.47.104, 52.116; 5.25.62, 34.87, 35.91–92, 37.97–98, 38.100, 52.137–38; App. *Mithr.* 93.

59. Strabo 14.5.2 (C.668–69), Flor. 1.41.1–7, App. *Mithr.* 92–93, Plut. *Pomp.* 24, Dio Cass. 36.20–23.

60. Dio Cass. 36.22.2–3.

61. Ibid. 36.23.1–2.

62. App. *Mithr.* 93, Plut. *Pomp.* 24.

63. App. *Mithr.* 92.

64. Plut. *Pomp.* 24.

65. Cf. Clavel-Lévêque (above, n. 52) 27–28.

66. Livy, *per.* 68; Plut. *Pomp.* 24; Cic. *De Orat.* 1.82; Jul. Obs. 44.

67. Sallust, *Hist.* Bk. 1, frr. 127–32 Maurenbrecher, Bk. 2 frr. 81, 87; Eutrop. 6.3; Livy, *per.* 90, 93; Oros. 5.23.21; App. *Mithr.* 93; Flor. 1.41.4–5; Cic. *II Verr.* 3.90.210 ff.; Strabo 12.6.2 (C. 568).

68. Vell. Pat. 2.31.3–4.

69. Cic. *II Verr.* 3.91.213–92.215.

70. Flor. 1.42.1–3; Livy, *per.* 97; cf. Ormerod 226–27.

71. Livy, *per.* 97; DS 40.1. Florus (42.7.1) asserts that the undeclared ulterior object of this expedition was the conquest of Crete, its excuse the fact that the Cretans had supported Mithridates.

72. Plut. *Ant.* 1, Dio Cass. 30–35.111.1.

73. Flor. 1.42.4: "totam insulam igni ferroque populatus." Cf. Plut. *Pomp.* 29; Dio Cass. 36.1a, 17a; Livy, *per.* 98–100; App. *Sic.* fr. 6.2 White; Vell. Pat. 2.34.1; Cic. *Pro Flac.* 6, 30, 33, *De Imp. Pomp.* 46; DS 40.1; Eutrop. 6.11.1; Oros. 6.4.2.

74. Plut. *Pomp.* 29 (anti-Pompeian); Dio Cass. 36.17a–19 (anti-Metellan); Livy, *per.* 99; Val. Max. 7.6.1.

75. Flor. 1.42.6: "nec quicquam tamen amplius de tam famosa uictoria quam cognomen Creticum reportauit." Cf. Greenhalgh, *Pompey: The Roman Alexander* 97–100.

76. Greenhalgh, ibid. 98.

77. But see, e.g., Van Ooteghem 200; J. M. Cobban, *Senate and Provinces 78–49 BC* (Cambridge, 1935) 113–14; and Ormerod, *CAH* IX 371, for appreciative estimates of his military achievement.

78. App. *Mithr.* 72–91 *passim*, Plut. *Luc.* 5–36 *passim*, Dio Cass. 36.1–16; cf. Will, *HP²* 2.493, 496, for a convenient conspectus of other minor scattered sources, and Sherwin-White 167 ff. for an up-to-date narrative of the campaign.

79. Plut. *Luc.* 20.

80. App. *Mithr.* 63.

81. Plut. *Luc.* 14, 39–43; Cic. *De Offic.* 1.39, *De Leg.* 3.13; Athen. 2.50f–51b, 6.274e–f, 12.543a; Plin. *HN* 9.170, 14.96, 15.102; cf. Van Ooteghem 166–99; Magie 1.350.

82. Plut. *Luc.* 37, *Cat. Min.* 29; Vell. Pat. 2.34.2; Plin. *HN* 14.96, 34.36; Cic. *Acad.* 2.3, *Pro Mur.* 37, 69; App. *Mithr.* 77; cf. Van Ooteghem 163 ff. Epigraphical evidence (dubious): Van Ooteghem 163 n. 1; Magie 2.1219 n. 60, and note his comment at 1.350: "Without his achievement his illustrious successor could not have won the victory which overthrew the great enemy of Rome." The wealth of Mithridates, duly paraded by Lucullus, is striking: it included a six-foot gold statue of the monarch himself.

83. Plut. *Pomp.* 25–26; Dio Cass. 36.23.4, 24.3, 34.3, 36a, 37.1; App. *Mithr.* 94; Vell. Pat. 2.31.1–2.

84. Plut. *Pomp.* 26; App. *Mithr.* 94 (25 *legati*, 270 ships); Livy, *per.* 99. Greenhalgh, *Pompey: The Roman Alexander* 90, assumes that each of the 24 *legati* "was to have the assistance of two quaestors," but the Greek—δύο δὲ ταμίαι παρῆσαν—will not really bear this interpretation.

85. Plut. *Pomp.* 29, Flor. 1.41.9–13, App. *Mithr.* 95.

86. Cic. *De Imp. Pomp.* 34; Plut. *Pomp.* 29; App. *Mithr.* 95; Dio Cass. 36.37.3; Livy, *per.* 99; Flor. 1.41.15; Eutrop. 6.12.1; Oros. 6.4.1.

87. Plut. *Pomp.* 27, Dio Cass. 36.37.2.

88. App. *Mithr.* 94.

89. Strabo 14.3.3 (C.665), Plut. *Pomp.* 28.

90. Flor. 1.41.15, Cic. *Pro Flac.* 28.

91. Plut. *Pomp.* 25.

92. Cic. *II Verr.* 5.26.66–28.73.

93. Vell. Pat. 2.32.4; Plut. *Pomp.* 28; Livy, *per.* 99; Flor. 1.41.14.

94. Serv. *ad Georg.* 4.127; cf. L. P. Wilkinson, *The Georgics of Virgil* (Cambridge, 1969) 174–75.

95. Dio Cass. 36.43.2; Cic. *Ad Fam.* 1.9.11, *De Imp. Pomp.* 68.

96. Cf. Cic. *Pro Mur.* 34.

97. Plut. *Pomp.* 31, *Luc.* 36; Dio Cass. 36.46.1; Vell. Pat. 2.33.2 ff.

98. Dio Cass. 36.45.4, App. *Mithr.* 98.

99. App. *Mithr.* 97–105, 111–12 (death and estimate); Dio Cass. 36.45–54, 37.1–5, 7a, 11–14; Plut. *Pomp.* 30–35; Joseph. *BJ* 1.138, *AJ* 14.53.

100. App. *Syr.* 49, 50, *Mithr.* 106; Plut. *Pomp.* 39; cf. Sherwin-White 211–12.

101. Just. 40.2.2.

102. Bevan, *House of Seleucus* 2.266–67; Downey, *History* 139 ff.

103. Just. 40.2.3–4; Dio Cass. 37.7a; App. *Syr.* 49.

104. Bevan, *House of Seleucus* 2.268.

105. Cf. Badian, *Roman Imperialism* 75, who argues that "peace could no longer be guaranteed without annexation," and Sherwin-White 212: "The collapse of the Seleucid authority had removed the sole cohesive power that held the rival dynasts together."

106. So Seager, *Pompey* 50, basing himself on Seyrig's interesting numismatic evidence from Antioch and Apamea, in *Syria* 27 (1950) 11 ff.

107. See in general Greenhalgh, *Pompey: The Roman Alexander* chap. 10, 147 ff., and bibliography, 242–44; a shorter but useful account in Seager, *Pompey* 52–55; Badian, *Roman Imperialism* 77 ff.

108. Badian, 78–81 with further bibliography. Pompey collected 36,000 talents in gold and silver from Mithridates alone. For a discussion of the treasures accumulated during this campaign, see Sherwin-White 207–8 with n. 53.

109. Badian, *Roman Imperialism* 78 ff.

110. Plin. *HN* 33.134: "nisi qui *redditu annuo* legionem tueri posset," cited by Badian, *Roman Imperialism* 82; cf., for slightly variant versions of this apothegm, Plut. *Crass.* 2, Cic. *De Offic.* 1.25. Pompey, as Badian says, *Publicans* 99, "owned much of the East that he had conquered."

111. Plin. *HN* 7.99, Flor. 1.40.31.

112. DS 1.83.

113. See, e.g., Juv. *Sat.* 15 *passim.*

114. Cic. *De Prov. Cons.* 4–9, *In Pison.* 37–41; cf. Val. Max. 8.1.6.

115. *Bell. Alex.* 33, Caes. *Bell. Civ.* 3.108.2. Both Cleopatra and Ptolemy XIII had been given the title of Philadelphos, hopefully but inaccurately: between these siblings there was no love lost.

116. Tarn, *CAH* X 111.

117. The apparent exceptions are, significantly, both in situations where the main object in view was, one way or another, political persuasion: the visit of Cn. Pompeius to Alexandria on his father's behalf in 49 (Plut. *Ant.* 25), and the fraught meeting with Octavian after Antony's suicide: Dio Cass. 51.12, Flor. 2.21.9 (cf. below, p. 662).

118. Richter, *Portraits* 3.269 and figs. 1857–64, rev. abridged ed. 237 with figs. 218–20 (a very dubious head in the Vatican, = Grant, *Cleopatra* fig. 22); Grant, ibid. figs. 18, 19, 20, 21 (better reproduced in Grant, *Julius Caesar* opposite p. 185; for the ascription of this, the Cherchell bust, see J. Charbonneaux, J. Carcopino, and A. Piganiol, in *Libyca* 2 [1954] 49–63), 29, 44.

119. Pascal, *Pensées* (Paris, 1670) no. 162.

120. See in particular the excellent reproduction of a Phoenician silver tetradrachm, ca. 34 B.C., when Cleopatra was in her mid-thirties, *CAH, Plates to Volume VII,* part 1 (1984) 7, fig. 4(d). Grant, *Cleopatra* 66, derives from the iconography "an impression of a *belle laide* with a rather large *mouth*" (my emphasis), a curious case of presumably unconscious displacement.

121. See Grant, *Cleopatra* 20; cf. A. B. Brett, *AJA* 41 (1937) 460 with fig. 6; H. Seyrig, *RA* (1968) 252 ff.

122. Plut. *Ant.* 25; cf. above, n. 117.

123. Dio Cass. 51.12, Flor. 2.21.9; contrast Plut. *Ant.* 83, and cf. Volkmann, *Cleopatra* 203–4.

124. Plut. *Ant.* 27: in addition to Greek she spoke Egyptian, Aramaic, Hebrew, Syriac, Ethiopian, Median, Parthian, and Troglodyte (whatever that may have been). *Mutatis mutandis*, the Alexandrian polyglot tradition, including Arabic, Coptic, Greek, French, and Italian, has persisted down the ages. As a linguist Cleopatra does not seem to have been in the same league as Mithridates VI (cf. p. 558); but by any standards hers was a remarkable achievement.

125. Orosius, 6.19.20, tells us that Cleopatra not only had a textile factory for making rugs and carpets, but hired a Roman senator, Q. Ovinius, to run it; this self-demeaning act got him executed in short order by Octavian, "quod obscenissime lanificio textrinoque reginae senator populi Romani praeesse non erubuerat." To challenge the class system could be a risky business.

126. Plut. *Caes.* 49: was the carpet, one wonders, from her own factory?

127. Plut. *Ant.* 26, Dio Cass. 48.24.2, App. *Bell. Civ.* 5.8, Socrates of Rhodes *ap.* Athen. 4.147f–148b. Plutarch, or his source, knew very well what was in her mind on this famous occasion: he explained the display at Tarsus by the fact that "she so despised and derided the man," οὕτω κατεφρόνησε καὶ κατεγέλασε τοῦ ἀνδρός.

128. Plut. *Ant.* 54.

129. Cf. Grant, *Cleopatra* 46–47; Bevan, *House of Ptolemy* 369 ff.

130. For a more favorable verdict, see, e.g., Huzar chap. 15, 253 ff.

131. Grant, *Cleopatra* 47–48 with reff.

132. Val. Max. 4.1.15, Caes. *Bell. Civ.* 3.110 *ad fin.*; cf. Becher 134–35.

133. Caes. *Bell. Civ.* 3.103, cf. 107; App. *Bell. Civ.* 2.84.

134. Grant, *Cleopatra* 48–53.

135. Strabo 17.1.11 (C.796).

136. For the numismatic evidence, see Grant, *Cleopatra* 53 with n. 76.

137. Strabo 17.1.11 (C.796); Caes. *Bell. Civ.* 3.103; Plut. *Caes.* 48, 49; Trog. *prol.* 40; App. *Bell. Civ.* 2.84.

138. Eutrop. 6.21, Ampel. 35.4; cf. Heinen, *Röm* 57 ff.; Badian, *JRS* 58 (1968) 259, reviewing Heinen. Ampelius is hardly a trustworthy source; Ilse Becher (p. 90) remarks of him that "diese Deutung auf die Liste der sachlichen Unrichtigkeiten und Anachronismen zu schreiben, die das Werk sonst aufweist, scheint mir nicht angängig," but there seems no doubt that his information in this case is correct.

139. Plut. *Pomp.* 74–80, *Caes.* 48; Caes. *Bell. Civ.* 3.102–4; App. *Bell. Civ.* 2.83–86; Dio Cass. 42.2–5; Flor. 2.13.51–52; Vell. Pat. 2.53.1–4; cf. Greenhalgh, *Pompey: The Republican Prince* chap. 10, esp. pp. 260–65. A long and florid account of Pompey's death is also given by Lucan, 8.33–872; but this (like the rest of the epic) is, in effect, romantic fiction, politically *parti pris* in a manner that one can only describe as Jacobean (if not Jacobin), and larded throughout with fashionable literary rhetoric. Since I consider the *Pharsalia* to possess rather less value as a source for the events of this period than does Xenophon's *Cyropaedia* for sixth-century Persian history, I have nowhere cited it as evidence. The arguments and analyses presented by two excellent articles, A. W. Lintott's "Lucan and the History of the Civil War," *CQ* 21 (1971) 488–505, and my former student R. C. Lounsbury's "History and Motive in Book Seven of Lucan's *Pharsalia*," *Hermes* 104 (1976) 210–39, both—though I suspect not intentionally—confirm me in this opinion.

140. Caes. *Bell. Civ.* 3.104.1.

141. *Bell. Alex.* 34.1; Caes. *Bell. Civ.* 3.106.1–5, 112.8; Dio Cass. 42.34.6; Livy, *per.* 112.

142. Caes. *Bell. Civ.* 3.103.2, Plut. *Caes.* 48, Strabo 17.1.41 (C.796).

143. Plut. *Caes.* 48; Dio Cass. 42.9.1, cf. 34.1; Oros. 6.15.29.

144. Caes. *Bell. Civ.* 3.107, Plut. *Caes.* 48–49, Dio Cass. 42.34.2–35.1, Flor. 2.13.56–58.

145. Dio Cass. 42.35.2.

146. Ibid. 42.35.4–6; cf. Gelzer, *Caesar* 248–49.

147. Cic. *Att.* 5.21.10–13, 6.1.5–8.

148. Caes. *Bell. Civ.* 3.107 (*argumentum ex silentio*); cf. Bicknell 325 ff., esp. 330–31.

149. Caes. *Bell. Civ.* 3.108–9, Dio Cass. 42.36.1–3, Plut. *Caes.* 49. There is no rational answer to the question why Caesar allowed himself to be put in jeopardy by this force. If he did not know of its existence, his intelligence had fallen off sadly since his Gallic campaigns. If he did, why did he ignore it? Because he despised all things Egyptian? But this was a mercenary army composed to a large extent of ex-legionaries (cf. p. 900 n. 24). Because he was besotted, to the exclusion of all else, by Cleopatra? Subsequent events make this highly im-

probable. Because he seriously overestimated his own authority in the palace? Possible, but a poor reflection on the judgment of an otherwise acute man.

150. *Bell. Alex.* 17–21, Dio Cass. 42.40.3–5, Plut. *Caes.* 49, Flor. 2.13.56–59.

151. Plut. *Caes.* 49, Dio Cass. 42.38.2, Oros. 6.15.31, Sen. *Dial.* 9.9.5, Aul. Gell. *NA* 7.17.3. The number of rolls lost is variously estimated at 400,000 or 700,000; both figures sound inflated. Calvisius (*ap.* Plut. *Ant.* 58) claimed that Antony later partly compensated the bookish Cleopatra for this public loss by turning over to her, *en bloc*, the 200,000 rolls of the royal library at Pergamon. Grant, *Cleopatra* 71, argues that not the Library itself, but a consignment of books on the docks was what got incinerated; the evidence, however, all goes the other way, and indeed is so interpreted by Gelzer, *Caesar* 249 n. 7, cited by Grant in support.

152. Caes. *Bell. Civ.* 3.112.

153. *Bell. Alex.* 4, Caes. *Bell. Civ.* 3.112, Dio Cass. 42.39.1.

154. *Bell. Alex.* 22–25, Dio Cass. 42.42.1–4.

155. *Bell. Alex.* 26–32; Plut. *Caes.* 49; Dio Cass. 42.41, 43; Flor. 2.13.60.

156. Livy, *per.* 112; *Bell. Alex.* 31; Dio Cass. 42.43.

157. Suet. *Div. Jul.* 52, App. *Bell. Civ.* 2.90.

158. *Bell. Alex.* 33; Suet. *Div. Jul.* 35.1, 52.1, 76.3; Dio Cass. 42.44.1–4, 43.19.2; App. *Bell. Civ.* 2.90; Strabo 17.1.11 (C.796). Grant, *Cleopatra* 83–85, discussing the evidence for paternity, renders a *non liquet* verdict; but the circumstantial evidence all points to Caesarion's having been Caesar's son. Antony informed the Senate (citing witnesses) that Caesar had acknowledged Caesarion (Suet. *Div. Jul.* 52.1). The doubts will all have been cast, and with good cause, by Octavian and his party. We may also legitimately ask ourselves, if a child born to Cleopatra shortly after Caesar's departure from Egypt was not his, whose was it? Despite hostile propaganda, Cleopatra seems to have been scrupulously faithful to both her Roman lovers (cf. p. 662 and n. 117 above).

159. Suet. *Div. Jul.* 52, Dio Cass. 43.27.3.

160. Suet. *Div. Jul.* 52, Dio Cass. 44.7.3.

161. Cic. *Att.* 15.15; cf. Becher 17–19.

162. Dio Cass. 43.27.3.

163. Ibid. 43.19.2–4.

164. Justinian, *Inst.* 1.10.

165. Macrob. *Sat.* 1.14.3; cf. E. Bickerman, *Chronology of the Ancient World* (London, 1968, 2nd. ed. 1980) 47. In 46 Caesar, acting as Pontifex Maximus, was obliged to intercalate no fewer than 90 days, for a grand annual total of 445 (Censorinus 20.8), in order to straighten things out.

166. Cic. *Att.* 14.8.1.

167. App. *Bell. Civ.* 4.61; Joseph. *AJ* 15.89, *Cont. Ap.* 2.58; Porph. *FGrH* 260 F 2, 16; Dio Cass. 47.31.5. Ptolemy XIV was still alive in July, but dead before September: Heinen, *Caesar* 178, citing *POxy.* 14.1629.

168. *OGIS* 194; App. *Bell. Civ.* 4.61, 63; Sen. *Quaest. Nat.* 4.2.

169. Dio Cass. 47.30.4, 31.5; App. *Bell. Civ.* 4.61, 5.8.

170. App. *Bell. Civ.* 4.59–62.

171. Ibid. 4.61, 63, 82.

172. Ibid. 4.63, 82; cf. Macurdy 193–94, correcting Bevan's view, *House of Ptolemy* 372–74, that Cleopatra remained neutral till the winner emerged.

173. Strabo 14.6.6 (C.685); cf. Bicknell 330 ff.

174. App. *Bell. Civ.* 4.61, 5.8–9.

175. Cf. Grant, *Cleopatra* 102–3.

176. Dio Cass. 47.31.5.

177. Plut. *Ant.* 24, 36; cf. *SIG*³ 760.

178. Cf. Grant, *Cleopatra* 38.

179. Plut. *Ant.* 26, Dio Cass. 48.24.2, Socrates of Rhodes *ap.* Athen. 4.147f–148b.

180. On Fulvia, see Plut. *Ant.* 10.

181. Suet. *Div. Aug.* 69: "quid te mutauit? quod reginam ineo?"

182. Plut. *Ant.* 28–29, Dio Cass. 48.24.3, App. *Bell. Civ.* 5.10–11, Flor. 2.11.1–3, Zonar. 10.22.

183. App. *Bell. Civ.* 5.9, Dio Cass. 48.24.2, Joseph. *AJ* 15.89.

184. So, rightly, Grant, *Cleopatra* 120.

185. Cf. Bicknell 334 ff.

186. App. *Bell. Civ.* 5.29–48 *passim.*

187. Plut. *Ant.* 30–31, App. *Bell. Civ.* 5.59.

188. Plut. *Ant.* 30, 33, 34; Just. 42.4.7–10; Dio Cass. 48.24.4–27.3, 39–41; 49.19–22.

189. Plut. *Ant.* 35, Dio Cass. 48.54, App. *Bell. Civ.* 5.93.

190. Plut. *Ant.* 35; App. *Bell. Civ.* 5.95, 135. Dio Cass. 48.54.2, probably reflecting an Augustan tradition, asserts that the legions were, in fact, duly dispatched.

191. Cf. Grant, *Cleopatra* 224.

192. Dio Cass. 48.54.5, App. *Bell. Civ.* 5.95, Plut. *Ant.* 35.

193. Will, *HP*² 2.545.

194. Plut. *Ant.* 36, Strabo 14.5.3 (C.669), Dio Cass. 49.32.1–5.

195. Cf. Meiggs 117; Grant, *Cleopatra* 138.

196. For the significance of the Helios title, see above, pp. 437–38, and also Grant, *Cleopatra* 142–44, for a discussion of the millenary implications of the sun cult, the promise of a new Golden Age.

197. Porph. *FGrH* 260 F 2, 17; cf. Magie 2.1287 n. 29; Grant, *Cleopatra* 141, 266 n. 20; Sherk, *Translated Documents* 88, pp. 110–11.

198. Plut. *Ant.* 37–51 *passim*, Vell. Pat. 2.82.1–3, Dio Cass. 49.25–31 *passim*, Flor. 2.20.10, Just. 42.5.3.

199. Plut. *Ant.* 53, Dio Cass. 49.33.4. Antony now had no need of Cleopatra's wiles to force him into a decision of this sort.

200. App. *Bell. Civ.* 5.144, Dio Cass. 49.18.4, Vell. Pat. 2.79.

201. Plut. *Ant.* 87.

202. Dio Cass. 49.40; Plut. *Ant.* 50, 56; Vell. Pat. 2.82.

203. Dio Cass. 41.1–3, cf. 49.32.4–5, 50.4–5; Plut. *Ant.* 54.

204. Cavafy, Ποιήματα Α΄ 35–36 = *Collected Poems* 76–77.

205. Ibid.: τί κούφια λόγια ἤσανε αὐτές ἡ βασιλεῖες.

206. Dio Cass. 50.4.1, 50.5 *passim*; Vell. Pat. 2.82.4.

207. Huzar 199.

208. Dio Cass. 49.41.4–6, Plut. *Ant.* 55.

209. *Oracula Sibyllina* 3.350–61, 367–80; cf. Carter 182 ff.

210. Grant, *Cleopatra* 168; cf. Macurdy 93 ff.; Sherk, *Translated Documents* 89, pp. 111–12.

211. Bevan, *House of Ptolemy* 377.

212. Dio Cass. 50.5.4; cf. Macurdy 204.

213. Cf. Grant, *Cleopatra* 169 and numismatic testimony there cited.

214. Plut. *Ant.* 58, Dio Cass. 50.3.3–5.

215. Dio Cass. 50.6.4, Plut. *Ant.* 60.

216. Becher chap. 3, 143 ff., gives a full conspectus of the evidence: see in particular Prop. 3.11.29–56, cf. 4.6.57–64; Virg. *Aen.* 8.696–713; Hor. *Odes* 1.37; and the rhetorical speech put in Octavian's mouth by Dio Cassius, 50.24.3–25.4, which certainly reflects the same tradition.

217. Hor. *Odes* 1.37.14.

218. Prop. 3.11.56.

219. Strabo 17.1.11 (C.797): καὶ τὴν Αἴγυπτον ἔπαυσε παροινουμένην.

220. Prop. 3.11.30, Dio Cass. 51.15.4.

221. Philostr. *Vit. Soph.* 1.4, p. 486 Kayser, cited by Grant, *Cleopatra* 181.

222. Dio Cass. 50.1.3–5, 5.1.

223. Plin. *HN* 33.50: "Messalla orator prodidit Antonium triumuirum aureis usum uasis in omnibus obscenis desideriis, pudendo crimine etiam Cleopatrae." In my more frivolous moments, convinced that Cleopatra would not have been so choosy, I like to picture the two of them in the royal suite, with a matching His and Hers set, gold-plated at the very least, sitting under the bed.

224. The propaganda was by no means all one-sided: Antony attacked Octavian for his low birth, for having been adopted by Caesar only after submitting to sodomization, for cowardice and incompetence in battle (that charge came close to the knuckle), for incurable womanizing (pot calling the kettle black), and anything else he could rake up. See Suet. *Div. Aug.* 2.3, 4.2 (low birth); 16.2 (cowardice); 69.1–2, 71.1 (womanizing); 78 (homosexuality and adoption); cf. Huzar chap. 14, 237 ff. As she reminds us, it was Octavian, that master propagandist, who won, and thus our evidence for Antony is bound to be *parti pris*; but Antony's mud was well aimed, and some of that stuck, too.

225. An excellent account in Carter chap. 16, 215 ff.

226. Plut. *Ant.* 74–86 *passim*, esp. 85–86; Dio Cass. 51.1–15 *passim*, esp. 14; Strabo 17.1.10 (C.795); Livy, *per.* 133; Galen 14.237 Kühn. These sources, while tending to agree on some kind of poison as Cleopatra's means of suicide (Dio Cassius insists that, apart from some small punctures in her arm, all else is guesswork), do not all give snakebite as the immediate cause.

227. Plut. *Ant.* 85; cf. Grant, *Cleopatra* 225 ff.

228. E.g., Hor. *Odes* 1.37.20–32.

229. Plut. *Ant.* 81, Dio Cass. 51.15.5. It was bad, as Areius remarked, in a nasty parody of Homer (*Il.* 2.204), to have too many Caesars. Walbank, *CAH* VII².1, 99–100, rightly emphasizes the irony of the Roman Republic eliminating the Eastern monarchies only to usher in a monarchy under another name that was to survive for some five hundred years.

230. Plut. *Ant.* 86. For the Egyptian cobra, *Naja haje* (called in Greek the ἀσπίς because of its shieldlike expanding hood), cf. Hdt. 4.191, Nic. *Ther.* 158.

231. See W. Spiegelberg, "Weshalb wählte Kleopatra den Tod durch Schlangenbiss?" *SBAW* 2 (1925) 1–6, esp. 3 ff.; cf. Becher chap. 8, 151 ff.

SELECT BIBLIOGRAPHY

This list records only secondary works cited in short forms in the notes. The absence of any name or title is no guarantee that it does not occur in the notes, where other items, not listed here, are given with full bibliographical information. Titles of journals are abbreviated below in general as in *L'Année Philologique*.

Aalders, G. J. D. *Political Thought in Hellenistic Times.* Amsterdam, 1976.

Abel, F. M. *Histoire de la Palestine.* Vol. 1, *De la conquête d'Alexandre jusqu'à la guerre juive.* Paris, 1952.

———. *Les Livres des Maccabées.* 2d ed. Paris, 1949.

Accame, S. *Il dominio romano in Grecia dalla guerra acaica ad Augusto.* Roman, 1946. [Reprint: 1972.]

Adams, W. L. "Cassander, Macedonia, and the Policy of Coalition, 323–301 B.C." Dissertation, University of Virginia. Charlottesville, 1974.

———. "Perseus and the Third Macedonian War." In Adams and Borza, eds., 237–56.

Adams, W. L., and E. N. Borza, eds. *Philip II, Alexander the Great and the Macedonian Heritage.* Washington, D.C., 1982.

Africa, T. W. "Aristonicus, Blossius, and the City of the Sun." *International Review of Social History* 6 (1961) 110–24.

———. *Phylarchus and the Spartan Revolution.* Berkeley and Los Angeles, 1961.

———. *Science and the State in Greece and Rome.* New York, 1968.

———. "Worms and the Death of Kings: A Cautionary Note on Disease and History." *ClAnt* 1 (1982) 1–17.

Allen, R. E. *The Attalid Kingdom: A Constitutional History.* Oxford, 1983.

Anson, E. M. "Discrimination and Eumenes of Cardia." *AncW* 3 (1980) 55–59.

———. "Eumenes of Cardia." Dissertation, University of Virginia, Charlottesville, 1975.

———. "The Siege of Nora: A Source Conflict." *GRByS* 18 (1977) 251–56.

Arnold, E. V. *Roman Stoicism.* London, 1911.

Arnott, W. G. "Herodas and the Kitchen Sink." *G&R* 18 (1971) 121–32.

———. *Menander.* Vol. 1. London, 1979. [Loeb ed.]

———. *Menander, Plautus and Terence.* Oxford, 1975.

———. "Moral Values in Menander." *Philologus* 125 (1981) 215–27.

———. "Young Lovers and Confidence Tricksters: The Rebirth of Menander." *University of Leeds Review* 13 (1970) 1–18.

Arrighetti, G. *Epicuro: Opere.* 2d ed. Turin, 1973.

Ashton, N. G. "The Naumachia near Amorgos in 322 B.C." *BSA* 72 (1977) 1–11.

Association Guillaume Budé. *Actes du VIIIᵉ Congrès, Paris, 5–10 avril 1968.* Paris, 1969.

Atkinson, K. M. T. "The Seleucids and the Greek Cities of Western Asia Minor." *Antichthon* 2 (1968) 32–57.

Austin, M. *The Hellenistic World from Alexander to the Roman Conquest: A Selection of Ancient Sources in Translation*. Cambridge, 1981.

Avi-Yonah, M. *Hellenism and the East: Contacts and Interrelations from Alexander to the Roman Conquest*. Jerusalem, 1978.

Aymard, A. *Études d'histoire ancienne*. Paris, 1967.

———. *Les premiers rapports de Rome et de la confédération achaienne*. Bordeaux, 1938.

Badian, E. "Alexander the Great and the Greeks of Asia." In *Ancient Society and Institutions: Studies Presented to Victor Ehrenberg on His 75th Birthday* 37–69. Oxford, 1966.

———. *Foreign Clientelae (264–70 B.C.)*. Oxford, 1958.

———. "Introduction." In *Polybius: The Histories*, tr. M. Chambers, ix–xlii. New York, 1966.

———. "Notes on Roman Policy in Illyria (230–201 B.C.)." In Badian, *Studies* 1–33. [Originally published in *PBSR* 20 (1952) 72–93.]

———. *Publicans and Sinners*. 2d ed. Ithaca, N.Y., 1983.

———. Review of M. J. Fontana, *Le lotte*. *Gnomon* 34 (1962) 381–87.

———. *Roman Imperialism in the Late Republic*. 2d ed. Ithaca, N.Y., 1968.

———. "Rome and Antiochus the Great: A Study in Cold War." In Badian, *Studies* 112–39. [Originally published in *CPh* 54 (1959) 81–99.]

———. "Rome, Athens, and Mithridates." *AJAH* 1 (1976) 105–28.

———. *Studies in Greek and Roman History*. Oxford, 1964.

———. "Sulla's Cilician Command." In Badian, *Studies* 157–78. [Originally published in *Athenaeum*, n.s., 37 (1959) 279–303.]

———. "The Testament of Ptolemy Alexander." *RhM* 110 (1967) 178–92.

———. *Titus Quinctius Flamininus: Philhellenism and Realpolitik*. Cincinnati, 1970.

———. "The Treaty Between Rome and the Achaean League." *JRS* 42 (1952) 76–80.

Bagnall, R. S. *The Administration of the Ptolemaic Possessions Outside Egypt*. Leiden, 1976.

Bagnall, R. S., and P. Derow, eds. *Greek Historical Documents: The Hellenistic Period*. Chico, Calif., 1981.

Bailey, C. *Epicurus: The Extant Remains*. Oxford, 1926. [Reprint: 1970.]

———. *The Greek Atomists and Epicurus*. Oxford, 1928. [Reprint: 1964.]

Barigazzi, A. *La formazione spirituale di Menandro*. Turin, 1965.

Bar-Kochva, B. *The Seleucid Army: Organisation and Tactics in the Great Campaigns*. Cambridge, 1976.

Barnes, J., J. Brunschwig, M. Burnyeat, and M. Schofield, eds. *Science and Speculation: Studies in Hellenistic Theory and Practice*. Cambridge and Paris, 1982.

Bartlett, J. R. *Jews in the Hellenistic World: Josephus, Aristeas, the Sibylline Oracles, Eupolemus*. Cambridge, 1985.

Beare, F. W. "Zeus in the Hellenistic Age." In W. S. McCullough, ed., *The Seed of Wisdom: Essays in Honour of T. J. Meek* 92–113. Toronto, 1964.

Becher, I. *Das Bild der Kleopatra in der griechischen und lateinischen Literatur*. Berlin, 1966.

Bell, H. I. *Cults and Creeds in Graeco-Roman Egypt*. 2d ed. Liverpool, 1954.

———. *Egypt from Alexander the Great to the Arab Conquest*. Oxford, 1948.

Bengtson, H. *Die Diadochen: Die Nachfolger Alexanders (323–281 v.Chr.)*. Munich, 1987.

———. *Griechische Geschichte: Von den Anfängen bis in die römische Kaiserzeit*. 4th ed. Munich, 1969.

———. *Herrschergestalten des Hellenismus*. Munich, 1975.

———. *Kleine Schriften zur alten Geschichte*. Munich, 1974.

———. *Die Strategie in der hellenistischen Zeit: Ein Beitrag zum antiken Staatsrecht*. 3 vols. Munich, 1937–52.

Béranger, J. "Grandeur et servitude du souverain hellénistique." *EL* 7 (1964) 3–16.

Bernard, P. "Aï Khanum on the Oxus." *PBA* 53 (1967) 71–95.

———. "Aux confines de l'Orient barbare: Aï Khanoum, ville coloniale grecque." *DossArch* 5 (1974) 99–114.

———. "Campagne de fouilles 1969 à Aï Khanoum en Afghanistan." *CRAI* (1970) 301–49.

———. "Campagne de fouilles de 1970 à Aï Khanoum (Afghanistan)." *CRAI* (1971) 385–453.

———. "Campagne de fouilles à Aï Khanoum (Afghanistan)." *CRAI* (1972) 605–32.

———. "Campagne de fouilles 1974 à Aï Khanoum (Afghanistan)." *CRAI* (1975) 167–97.

———. "Campagne de fouilles 1975 à Aï Khanoum (Afghanistan)." *CRAI* (1976) 287–322.

———. "Campagne de fouilles 1976–1977 à Aï Khanoum (Afghanistan)." *CRAI* (1978) 421–63.

———. "Campagne de fouilles 1978 à Aï Khanoum (Afghanistan)." *CRAI* (1980) 435–59.

———. "Fouilles de Aï Khanoum (Afghanistan): Campagnes de 1972 et 1973." *CRAI* (1974) 280–308.

———. "Quatrième campagne de fouilles à Aï Khanoum (Bactriane)." *CRAI* (1969) 313–55.

———. "Les traditions orientales dans l'architecture gréco-bactrienne." *JA* 264 (1976) 245–75. [Résumé in *Le plateau iranien et l'Asie centrale* (Paris, 1977) 263–65.]

Bernard, P., and H. P. Francfort. *Études de géographie historique sur la plaine d'Aï Khanoum (Afghanistan)*. Paris, 1978.

Bernini, U. "Archidamo e Cleomene III: Politica interna ed estera a Sparta (242–227 A.C.)." *Athenaeum*, n.s., 59 (1981) 439–58.

———. "Studi su Sparta ellenistica: Da Leonida II a Cleomene III." *QUCC* 27 (1978) 28–59.

Berthold, R. M. "Lade, Pergamum, and Chios. Operations of Philip V in the Aegean." *Historia* 24 (1975) 150–63.

———. *Rhodes in the Hellenistic Age*. Ithaca, N.Y., 1984.

Berve, H. *Die Herrschaft des Agathokles*. Munich, 1953.

———. *König Hieron II*. Munich, 1959.

———. *Die Tyrannis bei den Griechen*. 2 vols. Munich, 1967.

Bevan, E. R. *The House of Ptolemy: A History of Egypt under the Ptolemaic Dynasty*. London, 1927 [Reprint: 1968.]

———. *The House of Seleucus*. 2 vols. London, 1902.

Beye, C. R. *Epic and Romance in the Argonautica of Apollonius*. Carbondale, Ill., 1982.

Bianchi Bandinelli, R., ed. *Storia e civiltà dei Greci*. Vol. 4, parts 7, 8; vol. 5, parts 9, 10. Milan, 1977.

Bickerman, E. *The God of the Maccabees: Studies in the Meaning and Origin of the Maccabean Revolt*. Tr. H. R. Moehring. Leiden, 1979. [See also Bikerman.]

Bicknell, P. J. "Caesar, Antony, Cleopatra and Cyprus." *Latomus* 36 (1977) 325–42.

Bieber, M. *The Sculpture of the Hellenistic Age*. New York, 1955. [Rev. ed. 1961.]

Biers, W. R. *The Archaeology of Greece: An Introduction*. Ithaca, N.Y., 1980.

Bignone, E. *L'Aristotele perduto e la formazione filosofica di Epicuro*. 2 vols. Florence, 1936.

———. *Epicuro: Opere, frammenti, testimonianze sulla sua vita*. Bari, 1920. [Reprint: 1964.]

Bikerman, E. *Institutions des Séleucides*. Paris, 1938. [See also Bickerman.]

Boardman, J., and E. La Rocca. *Eros in Greece*. London, 1978.

Bogaert, R. *Banques et banquiers dans les cités grecques*. Leiden, 1968.

———. "Banquiers, courtiers,et prêts maritimes à Athènes et à Alexandrie." *CE* 40 (1965) 140–56.

———. "Le statut des banques en Égypte ptolémaïque." *AC* 50 (1981) 86–99.

Bollack, J. *La pensée du plaisir: Épicure, textes moraux, commentaires*. Paris, 1975.

Bollack, J., M. Bollack, and H. Wismann. *La lettre d'Épicure à Hérodote*. Paris, 1971.

Borza, E. N. "The Natural Resources of Macedonia." In Adams and Borza, eds., 1–20.

Bosworth, A. B. "The Death of Alexander the Great: Rumour and Propaganda." *CQ*, n.s., 21 (1971) 112–36.

Bouché-Leclercq, A. *L'astrologie grecque*. Paris, 1899. [Reprint: 1963.]

———. *Histoire des Lagides*. 4 vols. Paris, 1903–7.

——. *Histoire des Séleucides (323–64 avant J.–C.).* 2 vols. Paris, 1914.

Bowman, A. K. *Egypt after the Pharaohs, 332 B.C.–A.D. 642.* Berkeley and Los Angeles, 1986.

Boyle, A. J., ed. *Ancient Pastoral: Ramus Essays on Greek and Roman Pastoral Poetry.* Berwick, Victoria, 1975.

Brady, T. A. *The Reception of the Egyptian Cults of the Greeks (330–30 B.C.).* Philadelphia, 1935.

Breebaart, A. B. "King Seleucus I, Antiochus, and Stratonice." *Mnemosyne* 20 (1967) 154–64.

Bréhier, E. *Chrysippe et l'ancien Stoïcisme.* Paris, 1951.

Briant, P. *Antigone le Borgne: Les débuts de sa carrière et les problèmes de l'assemblée macédonienne.* Paris, 1973.

——. "Brigandage, dissidence et conquête en Asie achéménide et hellénistique." *DHA* 2 (1976) 163–258.

——. "Colonisation hellénistique et populations indigènes: La phase d'installation." *Klio* 60 (1978) 57–92.

——. "D'Alexandre le Grand aux Diadoques: Le cas d'Eumène de Kardia." Parts 1 and 2. *REA* 74 (1972) 32–73; 75 (1973) 43–81.

——. "Dans le monde hellénistique: Les royaumes à l'ouest de l'Euphrate." *DossArch* 5 (1974) 31–50.

Bringmann, K. "Die Verfolgung der jüdischen Religion durch Antiochos IV.: Ein Konflikt zwischen Judentum und Hellenismus?" *A&A* 26 (1980) 176–90.

Briscoe, J. "The Antigonids and the Greek States, 276–196 B.C." In Garnsey and Whittaker, eds., 145–57.

——. *A Commentary on Livy, Books XXXI–XXXIII.* Oxford, 1973.

——. *A Commentary on Livy, Books XXXIV–XXXVII.* Oxford, 1981.

——. "Eastern Policy and Senatorial Politics, 168–146 B.C." *Historia* 18 (1969) 49–70.

——. "Rome and the Class Struggle in the Greek States, 200–146 B.C." *P&P* 36 (1967) 3–20.

Brochard, V. C. L. *Les sceptiques grecs.* 2d ed. Paris, 1932.

Broughton, T. R. S. *Magistrates of the Roman Republic.* 2 vols. New York, 1951–52 [Reprint: 1968.]

——. "Roman Asia Minor." In Frank, ed., vol. 4, pt. 1, 505–90.

Brown, B. R. *Anticlassicism in Greek Sculpture of the Fourth Century B.C.* New York, 1973.

——. *Ptolemaic Paintings and Mosaics and the Alexandrian Style.* Cambridge, Mass., 1957.

Brulé, P. *La piraterie crétoise hellénistique.* Paris, 1978.

Brunt, P. "Alexander, Barsine, and Heracles." *RFIC* 103 (1975) 22–34.

Buller, J. L. "The Pathetic Fallacy in Hellenistic Pastoral." *Ramus* 10 (1981) 35–52.

Bundy, E. L. "The 'Quarrel Between Kallimachos and Apollonios,' Part 1: The Epilogue of Kallimachos's *Hymn to Apollo.*" *CSCA* 5 (1972) 39–94.

Bunge, J. G. "Antiochos Helios: Methoden und Ergebnisse der Reichspolitik Antiochos' IV. Epiphanes von Syrien im Spiegel seiner Münzen." *Historia* 24 (1975) 164–88.

——. "Die Feiern Antiochos' IV. Epiphanes in Daphne im Herbst 166 v.Chr." *Chiron* 6 (1976) 53–71.

——. "Münzen als Mittel politischen Propaganda: Antiochos IV. von Syrien." *StudClas* 16 (1974) 43–52.

——. "Die sogenannte Religionsverfolgung Antiochos' IV. Epiphanes und die griechischen Städte." *JSJ* 10 (1979) 155–65.

——. "Theos Epiphanes: Zu den ersten fünf Regierungsjahren Antiochos' IV. Epiphanes." *Historia* 23 (1974) 57–85.

——. "Untersuchungen zum Zweiten Makkabäerbuch." Dissertation, Bonn, 1971.

Burstein, S. M. "The Aftermath of the Peace of Apamea." *AJAH* 5 (1980) 1–12.

——. "Arsinoë II Philadelphos: A Revisionist View." In Adams and Borza, eds., 197–212.

——. "Lysimachus and the Greek Cities of Asia Minor: The Case of Miletus." *AncW* 3 (1980) 73–79.

―――. *Outpost of Hellenism: The Emergence of Heraclea on the Black Sea.* Berkeley and Los Angeles, 1976.

―――. *Translated Documents of Greece and Rome,* vol. 3, *The Hellenistic Age from the Battle of Ipsos to the Death of Kleopatra VII.* Cambridge, 1985.

Camp, J. M. *The Athenian Agora: Excavations in the Heart of Classical Athens.* London, 1986.

Carpenter, R. *Beyond the Pillars of Heracles.* New York, 1966.

Carrata Thomes, F. *La rivolta di Aristonico e le origini della provincia romana d'Asia.* Turin, 1968.

Carspecken, J. F. "Apollonius Rhodius and the Homeric Epic." *YClS* 13 (1952) 33–143.

Carter, J. M. *The Battle of Actium.* London, 1970.

Cary, M. *A History of the Greek World from 323 to 146 B.C.* London, 1932. [Rev. ed. 1968.]

Cary, M., and E. H. Warmington. *The Ancient Explorers.* London, 1929.

Casertano, M. "Origine, motivi e presenza della Tyche in Menandro (con particolare riferimento al Dyscolos)." *ALGP* 14/16 (1977–79) 258–74.

Casson, L. "The Grain Trade of the Hellenistic World." *TAPhA* 85 (1954) 168–87.

―――. *Ships and Seamanship in the Ancient World.* Princeton, 1971.

―――. *Travel in the Ancient World.* London, 1974.

Cavafy, C. P. *Collected Poems.* Ed. G. P. Savidis. Tr. E. Keeley and P. Sherrard. Princeton, 1975.

―――. Ποιήματα. 2 vols. Ed. G. P. Savidis. Athens, 1963.

Charbonneaux, J., R. Martin, and F. Villard. *Hellenistic Art, 330–50 B.C.* Tr. P. Green. London, 1973.

Ciani, M. G. "Apollonio Rodio: Gli studi moderni e le prospettive attuali." *A&R* 15 (1970) 80–88.

―――. "Scritto con mistero: Osservazioni sull' oscurità di Licofrone." *GIF* 25 (1973) 132–48.

Cohen, G. M. "The Diadochoi and the New Monarchies." *Athenaeum,* n.s., 52 (1974) 177–79.

―――. "The Marriage of Lysimachus and Nicaea." *Historia* 22 (1973) 354–56.

―――. *The Seleucid Colonies: Studies in Founding, Administration and Organisation.* Wiesbaden, 1978.

Cohen, M. R., and I. E. Drabkin. *A Source Book in Greek Science.* Cambridge, Mass., 1948.

Cohn-Haft, L. *The Public Physicians of Ancient Greece.* Northampton, Mass., 1956.

Collins, F. "The Macedonians and the Revolt of Aristonicus." *AncW* 3 (1980) 83–87.

Consolo Langher, S. N. "Agatocle: Il colpo di stato. *Quellenfrage* e ricostruzione storica." *Athenaeum,* n.s., 54 (1976) 382–429.

―――. "La politica di Agatocle e i caratteri della tradizione dal conflitto con Messana alla battaglia presso il fiume Himera (315–310 a.C.)." *Archivio Storico Messinese,* 3d ser., 26/27 (1975/76) 29–89.

―――. "La Sicilia dalla scomparsa di Timoleonte alla morte di Agatocle." In E. Gabba and G. Vallet, eds., *La Sicilia antica* 2.291–342. Naples, 1980.

―――. "Lo strategato di Agatocle e l'imperialismo siracusano sulla Sicilia greca nelle tradizione diodorea e trogiana (316–310 a.C.)." *Kokalos* 25 (1979 [1981]) 117–87.

Corpus Papyrorum Judaicarum. Ed. V. A. Tcherikover and A. Fuks. Cambridge, Mass., 1957–

Crombie, A. C., ed. *Scientific Change: Symposium on the History of Science, University of Oxford, 9–15 July 1961.* London, 1963.

Cunningham, I. C. *Herodas: Mimiambi.* Oxford, 1971.

Daszewski, W. A. *Corpus of Mosaics from Egypt,* I: Hellenistic and Early Roman Period. Mainz am Rheim, 1985.

Davies, J. K. *Athenian Propertied Families, 600–300 B.C.* Oxford, 1971.

Davis, N., and C. M. Kraay, *The Hellenistic Kingdoms: Portrait Coins and History.* London, 1973.

Davis, P. J., and R. Hersh. *The Mathematical Experience.* Boston, 1981.

Davisson, W. I., and J. E. Harper. *European Economic History.* Vol. 1, *The Ancient World.* New York, 1972.

Day, J. *An Economic History of Athens under Roman Domination*. New York, 1942.

Debevoise, N. C. *A Political History of Parthia*. Chicago, 1938.

Deininger, J. *Der politische Widerstand gegen Rom in Griechenland, 217–86 v.Chr.* Berlin, 1971.

Dell, H. J. "Antigonos III and Rome." *CPh* 62 (1967) 94–103.

Delplace, C. "Le contenu social et économique du soulèvement d'Aristonicos: Opposition entre riches et pauvres?" *Athenaeum*, n.s., 56 (1978) 20–53.

De Witt, N. W. *Epicurus and His Philosophy*. Minneapolis, 1954.

Dick, B. F. "Ancient Pastoral and the Pathetic Fallacy." *Comparative Literature* 20 (1968) 27–44.

Dijksterhuis, E. J. *Archimedes*. 2d rev. ed. Tr. C. Dikshoorn. Princeton, 1987.

Dilke, O. A. W. *Greek and Roman Maps*. London, 1985.

Dinsmoor, W. B. *The Architecture of Ancient Greece: An Account of Its Historic Development*. 3d ed. London, 1950.

Dodds, E. R. *The Greeks and the Irrational*. Berkeley and Los Angeles, 1951.

Dover, K. J. *Greek Homosexuality*. London, 1978.

———. *Theocritus: Select Poems*. London, 1971.

Downey, G. *Ancient Antioch*. Princeton, 1963.

———. *A History of Antioch in Syria, from Seleucus to the Arab Conquest*. Princeton, 1961.

Drachmann, A. G. *Ancient Oil-Mills and Presses*. Copenhagen, 1932.

———. *Ktesibios, Philon and Heron: A Study in Ancient Pneumatics*. Copenhagen, 1948.

———. *The Mechanical Technology of Greek and Roman Antiquity: A Study of the Literary Sources*. Copenhagen, 1963.

Dudley, D. R. "Blossius of Cumae." *JRS* 31 (1941) 94–99.

———. *A History of Cynicism, from Diogenes to the 6th Century A.D.* London, 1967. [Reprint: 1967.]

Dumont, J. C. "À propos d'Aristonicos." *Eirene* 5 (1966) 189–96.

Dunand, F. *Le culte d'Isis dans le bassin oriental de la Méditerranée*. 3 vols. Leiden, 1973.

Eadie, J. W., and J. Ober, eds. *The Craft of the Ancient Historian: Essays in Honor of Chester G. Starr*. Lanham, Md., and London, 1985.

Easterling, P. E., and B. M. W. Knox, eds. *The Cambridge History of Classical Literature*. Vol. 1: *Greek Literature*. Cambridge, 1985.

Eddy, S. K. *The King Is Dead: Studies in the Near Eastern Resistance to Hellenism, 334–31 B.C.* Lincoln, Nebr., 1961.

Edelstein, E. J., and L. Edelstein. *Asclepius: A Collection and Interpretation of the Testimonia*. 2 vols. Baltimore, 1945.

Edelstein, L. "The History of Anatomy in Antiquity." In *Ancient Medicine: Selected Papers*, ed. O. Temkin and C. L. Temkin, 247–301. Baltimore, 1967.

———. *The Meaning of Stoicism*. Cambridge, Mass., 1966.

Edelstein, L., and I. G. Kidd. *Posidonius*. Vol. 1, *The Fragments*. Cambridge, 1972.

Eisen, K. F. *Polybiosinterpretationen: Beobachtungen zu Prinzipien griechischer und römischer Historiographie bei Polybios*. Heidelberg, 1966.

Engel, R. *Untersuchungen zum Machtaufstieg des Antigonos I. Monophthalmos: Ein Beitrag zur Geschichte der frühen Diadochenzeit*. Kallmünz and Regensburg, 1978.

Engelmann, H. *The Delian Aretalogy of Sarapis*. Tr. E. Osers. Leiden, 1975.

Erren, M. *Die Phainomena des Aratos von Soloi: Untersuchungen zum Sach- und Sinnverständnis*. Wiesbaden, 1967.

Errington, R. M. "Alexander in the Hellenistic World." In E. Badian, ed., *Alexandre le Grand: Image et Réalité* 137–79. Entretiens sur l'antiquité classique, 22. Geneva, 1976.

———. "The Alleged Syro-Macedonian Pact and the Origins of the Second Macedonian War." *Athenaeum*, n.s., 49 (1971) 336–54.

———. *The Dawn of Empire*. London, 1971.

———. "Diodorus Siculus and the Chronology of the Early Diadochoi, 320–311 B.C." *Hermes* 105 (1977) 478–504.

———. "From Babylon to Triparadeisos, 323–320 B.C." *JHS* 90 (1970) 49–77.

———. "Philip V, Aratus, and the 'Conspiracy of Apelles.'" *Historia* 16 (1967) 19–36.

————. *Philopoemen*. Oxford, 1969.

Farrington, B. *The Faith of Epicurus*. London, 1967.

————. *Greek Science*. Rev. ed. Harmondsworth, 1961.

————. *Science and Politics in the Ancient World*. London, 1939.

Ferguson, J. *Callimachus*. Boston, 1980.

————. "The Epigrams of Callimachus." *G&R* 17 (1970) 64–80.

————. *The Heritage of Hellenism*. London, 1973.

————. *Utopias of the Classical World*. London, 1975.

Ferguson, W. S. "Demetrius Poliorcetes and the Hellenic League." *Hesperia* 17 (1948) 112–36.

————. *Hellenistic Athens: An Historical Essay*. New York, 1911. [Reprint: 1969.]

Festugière, A. J. *L'astrologie et les sciences occultes*. Vol. 1 of *La révélation d'Hermès Trismégiste*. Paris, 1944.

————. *Epicurus and His Gods*. Tr. C. W. Chilton. Oxford, 1955.

————. *La vie spirituelle en Grèce à l'époque hellénistique*. Paris, 1977.

Finley, M. I. *The Ancient Economy*. Berkeley and Los Angeles, 1973; 2nd ed. 1985.

————. *Ancient Slavery and Modern Ideology*. New York, 1980.

————. "Between Slavery and Freedom." In Finley, *Economy* 116–32. [Originally published in *CSSH* 6 (1964) 233–49.]

————. "Debt-Bondage and the Problem of Slavery." In Finley, *Economy* 150–66. [Originally published in French in *RD*, 4th ser., 43 (1965) 159–84.]

————. "Diogenes the Cynic." In *Aspects of Antiquity* 89–101. New York, 1968.

————. *Economy and Society in Ancient Greece*. Ed. B. D. Shaw and R. P. Saller. New York, 1980.

————. *A History of Sicily: Ancient Sicily to the Arab Conquest*. London, 1968, 2nd ed. 1979.

————. "The Servile Statuses of Ancient Greece." In Finley, *Economy* 133–49. [Originally published in *RIDA*, 3d ser., 7 (1960) 165–89.]

————. "The Slave Trade in Antiquity: The Black Sea and Danubian Regions." In Finley, *Economy* 167–75. [Originally published in *Klio* 40 (1962) 51–59.]

————. "Technological Innovation and Economic Progress in the Ancient World." In Finley, *Economy* 176–95, 274–75. [Originally published in *Economic History Review* 18 (1965) 29–45.]

————. "Utopianism Ancient and Modern." In *The Use and Abuse of History* 178–92. London, 1975.

————. "Was Greek Civilisation Based on Slave Labour?" In Finley, *Economy* 97–115. [Originally published in *Historia* 8 (1959) 145–64.]

————, ed. *Slavery in Classical Antiquity*. Cambridge, 1960, 2nd ed. 1968.

Finn, D., and C. Houser. *Greek Monumental Bronze Sculpture*. London, 1983.

Fischer, T. *Seleukiden und Makkabäer: Beiträge zur Seleukidengeschichte und zu den politischen Ereignissen in Judäa während der 1. Hälfte des 2. Jahrhunderts v.Chr.* Bochum, 1980.

————. *Untersuchungen zum Partherkrieg Antiochos' VII. im Rahmen der Seleukidengeschichte*. Munich, 1970.

————. "Zu Tryphon." *Chiron* 2 (1972) 201–13.

Fontana, M. J. *Le lotte per la successione di Alessandro Magno dal 323 al 315*. Palermo, 1960.

Forster, E. M. *Alexandria: A History and a Guide*. 3d ed. New York, 1961.

Frank, T., ed. *An Economic Survey of Ancient Rome*. 6 vols. Baltimore, 1933–40. [Reprint: 1959.]

Fraser, P. M. *Ptolemaic Alexandria*. 3 vols. Oxford, 1972.

Freeman, E. A. *The History of Sicily from the Earliest Times*. 4 vols. Oxford, 1891–94.

Fuks, A. "Agis, Cleomenes and Equality." *CPh* 57 (1962) 161–66.

————. "The Bellum Achaicum and Its Social Aspect." *JHS* 90 (1970) 78–89.

————. "Isokrates and the Social-Economic Situation in Greece." *AncSoc* 3 (1972) 17–44.

————. "Patterns and Types of Social-Economic Revolution in Greece from the Fourth to the Second Century B.C." *AncSoc* 5 (1974) 51–81.

————. "Slave War and Slave Troubles in Chios in the Third Century B.C." *Athenaeum*, n.s., 46 (1968) 102–11.

————. "Social Revolution in Greece in the Hellenistic Age." *PP* 111 (1966) 437–48.

————. "The Spartan Citizen-Body in the Mid-Third Century B.C. and Its Enlargement Proposed by Agis IV." *Athenaeum*, n.s., 40 (1962) 244–63.

Funck, B. "Zur Innenpolitik des Seleukos Nikator." *AAntHung* 22 (1974) 505–20.

Gabba, E., ed. *Polybe*. Entretiens sur l'antiquité classique, 20. Geneva, 1974.

Garlan, Y. *Recherches de poliorcétique grecque*. Paris, 1974.

————. "Signification historique de la piraterie grecque." *DHA* 4 (1978) 1–16.

————. *War in the Ancient World: A Social History*. Tr. J. Lloyd. London, 1975.

Garnsey, P. D. A., and C. R. Whittaker, eds. *Imperialism in the Ancient World*. Cambridge, 1978.

Garrison, D. H. *Mild Frenzy: A Reading of the Hellenistic Love Epigram*. Wiesbaden, 1978.

Geer, R. M. *Epicurus: Letters, Principal Doctrines, and Vatican Sayings*. Indianapolis, 1964.

Gelzer, M. *Caesar: Politician and Statesman*. Tr. P. Needham. Oxford, 1969.

————. *Über die Arbeitsweise des Polybios*. Heidelberg, 1956.

Giangrande, G. *L'humour des Alexandrins*. Amsterdam, 1975.

————. *Scripta minora Alexandrina*. Amsterdam, 1980–

Giangrande, L. "Les utopies hellénistiques." *CEA* 5 (1976) 17–33.

Giuliano, A. *La cultura artistica delle provincie della Grecia in età romana (Epirus, Macedonia, Achaia, 146 a.C.–267 d.C.)*. Rome, 1965.

————. *Urbanistica delle città greche*. 3d ed. Milan, 1978.

Glew, D. "Mithridates Eupator and Rome: A Study of the Background of the First Mithridatic War." *Athenaeum*, n.s., 55 (1977) 380–405.

————. "The Selling of the King: A Note on Mithridates Eupator's Propaganda in 88 B.C." *Hermes* 105 (1977) 253–56.

Goldberg, S. M. *The Making of Menander's Comedy*. Berkeley and Los Angeles, 1981.

Gomme, A. W., and F. H. Sandbach. *Menander: A Commentary*. Oxford, 1973.

Goodenough, E. R. "The Political Philosophy of Hellenistic Kingship." *YClS* 1 (1928) 55–102.

Gould, J. B. *The Philosophy of Chrysippus*. Leiden, 1970.

Gow, A. S. F. *Theocritus*. 2 vols. Cambridge, 1950.

Gow, A. S. F., and D. L. Page. *The Greek Anthology: Hellenistic Epigrams*. 2 vols. Cambridge, 1965–68.

Gow, J. *A Short History of Greek Mathematics*. Cambridge, 1884. [Reprint: 1968.]

Graillot, H. *Le culte de Cybèle mère des dieux à Rome et dans l'empire romain*. Paris, 1912.

Grandjean, Y. *Une nouvelle arétalogie d'Isis à Maronée*. Leiden, 1975.

Grant, M. *The Ancient Historians*. New York, 1970.

————. *Cleopatra*. London, 1972.

————. *Julius Caesar*. London, 1969.

Green, P. M. *Alexander of Macedon, 356–323 B.C.: A Historical Biography*. Harmondsworth, 1974, repr. Berkeley and Los Angeles, 1991.

————. "The First Sicilian Slave War." *P&P* 20 (1961) 10–29.

Greenhalgh, P. *Pompey: The Republican Prince*. London, 1981.

————. *Pompey: The Roman Alexander*. London, 1980.

Grimal, P. *Hellenism and the Rise of Rome*. London, 1968.

Gruen, E. S. "Aratus and the Achaean Alliance with Macedon." *Historia* 21 (1972) 609–25.

————. "Class Conflict and the Third Macedonian War." *AJAH* 1 (1976) 29–60.

————. "The Coronation of the Diadochoi." In Eadie and Ober, eds., 253–71.

————. *The Hellenistic World and the Coming of Rome*. 2 vols. Berkeley and Los Angeles, 1984.

————. "The Last Years of Philip V." *GRByS* 15 (1974) 221–46.

————. "Macedonia and the Settlement of 167 B.C." In Adams and Borza, eds., 257–67.

————. "Material Rewards and the Drive for Empire." In W. V. Harris, ed., *The Imperialism of Mid-Republican Rome: Proceedings of a Conference Held at the American Academy in Rome, Nov. 5–6, 1982* 59–88. Rome, 1984.

———. "The Origins of the Achaean War." *JHS* 96 (1976) 46–69.

———. "Rome and Rhodes in the Second Century B.C.: A Historiographical Inquiry." *CQ*, n.s., 25 (1975) 58–81.

———. "Rome and the Seleucids in the Aftermath of Pydna." *Chiron* 6 (1976) 73–95.

Guthrie, W. K. C. *A History of Greek Philosophy*. 6 vols. Cambridge, 1962–81.

———. *Orpheus and Greek Religion*. 2d ed. London, 1952.

Habicht, C. *Gottmenschentum und griechische Städte*. 2d ed. Munich, 1970.

———. "Die herrschende Gesellschaft in den hellenistischen Monarchien." *Vierteljahrschrift für Sozial- und Wirtschaftsgeschichte* 45 (1958) 1–16.

———. *Studien zur Geschichte Athens in hellenistischer Zeit*. Göttingen, 1982.

———. *Untersuchungen zur politischen Geschichte Athens im 3. Jahrhundert v.Chr.* Munich, 1979.

———. "Zur Geschichte Athens in der Zeit Mithridates." *Chiron* 6 (1976) 127–42.

Hadas, M. *Hellenistic Culture: Fusion and Diffusion*. New York, 1959.

———. "The Social Revolution in Third-Century Sparta." *CW* 26 (1932) 65–68, 73–76.

Hadley, R. A. "Royal Propaganda of Seleucus I and Lysimachus." *JHS* 94 (1974) 50–65.

Hahm, D. E. *The Origins of Stoic Cosmology*. Columbus, Ohio, 1977.

Halperin, D. M. *Before Pastoral: Theocritus and the Ancient Tradition of Bucolic Poetry*. New Haven, 1983.

Hammond, N. G. L. "Alexander's Veterans after His Death." *GRByS* 25 (1984) 51–61.

———. *Epirus*. Oxford, 1967.

Hammond, N. G. L., and G. T. Griffith. *A History of Macedonia*. Vol. 2, *550–336 B.C.* Oxford, 1979.

Hammond, N. G. L., and F. W. Walbank. *A History of Macedonia*. Vol. 3, *336–167 B.C.* Oxford, 1988.

Handley, E. W., ed. *The Dyskolos of Menander*. Cambridge, Mass., 1965.

Hands, A. R. *Charities and Social Aid in Greece and Rome*. London, 1968.

Hanfmann, G. M. A. "Hellenistic Art." *DOP* 17 (1963) 77–94.

Hansen, E. V. *The Attalids of Pergamon*. 2d ed. Ithaca, N.Y., 1971.

Harding, P. *Translated Documents of Greece and Rome*, vol. 2, *From the Peloponnesian War to the Battle of Ipsus*. Cambridge, 1985.

Harris, W. V. *War and Imperialism in Republican Rome, 327–70 B.C.* Oxford, 1979.

Hauben, H. "Antigonos' Invasion Plan for His Attack on Egypt in 306 B.C." *OLP* 6/7 (1975/76) 267–71.

———. *Callicrates of Samos: A Contribution to the Study of the Ptolemaic Admiralty*. Louvain, 1970.

———. "The First War of the Successors (321 B.C.): Chronological and Historical Problems." *AncSoc* 8 (1977) 85–120.

———. "Fleet Strength at the Battle of Salamis, 306 B.C." *Chiron* 6 (1976) 1–5.

———. "On the Chronology of the Years 313–311 B.C." *AJPh* 94 (1973) 256–67.

———. "Rhodes, Alexander and the Diadochi from 333/332 to 304 B.C." *Historia* 26 (1977) 307–39.

Havelock, C. *Hellenistic Art: The Art of the Classical World from the Death of Alexander the Great to the Battle of Actium*. London, 1971. [Rev. ed. 1981.]

Head, B. V., G. F. Hill, and J. Walker. *A Guide to the Principal Coins of the Greeks, from circa 700 B.C. to A.D. 270*. London, 1959.

Healy, J. F. *Mining and Metallurgy in the Greek and Roman World*. London, 1978.

Heath, T. L. *A History of Greek Mathematics*. 2 vols. Oxford, 1921. [Reprint: 1981.]

———. *A Manual of Greek Mathematics*. Oxford, 1931.

Heichelheim, F. M. *An Ancient Economic History*. Vol. 3. Leiden, 1970.

———. *Wirtschaftliche Schwankungen der Zeit von Alexander bis Augustus*. Jena, 1930.

Heinen, H. *Röm und Ägypten von 51 bis 47 v.Chr.: Untersuchungen zur Regierungszeit der 7. Cleopatra und des 13. Ptolemäers*. Tübingen, 1966.

———. *Untersuchungen zur hellenistischen Geschichte des 3. Jahrhunderts v.Chr., zur Geschichte des Zeit des Ptolemaios Keraunos und zum chremonideischen Krieg.* Wiesbaden, 1972.

———. "Zur Sklaverei in der hellenistischen Welt." Parts 1 and 2. *AncSoc* 7 (1976) 127–49; 8 (1977) 121–54.

Hengel, M. *Jews, Greeks, and Barbarians: Aspects of the Hellenisation of Judaism in the pre-Christian Period.* Tr. J. Bowden. Philadelphia, 1980. [Originally published Stuttgart, 1976.]

———. *Judaism and Hellenism: Studies in Their Encounter in Palestine During the Early Hellenistic Period.* 2 vols. Tr. J. Bowden. Philadelphia, 1974. [Originally published Tübingen, 1969.]

Herter, H. "Glück und Verhängnis: Über die altgriechische Tyche." In *Kleine Schriften* 76–90. Munich, 1975. [Originally published in *Hellas* 4 (1963) 1–16.]

Herzog-Hauser, G. "Tyche." In *RE* 7A:2 (1943) cols. 1643–89.

Heuss, A. "Antigonos Monophthalmos und die griechischen Städte." *Hermes* 73 (1938) 133–94.

———. *Stadt und Herrscher des Hellenismus.* Leipzig, 1937. [Rev. ed. 1963.]

Hicks, R. D. *Stoic and Epicurean.* New York, 1910 [Reprint: 1962.]

———, ed. *Diogenes Laertius: Lives of Famous Philosophers.* 2 vols. London, 1925.

Hinske, N., ed. *Alexandrien: Kulturbegegnungen dreier Jahrtausende im Schmelztiegel einer mediterranen Großstadt.* Mainz, 1981.

Hodges, H. *Technology in the Ancient World.* Harmondsworth, 1970.

Holden, A. *Greek Pastoral Poetry.* Harmondsworth, 1974.

Holleaux, M. *Études d'épigraphie et d'histoire grecques.* Ed. L. Robert. 6 vols. Paris, 1938–69.

———. *Rome, la Grèce et les monarchies hellénistiques au troisième siècle avant J.-C.* Paris, 1921.

Holm, A. *Geschichte Siciliens im Alterthum.* 3 vols. Leipzig, 1870–98.

Holt, F. L. *Alexander the Great and Bactria: The Formation of a Greek Frontier in Central Asia.* Leiden, 1988.

———. "Discovering the Lost History of Ancient Afghanistan: Hellenistic Bactria in Light of Recent Archaeological and Historical Research." *AncW* 9 (1984) 3–28.

———. "The Euthydemid Coinage of Bactria: Further Hoard Evidence from Ai Khanoum." *RN*, 6th ser., 23 (1981) 7–44, pls. 1–12.

Hopp, J. *Untersuchungen zur Geschichte der letzten Attaliden.* Munich, 1977.

Hornblower, J. *Hieronymus of Cardia.* Oxford, 1981.

Hoven, R. *Stoïcisme et stoïciens face au problème de l'audelà.* Paris, 1971.

Hultsch, F., ed. *Pappi Alexandrini Collectionis quae supersunt.* 3 vols. Berlin, 1876–78. [Reprint: 1965.]

Hunt, A. S., and C. C. Edgar. *Select Papyri*, vol. 1, *Non-literary (Private Affairs)*; vol. 2, *Non-Literary (Public Documents)*. London, 1932–34.

Hunt, H. A. K. *A Physical Interpretation of the Universe: The Doctrines of Zeno the Stoic.* Melbourne, 1976.

Hurst, A. *Apollonios de Rhodes: Manière et coherence. Contribution à l'étude de l'esthétique alexandrine.* Bern, 1967.

Huss, W. "Die Beziehungen zwischen Karthago und Ägypten in hellenistischer Zeit." *AncSoc* 10 (1979) 119–37.

———. *Untersuchungen zur Aussenpolitik Ptolemaios' IV.* Munich, 1976.

Hutchinson, G. O. *Hellenistic Poetry.* Oxford, 1988.

Huzar, E. G. *Mark Antony: A Biography.* Minneapolis, 1978.

Jaehne, A. "Politische Aktivität der Bevölkerung Alexandreias am Ende des 3. Jahrhunderts v.u.Z. (nach Polybios)." *Klio* 58 (1976) 405–23.

———. "Die syrische Frage, Seleukia in Pierien und die Ptolemäer." *Klio* 56 (1974) 501–19.

Jaekel, S. "Menander's Dyskolos: Sostratos the Secret Hero; or, The Idea of Humanity." *Eos* 67 (1979) 257–65.

Jardé, A. *Les céréales dans l'antiquité grecque: La production.* Paris, 1925.

Jebb, R. C. *The Characters of Theophrastus.* 2d ed. Rev. J. E. Sandys. London, 1909.

Jenkins, G. K. *Ancient Greek Coins*. London, 1972.

Johns, C. *Sex or Symbol: Erotic Images of Greece and Rome*. Austin, 1982.

Jones, A. H. M. *The Greek City from Alexander to Justinian*. Oxford, 1940.

———. *Sparta*. Oxford, 1967.

Jones, W. H. S. *Hippocrates*. Vols. 1, 2, 4. London, 1923–31. [See also Withington.]

Kavolis, V. M. *Artistic Expression: A Sociological Analysis*. Ithaca, N.Y., 1968.

Kiechle, F. *Sklavenarbeit und technischer Fortschritt im römischen Reich*. Wiesbaden, 1969.

Kirchner, J. *Prosopographia Attica*. 2 vols. Berlin, 1901–3. [Reprint: 1981.]

Kirk, G. S., and J. E. Raven. *The Presocratic Philosophers: A Critical History with a Selection of Texts*. Cambridge, 1957.

Kirk, G. S., J. E. Raven, and M. Schofield. *The Presocratic Philosophers*. 2d ed. Cambridge, 1983.

Klein, T. M. "Apollonius' Jason: Hero and Scoundrel." *QUCC* 42, n.s. 13 (1983), 115–26.

———. "Callimachus, Apollonius Rhodius, and the Concept of the Big Book." *Eranos* 73 (1975) 16–25.

———. "The Role of Callimachus in the Development of the Counter-Genre." *Latomus* 33 (1974) 217–31.

Knox, A. D. *Herodes, Cercidas, and the Greek Choliambic Poets (Except Callimachus and Babrius)*. London, 1929.

Koehler, H. *Die Nachfolge in der Seleukidenherrschaft und die parthische Haltung im römisch-pontischen Konflikt*. Bochum, 1978.

Koehnken, A. *Apollonios Rhodios und Theokrit: Die Hylas- und die Amyklosgeschichten beider Dichter und die Frage der Priorität*. Göttingen, 1965.

Körte, A., and A. Thierfelder. *Menander: Reliquiae*. Vol. 2. 2d ed. Leipzig, 1959.

Konet, R. J. "The Role of Tuche in Menander's Aspis." *CB* 52 (1976) 90–92.

Kraay, C. M., and M. Hirmer. *Greek Coins*. London, 1966.

Kreissig, H. "Landed Property in the 'Hellenistic' Orient." *Eirene* 15 (1977) 5–26.

———. "Prolegomena zu einer Wirtschaftsgeschichte des Seleukidenreiches." *Klio* 56 (1974) 521–27.

———. *Wirtschaft und Gesellschaft im Seleukidenreich: Die Eigentums- und die Abhängigkeitsverhältnisse*. Berlin, 1978.

Kudlien, F. *Der griechische Arzt im Zeitalter des Hellenismus: Seine Stellung in Staat und Gesellschaft*. Mainz and Wiesbaden, 1979.

———. "Medical and Popular Ethics in Greece and Rome." *CM* 5 (1970) 91–121.

———. *Die Sklaven in der griechischen Medizin der klassischen und hellenistischen Zeit*. Wiesbaden, 1968.

Kuhrt, A., and S. Sherwin-White, eds. *Hellenism in the East*. Berkeley and Los Angeles, 1987.

Kyrieleis, Helmut. *Die Bildnisse der Ptolemäer*. Berlin, 1975.

Laffranque, M. *Poseidonios d'Apamée: Essai de mise au point*. Paris, 1964.

Landels, J. G. *Engineering in the Ancient World*. Berkeley and Los Angeles, 1978.

Larsen, J. A. O. "The Aetolian-Achaean Alliance of ca. 238–220 B.C." *CPh* 70 (1975) 159–72.

———. *Greek Federal States*. Oxford, 1968.

———. "Phocis in the Social War of 220–217 B.C." *Phoenix* 19 (1965) 116–28.

———. *Representative Government in Greek and Roman History*. Berkeley and Los Angeles, 1955.

———. "Roman Greece." In Frank, ed., 261–435.

———. "Was Greece Free Between 196 and 146?" *CPh* 30 (1935) 193–214.

Launey, M. *Recherches sur les armées hellénistiques*. 2 vols. Paris, 1949–50.

Lawall, G. "Apollonius' Argonautica: Jason as Anti-Hero." *YClS* 19 (1966) 119–69.

———. "Herodas 6 and 7 Reconsidered." *CPh* 71 (1976) 165–69.

———. *Theocritus' Coan Pastorals: A Poetry Book*. Cambridge, Mass., 1967.

Lee, D. "Science, Philosophy and Technology in the Greco-Roman World." Parts 1 and 2. *G&R* 20 (1973) 65–78, 180–93.

Lefkowitz, M. R. "The Quarrel Between Callimachus and Apollonius." *ZPE* 40 (1980) 1–19.

Lehmann, G. A. *Untersuchungen zur historischen Glaubwürdigkeit des Polybios.* Münster, 1967.

Lepore, E. "Leostene e le origini della guerra lamiaca." *PP* 10 (1955) 161–85.

Leriche, P. "Aï Khanoum: Un rempart hellénistique en Asie centrale." *RA* (1974) 231–70.

Lesky, A. *A History of Greek Literature.* Tr. J. Willis and C. de Heer. London, 1966.

Lévêque, P. "Antigone le Borgne." *REG* 89 (1976) 604–10.

———. "De Timoléon à Pyrrhos." *Kokalos* 14/15 (1968/69) 135–56.

———. "La guerre à l'époque hellénistique." In J.-P. Vernant, ed., *Problèmes de la guerre en Grèce ancienne, à la mémoire d'André Aymard* 261–87. Paris, 1968.

———. *Pyrrhos.* Paris, 1957.

Levi, M. A. "Ricerche su schiavitù e lavoro tributario nel mondo ellenistico." *RIL* 108 (1974) 25–65.

Lewis, N. *Greeks in Ptolemaic Egypt.* Oxford, 1986.

Lloyd, G. E. R. *Early Greek Science: Thales to Aristotle.* London, 1970.

———. "Experiment in Early Greek Philosophy and Medicine." *PCPhS,* n.s., 10 (1964) 50–72.

———. *Greek Science after Aristotle.* New York, 1973.

———. *Magic, Reason, and Experience: Studies in the Origin and Development of Greek Science.* Cambridge, 1979.

———. "Observational Error in Later Greek Science." In Barnes et al., eds., 128–64.

———. "Saving the Appearances." *CQ,* n.s., 28 (1978) 202–22.

———. *Science, Folklore and Ideology: Studies in the Life Sciences in Ancient Greece.* Cambridge, 1983.

Lloyd-Jones, H. "A Hellenistic Miscellany." *SIFC* 77 (1984) 52–72.

Lloyd-Jones, H., and P. Parsons, eds. *Supplementum Hellenisticum.* Berlin, 1982.

Long, A. A. *Hellenistic Philosophy: Stoics, Epicureans, Sceptics.* London, 1974.

———, ed. *Problems in Stoicism.* London, 1971.

Longega, G. *Arsinoë II.* Rome, 1968.

Longrigg, J. "Superlative Achievement and Comparative Neglect: Alexandrian Medical Science and Modern Historical Research." *HS* 19 (1981) 155–200.

Lullies, R., and M. Hirmer. *Greek Sculpture.* 2d ed. Tr. M. Bullock. London, 1960.

Lyons, A. S., and R. J. Petrucelli. *Medicine: An Illustrated History.* New York, 1978.

Maass, E. *Arati Phaenomena.* Berlin, 1893. [Reprint: 1955.]

———. *Commentariorum in Aratum reliquiae.* Berlin, 1898. [Reprint: 1958.]

Mackendrick, P. *The Athenian Aristocracy, 399 to 31 B.C.* Cambridge, Mass., 1969.

Macurdy, G. H. *Hellenistic Queens: A Study of Woman-Power in Macedonia, Seleucid Syria, and Ptolemaic Egypt.* Baltimore, 1932.

Maehler, H. "Egypt under the Last Ptolemies." *BICS* 30 (1983) 1–18.

Magie, D. *Roman Rule in Asia Minor.* 2 vols. Princeton, 1950. [Reprint: 1975.]

Mair, A. W., and G. R. Mair. *Callimachus and Lycophron; Aratus.* London, 1921.

Majno, G. *The Healing Hand: Man and Wound in the Ancient World.* Cambridge, Mass., 1975.

Manni, E. "Agatocle e la politica estera di Siracusa." *Kokalos* 12 (1966) 144–62.

———. *Demetrio Poliorcete.* Rome, 1951.

Manuel, F. E., and F. P. Manuel. *Utopian Thought in the Western World.* Cambridge, Mass., 1979.

Marasco, G. "Cleomene III, i mercenari e gli iloti." *Prometheus* 5 (1979) 45–62.

———. "Polibio e i rapporti etolo-spartani durante i regni di Agide IV e Cleomene III." *Prometheus* 6 (1980) 153–80.

———. "La politica achea nel Peloponneso durante la guerra demetriaca." *A&R* 25 (1980) 113–22.

———. "Storia e propaganda durante la guerra cleomenica: Un episodio del III sec. a.C." *RSI* 92 (1980) 5–34.

Marcus, R., H. St J. Thackeray, and L. Feldman. *Josephus.* 9 vols. London, 1926–65.

Marinoni, E. "La capitale del regno di Seleuco I." *RIL* 106 (1972) 579–631.

Marsden, E. W. *Greek and Roman Artillery: Historical Development.* London, 1969.

———. *Greek and Roman Artillery: Technical Treatises.* Oxford, 1971.

———. "Polybius as a Military Historian." In Gabba, ed., 267–301.

Martin, R. *L'urbanisme dans la Grèce antique.* 2d ed. Paris, 1974.

Mastrocinque, A. *La Caria e la Ionia meridionale in epoca ellenistica (323–188 a.C.).* Rome, 1979.

———. "L'eleutheria e le città ellenistiche." *AIV* 135 (1977) 1–23.

———. "Eumene a Roma (172 a.C.) e le fronti del libro macedonico di Appiano." *AIV* 134 (1975/76) 25–40.

———. "I miti della sovranità e il culto dei diadochi." *AIV* 137 (1978/79) 71–82.

———. "Osservazioni sull'attività di Antioco III nel 197 e 196 a.C." *PP* 31 (1976) 307–22.

Mastromarco, G. *Il pubblico di Eronda.* Padua, 1979.

———. *The Public of Herondas.* Tr. M. Nardella. Amsterdam, 1984.

McCullough, W. S. *The History and Literature of the Palestinian Jews from Cyrus to Herod, 550 B.C. to 4 B.C.* Toronto, 1975.

McKay, K. J. *Erysichthon: A Callimachean Comedy.* Leiden, 1962.

———. *The Poet at Play: Kallimachos, The Bath of Pallas.* Leiden, 1962.

McShane, R. B. *The Foreign Policy of the Attalids of Pergamum.* Urbana, Ill., 1964.

Meiggs, R. *Trees and Timber in the Ancient Mediterranean World.* Oxford, 1982.

Meiggs, R., and D. Lewis. *A Selection of Greek Historical Inscriptions to the End of the Fifth Century B.C.* Oxford, 1969.

Meillier, C. *Callimaque et son temps.* Lille, 1979.

———. "Les poètes hellénistiques et la société." *IL* 22 (1970) 169–78.

Meloni, P. *Perseo e la fine della monarchia macedone.* Rome, 1953.

Mendels, D. "The Attitude of Antiochus III Towards the Class Struggle in Greece (192–191 B.C.)." *RSA* 8 (1978) 27–38.

———. "Messene 215 B.C.: An Enigmatic Revolution." *Historia* 29 (1980) 246–50.

———. "Polybius, Philip V, and the Socio-Economic Question in Greece." *AncSoc* 8 (1977) 155–74.

Meritt, B. D. "Mid-Third-Century Athenian Archons." *Hesperia* 50 (1981) 78–99.

Merker, I. L. "The Ptolemaic Officials and the League of the Islanders." *Historia* 19 (1970) 141–60.

———. "The Silver Coinage of Antigonos Gonatas and Antigonos Doson." *ANSMusN* 9 (1960) 39–52.

Mørkholm, O. *Antiochus IV of Syria.* Copenhagen, 1966.

———. "The Speech of Agelaus at Naupactus in 217 B.C." *C&M* 28 (1967 [1970]) 240–53.

Mogensen, E. "Herodas III Revisited." *Didaskalos* 5 (1977) 395–98.

Moke, D. F. "Eroticism in the Greek Magical Papyri: Selected Studies." Dissertation, University of Minnesota, 1975.

Momigliano, A. *Alien Wisdom: The Limits of Hellenisation.* Cambridge, 1975.

———. "Ebrei e Greci." *RSI* 88 (1976) 425–43.

———. *Essays in Ancient and Modern Historiography.* Oxford, 1977.

———. "Polibio, Posidonio e l'imperialismo romano." In Association G. Budé, *Actes du IXe Congrès, Rome 13–18 avril 1973* 1.184–94. Paris, 1975. [Cf. *AAT* 107 (1973), 693–707, for another version of the same article.]

Mooney, G. W., ed. *The Argonautica of Apollonius Rhodius.* London, 1912.

Moreau, J. *L'âme du monde de Platon aux stoïciens.* Paris, 1939. [Reprint: Hildesheim, 1971.]

Moretti, L. "Filosofia stoica ed evergetismo ellenistico." *Athenaeum*, n.s., 55 (1977) 82–87.

———. *Iscrizioni storiche ellenistiche.* 2 vols. Florence, 1967–76.

Morgan, M. G. "Metellus Macedonicus and the Province Macedonia." *Historia* 18 (1969) 422–46.

Mossé, C. *Athens in Decline, 404–86 B.C.* Tr. J. Stewart. London, 1973.

———. "Un tyran grec à l'époque hellénistique: Nabis 'roi' de Sparte." *CH* 9 (1964) 313–23.

———. *La tyrannie dans la Grèce antique.* Paris, 1969.

Mueller, O. *Antigonos Monophthalmos und "das Jahr der Könige."* Bonn, 1973.

Musti, D. *L'economia in Grecia.* Rome, 1981.

———. "Polibio e la democrazia." *ASNP* 36 (1967) 155–207.

———. *Polibio e l'imperialismo romano.* Naples, 1978.

———. "Polibio negli studi dell'ultimo ventennio (1950–1970)." *ANRW* 1.2 (1972) 1114–81.

———. "Problemi polibiani (rassegna di studi 1950–1964)." *PP* 20 (1965) 380–426.

———. "Lo stato dei Seleucidi: Dinastia, popoli, città da Seleuco I ad Antioco III." *SCO* 15 (1966) 61–197.

Narain, A. K. *The Indo-Greeks.* Oxford, 1957.

Neuburger, A. *The Technical Arts and Sciences of the Ancients.* Tr. H. L. Brose. London, 1930 [Reprint: 1969.]

Neugebauer, O. *The Exact Sciences in Antiquity.* 2d ed. Providence, R. I., 1957. [Reprint: 1969.]

———. *A History of Ancient Mathematical Astronomy.* 3 vols. Berlin, 1975.

Newell, E. T. *The Coinages of Demetrius Poliorcetes.* Oxford, 1927.

Nicolet, C. *Rome et la conquête du monde méditerranéen (264–27 a.C.).* 2 vols. Paris, 1977–78.

Niese, B. *Geschichte der griechischen und makedonischen Staaten seit der Schlacht bei Chaeronea.* 3 vols. Gotha, 1893–1903.

Nilsson, M. P. *Geschichte der griechischen Religion.* 2 vols. 3d ed. Munich, 1967–74.

Nock, A. D. *Conversion: The Old and the New in Religion from Alexander the Great to Augustine.* Oxford, 1933.

———. *Essays on Religion and the Ancient World.* 2 vols. Ed. Z. Stewart. Oxford, 1972.

Oliva, P. "Die Auslandpolitik Kleomenes III," *AAntHung* 16 (1968) 179–85.

Ollier, F. "Le philosophe stoïcien Sphairos et l'oeuvre réformatrice des rois de Sparte Agis IV et Cléomène III." *REG* 49 (1936) 536–70.

Olshausen, E. *Prosopographie der hellenistischen Königsgesandten.* Vol. 1, *Von Triparadeisos bis Pydna.* Louvain, 1974.

———. *Rom und Ägypten von 116 bis 51 v.Chr.* Erlangen and Nuremberg, 1963.

Onians, J. *Art and Thought in the Hellenistic Age: The Greek World View, 350–50 B.C.* London, 1979.

Die Oracula Sibyllina. Ed. J. Geffcken. Leipzig, 1902. [Reprint: 1967.]

Ormerod, H. A. *Piracy in the Ancient World.* Liverpool, 1924. [Reprint: 1978.]

Orrieux, C. *Les papyrus de Zénon: L'horizon d'un grec en Égypte au IIIe siècle avant J.-C.* Paris, 1983.

Orth, W. *Königlicher Machtanspruch und städtische Freiheit: Untersuchungen zu den politischen Beziehungen zwischen den ersten Seleukidenherrschern (Seleukos I., Antiochos I., Antiochos II.) und den Städten des westlichen Kleinasien.* Munich, 1977.

Otto, W., and H. Bengtson. *Zur Geschichte des Niederganges des Ptolemäerreiches: Ein Beitrag zur Regierungszeit des 8. und des 9. Ptolemäers.* Munich, 1938.

Page, D. L. *Select Papyri,* vol. 3, *Literary Papyri (Poetry).* London, 1941.

Parke, H. W. *Greek Oracles.* London, 1967.

Pearson, A. C., ed. *The Fragments of Zeno and Cleanthes.* London, 1891. [Reprint: 1973.]

Pédech, P. "Un grec à la découverte de Rome: L'exil de Polybe (167–150 av. J.-C.)." *Orpheus* 11 (1964) 123–40.

———. "Les idées religieuses de Polybe: Étude sur la religion gréco-romaine au IIe siècle av. J.-C." *RHR* 167 (1965) 35–68.

———. *La méthode historique de Polybe.* Paris, 1964.

———. "Polybe face à la crise romaine de son temps." In Association Guillaume Budé, *Actes du IXe Congrès, Rome, 13–18 avril 1973,* 195–201.

Peremans, W. "Ptolémée IV et les Égyptiens." In J. Bingen, ed., *Hommages à Claire Préaux* 393–402. Brussels, 1975.

Peters, F. E. *The Harvest of Hellenism: A History of the Near East from Alexander the Great to the Triumph of Christianity*. New York, 1970.

Pfeiffer, R. *History of Classical Scholarship from the Beginnings to the End of the Hellenistic Age*. Oxford, 1968.

———, ed. *Callimachus*. 2 vols. Oxford, 1949–53.

Phillips, E. D. *Greek Medicine*. London, 1973.

Piper, L. J. *The Spartan Twilight*. New Rochelle, N.Y., 1986.

Pleket, H. W. *Epigraphica*. 2 vols. Leiden, 1964–69.

———. "Technology and Society in the Graeco-Roman World." *Acta Historiae Neerlandica* 2 (1967) 1–25.

Pohlenz, M. *Die Stoa: Geschichte einer geistigen Bewegung*. 2 vols. Göttingen, 1955–59.

Pollitt, J. J. *The Ancient View of Greek Art: Criticism, History and Terminology*. New Haven, 1974.

———. *Art and Experience in Classical Greece*. Cambridge, 1972.

———. *Art in the Hellenistic Age*. Cambridge, 1986.

Pomeroy, S. B. *Goddesses, Whores, Wives, and Slaves*. New York, 1975.

———. *Women in Hellenistic Egypt from Alexander to Cleopatra*. New York, 1984.

Pozzi, F. "Le riforme economico-sociali e le mire tiranniche di Agide IV e Cleomene III, re di Sparta." *Aevum* 42 (1968) 383–402.

Préaux, C. "L'Alexandrie des Ptolémées." *CE* 53 (1978) 301–6. [Review of Fraser, *Ptolemaic Alexandria*.]

———. *La civilisation hellénistique*. 2d ed. Paris, 1965.

———. "De la Grèce classique à l'Égypte hellénistique: La banque témoin." *CE* 33 (1958) 243–55.

———. *L'économie royale des Lagides*. Brussels, 1939.

———. *Le monde hellénistique: La Grèce et l'Orient de la mort d'Alexandre à la conquête romaine de la Grèce (323–146 av. J.-C.)*. 2 vols. Paris, 1978.

———. "Polybe et Ptolémée Philopator." *CE* 40 (1965) 364–75.

———. "Réflexions sur l'entité hellénistique." *CE* 40 (1965) 129–39.

———. "Sur la stagnation de la pensée scientifique a l'époque hellénistique." *ASPap* 1 (1966) 235–50.

———. "Sur les causes de la décadence du monde hellénistique." In *Atti dell' XI Congresso internazionale de papirologia, Milano 2–8 settembre 1965* 475–98. Milan, 1966.

Preisigke, F., F. Bilabel, and E. Kiessling, eds. *Sammelbuch griechischer Urkunden aus Ägypten*. Strassburg, Berlin, and Heidelberg, 1913–

Protzmann, H. "Realismus und Idealität in Spätklassik und Frühhellenismus: Ein Kapitel künstlerischer Problemgeschichte der Griechen." *JDAI* 92 (1977) 169–203.

Rankin, H. D. *Sophists, Socrates and Cynics*. Beckenham, Kent, 1983.

Reesor, M. E. *The Political Theory of the Old and Middle Stoa*. New York, 1951.

Reinach, T. *Mithridate Eupator, roi de Pont*. Paris, 1890.

Reverdin, O., ed. *Grecs et barbares*. Entretiens sur l'antiquité classique, 8. Geneva, 1962.

Reymond, A. *Histoire des sciences exactes et naturelles dans l'antiquité gréco-romaine*. 2d ed. Paris, 1955.

———. *History of the Sciences in Greco-Roman Antiquity*. Tr. R. G. de Bray. London, 1927.

Rhodes, P. J. *A Commentary on the Aristotelian Athenaion Politeia*. Oxford, 1981.

Rice, E. E. *The Grand Procession of Ptolemy Philadelphus*. Oxford, 1983.

Richter, G. M. A. *The Portraits of the Greeks*. 3 vols. London, 1965. [Rev. and abr. R. R. R. Smith (London, 1984).]

———. *Three Critical Periods in Greek Sculpture*. Oxford, 1951.

Rigsby, K. J. "The Era of the Province of Asia." *Phoenix* 33 (1979) 39–47.

Rist, J. M. *Epicurus*. Cambridge, 1972.

———, ed. *The Stoics*. Berkeley and Los Angeles, 1978.

———. "Zeno and Stoic Consistency." *Phronesis* 22 (1977) 161–74.

————. *Stoic Philosophy*. Cambridge, 1977.

Ritchie, A. D. *Studies in the History and Methods of the Sciences*. Edinburgh, 1958.

Robertson, D. S. *Greek and Roman Architecture*. 2d ed. Cambridge, 1969.

Robertson, M. *A History of Greek Art*. 2 vols. Cambridge, 1975.

Romano, D. G. "The Panathenaic Stadium and Theater of Lykourgos: A Re-Examination of the Facilities on the Pnyx Hill." *AJA* 89 (1985) 441–54.

Rosenmeyer, T. G. *The Green Cabinet: Theocritus and the European Pastoral Lyric*. Berkeley and Los Angeles, 1969.

Rostovtzeff, M. *A Large Estate in Egypt in the Third Century* B.C. Madison, Wisc., 1922.

————. "Rhodes, Delos, and Hellenistic Commerce." *CAH* VIII 619–67.

————. *The Social and Economic History of the Hellenistic World*. 3 vols. Oxford, 1941.

Roveri, A. *Studi su Polibio*. Bologna, 1964.

Ruben, W. "Die Griechen in Indien." In E. C. Welskopf, ed., *Hellenische Poleis* 2.1085–97. Berlin, 1974.

Russell, D. S. *The Jews from Alexander to Herod*. Oxford, 1967.

de Ste Croix, G. E. M. *The Class Struggle in the Ancient Greek World*. London, 1981, corr. impr. 1983.

Sale, W. "The Popularity of Aratus." *CJ* 61 (1966) 160–64.

Salomone Gaggero, E. "La propaganda antiromana di Mitridate VI Eupatore in Asia Minore e in Grecia." In *Contributi di storia antica in onore di Albino Garzetto* 89–123. Genoa, 1977.

Sambursky, S. *The Physical World of the Greeks*. London, 1956.

————. *Physics of the Stoics*. London, 1959.

Samuel, A. E. *From Athens to Alexandria: Hellenism and Social Goals in Ptolemaic Egypt*. Louvain, 1983.

————. *Greek and Roman Chronology: Calendars and Years in Classical Antiquity*. Munich, 1972.

————. *Ptolemaic Chronology*. Munich, 1962.

Sandbach, F. H. *The Stoics*. London, 1975.

Sarikakis, T. C. "Συμβολὴ εἰς τὴν ἱστορίαν τῆς Ἠπείρου κατὰ τοὺς χρόνους τῆς ῥωμαϊκῆς κυριαρχίας (167–31 π.Χ.)." Ἀρχαιολογικὴ Ἐφημερίς, 1964 (1967), 105–19.

————. "Les Vêpres Éphésiennes de l'an 88 av. J.-C." Ἐπιστημονικὴ Ἐπετηρὶς τῆς φιλοσοφικῆς Σχολῆς τοῦ Ἀριστοτελείου Πανεπιστημίου Θεσσαλονίκης 15 (1976) 253–64.

Sarton, G. *A History of Science: Hellenistic Science and Culture in the Last Three Centuries* B.C. Cambridge, Mass., 1959.

Scarborough, J. "The Drug Lore of Asclepiades of Bithynia." *Pharmacy in History* 17 (1975) 43–57.

————. "Nicander's Toxicology." Part 1, "Snakes"; part 2, "Spiders, Scorpions, Insects and Myriapods." *Pharmacy in History* 19 (1977) 3–23; 21 (1979) 3–92.

————. "Theophrastus on Herbals and Herbal Remedies." *JHB* 11 (1978) 353–85.

Schiffman, I. "Griechische und orientalische Quellen der hellenistischen Polisorganisation im vorderasiatischen Bereich." *Klio* 60 (1978) 203–16.

Schmidt, W., ed. *Heronis Alexandrini opera quae supersunt omnia*. Vol. 1. Leipzig, 1899.

Schmidt, W., and L. Nix, eds. *Heronis Alexandrini opera quae supersunt omnia*. Vol. 2. Leipzig, 1900.

Schmitt. H. H. *Die Staatsverträge des Altertums*. Vol. 3, *Die Verträge der griechisch-römischen Welt von 338 bis 200 v.Chr.* Munich, 1969.

————. *Untersuchungen zur Geschichte Antiochos' des Grossen und seiner Zeit*. Wiesbaden, 1967.

Schneider, C. *Kulturgeschichte des Hellenismus*. 2 vols. Munich, 1967–69.

Schofield, M., M. Burnyeat, and J. Barnes, eds. *Doubt and Dogmatism: Studies in Hellenistic Epistemology*. Oxford, 1980.

Schürer, E. *The History of the Jewish People in the Age of Jesus Christ (175* B.C.–A.D. *135)*. 3 vols. Ed. and rev. G. Vermes et al. Edinburgh, 1973–79.

Schwertfeger, T. *Der achaiische Bund von 146–27 v.Chr.* Munich, 1974.

Scullard, H. H. *The Elephant in the Greek and Roman World.* London, 1974.

Seager, R. "The Freedom of the Greeks of Asia." *CQ*, n.s., 31 (1981) 106–12.

———. *Pompey: A Political Biography.* Oxford, 1979.

Sedlar, J. W. *India and the Greek World: A Study in the Transmission of Culture.* Totowa, N.J., 1980.

Sedley, D. "Epicurus and His Professional Rivals." In J. Bollack and A. Laks, eds., *Études sur l'Épicurisme antique* 121–59. Lille, 1976.

Segal, C. "Landscape into Myth: Theocritus's Bucolic Poetry." *Ramus* 4 (1975) 115–39. [Reprinted in C. Segal, *Poetry* 210–34.]

———. *Poetry and Myth in Ancient Pastoral.* Princeton, 1981.

Segal, E. "The φύσις of Comedy." *HSCP* 77 (1973) 129–36.

Seibert, J. *Historische Beiträge zu den dynastischen Verbindungen in hellenistischer Zeit.* Wiesbaden, 1967.

———. *Untersuchungen zur Geschichte Ptolemaios I.* Munich, 1969.

———. *Das Zeitalter der Diadochen.* Darmstadt, 1983.

Seltman, C. *Greek Coins.* 2d ed. London, 1955.

Shear, T. L. *Kallias of Sphettos and the Revolt of Athens in 286 B.C.* Princeton, 1978.

Sherk, R. K. *Roman Documents from the Greek East.* Baltimore, 1969.

———. *Translated Documents of Greece and Rome*, vol. 4, *Rome and the Greek East to the Death of Augustus.* Cambridge, 1984.

Sherwin-White, A. N. *Roman Foreign Policy in the East.* London, 1984.

Shimron, B. *Late Sparta and the Spartan Revolution, 243–146 B.C.* Buffalo, N.Y., 1972.

———. "Nabis of Sparta and the Helots." *CPh* 61 (1966) 1–7.

———. "Polybius and the Reforms of Cleomenes III." *Historia* 13 (1964) 147–55.

———. "Polybius on Rome: A Reconsideration of the Evidence." *SCI* 5 (1979/80) 94–117.

Showerman, G. *The Great Mother of the Gods.* Madison, Wisc., 1901. [Reprint: 1969.]

Simonetta, A. M. "A New Essay on the Indo-Greeks, the Sakas and the Pahlavas." *East and West* 9 (1958) 154 ff.

Simpson, R. H. "Antigonus, Polyperchon, and the Macedonian Regency." *Historia* 6 (1957) 371–73.

———. "Antigonus the One-Eyed and the Greeks." *Historia* 8 (1959) 385–409.

———. "The Historical Circumstances of the Peace of 311." *JHS* 74 (1954) 25–31.

———. "Ptolemaeus' Invasion of Greece in 313 B.C." *Mnemosyne* 8 (1955) 34–37.

Smith, R. R. R. "Greeks, Foreigners, and Roman Republican Portraits." *JRS* 71 (1981) 24–38. [See also Richter, *Portraits.*]

———. *Hellenistic Royal Portraits.* Oxford, 1988.

Smith, W. D. "Erasistratus' Dietetic Medicine." *BHM* 56 (1982) 398–409.

———. *The Hippocratic Tradition.* Ithaca, N.Y., 1979.

Spanneut, M. *Permanence du Stoïcisme: De Zénon à Malraux.* Gembloux, 1973.

Stambaugh, J. E. *Sarapis under the Early Ptolemies.* Leiden, 1972.

Stewart, A. *Attika: Studies in Athenian Sculpture of the Hellenistic Age.* London, 1979.

Stough, C. L. *Greek Skepticism: A Study in Epistemology.* Berkeley and Los Angeles, 1969.

Strodach, G. K. *The Philosophy of Epicurus: Letters, Doctrines, and Parallel Passages from Lucretius.* Evanston, Ill., 1963.

Swigart, R. "Theocritus' Pastoral Response to City Women." *BR* 21 (1973) 145–74.

Taeger, F. *Charisma: Studien zur Geschichte des antiken Herrscherkultes.* 2 vols. Stuttgart, 1957–60.

Talbert, R. J. A. *Timoleon and the Revival of Greek Sicily, 344–314 B.C.* Cambridge, 1975.

Tapp, E. J. "Polybius' Conception of History." *Prudentia* 4 (1972) 33–41.

Tarn, W. W. *Antigonus Gonatas.* London, 1913. [Reprint: 1969.]

———. *The Greeks in Bactria and India.* 2d ed. Cambridge, 1951.

Tarn, W. W., and G. T. Griffith. *Hellenistic Civilisation.* 3d ed. London, 1952.

Tcherikover, V. *Hellenistic Civilisation and the Jews.* Tr. S. Applebaum. New York, 1959.

Temkin, O. "Greek Medicine as Science and Craft." *Isis* 44 (1953) 213–25.

Texier, J.-G. *Nabis.* Paris, 1975.

———. "Nabis et les hilotes." *DHA* 1 (1974) 189–205.

Theiler, W. *Poseidonios: Die Fragmente.* 2 vols. Berlin and New York, 1982.

Thomas, I. B. *Selections Illustrating the History of Greek Mathematics.* 2 vols. London, 1939.

Thompson, D. J. *Memphis under the Ptolemies.* Princeton, 1988.

Thompson, E. A. *A Roman Reformer and Inventor: Being a New Text of the Treatise De rebus bellicis with a Translation and Introduction.* Oxford, 1952.

Thompson, H. A., and R. E. Wycherley. *The Athenian Agora*, vol. 14, *The Agora of Athens.* Princeton, 1972.

Tracy, S. V. "Athens in 100 B.C." *HSCP* 83 (1979) 213–36.

Travlos, J. *Pictorial Dictionary of Ancient Athens.* New York, 1971.

———. Πολεοδομικὴ ἐξέλιξις τῶν ᾿Αθηνῶν ἀπὸ τῶν προϊστορικῶν χρόνων μέχρι τῶν ἀρχῶν τοῦ 19ου αἰῶνος. Athens, 1960.

Treloar, A. "Ancient Greece and India." *Prudentia* 9 (1977) 81–96.

Treu, K. "Menanders Menschen als Polisbürger." *Philologus* 125 (1981) 211–14.

———. "Die Menschen Menanders: Kontinuität und Neuerung im hellenistischen Menschenbild." In *Der Mensch als Mass der Dinge: Studien zum griechischen Menschenbild in der Zeit der Blüte und Krise der Polis* 399–421. Berlin, 1976.

Trypanis, C. A. *Callimachus: Aetia, Iambi, Lyric Poems, Hecale, Minor Epic and Elegiac Poems, and Other Fragments.* London, 1975.

Turner, E. G. "L'érudition alexandrine et les papyrus." *CE* 37 (1962) 135–52.

———. "Menander and the New Society of His Time." *CE* 54 (1979) 106–26.

———, ed. *Ménandre.* Entretiens sur l'antiquité classique, 16. Geneva, 1970.

Unguru, S. "History of Ancient Mathematics: Some Reflections on the State of the Art." *Isis* 70 (1979) 555–65. [Cf. H. Freudenthal in *AHES* 16 (1976/77) 189–200, a reply to Unguru's earlier article in *AHES* 15 (1975/76) 67–114.]

Urban, R. "Das Heer des Kleomenes bei Sellasia." *Chiron* 3 (1973) 95–102.

———. *Wachstum und Krise des achäischen Bundes: Quellenstudien zur Entwicklung des Bundes von 280 bis 222 v.Chr.* Wiesbaden, 1979.

Usener, H. *Epicurea.* Leipzig, 1887.

Usher, S. *The Historians of Greece and Rome.* London, 1969.

Ussher, R. G. *The Characters of Theophrastus.* London, 1960.

———. "The Mimiamboi of Herodas." *Hermathena* 129 (1980) 67–76.

Van der Valk, M. *Researches on the Text and Scholia of the Iliad.* 2 vols. Leiden, 1963.

Van der Waerden, B. L. *Science Awakening.* Tr. A. Dresden. New York, 1961.

Van Ooteghem, J. *Lucius Licinius Lucullus.* Brussels, 1959.

Van Sickle, J. "Theocritus and the Development of the Conception of Bucolic Genre." *Ramus* 5 (1976) 18–44.

Van Straaten, M. *Panaetii Rhodii fragmenta.* 3d ed. Leiden, 1962.

———. *Panétius: Sa vie, ses écrits et sa doctrine, avec une édition des fragments.* Leiden, 1946.

Van't Dack, E., P. Van Dessel, and W. Van Gucht, eds. *Egypt and the Hellenistic World: Proceedings of the International Colloquium, Leuven, 24–26 May 1982.* Louvain, 1983.

Vartsos, J. A. "᾿Ακμὴ τοῦ Πύρρου καὶ ἐπέμβασις αὐτοῦ εἰς τὴν Μακεδονίαν." *Athena* 67 (1963/64) 87–106.

———. "Osservazioni sulla campagna di Pirro in Sicilia." *Kokalos* 16 (1970) 89–97.

Vavřínek, V. "On the Structure of Slave Revolts: The Revolt of Aristonicus." In P. Oliva and J. Burian, eds., *Soziale Probleme im Hellenismus und im römischen Reich* 203–12. Prague, 1973.

Veneroni, B. "Divagazioni sul quinto mimiambo di Eroda." *REG* 85 (1972) 310–30.

Vermaseren, M. J. *Cybele and Attis: The Myth and the Cult.* London, 1977.

———, ed. *Studies in Hellenistic Religions.* Leiden, 1979.

Vian, F., and E. Delage, eds. and trs. *Apollonios de Rhodes: Argonautiques.* 3 vols. Paris, 1974–81.

Vogt, J. *Ancient Slavery and the Ideal of Man.* Tr. T. Wiedemann. Cambridge, Mass., 1975.

Volkmann, H. "Die Basileia als *endoxos douleia.*" *Historia* 16 (1967) 155–61.

———. *Cleopatra: A Study in Politics and Propaganda.* Tr. T. J. Cadoux. London, 1958.

Von Staden, H. "Experiment and Experience in Hellenistic Medicine." *BICS* 22 (1975) 178–99.

———. *Herophilus: The Art of Medicine in Early Alexandria.* Edition, translation, and essays. Cambridge, 1989.

Walbank, F. W. *Aratus of Sicyon.* Cambridge, 1933.

———. *The Hellenistic World.* London, 1981.

———. *A Historical Commentary on Polybius.* 3 vols. Oxford, 1957–79.

———. *Philip V of Macedon.* Cambridge, 1940.

———. *Polybius.* Berkeley and Los Angeles, 1972.

———. "Polybius and the Roman State." *GRByS* 5 (1964) 239–60.

———. "Sea-Power and the Antigonids." In Adams and Borza, eds., 213–36.

———. *Selected Papers: Studies in Greek and Roman History and Historiography.* Cambridge, 1985.

———. "*Symploke*: Its Role in Polybius' Histories." *YClS* 24 (1975) 197–212.

Wallon, H. A. *Histoire de l'esclavage dans l'antiquité.* 2d ed. 3 vols. Paris, 1879.

Wardman, A. E. *Rome's Debt to Greece.* London, 1976.

Wasserstein, A. "Greek Scientific Thought." *PCPhS*, n.s., 8 (1962) 51–63.

Watson, G. *The Stoic Theory of Knowledge.* Belfast, 1966.

Webster, T. B. L. *The Art of Greece: The Age of Hellenism.* New York, 1966.

———. *The Birth of Modern Comedy of Manners.* Adelaide, 1959.

———. *Hellenistic Poetry and Art.* London, 1964.

———. *An Introduction to Menander.* Manchester, 1974.

———. *Studies in Menander.* Manchester, 1950.

Wehrli, C. *Antigone et Démétrios.* Geneva, 1969.

———. "Phila, fille d'Antipater et épouse de Démétrius, roi des Macédoniens." *Historia* 13 (1964) 140–46.

Welles, C. B. *Alexander and the Hellenistic World.* Toronto, 1970.

———. "Alexander's Historical Achievement." *G&R* 12 (1965) 216–28.

———. *Royal Correspondence in the Hellenistic Age: A Study in Greek Epigraphy.* New Haven, 1934.

Wendel, C., ed. *Scholia in Apollonium Rhodium vetera.* Berlin, 1935. [Reprint: 1958.]

Westermann, W. L. *The Slave Systems of Greek and Roman Antiquity.* Philadelphia, 1955. [Cf. the reviews of P. A. Brunt, *JRS* 48 (1958) 164–70, and G. E. M. de Ste Croix, *CR*, n.s., 7 (1957) 54–59.]

Westlake, H. D. "Eumenes of Cardia." In *Essays on the Greek Historians and Greek History* 313–30. Manchester, 1969.

———. *Timoleon and His Relations with Tyrants.* Manchester, 1952.

Wheeler, M. *Flames over Persepolis.* London, 1968.

White, K. D. *Greek and Roman Technology.* London, 1983.

———. "Some Thoughts on Greek Science and Contemporary Science." *Phrontisterion* 4 (1966) 26–31.

von Wilamowitz-Moellendorff, U. *Hellenistische Dichtung in der Zeit von Kallimachos.* 2 vols. Berlin, 1926.

Wilcken, U. *Urkunden der Ptolemäerzeit.* 2 vols. Berlin and Leipzig, 1922–57.

———. "Zur Entstehung des hellenistischen Königskultes." *Sitzungsberichte der preussischen Akademie der Wissenschaften, philos.-hist. Klasse* 28 (1938) 298–321.

Will, E. "Comment on écrit l'histoire hellénistique." *Historia* 27 (1978) 65–82.

———. *Histoire politique du monde hellénistique (323–30 v. J.-C.).* 2d ed. 2 vols. Nancy, 1979–82.

———. "Le monde hellénistique." In Will et al., 337–645.

———. "Le monde hellénistique et nous." *AncSoc* 10 (1979) 79–95.

Will, E., C. Mossé, and P. Goukowsky. *Le monde grec et l'Orient*. Paris, 1975.

Will, F. *Herondas*. New York, 1973.

Winkler, H. *Rom und Ägypten im 2. Jahrhundert v.Chr.* Leipzig, 1933.

Withington, E. T. *Hippocrates*. Vol. 3. London, 1928. [See also Jones, W. H. S.]

Witt, R. E. *Isis in the Graeco-Roman World*. London, 1971.

Woodcock, G. *The Greeks in India*. London, 1966.

Wycherley, R. E. *How the Greeks Built Cities*. 2d ed. London, 1962.

———. *The Stones of Athens*. Princeton, 1978.

Zanker, G. "The Nature and Origin of Realism in Alexandrian Poetry." *A&A* 29 (1983) 124–45.

———. *Realism in Alexandrian Poetry: A Literature and Its Audience*. London, 1987.

Zeller, E. *Stoics, Epicureans, and Sceptics*. Tr. O. J. Reichel. London, 1892.

Ziegler, K. "Polybios (1)" RE 21:2 (1952) cols. 1440–1578.

INDEX

Aalders, G. J. D., 614–15, 626, 631
Abdalonymus of Sidon, 116 (fig. 49)
Abydos, 307–8
Academy (*see also* Plato, Platonism; Skeptics), 49, 59, 61, 85, 88, 168, 307, 316, 455, 602, 603, 612; *akatalēpsia*, 607; Attalids support, 168; *bios theōrētikos*, reaction against, 605; dialectic, largely abandoned after 314 B.C., 604; *epochē*, 607; ethical concerns, 604, 610; *katorthōmata*, 607; mathematics, largely abandoned after 314 B.C., 604; merged with Stoic and Peripatetic philosophy, 609; New Academy, 449; practical morality, 605; public affairs, 604; radicalism, opposition to, 604; Skeptics, 602, 606–9; Stoics, disputes with, 607, 638; *synkatathesis*, 607; systematization of knowledge, 605; tyranny, opposition to, 604
Acarnania, 125, 253, 300, 306–7; Medeon, 253
Achaea, Achaeans, 139, 153, 256, 261, 278–79, 283, 287, 288, 450, 556; "Achaean era," 525
Achaean League, 133, 137, 138, 139, 151, 153, 248, 249, 254, 261; "Achaean War" (*bellum Achaicum*), 435, 448–52, 525, 568; Aetolian League and, 248–49, 252–53, 274; anti-Macedonianism, 144, 249, 253, 259; anti-Romanism, 276, 283; anti-Spartanism, 253; Antigonus Doson and, 250, 256, 258, 259–61, 383; Antiochus III

and, 274, 420; Argos and, 253, 258; Athens and, 153, 253, 255, 259, 449; Corinth, destruction at, 279, 310–11, 435; development and organization, 139–40, 248; Egypt, support from, 151, 153; Flamininus and, 428; franchise, Roman restrictions of, 525; Lycortas and, 273; Lydiades as commander-in-chief of, 253; Macedonia and, 252–53, 298; Mantineans sold into slavery by, 383; Megalopolis joins, 253; Oropus and, 449; patriotic nationalism of, 449; Pergamon, helps raise siege of, 420; Perseus and, 426; Philip V and, 297–98, 300, 309; Philopoemen and, 261, 273, 274, 283, 300, 423; Polybius and, 273–76, 283; Ptolemy III, financed by, 249, 258, 373; resuscitation of (280 B.C.), 133; Rome, relations with, 274, 275–76, 279, 280, 309, 310, 415, 418–19, 423–44, 448–52, 525; Sparta and, 153, 249, 252, 253, 256–61, 273, 302–3, 309, 310, 415–17, 418–19, 423, 424, 449–51; *synedria*, 525; *synodos*, 450–51; Third Macedonian War, 428; war against Cleomenes III, 256–61; "War of Demetrius," 249, 253
Achaeus, 195, 265, 289, 291–93, 295
Acheron, 405
Achillas, 664, 667
Achilles, 205, 207, 238, 242
Acontius, 180
Acragas, 220, 222, 230

Acrotatus of Sparta, 153
Actium, 138, 264, 585, 649, 679, 680 (map 30)
Adea-Eurydice, 12, 15, 19–20
Aden, 329
Adonis, 237, 243, 588, 590
Adramyttion, Gulf of, 164
Adriatic, 126, 216, 223, 296, 297, 299, 300, 305, 308, 429, 447; piracy in, 216, 253, 254, 296; trade route, 216, 253, 254
Aegean basin, 11, 26, 28, 89, 138, 141 (map 9), 150, 216, 240, 263, 303, 305, 306, 308, 378, 408, 447, 538, 558, 571, 576; piracy in, 296, 305, 558; policing of, 73
Aemilius Paullus, 164, 277, 311, 338, 376, 386, 415, 417, 432, 566–67; portraits, 566; triumph, 415, 556; victory at Pydna, 269, 275, 277, 318, 430, 448, 556, 566
Aeneas Tacticus, 392
Aenus, 424
Aeschines, 590
Aeschylus, 52, 65, 89, 111, 358, 387, 396, 398, 501; *Prometheus*, 398, 471, 643
Aetolia, Aetolians, 10, 11, 12, 126, 253, 261, 283, 298, 414; Antigonus Gonatas and, 153; Athenians and, 398; defeat Gauls at Delphi, 133, 140; Delphi, acquisition of, 593; Perseus and, 427; reputation as bandits and pirates, 127, 153, 299–300, 305; seize Phocis, 126
Aetolian League, 139, 249, 253–54, 286, 393, 525; Achaean League and, 248, 249, 253, 254, 259, 274, 286–87, 419; anti-Macedonianism, 144; Antiochus III

929

At the end of his *Juvenal*—a considerably shorter book
than this—the late Gilbert Highet, in evident relief,
printed the following hexameter: INDICE COMPLETO
SALTAT SCRIPTOR PEDE LAETO. Indexing *Alexander
to Actium* has left me practically past dancing; but I would
like, by way of *envoi*, to record my grateful thanks to
my students Kerri Cox and Michele Clement, who with
skilful precision converted my holograph slips into copy
for the printer. Perhaps it is worth recording that, in this
computer age, theirs is the only electronic assistance
I have had from start to finish.

Compositor: G&S Typesetters, Inc.
Text: 10/13 Bembo
Display: Bembo
Printer: C. J. Krehbiel Co.
Binder: C. J. Krehbiel Co.